For Reference

Not to be taken from this room

DATAPEDIA
of the United States
1790–2005

Second Edition

DATAPEDIA
of the United States
1790–2005
America Year by Year

Second Edition

Edited by George Thomas Kurian

PROPERTY OF GERMANNA
COMMUNITY COLLEGE LIBRARY

BERNAN

Lanham, MD

© 2001 George Thomas Kurian.

All rights reserved. No part of this work covered by the copyrights hereon may be reproduced or used in any form or by any means, whether graphic, electronic, or mechanical—including photocopying, recording, taping, or information storage and retrieval systems—without written permission from the publisher.

ISBN: 0-89059-256-X

ISSN:

Composed and printed by Automated Graphic Systems, Inc., White Plains, MD, in the United States of America on acid-free paper that meets the American National Standards Institute Z39-48 standard.

2002 2001   4 3 2 1

Bernan Press
4611-F Assembly Drive
Lanham, MD 20706
email: info@bernan.com

Table of Contents

SECTION G

CONSUMER INCOME AND EXPENDITURES

SECTION H

SOCIAL STATISTICS

SECTION J

LAND, WATER AND CLIMATE

viii   Contents

Introduction

Datapedia of the United States, Millennium Edition, presents the most significant historical statistics of the United States in 23 selected areas from 1776 to 2000. In some areas, such as demography, where projections are possible, the data are extended to 2010.

For the period up to 1970, the *Datapedia of the United States* is based entirely on *Historical Statistics of the United States from Colonial Times.* For the three decades from 1970 to 2000, it is based on the annual *Statistical Abstract of the United State*s as well as data scattered in numerous other publications. However, *Datapedia* is not merely a supplement to *Historical Statistics.* It selects the most important of the time series contained in *Historical Statistics* and presents them in a reader-friendly format with Highlights for each section and over 40 charts. In doing so, it brings together in one source the best available data on the United States from 1770 to 2000. Except in cases where a reader is seeking highly specialized data, *Datapedia* will serve as a complete and convenient statistical profile of the United States covering all its vital sectors.

All chapter divisions in *Historical Statistics* have been maintained in *Datapedia* in the same sequence. The table numbers also have been kept in an effort to make cross references and comparisons easier. Generally, only national data are shown. Some exceptions are made where regional or state statistics are useful for the correct interpretation of data or where national data in the subject field cannot be summarized effectively. Of course, in the early part of many series, the data are limited to the Atlantic Seaboard.

Historical Statistics of the United States, on which *Datapedia* is based, has an interesting history. The first edition, which covered the years from 1776 to 1945, was initiated by the Social Research Council following a proposal by the Bureau of Census to prepare a historical supplement to the *Statistical Abstract.* It was published in 1949. The second edition brought the coverage to 1957, again with the participation of the Social Research Council. Work on the third edition began in 1969 and was completed in 1976, bringing the coverage to 1970. This time the Bureau of Census undertook the project alone. It

included over 12,500 time series, a 50% increase over the last edition. There were also substantial changes in the scope and density of the data.

Statistics have become essential tools for historians, social scientists, political scientists, journalists, demographers, and marketers. Historical statistics, now named cliometrics, serve an even more important function. Contrary to popular notion, statistical data never become outdated or useless. True, data are perishable, like fruits, and have an active shelf life of only a few months or until new data are collected. But when preserved or pickled, they help to illuminate historical trends and explain cyclical phenomena that otherwise remain obscure. Some of the most interesting data in *Historical Statistics* are derived from little known 19th century documents and publications, but without them historians will be at a loss to understand why, for example, farm prices rose or fell, or why certain types of industrial changes took place the way they did. Historical statistical data also serve as touchstones on which political, economic, and social theories and assumptions can be tested.

The quality of the statistical tables spanning over two centuries is remarkably even. The collection of statistics was not considered as a primary function of the government in the early years of the republic and much of the data have been gathered from occasional and fugitive publications and documents. Much data also have been lost. But, because the catchment area was so small, the degree of accuracy was much higher. As the complexity of statistical operations grew, so did the techniques of collection and analysis. Finally, with the introduction of computers in the 20th century, number crunching became extremely sophisticated, providing us with raw and refined data of exceptionally high quality. Data collection also is beginning to be focused on a number of areas in which few statistics were collected before. Still, not all subjects are equally well-endowed with numbers. In some there is an embarrassment of riches, while in others one has to scrape the bottom of the barrel to obtain a few crumbs.

As in *Historical Statistics,* data are arranged for macro subjects in lettered chapters and micro subjects in numbered series within the chapter. Each series or column is assigned a unique letter and number. Most of the data are annual, but certain series are presented only for years in which a national census was held. In general, only absolute rather than derived data are included because one-dimensional aggregates at gross levels offer somewhat greater flexibility to the user. Criteria for inclusion vary, but in most cases are based on the quantity and quality of the data available and the extent to which they enhance our understanding of historical trends.

Datapedia owes its genesis to the strong commitment of Bernan Press and its director, Don Hagen, to the publication of innovative statistical reference books. My thanks are also due to Dr. Cornelia J. Strawser, F. Hill Slowinski, Dan Parham, Tamera L. Wells-Lee, Lorrent Smith, Jacalyn Houston, Anthony Nathe, Dr. Helmut Wendel, Gaston Gohou, and Cheryl Grim for their dedication to this project. Finally, I wish to thank my wife, Annie Kurian for her support and encouragement.

April 2001   —George Thomas Kurian

SECTION **A**

POPULATION

POPULATION

Highlights

Ten Fastest-Growing States: 1990–1998 Percent Population Change

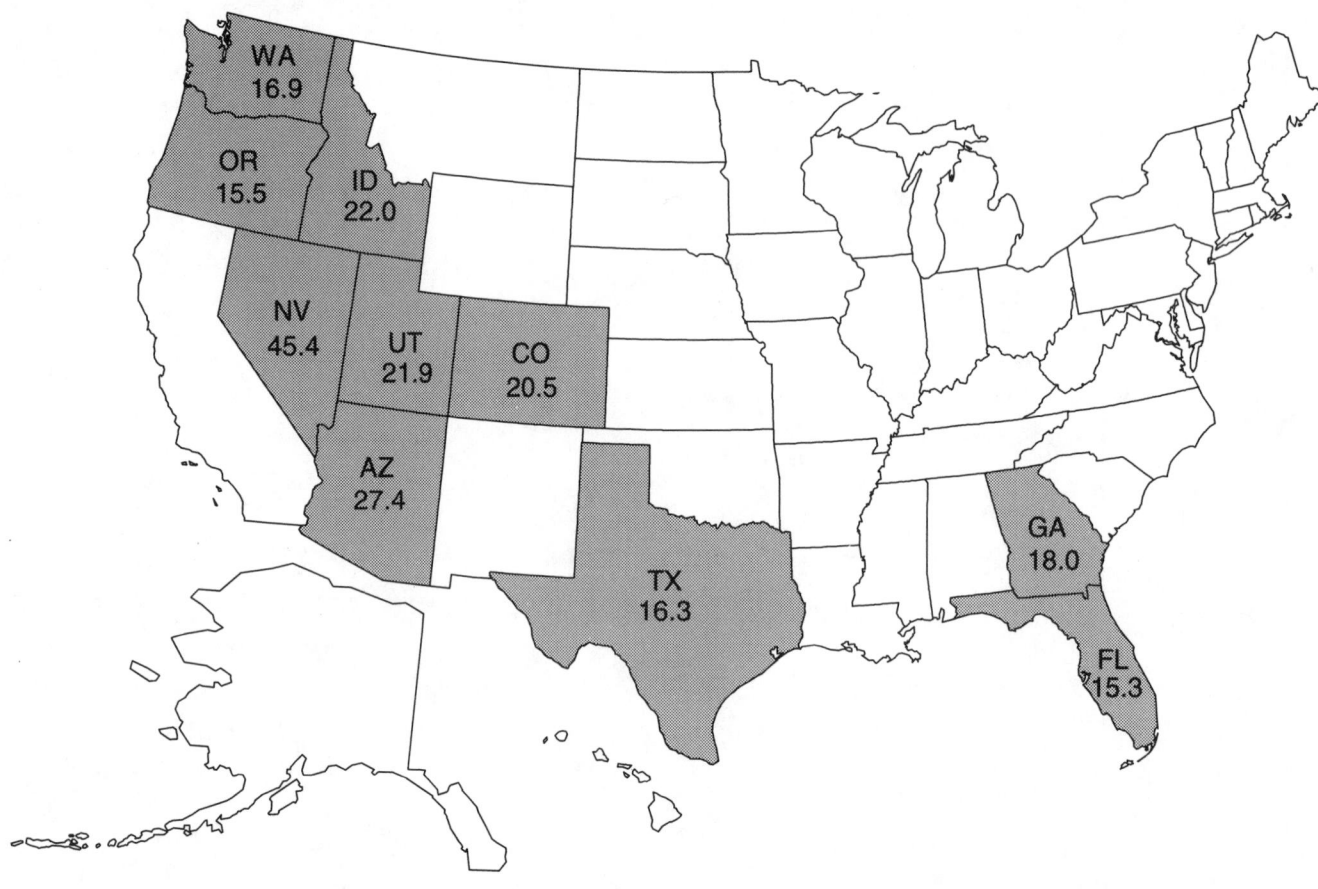

1 The Census of the United States was authorized by an act of Congress, dated March 1, 1790, providing for "the enumeration of the United States." The first census cost $44,377 and utilized the services of 17 marshals and 650 assistants. It counted a population of 3,939,326 in 16 states and the Ohio Territory. Virginia was the most populous state with 746,610 inhabitants, and Rhode Island the least with 68,825 inhabitants. New York City had a population of 33,131, Philadelphia 28,522, and Boston 18,320.

2 Between 1790 and 1990 the Center of Population moved from Maryland to Missouri.

Year	North Latitude	West Latitude	Approximate Location
1790	39° 16′ 30″	76° 11′ 12″	21 miles East of Baltimore MD
1850	35° 90′ 0″	81° 19′ 0″	23 miles SE of Parkersburg WV
1900	38° 9′ 36″	85° 48′ 54″	6 miles SE of Columbus IN
1950	38° 50′ 21″	89° 9′ 33″	8 miles NNW of Olney IL
1960	38° 55′ 58″	89° 12′ 35″	6.5 miles NW of Centralia IL
1970	38° 27′ 47″	89° 42′ 22″	5.3 miles SSE of Mescoutah IL
1980	38° 8′ 13″	90° 34′ 26″	0.25 miles West of De Soto MO
1990	37° 52′ 20″	91° 12′ 55″	9.7 miles SE of Steelville MO

3 Until 1830 people who were deaf, mute and blind were excluded from the census.

4 The fifth census in 1830 was the first in which the population of the United States exceeded 10 million; the first census in which the count exceeded 100 million was that of 1920 and the first in which the count exceeded 200 million was that of 1970.

5 The 1890 census was the first to utilize enumerating machines.

6 The first states to exceed 1 million in population were New York, Virginia, and Pennsylvania in 1820. The first state to exceed 5 million in population was New York in 1880.

7 New York City was the first city to exceed 1 million in population (exceeding Brooklyn which was then an independent city) in 1880.

8 Census counts are subject to a margin of error, estimated between 1.4% and 3.3%. The errors generally result from an undercount of certain segments of population.

9 Data on urban population were first published in 1870. Urban centers were defined as locations with a population of 8,000 or more. In 1880 and 1890 that figure was reduced to 4,000, and in 1900, to 2,500. This definition, with minor modifications, was accepted in later censuses up to and including 1940. In 1950 the Census Bureau adopted the concept of the urbanized area and delineated boundaries for unincorporated places. The urban population was defined as all persons living in urbanized areas, and outside these areas, in all places incorporated or unincorporated, which had 2,500 inhabitants or more. This definition has remained substantially unchanged in the following censuses. Minor modifications of this definition are employed in Alaska, New York, the New England states and Wisconsin.

10 Rural population is subdivided into two categories: rural farm and rural nonfarm. The definition of rural nonfarm is based on the size of the farm and the cash value of the farm produce.

11 The first attempt to define metropolitan population was made in the 1910 census. Metropolitan districts were defined for cities of 200,000 or more. Each metropolitan district included contiguous minor civil divisions that met certain rules of proximity and population density. In 1950, metropolitan districts were replaced by Standard Metropolitan Areas (SMAs), Consolidated Metropolitan Statistical Areas (CMSAs), and Primary Metropolitan Statistical Areas (PMSAs). These are defined in terms of entire counties, except in New England where the definitions are in terms of cities or towns. In general, an urbanized area is defined as a city (or twin cities) of 50,000 or more and the surrounding closely settled areas. From time to time new metropolitan areas are created and boundaries of others change. As a result, data over time may not be comparable.

12 The classification by race in censuses reflects common usage rather than strict biological stock. The data are obtained primarily through self-classification. The standard racial categories are White, Black, American Indian, Asian and Pacific Islander, and Hispanic (who may be Black or White). The 1990 census was the first to include an "other race" category that provided for a write-in entry. The Census of 1860 was the first in which American Indians were distinguished from other ethnic groups; however, it excluded those American Indians living on reservations.

13 Americans residing outside the United States numbered 6.29 million in 1990. The countries with the largest number of resident U. S. civilians were Mexico (495,000), Canada (278,000), France (126,000), Israel (124,000), Germany (107,000), the Philippines (109,000), Italy (102,000), the Dominican Republic (87,000) and Australia (65,000).

14 The population of the United States doubled five times between the first decennial census of 1790 and the 17th census in 1950. The first three doublings took 25 years each through 1865. The fourth required 35 years from 1865 to 1900. The fifth doubling took half a century to 1950. A sixth doubling appears improbable.

15 Between 1790 and 1850, the annual increase of population exceeded 3%, with the highest being 3.6% from 1800 to 1810. In the remaining five decades of the 19th century and the first decade of the 20th century, the rate of growth ranged from 2.7% to 2.1%. The growth rate slumped to 1.5% between 1910 and 1920, rose to 1.6% in the following decade, and then plummeted to 0.7% during the Depression in the 1930s. It rebounded to 1.9% in the 1950s (known as the Baby Boom) and was followed by a rate of 1.3% in the 1970s (the Baby Bust). 1969 was the first year that it dipped below 1% where it has remained, except for 1977 to 1980 and 1990 to 1993.

16 The highest decennial jump in population was 36.4% reported in the third census in 1810 followed by 35.9% in 1850, 35.6% in 1860, and 35.1% in 1800. The lowest was 7.2% reported in 1940, followed by 9.8% in 1990 and 11.4% in 1980.

17 The United States had more males than females until the end of World War II in 1945. Since then, the sex ratio has been in favor of females. However, more male children are born so that males are in the majority until age 24.

18 Urbanized areas accounted for 75.2% of the population and 74.5% of the housing units, but only 2.5% of the land area in 1990. The West was the most urbanized area, with 86.3% of its total population living in urbanized areas, followed by the Northeast (78.9%), the Midwest (71.7%), and the South (68.6%). The most urbanized state was California with 92.6%, followed by New Jersey (89.4%), Hawaii (89%), Nevada (88.3%), Arizona (87.5%), Utah (87%), Rhode Island (86%), Florida (84.8%), Illinois (84.6%), Massachusetts (84.3%), New York (84.3%), Colorado (82.4%), Maryland (81.3%), and Texas (80.3%). The least urbanized state was Vermont with 32.2%, followed by West Virginia (36.1%) and Mississippi (47.1%).

19 In 1790, the percentage of the urban population was 5.4%. In 1990, it was 75.2%.

20 In 1998, 142.7 million people (53% of the U. S. population) lived within 50 miles of a coast, a loss of 1% compared to 1970. Of the 53% of the population living on the coast, 23% lived on the Atlantic coast, 6% on the Gulf of Mexico, 10% on the Great Lakes and 14% on the Pacific Coast.

21 In the first census of 1790 the density of population was only 4.5 per square mile of land area. It reached 10.6 in 1860, 21.2 in 1890, 31 in 1910, 41.2 in 1930, 50.7 in 1950, 64 in 1980, and 76.4 in 1990. The state with the greatest density of population was New Jersey with 1,093.8 followed by Rhode Island with 945.9. The state with the least density of population was Alaska with 1.1.

22 Blacks comprised 12.7% of the population in 1998, compared to 15.7% in 1850. Nearly 52.8% of Blacks lived in the South, 19.1% in the Midwest, 18.7% in the Northeast, and 9.4% in the West.

23 Hispanics and Asians have a net growth at a rate of 3.6 and 3.4% respectively compared to 0.7% for Whites and 1.3% for Blacks.

24 Nevada has the fastest growing population, with a phenomenal growth rate of 45.4% from 1990 to 1998. Western states generally experienced greater population growths led by Arizona (27.4%), Idaho (22%), Utah (21.9%), Colorado (20.5%) and Washington (16.9%). Only one state lost population during this period,—Rhode Island by 1.5%. California, which ranked first in population in 1980, retained that rank in 1998, while New York lost its second rank to Texas, and Florida advanced from fourth to seventh.

25 California lost 2.082 million of its residents through emigration, New York lost 1.722 million, and Florida lost 1.035 million. The greatest gains through immigration were registered in Georgia (598,000), Texas (541,000), Arizona (519,000), and North Carolina (501,000).

26 The annual growth rate for Whites in 1998 was 0.6% compared to 1.3% for Blacks, 1.4% for American Indians, 3.4% for Asians and 3.6% for Hispanics.

27 Sixteen percent of the population is mobile. This means that people moved from their original house to a different house. Of these 6% to a different county and 3% to a different state. Poorer people tend to move more than wealthier people. Of those with a household income of less than $5,000, 23% moved compared to 10% of those with an income of more than $75,000.

28 Significant disparities exist in the regional distribution of races. While Whites are distributed fairly equally over the four main regions (Northeast, Midwest, South and West), 52.8% of Blacks are concentrated in the South and only 9.1% in the West. Nearly 47.6% of American Indians are found in the West and only 6.4% in the Northeast. Asians and Hispanics also are more numerous in the West, with 55.7% and 45.2% respectively. One third of all Hispanics live in California and another one-sixth in Texas. New York has the largest Black population (3.22 million) followed by California (2.45 million), Texas (2.43 million), Florida (2.2 million) and Georgia (2.1 million).

29 The number of senior citizens in the United States will grow from 34.7 million in 2000 to 39.4 million in 2010. Those from 48 to 64 years of age will grow in number from 60.9 million to 78.8 million, while those from 18 to 44 years of age will decrease from 108 million to 106 million during the same period. In 1998, there were 4.054 million senior citizens over the age of 85.

30 In 1996, there were 274 Metropolitan Statistical Areas (MSAs) and Consolidated Metropolitan Statistical Areas (CMSAs) inhabited by 79.9% of the population. Of these 47 had populations of a million or more, accounting for 139.2 million. New Jersey was the only state considered 100% metropolitan. Other states with a more than 90% metropolitan population included California (96.6%), Massachusetts (96.1%), Connecticut (95.6%), Rhode Island (93.8%), Florida (92.9%), Maryland (92.8%), and New York (92.8%). Vermont and Wyoming are the most rural states with 72.3% and 70.3% of their populations respectively in nonmetropolitan areas.

31 There are 19,355 incorporated places in the United States, of which 10 have more than a million inhabitants and 16,806 fewer than 10,000. Both categories lost population between 1970 and 1996, while those between 25,000 and 250,000 gained population. Incorporated places with a population between 50,000 and 99,999 have fared best.

32 Fifty-nine U.S. cities had double-digit growth rates between 1980 and 1996, led by Las Vegas with a growth rate of 40.9%.

33 In 1990, ten tribes accounted for 56.5% of the 1.878 million American Indian population: Cherokee (16.4%), Navajo (11.7%), Chippewa (5.5%), Sioux (5.5%), Choctaw (4.4%), Pueblo (2.8%), Apache (2.7%), Iroquois (2.6%), Lumbee (2.6%), and Creek (2.3%). Twenty-two point-one percent of American Indians live below the poverty level.

34 The percentage of foreign-born population increased only slightly from 6.9% in 1950 to 7.9% in 1990. Mexicans account for 35.7% of the foreign-born population.

35 Foreign-language speakers have been increasing in number in the United States since 1950: 17.3 million speak Spanish; 1.7 million speak French; 1.5 million speak German; 1.3 million speak Italian; and 1.2 million speak Chinese.

36 Of Americans of European ancestry, those of German descent are the most numerous—an estimated 57.9 million—followed by British/English (33.7 million), Italian (14.6 million), French (10.3 million), Polish (9.3 million), and Dutch (6.2 million).

37 Marriage remains the norm, but the percentage of married couples in the population declined from 65.5% in 1980 to 59.7% in 1998. The divorced segment of the population increased to 9.8% in 1998 from 6.2% in 1980.

38 Miscegenation has become more acceptable since 1980. Black/White marriages doubled during this period from 167,000 to 330,000, while White/Other Race marriages have increased from 450,000 to 975,000.

39 The average size of the American family declined from 3.14 members in 1970 to 2.62 in 1998. Of the total number of 70.8 million family households, 12.6 million are headed by females. Nonfamily households have become more common since the 1960s. Of the 31.6 million nonfamily households, 17.5 million are headed by females.

40 Seventy-three percent of White family households have two parents, compared to 38% of Black family households. Fifty-seven percent of Black family households are run by single mothers and 5% by single fathers.

Series A 1-5. Area and Population of the United States: 1790 to 1999

Year	Land area (square miles)	Resident population				Year	Land area (square miles)	Resident population			
		Number	Increase from preceding census		Per square mile of land area			Number	Increase from preceding census		Per square mile of land area
			Number	Percent[2]					Number	Percent[2]	
	1	**2**	**3**	**4**	**5**		**1**	**2**	**3**	**4**	**5**
1999 (July 1)[1]......	3 536 342	272 690 813	23 899 888	9.6	77.1	1890 (June 1)	2 969 640	62 947 714	12 791 931	25.5	21.2
1990 (Apr. 1)........	3 536 278	248 790 925	22 245 120	9.8	70.4	1880 (June 1)	2 969 640	50 155 783	10 337 334	26.0	16.9
1980 (Apr. 1)........	3 539 289	226 545 805	23 243 774	11.4	64.0	1870 (June 1)	2 969 640	[4] 39 818 449	8 375 128	26.6	13.4
1970 (Apr. 1)........	3 540 023	203 302 031	23 978 856	13.4	57.4						
1960 (Apr. 1)*......	3 540 911	179 323 175	28 625 814	19.0	50.6	1860 (June 1)	2 969.640	31 443 321	8 251 445	35.6	10.6
						1850 (June 1)	2 940.042	23 191 876	6 122 423	35.9	7.9
1960 (Apr. 1)[3]	2 968 054	178 464 236	27 766 875	18.4	60.1	1840 (June 1)	1 749 462	17 069 453	4 203 433	32.7	9.8
1950 (Apr. 1)........	2 974 726	150 697 361	19 028 086	14.5	50.7	1830 (June 1)	1 749 462	12 866 020	3 227 567	33.5	7.4
1940 (Apr. 1)........	2 977 128	131 669 275	8 894 229	7.2	44.2	1820 (Aug. 17)......	1 749 462	9 638 453	2 398 572	33.1	5.5
1930 (Apr. 1)........	2 977 128	122 775 046	17 064 426	16.1	41.2						
1920 (Jan. 1)........	2 969 451	105 710 620	13 738 354	14.9	35.6	1810 (Aug. 6)........	1 681 828	7 239 881	1 931 398	36.4	4.3
						1800 (Aug. 4)........	864 746	5 308 483	1 379 269	35.1	6.1
1910 (Apr. 15)......	2 969 565	91 972 266	15 977 691	21.0	31.0	1790 (Aug. 2)........	864 746	3 929 214	. . .	. . .	4.5
1900 (June 1).......	2 969 834	75 994 575	13 046 861	20.7	25.6						

* Denotes first year for which figures include Alaska and Hawaii.
1. 1999 figures are based on a postcensal estimate while all others are Decennial Census counts.
2. Based on interval since preceding census which is not always exactly 10 years.
3. Conterminous United States (excludes Alaska and Hawaii).
4. Revised to include adjustment of 1 260 078 for under enumeration in the southern states. Unrevised census count is 38 558 371.

Series A 6-8. Annual Population Estimates for the United States: 1790 to 1999

(In thousands)

Year	Total including Armed Forces overseas	Total resident population	Civilian resident population	Year	Total resident population	Year	Total resident population	Year	Total resident population
	6	**7**	**8**		**7**		**7**		**7**
1999.................	272 945	272 691	271 491	1939.................	130 880	1889.................	61 775	1839.................	16 684
1998.................	270 509	270 248	269 027	1938.................	129 825	1888.................	60 496	1838.................	16 264
1997.................	268 048	267 784	266 531	1937.................	128 825	1887.................	59 217	1837.................	15 843
1996.................	265 502	265 229	263 943	1936.................	128 053	1886.................	57 938	1836.................	15 423
1995.................	263 082	262 803	261 452	1935.................	127 250	1885.................	56 658	1835.................	15 003
1994.................	260 637	260 327	258 915	1934.................	126 374	1884.................	55 379	1834.................	14 582
1993.................	258 119	257 783	256 310	1933.................	125 579	1883.................	54 100	1833.................	14 162
1992.................	255 410	255 030	253 445	1932.................	124 840	1882.................	52 821	1832.................	13 742
1991.................	252 665	252 153	250 542	1931.................	124 040	1881.................	51 542	1831.................	13 321
1990.................	249 973	249 464	247 824	1930.................	123 077	1880.................	50 262	1830.................	12 901
1989.................	247 342	246 819	245 131	1929.................	121 767	1879.................	49 208	1829.................	12 565
1988.................	245 021	244 499	242 817	1928.................	120 509	1878.................	48 174	1828.................	12 237
1987.................	242 804	242 289	240 550	1927.................	119 035	1877.................	47 141	1827.................	11 909
1986.................	240 651	240 133	238 412	1926.................	117 397	1876.................	46 107	1826.................	11 580
1985.................	238 466	237 924	236 219	1925.................	115 829	1875.................	45 073	1825.................	11 252
1984.................	236 348	235 825	234 110	1924.................	114 109	1874.................	44 040	1824.................	10 924
1983.................	234 307	233 792	232 097	1923.................	111 947	1873.................	43 006	1823.................	10 596
1982.................	232 188	231 664	229 995	1922.................	110 049	1872.................	41 972	1822.................	10 268
1981.................	229 966	229 466	227 818	1921.................	108 538	1871.................	40 938	1821.................	9 939
1980.................	227 726	227 225	225 621	1920.................	106 461	1870.................	39 905	1820.................	9 618
1979.................	225 055	224 567	222 969	1919.................	[1] 104 514	1869.................	39 051	1819.................	9 379
1978.................	222 585	222 095	220 467	1918.................	[1] 103 208	1868.................	38 213	1818.................	9 139
1977.................	220 239	219 760	218 106	1917.................	[1] 103 268	1867.................	37 376	1817.................	8 899
1976.................	218 035	217 563	215 894	1916.................	101 961	1866.................	36 538	1816.................	8 659
1975.................	215 973	215 465	213 789	1915.................	100 546	1865.................	35 701	1815.................	8 419
1974.................	213 854	213 342	211 636	1914.................	99 111	1864.................	34 863	1814.................	8 179
1973.................	211 909	211 357	209 600	1913.................	97 225	1863.................	34 026	1813.................	7 939
1972.................	209 896	209 284	207 511	1912.................	95 335	1862.................	33 188	1812.................	7 700
1971.................	207 661	206 827	204 866	1911.................	93 863	1861.................	32 351	1811.................	7 460
1970.................	205 052	203 984	201 895	1910.................	92 407	1860.................	31 513	1810.................	7 224
1969.................	202 677	201 385	199 145	1909.................	90 490	1859.................	30 687	1809.................	7 031
1968.................	200 706	199 399	197 113	1908.................	88 710	1858.................	29 862	1808.................	6 838
1967.................	198 712	197 457	195 264	1907.................	87 008	1857.................	29 037	1807.................	6 644
1966.................	196 560	195 576	193 420	1906.................	85 450	1856.................	28 212	1806.................	6 451
1965.................	194 303	193 526	191 605	1905.................	83 822	1855.................	27 386	1805.................	6 258
1964.................	191 889	191 141	189 141	1904.................	82 166	1854.................	26 561	1804.................	6 065
1963.................	189 242	188 483	186 493	1903.................	80 632	1853.................	25 736	1803.................	5 872
1962.................	186 538	185 771	183 677	1902.................	79 163	1852.................	24 911	1802.................	5 679
1961.................	183 691	182 992	181 143	1901.................	77 584	1851.................	24 086	1801.................	5 486
1960.................	180 671	179 979	178 140	1900.................	76 094	1850.................	23 261	1800.................	5 297
1959*.................	177 830	177 135	175 277	1899.................	74 799	1849.................	22 631	1799.................	5 159
1959.................	177 073	176 289	174 521	1898.................	73 493	1848.................	22 018	1798.................	5 021
1958.................	174 141	173 320	171 485	1897.................	72 189	1847.................	21 406	1797.................	4 883
1957.................	171 274	170 371	168 400	1896.................	70 885	1846.................	20 794	1796.................	4 745
1956.................	168 221	167 306	165 373	1895.................	69 580	1845.................	20 182	1795.................	4 607
1955.................	165 275	164 308	162 311	1894.................	68 275	1844.................	19 569	1794.................	4 469
1954.................	162 391	161 164	159 059	1893.................	66 970	1843.................	18 957	1793.................	4 332
1953.................	159 565	158 242	155 975	1892.................	65 666	1842.................	18 345	1792.................	4 194
1952.................	156 954	155 687	153 292	1891.................	64 361	1841.................	17 733	1791.................	4 056
1951.................	154 287	153 310	151 009	1890.................	63 056	1840.................	17 120	1790.................	3 929
1950.................	151 684	151 235	150 203						
1949.................	149 188	148 665	147 578						
1948.................	146 631	146 093	145 168						
1947.................	144 126	143 446	142 566						
1946.................	141 389	140 054	138 385						
1945.................	139 928	132 481	127 573						
1944.................	138 397	132 885	126 708						
1943.................	136 739	134 245	127 499						

See footnotes at end of table.

Series A 6-8.   Annual Population Estimates for the United States: 1790 to 1999—Cont'd.
(In thousands)

Year	Total including Armed Forces overseas	Total resident population	Civilian resident population	Year	Total resident population	Year	Total resident population	Year	Total resident population
	6	7	8		7		7		7
1942....................	134 860	133 920	130 942						
1941....................	133 402	133 121	131 595						
1940....................	132 122	131 954	131 658						

* Denotes first year for which figures include Alaska and Hawaii.
1. Total population including Armed Forces overseas (in thousands): 1917 = 103 414; 1918 = 104 550; 1919 = 105 063; civilian population (in thousands): 1917 = 102 796; 1918 = 101 488; 1919 = 104 158.

Series A 23-25. Annual Estimates of the Population by Sex: 1900 to 2050

(In thousands. As of July 1. 1900–1939 and 1992–2050, resident population: 1940–1991, total population, including Armed Forces overseas. 1960–1991, preliminary)

Year	Total	Sex		Year	Total	Sex	
		Male	Female			Male	Female
	23	**24**	**25**		**23**	**24**	**25**
2050	403 687	206 640	197 047	1952	156 954	78 061	78 893
2025	337 815	172 806	165 009	1951	154 287	76 792	77 496
2020	324 927	166 071	158 856	1950	151 684	75 539	76 146
2015	312 268	159 524	152 744	1949	149 188	74 335	74 853
2010	299 862	153 183	146 679	1948	146 631	73 130	73 502
2005	287 716	147 018	140 698	1947	144 126	71 946	72 180
2000	275 372	134 720	140 652	1946	141 389	70 631	70 757
1999 *	272 945	133 496	139 450	1945	139 928	70 035	69 893
1998	270 509	132 255	138 254	1944	138 397	69 378	69 020
1997	268 048	131 012	137 036	1943	136 739	68 546	68 194
1996	265 502	129 743	135 759	1942	134 860	67 597	67 263
1995	263 082	128 538	134 544	1941	133 402	66 920	66 482
1994	260 637	127 321	133 316	1940	132 122	66 352	65 770
1993	258 119	126 083	132 036	1939	130 880	65 713	65 166
1992	255 410	124 756	130 653	1938	129 825	65 235	64 590
1991	252 665	123 408	129 256	1937	128 825	64 790	64 035
1990	249 973	122 075	127 899	1936	128 053	64 460	63 594
1989	247 342	120 739	126 603	1935	127 250	64 110	63 140
1988	245 021	119 550	125 472	1934	126 374	63 726	62 648
1987	242 804	118 416	124 388	1933	125 579	63 384	62 195
1986	240 651	117 324	123 327	1932	124 840	63 070	61 770
1985	238 466	116 217	122 249	1931	124 040	62 726	61 314
1984	236 348	115 142	121 206	1930	123 077	62 297	60 780
1983	234 307	114 113	120 195	1929	121 767	61 680	60 087
1982	232 188	113 052	119 135	1928	120 509	61 101	59 408
1981	229 966	111 956	118 010	1927	119 035	60 397	58 638
1980	227 726	110 859	116 867	1926	117 397	59 588	57 809
1979	225 055	109 584	115 472	1925	115 829	58 813	57 016
1978	222 585	108 424	114 161	1924	114 109	57 985	56 124
1977	220 239	107 335	112 905	1923	111 947	56 861	55 086
1976	218 035	106 309	111 727	1922	110 049	55 886	54 163
1975	215 973	105 366	110 607	1921	108 538	55 292	53 246
1974	213 854	104 391	109 463	1920	106 461	54 291	52 170
1973	211 909	103 506	108 402	1919	[1] 104 514	[2] 53 103	51 411
1972	209 896	102 591	107 305	1918	[1] 103 208	[2] 51 974	51 234
1971	207 661	101 567	106 094	1917	[1] 103 268	[2] 52 788	50 480
1970	205 052	100 354	104 698	1916	101 961	52 234	49 727
1969	202 677	99 287	103 390	1915	100 546	51 573	48 973
1968	200 706	98 426	102 280	1914	99 111	50 883	48 228
1967	198 712	97 564	101 148	1913	97 225	49 957	47 268
1966	196 560	96 620	99 941	1912	95 335	49 025	46 310
1965	194 303	95 609	98 694	1911	93 863	48 290	45 573
1964	191 889	94 518	97 371	1910	92 407	47 554	44 853
1963	189 242	93 303	95 939	1909	90 490	46 545	43 945
1962	186 538	92 066	94 472	1908	88 710	45 594	43 116
1961	183 691	90 740	92 952	1907	87 008	44 682	42 326
1960	180 671	89 320	91 352	1906	85 450	43 841	41 609
1959 *	177 830	87 995	89 834	1905	83 822	42 965	40 857
1959	177 073	87 621	89 453	1904	82 166	42 089	40 077
1958	174 141	86 236	87 905	1903	80 632	41 262	39 370
1957	171 274	84 892	86 382	1902	79 163	40 483	38 680
1956	168 221	83 434	84 786	1901	77 584	39 649	37 935
1955	165 275	82 030	83 246	1900	76 094	38 867	37 227
1954	162 391	80 647	81 744				
1953	159 565	79 295	80 270				

* Denotes first year for which figures include Alaska and Hawaii.
1. Estimates including Armed Forces overseas, in thousands: 1917 = 103 414; 1918 = 104 550; 1919 = 105 063.
2. Estimates including Armed Forces overseas, in thousands: 1917 = 52 934; 1918 = 53 316; 1919 = 53 658.

Series A 29-37. Annual Estimates of the Population, by Age: 1900 to 1998

(As of July 1. 1900–1939, resident population; 1940–1970, total population, including Armed Forces overseas.)

Year	Total	Under 5	5-14	15-24	25-34	35-44	45-54	55-64	65 and over
	29	**30**	**31**	**32**	**33**	**34**	**35**	**36**	**37**
1998	270 299 000	18 966 000	35 105 000	37 029 000	43 170 000	37 441 000	25 060 000	21 115 000	31 081 000
1997	267 744 000	19 097 000	38 840 000	36 623 000	39 544 000	44 005 000	33 622 000	21 817 000	34 198 000
1996	265 284 000	19 286 000	38 422 000	36 222 000	40 236 000	43 393 000	32 370 000	21 361 000	33 861 000
1995	262 890 000	19 535 000	37 933 000	36 224 000	40 835 000	42 570 000	31 109 000	21 141 000	33 544 000
1994	260 372 000	16 696 000	37 446 000	36 172 000	41 306 000	41 695 000	29 881 000	21 016 000	33 162 000
1993	257 795 000	19 670 000	36 922 000	36 197 000	41 837 000	40 809 000	28 665 000	20 918 000	32 777 000
1992	255 011 000	19 488 000	36 263 000	36 254 000	42 396 000	39 896 000	27 417 000	20 925 000	32 271 000
1991	252 106 000	19 185 000	35 854 000	36 404 000	42 867 000	39 280 000	25 748 000	21 004 000	31 764 000
1990	248 710 000	18 354 000	35 213 000	37 774 000	43 176 000	37 579 000	25 224 000	21 148 000	31 242 000
1980	226 109 000	16 348 000	34 942 000	42 487 000	37 082 000	25 634 000	22 799 000	21 148 000	25 669 000
1970	204 879 000	17 156 000	40 733 000	36 496 000	25 293 000	23 142 000	23 310 000	18 664 000	20 085 000
1969	202 677 000	17 376 000	40 884 000	35 236 000	24 681 000	23 383 000	23 047 000	18 390 000	19 680 000
1968	200 706 000	17 913 000	40 772 000	34 090 000	23 990 000	23 731 000	22 758 000	18 088 000	19 365 000
1967	198 712 000	18 563 000	40 496 000	33 196 000	23 156 000	24 038 000	22 440 000	17 752 000	19 071 000
1966	196 560 000	19 208 000	40 051 000	32 012 000	22 725 000	24 276 000	22 125 000	17 408 000	18 755 000
1965	194 303 000	19 824 000	39 426 000	30 773 000	22 465 000	24 447 000	21 839 000	17 077 000	18 541 000
1964	191 889 000	20 165 000	38 783 000	29 519 000	22 396 000	24 562 000	21 580 000	16 758 000	18 127 000
1963	189 242 000	20 342 000	38 124 000	28 223 000	22 410 000	24 584 000	21 346 000	16 436 000	17 778 000
1962	186 538 000	20 469 000	37 435 000	26 909 000	22 494 000	24 519 000	21 124 000	16 131 000	17 457 000
1961	183 691 000	20 522 000	37 031 000	25 242 000	22 692 000	24 392 000	20 875 000	15 847 000	17 089 000
1960	180 671 000	20 341 000	35.735 000	24 576 000	22 919 000	24 221 000	20 578 000	15 625 000	16 675 000
1959*	177 830 000	20 175 000	34 564 000	23 988 000	23 169 000	24 023 000	20 262 000	15 401 000	16 248 000
1959	177 073 000	20 055 000	34 390 000	23 890 000	23 062 000	23 917 000	20 189 000	15 357 000	16 213 000
1958	174 141 000	19 768 000	33 322 000	23 162 000	23 430 000	23 693 000	19 857 000	15 139 000	15 771 000
1957	171 274 000	19 379 000	32 515 000	22 311 000	23 737 000	23 496 000	19 513 000	14 973 000	15 353 000
1956	168 221 000	18 895 000	31 423 000	21 869 000	24 015 000	23 160 000	19 143 000	14 815 000	14 902 000
1955	165 275 000	18 467 000	30 248 000	21 667 000	24 175 000	22 818 000	18 824 000	14 586 000	14 489 000
1954	162 391 000	17 962 000	29 092 000	21 641 000	24 233 000	22 571 000	18 501 000	14 350 000	14 040 000
1953	159 565 000	17 548 000	27 880 000	21 658 000	24 233 000	22 359 000	18 171 000	14 135 000	13 582 000
1952	156 954 000	17 228 000	26 656 000	21 796 000	24 197 000	22 109 000	17 881 000	13 918 000	13 169 000
1951	154 287 000	17 252 000	25 055 000	22 018 000	24 085 000	21 833 000	17 623 000	13 654 000	12 768 000
1950	151 684 000	16 331 000	24 477 000	22 260 000	23 932 000	21 557 000	17 400 000	13 364 000	12 362 000
1949	149 188 000	15 607 000	23 770 000	22 570 000	23 729 000	21 187 000	17 260 000	13 145 000	11 921 000
1948	146 631 000	14 919 000	23 089 000	22 866 000	23 494 000	20 794 000	17 107 000	12 824 000	11 538 000
1947	144 126 000	14 406 000	22 257 000	23 122 000	23 236 000	20 421 000	16 970 000	12 528 000	11 185 000
1946	141 389 000	13 244 000	21 844 000	23 382 000	22 954 000	20 073 000	16 820 000	12 244 000	10 828 000
1945	139 928 000	12 979 000	21 599 000	23 705 000	22 734 000	19 787 000	16 642 000	11 988 000	10 494 000
1944	138 397 000	12 524 000	21 573 000	23 999 000	22 511 000	19 505 000	16 419 000	11 719 000	10 147 000
1943	136 739 000	12 016 000	21 699 000	24 065 000	22 194 000	19 226 000	16 199 000	11 472 000	9 867 000
1942	134 860 000	11 301 000	21 823 000	24 093 000	21 911 000	18 950 000	15 976 000	11 220 000	9 584 000
1941	133 402 000	10 850 000	22 089 000	24 074 000	21 691 000	18 692 000	15 759 000	10 959 000	9 288 000
1940	132 122 000	10 579 000	22 363 000	24 033 000	21 446 000	18 422 000	15 555 000	10 694 000	9 031 000
1939	130 880 000	10 148 000	22 701 000	23 819 000	21 176 000	18 178 000	15 336 000	10 487 000	8 764 000
1938	129 825 000	10 176 000	23 146 000	23 655 000	20 953 000	18 001 000	15 077 000	10 310 000	8 508 000
1937	128 825 000	10 009 000	23 564 000	23 487 000	20 723 000	17 866 000	14 785 000	10 132 000	8 258 000
1936	128 053 000	10 044 000	23 942 000	23 309 000	20 505 000	17 783 000	14 495 000	9 949 000	8 027 000
1935	127 250 000	10 170 000	24 213 000	23 130 000	20 275 000	17 712 000	14 208 000	9 739 000	7 804 000
1934	126 374 000	10 331 000	24 402 000	22 963 000	20 022 000	17 640 000	13 933 000	9 502 000	7 582 000
1933	125 579 000	10 612 000	24 531 000	22 820 000	19 750 000	17 569 000	13 684 000	9 249 000	7 363 000
1932	124 840 000	10 903 000	24 614 000	22 716 000	19 484 000	17 504 000	13 481 000	8 992 000	7 147 000
1931	124 040 000	11 179 000	24 629 000	22 617 000	19 242 000	17 412 000	13 296 000	8 735 000	6 928 000
1930	123 077 000	11 372 000	24 631 000	22 487 000	19 039 000	17 270 000	13 096 000	8 477 000	6 705 000
1929	121 767 000	11 734 000	24 470 000	22 151 000	18 941 000	16 921 000	12 761 000	8 315 000	6 474 000
1928	120 509 000	11 978 000	24 320 000	21 811 000	18 953 000	16 540 000	12 430 000	8 178 000	6 299 000
1927	119 035 000	12 111 000	24 152 000	21 430 000	18 948 000	16 172 000	12 092 000	8 003 000	6 127 000
1926	117 397 000	12 189 000	23 906 000	21 037 000	18 867 000	15 847 000	11 786 000	7 805 000	5 960 000
1925	115 829 000	12 316 000	23 614 000	20 691 000	18 720 000	15 576 000	11 521 000	7 605 000	5 786 000
1924	114 109 000	12 269 000	23 358 000	20 314 000	18 557 000	15 337 000	11 278 000	7 387 000	5 609 000

See footnotes at end of table.

Series A 29-37. Annual Estimates of the Population, by Age: 1900 to 1998—Cont'd.

(As of July 1. 1900–1939, resident population; 1940–1970, total population, including Armed Forces overseas.)

Year	Total	Under 5	Age group (in years)						
			5-14	15-24	25-34	35-44	45-54	55-64	65 and over
	29	**30**	**31**	**32**	**33**	**34**	**35**	**36**	**37**
1923	111 947 000	12 119 000	23 089 000	19 798 000	18 231 000	15 066 000	11 068 000	7 165 000	5 411 000
1922	110 049 000	12 031 000	22 788 000	19 402 000	17 924 000	14 823 000	10 899 000	6 951 000	5 231 000
1921	108 538 000	11 879 000	22 515 000	19 140 000	17 747 000	14 665 000	10 721 000	6 791 000	5 080 000
1920	106 461 000	11 631 000	22 158 000	18 821 000	17 416 000	14 382 000	10 505 000	6 619 000	4 929 000
1919	104 514 000	11 536 000	21 849 000	18 465 000	16 912 000	14 008 000	10 402 000	6 456 000	4 886 000
1918	103 208 000	11 606 000	21 732 000	18 071 000	16 445 000	13 879 000	10 293 000	6 356 000	4 826 000
1917	103 268 000	11 527 000	21 369 000	18 836 000	16 913 000	13 647 000	10 068 000	6 194 000	4 714 000
1916	101 961 000	11 442 000	21 008 000	18 872 000	16 776 000	13 388 000	9 846 000	6 026 000	4 603 000
1915	100 546 000	11 347 000	20 660 000	18 844 000	16 580 000	13 130 000	9 613 000	5 866 000	4 501 000
1914	99 111 000	11 244 000	20 816 000	18 796 000	16 370 000	12 875 000	9 398 000	5 711 000	4 401 000
1913	97 225 000	11 082 000	19 904 000	18 649 000	16 070 000	12 562 000	9 135 000	5 542 000	4 281 000
1912	95 335 000	10 915 000	19 503 000	18 477 000	15 772 000	12 252 000	8 875 000	5 372 000	4 169 000
1911	93 863 000	10 796 000	19 214 000	18 355 000	15 530 000	12 003 000	8 657 000	5 234 000	4 074 000
1910	92 407 000	10 671 000	18 950 000	18 212 000	15 274 000	11 759 000	8 454 000	5 101 000	3 986 000
1909	90 490 000	10 509 000	18 670 000	17 871 000	14 923 000	11 471 000	8 204 000	4 964 000	3 878 000
1908	88 710 000	10 364 000	18 440 000	17 526 000	14 585 000	11 202 000	7 974 000	4 840 000	3 779 000
1907	87 008 000	10 220 000	18 240 000	17 184 000	14 257 000	10 945 000	7 755 000	4 724 000	3 684 000
1906	85 450 000	10 092 000	18 067 000	16 864 000	13 952 000	10 705 000	7 554 000	4 621 000	3 595 000
1905	83 822 000	9 944 000	17 888 000	16 526 000	13 631 000	10 461 000	7 350 000	4 517 000	3 505 000
1904	82 166 000	9 791 000	17 697 000	16 178 000	13 315 000	10 211 000	7 150 000	4 410 000	3 414 000
1903	80 632 000	9 645 000	17 524 000	15 858 000	13 019 000	9 974 000	6 964 000	4 313 000	3 335 000
1902	79 163 000	9 502 000	17 360 000	15 555 000	12 737 000	9 745 000	6 788 000	4 220 000	3 256 000
1901	77 584 000	9 336 000	17 158 000	15 242 000	12 442 000	9 504 000	6 606 000	4 122 000	3 174 000
1900	76 094 000	9 181 000	16 966 000	14 951 000	12 161 000	9 273 000	6 437 000	4 026 000	3 099 000

* Denotes first year for which figures include Alaska and Hawaii.

Series A 91-104.   Resident Population, by Sex: 1790 to 2000

| Year | All races | | Year | All races | | Year | All races | |
| | Male | Female | | Male | Female | | Male | Female |
	91	**98**		**91**	**98**		**91**	**98**
2000	134 511 026	140 618 661	1982	112 579 409	119 085 049	1940	66 061 592	65 607 683
1999	133 276 559	139 414 254	1981	111 502 932	117 962 782	1930	62 137 080	60 637 966
1998	132 029 729	138 218 274						
1997	130 783 107	137 000 500	1980	110 398 730	116 825 951	1920	53 900 431	51 810 189
1996	129 504 353	135 724 219	1979	109 132 000	115 436 000	1910	47 332 277	44 639 989
			1978	107 963 000	114 132 000	1900	38 816 448	37 178 127
1995	128 293 712	134 509 564	1977	106 880 000	112 880 000	1890	32 237 101	30 710 613
1994	127 049 175	133 277 846	1976	105 859 000	111 704 000	1880	25 518 820	24 636 963
1993	125 787 805	131 994 803						
1992	124 423 544	130 606 155	1975	104 876 000	110 589 000	1870	19 493 565	19 064 806
1991	122 956 043	129 197 049	1974	103 890 000	109 451 000	1860	16 085 204	15 358 117
			1973	102 962 000	108 396 000	1850	11 837 660	11 354 216
1990	121 626 118	127 838 278	1972	101 984 000	107 300 000	1840	8 688 532	8 380 921
1989	120 277 515	126 541 715	1971	100 738 000	106 089 000	1830	6 532 489	6 333 531
1988	119 085 538	125 413 444						
1987	117 960 809	124 328 109	1970	99 291 000	104 692 000	1820	4 896 605	4 741 848
1986	116 865 159	123 267 728	1960 *	88 331 494	90 991 681	1810	(1)	(1)
			1960	87 864 510	90 599 726	1800	(1)	(1)
1985	115 729 534	122 194 261	1950	74 833 239	75 864 122	1790	(1)	(1)
1984	114 670 261	121 154 641						
1983	113 646 996	120 144 998						

* Denotes first year for which figures include Alaska and Hawaii.
1. Data by sex not available. See Series A 1-5 for total population.

Series A 143-151. Median Age of the Population, by Race and Sex: 1790 to 1998

Year	Total	All Races		Total	White		Total	Black	
		Male	Female		Male	Female		Male	Female
	143	144	145	146	147	148	149	150	151
1998	35.2	34.1	36.3	36.3	...	...	29.9	...	...
1997	34.9	33.8	36.1	36.0	...	...	29.7	...	...
1996	34.7	33.5	35.8	35.7	...	...	29.5	...	...
1995	34.3	33.2	35.5	35.4	...	...	29.2	...	...
1994	34.1	32.9	35.2	35.0	...	...	29.0	...	...
1993	33.7	32.6	34.9	34.7	...	...	28.7	...	...
1992	33.4	32.3	34.6	34.4	...	...	28.4	...	...
1991	33.1	31.9	34.3	34.1	...	...	28.2	...	...
1990	32.8	31.6	34.0	33.8	...	...	27.9	...	...
1989	32.6	31.6	33.8	33.6	32.5	34.7	27.7	26.3	29.1
1988	32.0	31.2	33.5	33.3	32.1	34.4	27.5	26.1	28.8
1987	31.7	30.9	33.3	33.0	31.9	34.2	27.2	25.8	28.5
1986	31.6	30.6	33.0	32.7	31.5	33.9	26.9	25.5	28.2
1985	31.5	30.3	32.7	32.4	31.2	33.6	26.6	25.2	27.8
1984	31.2	30.0	32.8	32.2	31.0	33.4	26.3	24.9	27.6
1983	30.9	29.6	32.2	31.8	30.5	33.1	25.8	24.4	27.2
1982	30.6	29.4	31.9	31.5	30.2	32.8	25.5	24.1	26.8
1981	30.3	29.1	31.6	31.2	29.9	32.5	25.2	23.9	26.5
1980	30.0	28.8	31.3	30.9	29.6	32.2	24.9	23.6	26.2
1979	29.8	38.9	31.3	30.9	29.7	32.2	24.6	23.5	25.9
1978	29.5	28.6	31.0	30.6	29.4	32.0	24.3	23.2	25.5
1977	29.2	28.2	30.6	30.3	29.0	31.6	24.1	22.9	25.2
1976	28.9	...	...	...	...	...	...	...	...
1975	28.8	27.6	30.3	29.6	28.4	31.0	23.4	22.2	24.6
1974	28.7	27.4	29.8	29.5	28.2	30.8	23.2	21.9	24.3
1973	28.4	...	...	...	...	...	...	...	...
1972	28.2	26.8	29.4	29.2	...	...	23.0	...	...
1971	28.0	...	...	...	...	...	...	...	...
1970	28.1	26.8	29.3	28.9	27.6	30.2	22.4	21.0	23.6
1960*	29.5	28.7	30.3	30.3	29.4	31.1	23.5	22.3	24.5
1960	29.6	28.7	30.4	30.3	29.5	31.2	23.5	22.3	24.5
1950	30.2	29.9	30.5	30.8	30.4	31.1	26.1	25.8	26.4
1940	29.0	29.1	29.0	29.5	29.5	29.5	25.3	25.3	25.3
1930	26.5	26.7	26.2	26.9	27.1	26.6	23.5	23.7	23.3
1920	25.3	25.8	24.7	25.6	26.1	25.1	22.3	22.8	22.0
1910	24.1	24.6	23.5	24.5	24.9	23.9	20.8	21.0	20.7
1900	22.9	23.3	22.4	23.4	23.8	22.9	19.5	19.5	19.5
1890	22.0	22.3	21.6	22.5	22.9	22.1	18.1	17.9	18.3
1880	20.9	21.2	20.7	21.4	21.6	21.1	...	...	...
1870	20.2	20.2	20.1	20.4	20.6	20.3	18.3	17.8	18.8
1860	19.4	19.8	19.1	19.7	20.1	19.3	17.5	17.5	17.5
1850	18.9	19.2	18.6	19.2	19.5	18.8	17.4	17.3	17.4
1840	17.8	17.9	17.8	17.9	18.0	17.8	17.6	17.5	17.6
1830	17.2	17.2	17.3	17.3	17.2	17.3	17.2	17.1	17.3
1820	16.7	16.6	16.8	16.6	16.5	16.6	17.2	17.1	17.4
1810	...	...	...	16.0	15.9	16.1	...	...	...
1800	...	...	...	16.0	15.7	16.3	...	...	...
1790	...	...	...	...	(1)	...	...	...	...

* Denotes first year for which figures include Alaska and Hawaii.
1. Median falls in the open-ended age group, 16 years and over, which includes 50.3 percent of the white male population.

Series A 160-171. Marital Status of the Population, by Age and Sex: 1890 to 1998
(Since 1940, marital status not reported is allocated on basis of other characteristics)

Year and age	Males, 18 years old and over						Females, 18 years old and over					
	Total	Never married	Married	Widowed	Divorced	Status not reported	Total	Never married	Married	Widowed	Divorced	Status not reported
	160	161	162	163	164	165	166	167	168	169	170	171
1998	95 000 000	25 500 000	58 600 000	2 600 000	8 300 000		102 400 000	21 000 000	59 300 000	11 000 000	11 100 000	
1996	92 700 000	24 900 000	57 600 000	2 500 000	7 800 000		100 400 000	20 000 000	58 800 000	11 100 000	10 500 000	
1995	92 000 000	24 600 000	57 700 000	2 300 000	7 400 000		99 600 000	19 300 000	58 900 000	11 100 000	10 300 000	
1994	91 200 000	24 700 000	57 000 000	2 200 000	7 200 000		98 800 000	19 500 000	58 100 000	11 100 000	10 100 000	
1992	88 700 000	23 200 000	56 200 000	2 500 000	6 800 000		96 600 000	18 600 000	57 100 000	11 300 000	9 600 000	
1991	87 800 000	22 900 000	55 900 000	2 400 000	6 600 000		95 800 000	18 500 000	56 800 000	11 300 000	9 200 000	
1990	86 900 000	22 400 000	55 800 000	2 300 000	6 300 000		95 000 000	17 900 000	56 700 000	11 500 000	8 800 000	
1989	85 800 000	22 200 000	55 300 000	2 300 000	6 000 000		94 000 000	17 800 000	56 200 000	11 500 000	8 500 000	
1988	84 800 000	21 500 000	55 200 000	2 300 000	6 700 000		92 900 000	17 400 000	56 100 000	11 200 000	8 200 000	
1987	83 700 000	21 100 000	54 900 000	2 100 000	5 600 000		91 900 000	17 100 000	55 600 000	11 100 000	8 000 000	
1986	82 800 000	20 900 000	54 300 000	2 200 000	5 500 000		90 900 000	16 600 000	54 900 000	11 300 000	8 100 000	
1985	81 500 000	20 500 000	53 500 000	2 100 000	5 300 000		89 900 000	16 400 000	54 400 000	11 400 000	7 800 000	
1984	80 500 000	20 500 000	53 000 000	2 100 000	4 900 000		88 900 000	16 400 000	54 100 000	11 100 000	7 400 000	
1983	79 300 000	19 900 000	52 900 000	1 900 000	4 600 000		87 700 000	16 000 000	53 800 000	10 900 000	7 000 000	
1982	78 100 000	19 100 000	52 500 000	1 900 000	4 600 000		85 600 000	15 300 000	53 600 000	10 800 000	6 900 000	
1981	76 900 000	18 400 000	52 100 000	1 900 000	4 400 000		85 200 000	14 800 000	53 200 000	10 800 000	6 400 000	
1980	75 700 000	18 000 000	51 800 000	2 000 000	3 900 000		83 800 000	14 300 000	52 800 000	10 800 000	6 000 000	
1979	72 700 000	17 000 000	50 300 000	1 900 000	3 500 000		80 600 000	13 600 000	51 200 000	10 400 000	5 400 000	
1978	71 500 000	16 100 000	50 100 000	1 900 000	3 400 000		79 300 000	13 000 000	50 900 000	10 100 000	5 300 000	
1977	70 300 000	15 400 000	49 900 000	1 900 000	3 200 000		77 900 000	12 200 000	50 900 000	10 000 000	4 900 000	
1976	69 100 000	14 700 000	49 800 000	1 800 000	2 800 000		76 700 000	11 500 000	50 800 000	10 000 000	4 400 000	
1975	67 900 000	14 100 000	49 400 000	1 800 000	2 500 000		75 300 000	11 000 000	50 300 000	10 100 000	4 000 000	
1974	66 500 000	13 300 000	49 000 000	1 800 000	2 300 000		74 000 000	10 500 000	50 000 000	9 800 000	3 600 000	
1973	65 200 000	12 700 000	48 600 000	1 900 000	1 900 000		72 800 000	10 100 000	49 500 000	9 800 000	3 200 000	
1972	64 200 000	12 500 000	48 000 000	1 800 000	1 700 000		71 500 000	9 800 000	49 000 000	9 600 000	3 000 000	
1971	63 700 000	12 600 000	47 200 000	1 900 000	1 800 000		70 700 000	9 900 000	48 100 000	9 700 000	2 800 000	

Year and age	Males, 14 years old and over						Females, 14 years old and over					
	Total	Never married	Married	Widowed	Divorced	Status not reported	Total	Never married	Married	Widowed	Divorced	Status not reported
	160	161	162	163	164	165	166	167	168	169	170	171
1970 Total 14 years and over	71 485 878	20 426 937	47 001 412	2 130 932	1 926 597		77 910 094	17 624 105	47 666 431	9 615 280	3 004 278	
14 years	2 136 818	2 111 778	20 768	2 451	1 821		2 049 056	2 019 680	22 010	5 421	1 945	
15-19 years	9 718 189	9 315 441	381 500	8 529	12 719		9 485 229	8 358 248	1 073 147	23 038	30 796	
15-17 years	6 071 485	5 986 895	74 740	5 057	4 793		5 825 133	5 553 582	250 529	12 382	8 640	
18 and 19 years	3 646 704	3 328 546	306 760	3 472	7 926		3 660 096	2 804 666	822 618	10 656	22 156	
20-24 years	7 761 209	4 207 592	3 329 772	12 878	110 967		8 354 509	3 030 876	5 054 321	56 508	212 804	
25-29 years	6 569 924	1 288 594	5 066 314	19 196	195 830		6 810 076	827 906	5 616 300	71 530	294 340	
30-34 years	5 607 593	601 868	4 803 203	19 574	182 948		5 868 858	435 897	5 055 678	86 494	290 789	
35-44 years	11 261 731	884 372	9 895 931	75 546	405 882		11 860 315	672 255	10 187 753	353 760	646 547	
45-54 years	11 138 181	711 099	9 813 513	186 144	427 425		11 996 408	662 506	9 728 095	942 796	663 011	
55-64 years	8 858 893	574 425	7 587 085	364 665	332 718		9 827 148	669 051	6 677 855	1 988 096	492 146	
65 years and over	8 433 330	631 768	6 103 326	1 441 949	256 287		11 658 495	947 686	4 251 272	6 087 637	371 900	
1960 *Total 14 years and over	61 315 358	15 313 822	42 630 422	2 071 910	1 299 204		64 961 189	12 320 199	42 905 285	7 880 607	1 855 098	
14 years	1 402 724	1 394 426	7 756	163	379		1 345 136	1 330 089	14 250	391	406	
15-19 years	6 698 837	6 437 186	254 377	1 784	5 490		6 588 597	5 528 745	1 033 804	4 751	21 297	
15-17 years	4 341 635	4 290 310	48 850	897	1 578		4 174 262	3 886 610	277 151	1 874	5 627	
18 and 19 years	2 357 202	2 146 876	205 527	887	3 912		2 417 335	1 642 135	756 653	2 877	15 670	
20-24 years	5 283 228	2 807 784	2 417 552	4 780	53 112		5 519 937	1 567 622	3 833 956	17 252	101 107	
25-29 years	5 333 282	1 111 768	4 117 072	9 548	94 894		5 537 104	582 114	4 772 006	37 047	145 937	
30-34 years	5 840 287	694 924	5 000 763	17 246	127 354		6 111 422	422 915	5 423 228	74 109	191 170	
35-44 years	11 739 191	948 784	10 410 091	76 436	303 880		12 336 341	748 766	10 741 606	374 216	471 753	
45-54 years	10 139 671	749 390	8 896 768	182 260	311 253		10 485 709	738 266	8 379 825	921 258	446 360	
55-64 years	7 569 153	605 187	6 351 408	380 508	232 050		8 138 691	648 264	5 375 362	1 819 043	296 022	
65 years and over	7 308 985	564 373	5 174 635	1 399 185	170 792		8 898 252	753 418	3 331 248	4 632 540	181 046	
1950 Total 14 years and over	54 601 105	14 399 840	36 866 055	2 263 850	1 071 360		57 102 295	11 418 335	37 576 800	6 734 275	1 372 885	
14 years	1 090 929	1 080 370	6 660	1 670	1 320		1 047 370	1 039 610	6 980	565	215	
15-19 years	5 323 470	5 146 610	166 955	4 995	4 910		5 321 755	4 412 565	887 615	5 260	16 315	

See footnotes at end of table.

Series A 160-171.   Marital Status of the Population, by Age and Sex: 1890 to 1998—Cont'd.

(Since 1940, marital status not reported is allocated on basis of other characteristics)

Year and age	Males, 14 years old and over Total	Never married	Married	Widowed	Divorced	Status not reported	Females, 14 years old and over Total	Never married	Married	Widowed	Divorced	Status not reported
	160	161	162	163	164	165	166	167	168	169	170	171
15-17 years..............	3 187 510	3 151 360	30 410	3 460	2 280		3 116 230	2 893 350	217 325	2 055	3 500	
18 and 19 years..........	2 135 960	1 995 250	136 545	1 535	2 630		2 205 525	1 519 215	670 290	3 205	12 815	
20-24 years.................	5 559 265	3 281 540	2 217 810	9 060	50 855		5 878 040	1 898 910	3 856 760	25 280	97 090	
25-29 years.................	5 904 975	1 404 860	4 381 375	15 485	103 255		6 277 480	833 040	5 227 960	57 490	158 990	
30-34 years.................	5 562 315	734 195	4 690 995	20 945	116 180		5 896 625	546 245	5 082 260	91 945	176 175	
35-44 years.................	10 402 195	996 570	9 046 675	94 865	264 085		10 837 650	900 480	9 140 055	409 250	387 865	
45-54 years.................	8 484 515	725 355	7 267 615	240 755	250 790		8 687 605	680 150	6 737 675	967 595	302 185	
55-64 years.................	6 540 100	551 185	5 320 670	495 140	173 105		6 633 170	525 405	4 310 160	1 636 660	160 945	
65 years and over........	5 734 250	479 155	3 767 300	1 380 935	106 860		6 522 600	581 930	2 327 335	3 540 230	73 105	
1940 Total												
14 years and over	50 553 748	17 593 379	30 192 334	2 143 612	624 423		50 549 176	13 935 866	30 090 488	5 700 202	822 620	
14 years	1 218 116	1 216 784	1 247	60	25		1 187 614	1 184 094	3 353	110	57	
15-19 years.................	6 180 153	6 073 165	104 935	1 031	1 022		6 153 370	5 425 023	713 940	6 423	8 984	
15-17 years.................	3 684 780	3 670 287	14 002	311	180		3 629 909	3 461 246	165 131	1 729	1 803	
18 and 19 years..........	2 495 373	2 402 878	90 933	720	842		2 523 461	1 962 777	548 809	4 694	7 181	
20-24 years.................	5 692 392	4 109 304	1 557 104	8 394	17 590		5 895 443	2 781 001	3 025 923	32 751	55 768	
25-29 years.................	5 450 662	1 964 118	3 417 046	20 973	48 525		5 645 976	1 288 092	4 185 325	71 878	100 681	
30-34 years.................	5 070 312	1 050 199	3 912 820	36 714	70 579		5 172 076	761 698	4 155 872	128 256	126 250	
35-44 years.................	9 164 794	1 283 994	7 551 974	155 405	173 421		9 168 426	950 876	7 430 791	537 584	249 175	
45-54 years.................	7 962 019	885 004	6 590 954	328 130	157 931		7 550 052	654 312	5 736 614	991 448	167 678	
55-64 years.................	5 409 180	577 170	4 245 427	488 620	97 963		5 163 025	462 407	3 254 768	1 365 044	80 806	
65 years and over........	4 406 120	433 641	2 810 827	1 104 285	57 367		4 613 194	429 363	1 583 902	2 566 708	33 221	
1930 Total												
14 years and over	45 035 691	16 143 512	26 311 682	2 022 588	488 688	69 221	43 970 842	12 465 795	26 159 771	4 728 565	572 574	44 137
14 years	1 206 486	1 205 662	761	42	21	X	1 175 899	1 171 393	4 241	167	98	X
15-19 years.................	5 757 825	5 645 359	100 362	1 513	1 348	9 243	5 794 290	5 032 174	731 967	12 337	12 371	5 441
15-17 years.................	3 493 718	3 482 706	10 553	281	178	X	3 465 118	3 279 560	179 404	3 284	2 870	X
18 and 19 years..........	2 264 107	2 162 653	89 809	1 232	1 170	9 243	2 329 172	1 752 614	552 563	9 053	9 501	5 441
20-24 years.................	5 336 815	3 779 443	1 500 493	17 657	221 990	17 322	5 533 563	2 547 057	2 857 665	56 375	62 464	10 002
25-29 years.................	4 860 180	1 785 413	2 977 004	39 013	50 229	8 521	4 973 428	1 079 923	3 697 645	102 041	89 124	4 695
30-34 years.................	4 561 786	965 945	3 468 176	59 493	62 669	5 503	4 558 635	603 048	3 715 648	148 571	88 219	3 149
35-44 years.................	8 816 319	1 261 705	7 189 452	218 881	137 180	9 101	8 382 521	839 130	6 832 581	547 562	157 650	5 598
45-54 years.................	6 803 569	776 863	5 551 146	357 047	111 471	7 042	6 214 514	564 466	4 673 539	872 676	98 874	4 959
55-64 years.................	4 367 500	442 505	3 407 751	445 262	66 499	5 483	4 029 398	360 188	2 499 285	1 119 802	45 881	4 242
65 years and over........	3 325 211	280 617	2 116 537	883 680	37 371	7 006	3 308 594	268 416	1 147 200	1 869 034	17 893	6 051
1920 Total												
14 years and over	37 861 085	13 969 763	21 823 326	1 754 302	234 519	79 175	36 134 659	10 608 384	21 301 014	3 909 736	272 736	42 789
14 years	1 033 297	1 029 971	3 173	118	35	X	1 012 968	1 007 088	5 554	269	57	X
15-19 years.................	4 673 792	4 567 770	96 374	1 830	759	7 059	4 756 764	4 137 650	596 542	12 239	6 017	4 316
15-17 years.................	2 828 546	2 815 533	12 521	384	108	X	2 861 030	2 711 081	145 390	3 091	1 468	X
18 and 19 years..........	1 845 246	1 752 237	83 853	1 446	651	7 059	1 895 734	1 426 569	451 152	9 148	4 549	4 316
20-24 years.................	4 527 045	3 200 623	1 280 318	20 511	10 280	15 313	4 749 976	2 164 051	2 483 697	65 414	28 582	8 232
25-29 years.................	4 538 233	1 789 721	2 662 124	51 470	22 856	12 062	4 548 258	1 048 285	3 336 501	117 389	41 243	4 842
30-34 years.................	4 130 783	995 869	3 023 357	74 454	28 080	9 023	3 940 410	588 119	3 155 854	152 893	40 188	3 356
35-44 years.................	7 359 904	1 188 586	5 873 308	220 700	63 592	13 718	6 730 934	767 882	5 426 434	485 493	75 027	6 098
45-54 years.................	5 653 095	677 420	4 580 056	329 976	56 162	9 481	4 845 398	464 838	3 587 794	739 058	48 562	5 146
55-64 years.................	3 461 865	337 592	2 697 429	386 587	34 249	6 008	3 069 807	257 029	1 878 478	906 362	23 451	4 487
65 years and over........	2 483 071	182 211	1 607 187	668 656	18 506	6 511	2 450 144	173 442	830 160	1 430 621	9 609	6 312
1910 Total												
14 years and over	33 247 336	13 455 690	18 066 188	1 466 839	155 604	103 015	30 904 861	9 826 911	17 667 119	3 167 432	184 621	58 778
14 years	935 974	934 980	898	82	14	X	912 148	908 435	3 482	198	33	X
15-19 years.................	4 527 282	4 448 067	51 877	1 110	347	25 881	4 536 321	3 985 764	513 239	10 261	3 650	23 407
15-17 years.................	2 688 370	2 667 874	4 990	252	70	15 184	2 683 806	2 543 264	121 803	2 697	867	15 175
18 and 19 years..........	1 838 912	1 780 193	46 887	858	277	10 697	1 852 515	1 442 500	391 436	7 564	2 783	8 232
20-24 years.................	4 580 290	3 432 161	1 100 093	18 815	6 732	22 489	4 476 694	2 163 683	2 225 362	55 354	20 370	11 925
25-29 years.................	4 244 348	1 816 137	2 353 525	45 092	15 503	14 091	3 935 655	981 556	2 823 935	95 385	29 153	5 626
30-34 years.................	3 656 768	951 820	2 611 244	65 339	19 068	9 297	3 315 417	535 170	2 619 959	128 942	28 109	3 237

Series A 160-171. Marital Status of the Population, by Age and Sex: 1890 to 1998—Cont'd.

(Since 1940, marital status not reported is allocated on basis of other characteristics)

Year and age	Males, 14 years old and over						Females, 14 years old and over					
	Total	Never married	Married	Widowed	Divorced	Status not reported	Total	Never married	Married	Widowed	Divorced	Status not reported
	160	161	162	163	164	165	166	167	168	169	170	171
35-44 years	6 153 366	1 026 502	4 873 153	198 701	42 688	12 322	5 504 321	628 516	4 410 310	411 896	49 269	4 330
45-54 years	4 488 929	499 751	3 658 931	286 222	36 502	7 523	3 881 059	331 573	2 904 043	610 386	31 934	3 123
55-64 years	2 674 403	222 950	2 112 699	312 420	21 675	4 659	2 379 698	167 991	1 479 454	714 452	15 200	2 601
65 years and over........	1 985 976	123 322	1 303 768	539 058	13 075	6.753	1 963 548	124 223	687 335	1 140 558	6 903	4 529
1900 Total 14 years and over	26 286 316	11 053 813	13 920 057	1 173 509	83 828	55 109	24 951 254	8 319 285	13 784 538	2 706 332	114 476	26 923
14 years	793 340	792 267	667	33	7	366	775 224	770 742	3 783	126	30	543
15-19 years	3 750 451	3 706 382	37 781	871	194	5 223	3 805 638	3 374 814	415 682	9 336	2 418	3 388
20-24 years	3 624 580	2 812 113	782 907	14 332	3 322	11 906	3 710 436	1 913 552	1 726 296	52 545	13 124	4 919
25-29 years	3 323 543	1 520 782	1 746 620	38 781	8 218	9 142	3 205 898	882 875	2 209 357	91 847	18 461	3 358
30-34 years	2 901 321	800 664	2 025 729	58 312	10 307	6 309	2 654 718	441 409	2 071 698	121 944	17 384	2 283
35-44 years	4 872 781	826 201	3 840 575	174 535	22 630	8 840	4 339 166	481 668	3 451 375	372 677	29 953	3 493
45-54 years	3 402 458	349 429	2 797 354	230 656	19 498	5 521	2 994 983	234 413	2 212 223	526 456	19 111	2 780
55-64 years	2 062 424	156 823	1 644 373	245 424	12 297	3 507	1 940 111	128 954	1 172 904	626 271	9 566	2 416
65 years and over........	1 555 418	89 152	1 044 051	410 565	7 355	4 295	1 525 080	90 858	521 220	905 130	4 129	3 743
1890 Total 14 years and over	21 397 501	9 331 617	11 176 124	811 110	48 708	29 942	20 239 343	6 906 714	11 101 645	2 144 496	71 584	14 904
14 years	723 158	723 015	23	X	1	119	695 801	694 281	1 411	17	12	80
15-19 years	3 248 711	3 230 935	16 746	137	28	965	3 308 852	2 987 949	313 983	4 845	1 101	974
20-24 years	3 104 893	2 505 460	585 748	7 610	1 468	4 607	3 091 783	1 601 266	1 444 712	36 456	6 931	2 418
25-29 years	2 698 311	1 240 797	1 421 407	26 601	4 340	5 166	2 529 466	641 988	1 805 064	69 965	10 588	1 861
30-34 years	2 425 664	642 827	1 728 930	43 777	5 832	4 298	2 152 966	326 306	1 717 204	96 797	11 161	1 498
35-44 years	3 705 648	568 511	2 997 030	120 796	12 837	6 474	3 346 031	330 139	2 698 266	296 302	18 899	2 425
45-54 years	2 627 024	239 928	2 213 901	157 920	11 393	3 882	2 430 878	171 454	1 796 979	447 370	13 080	1 995
55-64 years	1 630 373	111 144	1 342 414	166 686	7 835	2 294	1 499 997	86 573	905 627	499 420	6 721	1 656
65 years and over........	1 233 719	69 100	869 925	287 583	4 974	2 137	1 183 569	66 758	418 399	693 324	3 091	1 997

* Denotes first year for which figures include Alaska and Hawaii.
X Represents zero.

Series A 172-194. Population of Regions, by Race and Residence: 1790 to 1996
(In thousands)

Region and Year	Total population	Race			Residence	
		White	Black	Other	Urban	Rural
	172	175	176	177	178	179
Northeast						
1996	51 600	...	...	...	...	...
1995	51 500	...	...	...	...	...
1994	51 400	...	...	...	...	...
1993	51 277	...	...	...	...	...
1992	51 100	...	...	...	...	...
1991	50 964					
1990	50 809	42 069	5 613	5 214	40 092	10 717
1980	49 137	42 328	4 849	1 950	38 904	10 232
1970	49 041	44 311	4 344	386	39 450	9 591
1960	44 678	41 522	3 028	127	35 840	8 838
1950	39 478	37 399	2 018	61	31 373	8 105
1940	35 977	34 567	1 370	40	27 568	8 409
1930	34 427	33 237	1 147	43	26 707	7 720
1920	29 662	28 958	679	25	22 404	7 258
1910	25 869	25 361	484	23	18 563	7 305
1900	21 047	20 638	385	24	13 911	7 136
1890	17 407	17 122	270	15	10 266	7 141
1880	14 507	14 274	229	4	7 370	7 137
1870	12 299	12 117	180	2	5 448	6 851
1860	10 594	10 438	156	(Z)	3 787	6 807
1850	8 627	8 447	150	X	2 289	6 338
1840	6 761	6 619	142	X	1 253	5 508
1830	5 542	5 417	125	X	785	4 758
1820	4 360	4 246	114	X	480	3 880
1810	3 487	3 384	102	X	380	3 107
1800	2 636	2 553	83	X	245	2 391
1790	1 968	1 901	67	X	160	1 809
Midwest						
1996	62 100	...	...	...	...	...
1995	61 700	...	...	...	...	...
1994	61 400	...	...	...	...	...
1993	61 038	...	...	...	...	...
1992	60 628	...	...	...	...	...
1991	60 178					
1990	59 669	52 018	5 716	2 833	42 774	16 894
1980	58 666	52 195	5 337	1 334	41 466	17 388
1970	56 572	51 641	4 572	359	40 481	16 091
1960	51 619	48 003	3 446	170	35 481	16 138
1950	44 461	42 119	2 228	114	28 491	15 970
1940	40 143	38 640	1 420	83	23 437	16 706
1930	38 594	37 151	1 262	181	22 351	16 243
1920	34 020	33 164	793	62	17 776	16 244
1910	29 889	29 279	543	66	13 487	16 401
1900	26 333	25 776	496	61	10 165	16 168
1890	22 410	21 914	431	65	7 418	14 992
1880	17 364	16 961	386	17	4 198	13 166
1870	12 981	12 699	273	10	2 702	10 279
1860	9 097	8 900	184	13	1 263	7 833
1850	5 404	5 268	136	X	499	4 904
1840	3 352	3 262	89	X	129	3 222
1830	1 610	1 569	42	X	42	1 569
1820	859	841	18	X	10	850
1810	292	286	7	X	3	290
1800	51	50	1	X	X	51
South						
1996	93 100	...	...	...	...	...

See footnote at end of chart.

18

Series A 172-194. Population of Regions, by Race and Residence: 1790 to 1996—Cont'd.

(In thousands)

Region and Year	Total population	Race			Residence	
		White	Black	Other	Urban	Rural
	172	175	176	177	178	179
1995	92 000	...	...	...	...	...
1994	90 700	...	...	...	...	...
1993	89 417	...	...	...	...	...
1992	88 153	...	...	...	...	...
1991	86 911					
1990	85 446	65 582	15 829	8 452	58 656	26 790
1980	73 572	58 949	14 048	2 364	50 414	24 958
1970	62 795	50 420	11 970	405	40 540	22 255
1960	54 973	43 477	11 312	185	32 160	22 813
1950	47 197	36 850	10 225	122	22 956	24 241
1940	41 666	31 659	9 905	103	15 290	26 375
1930	37 858	27 674	9 362	882	12 904	24 953
1920	33 126	24 132	8 912	81	9 300	23 826
1910	29 389	20 547	8 749	92	6 623	22 767
1900	24 524	16 522	7 923	79	4 421	20 103
1890	20 028	13 193	6 761	74	3 261	16 767
1880	16 517	10 555	5 954	7	2 017	14 500
1870	12 288	7 863	4 421	4	1 497	10 791
1860	11 133	7 034	4 097	2	1 067	10 067
1850	8 983	5 630	3 352	X	744	8 239
1840	6 951	4 309	2 642	X	463	6 488
1830	5 708	3 546	2 162	X	301	5 407
1820	4 419	2 776	1 644	X	204	4 216
1810	3 461	2 191	1 268	X	143	3 318
1800	2 622	1 704	918	X	78	2 544
1790	1 961	1 271	690	X	42	1 919
West						
1996	58 500	...	...	...	...	...
1995	57 700	...	...	...	...	...
1994	56 900	...	...	...	...	...
1993	56 051	...	...	...	...	...
1992	55 146	...	...	...	...	...
1991	54 078					
1990	52 786	40 017	2 828	15 087	45 531	7 255
1980	43 172	34 890	2 262	6 020	36 211	6 961
1970	34 804	31 377	1 695	1 732	28 854	5 950
1960	28 053	25 830	1 086	1 137	21 787	6 266
1950	20 190	18 574	571	416	14 027	6 163
1940	14 379	13 350	171	363	8 409	5 969
1930	12 324	10 802	120	974	7 199	5 125
1920	9 214	8 567	79	258	4 773	4 440
1910	7 082	6 544	51	231	3 391	3 691
1900	4 309	3 873	30	188	1 718	2 591
1890	3 134	2 872	27	203	1 161	1 974
1880	1 801	1 612	12	144	544	1 257
1870	991	910	6	74	256	735
1860	619	551	4	64	99	520
1850	179	178	1	X	11	167

Z represents less than .5.
X represents 0.

Series A 195-209. Population of States, by Race: 1790 to 1998

(In thousands, except series A 196)

State and year	Total	Per square mile of land area	White	Black
	195	196	199	200
Alabama				
1998	4 352	85.8	3 177	1 132
1990	4 041	79.6	2 976	1 021
1980	3 894	76.7	2 873	996
1970	3 444	67.9	2 534	903
1960	3 267	64.2	2 284	980
1950	3 062	59.9	2 080	980
1940	2 833	55.5	1 849	983
1930	2 646	51.8	1 701	945
1920	2 348	45.8	1 447	901
1910	2 138	41.7	1 229	908
1900	1 829	35.7	1 001	827
1890	1 513	29.5	834	678
1880	1 263	24.6	662	600
1870	997	19.4	521	476
1860	964	18.8	526	438
1850	772	15.0	427	345
1840	591	11.5	335	256
1830	310	6.0	190	119
1820	128	2.5	85	42
1810 [1]	9	...	...	...
1800 [1]	1	...	...	...
Alaska				
1998	614	1.1	463	24
1990	550	1.0	415	22
1980	402	.7	310	14
1970	303	.5	237	9
1960	226	.4	179	7
1950	129	.2	93	X
1940 [2]	73	.1	39	(Z)
1930 [3]	59	.1	29	(Z)
1920	55	.1	28	(Z)
1910	64	.1	36	(Z)
1900	64	.1	30	(Z)
1890	32	...	4	...
1880	33	...	(Z)	...
Arizona				
1998	4 669	41.1	4 145	169
1990	3 665	32.3	2 963	111
1980	2 717	23.9	2 241	75
1970	1 775	15.6	1 605	53
1960	1 302	11.5	1 170	43
1950	750	6.6	655	26
1940	499	4.4	427	15
1930	436	3.8	379	11
1920	334	2.9	291	8
1910	204	1.8	171	2
1900	123	1.1	93	2
1890	88	.8	56	1
1880	40	.4	35	(Z)
1870	10	.1	10	(Z)
Arkansas				
1998	2 538	48.7	2 098	408
1990	2 351	45.1	1 945	374
1980	2 286	43.9	1 890	374
1970	1 923	37.0	1 566	352
1960	1 786	34.2	1 396	389
1950	1 910	36.3	1 482	427
1940	1 949	37.0	1 466	483
1930	1 854	35.2	1 375	478
1920	1 752	33.4	1 280	472
1910	1 574	30.0	1 131	443
1900	1 312	25.0	945	367
1890	1 128	21.5	819	309
1880	803	15.3	592	211
1870	484	9.2	362	122
1860	435	8.3	324	111
1850	210	4.0	162	48
1840	98	1.9	77	20
1830	30	0.6	26	5
1820	14	0.1	13	2
1810	1	...	...	...
California				
1998	32 667	209.4	25 965	2 456
1990	29 760	190.8	20 524	2 209
1980	23 668	151.7	18 031	1 819
1970	19 971	127.6	17 761	1 400
1960	15 717	100.4	14 455	884
1950	10 586	67.5	9 915	462
1940	6 907	44.1	6 597	124
1930	5 677	36.2	5 408	81
1920	3 427	22.0	3 265	39
1910	2 378	15.3	2 260	22
1900	1 485	9.5	1 403	11
1890	1 213	7.8	1 112	11
1880	865	5.5	767	6
1870	560	3.6	499	4
1860	380	2.4	323	4
1850	93	0.6	92	1
Colorado				
1998	3 971	38.3	3 666	172
1990	3 294	31.8	2 905	133
1980	2 890	27.9	2 571	102
1970	2 210	21.3	2 112	66
1960	1 754	16.9	1 701	40
1950	1 325	12.8	1 297	20
1940	1 123	10.8	1 107	12
1930	1 036	10	1 019	12
1920	940	9.1	924	11
1910	799	7.7	783	11
1900	540	5.2	529	9
1890	413	4.0	405	6
1880	194	1.9	191	2
1870	40	.4	39	(Z)
1860	34	.3	34	(Z)
Connecticut				
1998	3 274	675.7	2 882	304
1990	3 287	678.4	2 859	274
1980	3 108	641.3	2 799	217
1970	3 032	623.6	2 835	181
1960	2 535	520.6	2 424	107

See footnotes at end of table.

Series A 195-209. Population of States, by Race: 1790 to 1998—Cont'd.

(In thousands, except series A 196)

State and year	Total	Per square mile of land area	White	Black
	195	**196**	**199**	**200**
1950	2 007	409.7	1 952	53
1940	1 709	348.9	1 675	33
1930	1 607	328.0	1 577	29
1920	1 381	286.4	1 359	21
1910	1 115	231.3	1 099	15
1900	908	188.5	892	15
1890	746	154.8	733	12
1880	623	129.2	611	12
1870	537	111.5	528	10
1860	460	95.5	452	9
1850	371	76.9	363	8
1840	310	64.3	302	8
1830	298	61.8	290	8
1820	275	57.1	267	8
1810	262	54.3	255	7
1800	251	52.1	245	6
1790	238	49.4	233	6
Delaware				
1998	744	380.6	582	144
1990	666	340.8	535	112
1980	594	304.1	488	96
1970	548	276.5	466	78
1960	446	225.2	384	61
1950	318	160.8	274	44
1940	267	134.7	231	36
1930	238	120.5	206	33
1920	223	113.5	193	30
1910	202	103.0	171	31
1900	185	94.0	154	31
1890	168	85.7	140	28
1880	147	74.6	120	26
1870	125	63.6	102	23
1860	112	57.1	91	22
1850	92	46.6	71	20
1840	78	39.7	59	20
1830	77	39.1	58	19
1820	73	37.0	55	17
1810	73	37.0	55	17
1800	64	32.7	50	14
1790	59	30.1	46	13
Dist. of Columbia				
1998	523	8 519.9	180	326
1990	607	9 882.8	180	400
1980	638	10 394.6	172	449
1970	757	12 401.8	209	538
1960	764	12 523.9	345	412
1950	802	13 150.5	518	281
1940	663	10 870.3	474	187
1930	487	7 981.5	354	132
1920	483	7 292.9	327	110
1910	331	5 517.8	236	94
1900	279	4 645.3	192	87
1890	230	3 972.3	155	76
1880	178	3 062.5	118	60
1870	132	2 270.7	88	43
1860	75	1 294.5	61	14
1850	52	891.2	38	14
1840	34	485.7	24	10
1830	30	442.6	21	9
1820	23	367.1	16	7
1810	15	266.9	10	5
1800	8	156.6	6	2
Florida				
1998	14 916	276.2	12 319	2 268
1990	12 938	239.6	10 749	1 760
1980	9 747	180.5	8 185	1 343
1970	6 791	125.5	5 719	1 042
1960	4 952	91.5	4 064	880
1950	2 771	51.1	2 166	603
1940	1 897	35	1 382	514
1930	1 468	27.1	1 035	432
1920	968	17.7	638	329
1910	753	13.7	444	309
1900	529	9.6	297	231
1890	391	7.1	225	166
1880	269	4.9	143	127
1870	188	3.4	96	92
1860	140	2.6	78	63
1850	87	1.6	47	40
1840	54	1	28	27
1830	35	0.6	18	16
Georgia				
1998	7 642	131.9	5 293	2 181
1990	6 478	111.9	4 600	1 747
1980	5 463	94.3	3 947	1 465
1970	4 588	79	3 391	1 187
1960	3 943	67.8	2 817	1 123
1950	3 445	58.9	2 381	1 063
1940	3 124	53.4	2 038	1 085
1930	2 909	49.7	1 837	1 071
1920	2 896	49.3	1 689	1 206
1910	2 609	44.4	1 432	1 177
1900	2 216	37.7	1 181	1 035
1890	1 837	31.3	978	859
1880	1 542	26.3	817	725
1870	1 184	20.2	639	545
1860	1 057	18.0	592	466
1850	906	15.4	522	285
1840	691	11.8	408	284
1830	517	8.8	297	220
1820	341	5.8	190	151
1810	252	4.3	145	107
1800	163	1.5	102	60
1790	83	.6	53	30
Hawaii				
1998	1 193	185.7	395	35
1990	1 108	172.5	370	27
1980	965	150.2	319	17
1970	770	119.6	298	8
1960	633	98.5	202	5
1950	500	78.0	115	3

See footnotes at end of table.

Series A 195-209. Population of States, by Race: 1790 to 1998—Cont'd.

(In thousands, except series A 196)

State and year	Resident population		Race		State and year	Resident population		Race	
	Total	Per square mile of land area	White	Black		Total	Per square mile of land area	White	Black
	195	**196**	**199**	**200**		**195**	**196**	**199**	**200**
1940	423	66.0	104	(Z)	1850	988	27.5	977	11
1930	368	57.5	80	1	1840	686	19.1	679	7
1920	256	39.9	55	(Z)	1830	343	9.6	338	4
1910	192	30.0	44	1	1820	147	4.1	146	1
1900	154	24.0	29	(Z)	1810	25	0.6	24	1
Idaho					1800	6	(4)	5	(Z)
1998	1 229	14.8	1 191	7					
1990	1 007	12.2	950	3	**Iowa**				
1980	944	11.4	902	3	1998	2 862	51.2	2 761	57
1970	713	8.6	699	2	1990	2 777	49.7	2 683	48
1960	667	8.1	657	2	1980	2 914	52.1	2 839	42
					1970	2 825	50.5	2 783	33
1950	589	7.1	581	1	1960	2 758	49.2	2 729	25
1940	525	6.3	519	1					
1930	445	5.4	439	1	1950	2 621	46.8	2 600	20
1920	432	5.2	426	1	1940	2 538	45.3	2 521	17
1910	326	3.9	319	1	1930	2 471	44.1	2 453	17
					1920	2 404	43.2	2 384	19
1900	162	1.9	154	(Z)	1910	2 225	40	2 209	15
1890	89	1.1	82	(Z)					
1880	33	.4	29	(Z)	1900	2 232	40.2	2 219	13
1870	15	.2	11	(Z)	1890	1 912	34.4	1 901	11
					1880	1 625	29.2	1 615	10
Illinois					1870	1 194	21.5	1 188	6
1998	12 045	216.7	9 775	1 840	1860	675	12.1	674	1
1990	11 431	205.6	8 953	1 694					
1980	11 427	205.5	9 233	1 675	1850	192	3.5	192	(Z)
1970	11 110	199.4	9 600	1 426	1840	43	0.2	43	(Z)
1960	10 081	180.4	9 010	1 037	**Kansas**				
1950	8 712	155.8	8 046	646	1998	2 629	32.1	2 405	155
1940	7 897	141.2	7 504	387	1990	2 478	30.3	2 232	143
1930	7 631	136.4	7 295	329	1980	2 364	28.9	2 168	126
1920	6 485	115.7	6 299	182	1970	2 249	27.5	2 122	107
1910	5 639	100.6	5 527	109	1960	2 179	26.6	2 079	91
1900	4 822	86.1	4 735	85	1950	1 905	23.2	1 829	73
1890	3 826	68.3	3 768	57	1940	1 801	21.9	1 734	65
1880	3 078	55.0	3 031	46	1930	1 881	22.9	1 812	66
1870	2 540	45.4	2 511	29	1920	1 769	21.6	1 709	58
1860	1 712	30.6	1 704	8	1910	1 691	20.7	1 634	54
1850	851	15.2	846	5	1900	1 470	18.0	1 416	52
1840	476	8.5	472	4	1890	1 428	17.5	1 377	50
1830	157	2.8	155	2	1880	996	12.2	952	43
1820	55	1	54	1	1870	364	4.5	346	17
1810	12	0.1	12	1	1860	107	1.3	106	1
Indiana					**Kentucky**				
1998	5 899	164.5	5 338	491	1998	3 936	99.1	3 619	285
1990	5 544	154.6	5 021	432	1990	3 685	92.8	3 392	263
1980	5 490	153.1	5 004	415	1980	3 660	92.1	3 379	259
1970	5 195	143.9	4 820	357	1970	3 221	81.2	2 982	231
1960	4 662	128.8	4 389	269	1960	3 038	76.2	2 820	216
1950	3 934	108.7	3 759	174	1950	2 945	73.9	2 742	202
1940	3 428	94.7	3 305	122	1940	2 846	70.9	2 631	214
1930	3 239	89.4	3 126	112	1930	2 615	65.2	2 388	226
1920	2 930	81.3	2 849	81	1920	2 417	60.2	2 181	236
1910	2 701	74.9	2 640	60	1910	2 290	57.0	2 028	262
1900	2 516	70.1	2 459	58	1900	2 147	53.4	1 862	285
1890	2 192	61.1	2 147	45	1890	1 859	46.3	1 590	268
1880	1 978	55.1	1 939	39	1880	1 649	41.0	1 377	271
1870	1 681	46.8	1 656	25	1870	1 321	32.9	1 099	222
1860	1 350	37.6	1 339	11	1860	1 156	28.8	919	236

See footnotes at end of table.

Series A 195-209. Population of States, by Race: 1790 to 1998—Cont'd.

(In thousands, except series A 196)

State and year	Resident population		Race		State and year	Resident population		Race	
	Total	Per square mile of land area	White	Black		Total	Per square mile of land area	White	Black
	195	**196**	**199**	**200**		**195**	**196**	**199**	**200**
1850	982	24.4	761	221	1960	3 101	313.5	2 574	518
1840	780	19.4	590	190	1950	2 343	237.1	1 955	386
1830	688	17.1	519	170	1940	1 821	184.2	1 518	302
1820	564	14.0	435	129	1930	1 632	165	1 354	276
1810	407	10.1	324	82	1920	1 450	145.8	1 205	244
1800	221	5.5	180	41	1910	1 295	130.3	1 063	232
1790	74	1.8	61	13	1900	1 188	119.5	952	235
					1890	1 042	104.9	826	216
Louisiana					1880	935	94	725	210
1998	4 369	100.3	2 887	1 407	1870	781	78.6	605	175
1990	4 220	96.9	2 839	1 299					
1980	4 206	96.5	2 912	1 238	1860	687	69.1	516	171
1970	3 645	81.0	2 541	1 087	1850	583	58.6	418	165
1960	3 257	72.2	2 212	1 039	1840	470	47.3	318	152
					1830	447	45	291	156
1950	2 684	59.4	1 797	882	1820	407	41	260	147
1940	2 364	52.3	1 512	849					
1930	2 102	46.5	1 323	776	1810	381	38.3	235	145
1920	1 799	39.6	1 097	700	1800	342	34.4	216	125
1910	1 656	36.5	941	714	1790	320	32	209	111
1900	1 382	30.4	730	651	**Massachusetts**				
1890	1 119	24.6	558	559	1998	6 147	784.3	5 514	395
1880	940	20.7	455	484	1990	6 016	767.6	5 405	300
1870	727	16.0	362	364	1980	5 737	732	5 363	221
1860	708	15.6	357	350	1970	5 689	727.0	5 478	176
					1960	5 149	657.3	5 023	112
1850	518	11.4	255	262					
1840	352	7.8	158	194	1950	4 691	596.2	4 612	73
1830	216	4.8	89	126	1940	4 317	545.9	4 258	55
1820	153	3.4	74	80	1930	4 250	537.4	4 193	52
1810	77	2.2	34	42	1920	3 852	479.2	3 804	45
					1910	3 366	418.8	3 325	38
Maine									
1998	1 244	40.3	1 223	6	1900	2 805	349.0	2 770	32
1990	1 228	39.8	1 208	5	1890	2 239	278.5	2 215	22
1980	1 125	36.4	1 110	3	1880	1 783	221.9	1 764	19
1970	994	32.1	985	3	1870	1 457	181.3	1 443	14
1960	969	31.3	963	3	1860	1 231	153.1	1 221	10
1950	914	29.4	911	1	1850	995	123.7	985	9
1940	847	27.3	845	1	1840	738	91.7	729	9
1930	797	25.7	795	1	1830	610	75.9	603	7
1920	768	25.7	766	1	1820	523	65.1	516	7
1910	742	24.8	740	1	1810	472	58.7	465	7
1900	694	23.2	682	1	1800	423	52.6	417	6
1890	661	22.1	659	1	1790	379	47.1	373	5
1880	649	21.7	647	1					
1870	627	21	625	2	**Michigan**				
1860	628	21	627	1	1998	9 817	172.8	8 195	1 405
					1990	9 295	163.6	7 756	1 292
1850	583	19.5	582	1	1980	9 262	163.0	7 872	1 199
1840	502	16.8	500	1	1970	8 882	156.2	7 833	991
1830	399	13.4	398	1	1960	7 823	137.7	7 086	718
1820	298	10	297	1					
1810	229	7.7	228	1	1950	6 372	111.7	5 918	442
					1940	5 256	92.2	5 040	208
1800	152	5.1	151	1	1930	4 842	84.9	4 664	169
1790	97	3.2	96	1	1920	3 668	63.8	3 602	60
					1910	2 810	48.9	2 785	17
Maryland									
1998	5 135	525.3	3 487	1 428	1900	2 421	42.1	2 399	16
1990	4 781	489.2	3 394	1 190	1890	2 094	36.4	2 073	15
1980	4 217	431.4	3 159	958	1880	1 637	28.5	1 615	15
1970	3 924	396.6	3 195	699	1870	1 184	20.6	1 167	12

See footnotes at end of table.

Series A 195-209.   Population of States, by Race: 1790 to 1998—Cont'd.

(In thousands, except series A 196)

State and year	Resident population		Race		State and year	Resident population		Race	
	Total	Per square mile of land area	White	Black		Total	Per square mile of land area	White	Black
	195	**196**	**199**	**200**		**195**	**196**	**199**	**200**
1860	749	13.0	736	7	1910	3 293	47.9	3 135	157
1850	398	6.9	395	3	1900	3 107	45.2	2 945	161
1840	212	3.7	212	1	1890	2 679	39	2 528	150
1830	32	.2	31	(Z)	1880	2 168	31.6	2 023	145
1820	9	(4)	9	(Z)	1870	1 721	25	1 603	118
1810	5	.1	5	(Z)	1860	1 182	17.2	1 063	119
Minnesota					1850	682	9.9	592	90
1998	4 725	59.4	4 403	141	1840	384	5.6	324	60
1990	4 375	55.0	4 130	95	1830	140	2.1	115	26
1980	4 076	51.2	3 936	53	1820	67	1	56	11
1970	3 806	48.0	3 736	35	1810	20	(NA)	17	4
1960	3 414	43.1	3 372	22	**Montana**				
1950	2 982	37.3	2 954	14	1998	880	6.0	816	3
1940	2 792	34.9	2 769	10	1990	799	5.5	741	2
1930	2 564	32.0	2 543	9	1980	787	5.4	740	2
1920	2 387	29.5	2 369	9	1970	694	4.8	663	2
1910	2 076	25.7	2 059	7	1960	675	4.6	651	1
1900	1 751	21.7	1 737	5	1950	591	4.1	572	1
1890	1 310	16.2	1 296	4	1940	559	3.8	540	1
1880	781	9.7	777	2	1930	538	3.7	520	1
1870	440	5.4	438	1	1920	549	3.8	534	2
1860	172	2.1	169	(Z)	1910	376	2.6	361	2
1850	6	(4)	6	(Z)	1900	243	1.7	226	2
					1890	143	1.0	128	1
Mississippi					1880	39	.3	35	(Z)
1998	2 752	58.7	1 719	1 003	1870	21	.1	18	(Z)
1990	2 573	54.9	1 633	915					
1980	2 521	53.7	1 615	887	**Nebraska**				
1970	2 217	46.9	1 633	816	1998	1 663	21.6	1 559	67
1960	2 178	46	1 258	916	1990	1 578	20.5	1 487	57
					1980	1 570	20.4	1 490	48
1950	2 179	46.1	1 189	986	1970	1 485	19.4	1 433	40
1940	2 184	46.1	1 106	1 075	1960	1 411	18.4	1 375	29
1930	2 010	42.4	998	1 010					
1920	1 791	38.6	854	935	1950	1 326	17.3	1 301	19
1910	1 797	38.8	786	1 009	1940	1 316	17.2	1 298	14
					1930	1 378	18.0	1 360	14
1900	1 551	33.5	641	908	1920	1 296	16.9	1 279	13
1890	1 290	27.8	545	743	1910	1 192	15.5	1 180	8
1880	1 132	24.4	479	650					
1870	828	17.9	383	444	1900	1 066	13.9	1 057	6
1860	791	17.1	354	437	1890	1 063	13.8	1 047	9
					1880	452	5.9	450	2
1850	607	13.1	296	311	1870	123	1.6	122	1
1840	376	8.1	179	197	1860	29	.2	29	(Z)
1830	137	2.9	70	66					
1820	75	1.6	42	33	**Nevada**				
1810 [1]	31	0.4	23	17	1998	1 747	15.9	1 501	133
					1990	1 202	10.9	1013	79
1800 [1]	8	0.3	5	4	1980	801	7.3	700	51
					1970	489	4.4	448	28
Missouri					1960	285	2.6	263	13
1998	5 439	78.9	4 745	613					
1990	5 117	74.3	4 486	548	1950	160	1.5	150	4
1980	4 917	71.4	4 346	514	1940	110	1.0	104	1
1970	4 678	67.8	4 177	480	1930	91	.8	85	1
1960	4 320	62.6	3 923	391	1920	77	.7	71	(Z)
					1910	82	.7	74	1
1950	3 955	57.1	3 656	297					
1940	3 785	54.6	3 539	244	1900	42	.4	35	(Z)
1930	3 629	52.4	3 404	224	1890	47	.4	39	(Z)
1920	3 404	49.5	3 225	178	1880	62	.6	54	(Z)

See footnotes at end of table.

Series A 195-209.   Population of States, by Race: 1790 to 1998—Cont'd.

(In thousands, except series A 196)

State and year	Resident population		Race		State and year	Resident population		Race	
	Total	Per square mile of land area	White	Black		Total	Per square mile of land area	White	Black
	195	**196**	**199**	**200**		**195**	**196**	**199**	**200**
1870	42	.4	39	(Z)	1940	532	4.4	492	5
1860	7	.1	7	(Z)	1930	423	3.5	391	3
					1920	360	2.9	335	6
New Hampshire					1910	327	2.7	305	2
1998	1 185	132.1	1 160	9					
1990	1 109	123.7	1 087	7	1900	195	1.6	180	2
1980	921	102.6	910	4	1890	160	1.3	143	2
1970	736	81.7	733	3	1880	120	1.0	109	1
1960	607	67.2	604	2	1870	92	.7	90	(Z)
					1860 [5]	94	.4	83	(Z)
1950	533	59.1	532	1					
1940	492	54.5	491	(Z)	1850 [6]	62	.3	62	(Z)
1930	465	51.6	464	1					
1920	443	49.1	442	1	**New York**				
1910	431	47.7	430	1	1998	18 175	384.9	13 885	3 220
					1990	17 990	381.0	13 385	2 859
1900	412	45.6	411	1	1980	17 558	371.8	13 961	2 402
1890	377	41.7	376	1	1970	18 241	381.3	15 834	2 169
1880	347	38.4	346	1	1960	16 782	350.6	15 287	1 418
1870	318	35.2	318	1					
1860	326	36.1	326	(Z)	1950	14 830	309.3	13 872	918
					1940	13 479	281.2	12 880	571
1850	318	35.2	317	1	1930	12 588	262.6	12 153	413
1840	285	31.5	284	1	1920	10 385	217.9	10 172	198
1830	269	29.8	269	1	1910	9 114	191.2	8 967	134
1820	244	27	243	1					
1810	214	23.7	214	1	1900	7 269	152.5	7 157	99
					1890	6 003	126.0	5 924	70
1800	184	20.4	184	1	1880	5 083	106.7	5 016	65
1790	142	15.7	142	1	1870	4 383	92.0	4 330	52
					1860	3 881	81.4	3 832	49
New Jersey									
1998	8 115	1 093.8	6 452	1 188	1850	3 097	65.0	3 048	49
1990	7 730	1 042.0	6 130	1 037	1840	2 429	51.0	2 379	50
1980	7 365	992.7	6 127	925	1830 [7]	1 919	40.3	1 868	45
1970	7 171	953.1	6 350	770	1820	1 373	28.8	1 333	39
1960	6 067	805.5	5 539	515	1810	959	20.1	919	40
1950	4 835	642.8	4 512	319	1800	589	12.4	556	31
1940	4 160	553.1	3 931	227	1790	340	7.1	314	26
1930	4 041	537.3	3 830	209					
1920	3 156	420	3 037	117	**North Carolina**				
1910	2 537	337.7	2 446	90	1998	7 546	154.9	5 684	1 665
					1990	6 629	136.1	5 008	1 456
1900	1 884	250.7	1 812	70	1980	5 880	120.7	4 458	1 319
1890	1 445	192.3	1 397	48	1970	5 084	104.1	3 902	1 126
1880	1 131	150.5	1 092	39	1960	4 556	93.2	3 399	1 116
1870	906	120.6	875	31					
1860	672	89.4	647	25	1950	4 062	82.7	2 983	1 047
					1940	3 572	72.7	2 568	981
1850	490	65.2	466	24	1930	3 170	64.5	2 235	919
1840	373	49.7	352	22	1920	2 559	52.5	1 784	763
1830	321	42.7	300	21	1910	2 206	45.3	1 501	698
1820	278	36.9	258	20					
1810	246	32.7	227	19	1900	1 894	38.9	1 264	624
					1890	1 618	33.2	1 055	561
1800	211	28.1	194	17	1880	1 400	28.7	867	531
1790	184	24.5	170	14	1870	1 071	22.0	678	392
					1860	993	20.4	630	362
New Mexico									
1998	1 737	14.3	1 503	45	1850	869	17.8	553	316
1990	1 515	12.5	1 146	30	1840	753	15.5	485	269
1980	1 303	10.7	978	24	1830	738	15.1	473	265
1970	1 017	8.4	916	20	1820	639	13.1	419	220
1960	951	7.8	876	17	1810	556	11.4	376	179
					1800	478	9.8	338	140
1950	681	5.6	630	8	1790	394	8.1	288	106

See footnotes at end of table.

Series A 195-209.   Population of States, by Race: 1790 to 1998—Cont'd.

(In thousands, except series A 196)

State and year	Resident population Total	Per square mile of land area	Race White	Black
	195	196	199	200
North Dakota				
1998	638	9.3	599	4
1990	639	9.3	604	4
1980	653	9.5	626	3
1970	618	8.9	599	2
1960	632	9.1	620	1
1950	620	8.8	608	(Z)
1940	642	9.2	631	(Z)
1930	681	9.7	672	(Z)
1920	647	9.2	640	(Z)
1910	577	8.2	570	1
1990	319	4.5	312	(Z)
1890	191	2.7	182	(Z)
1880 [8]	37	0.9	133	(Z)
1970 [8]	2	0.1	13	(Z)
1860 [8]	5	(4)	3	X
Ohio				
1998	11 209	273.7	9 768	1 290
1990	10 847	264.9	9 522	1 155
1980	10 798	263.7	9 597	1 077
1970	10 657	260	9 647	970
1960	9 706	236.6	8 910	786
1950	7 947	193.8	7 428	513
1940	6 908	168	6 567	339
1930	6 647	161.6	6 335	309
1920	5 759	141.4	5 572	186
1910	4 767	117	4 655	111
1900	4 158	102.1	4 060	97
1890	3 672	90.1	3 585	87
1880	3 198	78.5	3 118	80
1870	2 665	65.4	2 602	63
1860	2 340	57.4	2 303	37
1850	1 980	48.6	1 955	25
1840	1 519	37.3	1 502	17
1830	938	23.3	928	10
1820	581	14.5	577	5
1810	231	5.7	229	2
1800	45	1.1	45	(Z)
Oklahoma				
1998	3 347	48.7	2 777	262
1990	3 146	45.8	2 584	234
1980	3 025	44	2 598	205
1970	2 559	37.2	2 280	172
1960	2 328	33.8	2 108	153
1950	2 233	32.4	2 033	146
1940	2 336	33.7	2 104	169
1930	2 396	34.6	2 131	172
1920	2 028	29.2	1 821	149
1910	1 657	23.9	1 445	138
1900	790	11.4	670	56
1890	259	3.7	173	22
Oregon				
1998	3 282	34.2	3 070	61
1990	2 842	29.6	2 637	46
1980	2 633	27.4	2 491	37
1970	2 092	21.7	2 032	26

State and year	Resident population Total	Per square mile of land area	Race White	Black
	195	196	199	200
1960	1 769	18.4	1 732	18
1950	1 521	15.8	1 497	12
1940	1 090	11.3	1 076	3
1930	954	9.9	939	2
1920	783	8.2	769	2
1910	673	7.0	655	1
1900	414	4.3	395	1
1890	318	3.3	302	1
1880	175	1.8	163	(Z)
1870	91	1.0	87	(Z)
1860	52	.5	52	(Z)
1850	12	(4)	13	(Z)
Pennsylvania				
1998	12 001	267.8	10 619	1 166
1990	11 882	265.1	10 520	1 090
1980	11 865	264.7	10 652	1 047
1970	11 801	262.3	10 738	1 017
1960	11 319	251.4	10 454	853
1950	10 498	233.1	9 854	638
1940	9 900	219.8	9 427	470
1930	9 631	213.8	9 196	431
1920	8 720	194.5	8 433	285
1910	7 665	171.0	7 468	194
1900	6 302	140.6	6 142	157
1890	5 258	117.3	5 148	108
1880	4 283	95.5	4 197	86
1870	3 522	78.6	3 457	65
1860	2 906	64.8	2 849	57
1850	2 312	51.6	2 258	54
1840	1 724	38.5	1 676	48
1830	1 348	30.1	1 310	38
1820	1 049	23.4	1 017	30
1810	810	18.1	787	23
1800	602	13.4	586	16
1790	434	9.7	424	10
Rhode Island				
1998	988	945.9	911	49
1990	1 003	960.3	917	39
1980	947	906.4	897	28
1970	950	902.5	915	25
1960	859	819.3	839	18
1950	792	748.5	777	14
1940	713	674.2	702	11
1930	687	649.8	677	10
1920	604	566.4	594	10
1910	543	508.5	532	10
1900	429	401.6	419	9
1890	346	323.8	338	7
1880	277	259.2	270	6
1870	217	203.7	212	5
1860	175	163.7	171	4
1850	148	138.3	144	4
1840	109	102	106	3
1830	97	91.1	94	4
1820	83	77.8	79	4

See footnotes at end of table.

Series A 195-209.   Population of States, by Race: 1790 to 1998—Cont'd.
(In thousands, except series A 196)

State and year	Resident population Total	Resident population Per square mile of land area	Race White	Race Black
	195	**196**	**199**	**200**
1810	77	72.1	73	4
1800	69	64.8	65	4
1790	69	64.5	65	4
South Carolina				
1998	3 836	127.4	2 645	1 147
1990	3 487	115.8	2 407	1 040
1980	3 121	103.7	2 147	949
1970	2 591	85.7	1 794	789
1960	2 383	78.7	1 551	829
1950	2 117	69.9	1 293	822
1940	1 900	62.1	1 084	814
1930	1 739	56.8	944	794
1920	1 684	55.2	819	865
1910	1 515	49.7	679	836
1900	1 340	44	558	782
1890	1 151	37.7	462	689
1880	996	32.6	391	604
1870	706	23.1	290	416
1860	704	23.1	291	412
1850	669	21.9	275	394
1840	594	19.5	259	335
1830	581	19.1	258	323
1820	503	16.5	237	265
1810	415	13.6	214	201
1800	346	11.3	196	149
1790	249	8.2	140	109
South Dakota				
1998	738	9.7	669	5
1990	696	9.2	638	3
1980	691	9.1	640	2
1970	666	8.8	630	2
1960	681	9	653	1
1950	653	8.5	629	1
1940	643	8.4	619	(Z)
1930	693	9.1	670	1
1920	637	8.3	619	1
1910	584	7.6	564	1
1900	402	5.2	381	(Z)
1890	349	4.5	328	1
1880 [8]	98	. . .	97	(Z)
1870 [8]	12	. . .	11	(Z)
1860 [8]	. . .	. . .	. . .	. . .
Tennessee				
1998	5 431	131.7	4 466	900
1990	4 877	118.3	4 048	778
1980	4 591	111.4	3 835	726
1970	3 926	94.9	3 294	621
1960	3 567	86.2	2 978	587
1950	3 292	78.8	2 760	531
1940	2 916	69.5	2 407	509
1930	2 617	62.4	2 139	478
1920	2 338	56.1	1 886	452
1910	2 185	52.4	1 711	473
1900	2 021	48.5	1 540	480
1890	1 768	42.4	1 337	531

State and year	Resident population Total	Resident population Per square mile of land area	Race White	Race Black
	195	**196**	**199**	**200**
1880	1 542	37.0	1 139	403
1870	1 259	30.2	936	322
1860	1 110	26.6	827	283
1850	1 003	24.1	757	246
1840	829	19.9	641	139
1830	682	16.4	536	146
1820	423	10.1	340	83
1810	262	6.3	216	46
1800	106	2.5	92	14
1790	36	.8	32	4
Texas				
1998	19 760	75.4	16 678	2 430
1990	16 987	64.9	12 775	2 022
1980	14 226	54.3	11 198	1 710
1970	11 199	42.7	9 717	1 399
1960	9 580	36.4	8 375	1 187
1950	7 711	29.3	6 727	977
1940	6 415	24.3	5 488	924
1930	5 825	22.1	4 967	855
1920	4 663	17.8	3 918	742
1910	3 897	14.8	3 205	690
1900	3 049	11.6	2 427	621
1890	2 236	8.5	1 746	488
1880	1 592	6.1	1 197	393
1870	819	3.1	565	253
1860	604	2.3	421	183
1850	213	.8	154	59
Utah				
1998	2 100	25.6	1 998	19
1990	1 723	21.0	1 616	12
1980	1 461	17.8	1 383	9
1970	1 059	12.9	1 032	7
1960	891	10.8	874	4
1950	689	8.4	677	3
1940	550	6.7	543	1
1930	508	6.2	500	1
1920	449	5.5	442	1
1910	373	4.5	367	1
1900	277	3.4	272	1
1890	211	2.6	206	1
1880	144	1.8	142	(Z)
1870	87	1.1	86	(Z)
1860	40	0.3	40	(Z)
1850	11	(4)	11	(Z)
Vermont				
1998	591	63.9	581	3
1990	563	60.8	555	2
1980	511	55.3	507	1
1970	444	47.9	443	1
1960	390	42	389	1
1950	378	40.7	377	(Z)
1940	359	38.7	359	(Z)
1930	360	38.8	359	1
1920	352	38.6	352	1
1910	356	39	354	2

See footnotes at end of table.

Series A 195-209.   Population of States, by Race: 1790 to 1998—Cont'd.

(In thousands, except series A 196)

State and year	Resident population Total	Resident population Per square mile of land area	Race White	Race Black	State and year	Resident population Total	Resident population Per square mile of land area	Race White	Race Black
	195	196	199	200		195	196	199	200
1900	344	37.7	343	1	1860 [11]	12	.1	11	(Z)
1890	332	36.4	331	1	1850 [9]	1	...	...	...
1880	332	36.4	331	1					
1870	331	36.2	330	1					
1860	315	34.5	314	1	**West Virginia**				
1850	314	34.4	313	1	1998	1 811	75.2	1 741	58
1840	292	32	291	1	1990	1 793	74.5	1 726	56
1830	281	30.8	280	1	1980	1 950	80.9	1 875	65
1820	236	25.9	235	1	1970	1 744	72.5	1 673	67
1810	218	23.9	217	1	1960	1 860	77.2	1 770	89
1800	154	16.9	154	1	1950	2 006	83.3	1 890	115
1790	85	9.4	85	(Z)	1940	1 902	79.0	1 784	118
					1930	1 729	71.8	1 614	115
					1920	1 464	60.9	1 377	86
Virginia					1910	1 221	50.8	1 157	64
1998	6 791	171.5	5 163	1 363					
1990	6 187	156.3	4 792	1 163	1900	959	39.9	915	43
1980	5 347	135	4 230	1 009	1890	763	31.8	730	33
1970	4 651	116.9	3 762	861	1880	618	25.7	593	26
1960	3 967	99.6	3 142	816	1870	442	18.4	424	18
					1860 [10]	377	...	...	...
1950	3 319	83.2	2 582	734					
1940	2 678	67.1	2 016	661	1850 [10]	302	...	...	...
1930	2 422	60.7	1 770	650	1840 [10]	225	...	...	...
1920	2 309	57.4	1 618	690	1830 [10]	177	...	...	...
1910	2 062	51.2	1 390	671	1820 [10]	137	...	...	...
					1810 [10]	105	...	...	...
1900	1 854	46.1	1 193	661					
1890	1 656	41.1	1 020	635	1800 [10]	79	...	...	...
1880	1 513	37.6	881	632	1790 [10]	56	...	...	...
1870	1 225	30.4	712	513					
1860 [10]	1 220	24.8	1 047	549	**Wisconsin**				
1850 [10]	1 119	22.1	895	527	1998	5 224	96.2	4 807	291
1840 [10]	1 025	19.3	748	502	1990	4 892	90.1	4 513	245
1830 [10]	1 044	18.9	701	520	1980	4 706	86.6	4 443	183
1820 [10]	938	16.6	610	465	1970	4 418	81.1	4 259	128
1810 [10]	878	15.2	557	426	1960	3 952	72.6	3 859	75
1800 [10]	808	13.7	518	367	1950	3 435	62.8	3 393	28
1790 [10]	692	11.6	442	306	1940	3 138	57.3	3 113	12
					1930	2 939	53.7	2 916	11
					1920	2 632	47.6	2 617	5
Washington					1910	2 334	42.2	2 321	3
1998	5 689	85.4	5 058	198					
1990	4 867	73.1	4 309	150	1900	2 069	37.4	2 058	3
1980	4 132	62.1	3 779	106	1890	1 693	30.6	1 681	2
1970	3 413	51.2	3 251	71	1880	1 315	23.8	1 310	3
1960	2 853	42.8	2 752	49	1870	1 055	19.1	1 051	2
					1860	776	14	774	1
1950	2 379	35.6	2 316	31					
1940	1 736	25.9	1 698	7	1850	305	5.5	305	1
1930	1 563	23.3	1 522	7	1840	31	0.4	31	(Z)
1920	1 357	20.3	1 320	7					
1910	1 142	17.1	1 109	6	**Wyoming**				
1900	518	7.8	496	3	1998	481	5.0	462	4
1890	357	5.3	341	2	1990	454	4.7	427	4
1880	75	1.1	67	(Z)	1980	470	4.8	446	3
1870	24	.4	22	(Z)	1970	332	3.4	323	3

See footnotes at end of table.

Series A 195-209.   Population of States, by Race: 1790 to 1998—Cont'd.

(In thousands, except series A 196)

State and year	Resident population		Race		State and year	Resident population		Race	
	Total	Per square mile of land area	White	Black		Total	Per square mile of land area	White	Black
	195	**196**	**199**	**200**		**195**	**196**	**199**	**200**
1960...	330	3.4	323	2	1910...	146	1.5	140	2
1950...	291	3	284	3	1900...	93	0.9	89	1
1940...	251	2.6	247	1	1890...	63	0.6	59	1
1930...	226	2.3	221	1	1880...	21	0.2	19	(Z)
1920...	194	2	190	1	1870...	9	0.1	9	(Z)

X Represents zero.
Z Less than 500.
1. Population of those parts of Mississippi Territory now in present State. Population per square mile, sex, race and age detail for Alabama included with Mississippi.
2. Census taken October 1, 1939.
3. Census taken October 1, 1929.
4. Less than 1/10 of a person.
5. Includes population of area taken to form part of Arizona Territory in 1863.
6. Data for Territory of New Mexico which included parts of present States of Arizona and New Mexico, and smaller parts of Colorado and Nevada.
7. Includes 5 602 persons for whom sex, race, and age detail are not available.
8. North and South Dakota comprised Dakota Territory. Population per square mile, sex and age detail for South Dakota included with North Dakota.
9. Population total of those parts of Oregon Territory taken to form part of Washington Territory in 1853 and 1859 excluded from Oregon included under Washington. Population per square mile, sex, race and age detail for Washington included with Oregon.
10. Sex, race and age detail for West Virginia, 1790-1860, included with Virginia.
11. Includes population of Idaho and parts of Montana and Wyoming.

Series A 210-262. Land Area of the United States, by States and Territories: 1790 to 2000

(In square miles)

Series No.	State or territory	Year of admission to state-hood	2000	1980	1970	1960	1950	1940	1930	1920	1910	1900	1890
210	United States..........	...	3 536 342	3 539 289	3 540 023	3 540 911	2 974 726	2 977 128	2 973 776	2 973 774	2 973 890	2 974 159	2 973 965
211	Alabama.................	1819	50 750	50 767	50 078	50 851	51 078	51 078	51 279	51 279	51 279	51 279	51 279
212	Alaska....................	1959	570 374	570 833	566 432	566 432	...	...	...	...	...	...	...
213	Arizona..................	1912	113 642	113 508	113 417	113 563	113 575	113 580	113 810	113 810	113 810	113 840	113 840
214	Arkansas................	1836	52 075	52 078	51 945	52 175	52 675	52 725	52 525	52 525	52 525	52 525	52 525
215	California...............	1850	155 973	156 299	156 361	156 537	156 740	156 803	155 652	155 652	155 652	156 092	155 900
216	Colorado	1876	103 730	103 595	103 766	103 794	103 922	103 967	103 658	103 658	103 658	103 658	103 658
217	Connecticut............	[1] 1788	4 845	4 872	4 862	4 870	4 899	4 899	4 820	4 820	4 820	4 820	4 820
218	Delaware................	[1] 1787	1 955	1 932	1 982	1 982	1 978	1 978	1 965	1 965	1 965	1 965	1 965
219	District of Columbia ...	...	61	63	61	61	61	61	62	60	60	60	58
220	Florida..................	1845	53 997	54 153	54 090	54 136	54 262	54 262	54 861	54 861	54 861	54 861	54 861
221	Georgia..................	[1] 1788	57 919	58 056	58 073	58 197	58 483	58 518	58 725	58 725	58 725	58 725	58 725
222	Hawaii....................	1959	6 423	6 425	6 425	6 425	...	...	...	...	...	...	...
223	Idaho.....................	1890	82 751	82 412	82 677	82 677	82 769	82 808	83 354	83 354	83 354	83 354	83 354
224	Illinois...................	1818	55 593	55 645	55 748	55 875	55 935	55 947	56 043	56 043	56 043	56 002	56 002
225	Indiana..................	1816	35 870	35 932	36 097	36 189	36 205	36 205	36 045	36 045	36 045	35 885	35 885
226	Iowa......................	1846	55 875	55 965	55 941	56 043	56 045	55 986	55 586	55 586	55 586	55 586	55 586
227	Kansas...................	1861	81 823	81 778	81 787	82 056	82 108	82 113	81 774	81 774	81 774	81 774	81 774
228	Kentucky................	1792	39 732	39 669	39 650	39 851	39 864	40 109	40 181	40 181	40 181	40 181	40 181
229	Louisiana...............	1812	43 566	44 521	44 930	45 131	45 162	45 177	45 409	45 409	45 409	45 409	45 409
230	Maine.....................	1820	30 865	30 995	30 920	30 933	31 040	31 040	29 895	29 895	29 895	29 895	29 895
231	Maryland................	[1] 1788	9 775	9 837	9 891	9 891	9 881	9 887	9 941	9 941	9 941	9 941	9 941
232	Massachusetts........	[1] 1788	7 838	7 824	7 826	7 833	7 867	7 907	8 039	8 039	8 039	8 039	8 039
233	Michigan................	1837	56 809	56 954	56 817	56 817	57 022	57 022	57 480	57 480	57 480	57 480	57 480
234	Minnesota	1858	79 617	79 548	79 289	79 289	80 009	80 009	80 858	80 858	80 858	80 858	80 858
235	Mississippi	1817	46 914	47 233	47 296	47 358	47 248	47 420	46 362	46 362	46 362	46 362	46 362
236	Missouri	1821	68 898	68 945	68 995	69 046	69 226	69 270	68 727	68 727	68 727	68 727	68 727
237	Montana.................	1889	145 556	145 388	145 587	145 603	145 878	146 316	146 131	146 131	146 201	146 201	146 201
238	Nebraska	1867	76 878	76 644	76 483	76 522	76 663	76 653	76 808	76 808	76 808	76 808	76 808
239	Nevada	1864	109 806	109 894	109 889	109 889	109 789	109 802	109 802	109 821	109 821	109 821	109 821
240	New Hampshire.......	[1] 1788	8 969	8 993	9 027	9 033	9 017	9 024	9 031	9 031	9 031	9 031	9 031
241	New Jersey.............	[1] 1787	7 419	7 468	7 521	7 532	7 522	7 522	7 514	7 514	7 514	7 514	7 514
242	New Mexico............	1912	121 365	121 335	121 412	121 445	121 511	121 511	122 503	122 503	122 503	122 503	122 503
243	New York................	[1] 1788	47 224	47 377	47 831	47 869	47 944	47 929	47 654	47 654	47 654	47 654	47 654
244	North Carolina	[1] 1789	48 718	48 843	48 798	48 880	49 097	49 142	48 740	48 740	48 740	48 740	48 740
245	North Dakota	1889	68 994	69 300	69 273	69 280	70 057	70 054	70 183	70 183	70 183	70 183	70 183
246	Ohio	1803	40 953	41 004	40 975	41 048	41 000	41 122	40 740	40 740	40 740	40 740	40 740
247	Oklahoma	1907	68 679	68 655	68 782	68 983	69 031	69 283	69 414	69 414	69 414	38 624	38 624
248	Oregon...................	1859	96 003	96 184	96 184	96 209	96 315	96 350	95 607	95 607	95 607	95 607	95 607
249	Pennsylvania	[1] 1787	44 820	44 888	44 966	45 025	45 045	45 045	44 832	44 832	44 832	44 832	44 832
250	Rhode Island	[1] 1790	1 045	1 055	1 049	1 049	1 058	1 058	1 067	1 067	1 067	1 067	1 067
251	South Carolina........	[1] 1788	30 111	30 203	30 225	30 280	30 305	30 594	30 495	30 495	30 495	30 495	30 495
252	South Dakota..........	1889	75 898	75 952	75 955	75 956	76 536	76 536	76 868	76 868	76 868	76 868	70 868
253	Tennessee..............	1796	41 220	41 155	41 328	41 366	41 797	41 961	41 687	41 687	41 687	41 687	41 687
254	Texas.....................	1845	261 914	262 017	262 134	262 970	263 513	263 644	262 398	262 398	262 398	262 398	262 398
255	Utah......................	1896	82 168	82 073	82 096	82 381	82 346	82 346	82 184	82 184	82 184	82 184	82 184
256	Vermont.................	1791	9 249	9 273	9 267	9 274	9 278	9 278	9 124	9 124	9 124	9 124	9 124
257	Virginia..................	[1] 1788	39 598	39 704	39 780	39 841	39 893	39 899	40 262	40 262	40 262	40 262	40 292
258	Washington.............	1889	66 582	66 511	66 570	66 663	66 786	66 977	66 836	66 836	66 836	66 836	66 836
259	West Virginia	1863	24 087	24 119	24 070	24 084	24 080	24 090	24 022	24 022	24 022	24 022	25 022
260	Wisconsin	1848	54 314	54 426	54 464	54 466	54 705	54 715	55 256	55 256	55 256	55 256	55 256
261	Wyoming................	1890	97 105	96 989	97 203	97 281	97 506	97 506	97 548	97 548	97 594	97 594	97 594
262	Indian Territory .... and unorganized territory	...	...	...	...	...	...	...	...	...	...	30 790	30 790
263	Other territory	...	...	...	...	...	...	...	...	...	...	...	...

See footnotes at end of table.

Series A 210-262. Land Area of the United States, by States and Territories: 1790 to 2000—Cont'd.

(In square miles)

Series No.	State or territory	1880	1870	1860	1850	1840	1830	1820	1810	1800	1790
210	United States	2 973 965	2 973 965	2 973 965	2 944 337	1 753 588	1 753 588	1 753 588	1 685 865	867 980	867 980
211	Alabama	51 279	51 279	51 279	51 279	51 279	51 279	51 279	...	...	...
212	Alaska	...	...	...	...	...	...	...	...	...	...
213	Arizona	113 840	113 840	...	...	...	...	...	...	...	...
214	Arkansas	52 525	52 525	52 525	52 525	52 525	52 525	105 275	...	...	...
215	California	155 900	155 900	155 900	155 900	...	...	...	...	...	...
216	Colorado	103 658	103 658	103 658	...	...	...	...	...	...	...
217	Connecticut	4 820	4 820	4 820	4 820	4 820	4 820	4 820	4 820	4 820	4 820
218	Delaware	1 965	1 965	1 965	1 965	1 965	1 965	1 965	1 965	1 965	1 965
219	District of Columbia	58	58	58	58	90	90	90	90	90	...
220	Florida	54 861	54 861	54 861	54 861	54 861	54 861	54 861	...	...	...
221	Georgia	58 725	58 725	58 725	58 725	58 725	58 725	58 725	58 725	111 877	145 196
222	Hawaii	...	...	...	...	...	...	...	...	...	...
223	Idaho	83 354	83 360	...	...	...	...	...	...	...	...
224	Illinois	56 002	56 002	56 002	56 002	56 002	56 002	56 002	192 381	...	...
225	Indiana	35 885	35 885	35 885	35 885	35 885	35 885	35 885	42 933	252 084	...
226	Iowa	55 586	55 586	55 856	55 856	191 656	...	...	...	...	...
227	Kansas	81 774	81 774	81 774	...	...	...	...	...	...	...
228	Kentucky	40 181	40 181	40 181	40 181	40 181	40 181	40 181	40 181	40 181	40 181
229	Louisiana	45 409	45 409	45 409	45 409	45 409	45 409	45 409	34 065	...	...
230	Maine	29 895	29 895	29 895	29 895	29 895	29 895	29 895	29 895	29 895	29 895
231	Maryland	9 941	9 941	9 941	9 941	9 941	9 941	9 941	9 941	9 941	9 999
232	Massachusetts	8 039	8 039	8 039	8 041	8 041	8 041	8 041	8 041	8 041	8 041
233	Michigan	57 480	57 480	57 480	57 480	57 480	186 052	186 052	42 625	...	...
234	Minnesota	80 858	80 858	80 858	163 457	...	...	...	...	...	...
235	Mississippi	46 362	46 362	46 362	46 362	46 362	46 362	46 362	97 641	33 319	...
236	Missouri	68 727	68 727	68 727	68 727	68 727	65 618	65 618	...	...	...
237	Montana	146 201	146 195	...	...	...	...	...	...	...	...
238	Nebraska	76 172	76 172	118 915	...	...	...	...	...	...	...
239	Nevada	109 821	109 821	61 260	...	...	...	...	...	...	...
240	New Hampshire	9 031	9 031	9 031	9 031	9 031	9 031	9 031	9 031	9 031	9 031
241	New Jersey	7 514	7 514	7 514	7 514	7 514	7 514	7 514	7 514	7 514	7 514
242	New Mexico	122 503	122 503	247 782	236 548	...	...	...	...	...	...
243	New York	47 654	47 654	47 654	47 652	47 652	47 652	47 652	47 652	47 652	47 652
244	North Carolina	48 740	48 740	48 740	48 740	48 740	48 740	48 740	48 740	48 740	48 740
245	North Dakota	...	...	...	...	...	...	...	...	...	...
246	Ohio	40 740	40 740	40 740	40 740	40 740	40 228	40 228	40 228	40 228	...
247	Oklahoma	...	...	...	...	...	...	...	...	...	...
248	Oregon	95 607	95 607	95 607	282 257	...	...	...	...	...	...
249	Pennsylvania	44 832	44 832	44 832	44 832	44 832	44 832	44 832	44 832	44 832	44 832
250	Rhode Island	1 067	1 067	1 067	1 067	1 067	1 067	1 067	1 067	1 067	1 067
251	South Carolina	30 495	30 495	30 495	30 495	30 495	30 495	30 495	30 495	30 495	30 495
252	South Dakota	...	...	...	...	...	...	...	...	...	...
253	Tennessee	41 687	41 687	41 687	41 687	41 687	41 687	41 687	41 687	41 687	46 977
254	Texas	262 398	262 398	262 398	262 398	...	...	...	...	...	...
255	Utah	82 184	82 184	122 887	230 610	...	...	...	...	...	...
256	Vermont	9 124	9 124	9 124	9 124	9 124	9 124	9 124	9 124	9 124	9 124
257	Virginia	40 262	40 262	64 284	64 284	64 252	64 252	64 252	64 252	64 252	64 284
258	Washington	66 836	66 836	183 254	...	...	...	...	...	...	...
259	West Virginia	24 022	24 002	...	...	...	...	...	...	...	...
260	Wisconsin	55 256	55 256	55 256	55 256	82 643	...	...	...	...	...
261	Wyoming	97 594	97 594	...	...	...	...	...	...	...	...
262	Indian Territory and unorganized territory	69 414	69 414	69 414	535 003	511 967	52 750	...	...	...	...
263	Other territory										
	NW of Ohio River	...	...	...	...	...	...	...	...	25 855	318 167
	S. of Tennessee	...	...	...	...	...	...	...	...	5 290	...
	Missouri Territory	...	...	...	...	...	608 565	608 565	777 940	...	...
	Dakota Territory	147 687	147 687	312 094	...	...	...	...	...	...	...

1. Year of ratification of Constitution; one of the original 13 States.

Series A 335-349.   Households, by Number of Persons: 1790 to 1998

(Number in thousands. As of March, except as noted)

Year	Number of households	Size of household							Percent distribution of number of households						
		1 person	2 persons	3 persons	4 persons	5 persons	6 persons	7 or more persons	1 person	2 persons	3 persons	4 persons	5 persons	6 persons	7 or more persons
	335	**336**	**337**	**338**	**339**	**340**	**341**	**342**	**343**	**344**	**345**	**346**	**347**	**348**	**349**
1998.....	102 528	26 327	32 965	17 331	15 358	7 048	2 232	1 267	26.3	33.0	17.3	15.4	7.0	2.2	1.3
1997.....	101 000	. . .	. . .	. . .	. . .	. . .	. . .	. . .	25.4	32.7	17.1	15.4	6.8	2.3	1.3
1996.....	98 927	. . .	. . .	. . .	. . .	. . .	. . .	. . .	24.9	32.5	16.7	15.1	6.6	2.4	1.4
1995.....	98 990	24 732	31 834	16 827	15 321	6 616	2 279	1 382	25	32	17	15	7	2	1
1994.....	97 100	23 611	31 211	16 898	15 073	6 749	2 186	1 379	23.6	31.2	16.9	15.1	6.7	2.2	1.4
1993.....	95 358	. . .	. . .	. . .	. . .	. . .	. . .	. . .	. . .	. . .	. . .	. . .	. . .	. . .	. . .
1992.....	94 652	23 974	30 734	16 398	14 710	6 389	2 126	1 338	24.0	30.7	16.4	14.7	6.4	2.1	1.3
1991.....	93 183	23 600	30 200	16 100	14 600	6 200	2 200	1 500	25.0	32.0	17.0	15.0	7.0	2.0	2.0
1990.....	93 300	23 000	30 100	16 100	14 500	6 200	2 100	1 300	24.5	32.3	17.5	15.7	6.7	2.2	1.2
1985.....	86 800	20 600	27 400	15 500	13 600	6 100	2 300	1 300	23.7	31.6	17.8	15.7	7.0	2.6	1.5
1980.....	80 800	18 300	25 300	14 100	12 700	6 100	2 500	1 800	22.5	31.3	17.5	15.8	7.6	3.2	2.2
1975.....	71 100	13 900	21 800	12 400	11 100	6 400	3 100	2 500	19.6	30.6	17.4	15.6	9.0	4.3	3.5
1970.....	62 874	10 692	18 129	10 903	9 935	6 532	3 505	3 178	17.0	28.8	17.3	15.8	10.4	5.6	5.1
1969.....	61 806	10 333	17 916	10 698	9 714	6 345	3 534	3 266	16.7	29.0	17.3	15.7	10.3	5.7	5.3
1968.....	60 446	9 743	17 272	10 513	9 565	6 281	3 605	3 467	16.1	28.6	17.4	15.8	10.4	6.0	5.7
1967.....	58 845	9 139	16 659	10 334	9 496	6 235	3 468	3 527	15.5	28.3	17.6	16.1	10.6	5.9	6.0
1966.....	58 092	9 044	16 589	9 939	9 414	6 223	3 446	3 446	15.6	28.6	17.1	16.2	10.7	5.9	5.9
1965.....	57 251	8 603	16 067	10 230	9 239	6 293	3 316	3 503	15.0	28.1	17.9	16.1	11.0	5.8	6.1
1964.....	55 996	7 800	15 579	10 007	9 539	6 311	3 364	3 396	13.9	27.8	17.9	17.0	11.3	6.0	6.1
1963.....	55 189	7 490	15 257	9 974	9 431	6 231	3 468	3 337	13.6	27.6	18.1	17.1	11.3	6.3	6.0
1962.....	54 652	7 458	15 429	10 056	9 328	6 004	3 361	3 016	13.6	28.2	18.4	17.1	11.0	6.1	5.5
1961.....	53 291	7 077	15 110	9 731	9 343	6 022	3 070	2 938	13.3	28.4	18.3	17.5	11.3	5.8	5.5
1960*...	52 610	6 871	14 616	9 941	9 277	6 064	2 976	2 865	13.1	27.8	18.9	17.6	11.5	5.7	5.4
1959.....	51 302	6 317	14 538	9 788	9 123	5 793	2 948	2 795	12.3	28.4	19.1	17.8	11.3	5.7	5.4
1958.....	50 402	6 078	14 303	9 715	8 933	5 609	3 002	2 762	12.1	28.4	19.3	17.7	11.1	6.0	5.5
1957.....	49 543	5 451	14 274	9 743	9 096	5 487	2 848	2 644	11.0	28.8	19.7	18.4	11.1	5.7	5.3
1956.....	48 785	5 396	13 827	9 936	9 152	5 287	2 624	2 563	11.1	28.3	20.4	18.8	10.8	5.4	5.3
1955.....	47 788	5 212	13 612	9 725	9 052	5 291	2 568	2 328	10.9	28.5	20.4	18.9	11.1	5.4	4.9
1954.....	46 893	5 032	13 249	9 776	8 820	5 170	2 521	2 325	10.7	28.3	20.8	18.8	11.0	5.4	5.0
1953[1]...	46 828	6 148	13 530	9 868	8 300	4 658	2 332	1 992	13.1	28.9	21.1	17.7	9.9	5.0	4.3
1952[2]...	45 464	5 388	13 460	9 908	8 106	4 378	2 142	2 082	11.9	29.6	21.8	17.8	9.6	4.7	4.6
1951[2]...	44 564	. . .	. . .	. . .	. . .	. . .	. . .	. . .	. . .	. . .	. . .	. . .	. . .	. . .	. . .
1950[1]...	43 468	4 737	12 529	9 808	7 729	4 357	2 196	2 113	10.9	28.8	22.6	17.8	10.0	5.1	4.9
1940[2]...	34 949	2 481	8 667	7 829	6 326	4 019	2 377	3 250	7.1	24.8	22.4	18.1	11.5	6.8	9.3
1930[2]...	29 905	2 357	6 983	6 227	5 235	3 574	2 273	3 255	7.9	23.4	20.8	17.5	12.0	7.6	10.9
1900.....	15 964	814	2 395	2 810	2 698	2 267	1 740	3 257	5.1	15.0	17.6	16.9	14.2	10.9	20.4
1890[3]...	12 690	457	1 675	2 119	2 132	1 916	1 472	2 919	3.6	13.2	16.7	16.8	15.1	11.6	23.0
1790.....	558	21	44	65	77	78	74	200	3.7	7.8	11.7	13.8	13.9	13.2	35.8

* Denotes first year for which figures include Alaska and Hawaii.
1. Covers related persons only; therefore, not strictly comparable with other years.
2. As of April.
3. As of June; includes a small number of quasi-households.

Series AA-1.   Resident Population Projections: 1999 to 2050

(In thousands [272,330 represents 272,330,000]. As of July 1. Each series shown assumes middle levels of fertility, life expectancy, and net immigration unless otherwise specified. Middle level components are shown in footnote 1)

Year	Middle series [1]	Lowest series [2]	Highest series [3]	Fertility		Life expectancy		Net immigration	
				Low	High	Low	High	Low	High
1999	272 330	269 861	274 865	271 678	272 915	272 006	272 697	270 835	273 910
2000	274 634	271 237	278 129	273 731	275 448	274 185	275 141	272 581	276 802
2005	285 981	276 990	295 318	283 299	288 471	284 647	287 467	280 949	291 287
2010	297 716	281 468	314 571	292 303	302 893	294 986	300 482	289 423	306 444
2015	310 134	285 472	335 597	301 444	318 595	305 539	314 376	298 356	322 508
2020	322 742	288 807	357 702	310 429	334 889	315 885	328 698	307 290	338 955
2025	335 050	290 789	380 781	318 575	351 554	325 530	343 023	315 709	355 318
2030	346 899	291 070	405 089	325 517	368 732	334 331	357 227	323 414	371 480
2040	369 980	287 685	458 444	336 407	405 660	350 592	385 898	337 416	403 986
2050	393 931	282 524	518 903	345 352	447 502	367 913	415 908	351 354	438 299

1. Total fertility rate in 2050 = 2 245; life expectancy in 2050 = 82.0 years; and annual net immigration = 820 000. These are middle level assumptions. For explanation of total fertility rate; see headnote, Table 96.
2. Total fertility rate in 2050 = 1 910; life expectancy in 2050 = 74.8 years; and annual net immigration = 300 000. These are lowest level assumptions.
3. Total fertility rate in 2050 = 2 580; life expectancy in 2050 = 89.4 years; and annual net immigration = 1 370 000. These are highest level assumptions.

SOURCE: U.S. Census Bureau, Current Population Reports, P25-1130.

Series AA-2.   Components of Population Change, 1980 to 1998, and Projections, 1999 to 2050

(226 546 represents 226 546 000. Resident population. The estimates prior to 1990 are consistent with the original 1990 census count of 248 709 873: Starting with 1990, estimates reflect the revised April 1, 1990, census count of 248 765 170 which includes count resolution corrections processed through August 1997, and does not include adjustments for census coverage errors except for adjustments estimated for the 1995 Census Test in Oakland, California; Patterson, New Jersey; and six Louisiana parishes. These adjustments amounted to a total of 55 297 persons)

| | | Calendar year | | | | | Rate per 1 000 midyear population | | | |
| | Population as of Jan. 1 (1 000) | Net increase [1] | | Births (1 000) | Deaths (1 000) | Net migration [3] (1 000) | Net growth rate [1] | Birth rate | Death rate | Net migration rate [3] |
Year		Total (1 000)	Percent [2]							
1980 [4]	226 546	1 900	0.8	2 743	1 463	724	11.1	16.0	8.6	4.2
1981	228 446	2 200	1.0	3 629	1 978	690	9.6	15.8	8.6	3.0
1982	230 645	2 157	0.9	3 681	1 975	595	9.3	15.9	8.5	2.6
1983	232 803	2 066	0.9	3 639	2 019	592	8.8	15.6	8.6	2.5
1984	234 868	2 070	0.9	3 669	2 039	589	8.8	15.6	8.6	2.5
1985	236 938	2 171	0.9	3 761	2 086	649	9.1	15.8	8.8	2.7
1986	239 109	2 158	0.9	3 757	2 105	661	9.0	15.6	8.8	2.8
1987	241 267	2 195	0.9	3 809	2 123	666	9.1	15.7	8.8	2.7
1988	243 462	2 243	0.9	3 910	2 168	662	9.2	16.0	8.9	2.7
1989	245 705	2 438	1.0	4 041	2 150	712	9.9	16.4	8.7	2.9
1990 [5]	248 143	2 535	1.0	4 148	2 155	[6] 542	10.2	16.6	8.6	[6] 2.2
1991	250 693	2 901	1.2	4 111	2 170	[6] 960	11.5	16.3	8.6	[6] 3.8
1992	253 594	2 886	1.1	4 065	2 176	997	11.3	15.9	8.5	3.9
1993	256 480	2 614	1.0	4 000	2 269	882	10.1	15.5	8.8	3.4
1994	259 094	2 483	1.0	3 953	2 279	810	9.5	15.2	8.8	3.1
1995	261 577	2 443	0.9	3 900	2 312	856	9.3	14.8	8.8	3.3
1996	264 021	2 482	0.9	3 891	2 315	905	9.4	14.7	8.7	3.4
1997	266 503	2 564	1.0	3 895	2 315	984	9.6	14.5	8.6	3.7
1998	269 067	2 559	1.0	3 888	2 308	979	9.5	14.4	8.5	3.6
PROJECTIONS [7]										
1999	271 166	2 316	0.9	3 896	2 401	820	8.5	14.3	8.8	3.0
2000	273 482	2 294	0.8	3 899	2 425	820	8.4	14.2	8.8	3.0
2005	284 847	2 278	0.8	4 001	2 543	820	8.0	14.0	8.9	2.9
2010	296 511	2 426	0.8	4 243	2 638	820	8.1	14.3	8.9	2.8
2015	308 875	2 521	0.8	4 450	2 749	820	8.1	14.3	8.9	2.6
2020	321 487	2 504	0.8	4 579	2 895	820	7.8	14.2	9.0	2.5
2025	333 838	2 414	0.7	4 679	3 085	820	7.2	14.0	9.2	2.4
2030	345 730	2 333	0.7	4 822	3 309	820	6.7	13.9	9.5	2.4
2040	368 823	2 319	0.6	5 248	3 749	820	6.3	14.2	10.1	2.2
2050	392 681	2 517	0.6	5 672	3 975	820	6.4	14.4	10.1	2.1

1. Prior to April 1, 1990, includes "error of closure" (the amount necessary to make the components of change add to the net change between censuses), for which figures are not shown separately.
2. Percent of population at beginning of period.
3. Covers net international migration and movement of Armed Forces, federally affiliated civilian citizens, and their dependents.
4. Data are for period April 1 to December 31.
5. Net change for 1990 excludes "error of closure" for the three months prior to the April 1 census date. Therefore, it may not equal the difference between the populations at the beginning of 1990 and 1991.
6. Data reflect movement of Armed Forces due to the Gulf War.
7. Based on middle series of assumptions. See footnote 1, Table 3.

SOURCE: U.S. Census Bureau, Current Population Reports, P25-1095 and P25-1130; and unpublished data.

PROPERTY OF GERMANNA
COMMUNITY COLLEGE LIBRARY

Series AA-3.   Center of Population: 1970 to 1990

(Prior to 1960, excludes Alaska and Hawaii. The median center is located at the intersection of two median lines, a north-south line constructed so that half of the Nation's population lives east and half lives west of it, and an east-west line selected so that half of the Nation's population lives north and half lives south of it. The mean center of population is that point at which an imaginary, flat, weightless, and rigid map of the United States would balance if weights of identical value were placed on it so that each weight represented the location of one person on the date of the census)

Year	Median center		Mean center		
	Latitude-N	Longitude	Latitude-N	Longitude-W	Approximate location
1790 (August 2)	. . .	. . .	39 16 30	76 11 12	In Kent County, MD, 23 miles E of Baltimore MD
1850 (June 1)..........................	. . .	. . .	38 59 00	81 19 00	In Wirt County, WV, 23 miles SE of Parkersburg, WV [1]
1900 (June 1)..........................	40 03 32	84 49 01	39 09 36	85 48 54	In Bartholomew County, IN, 6 miles SE of Columbus, IN
1950 (April 1)	40 00 12	84 56 51	38 50 21	88 09 33	In Richland County, IL, 8 miles NNW of Olney, IL
1960 (April 1)	39 56 25	85 16 60	38 35 58	89 12 35	In Clinton County, IL, 6.5 miles NW of Centralia, IL
1970 (April 1)	39 47 43	85 31 43	38 27 47	89 42 22	In St. Clair County, IL, 5.3 miles ESE of Mascoutah, IL
1980 (April 1)	39 18 60	86 08 15	38 08 13	90 34 26	In Jefferson County, MO, .25 mile W of DeSoto, MO
1990 (April 1)	38 57 55	86 31 53	37 52 20	91 12 55	In Crawford County, MO, 10 miles SE of Steelville, MO

1. West Virginia was set off from Virginia, Dec. 31, 1862, and admitted as a state, June 19, 1863.

SECTION B

VITAL STATISTICS AND HEALTH

Highlights

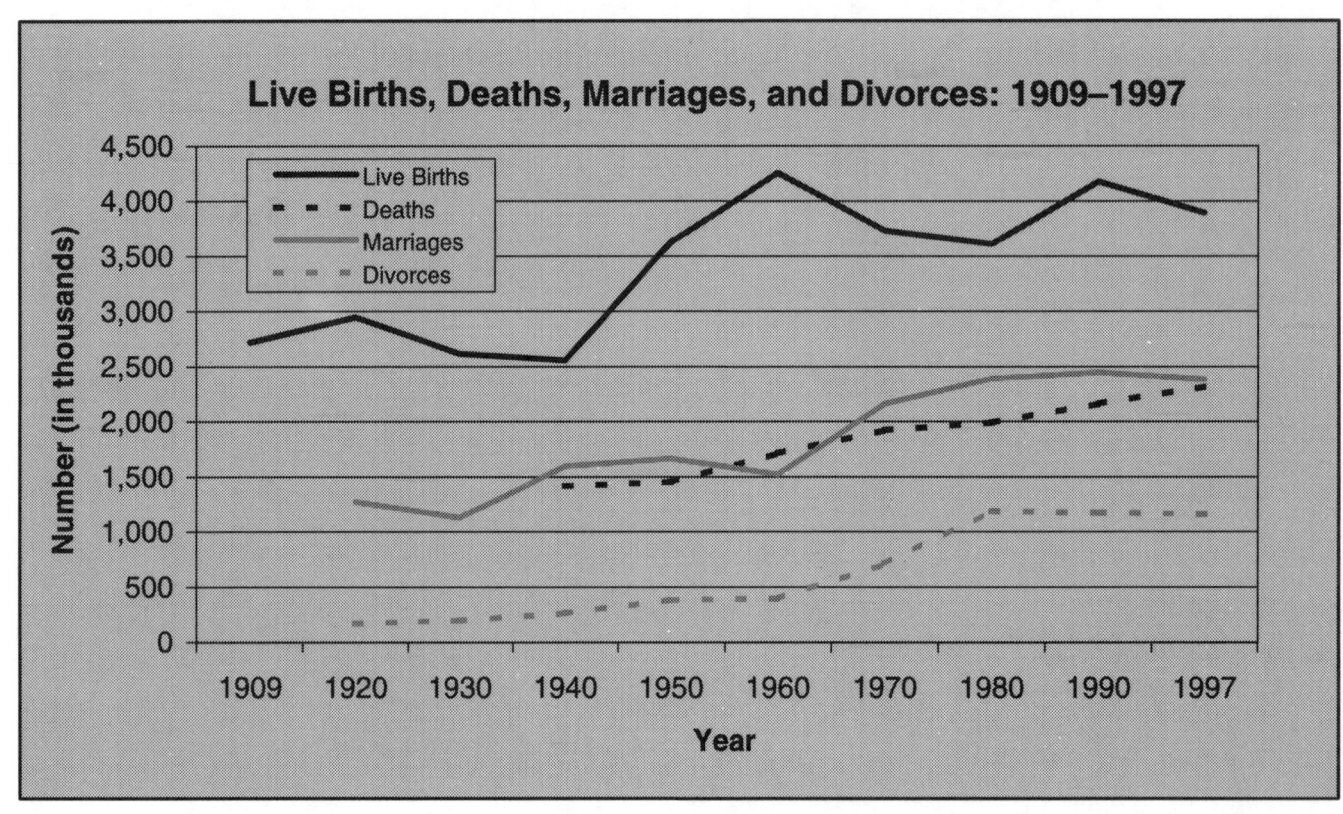

Live Births, Deaths, Marriages, and Divorces: 1909–1997

1 Vital statistics on the four key life events—births, deaths, marriages and divorces—are compiled by the National Center for Health Statistics, successor to the Office of Vital Statistics. From 1900 to 1946, the collection of these data was the responsibility of the Census Bureau.

2 Vital statistics are compiled on the basis of records received from the registration offices of all states, certain cities, and the District of Columbia. Reporting of these events is mandatory in many localities. The annual *Vital Statistics of the United States* summarizes these data, presenting final figures and an annual life table. A life table (also known as a mortality table) is an actuarial table and contains data on life expectancy and death.

3 The annual collection of mortality statistics began in 1900 and the collection of birth statistics in 1915. Since 1933, the entire United States has been included in birth- and death-registration areas. Alaska was added in 1959 and Hawaii in 1960. National statistics on fetal deaths have been compiled since 1922.

4 Birth statistics are based either on complete counts for states participating in the Vital Statistics Cooperative Program or on 50% samples. Mortality statistics are compiled in accordance with the World Health Organization (WHO) regulations based on *International Statistical Classification of Diseases, Injuries and Causes of Death.* The degree of accuracy of birth data is believed to be more than 99.1%. While death data may be nearly as complete as birth data, underreporting may be a problem in isolated areas. The reporting of fetal deaths is likely to be even less complete.

5 Since 1944, marriage and divorce statistics have been available on a uniform basis (i.e., the data are tabulated under standardized headings for all units). A census block for the collection of data on marriage registration was established in 1957 and for divorce registration in 1958.

6 Data on illegitimate births are based on estimates. In the 1930s, all states had a queried legitimacy or illegitimacy on birth certificates. This query was removed during the 1940s on grounds of confidentiality. As a result, the data suffered from potential misreporting. The term "illegitimate" was discarded and replaced by "Births to Unmarried Women" in the 1990 census.

7 Overall, four of the five vital statistics rates per 1,000 has dropped precipitously in the United States, and in all developed countries, since 1950. In the United States, the birth rate decreased from 24.1 to 14.6, the death rate from 9.6 to 8.6, the infant mortality rate from 29.2 to 7.1, and the marriage rate from 11.1 to 8.9. The only exception to this trend is the divorce rate, which increased from 2.6 to 4.3.

8 The difference in birth rates per 1,000 between White and Black women has narrowed since 1980. The relative rates in 1980 were 15.1 for Whites and 21.3 for Blacks, whereas the corresponding rates in 1996 were 14.1 and 17.8. This decrease is the result of a concomitant trend in fertility rates that dropped from 64.8 for Whites and 84.7 for Blacks in 1980 to 64.3 for Whites and 70.7 for Blacks in 1996.

9 There were fewer teenage mothers in 1996 than in 1980. Overall teenage births declined from 552,161 in 1980 to 489,211 in 1996. Of these births, 26% were to Black teenagers.

10 Utah has the highest birth rate of all states at 20.9, with a correspondingly high fertility rate of 88.5. Other states with high birth rates are Texas (17.2), Arizona (16.6), California (16.3), and Nevada (16.0).

11 The total fertility rate declined from an average of 3,449 (3,326 for Whites and 4,326 for Blacks) in 1960-64 to 2,040 (2,017 for Whites and 2,158 for Blacks). For Whites, this rate represents a rebound from 1976 when the fertility rate bottomed out at 1,738. The rate of natural increase has been negative for Whites since 1972, but it remains positive for Blacks with 3.7.

12 The percentage of children with low birth weights, defined as below 5 lbs. 8 oz., has increased from 6.8% in 1980 to 7.5% in 1997. A larger percentage of children born to teenage mothers and unmarried mothers have a lower birth weight (12.8% and 32.4% respectively).

13 The number of Caesarean deliveries rose steadily from 195,000 in 1970 to 797,000 in 1996. These deliveries are most common among women 35 years of age and older.

14 The number of abortions in the United States increased from 586,000 in 1972 (around the time of *Roe v Wade*), to 1,336,000 in 1996, although this figure represents a drop from the peak of 1,609,000 in 1990. Per 1,000 women (15 to 44 years of age), there were 22.9 abortions in 1996 compared to 29.4 in 1980. Nearly 49.2% of all pregnancies to Black women end in abortion, compared to 16.6% for Whites. Late-term abortions (also known as partial-birth abortions) after 13 weeks of gestation numbered 166,000.

15 In 1995, 21.4 million women used contraceptives. Of these women, 39.7% used nonsurgical means, such as the pill or condoms.

16 In 1998, among women who have ever married, 18.7% were childless. The percentage was slightly higher for White women (19.3%) than for Black women (13.6%).

17 Although Americans can expect to live 28.1 years longer than their ancestors did in 1900, the United States trails a number of other developed countries, including Japan, Sweden, Switzerland, Norway, Canada, France, Netherlands, Australia, Italy and Greece in longevity. In 2000, the life expectancy of men was 73 years and women 79.7 years, with an average of 76.4 years. Life expectancy for Blacks is seven years less than that of Whites: 64.6 for men and 74.7 for women, with an average of 69.7.

18 In the United States, 264 persons die every hour, or about 4.4 persons every minute. The death rate is fairly uniform in all states and regions, but is lowest in Alaska at 4.1 per 1,000.

19 Major cardiovascular diseases and malignancies are the leading causes of death in the United States, with crude death rates per 100,000 of 352.2 and 200.8, respectively. These rates have remained fairly steady over the years despite medical advances. Accidents are the leading cause of death for two age groups (1 to 14 and 15 to 24); cancer leads for people 45 to 64 years old; and heart disease is the number one cause of death for those over age 65. Motor vehicle accidents are the cause of death for 15.5 persons and suicides for 10.3 persons out of 100,000. Motor vehicle accident rates have shown a slight decline from 54,633 in 1989 to 42,400 in 1997, perhaps as a result of better-made cars and stricter laws against drunk driving.

20 Whites have a higher suicide rate (19.3 for males and 4.8 for females) than Blacks (12.0 for males and 2.3 for females). However, the rates are reversed for homicides, where Blacks have an extremely high rate (69.2 for males and 13.5 for females) compared to Whites (12.5 for males and 2.5 for females).

21 In a key area of vital statistics, the United States registered significant gains: Between 1980 and 1997, the infant mortality rate dropped from 12.6 to 7.1, maternal deaths from 9.2 to 7.6, and neonatal deaths from 8.5 to 4.7, all per 1,000 live births. However, the gap between Whites and Blacks continues to persist. Blacks have an infant mortality rate of 14.7 per 1,000 live births compared to 6.1 for Whites.

22 AIDS was first included as a cause of death in 1982. Since then, the number of AIDS-related deaths jumped from 3.266 in 1984 to 20,539 in 1997. Men make up three-fourths of the total and Blacks outnumber Whites by 10,256 to 6,990. In 1997, 58,492 AIDS cases were reported, down from 103,533 in 1990. New York leads in the number of reported AIDS cases with 13,189, followed by California 7,029 and Florida 6,098. Between 1981 and 1998 a total of 688,200 cases have been reported; nearly half of these cases are individuals in the 30- to 39-years-old range.

23 Between 1980 and 1996, 14,843 persons died of drug-related causes and 19,770 persons died of alcohol-related causes.

24 The median age at marriage rose for females from 20.6 in 1970 to 24.0 in 1990 and for males from 22.5 to 25.9 in the same period.

25 The median duration of marriage for divorced couples was 7.2 years in 1990. More divorced men and widowers remarry than divorced women and widows. Per 1,000 persons aged 15 and older, 76.2 divorcees and 5.2 widows remarry compared to 105.9 for divorced men and 23.8 widowers.

26 Healthcare expenditures are the fastest growing component of the Gross Domestic Product (GDP) increasing from $247.3 billion in 1970 to $1.092 trillion in 1997. Of this total, consumers spent $187.6 billion, private insurance $348 billion, and government $507.1 billion. The largest item in healthcare expenditures was hospital care $371.1 million, followed by physician services ($217.6 billion), dental services ($50.6 billion), and medication ($108.9 billion).

27 The federal government has provided hospital and medical care directly to specified groups of beneficiaries since 1798 when President John Adams signed into law the Act for the Relief of Sick and Disabled Seamen. Since that time, federally sponsored and financed medical care has been expanded to include such groups as Native Americans, Alaskan natives, veterans, narcotics addicts, and owners of commercial fishing boats. State, local and county governments also provide hospital and medical care for their residents.

28 Beginning in 1966, the Medicaid Program which was enacted as Title XIX of the Social Security Act, enabled states to provide a single health program for the indigent with federal financial participation. Medicaid offers five basic services: inpatient hospital care; outpatient hospital services; laboratory and X-ray services; nursing home services; and physicians' services. In addition, states may offer other services, such as prescription plans or dental care, for which they receive federal funds.

29 Federal health insurance for the aged (Medicare) became effective July 1, 1966, providing hospital and medical protection to an enrolled population aged 65 and over. It includes Part A (hospital program) and Part B (a supplementary program covering physicians' services, outpatient hospital services, therapy, tests, ambulance services, and certain medical supplies. The Part A program is financed on a self-supporting basis through a federal tax, the proceeds of which are placed in a trust fund. Part B is financed through monthly premium payments paid by enrollees and matched by the federal government.

30 The first medical school in the United States, the College of Philadelphia, Department of Medicine (now the University of Pennsylvania School of Medicine) was founded in 1765. The number of medical schools increased to three by 1800, 52 in 1850, and 162 in 1906. From 1906 to 1929 the number declined sharply because of tougher accreditation procedures by the American Medical Association's Council on Medical Education.

31 The first dental school, Baltimore College of Dental Surgery, was founded in 1840. Before that date physicians also practiced dentistry. From 1840 to 1880, dental practitioners learned their trade as apprentices, and it was not until 1880 that most states enacted laws requiring graduation from an accredited dental school.

32 Nursing education began in 1873 with the opening of three schools and by 1893, 70 were in operation. By 1923, all states had licensing bodies for the nursing profession.

33 The first physician in the American Colonies was Dr. Lawrence Bohune, physician of the London Company, who arrived in Virginia in 1610. The first physician in New England was Dr. Samuel Fuller, one of the signers of the Compact on board the *Mayflower* on November 21, 1620. The first American medical graduate was Dr. John Archer, who graduated with nine others from the University of Pennsylvania in 1768.

34 The first American dentist was Josiah Flagg, who, at the age of 18, began practicing dentistry in Boston in 1782.

35 The first trained nurse in the United States was Linda Ann Judson Richards, who graduated from the training school of the New England Hospital for Women and Children in 1873.

36 Disease notification began in the Colonial period was on a local basis, particularly in the port cities. It was limited to epidemics of pestilential diseases. Statewide notification was not required until 1883 when Michigan passed a law under which physicians were asked to report certain diseases to health officers or boards of health. Over the next three decades all states made similar requirements. In 1871, the federal government passed a law providing for the collection of such statistics. By 1912, the data were supplied by 19 states and the District of Columbia on diphtheria, measles, poliomyelitis, scarlet fever, tuberculosis, typhoid, and smallpox. None of these is now considered an important threat to public health. General statistics on health are collected and published by the National Center for Health Statistics in its *National Health Interview Survey* and *National Health and Nutrition Examination Surveys.* Data on diseases are compiled by the Public Health Service through its Centers for Disease Control in Atlanta and published in *Morbidity and Mortality Report.*

37 Per capita health expenditures quadrupled between 1970 and 1997 from $553 to $1,924. In 1997 physician's services consumed the largest amount at $515, followed by hospital services ($451) and medication ($334).

38 Of federal government expenditures on healthcare in 1997 (amounting to $485.5 billion), a little less than half ($214.5 billion) was accounted for by Medicare. Medicare expenditures have skyrocketed from $37.5 billion in 1980 to $241.2 billion in 1999 and are expected to reach $356.1 billion in 2005. The number of enrollees in the Medicare program was 38.4 million in 1997.

39 In 1997, 28.7 million Americans were enrolled in the Medicaid program. Of these, 15.3 million live below the poverty level.

40 Nineteen-point-two billion dollars was spent on medical research in the United States in 1999, compared to $2 million in 1970.

41 Health insurance premiums reached $348 billion in 1997. Insurance carriers met 90.1% of all hospital care expenditures and 76.2% of physicians' service costs.

42 Based on 1982 = 100, the Consumer Price Index of Medical Care Prices rose from 74.9 in 1970 to 242.1 in 1998. However, the rate of change has declined from 9.3% per annum in 1990 to 3.2 in 1998.

43 In 1997, 16.1% of the population, or 43.4 million people carried no medical insurance coverage of any kind and had no safety net. Texas leads the country with 24.9%

of its residents lacking health coverage, followed by Arizona and Arkansas, each at 24.5%.

44 The average American male visits his doctor 4.7 times a year and his dentist 1.9 times. The average American female, however, visits her doctor 6.1 times and her dentist 2.2 times.

45 There were 651 health maintenance organizations (HMOs) in the United States in 1998, compared to 235 in 1980. An HMO is a prepaid health plan offering comprehensive care to members through designated providers, with a fixed periodic payment for healthcare services and a requirement that members be in a plan for a specified period of time. A Group HMO delivers health services through a physician group that is controlled by the HMO or that contracts with one or more independent group practices for the same purpose. An Individual Practice Association (IPA) HMO contracts directly with physicians, associations of independent physicians or multispecialty group practices. The total revenue of these HMO's reached $421.3 billion in 1997 compared to $271.1 billion in 1990.

46 The number of professionally active physicians in the United States in 1997 was 684,600 of which 164,900 were foreign medical graduates, 527,000 were males, 164,900 were females, 458,200 were in an office-based practice, 145,300 were in a hospital-based practice, and 19,400 were in federal service. The number of dentists in the same year was 196,000 or 162 per 100,000. The number of registered active nurses in 1996 was 2.162 million, or 815 per 100,000.

47 The number of medical schools in the United States has remained steady since 1980 at between 125 (1997) and 127. These schools had a total enrollment of 16,935, a figure that also has remained steady since 1980. In 1997, 15,923 students graduated from these schools.

48 The mean net income of physicians has grown from $5,224 in 1929 to $12,324 in 1950, $97,000 in 1982, $155,800 in 1989 and $199,000 in 1996. Cardiovascular surgeons report the highest income, earning an average of $275,200 annually, while family practitioners earn the lowest at $139,100. Physicians carry a large malpractice insurance premium load, which, in the case of obstetricians and gynecologists averages $35,200 a year.

49 In 1997, there were 6,097 hospitals in the United States (down from 6,965 in 1980), of which only 3,287 have 100 beds or more. Of the total, community hospitals numbered 5,057, for-profits 797, psychiatric hospitals 601, and federal hospitals 285. Hospital beds numbered 1.035 million, or 3.9 per 1,000 persons. Of these beds, only 673,000 are in use on any given day. Hospitals employ 4.333 million persons and have annual expenditures of $342.3 billion (compared to $91.9 billion in 1980).

50 The average length of stay in a hospital is 4.9 days, down from 15.3 days in 1931, 10.1 days in 1953, and 7 days in 1980. Because of pressure from HMOs, patients are allowed to remain in hospital care for fewer days than before. For the same reason, more cases are treated on an outpatient or ambulatory basis. Outpatient visits numbered 520.6 million in 1997 compared to 263 million in 1980. Emergency visits in 1997 numbered 97.4 million.

51 The average cost per day of a hospital stay rose from $5.21 in 1946 to $10.67 in 1954, $21.00 in 1963, $45.01 in 1969, $53.95 in 1970, $134 in 1975, $245 in 1980, $460 in 1985, $687 in 1990, and $1,033 in 1997. The states with the highest costs per day were Alaska and California, and the lowest are South Dakota and Montana.

52 Organ transplants and grafts have become relatively common since the 1970s. In 1998, there were 2,992 heart transplants, 4,167 liver transplants, 12,307 kidney transplants, 928 lung transplants, 45,493 cornea grafts, 475,000 bone grafts and 9,000 skin grafts.

53 In 1995, there were 16,700 nursing homes (down from 19,100 in 1985), with 1,771,000 beds. Eleven thousand of these nursing homes are owned by proprietary for-profit corporations.

54 In 1994, there were 5,392 mental health facilities, of which 1,145 were mental hospitals. These facilities have 248,400 inpatient beds.

55 An average of 4.8 days per capita were lost annually in 1996 because of disability. An average student lost 4 school days annually and an average person spent 5.9 days in bed.

56 Unintentional injuries caused a loss of $478 billion in 1997, including wage and productivity losses, medical and administrative expenses, and damages. Of this amount, motor vehicle accidents accounted for $200.3 billion.

57 Millions of Americans suffer from various chronic conditions—33.6 million with arthritis, 8.2 million with visual impairments, 22 million with hearing impairments, 29.4 million with orthopedic impairments, 7.6 million with diabetes, 11.5 million with migraines, 20.6 million with heart conditions, 28.3 million with high blood pressure, 14.1 million with chronic bronchitis and 14.5 million with asthma.

58 Prosthetic devices are assistive technological devices that help the impaired to live as normal a life as possible. In 1994, 4.5 million Americans used anatomical devices, such as braces and artificial limbs; 7.3 million used mobility devices, such as wheelchairs (1.5 million) and crutches (575,000); and 4.4 million used hearing devices, such as hearing aids.

59 Antismoking campaigns have resulted in an across-the-board decline in cigarette smoking in all age groups 12 years and older from 38.7% in 1985 to 29.6% in 1997. During the same period, users of alcohol have declined from 60.2% to 51.4%. Blacks smoke more than Whites, and males more than females.

60 Marijuana and hashish remain the drugs of choice among 12-to-17-year olds, with 9.4% of persons in that age group acknowledging their use. Cocaine and crack come next. There are 10,867 substance abuse treatment facilities in the United States, which treated 929,166 clients. In 1997, 684,317 persons were identified as having serious drug addictions and 623,735 persons as having serious alcohol problems.

61 In 1999, 563,100 persons died from cancer, and 1.221 million new cases were reported. Of the new cases, 171,600 cases were lung cancer and 175,000 were female breast cancer.

62 Despite access to better health information, 34.8% of Americans 20 to 74 years old are overweight. Overweight is defined for men as body mass index greater than or equal to 27.8 kilograms/meter squared, and for women as body mass index greater than or equal to 27.3 kilograms/meter squared. Women are more overweight than men (35.9% to 33.7%). Black women are the most overweight at 53%. Other health indicators are equally troubling: 30.1% smoke, 37.5% have five or more drinks on any given day, and 22% sleep less than six hours a day. Only 19.6% engage in regular and sustained physical activity.

63 The annual consumption of red meat has declined from 132 pounds in 1970 to 111 pounds in 1997. Poultry has gained as a result, its consumption rising from 40.8 pounds to 64.8 pounds in the same period.

64 Soft drinks remain the most popular beverage, with annual consumption increasing from 35 gallons per capita to 53 gallons between 1980 and 1997. Fruit juices also have become popular, with annual per capita consumption rising from 7.4 gallons to 9.2 gallons. All other beverages have registered a decline during this period: coffee from 26.7 gallons to 23.5 gallons; milk from 27.6 gallons to 24.0 gallons; beer from 36.6 gallons to 33.9 gallons; wine from 3.2 gallons to 3.0 gallons, and distilled spirits from 3.0 gallons to 1.9 gallons.

Series B 1-4. Live Births, Deaths, Marriages and Divorces: 1909 to 1997

(In thousands. Birth, marriage and divorce figures represent estimates of all such events; death figures, the number of registered events)

Year	Live births [1,2]	Deaths [3]	Marriages	Divorces [4]	Year	Live births [1,2]	Deaths [3]	Marriages	Divorces [4]
	1	2	3	4		1	2	3	4
1997	3 895	2 315	2 384	1 163	1952	3 913	1 497	1 539	392
1996	3 891	2 315	2 344	1 150	1951	3 823	1 482	1 595	381
1995	3 900	2 312	1 954	973	1950	3 632	1 452	1 667	385
1994	3 979	2 286	2 362	1 191	1949	3 649	1 444	1 580	397
1993	4 000	2 269	2 334	1 187	1948	3 637	1 444	1 811	408
1992	4 065	2 176	2 362	1 215	1947	3 817	1 445	1 992	483
1991	4 111	2 170	2 371	1 187	1946	3 411	1 396	2 291	610
1990	4 179	2 162	2 448	1 175	1945	2 858	1 402	1 613	485
1989	4 041	2 050	2 404	1 163	1944	2 939	1 411	1 452	400
1988	3 910	2 168	2 396	1 167	1943	3 104	1 460	1 577	359
1987	3 809	2 123	2 403	1 166	1942	2 989	1 385	1 772	321
1986	3 757	2 105	2 407	1 178	1941	2 703	1 398	1 696	293
1985	3 761	2 086	2 413	1 190	1940	2 559	1 417	1 596	264
1984	3 669	2 039	2 477	1 169	1939	2 466	1 388	1 404	251
1983	3 639	2 019	2 336	1 158	1938	2 496	1 381	1 331	244
1982	3 681	1 975	2 456	1 170	1937	2 413	1 450	1 451	249
1981	3 629	1 978	2 422	1 213	1936	2 355	1 479	1 369	236
1980	3 612	1 990	2 390	1 189	1935	2 377	1 393	1 327	218
1979	3 494	1 914	2 331	1 181	1934	2 396	1 397	1 302	204
1978	3 333	1 928	2 282	1 130	1933	2 307	1 342	1 098	165
1977	3 327	1 900	2 178	1 091	1932	2 440	. . .	982	164
1976	3 168	1 909	2 155	1 083	1931	2 506	. . .	1 061	188
1975	3 144	1 893	2 153	1 036	1930	2 618	. . .	1 127	196
1974	3 160	1 934	2 230	977	1929	2 582	. . .	1 233	206
1973	3 137	1 973	2 284	915	1928	2 674	. . .	1 182	200
1972	3 258	1 964	2 282	845	1927	2 802	. . .	1 201	196
1971	3 556	1 928	2 190	773	1926	2 839	. . .	1 203	185
1970	3 731	1 921	2 163	708	1925	2 909	. . .	1 188	175
1969	3 600	1 922	2 145	639	1924	2 979	. . .	1 185	171
1968	3 502	1 930	2 069	584	1923	2 910	. . .	1 230	165
1967	[5]3 521	1 851	1 927	523	1922	2 882	. . .	1 134	149
1966	3 606	1 863	1 857	499	1921	3 055	. . .	1 164	160
1965	3 760	1 828	1 800	479	1920	2 950	. . .	1 274	171
1964	4 027	1 798	1 725	450	1919	2 740	. . .	. . .	. . .
1963	4 098	1 814	1 654	428	1918	2 948	. . .	. . .	. . .
1962	4 167	1 757	1 577	413	1917	2 944	. . .	. . .	. . .
1961	4 268	1 702	1 548	414	1916	2 964	. . .	. . .	. . .
1960 *	4 258	1 712	1 523	393	1915	2 965	. . .	. . .	. . .
1959 [6]	4 245	1 657	1 494	395	1914	2 966	. . .	. . .	. . .
1958	4 255	1 648	1 451	368	1913	2 869	. . .	. . .	. . .
1957	4 308	1 633	1 518	381	1912	2 840	. . .	. . .	. . .
1956	4 218	1 564	1 585	382	1911	2 809	. . .	. . .	. . .
1955	4 104	1 529	1 531	377	1910	2 777	. . .	. . .	. . .
1954	4 078	1 481	1 490	379	1909	2 718	. . .	. . .	. . .
1953	3 965	1 518	1 546	390					

* Denotes first year for which figures include Alaska and Hawaii.
1. 1959-1970, registered live births; 1909-1958, adjusted for under-registration.
2. Based on 50 percent sample for 1951-1954, 1956-1966 and 1968-1970.
3. Excludes fetal deaths.
4. Includes reported annulments.
5. Based on 20- to 50-percent sample.
6. Includes Alaska.

Series B 5-10. Birth Rate—Total and Fertility Rate for Women 15-44 Years Old, by Race: 1800 to 1997

(Based on estimated total live births per 1 000 population for specified group. Based on a 50-percent sample of births for 1951-1954, 1956-1966 and 1968-1970; on 20- to 50-percent sample for 1967. Prior to 1959, births adjusted for under-registration; thereafter, registered live births)

Year	Birth Rate, total population			Fertility Rate, women 15-44 years[1]			Year	Birth Rate, total population			Fertility Rate, women 15-44 years[1]		
	Total	White	Black	Total	White	Black		Total	White	Black	Total	White	Black
	5	6	7	8	9	10		5	6	7	8	9	10
1997	14.6	...	...	65.3	64.2	70.8	1947	26.6	26.1	31.2	113.3	111.8	125.9
1996	14.7	14.1	17.8	65.3	64.3	70.7	1946	24.1	23.6	38.4	101.9	100.4	113.9
1995	14.8	14.2	18.2	65.6	64.4	72.3	1945	20.4	19.7	26.5	85.9	83.4	106.0
1994	15.0	14.4	19.5	66.7	64.9	76.9	1944	21.2	20.5	27.4	88.8	86.3	108.5
1993	15.5	14.7	20.5	67.6	65.4	80.5	1943	22.7	22.1	28.3	94.3	92.3	111.0
1992	15.9	15.0	21.3	68.9	66.5	83.2	1942	22.2	21.5	27.7	91.5	89.5	107.6
1991	16.3	15.4	21.9	69.6	67.0	85.2	1941	20.3	19.5	27.3	83.4	80.7	105.4
1990	16.7	15.8	22.4	70.9	68.3	86.8	1940	19.4	18.6	26.7	79.9	77.1	102.4
1989	16.4	15.4	22.3	69.2	66.4	86.2	1939	18.8	18.0	26.1	77.6	74.8	100.1
1988	16.0	14.7	22.2	67.2	63.0	86.6	1938	19.2	18.4	26.3	79.1	76.5	100.5
1987	15.7	14.5	21.6	65.7	62.0	83.8	1937	18.7	17.9	26.0	77.1	74.4	99.4
1986	15.6	14.5	21.2	65.4	61.9	82.4	1936	18.4	17.6	25.1	75.8	73.3	95.9
1985	15.8	15.0	20.4	66.2	64.1	78.8	1935	18.7	17.9	25.8	77.2	74.5	98.4
1984	15.6	14.5	20.8	65.4	62.2	81.4	1934	19.0	18.1	26.3	78.5	75.8	100.4
1983	15.6	14.6	20.9	65.8	62.4	81.7	1933	18.4	17.6	25.5	76.3	73.7	97.3
1982	15.9	14.9	21.4	67.3	63.9	84.1	1932	19.5	18.7	26.9	81.7	79.0	103.0
1981	15.8	14.8	21.6	67.4	63.9	85.4	1931	20.2	19.5	26.6	84.6	82.4	102.1
1980	15.9	15.1	21.3	68.4	64.8	84.7	1930	21.3	20.6	27.5	89.2	87.1	105.9
1979	15.6	14.8	22.3	68.5	64.5	90.5	1929	21.2	20.5	27.3	89.3	87.3	106.1
1978	15.0	14.2	21.6	66.6	62.7	88.6	1928	22.2	21.5	28.5	93.8	91.7	111.0
1977	15.1	14.4	21.7	67.8	64.0	89.8	1927	23.5	22.7	31.1	99.8	97.1	121.7
1976	14.6	13.8	20.8	65.8	62.2	87.2	1926	24.2	23.1	33.4	102.6	99.2	130.3
1975	14.6	13.8	20.9	66.7	63.0	89.2	1925	25.1	24.1	34.2	106.6	103.3	134.0
1974	14.8	14.0	21.0	68.4	64.7	90.8	1924	26.1	25.1	34.6	110.9	107.8	135.6
1973	14.8	13.9	21.5	69.2	65.3	94.3	1923	26.0	25.2	33.2	110.5	108.0	130.5
1972	15.6	14.6	22.9	73.4	69.2	100.3	1922	26.2	25.4	33.2	111.2	108.8	130.8
1971	17.2	16.2	24.7	81.8	77.5	109.5	1921	28.1	27.3	35.8	119.8	117.2	140.8
1970	18.4	17.4	25.1	87.9	84.1	113.0	1920	27.7	26.9	35.0	117.9	115.4	137.5
1969	17.8	16.9	24.4	86.5	82.4	114.8	1919	26.1	25.3	32.4	111.2	...	...
1968	17.5	16.6	24.2	85.7	81.5	114.9	1918	28.2	27.6	33.0	119.8	...	...
1967 [2]	17.8	16.8	25.0	87.6	83.1	119.8	1917	28.5	27.9	32.9	121.0	...	...
1966	18.4	17.4	26.1	91.3	86.4	125.9	1916	29.1	28.5	...	123.4	121.8	...
1965	19.4	18.3	27.6	96.6	91.4	133.9	1915	29.5	28.9	...	125.0	123.2	...
1964	21.0	20.0	29.1	105.0	99.9	141.7	1914	29.9	29.3	...	126.6	124.6	...
1963 [3]	21.7	20.7	29.7	108.5	103.7	144.9	1913	29.5	28.8	...	124.7	122.4	...
1962 [3]	22.4	21.4	30.5	112.2	107.5	148.8	1912	29.8	29.0	...	125.8	123.3	...
1961	23.3	22.2	34.6	117.2	112.2	153.5	1911	29.9	29.1	...	126.3	123.6	...
1960 *	23.7	22.7	32.1	118.0	113.2	153.6	1910	30.1	29.2	...	126.8	123.8	...
1959 [4]	24.0	22.9	32.9	118.8	113.9	156.0	1909	30.0	29.2	...	126.8	123.6	...
1958	24.5	23.3	34.3	120.2	114.9	160.5	1900	32.3	30.1	...	...	130	...
1957	25.3	24.0	35.3	122.9	117.7	163.0	1890	...	31.5	...	...	137	...
1956	25.2	24.0	35.4	121.2	116.0	160.9	1880	39.8	35.2	...	...	155	...
1955	25.0	23.8	34.7	118.5	113.8	155.3	1870	...	38.3	...	...	167	...
1954	25.3	24.2	34.9	118.1	113.6	153.2	1860	44.3	41.4	...	...	184	...
1953	25.0	24.0	34.1	115.2	111.0	147.3	1850	...	43.3	...	...	194	...
1952	25.1	24.1	33.6	113.9	110.1	143.3	1840	51.8	48.3	...	...	222	...
1951	24.9	23.9	33.8	111.5	107.7	142.1	1830	...	51.4	...	...	240	...
1950	24.1	23.0	33.3	106.2	102.3	137.3	1820	55.2	52.8	...	...	260	...
1949	24.5	23.6	33.0	107.1	103.6	135.1	1810	...	54.3	...	...	274	...
1948	24.9	24.0	32.4	107.3	104.3	131.6	1800	...	55.0	...	...	278	...

* Denotes first year for which figures include Alaska and Hawaii.
1. Computed by relating total births, regardless of age of mother, to women aged 15-44 years.
2. For 1800-1970, Black and other.
3. Figures by race exclude New Jersey; state did not require reporting of race.
4. Includes Alaska.

Series B 11-19. Fertility Rate by Race: 1940 to 1999

(The total fertility rate is the number of births that 1,000 women would have in their lifetime if, at each year of age, they experienced the birth rates occurring in the specified year. A total fertility rate of 2,110 represents "replacement level" fertility for the total population under current mortality conditions (assuming no net immigration). Based on race of child through 1979; beginning 1980, based on race of mother. Prior to 1959, births adjusted for under registration; thereafter, registered live births. Based on 50-percent sample of births for 1951–1954, 1956–1966, and 1968–1970; on 20- to 50-percent sample for 1967)

Total Fertility Rate (1980–1999)

Year	Total	White	Black and Other	American Indian	Asian or Pacific Islander
	11	11	11	11	11
1999	2 075	2 063	2 149	2 050	1 931
1998	2 058	2 041	2 171	2 091	1 868
1997	2 033	2 009	2 154	2 048	1 926
1996	2 027	2 006	2 144	2 030	1 908
1995	2 019	1 989	2 175	2 034	1 924
1994	2 036	1 985	2 300	2 080	1 943
1993	2 046	1 982	2 385	2 141	1 936
1992	2 065	1 994	2 442	2 190	1 942
1991	2 073	1 996	2 480	2 169	1 956
1990	2 081	2 003	2 480	2 183	2 003
1989	2 014	1 931	2 433	2 247	1 948
1988	1 934	1 857	2 298	2 154	1 987
1987	1 872	1 805	2 198	2 099	1 886
1986	1 838	1 776	2 136	2 082	1 836
1985	1 844	1 787	2 109	2 128	1 885
1984	1 807	1 749	2 071	2 136	1 892
1983	1 799	1 741	2 066	2 181	1 944
1982	1 828	1 767	2 107	2 213	2 016
1981	1 812	1 748	2 118	2 090	1 976
1980	1 840	1 773	2 177	2 163	1 954

Total Fertility Rate (1960–1979)

Year	Total	White	Black	American Indian	Asian or Pacific Islander
	11	11	11	11	11
1979	1 808	1 716	2 263	...	...
1978	1 760	1 668	2 218	...	...
1977	1 790	1 703	2 251	...	...
1976	1 738	1 652	2 187	...	...
1975	1 774	1 686	2 243	...	...
1974	1 835	1 749	2 299	...	...
1973	1 879	1 783	2 411	...	...
1972	2 010	1 907	2 601	...	...
1971	2 267	2 161	2 902	...	...
1970	2 480	2 385	3 100	...	...
1969	2 465	2 360	3 043	...	...
1968	2 477	2 368	3 100	...	...
1967	2 573	2 453	3 312	...	...
1966	2 736	2 609	3 545	...	...
1965	2 928	2 780	3 829	...	...
1964	3 208	3 074	4 139	...	...
1963	3 333	3 190	...	...	...
1962	3 474	3 340	...	...	...
1961	3 629	3 502	4 542	...	...
1960	3 654	3 533	...	...	...

Total Fertility Rate (1940–1959)

Year	Total	White	Black	American Indian	Asian or Pacific Islander
	11	11	11	11	11
1959	3 670	3 544	...	...	...
1958	3 630	3 530	...	...	...
1957	3 680	3 580	...	...	...
1956	3 600	3 500	...	...	...
1955	3 500	3 400	...	...	...
1954	3 460	3 370	...	...	...
1953	3 350	3 270	...	...	...
1952	3 290	3 210	...	...	...
1951	3 200	3 120	...	...	...
1950	3 030	2 950	...	...	...
1949	3 040	2 960	...	...	...
1948	3 030	2 970	...	...	...
1947	3 180	3 170	...	...	...
1946	2 860	2 840	...	...	...
1945	2 420	2 380	...	...	...
1944	2 490	2 450	...	...	...
1943	2 640	2 610	...	...	...
1942	2 550	2 530	...	...	...
1941	2 330	2 280	...	...	...
1940	2 230	2 180	...	...	...

Total Fertility Rate (1917–1939)

Year	Total	White	Black	American Indian	Asian or Pacific Islander
	11	11	11	11	11
1939	2 172	2 120	...	...	...
1938	2 222	2 175	...	...	...
1937	2 173	2 121	...	...	...
1936	2 146	2 101	...	...	...
1935	2 189	2 141	...	...	...
1934	2 232	2 181	...	...	...
1933	2 172	2 126	...	...	...
1932	2 319	2 271	...	...	...
1931	2 402	2 369	...	...	...
1930	2 533	2 506	...	...	...
1929	2 532	2 506	...	...	...
1928	2 660	2 632	...	...	...
1927	2 824	2 783	...	...	...
1926	2 901	2 839	...	...	...
1925	3 012	2 949	...	...	...
1924	3 121	3 069	...	...	...
1923	3 101	3 063	...	...	...
1922	3 109	3 072	...	...	...
1921	3 326	3 282	...	...	...
1920	3 263	3 219	...	...	...
1919	3 068	3 025	...	...	...
1918	3 312	3 288	...	...	...
1917	3 333	3 312	...	...	...

NOTE: 1999 data are preliminary.

SOURCES:
Hauser, Robert. *Fertility Tables for Birth Cohorts by Color: United States 1901-1973.* (Rockville, MD: National Center for Health Statistics, 1976).
National Center for Health Statistics, Births: Preliminary Data for 1999, by S.A. Curtin and J.A. Martin. *National Vital Statistics Reports* 48, no. 14 (Hyattsville, MD: National Center for Health Statistics, 2000).
National Center for Health Statistics, Births: Final Data for 1998, by S.J. Ventura, J.A. Martin, S.C. Curtin, T.J. Mathews, and M.M. Park.
National Vital Statistics Reports 48, no. 3 (Hyattsville, MD: National Center for Health Statistics, 2000).
National Center for Health Statistics, *Vital Statistics of the United States, 1969, Volume I, Natality* (Rockville, MD: U.S. Department of Health and Human Services, 1974)

Series B 28-35. Birth Rates of Unmarried Women ages 15 to 44, by Age of Mother: 1950 to 1999

(Excludes births to nonresidents of the United States. Rates are live births per 1 000 unmarried females in specified group. Figures for age of mother not stated are distributed. Based on 5-percent sample of births for 1951–1954, 1956–1966, and 1968–1970; on 20- to 50-percent sample for 1967. Data prior to 1980 are estimated and based on the race of the child; 1980 and later, based on race of mother.)

| | Total | | Birth rates, by age of mother | | | | | | | White, total | | | Black | |
| | Births (1 000) | Birth rate, all ages | 15-19 years | 20-24 years | 25-29 years | 30-34 years | 35-39 years | 40-44 years | Year | Births (1 000) | Birth rate, all ages | Year | Births (1 000) | Birth rate, all ages |
Year	28	29	30	31	32	33	34	35		28	29		28	29
1999	1 305	43.9	...	...	...	...	...	...	1999	836.0	...	1999	417.0	...
1998	1 294	44.3	41.5	72.3	58.4	39.1	19.0	4.6	1998	821.4	37.5	1998	421.4	73.3
1997	1 257	44.0	42.2	71.0	56.2	39.0	19.0	4.6	1997	793.2	37.0	1997	415.1	73.4
1996	1 260	44.8	42.9	70.7	56.8	41.1	20.1	4.8	1996	795.4	37.6	1996	415.2	74.4
1995	1 254	45.1	44.4	70.3	56.1	39.6	19.5	4.7	1995	785.0	37.5	1995	421.5	75.9
1994	1 290	46.9	46.4	72.2	59.0	40.1	19.8	4.7	1994	794.3	38.3	1994	448.3	82.1
1993	1 240	45.3	44.5	69.2	57.1	38.5	19.0	4.4	1993	742.1	35.9	1993	452.5	84.0
1992	1 225	45.2	44.6	68.5	56.5	37.9	18.8	4.1	1992	722.0	35.2	1992	459.0	86.5
1991	1 214	45.2	44.8	68.0	56.5	38.1	18.0	3.8	1991	707.5	34.6	1991	463.8	79.5
1990	1 165	43.8	42.5	65.1	56.0	37.6	17.3	3.6	1990	669.7	32.9	1990	455.3	90.5
1989	1 094	41.6	40.1	61.2	52.8	34.9	16.0	3.4	1989	613.5	30.2	1989	442.4	90.7
1988	1 005	38.5	36.4	56.0	48.5	32.0	15.0	3.2	1988	557.4	27.4	1988	413.2	86.5
1987	933	36.0	33.8	52.6	44.5	29.6	13.5	2.9	1987	514.0	25.3	1987	387.5	82.6
1986	878	34.2	32.3	49.3	42.2	27.2	12.2	2.7	1986	480.5	23.9	1986	369.8	79.0
1985	828	32.8	31.4	46.5	39.9	25.2	11.6	2.5	1985	445.6	22.5	1985	356.2	77.0
1984	770	31.0	30.0	43.0	37.1	23.3	10.9	2.5	1984	403.0	20.6	1984	342.5	75.2
1983	738	30.3	29.5	41.8	35.5	22.4	10.2	2.6	1983	381.3	19.8	1983	333.2	76.2
1982	715	30.0	28.7	41.5	35.1	21.9	10.0	2.7	1982	365.6	19.3	1982	328.0	77.9
1981	687	29.5	27.9	41.1	34.5	20.8	9.8	2.6	1981	346.5	18.6	1981	321.4	79.4
1980	666	29.4	27.6	40.9	34.0	21.1	9.7	2.6	1980	329.0	18.1	1980	318.8	81.1
1979	598	27.2	26.4	37.7	29.9	17.7	8.4	2.3	1979	263.0	14.9	1979	315.8	83.0
1978	544	25.7	24.9	35.3	28.5	16.9	8.2	2.2	1978	233.6	13.7	1978	293.4	81.1
1977	516	25.6	25.1	34.0	27.7	16.9	8.4	2.4	1977	220.1	13.5	1977	281.6	82.6
1976	468	24.3	23.7	31.7	26.8	17.5	9.0	2.5	1976	197.1	12.6	1976	258.8	81.6
1975	448	24.5	23.9	31.2	27.5	17.9	9.1	2.6	1975	186.4	12.4	1975	249.6	84.2
1974	418	23.9	23.0	30.5	27.9	18.4	10.0	2.6	1974	168.5	11.7	1974	238.8	85.5
1973	407	24.3	22.7	31.5	29.6	20.3	10.8	3.0	1973	163.0	11.8	1973	234.5	88.6
1972	403	24.8	22.8	33.2	30.8	22.6	12.0	3.1	1972	160.5	11.9	1972	233.3	91.6
1971	401	25.5	22.3	35.5	34.5	25.2	13.3	3.5	1971	163.8	12.5	1971	229.0	96.1
1970	399	26.4	22.4	38.4	37.0	27.1	13.6	3.5	1970	175.1	13.9	1970	215.1	95.5
1969	361	24.8	20.4	37.3	37.9	27.0	13.5	3.6	1969	163.7	13.4			
1968	339	24.3	19.7	37.2	38.3	27.8	14.8	3.8	1968	155.2	13.1			
1967	318	23.7	18.5	38.1	41.1	28.9	15.3	4.0	1967	142.2	12.5			
1966	302	23.3	17.5	39.0	45.1	32.7	16.3	4.1	1966	132.9	11.9			
1965	291	23.4	16.7	39.6	49.1	37.2	17.4	4.5	1965	123.7	11.6			

See footnotes at end of chart.

Series B 28-35. Birth Rates of Unmarried Women ages 15 to 44, by Age of Mother: 1950 to 1999—Cont'd.

(Excludes births to nonresidents of the United States. Rates are live births per 1 000 unmarried females in specified group. Figures for age of mother not stated are distributed. Based on 5-percent sample of births for 1951–1954, 1956–1966, and 1968–1970; on 20- to 50-percent sample for 1967. Data prior to 1980 are estimated and based on the race of the child; 1980 and later, based on race of mother.)

Year	Total Births (1 000)	Total Birth rate, all ages	15-19 years	20-24 years	25-29 years	30-34 years	35-39 years	40-44 years	Year	White, total Births (1 000)	White, total Birth rate, all ages	Year	Black Births (1 000)	Black Birth rate, all ages
	28	**29**	**30**	**31**	**32**	**33**	**34**	**35**		**28**	**29**		**28**	**29**
1964	276	23.0	15.9	39.5	49.9	36.9	16.3	4.4	1964	114.3	11.0			
1963	259	22.5	15.3	39.9	48.8	33.1	16.1	4.3	1963	104.6	10.5			
1962	245	21.9	14.8	40.7	46.6	29.6	15.6	4.1	1962	94.7	9.8			
1961	240	22.7	16.0	41.4	46.4	28.2	15.4	3.9	1961	91.1	10.0			
1960	224	21.6	15.3	39.7	45.1	27.8	14.1	3.6	1960	82.5	9.2			
1959	221	21.9	15.5	40.2	44.1	28.1	14.1	3.3	1959	79.6	9.2			
1958	209	21.2	15.3	38.2	40.5	27.5	13.3	3.2	1958	74.6	8.8			
1957	202	21.0	15.8	37.3	36.8	26.8	12.1	3.1	1957	70.8	8.6			
1956	194	20.4	15.6	36.4	35.6	24.6	11.1	2.8	1956	67.5	8.3			
1955	183	19.3	15.1	33.5	33.5	22.0	10.5	2.7	1955	64.2	7.9			
1954	177	18.7	14.9	31.4	31.0	20.4	10.3	2.5	1954	62.7	. . .			
1953	161	16.9	13.9	28.0	27.6	17.3	9.0	2.4	1953	56.6	. . .			
1952	150	15.8	13.5	25.4	24.8	15.7	8.2	1.9	1952	54.1	. . .			
1951	147	15.1	13.2	23.2	22.8	14.6	7.6	2.2	1951	52.6	. . .			
1950	142	14.1	12.6	21.3	19.9	13.3	7.2	2.0	1950	53.5	6.1			

NOTE: 1999 data are preliminary.

SOURCES:
National Center for Health Statistics, Births: Preliminary Data for 1999, by S.A. Curtin and J.A. Martin. *National Vital Statistics Reports* 48, no. 14 (Hyattsville, MD: National Center for Health Statistics, 2000).
National Center for Health Statistics, Births: Final Data for 1998, by S.J. Ventura, J.A. Martin, S.C. Curtin, T.J. Mathews, and M.M. Park.
National Vital Statistics Reports 48, no. 3 (Hyattsville, MD: National Center for Health Statistics, 2000).
National Center for Health Statistics, Births: Final Data for 1997, by S.J. Ventura, J.A. Martin, S.C. Curtin, and T.J. Mathews.
National Vital Statistics Reports 47, no. 18 (Hyattsville, MD: National Center for Health Statistics, 1999).
National Center for Health Statistics, Report of Final Natality Statistics, 1996, by S.J. Ventura, J.A. Martin, S.C. Curtin, and T.J. Mathews.
Monthly Vital Statistics Report 46, no. 11, Supplement (Hyattsville, MD: National Center for Health Statistics, 1998).
National Center for Health Statistics, Report of Final Natality Statistics, 1995, by S.J. Ventura, J.A. Martin, S.C. Curtin, and T.J. Mathews.
Monthly Vital Statistics Report 45, no. 11, Supplement (Hyattsville, MD: National Center for Health Statistics, 1997).
National Center for Health Statistics, Advance Report of Final Natality Statistics, 1994, by S.J. Ventura, J.A. Martin, T.J. Mathews, and S.C. Clarke.
Monthly Vital Statistics Report 44, no. 11, Supplement (Hyattsville, MD: National Center for Health Statistics, 1996).
National Center for Health Statistics, *Vital Statistics of the United States*, 1993, Volume I, Natality (Hyattsville, MD: U.S. Department of Health and Human Services, 1999).
National Center for Health Statistics, *Vital Statistics of the United States*, 1979, Volume I, Natality (Hyattsville, MD: U.S. Department of Health and Human Services, 1984).
National Center for Health Statistics, *Vital Statistics of the United States*, 1969, Volume I, Natality (Rockville, MD: U.S. Department of Health and Human Services, 1974).
National Center for Health Statistics, *Vital Statistics of the United States*, 1963, Volume I, Natality (Washington, DC: U.S. Department of Health, Education, and Welfare, 1964).

Series B 107-115. Expectation of Life (in years) at Birth, by Race and Sex: 1900 to 2010
(Prior to 1929, for death-registration area only)

Year	Total			White			Black and other		
	Both sexes	Male	Female	Both sexes	Male	Female	Both sexes	Male	Female
	107	**108**	**109**	**110**	**111**	**112**	**113**	**114**	**115**
2010	77.9	74.4	81.3	78.3	74.9	81.7	...	...	...
2005	77.6	74.2	81.0	78.1	74.6	81.5	...	...	...
2000	77.0	73.5	80.4	77.5	74.0	80.9	...	...	...
1995	76.3	72.8	79.7	76.8	73.4	80.2	...	...	...
1997	76.5	73.6	79.2	77.1	74.3	73.9	...	...	...
1996	76.1	73.0	79.0	76.8	73.8	79.6	72.6	68.9	76.1
1995	75.8	72.5	78.9	76.5	73.4	79.6	71.9	67.9	75.7
1994	75.7	72.3	79.0	76.4	73.2	79.6	71.7	67.5	75.8
1993	75.5	72.2	78.8	76.3	73.1	79.5	71.5	67.3	75.5
1992	75.8	72.3	79.1	76.5	73.2	79.8	71.8	67.7	75.7
1991	75.5	72.0	78.9	76.3	72.9	79.6	71.5	67.3	75.5
1990	75.4	72.0	78.8	76.0	72.6	79.3	72.4	68.4	76.3
1989	75.3	71.8	78.6	76.0	72.7	79.2	71.2	67.1	75.2
1988	74.9	71.5	78.3	75.6	72.3	78.9	71.2	67.1	75.1
1987	75.0	71.5	78.4	75.6	72.2	78.9	71.3	67.3	75.2
1986	74.8	71.3	78.3	75.4	72.0	78.8	71.2	67.2	75.1
1985	74.7	71.2	78.2	75.3	71.9	78.7	71.2	67.2	75.0
1984	74.7	71.2	78.2	75.3	71.8	78.7	71.3	67.4	75.0
1983	74.6	71.0	78.1	75.2	71.7	78.7	71.3	67.4	74.9
1982	74.5	70.9	78.1	75.1	71.5	78.7	71.0	66.8	75.0
1981	74.2	70.4	77.8	74.8	71.1	78.4	70.3	66.1	74.4
1980	73.7	70.0	77.4	74.4	70.7	78.1	69.5	65.3	73.6
1979	73.9	70.0	77.8	74.6	70.8	78.4	69.8	65.4	74.1
1978	73.5	69.6	77.3	74.1	70.4	78.0	69.3	65.0	73.5
1977	73.3	69.5	77.2	74.0	70.2	77.9	68.9	64.7	73.2
1976	72.9	69.1	76.8	73.6	69.9	77.5	68.4	64.2	72.7
1975	72.6	68.8	76.6	73.4	69.5	77.3	68.0	63.7	72.4
1974	71.9	68.1	75.8	72.7	68.9	76.6	67.6	62.9	71.3
1973	71.3	67.6	75.3	72.2	68.4	76.1	65.9	61.9	70.1
1972	71.1	67.4	75.1	72.0	68.3	75.9	65.6	61.5	69.9
1971	71.1	67.4	75.0	72.0	68.3	75.8	65.6	61.6	69.7
1970	70.9	67.1	74.8	71.7	68.0	75.6	65.3	61.3	69.4
1969	70.5	66.8	74.3	71.3	67.8	75.1	64.3	60.5	68.4
1968	70.2	66.6	74.0	71.1	67.5	74.9	63.7	60.1	67.5
1967	70.5	67.0	74.2	71.3	67.8	75.1	64.6	61.1	68.2
1966	70.1	66.7	73.8	71.0	67.6	74.7	64.0	60.7	67.4
1965	70.2	66.8	73.7	71.0	67.6	74.7	64.1	61.1	67.4
1964	70.2	66.9	73.7	71.0	67.7	74.6	64.1	61.1	67.2
1963 [1]	69.9	66.6	73.4	70.8	67.5	74.4	63.6	60.9	66.5
1962 [1]	70.0	66.8	73.4	70.9	67.6	74.4	64.1	61.5	66.8
1961	70.2	67.0	73.6	71.0	67.8	74.5	64.4	61.9	67.0
1960 *	69.7	66.6	73.1	70.6	67.4	74.1	63.6	61.1	66.3
1959 [2]	69.9	66.8	73.2	70.7	67.5	74.2	63.9	61.3	66.5
1958	69.6	66.6	72.9	70.5	67.4	73.9	63.4	61.0	65.8
1957	69.5	66.4	72.7	70.3	67.7	73.7	63.0	60.7	65.5
1956	69.7	66.7	72.9	70.5	67.5	73.9	63.6	61.3	66.1
1955	69.6	66.7	72.8	70.5	67.4	73.7	63.7	61.4	66.1
1954	69.6	66.7	72.8	70.5	67.5	73.7	63.4	61.1	65.9
1953	68.8	66.0	72.0	69.7	66.8	73.0	62.0	59.7	64.5
1952	68.6	65.8	71.6	69.5	66.6	72.6	61.4	59.1	63.8
1951	68.4	65.6	71.4	69.3	66.5	72.4	61.2	59.2	63.4
1950	68.2	65.6	71.1	69.1	66.5	72.2	60.8	59.1	62.9
1949	68.0	65.2	70.7	68.8	66.2	71.9	60.6	58.9	62.7
1948	67.2	64.6	69.9	68.0	65.5	71.0	60.0	58.1	62.5
1947	66.8	64.4	69.7	67.6	65.2	70.5	59.7	57.9	61.9
1946	66.7	64.4	69.4	67.5	65.1	70.3	59.1	57.5	61.0
1945	65.9	63.6	67.9	66.8	64.4	69.5	57.7	56.1	59.6
1944	65.2	63.6	66.8	66.2	64.5	68.4	56.6	55.8	57.7

See footnotes at end of chart.

Series B 107-115. Expectation of Life (in years) at Birth, by Race and Sex: 1900 to 2010—Cont'd.

(Prior to 1929, for death-registration area only)

Year	Total			White			Black and other		
	Both sexes	Male	Female	Both sexes	Male	Female	Both sexes	Male	Female
	107	**108**	**109**	**110**	**111**	**112**	**113**	**114**	**115**
1943	63.3	62.4	64.4	64.2	63.2	65.7	55.6	55.4	56.1
1942	66.2	64.7	67.9	67.3	65.9	69.4	56.6	55.4	58.2
1941	64.8	63.1	66.8	66.2	64.4	68.5	53.8	52.5	55.3
1940	62.9	60.8	65.2	64.2	62.1	66.6	53.1	51.5	54.9
1939	63.7	62.1	65.4	64.9	63.3	66.6	54.5	53.2	56.0
1938	63.5	61.9	65.3	65.0	63.2	66.8	52.9	51.7	54.3
1937	60.0	58.0	62.4	61.4	59.3	63.8	50.3	48.3	52.5
1936	58.5	56.6	60.6	59.8	58.0	61.9	49.0	47.0	51.4
1935	61.7	59.9	63.9	62.9	61.0	65.0	53.1	51.3	55.2
1934	61.1	59.3	63.3	62.4	50.6	64.6	51.8	50.2	53.7
1933	63.3	61.7	65.1	64.3	62.7	66.3	54.7	53.5	56.0
1932	62.1	61.0	63.5	63.2	62.0	64.5	53.7	52.8	54.6
1931	61.1	59.4	63.1	62.6	60.8	64.7	50.4	49.5	51.5
1930	59.7	58.1	61.6	61.4	59.7	63.5	48.1	47.3	49.2
1929	57.1	55.8	58.7	58.6	57.2	60.3	46.7	45.7	47.8
1928	56.8	55.6	58.3	58.4	57.0	60.0	46.3	45.6	47.0
1927	60.4	59.0	62.1	62.0	60.5	63.9	48.2	47.6	48.9
1926	56.7	55.5	58.0	58.2	57.0	59.6	44.6	43.7	45.6
1925	59.0	57.6	60.6	60.7	59.3	62.4	45.7	44.9	46.7
1924	59.7	58.1	61.5	61.4	59.8	63.4	46.6	45.5	47.8
1923	57.2	56.1	58.5	58.3	57.1	59.6	48.3	47.7	48.9
1922	59.6	58.4	61.0	60.4	59.1	61.9	52.4	51.8	53.0
1921	60.8	60.0	61.8	61.8	60.8	62.9	51.5	51.6	51.3
1920	54.1	53.6	54.6	54.9	54.4	55.6	45.3	45.5	45.2
1919	54.7	53.5	56.0	55.8	54.5	57.4	44.5	44.5	44.4
1918	39.1	36.6	42.2	39.8	37.1	43.2	31.1	29.9	32.5
1917	50.9	48.4	54.0	52.0	49.3	55.3	38.8	37.0	40.8
1916	51.7	49.6	54.3	52.5	50.2	55.2	41.3	39.6	43.1
1915	54.5	52.5	56.8	55.1	53.1	57.5	38.9	37.5	40.5
1914	54.2	52.0	56.8	54.9	52.7	57.5	38.9	37.1	40.8
1913	52.5	50.3	55.0	53.0	50.8	55.7	38.4	36.7	40.3
1912	53.5	51.5	55.9	53.9	51.9	56.2	37.9	35.9	40.0
1911	52.6	50.9	54.4	53.0	51.3	54.9	36.4	34.6	38.2
1910	50.0	48.4	51.8	50.3	48.6	52.0	35.6	33.8	37.5
1909	52.1	50.5	53.8	52.5	50.9	54.2	35.7	34.2	37.3
1908	51.1	49.5	52.8	51.5	49.9	53.3	34.9	33.8	36.0
1907	47.6	45.6	49.9	48.1	46.0	50.4	32.5	31.1	34.0
1906	48.7	46.9	50.8	49.3	47.3	51.4	32.9	31.8	33.9
1905	48.7	47.3	50.2	49.1	47.6	50.6	31.3	29.6	33.1
1904	47.6	46.2	49.1	48.0	46.6	49.5	30.8	29.1	32.7
1903	50.5	49.1	52.0	50.9	49.5	52.5	33.1	31.7	34.6
1902	51.5	49.8	53.4	51.9	50.2	53.8	34.6	32.9	36.4
1901	49.1	47.6	50.6	49.4	48.0	51.0	33.7	32.2	35.3
1900	47.3	46.3	48.3	47.6	46.6	48.7	33.0	32.5	33.5

* Denotes first year for which figures include Alaska and Hawaii.
1. Excludes New Jersey; state did not require reporting of race.
2. Includes Alaska.

Series B 136-147. Fetal Death Ratio; Neonatal, Infant and Maternal Mortality Rates, by Race: 1915 to 1997

(Prior to 1933, for registration area only)

Year	Fetal death ratio per 1 000 live births [1]			Neonatal mortality rate per 1 000 live births			Infant mortality rate per 1 000 live births			Maternal mortality rate per 100 000 live births		
	Total	White	Black and other	Total	White	Black and other	Total	White	Black and other	Total	White	Black and other
	136	**137**	**138**	**139**	**140**	**141**	**142**	**143**	**144**	**145**	**146**	**147**
1997	...	...	...	4.8	4.0	7.7	7.2	6.0	11.8	...	...	...
1996	...	...	...	4.8	4.0	7.9	7.3	6.0	12.2	7.6	5.1	16.9
1995	...	...	...	4.9	4.1	8.1	7.6	6.3	12.6	7.1	4.2	18.5
1994	...	...	...	5.1	4.2	8.6	8.0	6.6	13.5	8.3	6.2	16.2
1993	(NA)	...	...	5.3	4.3	9.0	8.4	6.8	14.1	7.5	4.8	17.6
1992	7.4	6.3	11.7	5.4	4.3	9.2	8.5	6.9	14.4	7.8	5.0	18.2
1990	7.5	6.4	11.9	5.8	4.8	9.9	9.2	7.6	15.5	8.2	5.4	19.1
1989	7.5	6.4	11.4	6.2	5.1	10.3	9.8	8.1	16.3	7.9	5.6	16.5
1988	7.5	6.4	11.4	6.3	5.4	10.3	10.0	8.4	16.1	8.6	5.9	17.4
1987	7.7	6.7	11.5	6.5	5.5	10.7	10.1	8.5	16.5	6.6	5.1	12.0
1986	7.7	6.8	11.2	6.7	5.7	10.8	10.4	8.8	16.7	7.2	4.9	16.0
1985	7.9	7.0	11.3	7.0	6.0	11.0	10.6	9.2	16.8	7.8	5.2	18.1
1984	8.2	7.4	11.5	7.0	6.1	10.9	10.8	9.3	17.8	7.8	5.4	16.9
1983	8.5	7.5	12.4	7.3	6.3	11.4	11.2	9.6	17.8	8.0	5.9	16.3
1982	8.9	7.9	12.7	7.7	6.7	12.0	11.5	9.9	18.3	7.9	5.8	16.4
1981	9.0	8.0	12.8	8.0	7.0	12.5	11.9	10.3	18.8	8.5	6.3	17.3
1980	9.2	8.2	13.4	8.5	7.4	4.0	13.2	10.9	20.2	9.2	6.7	19.8
1979	9.4	8.4	13.8	8.9	7.9	12.9	13.1	11.4	19.8	9.6	6.4	22.7
1978	9.7	8.5	14.7	9.5	8.4	14.0	13.8	12.0	21.1	9.6	6.4	23.0
1977	9.9	8.7	14.6	9.9	8.7	14.7	14.1	12.3	21.7	11.2	7.7	26.0
1976	10.5	9.3	15.2	10.9	9.7	16.3	15.2	13.3	23.5	12.3	9.0	26.5
1975	10.7	9.5	16.0	11.6	10.4	16.8	16.1	14.2	24.2	12.8	9.1	29.0
1974	11.5	10.2	17.0	12.3	11.1	17.2	16.7	14.8	24.9	14.6	10.0	35.1
1973	12.2	10.8	18.6	13.0	11.8	17.9	17.7	15.8	26.2	15.2	10.7	34.6
1972	12.7	11.2	19.5	13.6	12.4	19.2	18.5	16.4	27.7	18.8	14.3	38.5
1971	13.4	11.8	21.2	14.2	13.0	19.6	19.1	17.1	28.5	18.8	13.0	45.3
1970	14.2	12.4	22.6	15.1	13.8	21.4	20.0	17.8	30.9	22.0	14.0	56.0
1969	14.1	12.4	22.5	15.6	14.2	22.5	20.9	18.4	32.9	22.0	15.0	56.0
1968	15.8	13.8	25.6	16.1	14.7	23.0	21.8	19.2	34.5	25.0	17.0	64.0
1967	15.6	13.5	25.8	16.5	15.0	23.8	22.4	19.7	35.9	28.0	20.0	70.0
1966	15.7	13.6	26.1	17.2	15.6	24.8	23.7	20.6	38.8	29.0	20.0	72.0
1965	16.2	13.9	27.2	17.7	16.1	25.4	24.7	21.5	40.3	32.0	21.0	84.0
1964	16.4	14.1	28.2	17.9	16.2	26.5	24.8	21.6	41.1	33.0	22.0	90.0
1963 [2]	15.8	13.7	26.7	18.2	16.7	26.1	25.2	22.2	41.5	36.0	24.0	97.0
1962 [2]	15.9	13.9	26.7	18.3	16.9	26.1	25.3	22.3	41.4	35.0	24.0	96.0
1961	16.1	14.1	27.0	18.4	16.9	26.2	25.3	22.4	40.7	37.0	25.0	101.0
1960 *	16.1	14.1	26.8	18.7	17.2	26.9	26.0	22.9	43.2	37.0	26.0	98.0
1959 [3]	16.2	14.2	27.3	19.0	17.5	27.7	26.4	23.2	44.0	37.0	26.0	102.0
1958	16.5	14.5	27.5	19.5	17.8	29.0	27.1	23.8	45.7	38.0	26.0	102.0
1957	16.3	14.5	26.8	19.1	17.5	27.8	26.3	23.3	43.7	41.0	28.0	118.0
1956	16.5	14.6	27.2	18.9	17.5	27.0	26.0	23.2	42.1	41.0	29.0	111.0
1955	17.1	15.2	28.4	19.1	17.7	27.2	26.4	23.6	42.8	47.0	33.0	130.0
1954	17.5	15.5	28.9	19.1	17.8	27.0	26.6	23.9	42.9	52.0	37.0	144.0
1953	17.8	15.9	29.6	19.6	18.3	27.4	27.8	25.0	44.7	61.0	44.0	166.0
1952	18.3	16.1	32.2	19.8	18.5	28.0	28.4	25.5	47.0	68.0	49.0	188.0
1951	18.8	16.7	32.1	20.0	18.9	27.3	28.4	25.8	44.8	75.0	55.0	201.0
1950	19.2	17.1	32.5	20.5	19.4	27.5	29.2	26.8	44.5	83.0	61.0	222.0
1949	19.8	17.5	34.6	21.4	20.3	28.6	31.3	28.9	47.3	90.0	68.0	235.0
1948	20.6	18.3	36.5	22.2	21.2	29.1	32.0	29.9	46.5	117.0	89.0	301.0
1947	21.1	18.7	39.6	22.8	21.7	31.0	32.2	30.1	48.5	135.0	109.0	335.0
1946	22.8	20.4	40.9	24.0	23.1	31.5	33.8	31.8	49.5	157.0	131.0	359.0
1945	23.9	21.4	42.0	24.3	23.3	32.0	38.3	35.6	57.0	207.0	172.0	455.0
1944	27.0	24.5	45.4	24.7	23.6	32.5	39.8	36.9	60.3	228.0	189.0	506.0
1943	26.7	24.2	46.2	24.7	23.7	32.9	40.4	37.5	62.5	245.0	211.0	510.0

See footnotes at end of table.

Series B 136-147. Fetal Death Ratio; Neonatal, Infant and Maternal Mortality Rates, by Race: 1915 to 1997—Cont'd.

(Prior to 1933, for registration area only)

Year	Fetal death ratio per 1 000 live births [1]			Neonatal mortality rate per 1 000 live births			Infant mortality rate per 1 000 live births			Maternal mortality rate per 100 000 live births		
	Total	White	Black and other	Total	White	Black and other	Total	White	Black and other	Total	White	Black and other
	136	137	138	139	140	141	142	143	144	145	146	147
1942	28.2	25.5	49.3	25.7	24.5	34.6	40.4	37.3	64.6	259.0	222.0	544.0
1941	29.9	26.5	54.0	27.7	26.1	39.0	45.3	41.2	74.8	317.0	266.0	678.0
1940	31.3	27.7	56.7	28.8	27.2	39.7	47.0	43.2	73.8	376.0	320.0	774.0
1939	32.0	28.2	59.0	29.3	27.8	39.6	48.0	44.3	74.2	404.0	353.0	762.0
1938	32.1	28.1	61.1	29.6	28.3	39.1	51.0	47.1	79.1	435.0	377.0	849.0
1937	33.4	29.2	63.2	31.3	29.7	42.1	54.4	50.3	83.2	489.0	436.0	858.0
1936	34.4	29.8	66.9	32.6	31.0	43.9	57.1	52.9	87.6	568.0	512.0	972.0
1935	35.8	31.1	68.7	32.4	31.0	42.7	55.7	51.9	83.2	582.0	531.0	946.0
1934	36.2	31.4	70.1	34.1	[4] 32.3	[4] 45.3	60.1	[4] 54.5	[4] 94.4	593.0	[4] 544.0	[4] 897.0
1933	37.0	32.2	71.1	34.0	[4] 32.1	[4] 45.8	58.1	[4] 52.8	[4] 91.3	619.0	[4] 564.0	[4] 967.0
1932	37.8	32.7	74.4	33.5	[4] 32.0	[4] 43.7	57.6	[4] 53.3	[4] 86.2	633.0	[4] 581.0	[4] 976.0
1931	38.2	33.4	74.1	34.6	33.2	45.2	61.6	57.4	93.1	661.0	601.0	1 114.0
1930	39.2	34.0	79.9	35.7	34.2	47.4	64.6	60.1	99.9	673.0	609.0	1 174.0
1929	39.5	34.4	79.7	36.9	35.6	47.3	67.6	63.2	102.2	695.0	631.0	1 199.0
1928	40.2	35.0	81.5	37.2	35.7	48.8	68.7	64.0	106.2	692.0	627.0	1 210.0
1927	38.8	34.8	74.8	36.1	35.0	46.1	64.6	60.6	100.1	647.0	594.0	1 133.0
1926	38.1	35.1	73.0	37.9	37.1	48.0	73.3	70.0	111.8	656.0	619.0	1 071.0
1925	38.1	35.1	73.1	37.8	36.8	49.5	71.7	68.3	110.8	647.0	603.0	1 162.0
1924	39.3	35.8	76.2	38.6	37.4	51.2	70.8	66.8	112.9	656.0	607.0	1 179.0
1923	38.9	35.9	71.8	39.5	38.6	49.9	77.1	73.5	117.4	665.0	626.0	1 095.0
1922	39.4	36.4	73.4	39.7	38.8	49.9	76.2	73.2	110.0	664.0	628.0	1 068.0
1921	...	...	...	39.7	38.7	50.3	75.6	72.5	108.5	682.0	644.0	1 077.0
1920	...	...	...	41.5	40.4	55.0	85.8	82.1	131.7	799.0	760.0	1 281.0
1919	...	...	...	41.5	40.3	55.2	86.6	83.0	130.5	737.0	696.0	1 244.0
1918	...	...	...	44.2	43.3	60.5	100.9	97.4	161.2	916.0	889.0	1 393.0
1917	...	...	...	43.4	42.6	58.0	93.8	90.5	150.7	662.0	632.0	1 177.0
1916	...	...	...	44.1	43.5	68.9	101.0	99.0	184.9	622.0	608.0	1 179.0
1915	...	...	...	44.4	...	...	99.9	98.6	181.2	608.0	601.0	1 056.0

* Denotes first year for which figures include Alaska and Hawaii.

1. Beginning in 1945, includes only deaths for which the period of gestation was given as 20 weeks or more or not stated. For earlier years, includes all fetal deaths, regardless of gestation. In 1945, ratios based on all fetal deaths, regardless of gestation, were: Total, 26.6; white, 24.1; black and other, 44.6.

2. Figures by race exclude New Jersey; state did not require reporting of race.

3. Includes Alaska.

4. Mexicans included with Black and other.

Series B 167-180. Death Rate, by Race and Sex: 1900 to 1997

(Number of deaths, excluding fetal deaths, per 1,000 population. Prior to 1933 for death-registration area only)

Year	Total	Death rate						Year	Total	Death rate					
		White			Black[1]					White			Black[1]		
		Both sexes	Male	Female	Both sexes	Male	Female			Both sexes	Male	Female	Both sexes	Male	Female
	167	168	169	170	171	172	173		167	168	169	170	171	172	173
1997	8.6	9.0	9.1	9.0	8.0	8.8	7.3	1947	10.1	9.9	11.4	8.5	11.4	12.5	10.3
1996	8.7	9.1	9.2	9.0	8.4	9.4	7.5	1946	10.0	9.8	11.2	8.5	11.1	12.2	10.0
1995	8.8	9.1	9.3	8.9	8.6	9.8	7.6	1945	10.6	10.4	12.5	8.6	11.9	13.5	10.5
1994	8.8	9.1	9.3	8.8	8.6	9.9	7.5	1944	10.6	10.4	12.2	8.8	12.4	13.8	11.1
1993	8.8	9.1	9.4	8.8	8.8	10.1	7.6	1943	10.9	10.7	12.2	9.2	12.8	14.0	11.6
1992	8.5	8.8	9.2	8.4	8.5	9.8	7.4	1942	10.3	10.1	11.4	8.7	12.7	14.0	11.4
1991	8.6	8.9	9.3	8.5	8.6	10.0	7.4	1941	10.5	10.2	11.4	8.9	13.5	14.8	12.2
1990	8.6	8.9	9.3	8.5	8.8	10.1	7.5	1940	10.8	10.4	11.6	9.2	13.8	15.1	12.6
1989	8.7	8.9	9.4	8.5	8.9	10.3	7.6	1939	10.6	10.3	11.3	9.2	13.5	14.7	12.4
1988	8.8	9.1	9.6	8.7	8.9	10.3	7.6	1938	10.6	10.3	11.3	9.2	14.0	15.2	12.9
1987	8.7	9.0	9.5	8.5	8.6	9.9	7.4	1937	11.3	10.8	12.0	9.6	14.9	16.4	13.4
1986	8.7	9.0	9.5	8.4	8.5	9.9	7.3	1936	11.6	11.1	12.3	9.9	15.4	16.9	13.9
1985	8.8	9.0	9.6	8.4	8.5	9.9	7.3	1935	10.9	10.6	11.6	9.5	14.3	15.6	13.0
1984	8.6	8.9	9.5	8.2	8.3	9.6	7.1	1934	11.1	10.6	11.7	9.6	14.8	16.0	13.5
1983	8.6	8.8	9.6	8.2	8.3	9.6	7.1	1933	10.7	10.3	11.2	9.3	14.1	15.1	13.1
1982	8.5	8.7	9.5	8.0	8.2	9.6	6.9	1932	10.9	10.5	11.3	9.6	14.5	15.4	13.5
1981	8.6	8.8	9.7	8.0	8.4	9.9	7.1	1931	11.1	10.6	11.5	9.6	15.5	16.5	14.5
1980	8.8	8.9	9.8	8.1	8.8	10.3	7.3	1930	11.3	10.8	11.7	9.8	16.3	17.4	15.3
1979	8.5	8.7	9.8	7.7	8.4	10.0	7.0	1929	11.9	11.3	12.2	10.4	16.9	18.0	15.8
1978	8.7	8.8	9.8	7.8	8.6	10.2	7.1	1928	12.0	11.4	12.3	10.5	17.1	18.0	16.2
1977	8.6	8.7	9.8	7.7	8.6	10.3	7.2	1927	11.3	10.8	11.6	10.0	16.4	17.2	15.6
1976	8.9	9.0	10.1	7.9	8.2	9.8	6.8	1926	12.1	11.6	12.3	10.8	17.8	18.7	16.9
1975	8.5	8.7	10.0	7.8	8.8	10.6	7.3	1925	11.7	11.1	11.8	10.4	17.4	18.2	16.6
1974	9.2	9.2	10.4	8.1	8.7	10.4	7.2	1924	11.6	11.0	11.8	10.3	17.1	17.9	16.3
1973	9.4	9.4	10.7	8.2	9.1	10.8	7.6	1923	12.1	11.7	12.3	11.0	16.5	17.0	16.0
1972	9.4	9.5	10.8	8.2	9.2	11.0	7.6	1922	11.7	11.3	11.9	10.7	15.2	15.7	14.8
1971	9.3	9.3	10.7	8.1	9.2	10.8	7.7	1921	11.5	11.1	11.6	10.6	15.5	15.7	15.4
1970	9.5	9.5	10.9	8.1	9.4	11.2	7.8	1920	13.0	12.6	13.0	12.1	17.7	17.8	17.5
1969	9.5	9.5	10.9	8.2	9.6	11.3	8.0	1919	12.9	12.4	13.0	11.8	17.9	18.1	17.8
1968	9.7	9.6	11.1	8.2	9.9	11.6	8.3	1918	18.1	17.5	19.3	15.8	25.6	26.7	24.4
1967	9.4	9.4	10.8	8.0	9.4	10.9	7.9	1917	14.0	13.5	14.6	12.4	20.4	21.4	19.4
1966	9.5	9.5	10.9	8.1	9.7	11.3	8.3	1916	13.8	13.4	14.4	12.4	19.1	19.9	18.4
1965	9.4	9.4	10.8	8.0	9.6	11.1	8.2	1915	13.2	12.9	13.7	12.0	20.2	20.8	19.5
1964	9.4	9.4	10.8	8.0	9.7	11.1	8.3	1914	13.3	13.0	13.9	12.1	20.2	20.9	19.4
1963 [2]	9.6	9.5	11.0	8.1	10.1	11.5	8.7	1913	13.8	13.5	14.5	12.5	20.3	21.0	19.6
1962 [2]	9.5	9.4	10.8	8.0	9.8	11.2	8.5	1912	13.6	13.4	14.3	12.4	20.6	21.3	19.7
1961	9.3	9.3	10.7	7.8	9.6	10.9	8.4	1911	13.9	13.7	14.5	12.8	21.3	21.9	20.6
1960 *	9.5	9.5	11.0	8.0	10.1	11.5	9.1	1910	14.7	14.5	15.4	13.6	21.7	22.3	21.0
1959 [3]	9.4	9.3	10.8	7.9	9.9	11.3	8.6	1909	14.2	14.0	14.9	13.2	21.8	22.3	21.2
1958	9.5	9.4	10.9	8.0	10.3	11.6	9.0	1908	14.7	14.5	15.3	13.6	22.4	22.8	22.0
1957	9.6	9.5	11.0	8.0	10.5	11.9	9.1	1907	15.9	15.7	16.8	14.5	24.3	25.0	23.5
1956	9.4	9.3	10.8	7.8	10.1	11.4	8.8	1906	15.7	15.5	16.5	14.4	24.2	24.7	23.6
1955	9.3	9.2	10.7	7.8	10.0	11.3	8.8	1905	15.9	15.7	16.5	14.8	25.5	26.8	24.3
1954	9.2	9.1	10.6	7.6	10.1	11.4	8.8	1904	16.4	16.2	17.1	15.3	26.1	27.6	24.7
1953	9.6	9.4	11.0	8.0	10.8	12.3	9.4	1903	15.6	15.4	16.2	14.6	24.5	25.5	23.4
1952	9.6	9.4	11.0	8.0	11.0	12.5	9.6	1902	15.5	15.3	16.2	14.4	23.6	24.8	22.3
1951	9.7	9.5	11.0	8.0	11.0	12.5	9.8	1901	16.4	16.2	17.1	15.4	24.3	25.6	23.1
1950	9.6	9.5	10.9	8.1	11.2	12.5	9.9	1900	17.2	17.0	17.7	16.3	25.0	25.7	24.4
1949	9.7	9.5	11.0	8.1	11.2	12.5	10.0								
1948	9.9	9.7	11.2	8.3	11.4	12.7	10.1								

* Denotes first year for which figures include Alaska and Hawaii.
1. From 1977 to date, Black only. For 1900-1976, Black and other. In 1970, the rates for Black only were 10.0 for both sexes; 11.9 for male; and 8.3 for female.
2. Excludes New Jersey; state did not require reporting of race.
3. Includes Alaska.

Series B 214-215. Marriage Rate: 1920 to 1997

Year	Per 1 000 population 214	Per 1 000 unmarried females[1] 215	Year	Per 1 000 population 214	Per 1 000 unmarried females[1] 215	Year	Per 1 000 population 214	Per 1 000 unmarried females[1] 215	Year	Per 1 000 population 214	Per 1 000 unmarried females[1] 215
1997	8.9	(NA)	1977	9.9	63.6	1957	8.9	78.0	1937	11.3	78.0
1996	8.8	49.7	1976	9.9	65.2	1956	9.5	82.4	1936	10.7	74.0
1995	8.9	50.8	1975	10.0	66.9	1955	9.3	80.9	1935	10.4	72.5
1994	9.1	51.5	1974	10.5	72.0	1954	9.2	79.8	1934	10.3	71.8
1993	9.0	52.3	1973	10.8	76.0	1953	9.8	83.7	1933	8.7	61.3
1992	9.3	53.3	1972	10.9	77.5	1952	9.9	83.2	1932	7.9	56.0
1991	9.4	54.2	1971	10.6	76.3	1951	10.4	86.6	1931	8.6	61.9
1990	9.8	54.5	1970	10.6	76.5	1950	11.1	90.2	1930	9.2	67.6
1989	9.7	54.2	1969	10.6	80.0	1949	10.6	86.7	1929	10.1	75.5
1988	9.8	54.6	1968	10.4	79.1	1948	12.4	98.5	1928	9.8	74.1
1987	9.9	55.7	1967	9.7	76.4	1947	13.9	106.2	1927	10.1	77.0
1986	10.0	56.2	1966	9.5	75.6	1946	16.4	118.1	1926	10.2	78.7
1985	10.1	57.0	1965	9.3	75.0	1945	12.2	83.6	1925	10.3	79.2
1984	10.5	59.5	1964	9.0	74.6	1944	10.9	76.5	1924	10.4	80.3
1983	10.5	59.9	1963	8.8	73.4	1943	11.7	83.0	1923	11.0	85.2
1982	10.6	61.4	1962	8.5	71.2	1942	13.2	93.0	1922	10.3	79.7
1981	10.6	61.7	1961	8.5	72.2	1941	12.7	88.5	1921	10.7	83.0
1980	10.6	61.4	1960*	8.5	73.5	1940	12.1	82.8	1920	12.0	92.0
1979	10.4	63.6	1959 [2]	8.5	73.6	1939	10.7	73.0			
1978	10.3	64.1	1958	8.4	72.0	1938	10.3	69.9			

* Denotes first year for which figures include Alaska and Hawaii.
1. 15 years old and over.
2. Includes Alaska.

Series B 216-220. Divorce Rate: 1920 to 1997
(Includes reported annulments)

Year	Divorce rate Per 1 000 population	Per 1 000 married females[1]	Median duration of marriage (years)	Year	Divorce rate Per 1 000 population	Per 1 000 married females[1]	Median duration of marriage (years)	Year	Divorce rate Per 1 000 population	Per 1 000 married females[1]	Median duration of marriage (years)
	216	217	218		216	217	218		216	217	218
1997	4.3	...	(NA)	1971	3.7	15.8	6.7	1945	3.5	14.4	...
1996	4.3	19.5	...	1970	3.5	14.9	6.7	1944	2.9	12.0	...
1995	4.9	19.8	...	1969	3.2	13.4	6.9	1943	2.6	11.0	...
1994	4.6	20.5	...	1968	2.9	12.5	7.0				
1993	4.6	20.5	...	1967	2.6	11.2	7.1	1942	2.4	10.1	...
1992	4.8	21.2	...	1966	2.5	10.9	7.1	1941	2.2	9.4	...
1991	4.7	20.9	...	1965	2.5	10.6	7.2	1940	2.0	8.8	...
1990	4.7	20.9	7.2	1964	2.4	10.0	7.4	1939	1.9	8.5	...
1989	4.7	20.4	7.2	1963	2.3	9.6	7.5	1938	1.9	8.4	...
1988	4.8	20.7	7.1	1962	2.2	9.4	7.3	1937	1.9	8.7	...
1987	4.8	20.8	7.0	1961	2.3	9.6	7.1	1936	1.8	8.3	...
1986	4.9	21.2	6.9	1960*	2.2	9.2	7.2	1935	1.7	7.8	...
1985	5.0	21.7	6.8	1959[2]	2.2	9.3	7.0	1934	1.6	7.5	...
1984	5.0	21.5	6.9	1958	2.1	8.9	6.4	1933	1.3	6.1	...
1983	5.0	21.3	7.0	1957	2.2	9.2	6.7	1932	1.3	6.1	...
1982	5.1	21.7	7.0	1956	2.3	9.4	6.5	1931	1.5	7.1	...
1981	5.3	22.6	7.0	1955	2.3	9.3	6.4	1930	1.6	7.5	...
1980	5.2	22.6	6.8	1954	2.4	9.5	6.4	1929	1.7	8.0	...
1979	5.3	22.8	6.8	1953	2.5	9.9	6.1	1928	1.7	7.8	...
1978	5.1	21.9	6.6	1952	2.5	10.1	6.1	1927	1.6	7.8	...
1977	5.0	21.1	6.6	1951	2.5	9.9	6.0	1926	1.6	7.5	...
1976	5.0	21.1	6.5	1950	2.6	10.3	5.8	1925	1.5	7.2	...
1975	4.9	20.3	6.5	1949	2.7	10.6	...	1924	1.5	7.2	...
1974	4.6	19.3	6.5	1948	2.8	11.2	...	1923	1.5	7.1	...
1973	4.3	18.2	6.6	1947	3.4	13.6	...	1922	1.4	6.6	...
1972	4.0	17.0	6.7	1946	4.3	17.9	...	1921	1.5	7.2	...
								1920	1.6	8.0	...

* Denotes first year for which figures include Alaska and Hawaii.
1. 15 years old and over. Population enumerated as of April 1 for 1940, 1950 and 1960 and estimated as of July 1 for all other years; includes Armed Forces abroad for 1941-1946.
2. Includes Alaska.

Series B 221-235. Total National Health Expenditures, by Type of Service: 1929 to 1997

(Calendar year data. Totals in million dollars.)

| Year | Total | Health services and supplies | | | | | | | | | | Research and medical-facilities construction | |
| | | Total | Hospital care | Physicians' services | Dentists' services | Other professional services[1] | Drugs and drug sundries[2] | Eyeglasses and appliances | Nursing home care | Government public health activities | Other health services | Research[2] | Construction |
	221	222	223	224	225	226	227	228	229	231	232	234	235
1997.....	1 092 400	1 057 500	371 100	217 600	50 600	61 900	108 900	13 900	82 800	38 500	29 900	18 000	16 900
1996.....	1 042 500	1 010 600	360 800	208 500	47 500	57 500	98 300	13 400	79 400	34 000	27 400	17 200	14 800
1995.....	993 700	963 100	347 200	201 900	45 000	53 600	88 900	13 100	75 500	30 400	25 100	16 700	13 900
1994.....	947 700	917 200	185 900	193 000	42 400	49 600	81 600	12 500	71 100	28 200	21 900	15 900	14 600
1993.....	898 500	869 500	175 900	185 900	39 500	46 100	76 200	12 300	66 400	25 300	18 000	14 500	14 500
1992.....	836 500	809 000	759 200	175 900	37 000	42 100	71 200	1 190	62 300	23 400	15 400	14 200	13 400
1991.....	761 700	736 800	282 300	759 200	33 300	38 300	65 600	11 200	57 200	21 400	13 600	12 900	12 000
1990.....	666 200	643 400	256 000	125 700	34 000	31 600	54 600	12 100	53 100	19 300	11 300	12 400	10 400
1989.....	602 800	582 100	232 600	113 600	31 600	27 100	50 600	11 400	47 700	18 300	9 700	11 000	9 600
1988.....	546 000	526 200	212 000	105 100	29 400	23 800	46 300	10 100	42 800	16 600	8 700	10 300	9 500
1987.....	494 100	476 800	194 200	93 000	27 100	21 100	43 200	9 100	39 700	14 600	7 800	9 000	8 200
1986.....	458 200	442 000	179 600	92 000	29 600	14 100	30 600	8 200	38 100	13 400	11 900	8 200	8 000
1985.....	422 600	407 200	168 300	74 000	23 300	16 600	36 200	7 100	34 100	12 300	6 400	7 800	7 600
1984.....	391 100	375 400	156 300	75 400	24 600	10 900	26 500	7 000	31 700	11 000	9 400	6 800	8 900
1983.....	357 200	341 800	146 800	64 800	21 700	9 300	24 500	6 200	29 400	9 900	8 300	6 200	9 200
1982.....	322 400	308 300	135 500	61 800	19 500	7 100	22 400	5 700	27 300	8 600	7 600	5 900	8 200
1981.....	286 600	273 500	118 000	54 800	17 300	6 400	21 300	5 700	24 200	7 700	6 900	5 700	7 500
1980.....	250 100	238 900	102 400	41 900	14 400	8 700	21 600	4 600	20 000	7 200	4 600	5 400	5 800
1979.....	215 000	204 500	86 100	40 200	13 300	4 700	17 200	4 600	17 600	6 200	5 100	4 800	5 700
1978.....	189 300	179 500	75 700	35 800	11 800	4 100	15 400	4 100	15 200	5 300	4 500	4 400	5 300
1977.....	162 600	153 900	65 600	32 200	10 000	3 200	12 500	2 100	12 600	3 700	4 300	3 700	5 100
1976.....	141 000	132 400	55 600	27 500	8 700	2 400	11 300	1 900	10 700	3 500	4 000	3 600	5 000
1975.....	132 700	124 300	52 100	24 900	8 200	2 600	11 900	3 200	10 100	3 200	3 700	3 300	5 100
1974.....	106 300	99 300	41 000	19 700	6 900	1 900	9 400	1 700	7 500	2 500	3 200	2 500	4 500
1973.....	99 069	...	38 270	18 200	5 970	1 900	9 300	2 091	7 050	1 905	3 643	2 484	4 258
1972.....	90 391	...	34 219	16 916	5 581	1 717	8 628	1 896	6 274	1 804	3 306	2 173	4 180
1971.....	81 294	...	30 552	15 835	5 068	1 547	7 821	1 839	5 446	1 811	2 897	1 954	3 845
1970.....	71 573	66 365	27 597	14 294	4 419	1 466	7 297	1 866	3 070	1 568	2 690	1 842	3 366
1969.....	64 142	59 351	24 093	12 654	4 047	1 313	6 812	1 765	2 650	1 316	2 592	1 818	2 973
1968.....	56 587	52 532	20 926	11 099	3 623	1 271	6 165	1 731	2 280	1 098	2 332	1 795	2 260
1967.....	50 696	46 987	18 145	10 287	3 360	1 158	5 652	1 609	1 858	942	2 099	1 703	2 006
1966.....	44 974	41 440	15 583	9 156	2 964	1 123	5 309	1 413	1 526	885	1 800	1 574	1 960
1965.....	40 468	37 087	13 605	8 745	2 808	1 038	4 850	1 230	1 328	698	1 492	1 469	1 912
1964.....	37 461	34 375	12 697	8 056	2 648	940	4 446	1 072	1 214	610	1 511	1 324	1 762
1963.....	33 530	30 890	11 709	6 891	2 277	921	4 235	952	891	540	1 380	1 184	1 456
1962.....	31 295	28 857	10 658	6 498	2 234	902	4 095	908	695	505	1 277	1 032	1 406
1961.....	28 783	26 766	9 921	5 895	2 067	882	3 824	804	606	452	1 320	844	1 174
1960.....	26 895	25 185	9 092	5 684	1 977	862	3 657	776	526	414	1 336	662	1 048
1959.....	24 878	23 354	8 177	5 481	1 894	801	3 525	722	434	428	1 138	526	998
1958.....	22 848	21 442	7 548	4 910	1 850	729	3 242	678	383	424	1 045	416	990
1957.....	21 108	19 885	6 892	4 419	1 737	673	3 010	678	368	415	1 011	344	879
1956.....	19 246	18 348	6 347	4 067	1 625	610	2 686	668	358	402	965	270	628
1955.....	17 745	16 884	5 900	3 689	1 508	562	2 384	604	312	377	924	210	651
1954.....	16 799	15 946	5 502	3 574	1 406	541	2 181	606	270	374	904	183	670
1953.....	15 745	14 895	5 085	3 278	1 234	499	2 152	612	248	378	911	164	686
1952.....	14 988	13 949	4 685	3 042	1 098	459	2 071	586	228	427	952	150	889
1951.....	13 992	12 912	4 254	2 868	997	426	1 989	551	207	416	883	134	946
1950.....	12 662	11 702	3 851	2 747	961	396	1 726	491	187	361	666	117	843
1949.....	11 576	10 811	3 557	2 633	920	371	1 557	458	168	338	539	105	660
1948.....	10 612	10 184	3 203	2 611	900	354	1 466	436	150	306	470	89	339
1940.....	3 987	3 868	1 011	973	419	174	637	189	33	153	112	3	116
1935.....	2 936	2 875	763	773	302	153	475	133	...	117	64	...	61
1929.....	3 649	3 436	663	1 004	482	252	606	133	...	96	91	...	213

1. Services of registered and practical nurses in private duty, visits of nurses, podiatrists, physical therapists, clinical psychologists, chiropractors, naturopaths and Christian Science practitioners.
2. Research expenditures of drug companies included in expenditures for drugs and drug sundries and excluded from research expenditures.

Series B 236-247. National and Personal Health Care Expenditures, by Source of Funds: 1929 to 1997

(In billions of dollars, except percent. Calendar year data.)

Year	National health expenditures — Amount	National health expenditures — Percent of gross national product	Personal health care expenditures — Private insurance benefits	Personal health care expenditures — Public expenditures
	236	237	245	247
1997	1 092 400	13.4	348 000	507 100
1996	1 042 500	13.6	337 100	481 400
1995	993 700	13.6	324 300	455 200
1994	947 700	13.6	315 100	422 800
1993	898 500	13.7	306 800	385 300
1992	836 500	13.4	285 500	353 000
1991	761 704	12.8	221 600	320 295
1990	666.2	12.2	216.8	268.6
1989	602.8	11.6	196.4	240.0
1988	546.0	11.2	174.4	215.1
1987	494.1	10.9	154.8	197.7
1986	454.8	10.7	143.2	180.3
1985	422.6	10.5	134.1	165.4
1984	389.6	10.3	123.7	150.8
1983	358.6	10.5	111.4	139.5
1982	326.1	10.3	100.5	127.0
1981	290.2	9.5	86.9	114.2
1980	250.1	9.2	73.4	98.1
1979	217.2	8.7	63.2	84.1
1978	193.7	8.6	55.0	73.6
1977	172.0	8.6	47.8	64.6
1976	152.2	8.5	39.7	56.9
1975	132.9	8.3	32.9	50.2
1974	116.1	7.9	27.8	42.8
1973	102.5	7.5	24.6	35.9
1972	92.3	7.6	21.9	31.8
1971	82.3	7.5	19.1	28.2
1970	71.6	7.3	15.7	21.9
1969	64.1	6.9	13.1	19.7
1968	56.6	6.5	11.3	17.5
1967	50.7	6.4	9.5	14.6
1966	44.9	6.0	9.1	9.5
1965	40.5	5.9	8.7	7.3
1964	37.5	5.9	7.8	6.9
1963	33.5	5.7	7.0	6.4
1962	31.3	5.6	6.3	6.0
1961	28.8	5.5	5.7	5.6
1960	26.9	5.3	5.0	5.2
1959	24.9	5.1	4.4	4.8
1958	22.8	5.1	3.9	4.5
1957	21.1	4.8	3.5	4.2
1956	19.2	4.6	3.0	3.9
1955	17.7	4.4	2.5	3.6
1954	16.8	4.6	2.2	3.4
1953	15.7	4.3	1.9	3.3
1952	15.0	4.3	1.6	3.3
1951	14.0	4.3	1.3	3.0
1950	12.7	4.5	1.0	2.4
1949	11.6	4.5	.8	2.0
1948	10.6	4.1	.6	1.8
1940	4.0	4.0	...	.6
1935	3.0	4.0	...	.4
1929	3.6	3.5	...	.3

Series B 275-290.   Physicians, Dentists and Nurses; and Medical, Dental and Nursing Schools: 1810 to 1997

(Census figures in italics. Figures for schools and students are for academic session ending in the specified year)

Year	Physicians [1] Number	Rate per 100 000 population	Medical schools [2] Number [3]	Students	Grad-uates	Dentists [4] Number	Rate per 100 000 population	Dental schools Number [5]	Students	Grad-uates	Active professional graduate nurses Number	Rate per 100 000 population	Professional nursing schools [6] Number	Students	Grad-uates
	275	276	278	279	280	281	282	283	284	285	286	287	288	289	290
1997...	756 700	282	125	67 276	15 923		...	54	16 570	...			1 508	238 244	...
1996...	737 800	278	125	66 970	15 907	196 000	61	54	16 552	3 810	2 162 000	815	1 516	261 219	94 757
1995...	720 300	274	125	67 072	15 888	194 000	61	54	16 353	3 908	2 116 000	805	1 501	268 350	97 052
1994...	684 400	262	126	66 629	15 555	191 000	60	54	16 250	3 875	2 044 000	785	1 493	270 228	94 870
1993...	670 300	260	126	66 142	15 466	187 000	60	55	15 980	3 778	1 976 000	767	1 484	257 983	88 149
1992...	653 100	255	126	65 602	15 365	183 000	60	55	15 882	3 918	1 907 000	748	1 484	237 598	80 839
1990...	615 400	246	127	65 016	15 398	173 000	59	58	16 412	4 233	1 790 000	713	1 457	201 458	66 088
1989...	645 000	261	142	71 600	17 200	168 000	59	58	16 200	4 300	1 666 000	675	1 457	201 000	62 000
1988...	629 000	257	142	71 900	17 500	164 000	58	58	17 100	4 600	1 648 000	674	1 442	185 000	65 000
1987...	612 000	253	142	72 300	17 400	161 000	58	58	17 900	4 700	1 627 000	671	1 465	183 000	71 000
1986...	595 000	248	142	72 800	17 700	158 000	58	59	18 700	5 000	1 589 000	662	1 469	194 000	77 000
1985...	577 000	243	142	73 200	17 800	156 000	58	60	19 600	5 400	1 544 000	649	1 473	218 000	82 000
1984...	...	...	142	73 600	17 600	153 000	57	60	20 600	5 300	1 486 000	630	1 477	237 000	80 000
1983...	542 000	232	142	73 500	17 100	150 000	56	60	21 400	5 800	1 439 000	616	1 466	251 000	77 000
1982...	523 000	222	142	72 600	17 000	147 000	55	60	22 200	5 400	1 380 111	595	1 432	242 000	74 000
1981...	505 000	217	142	71 600	16 800	144 000	54	60	22 600	5 600	1 327 000	578	1 401	235 000	74 000
1980...	487 000	214	141	70 100	16 200	141 000	54	60	22 800	5 300	1 273 000	560	1 385	231 000	76 000
1979...	472 000	207	138	66 500	16 000	138 000	53	60	22 200	5 400	1 200 000	534	1 374	235 000	77 000
1978...	454 000	201	124	64 300	15 400	136 000	52	59	21 500	5 300	...	...	1 340	239 000	78 000
1977...	438 000	196	126	61 900	14 500	133 000	52	59	21 000	5 200	1 028 000	468	1 339	245 000	78 000
1976...	426 000	194	123	59 600	14 300	...	52	59	20 800	5 300	961 000	449	1 349	250 000	78 000
1975...	409 000	190	123	59 300	13 900	127 000	50	59	20 800	5 000	961 000	446	1 360	250 000	75 000
1974...	394 000	182	121	53 700	12 200	...	...	58	19 400	4 500	857 000	404	1 359	233 000	68 000
1973...	382 000	178	114	50 100	11 000	122 000	48	56	18 400	4 200	815 000	390	1 363	213 000	59 000
1972...	371 000	174	115	46 000	10 000	120 000	47	52	17 300	4 000	780 000	376	1 350	188 000	52 000
1971...	359 000	174	110	42 600	9 400	118 000	47	53	16 600	3 800	723 000	353	1 343	165 000	47 000
1970...	348 328	166	107	39 666	8 799	118 175	58	53	16 008	3 700	700 000	345	1 328	150 795	43 639
1969...	338 942	163	104	37 712	8 486	115 610	57	52	15 408	3 433	680 000	338	1 287	145 588	42 196
1968...	330 732	161	100	36 368	8 400	113 636	57	50	14 955	3 457	659 000	331	2 262	141 948	41 555
1967...	322 045	158	95	35 212	8 148	112 152	56	49	14 421	3 360	640 000	325	1 219	139 070	38 237
1966...	313 559	156	93	34 516	7 934	111 130	56	49	14 020	3 198	621 000	319	1 191	135 702	35 125
1965...	305 115	153	93	34 089	7 803	109 301	56	49	13 876	3 181	613 188	319	1 153	129 629	24 686
1964...	297 089	159	92	33 595	7 691	107 820	56	48	13 691	3 213	582 000	306	1 142	124 744	35 259
1963...	289 188	149	92	33 072	7 631	106 230	56	48	13 576	3 233	...	...	1 128	123 861	32 398
1962...	270 136	145	92	32 633	7 530	105 252	56	47	13 513	3 207	550 000	297	1 118	123 012	31 186
1961...	...	...	92	32 232	7 500	103 596	56	47	13 580	3 290	...	...	1 123	118 849	30 267
1960...	274 833	148	*91	*31 999	*7 508	101 947	56	*47	*13 581	*3 253	*504 000	*282	*1 119	*115 057	*30 113
1959...	*236 818	*133	85	29 614	6 860	*100 615	*57	47	13 509	3 190	...	...	1 126	113 518	30 312
1958...	...	...	85	29 473	6 861	98 540	57	47	13 279	3 083	460 000	268	1 118	112 989	30 410
1957...	226 625	132	85	29 130	6 796	100 534	59	45	13 004	3 050	...	...	1 115	114 674	29 933
1956...	...		82	28 639	6 845	99 227	59	43	12 730	3 038	430 000	262	1 125	114 423	30 236
1955...	218 061	132	81	28 583	6 977	97 529	59	43	12 601	3 081	[7] 430 000	259	1 139	107 572	28 729
1954	214 200	132	80	28 227	6 861	95 883	59	43	12 516	3 084	[7] 389 600	244	1 141	103 019	28 539
1953...	210 900	132	79	27 688	6 668	93 726	59	42	12 370	2 945	...	...	1 148	102 019	29 308
1952...	207 900	132	79	27 076	6 080	91 638	58	42	12 169	2 975	...	...	1 167	102 550	29 016
1951...	205 500	133	79	26 186	6 135	...	...	42	11 891	2 830	...	...	1 183	103 433	28 794
1950...	203 400	134	79	25 103	5 553	89 441	59	41	11 460	2 565	[7] 375 000	249	1 203	98 712	25 790
1950...	191 947	128	...	...	...	74 855	50	...	...	...	...	...	...	...	...
1949...	201 277	135	78	23 670	5 094	...	...	41	10 132	1 574	...	...	1 215	88 817	21 379
1948...	...	...	77	22 739	5 543	...	...	40	8 996	1 755	...	...	1 245	91 643	34 268
1947...	...	...	77	23 900	6 389	82 990	58	40	8 287	2 225	...	...	1 253	106 900	40 744
1946...	...	...	77	23 216	5 826	...	...	39	7 274	2 666	...	...	1 271	128 828	36 195
1945...	...	...	77	24 028	5 136	...	...	39	*8 590	3 212	...	...	1 295	126 576	31 721
1944...	...	...	77	*48 195	*10 303	...	...	39	*9 014	2 470	...	...	1 307	112 249	28 276
1943...	...	...	76	22 631	5 223	...	...	39	*8 847	1 926	...	...	1 297	100 486	26 816
1942...	180 496	134	77	22 031	5 163	...	...	39	*8 355	1 784	...	...	1 299	91 457	25 613
1941...	...	...	77	21 379	5 275	...	...	39	7 720	1 568	...	...	1 303	87 588	24 889
1940...	175 163	133	77	21 271	5 097	...	...	39	7 407	1 757	[7] 284 200	216	1 311	85 156	23 600
1940...	165 989	126	...	...	...	69 921	53	...	...	...	...	...	...	...	...
1939...	...	...	77	21 302	5 089	...	...	39	7 331	1 794	...	...	1 328	82 095	22 485
1938...	169 628	131	77	21 587	5 194	...	...	39	7 184	1 704	...	...	1 349	74 305	20 655
1937...	...	...	77	22 095	5 377	...	...	39	7 397	1 739	...	...	1 389	73 286	20 400
1936...	165 163	129	77	22 564	5 183	...	...	39	7 306	1 736	...	...	1 417	69 589	18 600

See footnotes at end of chart.

Series B 275-290. Physicians, Dentists and Nurses; and Medical, Dental and Nursing Schools: 1810 to 1997—Cont'd.

(Census figures in italics. Figures for schools and students are for academic session ending in the specified year)

Year	Physicians [1] Number	Rate per 100 000 population	Medical schools [2] Number [3]	Students	Graduates	Dentists [4] Number	Rate per 100 000 population	Dental schools Number [5]	Students	Graduates	Active professional graduate nurses Number	Rate per 100 000 population	Professional nursing schools [6] Number	Students	Graduates
	275	276	278	279	280	281	282	283	284	285	286	287	288	289	290
1935...	...	...	77	22 888	5 101	...	...	39	7 175	1 840	...	...	1 472	67 533	19 600
1934...	161 359	128	77	22 799	5 035	...	...	39	7 160	1 864	...	...	...	...	...
1933...	...	...	77	22 466	4 895	...	...	39	7 508	1 986	...	...	...	...	...
1932...	...	...	76	22 135	4 936	...	...	38	8 031	1 840	...	...	1 781	84 290	25 312
1931...	156 406	126	76	21 982	4 735	...	...	38	8 129	1 842	...	...	1 844	100 419	25 971
1930...	...	...	76	21 597	4 565	...	...	38	7 813	1 561	7 214 300	174	...	...	...
1930...	153 803	125	...	...	...	71 055	58	...	...	...	...	...	...	...	...
1929...	152 503	125	76	20 878	4 446	...	...	40	8 200	2 442	...	...	1 885	78 771	23 810
1928...	...	...	80	20 545	4 262	67 334	56	40	...	2 563	...	...	...	...	...
1927...	149 521	126	80	19 662	4 035	...	...	40	10 333	2 642	...	...	1 797	77 768	18 623
1926...	...	...	79	18 840	3 962	...	...	44	...	2 610	...	...	...	...	...
1925...	147 010	127	80	18 200	3 974	64 481	56	43	11 863	2 590	...	...	...	...	...
1924...	...	...	79	17 728	3 562	...	...	43	...	3 422	...	...	...	...	...
1923...	145 966	130	80	16 960	3 120	...	...	45	13 099	3 271	...	...	...	...	...
1922...	...	...	81	15 635	2 520	...	...	45	...	1 765	...	...	...	...	...
1921...	145 404	134	83	14 466	3 186	...	...	45	11 745	1 795	...	...	...	...	...
1920...	...	...	85	13 798	3 047	...	...	46	...	906	7 103 900	98	1 755	54 953	14 980
1920...	144 977	137	...	...	...	56 152	53	...	...	...	...	...	...	...	...
1919...	...	...	85	13 052	2 656	...	...	46	...	3 587	...	...	...	...	...
1918...	147 812	141	90	13 630	2 670	...	...	46	...	3 345	...	...	...	...	...
1917...	...	...	96	13 764	3 379	45 988	44	46	...	3 010	...	...	...	...	...
1916...	145 241	142	95	14 012	3 518	...	...	49	...	2 835	...	...	...	...	...
1915...	...	...	96	14 891	3 536	...	...	49	...	2 388	...	...	1 509	46 141	11 118
1914...	142 332	144	102	16 502	3 594	42 606	43	48	...	2 254	...	...	...	...	...
1913...	...	...	107	17 015	3 981	...	...	51	...	2 022	...	...	...	...	...
1912...	137 199	144	118	18 412	4 483	38 866	41	52	...	1 940	...	...	...	...	...
1911...	...	...	122	19 786	4 273	...	...	54	...	1 742	...	...	...	...	...
1910...	135 000	146	131	21 526	4 440	37 684	41	54	...	1 646	7 50 500	55	1 129	32 636	8 140
1910...	151 132	164	...	...	...	39 997	43	...	...	...	...	...	...	...	...
1909...	134 402	149	140	22 145	4 515	...	...	56	...	1 761	...	...	...	...	...
1908...	...	...	151	22 602	4 741	36 670	41	55	...	2 005	...	...	...	...	...
1907...	...	...	159	24 276	4 980	...	...	55	...	1 724	...	...	...	...	...
1906...	134 688	158	162	25 204	5 364	35 238	41	55	...	1 519	...	...	...	...	...
1905...	...	...	158	26 147	5 600	...	...	55	...	2 621	...	...	862	19 824	5 795
1904...	128 950	157	160	28 142	5 747	32 204	39	56	...	2 168	...	...	...	...	...
1903...	...	...	160	27 615	5 698	...	...	55	...	2 198	...	...	...	...	...
1902...	123 196	156	160	27 501	5 009	28 109	36	56	...	2 294	...	...	...	...	...
1901...	...	...	160	26 417	5 444	...	...	57	...	2 304	...	...	...	...	...
1900...	119 749	157	160	25 171	5 214	25 189	33	57	...	2 091	...	...	432	11 164	3 456
1900...	132 002	173	...	...	...	29 665	39	...	...	...	...	...	...	...	...
1898...	115 524	157	...	...	...	23 911	33	54	...	1 894	...	...	...	...	...
1896...	104 554	147	...	...	...	20 063	28	48	...	1 432	...	...	...	...	...
1893...	103 090	154	...	...	...	...	...	37	...	...	...	...	...	...	...
1890...	100 180	159	133	15 404	4 454	...	...	31	...	960	...	...	35	1 552	471
1890...	104 805	166	...	...	...	17 498	28	...	...	...	...	...	...	...	...
1886...	87 521	151	...	...	...	...	...	23	...	473	...	...	...	...	...
1880...	82 000	163	100	11 826	3 241	...	...	14	...	315	...	...	15	323	157
1880...	85 671	171	...	...	...	12 314	25	...	...	...	...	...	...	...	...
1870...	60 000	150	75	...	...	...	...	10	...	147	...	...	...	...	...
1870...	64 414	162	...	...	...	7 988	20	...	...	...	...	...	...	...	...
1860...	55 055	175	65	...	...	5 606	18	3	...	64	...	...	...	...	...
1850...	40 755	176	52	...	...	2 923	13	2	...	17	...	...	...	...	...
1840...	...	...	35	...	...	1 000	6	1	...	...	...	...	...	...	...
1830...	...	...	20	...	...	300	2	...	...	...	...	...	...	...	...
1820...	...	...	10	...	...	100	1	...	...	...	...	...	...	...	...
1810...	...	...	5	...	...	50	1	...	...	...	...	...	...	...	...

* Denotes first year for which figures include Alaska and Hawaii.
1. Beginning 1960, includes osteopaths.
2. Beginning 1954, includes Puerto Rico; beginning 1960, includes osteopaths and their schools.
3. Approved medical and basic science schools.
4. Beginning 1958, excludes graduates of year stated.
5. For 1840 and 1926-1931, schools offering courses in dentistry; for 1850-1925, schools conferring degrees; for other years, schools in operation. Includes Puerto Rico.
6. Includes Hawaii and Puerto Rico beginning 1950 for number and students and 1952 for graduates.
7. Census estimate adjusted to exclude student nurses enumerated as graduates.

Series B 305-318.   Hospitals and Beds, by Type of Service and Ownership (AHA): 1946 to 1997

	Total		Non-Federal				Federal, all types		
			Long-term general and special		Psychiatric				Total beds per 1 000 population
Year	Hospitals	Beds	Hospitals	Beds	Hospitals	Beds	Hospitals	Beds	
	305	**306**	**309**	**310**	**311**	**312**	**315**	**316**	**317**
1997	6 097	1 035 000	125	17 000	601	100 000	285	62 000	3.9
1996	6 201	1 062 000	112	19 000	636	106 000	290	73 000	4.0
1995	6 291	1 081 000	112	19 000	657	110 000	299	78 000	4.1
1994	6 374	1 128 000	110	19 000	696	121 000	307	84 000	4.3
1993	6 467	1 163 000	117	21 000	741	131 000	316	87 000	4.5
1992	6 539	1 178 000	115	23 000	774	139 000	325	89 000	4.6
1991	6 634	1 197 000	126	25 000	800	150 000	334	95 000	4.7
1990	6 649	1 213 000	131	25 000	757	158 000	337	98 000	4.9
1989	6 720	1 224 000	138	27 000	741	160 000	340	100 000	5.1
1988	6 780	1 241 000	129	27 000	726	163 000	342	104 000	5.0
1987	6 821	1 261 000	131	28 000	684	165 000	342	109 000	5.3
1986	6 841	1 283 000	133	30 000	634	165 000	342	111 000	5.4
1985	6 872	1 318 000	128	31 000	610	169 000	343	112 000	5.5
1984	6 872	1 339 000	131	30 000	579	175 000	341	112 000	5.7
1983	6 888	1 350 000	131	30 000	564	185 000	342	113 000	5.8
1982	6 915	1 360 000	138	34 000	558	195 000	346	114 000	5.9
1981	6 933	1 362 000	146	35 000	549	202 000	348	116 000	6.0
1980	6 965	1 365 000	157	39 000	534	215 000	359	117 000	6.0
1979	6 988	1 372 000	165	40 000	527	224 000	361	117 000	6.1
1978	7 015	1 381 000	169	41 000	526	235 000	370	122 000	6.2
1977	7 099	1 407 000	189	45 000	541	261 000	377	124 000	6.4
1976	7 082	1 434 000	197	49 000	528	291 000	380	129 000	6.6
1975	7 156	1 466 000	215	51 000	544	330 000	382	132 000	6.8
1974	7 174	1 513 000	221	54 000	543	383 000	387	136 000	7.2
1973	7 123	1 535 000	229	57 000	543	422 000	397	142 000	7.3
1972	7 061	1 550 000	216	54 000	529	457 000	401	143 000	7.6
1971	7 097	1 556 000	218	54 000	513	469 000	407	148 000	7.5
1970	7 123	1 615 771	236	59 961	519	526 889	408	160 969	8.0
1969	7 144	1 649 663	260	63 075	509	570 550	415	169 681	8.3
1968	7 137	1 663 203	280	66 517	505	593 916	416	174 645	8.4
1967	7 172	1 671 125	331	80 311	470	609 075	416	175 065	8.5
1966	7 160	1 678 658	291	67 337	476	639 041	425	173 005	8.7
1965	7 123	1 703 522	283	65 897	483	685 175	443	173 962	8.9
1964	7 127	1 696 039	300	68 783	487	691 367	441	175 490	9.0
1963	7 138	1 701 839	323	73 525	499	714 661	446	176 318	9.1
1962	7 028	1 689 414	323	73 474	491	716 781	447	177 677	9.2
1961	6 923	1 669 789	321	70 536	483	714 622	437	177 554	9.2
1960	6 876	1 657 970	308	67 214	488	722 493	435	177 105	9.3
1959 *	6 845	1 612 822	330	68 323	459	688 410	438	178 820	9.2
1958	6 786	1 572 036	321	78 383	475	646 270	439	180 574	9.1
1957	6 818	1 588 691	340	77 608	452	641 455	437	183 002	9.2
1956	6 966	1 607 692	395	75 646	525	695 331	432	184 121	9.6
1955	6 956	1 604 408	402	76 278	542	707 162	428	183 162	9.8
1954	6 970	1 577 961	406	70 926	554	691 176	430	189 233	9.8
1953	6 978	1 580 654	406	68 039	541	691 855	435	202 604	10.0
1952	6 903	1 561 809	405	69 731	546	675 749	439	213 018	10.0
1951	6 832	1 521 959	394	62 768	551	655 932	422	214 597	9.9
1950	6 788	1 455 825	412	70 136	533	619 530	414	189 477	9.6
1949	6 277	1 435 288	395	79 145	507	614 465	376	186 764	9.7
1948	6 160	1 411 150	362	77 040	504	601 103	386	185 846	9.7
1947	6 173	1 400 318	385	84 758	499	580 273	403	199 771	9.8
1946	6 125	1 435 778	389	83 415	476	568 473	404	235 964	10.3

* Denotes first year for which figures include Alaska and Hawaii.

Series B 359-370. Average Daily Census and Admissions to Hospitals: 1946 to 1997
(In thousands)

Year	Average daily census 359	Admissions during year 360	Year	Average daily census 359	Admissions during year 360	Year	359	360	Year	359	360
1997	673	...	1983	1 027.9	38 900	1970	1 298	31 759	1957	1 320	22 993
1996	685	30 545				1969	1 346	30 729	1956	1 356	22 090
1995	710	30 722	1982	1 052.7	39 100	1968	1 378	29 766	1955	1 363	21 073
1994	745	30 843	1981	1 060.9	39 200				1954	1 343	20 345
1993	783	30 825	1980	1 059.7	38 900	1967	1 380	29 361	1953	1 342	20 184
			1979	1 043.4	37 800	1966	1 398	29 151			
1992	807	30 951	1978	1 041.9	37 200	1965	1 403	28 812	1952	1 336	19 624
1991	827.1	31 098				1964	1 421	28 266	1951	1 298	18 783
1990	843.7	36 820	1977	1 065.9	37 100	1963	1 430	27 502	1950	1 253	18 483
1989	...	...	1976	1 089.7	36 800				1949	1 240	17 224
1988	863.4	34 100	1975	1 124.9	36 200	1962	1 407	26 531	1948	1 241	16 821
			1974	1 187.4	35 500	1961	1 393	25 474			
1987	872.6	34 400	1973	1 189.0	34 400	1960	1 402	25 027	1947	1 190	17 689
1986	882.6	35 200				1959*	1 363	23 605	1946	1 142	15 675
1985	909.8	36 300	1972	1 208.9	33 300	1958	1 323	23 697			
1984	970.3	37 900	1971	1 236.8	32 700						

* Denotes first year for which figures include Alaska and Hawaii.

Series B 389-400. Hospital Expense Per Patient Day: 1946 to 1996
(In dollars. Covers hospitals accepted for registration by the American Hospital Association)

Year	Amount 389	Year	Amount 389	Year	Amount 389	Year	Amount 389
1996	...	1982	327	1970	53.95	1957	13.48
1995	958			1969	45.01		
1994	931	1981	284	1968	37.78	1956	12.16
1993	881	1980	245	1967	32.54	1955	11.24
1992	820	1979	217			1954	10.67
		1978	194	1966	27.94	1953	9.73
1991	752	1977	174	1965	25.29	1952	9.14
1990	687			1964	23.20		
1989	637	1976	153	1963	21.00	1951	8.26
1988	586	1975	134	1962	19.73	1950	7.98
1987	539	1974	114			1949	7.70
		1973	84	1961	18.46	1948	6.35
1986	501	1972	74	1960	16.46	1947	5.42
1985	460			1959*	15.65		
1984	411	1971	64	1958 [1]	14.74	1946	5.21
1983	369						

* Denotes first year for which figures include Alaska and Hawaii.
1. Includes Alaska.

Series B 413-422. Hospitals Expenses and Personnel: 1946 to 1997

Year	Total	Federal	Year	Total	Federal	Year	Total	Federal	Year	Total	Federal
	413	414		413	414		413	414		413	414
EXPENSES (mil. dol.)											
1997	342 300	22 700	1983	136 300	10 700	1970	25 556	2 483	1957	6 496	1 013
1996	330 500	22 300				1969	22 103	2 350	1956	6 017	968
1995	320 300	20 200	1982	123 200	9 500	1968	19 061	2 032	1955	5 594	837
1994	310 800	20 000	1981	107 100	8 600				1954	5 229	927
1993	301 500	19 600	1980	91 900	7 900	1967	16 395	1 795	1953	4 765	853
			1979	79 800	7 300	1966	14 198	1 633			
1992	282 500	18 200	1978	70 900	6 700	1965	12 948	1 568	1952	4 456	925
1991	258 500	16 800				1964	12 031	1 503	1951	3 913	743
1990	234 900	15 200	1977	63 600	6 200	1963	10 956	1 458	1950	3 651	712
1989	214 900	15 100	1976	56 000	5 300				1949	3 486	764
1988	196 700	14 600	1975	48 700	4 500	1962	10 129	1 408	1948	2 875	480
			1974	41 406	3 971	1961	9 387	1 308			
1987	178 700	13 700	1973	36 290	3 524	1960	8 421	1 134	1947	2 354	405
1986	165 200	13 100				1959*	7 789	1 119	1946	1 963	373
1985	153 300	12 300	1972	32 700	3 100	1958	7 133	1 051			
1984	144 100	11 200	1971	28 812	2 821						
PERSONNEL (1 000)											
1997	4 333	296	1983	3 707	286	1970	2 537	216	1957	1 401	186
1996	4 276	295				1969	2 426	213	1956	1 375	198
1995	4 273	301	1982	3 959	302	1968	2 309	210	1955	1 301	192
1994	4 270	301	1981	3 661	283				1954	1 246	195
1993	4 289	320	1980	3 492	279	1967	2 203	214	1953	1 169	198
			1979	3 382	273	1966	2 106	206			
1992	4 236	306	1978	3 280	277	1965	1 952	199	1952	1 119	206
1991	4 165	301				1964	1 887	193	1951	1 075	197
1990	4 063	303	1977	3 213	278	1963	1 840	206	1950	1 058	169
1989	3 937	288	1976	3 108	269				1949	963	161
1988	3 840	295	1975	3 023	256	1962	1 763	207	1948	939	154
			1974	2 919	244	1961	1 696	202			
1987	3 742	297	1973	2 769	238	1960	1 598	186	1947	883	161
1986	3 647	296				1959	1 520	179	1946	830	162
1985	3 625	299	1972	2 671	232	1958	1 465	181			
1984	3 630	290	1971	2 589	225						

* Denotes first year for which figures include Alaska and Hawaii.

Series B 448-452.   Index of Per Capita Consumption of Selected Nutrients: 1909 to 1985
(1967 = 100. Beginning 1941, civilian only)

Year	Protein 448	Fat 449	Carbo-hydrate 450	Year	Protein 448	Fat 449	Carbo-hydrate 450	Year	Protein 448	Fat 449	Carbo-hydrate 450
1985	106	112	110	1958	96	95	101	1933	92	89	117
1984	105	106	107	1957	97	94	100	1932	93	89	120
1983	104	107	106	1956	98	97	101	1931	94	90	123
1982	103	105	106					1930	95	89	127
1981	102	106	105	1955	97	97	101	1929	96	91	126
				1954	96	95	102	1928	96	90	129
1980	102	105	104	1953	97	95	103	1927	97	89	128
1979	104	109	108	1952	96	95	104	1926	96	89	128
1978	104	106	105	1951	95	93	105				
1977	104	105	105					1925	97	89	127
1976	105	107	105	1950	96	97	108	1924	98	90	127
				1949	96	93	107	1923	98	90	125
1975	100	98	101	1948	96	93	106	1922	96	86	129
1974	100	102	101	1947	99	95	110	1921	93	81	118
1973	100	103	103	1946	104	95	110				
1972	106	102	102					1920	95	82	123
1971	103	105	102	1945	104	92	112	1919	99	87	128
				1944	101	95	114	1918	99	86	124
1970	102	105	102	1943	102	95	115	1917	98	81	126
1969	102	103	102	1942	99	93	114	1916	98	84	126
1968	101	103	101	1941	96	96	119				
1967	100	100	100					1915	99	84	129
1966	99	98	99	1940	95	95	115	1914	100	85	129
				1939	94	93	118	1913	102	83	131
1965	98	97	99	1938	92	89	116	1912	104	83	131
1964	99	99	100	1937	92	89	116	1911	103	84	131
1963	98	97	99	1936	93	89	117				
1962	96	95	100					1910	104	83	133
1961	97	95	100	1935	90	85	117	1909	106	85	133
				1934	93	89	115				
1960	97	95	101								
1959	97	98	101								

Series BB1.   Per Capita Consumption of Selected Beverages, by Type: 1980 to 1997

(In gallons. Consumption represents the residual after exports; nonfood use and ending stocks are subtracted from the sum of beginning stocks, domestic production, and imports.)

Commodity	1980	1985	1990	1992	1993	1994	1995	1996	1997
Nonalcoholic	. . .	. . .	128.4	131.6	132.4	133.2	133.5	137.0	139.6
Milk (plain and flavored)	27.6	26.7	25.7	25.3	24.8	24.8	24.3	24.3	24.0
Whole	17.0	14.3	10.5	9.8	9.3	9.2	8.8	8.7	8.5
Reduced-fat, light, and skim	10.5	12.3	15.2	15.6	15.4	15.6	15.6	15.7	15.5
Tea	7.3	7.1	6.9	8.1	8.4	8.2	8.0	7.8	7.4
Coffee	26.7	27.4	26.9	25.9	23.5	21.1	20.5	22.5	23.5
Bottled water	2.4	4.5	8.0	8.2	9.4	10.7	11.6	12.5	13.1
Carbonated soft drinks	35.1	35.7	46.3	48.5	50.1	51.3	51.6	52.0	53.0
Diet	5.1	7.1	10.7	11.6	11.7	11.8	11.8	11.7	11.6
Regular	29.9	28.7	35.6	36.9	38.4	39.6	39.8	40.3	41.4
Fruit juices	7.4	7.8	7.9	8.6	8.5	8.8	8.7	8.9	9.2
Fruit drinks, cocktails, and ades	. . .	. . .	6.3	6.5	7.0	7.4	7.8	8.0	8.3
Canned iced tea	. . .	. . .	0.1	0.2	0.4	0.6	0.7	0.7	0.8
Vegetable juices	. . .	. . .	0.3	0.3	0.3	0.3	0.3	0.3	0.3
Alcoholic (adult population)	42.8	40.7	39.9	38.4	38.2	38.3	38.0	38.6	38.9
Beer	36.6	34.6	34.7	33.6	33.6	33.8	33.4	33.8	33.9
Wine [1]	3.2	3.5	3.0	2.7	2.6	2.6	2.7	2.9	3.0
Distilled spirits	3.0	2.6	2.2	2.0	2.0	1.9	1.9	1.9	1.9

1. Beginning 1985, includes wine coolers.

SOURCE of Tables 251 and 252: U.S. Dept. of Agriculture, Economic Research Service, Food Consumption, Prices, and Expenditures, annual; and Agricultural Outlook, monthly.

Series BB2. Nutrients in Foods Available for Civilian Consumption Per Capita Per Day: 1970 to 1994

(Computed by the Center for Nutrition Policy and Promotion (CNPP). Based on Economic Research Service (ERS) estimates of per capita quantities of food available for consumption from "Food Consumption, Prices, and, Expenditures," on imputed consumption data for foods no longer reported by ERS, and on CNPP estimates of quantities of produce from home gardens. Food supply estimates do not reflect loss of food or nutrients from further marketing or home processing. Enrichment and fortification levels of iron, thiamin, riboflavin, niacin, vitamin A, vitamin B_6, vitamin B_{12}, and ascorbic acid are included)

Nutrient	Unit	1970-79	1980-89	1990	1993	1994
Food energy	Calories	3 300	3 400	3 600	3 700	3 800
Carbohydrate	Grams	391	417	458	482	491
Protein	Grams	95	100	105	108	110
Total fat [1]	Grams	151	157	156	161	159
Saturated	Grams	52	53	51	52	52
Monounsaturated	Grams	61	63	63	66	65
Polyunsaturated	Grams	28	31	32	32	31
Cholesterol	Milligrams	440	420	400	410	410
Vitamin A	Micrograms RE [2]	1 530	1 510	1 530	1 530	1 520
Carotenes	Micrograms RE [2]	580	620	670	670	660
Vitamin E	Milligrams a-TE [3]	14.2	15.7	16.6	17.6	16.9
Vitamin C	Milligrams	109	114	111	122	124
Thiamin	Milligrams	2.1	2.4	2.6	2.7	2.7
Riboflavin	Milligrams	2.4	2.5	2.6	2.6	2.6
Niacin	Milligrams	23.6	26.4	28.0	29.0	29.0
Vitamin B_6	Milligrams	2.0	2.1	2.2	2.3	2.3
Folacin	Micrograms	289	303	311	329	331
Vitamin B_{12}	Micrograms	9.1	8.4	8.2	8.0	8.1
Calcium	Milligrams	880	900	940	950	960
Phosphorus	Milligrams	1 460	1 530	1 620	1 650	1 680
Magnesium	Milligrams	320	340	370	380	380
Iron	Milligrams	18.7	18.2	20.2	20.9	21.2
Zinc	Milligrams	12.1	12.3	12.7	13.0	13.2
Copper	Milligrams	1.6	1.7	1.8	1.9	1.9
Potassium	Milligrams	3 470	3 530	3 650	3 750	3 780

1. Includes other types of fat not shown separately.
2. Retinol equivalents.
3. Alpha-Tocopherol equivalents.

SOURCE: U.S. Dept. of Agriculture, Center for Nutrition Policy and Promotion. Data published by Economic Research Service in Food Consumption, Prices, and Expenditures, annual.

Series BB3. Current Cigarette Smoking: 1985 to 1995

(In percent. Prior to 1994, a current smoker is a person who has smoked at least 100 cigarettes and who now smokes. Beginning 1994, definition includes persons who smoke only "some days." Excludes unknown smoking status. Based on the National Health Interview Survey)

Sex, age, and race	1985	1990	1994	1995	Sex, age, and race	1985	1990	1994	1995
Total smokers	30.1	25.5	25.5	24.7					
Male, total	32.6	28.4	28.2	27.0	Female, total	27.9	22.8	23.1	22.6
18 to 24 years	28.0	26.6	29.8	27.8	18 to 24 years	30.4	22.5	25.2	21.8
25 to 34 years	38.2	31.6	31.4	. . .	25 to 34 years	32.0	28.2	28.8	. . .
35 to 44 years	37.6	34.5	33.2	. . .	35 to 44 years	31.5	24.8	26.8	. . .
45 to 64 years	33.4	29.3	28.3	27.1	45 to 64 years	29.9	24.8	22.8	24.0
65 years and over	19.6	14.6	13.2	14.3	65 years and over	13.5	11.5	11.1	11.5
White, total	31.7	28.0	27.7	. . .	White, total	27.7	23.4	23.7	. . .
18 to 24 years	28.4	27.4	31.8	. . .	18 to 24 years	31.8	25.4	28.5	. . .
25 to 34 years	37.3	31.6	32.5	. . .	25 to 34 years	32.0	28.5	30.2	. . .
35 to 44 years	36.6	33.5	32.0	. . .	35 to 44 years	31.0	25.0	27.1	. . .
45 to 64 years	32.1	28.7	26.9	. . .	45 to 64 years	29.7	25.4	23.2	. . .
65 years and over	18.9	13.7	11.9	. . .	65 years and over	13.3	11.5	11.1	. . .
Black, total	39.9	32.5	33.7	. . .	Black, total	31.0	21.2	21.7	. . .
18 to 24 years	27.2	21.3	18.7	. . .	18 to 24 years	23.7	10.0	11.8	. . .
25 to 34 years	45.6	33.8	29.8	. . .	25 to 34 years	36.2	29.1	24.8	. . .
35 to 44 years	45.0	42.0	44.5	. . .	35 to 44 years	40.2	25.5	28.2	. . .
45 to 64 years	46.1	36.7	41.2	. . .	45 to 64 years	33.4	22.6	23.5	. . .
65 years and over	27.7	21.5	25.6	. . .	65 years and over	14.5	11.1	13.6	. . .

SOURCE: U.S. National Center for Health Statistics, Health United States, 1996-97 and Injury Chartbook, 1997, and U.S. Centers for Disease Control and Prevention, Morbidity and Mortality Weekly Report, Vol. 46, No. 51, December 26, 1997.

Series BB4.   Drug Use, by Type of Drug and Age Group: 1985 to 1997

(In percent. Current users are those who used drugs at least once within month prior to this study. Based on national samples of respondents residing in households. Subject to sampling variability; see source)

Age and type of drug	Ever used					Current user				
	1985	1990	1995	1996	1997	1985	1990	1995	1996	1997
12 YEARS OLD AND OVER										
Marijuana and hashish	29.4	30.5	31.0	32.0	32.9	9.7	5.4	4.7	4.7	5.1
Cocaine..	11.2	11.2	10.3	10.3	10.5	3.0	0.9	0.7	0.8	0.7
Crack	. . .	1.5	1.8	2.2	1.9	. . .	0.3	0.2	0.3	0.3
Inhalants	7.9	5.7	5.7	5.6	5.7	0.6	0.4	0.4	0.4	0.4
Hallucinogens	6.9	7.9	9.5	9.7	9.6	1.2	0.4	0.7	0.6	0.8
PCP	2.0	2.0	3.2	3.2	3.0	. . .	. . .	—	0.1	0.1
LSD	4.6	5.8	7.5	7.7	7.8	. . .	. . .	0.3	0.2	0.2
Heroin	0.9	0.8	1.2	1.1	0.9	0.1	—	0.1	0.1	0.2
Stimulants [1]	7.3	5.5	4.9	4.7	4.5	1.8	0.6	0.4	0.4	0.3
Sedatives [1]	4.8	2.8	2.7	2.3	1.9	0.5	0.2	0.2	0.1	0.1
Tranquilizers [1]	7.6	4.0	3.9	3.6	3.2	2.2	0.6	0.4	0.4	0.4
Analgesics [1]	7.6	6.3	6.1	5.5	4.9	1.4	0.9	0.6	0.6	0.7
Alcohol	84.9	82.2	82.3	82.6	81.9	60.2	52.6	52.2	51.0	51.4
Cigarettes....................................	78.0	75.4	71.8	71.6	70.5	38.7	32.6	28.8	28.9	29.6
Smokeless tobacco.......................	. . .	17.5	17.0	17.0	17.3	. . .	3.9	3.3	3.2	3.2
12 to 17 YEARS OLD										
Marijuana and hashish	20.1	12.7	16.2	16.8	18.9	10.2	4.4	8.2	7.1	9.4
Cocaine...	4.7	2.6	2.0	1.9	3.0	1.5	0.6	0.8	0.6	1.0
Alcohol	56.1	48.8	40.6	38.8	39.7	41.2	32.5	21.1	18.8	20.5
Cigarettes.....................................	50.7	45.1	38.1	36.3	38.7	29.4	22.4	20.2	18.3	19.9
18 TO 25 YEARS OLD										
Marijuana and hashish	57.6	50.4	41.4	44.0	41.5	21.7	12.7	12.0	13.2	12.8
Cocaine...	24.3	19.3	9.8	10.2	8.9	8.1	2.3	1.3	2.0	1.2
Alcohol	. . .	87.6	84.4	83.8	83.5	70.1	62.8	61.3	60.0	58.4
Cigarettes.....................................	75.3	70.7	67.7	68.5	67.7	47.4	40.9	35.3	38.3	40.6
26 TO 34 YEARS OLD										
Marijuana and hashish	54.1	56.5	51.8	50.5	47.9	19.0	9.5	6.7	6.3	6.0
Cocaine...	23.6	25.4	21.6	20.9	18.4	6.3	1.9	1.2	1.5	0.9
Alcohol	. . .	. . .	90.1	90.3	88.9	70.6	64.4	63.0	61.6	60.2
Cigarettes.....................................	84.7	84.1	75.8	73.8	72.8	45.7	42.4	34.7	35.0	33.7
35 YEARS OLD AND OVER										
Marijuana and hashish	13.9	19.6	25.3	27.0	29.4	2.6	2.4	1.8	2.0	2.6
Cocaine...	4.1	5.9	8.6	8.9	9.9	0.5	0.2	0.4	0.4	0.5
Alcohol	. . .	83.5	87.1	87.8	87.0	57.5	49.5	52.6	51.7	52.8
Cigarettes.....................................	82.2	79.0	77.5	77.8	76.0	35.5	28.9	27.2	27.0	27.9

— Represents or rounds to zero.
1. Nonmedical use; does not include over-the-counter drugs.

SOURCE: U.S. Substance Abuse and Mental Health Services Administration, National Household Survey on Drug Abuse, annual.

Series BB5. AIDS Cases Reported, by Patient Characteristic: 1981 to 1998

(Provisional. For cases reported in the year shown. Data shown for 1990 and 1994-97 are as reported through December 1997; data for 1981-98 and 1998 are as reported through December 1998 and include Puerto Rico, Virgin Islands, Guam, and U.S. Pacific Islands. For data on AIDS deaths, see Table 142. Data are subject to retrospective changes and may differ from those data in Table 226)

Characteristic	1981-98, total	1990	1994	1995	1996	1997	1998
Total [1]	688 200	41 529	77 103	70 864	66 497	58 443	48 269
Age:							
Under 5 years old	6 574	583	751	554	482	306	. . .
5 to 12 years old	1 887	137	220	189	168	145	. . .
13 to 19 years old	3 423	167	385	380	375	354	. . .
20 to 29 years old	117 717	7 854	12 321	10 866	9 655	8 130	. . .
30 to 39 years old	310 196	18 798	34 775	31 731	29 647	25 693	. . .
40 to 49 years old	176 239	9 725	20 505	19 446	18 818	16 957	. . .
50 to 59 years old	52 437	2 926	5 894	5 560	5 290	4 951	. . .
60 years old and over	19 724	1 253	2 050	1 924	1 858	1 733	. . .
Sex:							
Male	574 783	36 667	63 301	57 451	52 969	45 696	37 076
Female	113 414	4 862	13 802	13 413	13 528	12 747	11 190
Race/ethnic group:							
Non-Hispanic White	304 094	22 258	32 729	29 386	26 172	20 170	16 118
Non-Hispanic Black	251 408	13 199	30 923	29 060	28 639	26 995	21 752
Hispanic	124 841	5 657	12 556	11 544	10 796	10 387	9 650
Other/unknown	7 857	415	895	874	890	891	749
Transmission category:							
Males, 13 years and over	570 425	36 277	62 820	57 082	52 630	45 440	36 886
Men who have sex with men	326 051	23 797	35 255	30 953	27 460	20 894	16 642
Injecting drug use	126 889	6 957	15 124	13 329	11 801	9 737	7 869
Men who have sex with men and injecting drug use	43 640	2 809	4 529	3 805	3 153	2 262	1 984
Hemophilia/coagulation disorder	4 663	332	482	426	304	180	145
Heterosexual contact [2]	15 346	260	1 886	1 930	2 348	2 087	1 979
Heterosexual contact with injecting drug user	8 015	457	932	874	827	703	631
Transfusion [3]	4 784	449	369	341	270	217	156
Undetermined [4]	41 037	1 216	4 243	5 424	6 467	9 360	7 480
Females, 13 years and over	109 311	4 529	13 295	13 017	13 195	12 530	10 998
Injecting drug use	46 804	2 325	5 907	5 290	4 728	4 044	3 201
Hemophilia/coagulation disorder	248	16	28	26	22	16	17
Heterosexual contact [2]	24 897	506	3 431	3 518	3 781	3 293	2 913
Heterosexual contact with injecting drug user	18 231	1 035	2 029	1 873	1 870	1 349	1 212
Transfusion [3]	3 598	335	310	271	266	181	137
Undetermined [4]	15 533	312	1 590	2 039	2 528	3 647	3 518

1. Includes unknown, not shown separately.
2. Includes persons who have had heterosexual contact with a person with human immunodeficiency virus (HIV) infection or at risk of HIV infection.
3. Receipt of blood transfusion, blood components, or tissue.
4. Includes persons for whom risk information is incomplete (because of death, refusal to be interviewed, or loss to followup), persons still under investigation, men reported only to have had heterosexual contact with prostitutes, and interviewed persons for whom no specific risk is identified.

SOURCE: U.S. Centers for Disease Control and Prevention, Atlanta, GA, HIV/AIDS Surveillance Reports, semiannual.

Series BB6.   Abortions—Number, Rate, and Ratio, by Race: 1975 to 1996

| | All races | | | | White | | | | Black and other | | | |
| | Women 15-44 years old (1 000) | Abortions | | | Women 15-44 years old (1 000) | Abortions | | | Women 15-44 years old (1 000) | Abortions | | |
Year		Number (1 000)	Rate per 1 000 women	Ratio per 1 000 live births [1]		Number (1 000)	Rate per 1 000 women	Ratio per 1 000 live births [1]		Number (1 000)	Rate per 1 000 women	Ratio per 1 000 live births [1]
1996....................	59 606	1 366	22.9	351	48 120	800	16.6	259	11 486	566	49.2	701
1995....................	59 442	1 364	22.9	351	48 140	820	17.0	265	11 302	544	48.1	686
1994 [2]....................	59 284	1 431	24.1	364	48 121	861	17.9	277	11 163	570	51.1	699
1993 [2]....................	59 143	1 500	25.4	378	48 137	911	18.9	291	11 007	589	53.5	700
1992....................	59 020	1 529	25.9	380	48161	943	19.6	298	10 859	585	53.9	681
1991....................	59 080	1 557	26.3	379	48 406	982	20.3	303	10 674	574	53.8	661
1990 [2]....................	58 700	1 609	27.4	389	48 224	1 039	21.5	318	10 476	570	54.4	655
1989 [2]....................	58 365	1 567	26.8	380	48 104	1 006	20.9	309	10 261	561	54.7	650
1988....................	58 192	1 591	27.3	401	48 325	1 026	21.2	333	9 867	565	57.3	638
1987....................	57 964	1 559	27.1	405	48 288	1 017	21.1	338	9 676	542	56.0	648
1986 [2]....................	57 483	1 574	27.4	416	48 010	1 045	21.8	350	9 473	529	55.9	661
1985....................	56 754	1 589	28.0	422	47 512	1 076	22.6	360	9 242	513	55.5	659
1984....................	56 061	1 577	28.1	423	47 023	1 087	23.1	366	9 038	491	54.3	646
1983 [2]....................	55 340	1 575	28.5	436	46 506	1 084	23.3	376	8 834	491	55.5	670
1982....................	54 679	1 574	28.8	428	46 049	1 095	23.8	373	8 630	479	55.5	646
1981....................	53 901	1 577	29.3	430	45 494	1 108	24.3	377	8 407	470	55.9	645
1980....................	53 048	1 554	29.3	428	44 942	1 094	24.3	376	8 106	460	56.5	642
1979....................	52 016	1 498	28.8	420	44 266	1 062	24.0	373	7 750	435	56.2	625
1975....................	47 606	1 034	21.7	331	40 857	701	17.2	276	6 749	333	49.3	565

1. Live births are those which occurred from July 1 of year shown through June 30 of the following year (to match time of conception with abortions). Births are classified by race of child 1972–1988, and by race of mother after 1988.
2. Total numbers of abortions in 1983 and 1986 have been estimated by interpolation; 1989, 1990, 1993, and 1994 have been estimated using trends in CDC data.

MIGRATION
Highlights

1 The continuous record of immigration into the United States began with the Act of 1819. This Act required the captain or master of a vessel arriving at a U.S. port to deliver to the local collector of customs a list or manifest of all passengers taken on board, designating the age, sex, nationality, and occupation of each passenger, as well as the number of passengers who died during the passage. Copies of the manifests were transmitted to the Secretary of State, who reported the information periodically to Congress. Although the reporting of alien arrivals had also been required by the Act of 1798 (which expired in 1817), the number of arrivals prior to 1819 is not known. William J. Bromwell, author of *History of Immigration to the United States,* estimates the number of foreign arrivals between the close of the Revolutionary War and 1819 at 250,000. Immigration statistics were compiled by the Department of State from 1820 to 1870, by the Treasury Department's Bureau of Statistics from 1867 to 1895 and since 1892 by the Office or Bureau of Immigration ((later the Immigration and Naturalization Service). Annual reports have presented the data on immigration statistics since 1892 with the exception of 1942, when no report was issued because of wartime conditions. Since 1820, reporting on immigration data has undergone many changes. Only arrivals by vessels at Atlantic and Gulf ports were included until 1850 when Pacific ports were added. During the Civil War, Southern ports under Confederate control were excluded. Later, the reporting area was expanded to include outlying possessions: Alaska from 1871 (although irregularly until 1904), Hawaii from 1901, Puerto Rico from 1902 and the Virgin Islands from 1942. The government did not require arrivals at land borders to be counted until 1904, when land border stations were established. By 1908, such arrivals were fully incorporated into the annual totals. In any case, until the first decade of the 20th century, there were few Canadian or Mexican immigrants in the United States.

2 Since 1933, aliens arriving in the United States have been classified as immigrants or nonimmigrants. Immigrants are nonresident aliens admitted to the United States for permanent residence. Until July 1, 1968, they were further classified into quota and nonquota immigrants. The former were subject to the established quotas of Eastern Hemisphere countries, while nonquota immigrants included natives of the Western Hemisphere and certain groups of special immigrants (classes of immigrants admitted to the United States for political reasons). Since July 1, 1968, this distinction has been abolished in favor of numerical ceilings for regions and countries, but the category of special immigrants has been retained. The collection of data on emigrants has been suspended since 1957. Net immigration data suffer from lack of reliable emigration figures, as well as conflicts in the enumeration of nonimmigrant arrivals.

3 From 1925 to 1929, the annual immigration quota of 164,667 was based on 2% of foreign-born residents of the United States as determined by the 1890 census. The national origin formula provided that the annual quota equal one-sixth of 1% of the number of White inhabitants of the continental United States in 1920, less Western Hemisphere immigrants and their descendants. The annual quota for each nationality was then determined by the same ratio to 150,000 as the number of inhabitants living in the continental United States in 1920 to the total inhabitants (with a minimum of 100). The Act of 1965 replaced the quota system with an annual numerical limitation of 170,000 on the Eastern Hemisphere and 120,000 on the Western Hemisphere, with a ceiling of 20,000 for each country of origin.

4 Before 1882, various state laws excluded certain aliens from admission, such as paupers, felons, and the diseased. The first Chinese Exclusion Law, passed in 1882, also excluded lunatics, idiots, and those likely to become public charges. Nine years later, Congress passed a much broader exclusion law in the Act of 1891. Statistics on excluded aliens were first compiled in 1892. Subsequent acts, principally those of 1917 and 1952, extended the excluded categories to anarchists, criminals, drug traffickers, subversives and mental and physical defectives. However, landed immigrants enjoy all the judicial protection of citizens and may appeal deportation and expulsion orders.

5 Since the first naturalization statute of 1790, there have been three requirements for immigrants seeking U. S. citizenship: (1) residence in the United States for five years, (2) a good moral character; and (3) an oath to support the Constitution. The residence requirement is only three years for a spouse of a U. S. citizen. Before 1906, individual

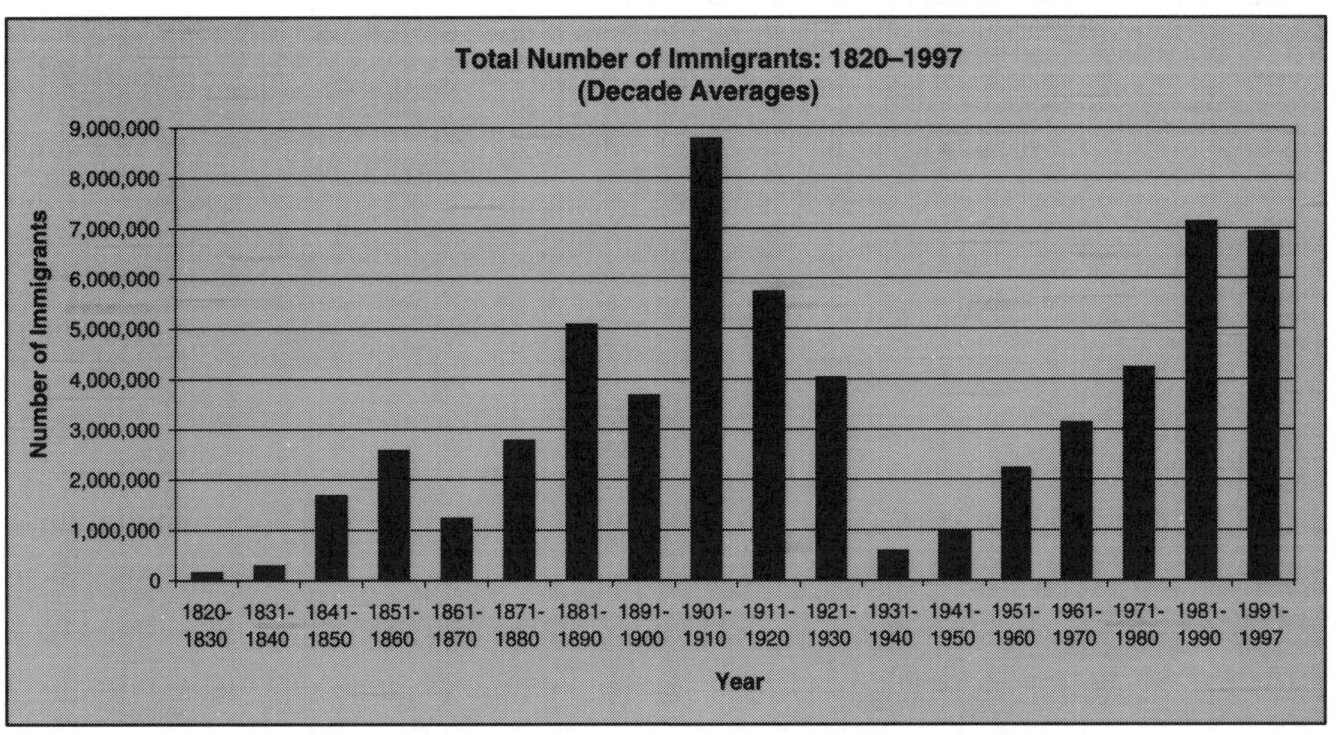

Total Number of Immigrants: 1820–1997
(Decade Averages)

courts kept naturalization records, but no national data were compiled. Since 1906, all courts have been required to file petitions and certificates of naturalization with the Bureau of Immigration and Naturalization.

6 While most European countries were represented in the immigration totals in the early 19th century, the first immigrant from Korea arrived only in 1948, from the Philippines in 1936, from Japan in 1861, and from Australia in 1870.

7 The annual number of legal immigrants exceeded one million in eight years: 1905, 1906, 1907, 1910, 1913, 1914, 1989, and 1990. There is no official count of illegal immigrants.

8 The Refugee Act of 1980 provides for the admission of refugees and asylum-seekers based on United Nations guidelines. Authorized admission ceilings are set annually by the President of the United States in consultation with Congress. After one year of residence, refugees are eligible

for immigrant status. Beginning in 1966, Cubans admitted or paroled (admitted without immigration visa) into the United States after 1959 and present in the United States for at least two years could obtain permanent resident status. The Refugee Act of 1980 reduced the residency requirement to one year. In addition, the 125,000 Cuban immigrants admitted to the United States as part of the Muriel boatlift were eligible to become immigrants. Since 1977, refugees from Vietnam, Laos, and Cambodia have been eligible to apply for permanent resident status after living for at least two years (later reduced to one year) in the United States. Other refugee streams have been permitted into the United States under the Refugee Relief Act of 1958 and the Refugees-Escapees-Parolees Act of 1960. A total of 1,013,620 refugees were admitted in the 1980s and 748,122 between 1991 and 1997.

9 The number of illegal immigrants in the United States is estimated at 7,855,600. Mexicans make up 34% of this total.

Series C 89-119. Immigrants, by Country: 1820 to 1997

(For years ending Sept. 30 from 1977 to date; prior to that, years ending June 30, except: 1820–1831 and 1844–1849, years ending Sept. 30; 1833–1842 and 1851–1867, years ending Dec. 31; 1832 covers 15 months ending Dec. 31; 1843, 9 months ending Sept. 30; 1850, 15 months ending Dec. 31; 1868, 6 months ending June 30, 1990–1997, by country of birth; 1906–1989, country of last permanent residence; prior to 1906, countries from which the immigrants came.)

Year	All Countries [1]	Europe					Commonwealth of Independent States [4]	Italy
		Total	Northwestern Europe		Central Europe			
			United Kingdom [2]	Ireland [2]	Germany [3]	Poland		
	89	**90**	**91**	**92**	**95**	**96**	**98**	**100**
1997	798 378	119 900	10 700	1 000	. . .	12 000	. . .	. . .
1996	915 900	147 600	13 600	1 700	6 700	15 800	62 800	2 500
1995	720 461	128 200	12 400	5 300	6 200	13 800	54 500	2 200
1994	804 416	160 900	16 300	17 300	7 000	28 000	63 400	2 300
1993	904 292	158 300	18 800	13 600	7 300	27 800	58 600	2 500
1992	973 977	145 400	20 000	12 200	9 900	25 500	43 600	2 600
1991	1 827 167	135 200	13 900	4 800	6 500	19 200	57 000	2 600
1990	1 536 486	112 400	15 900	10 300	7 500	20 500	25 500	3 300
1981-1990	7 338 100	761 550	159 200	32 000	91 960	83 300	58 700	67 300
1971-1980	4 493 300	800 400	137 400	11 500	74 400	37 200	39 000	129 400
1970	373 326	110 653	14 089	1 583	10 632	2 013	836	27 369
1969	358 579	114 052	15 072	1 981	10 380	2 115	574	27 033
1968	454 448	129 022	26 025	2 995	16 590	3 676	974	25 882
1967	361 972	128 775	23 004	2 765	16 595	4 356	876	28 487
1966	323 040	115 898	18 777	3 267	17 654	8 490	768	26 447
1965	296 697	101 468	24 135	5 187	22 432	7 093	632	10 874
1964	292 248	108 215	25 758	6 055	24 494	7 097	763	12 769
1963	306 260	109 066	22 708	5 746	24 727	6 785	591	16 175
1962	283 763	103 989	18 066	5 118	21 477	5 660	753	20 119
1961	271 344	108 532	18 719	5 738	25 815	6 254	996	18 956
1960	265 398	120 178	19 967	6 918	29 452	4 216	856	13 369
1959	260 686	138 191	18 325	6 595	32 039	2 800	775	16 804
1958	253 265	115 198	24 147	9 134	29 498	1 470	641	23 115
1957	326 867	169 625	24 020	8 227	60 353	571	663	19 624
1956	321 625	156 866	19 008	5 607	44 409	263	643	40 430
1955	237 790	110 591	15 761	5 222	29 596	129	523	30 272
1954	208 177	92 121	16 672	4 655	33 098	67	475	13 145
1953	170 434	82 352	16 639	4 304	27 329	136	609	8 432
1952	265 520	193 626	22 177	3 526	104 236	235	548	11 342
1951	205 717	149 545	14 898	3 144	87 755	98	555	8 958
1950	249 187	199 115	12 755	5 842	128 592	696	526	12 454
1949	188 317	129 592	21 149	8 678	55 284	1 673	694	11 695
1948	170 570	103 544	26 403	7 534	19 368	2 447	897	16 075
1947	147 292	83 535	23 788	2 574	13 900	745	761	13 866
1946	108 721	52 852	33 552	1 816	2 598	335	153	2 636
1945	38 119	5 943	3 029	427	172	195	98	213
1944	28 551	4 509	1 321	112	238	292	157	120
1943	23 725	4 920	974	165	248	394	159	49
1942	28 781	11 153	907	83	2 150	343	197	103
1941	51 776	26 541	7 714	272	4 028	451	665	450
1940	70 756	50 454	6 158	839	21 520	702	898	5 302
1939	82 998	63 138	3 058	1 189	33 515	3 072	1 021	6 570
1938	67 895	44 495	2 262	1 085	17 199	2 403	960	7 712
1937	50 244	31 863	1 726	531	10 895	1 212	629	7 192
1936	36 329	23 480	1 310	444	6 346	869	378	6 774
1935	34 956	22 778	1 413	454	5 201	1 504	418	6 566
1934	29 470	17 210	1 305	443	4 392	1 032	607	4 374
1933	23 068	12 383	979	338	1 919	1 332	458	3 477
1932	35 576	20 579	2 057	539	2 670	1 296	636	6 662
1931	97 139	61 909	9 110	7 305	10 401	3 604	1 396	13 399
1930	241 700	147 438	31 015	23 445	25 569	9 231	2 772	22 327
1929	279 678	158 598	21 327	19 921	46 751	9 002	2 450	18 008
1928	307 255	158 513	19 958	25 268	45 778	8 755	2 652	17 728
1927	335 175	168 368	23 669	28 545	48 513	9 211	2 933	17 297
1926	304 488	155 562	25 528	24 897	50 421	7 126	3 323	8 253

See footnotes on next page.

Series C 89-119. Immigrants, by Country: 1820 to 1997—Cont'd.

(For years ending Sept. 30 from 1977 to date; prior to that, years ending June 30, except: 1820–1831 and 1844–1849, years ending Sept. 30; 1833–1842 and 1851–1867, years ending Dec. 31; 1832 covers 15 months ending Dec. 31; 1843, 9 months ending Sept. 30; 1850, 15 months ending Dec. 31; 1868, 6 months ending June 30, 1990–1997, by country of birth; 1906–1989, country of last permanent residence; prior to 1906, countries from which the immigrants came.)

		Europe					Commonwealth	
			Northwestern Europe		Central Europe		of Independent	
Year	All Countries [1]	Total	United Kingdom [2]	Ireland [2]	Germany [3]	Poland	States [4]	Italy
	89	90	91	92	95	96	98	100
1925	294 314	148 366	27 172	26 650	46 068	5 341	3 121	6 203
1924	706 896	364 339	59 490	17 111	75 091	28 806	20 918	56 246
1923	522 919	307 920	45 759	15 740	48 277	26 538	21 151	46 674
1922	309 556	216 385	25 153	10 579	17 931	28 635	19 910	40 319
1921	805 228	652 364	51 142	28 435	6 803	95 089	10 193	222 260
1920	430 001	246 295	38 471	9 591	1 001	4 813	1 751	95 145
1919	141 132	24 627	6 797	474	52	(5)	1 403	1 884
1918	110 618	31 063	2 516	331	447	(5)	4 242	5 250
1917	295 403	133 083	10 735	5 406	1 857	(5)	12 716	34 596
1916	298 826	145 699	16 063	8 639	2 877	(5)	7 842	33 665
1915	326 700	197 919	27 237	14 185	7 799	(5)	26 187	49 688
1914	1 218 480	1 058 391	48 729	24 688	35 734	5 255 660	283 738	
1913	1 197 892	1 055 855	60 328	27 876	34 329	(5)	291 040	265 542
1912	838 172	718 875	57 148	25 879	27 788	(5)	162 395	157 134
1911	878 587	764 757	73 384	29 112	32 061	5 158 721	182 882	
1910	1 041 570	926 291	68 941	29 855	31 283	(5)	186 792	215 537
1909	751 786	654 875	46 793	25 033	25 540	(5)	120 460	183 218
1908	782 870	691 901	62 824	30 556	32 309	(5)	156 711	128 503
1907	1 285 349	1 199 566	79 037	34 530	37 807	(5)	258 943	285 731
1906	1 100 735	1 018 365	67 198	34 995	37 564	(5)	215 665	273 120
1905	1 026 499	974 273	84 189	52 945	40 574	(5)	184 897	221 479
1904	812 870	767 933	51 448	36 142	46 380	(5)	145 141	193 296
1903	857 046	814 507	33 637	35 310	40 086	(5)	136 093	230 622
1902	648 743	619 068	16 898	29 138	28 304	(5)	107 347	178 375
1901	487 918	469 237	14 985	30 561	21 651	(5)	85 257	135 996
1900	448 572	424 700	12 509	35 730	18 507	(5)	90 787	100 135
1899	311 715	297 349	13 456	31 673	17 476	(5)	60 982	77 419
1898	229 299	217 786	12 894	25 128	17 111	4 726	29 828	58 613
1897	230 832	216 397	12 752	28 421	22 533	4 165	25 816	59 431
1896	343 267	329 067	24 656	40 262	31 885	691	51 445	68 060
1895	258 536	250 342	28 833	46 304	32 173	790	35 907	35 427
1894	285 631	277 052	22 520	30 231	53 989	1 941	39 278	42 977
1893	439 730	429 324	35 189	43 578	78 756	16 374	42 310	72 145
1892	579 663	570 876	42 215	51 383	119 168	40 536	81 511	61 631
1891	560 319	546 085	66 605	55 706	113 554	27 497	47 426	76 055
1890	455 302	445 680	69 730	53 024	92 427	11 073	35 598	52 003
1889	444 427	434 790	87 992	65 557	99 538	4 922	33 916	25 307
1888	546 889	538 131	108 692	73 513	109 717	5 826	33 487	51 558
1887	490 109	482 829	93 378	68 370	106 865	6 128	30 766	47 622
1886	334 203	329 529	62 929	49 619	84 403	3 939	17 800	21 315
1885	395 346	353 083	57 713	51 795	124 443	3 085	17 158	13 642
1884	518 592	453 686	65 950	63 344	179 676	4 536	12 689	16 510
1883	603 322	522 587	76 606	81 486	194 786	2 011	9 909	31 792
1882	788 992	648 186	102 991	76 432	250 630	4 672	16 918	32 159
1881	669 431	528 545	81 376	72 342	210 485	5 614	5 041	15 401
1880	457 257	348 691	73 273	71 603	84 638	2 177	5 014	12 354
1879	177 826	134 259	29 955	20 013	34 602	489	4 453	5 791
1878	138 469	101 612	22 150	15 932	29 313	547	3 048	4 344
1877	141 857	106 195	23 581	14 569	29 298	533	6 599	3 195
1876	169 986	120 920	29 291	19 575	31 937	925	4 775	3 015
1875	227 498	182 961	47 905	37 957	47 769	984	7 997	3 631
1874	313 339	262 783	62 021	53 707	87 291	1 795	4 073	7 666
1873	459 803	397 541	89 500	77 344	149 671	3 338	1 634	8 757
1872	404 806	352 155	84 912	68 732	141 109	1 647	1 018	4 190
1871	321 350	265 145	85 455	57 439	82 554	535	673	2 816

See footnotes on next page.

Series C 89-119. Immigrants, by Country: 1820 to 1997—Cont'd.

(For years ending Sept. 30 from 1977 to date; prior to that, years ending June 30, except: 1820–1831 and 1844–1849, years ending Sept. 30; 1833–1842 and 1851–1867, years ending Dec. 31; 1832 covers 15 months ending Dec. 31; 1843, 9 months ending Sept. 30; 1850, 15 months ending Dec. 31; 1868, 6 months ending June 30, 1990–1997, by country of birth; 1906–1989, country of last permanent residence; prior to 1906, countries from which the immigrants came.)

		Europe					Commonwealth of Independent States [4]	Italy
			Northwestern Europe		Central Europe			
Year	All Countries [1]	Total	United Kingdom [2]	Ireland [2]	Germany [3]	Poland		
	89	90	91	92	95	96	98	100
1870	387 203	328 626	103 677	56 996	118 225	223	907	2 891
1869	352 768	315 963	84 438	40 786	131 042	184	343	1 489
1868	138 840	130 090	24 127	32 068	55 831	X	141	891
1867	315 722	283 751	52 641	72 879	133 426	310	205	1 624
1866	318 568	278 916	94 924	36 690	115 892	412	287	1 382
1865	248 120	214 048	82 465	29 772	83 424	528	183	924
1864	193 418	185 233	53 428	63 523	57 276	165	256	600
1863	176 282	163 733	66 882	55 916	33 162	94	77	547
1862	91 985	83 710	24 639	23 351	27 529	63	79	566
1861	91 918	81 200	19 675	23 797	31 661	48	34	811
1860	153 640	141 209	29 737	48 637	54 491	82	65	1 019
1859	121 282	110 949	26 163	35 216	41 784	106	91	932
1858	123 126	111 354	28 956	26 873	45 310	9	246	1 240
1857	251 306	216 224	58 479	54 361	91 781	124	25	1 007
1856	200 436	186 083	44 658	54 349	71 028	20	9	1 365
1855	200 877	187 729	47 572	49 627	71 918	462	13	1 052
1854	427 833	405 542	58 647	101 606	215 009	208	2	1 263
1853	368 645	361 576	37 576	162 649	41 946	33	3	555
1852	371 603	362 484	40 699	159 548	145 918	110	2	351
1851	379 466	369 510	51 487	221 253	72 482	10	1	447
1850	369 980	308 323	51 085	164 004	78 896	5	31	431
1849	297 024	286 501	55 132	159 398	60 235	4	44	209
1848	226 527	218 025	35 159	112 934	58 465	X	1	241
1847	234 968	229 117	23 302	105 536	74 281	8	5	164
1846	154 416	146 315	22 180	51 752	57 561	4	248	151
1845	114 371	109 301	19 210	44 821	34 355	6	1	137
1844	78 615	74 745	14 353	33 490	20 731	36	13	141
1843	52 496	49 013	8 430	19 670	14 441	17	6	117
1842	104 565	99 945	22 005	51 342	20 370	10	28	100
1841	80 289	76 216	16 188	37 772	15 291	15	174	179
1840	84 066	80 126	2 613	39 430	29 704	5	X	37
1839	68 069	64 148	10 271	23 963	21 028	46	7	84
1838	38 914	34 070	5 420	12 645	11 683	41	13	86
1837	79 340	71 039	12 218	28 508	23 740	81	19	36
1836	76 242	70 465	13 106	30 578	20 707	53	2	115
1835	45 374	41 987	8 970	20 927	8 311	54	9	60
1834	65 365	57 510	10 490	24 474	17 686	54	15	105
1833	58 640	29 111	4 916	8 648	6 988	1	159	1 699
1832	60 482	34 193	5 331	12 436	10 194	34	52	3
1831	22 633	13 039	2 475	5 772	2 413	X	1	28
1830	23 322	7 217	1 153	2 721	1 976	2	3	9
1829	22 520	12 523	3 179	7 415	597	X	1	23
1828	27 382	24 729	5 352	12 488	1 851	1	7	34
1827	18 875	16 719	4 186	9 766	432	1	19	35
1826	10 837	9 751	2 319	5 408	511	X	4	57
1825	10 199	8 543	2 095	4 888	450	1	10	75
1824	7 912	4 965	1 264	2 345	230	4	7	45
1823	6 354	4 016	1 100	1 908	183	3	7	33
1822	6 911	4 418	1 221	2 267	148	3	10	35
1821	9 127	5 936	3 210	1 518	383	1	7	63
1820	8 385	7 691	2 410	3 614	968	5	14	30

X Represents zero.
1. For 1820–1867 excludes returning citizens.
2. Prior to 1926, data for Northern Ireland included Ireland. Since 1995, data for the United Kingdom refer to England, Scotland, Wales, and Northern Ireland.
3. Includes Austria, 1938 to 1945.
4. Comprises former Soviet Union.
5. Between 1899 and 1919, included with Austria-Hungary, Germany, and Russia.

Series C 89-119. Immigrants, by Country: 1820 to 1997—Cont'd.

(For years ending Sept. 30 from 1977 to date; prior to that, years ending June 30, except: 1820–1831 and 1844–1849, years ending Sept. 30; 1833–1842 and 1851–1867, years ending Dec. 31; 1832 covers 15 months ending Dec. 31; 1843, 9 months ending Sept. 30; 1850, 15 months ending Dec. 31; 1868, 6 months ending June 30, 1990–1997, by country of birth; 1906–1989, country of last permanent residence; prior to 1906, countries from which the immigrants came.)

Year	Asia							America		
	Total	Turkey in Asia [1]	China [2]	India	Japan [3]	Korea [4]	Philippines	Total	Canada and Newfoundland [5]	Mexico
	102	103	104	105	106	107	108	110	111	112
1997	265 800	3 100	47 900	38 100	5 100	14 200	49 100	360 400	11 600	146 900
1996	307 800	3 700	55 100	44 900	6 000	18 200	55 900	402 300	15 800	163 600
1995	267 900	2 900	44 800	34 700	4 837	16 000	51 000	277 200	12 900	89 900
1994	292 600	1 800	64 000	34 900	6 093	16 000	53 500	319 600	16 100	111 400
1993	358 000	2 200	79 900	40 100	6 908	18 000	63 500	355 300	17 200	126 600
1992	357 000	2 500	55 300	36 700	11 028	19 400	61 000	439 400	15 200	213 800
1991	358 500	2 500	46 300	45 100	5 049	26 500	63 600	1 290 900	13 500	946 200
1990	338 600	2 500	47 000	30 700	5 734	32 300	63 800	1 043 400	16 800	679 100
1981-1990	2 738 000	23 200	346 700	250 800	47 100	333 700	548 800	3 615 200	156 900	1 655 800
1971-1980	1 588 200	13 400	124 300	164 100	49 800	267 600	355 000	1 982 700	169 900	640 300
1970	90 215	495	6 427	8 795	4 731	8 888	30 507	161 727	26 850	44 821
1969	72 959	556	5 264	5 205	4 095	5 854	20 263	164 045	29 303	45 748
1968	56 298	325	4 851	4 165	3 810	3 592	16 086	262 736	41 716	44 716
1967	57 574	491	7 118	4 129	4 125	3 845	10 336	170 235	34 768	43 034
1966	40 113	365	2 948	2 293	3 468	2 414	5 894	162 551	37 273	47 217
1965	20 040	365	1 611	467	3 294	2 139	2 963	171 019	50 035	40 686
1964	21 279	331	2 684	488	3 774	2 329	2 862	158 644	51 114	34 448
1963	23 242	307	1 605	965	4 147	2 560	3 483	169 966	50 509	55 986
1962	20 249	304	1 356	390	4 054	1 463	3 354	155 871	44 272	55 805
1961	19 495	296	900	292	4 490	1 442	2 628	139 580	47 470	41 476
1960	21 604	200	1 380	244	5 699	1 410	2 791	119 525	46 668	32 708
1959	25 259	229	1 702	351	6 248	1 614	2 503	93 061	34 599	22 909
1958	20 870	197	1 143	323	6 847	1 470	2 034	113 132	45 143	26 791
1957	20 008	77	2 098	196	6 829	577	1 874	134 160	46 354	49 321
1956	17 327	48	1 386	185	5 967	579	1 792	144 713	42 363	61 320
1955	10 935	54	568	194	4 150	263	1 598	110 436	32 435	43 702
1954	9 970	33	254	144	3 846	175	1 234	95 587	34 873	30 645
1953	8 231	13	528	104	2 579	75	1 074	77 650	36 283	17 183
1952	9 328	12	263	123	3 814	47	1 179	61 049	33 354	9 079
1951	7 149	3	335	109	271	21	3 228	47 631	25 880	6 153
1950	4 508	13	1 280	121	100	24	729	44 191	21 885	6 744
1949	7 595	40	3 415	175	529	39	1 157	49 334	25 156	8 083
1948	11 907	16	7 203	263	423	44	1 168	52 746	25 485	8 384
1947	6 733	22	3 191	432	131	...	910	52 753	24 342	7 558
1946	2 108	16	252	425	14	...	475	46 066	21 344	7 146
1945	461	13	71	103	1	...	19	29 646	11 530	6 702
1944	231	15	50	41	4	...	4	23 084	10 143	6 598
1943	342	36	65	71	20	...	8	18 162	9 761	4 172
1942	615	31	179	36	44	...	51	16 377	10 599	2 378
1941	1 971	16	1 003	94	289	...	170	22 445	11 473	2 824
1940	2 050	7	643	52	102	...	137	17 822	11 078	2 313
1939	2 281	15	642	36	102	...	119	17 139	10 813	2 640
1938	2 492	11	613	34	93	...	116	20 486	14 404	2 502
1937	1 149	13	293	47	132	...	84	16 903	12 011	2 347
1936	793	20	273	13	91	...	72	11 786	8 121	1 716
1935	682	31	229	32	88	...	(6)	11 174	7 782	1 560
1934	597	22	187	28	86	...	...	11 409	7 945	1 801
1933	552	27	148	44	75	...	...	9 925	6 187	1 936
1932	1 931	43	750	87	526	...	...	12 577	8 003	2 171
1931	3 345	139	1 150	123	653	...	...	30 816	22 183	3 333
1930	4 535	118	1 589	110	837	...	...	88 104	65 254	12 703
1929	3 758	70	1 446	103	771	...	...	116 177	66 451	40 154
1928	3 880	80	1 320	102	550	...	...	144 281	75 281	59 016
1927	3 669	73	1 471	102	723	...	...	161 872	84 580	67 721
1926	3 413	37	1 751	93	654	...	...	144 393	93 368	43 316

See footnotes at end of chart.

Series C 89-119. Immigrants, by Country: 1820 to 1997—Cont'd.

(For years ending Sept. 30 from 1977 to date; prior to that, years ending June 30, except: 1820–1831 and 1844–1849, years ending Sept. 30; 1833–1842 and 1851–1867, years ending Dec. 31; 1832 covers 15 months ending Dec. 31; 1843, 9 months ending Sept. 30; 1850, 15 months ending Dec. 31; 1868, 6 months ending June 30, 1990–1997, by country of birth; 1906–1989, country of last permanent residence; prior to 1906, countries from which the immigrants came.)

Year	Asia							America		
	Total	Turkey in Asia [1]	China [2]	India	Japan [3]	Korea [4]	Philippines	Total	Canada and Newfoundland [5]	Mexico
	102	103	104	105	106	107	108	110	111	112
1925	3 578	51	1 937	65	723	...	...	141 496	102 753	32 964
1924	22 065	2 820	6 992	183	8 801	...	...	318 855	200 690	89 336
1923	13 705	2 183	4 986	257	5 809	...	...	199 972	117 011	63 768
1922	14 263	1 998	4 406	360	6 716	...	...	77 448	46 810	19 551
1921	25 034	11 735	4 009	511	7 878	...	...	124 118	72 317	30 758
1920	17 505	5 033	2 330	300	9 432	...	...	162 666	90 025	52 361
1919	12 674	19	1 964	171	10 064	...	...	102 286	57 782	29 818
1918	12 701	43	1 795	130	10 213	...	...	65 418	32 452	18 524
1917	12 756	393	2 237	109	8 991	...	...	147 779	105 399	17 869
1916	13 204	1 670	2 460	112	8 680	...	...	137 424	101 551	18 425
1915	15 211	3 543	2 660	161	8 613	...	...	111 206	82 215	12 340
1914	34 273	21 716	2 502	221	8 929	...	...	122 695	86 139	14 614
1913	35 358	23 955	2 105	179	8 281	...	...	103 907	73 802	11 926
1912	21 449	12 788	1 765	175	6 114	...	...	95 926	55 990	23 238
1911	17 428	10 229	1 460	524	4 520	...	...	94 364	56 830	19 889
1910	23 533	15 212	1 968	1 696	2 720	...	...	89 534	56 555	18 691
1909	12 904	7506	1 943	203	3 111	...	...	82 208	51 941	16 251
1908	28 365	9 753	1 397	1 040	15 803	...	...	59 997	38 510	6 067
1907	40 524	8 053	961	898	30 226	...	...	41 762	19 918	1 406
1906	22 300	6 354	1 544	216	13 835	...	...	24 613	5 063	1 997
1905	23 925	6 157	2 166	190	10 331	...	...	25 217	2 168	2 637
1904	26 186	5 235	4 309	261	14 264	...	...	16 420	2 837	1 009
1903	29 966	7 118	2 209	94	19 968	...	...	11 023	1 058	528
1902	22 271	6 223	1 649	93	14 270	...	...	6 698	636	709
1901	13 593	5 782	2 459	22	5 269	...	...	4 416	540	347
1900	17 946	3 962	1 247	9	12 635	...	...	5 455	396	237
1899	8 972	4 436	1 660	17	2 844	...	...	4 316	1 322	161
1898	8 637	4 275	2 071	X	2 230	...	...	2 627	352	107
1897	9 662	4 732	3 363	X	1 526	...	...	4 537	291	91
1896	6 764	4 139	1 441	X	1 110	...	...	7 303	278	150
1895	4 495	2 767	539	X	1 150	...	...	3 508	244	116
1894	4 690	X	1 170	X	1 931	...	...	3 551	194	109
1893	2 392	X	472	X	1 380	...	...	2 593	(7)	(8)
1892	(7)	...	...	...	...	...	...	(7)	(7)	(8)
1891	7 678	2 488	2 836	42	1 136	...	...	5 082	234	(8)
1890	4 448	1 126	1 716	43	691	...	...	3 833	183	(8)
1889	1 725	593	118	59	640	...	...	5 459	28	(8)
1888	843	273	26	20	404	...	...	5 402	15	(8)
1887	615	208	10	32	229	...	...	5 270	9	(8)
1886	317	15	40	17	194	...	...	3 026	17	(8)
1885	198	...	22	34	49	...	...	41 203	38 336	323
1884	510	...	279	12	20	...	...	63 339	60 626	430
1883	8 113	...	8 031	9	27	...	...	71 729	70 274	469
1882	39 629	...	39 579	10	5	...	...	100 129	98 366	366
1881	11 982	5	11 890	33	11	...	...	127 577	125 450	325
1880	5 839	4	5 802	21	4	...	...	101 692	99 744	492
1879	9 660	31	9 604	15	4	...	...	33 043	31 286	556
1878	9 014	7	8 992	8	2	...	...	27 204	25 592	465
1877	10 640	3	10 594	17	7	...	...	24 065	22 137	445
1876	22 943	8	22 781	25	4	...	...	24 686	22 505	631
1875	16 499	1	16 437	19	3	...	...	26 640	24 097	610
1874	13 838	6	13 776	17	21	...	...	35 339	33 020	386
1873	20 325	3	20 292	15	9	...	...	40 335	37 891	606
1872	7 825	X	7 788	12	17	...	...	42 205	40 204	569

See footnotes at end of chart.

Series C 89-119. Immigrants, by Country: 1820 to 1997—Cont'd.

(For years ending Sept. 30 from 1977 to date; prior to that, years ending June 30, except: 1820–1831 and 1844–1849, years ending Sept. 30; 1833–1842 and 1851–1867, years ending Dec. 31; 1832 covers 15 months ending Dec. 31; 1843, 9 months ending Sept. 30; 1850, 15 months ending Dec. 31; 1868, 6 months ending June 30, 1990–1997, by country of birth; 1906–1989, country of last permanent residence; prior to 1906, countries from which the immigrants came.)

Year	Asia					America		
	Total	Turkey in Asia [1]	China [2]	India	Japan [3]	Total	Canada and Newfoundland [5]	Mexico
	102	103	104	105	106	110	111	112
1871	7 240	4	7 135	14	78	48 835	47 164	402
1870	15 825	X	15 740	24	48	42 658	40 414	463
1869	12 949	2	12 874	3	63	23 767	21 120	320
1868	5 171	...	5 157	X	X	3 415	2 785	129
1867	3 961	...	3 863	2	67	24 715	23 379	292
1866	2 411	...	2 385	17	7	33 582	32 180	239
1865	2 947	...	2 942	5	X	22 778	21 586	193
1864	2 982	...	2 975	6	X	4 607	3 636	99
1863	7 216	...	7 214	1	X	4 147	3 464	96
1862	3 640	...	3 633	5	X	4 175	3 275	142
1861	7 528	...	7 518	6	1	2 763	2 069	218
1860	5 476	...	5 467	5	...	6 343	4 514	229
1859	3 461	...	3 457	2	...	5 466	4 163	265
1858	5 133	...	5 128	5	...	5 821	4 603	429
1857	5 945	...	5 944	1	...	6 811	5 670	133
1856	4 747	...	4 733	13	...	9 058	6 493	741
1855	3 540	...	3 526	6	...	9 260	7 761	420
1854	13 100	...	13 100	X	...	8 533	6 891	446
1853	47	...	42	5	...	6 030	5 424	162
1852	4	...	X	4	...	7 695	6 352	72
1851	2	...	X	2	...	9 703	7 438	181
1850	7	...	3	4	...	15 768	9 376	597
1849	11	...	3	8	...	8 904	6 890	518
1848	8	...	X	6	...	7 989	6 473	24
1847	12	...	4	8	...	5 231	3 827	62
1846	11	...	7	4	...	5 525	3 855	222
1845	6	...	6	X	...	5 035	3 195	498
1844	6	...	3	1	...	3 740	2 711	197
1843	11	...	3	2	...	2 854	1 502	398
1842	7	...	4	2	...	3 994	2 078	403
1841	3	...	2	1	...	3 429	1 816	352
1840	1	...	X	1	...	3 815	1 938	395
1839	...	...	X	X	...	3 617	1 926	353
1838	1	...	X	1	...	2 990	1 476	211
1837	11	...	X	11	...	3 628	1 279	627
1836	4	...	X	4	...	4 936	2 814	798
1835	17	...	8	8	...	3 312	1 193	1 032
1834	6	...	X	6	...	2 779	1 020	885
1833	3	...	X	3	...	3 282	1 194	779
1832	4	...	X	4	...	2 871	608	827
1831	1	...	X	1	...	2 194	176	692
1830	...	...	X	X	...	2 296	189	983
1829	2	...	1	1	...	3 299	409	2 290
1828	3	...	X	3	...	2 090	267	1 089
1827	1	...	X	1	...	580	165	127
1826	1	...	X	1	...	831	223	106
1825	1	...	1	X	...	846	314	68
1824	1	...	X	1	...	559	155	110
1823	...	...	X	X	...	382	167	35
1822	1	...	X	1	...	378	204	5
1821	...	...	X	X	...	303	184	4
1820	5	...	1	1	...	387	209	1

See footnotes at end of chart.

Series C 89-119. Immigrants, by Country: 1820 to 1997—Cont'd.

(For years ending Sept. 30 from 1977 to date; prior to that, years ending June 30, except: 1820-1831 and 1844-1849, years ending Sept. 30; 1833-1842 and 1851-1867, years ending Dec. 31; 1832 covers 15 months ending Dec. 31; 1843, 9 months ending Sept. 30; 1850, 15 months ending Dec. 31; 1868, 6 months ending June 30, 1990-1997, by country of birth; 1906-1989, country of last permanent residence; prior to 1906, countries from which the immigrants came.)

Year	Africa, total	Year	Africa, total	Year	Africa, total	Year	Africa, total
	115		**115**		**115**		**115**
1997	47 800	1939	218	1899	51	1859	11
1996	52 900	1938	174	1898	48	1858	17
1995	42 500	1937	155	1897	37	1857	25
1994	26 700	1936	105	1896	21	1856	6
1993	27 800						
		1935	118	1895	36	1855	14
1992	27 100	1934	104	1894	24	1854	. . .
1991	36 200	1933	71	1893	(7)	1853	8
1990	35 900	1932	186	1892	(7)	1852	. . .
1981-1990	176 900	1931	417	1891	103	1851	3
1971-1980	80 800						
		1930	572	1890	112	1850	. . .
1970	7 099	1929	509	1889	187	1849	3
1969	4 460	1928	475	1888	65	1848	10
1968	3 220	1927	520	1887	40	1847	. . .
1967	2 577	1926	529	1886	122	1846	1
1966	1 967						
		1925	412	1885	112	1845	4
1965	1 949	1924	900	1884	59	1844	14
1964	2 015	1923	548	1883	67	1843	6
1963	1 982	1922	520	1882	60	1842	3
1962	1 834	1921	1 301	1881	33	1841	14
1961	1 851						
		1920	648	1880	18	1840	6
1960	1 925	1919	189	1879	12	1839	10
1959	1 992	1918	299	1878	18	1838	10
1958	2 008	1917	566	1877	16	1837	2
1957	1 600	1916	894	1876	89	1836	6
1956	1 351						
		1915	934	1875	54	1835	14
1955	1 203	1914	1 539	1874	58	1834	1
1954	1 248	1913	1 409	1873	28	1833	1
1953	989	1912	1 009	1872	41	1832	2
1952	931	1911	956	1871	24	1831	2
1951	845						
		1910	1 072	1870	31	1830	2
1950	849	1909	858	1869	72	1829	1
1949	995	1908	1 411	1868	3	1828	6
1948	1 027	1907	1 486	1867	25	1827	4
1947	1 284	1906	712	1866	33	1826	. . .
1946	1 516						
		1905	757	1865	49	1825	1
1945	406	1904	686	1864	37	1824	. . .
1944	112	1903	176	1863	3	1823	. . .
1943	141	1902	37	1862	12	1822	. . .
1942	473	1901	173	1861	47	1821	2
1941	564						
		1900	30	1860	126	1820	1
1940	202						

X Represents zero.
1. No record of immigration from Turkey in Asia until 1869.
2. Beginning 1957, includes Taiwan.
3. No record of immigration from Japan until 1861.
4. No record of immigration from Korea prior to 1948.
5. Prior to 1920, Canada and Newfoundland were recorded as British North America, and for 1820-1898, included all British North American possessions. Land arrivals not completely enumerated until 1908.
6. Philippines included in "All other countries" prior to 1936.
7. Included in "All other countries."
8. No record of immigration from Mexico for 1886 to 1893. Land arrivals not completely enumerated until 1908.

Series C 158-161.   Formal Removals and Voluntary Departures of Aliens: 1892 to 1998

(For federal fiscal years. Formal removals include deportations, exclusions, and removals.)

Year	Aliens expelled		Year	Aliens expelled			Year	Aliens deported
	Formal removals	Voluntary departures		Total	Deported	Required to depart		
	159	160		158	159	160		159
1998	172 547	1 569 817	1960	59 625	6 829	52 796	1917	1 853
1997	114 292	1 440 580	1959	64 598	7 988	56 610	1916	2 781
1996	69 588	1 573 372	1958	67 742	7 142	60 600		
1995	50 873	1 313 711	1957	68 461	5 082	63 379	1915	2 564
1994	45 621	1 029 052	1956	88 188	7 297	80 891	1914	4 610
							1913	3 461
1993	42 469	1 243 334	1955	247 797	15 028	232 769	1912	2 456
1992	43 671	1 105 829	1954	1 101 228	26 951	1 074 277	1911	2 788
1991	33 189	1 061 105	1953	905 236	19 845	885 391		
1990	30 039	1 022 533	1952	723 959	20 181	703 778	1910	2 695
1989	34 427	830 890	1951	686 713	13 544	673 169	1909	2 124
							1908	2 069
1988	25 829	911 790	1950	579 105	6 628	572 477	1907	995
1987	24 336	1 091 203	1949	296 337	20 040	276 297	1906	676
1986	24 592	1 586 320	1948	217 555	20 371	197 184		
1985	23 105	1 041 296	1947	214 543	18 663	195 880	1905	845
1984	18 696	909 833	1946	116 320	14 375	101 945	1904	779
							1903	547
1983	19 211	931 600	1945	80 760	11 270	69 490	1902	465
1982	15 216	812 572	1944	39 449	7 179	32 270	1901	363
1981	17 379	823 875	1943	16 154	4 207	11 947		
1980	18 013	719 211	1942	10 613	3 709	6 904	1900	356
1979	26 825	966 137	1941	10 938	4 407	6 531	1899	263
							1898	199
1978	29 277	975 515	1940	15 548	6 954	8 594	1897	263
1977	31 263	867 015	1939	17 792	8 202	9 590	1896	238
1976	29 226	765 094	1938	18 553	9 275	9 278		
1975	24 432	655 814	1937	17 617	8 829	8 788	1895	277
1974	19 413	718 740	1936	17 446	9 195	8 251	1894	417
							1893	577
1973	17 346	568 005	1935	16 297	8 319	7 978	1892	637
1972	16 883	450 927	1934	16 889	8 879	8 010		
1971	18 294	370 074	1933	30 212	19 865	10 347		
1970	17 469	303 348	1932	30 201	19 426	10 775		
1969	11 030	240 958	1931	29 861	18 142	11 719		
1968	9 590	179 952	1930	28 018	16 631	11 387		
1967	9 728	142 343	1929	38 796	12 908	25 888		
1966	9 680	123 683	1928	31 571	11 625	19 946		
1965	10 572	95 263	1927	26 674	11 662	15 012		
1964	9 167	73 042	1926	10 904	10 904	. . .		
1963	7 763	69 392	1925	9 495	9 495	. . .		
1962	8 025	54 164	1924	6 409	6 409	. . .		
1961	8 181	52 383	1923	3 661	. . .			
			1922	4 345	4 345	. . .		
			1921	4 517	4 517	. . .		
			1920	2 762	2 762	. . .		
			1919	3 068	3 068	. . .		
			1918	1 569	1 569	. . .		

LABOR
Highlights

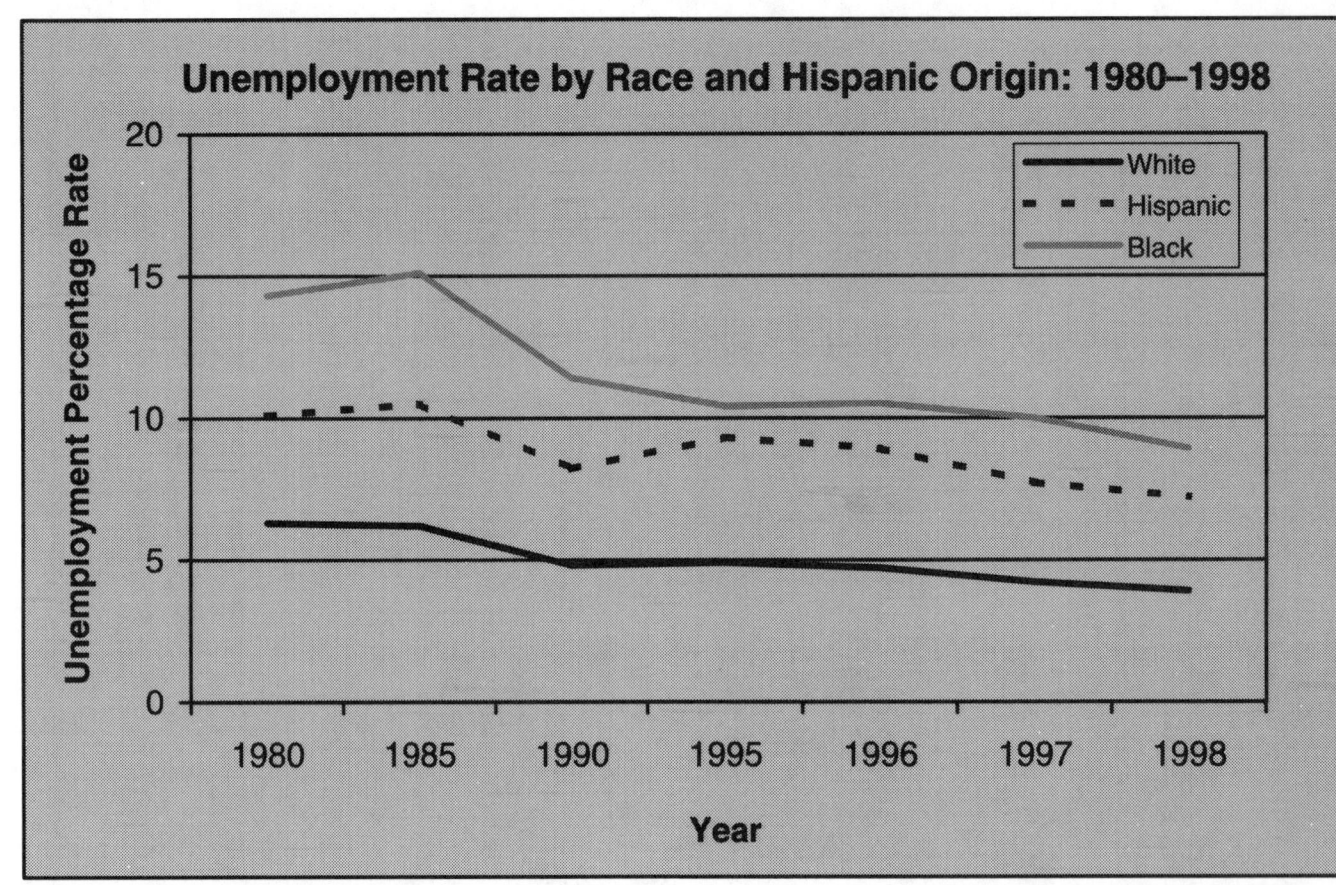

Unemployment Rate by Race and Hispanic Origin: 1980–1998

Legend: White, Hispanic, Black

X-axis: Year (1980, 1985, 1990, 1995, 1996, 1997, 1998)
Y-axis: Unemployment Percentage Rate (0 to 20)

1 The techniques for measuring labor force (or work force) data were developed during the late 1930s by the Works Projects Administration (WPA). For every week containing the 12th day of the month, the Bureau of the Census collects data for the Bureau of Labor Statistics. This dataset is part of the former Current Population Survey and is based on a scientifically designed sample of households. The survey includes all employed and unemployed persons as well as self-employed persons, unpaid family workers and domestic servants, and others who do not ordinarily appear on the payrolls of any establishment. Labor force data are also collected in the decennial censuses.

2 The concepts of employment, unemployment, and labor have changed over the years. By current definitions,

employed persons are those who work as paid employees or in their own businesses or professions, or on their farms, or who work 15 hours or more as unpaid workers in a family enterprise. It also includes those who are temporarily absent from work or business because of illness, vacation, bad weather, labor-management disputes, or personal reasons. Volunteer workers are excluded. Unemployed persons are those who do not work during the survey week, but who make efforts to secure a job and are available for work. The civilian labor force (persons 14 years and over until 1966 and over 16 years thereafter) is the sum of the employed and the unemployed. Data on the size of the armed forces is obtained from the Department of Defense and added to the civilian labor force to obtain the Total Labor Force. For years prior to 1940 (when detailed labor force data became available for the whole nation) the data are based on Stanley Legerbott's *Manpower in Economic Growth: The American Record Since 1800*. Legerbott obtained his data by interpolating between detailed worker rates in the census years and applying the resultant series to unpublished census estimates of population. The gainful worker concept differs from other concepts in that its primary purpose is a count of occupations and occupational status rather than employment. It excludes students as well as women doing housework, but includes retired people who report their former line of work.

3 The most sensitive labor force data relate to unemployment. Because they are based on reports of unemployment insurance claims, rates may be generally lower than actual unemployment. They exclude those long-term unemployed who have become discouraged and opted out of the employment market. In earlier years, unemployment estimates were calculated as a residual, that is, the total number of employed persons was deducted from the total civilian labor force. The unemployment rate presents the data on unemployed persons as a percentage of the civilian labor force. The lowest unemployment rate (that is, the closest the United States ever came to the concept of full employment) was achieved in 1944 during wartime (1.2%), the highest rates were in 1894 (18.3%) and in 1939 (17.2%).

4 Economically Active Population is a concept developed by David L. Caplan and M. Claire Casey. It refers to both employed and unemployed workers in the civilian labor force 10 years old and over before 1940, and 14 years and over since 1940. It is similar to the gainful workers concept, which is also based on occupation and marketable skills rather than on employment. The occupational classification system is generally comparable with the system used in the *Dictionary of Occupational Titles*.

5 The most common range of wages for agricultural laborers in the United States in the 19th century was from $8 to $12 per month, the same range that prevails in many Third World countries today. Data on wages after the Civil War and before 1900 come from a number of published reports, such as Joseph D. Weeks's *Report on the Statistics of Wages in the Manufacturing Industries* (1886) and the *Aldrich Reports on Wholesale Prices, on Wages and on Transportation* (1893). Since 1939, private industry employment and payrolls are based principally upon records of the Social Security Programs.

6 The average weekly hours worked and paid for differ from average hours worked per week, both during times of substantial unemployment as well as times of relative full employment because of the overtime element. The widespread adoption of paid vacations of increasing length and the increasing number of paid holidays raised average weekly hours paid for, while keeping the average weekly hours worked low.

7 The Bureau of Labor Statistics monitors and publishes biennial data on labor unions, their membership dues, collective agreements and voting rights. Union membership figures are available since 1951 and include the AFL-CIO, the principal labor federation, and independent labor unions. The decline in union membership has consequences not merely in U.S. industry but also in U. S. politics.

8 Data on work stoppages, including strikes and lockouts, were first published in 1881 and at five-year intervals thereafter with the exception of the period from1906 to 1913. This seven-year lapse occurred while the charge of collecting labor statistics was moved from the Bureau of Labor (which collected these data from 1881 to 1905) to the Department of Labor, which was officially founded in 1913. During the transition period there was no government agency for the collection of labor statistics. Until 1927 these data were quite fragmentary and based on press reports and other secondary sources.

9 Compilation of work injury statistics began in 1910 for the iron and steel industry and by 1925 covered 24 industries. Since 1920, reports have been standardized with the injury-frequency rate defined as the average number of disabling injuries per million people-hours worked.

10 In 1998, the civilian labor force consisted of 137,673,000 persons or 67.1% of the population. The highest participation rate (92.5%) is found among males 25 to 34 years of age while the lowest (8.7%) is found among women 65 years and older. White male participation rate (75.6% in 1998) has been historically higher than that of Black male participation rate (69.0% in 1998). The civilian labor force participation is expected to grow to 69% in 2005, but the increase will come not from men but from women.

11 Marital status makes a difference in the participation rates of men and women. The participation rate for single women (68.5%) is higher than that for married women (61.2%). The figures are reversed for men, with single men having a lower rate (73.3%) than that for married men (77.6%).

12 While the average work week was 39.2 hours in 1998, nearly 10.6 million people work for more than 60 hours every week and 14.5 million people work between 48 and 49 hours. Nearly 7.9 million people hold multiple jobs, and 33.1 million people hold part-time jobs.

13 One of the fastest growing sectors of the employment market is that of self-employed persons with home-based businesses. Their number in 1997 was 4.125 million, almost equally distributed between men (2.1 million) and women (1.9 million). Minorities have not been prominent in these businesses, the overwhelming majority of which are White. Black home-based businesses number 135,000 and Hispanic businesses 156,000.

14 The percentage of workers who have not completed high school declined from 36.1% in 1970 to 10.7% in 1998, while the percentage of college graduates rose from 14.1% to 29.1%

15 Men, women, and minorities have certain niches in employment. Women are more numerous in social services (81.8%), elementary and secondary schools (75.3%), health services (79%), hospitals (76.3%), and personal services (70.3%), but are far fewer in manufacturing (9.4%), and automobile services (13.5%). Similarly Blacks have more than their population percentage in transportation, communication and utilities (15.1%), personnel supply services (20.8%), protective services (26.0%), hotels and lodging (15.4%), and social services (17.5%). The wage disparity between men and women is a reflection of the genderization of employment sectors and the concentration of women in lower paying jobs.

16 Unemployment was at a historic low in 1998 at 4.5%, but this rate masks serious disparities between certain age groups. Among Blacks 16 to 19 years old, the unemployment rate is 27.6%, and among all males in that same age group it is 16.2%. Unemployment is also higher among certain sectors, such as agriculture (8.3%), and construction (7.5%). Certain states, such as West Virginia (6.6%), Hawaii, and New Mexico (6.2%) have higher than the national average unemployment, while Minnesota has only 2.5% and New Hampshire and Virginia have 2.9% each.

17 More than 49.8% of workers use computers in their jobs. Computer use is most widespread in executive, administrative and managerial work (77.5%), college and university teaching (79.9%), technical support (75.1%), and administrative and clerical support (77.6%).

18 Output per hour in the business sector has kept pace with real hourly compensation. With 1992 as the base, the index of output per hour in the business sector was 107.3 in 1998 and the index of real hourly compensation was 103.

19 In 1998, 130,000 persons failed to show up at work because of bad weather, compared to 128,000 in 1970.

20 The Index of Help Wanted Advertising in Newspapers (1987 = 100) has declined to 87 in 1997, when 6.5 million openings were advertised nationally.

21 The average hourly earnings, including overtime doubled in private industry since 1980. In 1997 it was highest in construction ($16.95) and manufacturing ($16.56) and lowest in retail trade ($8.75). Overall annual compensation was highest in construction ($61,303), electric, gas, and sanitary services ($65,228) and communication ($63,107). It was lowest in agriculture, forestry and fishing ($22,892) and retail trade ($22,484). Highest average annual pay is received in New York ($38,497), Connecticut ($38,895) and New Jersey ($37,513) and the lowest in Montana ($21,947) and North Dakota ($22,047).

22 In constant 1996 dollars, the minimum wage has moved up only slightly from $4.37 in 1954 to $4.75 in 1996, although in current dollars it has increased from $0.75 to $4.75.

23 In 1992, supplementary benefits added $5.02 to the payroll for every hour worked. Of these benefits, paid leave accounted for $1.16.

24 The jobs with the fastest potential growth rate until 2001 are home health aids, systems analysts and computer scientists, personal and home care aides, medical assistants, human service workers, radiologic technologists and technicians, medical secretaries, psychologists, travel agents, correction officers, flight attendants, computer programmers, management analysts and child care workers. The jobs with the fastest potential decline during the same period are: electrical and electronic equipment assemblers, textile machine operators, telephone and cable TV line installers and repairers, machine tool cutting operators, private household cleaners and servants, machine forming operators, switchboard operators, farmers and farm workers, garment sewing machine operators, and typists and word processors.

25 In 1997, there were 43,300 job-related deaths and 9.6 million work-related disabling injuries leading to the loss of 420 million days of production time.

26 Two-point-nine million cases of workplace violence were reported between 1992 and 1996. Whites are more prone to workplace violence than Blacks and males more than females. Law enforcement officials suffer most from workplace violence.

27 Workplace stoppages, such as strikes and lockouts, once a permanent fixture of the industrial landscape, have become scarce. In 1998 there were only 34 work stoppages involving 387,000 workers and the loss of 5.116 million workdays compared to 424 work stoppages in 1974 involving 1,796,000 workers and the loss of 31.8 million workdays. American workers are more satisfied with their work conditions and pay than they have ever been in this century.

28 Labor Union membership has declined overall from 17.1 million in 1983 to 16.2 million in 1998. Most of the decline is in the private sector where union membership is down from 11.9 million in 1983 to 9.3 million in 1998. This decline is partially offset by a slight increase in union membership in the public sector from 5.7 million to 6.9 million in the same period.

Series D 11-25.   Labor Force Status of the Population: 1870 to 1998

(In thousands of persons 16 years and older, except as noted. Annual estimates are averages of monthly figures. Alaska and Hawaii are included beginning in 1960. Introduction of decennial census data and other improvements in estimation procedures in a number of years result in some year-to-year discontinuities.)

Year	Non-institutional population [1]	Total labor force [2]	Total civilian labor force	Employed—Agriculture	Employed—Nonagriculture	Unemployed	Total not in labor force
	11	12	14	16	17	18	19
1998	205 220	(NA)	131 463	3 378	128 085	6 210	67 547
1997	203 133	(NA)	129 558	3 399	126 159	6 739	66 837
1996	200 591	(NA)	126 708	3 443	123 264	7 236	66 647
1995	198 584	(NA)	124 900	3 440	121 460	7 404	66 280
1994	196 814	(NA)	123 060	3 409	119 651	7 996	65 758
1993	194 838	(NA)	120 259	3 115	117 144	8 940	65 638
1992	192 805	(NA)	118 492	3 247	115 245	9 613	64 700
1991	191 329	(NA)	116 877	3 269	114 449	8 628	64 578
1990	189 686	(NA)	117 914	3 223	115 570	7 047	63 324
1989	188 081	(NA)	117 342	3 199	114 142	6 528	62 523
1988	186 322	123 893	114 968	3 169	111 800	6 701	62 944
1987	184 490	122 122	112 440	3 208	109 232	7 425	62 888
1986	182 293	120 079	109 597	3 163	106 434	8 237	62 752
1985	179 912	117 695	107 150	3 179	103 971	8 312	62 744
1984	178 080	115 763	105 005	3 321	101 685	8 539	62 839
1983	175 891	113 750	100 834	3 383	97 450	10 717	62 665
1982	173 939	112 384	99 526	3 401	96 125	10 678	62 067
1981	171 775	110 812	100 397	3 368	97 030	8 273	61 460
1980	169 349	109 042	99 303	3 364	95 938	7 637	60 806
1979	166 400	107 050	98 824	3 347	95 477	6 137	59 900
1978	163 541	104 368	96 048	3 387	92 661	6 202	59 659
1977	160 689	101 142	92 017	3 283	88 734	6 991	60 025
1976	157 818	98 302	88 752	3 331	85 421	7 406	59 991
1975	154 831	95 955	85 846	3 408	82 438	7 929	59 377
1974	150 800	94 179	91 000	3 515	83 279	5 156	58 171
1973	148 300	91 756	88 700	3 470	81 594	4 365	57 667
1972	145 800	89 484	86 500	3 484	78 669	4 882	57 091
1971	142 600	87 198	84 100	3 394	75 972	5 016	55 834
1970	140 182	85 959	82 771	3 463	75 215	4 093	54 315
1969	137 841	84 240	80 734	3 606	74 296	2 832	53 602
1968	135 562	82 272	78 737	3 817	72 103	2 817	53 291
1967	133 319	80 793	77 347	3 844	70 527	2 975	52 527
1966	131 180	78 893	75 770	3 979	68 915	2 875	52 288
1965	129 236	77 178	74 455	4 361	66 726	3 366	52 058
1964	127 224	75 830	73 091	4 523	64 782	3 786	51 394
1963	125 154	74 571	71 833	4 687	63 076	4 070	50 583
1962	122 981	73 442	70 614	4 944	61 759	3 911	49 539
1961	121 343	73 031	70 459	5 200	60 546	4 714	48 312
1960 *	119 759	72 142	69 628	5 458	60 318	3 852	47 617
1959	117 881	70 921	68 369	5 565	59 065	3 740	46 960
1958	116 363	70 275	67 639	5 586	57 450	4 602	46 088
1957	115 065	69 729	66 929	5 947	58 123	2 859	45 336
1956	113 811	69 409	66 552	6 283	57 517	2 750	44 402
1955	112 732	68 072	65 023	6 449	55 724	2 852	44 660
1954	111 671	66 993	63 643	6 206	53 903	3 532	44 678
1953	110 601	66 560	63 015	6 261	54 922	1 834	44 041
1952	108 823	65 730	62 138	6 501	53 753	1 883	43 093
1951	107 721	65 117	62 017	6 726	53 239	2 055	42 604
1950	106 645	63 858	62 208	7 160	51 760	3 288	42 787
1949	105 611	62 903	61 286	7 656	49 990	3 637	42 708
1948	104 527	62 080	60 621	7 629	50 713	2 276	42 447
1947	103 418	60 941	59 350	7 891	49 148	2 311	42 477
Decennial census:							
1970 (April)	139 130	82 049	80 051	2 750	73 804	3 497	57 082
1960 (April) *[3]	124 517	69 877	68 144	4 257	60 383	3 505	54 639
1950 (April) [3]	110 267	59 643	58 646	[4] 6 876	[4] 48 912	2 858	50 624
1940 (April) [3]	[4] 100 147	53 011	52 705	8 449	36 621	7 635	[4] 47 136

See footnotes at end of table.

Series D 11-25.   Labor Force Status of the Population: 1870 to 1998—Cont'd.

(In thousands of persons 16 years and older, except as noted. Annual estimates are averages of monthly figures. Alaska and Hawaii are included beginning in 1960. Introduction of decennial census data and other improvements in estimation procedures in a number of years result in some year-to-year discontinuities.)

Year	Non-institutional population [1]	Total labor force [2]	Total civilian labor force	Employed— Agriculture	Employed— Nonagriculture	Unemployed	Total not in labor force
	11	12	14	16	17	18	19
1930 (April) [5]............................	98 723	48 830	. . .	10 472	38 358	. . .	49 893
1920 (Jan.) [5]............................	82 739	41 614	. . .	10 666	30 948	. . .	41 125
1910 (April) [5]............................	71 580	38 167	. . .	12 388	25 779	. . .	33 413
1900 (June) [5]............................	57 950	29 073	. . .	10 382	18 691	. . .	28 877
1890 (June) [5]............................	47 414	23 318	. . .	9 148	14 170	. . .	24 095
1880 (June) [5]............................	36 762	17 392	. . .	7 714	9 678	. . .	19 370
1870 (June) [5]............................	28 229	12 506	. . .	5 949	6 557	. . .	15 723

* Denotes first year for which figures include Alaska and Hawaii.
1. 1870-1930, total population includes institutional.
2. 1940-1970, includes Armed Forces.
3. Data for persons 14 years old and older.
4. Estimated from data based on different sample.
5. Data for persons 10 years old and over reporting a gainful occupation.

Series D 85-86.   Unemployment: 1890 to 1998
(Annual percentages)

Year	Percent of civilian labor force 86	Year	Percent of civilian labor force 86	Year	Percent of civilian labor force 86	Year	Percent of civilian labor force 86	Year	Percent of civilian labor force 86
1998	4.5	1975	6.9	1953	2.9	1931	15.9	1910	5.9
1997	4.9	1974	5.6	1952	3.0	1930	8.7	1909	5.1
1996	5.4			1951	3.3	1929	3.2		
1995	5.6	1973	4.9	1950	5.3			1908	8.0
1994	6.1	1972	5.6	1949	5.9	1928	4.2	1907	2.8
		1971	5.9			1927	3.3	1906	1.7
1993	6.9	1970	4.9	1948	3.8	1926	1.8	1905	4.3
1992	7.5	1969	3.5	1947	3.9	1925	3.2	1904	5.4
1991	6.8			1946	3.9	1924	5.0		
1990	5.6	1968	3.6	1945	1.9			1903	3.9
1989	5.3	1967	3.8	1944	1.2	1923	2.4	1902	3.7
		1966	3.8			1922	6.7	1901	4.0
1988	5.5	1965	4.5	1943	1.9	1921	11.7	1900	5.0
1987	6.2	1964	5.2	1942	4.7	1920	5.2	1899	6.5
1986	7.0			1941	9.9	1919	1.4		
1985	7.2	1963	5.7	1940	14.6			1898	12.4
1984	7.5	1962	5.5	1939	17.2	1918	1.4	1897	14.5
		1961	6.7			1917	4.6	1896	14.4
1983	9.6	1960 *	5.5	1938	19.0	1916	5.1	1895	13.7
1982	9.7	1959	5.5	1937	14.3	1915	8.5	1894	18.4
1981	7.6			1936	16.9	1914	7.9		
1980	7.1	1958	6.8	1935	20.1			1893	11.7
1979	5.8	1957	4.3	1934	21.7	1913	4.3	1892	3.0
		1956	4.1			1912	4.6	1891	5.4
1978	6.1	1955	4.4	1933	24.9	1911	6.7	1890	4.0
1977	7.1	1954	5.5	1932	23.6				
1976	7.7								

* Denotes first year for which figures include Alaska and Hawaii.

Series D 87-101. Unemployment Rates for Selected Groups in the Labor Force: 1947 to 1998

(Unemployment in a specified group as a percent of persons 16 years and over in that group in the civilian labor force)

Year	All civilian workers			White	Black	Year	All civilian workers			White	Black[1]
	Total	Male	Female	Total	Total		Total	Male	Female	Total	Total
	87	88	89	90	93		87	88	89	90	93
1998	4.5	4.4	4.6	3.9	8.9	1972	5.6	5.0	6.6	5.1	10.4
1997	4.9	4.9	5.0	4.2	10.0	1971[1]	5.9	5.3	6.9	5.4	9.9
1996	5.4	5.4	5.4	4.7	10.5	1970	4.9	4.4	5.9	4.5	8.2
1995	5.6	5.6	5.6	4.9	10.4	1969	3.5	2.8	4.7	3.1	6.4
1994	6.1	6.2	6.0	5.3	11.5						
						1968	3.6	2.9	4.8	3.2	6.7
1993	6.9	7.2	6.6	6.1	13.0	1967	3.8	3.1	5.2	3.4	7.4
1992	7.5	7.9	7.0	6.6	14.2	1966	3.8	3.2	4.8	3.4	7.3
1991	6.8	7.2	6.4	6.1	12.4	1965	4.5	4.0	5.5	4.1	8.1
1990	5.6	5.7	5.5	4.8	11.3	1964	5.2	4.6	6.2	4.6	9.6
1989	5.3	5.2	5.4	4.5	11.4						
						1963	5.7	5.2	6.5	5.0	10.8
1988	5.5	5.5	5.6	4.7	11.7	1962	5.5	5.2	6.2	4.9	10.9
1987	6.2	6.2	6.2	5.3	13.0	1961	6.7	6.4	7.2	6.0	12.4
1986	7.0	6.9	7.1	6.0	14.5	1960	5.5	5.4	5.9	5.0	10.2
1985	7.2	7.0	7.4	6.2	15.1	1959	5.5	5.2	5.9	4.8	10.7
1984	7.5	7.4	7.6	6.5	15.9						
						1958	6.8	6.8	6.8	6.1	12.6
1983	9.6	9.9	9.2	8.4	19.5	1957	4.3	4.1	4.7	3.8	7.9
1982	9.7	9.9	9.4	8.6	18.9	1956	4.1	3.8	4.8	3.6	8.3
1981	7.6	7.4	7.9	6.7	15.6	1955	4.4	4.2	4.9	3.9	8.7
1980	7.1	6.9	7.4	6.3	14.3	1954	5.5	5.3	6.0	5.0	9.9
1979	5.8	5.1	6.8	5.1	12.3						
						1953	2.9	2.8	3.3	2.7	4.5
1978	6.1	5.3	7.2	5.2	12.8	1952	3.0	2.8	3.6	2.8	5.4
1977	7.1	6.3	8.2	6.2	14.0	1951	3.3	2.8	4.4	3.1	5.3
1976	7.7	7.1	8.6	7.0	14.0	1950	5.3	5.1	5.7	4.9	9.0
1975	8.5	7.9	9.3	7.8	14.8	1949	5.9	5.9	6.0	5.6	8.8
1974	5.6	4.9	6.7	5.0	10.5						
						1948	3.8	3.6	4.1	3.5	5.9
1973	4.9	4.2	6.0	4.3	9.4	1947	3.9	4.0	3.7	. . .	. . .

1. In 1971 and earlier years, "Black and other" (including Asian, Native American, Alaskan Natives, and Pacific Islanders); in 1972, the unemployment rate for "Black and other" was 10.0 percent.

Series D 102-115. Unemployment Rates, by Industry: 1948 to 1999

(Unemployment in a specified group as a percent of persons 16 years and over in that group in the civilian labor force)

Year	Total unemployed[1]	Experienced wage and salary workers								Government
		Agriculture	Wage and salary workers in private nonagricultural industries							
			Mining	Construction	Manufacturing	Transportation and public utilities	Wholesale and retail trade	Finance, insurance, real estate	Service industries	
	102	104	106	107	108	111	112	113	114	115
1999	4.0	8.9	5.7	7.0	3.6	3.0	5.2	2.3	4.0	2.2
1998	4.5	8.3	3.2	7.5	3.9	3.4	5.5	2.5	4.5	2.3
1997	4.9	9.1	3.8	9.0	4.2	3.5	6.2	3.0	4.6	2.6
1996	5.4	10.2	5.1	10.1	4.8	4.1	6.4	2.7	5.4	2.9
1995	5.6	11.1	5.2	11.5	4.9	4.5	6.5	3.3	5.4	2.9
1994	6.1	11.3	5.4	11.8	5.6	4.8	7.4	3.6	5.9	3.4
1993	6.8	11.7	7.4	14.4	7.2	5.1	7.8	4.1	6.1	3.3
1992	7.5	12.5	8.0	16.8	7.8	5.5	8.4	4.6	6.5	3.6
1991	6.8	11.8	7.8	15.5	7.3	5.3	7.6	4.0	5.7	3.3
1990	5.6	9.8	4.8	11.1	5.8	3.9	6.4	3.0	5.0	3.7
1989	5.3	9.6	5.8	10.0	5.1	3.9	6.0	3.1	4.8	2.7
1988	5.5	10.6	7.9	10.6	5.3	3.9	6.2	3.0	4.9	2.8
1987	6.2	10.5	10.0	11.6	6.0	4.5	6.9	3.1	5.4	3.5
1986	7.0	12.5	13.5	13.1	7.1	5.1	7.6	3.5	6.1	3.6
1985	7.2	13.2	9.5	13.1	7.7	5.1	7.6	3.5	6.2	3.9
1984	7.5	13.5	10.0	14.3	7.5	5.5	8.0	3.7	6.6	4.5
1983	9.6	16.0	17.0	18.4	11.2	7.4	10.0	4.5	7.9	5.3
1982	9.7	14.7	13.4	20.0	12.3	6.8	10.0	4.7	7.6	4.9
1981	7.6	12.1	6.0	15.6	8.3	5.2	8.1	3.5	6.6	4.7
1980	7.1	11.0	6.4	14.1	8.5	4.9	7.4	3.4	5.9	4.1
1979	5.8	9.3	4.9	10.3	5.6	3.7	6.5	3.0	5.5	3.7
1978	6.0	8.9	4.2	10.6	5.5	3.7	6.9	3.1	5.7	3.9
1977	7.0	11.2	3.8	12.7	6.7	4.7	8.0	3.8	6.6	4.2
1976	7.7	11.8	4.6	15.5	7.9	5.0	8.6	4.3	7.2	4.4
1975	8.5	10.4	4.1	18.0	10.9	5.6	8.7	4.9	7.1	4.1
1974	5.6	7.5	3.0	10.7	5.8	3.3	6.5	3.1	5.2	3.0
1973	4.9	7.0	2.9	8.9	4.4	3.0	5.7	2.7	4.8	2.7
1972	5.6	7.7	3.2	10.3	5.6	3.5	6.4	3.4	5.3	3.0
1971	5.9	7.9	4.0	10.4	6.8	3.8	6.4	3.3	5.6	2.9
1970	4.9	7.5	3.1	9.7	5.6	3.2	5.3	2.8	4.7	2.2
1969	3.5	6.1	2.9	6.0	3.3	2.2	4.1	2.1	3.5	1.9
1968	3.6	6.3	3.1	6.9	3.3	2.0	4.0	2.2	3.7	1.8
1967	3.8	6.9	3.4	7.4	3.7	2.4	4.2	2.5	3.9	1.8
1966	3.8	6.6	3.7	8.0	3.2	2.1	4.4	2.1	3.9	1.8
1965	4.5	7.6	5.4	10.1	4.0	2.9	5.0	2.3	4.6	1.9
1964	5.2	9.7	6.7	11.2	5.0	3.5	5.7	2.6	5.3	2.1
1963	5.7	9.2	7.2	13.3	5.7	4.2	6.2	2.7	5.7	2.2
1962	5.5	7.5	7.8	13.5	5.8	4.1	6.3	3.0	5.5	2.1
1961	6.7	9.6	11.1	15.7	7.8	5.3	7.3	3.3	6.2	2.5
1960	5.5	8.3	9.7	13.5	6.2	4.6	5.9	2.4	5.1	2.4
1959	5.5	9.1	9.7	13.4	6.1	4.4	5.8	2.5	5.3	2.2
1958	6.8	10.3	11.0	15.3	9.3	6.1	6.8	2.9	5.7	2.5
1957	4.3	6.9	5.9	10.9	5.1	3.3	4.5	1.8	4.2	1.9
1956	4.1	7.4	6.8	10.0	4.7	3.0	4.5	1.8	4.6	1.7
1955	4.4	7.2	9.1	10.9	4.7	4.0	4.7	2.4	5.2	2.0
1954	5.5	9.0	14.4	12.9	7.1	5.6	5.7	2.3	5.5	2.2
1953	2.9	5.6	4.6	7.2	3.1	2.2	3.4	1.8	3.4	1.5
1952	3.0	4.8	3.8	6.7	3.5	2.3	3.5	1.8	3.6	1.6
1951	3.3	4.4	4.0	7.2	3.9	2.3	3.9	1.5	4.2	1.8
1950	5.3	9.0	6.7	12.2	6.2	4.6	6.0	2.2	6.4	3.0
1949	5.9	7.1	8.9	14.0	8.0	5.9	6.2	2.1	6.8	3.1
1948	3.8	5.5	3.1	8.7	4.2	3.5	4.7	1.8	4.8	2.2

1. Also includes the self-employed, unpaid family workers and those with no previous work experience, not shown separately.

Series D 167-181.   Labor Force and Employment, by Industry: 1800 to 1998
(In thousands of persons 10 years old and over)

| Year | Labor force | Employment | | | | |
| | | Agriculture | Mining | Construction | Manufacturing | Trade |
	167	170	172	173	174	177
1998	129 210	3 378	575	5 965	18 716	25 353
1997	126 089	3 399	592	5 686	18 657	25 754
1996	123 051	3 443	580	5 418	18 495	26 669
1995	120 631	3 440	581	5 160	18 524	27 565
1994	117 572	3 409	601	4 986	18 321	28 079
1993	113 828	3 115	610	4 668	18 075	28 659
1992	111 848	3 247	635	4 492	18 104	29 300
1991	116 877	3 233	733	7 087	20 434	24 055
1990	117 914	3 186	730	7 696	21 284	24 269
1989	117 342	3 199	719	7 680	21 652	24 230
1988	114 968	3 169	753	7 603	21 320	23 663
1987	112 440	3 208	818	7 456	20 935	23 392
1986	109 597	3 163	880	7 288	20 962	22 813
1985	107 150	3 179	939	6 987	20 879	22 296
1984	105 005	3 321	957	6 665	20 995	21 979
1983	100 634	3 541	921	6 149	19 946	21 145
1982	99 526	3 571	1 028	5 756	20 286	20 758
1981	100 397	3 518	1 118	6 060	21 817	20 524
1980	99 303	3 364	979	6 215	21 942	20 191
1979	96 945	3 455	865	6 299	22 137	19 672
1978	94 373	3 501	828	6 043	21 497	19 253
1977	90 546	3 383	814	5 504	20 637	18 706
1976	87 485	3 417	770	5 162	20 044	18 025
1975	84 783	3 476	732	5 015	19 275	17 470
1974	85 936	3 588	655	5 454	20 879	17 253
1973	80 285	3 452	638	4 028	20 054	16 665
1972	81 702	3 585	597	5 246	19 866	16 470
1970	78 678	3 463	516	4 818	20 746	15 008
1960	74 060	5 970	709	3 640	17 145	14 051
1950	65 470	7 870	901	3 029	15 648	12 152
1940	56 290	9 575	925	1 876	11 309	9 328
1930	48 830	10 560	1 009	1 988	9 884	8 122
1920	41 610	10 790	1 180	1 233	11 190	5 845
1910	37 480	11 770	1 068	1 949	8 332	5 320
1900	29 070	11 680	637	1 665	5 895	3 970
1890	23 320	9 960	440	1 510	4 390	2 960
1880	17 390	8 920	280	900	3 290	1 930
1870	12 930	6 790	180	780	2 470	1 310
1860	11 110	5 880	176	520	1 530	890
1850	8 250	4 520	102	410	1 200	530
1840	5 660	3 570	32	290	500	350
1830	4 200	2 965	22	. . .	. . .	. . .
1820	3 135	2 470	13	. . .	. . .	. . .
1810	2 330	1 950	11	. . .	75	. . .
1800	1 900	1 400	10	. . .	. . .	. . .

Series D 722-727. Average Annual Earnings of Employees: 1929 to 1997

Year	Full-time employees (OBE-BEA) [1]	Year	Full-time employees (OBE-BEA) [1]	Year	Full-time employees (OBE-BEA) [1]	Year	Full-time employees (OBE-BEA) [1]	Year	Full-time employees (OBE-BEA) [1]
	722		722		722		722		722
1997	33 429	1982	18 488	1967	6 230	1953	3 581	1940	1 299
1996	32 040	1981	17 218	1966	5 967			1939	1 264
1995	30 902	1980	15 757	1965	5 710	1952	3 402	1938	1 230
1994	29 922	1979	14 376	1964	5 503	1951	3 217		
1993	29 351	1978	13 287	1963	5 243	1950	2 992	1937	1 258
						1949	2 844	1936	1 184
1992	28 667	1977	12 379	1962	5 065	1948	2 786	1935	1 137
1991	27 192	1976	11 620	1961	4 884			1934	1 091
1990	25 889	1975	10 836	1960	4 743	1947	5 589	1933	1 048
1989	24 766	1974	9 994	1959	4 594	1946	2 359		
1988	24 032	1973	9 298	1958	4 375	1945	2 190	1932	1 120
						1944	2 109	1931	1 275
1987	22 913	1972	8 610	1957	4 230	1943	1 951	1930	1 368
1986	21 935	1971	. . .	1956	4 055			1929	1 405
1985	21 079	1970	7 564	1955	3 851	1942	1 709		
1984	20 168	1969	7 095	1954	3 667	1941	1 443		
1983	19 330	1968	6 657						

1. OBE = Office of Business Economics (1929-1967);
BEA = Bureau of Economic Analysis (1928-1970).

Series D 802-810. Earnings and Hours of Production Workers in Manufacturing: 1909 to 1999

Year	All manufacturing			Year	All manufacturing			Year	All manufacturing		
	Average hourly earnings	Average weekly hours	Average weekly earnings $		Average hourly earnings	Average weekly hours	Average weekly earnings $		Average hourly earnings	Average weekly hours	Average weekly earnings $
	802	803	804		802	803	804		802	803	804
1999	13.91	41.7	580.05	1969	3.19	40.6	129.51	1939	.63	37.7	23.64
1998	13.49	41.7	562.53	1968	3.01	40.7	122.51	1938	.62	35.6	22.07
1997	13.17	42.0	553.14	1967	2.82	40.6	114.49	1937	.62	38.6	23.82
1996	12.77	41.6	531.23	1966	2.71	41.4	112.19	1936	.55	39.2	21.56
1995	12.37	41.6	514.59	1965	2.61	41.2	107.53	1935	.54	36.6	19.91
1994	12.07	42.0	506.94	1964	2.53	40.7	102.97	1934	.53	34.6	18.20
1993	11.74	41.4	486.04	1963	2.46	40.5	99.63	1933	.44	38.1	16.65
1992	11.46	41.0	469.86	1962	2.39	40.4	96.56	1932	.44	38.3	16.89
1991	11.18	40.7	455.03	1961	2.32	39.8	92.34	1931	.51	40.5	20.64
1990	10.83	40.8	441.86	1960	2.26	39.7	89.72	1930	.55	42.1	23.00
1989	10.48	41.0	429.68	1959*	2.19	40.3	88.26	1929	.56	44.2	24.76
1988	10.19	41.1	418.81	1958	2.11	39.2	82.71	1928	.56	44.4	24.70
1987	9.91	41.0	406.31	1957	2.05	39.8	81.59	1927	.54	45.0	24.47
1986	9.73	40.7	396.01	1956	1.95	40.4	78.78	1926	.54	45.0	24.38
1985	9.54	40.5	386.37	1955	1.86	40.7	75.70	1925	.54	44.5	24.11
1984	9.19	40.7	374.03	1954	1.78	39.6	70.49	1924	.54	43.7	23.67
1983	8.83	40.1	354.08	1953	1.74	40.5	70.47	1923	.52	45.6	23.56
1982	8.49	38.9	330.26	1952	1.65	40.7	67.16	1922	.48	44.2	21.28
1981	7.99	39.8	318.00	1951	1.56	40.6	63.34	1921	.51	43.1	21.94
1980	7.27	39.7	288.62	1950	1.44	40.5	58.32	1920	.55	47.4	26.02
1979	6.70	40.2	269.34	1949	1.38	39.1	53.88	1919	.47	46.3	21.84
1978	6.17	40.4	249.27	1948	1.33	40.0	53.12	1918	. . .	. . .	19.12
1977	5.68	40.3	228.90	1947	1.22	40.4	49.17	1917	. . .	. . .	14.97
1976	5.22	40.1	209.32	1946	1.08	40.3	43.32	1916	. . .	. . .	12.63
1975	4.83	39.5	190.79	1945	1.02	43.5	44.20	1915	. . .	. . .	11.22
1974	4.42	40.0	176.80	1944	1.01	45.2	45.70	1914	.22	49.4	10.92
1973	4.09	40.7	166.46	1943	.96	45.0	43.07	1909	.19	51.0	9.74
1972	3.82	40.5	154.71	1942	.85	43.1	36.68				
1971	3.57	39.9	142.44	1941	.73	40.6	29.48				
1970	3.35	39.8	133.33	1940	.66	38.1	24.96				

* Denotes first year for which figures include Alaska and Hawaii.

Series D 946-951. Labor Union Membership as Percent of Total Employment: 1930 to 1996

(In thousands, except percent)

Year	Total union member-ship 946	Percent of employed 951	Year	Total union member-ship 946	Percent of employed 951	Year	Total union member-ship 946	Percent of employed 951	Year	Total union member-ship 946	Percent of employed 951
1996	16 269	14.5	1978	23 306	19.7	1961	17 328	30.2	1944	14 621	33.8
1995	16 360	14.9	1977	. . .	. . .	1960	18 117	* 31.4	1943	13 642	31.1
1994	16 748	15.5				1959	18 169	32.1	1942	10 762	25.9
1993	16 598	14.9	1976	21 171	20.3	1958	18 081	33.2			
1992	16 390	14.5	1975	. . .	. . .	1957	18 431	32.8	1941	10 489	27.9
			1974	23 408	21.7				1940	8 944	26.9
1991	16 568	16.1	1973	. . .	. . .	1956	18 477	33.4	1939	8 980	28.6
1990	. . .	. . .	1972	20 893	21.8	1955	17 749	33.2	1938	8 265	27.5
1989	16 960	16.4				1954	17 955	34.7	1937	7 218	22.6
1988	17 002	16.8	1971	. . .	. . .	1953	17 860	33.7			
1987	16 913	17.0	1970	20 752	27.4	1952	16 750	32.5	1936	4 164	13.7
			1969	20 382	27.1				1935	3 728	13.2
1986	16 975	18.0	1968	20 258	27.9	1951	16 750	33.3	1934	3 249	11.9
1985	16 996	18.8	1967	19 712	27.9	1950	15 000	31.5	1933	2 857	11.3
1984	17 340	17.9				1949	15 000	32.6	1932	3 226	12.9
1983	17 717	20.1	1966	19 181	28.1	1948	15 000	31.9			
1982	. . .	. . .	1965	18 519	28.4	1947	15 414	33.7	1931	3 526	12.4
			1964	17 976	28.9				1930	3 632	11.6
1981	. . .	. . .	1963	17 586	29.2	1946	14 974	34.5			
1980	22 811	25.2	1962	17 630	29.8	1945	14 796	35.5			
1979	. . .	. . .									

* Denotes first year for which figures include Alaska and Hawaii.
1. Excludes Canadian members.

Series D 970-985.   Work Stoppages, Workers Involved, and Days Idle: 1927 to 1996

(From 1971, excludes work stoppages involving fewer than 1,000 workers and lasting less than one day[1])

Year	Work stoppages and man-days idle				Year	Work stoppages and man-days idle			
	Stoppage beginning in year		Days idle			Stoppage beginning in year		Days idle	
	Number	Workers involved, number (1 000)	Number (1 000)	% of estimated total working time		Number	Workers involved, number (1 000)	Number (1 000)	% of estimated total working time
	970	**971**	**973**	**974**		**970**	**971**	**973**	**974**
1996	37	273	4 887	0.02	1961	3 367	1 450	16 300	0.11
1995	31	192	5 771	0.02	1960	3 333	1 320	19 100	0.14
1994	45	322	5 020	0.02	1959 *	3 708	1 880	69 000	0.50
1993	35	182	3 981	0.01	1958	3 694	2 060	23 900	0.18
1992	35	364	3 989	0.01	1957	3 673	1 390	16 500	0.12
1991	40	392	4 584	0.02	1956	3 825	1 900	33 100	0.24
1990	44	185	5 926	0.02	1955	4 320	2 650	28 200	0.22
1989	51	452	16 996	0.07	1954	3 468	1 530	22 600	0.18
1988	40	118	4 364	0.02	1953	5 091	2 400	28 300	0.22
1987	46	174	4 469	0.02	1952	5 117	3 540	59 100	0.48
1986	69	533	11 861	0.05	1951	4 737	2 220	22 900	0.18
1985	54	324	7 079	0.03	1950	4 843	2 410	38 800	0.33
1984	62	376	8 499	0.04	1949	3 606	3 030	50 500	0.44
1983	81	909	17 461	0.08	1948	3 419	1 960	34 100	0.28
1982	96	656	9 061	0.04	1947	3 693	2 170	34 600	0.30
1981	145	729	16 908	0.07	1946	4 985	4 600	116 000	1.04
1980	187	795	20 844	0.09	1945	4 750	3 470	38 000	0.31
1979	295	1 021	20 409	0.09	1944	4 956	2 120	8 720	0.07
1978	219	1 006	23 774	0.11	1943	3 752	1 980	13 500	0.10
1977	298	1 212	21 258	0.10	1942	2 968	840	4 180	0.04
1976	231	1 519	23 962	0.12	1941	4 288	2 360	23 000	0.23
1975	235	965	17 563	0.09	1940	2 508	577	6 700	0.08
1974	424	1 796	31 809	0.16	1939	2 613	1 170	17 800	0.21
1973	317	1 400	16 260	0.08	1938[2]	2 772	688	9 150	.15
1972	250	975	16 764	0.09	1937	4 740	1 860	28 400	.43
1971	298	2 516	35 538	0.19	1936	2 172	789	13 900	.21
1970[1]	5 716	3 305	66 414	0.37	1935	2 014	1 120	15 500	.29
1969	5 700	2 481	42 869	0.24	1934	1 856	1 470	19 600	.38
1968	5 045	2 649	49 018	0.28	1933	1 695	1 170	16 900	.36
1967	4 595	2 870	42 100	0.25	1932	841	324	10 500	.23
1966	4 405	1 960	25 400	0.15	1931	810	342	6 890	.11
1965	3 963	1 550	23 300	0.15	1930	637	183	3 320	.05
1964	3 655	1 640	22 900	0.15	1929	921	289	5 350	.07
1963	3 362	941	16 100	0.11	1928	604	314	12 600	.17
1962	3 614	1 230	18 600	0.13	1927	707	330	26 200	.37

* Denotes first year for which figures include Alaska and Hawaii.
1. In 1970, the number of stoppages involving 1,000 workers or more was 381; number of workers involved 2,468,000; days idle, 52,761,000; and percent of estimated working time lost, 0.29.
2. Before 1939, percent of estimated total working time in private nonfarm economy. In 1939, that percent was 0.28.

Series D 1029-1036. Work Injury Frequency Rates in Manufacturing and Mining: 1922 to 1997

(Rate is average number of disabling injuries per million man-hours worked)

Year	Manu-facturing [1]	Mining	Year	Manu-facturing [1]	Mining	Year	Manu-facturing [1]	Mining	Year	Manu-facturing [1]	Mining
	1029	1030		1029	1030		1029	1030		1029	1030
1998	9.7	4.9	1977	13.1	10.9	1957	11.4	35.8	1937	17.8	70.5
1997	10.3	5.9	1976	13.3	11.0	1956	12.0	37.1	1936	16.6	70.2
1996	10.6	5.4	1975	13.0	11.0	1955	12.1	38.3	1935	17.9	72.7
1995	11.6	6.2	1974	14.6	10.2	1954	11.9	37.7	1934	20.2	73.8
1994	12.2	6.3	1973	15.3	12.5	1953	13.4	40.3	1933	19.3	71.7
1993	12.1	6.8	1972	15.6	...	1952	14.3	43.6	1932	19.6	74.8
1992	12.5	7.3	1971	...	...	1951	15.5	45.1	1931	18.9	79.9
1991	12.7	7.4	1970	15.2	28.9	1950	14.7	46.3	1930	23.1	...
1990	13.2	8.3	1969	14.8	28.0	1949	14.5	48.3	1929	24.0	...
1989	13.1	8.5	1968	14.0	27.8	1948	17.2	53.2	1928	22.5	...
1988	13.1	8.8	1967	14.0	28.0	1947	18.8	55.8	1927	22.6	...
1987	11.9	8.5	1966	13.6	28.4	1946	19.9	58.0	1926	24.2	...
1986	10.6	7.4	1965	12.8	28.3	1945	18.6	55.5	1925	...	...
1985	10.4	8.4	1964	12.3	28.8	1944	18.4	57.2	1924	...	...
1984	10.6	9.7	1963	11.9	28.8	1943	20.0	59.4	1923	...	...
1983	10.0	8.4	1962	11.9	28.6	1942	19.9	61.2	1922	...	...
1982	10.2	10.5	1961	11.8	29.5	1941	18.1	63.2			
1981	11.5	11.8	1960	12.0	29.8	1940	15.3	65.2			
1980	12.2	11.2	1959	12.4	29.2	1939	14.9	64.8			
1979	13.3	11.4	1958	[2] 11.4	[3] 31.9	1938	15.1	67.5			
1978	13.2	11.5									

1. Prior to 1987, excludes petroleum refining, smelting and refining of nonferrous metals, cement and lime manufacturing and coke production.
2. Industry definition revised to conform to the 1957 edition of the Standard Industrial Classification Manual. Comparisons to prior years should be made with caution.
3. Beginning 1958, includes data on sand and gravel operations.

Series DD-1. Federal Minimum Wage Rates: 1954 to 1996

Year	Value of the minimum wage [1]		Year	Value of the minimum wage [1]	
	Current dollars	Constant (1996) dollars [2]		Current dollars	Constant (1996) dollars [2]
1954	0.75	4.37	1976	2.30	6.34
1955	0.75	4.39	1977	2.30	5.95
1956	1.00	5.77	1978	2.65	6.38
1957	1.00	5.58	1979	2.90	6.27
1958	1.00	5.43	1980	3.10	5.90
1959	1.00	5.39	1981	3.35	5.78
1960	1.00	5.30	1982	3.35	5.45
1961	1.15	6.03	1983	3.35	5.28
1962	1.15	5.97	1984	3.35	5.06
1963	1.25	6.41	1985	3.35	4.88
1964	1.25	6.33	1986	3.35	4.80
1965	1.25	6.23	1987	3.35	4.63
1966	1.25	6.05	1988	3.35	4.44
1967	1.40	6.58	1989	3.35	4.24
1968	1.60	7.21	1990	3.80	4.56
1969	1.60	6.84	1991	4.25	4.90
1970	1.60	6.47	1992	4.25	4.75
1971	1.60	6.20	1993	4.25	4.61
1972	1.60	6.01	1994	4.25	4.50
1973	1.60	5.65	1995	4.25	4.38
1974	2.00	6.37	1996	4.75	4.75
1975	2.10	6.12			

1. Effective September 1, 1997, the Federal minimum wage rose to $5.15; $5.03 in constant 1996 dollars.
2. Adjusted for inflation using the CPI-U.

SOURCE: U.S. Employment Standards Administration, Internet site <http://www.dol.gov/esa/public/minwage/main.htm> (accessed 25 May 1999).

Series DD3. Self-Employed Workers, by Industry and Occupation: 1970 to 1998

(In thousands (7 031 represents 7 031 000). For civilian noninstitutional population 16 years old and over. Annual averages of monthly figures. Based on the Current Population Survey)

Item	1970	1980	1990 [1]	1994 [1]	1995	1996	1997 [1]	1998 [1]
Total self-employed..............................	7 031	8 642	10 097	10 648	10 482	10 490	10 513	10 303
Industry: Agriculture	1 810	1 642	1 378	1 645	1 580	1 518	1 457	1 341
Nonagriculture	5 221	7 000	8 719	9 003	8 902	8 971	9 056	8 962
Mining..	14	28	24	13	16	15	14	21
Construction..	687	1 173	1 457	1 506	1 460	1 496	1 492	1 519
Manufacturing	264	358	427	426	433	406	422	428
Transportation and public utilities......................	196	282	301	385	396	432	438	430
Trade..	1 667	1 899	1 851	1 906	1 772	1 760	1 761	1 640
Finance, insurance, and real estate	254	458	630	625	660	674	629	609
Services	2 140	2 804	4 030	4 142	4 166	4 189	4 300	4 317
Occupation:								
Managerial and professional specialty	...	...	3 050	3 106	3 147	3 288	3 432	3 400
Technical, sales, and administrative support	...	...	2 240	2 380	2 341	2 304	2 219	2 117
Service occupations	...	...	1 207	1 178	1 190	1 198	1 179	1 198
Precision production, craft, and repair	...	...	1 675	1 740	1 618	1 595	1 651	1 697
Operators, fabricators, and laborers	...	...	567	639	631	634	629	584
Farming, forestry, and fishing.................................	...	...	1 358	1 605	1 556	1 471	1 403	1 307

1. Data not strictly comparable with earlier years because of changes in classifications and methods and introduction of decennial census data.

SOURCE: U.S. Bureau of Labor Statistics, Bulletin 2307; Employment and Earnings, monthly, January issues; and unpublished data.

Series DD4. Marital Status of Women in the Civilian Labor Force: 1960 to 1998

(Annual averages of monthly figures (23 240 represent 23 240 000). For civilian noninstitutional population 16 years old and over. Based on the Current Population Survey)

Year	Female labor force (1 000)				Female participation rate [3]			
	Total	Single	Married [1]	Other [2]	Total	Single	Married [1]	Other [2]
1960	23 240	5 410	12 893	4 937	37.7	58.6	31.9	41.6
1965	26 200	5 976	14 829	5 396	39.3	54.5	34.9	40.7
1970	31 543	7 265	18 475	5 804	43.3	56.8	40.5	40.3
1975	37 475	9 125	21 484	6 866	46.3	59.8	44.3	40.1
1980	45 487	11 865	24 980	8 643	51.5	64.4	49.9	43.6
1982	47 755	12 460	25 971	9 324	52.6	65.1	51.1	44.8
1983	48 503	12 659	26 468	9 376	52.9	65.0	51.8	44.4
1984	49 709	12 867	27 199	9 644	53.6	65.6	52.8	44.7
1985	51 050	13 163	27 894	9 993	54.5	66.6	53.8	45.1
1986	52 413	13 512	28 623	10 277	55.3	67.2	54.9	45.6
1987	53 658	13 885	29 381	10 393	56.0	67.4	55.9	45.7
1988	54 742	14 194	29 921	10 627	56.6	67.7	56.7	46.2
1989	56 030	14 377	30 548	11 104	57.4	68.0	57.8	47.0
1990 [4]	56 829	14 612	30 901	11 315	57.5	66.7	58.4	47.2
1991	57 178	14 681	31 112	11 385	57.4	66.2	58.5	46.8
1992	58 141	14 872	31 700	11 570	57.8	66.2	59.3	47.1
1993	58 795	15 031	31 980	11 784	57.9	66.2	59.4	47.2
1994 [4]	60 239	15 333	32 888	12 018	58.8	66.7	60.7	47.5
1995	60 944	15 467	33 359	12 118	58.9	66.8	61.0	47.4
1996	61 857	15 842	33 618	12 397	59.3	67.1	61.2	48.1
1997 [4]	63 036	16 492	33 802	12 742	59.8	67.9	61.6	48.6
1998 [4]	63 714	17 087	33 857	12 771	59.8	68.5	61.2	48.8

1. Husband present.
2. Widowed, divorced, or separated.
3. Labor force as a percent of civilian noninstitutional population in group.
4. Data not strictly comparable with earlier years because of changes in classification and methods and introduction of decennial census data.

SOURCE: U.S. Bureau of Labor Statistics, Bulletin 2307; and unpublished data.

NATIONAL INCOME AND WEALTH

NATIONAL INCOME AND WEALTH

Highlights

1 The earliest statistics of prices were compiled by Samuel Blodgett, Jr., in *Economica: A Statistical Manual of the United States of America,* published in 1806. It includes a collection of prices for 16 important commodities in five markets for the years 1785 to 1805. The first serious attempt to summarize price data in the form of index numbers was made by Horatio C. Burchard, Director of the Mint, in his report to the Secretary of the Treasury in 1881. In 1886, a special report containing retail prices for about 60 "necessaries of life," was included in volume 20 of the Tenth Census. In 1891, a Senate Resolution led Roland P. Falkner to collect a voluminous body of data covering wholesale prices from 1840-1891, and retail prices for the 28-month period ending September 1891. This information was published in the Aldrich Reports. In 1900, Falkner extended his indexes to 1899 with quotations for 142 articles, collected by the Department of Labor.

In 1902, the Department of Labor began publishing its *Index of Wholesale Prices,* which it has published continuously to the present day. In addition to this series, John R. Commons published an *Index of Wholesale Prices* for 1878 to 1900 in his *Quarterly Bulletin of the Bureau of Economic Research.* Bradstreet's Index of Wholesale Prices for about 96 commodities was established in 1897 and included data beginning with 1890. Dun's Index numbers of Wholesale Prices for about 350 commodities was published in *Dun's Review* beginning in 1901 and extending back to 1860. Walter B. Smith and Arthur H. Cole computed wholesale commodity price indexes covering 1792 to 1862 for *Fluctuations in American Business, 1790-1860,* published by Harvard University Press in 1935. It covered Boston, New York, and Philadelphia.

The most extensive historical price investigations, however, were undertaken under the auspices of the International Scientific Committee on Price History. They were summarized in *Wholesale Commodity Prices in the United States, 1700-1861,* published by Harvard University Press in 1938. Wholesale price indexes were compiled by Frederick C. Mills for economically significant commodities. Part of this series was first published by the National Bureau of Economic Research for 1830 to 1931 in *Economic Tendencies in the United States.* (Wholesale prices are compiled from prices in primary markets and pertain to the first major commercial transaction for each commodity. The quotations are generally selling prices of manufacturers or producers or the selling price on an organized exchange or at a central market). The current price index was begun in 1952 and spliced to the former series. While the 1952 revision did not alter the conceptual definition of the index, it did adopt major changes in coverage and methods. The list of priced commodities was expanded from 947 to 1,800 in 1952, 2,450 in 1970, and 10,000 in 1998. The index is currently known as the Producer Price Index. The base years have changed from 1890 to 1899 to 1913, 1926, 1967, and 1982. The weighting factors for each commodity represent the value of shipments for the specific commodity priced and for all others in the same group known to have similar price movements. The indexes are calculated as averages of relatives weighted by value of shipments. Changes in quality are factored into the index.

2 The volume of information available for wholesale prices is not matched at the retail level, especially for the early years. The official Consumer Price Index (CPI) was initiated by the Bureau of Labor Statistics (BLS) in 1904 with a food index covering the years 1890 to 1893. The Food Index was continued until the end of World War I, when it became one component group of a comprehensive Cost of Living Index. Since then, the index has been expanded in scope, resulting in an improvement in the quality of data. At present the index is issued monthly. From 1918 to 1958, the National Industrial Conference Board also compiled a consumer price index. Consumer price data before 1913 are extremely patchy. The only cost of living indexes computed from retail price data before 1913 are Wesley C. Mitchell's *Relative Cost of Living for 1860 to 1880,* Ethel Hoover's *Consumer Price Index for 1851 to 1880* and Rees' *Cost of Living Index, 1890-1914.* These indexes were compiled from newspapers and other sources, and their reliability is affected by changes in quality, incomplete files, nominal prices, changes in consumer tastes, and demographic and other changes. In 1919, the BLS began the publication of complete indexes at semiannual intervals. The first major revision of the Consumer Price Index occur-

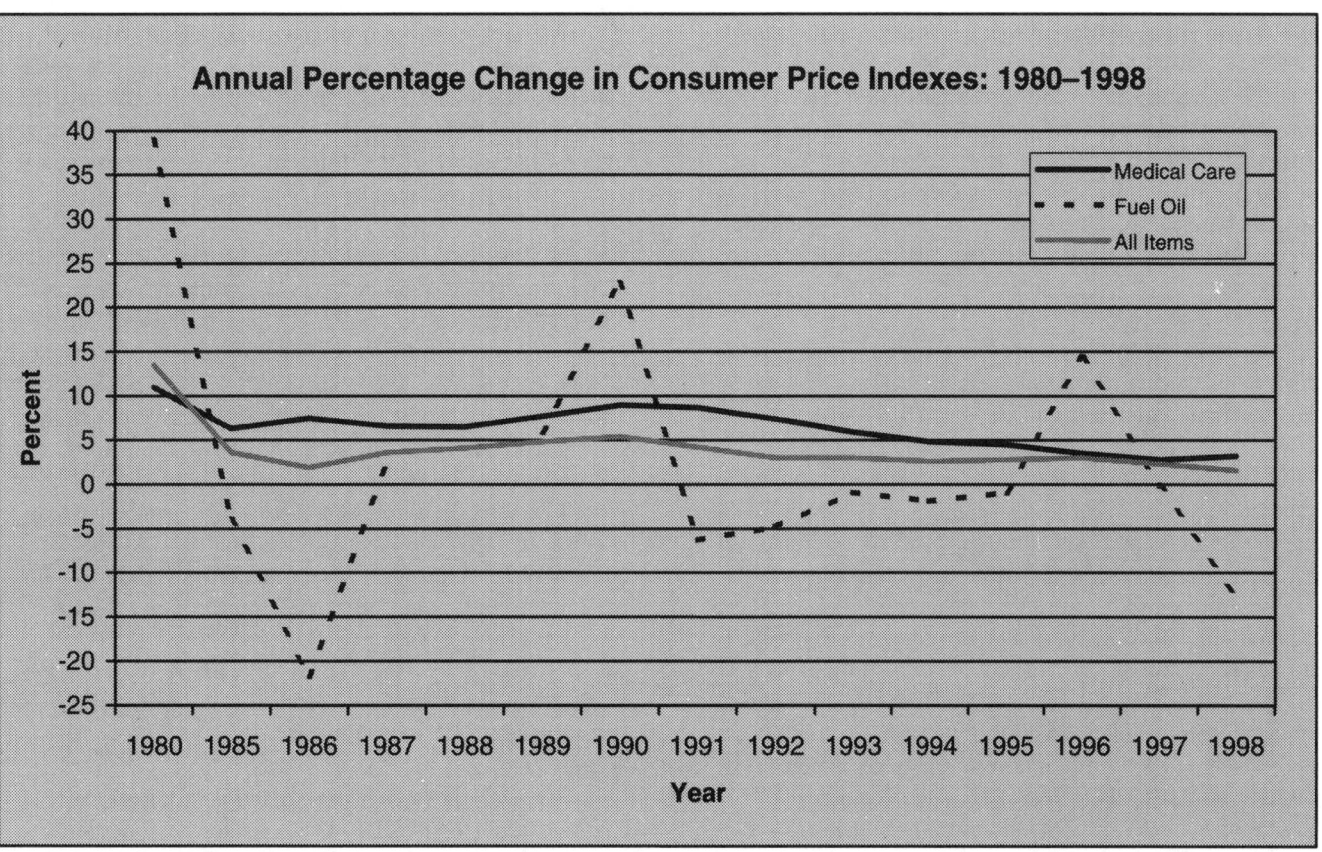

Annual Percentage Change in Consumer Price Indexes: 1980–1998

red in 1940, with subsequent revisions in 1953, 1964, 1978, 1987 and 1998. The last revision changed the base year to 1982 to 1984. The BLS publishes CPIs for two population groups: CPI-W covering urban wage-earners and clerical workers who comprise about 32% of the population, and CPI-U for all urban consumers, including groups excluded from CPI-W. such as the unemployed, self-employed, retirees, professionals, and managers. The current CPI is based on a market basket of goods and services, including food, clothing, shelter, fuels, transportation, healthcare, and so on. It is based on data collected from 85 areas across the country (up from 40 in 1952, 46 in 1953, 50 in 1964, and 56 in 1966) and from more than 50,000 housing units and 23,000 establishments. The BLS publishes a national index as well as separate indexes for regions, area-size classes and 26 local areas or MSAs. In calculating the index, each item is assigned a weight to account for its relative importance in consumer budgets. Price changes for the various items in each location are then averaged. Local data are then combined to obtain a city average.

The percent change in the CPI from month to month or relative to the same month in the previous year is known as the inflation rate. PPI and CPI show the same general pattern of inflation but the latter is more volatile. The PPI is generally the leading indicator and often tends to foreshadow trends that later occur in the CPI. Other measures of inflation include the Index of Industrial Materials Prices, the Dow Jones Commodity Spot Price Index, Futures Price Index, Employment Cost Index, Hourly Compensation Index, and the Unit Labor Cost Index.

3 Income and expenditures represent two facets of an economy and are commonly measured by the Gross National Product (GNP) and the Gross Domestic Product (GDP). In 1991, the Bureau of Economic Analysis began featuring GDP rather than GNP as the measure of national production because it is the more appropriate measure for short-term monitoring of the economy and also because it facilitates international comparisons. GDP is the primary measure of production in the System of National Accounts and is the total national output of goods and services valued at market prices. It includes purchases of goods and services by consumers and government, gross private domestic investment, and net exports of goods and services. GDP measures the output attributable to all labor and property supplied by U. S. residents. It differs from national income mainly in that GNP includes allowances for depreciation and for indirect business taxes. The dollar levels of GDP and GNP differ little but percentage changes may differ more significantly. The annual rates of growth of real GNP have been slightly less than the annual rates of growth of real GDP for most years. The short-term differences are greater and tend to fluctuate more. National income is the aggregate of labor and property earnings which arise in the current production of goods and services. It is the sum of employee compensation, proprietors' income, rental income of persons, corporate profits and net interest. It measures the total factor cost of the goods and services produced by the economy. Capital consumption adjustment for corporations, sole proprietorships and partnerships is the difference between capital consumption claimed on income tax returns and capital consumption allowances measured at straight-line depreciation, consistent service lives, and replacement cost. Personal income is the current income received by persons from all sources minus their contributions for social insurance (including transfers from government, such as Social Security, but excluding interpersonal transfers). Disposable personal income (income available for spending or saving) is personal income less personal tax and nontax payments.

4 In recent years, discussion has focused on the limitations of the standard measurements of national income and wealth. First, national product is primarily a measure of the output of the market economy. No account is taken of the value of homemakers' services, home repairs, or noncommercial recreation. Second, there is no agreement on what goods should be properly considered the end products of the economy. As ordinarily constituted, national product includes all items of consumer expenditure, including expenditures on commuting and labor union dues, which are not end products in themselves. It also overstates the growth of the economy because it includes defense expenditures, as well as police and fire protection. Third, because of the techniques used in adjusting for price changes, national product fails to reflect fully the changes in the quality of goods. The limitation tends to understate economic growth. Fourth, aggregate figures on national product mask changes in the distribution of income between rich and poor, the age-composition of the population, and people-hours spent in economic activity.

5 As part of a comprehensive revision in 1996, BEA replaced its fixed-weight (1987 dollars) index as the featured measure of real GDP with an index based on chain-type annual weights. Under the new system, changes in real output and prices are calculated as the average of changes based on weights for the current and preceding years. (Components of real output are weighted by price, and components of price are weighted by output). These annual changes are "chained" (multiplied) together to form a time series that allows for the effects of changes in relative prices and changes in the composition of output over time. The new output indexes and new price indexes are expressed as 1992 = 100.

6 The primary source of national income and product data is the *Survey of Current Business,* published monthly by the Department of Commerce. Detailed historical data appear in the two-volume *National Income and Product Accounts of the United States.* For earlier periods, the classic sources are Simon Kuznets' *National Income and Its Composition, 1919-1983; Capital in the American Economy: Its Formation and Financing; National Product Since 1869,* and *Enterprise and Social Progress;* Willford I. King's *The Wealth and Income of the People of the United States*; and Robert F. Martin's *National Income in the United States, 1799-1938.*

7 Generally speaking, national saving equals national income minus national consumption and is identical to net national investment. Although data on saving are imperfect for statistical and conceptual reasons, they throw important light on the nature of the different groups of savers and the varius forms of savings.

8 The Poverty Index was devised by the Social Security Administration in 1964 and revised by the Federal Inter-Agency Committee in 1969 and 1980. It is based solely on money income and does not include noncash benefits, such as food stamps, Medicaid, and public housing. The Poverty Threshold is updated every year to reflect changes in the Consumer Price Index. In 1980, it was $4,290 for one person under 65, $3,949 for one person over 65, and $11,269 for six persons. In 1983 the matrix was expanded to nine persons. In 1997, the Poverty Threshold was $8,183 for one person, ($8,350 for a person under 65 and $7,698 for a person over 65), going up to $32,566 for nine persons.

9 The GDP passed the $1 trillion mark in 1970 and the $8 trillion mark in 1997. In 1998, it was $8.511 trillion, the largest national GDP in the world.

10 Services have overtaken manufacturing as the largest contributor to GDP. There are four trillion dollar sectors: services led by $1.656 trillion; followed by FIRE (Finance, Insurance, Real Estate), ($1.024 trillion), Manufacturing ($1.378 trillion), and Government ($1.027 trillion). The other sectors are Retail Trade ($712.9 billion), Transportation and Public Utilities ($676.3 billion), Wholesale Trade, ($562.8 billion), and agriculture ($131.7 billion).

11 The annual growth rate of GDP has remained fairly consistent throughout the 1990s growing by between 3% (1991) and 5.9% (1994 and 1997). The growth rate was buttressed by strong showing by consumption expenditures on services and gross private domestic investment.

12 The Gross State Product is the gross market value of goods and services and is the state counterpart of the GDP. The states with the highest GSP in 1996 are California ($962.7 billion) New York ($613.3 billion), and Texas ($551.8 billion). The states with the lowest GSP were Vermont ($14.6 billion), North Dakota ($15.7 billion), and Wyoming ($16.8 billion).

13 Manufacturing is strongest in California ($138.7 billion), Texas ($90.8 billion), and Ohio ($80.7 billion). California leads across the board in all sectors and accounts for more than 12% of the national GDP.

14 Of personal consumption expenditures totaling $5.493 trillion in 1997, the largest item was medical care ($957 billion), followed by food ($832 billion), housing ($829 billion), transportation ($636 billion), household oper-

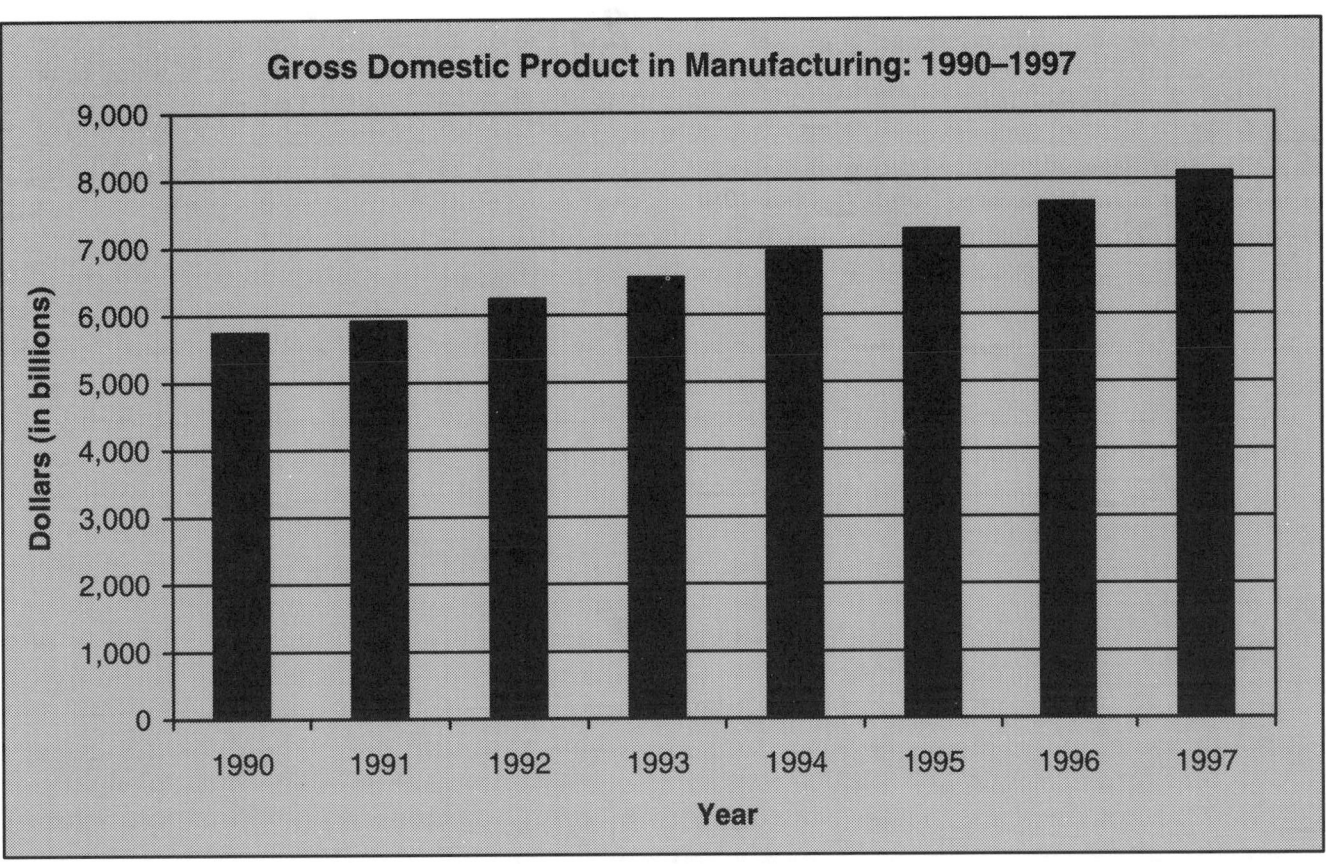

Gross Domestic Product in Manufacturing: 1990–1997

ation ($620 billion), recreation ($462 billion), personal business ($459 billion), clothing, accessories, and jewelry ($353 billion), religious and welfare activities ($157 billion), and education and research ($129 billion).

15 In 1998, saving reached $1.458 trillion, of which gross private saving was $1.090 trillion. Gross government saving was $377.6 billion of which the federal portion was $142.5 billion.

16 In 1998, total personal income in the United States was $7.126 trillion of which wage and salary disbursements accounted for $4.149 trillion, proprietors' income $577.2 billion, rental income $177.2 billion, personal dividend income $263.1 billion, and personal interest income $764.8 billion.

17 The personal income per capita, one of the key indicators of prosperity, was $26,412 in 1998, up from $19,156 in 1990. Connecticut was the top state in this category with a per capita income of $37,598, followed by New Jersey ($33,937), Massachusetts ($32,797), New York ($31,734), Maryland ($29,943), Delaware ($29,814), New Hampshire ($29,290), Illinois ($28,873), Colorado ($28,657), and Washington ($27,961). The three states with the lowest per capita income are Mississippi ($18,958), West Virginia ($19,362), and New Mexico ($19,936).

18 In 1998, an average family spent $34,819 annually on household needs. Of these, the largest items were housing ($11,272), transportation ($6,457), food ($4,801), healthcare ($1,841), entertainment ($1,813), personal insurance and pensions ($3,223), reading ($164), and alcoholic beverages ($309).

19 Asian households receive the highest median money income ($45,249). Whites are next with $38,972, Hispanics third with $26,628, and Blacks last with $25,050. The gap between Blacks on the one hand, and Asians and Whites on the other, increased since 1970.

20 The gap between the rich and the poor widened in the 1990s. In 1970, the share of aggregate income received by the lowest fifth was 5.4% while that of the highest fifth was 40.9%. In 1997, the share of aggregate income received by the lowest fifth was 9.9% and that of the highest fifth 47.2%. Nearly half the aggregate income is received by the top 20% of the population. In dollar terms, the highest fifth families have an average annual income of $137,080 and the lowest fifth $20,586. In racial terms, the disparities are even more stark: 14.5 million White families receive more than $75,000 annually in contrast to only 832,000 Black families.

21 Twenty-six-point-five percent of Black families and 27.1% of Hispanic families live below the poverty level compared to 11% of White families and 14% of Asian families. The states with the largest percentages of persons below the poverty level are New Mexico (21.2%), Arkansas (19.7%), and California (16.6%).

22 The mean net worth, measured in constant dollars, of an American family has declined from $225,900 in 1980 to $208,100 in 1995.

23 The net stock of fixed tangible personal and institutional wealth in 1997 was $24.8 trillion, of which the private sector accounted for $17.3 trillion.

Series F 1-5. Gross National Product, Total and Per Capita, in Current and Chained (1996) Dollars: 1869-1999

Year	Current Price		Chained (1996) dollars	
	Gross national product Bill. Dol.	Gross national income per capita Dollars	Gross national product Bill. Dol.	Gross national income per capita Dollars
	1	1	1	1
1999	9 288.2	34 023	8 868.3	32 485
1998	8 786.7	32 476	8 515.1	31 472
1997	8 325.4	31 055	8 168.1	30 468
1996	7 831.2	29 496	7 831.2	29 496
1995	7 420.9	28 209	7 564	28 752
1994	7 071.1	27 132	7 364.3	28 257
1993	6 666.7	25 829	7 087.8	27 461
1992	6 342.3	24 833	6 905.8	27 039
1991	6 010.9	23 789	6 703.4	26 530
1990	5 832.2	23 331	6 740	26 962
1989	5 509.4	22 270	6 615.5	26 742
1988	5 126.8	20 921	6 391.1	26 080
1987	4 756.2	19 586	6 130.8	25 246
1986	4 468.3	18 565	5 932.5	24 649
1985	4 238.4	17 771	5 750.9	24 112
1984	3 968.1	16 786	5 553.8	23 494
1983	3 571.8	15 242	5 184.9	22 126
1982	3 295.7	14 192	4 973.6	21 418
1981	3 166.1	13 765	5 075.4	22 066
1980	2 830.8	12 431	4 962.3	21 791
1979	2 599.3	11 547	4 973.9	22 096
1978	2 318	10 412	4 805.3	21 584
1977	2 052.1	9 315	4 556.6	20 685
1976	1 841	8 442	4 351.4	19 953
1975	1 648.4	7 632	4 117.7	19 065
1974	1 516.7	7 091	4 142.3	19 366
1973	1 398.2	6 597	4 161	19 633
1972	1 249.1	5 950	3 925.7	18 701
1971	1 136.2	5 471	3 722.9	17 925
1970	1 046.1	5 101	3 600.6	17 556
1969	991.5	4 891	3 594.1	17 728
1968	917.6	4 571	3 489.8	17 384
1967	839.5	4 224	3 330.4	16 757
1966	794.5	4 041	3 248.9	16 526
1965	725.5	3 733	3 051.7	15 702
1964	669.4	3 488	2 868.5	14 946
1963	623.2	3 292	2 710.8	14 320
1962	590.7	3 166	2 598	13 924
1961	549.3	2 990	2 448.8	13 327
1960	530.6	2 935	2 391.9	13 232
1959	510.3	2 881	2 332.8	13 170
1958	470.7	2 703	2 176.3	12 497
1957	464.7	2 713	2 199.6	12 843
1956	440.8	2 620	2 156	12 816
1955	417.8	2 528	2 113	12 785
1954	383.3	2 360	1 972.5	12 147
1953	381.9	2 393	1 985.1	12 441
1952	360.7	2 298	1 899.2	12 100
1951	341.5	2 213	1 826.3	11 837
1950	295.8	1 950	1 695.6	11 179
1949	269	1 803	1 559.1	10 451
1948	271.1	1 849	1 569	10 700
1947	245.6	1 704	1 502.7	10 426
1946	223	1 577	1 511	10 687
1945	223.4	1 597	1 697.1	12 128
1944	220.1	1 590	1 718.8	12 419
1943	198.8	1 454	1 588.2	11 615

See footnotes at end of chart.

Series F 1-5.   Gross National Product, Total and Per Capita, in Current and Chained (1996) Dollars: 1869-1999—Cont'd.

Year	Current Price		Chained (1996) dollars	
	Gross national product Bill. Dol.	Gross national income per capita Dollars	Gross national product Bill. Dol.	Gross national income per capita Dollars
	1	1	1	1
1942	162.2	1 203	1 364.8	10 120
1941	127.2	954	1 153.8	8 649
1940	101.7	770	984.5	7 451
1939	92.5	706	908	6 930
1938	86.5	666	840	6 463
1937	92.3	716	869.9	6 745
1936	84	655	825.5	6 440
1935	73.7	579	731.9	5 747
1934	66.3	524	671.4	5 308
1933	56.7	451	606.8	4 828
1932	59.2	474	616.1	4 931
1931	77.1	621	708.8	5 709
1930	92	747	757.9	6 152
1929	104.5	857	828.9	6 801

Year	Current Price		Chained (1958) dollars	
	Gross national product	Gross national income per capita	Gross national product	Gross national income per capita
	1	1	1	1
1929	104.5	857	203.6	1 671
1928*	97	805	190.9	1 584
1927	94.9	797	189.9	1 594
1926	97	826	190	1 619
1925	93.1	804	179.4	1 549
1924	84.7	742	165.5	1 450
1923	85.1	760	165.9	1 482
1922	74.1	673	148	1 345
1921	69.6	641	127.8	1 177
1920	91.5	860	140	1 315
1919	84	804	146.4	1 401
1918	76.4	740	151.8	1 471
1917	60.4	585	135.2	1 310
1916	48.3	473	134.3	1 317
1915	40	398	124.5	1 238
1914	38.6	389	125.6	1 267
1913	39.6	407	131.4	1 351
1912	39.4	413	130.2	1 366
1911	35.8	382	123.2	1 313
1910	35.3	382	120.1	1 299
1909	33.4	369	116.8	1 290
1908	27.7	312	100.2	1 130
1907	30.4	349	109.2	1 255
1906	28.7	336	107.5	1 258
1905	25.1	299	96.3	1 149
1904	22.9	279	89.7	1 092
1903	22.9	284	90.8	1 126
1902	21.6	273	86.5	1 093
1901	20.7	267	85.7	1 105
1900	18.7	246	76.9	1 011
1899	17.4	233	74.8	1 000
1898	15.4	210	68.6	933
1897	14.6	202	67.1	930
1896	13.3	188	61.3	865
1895	13.9	200	62.6	900

See footnotes at end of chart.

Series F 1-5. Gross National Product, Total and Per Capita, in Current and Chained (1996) Dollars: 1869-1999—Cont'd.

Year	Current Price		Chained (1958) dollars	
	Gross national product	Gross national income per capita	Gross national product	Gross national income per capita
	1	1	1	1
1894	12.6	185	55.9	819
1893	13.8	206	57.5	859
1892	14.3	218	60.4	920
1891	13.5	210	55.1	856
1890	13.1	208	52.7	836
1889	12.5	202	49.1	795
1879-1888**	11.2	205	42.4	774
1869-1878**	7.4	170	23.1	531

* From 1869 to 1928, the chained prices are 1958 dollars
** Decade average

Series F 17-30. Per Capita Income and Product Series for Selected Items in Current and Chained Prices: 1929 to 1999

(In dollars. Based on estimated population as of July 1, including Armes Forces abroad)

Year	Current dollars				Year	Chained (1996) dollars		
	Gross domestic product	Personal income	Disposable personal income	Personal consumption expenditures		Gross domestic product	Disposable personal income	Personal consumption expenditures
	17	18	19	20				
1999	34 063	28 534	24 314	22 962	1999	32 512	23 191	21 901
1998	32 489	27 317	23 359	21 625	1998	31 474	22 672	20 989
1997	31 029	25 876	22 262	20 625	1997	30 436	21 838	20 232
1996	29 428	24 660	21 385	19 727	1996	29 428	21 385	19 727
1995	28 131	23 571	20 613	18 888	1995	28 676	21 055	19 294
1994	27 068	22 593	19 820	18 097	1994	28 194	20 709	18 910
1993	25 735	21 735	19 121	17 259	1993	27 363	20 384	18 399
1992	24 741	21 105	18 616	16 482	1992	26 938	20 318	17 989
1991	23 691	20 126	17 710	15 717	1991	26 423	19 919	17 677
1990	23 215	19 614	17 176	15 327	1990	26 834	20 058	17 899
1989	22 188	18 593	16 235	14 539	1989	26 646	19 833	17 760
1988	20 845	17 433	15 312	13 697	1988	25 987	19 522	17 463
1987	19 529	16 317	14 246	12 787	1987	25 174	18 870	16 938
1986	18 501	15 425	13 555	12 029	1986	24 565	18 641	16 541
1985	17 664	14 738	12 941	11 373	1985	23 970	18 229	16 020
1984	16 636	13 853	12 215	10 569	1984	23 288	17 799	15 401
1983	15 085	12 576	11 036	9 757	1983	21 902	16 673	14 741
1982	14 035	11 922	10 364	8 954	1982	21 184	16 328	14 105
1981	13 614	11 301	9 773	8 453	1981	21 830	16 265	14 069
1980	12 276	10 205	8 869	7 741	1980	21 521	16 063	14 021
1979	11401	9 247	8 033	7 091	1979	21 821	16 120	14 230
1978	10 313	8 302	7 253	6 425	1978	21 383	15 845	14 035
1977	9 221	7 432	6 519	5 803	1977	20 481	15 256	13 583
1976	8 363	6 765	5 960	5 272	1976	19 771	14 873	13 155
1975	7 571	6 166	5 470	4 771	1975	18 911	14 393	12 551
1974	7 017	5 730	5 013	4 359	1974	19 163	14 268	12 407
1973	6 537	5 254	4 619	4 022	1973	19 456	14 496	12 626
1972	5 909	4 736	4 138	3 671	1972	18 570	13 692	12 149
1971	5 434	4 358	3 860	3 382	1971	17 804	13 218	11 581
1970	5 069	4 101	3 591	3 164	1970	17 446	12 823	11 300
1969	4 860	3 851	3 329	2 987	1969	17 616	12 451	11 171
1968	4 540	3 559	3 119	2 783	1968	17 266	12 196	10 881
1967	4 197	3 272	2 899	2 559	1967	16 646	11 776	10 396
1966	4 015	3 085	2 742	2 451	1966	16 416	11 417	10 204
1965	3 705	2 868	2 567	2 286	1965	15 583	10 965	9 764
1964	3 462	2 688	2 412	2 145	1964	14 831	10 456	9 300
1963	3 268	2 541	2 249	2 024	1963	14 212	9 886	8 896
1962	3 143	2 454	2 174	1 950	1962	13 821	9 666	8 668
1961	2 970	2 342	2 081	1 865	1961	13 236	9 361	8 388
1960	2 918	2 283	2 026	1 838	1960	13 148	9 210	8 358
1959	2 865	2 224	1 983	1 796	1959	13 092	9 167	8 303
1958	2 687	2 125	1 899	1 703	1958	12 420	8 922	7 999
1957	2 694	2 098	1 867	1 675	1957	12 751	8 988	8 068
1956	2 603	2 021	1 800	1 616	1956	12 728	8 930	8 018
1955	2 512	1 917	1 715	1 567	1955	12 703	8 675	7 928
1954	2 347	1 818	1 629	1 481	1954	12 073	8 276	7 524
1953	2 381	1 834	1 622	1 463	1953	12 371	8 319	7 503
1952	2 285	1 759	1 552	1 400	1952	12 024	8 071	7 279
1951	2 201	1 677	1 499	1 352	1951	11 764	7 953	7 176
1950	1 940	1 516	1 388	1 270	1950	11 119	7 863	7 192
1949	1 794	1 396	1 281	1 199	1949	10 396	7 343	6 872
1948	1 838	1 440	1 307	1 196	1948	10 639	7 433	6 807
1947	1 696	1 333	1 194	1 126	1947	10 374	7 183	6 775
1946	1 572	1 269	1 145	1 020	1946	10 648	7 599	6 768
1945	1 594	1 229	1 087	856	1945	12 101	7 729	6 088

Series F 17-30. Per Capita Income and Product Series for Selected Items in Current and Chained Prices: 1929 to 1999—Cont'd.

(In dollars. Based on estimated population as of July 1, including Armes Forces abroad)

Year	Current dollars				Year	Chained (1996) dollars		
	Gross domestic product	Personal income	Disposable personal income	Personal consumption expenditures		Gross domestic product	Disposable personal income	Personal consumption expenditures
	17	18	19	20				
1944	1 587	1 201	1 072	784	1944	12 386	7 920	5 793
1943	1 451	1 114	990	729	1943	11 582	7 737	5 698
1942	1 199	918	880	659	1942	10 084	7 507	5 623
1941	950	722	703	607	1941	8 612	6 739	5 822
1940	767	595	581	539	1940	7 423	5 912	5 486
1939	702	558	545	513	1939	6 896	5 589	5 259
1938	662	528	512	494	1938	6 429	5 201	5 022
1937	712	576	560	518	1937	6 713	5 556	5 145
1936	653	537	525	485	1936	6 417	5 400	4 990
1935	576	475	465	439	1935	5 718	4 827	4 558
1934	522	425	417	407	1934	5 284	4 430	4 324
1933	449	373	365	366	1933	4 800	4 063	4 065
1932	471	400	393	390	1932	4 897	4 214	4 186
1931	617	528	517	489	1931	5 667	4 896	4 626
1930	741	621	605	570	1930	6 101	5 109	4 808
1929	851	700	683	635	1929	6 746	5 516	5 134

Series F 192-209. National Income by Sector, Legal Form of Organization, and Type of Income: 1929 to 1999

(In billions of dollars)

Year	National income (192)	Domestic business (193)	Corporate business, including mutual — Total (194)	Corp. — Compensation of employees (195)	Corp. — Corporate profits with inventory valuation and capital consumption on adj. (196)	Corp. — Net interest (197)	Sole proprietorships and partnerships — Total (198)	Sole — Compensation of employees (199)	Sole — Proprietors' income with inventory valuation and capital consumption on adj. (200)	Sole — Net interest (201)	Other private business — Total (202)	Other — Compensation of employees (203)	Other — Proprietors' income with inventory valuation and capital consumption on adj.	Other — Rental income of persons with capital consumption on adj. (204)	Other — Net interest (205)	Government enterprises (206)	General government (207)	Households and institutions (208)	Rest of the world (209)
1999	7 469.7	6 224.3	4 492.3	3 585.2	744.6	162.5	1 125.1	345.0	659.9	120.2	508.4	20.0	3.5	143.4	341.5	98.5	854.7	401.7	-11.0
1998	7 038.1	5 837.5	4 220.1	3 351.4	711.5	157.1	1 041.5	320.0	617.3	104.2	480.5	18.5	3.4	135.4	323.2	95.4	818.9	385.1	-3.5
1997	6 618.4	5 458.1	3 952.1	3 098.1	723.1	130.8	953.2	295.8	577.8	79.6	460.2	16.4	3.3	128.3	312.2	92.6	790.0	363.2	7.1
1996	6 210.4	5 084.3	3 658.2	2 912.2	653.2	92.8	890.9	274.3	541.7	74.9	445.0	15.5	3.1	129.7	296.8	90.2	759.4	348.6	18.1
1995	5 876.7	4 790.2	3 445.6	2 776.5	576.8	92.4	832.5	261.2	494.9	76.4	423.8	14.8	2.8	117.9	288.2	88.4	735.8	330.3	20.3
1994	5 556.8	4 509.7	3 234.9	2 646.0	496.0	92.9	793.1	243.7	473.6	75.9	395.7	14.6	3.0	110.3	267.8	86.0	717.0	313.3	16.8
1993	5 251.9	4 234.7	3 018.6	2 500.4	433.4	84.4	758.3	228.9	459.0	70.4	376.1	14.2	2.9	90.9	268.2	81.7	695.8	297.0	24.4
1992	4 994.9	4 020.0	2 860.0	2 385.5	384.4	90.1	722.8	216.3	431.7	74.8	356.2	13.8	2.6	63.3	276.5	81.2	671.8	279.5	23.4
1991	4 756.6	3 829.3	2 731.4	2 259.7	356.9	114.8	671.8	205.5	381.8	84.5	349.5	13.3	2.4	56.4	277.4	76.7	645.1	257.5	24.7
1990	4 642.1	3 765.8	2 687.7	2 217.6	335.9	134.3	671.4	202.1	378.8	90.5	333.5	13.1	2.2	49.1	269.1	73.2	609.4	237.9	29.0
1989	4 392.1	3 589.8	2 570.2	2 101.4	331.4	137.4	644.1	189.3	359.6	95.1	308.3	12.6	2.1	40.5	253.1	67.2	567.3	214.6	20.4
1988	4 151.1	3 404.9	2 456.3	1 995.4	348.3	112.5	593.5	175.8	336.7	81.0	291.3	11.8	2.1	44.1	233.3	64.0	532.6	195.1	18.4
1987	3 803.4	3 116.4	2 264.5	1 858.8	298.6	107.0	526.5	154.4	302.0	70.1	266.6	11.6	1.9	35.8	217.3	58.9	499.9	173.3	13.7
1986	3 525.8	2 885.4	2 079.3	1 732.7	261.0	85.6	503.5	148.2	276.8	78.5	247.1	11.1	1.8	32.2	202.0	55.6	471.1	153.7	15.5
1985	3 380.4	2 769.9	2 002.2	1 634.7	284.0	83.4	479.5	141.3	265.1	73.2	234.6	10.7	2.0	39.1	182.9	53.6	444.3	141.0	25.4
1984	3 162.3	2 584.7	1 876.3	1 523.0	272.8	80.5	444.7	131.6	245.3	67.7	214.5	10.0	2.2	39.5	162.8	49.3	411.0	131.2	35.3
1983	2 796.5	2 264.6	1 658.4	1 373.3	218.6	66.4	367.8	119.5	193.7	54.7	192.5	9.2	1.7	36.9	144.6	46.0	375.8	119.2	36.9
1982	2 603.0	2 105.2	1 537.3	1 299.4	168.5	69.4	343.4	114.1	178.2	51.1	181.8	8.6	1.7	39.6	131.9	42.8	353.1	108.2	36.4
1981	2 497.1	2 039.3	1 494.8	1 243.5	189.3	62.0	338.8	110.5	184.6	43.7	165.0	8.2	1.6	39.6	115.6	40.6	325.5	97.6	34.7
1980	2 243.0	1 824.9	1 334.1	1 122.3	163.0	48.7	314.8	103.3	176.1	35.4	140.2	7.5	1.5	31.3	99.8	35.8	295.7	87.1	35.3
1979	2 075.6	1 699.1	1 243.1	1 023.1	187.9	32.0	307.4	95.8	182.3	29.3	117.3	6.9	1.4	24.5	84.5	31.4	266.3	77.3	32.9
1978	1 860.2	1 523.6	1 116.9	901.7	194.4	20.9	277.9	85.3	168.8	23.7	100.4	6.2	1.2	22.4	70.6	28.4	244.8	69.7	22.1
1977	1 635.8	1 327.7	971.0	784.6	171.8	14.5	244.7	76.8	147.2	20.7	86.1	5.7	1.1	20.4	58.9	25.9	225.1	62.4	20.7
1976	1 456.4	1 175.8	850.6	695.1	144.0	11.5	223.0	71.6	133.2	18.2	78.1	5.1	1.1	21.5	50.4	24.0	206.4	57.1	17.1
1975	1 302.2	1 047.4	750.2	614.8	118.4	17.0	202.5	65.8	120.6	16.2	72.5	4.7	1.0	22.0	44.8	22.2	189.6	52.0	13.2
1974	1 211.9	979.3	700.6	587.4	97.0	16.2	191.1	62.3	114.6	14.2	68.4	4.4	0.9	23.0	40.2	19.3	169.8	47.1	15.7
1973	1 127.4	916.3	653.0	533.9	109.1	10.0	183.8	58.1	114.5	11.3	62.7	4.1	0.7	23.1	34.7	16.8	155.4	43.0	12.7
1972	1 000.4	809.7	581.0	472.5	100.2	8.2	157.2	51.6	97.1	8.5	56.3	3.8	0.6	21.6	30.3	15.2	143.1	38.9	8.7
1971	903.9	729.7	521.3	425.2	87.3	8.8	142.5	49.6	85.6	7.3	51.9	3.4	0.5	21.2	26.7	14.0	130.9	35.6	7.7
1970	837.5	679.2	484.0	400.2	74.5	9.2	134.5	49.1	79.4	6.0	47.9	3.2	0.5	20.3	23.9	12.8	119.4	32.4	6.4
1969	802.7	659.6	471.7	378.6	87.1	6.0	131.3	48.1	78.4	4.9	45.6	3.0	0.5	20.3	21.8	11.0	107.5	29.5	6.2
1968	743.6	613.6	435.0	341.3	90.9	2.8	125.4	46.4	75.0	4.0	43.3	2.8	0.5	20.2	19.9	9.9	97.8	26.1	6.2
1967	681.7	565.4	396.2	308.4	84.8	3.0	118.8	44.5	70.6	3.6	41.5	2.6	0.5	20.4	18.1	8.9	87.4	23.4	5.5
1966	646.7	541.8	377.6	288.5	87.4	1.6	116.2	43.9	69.1	3.3	39.8	2.3	0.5	19.9	17.0	8.3	78.4	21.3	5.2
1965	589.6	495.6	341.6	259.8	81.2	0.6	108.8	41.3	64.8	2.8	37.5	2.1	0.5	19.2	15.7	7.7	69.3	19.3	5.4

Series F 192-209. National Income by Sector, Legal Form of Organization, and Type of Income: 1929 to 1999—Cont'd.

(In billions of dollars)

Year	National income	Domestic business	Corporate business, including mutual — Total	Corp. — Compensation of employees	Corp. — Corporate profits with inventory valuation and capital consumption on adj.	Corp. — Net interest	Sole prop. and partnerships — Total	Sole prop. — Compensation of employees	Sole prop. — Proprietors' income with inventory valuation and capital consumption on adj.	Sole prop. — Net interest	Other private business — Total	Other — Compensation of employees	Other — Proprietors' income with inventory valuation and capital consumption on adj.	Other — Rental income of persons with capital consumption on adj.	Other — Net interest	Government enterprises	General government	Households and institutions	Rest of the world
	192	193	194	195	196	197	198	199	200	201	202	203		204	205	206	207	208	209
1964	542.1	454.8	309.7	239.2	70.4	0.1	102.7	40.1	60.2	2.4	35.4	2.0	0.5	18.6	14.3	7.1	64.4	17.9	5.0
1963	504.4	423.8	286.1	222.7	63.6	-0.1	97.3	38.1	57.3	1.9	33.8	1.9	0.4	18.5	12.9	6.6	59.3	16.7	4.6
1962	477.1	401.8	268.9	211.0	57.8	0.1	94.9	37.2	56.0	1.6	31.9	1.8	0.4	17.8	11.9	6.1	55.5	15.6	4.2
1961	442.5	372.8	245.6	195.6	50.1	-0.1	91.8	36.5	54.0	1.4	29.7	1.7	0.4	16.9	10.7	5.7	51.6	14.5	3.6
1960	427.5	362.4	239.4	190.7	49.2	-0.5	89.7	37.0	51.5	1.2	27.8	1.5	0.3	16.2	9.8	5.5	48.1	13.9	3.2
1959	411.5	351.3	230.8	180.3	51.0	-0.5	89.7	37.1	51.4	1.2	25.9	1.4	0.3	15.2	8.9	5.0	44.9	12.4	2.9
1958	377.3	320.1	204.0	164.0	39.9	0.2	87.4	35.2	51.1	1.2	23.9	1.4	0.3	14.5	7.8	4.7	42.9	11.5	2.7
1957	375.0	321.5	210.1	166.5	43.9	-0.4	85.3	35.2	49.0	1.0	21.9	1.3	-0.1	13.8	6.9	4.2	39.8	10.6	3.2
1956	358.7	308.7	202.4	158.2	44.5	-0.4	82.0	34.1	47.0	0.9	20.3	1.3	0.0	13.1	5.9	4.0	37.2	9.9	2.9
1955	338.5	292.1	190.5	144.7	46.1	-0.3	78.6	32.2	45.5	0.8	19.2	1.3	0.0	12.8	5.2	3.8	34.8	9.1	2.5
1954	308.4	265.0	167.9	132.3	35.9	-0.2	75.5	31.2	43.5	0.8	18.1	1.2	0.0	12.5	4.5	3.6	33.0	8.1	2.2
1953	308.2	266.0	170.5	134.0	36.9	-0.4	75.5	31.4	43.3	0.7	16.6	1.2	0.0	11.5	3.9	3.5	32.4	7.8	2.0
1952	293.3	252.4	158.9	123.1	36.5	-0.6	74.9	29.9	44.4	0.7	15.0	1.1	0.0	10.5	3.5	3.5	31.5	7.2	2.1
1951	278.7	242.1	152.7	114.6	38.6	-0.5	72.7	28.2	43.9	0.7	13.6	1.1	0.0	9.5	3.1	3.0	27.7	6.9	2.0
1950	241.0	211.8	132.4	98.7	34.1	-0.4	64.4	25.3	38.6	0.6	12.3	1.0	0.0	8.7	2.7	2.7	21.2	6.5	1.5
1949	216.7	189.3	115.9	88.8	27.5	-0.3	59.9	23.6	35.7	0.5	11.0	0.8	0.0	7.8	2.3	2.6	20.1	5.9	1.3
1948	223.3	198.1	120.4	91.1	29.6	-0.3	64.9	24.0	40.4	0.4	10.5	0.8	0.0	7.6	2.1	2.3	18.1	5.6	1.5
1947	198.6	174.6	104.7	82.1	22.5	0.0	58.4	22.4	35.6	0.4	9.5	0.7	0.0	7.0	1.8	2.0	17.6	5.1	1.2
1946	182.3	154.7	86.3	69.9	16.7	-0.2	57.2	20.4	36.6	0.3	9.3	0.6	0.0	7.0	1.6	1.9	22.4	4.5	0.7
1945	183.3	143.5	84.1	64.1	19.8	0.2	49.6	17.6	31.7	0.3	8.2	0.5	0.0	6.1	1.6	1.6	35.3	4.1	0.4
1944	184.3	147.9	91.6	67.1	24.2	0.3	46.8	16.2	30.3	0.3	8.0	0.5	0.0	5.9	1.6	1.5	32.3	3.7	0.5
1943	171.4	142.1	88.8	64.1	24.1	0.5	44.1	14.6	29.1	0.4	7.8	0.5	0.0	5.6	1.7	1.5	25.6	3.2	0.4
1942	137.6	119.0	73.2	52.8	19.7	0.7	37.3	12.7	24.1	0.5	7.3	0.4	0.0	5.0	1.8	1.2	15.2	2.9	0.5
1941	104.3	91.8	56.9	41.6	14.6	0.7	27.6	9.8	17.3	0.5	6.2	0.4	0.0	4.0	1.9	1.1	9.5	2.5	0.5
1940	81.1	70.5	42.8	32.9	9.2	0.8	21.1	7.8	12.9	0.5	5.5	0.3	0.0	3.4	1.8	1.0	7.8	2.4	0.4
1939	72.9	62.5	36.7	29.8	5.9	1.0	19.4	7.2	11.7	0.5	5.4	0.3	0.0	3.3	1.8	0.9	7.6	2.3	0.4
1938	67.4	57.1	32.6	27.3	4.3	1.1	18.5	6.8	11.2	0.5	5.2	0.3	0.0	3.1	1.8	0.9	7.7	2.2	0.4
1937	74.0	64.4	38.1	30.5	6.5	1.1	20.7	7.1	13.1	0.5	4.7	0.3	0.0	2.6	1.9	0.9	6.9	2.3	0.4
1936	65.8	56.2	33.3	26.3	5.8	1.1	17.7	6.2	11.0	0.5	4.4	0.2	0.0	2.3	1.9	0.8	7.3	2.0	0.3
1935	57.9	49.7	28.0	23.1	3.6	1.3	16.7	5.5	10.7	0.5	4.3	0.2	0.0	2.2	1.9	0.8	6.0	1.9	0.3
1934	50.2	42.5	24.5	21.0	2.2	1.3	13.1	5.0	7.6	0.6	4.2	0.2	0.0	2.1	1.9	0.7	5.6	1.8	0.3
1933	41.4	34.7	18.7	18.0	-0.3	1.0	10.8	4.4	5.8	0.6	4.5	0.2	0.0	2.5	1.9	0.6	4.7	1.7	0.3
1932	43.9	37.2	19.9	19.0	-0.4	1.3	11.2	4.8	5.6	0.7	5.4	0.2	0.0	3.2	2.0	0.7	4.5	1.9	0.4
1931	60.4	52.9	29.6	25.4	2.8	1.4	16.3	6.4	9.1	0.8	6.3	0.2	0.0	4.0	2.1	0.8	4.7	2.3	0.5
1930	75.6	67.6	39.4	30.8	7.1	1.4	20.3	7.8	11.7	0.8	7.2	0.3	0.0	4.9	2.0	0.8	4.6	2.7	0.7
1929	86.8	78.8	45.9	34.2	10.4	1.3	24.2	8.6	14.9	0.6	8.0	0.3	0.0	5.6	2.1	0.8	4.4	2.9	0.8

SOURCE: U.S. Bureau of Economic Analysis, National Income and Product Accounts of the United States.

Series F 226-237. National Income Without Capital Consumption Adjustment by Industry Group: 1929 to 1999

(In billions of dollars)

Year	Total	Domestic industries	Private industries	Agriculture, forestry, and fisheries	Mining	Contract con-struction	Manu-facturing	Whole-sale and retail trade	Finance, insurance and real estate	Transpor-tation	Communi-cation and public utilities	Services	Govern-ment and govern-ment enter-prises	Rest of the world
	226			**227**	**228**	**229**	**230**	**231**	**232**	**233**	**234**	**235**	**236**	**237**
1999.....	7 439.2	7 450.2	6 497	109.2	51.3	381.8	1 193.3	1 077	1 366.9	236.9	297.8	1 782.9	953.2	-11
1998.....	7 009.3	7 012.8	6 098.5	102.5	54.5	346.4	1 153.7	1 010.4	1 285.2	225.1	272.8	1 648	914.3	-3.5
1997.....	6 599.6	6 592.6	5 709.9	101.6	58.2	309.3	1 119.3	933.6	1 197.1	207.2	266.5	1 517.2	882.6	7.1
1996.....	6 206.4	6 188.3	5 338.7	101.9	50.7	290.3	1 073.9	864.5	1 088	194.7	266.9	1 407.8	849.6	18.1
1995.....	5 884.4	5 864	5 039.9	86.9	45.7	266.7	1 058.5	810	1 013.5	183.9	256.7	1 318.1	824.2	20.3
1994.....	5 576.4	5 559.6	4 756.6	93.7	43.9	252.8	1 006	774.7	932.7	176.6	246.6	1 229.5	803	16.8
1993.....	5 267.9	5 243.5	4 466	91.9	40.5	228.3	929.1	721.5	897.1	163.2	229.1	1 165.4	777.5	24.4
1992.....	5 018.2	4 994.8	4 241.8	90.7	39.7	215.6	886	698.7	841.5	152.9	213.2	1 103.6	753	23.4
1991.....	4 769.1	4 744.4	4 022.6	83.6	40.2	214.6	863.9	667.3	786.4	146.1	205	1 015.6	721.8	24.7
1990.....	4 640.5	4 611.6	3 929	89	40.8	230.5	879	651.3	738.5	138.7	191.8	969.5	682.6	29
1989.....	4 366.9	4 346.5	3 712.1	85.5	36.2	227.1	853.4	630.6	691.6	133.7	180	873.8	634.5	20.4
1988.....	4 112.1	4 093.6	3 497.1	78.2	35.9	218.9	822.2	591.4	651.5	132.7	170.9	795.3	596.5	18.4
1987.....	3 760.3	3 746.6	3 187.9	78.9	28.6	202.9	739.8	546	599.7	123.4	162.8	705.9	558.8	13.7
1986.....	3 475.8	3 460.3	2 933.6	70.7	28.4	191.8	686.8	522.4	528.8	115.5	152.4	636.8	526.7	15.5
1985.....	3 318.1	3 292.8	2 795	69	40.1	171.8	691.3	499.5	484.9	107.3	148	583	497.8	25.4
1984.....	3 126.5	3 091.1	2 630.8	70.2	43.8	153	672.5	470.7	439.6	106.6	143.4	531.1	460.3	35.3
1983.....	2 788.1	2 751.2	2 329.4	54.7	40.3	128.2	598	416.1	397.6	93.3	130.5	470.6	421.8	36.9
1982.....	2 620.2	2 583.7	2 187.9	61.2	50.2	119.2	576.7	386.8	355.2	86.5	126	426.2	395.8	36.4
1981.....	2 523.4	2 488.7	2 122.6	63.5	51.7	121.3	594.1	371.8	334.1	88.4	110.3	387.5	366.1	34.7
1980.....	2 282.9	2 247.6	1 916	52.2	45.7	120.9	536.6	336.4	300.9	83.5	94.7	345.1	331.6	35.3
1979.....	2 107.5	2 074.6	1 776.9	58.6	33.1	117.9	518.4	317.1	266.3	78.7	81.7	304.9	297.7	32.9
1978.....	1 885	1 862.9	1 589.7	51.1	27.5	104.6	471.7	285	232.2	71.3	77.1	269.1	273.2	22.1
1977.....	1 656	1 635.4	1 384.4	42.9	25.2	88.4	416.7	252	194.7	62.9	67.7	233.8	251	20.7
1976.....	1 476.2	1 459	1 228.6	42.7	21.5	79.8	366.6	227.9	168.7	56.1	60.7	204.6	230.4	17.1
1975.....	1 317.9	1 304.7	1 092.9	44.4	20.9	69.7	318	205	152	48	53.5	181.5	211.8	13.2
1974.....	1 217.6	1 201.9	1 012.9	43.4	16.7	69.5	302.3	184.7	140.2	47.6	45.2	163.3	189	15.7
1973.....	1 127.2	1 114.5	942.3	46.6	11.2	65.1	286.1	169.7	129.9	42.8	42.4	148.5	172.2	12.7
1972.....	999.4	990.7	832.5	32.2	9.3	57.3	253.2	152.5	118.4	38.2	39.1	132.2	158.3	8.7
1971.....	904	896.3	751.4	27	8.4	51.8	227.4	138.9	108.6	34.4	35.7	119.1	144.9	7.7
1970.....	836.1	829.7	697.5	25.6	8.3	47.2	215.9	128.3	97.8	31.2	33.1	110.1	132.2	6.4
1969.....	799.7	793.5	675.1	24.8	7.3	44.9	222.7	121.2	91.8	29.9	31.2	101.3	118.4	6.2
1968.....	740.4	734.2	626.5	22.5	7.1	40.1	211.9	111.7	85.2	28	28.8	91.2	107.7	6.2
1967.....	677.7	672.2	575.9	21.7	6.4	36.7	194.7	101.8	78.7	26	26.6	83.3	96.3	5.5
1966.....	642.5	637.3	550.6	22.7	6.3	35.1	190.7	95.2	74.1	25.5	25.4	75.7	86.7	5.2
1965.....	585.2	579.8	502.9	21.2	6.1	32.1	172	88.2	68.2	23.7	23.3	68	76.9	5.4
1964.....	538.1	533.1	461.5	18.4	6	29.3	154.9	82.5	63.7	21.8	22	62.9	71.5	5
1963.....	501.1	496.6	430.6	19	5.8	26.7	144.4	75.8	60	20.6	20.5	57.6	66	4.6
1962.....	475.1	470.9	409.3	19	5.5	25	136.5	72.7	57.6	19.6	19.3	54	61.6	4.2
1961.....	443.5	439.8	382.5	18.6	5.6	23.3	125.3	68.3	54.4	18.7	18.2	50.2	57.3	3.6
1960.....	429.2	425.9	372.4	17.7	5.6	22.3	125.5	66.7	51.6	18.5	17.4	47	53.5	3.2
1959.....	413.6	410.8	360.9	16.9	5.5	21.8	124.6	65.4	48.3	18.2	16	44.1	49.9	2.9
1958.....	380.1	377.4	329.8	18.9	5.7	20	108.2	60.1	45.1	16.9	14.7	40.2	47.6	2.7
1957.....	378	374.8	330.8	16.7	6.6	20.5	116.6	59	41.9	17.8	13.8	38.1	44	3.2
1956.....	361.4	358.5	317.3	16.5	6.6	19.6	113.4	56.3	39.3	17.3	12.9	35.3	41.2	2.9
1955.....	340.4	337.9	299.3	16.5	5.9	17.6	108.2	53.5	37.1	16.2	12	32.3	38.6	2.5
1954.....	311.6	309.4	272.8	17.5	5.3	16.5	94.9	49.4	34.5	14.8	11.1	28.8	36.6	2.2
1953.....	312.5	310.5	274.6	18.1	5.5	16.4	100.6	48.3	31.7	16	10.3	27.7	35.9	2
1952.....	298.5	296.3	261.3	20.3	5.5	15.9	92.7	47.5	28.8	15.6	9.4	25.7	35	2.1
1951.....	284.3	282.3	251.5	21.2	5.8	14.7	90.5	45.8	26.1	15.1	8.5	24	30.7	2
1950.....	245.8	244.2	220.3	18.3	5.3	12.4	76.4	41.4	23.8	13.4	7.3	22	23.9	1.5
1949.....	221.5	220.1	197.5	17.3	4.5	10.9	64.9	39.2	21.4	12.1	6.7	20.4	22.7	1.3
1948.....	228.3	226.8	206.4	22.2	5.4	11	68.8	40.1	20.1	12.8	6	20	20.4	1.5
1947.....	202.9	201.7	182.1	19.3	4.3	8.5	59.6	37.7	18	11.6	5.1	18.1	19.6	1.2

See footnotes at end of chart.

Series F 226-237. National Income Without Capital Consumption Adjustment by Industry Group: 1929 to 1999—Cont'd.

(In billions of dollars)

Year	Total	Domestic industries	Private industries	Agriculture, forestry, and fisheries	Mining	Contract con-struction	Manu-facturing	Whole-sale and retail trade	Finance, insurance and real estate	Transpor-tation	Communi-cation and public utilities	Services	Govern-ment and govern-ment enter-prises	Rest of the world
	226			227	228	229	230	231	232	233	234	235	236	237
1946.....	185.9	185.2	160.9	18.5	3	6.5	49.2	34.7	17.1	10.4	4.8	16.6	24.3	0.7
1945.....	183.7	183.4	146.4	15.7	2.8	4.3	52.2	28.1	14.5	10.5	4.2	14.1	36.9	0.4
1944.....	184.8	184.4	150.6	15.2	3	4.1	60.3	25.9	13.7	11.2	4	13.1	33.8	0.5
1943.....	172.5	172.1	145	15	2.8	5.5	58.3	24	13	10.8	4	11.8	27.1	0.4
1942.....	139.2	138.7	122.4	12.7	2.6	6.5	45.5	20.6	12	8.6	3.7	10.2	16.4	0.5
1941.....	105.9	105.4	94.9	8.5	2.4	4.2	33.2	17.5	10.6	6.3	3.3	8.8	10.6	0.5
1940.....	82.5	82.2	73.4	6.2	1.9	2.6	22.5	14.7	9.5	5	3	8	8.8	0.4
1939.....	74.1	73.7	65.1	6.1	1.6	2.3	18.1	12.7	9.2	4.6	2.9	7.5	8.6	0.4
1938.....	68.8	68.4	59.8	6.1	1.6	2	15.1	12.3	8.9	4.1	2.7	7.2	8.6	0.4
1937.....	75.2	74.8	67	7.7	2	2.1	19.5	12.5	8.3	4.6	2.7	7.5	7.8	0.4
1936.....	66.4	66.1	58	5.9	1.6	2	16.3	11	7.7	4.3	2.5	6.8	8.2	0.3
1935.....	58.5	58.2	51.4	6.7	1.2	1.3	13.3	9.6	7.1	3.7	2.3	6.1	6.8	0.3
1934.....	50.8	50.6	44.3	4.3	1.2	1.1	11	8.5	6.7	3.4	2.2	5.7	6.3	0.3
1933.....	41.6	41.3	36	3.9	0.6	0.8	7.7	5.9	6.9	3.1	2	5.1	5.4	0.3
1932.....	44.2	43.8	38.6	3.6	0.7	1.1	7.3	6.9	8	3.2	2.3	5.6	5.2	0.4
1931.....	61	60.5	55.1	5.3	1	2.2	12.5	10.2	9.7	4.4	2.6	7.2	5.5	0.5
1930.....	76.7	76	70.7	6.6	1.7	3.2	18.3	12.7	11.6	5.6	2.8	8.3	5.3	0.7
1929.....	88.2	87.4	82.3	8.7	2.1	3.8	22	13.9	13.7	6.6	2.8	8.8	5.1	0.8

SOURCE: U.S. Bureau of Economic Analysis, National Income and Product Accounts of the United States.

Series F 297-348. Personal Income by States: 1929 to 1998

Year	Alabama	Alaska	Arizona	Arkansas	Cali-fornia	Colorado	Connecti-cut	Delaware	Florida	Georgia	Hawaii	Idaho	Illinois	Indiana
	298	**299**	**300**	**301**	**302**	**303**	**304**	**305**	**307**	**308**	**309**	**310**	**311**	**312**
						TOTAL INCOME (millions of dollars)								
1998	93 300	15 800	107 700	51 600	898 400	113 800	123 100	22 200	385 600	191 200	31 200	25 900	347 800	142 900
1997	89 300	15 200	100 200	49 400	846 800	105 100	117 200	20 900	364 000	178 900	30 500	24 700	332 000	136 100
1996	85 700	14 900	92 900	47 500	801 500	95 900	108 700	20 000	347 100	167 000	29 800	23 200	315 100	131 100
1995	81 300	14 400	86 500	44 500	754 800	90 900	104 600	18 400	321 500	156 000	29 400	22 100	298 200	124 000
1994	76 000	14 400	77 400	41 400	707 000	81 600	96 300	16 100	302 400	142 900	28 400	20 700	279 500	117 200
1993	71 600	13 800	71 300	38 800	683 500	76 600	92 300	15 300	283 400	132 900	27 400	19 300	263 600	109 600
1992	67 100	12 700	65 600	37 000	656 800	69 800	88 500	14 800	261 600	122 400	24 600	17 100	251 300	102 200
1991	63 700	12 500	61 500	35 000	636 500	65 600	85 200	13 800	250 700	115 000	24 200	16 000	240 400	96 600
1990	60 700	11 900	58 900	33 400	619 800	62 300	83 500	13 400	241 800	110 900	22 700	15 400	233 800	94 000
1989	56 100	11 400	56 200	31 000	579 200	58 200	79 900	12 400	223 600	103 300	20 500	13 900	219 400	88 800
1988	52 600	10 100	52 200	29 100	535 700	54 400	75 000	11 500	203 800	96 900	18 500	12 700	204 000	81 800
1987	48 800	9 600	48 500	27 500	493 000	51 400	68 300	10 800	187 400	89 000	17 000	11 800	190 400	77 000
1986	45 700	9 800	44 900	26 100	453 400	49 400	62 400	9 800	171 000	82 100	15 600	11 200	179 100	72 200
1985	43 000	9 800	41 000	24 800	422 600	47 500	57 900	9 100	158 400	75 400	14 600	10 900	170 000	68 300
1984	39 800	8 600	35 500	22 800	367 500	43 700	51 600	8 300	137 800	66 800	13 300	10 200	158 000	64 900
1983	36 500	8 200	31 600	20 800	333 700	40 100	46 900	7 600	123 800	59 600	12 400	9 400	142 400	57 900
1982	34 100	7 400	29 100	19 400	310 700	37 400	43 400	7 100	114 400	54 000	11 600	8 700	138 500	54 800
1981	32 500	6 200	27 500	18 700	292 100	33 900	40 300	6 600	105 900	50 200	10 900	8 500	132 900	53 500
1980	29 200	5 100	24 000	16 700	259 600	29 000	36 500	6 200	88 700	44 200	9 800	7 600	120 400	49 200
1979	26 300	4 600	20 300	14 800	225 000	24 800	31 000	5 600	75 600	38 500	8 500	6 700	110 300	46 900
1978	23 400	4 400	17 400	13 500	197 300	21 400	27 600	5 000	64 500	34 100	7 400	6 000	98 300	41 400
1977	20 700	4 300	14 900	11 900	173 200	18 800	25 100	4 500	56 500	30 400	6 800	5 100	87 300	36 900
1976	. . .	. . .	. . .	. . .	. . .	. . .	. . .	. . .	. . .	. . .	. . .	. . .	. . .	. . .
1975	16 800	3 800	11 900	9 500	139 500	15 200	21 100	3 800	46 600	24 800	5 700	4 200	75 400	29 800
1974	15 100	2 300	11 100	8 700	126 100	13 800	19 900	3 600	43 800	23 200	5 100	3 900	69 800	27 700
1973	13 700	2 000	9 700	8 100	113 700	12 300	18 300	3 300	37 800	20 900	4 600	3 400	64 800	26 500
1972	11 700	1 700	8 400	6 600	102 400	10 500	16 500	2 800	30 400	18 200	4 000	2 700	57 700	23 200
1971	10 800	1 500	7 300	6 000	94 100	9 500	15 300	2 600	27 600	16 800	3 700	2 500	53 400	21 100
1970	10 053	1 404	6 507	5 527	89 312	8 541	14 803	2 466	25 275	15 269	3 476	2 352	50 023	19 539
1969	9 163	1 250	5 765	5 004	83 067	7 623	13 819	2 271	22 542	14 347	3 044	2 148	47 233	19 110
1968	8 369	1 111	5 062	4 597	76 720	6 855	12 674	2 070	19 791	12 784	2 700	1 885	43 653	17 413
1967	7 659	1 022	4 516	4 236	69 807	6 122	11 703	1 882	17 451	11 541	2 414	1 790	40 627	16 002
1966	7 245	916	4 110	3 999	65 002	5 697	10 657	1 790	15 683	10 568	2 220	1 681	38 266	15 278
1965	6 713	855	3 773	3 577	60 104	5 295	9 765	1 704	14 182	9 531	2 014	1 668	35 070	14 067
1964	6 108	788	3 529	3 387	56 471	4 984	9 004	1 561	12 976	8 635	1 907	1 459	32 188	12 640
1963	5 666	702	3 362	3 104	52 522	4 745	8 449	1 453	11 859	7 895	1 772	1 409	30 174	11 869
1962	5 274	664	3 177	2 899	48 948	4 559	7 999	1 350	11 050	7 280	1 676	1 410	28 948	11 214
1961	5 025	633	2 905	2 704	45 601	4 294	7 447	1 275	10 248	6 746	1 595	1 310	27 486	10 542
1960	4 887	647	2 681	2 461	42 913	4 018	7 122	1 244	9 739	6 477	1 476	1 238	26 689	10 271
1959	4 699	562	2 455	2 421	40 955	3 752	6 785	1 202	9 303	6 211	1 315	1 227	25 751	9 817
1958	4 442	528	2 220	2 210	37 321	3 524	6 446	1 135	8 453	5 767	1 178	1 161	24 353	9 192
1957	4 261	537	2 028	2 091	35 497	3 365	6 398	1 125	7 730	5 531	1 114	1 104	24 056	9 187
1956	4 005	548	1 861	2 035	33 177	3 066	6 029	1 124	6 972	5 350	1 041	1 047	23 024	8 875
1955	3 761	505	1 655	1 970	30 378	2 804	5 552	980	6 070	5 000	972	951	21 167	8 265
1954	3 314	495	1 514	1 810	27 682	2 566	5 160	857	5 328	4 536	908	902	19 933	7 653
1953	3 432	511	1 478	1 842	27 002	2 528	5 087	835	5 050	4 581	896	899	19 812	8 073
1952	3 287	494	1 399	1 823	25 214	2 498	4 710	782	4 554	4 447	865	932	18 608	7 326
1951	3 077	448	1 230	1 763	22 756	2 313	4 335	731	4 048	4 122	793	850	17 711	6 938
1950	2 691	322	1 006	1 575	19 774	1 970	3 779	684	3 599	3 574	692	764	15 948	5 998
1949	2 446	. . .	906	1 474	17 878	1 820	3 374	586	3 177	3 150	685	712	14 607	5 388
1948	2 571	. . .	879	1 597	17 633	1 810	3 450	537	3 043	3 154	723	725	15 521	5 624
1940	792	. . .	251	496	5 802	615	1 511	275	971	1 047	. . .	235	5 958	1 889
1929	852	. . .	255	567	5 505	649	1 585	245	758	1 014	. . .	235	7 291	1 983

Series F 297-348. Personal Income by States: 1929 to 1998—Cont'd.

Year	Alabama	Alaska	Arizona	Arkansas	California	Colorado	Connecticut	Delaware	Florida	Georgia	Hawaii	Idaho	Illinois	Indiana
	298	299	300	301	302	303	304	305	307	308	309	310	311	312

PER CAPITA INCOME (dollars)

Year	Alabama	Alaska	Arizona	Arkansas	California	Colorado	Connecticut	Delaware	Florida	Georgia	Hawaii	Idaho	Illinois	Indiana
1998	21 442	25 675	23 060	20 346	27 503	28 657	3 758	29 814	25 852	25 020	26 137	21 081	28 873	24 219
1997	20 672	24 969	21 998	19 595	26 314	27 015	35 863	28 493	24 799	23 882	25 598	20 392	27 688	23 202
1996	20 055	24 558	20 989	18 928	25 144	25 084	33 189	27 622	24 104	22 709	25 159	19 539	26 598	22 440
1995	19 041	23 971	20 078	17 934	23 983	24 304	32 073	25 603	22 676	21 696	24 848	18 961	25 135	21 427
1994	18 010	23 788	19 001	16 898	22 493	22 333	29 402	22 828	21 667	20 251	24 057	18 231	23 784	20 378
1993	17 129	23 070	18 085	15 995	21 895	21 498	28 151	21 852	20 650	19 249	23 504	17 512	22 560	19 213
1992	16 518	22 258	17 468	15 572	21 593	20 585	27 338	21 208	19 664	18 495	22 476	16 679	21 784	18 415
1991	15 567	21 932	16 401	14 753	20 952	19 440	25 881	20 349	18 880	17 364	21 306	15 401	20 824	17 217
1990	14 998	21 646	16 006	14 176	20 689	18 860	25 395	20 095	18 539	17 045	20 361	15 250	20 433	16 921
1989	13 625	21 656	15 802	12 901	19 929	17 553	24 683	18 483	17 647	16 053	18 472	13 707	18 824	15 779
1988	12 814	19 237	14 995	12 141	18 915	16 471	23 190	17 347	16 515	15 280	16 840	12 652	17 567	14 721
1987	11 982	18 282	14 355	11 385	17 749	15 624	21 288	16 319	15 538	14 316	15 540	11 838	16 366	13 894
1986	11 293	18 378	13 679	11 025	16 792	15 114	19 547	15 498	14 622	13 454	14 683	11 172	15 503	13 124
1985	10 698	18 785	12 957	10 525	16 035	14 699	18 227	14 547	13 935	12 616	13 900	10 817	14 730	12 424
1984	9 981	17 155	11 629	9 724	14 344	13 742	16 369	14 111	12 553	11 441	12 761	10 174	13 728	11 799
1983	9 229	17 225	10 653	8 936	13 256	12 771	14 945	12 615	11 593	10 389	12 115	9 534	12 401	10 570
1982	8 683	16 854	10 050	8 432	12 617	12 242	13 963	11 828	10 927	9 654	11 590	9 008	12 012	10 057
1981	8 284	14 904	9 871	8 178	12 064	11 389	12 844	11 033	10 438	9 012	11 068	8 875	11 616	9 748
1980	7 704	13 835	9 172	7 465	11 603	10 598	12 112	10 249	9 764	8 348	10 617	8 569	10 837	9 245
1979	6 976	11 252	8 305	6 785	9 913	8 945	9 959	9 557	8 532	7 515	9 353	7 446	9 823	8 686
1978	6 247	10 851	7 374	6 183	8 850	8 001	8 914	8 604	7 505	6 700	8 380	6 813	8 745	7 696
1977	5 622	10 586	6 509	5 540	7 911	7 160	8 061	7 697	6 684	6 014	7 677	5 980	7 768	6 921
1976	. . .	. . .	. . .	. . .	. . .	. . .	. . .	. . .	. . .	. . .	. . .	. . .	. . .	. . .
1975	4 634	9 673	5 364	4 527	6 580	6 006	6 795	6 573	5 634	5 029	6 711	5 205	6 734	5 612
1974	4 198	7 023	4 989	4 280	5 997	5 343	6 471	6 227	5 235	4 662	5 882	4 934	6 337	5 263
1973	3 864	5 926	4 687	3 956	5 508	4 966	5 931	5 813	4 820	4 343	5 525	4 381	5 801	4 998
1972	3 333	5 162	4 300	3 357	5 002	4 449	5 342	4 983	4 188	3 846	4 995	3 635	5 126	4 391
1971	3 087	4 875	3 913	3 078	4 640	4 153	4 995	4 673	3 930	3 599	4 738	3 409	4 775	4 027
1970	2 913	4 603	3 631	2 869	4 467	3 839	4 871	4 483	3 692	3 318	4 562	3 280	4 492	3 752
1969	2 664	4 223	3 319	2 616	4 214	3 519	4 606	4 205	3 394	3 153	4 097	3 038	4 279	3 716
1968	2 429	3 899	3 010	2 417	3 956	3 233	4 276	3 876	3 077	2 852	3 755	2 712	3 970	3 419
1967	2 215	3 675	2 743	2 228	3 640	2 982	3 987	3 585	2 796	2 618	3 409	2 602	3 711	3 167
1966	2 092	3 380	2 547	2 106	3 447	2 839	3 671	3 469	2 569	2 413	3 185	2 440	3 531	3 056
1965	1 950	3 154	2 382	1 888	3 234	2 668	3 418	3 362	2 382	2 200	2 885	2 431	3 280	2 858
1964	1 799	2 997	2 268	1 785	3 111	2 530	3 218	3 141	2 245	2 028	2 813	2 145	3 042	2 603
1963	1 687	2 744	2 210	1 655	2 973	2 451	3 098	3 009	2 107	1 892	2 641	2 062	2 901	2 473
1962	1 587	2 699	2 180	1 564	2 867	2 401	3 022	2 879	2 025	1 782	2 567	2 038	2 816	2 368
1961	1 515	2 659	2 065	1 497	2 764	2 329	2 880	2 765	1 955	1 680	2 481	1 916	2 713	2 229
1960	1 493	2 824	2 030	1 376	2 704	2 271	2 800	2 772	1 946	1 637	2 366	1 846	2 646	2 198
1959	1 467	2 507	1 947	1 378	2 648	2 194	2 689	2 725	1 935	1 606	2 156	1 867	2 579	2 128
1958	1 405	2 357	1 861	1 280	2 508	2 114	2 635	2 621	1 826	1 516	1 981	1 797	2 463	2 006
1957	1 371	2 323	1 802	1 207	2 489	2 023	2 712	2 641	1 768	1 469	1 944	1 720	2 488	2 028
1956	1 304	2 446	1 767	1 194	2 419	1 887	2 603	2 754	1 723	1 445	1 900	1 667	2 416	1 991
1955	1 233	2 273	1 677	1 142	2 313	1 814	2 414	2 519	1 620	1 375	1 838	1 539	2 243	1 894
1954	1 099	2 300	1 623	1 044	2 172	1 718	2 294	2 328	1 520	1 259	1 802	1 503	2 154	1 795
1953	1 124	2 492	1 654	1 035	2 204	1 767	2 346	2 379	1 526	1 288	1 795	1 509	2 186	1 930
1952	1 071	2 612	1 662	992	2 167	1 830	2 263	2 293	1 442	1 241	1 748	1 588	2 078	1 766
1951	1 006	2 836	1 566	927	2 044	1 745	2 137	2 209	1 359	1 167	1 580	1 443	2 015	1 694
1950	880	2 384	1 330	825	1 852	1 487	1 875	2 132	1 281	1 034	1 386	1 295	1 825	1 512
1949	815	. . .	1 270	800	1 730	1 406	1 660	1 853	1 191	947	1 354	1 249	1 685	1 361
1948	866	. . .	1 274	875	1 752	1 433	1 713	1 720	1 180	968	1 407	1 315	1 815	1 451
1940	278	. . .	502	254	835	544	885	1 023	507	336	. . .	450	754	550
1929	322	. . .	593	306	995	644	994	1 037	525	349	. . .	502	959	615

Series F 297-348. Personal Income by States: 1929 to 1998—Cont'd.

Year	Iowa	Kansas	Kentucky	Louisiana	Maine	Maryland	Massa-chusetts	Michigan	Minnesota	Mississippi	Missouri	Montana	Nebraska	Nevada
	313	314	315	316	317	318	319	320	321	322	323	324	325	326
TOTAL INCOME (millions of dollars)													
1998......	68 500	65 700	84 700	93 300	28 600	153 800	201 600	253 800	130 000	52 200	132 800	17 800	41 200	47 500
1997......	66 000	62 400	80 400	89 100	27 200	146 100	191 000	244 100	123 000	49 400	127 800	17 300	39 100	44 500
1996......	64 300	59 900	76 500	86 200	25 900	138 100	179 400	238 000	119 100	47 500	122 500	16 700	38 100	40 800
1995......	58 000	55 300	71 700	81 500	24 700	131 300	170 200	226 200	109 300	44 600	115 000	15 900	34 400	37 500
1994......	57 300	53 400	68 100	76 200	24 400	124 800	154 800	212 100	102 500	62 300	109 300	15 300	33 200	35 000
1993......	51 600	50 300	64 100	71 300	23 300	118 500	146 900	194 700	94 900	38 900	102 400	14 600	31 700	31 600
1992......	51 400	48 900	62 100	67 400	22 500	112 800	144 300	184 100	89 800	36 800	97 800	13 200	30 600	26 900
1991......	48 900	46 200	57 700	64 400	21 400	107 300	137 300	175 000	84 700	34 600	92 000	13 000	28 400	24 600
1990......	48 100	44 900	55 300	61 200	21 200	105 000	135 800	171 200	82 200	33 000	89 600	12 200	27 600	23 300
1989......	44 000	41 500	51 200	56 600	19 900	98 600	131 100	161 800	76 900	30 700	84 100	11 300	24 900	21 400
1988......	40 500	39 200	47 700	53 900	18 100	90 800	123 100	151 400	71 000	29 000	78 800	10 400	23 400	18 800
1987......	40 300	37 400	44 900	51 200	16 600	82 200	112 100	141 600	67 600	27 000	74 900	10 000	22 800	18 500
1986......	38 000	35 700	42 000	50 500	15 100	75 600	102 900	135 300	63 200	25 400	70 600	9 600	21 700	14 900
1985......	36 200	33 800	40 100	50 700	13 900	70 200	95 000	127 200	59 300	24 200	66 700	9 100	20 800	13 800
1984......	35 200	32 500	38 600	48 400	12 300	61 400	84 500	113 600	55 000	23 000	60 700	8 400	19 700	12 000
1983......	31 100	29 400	34 900	45 500	11 300	56 200	76 500	104 100	49 300	21 100	54 800	8 100	17 800	11 100
1982......	31 300	28 300	32 800	44 700	10 300	52 200	69 900	99 700	46 200	19 800	50 400	7 700	16 900	10 600
1981......	31 300	26 800	31 400	42 000	9 600	49 100	64 900	97 900	43 900	18 800	48 200	7 400	16 300	10 000
1980......	27 300	23 600	27 900	35 600	8 900	44 200	58 200	92 300	39 700	16 600	44 300	6 700	14 700	8 600
1979......	24 900	21 500	25 900	30 000	7 700	38 000	51 000	85 300	35 600	15 000	39 600	5 800	13 100	7 200
1978......	22 800	18 800	23 100	26 300	6 900	34 400	46 600	77 600	31 500	13 800	35 700	5 500	11 600	6 000
1977......	19 800	16 600	20 600	23 200	6 200	31 300	42 000	69 600	28 300	12 000	31 900	4 700	10 500	5 100
1976......	. . .	. . .	. . .	. . .	. . .	. . .	. . .	. . .	. . .	. . .	. . .	. . .	. . .	. . .
1975......	16 900	13 600	16 600	18 300	5 000	26 400	35 300	54 600	22 700	9 500	26 100	4 000	9 100	3 900
1974......	15 100	12 500	14 900	16 500	4 800	24 300	33 400	53 500	21 200	8 800	24 100	3 600	8 100	3 500
1973......	15 300	12 100	13 500	14 800	4 200	22 200	30 600	50 200	20 000	8 200	23 000	3 400	8 100	3 100
1972......	12 400	10 400	11 900	13 100	3 700	19 900	28 200	43 700	16 900	6 900	20 000	2 800	6 600	2 700
1971......	11 100	9 500	10 800	12 000	3 400	18 100	26 300	29 900	15 600	6 300	18 600	2 600	6 100	2 500
1970......	10 609	8 635	10 008	11 180	3 255	16 856	24 731	36 993	14 709	5 753	17 682	2 438	5 653	2 195
1969......	9 907	8 138	9 214	10 364	2 986	15 437	22 926	35 782	13 509	5 262	16 140	2 200	5 297	2 047
1968......	9 132	7 528	8 518	9 887	2 762	14 020	21 049	32 831	12 205	4 848	15 074	2 029	4 653	1 792
1967......	8 509	6 902	7 772	9 052	2 544	12 590	19 286	29 667	11 150	4 425	13 832	1 915	4 413	1 581
1966......	8 315	6 599	7 202	8 247	2 431	11 668	17 715	28 206	10 366	4 122	12 874	1 875	4 242	1 510
1965......	7 559	6 030	6 553	7 412	2 262	10 681	16 421	25 860	9 523	3 743	11 975	1 722	3 851	1 434
1964......	6 643	5 581	5 996	6 799	2 090	9 749	15 392	23 005	8 604	3 420	11 028	1 592	3 481	1 353
1963......	6 347	5 327	5 751	6 298	1 923	8 959	14 514	21 039	8 303	3 289	10 407	1 587	3 340	1 265
1962......	6 001	5 183	5 444	5 908	1 876	8 342	13 878	19 568	7 858	2 976	9 896	1 581	3 274	1 122
1961......	5 742	4 945	5 139	5 589	1 808	7 800	13 220	18 243	7 570	2 819	9 415	1 371	3 046	911
1960......	5 473	4 714	4 807	5 417	1 788	7 285	12 657	18 318	7 227	2 630	9 142	1 383	2 988	829
1959......	5 317	4 484	4 667	5 361	1 686	6 952	12 123	17 588	6 787	2 569	8 936	1 344	2 757	770
1958......	5 200	4 443	4 441	5 105	1 637	6 567	11 438	16 603	6 585	2 349	8 461	1 370	2 713	711
1957......	5 077	4 006	4 291	5 028	1 583	6 314	11 074	16 870	6 135	2 172	8 053	1 297	2 615	673
1956......	4 580	3 804	4 107	4 547	1 534	5 976	10 497	16 529	5 778	2 141	7 844	1 241	2 274	625
1955......	4 307	3 626	3 866	4 114	1 449	5 467	9 891	15 900	5 483	2 102	7 450	1 178	2 191	604
1954......	4 525	3 597	3 692	3 881	1 314	5 069	9 293	14 354	5 202	1 875	6 974	1 079	2 253	519
1953......	4 200	3 434	3 752	3 858	1 298	5 041	9 179	14 741	5 079	1 943	6 948	1 096	2 125	480
1952......	4 338	3 524	3 587	3 636	1 291	4 721	8 675	13 050	4 823	1 907	6 576	1 075	2 187	440
1951......	4 127	3 077	3 361	3 336	1 188	4 318	8 344	12 176	4 660	1 796	6 245	1 049	2 067	378
1950......	3 897	2 765	2 881	3 021	1 087	3 772	7 654	10 895	4 227	1 643	5 672	962	1 978	327
1949......	3 392	2 477	2 659	2 857	1 060	3 392	6 971	9 627	3 846	1 441	5 196	788	1 697	286
1948......	4 042	2 523	2 788	2 679	1 084	3 331	7 012	9 691	4 106	1 639	5 338	876	1 909	283
1940......	1 274	756	908	852	437	1 304	3 367	3 595	1 475	470	1 974	316	573	101
1929......	1 449	1 013	1 026	863	476	1 265	3 855	3 809	1 548	573	2 287	315	827	81

Series F 297-348. Personal Income by States: 1929 to 1998—Cont'd.

Year	Iowa	Kansas	Kentucky	Louisiana	Maine	Maryland	Massa-chusetts	Michigan	Minnesota	Mississippi	Missouri	Montana	Nebraska	Nevada
	313	314	315	316	317	318	319	320	321	322	323	324	325	326
						PER CAPITA INCOME (dollars)								
1998......	23 925	24 981	21 506	21 346	22 952	29 943	32 797	25 857	27 510	18 958	24 427	20 172	24 754	27 200
1997......	23 120	23 972	20 570	20 458	21 937	28 674	31 239	24 956	26 243	18 098	23 629	19 660	23 618	26 514
1996......	22 560	23 281	19 687	19 824	20 826	27 221	29 439	24 810	25 580	17 441	22 864	19 047	23 047	25 451
1995......	20 412	21 481	18 601	18 826	19 995	26 141	28 097	23 407	23 736	16 574	21 540	18 286	21 029	24 541
1994......	20 265	20 896	17 807	17 651	19 663	24 933	25 616	22 333	22 453	15 838	20 717	17 865	20 488	24 023
1993......	18 275	19 849	16 889	16 612	18 780	23 908	24 410	20 584	20 979	14 745	19 557	17 373	19 672	22 894
1992......	18 148	19 210	16 418	15 876	18 137	23 186	23 588	19 707	20 485	14 070	18 949	16 361	19 189	21 972
1991......	17 505	18 511	15 539	15 143	17 306	22 080	22 897	18 679	19 107	13 343	17 842	16 043	17 852	19 175
1990......	17 301	18 104	14 992	14 528	17 183	21 857	22 555	18 378	18 731	12 830	17 479	15 304	17 490	19 049
1989......	15 487	16 498	13 743	12 921	16 248	21 013	22 174	17 444	17 657	11 724	16 292	14 078	15 446	19 269
1988......	14 316	15 688	12 792	12 238	15 045	19 639	20 898	16 391	16 472	11 055	15 331	12 870	14 569	17 849
1987......	13 859	14 962	11 963	11 439	13 985	18 231	19 140	15 473	15 716	10 250	14 582	12 331	13 976	16 381
1986......	13 335	14 503	11 268	11 233	12 846	16 934	17 635	14 807	14 995	9 663	13 946	11 726	13 572	15 453
1985......	12 619	13 812	10 768	11 302	11 903	15 970	16 305	14 001	14 144	9 249	13 250	11 015	12 967	14 693
1984......	12 090	13 319	10 374	10 850	10 678	14 111	14 574	12 518	13 219	8 857	12 129	10 216	12 280	13 216
1983......	10 697	12 102	9 396	10 262	9 861	13 047	13 260	11 476	11 901	8 155	11 029	9 945	11 175	12 441
1982......	10 638	11 743	9 097	10 048	9 278	12 261	12 285	10 748	11 277	7 775	10 469	9 618	10 885	11 902
1981......	10 749	11 237	8 567	9 778	8 494	11 522	11 248	10 620	10 684	7 414	10 911	9 252	10 331	11 816
1980......	9 537	9 941	8 022	8 682	8 218	10 790	10 612	10 165	10 062	6 926	9 298	8 924	9 274	11 421
1979......	8 589	9 055	7 342	7 477	7 057	9 150	8 844	9 269	8 760	6 167	8 132	7 412	8 341	10 204
1978......	7 873	8 001	6 615	6 640	6 333	8 306	8 063	8 442	7 847	5 736	7 342	7 051	7 391	9 032
1977......	6 878	7 134	5 945	5 913	5 734	7 572	7 258	7 619	7 129	5 030	6 654	6 125	6 720	7 988
1976......	. . .	. . .	. . .	. . .	. . .	. . .	. . .	. . .	. . .	. . .	. . .	. . .	. . .	. . .
1975......	5 907	5 955	4 882	4 808	4 762	6 401	6 071	6 008	5 785	4 042	5 475	5 387	5 887	6 636
1974......	5 302	5 406	4 470	4 310	4 439	5 881	5 731	5 928	5 450	3 764	5 056	4 776	4 877	6 073
1973......	5 347	5 338	4 050	3 950	4 040	5 446	5 268	5 540	5 144	3 546	4 831	4 626	5 299	5 712
1972......	4 318	4 593	3 601	3 528	3 571	4 897	4 870	4 817	4 332	3 063	4 206	3 897	4 341	5 215
1971......	3 877	4 192	3 306	3 252	3 375	4 522	4 562	4 430	4 032	2 788	3 940	3 629	4 030	4 822
1970......	3 749	3 841	3 104	3 068	3 272	4 281	4 340	4 156	3 848	2 596	3 768	3 498	3 794	4 452
1969......	3 532	3 639	2 881	2 864	3 010	3 991	4 058	4 075	3 595	2 370	3 478	3 170	3 594	4 264
1968......	3 258	3 397	2 666	2 744	2 779	3 675	3 747	3 775	3 296	2 185	3 300	2 899	3 172	3 862
1967......	3 047	3 141	2 450	2 528	2 534	3 351	3 448	3 438	3 047	1 986	3 047	2 731	3 029	3 521
1966......	3 011	3 000	2 288	2 323	2 433	3 158	3 200	3 314	2 866	1 836	2 846	2 652	2 914	3 385
1965......	2 757	2 733	2 087	2 120	2 269	2 967	2 985	3 094	2 651	1 667	2 681	2 439	2 618	3 229
1964......	2 419	2 527	1 916	1 973	2 105	2 792	2 825	2 810	2 418	1 526	2 483	2 255	2 349	3 177
1963......	2 310	2 403	1 857	1 865	1 937	2 646	2 716	2 611	2 351	1 466	2 370	2 258	2 263	3 185
1962......	2 182	2 323	1 768	1 766	1 887	2 556	2 637	2 467	2 237	1 327	2 271	2 264	2 236	3 188
1961......	2 083	2 232	1 683	1 700	1 817	2 456	2 533	2 311	2 182	1 278	2 165	1 969	2 107	2 893
1960......	1 986	2 159	1 581	1 662	1 834	2 340	2 453	2 338	2 110	1 205	2 113	2 036	2 108	2 848
1959......	1 948	2 076	1 556	1 671	1 772	2 268	2 369	2 264	2 016	1 202	2 099	2 009	1 974	2 760
1958......	1 920	2 074	1 500	1 618	1 734	2 202	2 283	2 165	1 988	1 126	2 021	2 057	1 962	2 645
1957......	1 869	1 882	1 465	1 614	1 679	2 198	2 247	2 229	1 874	1 040	1 922	1 944	1 876	2 588
1956......	1 694	1 795	1 417	1 500	1 635	2 216	2 146	2 214	1 783	1 026	1 884	1 891	1 628	2 502
1955......	1 608	1 732	1 328	1 396	1 552	1 994	2 026	2 183	1 729	1 020	1 802	1 852	1 594	2 549
1954......	1 723	1 762	1 272	1 346	1 417	1 888	1 893	2 031	1 671	908	1 715	1 729	1 681	2 437
1953......	1 598	1 722	1 293	1 346	1 421	1 964	1 910	2 161	1 665	923	1 728	1 779	1 612	2 462
1952......	1 652	1 783	1 229	1 279	1 411	1 888	1 866	1 962	1 592	886	1 656	1 786	1 668	2 429
1951......	1 577	1 578	1 143	1 205	1 297	1 769	1 793	1 874	1 548	830	1 556	1 761	1 571	2 249
1950......	1 485	1 443	981	1 120	1 186	1 602	1 633	1 701	1 410	755	1 431	1 622	1 490	2 018
1949......	1 316	1 287	933	1 084	1 174	1 456	1 470	1 520	1 310	691	1 339	1 385	1 304	1 823
1948......	1 590	1 333	990	1 032	1 235	1 467	1 500	1 560	1 431	790	1 389	1 616	1 509	1 814
1940......	502	423	317	360	515	709	780	676	529	216	521	566	436	890
1929......	589	543	394	414	597	780	912	794	602	287	631	801	602	896

Series F 297-348. Personal Income by States: 1929 to 1998—Cont'd.

Year	New Hampshire	New Jersey	New Mexico	New York	North Carolina	North Dakota	Ohio	Oklahoma	Oregon	Pennsyl-vania	Rhode Island	South Carolina	South Dakota	Tennessee
	327	328	329	330	331	332	333	334	335	336	337	338	339	340
						TOTAL INCOME (millions of dollars)								
1998......	34 400	275 400	34 600	576 800	181 400	13 800	281 700	70 500	81 300	321 500	26 500	81 700	16 300	127 900
1997......	32 500	260 700	33 300	548 900	172 200	12 900	270 500	67 400	77 600	308 300	25 300	77 700	15 500	121 900
1996......	30 800	248 100	32 200	523 400	161 200	13 300	263 000	63 900	72 600	297 400	24 500	73 100	15 800	115 800
1995......	29 000	235 400	30 400	500 600	150 900	11 600	247 400	60 700	67 900	280 100	23 300	69 500	13 800	110 500
1994......	26 000	221 600	28 300	472 400	139 100	11 800	232 300	57 800	63 000	269 100	22 200	64 800	14 100	100 800
1993......	25 100	211 200	26 400	450 600	129 800	10 900	217 900	55 000	59 000	256 000	21 200	61 200	12 800	93 900
1992......	25 500	206 100	24 300	426 400	120 900	10 700	205 200	52 000	54 200	243 200	20 400	57 600	11 800	87 100
1991......	23 100	196 900	23 000	405 500	112 100	10 200	196 000	50 200	51 400	228 800	18 900	54 900	11 500	80 900
1990......	23 100	192 500	21 700	398 400	108 200	9 800	190 800	48 600	49 200	222 100	18 900	53 000	11 100	77 500
1989......	22 400	183 900	20 100	378 300	99 900	9 000	178 600	45 600	44 900	207 900	17 900	47 900	9 800	72 600
1988......	21 100	171 800	18 700	352 100	92 400	8 200	167 600	43 000	41 000	193 600	16 800	44 700	9 000	68 100
1987......	18 500	156 100	17 800	320 900	85 400	8 700	157 600	41 100	38 200	181 600	15 300	41 100	8 900	62 500
1986......	16 800	143 300	16 900	299 300	78 700	8 400	148 900	40 500	35 800	169 900	14 200	38 200	8 400	57 500
1985......	15 300	133 300	16 200	280 300	73 000	8 200	142 000	40 200	34 000	160 800	13 300	35 800	7 800	53 600
1984......	12 800	114 800	14 700	250 400	66 300	8 600	132 400	38 700	31 000	146 900	12 200	33 200	7 800	49 100
1983......	11 600	104 500	13 500	229 900	59 600	7 900	125 000	36 200	28 700	136 400	11 200	29 900	6 900	44 600
1982......	10 200	97 600	12 500	217 200	54 400	7 300	115 100	36 100	27 400	130 000	10 300	27 200	6 700	41 400
1981......	9 400	90 800	11 600	201 900	51 500	7 200	110 900	32 900	26 700	123 800	9 700	25 800	6 400	39 400
1980......	8 400	80 700	10 200	180 600	46 000	5 700	102 400	27 600	24 600	112 200	9 000	22 700	5 400	35 500
1979......	7 300	71 100	9 100	160 600	41 300	5 100	94 200	23 800	22 300	100 400	7 700	20 600	5 100	32 000
1978......	6 300	64 600	7 900	146 700	36 800	4 900	84 000	20 000	19 200	90 900	7 000	18 200	4 700	28 300
1977......	5 500	58 600	7 000	135 100	32 800	4 000	75 800	17 800	16 700	82 600	6 300	16 200	4 100	24 900
1976......	...	...	...	...	...	...	...	...	...	...	...	...	...	...
1975......	4 400	49 800	5 500	117 800	26 900	3 800	62 000	14 300	13 200	69 300	5 300	13 100	3 400	20 000
1974......	4 000	45 800	4 600	111 500	24 800	3 600	59 200	12 400	12 000	64 500	5 000	12 000	3 200	18 800
1973......	3 700	43 000	4 300	104 200	22 600	3 600	54 500	11 600	10 800	59 400	4 700	10 600	3 300	16 900
1972......	3 200	37 800	3 900	97 700	19 400	2 400	48 700	10 000	9 400	53 000	4 300	9 200	2 500	14 700
1971......	2 900	35 100	3 400	91 700	17 700	2 200	44 800	9 100	8 500	49 300	4 000	8 300	2 300	13 200
1970......	2 779	33 347	3 173	86 070	16 383	1 928	42 665	8 617	7 765	46 593	3 748	7 691	2 080	12 118
1969......	2 475	30 423	2 908	80 923	15 036	1 867	40 424	7 827	7 276	43 301	3 453	6 985	1 995	11 231
1968......	2 286	27 987	2 656	75 041	13 566	1 656	37 098	7 224	6 631	39 938	3 270	6 353	1 886	10 214
1967......	2 079	25 638	2 463	68 657	12 288	1 596	33 788	6 675	6 096	37 062	2 988	5 728	1 731	9 280
1966......	1 905	23 862	2 380	63 717	11 341	1 568	32 201	6 154	5 760	34 783	2 740	5 303	1 681	8 663
1965......	1 728	22 105	2 269	59 487	10 092	1 505	29 383	5 668	5 333	31 943	2 504	4 702	1 528	7 850
1964......	1 601	20 515	2 115	55 987	9 292	1 288	26 878	5 231	4 892	29 936	2 346	4 253	1 320	7 138
1963......	1 510	19 372	2 031	52 559	8 606	1 292	25 189	4 889	4 553	27 876	2 193	3 928	1 350	6 640
1962......	1 442	18 430	1 969	50 535	8 154	1 370	24 208	4 698	4 287	26 918	2 110	3 733	1 407	6 255
1961......	1 356	17 333	1 871	47 821	7 596	964	23 008	4 561	4 046	25 747	1 964	3 450	1 227	5 881
1960......	1 300	16 526	1 799	46 178	7 123	1 087	22 762	4 358	3 939	25 451	1 895	3 283	1 218	5 521
1959......	1 237	15 849	1 759	44 301	6 712	949	22 035	4 137	3 804	24 719	1 844	3 119	981	5 394
1958......	1 132	14 823	1 618	41 715	6 263	1 030	20 637	4 000	3 556	23 594	1 748	2 885	1 094	5 025
1957......	1 102	14 550	1 442	40 818	5 980	905	20 959	3 744	3 416	23 414	1 701	2 810	1 068	4 872
1956......	1 035	13 719	1 284	38 608	5 935	881	19 992	3 591	3 422	22 295	1 674	2 697	914	4 671
1955......	983	12 688	1 181	36 453	5 571	848	18 762	3 390	3 198	20 669	1 614	2 599	857	4 374
1954......	915	11 957	1 077	34 275	5 120	766	17 397	3 193	2 961	19 515	1 523	2 434	916	4 105
1953......	884	11 750	1 048	33 206	5 040	757	17 423	3 201	2 990	19 938	1 531	2 615	892	4 080
1952......	833	10 934	1 004	31 396	4 851	740	15 942	3 087	2 966	18 617	1 446	2 527	828	3 810
1951......	792	10 151	936	30 009	4 691	794	14 894	2 837	2 784	17 752	1 384	2 321	942	3 645
1950......	704	8 934	811	27 841	4 219	782	12 930	2 547	2 482	16 189	1 262	1 886	814	3 295
1949......	671	8 131	719	26 046	3 675	674	11 749	2 460	2 251	14 553	1 151	1 724	689	3 001
1948......	668	8 063	655	26 051	3 732	813	12 269	2 390	2 278	14 716	1 175	1 779	916	3 037
1940......	281	3 406	198	11 724	1 155	218	4 575	851	671	6 408	531	572	231	982
1929......	320	3 705	160	14 171	1 044	246	5 179	1 076	652	7 546	596	467	288	976

Series F 297-348. Personal Income by States: 1929 to 1998—Cont'd.

Year	New Hampshire	New Jersey	New Mexico	New York	North Carolina	North Dakota	Ohio	Oklahoma	Oregon	Pennsyl-vania	Rhode Island	South Carolina	South Dakota	Tennessee
	327	**328**	**329**	**330**	**331**	**332**	**333**	**334**	**335**	**336**	**337**	**338**	**339**	**340**
							PER CAPITA INCOME (dollars)							
1998......	29 022	33 937	19 936	31 734	24 036	21 675	25 134	21 072	24 766	26 792	26 797	21 309	22 114	23 559
1997......	27 766	32 356	19 298	30 250	23 168	20 103	21 463	20 305	23 920	25 670	25 667	20 508	21 076	22 699
1996......	26 520	31 053	18 770	28 782	22 010	20 710	23 537	19 350	22 668	24 668	24 765	19 755	21 516	21 764
1995......	25 313	29 568	18 029	27 587	20 996	18 149	22 217	18 544	21 618	23 268	23 520	18 789	18 724	21 109
1994......	23 434	28 038	17 106	25 999	19 669	18 546	20 928	17 744	20 419	22 324	22 251	17 695	19 577	19 482
1993......	22 357	26 876	16 346	24 824	18 670	17 072	19 696	17 026	19 437	21 281	21 244	16 861	17 879	18 439
1992......	21 840	26 111	15 538	24 128	17 831	17 098	18 945	16 460	18 667	20 610	20 206	16 200	17 280	17 647
1991......	20 951	25 372	14 844	22 456	16 642	16 088	17 916	15 827	17 592	19 128	18 840	15 420	16 392	16 325
1990......	20 773	24 881	14 254	22 129	16 266	15 355	17 568	15 451	17 182	18 679	18 809	15 141	15 890	15 868
1989......	20 267	23 778	13 140	21 073	15 198	13 563	16 373	14 154	15 919	17 269	17 950	13 634	13 685	14 694
1988......	19 410	22 265	12 401	19 663	14 243	12 342	15 427	13 306	14 811	16 135	16 870	12 907	12 599	13 895
1987......	18 032	20 303	11 872	17 906	13 284	12 641	14 529	12 481	13 850	15 103	15 644	12 070	12 370	12 913
1986......	16 396	18 793	11 459	16 821	12 423	12 440	13 857	12 249	13 239	14 281	14 589	11 286	11 803	11 984
1985......	15 367	17 618	11 197	15 773	11 662	11 951	13 176	12 139	12 628	13 554	13 779	10 729	11 029	11 252
1984......	13 148	15 282	10 330	14 121	10 758	12 461	12 314	11 745	11 582	12 343	12 730	10 075	11 049	10 400
1983......	12 109	14 000	9 656	13 014	9 805	11 664	11 218	10 988	10 768	11 468	11 694	9 168	9 851	9 515
1982......	11 189	13 089	9 301	12 222	9 148	10 877	10 664	11 084	10 168	10 939	10 937	8 605	9 366	9 013
1981......	10 051	12 230	8 707	11 473	8 648	10 911	10 274	10 606	10 017	10 423	10 129	8 128	9 245	8 516
1980......	9 788	11 573	8 169	10 721	7 999	8 538	9 723	9 393	9 866	9 891	9 518	7 589	8 217	8 030
1979......	8 231	9 702	7 294	9 098	7 359	7 774	8 775	8 226	8 842	8 559	8 266	7 027	7 334	7 299
1978......	7 277	8 818	6 505	8 267	6 607	7 478	7 812	6 951	7 839	7 733	7 526	6 242	6 841	6 489
1977......	6 536	7 994	5 857	7 537	5 935	6 190	7 084	6 346	7 007	7 011	6 775	5 628	5 957	5 785
1976......	. . .	. . .	. . .	. . .	. . .	. . .	. . .	. . .	. . .	. . .	. . .	. . .	. . .	. . .
1975......	5 431	6 786	4 836	6 523	4 943	5 896	5 771	5 233	5 764	5 832	5 705	4 665	4 995	4 823
1974......	5 143	6 384	4 137	6 244	4 612	5 547	5 549	4 566	5 270	5 490	5 376	4 258	4 218	4 484
1973......	4 615	5 874	3 877	5 720	4 258	5 730	5 070	4 331	4 845	5 010	4 869	3 885	4 771	4 124
1972......	4 092	5 126	3 656	5 319	3 721	3 718	4 512	3 802	4 296	4 447	4 399	3 448	3 716	3 640
1971......	3 796	4 811	3 298	5 000	3 424	3 538	4 175	3 515	3 959	4 147	4 126	3 142	3 441	3 300
1970......	3 745	4 635	3 117	4 714	3 218	3 120	3 992	3 350	3 694	3 943	3 941	2 963	3 124	3 082
1969......	3 418	4 288	2 877	4 470	2 989	3 006	3 827	3 088	3 528	3 688	3 705	2 718	2 987	2 882
1968......	3 224	3 995	2 672	4 157	2 711	2 667	3 528	2 886	3 309	3 402	3 546	2 483	2 819	2 634
1967......	2 982	3 701	2 463	3 828	2 481	2 549	3 245	2 682	3 081	3 173	3 287	2 261	2 580	2 405
1966......	2 797	3 483	2 364	3 571	2 316	2 424	3 117	2 508	2 925	2 982	3 048	2 104	2 461	2 267
1965......	2 556	3 267	2 242	3 354	2 075	2 319	2 880	2 323	2 753	2 749	2 804	1 885	2 208	2 067
1964......	2 414	3 089	2 102	3 183	1 935	1 985	2 666	2 138	2 591	2 599	2 650	1 719	1 883	1 893
1963......	2 326	2 966	2 053	3 010	1 815	2 006	2 522	2 004	2 457	2 440	2 504	1 597	1 906	1 786
1962......	2 282	2 890	2 011	2 921	1 732	2 151	2 438	1 936	2 358	2 371	2 422	1 541	1 996	1 703
1961......	2 193	2 767	1 939	2 803	1 629	1 504	2 335	1 917	2 264	2 260	2 289	1 432	1 770	1 624
1960......	2 135	2 708	1 886	2 742	1 558	1 714	2 338	1 865	2 223	2 247	2 216	1 372	1 783	1 544
1959......	2 076	2 635	1 914	2 655	1 506	1 536	2 278	1 807	2 179	2 200	2 152	1 329	1 471	1 532
1958......	1 948	2 517	1 826	2 513	1 431	1 699	2 150	1 764	2 070	2 134	2 038	1 252	1 668	1 448
1957......	1 927	2 536	1 702	2 493	1 369	1 479	2 227	1 641	1 996	2 137	1 998	1 236	1 603	1 419
1956......	1 829	2 443	1 593	2 396	1 377	1 437	2 171	1 580	2 016	2 032	1 993	1 210	1 365	1 368
1955......	1 765	2 306	1 504	2 283	1 313	1 378	2 081	1 507	1 927	1 889	1 962	1 181	1 293	1 281
1954......	1 651	2 231	1 412	2 167	1 239	1 254	1 961	1 445	1 821	1 804	1 866	1 119	1 398	1 222
1953......	1 616	2 247	1 386	2 139	1 223	1 244	2 028	1 467	1 867	1 870	1 878	1 199	1 376	1 229
1952......	1 557	2 134	1 367	2 067	1 181	1 217	1 926	1 391	1 875	1 773	1 804	1 160	1 282	1 137
1951......	1 497	2 028	1 306	2 015	1 139	1 314	1 848	1 284	1 789	1 697	1 765	1 071	1 438	1 081
1950......	1 323	1 834	1 177	1 873	1 037	1 263	1 620	1 143	1 620	1 541	1 605	893	1 242	994
1949......	1 259	1 663	1 117	1 749	940	1 130	1 474	1 169	1 573	1 401	1 437	850	1 091	927
1948......	1 284	1 689	1 084	1 797	973	1 401	1 558	1 144	1 621	1 431	1 493	891	1 497	944
1940......	571	816	373	871	323	340	660	366	618	648	739	301	360	334
1929......	685	929	381	1 164	333	365	782	454	689	776	871	269	417	375

Series F 297-348. Personal Income by States: 1929 to 1998—Cont'd.

Year	Texas	Utah	Vermont	Virginia	Washington	West Virginia	Wisconsin	Wyoming
	341	342	343	344	345	346	347	348
TOTAL INCOME (millions of dollars)								
1998	493 100	44 100	14 300	196 000	159 100	35 100	131 000	11 100
1997	459 600	41 700	13 500	175 900	148 500	34 000	125 100	10 800
1996	421 700	38 300	13 000	166 400	137 400	33 700	120 100	10 200
1995	398 600	36 000	12 400	158 100	128 600	31 800	112 800	9 900
1994	364 900	32 500	11 700	140 800	120 800	31 400	106 800	9 700
1993	345 000	30 000	11 200	140 200	114 500	29 400	99 900	9 300
1992	315 900	27 800	10 700	131 600	104 800	27 300	93 800	8 100
1991	300 200	25 700	10 100	125 600	97 600	25 500	89 400	7 900
1990	285 100	24 200	9 900	122 400	92 200	24 600	86 300	7 400
1989	266 800	22 300	9 300	115 400	84 000	22 900	80 100	6 900
1988	248 300	20 700	8 500	106 500	76 100	21 700	74 300	6 600
1987	232 800	19 100	7 800	97 500	70 800	20 900	. . .	. . .
1986	225 200	18 300	7 200	89 400	66 300	20 300	. . .	. . .
1985	220 700	17 500	6 600	82 500	62 000	19 500	62 900	6 500
1984	202 000	16 100	5 700	73 600	55 400	19 200	58 700	6 400
1983	183 800	14 600	5 200	67 900	52 300	18 000	53 700	6 100
1982	174 500	13 800	4 900	60 600	49 100	17 100	51 000	6 200
1981	161 300	12 900	4 600	56 700	47 100	16 200	48 800	6 000
1980	136 100	11 200	4 000	50 300	42 700	15 200	44 100	5 200
1979	115 700	9 800	3 600	44 700	37 000	14 000	39 700	4 300
1978	100 200	8 700	3 200	39 200	31 900	12 000	35 500	3 900
1977	87 300	7 500	2 800	35 200	27 500	11 100	32 000	3 100
1976	. . .	. . .	. . .	. . .	. . .	. . .	. . .	. . .
1975	68 300	5 900	2 300	28 700	22 400	8 900	25 500	2 300
1974	59 700	5 200	2 100	26 200	19 900	7 800	24 000	1 900
1973	53 900	4 700	1 900	23 600	17 700	7 100	21 700	1 700
1972	47 100	4 200	1 800	20 300	15 400	6 400	19 000	1 500
1971	42 600	3 800	1 700	18 400	14 200	5 800	17 500	1 300
1970	40 240	3 451	1 480	17 000	13 730	5 320	16 818	1 268
1969	36 678	3 116	1 426	15 461	13 118	4 780	15 299	1 112
1968	33 309	2 892	1 305	14 123	12 067	4 487	14 208	997
1967	30 019	2 672	1 178	12 741	10 890	4 251	13 094	932
1966	27 676	2 517	1 089	11 684	9 876	3 994	12 442	893
1965	24 956	2 356	956	10 718	8 627	3 728	11 345	854
1964	23 116	2 220	856	9 905	8 058	3 492	10 449	825
1963	21 646	2 156	798	8 983	7 736	3 266	9 665	813
1962	20 576	2 071	777	8 443	7 599	3 124	9 396	795
1961	19 615	1 910	731	7 777	7 051	3 031	8 885	776
1960	18 588	1 774	715	7 340	6 680	2 987	8 619	750
1959	18 047	1 678	672	6 995	6 514	2 968	8 376	717
1958	17 175	549	626	6 591	6 114	2 887	7 755	677
1957	16 538	1 482	619	6 349	5 912	2 967	7 547	645
1956	15 472	1 381	598	6 084	5 583	2 768	7 211	605
1955	14 438	1 272	549	5 638	5 306	2 492	6 682	570
1954	13 504	1 165	526	5 338	5 035	2 347	6 212	533
1953	13 196	1 166	521	5 292	4 934	2 473	6 265	549
1952	12 837	1 116	496	5 150	4 697	2 462	6 093	547
1951	11 914	1 053	482	4 763	4 414	2 365	5 837	556
1950	10 486	911	425	4 070	3 995	2 146	6 078	484
1949	9 839	835	396	3 648	3 600	1 994	4 633	445
1948	9 142	810	407	6 624	3 608	2 126	4 701	429
1940	2 762	266	183	1 245	1 140	767	1 734	151
1929	2 764	283	224	1 053	1 165	790	2 007	152

Series F 297-348. Personal Income by States: 1929 to 1998—Cont'd.

Year	Texas	Utah	Vermont	Virginia	Washington	West Virginia	Wisconsin	Wyoming
	341	**342**	**343**	**344**	**345**	**346**	**347**	**348**
			PER CAPITA INCOME (dollars)					
1998	24 957	21 019	24 175	27 385	27 961	19 362	25 079	23 167
1997	23 707	20 185	23 017	26 109	26 451	18 724	24 048	22 596
1996	22 045	19 156	22 124	24 925	24 838	18 444	23 269	21 245
1995	21 320	18 054	21 246	23 943	23 677	17 441	21 960	20 685
1994	19 857	17 043	20 224	22 594	22 610	17 208	21 019	20 436
1993	19 145	16 136	19 437	21 653	21 774	16 169	19 806	19 719
1992	18 460	15 501	18 809	20 934	21 233	15 554	19 103	18 896
1991	17 305	14 529	17 747	19 976	19 442	14 174	18 046	17 118
1990	16 717	13 985	17 506	19 701	18 777	13 744	17 590	16 283
1989	15 702	13 079	16 371	18 927	17 647	12 345	16 449	14 508
1988	14 753	12 225	15 268	17 712	16 364	11 578	15 378	13 720
1987	13 734	11 532	14 256	16 531	15 535	10 959	14 652	12 819
1986	13 494	10 968	13 320	15 423	14 866	10 587	13 923	12 723
1985	13 476	10 653	12 376	14 468	14 076	10 073	13 234	12 834
1984	12 636	9 719	10 692	13 067	12 728	9 846	12 309	12 586
1983	11 686	9 005	9 957	12 122	12 162	9 160	11 311	11 920
1982	11 378	8 714	9 516	11 386	11 682	8 970	10 777	12 157
1981	10 954	8 478	8 877	10 450	11 163	8 336	10 227	12 217
1980	9 798	7 952	8 577	9 827	10 725	7 915	9 845	11 339
1979	8 649	7 185	7 280	8 605	9 435	7 470	8 419	9 657
1978	7 697	6 622	6 541	7 624	8 450	6 456	9 597	9 096
1977	6 803	5 923	5 823	6 865	7 528	5 986	6 890	7 562
1976	. . .	. . .	. . .	. . .	. . .	. . .	. . .	. . .
1975	5 583	4 903	4 923	5 770	6 300	4 968	5 616	6 127
1974	4 790	4 452	4 588	5 265	5 651	4 390	5 210	5 156
1973	4 558	4 096	4 185	4 868	5 151	3 974	4 781	4 696
1972	4 045	3 745	3 865	4 258	4 476	3 574	4 207	4 345
1971	3 726	3 442	3 638	3 899	4 132	3 275	3 912	3 929
1970	3 576	3 228	3 311	3 653	4 022	3 047	3 794	3 796
1969	3 321	2 976	3 262	3 351	3 924	2 738	3 495	3 380
1968	3 079	2 810	3 035	3 098	3 690	2 545	3 270	3 077
1967	2 832	2 622	2 785	2 826	3 431	2 403	3 043	2 895
1966	2 638	2 495	2 638	2 622	3 231	2 250	2 911	2 765
1965	2 405	2 377	2 365	2 430	2 908	2 087	2 681	2 571
1964	2 251	2 270	2 146	2 273	2 721	1 943	2 509	2 435
1963	2 131	2 213	2 010	2 101	2 618	1 819	2 350	2 419
1962	2 047	2 162	1 976	2 020	2 583	1 727	2 321	2 386
1961	1 997	2 041	1 875	1 899	2 447	1 658	2 216	2 304
1960	1 931	1 971	1 839	1 842	2 340	1 612	2 175	2 267
1959	1 919	1 929	1 736	1 770	2 309	1 600	2 153	2 239
1958	1 856	1 833	1 648	1 684	2 205	1 565	2 018	2 148
1957	1 823	1 794	1 647	1 652	2 170	1 610	1 991	2 054
1956	1 752	1 707	1 586	1 634	2 092	1 491	1 927	1 938
1955	1 667	1 625	1 463	1 571	2 038	1 326	1 816	1 857
1954	1 611	1 554	1 395	1 501	2 001	1 232	1 722	1 818
1953	1 583	1 578	1 374	1 488	2 001	1 282	1 787	1 892
1952	1 544	1 542	1 324	1 470	1 919	1 258	1 757	1 866
1951	1 469	1 491	1 275	1 387	1 821	1 192	1 697	1 911
1950	1 349	1 309	1 121	1 228	1 674	1 065	1 477	1 668
1949	1 291	1 244	1 074	1 108	1 569	1 033	1 366	1 605
1948	1 199	1 241	1 133	1 130	1 600	1 120	1 418	1 595
1940	430	482	505	458	655	402	552	606
1929	480	558	625	434	749	460	684	683

Series F 552-565. Sources and Uses of Savings: 1929 to 1999

(In billions of dollars)

Year	Gross saving						Gross investment			Statistical discrepancy	Gross saving as a percentage of Gross National Product
	Total	Personal saving	Undis- tributed corporate	Capita con- sumption	Government saving		Private domestic	Govern- ment	Net foreign		
					Federal	State and local					
	552	553	556	558	559	560	561	562	563	564	565
1999	1 717.6	147.6	229.4	961.4	217.3	156.8	1 650.1	308.7	-313.2	-71.9	18.5
1998	1 654.4	265.4	218.9	889.4	137.4	141.2	1 549.9	278.8	-199.1	-24.8	18.8
1997	1 502.3	252.9	261.3	832.4	33.4	125.1	1 390.5	264.6	-123.1	29.7	18
1996	1 349.3	272.1	232.7	782	-51.5	110.4	1 242.7	250.1	-110.7	32.8	17.2
1995	1 257.5	302.4	203.6	743.6	-108	99.4	1 143.8	238.2	-98	26.5	16.9
1994	1 155.9	315.5	151.6	714.6	-130.9	87.5	1 097.1	225.6	-108.3	58.5	16.3
1993	1 039.4	350.8	142	660.1	-195.4	75.4	955.1	220.9	-72.9	63.8	15.6
1992	1 007.4	413.7	124.4	642.2	-222.2	65	866.6	223.1	-38.7	43.7	15.9
1991	1 015.8	371.7	119.2	608	-142.3	59.1	800.2	220.3	14.9	19.6	16.9
1990	977.7	334.3	102.4	579.5	-104.3	65.7	861.7	215.8	-69.2	30.6	16.8
1989	967.6	301.8	99.2	554	-65.6	78.1	872.9	197.7	-86.7	16.3	17.6
1988	936.2	292.3	138.3	512.4	-77.2	70.5	821.1	186.2	-113.2	-42.2	18.3
1987	810.4	252.8	107.3	478.2	-91.6	63.7	781.5	184.3	-152	3.3	17
1986	735.9	267.8	88	450.8	-139.2	68.7	747.2	173.2	-140.6	43.9	16.5
1985	772.5	282.6	128.3	422.6	-127.9	67	736.3	158.8	-110.9	11.7	18.2
1984	769.4	306.5	124.7	393.6	-121.6	66.2	735.5	139.4	-87	18.6	19.4
1983	608	227.8	93.2	372.7	-131.5	45.7	564.2	122.8	-32	47	17
1982	625.7	262.2	61.9	357.4	-93.1	37.2	516.1	112.3	-0.2	2.5	19
1981	656.5	243.7	64.1	323.8	-18.9	43.8	570.8	106.9	6.3	27.5	20.7
1980	555.5	205.6	49.6	282.6	-22.8	40.6	477.9	100.3	11.4	33.9	19.6
1979	544.9	165.8	77	244.9	16.6	40.5	490.6	88.5	1.4	35.7	21
1978	481.6	145.4	82.9	210.7	-0.6	43.1	436	77.1	-10.4	21	20.8
1977	398.2	125.6	73.1	184.4	-20.6	35.7	361.3	67.5	-9	21.6	19.4
1976	342.7	122.1	57.3	164.5	-29.9	28.6	292	66.4	8.9	24.5	18.6
1975	298.4	125.2	49.1	149.2	-47.7	22.7	230.2	64.5	21.4	17.7	18.1
1974	304	114.3	29.5	126.9	6.4	27	249.4	57.4	7.1	10	20
1973	294.6	102.5	44.8	109.1	8.3	30	244.5	49.4	8.7	8	21.1
1972	241.6	76.9	41.1	99.4	-3.8	28.4	207.6	46.3	-3.6	8.7	19.3
1971	211.4	80.1	32.4	89.8	-9.5	18.2	178.2	44	0.6	11.3	18.6
1970	194.3	69.5	23	81.9	2.3	17.6	152.4	44.8	4	6.9	18.6
1969	199.8	52.6	29.8	74.6	25.5	17.3	156.4	44.4	1.8	2.9	20.1
1968	183.3	52.7	33.6	67.5	13.8	15.8	141.2	44.7	1.7	4.3	20
1967	171.1	54	35.4	61.4	5.8	14.5	128.6	43.8	3.5	4.8	20.4
1966	169.1	44.5	37.6	56.3	16.1	14.6	131.3	40.4	3.9	6.4	21.3
1965	158.1	42.7	34.9	51.8	16	12.7	118.2	35.6	6.2	1.9	21.8
1964	143	40.5	28.6	48.4	13.4	12.1	102.1	34.6	7.5	1.2	21.4
1963	132.8	33.1	25.2	45.9	17.5	11	93.8	33.6	5	-0.4	21.3
1962	124.6	33.5	22.6	44.3	14	10.2	88.1	33.3	3.9	0.7	21.1
1961	113.9	31.9	16.8	42.8	13.5	9	78.2	31.3	4.3	-0.2	20.7
1960	110.9	26.4	16.3	41.8	17.8	8.7	78.9	28.3	3.2	-0.6	20.9
1959	105.8	26.5	17.5	40.2	13.6	8	78.5	29.3	-1.2	0.8	20.7
1958	90.1	28.2	11.9	38.8	4.5	6.8	64.5	26.5	0.9	1.7	19.1
1957	99	26.8	13.8	37.3	13.1	8	70.5	24.4	4.8	0.6	21.3
1956	98.6	25.4	14.1	34.4	16.8	7.9	72	22.9	2.8	-0.9	22.4
1955	87.4	19.5	16	31	14.4	6.5	69	21	0.4	3.1	20.9
1954	72.7	19.8	11	29.3	6.6	6.1	53.8	22.5	0.2	3.9	19
1953	74.6	21.3	9.5	28	9.5	6.3	56.4	24	-1.3	4.6	19.5
1952	73.8	20.6	10.4	26.6	10.6	5.7	54	22.3	0.6	3.1	20.5
1951	74.8	19.7	9.3	24.9	15.8	5.1	60.2	17.6	0.9	3.9	21.9
1950	60.3	15.2	8.6	21.7	11.4	3.4	54.1	9.8	-1.8	1.7	20.4
1949	45.6	10	11.1	20.1	1	3.5	36.9	9.7	0.9	1.8	17
1948	58.3	14.1	11.4	18.3	11.2	3.3	48.1	7	2.4	-0.7	21.5
1947	46.8	8.1	5.9	15.6	14.1	3.2	35	4.6	9.3	2.1	19
1946	38.9	16.3	2.7	12.7	4.3	3	31.1	3.5	4.9	0.7	17.4
1945	29.6	31.4	4.8	10.7	-20.2	2.9	10.8	24.1	-1.3	4	13.3

See footnotes at end of chart.

Series F 552-565. Sources and Uses of Savings: 1929 to 1999—Cont'd.

(In billions of dollars)

Year	Gross saving						Gross investment			Statistical discrepancy	Gross saving as a percentage of Gross National Product
	Total	Personal saving	Undis- tributed corporate	Capita con- sumption	Government saving		Private domestic	Govern- ment	Net foreign		
					Federal	State and local					
	552	553	556	558	559	560	561	562	563	564	565
1944	39.8	39	7	10.4	-19.4	3	7.8	36.6	-2	2.6	18.1
1943	44.8	34.9	6	10.2	-9.3	2.9	6.1	39.1	-2.1	-1.7	22.5
1942	39.8	29	4.4	10.2	-6.6	2.9	10.4	28.5	-0.1	-0.9	24.5
1941	29.7	11.7	2.9	9	3	3.1	18.1	10.8	1.3	0.5	23.4
1940	18.3	4.5	2.6	8	0.1	3	13.6	4.4	1.5	1.2	18
1939	13.5	3.4	1	7.7	-1.7	3	9.3	4.5	1	1.4	14.5
1938	11.6	1.5	0.4	7.8	-0.9	2.9	7.1	4.2	1.2	0.8	13.5
1937	16.1	4.5	0.6	7.5	0.6	3	12.2	3.8	0.2	0.1	17.4
1936	11.3	4.3	0	6.8	-2.9	3.2	8.6	4.1	-0.1	1.3	13.5
1935	9.5	2.6	0	6.6	-1.6	1.9	6.7	2.8	-0.1	-0.1	12.9
1934	6.2	0.6	-1	6.6	-1.9	2	3.7	2.7	0.4	0.5	9.4
1933	3.1	-0.7	-2.9	6.3	-0.7	1.1	1.7	1.9	0.2	0.7	5.5
1932	3.1	-0.4	-3.3	6.7	-1.2	1.3	1.3	2.1	0.2	0.5	5.3
1931	8.2	2.6	-1.8	7.7	-1.9	1.7	5.9	3	0.2	0.9	10.7
1930	14.9	3.2	1	8.3	0.4	2.1	10.8	3.2	0.7	-0.3	16.2
1929	19.2	3.9	3.4	8.4	1.3	2.2	16.5	2.8	0.8	0.9	18.4

SOURCE: U.S. Bureau of Economic Analysis, National Income and Product Accounts of the United States.

Series FF-1. Persons Below Poverty Level and Below 125 Percent of Poverty Level: 1960 to 1997

(Persons as of March of the following year. Based on Current Population Survey)

Year	Number below poverty level (1 000)					Percent below poverty level					Below 125 percent of poverty level	
	All races [1]	White	Black	Asian and Pacific Islander	Hispanic [2]	All races [1]	White	Black	Asian and Pacific Islander	Hispanic [2]	Number (1 000)	Percent of total population
1960	39 851	28 309	. . .	. . .	. . .	22.2	17.8	. . .	. . .	. . .	54 560	30.4
1970	25 420	17 484	7 548	. . .	. . .	12.6	9.9	33.5	. . .	. . .	35 624	17.6
1975	25 877	17 770	7 545	. . .	2 991	12.3	9.7	31.3	. . .	26.9	37 182	17.6
1976	24 975	16 713	7 595	. . .	2 783	11.8	9.1	31.1	. . .	24.7	35 509	16.7
1977	24 720	16 416	7 726	. . .	2 700	11.6	8.9	31.3	. . .	22.4	35 659	16.7
1978	24 497	16 259	7 625	. . .	2 607	11.4	8.7	30.6	. . .	21.6	34 155	15.8
1979	26 072	17 214	8 050	. . .	2 921	11.7	9.0	31.0	. . .	21.8	36 616	16.4
1980	29 272	19 699	8 579	. . .	3 491	13.0	10.2	32.5	. . .	25.7	40 658	18.1
1981	31 822	21 553	9 173	. . .	3 713	14.0	11.1	34.2	. . .	26.5	43 748	19.3
1982	34 398	23 517	9 697	. . .	4 301	15.0	12.0	35.6	. . .	29.9	46 520	20.3
1983	35 303	23 984	9 882	. . .	4 633	15.2	12.1	35.7	. . .	28.0	47 150	20.3
1984	33 700	22 955	9 490	. . .	4 806	14.4	11.5	33.8	. . .	28.4	45 288	19.4
1985	33 064	22 860	8 926	. . .	5 236	14.0	11.4	31.3	. . .	29.0	44 166	18.7
1986	32 370	22 183	8 983	. . .	5 117	13.6	11.0	31.1	. . .	27.3	43 486	18.2
1987	32 221	21 195	9 520	1 021	5 422	13.4	10.4	32.4	16.1	28.0	43 032	17.9
1988	31 745	20 715	9 356	1 117	5 357	13.0	10.1	31.3	17.3	26.7	42 551	17.5
1989	31 528	20 785	9 302	939	5 430	12.8	10.0	30.7	14.1	26.2	42 653	17.3
1990	33 585	22 326	9 837	858	6 006	13.5	10.7	31.9	12.2	28.1	44 837	18.0
1991	35 708	23 747	10 242	996	6 339	14.2	11.3	32.7	13.8	28.7	47 527	18.9
1992	38 014	25 259	10 827	985	7 592	14.8	11.9	33.4	12.7	29.6	50 592	19.7
1993	39 265	26 226	10 877	1 134	8 126	15.1	12.2	33.1	15.3	30.6	51 801	20.0
1994	38 059	25 379	10 196	974	8 416	14.5	11.7	30.6	14.6	30.7	50 401	19.3
1995	36 425	24 423	9 872	1 411	8 574	13.8	11.2	29.3	14.6	30.3	48 761	18.5
1996	36 529	24 650	9 694	1 454	8 697	13.7	11.2	28.4	14.5	29.4	49 310	18.5
1997	35 574	24 396	9 116	1 468	8 308	13.3	11.0	26.5	14.0	27.1	47 853	17.8

1. Includes other races not shown separately.
2. Persons of Hispanic origin may be of any race.

SOURCE: U.S. Census Bureau, Current Population Reports, P60-201.

Series FF-2. GDP in Current and Chained (1996) Dollars: 1929 to 1999

(In Billions of dollars)

Item	1929	1930	1931	1932	1933	1934	1935	1936	1937	1938
CURRENT DOLLARS										
Gross domestic product	103.7	91.3	76.6	58.8	56.4	66.0	73.3	83.7	91.9	86.1
Personal consumption expenditures	77.5	70.2	60.7	48.7	45.9	51.5	55.9	62.2	66.8	64.2
Durable goods	9.2	7.2	5.5	3.6	3.5	4.2	5.1	6.3	6.9	5.7
Nondurable goods	37.7	34.0	29.0	22.7	22.3	26.7	29.3	32.9	35.2	34.0
Services	30.5	29.0	26.3	22.4	20.2	20.5	21.5	23.0	24.7	24.6
Gross private domestic investment	16.5	10.8	5.9	1.3	1.7	3.7	6.7	8.6	12.2	7.1
Fixed investment	14.9	11.0	7.0	3.6	3.1	4.3	5.6	7.5	9.5	7.7
Change in private inventories	1.5	-0.2	-1.1	-2.4	-1.4	-0.6	1.1	1.2	2.6	-0.6
Net exports of goods and services	0.4	0.3	0.0	0.0	0.1	0.3	-0.2	-0.2	0.0	0.9
Exports	5.9	4.4	2.9	2.0	2.0	2.6	2.8	3.0	4.0	3.8
Imports	5.6	4.1	2.9	1.9	1.9	2.2	3.0	3.2	4.0	2.8
Government consumption expenditures and gross investment	9.4	10.0	9.9	8.8	8.7	10.6	10.9	13.1	12.8	13.8
Federal	1.7	1.8	1.8	1.8	2.3	3.2	3.3	5.5	5.0	5.6
National defense	0.9	0.9	0.9	0.9	0.9	0.8	1.0	1.2	1.3	1.4
State and local	7.7	8.2	8.1	7.0	6.5	7.3	7.6	7.6	7.8	8.2
CHAINED (1996) DOLLARS										
Gross domestic product	822.2	751.5	703.6	611.8	603.3	668.3	728.3	822.5	865.8	835.6
Personal consumption expenditures	625.7	592.3	574.3	523.0	511.0	546.9	580.6	639.6	663.5	652.6
Durable goods	...	...	...	...	...	...	...	...	...	...
Nondurable goods	...	...	...	...	...	...	...	...	...	...
Services	...	...	...	...	...	...	...	...	...	...
Gross private domestic investment	93.6	62.5	39.2	11.8	17.5	31.6	58.4	74.9	93.6	61.9
Fixed investment	...	...	...	...	...	...	...	...	...	...
Change in private inventories	...	...	...	...	...	...	...	...	...	...
Net exports of goods and services	...	...	...	...	...	...	...	...	...	...
Exports	35.8	29.6	24.6	19.3	19.4	21.5	22.7	23.9	30.1	29.8
Imports	46.3	40.3	35.1	29.2	30.4	31.0	40.7	40.2	45.2	35.2
Government consumption expenditures and gross investment	110.1	121.3	126.6	122.4	118.0	133.0	137.0	158.9	153.2	164.6
Federal	...	...	...	...	...	...	...	...	...	...
National defense	...	...	...	...	...	...	...	...	...	...
State and local	...	...	...	...	...	...	...	...	...	...

Item	1939	1940	1941	1942	1943	1944	1945	1946	1947	1948
CURRENT DOLLARS										
Gross domestic product	92.0	101.3	126.7	161.8	198.4	219.7	223.0	222.3	244.4	269.6
Personal consumption expenditures	67.2	71.2	81.0	88.9	99.7	108.5	119.8	144.2	162.3	175.4
Durable goods	6.7	7.8	9.7	6.9	6.5	6.7	8.0	15.8	20.4	22.9
Nondurable goods	35.1	37.0	42.9	50.8	58.6	64.3	71.9	82.7	90.9	96.6
Services	25.4	26.4	28.5	31.3	34.6	37.4	40.0	45.8	51.0	55.9
Gross private domestic investment	9.3	13.6	18.1	10.4	6.1	7.8	10.8	31.1	35.0	48.1
Fixed investment	9.1	11.2	13.8	8.5	6.9	8.7	12.3	25.1	35.5	42.4
Change in private inventories	0.2	2.4	4.3	1.9	-0.7	-0.9	-1.5	6.0	-0.6	5.7
Net exports of goods and services	0.8	1.4	1.0	-0.3	-2.4	-2.2	-0.9	7.1	10.8	5.4
Exports	3.9	4.8	5.4	4.3	3.9	4.8	6.7	14.1	18.7	15.5
Imports	3.1	3.4	4.4	4.6	6.3	6.9	7.5	7.0	7.9	10.1
Government consumption expenditures and gross investment	14.7	15.1	26.6	62.8	94.9	105.5	93.2	39.8	36.4	40.6
Federal	5.9	6.4	17.9	54.1	86.5	97.0	84.2	29.0	22.6	24.2
National defense	1.5	2.5	14.3	51.2	84.2	94.6	82.1	25.3	18.2	18.4
State and local	8.9	8.7	8.7	8.7	8.5	8.5	9.0	10.8	13.9	16.5
CHAINED (1996) DOLLARS										
Gross domestic product	903.5	980.7	1 148.8	1 360.0	1 583.7	1 714.1	1 693.3	1 505.5	1 495.1	1 560.0
Personal consumption expenditures	689.0	724.9	776.7	758.3	779.1	801.7	851.8	956.9	976.4	998.1
Durable goods	...	...	...	...	...	...	...	...	...	...
Nondurable goods	...	...	...	...	...	...	...	...	...	...
Services	...	...	...	...	...	...	...	...	...	...
Gross private domestic investment	79.6	110.9	135.4	71.6	42.3	52.2	69.0	175.0	168.6	215.3
Fixed investment	...	...	...	...	...	...	...	...	...	...
Change in private inventories	...	...	...	...	...	...	...	...	...	...
Net exports of goods and services	...	...	...	...	...	...	...	...	...	...
Exports	31.4	35.7	36.7	24.1	20.1	21.6	30.5	66.5	75.9	59.8
Imports	36.9	37.8	46.5	42.2	53.2	55.7	59.2	49.1	46.6	54.4
Government consumption expenditures and gross investment	179.7	182.4	303.0	711.1	1 059.9	1 195.6	1 041.0	359.7	307.1	328.9
Federal	...	...	...	...	...	...	...	...	...	...
National defense	...	...	...	...	...	...	...	...	...	...
State and local	...	...	...	...	...	...	...	...	...	...

See footnote at end of chart.

Series FF-2. GDP in Current and Chained (1996) Dollars: 1929 to 1999—Cont'd.
(In Billions of dollars)

	1949	1950	1951	1952	1953	1954	1955	1956	1957	1958
CURRENT DOLLARS										
Gross domestic product	267.7	294.3	339.5	358.6	379.9	381.1	415.2	438.0	461.5	467.9
Personal consumption expenditures	178.8	192.7	208.6	219.7	233.4	240.5	259.0	271.9	287.0	296.6
Durable goods	25.1	30.7	29.9	29.3	32.7	31.9	38.8	38.1	40.0	37.4
Nondurable goods	94.9	98.2	109.2	114.7	117.8	119.7	124.7	130.8	137.1	141.7
Services	58.9	63.7	69.6	75.6	82.9	88.9	95.4	102.9	109.9	117.4
Gross private domestic investment	36.9	54.1	60.2	54.0	56.4	53.8	69.0	72.0	70.5	64.5
Fixed investment	39.6	48.3	50.3	50.5	54.5	55.8	64.0	68.1	69.7	64.9
Change in private inventories	-2.7	5.8	9.9	3.5	1.9	-1.9	5.0	3.9	0.8	-0.4
Net exports of goods and services	5.2	0.7	2.4	1.0	-0.8	0.3	0.4	2.3	4.0	0.4
Exports	14.4	12.3	17.0	16.3	15.2	15.7	17.6	21.2	23.9	20.4
Imports	9.2	11.6	14.6	15.3	16.0	15.4	17.2	18.9	19.9	20.0
Government consumption expenditures and gross investment	46.8	46.9	68.3	83.9	90.8	86.5	86.8	91.8	100.1	106.5
Federal	27.6	26.0	45.0	59.2	64.4	57.3	54.9	56.7	61.3	63.9
National defense	19.9	19.6	39.3	52.4	56.0	49.3	47.0	49.3	53.7	55.5
State and local	19.2	20.9	23.3	24.7	26.4	29.2	31.9	35.1	38.8	42.6
CHAINED (1996) DOLLARS										
Gross domestic product	1 550.9	1 686.6	1 815.1	1 887.3	1 973.9	1 960.5	2 099.5	2 141.1	2 183.9	2 162.8
Personal consumption expenditures	1 025.3	1 090.9	1 107.1	1 142.4	1 197.2	1 221.9	1 310.4	1 348.8	1 381.8	1 393.0
Durable goods	...	...	...	...	...	...	...	...	...	...
Nondurable goods	...	...	...	...	...	...	...	...	...	...
Services	...	...	...	...	...	...	...	...	...	...
Gross private domestic investment	164.3	232.5	233.2	211.1	221.0	210.8	262.1	258.6	247.4	226.5
Fixed investment	...	...	...	...	...	...	...	...	...	...
Change in private inventories	...	...	...	...	...	...	...	...	...	...
Net exports of goods and services	...	...	...	...	...	...	...	...	...	...
Exports	59.2	51.8	63.5	60.6	56.5	59.3	65.6	76.5	83.1	71.8
Imports	52.5	62.0	64.5	70.1	76.7	72.9	81.7	88.4	92.1	96.4
Government consumption expenditures and gross investment	367.3	367.4	500.0	605.1	647.5	602.9	580.4	580.8	606.7	626.2
Federal	...	...	...	...	...	...	...	...	...	...
National defense	...	...	...	...	...	...	...	...	...	...
State and local	...	...	...	...	...	...	...	...	...	...

	1959	1960	1961	1962	1963	1964	1965	1966	1967	1968
CURRENT DOLLARS										
Gross domestic product	507.4	527.4	545.7	586.5	618.7	664.4	720.1	789.3	834.1	911.5
Personal consumption expenditures	318.1	332.3	342.7	363.8	383.1	411.7	444.3	481.8	508.7	558.7
Durable goods	42.7	43.3	41.8	46.9	51.6	56.7	63.3	68.3	70.4	80.8
Nondurable goods	148.5	152.9	156.6	162.8	168.2	178.7	191.6	208.8	217.1	235.7
Services	127.0	136.1	144.3	154.1	163.4	176.4	189.5	204.7	221.2	242.3
Gross private domestic investment	78.5	78.9	78.2	88.1	93.8	102.1	118.2	131.3	128.6	141.2
Fixed investment	74.6	75.7	75.2	82.0	88.1	97.2	109.0	117.7	118.7	132.1
Change in private inventories	3.9	3.2	3.0	6.1	5.6	4.8	9.2	13.6	9.9	9.1
Net exports of goods and services	-1.7	2.4	3.4	2.4	3.3	5.5	3.9	1.9	1.4	-1.3
Exports	20.6	25.3	26.0	27.4	29.4	33.6	35.4	38.9	41.4	45.3
Imports	22.3	22.8	22.7	25.0	26.1	28.1	31.5	37.1	39.9	46.6
Government consumption expenditures and gross investment	112.5	113.8	121.5	132.2	138.5	145.1	153.7	174.3	195.3	212.8
Federal	67.4	65.9	69.5	76.9	78.5	79.8	82.1	94.4	106.8	114.0
National defense	56.0	55.2	58.1	62.8	62.7	61.8	62.4	73.8	85.8	92.2
State and local	45.1	47.9	52.0	55.3	59.9	65.3	71.6	79.9	88.6	98.8
CHAINED (1996) DOLLARS										
Gross domestic product	2 319.0	2 376.7	2 432.0	2 578.9	2 690.4	2 846.5	3 028.5	3 227.5	3 308.3	3 466.1
Personal consumption expenditures	1 470.7	1 510.8	1 541.2	1 617.3	1 684.0	1 784.8	1 897.6	2 006.1	2 066.2	2 184.2
Durable goods	...	...	...	...	...	...	...	...	...	...
Nondurable goods	...	...	...	...	...	...	...	...	...	...
Services	...	...	...	...	...	...	...	...	...	...
Gross private domestic investment	272.9	272.8	271.0	305.3	325.7	352.6	402.0	437.3	417.2	441.3
Fixed investment	...	...	...	...	...	...	...	...	...	...
Change in private inventories	...	...	...	...	...	...	...	...	...	...
Net exports of goods and services	...	...	...	...	...	...	...	...	...	...
Exports	72.4	87.5	88.9	93.7	100.7	114.2	116.5	124.3	127.0	136.3
Imports	106.6	108.0	107.3	119.5	122.7	129.2	142.9	164.2	176.2	202.4
Government consumption expenditures and gross investment	661.4	661.3	693.2	735.0	752.4	767.1	791.1	862.1	927.1	956.6
Federal	...	...	...	...	...	...	...	...	...	...
National defense	...	...	...	...	...	...	...	...	...	...
State and local	...	...	...	...	...	...	...	...	...	...

See footnote at end of chart.

Series FF-2. GDP in Current and Chained (1996) Dollars: 1929 to 1999—Cont'd.

(In Billions of dollars)

	1969	1970	1971	1972	1973	1974	1975	1976	1977	1978
CURRENT DOLLARS										
Gross domestic product	985.3	1 039.7	1 128.6	1 240.4	1 385.5	1 501.0	1 635.2	1 823.9	2 031.4	2 295.9
Personal consumption expenditures	605.5	648.9	702.4	770.7	852.5	932.4	1 030.3	1 149.8	1 278.4	1 430.4
Durable goods	85.9	85.0	96.9	110.4	123.5	122.3	133.5	158.9	181.2	201.7
Nondurable goods	253.2	272.0	285.5	308.0	343.1	384.5	420.7	458.3	497.2	550.2
Services	266.4	292.0	320.0	352.3	385.9	425.5	476.1	532.6	600.0	678.4
Gross private domestic investment	156.4	152.4	178.2	207.6	244.5	249.4	230.2	292.0	361.3	436.0
Fixed investment	147.3	150.4	169.9	198.5	228.6	235.4	236.5	274.8	339.0	410.2
Change in private inventories	9.2	2.0	8.3	9.1	15.9	14.0	-6.3	17.1	22.3	25.8
Net exports of goods and services	-1.2	1.2	-3.0	-8.0	0.6	-3.1	13.6	-2.3	-23.7	-26.1
Exports	49.3	57.0	59.3	66.2	91.8	124.3	136.3	148.9	158.8	186.1
Imports	50.5	55.8	62.3	74.2	91.2	127.5	122.7	151.1	182.4	212.3
Government consumption expenditures and gross investment	224.6	237.1	251.0	270.1	287.9	322.4	361.1	384.5	415.3	455.6
Federal	116.1	116.4	117.6	125.6	127.8	138.2	152.1	160.6	176.0	191.9
National defense	92.6	90.9	89.0	93.5	93.9	99.7	107.9	113.2	122.6	132.0
State and local	108.5	120.7	133.5	144.4	160.1	184.2	209.0	223.9	239.3	263.8
CHAINED (1996) DOLLARS										
Gross domestic product	3 571.4	3 578.0	3 697.7	3 898.4	4 123.4	4 099.0	4 084.4	4 311.7	4 511.8	4 760.6
Personal consumption expenditures	2 264.8	2 317.5	2 405.2	2 550.5	2 675.9	2 653.7	2 710.9	2 868.9	2 992.1	3 124.7
Durable goods	...	...	...	...	...	...	...	...	...	...
Nondurable goods	...	...	...	...	...	...	...	...	...	...
Services	...	...	...	...	...	...	...	...	...	...
Gross private domestic investment	466.9	436.2	485.8	543.0	606.5	561.7	462.2	555.5	639.4	713.0
Fixed investment	...	...	...	...	...	...	...	...	...	...
Change in private inventories	...	...	...	...	...	...	...	...	...	...
Net exports of goods and services	...	...	...	...	...	...	...	...	...	...
Exports	143.7	159.3	160.4	173.5	211.4	231.6	230.0	243.6	249.7	275.9
Imports	213.9	223.1	235.0	261.3	273.4	267.2	237.5	284.0	315.0	342.3
Government consumption expenditures and gross investment	952.5	931.1	913.8	914.9	908.3	924.8	942.5	943.3	952.7	982.2
Federal	...	...	...	...	...	...	...	...	...	...
National defense	...	...	...	...	...	...	...	...	...	...
State and local	...	...	...	...	...	...	...	...	...	...

	1979	1980	1981	1982	1983	1984	1985	1986	1987	1988
CURRENT DOLLARS										
Gross domestic product	2 566.4	2 795.6	3 131.3	3 259.2	3 534.9	3 932.7	4 213.0	4 452.9	4 742.5	5 108.3
Personal consumption expenditures	1 596.3	1 762.9	1 944.2	2 079.3	2 286.4	2 498.4	2 712.6	2 895.2	3 105.3	3 356.6
Durable goods	214.4	214.2	231.3	240.2	281.2	326.9	363.3	401.3	419.7	450.2
Nondurable goods	624.4	696.1	758.9	787.6	831.2	884.7	928.8	958.5	1 015.3	1 082.9
Services	757.4	852.7	954.0	1 051.5	1 174.0	1 286.9	1 420.6	1 535.4	1 670.3	1 823.5
Gross private domestic investment	490.6	477.9	570.8	516.1	564.2	735.5	736.3	747.2	781.5	821.1
Fixed investment	472.7	484.2	541.0	531.0	570.0	670.1	714.5	740.7	754.3	802.7
Change in private inventories	18.0	-6.3	29.8	-14.9	-5.8	65.4	21.8	6.6	27.1	18.5
Net exports of goods and services	-24.0	-14.9	-15.0	-20.5	-51.7	-102.0	-114.2	-131.9	-142.3	-106.3
Exports	228.7	278.9	302.8	282.6	277.0	303.1	303.0	320.3	365.6	446.9
Imports	252.7	293.8	317.8	303.2	328.6	405.1	417.2	452.2	507.9	553.2
Government consumption expenditures and gross investment	503.5	569.7	631.4	684.4	735.9	800.8	878.3	942.3	997.9	1 036.9
Federal	211.6	245.3	281.8	312.8	344.4	376.4	413.4	438.7	460.4	462.6
National defense	146.7	169.6	197.8	228.3	252.5	283.5	312.4	332.2	351.2	355.9
State and local	291.8	324.4	349.6	371.6	391.5	424.4	464.9	503.6	537.5	574.3
CHAINED (1996) DOLLARS										
Gross domestic product	4 912.1	4 900.9	5 021.0	4 919.3	5 132.3	5 505.2	5 717.1	5 912.4	6 113.3	6 368.4
Personal consumption expenditures	3 203.2	3 193.0	3 236.0	3 275.5	3 454.3	3 640.6	3 820.9	3 981.2	4 113.4	4 279.5
Durable goods	...	...	...	...	...	...	...	...	455.2	481.5
Nondurable goods	...	...	...	...	...	...	...	...	1 274.5	1 315.1
Services	...	...	...	...	...	...	...	...	2 379.3	2 477.2
Gross private domestic investment	735.4	655.3	715.6	615.2	673.7	871.5	863.4	857.7	879.3	902.8
Fixed investment	...	...	...	...	...	...	...	...	856	887.1
Change in private inventories	...	...	...	...	...	...	...	...	29.6	18.4
Net exports of goods and services	...	...	...	...	...	...	...	...	-156.2	-112.1
Exports	302.4	334.8	338.6	314.6	306.9	332.6	341.6	366.8	408.0	473.5
Imports	347.9	324.8	333.4	329.2	370.7	461.0	490.7	531.9	564.2	585.6
Government consumption expenditures and gross investment	1 001.1	1 020.9	1 030.0	1 046.0	1 081.0	1 118.4	1 190.5	1 255.2	1 292.5	1 307.5
Federal	...	...	...	...	...	...	...	...	597.8	586.9
National defense	...	...	...	...	...	...	...	...	450.2	446.8
State and local	...	...	...	...	...	...	...	...	695.6	721.4

See footnote at end of chart.

Series FF-2.   GDP in Current and Chained (1996) Dollars: 1929 to 1999—Cont'd.

(In Billions of dollars)

	1989	1990	1991	1992	1993	1994	1995	1996	1997	1998	1999
CURRENT DOLLARS											
Gross domestic product	5 489.1	5 803.2	5 986.2	6 318.9	6 642.3	7 054.3	7 400.5	7 813.2	8 318.4	8 790.2	9 299.2
Personal consumption expenditures	3 596.7	3 831.5	3 971.2	4 209.7	4 454.7	4 716.4	4 969.0	5 237.5	5 529.3	5 850.9	6 268.7
Durable goods	467.8	467.6	443.0	470.8	513.4	560.8	589.7	616.5	642.5	693.9	761.3
Nondurable goods	1 165.4	1 246.1	1 278.8	1 322.9	1 375.2	1 438.0	1 497.3	1 574.1	1 641.6	1 707.6	1 845.5
Services	1 963.5	2 117.8	2 249.4	2 415.9	2 566.1	2 717.6	2 882.0	3 047.0	3 245.2	3 449.3	3 661.9
Gross private domestic investment	872.9	861.7	800.2	866.6	955.1	1 097.1	1 143.8	1 242.7	1 390.5	1 549.9	1 650.1
Fixed investment	845.2	847.2	800.4	851.6	934.0	1 034.6	1 110.7	1 212.7	1 327.7	1 472.9	1 606.8
Change in private inventories	27.7	14.5	-0.2	15.0	21.1	62.6	33.0	30.0	62.9	77.0	43.3
Net exports of goods and services	-80.7	-71.4	-20.7	-27.9	-60.5	-87.1	-84.3	-89.0	-89.3	-151.5	-254.0
Exports	509.0	557.2	601.6	636.8	658.0	725.1	818.6	874.2	966.4	966.0	990.2
Imports	589.7	628.6	622.3	664.6	718.5	812.1	902.8	963.1	1 055.8	1 117.5	1 244.2
Government consumption expenditures and gross investment	1 100.2	1 181.4	1 235.5	1 270.5	1 293.0	1 327.9	1 372.0	1 421.9	1 487.9	1 540.9	1 634.4
Federal	482.6	508.4	527.4	534.5	527.3	521.1	521.5	531.6	538.2	540.6	568.6
National defense	363.2	374.9	384.5	378.5	364.9	355.1	350.6	357.0	352.6	349.2	365.0
State and local	617.7	673.0	708.1	736.0	765.7	806.8	850.5	890.4	949.7	1 000.3	1 065.8
CHAINED (1996) DOLLARS											
Gross domestic product	6 591.8	6 707.9	6 676.4	6 880.0	7 062.6	7 347.7	7 543.8	7 813.2	8 159.5	8 515.7	8 875.8
Personal consumption expenditures	4 393.7	4 474.5	4 466.6	4 594.5	4 748.9	4 928.1	5 075.6	5 237.5	5 423.9	5 678.7	5 978.8
Durable goods	491.7	487.1	454.9	479	518.3	557.7	583.5	616.5	657.3	727.3	817.8
Nondurable goods	1 351	1 369.6	1 364	1 389.7	1 430.3	1 485.1	1 529	1 574.1	1 619.9	1 684.8	1 779.4
Services	2 546	2 616.2	2 651.8	2 729.7	2 802.5	2 886.2	2 963.4	3 047	3 147	3 269.4	3 390.8
Gross private domestic investment	936.5	907.3	829.5	899.8	977.9	1 107.0	1 140.6	1 242.7	1 393.3	1 566.8	1 669.7
Fixed investment	911.2	894.6	832.5	886.5	958.4	1 045.9	1 109.2	1 212.7	1 328.6	1 485.3	1 621.4
Change in private inventories	29.6	16.5	-1	17.1	20	66.8	30.4	30	63.8	80.2	45.3
Net exports of goods and services	-79.4	-56.5	-15.8	-19.8	-59.1	-86.5	-78.4	-89	-113.3	-221	-322.4
Exports	529.4	575.7	613.2	651.0	672.7	732.8	808.2	874.2	981.5	1 003.6	1 033.0
Imports	608.8	632.2	629.0	670.8	731.8	819.4	886.6	963.1	1 094.8	1 224.6	1 355.3
Government consumption expenditures and gross investment	1 343.5	1 387.3	1 403.4	1 410.0	1 398.8	1 400.1	1 406.4	1 421.9	1 455.4	1 486.4	1 536.1
Federal	594.7	606.8	604.9	595.1	572	551.3	536.5	531.6	529.6	526.9	540.1
National defense	443.3	443.2	438.4	417.1	394.7	375.9	361.9	357	347.7	341.7	348.5
State and local	749.5	781.1	798.9	815.3	827	848.9	869.9	890.4	925.8	959.2	995.6

SOURCE: U.S. Bureau of Economic Analysis, National Income and Product Accounts of the United States.

Series FF-3. Current-Cost Net Stock of Fixed Assets and Consumer Durable Goods: 1925–1999

(Billions of dollars; yearend estimates)

Year	Total	Private fixed assets					Government fixed assets			Consumer durable goods
		Total	Nonresidential			Residential	Total	Federal	State and local	
			Total	Equipment and software	Structures					
1999	27 865.8	19 882.3	10 046.6	4 010.9	6 035.7	9 835.7	5 422.8	1 428.6	3 994.3	2 560.7
1998	26 245.6	18 670.3	9 478.5	3 729.4	5 749.0	9 191.8	5 144.5	1 382.8	3 761.8	2 430.8
1997	24 924.8	17 653.1	9 006.8	3 519.8	5 487.0	8 646.3	4 942.9	1 367.0	3 575.9	2 328.8
1996	23 701.0	16 722.5	8 527.2	3 352.2	5 175.0	8 195.3	4 724.8	1 343.2	3 381.5	2 253.7
1995	22 617.0	15 908.5	8 124.2	3 182.8	4 941.4	7 784.2	4 533.0	1 314.4	3 218.6	2 175.6
1994	21 617.7	15 203.7	7 731.5	2 992.4	4 739.1	7 472.2	4 322.4	1 279.2	3 043.2	2 091.6
1993	20 396.6	14 318.0	7 327.1	2 828.6	4 498.5	6 991.0	4 085.6	1 229.0	2 856.7	1 993.0
1992	19 384.8	13 582.6	6 986.8	2 708.2	4 278.6	6 595.8	3 894.6	1 176.0	2 718.6	1 907.5
1991	18 614.5	13 021.5	6 760.5	2 622.8	4 137.7	6 261.0	3 732.4	1 129.8	2 602.6	1 860.6
1990	18 186.5	12 760.3	6 622.7	2 541.9	4 080.7	6 137.7	3 611.6	1 087.1	2 524.5	1 814.6
1989	17 363.9	12 197.2	6 285.1	2 400.2	3 884.8	5 912.2	3 438.7	1 039.5	2 399.3	1 727.9
1988	16 423.1	11 540.9	5 934.8	2 264.9	3 669.9	5 606.1	3 262.2	985.9	2 276.3	1 620.0
1987	15 458.3	10 857.3	5 574.0	2 130.6	3 443.4	5 283.3	3 102.6	929.5	2 173.2	1 498.4
1986	14 605.0	10 266.6	5 298.8	2 035.1	3 263.7	4 967.8	2 948.6	895.5	2 053.1	1 389.8
1985	13 705.3	9 657.8	5 056.4	1 920.6	3 135.8	4 601.3	2 782.1	855.6	1 926.5	1 265.5
1984	13 005.0	9 163.5	4 794.6	1 814.4	2 980.2	4 368.9	2 668.6	826.5	1 842.1	1 173.0
1983	12 327.7	8 667.6	4 532.8	1 724.2	2 808.5	4 134.8	2 567.2	791.3	1 775.9	1 092.9
1982	11 918.7	8 376.1	4 402.7	1 665.7	2 737.0	3 973.4	2 508.5	752.5	1 756.0	1 034.1
1981	11 318.7	7 949.7	4 145.8	1 575.6	2 570.2	3 804.0	2 371.3	709.1	1 662.2	997.6
1980	10 294.0	7 212.7	3 675.9	1 420.1	2 255.8	3 536.8	2 150.7	652.7	1 497.9	930.6
1979	9 061.7	6 339.9	3 202.6	1 220.9	1 981.7	3 137.3	1 877.0	586.7	1 290.2	844.8
1978	7 876.1	5 473.0	2 772.7	1 048.0	1 724.8	2 700.2	1 650.4	528.4	1 122.0	752.8
1977	6 969.0	4 787.4	2 449.0	920.3	1 528.7	2 338.5	1 513.8	493.2	1 020.6	667.8
1976	6 235.8	4 207.5	2 204.0	818.9	1 385.1	2 003.4	1 426.0	470.4	955.6	602.3
1975	5 717.5	3 815.2	2 010.1	740.5	1 269.6	1 805.1	1 352.2	436.5	915.7	550.1
1974	5 276.0	3 489.4	1 821.7	648.8	1 172.9	1 667.7	1 286.5	411.4	875.2	500.0
1973	4 456.4	2 968.2	1 500.4	525.2	975.1	1 467.8	1 054.0	363.9	690.2	434.2
1972	3 946.4	2 613.5	1 334.6	468.4	866.2	1 278.9	940.3	338.2	602.1	392.5
1971	3 586.8	2 366.4	1 225.6	434.5	791.1	1 140.8	858.0	308.6	549.4	362.4
1970	3 258.8	2 129.6	1 113.9	404.6	709.3	1 015.7	788.6	290.9	497.6	340.6
1969	2 998.6	1 973.7	1 013.2	368.2	645.0	960.5	707.8	271.7	436.1	317.1
1968	2 748.4	1 815.7	918.6	332.5	586.1	897.1	642.3	256.2	386.1	290.4
1967	2 501.8	1 649.2	838.1	300.8	537.2	811.1	591.3	243.5	347.7	261.4
1966	2 324.0	1 538.7	778.0	273.8	504.2	760.7	546.3	228.1	318.2	239.0
1965	2 141.8	1 418.1	714.5	246.0	468.5	703.6	505.0	216.9	288.1	218.6
1964	2 011.9	1 330.3	668.4	228.5	439.9	661.9	474.7	210.0	264.7	207.0
1963	1 894.8	1 245.5	632.8	215.7	417.1	612.7	452.8	204.7	248.1	196.5
1962	1 826.5	1 209.0	611.5	206.5	405.1	597.5	431.3	198.7	232.6	186.2
1961	1 752.2	1 167.4	591.4	199.0	392.4	576.0	404.9	187.6	217.3	179.9
1960	1 693.7	1 131.4	575.9	194.8	381.0	555.6	385.5	180.5	205.0	176.8
1959	1 643.1	1 099.4	564.9	188.7	376.3	534.5	372.2	176.5	195.7	171.5
1958	1 582.3	1 055.2	543.2	179.7	363.5	512.0	361.6	172.3	189.3	165.6
1957	1 527.7	1 022.7	526.4	172.8	353.6	496.3	343.0	165.9	177.1	162.0
1956	1 457.6	976.1	494.6	158.8	335.7	481.6	328.9	159.8	169.1	152.6
1955	1 343.8	905.7	448.4	142.2	306.2	457.2	296.5	147.4	149.1	141.6
1954	1 249.7	842.2	415.0	129.6	285.5	427.2	275.4	141.2	134.3	132.1
1953	1 195.9	808.0	401.7	123.5	278.2	406.2	259.7	131.1	128.6	128.3
1952	1 150.5	776.3	386.4	115.5	270.9	390.0	254.1	124.2	129.9	120.0
1951	1 085.9	735.9	365.9	108.3	257.6	370.0	236.9	114.3	122.6	113.1
1950	984.2	671.5	332.0	96.9	235.1	339.5	211.7	102.7	109.0	101.0
1949	896.6	611.5	304.1	85.3	218.8	307.4	199.6	103.0	96.6	85.5
1948	873.0	582.2	291.5	77.2	214.2	290.8	214.2	113.0	101.2	76.5
1947	811.0	529.5	263.7	65.2	198.5	265.8	214.7	121.7	93.0	66.9
1946	695.5	445.7	221.1	52.1	169.0	224.7	194.2	116.6	77.6	55.6
1945	609.4	374.8	184.5	42.6	141.9	190.3	186.7	117.4	69.2	47.9
1944	564.8	344.1	167.3	37.4	129.9	176.7	173.5	106.8	66.7	47.2
1943	522.4	326.3	162.1	36.3	125.8	164.2	150.9	82.7	68.2	45.2
1942	470.0	310.4	158.4	36.7	121.8	152.0	118.0	50.9	67.1	41.6
1941	411.1	289.5	148.5	35.8	112.7	141.0	84.4	24.4	60.0	37.2
1940	361.9	262.2	133.9	31.7	102.2	128.3	67.4	15.7	51.7	32.3

Series FF-3. Current-Cost Net Stock of Fixed Assets and Consumer Durable Goods: 1925–1999—Cont'd.

(Billions of dollars; yearend estimates)

Year	Total	Private fixed assets					Government fixed assets			Consumer durable goods
		Total	Nonresidential			Residential	Total	Federal	State and local	
			Total	Equipment and software	Structures					
1939	336.0	245.1	126.6	29.4	97.2	118.5	61.4	14.0	47.4	29.5
1938	327.2	239.6	125.5	28.9	96.5	114.2	59.1	13.4	45.7	28.5
1937	323.2	237.6	126.3	28.8	97.4	111.3	57.0	12.6	44.4	28.7
1936	303.9	222.9	119.3	26.3	93.0	103.6	54.0	11.4	42.6	27.1
1935	282.2	208.0	112.3	24.8	87.5	95.7	48.5	9.9	38.6	25.7
1934	275.7	204.4	110.4	24.8	85.6	94.0	45.6	8.6	37.0	25.7
1933	265.2	197.9	107.7	24.6	83.2	90.1	41.6	7.6	34.0	25.8
1932	255.8	193.8	107.6	25.6	81.9	86.3	35.5	6.7	28.8	26.5
1931	280.3	214.3	116.8	28.3	88.5	97.4	35.9	6.8	29.1	30.1
1930	315.8	242.0	129.2	30.7	98.5	112.8	39.5	7.5	32.0	34.4
1929	331.1	254.0	135.5	31.9	103.6	118.5	40.6	7.9	32.7	36.5
1928	326.0	249.8	135.2	31.4	103.8	114.5	40.5	8.5	32.1	35.7
1927	315.8	241.4	133.1	30.9	102.2	108.3	39.7	8.7	31.0	34.6
1926	307.2	234.9	130.0	29.9	100.1	104.9	38.9	9.0	29.9	33.5
1925	297.0	227.0	126.5	28.3	98.2	100.5	38.0	9.2	28.9	32.0

Series FF-4. Chain-Type Quantity Indexes for Net Stock of Fixed Assets and Consumer Durable Goods: 1925–1999

(Index numbers, 1996 = 100; yearend estimates)

Year	Total	Private fixed assets					Government fixed assets			Consumer durable goods
		Total	Nonresidential			Residential	Total	Federal	State and local	
			Total	Equipment and software	Structures					
1999	110.1	110.2	112.4	122.2	106.5	107.8	105.8	99.8	108.1	119.2
1998	106.3	106.4	107.8	113.2	104.4	105.0	103.6	99.5	105.2	111.0
1997	102.9	103.0	103.6	106.0	102.0	102.3	101.8	99.6	102.6	104.7
1996	100.0	100.0	100.0	100.0	100.0	100.0	100.0	100.0	100.0	100.0
1995	97.4	97.3	97.0	94.9	98.3	97.7	98.2	99.4	97.8	95.9
1994	95.1	95.0	94.4	90.5	97.0	95.6	96.7	99.4	95.6	92.3
1993	93.0	92.9	92.3	86.9	95.9	93.5	95.2	99.5	93.5	88.9
1992	91.0	91.0	90.6	84.3	94.8	91.5	93.6	99.1	91.4	86.2
1991	89.5	89.5	89.2	82.6	93.8	89.8	91.8	98.1	89.3	84.7
1990	88.1	88.1	87.8	81.2	92.3	88.5	89.8	96.8	87.0	84.0
1989	86.0	86.2	85.8	79.2	90.3	86.6	87.7	95.1	84.8	81.1
1988	83.7	84.1	83.7	76.9	88.4	84.5	85.8	93.4	82.8	77.2
1987	81.4	81.9	81.7	74.7	86.4	82.2	84.0	91.5	80.9	72.9
1986	79.0	79.8	79.7	72.9	84.4	79.9	81.9	88.7	79.2	68.6
1985	76.5	77.5	77.5	70.5	82.2	77.5	79.9	86.0	77.4	63.9
1984	74.0	75.1	74.7	67.7	79.5	75.5	78.0	83.6	75.8	59.9
1983	71.8	72.8	72.1	64.8	77.1	73.5	76.5	81.8	74.4	56.4
1982	70.1	71.1	70.4	63.2	75.4	71.9	75.4	80.4	73.3	54.3
1981	68.9	69.7	68.5	61.9	73.0	71.0	74.3	79.5	72.3	53.5
1980	67.2	67.7	65.9	59.3	70.5	69.8	73.2	78.8	71.0	52.6
1979	65.4	65.7	63.5	56.6	68.2	68.2	71.9	78.2	69.3	51.6
1978	63.2	63.2	60.8	53.0	66.2	66.0	70.6	77.9	67.7	49.3
1977	60.9	60.8	58.3	49.6	64.5	63.6	69.5	77.9	66.1	46.5
1976	59.0	58.8	56.4	47.0	63.2	61.4	68.6	78.0	64.8	43.8
1975	57.4	57.2	54.9	45.2	61.9	59.7	67.5	78.2	63.2	41.5
1974	56.1	55.8	53.4	43.6	60.6	58.5	66.4	78.4	61.6	40.1
1973	54.4	53.9	51.3	40.9	58.9	56.9	65.3	78.9	59.9	38.4
1972	52.3	51.6	49.0	38.0	57.1	54.6	64.3	79.7	58.2	35.6
1971	50.3	49.6	47.1	35.9	55.5	52.4	63.1	79.9	56.4	33.4
1970	48.7	47.9	45.6	34.4	53.9	50.5	62.0	81.0	54.4	31.7
1969	47.2	46.3	43.8	32.7	52.2	49.1	60.6	81.4	52.4	30.4
1968	45.4	44.6	41.9	30.6	50.5	47.6	59.0	81.5	50.0	28.6
1967	43.6	42.9	40.1	28.8	48.9	46.1	57.0	81.0	47.4	26.5
1966	41.9	41.4	38.4	27.0	47.2	44.9	54.8	79.5	44.9	24.9
1965	40.1	39.8	36.4	24.9	45.5	43.6	52.8	78.1	42.6	23.1
1964	38.4	38.1	34.7	23.2	43.9	42.1	51.0	77.3	40.4	21.4
1963	37.0	36.7	33.5	22.1	42.7	40.4	49.2	76.1	38.4	20.2
1962	35.6	35.5	32.5	21.2	41.6	38.9	47.4	74.6	36.5	19.3
1961	34.4	34.4	31.6	20.5	40.6	37.5	45.6	72.4	34.8	18.5
1960	33.4	33.4	30.9	20.1	39.6	36.3	43.8	70.5	33.1	18.2
1959	32.4	32.4	30.0	19.5	38.6	35.1	42.3	69.0	31.6	17.6
1958	31.3	31.4	29.3	19.0	37.7	33.8	40.7	67.0	30.0	17.0
1957	30.5	30.7	28.8	18.8	36.9	32.8	39.2	65.8	28.5	16.9
1956	29.5	29.7	27.9	18.0	35.9	31.7	38.0	65.0	27.1	16.1
1955	28.5	28.7	26.9	17.2	34.8	30.6	36.8	64.1	25.8	15.5
1954	27.4	27.6	26.0	16.4	33.9	29.3	35.6	62.9	24.6	14.3
1953	26.4	26.7	25.4	15.9	33.1	28.3	34.1	60.6	23.4	13.6
1952	25.3	25.9	24.6	15.1	32.4	27.3	32.4	56.8	22.5	12.7
1951	24.4	25.0	23.9	14.4	31.7	26.3	30.8	53.2	21.7	12.1
1950	23.4	24.2	23.1	13.6	31.0	25.3	29.6	51.1	20.9	11.3
1949	22.5	23.2	22.4	12.7	30.4	24.1	30.0	54.5	20.2	9.9
1948	21.9	22.4	21.7	11.9	29.9	23.2	30.5	58.0	19.5	9.0
1947	21.4	21.5	20.8	10.6	29.4	22.2	32.2	65.0	19.1	8.1
1946	21.0	20.6	19.9	9.3	29.0	21.4	34.4	73.4	18.9	7.1
1945	20.9	20.0	19.2	8.4	28.5	20.9	37.0	82.6	18.9	6.4
1944	20.5	19.9	18.9	7.8	28.5	20.9	35.1	75.6	19.1	6.5
1943	19.6	19.9	18.9	7.6	28.7	21.0	29.8	56.6	19.3	6.7

Series FF-4. Chain-Type Quantity Indexes for Net Stock of Fixed Assets and Consumer Durable Goods: 1925–1999—Cont'd.

(Index numbers, 1996 = 100; yearend estimates)

Year	Total	Private fixed assets					Government fixed assets			Consumer durable goods
		Total	Nonresidential			Residential	Total	Federal	State and local	
			Total	Equipment and software	Structures					
1942	18.5	20.0	19.2	7.7	29.0	21.0	23.4	34.2	19.4	6.9
1941	17.5	20.1	19.3	7.8	29.2	21.0	18.2	17.0	19.4	6.9
1940	16.8	19.7	19.0	7.4	29.1	20.6	16.2	11.7	19.0	6.7
1939	16.5	19.5	18.8	7.1	29.1	20.3	15.5	10.8	18.4	6.4
1938	16.2	19.4	18.8	7.1	29.2	20.0	14.7	10.2	17.5	6.2
1937	16.1	19.4	18.9	7.1	29.3	19.9	14.1	9.6	16.7	6.2
1936	15.8	19.2	18.7	6.8	29.2	19.8	13.4	8.9	16.1	5.9
1935	15.5	19.1	18.6	6.6	29.3	19.7	12.7	8.2	15.4	5.8
1934	15.5	19.2	18.7	6.6	29.6	19.6	12.3	7.4	15.0	5.8
1933	15.5	19.4	19.0	6.9	29.8	19.7	11.8	6.9	14.7	6.0
1932	15.7	19.7	19.5	7.3	30.2	19.8	11.5	6.5	14.4	6.3
1931	15.9	19.9	19.9	7.8	30.4	19.9	11.1	6.3	13.8	6.5
1930	15.8	19.9	20.0	8.0	30.3	19.8	10.5	6.1	13.0	6.6
1929	15.5	19.7	19.6	7.9	29.7	19.7	9.9	6.1	12.1	6.5
1928	15.0	19.2	19.0	7.6	28.9	19.3	9.4	6.1	11.3	6.2
1927	14.5	18.6	18.6	7.4	28.2	18.7	8.9	6.2	10.6	5.9
1926	14.0	18.1	18.0	7.2	27.4	18.0	8.6	6.2	10.0	5.7
1925	13.5	17.4	17.5	6.9	26.6	17.2	8.2	6.3	9.5	5.4

CONSUMER INCOME AND EXPENDITURES
Highlights

1 Reasonably reliable nationwide estimates of income distribution are available only from the 1940s when the minimum income requirement for filing income tax returns was substantially lowered to cover the vast majority of the population. Annual tabulations of tax-return data began during World War I but initially covered only a small fraction of the upper-income population. Sample field surveys of family incomes covering all income and occupation groups were introduced in the 1930s. Estimates of income distribution before the 1940s were pieced together from sample surveys in *American Studies of the Distribution of Wealth and Income by Size* (1939) by C. L. Merwin, *The Present Distribution of Wealth in the United States* (1896) by Charles B. Spahr, *Wealth and Income of the People of the United States* (1915) by Willford I. King, *Income in the United States* (1921/22) by W. C. Mitchell, W. I. King, F. R. Maucaulay and O. W. Knauth, and *America's Capacity to Consume* (1934) by Maurive Leven, H. H. Moulton and Clark Warburton. *The Consumer Purchase Study* (1935-36) conducted by the National Resources Committee under Hildegarde Kneeland was the first sample field survey in which income data were collected from all types of families. Based largely on 300,000 family income schedules, it represented a marked improvement over earlier estimates by providing data for numerous subgroups classified by occupation, community, region, color and family size. *The Survey of Spending and Saving in Wartime* is the only other pre-World War II source on the distribution of family income nationwide. The 1940 decennial census was the first to include income questions, making it possible to compare prewar and postwar income levels. For the post-World War II years, income data are available from two sources: the annual Current Population Surveys of the Census Bureau and the annual surveys of consumer finances conducted by the Survey Research Center of the University of Michigan. In addition, all censuses since 1950 provide detailed information on the level of total money income, as well as wage and salary income, classified by demographic and socioeconomic characteristics and cross-classified by sex, race and occupation, and industry groups. Complementing these sources are income and expenditure surveys conducted by the Bureau of Labor Statistics for selected population groups, studies of farm family income by the Department of Agriculture, and, since 1937, surveys of income distributions of workers covered under the Old Age, Survivors, Disability and Health Insurance (OASDHI) program. The much broader coverage of Federal Individual Income Tax Returns since World War II has made it possible to measure changes in relative income distribution over time. As part of its national income work, the Bureau of Economic Analysis, formerly the Office of Business Economics, publishes a personal income series by combining census and income tax data. To derive meaningful comparisons over time, the data for the prewar period have been adjusted to make them compatible with the postwar data. Direct compatibility among income distribution series has not been fully achieved because of variations in definitions and coverage. Definitional differences apply to the basic unit of classification, the income measure, the time period and the family unit.

2 Collection of data on consumer expenditures began in the United States in the 1870s. The most substantial of these studies was made for Massachusetts by Carroll D. Wright in 1875. The usefulness of the data gathered in this study led Congress to request that further studies of this type on a broader base be conducted by the newly formed U.S. Bureau of Labor (of which Wright was made commissioner). The data on food expenditures obtained in the 1901 survey were used to devise an index of food prices purchased by workers. During that period, the need for a more inclusive index of retail prices became clearer because food prices rose much faster than those of many other commodities and rent. A nationwide study of the expenditures of wage earners and clerical workers was undertaken in 1918. The survey was first undertaken in seacoast cities (because of the number of wage disputes in shipbuilding centers) but later was expanded to other industrial centers. The first study of overall consumer expenditures of farm families was made in Livingstone County in New York State in 1909. Dramatic increases in industrial and agricultural productivity and the collapse of the economy in 1929 led a number of economists to study the factors affecting consumer expenditures and to estimate changes in consumption

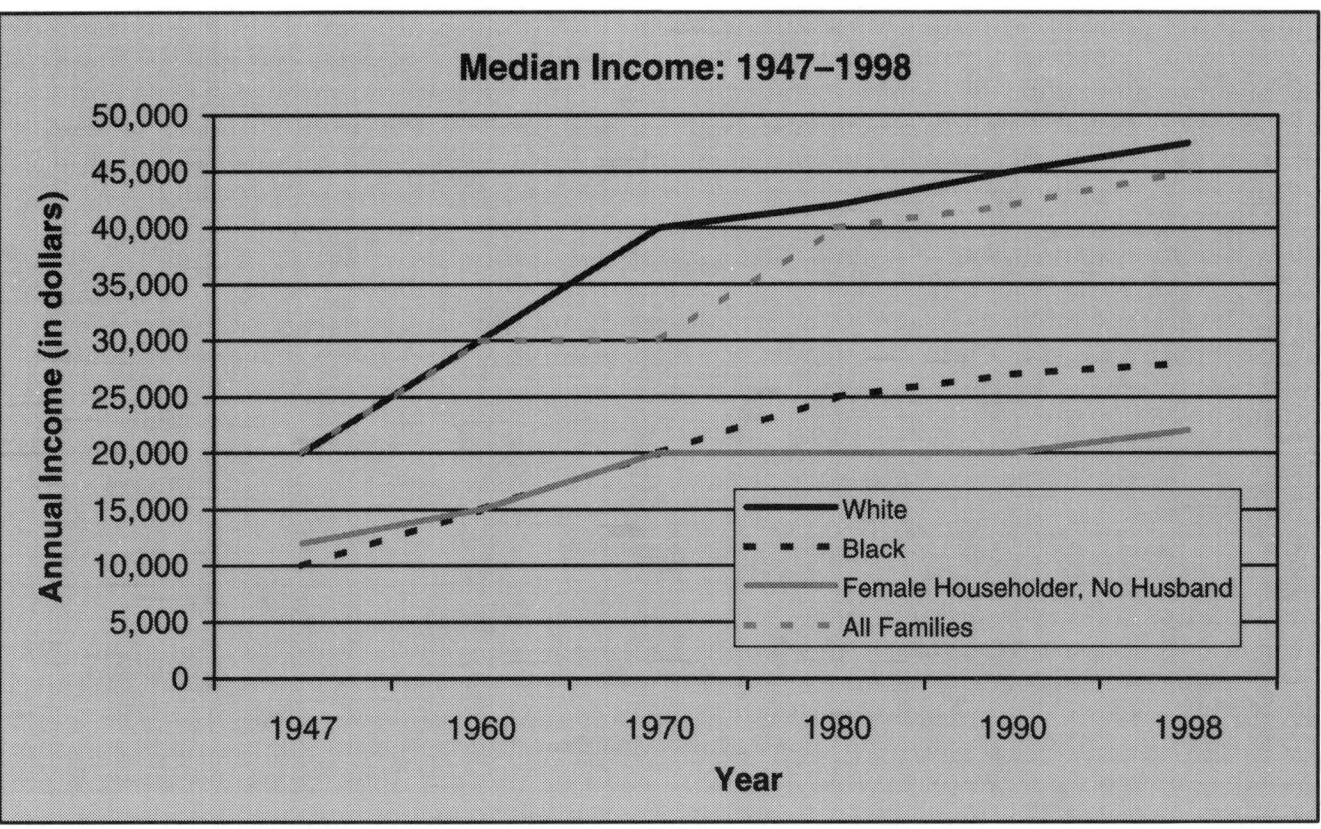

Median Income: 1947–1998

Annual Income (in dollars) / Year

White
Black
Female Householder, No Husband
All Families

patterns over time. The pioneer investigation in this field was presented in Simon Kuznets' *Commodity Flow and Capital Formation* (1938). It showed national aggregates for four types of consumer goods and services. The Brookings Institution published estimates of expenditure patterns at different income levels for farm and nonfarm families in 1934 and for single individuals in 1929. In the middle 1930s, two national cross-section studies of consumer expenditure patterns were undertaken. The first, conducted by the Bureau of Labor Statistics, covered employed city wage and clerical workers and was initiated to provide a new list of items and weights for the Consumer Price Index. The second, the *Study of Consumer Purchases*, was conducted jointly by the Bureau of Labor Statistics and the Bureau of Home Economics of the Department of Agriculture. The results of the second study were used by the National Resources Planning Board as the basis for a national estimate of consumer expenditures. The first detailed estimates and aggregate consumer expenditures in goods and services appeared in *High-Level Consumption* by William H. Lough in 1935 and covered the period from 1909 to 1931. Data for later years were revised and extended in *Outlay and Income in the United States, 1921-1938*, by Harold Barger and in *America's Needs and Resources* (1947) by J. Frederic Dewhurst. The first detailed estimates by the Department of Commerce of consumer expenditures for commodities and services were published in the *Survey of Current Business* in June 1944. As defined by the Department of Commerce, consumer expenditures represent the market value of purchases of goods and services by individuals and nonprofit institutions as well as the value of food, clothing, housing, and financial services received by them as income in kind. Rental value of owner-occupied houses is included, but purchases of dwellings, which are classified as capital goods, are not. Other national sample surveys include the Surveys of Consumer Finances, conducted for the Board of Governors of the Federal Reserve System by the Consumer Research Center of the University of Michigan, and the Household Food Consumption Surveys of the Department of Agriculture.

3 Based on 1982-1984 = 100, the Consumer Price Index in 1998 was 163. The rise was highest in medical care (242.1), shelter (182.1), and food (160.7). It was lowest in fuel oil (84.8), telephone services (100.7), and energy (102.9). The U. S. city average CPI was 163.0, with wide rational variations. It was highest in New York-Northern New Jersey-Long Island ((173.6) and Boston-Lawrence-Salem (171.7), and lowest in Washington-Baltimore (102.1). By selected products and services, the highest rise was for fresh fruits and vegetables (231.2), cable television (245.2), refuse collection (256.7), cereals (189.9), automobile insurance (254.3), airline fares (205.3), medical care (242.1), tobacco products (274.8) and college tuition (306.5).

4 The weekly food cost of a family of two has gone up from a range of $48.10 to $92.70 in 1990 to $58.40 to $113.50 in 1998. Relative cost for a family of four has

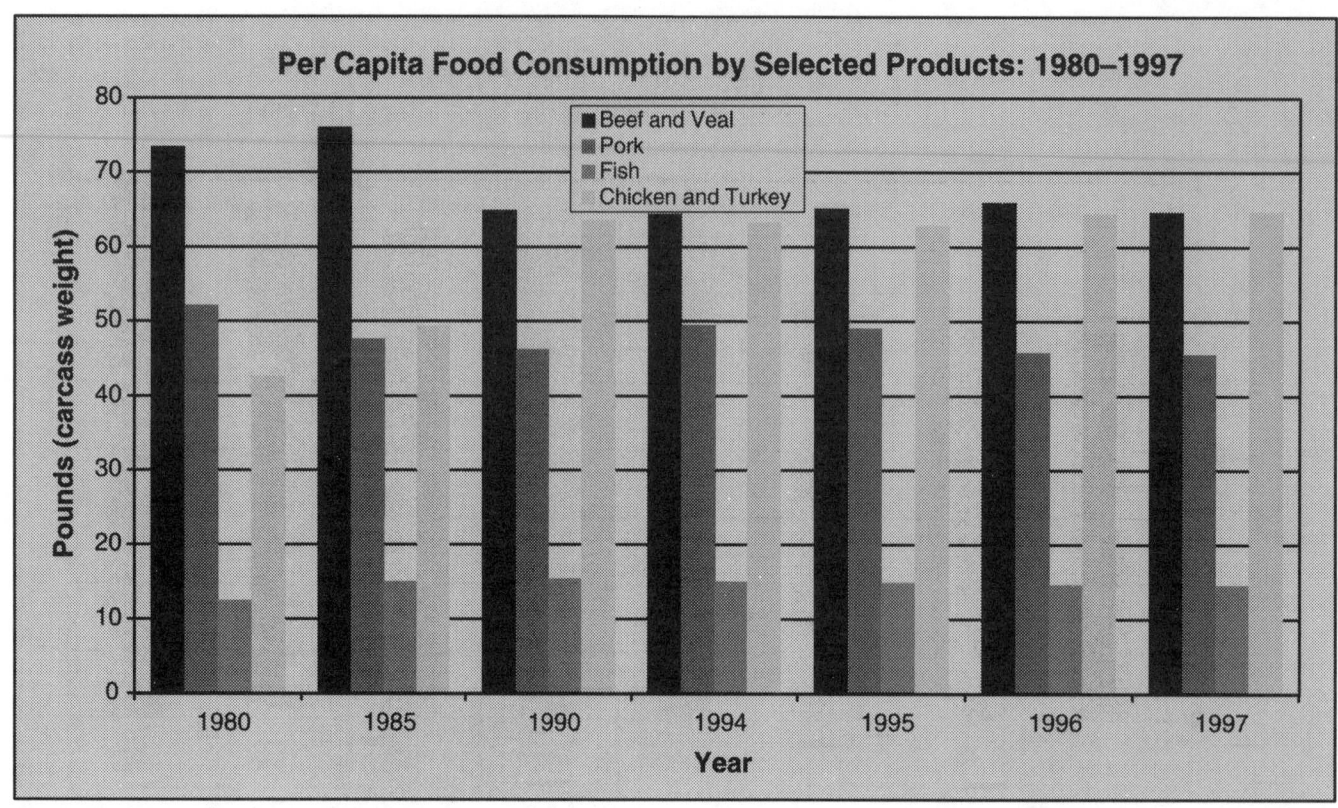

Per Capita Food Consumption by Selected Products: 1980–1997

gone up in the same period from $80.10 to 154.40 to $97.90 to $188.60.

5 Although the annual percentage rise in consumer prices in the United States was only 2.3 in 1997, it has one of the highest rates in the OECD, all countries of which, except five, have much lower rates. For example, Sweden had an annual percentage rise of 0.9 and Switzerland of 0.5.

6 Based on a nationwide average of 100, the most expensive housing was in New York (442.6), Oakland, California (266.1) and Boston (213.8). The cheapest housing was in Albany, Georgia (73.9), San Angelo, Texas (77.3) and Gadsden, Alabama (76.2).

7 The purchasing power of the dollar has declined substantially since 1950. With 1982 = $1.00, the purchasing power of the dollar was $3.456 measured by producer prices and $4.151 measured by consumer prices in 1950. In 1998, the relative values were $0.766 and $0.66.

135

Series G 179-188. Number and Median Money Income of Families and Unrelated Individuals: 1947 to 1997

(Income for calendar year shown)

Year	Total median income $	Year	Total median income $	Year	Total median income $	Year	Total median income $	Year	Total median income $	Year	Total median income $
	179		**179**		**179**		**179**		**179**		**179**
1997	44 658	1982	23 433	1972	11 116	1962	5 956	1952	3 890		
1996	42 300	1981	22 388	1971	10 285	1961	5 737	1951	3 709		
1995	40 611	1980	21 023	1970	9 867	1960	5 620	1950	3 319		
1994	38 782	1979	19 587	1969	9 433	1959	5 417	1949	3 107		
1993	36 959	1978	17 640	1968	8 633	1958	5 087	1948	3 187		
1992	36 573	1977	16 009	1967	7 933	1957	4 971	1947	3 031		
1991	35 939	1976	14 958	1966	7 532	1956	4 783				
1990	35 353	1975	13 719	1965	6 957	1955	4 421				
1989	34 213	1974	12 902	1964	6 569	1954	4 173				
1988	32 191	1973	12 051	1963	6 249	1953	4 233				
1987	30 970										
1986	29 458										
1985	27 735										
1984	26 433										
1983	24 580										

Series G 416-469. Personal Consumption Expenditures by Major Type of Product: 1946 to 1999

(In billions of dollars)

Year	Total	Durable goods	Motor vehicles and parts	Furniture and household equipment	Other	Non-durable goods	Food and beverages	Clothing and shoes	Gasoline, fuel oil, and other energy goods	Other	Services	Housing	Household operation	Trans-portation	Medical care	Recre-ation	Other
1999	6 268.7	761.3	320.7	288.5	152.0	1 845.5	897.8	307.0	142.7	498.0	3 661.9	906.2	360.2	256.5	943.6	237.1	958.4
1998	5 850.9	693.9	288.8	266.1	139.0	1 707.6	845.8	286.4	128.0	447.4	3 449.3	858.2	345.6	244.5	898.6	218.7	883.7
1997	5 529.3	642.5	264.2	248.9	129.4	1 641.6	812.2	271.7	143.2	414.5	3 245.2	810.5	333.0	234.4	854.6	206.2	806.5
1996	5 237.5	616.5	256.3	236.9	123.3	1 574.1	786.0	258.6	139.7	389.8	3 047.0	772.5	317.3	214.2	814.4	191.1	737.5
1995	4 969.0	589.7	249.3	225.0	115.4	1 497.3	755.8	247.8	127.4	366.4	2 882.0	740.8	298.1	197.7	780.7	176.0	688.7
1994	4 716.4	560.8	242.3	211.2	107.2	1 438.0	728.2	240.7	122.5	346.6	2 717.6	704.7	284.0	180.9	737.3	160.0	650.7
1993	4 454.7	513.4	222.1	192.4	98.9	1 375.2	697.9	231.1	119.4	326.8	2 566.1	666.5	268.9	166.2	700.6	151.2	612.6
1992	4 209.7	470.8	200.2	178.7	91.9	1 322.9	669.3	221.9	117.1	314.7	2 415.9	641.3	248.3	155.0	652.6	139.1	579.5
1991	3 971.2	443.0	182.8	171.5	88.7	1 278.8	657.6	208.7	114.8	297.8	2 249.4	616.0	238.6	142.8	591.0	126.4	534.5
1990	3 831.5	467.6	206.4	171.4	89.8	1 246.1	636.9	204.1	120.2	285.0	2 117.8	585.6	227.6	141.8	540.6	120.8	501.5
1989	3 596.7	467.8	211.4	171.4	84.9	1 165.4	591.9	198.9	108.9	265.7	1 963.5	546.4	221.3	136.6	479.2	110.1	469.9
1988	3 356.6	450.2	206.1	163.6	80.5	1 082.9	553.5	185.5	99.3	244.5	1 823.5	511.9	208.4	129.9	429.9	99.0	444.4
1987	3 105.3	419.7	193.1	153.4	73.2	1 015.3	515.3	174.4	96.6	229.1	1 670.3	476.4	196.9	118.2	381.8	87.1	409.3
1986	2 895.2	401.3	192.4	143.0	66.0	958.5	492.0	163.1	91.4	211.9	1 535.4	442.0	188.9	107.3	346.8	81.5	368.9
1985	2 712.6	363.3	175.7	128.5	59.0	928.8	467.6	152.1	110.8	198.2	1 420.6	406.8	182.2	100.0	322.5	75.6	333.6
1984	2 498.4	326.9	152.5	119.0	55.4	884.7	447.4	142.5	108.4	186.3	1 286.9	370.3	169.8	90.0	294.6	67.9	294.4
1983	2 286.4	281.2	126.9	106.6	47.7	831.2	423.8	130.9	106.7	169.8	1 174.0	338.7	157.6	79.4	267.9	61.7	268.9
1982	2 079.3	240.2	102.9	93.4	43.9	787.6	403.4	120.5	108.6	155.2	1 051.5	313.0	143.0	70.9	239.3	54.9	230.4
1981	1 944.2	231.3	95.8	92.1	43.4	758.9	383.5	117.2	113.7	144.5	954.0	287.7	127.3	68.7	213.0	49.3	208.0
1980	1 762.9	214.2	87.0	86.7	40.5	696.1	356.0	107.3	102.1	130.6	852.7	255.1	114.2	64.7	181.2	42.8	194.6
1979	1 596.3	214.4	93.5	82.7	38.2	624.4	324.7	101.2	80.6	118.0	757.4	226.5	101.0	59.1	158.1	38.3	174.5
1978	1 430.4	201.7	93.1	74.3	34.3	550.2	289.6	94.3	61.6	104.7	678.4	201.7	92.1	53.5	140.0	34.5	156.7
1977	1 278.4	181.2	83.5	67.2	30.5	497.2	262.7	84.1	58.0	92.4	600.0	179.5	82.7	49.2	122.6	31.4	134.6
1976	1 149.8	158.9	71.3	60.2	27.4	458.3	242.5	76.6	53.2	86.0	532.6	161.5	73.1	41.3	106.5	28.4	121.7
1975	1 030.1	133.5	54.8	54.5	24.2	420.7	223.2	70.8	48.1	78.5	476.1	147.0	64.3	35.7	93.4	25.4	110.3
1974	932.4	122.3	49.5	51.5	21.3	384.5	201.8	66.0	44.0	72.7	425.5	134.1	56.0	33.3	80.4	22.5	99.1
1973	852.5	123.5	56.1	47.9	19.5	343.1	179.6	62.5	34.4	66.6	385.9	122.7	50.2	31.2	71.5	19.7	90.5
1972	770.7	110.4	51.1	42.4	16.9	308.0	161.4	56.4	29.5	60.8	352.3	112.1	45.7	29.8	63.9	17.6	83.3
1971	702.4	96.9	44.5	37.8	14.6	285.5	149.7	51.7	27.7	56.4	320.0	102.7	41.3	27.1	56.9	16.3	75.7
1970	648.9	85.0	35.5	35.7	13.7	272.0	143.8	47.8	26.3	54.1	292.0	94.0	37.9	23.7	50.4	15.1	70.9
1969	605.5	85.9	38.4	34.7	12.9	253.2	131.5	46.5	25.0	50.2	266.4	86.8	35.2	20.9	44.8	13.8	64.9
1968	558.7	80.8	36.1	32.9	11.8	235.7	122.2	43.2	23.3	47.0	242.3	79.7	32.4	18.9	39.2	12.5	59.6
1967	508.7	70.4	30.0	30.0	10.4	217.1	112.5	39.2	21.9	43.5	221.2	74.1	30.2	17.3	33.9	11.1	54.7
1966	481.8	68.3	30.3	28.2	9.8	208.8	109.3	37.4	20.7	41.4	204.7	69.5	28.2	15.9	30.7	10.4	50.0
1965	444.3	63.3	29.9	25.1	8.2	191.6	100.7	34.1	19.2	37.6	189.5	65.4	26.5	14.5	27.9	9.6	45.5
1964	411.7	56.7	26.0	23.2	7.5	178.7	93.6	32.4	17.7	35.0	176.4	61.4	25.0	13.4	25.8	9.1	41.6
1963	383.1	51.6	24.4	20.7	6.6	168.2	88.3	29.8	17.0	33.1	163.4	58.0	23.6	12.7	22.6	8.5	37.9
1962	363.8	46.9	21.5	19.3	6.1	162.8	86.1	29.0	16.4	31.4	154.1	54.7	22.4	12.2	20.8	8.0	35.9
1961	342.7	41.8	17.8	18.3	5.7	156.6	84.0	27.6	15.8	29.2	144.3	51.2	21.2	11.7	18.7	7.5	34.0
1960	332.3	43.3	19.7	18.0	5.7	152.9	82.3	27.0	15.8	27.7	136.1	48.2	20.3	11.2	17.6	6.9	32.0

See footnotes at end of chart.

Series G 416-469. Personal Consumption Expenditures by Major Type of Product: 1946 to 1999—Cont'd.

(In billions of dollars)

Year	Total	Durable goods	Motor vehicles and parts	Furniture and household equipment	Other	Non-durable goods	Food and beverages	Clothing and shoes	Gasoline, fuel oil, and other energy goods	Other	Services	Housing	Household operation	Trans-portation	Medical care	Recre-ation	Other
1959	318.1	42.7	18.9	18.1	5.7	148.5	80.7	26.4	15.3	26.1	127.0	45.0	18.7	10.5	16.4	6.4	29.9
1958	296.6	37.4	15.1	16.9	5.4	141.7	77.9	24.9	14.8	24.2	117.4	42.0	17.5	9.7	14.8	5.8	27.6
1957	287.0	40.0	17.6	17.2	5.2	137.1	75.1	24.5	14.3	23.2	109.9	39.3	16.4	9.4	13.4	5.6	25.8
1956	271.9	38.1	15.8	17.3	5.0	130.8	71.4	24.4	13.3	21.7	102.9	36.7	15.4	8.9	12.2	5.6	24.1
1955	259.0	38.8	17.7	16.4	4.6	124.7	68.6	23.3	12.4	20.4	95.4	34.4	14.2	8.5	11.3	5.2	22.0
1954	240.5	31.9	12.8	14.8	4.3	119.7	66.8	22.3	11.4	19.3	88.9	32.3	12.7	8.2	10.6	4.8	20.3
1953	233.4	32.7	13.9	14.7	4.1	117.8	65.4	22.2	10.9	19.4	82.9	29.9	12.1	8.0	9.6	4.5	18.8
1952	219.7	29.3	11.4	14.0	3.9	114.7	64.1	22.0	10.2	18.4	75.6	27.0	11.2	7.3	8.6	4.3	17.3
1951	208.6	29.9	12.2	14.1	3.6	109.2	60.7	21.3	9.6	17.6	69.6	24.3	10.4	6.8	7.7	4.0	16.3
1950	192.7	30.7	13.7	13.7	3.3	98.2	53.9	19.6	8.9	15.8	63.7	21.7	9.5	6.2	7.2	3.9	15.2
1949	178.8	25.1	10.6	11.3	3.2	94.9	52.5	19.3	8.4	14.7	58.9	19.6	8.6	5.9	6.7	3.8	14.2
1948	175.4	22.9	8.0	11.5	3.4	96.6	54.2	20.1	8.2	14.1	55.9	17.9	8.1	5.8	6.6	3.8	13.8
1947	162.3	20.4	6.6	10.6	3.3	90.9	52.3	18.8	7.0	12.8	51.0	16.0	7.5	5.3	5.7	3.8	12.7
1946	144.2	15.8	4.1	8.4	3.2	82.7	47.4	18.2	5.9	11.3	45.8	14.2	6.8	5.0	4.7	3.7	11.4

SOURCE: U.S. Bureau of Economic Analysis, National Income and Product Accounts of the United States.

Series G 881-915. Apparent Civilian Per Capita Consumption of Foods: 1849 to 1997

(In pounds, except eggs. Calendar years, except as noted)

Year	Meats (carcass weight)			Fish (edible weight)	Edible fats and oils			Fruits		
	Total	Beef and veal	Pork, excluding lard		Total [1] (fat content)	Margarine [2] (actual weight)	Butter, farm and factory (actual weight)	Fresh (farm weight)		Apples
								Total [3]	Citrus [4]	
	881	882	883	885	886	888	889	890	891	892
1997	111.0	64.7	45.6	14.5	65.6	8.6	4.2	133.2	26.8	18.5
1996	112.8	66.0	45.9	14.7	65.8	9.2	4.3	129.0	24.9	19.0
1995	115.1	65.2	49.0	14.9	66.9	9.2	4.5	126.1	24.1	19.0
1994	114.7	64.4	49.5	15.1	68.6	9.9	4.8	126.5	25.0	19.6
1993	112.1	62.3	48.9	14.9	68.3	11.1	4.7	124.9	26.0	19.2
1992	114.1	63.6	49.5	14.7	65.7	11.0	4.4	123.5	24.4	19.3
1991	111.9	63.9	46.9	14.8	63.9	10.6	4.4	113.2	19.1	18.2
1990	112.3	64.9	46.3	15.5	62.7	10.9	4.4	92.3	22.6	19.8
1989	115.9	66.4	48.4	15.6	61.1	10.2	4.4	99.2	24.9	21.6
1988	119.5	69.7	48.8	15.2	63.0	10.3	4.5	99.2	26.4	20.0
1987	117.4	70.8	45.6	16.2	62.9	10.5	4.7	101.1	25.8	21.3
1986	122.2	76.0	45.2	15.5	64.3	11.4	4.6	95.9	26.1	18.2
1985	124.9	76.1	47.7	15.1	64.3	10.8	4.9	89.3	22.6	17.5
1984	151.9	79.9	61.5	13.7	58.6	10.4	4.9	91.7	24.0	18.6
1983	152.3	79.8	61.9	13.1	60.0	10.4	4.9	93.2	29.5	18.5
1982	147.0	78.5	58.5	12.3	58.2	11.0	4.3	87.6	24.8	17.7
1981	154.4	78.7	64.9	12.9	57.7	11.1	4.2	83.1	24.1	16.1
1980	126.4	73.4	52.1	12.5	57.2	11.3	4.5	90.0	28.9	19.2
1979	177.8	107.5	68.8	13.0	55.8	11.2	4.5	83.3	24.5	17.0
1978	182.7	120.8	60.3	13.4	54.6	11.2	4.4	81.5	26.5	15.8
1977	190.0	127.8	60.5	12.7	53.0	11.4	4.3	82.0	26.2	17.0
1976	192.1	131.6	58.7	12.9	54.8	11.9	4.3	85.5	29.0	18.7
1975	180.5	123.7	54.8	12.2	52.6	11.0	4.7	85.0	29.4	19.5
1974	188.0	119.1	66.6	12.0	53.5	11.3	4.6	78.3	27.3	15.8
1973	175.7	111.4	61.6	12.7	54.4	11.3	4.8	75.6	27.3	14.5
1972	189.0	118.3	67.4	12.5	54.2	11.3	4.9	77.0	27.2	17.4
1971	191.8	115.7	73.0	11.5	52.2	11.1	5.1	79.8	29.2	16.2
1970	186.3	116.6	66.4	14.8	53.2	11.0	5.3	81.0	28.6	18.3
1969	182.5	114.1	65.0	14.2	51.9	10.8	5.4	79.0	28.3	14.9
1968	183.2	113.3	66.2	14.0	51.2	10.8	5.7	78.3	26.3	15.7
1967	178.3	110.3	64.1	13.6	49.4	10.5	5.5	80.9	31.6	16.2
1966	170.9	108.8	58.1	13.9	49.7	10.5	5.7	81.4	29.1	16.1
1965	167.1	104.7	58.7	13.9	47.8	9.9	6.4	81.1	29.1	16.3
1964	174.7	105.1	65.4	13.5	47.6	9.7	6.9	78.7	26.2	17.9
1963	169.7	99.4	65.4	13.7	46.3	9.6	6.9	74.5	22.1	16.7
1962	163.1	94.4	63.5	13.6	45.7	9.3	7.3	83.4	29.5	17.4
1961	160.5	93.4	62.0	13.7	45.1	9.4	7.4	88.6	30.8	16.4
1960 *	160.9	91.2	64.9	13.2	45.3	9.4	7.5	93.4	33.7	18.3
1959	159.5	87.1	67.6	13.7	46.2	9.2	7.9	95.7	34.0	21.1
1958	151.6	87.2	60.2	13.3	45.3	9.0	8.3	94.0	31.0	22.5
1957	158.7	93.4	61.1	12.8	44.4	8.6	8.3	96.7	37.1	19.3
1956	166.7	94.9	67.3	12.9	45.2	8.2	8.7	98.9	39.1	18.9
1955	162.8	91.4	66.8	12.9	45.9	8.2	9.0	99.4	41.8	19.6
1954	154.7	90.1	60.0	13.5	45.5	8.5	8.9	105.1	42.0	20.0
1953	155.3	87.1	63.5	13.6	44.1	8.1	8.5	109.4	44.1	20.9
1952	146.0	69.4	72.4	13.3	44.1	7.9	8.6	114.4	45.1	21.6
1951	138.0	62.7	71.9	13.2	42.1	6.6	9.6	118.0	45.8	25.7
1950	144.6	71.4	69.2	13.8	45.9	6.1	10.7	108.8	41.7	22.7
1949	144.6	72.8	67.7	12.9	42.5	5.8	10.5	122.9	47.9	24.7
1948	145.5	72.6	67.8	13.1	42.6	6.1	10.0	131.6	54.4	26.3
1947	155.3	80.4	69.6	12.3	42.0	5.0	11.2	143.7	62.2	25.4
1946	154.1	71.6	75.8	12.8	40.0	3.9	10.5	133.9	59.1	23.0
1945	145.2	71.3	66.6	11.9	39.1	4.1	10.9	139.9	66.6	22.9
1944	154.2	68.0	79.5	10.7	40.9	3.9	11.9	140.1	68.2	25.5
1943	146.8	61.5	78.9	9.9	41.5	3.9	11.8	118.4	60.3	24.9
1942	140.3	69.4	63.7	10.7	44.9	2.8	15.9	130.0	57.7	28.1
1941	143.7	68.5	68.4	13.2	47.6	2.8	16.1	146.0	57.7	31.7

See footnotes at end of chart.

Series G 881-915. Apparent Civilian Per Capita Consumption of Foods: 1849 to 1997—Cont'd.

(In pounds, except eggs. Calendar years, except as noted)

Year	Meats (carcass weight)			Fish (edible weight)	Edible fats and oils			Fruits		
	Total	Beef and veal	Pork, excluding lard		Total [1] (fat content)	Margarine [2] (actual weight)	Butter, farm and factory (actual weight)	Fresh (farm weight)		Apples
								Total [3]	Citrus [4]	
	881	882	883	885	886	888	889	890	891	892
1940	142.4	62.3	73.5	13.0	46.4	2.4	17.0	139.1	56.7	29.7
1939	133.6	62.3	64.7	12.7	46.4	2.3	17.4	148.2	61.4	30.7
1938	127.1	62.0	58.2	12.8	45.3	3.0	16.6	131.7	49.1	28.2
1937	126.2	63.8	55.8	13.8	45.5	3.1	16.8	138.6	44.5	33.6
1936	130.6	68.9	55.1	13.7	45.7	3.1	16.8	125.6	46.2	27.6
1935	117.4	61.7	48.4	12.5	44.1	3.0	17.6	133.2	44.6	32.9
1934	143.9	73.2	64.4	11.2	44.5	2.1	18.6	116.3	39.8	25.3
1933	136.1	58.6	70.7	10.7	43.0	1.9	18.2	124.8	39.4	40.0
1932	131.1	53.3	70.7	10.4	42.9	1.6	18.5	125.9	36.7	39.2
1931	130.7	55.2	68.4	10.8	44.4	1.9	18.3	160.3	42.3	51.7
1930	129.0	55.3	67.0	12.2	. . .	2.6	17.6	129.9	31.2	42.1
1929	131.2	56.0	69.6	13.9	. . .	2.9	17.6	139.2	39.8	39.7
1928	131.6	55.2	70.9	14.1	. . .	2.6	17.6	146.1	29.5	48.9
1927	134.9	61.9	67.7	14.2	. . .	2.3	18.3	126.0	32.2	37.4
1926	138.0	68.5	64.1	13.4	. . .	2.0	18.3	160.8	31.4	62.3
1925	140.1	68.1	66.8	13.1	. . .	2.0	18.1	132.2	28.9	46.3
1924	147.3	68.1	74.0	13.0	. . .	2.0	17.8	148.0	33.9	54.1
1923	147.6	67.8	74.2	12.7	. . .	2.0	17.8	144.5	32.5	54.7
1922	137.7	66.9	65.7	13.3	. . .	1.7	17.1	144.8	24.6	57.5
1921	134.0	63.1	64.8	12.5	. . .	2.0	16.3	112.8	30.5	36.1
1920	136.0	67.1	63.5	13.8	. . .	3.4	14.9	142.6	26.0	63.0
1919	138.9	69.3	63.9	13.6	. . .	3.4	15.2	122.3	23.5	45.2
1918	141.6	75.8	61.0	12.9	. . .	3.3	14.1	119.6	16.5	56.9
1917	135.3	71.9	58.9	12.9	. . .	2.7	15.7	129.8	22.0	56.1
1916	140.1	65.3	69.0	13.0	. . .	1.8	17.3	133.7	22.0	63.9
1915	134.9	62.3	66.5	13.2	. . .	1.4	17.2	154.5	23.1	69.0
1914	140.0	67.8	65.1	13.7	. . .	1.4	17.0	160.4	24.1	71.8
1913	143.7	69.6	66.9	13.5	. . .	1.5	16.5	130.2	16.6	59.3
1912	145.9	71.5	66.7	13.3	. . .	1.5	16.6	156.5	18.5	74.6
1911	151.9	75.6	69.0	13.3	. . .	1.1	18.6	152.6	19.8	73.5
1910	146.4	77.6	62.3	13.2	. . .	1.6	18.3	134.7	17.8	59.4
1909	155.2	81.5	67.0	13.0	. . .	1.2	17.8	135.0	16.2	62.2
1908	163.3	79.3	77.7	. . .	. . .	1.0	19.7	. . .	. . .	. . .
1907	158.2	77.8	74.1	. . .	. . .	.9	17.6	. . .	. . .	. . .
1906	155.6	78.3	71.0	. . .	. . .	.8	17.8	. . .	. . .	. . .
1905	155.2	77.9	71.0	. . .	. . .	.6	19.9	. . .	. . .	. . .
1904	152.7	75.6	70.6	. . .	. . .	.6	18.5	. . .	. . .	. . .
1913	152.1	77.0	68.2	. . .	. . .	.6	18.3	. . .	. . .	. . .
1902	144.8	71.0	66.7	. . .	. . .	.9	17.6	. . .	. . .	. . .
1901	151.1	73.3	70.8	. . .	. . .	1.6	20.0	. . .	. . .	. . .
1900	150.7	72.3	71.9	. . .	. . .	1.3	20.1	. . .	. . .	. . .
1899	150.7	72.4	71.8	. . .	. . .	1.4	19.6	. . .	. . .	. . .

* Denotes first year for which figures include Alaska and Hawaii.
1. Computed from unrounded numbers.
2. Prior to 1909, data are for year beginning July.
3. Beginning in 1934, excludes apples from non-commercial areas. Citrus fruits on crop year basis, 1941 to date.
4. Beginning 1941, year begins October or November prior to year indicated.

Year	Butter (actual weight)	Year	Butter (actual weight)	Year	Butter (actual weight)	Year	Butter (actual weight)	Year	Butter (actual weight)	Year	Butter (actual weight)
	889		889		889		889		889		889
1898	19.8	1892	15.9	1886	16.8	1881	15.2	1876	14.5	1871	11.7
1897	20.8	1891	16.7	1885	16.1	1880	15.5	1875	12.4	1870	10.7
1896	22.2	1890	18.2	1884	15.3	1879	15.6	1874	13.4	1869	13.6
1895	18.4	1889	20.5								
1894	15.4			1883	15.2	1878	14.6	1873	13.4	1859	14.8
		1888	16.0	1882	13.9	1877	14.4	1872	10.6	1849	13.7
1893	15.5	1887	16.3								

Series G 881-915.   Apparent Civilian Per Capita Consumption of Foods: 1849 to 1997—Cont'd.

(In pounds, except eggs. Calendar years, except as noted)

| Year | Potatoes (farm weight) | Fresh vegetables (farm weight) | Dairy products | | | Eggs (number) | Chicken and turkey [2] (ready-to-cook) | Wheat flour | Peanuts (shelled) [3] | Coffee (greenbean basis) |
			Fluid milk and cream [1]	Cheese	Ice cream (product weight)					
	897	899	905	907	908	909	910	912	914	915
1997.........	47.9	185.6	...	28.0	16.2	239	64.8	149.7	5.8	9.3
1996.........	50.0	181.8	...	27.7	15.9	237	64.4	148.8	5.7	9.0
1995.........	49.2	175.1	223.8	27.3	15.7	235	62.9	141.8	5.7	8.0
1994.........	50.3	177.4	225.4	26.8	16.1	238	63.3	144.5	5.8	8.2
1993.........	49.3	171.9	225.7	26.2	16.1	235.6	62.5	143.3	6.0	9.1
1992.........	48.6	171.1	230.5	26.0	16.3	235.0	60.8	138.8	6.2	10.0
1991.........	46.4	163.3	233	25.0	16.3	233.7	58.3	136.9	6.5	10.3
1990.........	127.2	111.0	233.2	24.7	15.7	233	63.6	137.8	6.0	10.2
1989.........	126.7	112.9	236.4	23.9	16.1	236	60.8	129.2	7.0	10.3
1988.........	122.2	109.6	234.6	23.7	17.3	246	57.4	130.0	6.9	9.8
1987.........	125.7	105.7	238.5	24.1	18.4	254	55.5	129.9	6.4	10.2
1986.........	125.7	99.3	240.5	23.1	18.4	254	51.3	125.7	6.4	10.5
1985.........	122.4	100.2	241.0	22.5	18.1	255	49.4	124.7	6.3	10.5
1984.........	121.9	100.3	236.0	21.4	18.1	259	66.5	118.1	6.0	10.1
1983.........	118.4	92.6	236.1	20.5	18.0	260	64.6	117.4	5.9	10.2
1982.........	114.8	95.9	235.7	19.9	17.6	264	63.5	116.7	5.9	10.2
1981.........	69.6	71.5	240.6	18.2	17.4	264	62.0	115.8	5.5	10.3
1980.........	114.3	92.7	245.6	17.5	17.5	271	42.6	116.9	4.8	10.3
1979.........	116.0	105.9	254.0	17.2	17.1	278	60.5	117.0	6.8	11.3
1978.........	119.0	103.6	257.0	17.0	17.4	273	55.8	115.0	6.8	10.5
1977.........	120.0	101.6	260.0	16.1	17.5	268	53.2	115.0	6.3	9.4
1976.........	114.0	100.9	264.0	15.7	17.9	270	51.8	119.0	6.2	12.5
1975.........	122.2	89.9	261.4	14.3	18.6	276	48.9	114.5	6.0	12.2
1974.........	116.0	105.0	244.0	14.6	17.5	287	49.9	106.0	6.4	12.8
1973.........	116.0	100.0	257.0	13.7	17.5	294	49.2	109.0	6.6	13.7
1972.........	119.0	98.3	263.0	13.2	17.4	307	51.0	109.0	6.2	13.9
1971.........	119.0	99.2	259.0	12.2	17.5	314	49.8	110.0	5.9	13.3
1970.........	91.0	98.9	264.0	11.5	17.7	319	49.5	110	5.9	13.8
1969.........	92.0	98.9	272.0	11.0	18.0	318	47.4	112	5.9	14.2
1968.........	94.0	98.7	280.0	10.6	18.4	321	45.4	112	5.8	14.9
1967.........	92.0	98.1	285.0	10.1	17.8	324	45.8	112	5.7	14.8
1966.........	96.0	96.0	297.0	9.8	18.2	314	43.9	112	5.5	14.5
1965.........	93.0	98.6	302.0	9.6	18.5	314	40.9	113	5.6	14.8
1964.........	96.0	98.6	304.0	9.4	18.3	318	38.5	114	5.3	15.3
1963.........	100.0	101.4	307.0	9.2	18.0	318	37.5	114	5.0	15.7
1962.........	98.0	101.4	308.0	9.2	17.9	327	37.0	115	4.9	15.9
1961.........	102.0	103.8	312.0	8.6	18.0	329	37.4	118	4.9	15.8
1960 *........	101.0	105.9	322.0	8.3	18.3	335	34.2	118	4.9	15.8
1959.........	101.0	102.3	330.0	8.0	18.7	352	35.2	120	4.7	15.9
1958.........	101.0	103.7	337.0	8.1	17.8	354	34.0	121	4.5	15.5
1957.........	106.0	106.4	344.0	7.7	18.0	362	31.4	119	4.5	15.7
1956.........	99.0	107.0	348.0	8.0	18.0	369	29.6	121	4.4	15.8
1955.........	106.0	105.2	348.0	7.9	18.0	371	26.3	123	4.1	15.3
1954.........	106.0	107.2	346.0	7.9	17.4	376	28.1	126	4.2	14.7
1953.........	106.0	109.1	346.0	7.5	18.0	379	26.7	128	4.4	16.9
1952.........	101.0	111.6	350.0	7.6	17.9	390	26.8	131	4.4	16.9
1951.........	113.0	111.9	350.0	7.2	17.4	393	26.1	133	4.6	16.6
1950.........	106	115.2	348.0	7.7	17.2	389	24.7	135	4.5	16.1
1949.........	110	116.2	352.0	7.3	17.6	383	22.9	136	4.1	18.7
1948.........	105	123.0	355.0	6.9	18.5	389	21.4	137	4.6	18.4
1947.........	125	122.4	369.0	6.9	20.1	383	21.7	139	4.5	17.4
1946.........	123	129.9	389.0	6.7	23.1	379	23.1	156	5.3	20.1
1945.........	122	134.3	399.0	6.7	15.7	403	25.1	161	6.6	16.4
1944.........	136	123.9	381.0	4.9	14.3	354	23.1	149	6.0	15.8
1943.........	125	116.7	371.0	4.9	13.1	347	25.7	163	5.7	12.9
1942.........	127	119.0	354.0	6.4	15.8	318	20.7	157	6.2	13.6
1941.........	128	113.8	334.0	5.9	13.6	311	18.3	156	4.8	15.9

See footnotes at end of chart.

Series G 881-915. Apparent Civilian Per Capita Consumption of Foods: 1849 to 1997—Cont'd.

(In pounds, except eggs. Calendar years, except as noted)

Year	Potatoes (farm weight)	Fresh vegetables (farm weight)	Dairy products			Eggs (number)	Chicken and turkey [2] (ready-to-cook)	Wheat flour	Peanuts (shelled) [3]	Coffee (greenbean basis)
			Fluid milk and cream [1]	Cheese	Ice cream (product weight)					
	897	899	905	907	908	909	910	912	914	915
1940	123	116.9	331.0	6.0	11.4	319	17.0	155	5.0	15.5
1939	122	116.6	332.0	6.0	11.0	313	16.6	158	4.4	14.9
1938	129	114.5	329.0	5.9	10.4	310	15.0	160	4.3	14.9
1937	126	111.0	331.0	5.5	10.6	308	15.9	159	4.4	13.3
1936	130	112.5	330.0	5.4	9.5	289	15.9	163	4.6	13.7
1935	142	111.2	326.0	5.3	8.1	280	14.8	158	4.0	13.4
1934	135	115.2	322.0	4.9	7.1	289	15.3	157	3.3	12.3
1933	132	104.5	337.0	4.6	6.1	296	16.7	162	3.6	12.8
1932	134	108.8	339.0	4.4	6.3	313	16.0	170	4.1	12.4
1931	136	108.3	335.0	4.5	8.6	333	15.5	169	4.4	13.0
1930	132	111.9	337.0	4.7	9.8	331	17.2	171	3.2	12.5
1929	159	112.6	340.0	4.7	10.7	334	15.7	177	4.1	12.2
1928	147	104.2	337.0	4.4	9.9	338	14.6	179	3.8	11.9
1927	141	106.0	336.0	4.6	9.9	342	15.2	181	3.9	12.2
1926	128	100.6	338.0	4.6	9.5	339	14.2	182	3.4	12.4
1925	157	101.3	337.0	4.7	9.7	318	14.3	180	3.6	10.6
1924	154	100.9	336.0	4.6	8.8	324	13.7	180	3.5	12.2
1923	174	90.1	328.0	4.5	9.0	326	14.6	180	3.2	12.6
1922	143	92.8	342.0	4.3	8.2	316	14.2	180	2.7	11.8
1921	156	82.2	346.0	4.2	7.6	300	13.4	167	2.7	12.0
1920	140	95.0	348.0	4.0	7.6	299	13.7	179	3.0	11.7
1919	152	76.6	335.0	4.2	6.8	303	14.2	192	4.6	11.8
1918	174	...	361.0	3.9	6.4	284	13.3	179	2.8	10.0
1917	146	...	328.0	3.7	4.8	281	13.3	191	4.2	12.1
1916	143	...	315.0	3.8	4.3	299	13.8	204	2.8	11.5
1915	185	...	318.0	4.1	3.9	313	14.4	205	2.8	10.6
1914	157	...	321.0	4.2	3.4	295	14.5	207	2.5	9.2
1913	189	...	342.0	4.2	3.0	303	14.5	209	2.5	9.0
1912	179	...	355.0	3.9	2.7	312	14.9	211	2.3	10.8
1911	157	...	301.0	4.0	2.3	329	15.6	213	2.3	8.3
1910	198	...	315.0	4.3	1.9	306	15.5	214	2.5	9.2
1909	187	...	343.0	3.8	1.6	293	14.7	217	2.4	...

1. Cream included on whole-milk equivalent basis.
2. Chicken only, 1909-1928, but turkey consumption very small during that time.
3. September-August year through 1939; August-July year, thereafter.

Year	Cheese 907	Year	Cheese 907	Year	Cheese 907	Year	Cheese 907	Year	Cheese 907	Year	Cheese 907
1908	3.8	1898	3.4	1888	3.5	1878	3.5	1873	2.9	1859	2.9
1907	3.5	1897	3.6	1887	3.2	1877	2.7	1872	3.0	1849	4.1
1906	3.5	1896	2.9	1886	2.8	1876	2.6	1871	2.4		
1905	4.1	1895	2.9	1885	3.0	1875	3.1	1870	3.2		
1904	4.1	1894	2.9	1884	3.1	1874	2.6	1869	3.0		
1903	4.0	1893	2.9	1883	3.3						
1902	4.0	1892	3.7	1882	3.1						
1901	4.5	1891	3.5	1881	3.2						
1900	3.7	1890	3.8	1880	2.7						
1899	3.7	1889	3.5	1879	2.2						

Series GG-1. Families by Total Money Income, Race, and Hispanic Origin of Householder: 1967 to 1999

(Families as of March of the following year. Income in 1999 CPI-U adjusted dollars. Before 1983, constant dollar entries are based on the CPI-U-X1)

Race and Hispanic origin of house-holder and year	Number -1,000	Total	Under $5,000	$5,000 to $9,999	$10,000 to $14,999	$15,000 to $24,999	$25,000 to $34,999	$35,000 to $49,999	$50,000 to $74,999	$75,000 to $99,999	$100,000 and over	Value (dollars)	Standard error (dollars)
ALL RACES													
1999	72 031	100	2.4	3.3	4.8	12	11.9	16.5	21.2	12.7	15.2	48 950	300
1998	71 551	100	2.6	3.7	5.1	12.1	12.5	16.4	21.7	11.9	14	47 769	246
1997	70 884	100	2.7	3.9	5.3	12.7	12.4	17.3	21.4	11.5	12.9	46 262	266
1996	70 241	100	2.6	4.5	5.6	12.6	13.1	17.2	21.5	10.9	11.9	44 916	222
1995	69 597	100	2.4	4.1	5.8	13	13.4	17.6	21.2	11	11.4	44 395	232
1990	66 322	100	2.5	4.2	5.4	12.3	13.2	18.6	21.8	11.4	10.7	45 064	216
1985	63 558	100	2.6	4.5	5.7	13.5	13.5	18.9	21.8	10.8	8.7	42 943	232
1980	60 309	100	2	4.1	6.1	13.6	14	20.3	23.5	9.5	6.9	42 557	182
1975	56 245	100	1.7	4.2	6.6	14.3	14.7	22.1	23	8.2	5.2	40 669	154
1970	52 227	100	2.2	4.4	5.9	13.9	15.9	24	21.8	7.2	4.7	39 802	(NA)
1967	50 111	100	2.4	5.4	6.7	14.9	18.3	24.4	19	5.2	3.6	36 409	(NA)
WHITE													
1999	60 256	100	1.8	2.6	4.2	11.6	11.8	16.7	22.1	13.3	16	51 224	258
1998	60 077	100	2	2.9	4.6	11.3	12.5	16.7	22.5	12.4	15.1	50 106	289
1997	59 515	100	2.1	3.1	4.7	12.1	12.3	17.4	22.2	12.3	13.9	48 531	258
1996	58 934	100	1.8	3.5	4.9	12	13.1	17.6	22.5	11.6	12.8	47 523	282
1995	58 872	100	1.8	3.2	5.2	12.5	13.3	17.9	22.2	11.6	12.4	46 619	280
1990	56 803	100	1.8	3.2	4.6	11.9	13.2	19	22.8	12	11.5	47 055	227
1985	54 991	100	2.1	3.5	5	12.8	13.4	19.4	22.8	11.4	9.5	45 136	243
1980	52 710	100	1.6	3.2	5.2	12.9	13.9	20.9	24.7	10.1	7.5	44 340	190
1975	49 873	100	1.4	3.4	5.7	13.7	14.6	22.7	24.1	8.7	5.6	42 296	154
1970	46 535	100	1.9	3.7	5.3	13	15.8	24.8	22.9	7.6	5.1	41 291	(NA)
1967	44 814	100	2	4.7	5.9	14	18.4	25.4	20.1	5.5	3.9	37 791	(NA)
BLACK													
1999	8 664	100	6.3	8.3	9.1	16	13.6	15.3	15.8	8.1	7.5	31 778	603
1998	8 452	100	6.3	9.3	9	18.1	13.4	14.9	16.1	7.2	5.6	30 053	729
1997	8 408	100	6.6	9.8	9.5	17.7	13.6	15.8	16.3	5.9	4.8	29 690	626
1996	8 455	100	7.2	10.8	10.2	17.2	14	15.4	15.3	5.5	4.4	28 162	500
1995	8 055	100	6.9	10.8	10.2	17.2	14.4	15.8	14.4	6.4	3.9	28 389	676
1990	7 471	100	7.7	11.6	11.3	15.6	13.5	16.2	14.5	5.9	3.7	27 307	485
1985	6 921	100	6.5	12.8	10.8	18.8	14	15.5	13.7	5.6	2.4	25 991	474
1980	6 317	100	5.2	11.1	13.3	19.5	14.5	16.2	13.7	4.6	1.8	25 656	551
1975	5 586	100	3.9	11.2	14.1	19.7	16.4	16.8	13.4	3.5	1.1	26 024	373
1970	4 928	100	5.1	11.2	12.1	21.5	17.4	17	11.7	3	1.1	25 329	(NA)
1967	4 589	100	6.2	12.2	14.5	23.4	17.7	14.6	8.2	2.1	1	22 373	(NA)
ASIAN AND PACIFIC ISLANDER													
1999	2 506	100	2.8	3.8	4.8	9	9.1	14.8	18.5	12.8	24.3	56 316	1 656
1998	2 459	100	3.6	3.7	3.6	9.4	10.3	15.3	20.2	15	19	53 993	1 838
1997	2 381	100	2.9	2.5	5.2	8.7	9.6	17.5	21.4	13.8	18.3	53 820	1 865
1996	2 247	100	3.9	3.5	4.9	9.7	10.5	15.4	19.8	14	18.2	52 141	2 025
1995	2 125	100	2.7	4.3	6	9.6	11.3	15.7	22.1	12.8	15.5	50 675	1 175
1990	1 536	100	3.3	2.9	3.9	10.8	10.3	14.7	21.5	15.3	17.3	53 851	2 002

Series GG-1. Families by Total Money Income, Race, and Hispanic Origin of Householder: 1967 to 1999—Cont'd.

(Families as of March of the following year. Income in 1999 CPI-U adjusted dollars. Before 1983, constant dollar entries are based on the CPI-U-X1)

Race and Hispanic origin of householder and year	Number -1,000	Total	Under $5,000	$5,000 to $9,999	$10,000 to $14,999	$15,000 to $24,999	$25,000 to $34,999	$35,000 to $49,999	$50,000 to $74,999	$75,000 to $99,999	$100,000 and over	Value (dollars)	Standard error (dollars)
HISPANIC ORIGIN													
1999....................	7 561	100	4.3	5.7	8.9	19.7	15.9	16.7	15.9	7.3	5.5	31 663	490
1998....................	7 273	100	4.8	7	10.1	18.8	17	16	15.2	5.8	5.4	30 262	581
1997....................	6 961	100	4.9	8.1	10.6	19.9	15.3	17	13.1	6	5	29 211	652
1996....................	6 631	100	4.6	9.1	10.9	20.3	16.1	15.9	13.2	5.6	4.3	27 798	526
1995....................	6 287	100	4.9	9.3	11.3	21.4	16	15.1	13.4	4.8	3.8	26 859	607
1990....................	4 981	100	4.3	8.4	10.8	18.8	15.5	17.7	14.6	5.9	4	29 867	722
1985....................	4 206	100	4	9.1	11.1	19.2	15.6	17.6	14.5	6	3	29 460	758
1980....................	3 235	100	3.6	7.7	10.3	20.2	16.9	17.8	16.2	4.6	2.6	29 790	795
1975....................	2 499	100	3	9.1	10.5	21.4	17.4	20.8	13.2	3.1	1.5	28 313	679
1972....................	2 312	100	2.5	6	9.9	21	20.6	22	12.8	3.5	1.8	30 704	(NA)
NONHISPANIC WHITE													
1999....................	53 071	100	1.5	2.2	3.6	10.5	11.2	16.7	22.9	14.2	17.5	54 121	355
1998....................	53 107	100	1.7	2.4	3.8	10.3	11.9	16.8	23.5	13.3	16.4	52 747	266
1997....................	52 875	100	1.7	2.4	4	11.1	11.9	17.5	23.3	13.1	15	51 522	321
1996....................	52 625	100	1.6	2.9	4.2	11	12.7	17.8	23.6	12.4	13.8	49 930	268
1995....................	52 861	100	1.4	2.5	4.5	11.4	13	18.2	23.2	12.4	13.3	49 212	277
1990....................	52 038	100	1.5	2.7	4	11.2	13	19.1	23.6	12.6	12.2	48 742	279
1985....................	50 912	100	1.9	3.1	4.6	12.3	13.3	19.5	23.5	11.8	10	46 538	247
1980....................	49 584	100	1.5	2.9	4.9	12.5	13.7	21.1	25.2	10.4	7.8	45 215	213
1975....................	47 447	100	1.3	3.1	5.5	13.3	14.4	22.7	24.7	9	5.8	43 023	220
1972....................	46 213	100	1.5	3.1	4.9	12.3	14.5	23.2	24.5	9.6	6.5	43 879	188

SOURCE: U.S. Census Bureau, Current Population Survey.

Series GG-2. Share of Aggregate Income Received by Each Fifth and Top Five Percent of Households (All Races): 1967 to 1999

(Households as of March of the following year)

Year	Shares of aggregate income			Third fifth	Fourth fifth	Highest fifth	Top 5 percent
	Number (thous.)	Lowest fifth	Second fifth				
1999	104 705	3.6	8.9	14.9	23.2	49.4	21.5
1998	103 874	3.6	9	15	23.2	49.2	21.4
1997	102 528	3.6	8.9	15	23.2	49.4	21.7
1996	101 018	3.7	9	15.1	23.3	49	21.4
1995	99 627	3.7	9.1	15.2	23.3	48.7	21
1994	98 990	3.6	8.9	15	23.4	49.1	21.2
1993	97 107	3.6	9	15.1	23.5	48.9	21
1992	96 426	3.8	9.4	15.8	24.2	46.9	18.6
1991	95 669	3.8	9.6	15.9	24.2	46.5	18.1
1990	94 312	3.9	9.6	15.9	24	46.6	18.6
1989	93 347	3.8	9.5	15.8	24	46.8	18.9
1988	92 830	3.8	9.6	16	24.3	46.3	18.3
1987	91 124	3.8	9.6	16.1	24.3	46.2	18.2
1986	89 479	3.9	9.7	16.2	24.5	45.7	17.5
1985	88 458	4	9.7	16.3	24.6	45.3	17
1984	86 789	4.1	9.9	16.4	24.7	44.9	16.5
1983	85 290	4.1	10	16.5	24.7	44.7	16.4
1982	83 918	4.1	10.1	16.6	24.7	44.5	16.2
1981	83 527	4.2	10.2	16.8	25	43.8	15.6
1980	82 368	4.3	10.3	16.9	24.9	43.7	15.8
1979	80 776	4.2	10.3	16.9	24.7	44	16.4
1978	77 330	4.3	10.3	16.9	24.8	43.7	16.2
1977	76 030	4.4	10.3	17	24.8	43.6	16.1
1976	74 142	4.4	10.4	17.1	24.8	43.3	16
1975	72 867	4.4	10.5	17.1	24.8	43.2	15.9
1974	71 163	4.4	10.6	17.1	24.7	43.1	15.9
1973	69 859	4.2	10.5	17.1	24.6	43.6	16.6
1972	68 251	4.1	10.5	17.1	24.5	43.9	17
1971	66 676	4.1	10.6	17.3	24.5	43.5	16.7
1970	64 374	4.1	10.8	17.4	24.5	43.3	16.6
1969	62 874	4.1	10.9	17.5	24.5	43	16.6
1968	62 214	4.2	11.1	17.5	24.4	42.8	16.6
1967	60 813	4	10.8	17.3	24.2	43.8	17.5

SOURCE: U.S. Census Bureau, March Current Population Survey.

Series GG-3. Share of Aggregate Income Received by Each Fifth and Top Five Percent of Families (All Races): 1947 to 1999

(Families as of March of the following year)

Year	Share of aggregate income					
	Lowest fifth	Second fifth	Third fifth	Fourth fifth	Highest fifth	Top 5 percent
1999	4.3	9.9	15.6	23	47.2	20.3
1998	4.2	9.9	15.7	23	47.3	20.7
1997	4.2	9.9	15.7	23	47.2	20.7
1996	4.2	10	15.8	23.1	46.8	20.3
1995	4.4	10.1	15.8	23.2	46.5	20
1994	4.2	10	15.7	23.3	46.9	20.1
1993	4.1	9.9	15.7	23.3	47	20.3
1992	4.3	10.5	16.5	24	44.7	17.6
1991	4.5	10.7	16.6	24.1	44.2	17.1
1990	4.6	10.8	16.6	23.8	44.3	17.4
1989	4.6	10.6	16.5	23.7	44.6	17.9
1988	4.6	10.7	16.7	24	44	17.2
1987	4.6	10.7	16.8	24	43.8	17.2
1986	4.7	10.9	16.9	24.1	43.4	16.5
1985	4.8	11	16.9	24.3	43.1	16.1
1984	4.8	11.1	17.1	24.5	42.5	15.4
1983	4.9	11.2	17.2	24.5	42.4	15.3
1982	5	11.3	17.2	24.4	42.2	15.3
1981	5.3	11.4	17.5	24.6	41.2	14.4
1980	5.3	11.6	17.6	24.4	41.1	14.6
1979	5.4	11.6	17.5	24.1	41.4	15.3
1978	5.4	11.7	17.6	24.2	41.1	15.1
1977	5.5	11.7	17.6	24.3	40.9	14.9
1976	5.6	11.9	17.7	24.2	40.7	14.9
1975	5.6	11.9	17.7	24.2	40.7	14.9
1974	5.7	12	17.6	24.1	40.6	14.8
1973	5.5	11.9	17.5	24	41.1	15.5
1972	5.5	11.9	17.5	23.9	41.4	15.9
1971	5.5	12	17.6	23.8	41.1	15.7
1970	5.4	12.2	17.6	23.8	40.9	15.6
1969	5.6	12.4	17.7	23.7	40.6	15.6
1968	5.6	12.4	17.7	23.7	40.5	15.6
1967	5.4	12.2	17.5	23.5	41.4	16.4
1966	5.6	12.4	17.8	23.8	40.5	15.6
1965	5.2	12.2	17.8	23.9	40.9	15.5
1964	5.1	12	17.7	24	41.2	15.9
1963	5	12.1	17.7	24	41.2	15.8
1962	5	12.1	17.6	24	41.3	15.7
1961	4.7	11.9	17.5	23.8	42.2	16.6
1960	4.8	12.2	17.8	24	41.3	15.9
1959	4.9	12.3	17.9	23.8	41.1	15.9
1958	5	12.5	18	23.9	40.6	15.4
1957	5.1	12.7	18.1	23.8	40.4	15.6
1956	5	12.5	17.9	23.7	41	16.1
1955	4.8	12.3	17.8	23.7	41.3	16.4
1954	4.5	12.1	17.7	23.9	41.8	16.3
1953	4.7	12.5	18	23.9	40.9	15.7
1952	4.9	12.3	17.4	23.4	41.9	17.4
1951	5	12.4	17.6	23.4	41.6	16.8
1950	4.5	12	17.4	23.4	42.7	17.3
1949	4.5	11.9	17.3	23.5	42.7	16.9
1948	4.9	12.1	17.3	23.2	42.4	17.1
1947	5	11.9	17	23.1	43	17.5

SOURCE: U.S. Census Bureau, March Current Population Survey.

SECTION H

SOCIAL STATISTICS

Highlights

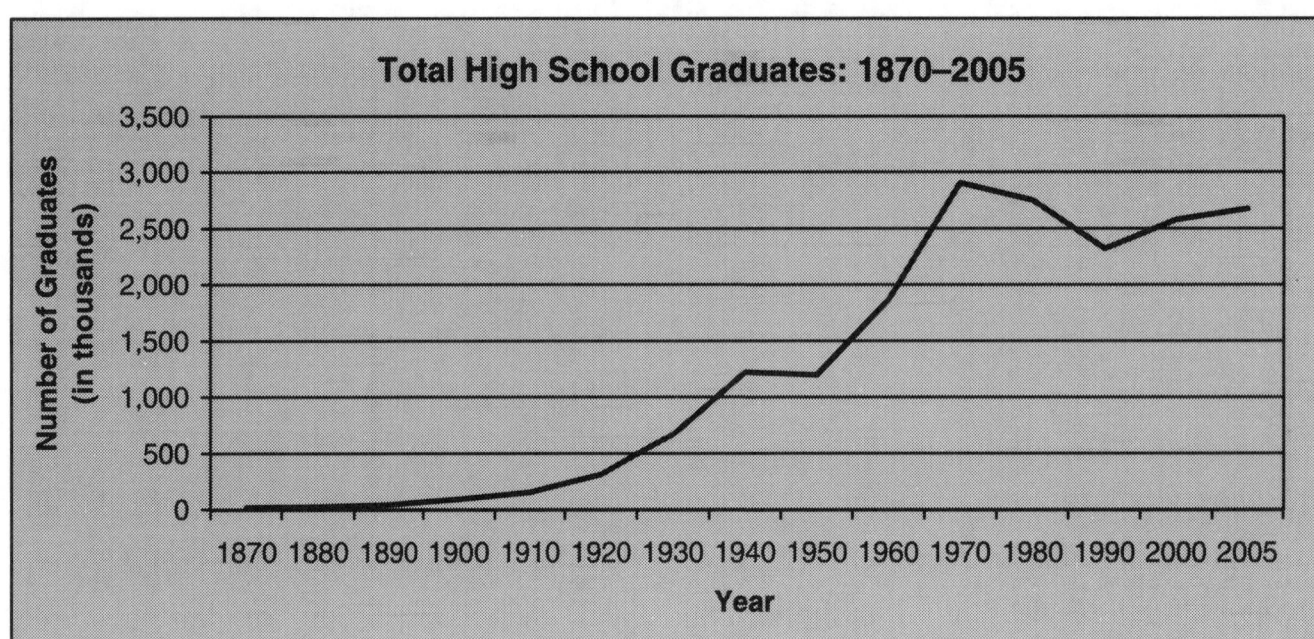

Total High School Graduates: 1870–2005

1 The United States adopted the concepts of Social Security and Welfare much later than other Western democracies. Throughout the 19th century, social welfare activities remained a local responsibility. Following public support of education in Massachusetts and other states, state intervention was extended to health programs, care of blind and orphaned people, worker's compensation, and retirement pensions. It was not until the Social Security Act of 1935 that the federal government participated in any major way in permanent welfare programs for the general population. The Act established a national system of old age insurance and provided federal grants-in-aid to the states for public assistance, maternal and child health and welfare services, general public health services, and vocational rehabilitation services. The Social Security Administration administers many of these programs, and its annual and monthly reports carry an enormous volume of statistical data.

2 Total social welfare expenditures have risen from $493 billion in 1980 to $1.5 trillion in 1995. The federal share of these expenditures declined from 62% in 1980 to 59%. Per capita social welfare expenditures were $5,622 in 1995 compared to $2,126 in 1980. In 1995, social insurance

accounted for 46.8% and public aid 16.8%. In 1995, social welfare expenditures accounted for 20.9% of total GDP and 67.5% of total government outlay.

3 Of 102.528 million households in the United States in 1997, 7.256 million received food stamps, 7.585 million received school lunches, 4.778 million received public housing and 13.589 million received medicaid.

4 In 1998, 179.1 million persons covered by Social Security, of whom 27.5 million were over age 65. The annual maximum taxable earnings were $68,400. The total Social Security payments in 1996 were $361.9 billion, and the average monthly benefit $765.00.

5 In 1995, there were 693,400 pension plans, of which 623,900 were defined contribution plans and 69,500 defined benefit plans. The total number of participants was 87.5 million.

6 In 1994, there were 174,945 401(K) plans, with assets of $674.681 billion.

7 In 1998, 17.157 million persons received work disability benefits, representing 10% of the civilian labor force.

8 In 1998, 19.8 million persons participated in federal food stamp programs.

9 Of the 13,739,000 custodial parents who were awarded child support in 1995, 2.198 million did not receive any payments. Thirty-nine-point-four percent of custodial parents live below poverty level.

10 In 1996, there were 142,374 foster homes in the United States for 483,629 children. The greatest percentage of children in foster homes is found in Illinois (17.3%), California (11.8%), New York (11.7%), and Rhode Island (11.6%).

11 Forty-eight-point-eight percent of the population does some voluntary work; more women volunteer than men (52.2% vs 45.1%), and more Whites than Blacks (51.9% vs 35.3%). Approximately one-quarter of voluntary work is church-related.

12 In 1997, Americans spent $143.5 billion on charity, of which $109.3 billion came from individuals. Nearly 75% of private philanthropy is earmarked for religion, 21.5% for education, 14% for health, and 10.6% for arts culture and humanities. The Census Bureau does not distinguish between religious organizations and religion-affiliated charities. Religion itself is considered a charity, even if it does not engage in what is generally considered as charitable work. Of the total number of households, approximately one-quarter does not contribute anything to charity.

13 There were 44,146 foundations in the United States in 1997, of which 165 had assets of more than $250 million, 227 had assets between $100 million and $250 million, and 385 had assets between $50 million and $100 million. These foundations made annual grants in 1997 of $7.945 billion, of which 23.9% went to education, 16.7% to health, 15.4% to human services, and 12.7% to arts, culture, and humanities.

14 In 1995, 60% of America's 21.4 million children under six years of age were in childcare arrangements other than in the parental home: 21% were in the care of relatives; 18% in the care of babysitters other than relatives; and 31% in organized childcare facilities. In 7.6% of cases, the mother cared for the child at work.

15 In 1998, there were 98,374 licensed childcare centers and 290,817 licensed family childcare providers.

16 Educational statistics have been collected and issued by the Office of Education from 1870 to 1953, by the Department of Health, Education, and Welfare from 1953 to 1979, and by the Department of Education from 1979 to the present. From 1870 to 1917, these statistics were included in the *Annual Report of the United States Commissioner of Education* and from 1918 to 1958 in the *Biennial Survey of Education*. Since 1962, the National Center for Educational Statistics has published summary data on education in two annual publications: *Digest of Educational Statistics* and *Condition of Education*. Two problems that arise in the study of educational statistics are inconsistencies in the definitions of terms and procedures, and a lack of timeliness. School authorities are not compelled by law to report to the Office of Education, but the vast majority of them do so voluntarily. Nonpublic schools under the operational control of private individuals and groups have reported their data in a slightly different format over the years, making this data incomparable with public school data. Enrollment information is collected on a state-by-state basis and represents a cumulative count of the total number of pupils registered at any time during the school year in each state. Pupils enrolled in more than one state in a school year are counted more than once, resulting in inflated totals.

17 The first school in the United States was established by the Dutch West India Company on Manhattan Island in 1633, with Adam Roelantsen as its first master. In 1783, the schools name was changed to Collegiate School. The first school committee or board was elected in Dorchester, Massachusetts, in 1645. The first school to operate on a one class to one room basis was set up in Quincy, Massachusetts, in 1846. The first school superintendent, Roswell William Haskins, was appointed in 1836 in Buffalo, New York. The Compulsory School Law, the first piece of educational legislation, was passed on June 14, 1642, by Massachusetts. According to the records of the Governor and Company of Massachusetts Bay, the legislation stated that "This Court, taking into consideration the great neglect of many parents and masters in training up their children in learning and labor and other employments which may be profitable to the Commonwealth, so hereupon order and decree that in every town the chosen men appointed for managing the prudential affairs of the same shall henceforth stand charged with the care of the redress of this evil." On November 11, 1647, Massachusetts ordered that "every town in this jurisdiction, after the Lord has increased them to the number of 50 householders, shall then forthwith appoint one within their town to teach all such children as shall resort to him to write and read, whose wages shall be paid either by the parents or masters of such children, or by the inhabitants in general." In 1852 the governor of Massachusetts ordered that children between the ages of 8 and 14 must attend school for 12 weeks in the year, six of which must be consecutive.

The first public school tax was an act providing "for the establishment of free schools," enacted January 15, 1825 by the State of Illinois. The tax was levied at the rate of 2%. The first schoolbook was the *New England Primer* (1689-90) printed by R. Pierce and sold by Benjamin Har-

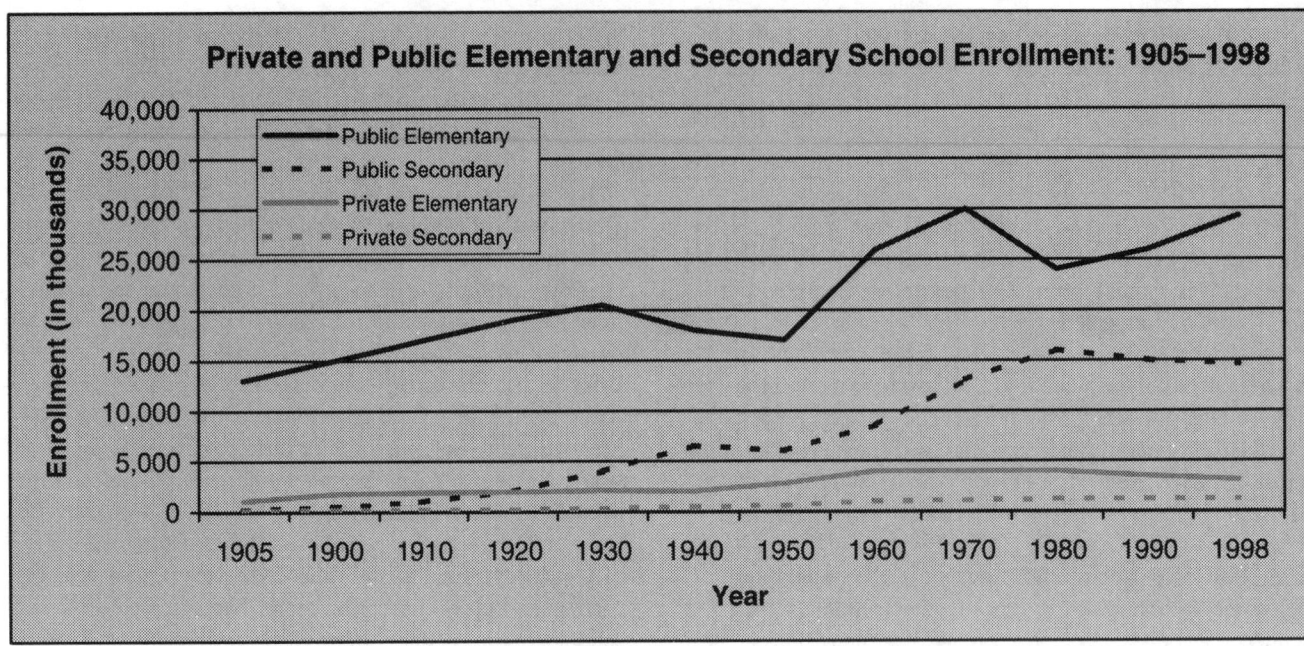

Private and Public Elementary and Secondary School Enrollment: 1905–1998

ris at the London Coffee House in Boston. Middlesex County Association for the Improvement of Common Schools was the first local education association organized in Middlesex, Connecticut, in May 1799. The first national education association, the American Institute of Instruction, was founded in Boston in 1830. The oldest educational magazine, the *Juvenile Mirror,* first appeared in New York City in 1811.

18 The Department of Education was founded by Act of Congress on March 2, 1867 as an agency for the "purpose of collecting such statistics and facts as shall show the condition and progress of education in the several states and territories, and of diffusing such information respecting the organization and management of school systems and methods of teaching as shall aid the people of the United States in the establishment and maintenance of efficient school systems and otherwise promote the cause of education." The first commissioner was Henry Barnard. The Act of July 28, 1868 abolished the Department of Education and created in its stead the Office of Education in the Department of Interior.

19 The first college in the United States was Harvard College, founded in 1636. It received £400 from the General Court of Massachusetts Bay and £800 and 300 books from the estate of John Harvard. The first commencement, held in 1642, was presided over by Henry Dunster, the college's first president, who served from 1640 to 1654. Georgetown College, the first Catholic college, was established in Washington DC in 1791. The first city college, the College of Charleston in Charleston, South Carolina, was founded in 1770, chartered in 1785, and opened in 1790. Oberlin Collegiate Institute, the first coeducational college, opened in 1833. The first college to receive a royal

charter was the Royal College of William and Mary in 1693. The first college for women was Mount Holyoke Seminary in South Hadley, Massachusetts, founded in 1837. The Cooper Union in New York City was the first college to prohibit discrimination on account of race, religion, or color in 1851. The first state university was the University of Georgia in Athens, Georgia, chartered in 1785 and opened in 1801. Lincoln University, the first Black university, was chartered in 1854 as Ashmun Institute in Chester County, Pennsylvania. The first educational institution legally designated as a university was the University of the State of Pennsylvania in 1791, known now as the University of Pennsylvania. The first university founded by a federal land grant was Ohio University in Athens, Ohio, chartered in 1804 and opened in 1808. The first college alumni association was the Society of Alumni of Williams College, Williamstown, Massachusetts, founded in 1821. Yale University awarded the first doctorates in 1861 to Eugene Schuyler, James Morris Whiton, and Arthur Williams Wright.

20 In 2000, there are 68.409 million pupils enrolled at all levels of education, of which, 53.446 million (86.9%) are enrolled in schools; 47.440 million pupils are enrolled in public schools K through 12 and 6.006 million in private schools K through 12; 11.7 million in public colleges; and 3.263 in private colleges. Total enrollment in schools and colleges is expected to reach 70.351 million in 2008, of which public schools will account for 60.735 million, or 86.3%. Between 1975 and 1980, total school and college enrollment dropped from 61 million to 58.3 million, but then picked up again in the 1990s.

21 Education ranks among the largest expenditure items in national and state budgets. Elementary and secondary education cost $351.3 billion and colleges and university education cost $232 billion, for a total of $583.8 billion in 1997, compared to $131.342 billion in 1960.

22 The number of high school graduates rose only marginally in the 1990s from 2.5 million in 1990 to 2.7 million in 2000, reflecting the ripple effects of the baby bust years (1968 to 1978).

23 Higher education had a healthy growth rate through 2000. Of the total enrollment of 14.889 million in 2000, males made up 6.442 million (43.26%) and females 8.447 million (56.74%). Females were in a minority in higher education until 1980. In 1960 male enrollment was 2.3 million compared to female enrollment of 1.2 million. Female majority status in college enrollment that began in the 1980s and has continued ever since. Male enrollment actually dropped between 1990 and 1997. Of total enrollment, 11.626 million (78%) are enrolled in public institutions and 3.263 million (22%) in private institutions; 12. 9 million are in undergraduate programs, 1.7 million in graduate programs, and 269,000 in first-time professional programs. Of the total 2.254 million degrees conferred, 1.173 million were bachelor's, 418,000 master's, and 47,000 doctorates. The total faculty strength is 947,000 of which 673,000 (71%) are in public institutions. This reflects a higher facuty/student ratio in private institutions.

24 In 1997, the age-specific enrollment rate of Blacks was higher than of Whites (58.4% versus 54.8%), but that of Hispanics is lower at 50.8%.

25 In terms of educational attainment, Asians have the highest level with 42.2%, followed by Whites with 25%, Blacks with 14.7%, and Hispanics with 11%.

26 Blacks have made dramatic gains in education as a result of federal programs. In 1950 only 12.9% of Blacks over 25 were high school graduates and only 2.1% held college degrees. By 1998 the relative numbers increased to 78% and 14.7%. Black men, however, trail black women in college attainment (13.9% vs. 15.4%).

27 Southern states are much less successful in the educational attainment of their citizens than Northern states. In terms of the percentage of persons with high school diplomas, Arkansas is at the bottom with 76.8%. Other Southern states with less than the national average of 82.8% are Alabama, Kentucky, Louisiana, Mississippi, New Mexico, South Carolina, Tennessee, Texas, and West Virginia. The states leading in educational attainment at the high school level are Alaska (90.6%) and Wyoming (90%). The leading states in college educational attainment are Colorado (34%), Maryland (31.8%), Connecticut (31.4%), Massachusetts and Minnesota (31% each), Virginia (30.3%) and New Jersey (30.1%)

28 Between 1996 and 1997, 45.1% of elementary schools, 74.1% of middle schools, and 76.9% of high schools reported criminal incidents. Of these, 4.2%, 18.7%, and 20.6% were serious. Schools with more than 50% minority enrollment reported 68.3% of the incidents. There were 3.347 million crimes committed against students in 1996, of which 255,000 were serious crimes. Per 1,000 students, the crime rate against students was 128.

29 Preprimary school enrollment in 1997 was 7.861 million, of which 4.438 million were in nursery schools and 3.422 million in kindergarten. Black enrollment rate is higher than that of Whites at this level (68.6% vs. 64.1%). More children are enrolled in private nursery schools than public ones (2.231 million vs. 2.207 million). However, more children are enrolled in public kindergartens than private ones (2.847 million versus 575,000).

30 Of total expenditures on school education in 1998, which were $323.879 billion, state governments bear 49.4%, local governments 43.8%, and the federal government 6.8% of the cost. Current expenditure per pupil enrolled is $6,842 compared to $2,050 in 1980.

31 In 1998, there were 3.087 million instructional staff in schools, of which 2.705 million were classroom teachers. The average salary of a classroom teacher has risen from $15,970 in 1980 to $39,385 in 1998. Teacher salaries are highest in Alaska ($51,700), Connecticut ($50,500) and New Jersey ($50,400). They are lowest in South Dakota ($27,300), North Dakota ($28,200), Mississippi ($29,500), and Louisiana ($29,700). Of all teachers, 12.2% moonlight all year and 8.4% moonlight during their summer break.

32 Of the total number of 88,223 schools, 61,805 are elementary schools, 21,307 secondary schools, and 5,111 combined and other schools. There are 176 schools with more than 3,000 pupils and 8,116 schools with fewer than 100 pupils.

33 One of the determinants of the quality of education is the pupil–teacher ratio. This ratio has always been higher in private schools at all levels, but the federal government is now engaged in an effort to reduce overcrowding in public schools and to appoint more teachers. Since 1960, the pupil–teacher ratio has improved in public elementary school from 28.4 to 18.9 and in public secondary schools from 21.7 to 14.7. The corresponding rates for private elementary and secondary schools are 16.3 and 11.4 respectively.

34 Schools are among the largest users of computers in the United States. During the 1998-1999 school year, there were 8.9 million computers in schools or 5.9 students per computer. Eighty-seven-point-nine percent of schools have internet access.

35 Of the 41.622 million school students in 1993-1994, 40.9% participate in special programs: 3.07% in bilingual education; 3.97% in English as a second language; 10.88% in remedial reading; 6.90% in remedial mathematics; 6.88% in programs for the impaired; 6.43% in programs for the gifted and talented; 0.27% in diagnostic and pre-scriptive programs; and 2.50% in extended day programs. In 1998, 5.339 million students had some impairment that required special instruction. Of these, 51% had specific learning disabilities, 19.8% speech or language impair-ments, 11% mental retardation, and 8.5% serious emotional disturbances.

36 Catholic school systems in the United States have been downsizing since the 1960s. In 1998, there were 6,990 Catholic elementary schools enrolling 2,013,000 pupils and 2,192 Catholic secondary schools enrolling 1,081,000 pupils, compared to 10,133 elementary schools enrolling 3,860,000 pupils and 1,227 secondary schools enrolling 636,000 pupils in 1967.

37 Scholastic Assessment Test (SAT) scores have been declining. This reflects a slippage in national educational standards. In 1967, average SAT scores were 543 for verbal (540 for males and 545 for females) and 516 for math (535 for males and 495 for females). The relative scores in 1998 were 505 for verbal (509 for males and 502 for females) and 512 for math (531 for males and 496 for females). Only 21% scored 600 or above in verbal and 23.7% in math, while 16.1% scored below 400 in verbal and 15.3% in math.

38 American College Testing (ACT) scores inched higher from 19.9% in 1967 to 21% in 1997, but males did better than females (21.2% for males vs. 20.9% for females). Males did better in math and science reasoning while females did better in English and reading. On profi-ciency tests, Blacks trailed Whites in reading, writing, his-tory, geography, science and mathematics by substantial margins.

39 Spanish and French are the most popular foreign lan-guages in schools, preferred by 40.6% and 27.2% respec-tively. German is a distant third at 9.3%.

40 Hispanic students lead in the percentage of status dropouts, that is, the percentage of the population who have not completed high school and are not enrolled. While the White dropout rate is 12.4% (13.8% for males and 10.9% for females), and the Black dropout rate is 16.7% (17.5% for males and 16.1% for females), the Hispanic rate is 30.6% (33.2% for males and 27.6% for females).

41 More high school graduates enroll in higher educa-tion institutions compared to the 1960s. In 1997, 67% of high school graduates went on to college (63.5% male, 70.3% female, 67.5% White, and 59.6% Black), compared to 45.1% of high school graduates in 1960 (54% males, 37.9% females, and 45.8% White).

42 In 1998 481,000 foreign (nonimmigrant) students were enrolled in U. S. colleges and universities. Of these 23,000 were from Africa, 308,000 from Asia, 72,000 from Europe and 51,000 from Latin America. Of the large Asian contingent, 47,000 came from Japan, 43,000 from South Korea, 34,000 from India, and 31,000 from China. Of all foreign students, 16% are studying engineering, 8% science and 21% business.

43 Of the 3,706 institutions of higher education in the United States in 1995, 2,244 were four-year institutions and 1,462 two-year institutions.

44 Of the higher education current funds revenues of $197.7 billion, 27.9% came from tuition and fees, 12.0% from the federal government, 23% from state governments, and 9.5% from auxiliary enterprises. Other sources of col-lege and university revenues are private gifts and grants ($5.0 billion), endowment earnings ($721 million), educa-tional activities ($3.5 billion), and hospitals ($12.2 billion). The market value of college and university endowments in 1995 was $128.8 billion.

45 With 1983 = 100, the Higher Education Price Index increased from 39.5 in 1970 to 178.6 in 1997. During the same time period, the personnel compensation component of the price index grew from 42.1 to 189, and the services and equipment component from 31.9 to 148. The highest jump was in library acquisitions, which grew from 25.7 to 260.9.

46 Federal financial assistance for college and univer-sity students in the form of loans and grants totaled $41.9 billion awarded to 15.3 million students in 1999.

47 Charges, including tuition, room, and board, were $6,788 (compared to $3,408 in 1985) in public institutions and $18,745 in private institutions (compared to $8,203 in 1985) in 1998.

48 Voluntary financial support for higher education rose to $16 billion annually in 1998 from $1.7 billion in 1970. The increase includes $13.150 billion from individuals and alumnae, $3 billion from business corporations, and $3.2 billion from foundations.

49 The 12 most popular languages on campuses are Spanish (606,300), French (205,400), German (96,300), Ital-ian (43,800), Japanese (44,700), Russian (24,700), Latin (25,900), Chinese (26,500), Greek (16,300), Hebrew (13,100), Portuguese (6,500), and Arabic (4,400).

50 Of college freshmen in 1998, 33% were A to A + students in high school, 54% B to B + students, and 13%

C to C+ students. By political orientation, 21% were liberal, 57% middle of the road and 19% conservative.

51 In 1996, 2.248 million students earned degrees from colleges and universities. Of that total, 44.2% were male (compared to 65.8% male in 1960). More women than men received associate's, bachelor's, and master's degrees, but men have a substantial lead in first professional (45,000 vs. 32,000) and doctoral (27,000 vs. 18,000) degrees.

52 The most popular fields of study at the baccalaureate level are business and management (19.4%), social sciences (10.8%), education (9.0%), health sciences (7.2%), and psychology (6.2%). At the master's level, the most popular fields of study are education (26.1%), business management (23.1%), health sciences (8.2%), engineering (7.0%), and public administration (5.9%).

53 In 1996, 15,341 medical degrees (40.9% female) were conferred by medical schools, 3,697 dental degrees (35.8% female) by dental schools, 39,828 law degrees (43.5% female) by law schools, and 5,879 theological degrees (25.2% female) by seminaries.

54 Blacks trail Whites in degrees earned at all levels. Blacks earn only 9.3% of associate's degrees, 7.8% of bachelor's degrees, 6.4% of master's degrees, 3.7% of doctorates, and 6.5% of first professional degrees.

55 Nonresident aliens earn 25.6% of all doctoral degrees and 11.8% of the master's degrees. Their doctoral share is highest in engineering, mathematics and computer and information science.

56 In 1997, there were 37,591 libraries of all kinds in the United States, including 9,815 public libraries, 4,700 academic libraries, 9,898 special libraries, and 1,897 government libraries. Academic libraries had a combined holding of 792,707,000 volumes, to which 22,450,000 volumes are added every year at a cost of $1.374 billion. With 12 million volumes, Harvard University has the largest university library.

57 National statistics on religious bodies were compiled and published between 1850 and 1936 by the Bureau of the Census, and since then by the magazine *Christian Herald* (now defunct), the *Yearbook of American and Canadian Churches* (Abingdon Press) as well as decennially in *Churches and Church Membership* by the Glenmary Research Center in Atlanta. Practically all national religious bodies compile reports or estimates from time to time based on records kept by local houses of worship. Many of the larger denominations also publish these figures periodically. The data gathered by the denominations are designed primarily for their own use, and thus, vary in scope and nature. Further, local records are kept by people untrained in statistical methods, and as a result, may suffer in consistency. Denominations also differ in their definitions of membership; accordingly, there are variations also in the bases of compilation. For instance, the Eastern Orthodox churches report estimates of the total number of persons within their cultural and nationality groups; Jews, the number of ethnic Jews in the community; Roman Catholics, Lutherans and Episcopals the total number of baptized persons (including infants); and evangelical Protestants, those who have attained full membership and are active members and tithers. One denomination, the Church of Christ, Scientist, forbids the enumeration of its members as contrary to Scripture and ceased reporting its membership figures after 1936. The total number of unreported membership is estimated at less than 1%. Another point to bear in mind is that these figures relate to formal membership and not to belief. Orthodoxy cannot be measured in numbers. The number of those who subscribe to some valid religious beliefs could conceivably be higher than membership numbers.

58 Religious statistics were included in nine censuses from 1850 to 1936. The early ones included the number of members as well as the number and value of edifices, but the 1880 data were not published. In 1906, the *Census of Religious Bodies*, published in two parts, was the first compiled by means of a questionnaire, to which 99% of those asked mailed returns. The compilation of 1926 is regarded by students of religious statistics as the most adequate ever made. It reported a total membership of 50,495,104 (43% of the resident population), compared to 42,954,512 in 1916. The total reported religious membership was 147,607,000 in 1989 (59% of total resident population.). The figures appear to contradict the popular perception that institutional religion is in decline.

59 In 1990, church-affiliated Christians made up slightly less than half of the national population at 49.3%. By region, the highest proportion of Christians was found in the Northeast (55%), followed by the Midwest (53%), the South (49.8%), and the West (37%). The states with the highest number of professing Christians were Utah (75.1%), Rhode Island (75%), North Dakota (73.8%), South Dakota (66.9%), Minnesota (64.9%), Wisconsin (64.4%), Massachusetts (64%), and Nebraska (63.1%). Christians formed more than half the population in Iowa (61.1%), Connecticut (60.8%), Pennsylvania (60.5%), New Mexico (58.9%), Oklahoma (57.9%), Alabama (57.3%), Louisiana (57.2%), Arkansas (56.1%), Mississippi (54.9%), Illinois (54.7%), Texas (54.5%), Kentucky (54.1%), Tennessee (54.1%), North Carolina (53.4%), Kansas (53.4%), New Jersey (53.3%), Missouri (53.1%), South Carolina (51.3%), and Idaho (50%). Generally, Western states have a very low church membership. The states with the lowest percentage of Christians were Nevada (29.1%), Alaska (30.6%), Washington (30.9%), Hawaii (33.1%), California (34.1%), Oregon (35.9%), and Colorado (36.4%). Jews comprise 2.4% of the national population with the highest

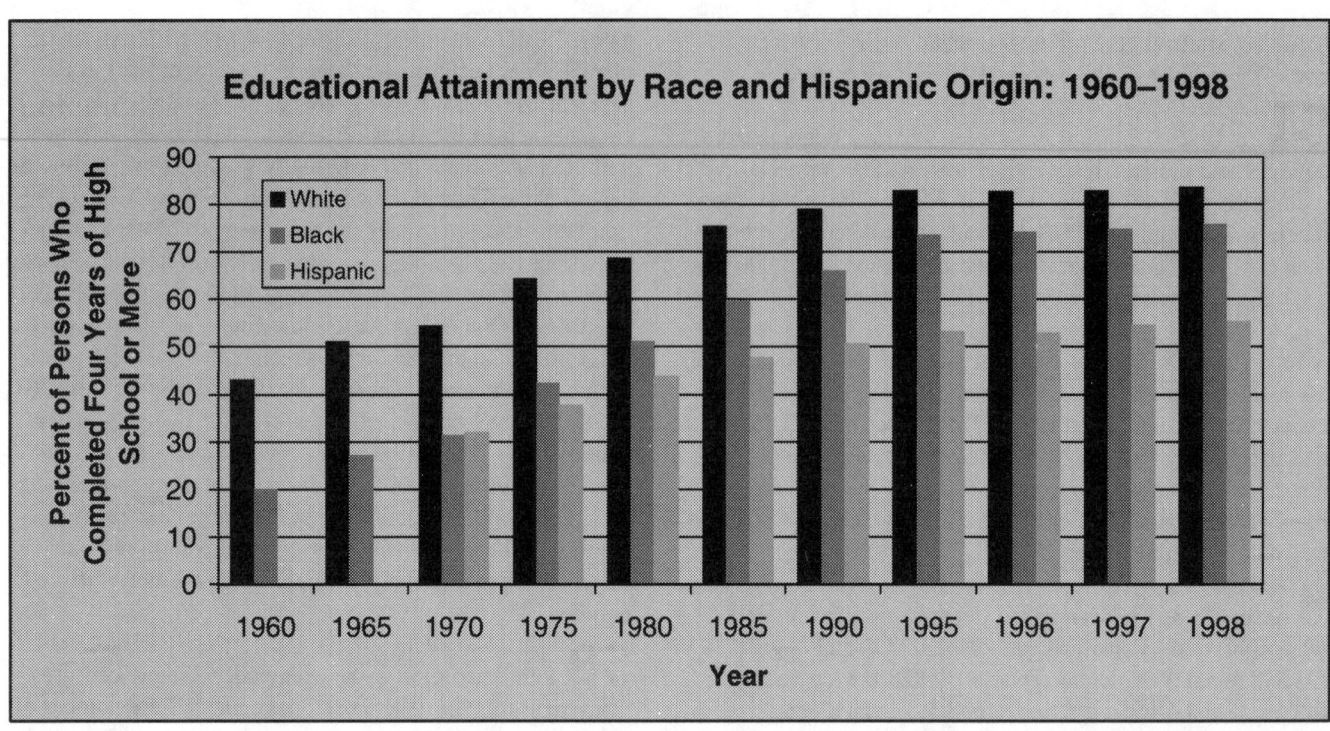

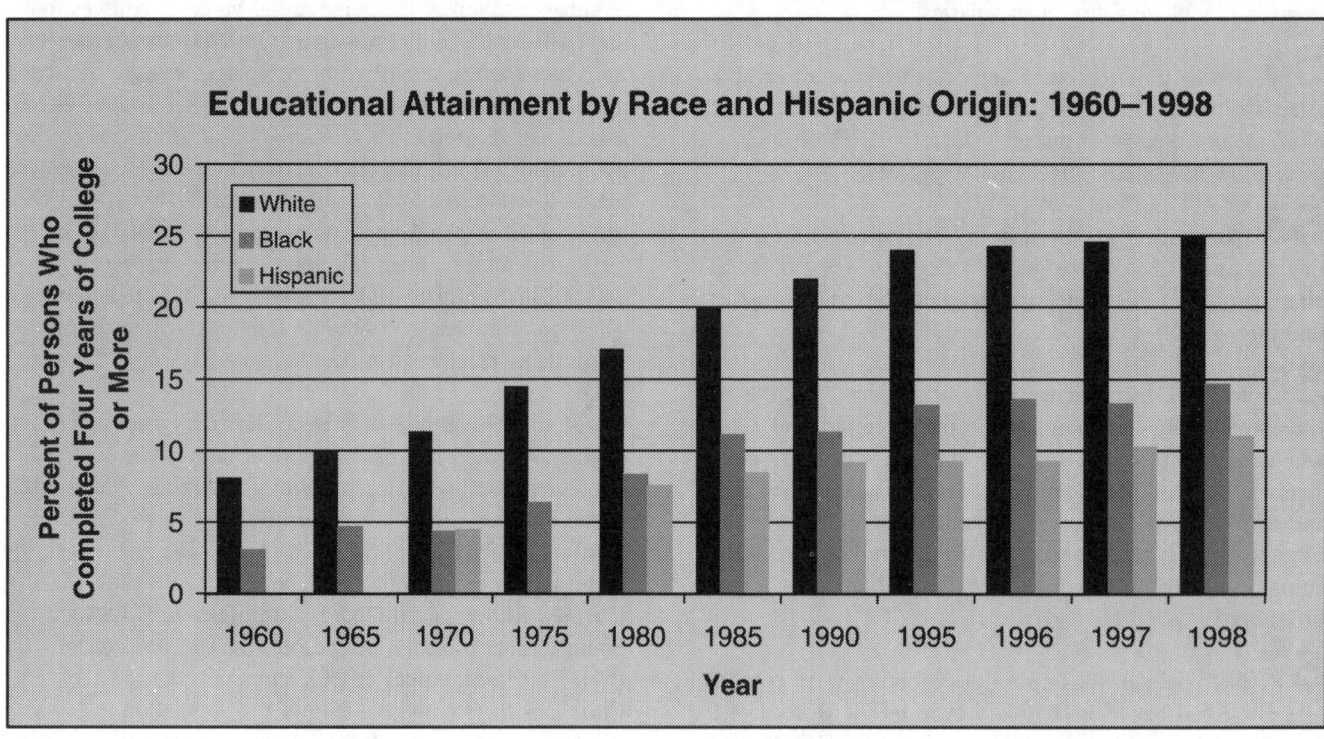

concentration in New York (10.3%). Other states with large Jewish concentrations were Florida, Massachusetts, and Maryland. In 31 states, Jews make up less than 1% of the population. The Jewish share of the population has consistently dropped from the early decades of the century when it formed more than 5% of the population. The main reasons for this decline are the rise in the immigration of non-Jews and the growing intermarriage of Jews with gentiles. Despite all the talk of pluralism, other religions are not statistically significant.

60 Roman Catholics made up the largest single denomination in the United States in 1995, with a membership roll of 61.2 million. Other large denominations were Southern Baptist (15.9 million), Methodist (8.9 million), Presbyterians (4.0 million), Lutherans (2.6 million), Evangelical Lutherans (5.2 million), Episcopals (2.4 million), Mormons (4.9 million), Church of God in Christ (5.5 million) and Assemblies of God (2.4 million).

61 The percentage of persons holding no religious beliefs grew from 3% in 1957 to 11% in 1990. Such disaffiliation was most severe among Protestants (56% in 1990 compared to 66% in 1957), but much less prevalent among Roman Catholics (25% in 1990 compared to 26% in 1957).

62 In 1990, the total number of pastors, priests, and other religious leaders was estimated at 340,094 serving 350,337 religious bodies. The number of religious edifices reported in the 1936 census was 142,487.

63 Statistics on recreation have not been generally compiled and published systematically. One major difficulty is in defining the term "recreation"; another is that even the compiled data remain in the files of the collecting agency. The National Park Service is the most dependable source. Since 1850, it has administered the large areas set aside for recreational purposes by Congress or by executive order. These include National Parks, National Seashores, National Monuments, National Historical and Military Areas, and National Parkways. Data on municipal parks and state parks come from the National Recreation and Park Association and data on national forests from the Forest Service.

64 In 1997, the National Park System included 77,457,000 acres, of which national parks accounted for 49,384,000 acres. The system had 275.3 million visitors.

65 In 1997, per capita annual expenditure was $164 on published materials and $1,813 on entertainment of all kinds. Motion pictures generated $63 billion in revenues, amusement and recreation services (including theaters, dance studios, bands and orchestras, bowling centers and commercial sports) $93.7 billion, and other amusement and recreation services (including physical fitness centers, public golf courses, and amusements parks) $51.6 billion.

66 In 1997, Americans purchased 2.1 billion books worth $26.450 billion, compared to 1.7 billion books worth $9.8 billion. General retailers accounted for $11.9 billion, college stores, $4.7 billion, libraries and institutions $2.2 billion, schools $3.4 billion, and direct mail $3.8 billion.

67 In 1998, consumers spent $13.7 billion on sound recordings (compared to $7.5 billion in 1990). Rock was the most popular genre, accounting for $25.7 billion, followed by country ($14.1 billion), rhythm and blues ($12.8 billion), pop ($10 billion), rap (9.7 billion), Gospel ($6.3 billion), classical ($3.3 billion) and jazz ($1.9 billion).

68 Household pet ownership was at an all-time high in 1996, when there were 31.2 million dog-owning families with 52.9 million dogs, 27 million cat-owning families with 59.1 million cats, and 4.6 million bird-owning families with12.6 million birds. In addition, individuals owned 4 million horses.

69 Lawn and garden expenditures reached $2.6 billion in 1997, of which lawn care cost $6.3 billion.

70 In 1996, there were 35,246,000 anglers, 13,975,000 hunters, and 62,868,000 wildlife watchers.

71 Attendance at major league baseball in 1997 was 64.9 million, almost equally divided between the National League and the American League. The average salary of a major league baseball player was $1.337 million compared to $371,000 in 1985.

72 In 1997, there were 27 professional basketball teams and 865 NCAA men's and 879 women's college teams. Total attendance at professional basketball games was 21.677 million. The average professional player's salary was $2.2 million, compared to $325,000 in 1985.

73 In 1997, there were 28 professional football teams and 581 college teams. The average professional player's salary was $725,000 compared to $194,000 in 1985.

74 Horse racing has lost much of its popularity in the 1990s. Horse racing days declined from 13,745 in 1985 to 11,958 in 1997 and attendance dropped from 73.346 million to 41.846 million. However, a parimutuel turnover showed an upturn from $12.2 billion to $15.2 billion.

75 In 1997, there were 14,602 golf courses in the United States catering to 26.4 million golfers. Of the total number of golf courses, 4,257 were private. In 1998, sales of golf equipment were $4.0 billion.

76 In 1997, there were 245,000 tennis courts serving 19.5 million players. In 1998, sales of tennis equipment were $335 million.

77 In 1997, there were 133,000 bowling lanes serving 91 million participants. More women (49.2 million) bowl than men (41.8 million).

78 In 1997, there were 32,000 motion picture theaters in the United States attended by 1.3 billion people. Total box-office receipts were $6.3 billion. The average admission price has gone up from $2.05 in 1985 to $4.59 in 1997.

79 In 1997, there were 16.284 million boats, and retail expenditures on boating was $19.6 billion.

80 Sales of sporting goods reached $66.4 billion in 1998. Of this, athletic and sport clothing and athletic and sport footwear accounted for $26.099 billion.

81 Sales of bicycles and related supplies increased from $2.4 billion in 1990 to $3.1 billion in 1998.

82 Next to reading literature (63%) and visiting historical parks (47%), the most popular arts activities are visiting museums (35%), and attending musical plays (25%), classical musical performances and nonmusical plays (16% each), jazz performances (12%), ballet (6%), and opera (5%).

83 The most popular participatory arts and crafts activity are weaving (28%), photography (17%), drawing (16%) pottery (15%), and modern dancing (13%).

84 In 1997, there were 36 new theatrical productions attended by 10.6 million persons that grossed $499 million in ticket sales. Broadway road tours were attended by 18 million people and grossed $782 million. There were 197 nonprofit professional theaters whose 2,295 productions and 51,453 performances were attended by 17.2 million people.

85 In 1997, there were 92 professional opera companies whose 2,137 performances were attended by 6.9 million people.

86 In 1997, symphony orchestras staged 26,906 performances attended by 31.9 million people and grossed 575.5 million in revenues.

87 The 10 most popular sports activities are exercise walking, swimming, bicycle riding, camping, fishing, bowling, exercising with equipment, basketball, jogging, and aerobic exercising. More women than men exercised by walking, swimming and aerobic exercising. Among men the most popular activities were swimming, bicycle riding, and fishing.

88 Information on travel is compiled annually by the Bureau of Economic Analysis and published periodically in the *Survey of Current Business*. Statistics on arrivals in the United States are reported by the U. S. Travel and Tourism Administration, while those on departures are reported in *International Air Travel Statistics*. Data on domestic travel are published by the Travel Data Center.

89 In 1997, there were 47.754 million foreign visitors to the United States generating $94.163 billion. In the same year, 52,735 Americans visited foreign countries, spending $69.455 billion. Foreign visitors spend more per capita in the United States than Americans spend abroad because of the dollar's strength.

90 Of Americans visiting foreign countries, 31.1 million went to Canada and Mexico and 9.8 million to Europe. Of foreign travelers to the United States, nearly half came from Canada and Mexico and 10.3 million from Europe.

91 Domestic travel generated $386.1 billion in 1996. The states with the largest internal tourism revenues were California ($50.2 billion), Florida ($33.3 billion), Texas ($24.6 billion), New York ($23.1 billion), and Illinois ($16.9 billion).

92 In 1997, Americans took 388.6 million vacation trips, 443.2 million pleasure trips, and 715.9 million business trips. During pleasure trips, 80% traveled by car and 16% traveled by air, and 39% stayed in a motel/hotel. The average nights per trip declined from 5.6 in 1985 to 3.8 in 1997 and the average miles per trip from 1,010 in 1985 to 901 in 1997.

93 Under the U.S. Constitution, law enforcement is a function of state and municipal governments. Crimes under federal jurisdiction include offenses against the U. S. government, and against or by its employees while engaged on official duties, as well as offenses that involve the crossing of state lines or interference with interstate commerce. Excluding the military and federal jurisdictions, there are 51 separate criminal law jurisdictions, one in each of the 50 states and one in the District of Columbia. Each of these has its own criminal law and procedure and its own law enforcement agencies with substantial differences in penalties for like offenses. While almost all of them follow the Anglo-Saxon Common Law, Louisiana's legal heritage, for example, is largely French and Continental.

94 The major sources of law enforcement and criminal justice data are the Federal Bureau of Investigation (FBI) and the Bureau of Justice Statistics. The latter has emerged in recent years as an incomparable data provider, publishing such reports as *Sourcebook of Criminal Justice Statistics, Criminal Victimization in the United States, Prisoners in State and Federal Institutions, Children in Custody, National Surveys of Courts, Census of State Correctional Facilities, Survey of Prison Inmates, Parole in the United States, Capital Punishment,* and *Expenditure and Employment Data for the Criminal Justice System.* The FBI's major publication is *Crime in the United States,* which grew out of the Uniform Crime Reporting Program initiated in 1930 by the International Association of Chiefs of Police. In 1958, a special committee was appointed to study the program. Their report made 22 recommendations that were incorporated in the *Uniform Crime Reports,* beginning with the 1958 issue. Its major innovations were the Crime Index and the Crime Rates per 100,000. Offenses are divided into two groups, designated Part I and Part II. Part I offenses make up the Crime Index. The original seven FBI Index offenses are murder, nonnegligent manslaughter, forcible rape, robbery, aggravated assault, burglary, larceny, and motor vehicle theft. Arson was added as the eighth Index offense in 1979. The FBI Reports are complemented by the National Crime Survey (NCS) of the Bureau of Justice Statistics. NCS data come directly from the victims and include offenses reported to the police as well as those not reported. When an offense involves more than one criminal act, it is counted only once under the more serious category.

95 The earliest statistics on the courts were collected and published by the Bureau of the Census from 1932 to 1945. There are several types of courts with varying degrees of jurisdiction: original, appellate, general and limited or special. The 94 federal courts of original jurisdiction are known as the District Courts.

96 Statistics on prisoners were collected by the Bureau of the Census in connection with each decennial census of population from 1850 to 1890. Independent enumerations of prisoners were made in 1904, 1910, 1923, and 1933. The first nationwide collection of data was made in 1926 by the Bureau of the Census, which published an annual summary until 1950. From 1950 to 1971 the data were published by the FBI, from 1971 to 1979 by the Law Enforcement Assistance Administration, and since 1979 by the Bureau of Justice Statistics.

97 Throughout the 1990s crime rates have declined, although not as dramatically as reported in the media. From 1987 to 1997, the overall decline was 7.2% reflecting the drop in crime rate per 100,000 from 5,550 in 1987 to 4,927 in 1997. But violent crime actually rose from 609 per 100,000 to 610. The murder rate showed the steepest drop (14%), followed by robbery (-10.3%), and rape (-4.2%), although aggravated assault rose 12.9%. The states with the highest violent crime rate per 100,000 are Florida (1,024), South Carolina (990), Louisiana (856), Illinois (861), New Mexico (853), Maryland (847), California (798), and Nevada (799). The District of Columbia tops all states with a relative rate of 2,024. The states with the lowest crime rates are South Dakota (87), New Hampshire (113), Vermont (120) and Maine (121).

98 Among cities, the highest crime rate are recorded in Atlanta (13,921), St. Louis (13,576), Miami (12,828), Tampa (12,260), Detroit (11,669), Oklahoma City (11,655), Minneapolis (11,439) Portland, Oregon (11,199), and Nashville (11,091). Among the cities with the lowest crime rates are San Jose, California ((3,870), and New York (4,861).

99 Beginning in 1988, more Black males became homicide victims than White males. In 1996, 8,183 Black males were murdered, compared to 7,570 White males. The Black male homicide rate is 51.5 per 100,000, compared to 7.9 for White males. Black females also have a higher homicide rate than White females (10.2 vs. 2.5).

100 In 1997, 8,049 hate crimes were reported by 11,211 law enforcement agencies. Of these, 3,120 were directed against Blacks, 1,087 against Jews, and 1,081 against homosexuals.

101 In 1997, there were 8.971 million personal crimes and 25.817 million property crimes. Of the latter, 4.6 million were household burglaries and 1.4 million auto thefts.

102 In 1997, 99,342 juveniles were arrested for violent crimes and 154,540 for drug abuse.

103 In 1997, 11.521 million persons were arrested. Of these, 7.608 million were White and 3.644 million were Black. Males made up 78.9% of the arrestees and juveniles under 18 17.3%. Persons arrested for nonserious crimes numbered 9.469 million of which 81,700 were arrested for prostitution, 1.242 million for drug violations, 966,100 for driving while under the influence, 90,800 for forgery and counterfeiting, 323,100 for fraud and 12,700 for embezzlement.

104 The government has been waging a losing war on drugs for many decades. In 1996, 3,794,034 pounds of drugs were seized by the Drug Enforcement Administration, compared to 1,238,425 pounds in 1990. Drug arrest rates for drug abuse violations soared to 602.5 per 100,000 in 1997 compared to 435.3 in 1990.

105 In 1995, 1.336 million illegal aliens were apprehended by the Border Police compared to 766,600 in 1980. Of these, 1.324 million were deported, and $686.6 million worth of narcotics were seized.

106 In 1996, state and local agencies employed 663,535 full-time, sworn police officers, or 25 per 10,000 population. Per capita, New York had the most police officers per 10,000 (39), followed by Louisiana (37) and New Jersey (35). Sixteen federal agencies employed 74,493 law enforcement officers. Of these four agencies employed 59%: Immigration and Naturalization Service (12,403); federal Bureau of Prisons (11,329); Federal Bureau of Investigation (10,389); and U. S. Customs Service (9,749). Other major federal law enforcement agencies include Drug Enforcement Administration (2,946), U. S. Marshals Service (2,650), Bureau of Alcohol, Tobacco and Firearms (1,869), and the U.S. Secret Service (3,185).

107 In 1996, there were 18,769 general purpose law enforcement agencies in the United States of which 13,578 were local agencies.

108 The number of police officers killed annually in the line of duty ranges from a high of 345 in 1989 to 112 in 1996. More police officers are killed in the South than in any other region.

109 The National Victimization Rate is 39.2 per 1,000. In 1997, one in every 25 Americans was the victim of a violent crime, and 23.7% of all households were touched by at least one criminal incident. Blacks were more often victimized than Whites (49% vs. 38.3%). Most crimes, including 41.2% of robberies and 20% of assaults, take place on the street, but 35% of rapes take place in the home of the victim. Of all criminal incidents, 31.7% involved firearms and 26.6% handguns.

110 In 1997, the Supreme Court docket consisted of 7,692 cases, of which 2,432 were appellate cases. Total cases available for argument were 138, but only 93 were decided by a signed opinion.

111 The U. S. Courts of Appeals heard 52,571 cases, of which 10,740 were criminal cases and 8,710 were civil cases. The median time for disposal of cases was 11.1 months compared to 8.9 months in 1980. U. S. District courts handled 265,200 civil cases and 48,700 criminal cases. Fifty-four-point-five percent of criminal cases ended in conviction.

112 In 1996, 456 federal officials, 109 state officials, and 219 local officials were indicted for corruption. A total 902 officials were convicted, including those who were not public officials, but were involved in their malfeasance.

113 In 1996, 1.758 million delinquency cases were disposed of by juvenile courts. Of these, 137,000 involved violent offenses. Per 1,000 youths at risk, the Black rate is 124.1 and the White rate 51.0.

114 In 1997, 798,358 child abuse and neglect cases were reported. Of these, 97,425 cases involved sexual abuse, 436,630 neglect, 195,517 physical abuse, and 49,146 emotional maltreatment.

115 In 1997, there were 567,079 jail inmates (excluding state and federal prisons), of whom 246,200 were Black and 396,500 were White. In the same year, state and federal prisoners totaled 1,123,478. Of the total number of 494,349 persons in prison for violent crimes, 122,435 were murderers. The total of all persons on probation or parole and in jails and prisons in 1997 was 5.690 million or 2.1% of the resident population.

116 In 1997, there were 3,335 prisoners under sentence of death. Of these 1,876 were White and 1,459 were Black. Nearly half of them had been on death row for more than 72 months, pending exhaustion of the appellate process. Between 1930 and 1937, 4,291 prisoners were executed, including 2,201 Blacks and 1,971 Whites. Those executed for murder numbered 3,691 (1,770 Blacks and 1,884 Whites). The vast majority of the prisoners executed for rape are Black (405 vs. 48 for Whites). Of the 68 prisoners executed in 1998, Texas accounted for 20 and Virginia for 13.

117 The total number of fires reported in 1997 was 8.525 million, including 4.585 million homes. The total property loss was estimated at $11.372 billion.

Series H 1-31. Social Welfare Expenditures Under Public Programs: 1890 to 1995

(In millions of dollars. Fiscal years)

Year	Total expenditures			Total social insurance	Total public aid	Health and medical programs[3]	Total education	Total veterans' programs	Housing	Total other social welfare
	Total	Percent of gross national product[1]	Percent of all government expenditures[2]							
	1	2	3	5	14	16	17	21	27	28
1995	1 505 000	20.9	67.5	705 000	254 000	86 000	366 000	39 000	29 000	27 000
1994	1 436 000	21.0	64.5	684 000	238 000	80 000	344 000	38 000	27 000	25 000
1993	1 367 000	21.1	66.6	659 000	221 000	75 000	332 000	36 000	21 000	23 000
1992	1 267 000	20.6	63.7	619 000	208 000	70 000	292 000	36 000	21 000	22 000
1991	1 159 000	19.8	60.3	561 000	181 000	. . .	277 000	33 000	. . .	20 000
1990	1 049 000	18.5	58.2	514 000	147 000	61 000	258 000	31 000	19 000	18 000
1989	956 000	18.6	53.0	468 055	127 475	. . .	238 631	30 104	. . .	16 609
1988	886 000	18.5	52.8	434 048	118 495	. . .	219 382	29 254	. . .	15 480
1987	833 000	18.8	53.4	415 023	110 695	. . .	201 540	28 051	. . .	15 278
1986	782 786	18.5	52.2	390 769	104 602	. . .	189 276	27 445	. . .	14 161
1985	731 000	18.5	52.2	372 529	98 086	39 000	172 103	27 042	13 000	13 552
1984	678 116	18.2	52.8	341 120	91 661	. . .	157 189	26 275	. . .	13 295
1983	643 437	19.3	54.5	331 161	86 644	. . .	141 815	25 802	. . .	12 466
1982	595 869	19.4	55.7	302 615	80 852	. . .	133 874	24 708	. . .	11 654
1981	550 841	18.6	56.9	267 395	82 424	. . .	128 145	23 441	. . .	11 983
1980	492 000	18.4	57.1	229 754	71 799	27 000	121 050	21 446	7 000	13 599
1979	430 280	17.5	58.4	194 288	64 622	. . .	109 262	20 602	. . .	11 076
1978	394 377	19.3	57.8	175 090	59 394	. . .	101 519	19 744	. . .	10 563
1977	360 602	19.6	59.4	160 883	53 266	. . .	93 878	19 015	. . .	9 071
1976	331 955	20.4	60.3	145 703	48 693	. . .	87 730	18 958	. . .	8 472
1975	289 000	19.0	56.6	123 013	41 308	. . .	80 834	17 019	. . .	6 947
1974	239 397	17.6	58.5	99 002	31 520	. . .	70 534	14 112	. . .	6 722
1973	213 942	17.3	55.5	86 166	28 691	. . .	64 734	13 026	. . .	5 698
1972	191 357	17.2	53.2	74 809	26 078	. . .	59 385	11 522	. . .	5 364
1971	171 908	16.9	51.7	66 369	21 262	. . .	56 705	10 456	. . .	4 983
1970	145 893	15.3	47.8	54 676	16 488	9 753	50 848	9 018	701	4 409
1969	127 149	14.1	44.7	48 772	13 439	9 006	43 673	7 934	532	3 792
1968	113 840	13.8	43.2	42 740	11 092	8 459	40 590	7 247	428	3 285
1967	99 710	12.9	42.4	37 339	8 811	7 628	35 808	6 898	378	2 848
1966	88 000	12.2	43.4	31 934	7 301	6 938	32 825	6 358	335	2 309
1965	77 175	11.8	42.4	28 123	6 283	6 246	28 108	6 031	318	2 066
1964	71 491	11.7	40.0	26 971	5 642	6 004	24 989	5 862	278	1 746
1963	66 766	11.6	39.5	26 614	5 296	5 594	22 671	5 751	248	1 593
1962	62 659	11.6	39.4	24 194	4 945	5 230	21 005	5 654	217	1 415
1961	58 236	11.5	39.3	22 365	4 444	4 927	19 337	5 624	196	1 343
1960	52 293	10.6	38.0	19 307	4 101	4 464	17 626	5 479	177	1 139
1959	49 821	10.6	(4)	18 287	3 998	4 401	16 498	5 472	156	1 010
1958	45 457	10.3	(4)	15 957	3 615	4 091	15 313	5 427	134	920
1957	39 350	9.1	(4)	12 472	3 309	3 776	13 732	5 119	120	823
1956	35 131	8.6	(4)	10 646	3 115	3 307	12 154	5 061	112	735
1955	32 640	8.6	32.7	9 835	3 003	3 103	11 157	4 834	89	619
1954	29 547	8.2	(4)	8 265	2 788	3 099	10 084	4 631	67	612
1953	27 045	7.5	(4)	6 607	2 728	3 190	9 231	4 735	51	503
1952	25 576	7.6	(4)	5 671	2 585	3 331	8 246	5 256	37	451
1951	24 055	7.7	(4)	4 772	2 592	2 783	7 415	5 996	35	462
1950	23 508	8.9	37.6	4 947	2 496	2 064	6 674	6 866	15	448
1949	21 165	8.1	(4)	4 186	2 089	1 753	5 807	6 927	8	396
1948	18 652	7.6	(4)	3 603	1 702	1 416	4 897	6 638	27	369
1947	17 337	7.8	(4)	4 160	1 442	1 367	4 089	5 683	281	316
1946	12 798	6.1	(4)	3 652	1 151	1 904	3 297	2 403	159	233
1945	9 205	4.4	8.4	1 409	1 031	2 354	3 076	1 126	11	198
1944	8 228	4.1	(4)	1 256	1 032	2 225	2 800	720	13	182
1943	8 283	4.7	(4)	1 259	1 550	1 886	2 793	623	14	159
1942	8 609	6.1	(4)	1 376	2 777	949	2 694	645	14	154
1941	8 953	8.0	(4)	1 330	3 524	724	2 617	613	9	136
1940	8 795	9.2	49.0	1 272	3 597	616	2 561	629	4	116

See footnotes at end of chart.

Series H 1-31.   Social Welfare Expenditures Under Public Programs: 1890 to 1995—Cont'd.

(In millions of dollars. Fiscal years)

| Year | Total expenditures | | | Total social insurance | Total public aid | Health and medical pro- grams[3] | Total education | Total veterans' programs | Housing | Total other social welfare |
	Total	Percent of gross national product[1]	Percent of all government expendi- tures[2]							
	1	**2**	**3**	**5**	**14**	**16**	**17**	**21**	**27**	**28**
1939	9 213	10.5	(4)	1 181	4 230	575	2 504	606	3	114
1938	7 924	9.0	(4)	849	3 233	540	2 563	627	4	108
1937	7 858	9.1	(4)	545	3 436	500	2 376	893	3	105
1936	10 184	13.2	(4)	456	3 079	454	2 228	3 826	42	101
1935	6 548	9.5	48.6	406	2 998	427	2 008	597	13	99
1934	5 832	9.7	(4)	362	2 531	400	1 914	530	(2)	96
1933	4 462	7.9	(4)	344	689	418	2 104	819	. . .	89
1932	4 303	6.4	(4)	355	256	435	2 352	825	. . .	81
1931	4 201	5.1	(4)	368	164	406	2 440	744	. . .	79
1930	4 085	4.2	(4)	361	78	378	2 523	668	. . .	78
1929	3 921	3.9	36.3	342	60	351	2 434	658	. . .	76
1913	1 000	2.5	34.0	15	(5)	150	525	196	. . .	[5]114
1890	318	2.4	38.0	. . .	(5)	18	146	113	. . .	[5]41

Z Less than $500 000.
1. Gross national product for 1970 and earlier.
2. Government expenditures exclude workmen's compensation and temporary disability insurance payments made through private insurance carriers and self-insurers although these (payable under statutory provisions) are included as social welfare expenditures, series H 1.
3. Excludes health and medical program parts of social insurance, public aid, veterans, and other social welfare.
4. Not computed.
5. "Public aid" included with "Other social welfare."

Series H 48-56.   Estimated Workers Under Social Insurance Programs: 1934 to 1991

(In millions. As of December except as indicated. OASDHI = Old Age, Survivors, Disability and Health Insurance)

| Year | Paid civilian population [1] | Retirement systems | | | Workers' compensation | Unemployment insurance [4] | Temporary disability insurance [5] |
| | | OASDHI [2] | Railroad retirement | Public employee [3] | | | |
	49	51	52	53	54	55	56
1991	116.2	110.5	0.3	7.1	95.1	106.0	...
1990	117.0	110.2	0.3	7.2	96.7	109.5	...
1989	117.4	110.5	0.3	7.1	95.3	108.8	22.2
1988	115.6	108.7	0.3	7.0	92.8	106.9	21.8
1987	113.3	106.3	0.3	6.9	90.0	103.7	21.6
1986	110.2	102.9	0.3	6.2	87.2	100.2	20.3
1985	107.7	100.3	0.3	6.0	85.1	98.2	19.8
1984	105.5	98.0	0.4	6.0	83.4	95.8	19.3
1983	102.2	92.7	0.4	6.4	80.5	91.3	18.7
1982	98.4	88.9	0.4	6.4	78.1	87.9	18.1
1981	99.0	89.5	0.5	6.4	79.8	89.9	18.4
1980	98.9	89.3	0.5	6.6	79.1	87.2	18.4
1979	98.6	...	...	...	...	...	...
1978	93.9	...	0.6	5.5	78.1	82.9	18.0
1977	92.2	83.5	0.5	5.5	74.2	75.8	16.7
1976	89.0	79.7	0.5	5.5	70.9	72.1	16.2
1975	86.2	75.7	0.5	5.5	68.6	69.7	16.7
1974	87.1	75.2	0.6	5.5	67.8	69.5	15.7
1973	85.9	75.6	0.6	5.3	68.6	69.0	16.0
1972	83.5	72.6	0.6	5.2	63.4	66.0	16.0
1971	81.5	69.8	0.6	5.2	60.5	57.1	14.8
1970	77.8	69.1	0.6	5.5	59.0	55.8	14.6
1970 [1]	70.8	69.2	0.6	4.8	58.7	55.8	14.6
1969	71.0	68.6	0.7	4.6	60.0	57.0	14.8
1968	68.8	67.1	0.7	4.5	58.3	55.5	14.2
1967	67.3	65.7	0.7	4.6	56.3	53.8	14.0
1966	65.7	64.9	0.7	4.6	55.1	52.8	13.7
1965	63.6	62.8	0.8	4.1	52.5	50.3	13.3
1964	60.8	60.1	0.8	3.9	50.0	47.9	12.7
1963	59.1	58.5	0.8	3.7	48.2	46.3	12.5
1962	58.0	57.3	0.8	4.0	46.8	45.4	12.3
1961	56.3	56.1	0.8	4.0	46.0	44.6	11.8
1960*	55.3	55.7	0.9	3.9	44.6	43.7	11.3
1959	55.1	55.4	0.9	3.8	45.1	44.1	11.4
1958	53.7	53.4	1.0	3.9	42.7	42.6	11.0
1957	53.9	53.7	1.1	3.9	43.1	43.2	11.2
1956	54.1	53.2	1.2	4.5	44.1	43.8	11.5
1955	53.4	51.8	1.3	4.7	42.9	41.7	11.2
1954	50.0	45.3	1.2	4.6	40.4	37.2	10.7
1954 (monthly average)	49.8	45.3	1.2	4.5	39.7	36.6	10.6
1949 (monthly average)	45.9	34.3	1.4	4.4	35.3	33.1	5.3
1944 (monthly average)	41.9	30.8	1.7	4.7	33.0	31.6	.2
1939 (monthly average)	33.2	24.0	1.2	2.0	22.0	22.4	...
1934 (monthly average)	28.9	...	...	1.4	17.0	...	...

* Denotes first year for which figures include Alaska and Hawaii.
1. 1970 [earlier value] and earlier, paid employees in civilian labor force.
2. Beginning 1955, includes persons covered under both a government retirement system and OASDHI (about 5.3 million in December 1970); excludes persons whose coverage was authorized on an elective or optional basis but not in effect (about 3.5 million in December 1970); also excludes railroad employees jointly covered by OASDHI and their own retirement program.
3. Excludes persons covered under both a government retirement system and OASDHI; see footnote 2.
4. State, railroad and federal employee programs.
5. State and railroad programs. Excludes government employees covered by sick-leave provisions.

Series H 346-367.   Public Assistance—Payments, Recipients and Average Monthly Payments: 1936 to 1997

(As of December. Through 1942, conterminous U.S. only; thereafter, data include Alaska and Hawaii; beginning 1950, Puerto Rico and Virgin Islands; beginning 1959, Guam; Public assistance for the aged, blind, and disabled encompass the Supplemental Security Income program, not Social Security—OASDHI)

Year	Payments for year[1] (mil. dollars)				Number of recipients (1,000)				Average monthly payment per recipient (dollars)			
	Old age assistance	Aid to the blind	Aid to the permanently and totally disabled	Aid to families with dependent children[2]	Old-age assistance	Aid to the blind	Aid to the permanently and totally disabled	Aid to families with dependent children[2]	Old-age assistance	Aid to the blind	Aid to the permanently and totally disabled	Aid to families with dependent children[2]
	350	351	352	353	355	356	357	358	362	363	364	365
1997	4 532	375	24 006	22 031	1 363	81	5 052	3 740	268	382	373	490
1996	4 507	372	23 906	20 614	1 413	82	5 119	4 434	261	379	391	387
1995	4 467	375	22 782	21 609	1 446	84	4 984	4 791	251	370	389	375
1994	4 367	372	21 131	22 827	1 466	85	4 745	5 035	243	364	384	378
1993	4 248	375	19 928	22 688	1 475	85	4 424	5 012	237	359	381	377
1992	4 140	371	17 711	21 656	1 471	85	4 010	4 829	227	362	407	374
1990	3 736	334	12 521	19 067	1 454	84	3 279	4 218	213	342	337	392
1989	3 476	316	11 180	17 466	1 439	83	3 071	3 875	199	320	309	383
1988	3 299	302	10 177	16 827	1 433	83	2 948	3 752	188	306	294	379
1987	3 194	291	9 458	16 373	1 455	83	2 486	3 734	181	297	287	365
1986	3 096	277	8 700	16 033	1 473	83	2 713	3 777	174	287	282	358
1985	3 035	264	7 755	15 196	1 504	82	2 551	3 721	164	274	261	341
1984	2 973	249	7 143	14 505	1 530	81	2 419	3 674	158	265	256	335
1983	2 814	229	6 357	13 838	1 515	79	2 307	3 721	158	256	245	321
1982	2 824	217	5 909	12 878	1 549	77	2 231	3 596	146	242	229	310
1981	2 818	206	5 566	12 981	1 678	79	2 262	3 833	138	228	214	302
1980	2 734	190	5 014	12 475	1 808	78	2 256	3 843	128	213	198	288
1979	2 526	166	4 381	11 069	1 872	77	2 201	3 560	123	212	182	271
1978	2 433	152	3 966	10 730	1 968	77	2 172	3 488	100	164	155	256
1977	2 448	146	3 709	10 604	2 051	77	2 109	3 547	97	159	150	250
1976	2 508	138	3 422	10 141	2 148	76	2 012	3 585	94	153	146	242
1975	2 605	131	3 142	9 211	2 307	74	1 933	3 568	91	147	141	229
1974	2 503	130	2 602	7 917	2 286	75	1 636	3 323	92	143	144	216
1973	1 743	104	1 610	7 212	1 852	78	1 217	3 156	78	111	110	195
1972	1 894	105	1 393	7 020	2 933	80	1 169	3 123	80	113	106	192
1971	1 923	100	1 085	5 653	2 024	80	1 068	2 918	78	106	102	191
1970	1 866	98	1 000	4 853	2 082	81	935	2 552	77.65	104.35	97.65	187.95
1969	1 850	94	827	3 565	2 074	81	803	1 875	73.90	98.75	90.15	176.05
1968	1 779	91	692	2 851	2 027	81	702	1 522	69.55	92.15	82.65	168.15
1967	1 859	90	612	2 280	2 073	83	646	1 297	70.15	90.45	80.60	161.70
1966	1 908	90	566	1 924	2 073	84	588	1 127	68.05	86.85	74.75	150.10
1965	2 046	90	561	1 809	2 087	85	557	1 054	63.10	81.35	66.50	136.95
1964	2 039	98	473	1 634	2 120	95	509	1 012	63.65	76.15	62.25	131.30
1963	2 023	96	415	1 466	2 152	97	464	954	62.80	73.95	59.85	122.40
1962	1 955	94	359	1 386	2 183	99	428	932	61.55	71.95	58.50	119.10
1961	1 886	93	316	1 228	2 229	103	389	916	57.60	68.05	57.05	114.65
1960	1 922	94	287	1 056	2 305	107	369	803	58.90	67.45	56.15	108.35
1959	1 875	90	259	995	2 370	108	346	776	56.70	65.60	54.15	103.70
1958	1 824	87	228	891	2 438	110	325	755	56.95	63.55	53.80	100.40
1957	1 768	83	200	750	2 480	108	290	667	55.50	62.20	52.35	95.15
1956	1 671	77	176	660	2 499	107	266	615	53.25	60.00	50.70	91.50
1955	1 606	71	156	633	2 538	104	241	602	50.05	55.55	48.75	85.50
1954	1 590	68	137	590	2 553	102	222	604	48.70	54.35	48.35	83.70
1953	1 597	66	116	559	2 582	100	192	547	48.90	54.05	47.90	82.30
1952	1 527	61	91	551	2 635	98	161	596	48.80	53.50	48.40	82.10
1951	1 469	56	58	559	2 701	97	124	592	44.55	48.05	46.45	75.80
1950	1 485	53	8	556	2 786	97	69	651	43.05	46.00	44.10	71.45
1949	1 373	48	...	472	2 736	93	X	599	44.75	46.10	X	74.20
1948	1 128	41	...	363	2 498	86	X	475	42.00	43.55	X	71.90
1947	986	36	...	294	2 332	81	X	416	37.40	39.60	X	63.00

See footnotes at end of chart.

Series H 346-367. Public Assistance—Payments, Recipients and Average Monthly Payments: 1936 to 1997—Cont'd.

(As of December. Through 1942, conterminous U.S. only; thereafter, data include Alaska and Hawaii; beginning 1950, Puerto Rico and Virgin Islands; beginning 1959, Guam; Public assistance for the aged, blind, and disabled encompass the Supplemental Security Income program, not Social Security—OASDHI)

Year	Payments for year[1] (mil. dollars)				Number of recipients (1,000)				Average monthly payment per recipient (dollars)			
	Old age assistance	Aid to the blind	Aid to the permanently and totally disabled	Aid to families with dependent children[2]	Old-age assistance	Aid to the blind	Aid to the permanently and totally disabled	Aid to families with dependent children[2]	Old-age assistance	Aid to the blind	Aid to the permanently and totally disabled	Aid to families with dependent children[2]
	350	351	352	353	355	356	357	358	362	363	364	365
1946	820	31	. . .	208	2 196	77	X	346	35.30	36.65	X	62.25
1945	726	27	. . .	150	2 056	71	X	274	30.90	33.50	X	52.05
1944	691	25	. . .	135	2 066	72	X	254	28.45	29.30	X	45.60
1943	650	25	. . .	140	2 149	76	X	272	26.65	27.95	X	41.55
1942	593	25	. . .	158	2 230	79	X	349	23.35	26.55	X	36.25
1941	540	23	. . .	153	2 238	77	X	391	21.25	25.80	X	33.65
1940	473	22	. . .	133	2 070	73	X	372	20.25	25.35	X	32.40
1939	434	20	. . .	115	1 912	70	X	316	19.30	25.45	X	31.75
1938	395	19	. . .	98	1 779	67	X	281	19.55	25.20	X	31.95
1937	310	16	. . .	71	1 579	56	X	229	19.45	27.20	X	31.50
1936	156	13	. . .	50	1 108	45	X	162	18.80	26.10	X	29.85

X Represents zero.
1. Beginning 1950, includes vendor payments for medical care.
2. In 1996-1997, converted to "Temporary Assistance for Needy Families." "Recipients" is number of families (not of persons) and "monthly payment per recipient" is per family.

Series H 398-411. Private Philanthropy—Estimated Fund Flows by Donors and Recipients: 1929 to 1998

(In billions of dollars)

| Year | Philanthropy payments by donors | | | | | Philanthropy revenues of recipients | | |
	Individuals	Charitable bequests	Corporation contributions	Foundation grants	Total	Religious organizations	Education	Hospitals and health
	399	**400**	**401**	**402**	**405**	**406**	**408**	**409**
1998	134.8	13.6	9.0	17.1	174.5	76.1	24.6	16.9
1997	122.9	12.6	8.2	13.9	157.7	72.7	22.2	14.0
1996	107.6	11.5	7.5	12.0	133.5	70.7	19.2	13.9
1995	95.4	10.7	7.3	10.6	124.0	66.3	17.6	12.6
1994	92.5	10.0	7.0	9.7	119.2	60.2	16.6	11.5
1993	92.0	8.5	6.5	9.5	116.5	56.3	15.4	10.8
1992	87.7	8.2	5.9	8.6	110.4	54.9	14.3	10.2
1991	84.3	7.8	5.2	7.7	105.0	50.0	13.5	9.7
1990	81.0	7.8	5.5	7.2	101.4	49.8	12.4	9.9
1989	79.5	7.0	5.5	6.6	98.4	47.8	11.0	9.9
1988	80.1	6.6	5.3	6.2	98.4	45.2	10.2	9.6
1987	72.3	6.6	5.5	5.9	90.3	43.5	9.8	9.2
1986	67.6	5.7	5.1	5.4	83.9	41.7	9.4	8.4
1985	57.4	4.8	4.6	4.9	71.7	38.2	8.2	7.7
1984	56.5	4.0	4.3	4.0	68.8	35.6	7.3	6.8
1983	52.1	3.9	3.7	3.6	63.2	31.8	6.7	6.7
1982	48.5	5.2	2.9	3.2	59.8	28.1	6.0	6.2
1981	46.4	3.6	2.5	3.1	55.6	25.1	5.8	5.8
1980	40.7	2.9	2.3	2.8	48.7	22.2	5.0	5.3
1979	36.5	2.2	2.3	2.2	43.3	20.1	6.0	6.0
1978	32.8	2.6	2.1	2.6	40.1	18.5	5.6	5.5
1977	29.3	3.0	1.7	2.0	36.0	16.9	4.8	4.9
1976	26.6	2.4	1.5	2.1	32.5	14.2	4.5	4.9
1975	23.5	2.2	1.2	2.0	28.6	12.8	4.0	4.4
1974	22.3	2.1	1.2	2.1	27.7	11.9	4.1	4.3
1973	20.4	2.0	1.2	2.0	25.6	10.5	4.1	4.2
1972	16.9	2.7	.8	2.2	22.6	9.7	3.5	3.6
1971	15.0	3.0	1.0	2.1	21.0	8.5	3.4	3.5
1970	14.0	2.1	.8	1.5	18.1	6.9	2.5	2.4
1969	13.3	2.1	1.1	1.2	17.0	6.5	2.4	2.3
1968	12.5	1.9	1.0	1.2	16.0	6.3	2.3	2.1
1967	11.3	1.7	.8	1.2	15.3	6.4	2.0	1.9
1966	10.6	1.5	.8	1.1	14.0	5.9	2.0	1.7
1965	10.0	1.3	.8	1.1	13.5	5.9	2.0	1.6
1964	9.5	1.2	.7	1.0	12.5	5.3	1.8	1.5
1963	8.9	1.0	.7	.8	12.0	5.0	1.6	1.3
1962	8.6	.9	.6	.8	11.3	4.8	1.5	1.2
1961	8.1	.9	.5	.7	10.7	4.7	1.3	1.1
1960	7.9	1.0	.5	.7	10.0	4.5	1.2	.9
1959	7.3	.8	.5	.6	...	...	...	...
1958	7.2	.7	.4	.6	8.6	4.0	1.1	.8
1957	6.7	.6	.4	.7	...	...	...	...
1956	6.3	.5	.4	.6	7.5	3.5	.9	.9
1955	5.8	.5	.4	.3	6.8	3.2	.8	.6
1954	5.3	.4	.3	.2	...	...	...	...
1953	5.2	.4	.5	.2	...	...	...	...
1952	4.8	.3	.4	.1	...	...	...	...
1951	4.3	.3	.3	.1	...	...	...	...
1950	3.8	.3	.3	.1	4.4	2.0	.4	.5
1949	3.5	.2	.2	.1	...	...	...	...
1948	3.4	.3	.2	.1	...	...	...	...
1947	3.1	.2	.2	.1	...	...	...	...
1946	2.7	.2	.2	.1	...	...	...	...
1945	2.4	.2	.3	.1	2.6	1.0	.2	.3
1944	2.2	.2	.2	.1	...	...	...	...

See footnotes at end of chart.

Series H 398-411. Private Philanthropy—Estimated Fund Flows by Donors and Recipients: 1929 to 1998—Cont'd.

(In billions of dollars)

Year	Philanthropy payments by donors					Philanthropy revenues of recipients		
	Individuals	Charitable bequests	Corporation contributions	Foundation grants	Total	Religious organizations	Education	Hospitals and health
	399	**400**	**401**	**402**	**405**	**406**	**408**	**409**
1943	2.1	.2	.2	.1	. . .	. . .	. . .	. . .
1942	1.7	.2	.1	.1	. . .	. . .	. . .	. . .
1941	1.3	.2	.1	.1	. . .	. . .	. . .	. . .
1940	1.1	.1	X	.1	1.2	.6	.2	.1
1939	1.0	.2	X	.1	. . .	. . .	. . .	. . .
1938	.9	.2	X	.1	. . .	. . .	. . .	. . .
1937	.9	.1	X	.1	. . .	. . .	. . .	. . .
1936	.8	.1	X	.1	. . .	. . .	. . .	. . .
1935	.7	.1	X	.1	1.0	.5	.1	X
1934	.7	.1	X	.1	. . .	. . .	. . .	. . .
1933	.6	.1	X	.1	. . .	. . .	. . .	. . .
1932	.6	.2	X	.1	. . .	. . .	. . .	. . .
1931	.7	.2	X	.1	. . .	. . .	. . .	. . .
1930	.8	.2	X	.1	1.4	.8	.2	.1
1929	.9	.2	X	.1	. . .	. . .	. . .	. . .

X Less than .05 billion.

Series H 412-432. Kindergarten Elementary and Secondary Schools and Enrollment: 1870 to 2008

	Schools[1]			Enrollment			
				Public day schools		Nonpublic school[1]	
School year ending x	School district[1]	Elementary public	Secondary public	Elementary public	Secondary public	Elementary public	Secondary public
	412	414	416	422	424	427	429
	...	...	...	*1 000*	*1 000*	*1 000*	*1 000*
2008	...	...	...	33 455	14 746	4 579	1 488
2007	...	...	...	33 489	14 854	4 584	1 498
2006	...	...	...	33 584	14 785	4 587	1 491
2005	...	...	...	33 756	14 579	4 620	1 471
2004	...	...	...	33 958	14 263	4 648	1 439
2003	...	...	...	34 124	13 951	4 671	1 407
2002	...	...	...	34 124	13 800	4 671	1 392
2001	...	...	...	34 055	13 643	4 661	1 376
2000	...	...	...	33 903	13 537	4 640	1 366
1999	...	...	...	33 722	13 420	4 616	1 354
1998	14 822	...	...	33 522	13 270	4 588	1 339
1997	14 891	...	...	32 951	13 003	4 545	1 322
1996	14 910	59 680	21 307	32 759	12 834	4 486	1 297
1995	14 947	...	...	32 341	12 500	4 431	1 269
1994	15 052			31 898	12 213	4 360	1 236
1993	15 212	...	...	31 504	11 961	4 280	1 191
1992	15 360	59 680	19 995	31 088	11 735	4 212	1 163
1991	15 439	...	...	...	...	...	...
1990	15 449	...	...	25 614	15 412	4 066	1 129
1989	15 513	...	...	24 620	15 906	4 162	1 193
1988	15 571	61 500	22 800	24 415	15 774	4 036	1 206
1987	15 684	61 500	22 900	24 304	15 703	4 232	1 247
1986	15 739	60 800	23 400	24 150	15 603	4 116	1 336
1985	15 812	...	...	24 229	15 193	4 195	1 362
1984	15 857	58 800	23 900	24 095	15 193	4 300	1 400
1983	15 909	...	...	23 949	15 303	4 315	1 400
1982	15 959	...	...	23 823	15 742	4 200	1 400
1981	16 001	...	...	24 087	15 957	4 100	1 400
1980	16 044	61 100	24 400	24 196	16 681	3 992	1 339
1979	...	64 400	24 200	24 547	17 104	3 700	1 300
1978	...	62 000	24 500	25 018	17 534	3 732	1 353
1977	...	62 600	25 400	24 954	18 623	3 797	1 343
1976	...	62 600	25 400	25 427	18 884	3 825	1 342
1975	...	63 600	25 700	25 656	19 164	3 700	1 300
1974	...	65 100	25 900	26 394	18 679	3 700	1 300
1973	...	64 900	25 900	26 443	19 001	3 700	1 300
1972	...	...	...	27 312	18 414	3 700	1 300
1971	...	65 800	25 400	27 882	18 389	3 900	1 300
1970[3]	17 995	65 800	25 352	29 996	13 022	4 100	1 400
1968	22 010	70 879	27 011	29 775	12 488	4 600	1 400
1966	26 983	73 216	26 597	28 315	11 597	4 763	1 329
1964	31 705	77 584	26 431	27 172	10 883	4 796	1 287
1962	35 676	81 910	25 350	26 622	9 566	4 521	1 120
1960*	40 520	91 853	25 784	25 679	8 485	4 286	1 035
1958	47 594	95 446	25 507	23 897	7 860	3 944	931
1956	54 859	104 427	26 046	22 726	6 873	3 623	823
1954	63 057	110 875	25 637	21 072	6 290	3 275	747
1952	71 094	123 763	23 746	19 409	5 882	2 922	656
1950	83 718	128 225	24 542	18 353	5 725	2 575	672
1948	94 926	146 760	25 484	17 302	5 653	2 269	602
1946	101 382	160 227	24 314	16 905	5 622	2 213	565
1944	111 383	169 905	28 973	17 016	5 554	2 022	421
1942	115 493	183 112	25 123	17 549	6 388	2 085	483
1940	117 108	...	...	18 237	6 601	2 096	458
1938	119 001	221 660	25 467	19 141	6 227	2 252	437

See footnotes at end of chart.

Series H 412-432. Kindergarten Elementary and Secondary Schools and Enrollment: 1870 to 2008—Cont'd.

| | Schools[1] | | | Enrollment | | | |
| | | | | Public day schools | | Nonpublic school[1] | |
School year ending x	School district[1]	Elementary public	Secondary public	Elementary public	Secondary public	Elementary public	Secondary public
	412	**414**	**416**	**422**	**424**	**427**	**429**
1936	...	232 174	25 652	19 786	5 975	2 253	387
1934	...	236 236	24 714	20 163	5 669	2 371	360
1932	127 531	232 750	26 409	20 434	5 140	2 384	403
1930	...	238 306	23 930	20 556	4 399	2 255	341
1928	...	...	...	20 573	3 911	2 235	341
1926	...	...	...	20 311	3 757	...	...
1924	...	...	...	20 289	3 390	...	...
1922	...	...	...	19 837	2 873	...	...
1920	...	...	...	18 897	2 200	1 456	214
1918	...	...	...	18 920	1 934	...	...
1916	...	...	...	18 896	1 456	...	...
1915	...	...	...	18 375	1 329	...	...
1914	...	...	...	17 935	1 219	...	...
1913	...	...	...	17 474	1 135	...	...
1912	...	...	...	17 078	1 105	...	...
1911	...	...	...	17 050	985	...	...
1910	...	...	...	16 899	915	1 440	117
1909	...	...	...	16 665	841	...	...
1908	...	...	...	16 292	770	...	...
1907	...	...	...	16 140	751	...	...
1906	...	...	...	15 919	723	...	...
1905	...	...	...	15 789	680	...	...
1904	...	...	...	15 620	636	...	...
1903	...	...	...	15 417	592	...	...
1902	...	...	...	15 367	551	...	...
1901	...	...	...	15 161	542	...	...
1900	...	...	...	14 984	519	1 147	111
1899	...	...	...	14 700	476	...	...
1898	...	...	...	14 654	450	...	...
1897	...	...	...	14 414	409	...	...
1896	...	...	...	14 118	380	...	...
1895	...	...	...	13 894	350	...	...
1894	...	...	...	13 706	289	...	...
1893	...	...	...	13 229	254	...	...
1892	...	...	...	13 016	240	...	...
1891	...	...	...	12 839	212	...	...
1890	...	...	...	12 520	203	1 662	95
1889	...	...	...	...	...	...	...
1888	...	...	...	...	...	...	...
1887	...	...	...	...	...	...	...
1886	...	...	...	...	...	...	...
1885	...	...	...	...	...	...	...
1884	...	...	...	...	...	...	...
1883	...	...	...	...	...	...	...
1882	...	...	...	...	...	...	...
1881	...	...	...	...	...	...	...
1880	...	...	...	9 757	110	...	...
1879	...	...	...	...	...	...	...
1878	...	...	...	...	...	...	...
1877	...	...	...	...	...	...	...
1876	...	...	...	...	...	...	...
1875	...	...	...	...	...	...	...
1874	...	...	...	...	...	...	...
1873	...	...	...	...	...	...	...
1872	...	...	...	...	...	...	...

See footnotes at end of chart.

Series H 412-432. Kindergarten Elementary and Secondary Schools and Enrollment: 1870 to 2008—Cont'd.

School year ending x	Schools[1]			Enrollment			
				Public day schools		Nonpublic school[1]	
	School district[1]	Elementary public	Secondary public	Elementary public	Secondary public	Elementary public	Secondary public
	412	**414**	**416**	**422**	**424**	**427**	**429**
1871	...	...	...	7 481	80	...	...
1870	...	...	...	...	...	...	...

* Denotes first year for which figures include Alaska and Hawaii.
1. Data for nonpublic schools for most years are partly estimated.
2. Includes operating and nonoperating districts.
3. Statistics are for 1970-71.

Series H 492-507. Public Elementary and Secondary School Expenditures: 1870 to 1998

(In millions of dollars)

School year ending	Total expenditures, all schools	School year ending x	Total expenditures, all schools	School year ending x	Total expenditures, all schools	School year ending x	Total expenditures, all schools	School year ending x	Total expenditures, all schools	School year ending x	Total expenditures, all schools	School year ending x	Total expenditures, all schools
	492		**492**		**492**		**492**		**492**		**492**		**492**
1998	323 879	1981	104 125	1958	13 569	1924	1 821	1903	251	1886	113
1997	308 077	1980	96 105	1956	10 955	1922	1 581	1902	238	1885	110
1996	292 323	1979	88 712	1954	9 092	1920	1 036	1901	228	1884	103
1995	276 502	1978	80 444	1952	7 344	1918	764	1900	215	1883	97
1994	262 485	1977	74 194	1950	5 838	1916	641	1899	200	1882	89
1993	248 786	1976	70 601	1948	4 311	1915	605	1898	194	1881	84
1992	236 750	1975	64 846	1946	2 907	1914	555	1897	188	1880	78
1991	227 459	1974	59 800	1944	2 453	1913	522	1896	183	1879	76
1990	209 698	1973	55 100	1942	2 323	1912	483	1895	176	1878	79
1989	191 378	1972	51 400	1940	2 344	1911	447	1894	173	1877	79
1988	175 700	1971	47 600	1938	2 233	1910	426	1893	164	1876	83
1987	163 091	1970	40 683	1936	1 969	1909	401	1892	156	1875	84
1986	152 187	1968	32 977	1934	1 720	1908	371	1891	147	1874	80
1985	139 382	1966	26 248	1932	2 175	1907	337	1890	141	1873	76
1984	127 500	1964	21 325	1930	2 317	1906	308	1889	133	1872	74
1983	118 425	1962	18 373	1928	2 184	1905	292	1888	124	1871	69
1982	111 186	1960*	15 613	1926	2 026	1904	273	1887	116	1870	63

* Denotes first year for which figures include Alaska and Hawaii.

Series H 520-530. Public Elementary and Secondary Schools—Attendance and Instructional Staff: 1870 to 1998

| School year ending x | Average daily attendance | Instructional staff | | School year ending x | Average daily attendance | Instructional staff | | School year ending x | Average daily attendance | Instructional staff | |
| | | Average annual salary in current dollars[1] | Total classroom teachers and other nonsupervisory staff[2] | | | Average annual salary in current dollars[1] | Total classroom teachers and other nonsupervisory staff[2] | | | Average annual salary in current dollars[1] | Total classroom teachers and other nonsupervisory staff[2] |
	520	524	526		520	524	526		520	524	526
	1 000		*1 000*		*1 000*		*1 000*		*1 000*		*1 000*
1998	42 764	41 598	3 087	1956	27 740	4 156	1 149	1901	10 716	...	432
1997	42 143	40 562	3 042	1954	25 644	3 825	1 042	1900	10 633	325	423
1996	41 477	39 465	2 970	1952	23 257	3 450	963	1899	10 389	...	414
1995	40 794	38 331	2 929	1950	22 284	3 010	914	1898	10 356	...	411
1994	40 144	37 446	2 865	1948	20 910	2 639	861	1897	10 053	...	405
1993	39 605	36 460	2 811	1946	19 849	1 995	831	1896	9 781	...	400
1992	38 927	35 552	2 763	1944	19 603	1 728	828	1895	9 549	286	398
1991	38 181	34 401	2 746	1942	21 031	1 507	859	1894	9 188	...	389
1990	37 573	32 638	2 685	1940	22 042	1 441	875	1893	8 856	...	383
1989	37 178	30 850	2 652	1938	22 298	1 374	877	1892	8 561	...	374
1988	37 062	29 219	2 605	1936	22 299	1 283	871	1891	8 329	...	368
1987	36 905	27 706	2 563	1934	22 458	1 227	847	1890	8 154	252	364
1986	36 681	26 362	2 519	1932	22 245	1 417	872	1889	8 006	...	357
1985	36 530	24 666	2 473	1930	21 265	1 420	854	1888	7 907	...	347
1984	36 508	21 900	2 144	1928	20 608	1 364	832	1887	7 682	...	339
1983	36 752	20 700	2 134	1926	19 856	1 277	814	1886	7 526	...	331
1982	37 072	19 300	2 158	1924	19 132	1 227	761	1885	7 298	224	326
1981	37 857	17 600	2 192	1922	18 432	1 166	723	1884	7 056	...	314
1980	38 411	15 970	2 521	1920	16 150	871	680	1883	6 652	...	304
1979	39 100	15 000	2 199	1918	15 549	635	651	1882	6 331	...	299
1978	40 200	14 200	2 208	1916	15 359	563	622	1881	6 146	...	294
1977	...	13 400	2 186	1915	14 986	543	604	1880	6 144	195	287
1976	41 300	12 600	2 196	1914	14 216	525	580	1879	5 876	...	280
1975	41 476	11 700	2 171	1913	13 614	512	565	1878	5 783	...	277
1974	41 400	10 800	2 155	1912	13 302	492	547	1877	5 427	...	267
1973	...	10 200	2 109	1911	12 872	466	534	1876	5 291	...	260
1972	42 300	9 700	2 070	1910	12 827	485	523	1875	5 248	...	258
1971	...	9 300	2 063	1909	12 685	...	506	1874	5 051	...	248
1970	41 934	8 840	2 131	1908	12 154	...	495	1873	4 745	...	238
1968	40 828	7 885	1 957	1907	11 926	...	481	1872	4 659	...	230
1966	39 154	6 935	1 786	1906	11 712	...	466	1871	4 545	...	220
1964	37 405	6 240	1 625	1905	11 482	386	460	1870	4 077	189	201
1962	34 682	5 700	1 504	1904	11 318	...	455				
1960*	32 477	5 174	1 387	1903	11 055	...	449				
1958	29 722	4 702	1 261	1902	11 064	...	442				

* Denotes first year for which figures include Alaska and Hawaii.

1. Prior to 1920, computed for teaching positions only; beginning 1920, also includes supervisors and principals. From 1971 through 1984, represents classroom teachers only. In 1980, average salary for instructional staff was $16,715.

2. Prior to 1938, number of different persons employed rather than number of positions. Includes librarians and guidance and psychological personnel. From 1971 through 1984, represents classroom teachers only. From 1985 forward, represents total instructional staff. In 1985, the number of classroom teachers was 2,175,000.

Series H 535-544. Catholic Elementary and Secondary Schools: 1920 to 1998

(In thousands except number of schools)

Year[1]	Elementary schools					Secondary schools				
	Number	Pupils enrolled	Teachers			Number	Pupils enrolled	Teachers		
			Total	Religious	Lay			Total	Religious	Lay
	535	**536**	**537**	**538**	**539**	**540**	**541**	**542**	**543**	**544**
1998	6 990	2 013	[2]106	8	98	1 227	636	47	4	43
1997	7 004	2 015	[2]106	7	98	1 219	634	47	5	42
1996	7 005	2 014	[2]108	8	99	1 226	631	46	5	41
1995	7 022	2 011	[2]119	10	109	1 228	624	48	6	42
1994	7 055	2 004	118	11	107	1 238	615	47	6	40
1993	7 114	1 992	112	12	100	1 231	585	45	7	38
1992	7 174	1 984	110	11	98	1 249	584	45	6	38
1991	7 239	1 964	109	12	96	1 269	587	44	6	37
1990	7 291	1 884	91	11	80	1 296	592	40	6	34
1989	7 395	1 893	94	12	82	1 324	606	43	8	35
1988	7 501	1 912	94	14	80	1 362	639	44	8	36
1987	7 601	1 942	93	15	78	1 391	681	47	10	37
1986	7 693	1 998	94	17	77	1 409	728	48	10	38
1985	7 811	2 061	97	18	79	1 434	760	50	11	39
1984	7 891	2 120	100	20	80	1 449	782	50	12	38
1983	7 937	2 180	99	21	78	1 464	788	48	12	36
1982	7 950	2 225	97	22	75	1 482	801	49	13	36
1981	7 996	2 266	97	24	73	1 498	828	49	14	35
1980	8 043	2 269	97	25	72	1 516	837	49	14	35
1979	8 100	2 293	98	27	70	1 540	846	50	15	35
1978	8 159	2 365	99	29	70	1 564	853	49	16	33
1977	8 204	2 421	100	32	68	1 593	867	51	18	33
1976	8 281	2 483	100	34	66	1 623	882	51	19	32
1975	8 340	2 525	99	35	64	1 653	890	50	20	30
1974	8 437	2 602	100	38	62	1 690	902	50	21	29
1973	8 569	2 714	103	41	62	1 728	907	51	23	29
1972	8 766	2 874	105	44	61	1 790	927	51	23	27
1971	8 982	3 076	106	47	59	1 857	959	53	26	27
1970	9 362	3 355	112	52	60	1 981	1 008	55	29	26
1969	9 695	3 607	110	56	54	2 076	1 051	53	29	23
1968	10 113	3 860	[2]126	68	58	2 192	1 081	[2]57	33	23
1967	10 350	4 106	[2]124	70	53	2 277	1 093	[2]55	34	21
1966	10 769	4 375	120	74	46	2 463	1 110	56	36	20
1965	10 879	4 492	120	76	44	2 413	1 082	57	38	19
1964	10 832	4 534	118	76	42	2 417	1 067	53	36	18
1963	10 775	4 546	115	77	38	2 430	1 044	51	35	16
1962	10 676	4 485	112	77	36	2 502	1 1009	47	34	13
1961	10 631	4 445	111	78	33	2 376	938	47	34	14
1960	10 501	4 373	108	79	29	2 392	880	44	33	11
1956	9 615	3 571	85	71	14	2 311	705	35	28	7
1954	9 279	3 235	77	67	9	2 296	624	32	26	6
1952	8 880	2 842	72	66	6	2 180	549	29	24	5
1950	8 589	2 561	67	62	5	2 189	506	28	23	5
1948	8 285	2 305	62	59	3	2 150	483	27	23	4
1947	. . .	. . .	. . .	. . .	. . .	2 111	467	27	23	4
1940	7 944	2 035	60	. . .	. . .	2 105	361	21	. . .	. . .
1936	7 929	2 103	59	55	3	1 946	285	17	14	3
1930	7 923	2 223	58	53	5	. . .	. . .	. . .	. . .	. . .
1920	6 551	796	42	. . .	. . .	1 552	130	8	. . .	. . .

1. Prior to 1958 data for school year ending; thereafter for October of year shown.
2. Includes part-time teachers.

Series H 598-601. High School Graduates: 1870 to 2005

(In thousands)

Year of graduation	Total number	Year of graduation	Total number	Year of graduation	Total number	Year of graduation	Total number	Year of graduation	Total number	Year of graduation	Total number
	598		**598**		**598**		**598**		**598**		**598**
2005	2 675	1979	2 801	1958	1 506	1929	632	1909	142	1889	39
2000	2 576	1978	2 825	1957	1 446	1928	597	1908	129	1888	33
1998	2 433.4	1977	2 840	1956	1 415	1927	579	1907	127	1887	32
1997	2 433	1976	2 844	1954	1 276	1926	561	1906	126	1886	33
1996	2 304	1975	2 823	1952	1 197	1925	528	1905	119	1885	32
1995	2 273.5	1974	2 771	1950	1 200	1924	494	1904	112	1884	31
1994	2 255	1973	2 737	1948	1 190	1923	426	1903	105	1883	28
1993	2 215	1972	2 706	1946	1 080	1922	357	1902	99	1882	27
1992	2 193	1971	2 643	1944	1 019	1921	334	1901	97	1881	25
1991	2 210	1970	2 906	1942	1 242	1920	311	1900	95	1880	24
1990	2 324	1969	2 839	1940	1 221	1919	298	1899	90	1879	23
1989	2 456.2	1968	2 702	1938	1 120	1918	285	1898	84	1878	22
1988	2 500.2	1967	2 680	1937	1 068	1917	272	1897	80	1877	21
1987	2 428.8	1966	2 672	1936	1 015	1916	259	1896	76	1876	20
1986	2 382.6	1965	2 665	1935	965	1915	240	1895	72	1875	20
1985	2 414.6	1964	2 290	1934	915	1914	219	1894	65	1874	19
1984	2 495	1963	1 950	1933	871	1913	200	1893	59	1873	18
1983	2 600	1962	1 925	1932	827	1912	181	1892	53	1872	17
1982	2 711	1961	1 971	1931	747	1911	168	1891	48	1871	17
1981	2 725	1960	1 864	1930	667	1910	156	1890	44	1870	16
1980	2 748	1959	1 639								

Series H 689-699.   Institutions of Higher Education—Number and Faculty: 1870 to 1995

School year ending x	Number of institutions			Faculty	School year ending x	Number of institutions			Faculty
	Total	2-year colleges[1]	4-year colleges			Total	2-year colleges[1]	4-year colleges	
	689	690	693	696		689	690	693	696
1995	3 706	1 462	2 244	932 000	1962	2 003	524	1 479	424 862
1994	3 688	1 473	2 215	915 000	1960*	1 959	508	1 451	380 554
1993	3 632	1 442	2 190	915 000	1958	1 894	490	1 404	344 525
1992	3 638	1 469	2 169	877 000	1956	1 850	467	1 383	298 910
1991	3 601	1 444	2 157	826 000	1954	1 862	518	1 344	265 911
1990[2]	3 559	1 418	2 141	817 000	1952	1 891	511	1 380	244 488
1989	3 535	1 408	2 127	824 000	1950	1 863	518	1 345	246 722
1988	3 565	1 436	2 129	804 000	1948	1 788	472	1 316	223 660
1987	3 587	1 452	2 135	793 000	1946	1 768	464	1 304	165 324
1986	3 406	1 336	2 070	722 000	1944	1 650	413	1 237	150 980
1985	3 340	1 311	2 029	715 000	1942	1 769	461	1 308	151 066
1984	3 331	1 306	2 205	717 000	1940	1 708	456	1 252	146 929
1983	3 284	1 271	2 013	724 000	1938	1 690	453	1 237	135 989
1982	3 280	1 296	1 984	865 000	1936	1 628	415	1 213	121 036
1981	3 253	1 274	1 979	865 000	1934	1 418	322	1 096	108 873
1980[3]	3 231	1 274	1 957	686 000	1932	1 478	342	1 136	[4]100 789
1979	3 152	1 195	1 957	823 000	1930	1 409	277	1 132	82 386
1978	3 134	1 193	1 941	809 000	1928	1 410	248	1 162	. . .
1977	2 826	1 018	1 808	812 000	1926	1 377	153	1 224	. . .
1976	2 785	1 002	1 783	793 000	1924	1 295	132	1 163	. . .
1975	3 026	1 128	1 898	781 000	1922	1 162	80	1 082	. . .
1974	2 747	1 003	1 744	695 000	1920	1 041	52	989	48 615
1973	2 720	1 003	1 717	634 000	1918	980	46	934	. . .
1972	2 665	964	1 701	590 000	1916	. . .	. . .	. . .	. . .
1971	2 606	931	1 695	596 000	1910	951	. . .	. . .	36 480
1970	2 525	886	1 689	. . .	1900	977	. . .	. . .	23 868
1968	2 374	786	1 588	. . .	1890	998	. . .	. . .	15 809
1966	2 230	622	1 608	596 400	1880	811	. . .	. . .	11 552
1964	2 139	644	1 495	494 514	1870	563	. . .	. . .	5 553

* Denotes first year for which figures include Alaska and Hawaii.
1. Beginning 1950, includes 2-year normal schools. Beginning 1964, includes institutions which do not offer courses creditable toward a bachelor's degree.
2. Data beginning 1990 not comparable with previous years, due to revised survey methods.
3. Beginning 1980, number of institutions includes count of branch campuses.
4. Full-time equivalent; total number of different persons not tabulated.

Series H 700-715. Institutions of Higher Education—Total Enrollment: 1946 to 1997

(In thousands, as of fall)

Year	Total enrollment					Year	Total enrollment				
	Number	Male	Female	4-year institution	2-year institution		Number	Male	Female	4-year institution	2-year institution
	700	**702**	**703**	**704**	**705**		**700**	**702**	**703**	**704**	**705**
1997	14 345	6 330	8 015	8 875	5 471	1972	9 215	5 239	3 976	6 459	2 756
1996	14 300	6 344	7 956	8 803	5 497	1971	8 949	5 207	3 742	6 369	2 579
1995	14 262	6 343	7 919	8 769	5 493	1970	8 581	5 044	3 537	6 262	2 319
1994	14 279	6 372	7 907	8 749	5 530	1969	8 005	4 746	3 258	5 937	2 068
1993	14 305	6 427	7 877	8 739	5 566	1968	7 513	4 478	3 035	5 721	1 792
1992	14 486	6 524	7 963	8 765	5 722	1967	6 912	4 133	2 779	5 399	1 513
1991	14 359	6 502	7 857	8 707	5 652	1966	6 390	3 856	2 534	5 064	1 326
1990	13 819	6 284	7 535	8 579	5 240	1965	5 921	3 630	2 291	4 748	1 173
1989	13 539	6 190	7 349	8 388	5 151	1964	5 280	3 249	2 031	. . .	. . .
1988	13 055	6 002	7 053	8 180	4 875	1963	4 780	2 962	1 818	. . .	. . .
1987	12 767	5 932	6 835	7 990	4 776	1961 `	4 145	2 586	1 559	. . .	. . .
1986	12 504	5 885	6 619	7 824	4 680	1959	3 640	2 333	1 307	. . .	. . .
1985	12 247	5 818	6 429	7 716	4 531	1957	3 324	2 171	1 153	. . .	. . .
1984	12 242	5 864	6 378	7 711	4 531	1956[1]	2 918	1 911	1 007	2 571	347
1983	12 465	6 024	6 441	7 741	4 723	1954[1]	2 446	1 563	883	2 164	282
1982	12 426	6 031	6 394	7 654	4 772	1952[1]	2 134	1 380	754	1 896	238
1981	12 372	5 975	6 397	7 655	4 716	1950[1]	2 281	1 560	721	2 064	217
1980	12 097	5 874	6 223	7 571	4 526	1948[1]	2 403	1 709	694	2 192	211
1979	11 570	5 683	5 887	7 353	4 217	1946[1]	2 078	1 418	661	. . .	. . .
1978	11 260	5 641	5 619	7 232	4 028						
1977	11 286	5 789	5 497	7 243	4 043						
1976	11 012	5 811	5 201	7 129	3 883						
1975	11 185	6 149	5 036	7 215	3 970						
1974	10 224	5 622	4 601	6 820	3 404						
1973	9 602	5 371	4 231	6 590	3 012						

* Denotes first year for which figures include Alaska and Hawaii.
1. For 1956 and earlier years, degree-credit enrollment only.

Series H 728-738. Institutions of Higher Education—Current Fund Expenditures: 1930 to 1996

(In millions of dollars)

School year ending X	Total current fund expenditures	Educational and general expenditures									Auxiliary enterprises and activities
		Total	Administration and general expense	Instruction and departmental research	Organized research [1]	Libraries	Plant operation and maintenance	Organized activities related to instructional departments [2]	Extension and public services	Scholarships and fellowships	
	728	729	730	731	732	733	734	735	736	737	738
1996	189 986	150 927	27 683	57 573	17 518	4 299	12 258	9 010	7 045	13 139	17 569
1995	182 969	144 158	25 905	55 720	17 110	4 166	11 746	8 112	6 691	12 285	17 205
1994	173 351	136 023	24 489	52 776	16 118	3 908	11 368	7 769	6 242	11 238	16 429
1993	165 241	128 978	23 415	50 341	15 291	3 685	10 784	7 388	5 935	10 148	15 562
1992	156 189	121 567	21 984	47 997	14 262	3 596	10 347	6 981	5 489	9 060	14 966
1991	146 088	114 140	20 752	45 496	13 444	3 344	10 063	6 707	5 076	7 551	14 272
1990	134 656	105 585	19 062	42 146	12 506	3 254	9 458	6 183	4 690	6 656	13 204
1989	123 867	96 803	17 310	38 813	11 432	3 010	8 740	5 894	4 227	5 919	12 280
1988	113 786	89 157	16 171	35 834	10 351	2 836	8 231	5 305	3 786	5 325	11 400
1987	105 764	82 958	15 061	33 711	9 352	2 441	7 819	5 134	3 448	4 776	11 037
1986	97 536	76 128	13 914	31 032	8 437	2 551	7 605	4 116	3 120	4 160	10 528
1985	89 951	70 061	12 765	28 777	7 552	2 362	7 345	3 712	2 861	3 670	10 012
1984	81 993	63 741	11 561	26 436	6 724	2 231	6 730	3 300	2 499	3 302	9 250
1983	75 936	58 929	10 412	24 673	6 265	2 040	6 392	3 047	2 320	2 923	8 614
1982	70 339	54 849	9 648	22 963	5 930	1 922	5 979	2 734	2 204	2 685	7 998
1981	64 053	50 074	8 682	20 733	5 658	1 759	5 350	2 513	2 058	2 505	7 288
1980	56 914	44 543	7 621	18 497	5 099	1 624	4 700	2 253	1 817	2 200	6 486
1979	50 721	39 833	6 832	16 663	4 448	1 427	4 179	2 044	1 593	1 945	5 750
1978	45 971	36 257	6 177	15 336	3 920	1 349	3 795	1 781	1 425	1 839	5 261
1977	42 600	33 152	5 591	14 031	3 600	1 250	3 437	1 545	1 343	1 770	4 858
1976	38 903	30 599	5 240	13 095	3 287	1 224	3 083	1 249	1 239	1 636	4 477
1975	35 058	27 548	4 495	11 798	3 126	1 002	2 788	1 254	1 098	1 450	4 074
1974	30 713	24 654	4 201	10 219	2 480	939	2 494	838	731	1 396	3 613
1973	27 956	22 400	3 713	9 244	2 394	841	2 141	791	670	1 322	3 338
1972	25 560	20 442	3 344	8 443	2 265	764	1 928	779	616	1 241	3 178
1971	23 375	18 715	2 984	7 804	2 209	716	1 730	693	588	1 098	2 988
1970	21 043	16 845	2 628	6 884	2 144	653	1 542	648	593	985	2 769
1969	18 482	14 718	2 278	5 942	2 034	572	1 338	535	537	815	2 539
1968	16 481	12 847	1 739	5 139	1 933	493	1 127	351	598	712	2 302
1966	12 509	10 377	1 251	3 756	2 448	346	845	558	438	426	1 888
1964	9 178	7 725	958	2 802	1 973	237	686	459	297	300	1 452
1962	7 155	5 997	730	2 202	1 474	177	564	375	244	229	1 158
1960*	5 601	4 685	583	1 793	1 022	135	470	294	206	172	916
1958	4 510	3 734	474	1 466	728	110	406	238	175	130	775
1956	3 499	2 862	355	1 141	501	86	324	222	138	95	638
1954	2 883	2 345	288	961	373	73	278	187	112	74	538
1952	2 471	1 960	234	823	318	61	240	148	97	39	478
1950	2 246	1 706	213	781	225	56	225	119	87	(4)	476
1948	1 883	1 392	172	658	159	44	202	85	71	(4)	439
1946	1 088	820	105	375	87	27	111	61	55	(4)	242
1944	974	754	70	334	59	20	81	48	44	(4)	199
1942	738	572	67	299	34	20	73	38	43	(4)	137
1940	675	522	63	280	27	19	70	27	35	(4)	124
1938	614	475	56	253	25	18	63	24	34	(4)	116
1936	541	420	48	225	22	16	57	20	29	(4)	95
1934	469	370	43	203	17	13	51	14	20	(4)	79
1932	537	421	47	233	22	11	57	21	24	(4)	91
1930	507	378	43	221	18	10	61	(3)	25	(4)	3

*Denotes first year for which figures include Alaska and Hawaii.
1. From 1930 through 1966, includes federally funded research and development centers; after 1966, such research and development not shown here but included in series H 728.
2. Academic support excluding expenditures for libraries; from 1920 through 1966, includes hospitals; after 1966, hospitals not shown here but included in series H 728.
3. Not tabulated separately; probably included in series H 728.
4. Before 1952, values not shown separately but included in series H 728.

Series H 751-765.   Institutions of Higher Education—Degrees Conferred by Sex: 1870 to 1996

School year ending X	Total all degrees	Bachelor's or first professional		Master's or second professional		Doctor's or equivalent	
		Male	Female	Male	Female	Male	Female
	751	753	754	758	759	762	763
1996	2 248 000	522 000	642 000	179 000	227 000	27 000	18 000
1995	2 218 000	526 000	634 000	179 000	219 000	27 000	18 000
1994	2 206 000	532 000	637 000	176 000	211 000	27 000	17 000
1993	2 167 000	533 000	632 000	169 000	200 000	26 000	16 000
1992	2 108 000	521 000	616 000	162 000	191 000	26 000	15 000
1991	2 025 000	504 000	590 000	156 000	181 000	25 000	15 000
1990	1 916 000	485 000	558 000	149 000	170 000	24 000	14 000
1989	1 870 000	483 000	535 000	149 000	161 000	23 000	13 000
1988	1 834 000	477 000	518 000	145 000	154 000	23 000	12 000
1987	1 825 000	481 000	510 000	141 000	148 000	22 000	12 000
1986	1 830 000	486 000	502 000	144 000	145 000	22 000	12 000
1985	1 828 000	483 000	497 000	143 000	143 000	22 000	11 000
1984	1 819 000	482 000	492 000	144 000	141 000	22 000	11 000
1983	1 822 000	479 000	490 000	145 000	145 000	22 000	11 000
1982	1 788 000	473 000	480 000	146 000	150 000	22 000	10 000
1981	1 752 000	470 000	465 000	147 000	149 000	23 000	10 000
1980	1 731 000	474 000	456 000	151 000	147 000	23 000	10 000
1979	1 727 000	477 000	444 000	153 000	148 000	24 000	9 000
1978	1 744 000	487 000	434 000	161 000	150 000	24 000	8 000
1977	1 741 000	496 000	424 000	168 000	149 000	25 000	8 000
1976	1 726 000	505 000	421 000	167 000	145 000	26 000	8 000
1975	1 666 000	505 000	418 000	162 000	131 000	27 000	7 000
1974	1 653 000	527 000	418 000	158 000	119 000	27 000	6 000
1973	1 586 000	518 000	404 000	109 000	120 000	29 000	6 000
1972	1 509 000	501 000	387 000	150 000	102 000	28 000	5 000
1971	1 393 000	476 000	364 000	138 000	92 000	28 000	5 000
1970	1 065 391	484 174	343 060	125 624	82 667	25 890	3 976
1969	984 129	444 380	319 805	121 531	72 225	22 752	3 436
1968	866 548	390 507	276 203	113 519	63 230	20 183	2 906
1967	768 871	353 349	237 198	103 092	54 615	18 163	2 454
1966	709 832	328 853	222 194	93 063	47 485	16 121	2 116
1965	663 622	316 286	213 717	77 544	39 608	14 692	1 775
1964	614 194	296 676	197 477	70 339	35 212	12 955	1 535
1963	551 810	271 882	171 636	64 198	31 272	11 448	1 374
1962	514 323	259 507	154 780	59 710	28 704	10 377	1 245
1961	487 513	253 077	142 171	55 267	26 423	9 463	1 112
1960*	476 704	252 996	136 187	51 965	25 727	8 801	1 028
1959	461 823	252 517	127 414	48 360	24 172	8 371	989
1958	438 030	241 560	121 942	44 229	21 357	7 978	964
1957	409 132	221 650	116 786	41 329	20 611	7 817	939
1956	377 698	198 615	110 899	39 393	19 888	8 018	885
1955	352 881	182 839	103 002	38 739	19 461	8 014	826
1954	357 327	186 884	104 624	38 147	18 676	8 181	815
1953	372 315	199 793	103 256	40 946	20 213	7 515	792
1952	401 203	225 981	104 005	43 557	19 977	6 969	714
1951	454 960	278 240	104 306	46 196	18 881	6 663	674
1950	496 874	328 841	103 217	41 220	16 963	5 990	643
1949	421 282	263 608	101 884	35 212	15 529	4 527	522
1948	317 607	175 615	95 571	28 931	13 501	3 496	493
1946	157 349	58 664	77 510	9 484	9 725	1 580	386
1944	141 582	55 865	69 998	5 711	7 703	1 880	425
1942	213 491	103 889	81 457	14 179	10 469	3 036	461
1940	216 521	109 546	76 954	16 508	10 233	2 861	429
1938	189 503	97 678	67 265	13 400	8 228	2 502	430
1936	164 197	86 067	57 058	11 503	6 799	2 370	400
1934	157 279	82 341	53 815	11 516	6 777	2 456	374
1932	160 084	83 271	54 792	12 210	7 157	2 247	407
1930	139 752	73 615	48 869	8 925	6 044	1 946	353
1928	124 995	67 659	43 502	7 727	4 660	1 249	198

See footnotes at end of table.

Series H 751-765. Institutions of Higher Education—Degrees Conferred by Sex: 1870 to 1996—Cont'd.

School year ending X	Total all degrees	Bachelor's or first professional		Master's or second professional		Doctor's or equivalent	
		Male	Female	Male	Female	Male	Female
	751	753	754	758	759	762	763
1926	108 407	62 218	35 045	6 202	3 533	1 216	193
1924	92 097	54 908	27 875	5 515	2 701	939	159
1922	68 488	41 306	20 362	4 304	1 680	708	128
1920	53 516	31 980	16 642	2 985	1 294	522	93
1918	42 041	26 269	12 316	1 806	1 094	491	65
1916	49 823	31 852	13 398	2 934	972	586	81
1915	48 100	31 417	12 495	2 638	939	549	62
1914	48 097	32 183	12 085	2 256	1 014	486	73
1913	45 959	31 312	11 084	2 021	1 004	481	57
1912	42 943	29 560	9 848	2 215	820	436	64
1911	40 434	28 547	8 934	1 821	635	449	48
1910	39 755	28 762	8 437	1 555	558	399	44
1909	40 531	29 433	8 459	1 713	475	397	54
1908	36 162	26 376	7 424	1 511	460	339	52
1907	34 202	25 269	6 965	1 215	404	320	29
1906	34 189	25 215	6 804	1 366	421	358	25
1905	33 813	24 934	6 585	1 538	387	341	28
1904	32 514	24 237	6 264	1 340	339	302	32
1903	31 962	23 872	6 035	1 385	333	302	35
1902	31 117	23 225	5 741	1 464	394	264	29
1901	30 790	23 099	5 582	1 405	339	334	31
1900	29 375	22 173	5 237	1 280	303	359	23
1899	27 867	21 064	4 916	1 275	267	327	18
1898	26 816	20 358	4 694	1 188	252	285	39
1897	26 963	20 550	4 681	1 163	250	299	20
1896	26 342	20 076	4 517	1 213	265	236	35
1895	25 712	19 723	4 383	1 124	210	247	25
1894	23 352	17 917	3 933	1 013	210	261	18
1893	19 989	15 342	3 325	...	...	...	...
1892	17 722	13 840	2 962	...	...	...	...
1891	17 803	13 902	2 938	...	...	...	...
1890	16 703	12 857	2 682	...	...	147	2
1889	16 305	12 397	2 623	...	...	...	...
1888	16 383	12 562	2 694	...	...	...	...
1887	14 402	11 008	2 394	...	...	...	...
1886	14 040	10 731	2 366	...	...	...	...
1885	15 882	12 043	2 691	...	...	...	...
1884	13 732	10 408	2 357	...	...	...	...
1883	16 029	12 294	2 822	...	...	...	...
1882	15 928	12 168	2 830	...	...	...	...
1881	15 830	12 035	2 836	...	...	...	...
1880	13 829	10 411	2 485	...	...	51	3
1879	13 036	9 808	2 273	...	...	...	...
1878	12 381	9 416	2 117	...	...	...	...
1877	10 915	8 329	1 816	...	...	...	...
1876	12 871	9 911	2 094	...	...	...	...
1875	12 616	9 905	2 027	...	...	...	...
1874	12 366	9 593	1 900	...	...	...	...
1873	11 723	9 070	1 737	...	...	...	...
1872	8 660	6 626	1 226	...	...	...	...
1871	12 370	10 484	1 873	...	...	...	...
1870	9 372	7 993	1 378	...	...	1	...

*Denotes first year for which figures include Alaska and Hawaii.

Series H 806-828. National Parks, Monuments and Allied Areas—Area and Visits: 1850 to 1998

(For years ending Sept. 30 prior to 1941; thereafter, for years ending Dec. 31 or as of Jan. 1 of the following year. Includes areas in Alaska, Hawaii, Virgin Islands and Puerto Rico.)

| Year | Total enumerated areas[1] | | National parks | | National monuments visits | National historical and commemorative archaelogical areas[3] visits | National parkways visits |
	Area	Visits[2]	Area	Visits[2]			
	807	808	810	811	814	817	820
	1 000 *acres*	*1 000*	*1 000* *acres*	*1 000*	*1 000*	*1 000*	*1 000*
1998	77 654	286 700	49 416	64 500	23 600	74 200	32 800
1997	77 457	275 300	49 384	65 300	24 100	63 000	31 600
1996	77 458	265 800	49 315	63 100	23 600	59 000	30 900
1995	77 355	269 600	49 307	64 800	23 500	56 900	31 300
1994	74 905	268 600	48 111	63 000	23 600	59 500	29 300
1993	75 515	273 100	45 521	59 800	26 500	61 900	30 400
1992	76 492	274 700	46 208	58 700	26 600	63 300	30 700
1991	76 607	267 800	46 135	57 400	25 800	61 000	26 800
1990	76 362	258 700	46 089	57 700	23 900	57 500	29 100
1989	76 331	269 400	46 081	57 400	23 700	63 900	31 200
1988	76 176	282 500	45 995	56 400	23 200	61 200	42 000
1987	75 970	287 200	45 875	56 600	23 500	68 600	39 300
1986	75 863	281 100	45 791	53 500	21 200	65 500	41 600
1985	75 749	263 400	45 739	50 000	15 900	61 900	40 000
1984	74 913	248 600	45 454	49 700	15 800	63 600	37 900
1983	74 846	243 600	45 427	50 000	16 200	57 300	37 700
1982	74 800	244 100	45 414	49 600	16 200	62 300	36 100
1981	73 665	329 700	44 470	63 300	17 100	95 000	43 800
1980	70 936	300 300	15 801	60 200	16 300	88 500	40 200
1979	70 797	282 400	15 684	57 500	16 800	83 900	35 000
1978	70 541	283 100	15 679	62 900	19 100	88 400	37 700
1977	29 571	262 600	15 374	62 000	18 500	85 500	36 200
1976	29 389	267 700	15 365	60 600	19 300	82 800	30 900
1975	29 091	238 800	15 344	58 800	17 300	75 700	36 000
1974	29 031	217 400	14 777	53 100	15 200	72 900	18 100
1973	29 117	215 600	14 740	54 700	16 300	71 600	13 000
1972	28 878	211 600	14 730	54 400	16 300	72 600	30 900
1971	28 731	200 543	14 470	49 115	15 913	75 182	27 671
1970	28 543	172 005	14 307	[4]45 879	17 304	46 593	27 818
1969	28 460	163 990	14 275	42 519	14 610	47 052	26 678
1968	27 971	150 836	14 212	42 515	14 206	43 838	23 919
1967	27 187	139 676	13 664	39 641	13 741	40 403	21 130
1966	26 551	133 081	13 628	38 556	13 144	43 030	15 925
1965	26 549	121 312	13 619	36 566	12 286	39 022	12 977
1964	26 102	111 386	13 566	34 047	12 164	34 847	11 478
1963	25 869	102 711	13 338	33 438	11 676	30 786	12 523
1962	26 003	97 045	13 333	32 191	11 752	27 958	11 835
1961	25 958	86 663	13 211	27 906	10 922	26 356	9 733
1960	25 704	79 229	13 208	26 630	10 738	21 820	8 983
1959	24 497	68 901	13 205	22 392	10 696	15 437	8 952
1958	24 398	65 461	13 106	21 672	9 734	14 076	8 131
1957	24 410	68 016	13 136	20 903	9 351	15 582	7 890
1956	24 398	61 602	13 131	20 055	8 769	13 543	7 438
1955	23 924	56 573	12 670	18 830	7 953	12 605	6 700
1954	23 908	54 210	12 641	17 969	7 805	12 587	6 067
1953	23 902	52 268	12 640	17 372	7 540	12 593	5 693
1952	23 840	47 379	12 589	17 143	6 807	11 979	3 558
1951	23 702	37 106	12 557	15 079	6 187	10 590	2 449
1950	23 836	33 253	12 222	13 919	5 310	9 476	1 996

See footnotes at end of chart.

Series H 806-828. National Parks, Monuments and Allied Areas—Area and Visits: 1850 to 1998—Cont'd.

(For years ending Sept. 30 prior to 1941; thereafter, for years ending Dec. 31 or as of Jan. 1 of the following year. Includes areas in Alaska, Hawaii, Virgin Islands and Puerto Rico.)

Year	Total enumerated areas[1]		National parks		National monuments visits	National historical and commemorative archaelogical areas[3] visits	National parkways visits
	Area	Visits[2]	Area	Visits[2]			
	807	**808**	**810**	**811**	**814**	**817**	**820**
1949	22 976	31 736	11 420	12 968	4 923	8 778	1 422
1948	22 955	29 859	11 347	11 293	4 438	7 849	1 510
1947	22 824	25 534	11 347	10 674	4 027	7 575	1 247
1946	22 424	21 752	11 062	8 991	3 603	6 734	1 262
1945	22 126	11 714	11 061	4 538	2 512	3 694	383
1944	22 107	8 340	11 055	2 646	1 851	3 310	268
1943	21 061	6 828	10 303	2 054	1 578	2 851	131
1942	20 886	9 371	10 300	3 815	1 832	3 130	256
1941	20 817	21 237	10 285	8 459	3 745	7 292	896
1940	20 762	16 755	10 258	7 358	2 817	5 924	. . .
1939	19 892	15 531	9 459	6 854	2 592	5 472	. . .
1938	18 647	16 331	9 409	6 619	2 364	6 784	. . .
1937	16 537	15 133	8 750	6 705	1 966	6 073	. . .
1936	15 433	11 990	8 692	5 791	1 681	4 518	. . .
1935	15 115	7 676	8 486	4 056	1 332	2 288	. . .
1934	15 244	6 337	8 532	3 517	1 386	1 434	. . .
1933	15 140	3 482	8 435	2 867	523	91	. . .
1932	12 968	3 755	8 417	2 949	406	400	. . .
1931	12 523	3 545	8 027	3 153	392	. . .	. . .
1930	10 581	3 247	7 797	2 775	472	. . .	. . .
1929	10 538	3 248	7 755	2 757	491	. . .	. . .
1928	10 359	3 025	7 581	2 569	456	. . .	. . .
1927	10 320	2 798	7 570	2 381	417	. . .	. . .
1926	10 249	2 315	7 501	1 942	373	. . .	. . .
1925	9 987	2 055	7 286	1 762	292	. . .	. . .
1924	8 813	1 671	7 278	1 424	247	. . .	. . .
1923	8 790	1 494	7 278	1 281	213	. . .	. . .
1922	8 781	1 216	7 278	1 045	172	. . .	. . .
1921	8 452	1 172	6 950	1 007	164	. . .	. . .
1920	8 452	1 058	6 950	920	139	. . .	. . .
1919	8 372	811	6 873	757	54	. . .	. . .
1918	7 554	455	6 255	452	3	. . .	. . .
1917	7 491	491	6 254	488	2	. . .	. . .
1916	5 984	358	4 742	356	2	. . .	. . .
1915	5 880	335	4 666	335	1	. . .	. . .
1914	5 986	240	4 437	240	1	. . .	. . .
1913	5 984	252	4 437	252	(Z)	. . .	. . .
1912	5 977	230	4 431	229	(Z)	. . .	. . .
1911	5 978	224	4 431	224	(Z)	. . .	. . .
1910	5 998	199	4 431	199	. . .	. . .	. . .
1909	5 013	86	3 449	86	. . .	. . .	. . .
1908	4 363	69	3 449	69	. . .	. . .	. . .
1907	3 547	61	3 444	61	. . .	. . .	. . .
1906	3 265	31	3 251	31	. . .	. . .	. . .
1905	3 471	141	3 457	141	. . .	. . .	. . .
1904	3 471	121	3 457	121	. . .	. . .	. . .
1903	3 470	. . .	3 456	. . .	. . .	. . .	. . .
1902	3 459	. . .	3 445	. . .	. . .	. . .	. . .
1901	3 300	. . .	3 286	. . .	. . .	. . .	. . .
1900	3 300	. . .	3 286	. . .	. . .	. . .	. . .

See footnotes at end of chart.

Series H 806-828. National Parks, Monuments and Allied Areas—Area and Visits: 1850 to 1998—Cont'd.

(For years ending Sept. 30 prior to 1941; thereafter, for years ending Dec. 31 or as of Jan. 1 of the following year. Includes areas in Alaska, Hawaii, Virgin Islands and Puerto Rico.)

Year	Total enumerated areas[1]		National parks		National monuments visits	National historical and commemorative archaeological areas[3] visits	National parkway visits
	Area	Visits[2]	Area	Visits[2]			
	807	808	810	811	814	817	82...
1899	3 300	. . .	3 286	. . .	. . .	. . .	. . .
1898	3 287	. . .	3 274	. . .	. . .	. . .	. . .
1897	3 287	. . .	3 274	. . .	. . .	. . .	. . .
1896	3 287	. . .	3 274	. . .	. . .	. . .	. . .
1895	3 287	. . .	3 274	. . .	. . .	. . .	. . .
1894	3 058	. . .	3 052	. . .	. . .	. . .	. . .
1893	3 058	. . .	3 052	. . .	. . .	. . .	. . .
1892	3 058	. . .	3 052	. . .	. . .	. . .	. . .
1891	3 058	. . .	3051	. . .	. . .	. . .	. . .
1890	2 889	. . .	2 889	. . .	. . .	. . .	. . .
1872-1889[5]	1 921	. . .	1 921	. . .	. . .	. . .	. . .
1850-1871[6]	1	. . .	1	. . .	. . .	. . .	. . .

Z Less than 500.

1. Not the same as the "national park system." Definition of the latter has changed from time to time. For 1850-1962 series H 806-808 are merely totals of the other items listed; thereafter, totals include other national parks and allied areas not shown separately, as follows (as of year end or Jan. 1 of the following year): 1970, 16 areas, 100 thousand acres and 4 742 visits; 1969, 13 areas, 94 thousand acres and 2 415 thousand visits; 1968, 14 areas, 128 thousand acres and 1 790 thousand visits; 1967, 10 areas, 48 thousand acres and 2 393 thousand visits; 1966, 10 areas, 23 thousand acres and 2 296 thousand visits; 1965, 1 area, 18 acres and 1 673 thousand visits; 1964, 1 area, 18 acres and 1 840 thousand visits; 1963, 1 area, 18 acres and no reported visits.
2. Beginning 1964, includes visits to the White House.
3. Includes national historical parks, national military parks, national battlefields, national battlefield parks, national battlefield sites, national cemeteries, national historic sties, national memorials, and one national memorial park. Does not include historical areas established under the Antiquities Act of 1906 and designated national monuments nor the White House.
4. Includes visits to two National Recreation Areas adjacent to North Cascades National Park.
5. Yellowstone National Park, the first national park established 1872.
6. Hot Springs Reservation set aside by the federal government in 1832 and established as a national park in 1921. Initial federal acreage was much greater than indicated but over a period of years was subdivided into tracts and sold some 900-odd acres being permanently reserved to the federal government. These series begin with 1850, the first year following the establishment of the Department of the Interior.

Series H 836-848. State Parks—Acreage, Expenditures, Funds, Revenue, Employees and Attendance: 1939 to 1997

Year	Total			Year	Total			Year	Total		
	Acreage[1]	Expenditures[2]	Attendance[2]		Acreage[1]	Expenditures[2]	Attendance[2]		Acreage[1]	Expenditures[2]	Attendance[2]
	836	839	846		836	839	846		836	839	846
	1 000 acres	$1 000	1 000		1 000 acres	$1 000	1 000		1 000 acres	$1 000	1 000
1997	12 484	1 322 991	783 400	1977	. . .	. . .	. . .	1954	5 005	49 134	166 427
1995	11 807	1 245 779	745 602	1976	. . .	. . .	. . .	1953	4 876	49 565	159 116
1992	11 831	1 086 631	724 805	1975	9 838	649 000	566 000	1952	4 928	40 469	149 255
1991	11 148	1 094 573	736 897	1974	. . .	. . .	. . .	1951	4 877	38 545	120 722
1990	11 238	1 060 158	722 819	1973	. . .	. . .	. . .	1950	4 657	36 399	114 291
1989	11 061	981 760	762 842	1972	. . .	. . .	. . .	1949	. . .	31 921	106 792
1988	10 820	903 426	710 342	1971	. . .	. . .	. . .	1948	. . .	32 059	105 248
1987	13 752	848 290	694 432	1970	8 555	386 752	482 536	1947	. . .	25 991	109 995
1986	13 726	799 851	675 465	1967	7 352	279 520	391 063	1946	4 634	15 445	92 507
1985	10 128	101 500	661 916	1962	5 763	108 881	284 795	1945	. . .	10 564	57 649
1984	10 148	892 000	665 524	1961	5 799	110 101	273 484	1944	. . .	6 466	39 668
1983	9 936	838 000	644 843	1960	5 602	87 373	259 001	1943	. . .	6 570	38 306
1982	9 912	888 000	631 031	1959*	5 681	88 268	255 310	1942	. . .	9 373	70 359
1981	9 326	968 000	618 080	1958	5 406	73 222	237 329	1941	4 260	10 022	97 489
1980	9 468	993 000	548 912	1957	5 248	74 008	216 780	1940	. . .	9 443	. . .
1979	9 411	1 078 000	609 010	1956	5 165	65 844	200 705	1939	. . .	7 429	. . .
1978	. . .	. . .	. . .	1955	5 086	55 093	183 188				

* Denotes first year for which figures include Alaska and Hawaii.
1. Excludes state forests, wildlife refuges and waysides not administered by state park agencies.
2. Detail may not add to total because some states did not report detail.

Series H 862-877. Participation in Selected Recreational Activities: 1901 to 1998

Year	Horseracing			Major league baseball attendance[1]			Motion Pictures[1]	Paid hunting and fishing license holders[2]	
	Racing days	Attendance[1]	Parimutuel turnover	American League	National League	World Series	Average weekly box office receipts	Hunting	Fishing
	865	866	867	868	869	870	873	875	876
			1 000	Mil. dol.	1 000	1 000	1 000	Mil. dol.	Millions	Millions
1998	(NA)	(NA)	(NA)	31 948	38 424	243	6 949		
1997	11 958	41 846	15 220	31 283	31 885	404	6 366	. . .	. . .
1996	12 457	43 367	14 902	29 718	30 379	268	5 912	. . .	. . .
1995	13 243	38 934	14 592	25 359	25 110	286	5 494	32.1	37.9
1994	13 082	42 065	14 143	24 202	25 808	. . .	5 396	31.6	37.9
1993	13 237	45 688	13 718	33 333	36 924	344	5 154	31.6	37.9
1992	13 644	49 275	14 078	31 760	24 113	311	4 871	31.3	37.4
1991	(NA)	(NA)	14 094	32 118	24 696	373	4 803	30.7	37.0
1990	13 841	63 803	7 162	30 332	24 492	209	5 022	30.0	37.0
1989	14 240	69 551	13 867	29 849	25 324	223	5 033	29.3	36.6
1988	14 285	69 949	13 616	28 500	24 499	260	4 458	30.0	36.8
1987	14 208	70 015	13 122	27 277	24 734	387	4 253	28.8	36.5
1986	13 853	70 580	12 421	25 173	22 333	322	3 778	27.9	35.9
1985	13 745	73 346	12 222	24 532	22 292	327	3 749	27.7	35.7
1984	13 683	74 076	12 032	23 961	20 781	272	2 749	28.5	36.1
1983	13 545	75 693	11 733	23 991	21 549	304	2 115	28.9	37.8
1982	13 523	76 858	11 888	23 080	21 507	385	3 453	28.3	37.2
1981	13 464	75 463	11 677	14 066	12 478	338	2 966	27.9	37.9
1980	13 133	74 690	11 218	21 890	21 124	325	2 749	27.0	35.2
1979	13 160	72 783	10 728	22 372	21 178	368	2 821	26.4	35.4
1978	13 147	75 324	10 029	20 530	20 107	337	2 643	25.8	32.8
1977	13 300	75 987	9 698	19 640	19 070	338	2 672	25.4	34.0
1976	13 570	79 307	9 421	14 658	16 661	223	2 036	25.2	34.9
1975	13 110	78 662	7 862	13 189	16 600	308	2 115	25.9	34.7
1974	12 211	74 948	7 513	13 016	16 978	308	1 908	25.1	34.3
1973	11 805	75 016	7 027	13 434	16 675	260	1 500	23.3	33.5
1972	11 478	70 807	6 401	11 438	15 530	363	1 375	22.2	33.0
1971	10 792	73 619	6 350	11 869	17 325	351	1 214	22.9	32.4
1970	9 962	69 704	5 977	12 085	16 662	253	. . .	22.2	31.1
1969	9 539	68 099	5 723	12 135	15 095	272	. . .	21.6	29.9
1968	9 051	65 460	5 310	11 317	11 785	380	. . .	20.9	28.8
1967	8 621	63 373	4 922	11 337	12 971	304	. . .	20.2	27.1
1966	8 384	63 577	4 784	10 167	15 015	221	. . .	19.6	26.3
1965	8 051	62 887	4 615	8 861	13 581	364	44	19.4	25.0
1964	7 561	60 595	4 402	9 235	12 045	322	44	19.1	24.5
1963	7 136	55 754	3 975	9 095	11 382	247	42	18.7	24.0
1962	6 532	50 582	3 669	10 015	11 360	377	43	18.2	23.1
1961	6 280	49 560	3 467	10 163	8 732	223	42	[3]18.2	23.1
1960	6 099	46 879	3 358	9 227	10 685	350	40	*[3]18.4	*23.3
1959	5 963	45 451	3 246	9 149	9 995	421	42	[3]11.9	19.9
1958	5 348	43 373	3 039	7 296	10 165	394	40	14.8	20.2
1957	5 187	41 365	2 937	8 196	8 820	395	45	14.9	19.3
1956	5 052	39 871	2 791	7 894	8 650	346	47	14.5	18.7
1955	4 899	38 503	2 592	8 943	7 674	362	46	14.2	18.9
1954	4 734	38 637	2 515	7 922	8 014	252	49	14.1	18.6
1953	4 656	38 249	2 556	6 964	7 420	307	46	14.8	17.7
1952	4 397	35 065	2 326	8 294	6 339	341	51	13.9	17.1
1951	4 114	31 865	1 934	8 883	7 244	342	54	12.6	16.0
1950	4 018	29 251	1 638	9 142	8 321	196	60	12.6	15.3
1949	3 702	. . .	1 599	10 731	9 485	237	70	12.8	15.5
1948	. . .	. . .	. . .	11 150	9 771	358	90	11.4	14.1
1947	. . .	. . .	. . .	9 486	10 388	390	90	12.1	12.6
1946	. . .	. . .	. . .	9 621	8 902	250	90	9.9	11.1
1945	. . .	. . .	. . .	5 580	5 261	333	85	8.2	8.3
1944	. . .	. . .	. . .	4 798	3 975	207	85	7.5	7.8

See footnotes at end of chart.

Series H 862-877. Participation in Selected Recreational Activities: 1901 to 1998—Cont'd.

Year	Horseracing			Major league baseball attendance[1]			Motion Pictures[1]	Paid hunting and fishing license holders[2]	
	Racing days	Attendance[1]	Parimutuel turnover	American League	National League	World Series	Average weekly box office receipts	Hunting	Fishing
	865	**866**	**867**	**868**	**869**	**870**	**873**	**875**	**876**
1943	...	...	...	3 697	3 769	277	85	8.1	8.0
1942	...	...	...	4 200	4 353	277	85	8.5	8.4
1941	...	...	...	4 912	4 778	236	85	7.9	8.0
1940	...	...	...	5 434	4 390	282	80	7.6	7.9
1939	...	...	...	4 271	4 707	184	85	7.5	7.9
1938	...	...	...	4 446	4 561	201	85	6.9	7.4
1935	...	...	...	3 688	3 657	287	80	6.0	5.1
1934	...	...	...	3 764	3 200	282	70	5.9	4.9
1933	...	...	...	2 926	3 163	163	60	5.7	4.9
1932	...	...	...	3 133	3 841	192	60	5.8	...
1931	...	...	...	3 883	4 584	232	75	6.4	...
1930	...	...	...	4 686	5 447	213	90	6.9	...
1929	...	...	...	4 662	4 926	190	80	6.4	...
1928	...	...	...	4 221	4 881	199	65	6.5	...
1927	...	...	...	4 613	5 310	202	57	6.0	...
1926	...	...	...	4 913	4 920	328	50	5.3	...
1925	...	...	...	5 187	4 354	283	46	4.9	...
1924	...	...	...	5 255	4 341	284	46	4.4	...
1923	...	...	...	4 603	4 070	301	43	4.3	...
1922	...	...	...	4 874	3 942	186	40	...	...
1921	...	...	...	4 620	3 987	270	...	...	...
1920	...	...	...	5 084	4 037	174	...	...	...
1919	...	...	...	3 654	2 878	237	...	...	...
1918	...	...	...	1 708	1 372	186	...	...	...
1917	...	...	...	2 859	2 361	129	...	...	...
1916	...	...	...	3 452	3 052	163	...	...	...
1915	...	...	...	2 435	2 430	143	...	...	...
1914	...	...	...	2 748	1 707	111	...	...	...
1913	...	...	...	3 527	2 832	151	...	...	...
1912	...	...	...	3 264	2 736	252	...	...	...
1911	...	...	...	3 340	3 232	180	...	...	...
1910	...	...	...	3 271	3 495	124	...	...	...
1909	...	...	...	3 740	3 496	145	...	...	...
1908	...	...	...	3 611	3 512	62	...	...	...
1907	...	...	...	3 399	2 640	78	...	...	...
1906	...	...	...	2 938	2 781	100	...	...	...
1905	...	...	...	3 121	2 734	92	...	...	...
1904	...	...	...	3 024	2 664	...	...	...	...
1903	...	...	...	2 345	2 390	100	...	...	...
1902	...	...	...	2 206	1 683	...	...	...	...
1901	...	...	...	1 684	1 920	...	...	...	...

*Denotes first year for which figures include Alaska and Hawaii.
1. Excludes Alaska and Hawaii for all years.
2. Beginning 1960, includes multiple counting of license holders who bought one or more nonresident licenses as well as a license for their own home state.
3. Excludes Colorado, Michigan, Minnesota and Wisconsin.

Series H 878-893. Personal Consumption Expenditures for Recreation: 1909 to 1999

(millions of dollars)

Year	Total	Nondurable toys and sport supplies	Wheel goods, durable toys, sport equipment, boats and pleasure aircraft	Video and audio goods, including radio and television receivers, records, musical instruments	Radio and television repairs	Admissions to specified spectator amusements				Clubs and fraternal organizations, except insurance	Commercial participant amusements	Parimutuel net receipts	Books and maps	Magazines, newspapers and sheet music	Flowers, seeds and potted plants
						Total	Motion picture theaters	Legitimate theater entertainment (plays, operas, etc.) or non-profit institutions, except athletics	Spectator sports						
	878	879	880	881	882	883	884	885	886	887	888	889	890	891	892
1999	534 900	63 100	51 300	99 100	3 900	25 800	7 400	10 200	8 200	15 800	63 100	3 800	29 800	37 000	17 500
1998	489 800	57 300	46 400	90 700	4 000	23 600	6 900	9 100	7 600	15 000	56 400	3 700	27 800	32 500	16 300
1997	456 600	53 200	42 800	83 700	4 000	22 100	6 300	8 600	7 100	14 600	52 800	3 600	26 300	29 100	15 300
1996	429 600	50 600	40 500	80 000	3 700	20 700	5 800	8 000	6 900	14 000	48 300	3 500	24 900	27 600	14 900
1995	401 600	47 200	38 500	77 000	3 600	19 200	5 500	7 600	6 100	12 700	43 900	3 500	23 100	26 200	13 800
1994	368 700	43 400	35 200	71 000	3 300	18 200	5 200	7 200	5 800	11 800	38 600	3 400	20 800	24 900	13 200
1993	340 100	39 500	32 500	62 600	3 300	17 500	5 000	6 800	5 700	11 100	34 000	3 300	18 800	23 100	12 500
1992	313 800	36 500	30 100	57 000	3 400	16 100	4 900	6 000	5 100	10 200	29 900	3 400	17 100	22 000	12 000
1991	295 300	34 600	29 500	55 100	3 400	15 600	5 200	5 400	4 900	9 500	25 700	3 400	16 400	22 100	11 000
1990	284 900	32 800	29 700	52 900	3 700	14 800	5 100	5 200	4 500	8 700	24 600	3 500	16 200	21 600	10 900
1989	268 200	30 700	29 300	52 400	3 700	13 300	4 600	4 400	4 300	8 000	21 800	3 300	15 000	20 100	10 500
1988	248 400	27 700	27 700	50 800	3 800	11 900	3 900	4 400	3 600	7 100	19 800	3 400	14 200	19 200	9 700
1987	224 500	25 300	25 600	46 200	3 500	10 800	3 400	4 000	3 400	6 700	17 300	3 000	13 000	17 600	9 200
1986	204 700	22 900	23 000	41 800	3 200	10 500	3 300	3 900	3 300	6 100	16 000	2 900	11 400	16 500	7 700
1985	187 600	21 400	21 200	35 900	3 200	9 700	3 200	3 200	3 300	5 500	15 100	2 800	10 600	15 900	6 900
1984	172 900	20 500	20 400	32 000	2 800	9 700	3 400	2 800	3 500	4 700	13 800	2 800	10 000	15 700	6 500
1983	155 000	18 400	16 900	28 500	2 800	8 700	3 200	2 400	3 100	4 400	12 900	2 600	9 000	14 600	6 000
1982	138 900	17 100	16 300	23 000	2 600	8 000	3 100	2 100	2 700	4 100	11 600	2 600	8 000	13 800	5 700
1981	129 500	16 000	16 400	22 200	2 500	7 100	2 700	2 000	2 400	3 400	10 800	2 500	7 300	13 000	5 300
1980	116 700	14 600	15 600	20 600	2 500	6 600	2 600	1 800	2 300	2 900	9 100	2 300	6 500	12 000	4 700
1979	108 400	13 600	16 200	19 400	2 400	6 400	2 800	1 500	2 100	2 500	8 000	2 100	5 700	10 900	4 200
1978	95 900	12 300	14 100	17 300	2 400	5 900	2 800	1 300	1 800	2 100	7 200	2 000	5 000	9 100	3 600
1977	85 500	10 800	12 800	15 800	2 500	5 000	2 400	1 100	1 600	2 200	6 400	1 900	4 100	7 700	2 900
1976	78 200	10 000	11 400	14 800	2 300	4 400	2 100	900	1 400	2 100	5 600	1 800	3 600	7 000	2 900
1975	70 500	9 000	10 100	13 500	2 200	4 300	2 200	800	1 300	2 000	4 900	1 700	3 600	6 400	2 700
1974	63 400	8 200	9 000	12 100	2 000	4 000	2 000	700	1 200	1 800	4 200	1 600	3 200	5 900	2 600
1973	57 600	7 400	8 500	11 300	1 900	3 500	1 600	600	1 200	1 600	3 500	1 400	3 100	5 300	2 300
1972	51 500	6 600	7 400	10 100	1 700	3 500	1 700	600	1 200	1 500	3 000	1 300	2 900	4 800	2 200
1971	46 000	5 800	5 600	8 900	1 500	3 500	1 700	500	1 200	1 500	2 600	1 200	3 000	4 400	1 900
1970	43 100	5 500	5 200	8 500	1 400	3 300	1 600	500	1 100	1 500	2 400	1 100	2 900	4 100	1 800
1969	40 000	5 200	5 200	8 000	1 300	3 100	1 500	500	1 100	1 500	2 100	1 000	2 300	3 700	1 700
1968	36 700	4 800	4 800	7 600	1 200	2 900	1 400	500	1 000	1 400	1 900	900	2 000	3 400	1 700
1967	33 100	4 300	4 100	7 000	1 100	2 500	1 200	500	800	1 300	1 800	900	1 900	3 300	1 500
1966	30 900	4 000	3 600	6 300	1 000	2 400	1 200	400	700	1 300	1 700	800	1 800	3 200	1 400
1965	26 900	3 600	2 900	5 100	1 000	2 200	1 200	400	700	1 200	1 600	800	1 700	2 700	1 300
1964	24 600	3 400	2 500	4 300	1 000	2 000	1 000	400	600	1 100	1 600	800	1 600	2 500	1 100
1963	22 500	3 100	2 200	3 700	1 000	1 900	1 000	400	500	1 100	1 500	700	1 400	2 500	1 000
1962	20 800	2 900	2 000	3 400	1 000	1 900	1 000	400	500	1 000	1 400	700	1 300	2 300	900
1961	19 300	2 700	2 000	3 200	900	1 800	1 000	300	400	1 000	1 200	600	1 200	2 000	700
1960	18 500	2 500	2 000	3 000	900	1 800	1 000	300	400	900	1 100	500	1 100	2 200	700
1959	17 700	2 400	2 000	3 100	800	1 700	1 000	300	300	900	900	500	1 100	2 100	600
1958	16 300	2 100	1 900	2 800	800	1 700	1 100	300	300	800	700	500	1 000	2 100	600
1957	15 900	2 000	1 700	2 900	700	1 800	1 200	300	300	800	600	400	1 000	2 000	600
1956	15 500	2 000	1 600	3 000	600	2 100	1 500	300	200	700	600	400	1 000	1 900	600
1955	14 600	1 800	1 400	2 900	600	2 000	1 500	200	200	700	500	400	900	1 900	600
1954	13 600	1 600	1 200	2 800	500	1 800	1 400	200	200	600	500	400	800	1 800	600
1953	13 100	1 700	1 100	2 600	500	1 700	1 300	200	200	600	400	400	800	1 800	600
1952	12 300	1 700	1 000	2 400	400	1 700	1 300	200	200	600	400	300	800	1 700	500
1951	11 700	1 700	900	2 200	400	1 800	1 300	200	200	600	400	300	800	1 600	500
1950	11 200	1 400	900	2 400	300	1 800	1 400	200	200	500	400	200	700	1 500	500

Series H 878-893. Personal Consumption Expenditures for Recreation: 1909 to 1999—Cont'd.
(millions of dollars)

Year	Total	Nondura-ble toys and sport supplies	Wheel goods, durable toys, sport equipment, boats and pleasure aircraft	Video and audio goods, including radio and television receivers, records, musical instruments	Radio and television repairs	Admissions to specified spectator amusements				Clubs and fraternal organiza-tions, except insurance	Commer-cial partici-pant amuse-ments	Parimutuel net receipts	Books and maps	Magazines, news-papers and sheet music	Flowers, seeds and potted plants
						Total	Motion picture theaters	Legitimate theater entertain-ment (plays, operas, etc.) or non-profit institutions, except athletics	Spectator sports						
	878	879	880	881	882	883	884	885	886	887	888	889	890	891	892
1949	10 000	1 200	800	1 700	200	1 900	1 500	200	200	500	400	200	600	1 500	500
1948	9 700	1 100	1 000	1 500	200	1 900	1 500	200	200	500	300	300	600	1 400	400
1947	9 300	900	1 000	1 400	100	2 000	1 600	200	200	500	300	300	500	1 200	400
1946	8 600	800	800	1 100	100	2 100	1 700	200	200	400	300	200	600	1 100	400
1945	6 200	600	400	300	100	1 700	1 500	100	100	300	200	200	500	1 000	400
1944	5 400	500	300	300	100	1 600	1 300	100	100	300	200	100	500	900	300
1943	5 000	400	300	400	100	1 500	1 300	100	100	300	200	100	400	800	300
1942	4 700	400	300	600	. . .	1 200	1 000	100	100	200	200	100	300	700	200
1941	4 300	400	300	600	. . .	1 000	800	100	100	200	200	100	300	600	200
1940	3 800	300	300	500	. . .	900	700	100	100	200	200	100	200	600	200
1939	3 500	300	200	400	. . .	800	700	100	100	200	200	. . .	200	600	200
1938	3 300	300	200	300	. . .	800	700	100	100	200	100	. . .	200	500	200
1937	3 400	300	200	400	. . .	800	700	100	100	200	200	. . .	200	500	200
1936	3 000	200	200	300	. . .	800	600	100	100	200	100	. . .	200	500	200
1935	2 600	200	100	200	. . .	700	600	. . .	100	200	100	. . .	200	500	100
1934	2 500	200	100	200	. . .	600	500	. . .	100	200	100	. . .	200	400	100
1933	2 200	200	100	200	. . .	600	500	. . .	100	200	100	. . .	200	400	100
1932	2 500	200	100	300	. . .	600	500	100	. . .	300	100	. . .	200	400	100
1931	3 300	300	200	500	. . .	900	700	100	100	300	100	. . .	300	500	100
1930	4 000	300	200	900	. . .	900	700	100	100	300	200	. . .	300	500	200
1929	4 400	300	200	1 000	. . .	900	700	100	100	300	200	. . .	300	500	200

Series H 921-940.   Travel to Foreign Countries—Travelers and Expenditures: 1919 to 1998

(Travelers in thousands; expenditures in millions of dollars)

Year	Total overseas travelers¹ 921	Total expenditures abroad² 931	Year	Total overseas travelers¹ 921	Total expenditures abroad² 931	Year	Total overseas travelers¹ 921	Total expenditures abroad² 931	Year	Total overseas travelers¹ 921	Total expenditures abroad² 931
1998	23 069	56 105	1978	7 790	8 475	1958	1 398	1 460	1938	370	303
1997	21 634	52 051	1977	7 390	7 451	1957	1 369	1 372	1937	435	348
1996	19 786	48 048	1976	6 897	6 856	1956	1 239	1 275	1936	381	297
1995	19 059	44 916	1975	6 354	6 417	1955	1 075	1 153	1935	314	245
1994	18 149	43 782	1974	6 467	5 980	1954	912	1 009	1934	302	218
1993	17 102	40 713	1973	6 933	5 371	1953	827	929	1933	300	199
1992	15 965	38 552	1972	6 790	4 944	1952	772	840	1932	393	259
1991	14 521	35 322	1971	5 667	4 311	1951	684	757	1931	438	341
1990	15 990	37 349	1970	5 260	3 973	1950	676	754	1930	538	463
1989	14 791	33 416	1969	4 623	3 407	1949	573	700	1929	517	483
1988	14 443	32 114	1968	3 885	3 030	1948	495	631	1928	518	448
1987	13 616	30 022	1967	3 425	3 207	1947	435	573	1927	471	400
1986	12 038	26 746	1966	2 975	2 657	1946	329	457	1926	433	372
1985	12 696	25 155	1965	2 623	2 438	1945	117	298	1925	408	347
1984	11 690	23 305	1964	2 220	2 211	1944	75	225	1924	351	303
1983	9 628	13 149	1963	1 990	2 114	1943	57	173	1923	291	260
1982	8 510	12 394	1962	1 767	1 939	1942	71	155	1922	320	243
1981	8 040	11 479	1961	1 575	1 785	1941	170	212	1921	294	200
1980	8 163	10 397	1960	1 634	1 750	1940	156	190	1920	302	190
1979	7 835	9 413	1959	1 516	1 610	1939	282	290	1919	152	123

1. Excludes the following: travel to Canada and Mexico; travel between conterminous United States and Alaska, Hawaii, Puerto Rico and Virgin Islands; cruise travelers; military personnel and other government employees and their dependents stationed abraoad and U.S. citizens residing abroad.
2. Includes shore expenditures of cruise travelers; excludes travel expenditures of military personnel and other government employees and their dependents stationed abroad and U.S. citizens residing abroad.

Series H 941-951.   Foreign Visitors to the United States—Number and Receipts: 1919 to 1998

(Visitors' data are for years ending June and, except for 1933 and 1934, exclude Canada and Mexico. Receipts data excludes transocean fares)

Year	Total visitors (1 000) 941	Total receipts (million dollars) 945	Year	Total visitors (1 000) 941	Total receipts (million dollars) 945	Year	Total visitors (1 000) 941	Total receipts (million dollars) 945	Year	Total visitors (1 000) 941	Total receipts (million dollars) 945
1998	23 698	71 250	1978	5 764	4 717	1958	447	825	1938	98	130
1997	24 194	73 301	1977	4 509	3 709	1957	419	785	1937	96	135
1996	22 658	69 751	1976	4 456	3 332	1956	345	705	1936	81	117
1995	20 639	63 395	1995	20 639	63 395	1955	328	654	1935	69	101
1994	18 458	58 417	1974	3 700	2 478	1954	307	595	1934	75	81
1993	18 662	57 875	1973	3 554	1 510	1953	287	574	1933	60	66
1992	17 791	54 742	1972	2 861	1 169	1952	296	550	1932	49	65
1991	16 155	48 384	1971	2 490	965	1951	255	473	1931	66	94
1990	15 059	43 007	1970	2 193	2 330	1950	242	419	1930	83	129
1989	13 999	36 205	1969	1 894	2 058	1949	258	392	1929	78	139
1988	12 512	29 434	1968	1 825	1 775	1948	282	334	1928	78	121
1987	10 434	18 032	1967	1 431	1 646	1947	229	342	1927	73	114
1986	8 860	15 642	1966	1 274	1 590	1946	117	257	1926	70	110
1985	7 537	13 079	1965	1 130	1 380	1945	102	162	1925	65	83
1984	7 528	12 533	1964	937	1 207	1944	70	117	1924	79	77
1983	7 873	6 289	1963	780	1 015	1943	50	84	1923	65	71
1982	8 761	6 671	1962	671	957	1942	42	82	1922	53	61
1981	9 069	6 466	1961	602	885	1941	46	70	1921	75	76
1980	8 200	5 566	1960	572	919	1940	81	95	1920	81	67
1979	7 230	6 051	1959	520	902	1939	100	135	1919	47	56

Series H 952-961. Crimes and Crime Rates, by Type: 1957 to 1998

(In thousands, except rate. Data refer to offenses known to the police. Rates are based on Bureau of the Census population data, excluding Armed Forces abroad)

Year	Total	Violent crime					Property crime			
		Total	Murder and non-negligent manslaughter	Forcible rape	Robbery	Aggravated assult	Total	Burglary	Larceny, $50 and over	Auto theft
	952	**953**	**954**	**955**	**956**	**957**	**958**	**959**	**960**	**961**
	NUMBER OF OFFENSES									
1998	12 476	1 531	16.9	93.1	447	974	10 945	2 330	7 374	1 241
1997	13 175	1 635	18.2	96.1	498	1 022	11 540	2 461	7 744	1 354
1996	13 494	1 689	19.7	96.3	536	1 037	11 805	2 506	7 905	1 394
1995	13 863	1 799	21.6	97.5	581	1 099	12 064	2 594	7 998	1 472
1994	13 990	1 858	23.3	102.2	619	1 113	12 132	2 713	7 880	1 539
1993	14 145	1 926	24.5	106.0	660	1 136	12 219	2 835	7 821	1 563
1992	14 438	1 932	23.8	109.1	672	1 127	12 506	2 980	7 915	1 611
1991	14 873	1 912	24.7	106.6	688	1 093	12 961	3 157	8 142	1 662
1990	14 476	1 820	23.4	102.6	639	1 055	12 656	3 074	7 946	1 636
1989	14 251	1 646	21.5	94.5	578	952	12 605	3 168	7 872	1 565
1988	13 923	1 566	20.7	92.5	543	910	12 357	3 218	7 706	1 433
1987	13 509	1 484	20.1	91.1	518	855	12 025	3 236	7 500	1 289
1986	13 212	1 489	20.6	91.5	543	834	11 723	3 241	7 257	1 224
1985	12 431	1 329	19.0	88.7	498	723	11 103	3 073	6 926	1 103
1984	11 882	1 273	18.7	84.2	485	685	10 609	2 984	6 592	1 032
1983	12 109	1 258	19.3	78.9	507	653	10 851	3 130	6 713	1 008
1982	12 974	1 322	21.0	78.8	553	669	11 652	3 447	7 143	1 062
1981	13 424	1 362	22.5	82.5	593	664	12 062	3 780	7 194	1 088
1980	13 408	1 345	23.0	83.0	566	673	12 064	3 795	7 137	1 132
1979	12 153	1 179	21.5	76.0	467	614	10 974	3 299	6 578	1 097
1978	11 141	1 062	19.6	67.1	417	558	10 080	3 104	5 983	992
1977	10 936	1 010	19.1	63.0	405	523	9 926	3 052	5 906	968
1976	11 305	987	18.8	56.7	420	491	10 318	3 090	6 271	958
1975	11 257	1 026	20.5	56.1	465	485	10 230	3 252	5 978	1 001
1974	10 253	975	20.7	55.4	442	456	9 279	3 039	5 263	977
1973	8 718	875	19.6	51.4	384	421	7 842	2 566	4 348	929
1972	8 249	835	18.7	46.9	376	393	7 414	2 376	4 151	887
1971	8 588	817	17.8	42.3	388	369	7 772	2 399	4 424	948
1970	5 581	733	16	38	348	331	4 848	2 177	1 750	922
1969	5 013	657	15	37	297	308	4 357	1 956	1 528	872
1968	4 477	590	14	31	262	283	3 887	1 835	1 274	778
1967	3 811	496	12	27	202	254	3 316	1 611	1 049	655
1966	3 272	426	11	26	157	233	2 846	1 392	897	557
1965	2 937	384	10	23	138	213	2 553	1 266	794	493
1964	2 762	361	9	21	130	201	2 401	1 198	734	470
1963	2 442	314	9	17	116	172	2 128	1 072	650	405
1962	2 219	299	8	17	110	163	1 920	982	574	364
1961	2 088	287	9	17	106	155	1 801	937	530	334
1960*	2 020	286	9	17	107	153	1 734	900	507	326
1959	1 630	223	9	15	75	124	1 408	698	416	294
1958	1 573	212	8	15	75	114	1 362	685	394	283
1957	1 422	199	8	¹13	67	111	1 224	604	355	265
	RATE PER 100 000 INHABITANTS									
1998	4 615	566	6.3	34.4	165	360	4 049	862	2 728	459
1997	4 930	610.8	6.8	35.9	186	382	4 318	919	2 886	505
1996	5 086	636.5	7.4	36.3	201	390	4 450	944	2 979	525
1995	5 275	684.6	8.2	37.1	220	418	4 591	987	3 043	560
1994	5 373	713.6	9.0	39.3	237	427	4 660	1 042	3 026	591
1993	5 484	746.8	9.5	41.1	255	440	4 737	1 099	3 032	606
1992	5 660	757.5	9.3	42.8	263	441	4 902	1 168	3 103	631
1991	5 897	758.1	9.8	42.3	272	433	5 139	1 252	3 228	659
1990	5 820	732	9.4	41.2	257	424	5 089	1 236	3 195	658
1989	5 741	663	8.7	38.1	233	383	5 078	1 276	3 171	630
1988	5 664	637	8.4	37.6	221	370	5 027	1 309	3 135	583

See footnotes at end of chart.

Series H 952-961. Crimes and Crime Rates, by Type: 1957 to 1998—Cont'd.

(In thousands, except rate. Data refer to offenses known to the police. Rates are based on Bureau of the Census population data, excluding Armed Forces abroad)

Year	Total	Violent crime					Property crime			
		Total	Murder and non-negligent manslaughter	Forcible rape	Robbery	Aggravated assult	Total	Burglary	Larceny, $50 and over	Auto theft
	952	953	954	955	956	957	958	959	960	961
1987	5 550	610	8.3	37.4	213	351	4 940	1 330	3 081	529
1986	5 480	618	8.6	37.9	225	346	4 863	1 345	3 010	508
1985	5 207	557	7.9	37.1	209	303	4 651	1 287	2 901	462
1984	5 031	539	7.9	35.7	205	290	4 492	1 264	2 791	437
1983	5 175	538	8.3	33.7	217	279	4 637	1 338	2 869	431
1982	5 604	571	9.1	34.0	239	289	5 033	1 489	3 085	459
1981	5 858	594	9.8	36.0	259	290	5 264	1 650	3 140	475
1980	5 950	597	10.2	36.8	251	299	5 353	1 684	3 167	502
1979	5 521	535	9.7	34.5	212	279	4 986	1 499	2 988	499
1978	5 109	487	9.0	30.8	191	256	4 622	1 424	2 744	455
1977	5 055	467	8.8	29.1	187	242	4 588	1 411	2 730	448
1976	5 266	460	8.8	26.4	196	229	4 807	1 439	2 921	446
1975	5 282	482	9.6	26.3	218	227	4 806	1 526	2 805	469
1974	4 850	461	9.8	26.2	209	216	4 389	1 438	2 490	462
1973	4 154	417	9.4	24.5	183	201	3 737	1 223	2 072	443
1972	3 961	401	9.0	22.5	181	189	3 560	1 141	1 994	426
1971	4 165	396	8.6	20.5	188	179	3 769	1 164	2 146	460
1970	2 747	361	8	19	171	163	2 836	1 071	861	454
1969	2 483	325	7	18	147	152	2 158	969	757	432
1968	2 240	295	7	16	131	142	1 945	918	637	389
1967	1 926	251	6	14	102	129	1 676	814	530	331
1966	1 671	218	6	13	80	119	1 453	711	458	285
1965	1 516	198	5	12	71	110	1 317	653	410	255
1964	1 443	189	5	11	68	105	1 255	626	383	245
1963	1 295	167	5	9	62	91	1 129	569	345	215
1962	1 194	161	5	9	59	88	1 033	528	309	196
1961	1 141	157	5	9	58	85	984	512	290	182
1960*	1 126	160	5	10	60	85	967	502	283	182
1959	918	126	5	9	42	70	792	393	234	165
1958	904	121	5	8	43	65	781	393	226	162
1957	835	117	5	[1]8	39	65	719	355	208	156

* Denotes first year for which figures include Alaska and Hawaii.
1. Includes statutory cases.

Series H 962-970   Federal Drug Seizures, by Type of Drug: 1990 to 1999

(In pounds. For fiscal years ending in year shown. Reflects the combined drug seizure effort of the Drug Enforcement Administration, the Federal Bureau of Investigation, the U.S. Customs Services, and beginning October 1993 the U.S. Border Patrol within the jurisdiction of the United States as well as maritime seizures by the U.S. Coast Guard. Based on reports to the Federal-wide Drug Seizure System, which eliminates duplicate reporting of a seizure involving more than one Federal agency.)

Drug	1990	1991	1992	1993	1994	1995	1996	1997	1998	1999
Total	1 238 425	1 591 277	1 881 693	1 845 998	2 397 037	2 913 227	3 181 573	3 338 276	834 096	4 949 878
Heroin	1 704	3 067	2 552	3 516	2 883	2 971	3 121	3 121	3 519	2 791
Cocaine	235 891	246 318	304 086	244 315	309 928	233 447	252 329	252 329	265 997	290 756
Cannabis	500 415	670 946	787 527	799 083	1 042 113	1 338 405	154 413	1 541 913	1 782 290	2 328 166
Marijuana	483 353	499 097	783 479	773 004	1 040 999	1 306 528	1 429 786	1 488 362	81 694	2 326 484
Hashish	17 062	171 849	4 048	26 080	1 114	31 876	32 096	53 051	596	1 681

Source: U.S. Drug Enforcement Administration, unpublished data from Federal-wide Drug Seizure System.

Series H 971-986.   Suicides: 1900 to 1997

(Refers only to deaths occurring within the United States. Rates per 100 000 resident population; for population bases used in computing rates, see series A 7)

Year	Suicides Number (979)	Rate (980)	Year	Suicides Number (979)	Rate (980)	Year	Suicides Number (979)	Rate (980)	Year	Suicides Number (979)	Rate (980)
1997	30 535	11.1	1972	25 004	12.6	1947	16 538	11.5	1923	11 096	11.5
1996	30 903	11.6	1971	24 092	11.7	1946	16 152	11.5	1922	10 876	11.7
1995	31 284	11.8	1970	23 480	11.6	1945	14 782	11.2	1921	10 906	12.4
1994	31 142	12.4	1969	22 364	11.1	1944	13 231	10.0	1920	8 790	10.2
1993	31 102	12.1	1968	21 372	10.7	1943	13 725	10.2	1919	9 543	11.5
1992	30 484	11.7	1967	21 325	10.8	1942	16 117	12.0	1918	9 685	12.3
1991	30 810	11.9	1966	21 281	10.9	1941	17 102	12.8	1917	9 157	13.0
1990	30 906	12.3	1965	21 507	11.1	1940	18 907	14.4	1916	9 181	13.7
1989	30 232	12.2	1964	20 588	10.8	1939	18 511	14.1	1915	10 011	16.2
1988	30 407	12.4	1963	20 825	11.0	1938	19 802	15.3	1914	9 802	16.1
1987	30 796	12.7	1962	20 207	10.9	1937	19 294	15.0	1913	8 932	15.4
1986	30 904	12.8	1961	18 999	10.4	1936	18 294	14.3	1912	8 549	15.6
1985	29 453	12.3	1960*	19 041	10.6	1935	18 214	14.3	1911	8 612	16.0
1984	29 286	11.9	1959[1]	18 633	10.6	1934	18 828	14.9	1910	7 283	15.3
1983	28 295	12.1	1958	18 519	10.7	1933	19 993	15.9	1909	7 061	16.0
1982	28 242	12.2	1957	16 632	9.8	1932	20 646	17.4	1908	6 506	16.8
1981	27 596	12.0	1956	16 727	10.0	1931	19 807	16.8	1907	5 027	14.5
1980	26 869	11.9	1955	16 760	10.2	1930	18 323	15.6	1906	4 323	12.8
1979	27 206	12.1	1954	16 356	10.1	1929	16 045	13.9	1905	2 940	13.5
1978	27 300	12.5	1953	15 947	10.1	1928	15 390	13.5	1904	2 611	12.2
1977	28 681	13.3	1952	15 567	10.0	1927	14 096	13.2	1903	2 371	11.3
1976	26 934	12.5	1951	15 909	10.4	1926	13 082	12.6	1902	2 124	10.3
1975	27 100	12.7	1950	17 145	11.4	1925	12 209	12.0	1901	2 105	10.4
1974	25 683	12.1	1949	16 993	11.4	1924	11 846	11.9	1900	2 036	10.2
1973	25 118	12.0	1948	16 354	11.2						

* Denotes first year for which figures include Alaska and Hawaii.
1. Includes Alaska.

Series H 987-998. Police Officers Killed: 1945 to 1998
(Covers law enforcement officers killed in line of duty.)

Year	Total killed	Year	Total killed	Year	Total killed	Year	Total killed
	987		**987**		**987**		**987**
1998	142	1983	152	1968	123	1953	63
1997	132	1982	164	1967	123	1952	63
1996	112	1981	157	1966	99	1951	64
1995	133	1980	165	1965	83	1950	36
1994	141	1979	165	1964	88	1949	55
1993	129	1978	146	1963	83	1948	64
1992	130	1977	123	1962	78	1947	67
1991	124	1976	140	1961	71	1946	82
1990	133	1975	185	1960	48	1945	59
1989	145	1974	179	1959	49		
1988	155	1973	176	1958	49		
1987	148	1972	157	1957	45		
1986	133	1971	181	1956	46		
1985	148	1970	146	1955	55		
1984	147	1969	125	1954	61		

Series H 999-1011. Persons Arrested, by Sex and Age: 1932 to 1998
(In thousands)

Year	Persons arrested[1]	Male	Under 18 years	Year	Persons arrested[1]	Male	Under 18 years	Year	Persons arrested[1]	Male	Under 18 years
	999	**1004**	**1006**		**999**	**1004**	**1006**		**999**	**1004**	**1006**
1998	11 231			1973	6 500	5 502	1 717	1951	831	746	37
1997	11 521	9 090	3 037	1972	7 013	5 956	1 794	1950	794	717	35
1995	11 416	9 087	2 089	1971	6 967	5 923	1 797	1949	792	713	33
1993	11 766	9 471	2 011	1970	6 257	5 624	1 661	1948	760	683	32
1991	10 744	8 734	1 750	1969	5 577	5 058	1 500	1947	734	659	34
1990	11 250	9 180	1 755	1968	5 349	4 891	1 457	1946	645	577	38
1989	11 261	9 234	1 745	1967	5 265	4 830	1 340	1945	544	460	50
1988	10 150	8 749	1 634	1966	4 798	4 407	1 149	1944	489	405	47
1987	10 796	8 882	1 781	1965	4 743	4 432	1 074	1943	491	412	48
1986	10 392	8 586	1 748	1964	4 381	4 138	961	1942	586	516	38
1985	10 290	8 499	1 763	1963	4 259	3 997	789	1941	631	573	37
1984	8 922	7 433	1 538	1962[2]	3 923	3 645	653	1940	609	557	35
1983	10 287	8 582	1 726	1961[2]	3 608	3 418	567	1939	577	533	36
1982	10 062	8 425	1 805	1960[2]	3 499	3 272	527	1938	554	517	36
1981	10 296	8 633	2 036	1959[2]	2 613	2 334	321	1937	520	484	33
1980	9 703	8 170	2 026	1958[2]	2 340	2 092	284	1936	462	428	26
1979	9 506	8 011	2 143	1957[2]	2 069	1 849	254	1935	392	365	23
1978	9 775	8 227	2 279	1956[2]	2 071	1 845	234	1934	344	320	19
1977	9 029	7 581	2 170	1955[2]	1 862	1 657	196	1933	320	297	18
1976	7 912	6 672	1 973	1954[2]	1 689	1 503	164	1932[3]	...	257	15
1975	8 014	6 752	2 078	1953[2]	1 791	1 597	150				
1974	6 179	5 185	1 683	1952[2]	1 111	991	86				

1. Each person arrested is counted rather than the number of charges filed against one person. Includes persons for whom age was not known. Prior to 1952, arrest data determined by examination of ingerprint cards.
2. City arrest data.
3. February 1 through December 31.

Series H 1012-1027. Criminal Justice System—Public Expenditures, by Level of Government: 1902 to 1996

(In millions of dollars)

Year	All governments				Federal government			
	Total[1]	Police protection	Judicial activities	Correction	Total[1]	Police protection	Judicial activities	Correction
	1012	1013	1014	1015	1016	1017	1018	1019
1996	. . .	51 505	. . .	40 575	. . .	6 872	. . .	3 065
1994	. . .	45 973	. . .	34 857	. . .	7 328	. . .	2 587
1992	. . .	41 248	. . .	31 017	. . .	6 703	. . .	2 411
1991	. . .	38 942	. . .	29 297	. . .	6 170	. . .	1 941
1988	60 980	27 956	7 618	19 119	7 794	3 555	1 158	1 226
1987	51 428	24 684	. . .	16 638	. . .	. . .	. . .	. . .
1986	46 947	22 685	. . .	14 957	. . .	. . .	. . .	. . .
1985	45 607	22 014	5 780	13 034	5 819	2 768	852	779
1984	. . .	. . .	. . .	. . .	. . .	. . .	. . .	. . .
1983	39 680	20 648	8 621	10 411	4 844	2 745	1 523	576
1982	35 839	19 022	7 771	9 047	4 269	2 366	1 390	513
1981	24 691	16 822	. . .	7 869	2 317	1 904	. . .	413
1980	22 064	15 163	. . .	6 901	2 126	1 739	. . .	387
1979	26 028	13 917	5 628	6 040	3 379	2 053	876	354
1978	24 132	13 120	5 051	5 523	3 122	1 952	746	337
1977	21 574	11 865	4 267	4 934	2 779	1 765	616	299
1976	19 681	11 028	3 807	4 386	2 450	1 612	472	256
1975	17 249	9 786	3 281	3 843	2 189	1 461	429	217
1974	14 954	8 512	1 708	3 240	1 961	1 222	136	215
1973	12 985	7 624	1 579	2 740	1 629	1 089	118	171
1972	11 721	6 903	1 491	2 422	1 492	962	179	133
1971	10 517	6 165	1 358	2 291	1 448	805	134	121
1970	8 571	5 081	1 190	1 706	978	589	129	83
1969	7 340	4 430	1 002	1 462	800	492	106	71
1968	6 070	3 725	976	1 369	445	290	90	65
1967	5 424	3 331	894	1 199	429	282	87	60
1966	4 903	3 033	793	1 077	393	257	79	57
1965	4 574	2 792	748	1 034	377	243	75	59
1964	4 222	2 586	697	939	342	220	66	56
1963	4 009	2 440	693	876	358	209	94	55
1962	3 795	2 326	628	841	304	196	57	51
1961	3 613	2 210	593	810	298	193	58	47
1960	3 349	2 030	597	722	291	173	74	44
1959	3 149	1 880	561	708	275	170	68	37
1958	2 861	1 769	519	573	261	159	63	39
1957	2 655	1 624	481	550	252	155	62	35
1956	2 434	1 487	447	500	250	156	61	33
1955	2 231	1 359	409	463	206	129	49	28
1954	2 080	1 254	399	427	210	124	56	30
1953	. . .	1 160	. . .	. . .	. . .	122	. . .	. . .
1952	. . .	1 080	. . .	365	. . .	141	. . .	28
1951	. . .	. . .	. . .	. . .	. . .	104	. . .	. . .
1950	. . .	864	. . .	. . .	. . .	88	. . .	. . .
1948	. . .	724	. . .	. . .	. . .	80	. . .	. . .
1947	. . .	. . .	. . .	. . .	. . .	. . .	. . .	. . .
1946	. . .	549	. . .	. . .	. . .	70	. . .	. . .
1945	. . .	. . .	. . .	. . .	. . .	. . .	. . .	. . .
1944	. . .	497	. . .	. . .	. . .	83	. . .	. . .
1942	. . .	444	. . .	. . .	. . .	50	. . .	. . .
1940	. . .	386	. . .	. . .	. . .	21	. . .	. . .
1938	. . .	378	. . .	. . .	. . .	19	. . .	. . .
1936	. . .	331	. . .	. . .	. . .	17	. . .	. . .
1932	. . .	349	. . .	. . .	. . .	31	. . .	. . .
1927	. . .	290	. . .	. . .	. . .	20	. . .	. . .
1922	. . .	204	. . .	. . .	. . .	14	. . .	. . .
1913	. . .	92	. . .	. . .	. . .	3	. . .	. . .
1902	. . .	50	. . .	. . .	. . .	X	. . .	. . .

See footnotes at the end of chart.

Series H 1012-1027. Criminal Justice System—Public Expenditures, by Level of Government: 1902 to 1996—Cont'd.

(In millions of dollars)

Year	State governments				Local government			
	Total[1]	Police protection	Judicial activities	Correction	Total[1]	Police protection	Judicial activities	Correction
	1020	1021	1022	1023	1024	1025	1026	1027
1996	...	6 499	...	25 294	...	38 184	...	12 216
1994	...	5 325	...	21 266	...	33 320	...	11 004
1992	...	4 863	...	18 306	...	29 682	...	10 300
1991	...	4 785	...	17 807	...	27 986	...	9 550
1988	22 120	4 513	3 071	12 671	33 535	20 333	3 688	6 530
1987	...	...	...	...	...	...	...	...
1986	...	...	...	...	...	...	...	...
1985	16 013	3 511	2 262	8 884	25 373	16 026	2 841	4 316
1984	...	...	...	...	...	...	...	...
1983	11 709	2 630	2 756	6 323	23 127	15 273	4 342	3 512
1982	10 649	2 486	2 606	5 557	20 922	14 170	3 775	2 976
1981	7 085	2 241	...	4 844	15 289	12 677	...	2 612
1980	6 285	2 027	...	4 258	13 653	11 397	...	2 256
1979	8 463	2 150	1 318	3 824	15 401	9 882	1 903	2 197
1978	6 888	1 892	1 497	3 177	14 322	9 276	2 809	2 009
1977	5 812	1 800	1 026	2 847	12 983	8 300	2 626	1 788
1976	5 204	1 696	903	2 475	12 027	7 720	2 432	1 654
1975	4 612	1 512	779	2 193	10 449	6 813	2 073	1 434
1974	3 906	1 308	439	1 813	9 092	5 982	1 223	1 213
1973	3 304	1 132	386	1 534	8 052	5 403	1 075	1 035
1972	2 948	903	346	1 378	7 281	4 948	965	911
1971	2 291	932	327	1 387	6 663	4 489	912	895
1970	2 134	689	282	1 051	5 454	3 803	779	572
1969	1 849	621	236	914	4 691	3 317	660	477
1968	1 622	541	209	872	4 003	2 894	677	432
1967	1 381	441	193	747	3 615	2 609	614	392
1966	1 224	385	175	664	3 286	2 391	539	356
1965	1 135	348	155	632	3 062	2 201	518	343
1964	1 042	315	141	586	2 838	2 051	490	297
1963	960	297	127	536	2 691	1 934	472	285
1962	902	276	118	508	2 589	1 854	453	282
1961	849	261	109	479	2 466	1 756	426	284
1960	769	245	99	425	2 289	1 612	424	253
1959	733	228	92	413	2 141	1 482	401	258
1958	671	214	87	370	1 929	1 396	369	164
1957	584	179	77	328	1 819	1 290	342	187
1956	526	159	72	295	1 658	1 172	314	172
1955	475	139	68	268	1 550	1 091	292	167
1954	446	130	66	250	1 424	1 000	277	147
1953	418	119	61	238	...	919	...	...
1952	386	106	57	223	...	833	...	114
1951	365	97	53	215	...	...	...	...
1950	332	85	49	198	...	691	...	...
1948	...	65	...	153	...	579	...	...
1947	...	...	...	107	...	...	...	...
1946	...	45	...	97	...	434	...	...
1945	...	...	...	82	...	...	...	...
1944	159	41	35	83	...	373	...	...
1942	...	40	...	80	...	354	...	...
1940	...	34	...	86	...	331	...	...
1938	...	30	...	85	...	329	...	...
1936	...	19	...	73	...	295	...	...
1932	...	15	...	87	...	303	...	...
1927	...	7	...	64	...	263	...	...
1922	...	4	...	64	...	186	...	...
1913	...	1	...	28	...	88	...	...
1902	...	X	...	14	...	50	...	...

X Represents zero.
1. Beginning 1969, legal services and prosecution and indigent defense included in totals.

192

Series H 1028-1062 Lawyers—Selected Characteristics: 1948 to 1998

(Data based on editions of Martindale-Hubbell Law Directory. Represents all persons who are members of the bar)

Series No.	Characteristic	1948	1951	1954	1957	1960	1963	1966	1970	1980	1985	1989	1991	1992	1994	1996	1998
1028	All lawyers[1]	...	221 605	241 514	262 320	285 933	296 069	316 856	355 242	542 205	655 191	723 189	805 872	788 000	861 000	911 000	957 000
1033	Male	168 113	199 052	216 564	229 433	245 897	261 639	281 336	315 715	498 019	569 649	606 768	646 495	619 368	647 472	646 810	683 298
1034	Female	2 997	5 059	5 036	6 350	6 488	7 143	8 068	9 103	44 185	85 542	116 421	159 377	168 632	213 528	264 190	273 702
	Status in practice[2]																
1046	Government	14 143	19 910	21 279	24 245	25 621	29 314	31 280	35 803	50 490	53 035	57 742	66 227	...	...	...	...
1047	Federal	...	8 314	9 040	12 458	13 045	15 113	16 284	18 710	20 132	10 989	23 042	27 985	...	...	...	...
1048	State	...	3 577	3 561	4 000	4 316	6 486	7 416	9 293	30 358	33 046	34 700	38 242	...	...	...	...
1049	City or county	8 013	8 019	8 678	7 787	8 260	7 715	7 580	7 800	...	...	...	...	...	...	...	...
1050	Judicial	7 130	7 471	7 903	7 910	8 180	8 748	9 712	10 349	19 160	21 677	19 071	21 536	...	...	...	...
1051	Federal	...	675	621	769	599	707	800	878	2 611	3 003	2 551	3 119	...	...	...	...
1052	State or county	...	4 561	5 041	5 056	5 301	5 712	6 823	7 548	16 549	18 674	16 520	18 417	...	...	...	...
1053	City	...	2 235	2 241	2 085	2 280	2 329	2 089	1 923	...	...	...	...	...	...	...	...
1054	Private practice	152 649	176 995	189 423	188 955	192 353	200 586	212 662	236 085	370 111	460 206	519 941	587 289	...	...	...	...
1058	Salaried	5 555	12 997	16 648	21 054	25 198	29 510	33 222	40 486	73 862	83 843	85 671	93 849	...	...	...	...
1059	Private industry	...	11 274	15 063	18 911	22 533	26 492	29 405	33 593	54 626	63 622	66 627	71 022	...	...	...	...
1060	Educational institutions	...	1 213	1 351	1 504	1 798	2 100	2 717	3 732	6 606	7 254	7 575	8 177	...	...	...	...
1061	Other private employment	...	510	234	639	867	918	1 100	3 161	12 630	12 967	11 469	14 650	...	...	...	...

1. Includes lawyers not reporting and an adjustment (subtraction) for duplications.
2. In some cases, if more than one subentry was applicable, the person was counted in each.

Series H 1063-1078. U.S. Supreme Court—Cases Filed and Disposed of During October Terms: 1940 to 1997

(In thousands, except rate)

Year	Total cases		Year	Total cases		Year	Total cases		Year	Total cases	
	Filed	Opinions disposed of		Filed	Opinions disposed of		Filed	Opinions disposed of		Filed	Opinions disposed of
	1063	**1065**		**1063**	**1065**		**1063**	**1065**		**1063**	**1065**
1997	7 692	138	1982	5 079	331	1967	3 106	462	1953	1 302	170
1996	7 602	140	1981	5 311	321	1966	2 752	402	1952	1 283	193
1995	7 565	145	1980	5 144	264	1965	2 774	338	1951	1 234	197
1994	8 100	136	1979	4 781	285	1964	2 288	275	1950	1 181	191
1993	7 786	145	1978	4 731	291	1963	2 294	393	1949	1 270	202
1992	7 245	166	1977	4 704	290	1962	2 373	388	1948	1 465	238
1991	6 770	196	1976	4 731	302	1961	2 185	264	1947	1 295	208
1990	6 316	201	1975	4 761	314	1960	1 940	282	1946	1 510	256
1989	5 746	275	1974	4 688	287	1959	1 862	249	1945	1 316	215
1988	5 657	301	1973	5 079	309	1958	1 819	275	1944	1 237	274
1987	5 268	239	1972	4 640	308	1957	1 639	323	1943	997	210
1986	5 123	319	1971	4 533	296	1956	1 802	266	1942	984	259
1985	5 158	317	1969	3 405	347	1955	1 644	246	1941	1 178	376
1984	5 006	309	1968	3 271	346	1954	1 397	196	1940	977	281
1983	5 100	331									

Source: Office of the Clerk, Supreme Court of the U.S.

Series H 1097-1111. U.S. District Courts—Civil and Criminal Cases: 1941 to 1997

(For years ending June 30)

Year	Civil cases			Criminal cases — Defendants disposed of			
	Total cases commenced	Total cases terminated	Cases commenced[1]	Not convicted	Convicted — Total	Convicted — Imprisonment	Convicted — Probation[2]
	1097	1098	1099	1101	1105	1108	1109
1997	265 200	249 000	48 700	7 500	54 500	39 900	11 900
1996	272 700	246 400	47 100	8 500	51 000	36 500	11 600
1995	239 000	226 100	44 200	9 000	46 300	31 700	11 500
1994	236 000	228 900	44 900	10 000	51 100	34 500	12 800
1993	228 600	225 200	45 700	9 200	50 400	34 200	12 600
1992	226 900	239 600	47 500	10 000	48 400	31 100	13 100
1991	207 700	211 700	45 100	10 000	46 800	29 200	13 800
1990	217 900	213 400	46 500	9 800	46 700	27 800	14 200
1989	233 500	234 600	44 900	10 100	44 500	24 900	15 000
1988	239 600	238 100	43 500	9 900	42 900	22 500	16 100
1987	239 000	237 500	42 200	10 200	43 900	23 300	16 000
1986	254 800	265 800	40 400	9 300	40 700	20 600	15 200
1985	273 700	268 600	38 500	8 800	38 500	18 700	14 400
1984	261 500	241 800	35 900	8 400	36 100	17 700	13 900
1983	241 800	213 600	34 900	7 700	35 600	17 900	14 100
1982	206 200	185 500	31 600	8 200	32 300	15 900	12 700
1981	180 600	172 900	30 400	8 300	29 900	13 700	12 200
1980	168 800	155 000	28 000	8 000	28 600	13 200	11 100
1979	154 700	140 000	31 500	8 300	32 900	14 600	13 500
1978	138 800	123 200	34 600	9 400	36 500	17 400	14 500
1977	130 600	115 500	39 800	11 700	41 500	19 600	16 100
1976	130 600	108 600	39 100	11 500	40 100	18 500	18 200
1975	117 300	103 800	41 100	11 800	37 400	17 300	17 900
1974	103 500	96 700	37 700	11 800	36 200	17 200	16 600
1973	98 560	97 402	40 367	11 741	34 983	17 540	15 026
1972	96 173	94 256	47 043	12 296	37 220	16 832	15 395
1971	93 396	85 368	41 290	12 512	32 103	14 378	13 243
1970	87 321	80 435	39 959	8 178	28 178	12 415	11 387
1969	77 193	73 354	35 413	5 993	26 803	12 847	9 991
1968	71 449	68 873	32 571	6 169	25 674	12 610	9 820
1967	70 961	70 172	32 207	5 191	26 344	13 085	9 435
1966	70 906	66 184	31 494	4 661	27 314	13 282	10 256
1965	67 678	65 478	33 334	4 961	28 757	13 668	10 779
1964	66 930	63 954	30 268	4 211	29 170	13 273	11 634
1963	63 630	62 379	39 920	5 042	29 803	13 639	12 047
1962	61 836	57 996	37 665	4 599	28 511	14 042	11 071
1961	58 293	55 416	28 460	4 046	28 625	14 162	10 714
1960	59 284	61 829	28 137	3 784	26 728	13 433	10 391
1959	57 800	62 172	28 729	3 696	27 033	13 648	10 726
1958	67 115	61 285	28 897	3 661	26 808	13 288	10 903
1957	62 380	63 568	28 120	3 471	26 254	12 986	10 760
1956	62 394	67 700	28 739	4 244	27 567	12 854	11 759
1955	59 375	58 974	35 310	5 135	33 855	16 889	14 021
1954	59 461	59 903	41 808	4 848	38 141	18 483	16 856
1953	64 001	57 490	37 291	4 289	33 473	15 637	15 118
1952	58 428	53 150	37 950	3 834	34 788	15 379	17 018
1951	51 600	52 119	38 670	4 066	37 000	14 963	19 271
1950	54 622	53 259	36 383	4 173	33 502	14 435	16 046
1949	53 421	48 396	34 432	4 190	32 074	14 204	14 690
1948	46 725	48 791	32 097	4 862	29 380	12 961	13 422
1947	58 956	54 515	33 652	5 527	31 108	14 375	12 612
1946	67 835	61 000	33 203	6 597	29 885	14 353	11 446
1945	60 965	52 300	39 429	7 536	34 117	16 311	13 153
1944	38 499	37 086	39 621	…	…	…	…
1943	36 789	36 044	36 588	…	…	…	…
1942	38 140	38 352	33 294	…	…	…	…
1941	38 477	38 561	31 823	…	…	…	…

1. Excludes transfers.
2. Includes probation and suspended sentence.
Source: Administrative Office of the U.S. Courts, "Statistical Tables for Federal Judiciary."

Series H 1112-1118. U.S. District Courts—Trials: 1944 to 1992

(For years ending June 30. Through 1960, trials commenced; thereafter, trials completed)

Year	Total trials	Civil trials			Criminal trials		
		Total	Nonjury	Jury	Total	Nonjury	Jury
	1112	1113	1114	1115	1116	1117	1118
1992	19,992	10,527	6,289	4,238	9,465	3,832	5,633
1991	19,949	11,024	6,507	4,517	8,925	3,678	5,247
1990	20,433	11,502	6,737	4,765	8,931	3,870	5,061
1989	20,102	12,085	6,878	5,207	8,017	3,553	4,464
1988	19,901	12,536	7,088	5,448	7,365	3,215	4,150
1987	19,985	13,162	7,597	5,565	6,823	2,912	3,911
1986	20,242	13,276	8,054	5,222	6,966	3,066	3,900
1985	20,729	14,254	8,817	5,437	6,475	2,778	3,697
1984	20,830	14,374	9,037	5,337	6,456	2,823	3,633
1983	21,345	14,689	9,712	4,977	6,856	3,003	3,653
1982	21,397	14,753	10,074	4,679	6,644	3,076	3,568
1981	21,239	14,697	10,047	4,650	6,542	2,962	3,580
1980	19,825	13,191	9,254	3,937	6,634	3,216	3,418
1979	18,563	11,764	8,348	3,416	6,799	3,132	3,667
1978	18,851	11,515	8,326	3,189	7,336	3,344	3,992
1977	18,827	11,605	7,792	3,813	7,222	2,661	4,561
1976	19,580	11,656	8,098	3,558	7,924	2,773	5,151
1975	19,236	11,603	7,903	3,700	7,633	2,726	4,907
1974	18,572	10,972	7,403	3,569	7,600	2,753	4,847
1973	19,467	10,896	7,289	3,607	8,571	2,927	5,644
1972	18,780	10,962	7,285	3,677	7,818	2,968	4,850
1971	17,549	10,093	6,600	3,493	7,456	2,923	4,533
1970	16,032	9,449	6,078	3,371	6,583	2,357	4,226
1969	14,397	8,834	5,619	3,215	5,563	1,883	3,680
1968	14,221	8,688	5,478	3,210	5,533	1,800	3,733
1967	12,500	8,095	4,472	3,353	4,405	1,345	3,060
1966	12,193	7,783	4,607	3,176	4,410	1,239	3,171
1965	11,485	7,613	4,459	3,154	3,872	1,143	2,729
1964	11,079	7,155	4,063	3,092	3,924	1,076	2,848
1963	10,960	7,095	3,925	3,170	3,865	1,159	2,706
1962	10,048	6,260	3,335	2,925	3,788	1,090	2,698
1961	9,594	6,156	3,245	2,911	3,438	982	2,456
1960	9,998	6,488	3,453	3,035	3,510	1,008	2,502
1959	10,293	6,896	3,566	3,330	3,397	1,033	2,364
1958	10,888	7,057	3,666	3,391	3,831	1,326	2,505
1957	10,443	6,884	3,595	3,289	3,559	1,214	2,345
1956	11,198	7,341	3,811	3,530	3,857	1,319	2,538
1955	11,138	7,049	4,110	2,939	4,089	1,351	2,738
1954	11,275	6,958	4,182	2,776	4,317	1,493	2,824
1953	10,768	6,861	4,272	2,589	3,907	1,361	2,546
1952	10,073	6,668	4,179	2,489	3,405	1,167	2,238
1951	9,878	6,962	4,492	2,470	2,916	1,035	1,881
1950	9,572	6,539	4,276	2,263	3,033	961	2,072
1949	9,282	6,426	4,149	2,277	2,856	997	1,859
1948	8,905	6,156	4,204	1,952	2,749	892	1,857
1947	8,818	5,850	3,989	1,861	2,968	1,112	1,856
1946	9,030	5,220	3,633	1,587	3,810	1,250	2,560
1945	9,779	5,265	3,561	1,704	4,514	1,503	3,011
1944	9,951	5,025	2,702	2,323	4,926	1,819	3,107

Series H 1119-1124. Juvenile Court—Cases Handled: 1940 to 1996

(In thousands, except rate)

Year	Delinquency cases, 10 to 17 years old	
	Total[1]	Rate per 1 000 population
	1123	1124
1996	1 758	61.8
1995	1 703	60.7
1994	1 605	58.2
1993	1 515	55.8
1992	1 484	55.8
1991	1 413	54.4
1990	1 320	51.7
1989	1 236	49.1
1988	1 190	47.0
1987	1 181	46.2
1986	1 180	45.5
1985	1 112	42.2
1984	1 034	38.7
1983	1 030	38.3
1982	1 073	39.1
1981	1 100	39.1
1980	1 093	38.3
1979	1 048	36.2
1978	1 023	34.6
1977	1 076	35.8
1976	1 077	35.1
1975	1 050	33.8
1974	1 252	37.5
1973	1 143	34.2
1972	1 112	33.6
1971	1 125	34.1
1970	1 052	32.3
1969	989	30.7
1968	900	28.5
1967	811	26.3
1966	745	24.7
1965	697	23.6
1964	686	23.5
1963	601	21.4
1962	555	20.6
1961	503	19.3
1960	510	20.1
1959	483	19.6
1958	470	20.0
1957	440	19.8
1956	520	25.2
1955	431	21.4
1954	395	20.2
1953	374	19.7
1952	332	18.2
1951	298	16.8
1950	280	16.1
1949	272	15.6
1948	254	14.9
1947	262	15.1
1946	295	16.9
1945	344	19.6
1944	330	18.6
1943	344	18.7
1942	250	13.4
1941	224	11.8
1940	200	10.5

1. For 1940-1956, includes traffic cases.
Source: National Center for Juvenile Justice, Pittsburgh, PA, "Juvenile Court Statistics."

Series H 1135-1143. Federal and State Institutions—Prisoners: 1926 to 1997

(Prisoners in institutions for adult offenders only.)

Year	Prisoners present (at end of year)			Year	Prisoners present (at end of year)			Year	Prisoners present (at end of year)		
	Total	Federal institutions	State institutions		Total	Federal institutions	State institutions		Total	Federal institutions	State institutions
	1135	1136	1137		1135	1136	1137		1135	1136	1137
1997	1 197 590	...	...	1973	204 211	22 815	181 396	1949	163 749	16 868	146 881
1996	1 138 984	...	...	1972	196 183	21 713	174 470	1948	155 977	16 328	139 649
1995	1 085 363	83 663	1 001 700	1971	198 061	20 948	177 113	1947	151 304	17 146	134 158
1994	1 016 691	79 795	936 896	1970	196 429	20 038	176 391	1946	140 079	17 622	122 457
1993	932 074	74 399	857 675	1969	196 007	19 623	176 384	1945	133 649	18 638	115 011
1992	846 277	65 706	780 571	1968	187 914	19 703	168 211	1944	132 456	18 139	114 317
1991	789 610	59 696	732 914	1967	194 896	19 579	175 317	1943	137 220	16 113	121 107
1990	739 980	50 810	688 084	1966	199 654	19 245	180 409	1942	150 384	16 623	133 761
1989	680 907	47 168	633 739	1965	210 895	21 040	189 855	1941	165 439	18 465	146 974
1988	603 732	42 738	560 994	1964	214 336	21 709	192 627	1940	173 706	19 260	154 446
1987	560 812	39 523	521 289	1963	217 283	23 128	194 155	1939	179 818	19 730	160 088
1986	522 084	36 531	485 553	1962	218 830	23 944	194 886	1938	159 382	17 083	142 299
1985	480 568	32 695	447 873	1961	220 149	23 696	196 453	1937	149 357	15 309	134 048
1984	443 398	27 602	415 796	1960	212 957	23 218	189 739	1936	143 573	15 373	128 200
1983	419 820	26 331	393 015	1959	207 446	22 492	184 954	1935	144 665	14 777	129 888
1982	394 374	23 652	371 864	1958	205 493	21 549	183 944	1934	138 220	12 080	126 140
1981	353 167	22 169	331 505	1957	195 256	20 420	174 836	1933	136 947	10 851	126 096
1980	315 974	20 611	295 363	1956	189 421	20 134	169 287	1932	137 183	12 282	124 901
1979	301 470	22 588	278 882	1955	185 780	20 088	165 692	1931	137 082	12 964	124 118
1978	294 396	26 391	268 005	1954	182 848	20 003	162 845	1930	127 495	12 181	115 314
1977	285 456	28 650	256 806	1953	173 547	19 363	154 184	1929	120 496	12 964	107 532
1976	262 833	26 980	235 853	1952	168 200	18 014	150 186	1928	116 626	8 204	108 422
1975	240 593	24 131	216 462	1951	165 640	17 395	148 245	1927	106 517	7 722	98 795
1974	218 466	22 361	196 105	1950	166 123	17 134	148 989	1926	96 125	6 803	89 322

Source: U.S. Bureau of Justice Statistics, "Prisoners in State and Federal Institutions on December 3."

Series H 1155-1167. Prisoners Executed Under Civil Authority, by Race and Offense: 1930 to 1998

(Prior to 1960, excludes Alaska and Hawaii except for three federal executions in Alaska: 1939, 1948 and 1950)

Year	All offenses			Year	All offenses			Year	All offenses		
	Total	White	Black		Total	White	Black		Total	White	Black
	1155	1156	1157		1155	1156	1157		1155	1156	1157
1998	68	48	18	1969	X	X	X	1949	119	50	67
1997	74	45	27	1968	X	X	X	1948	119	35	82
1996	45	31	14	1967	2	1	1	1947	153	42	111
1995	56	33	22	1966	1	1	X	1946	131	46	84
1994	31	20	11	1965	7	6	1	1945	117	41	75
1993	38	23	14	1964	15	8	7	1944	120	47	70
1992	31	19	11	1963	21	13	8	1943	131	54	74
1991	14	7	7	1962	47	28	19	1942	147	67	80
1990	23	16	7	1961	42	20	22	1941	123	59	63
1989	16	8	8	1960	56	21	35	1940	124	49	75
1988	11	6	5	1959	49	16	33	1939	160	80	77
1987	25	13	12	1958	49	20	28	1938	190	96	92
1986	18	11	7	1957	65	34	31	1937	147	69	74
1985	18	11	7	1956	65	21	43	1936	195	92	101
1984	21	13	8	1955	76	44	32	1935	199	119	77
1983	5	4	1	1954	81	38	42	1934	168	65	102
1982	2	1	1	1953	62	30	31	1933	160	77	81
1981	1	1	X	1952	83	36	47	1932	140	62	75
1971-1980	3	3	X	1951	105	57	47	1931	153	77	72
1970	X	X	X	1950	82	40	42	1930	155	90	65

X Represents zero.
Source: Through 1978, U.S. Law Enforcement Assistance Administration; thereafter, U.S. Bureau of Justice Statistics, "Correctional Population in the U.S." and "Capital Punishment."

Series HH-1 Social Security—Covered Employment, Earnings, and Contribution Rates: 1980 to 1998

(140.4 represents140 400 000. Includes Puerto Rico,Virgin Islands, American Samoa, and Guam Represents all reported employment. Data are estimated. OASDHI = Old-age, survivors, disability, and health insurance; SMI = Supplementary medical insurance)

Item	Unit	1980	1985	1990	1992	1993	1994	1995	1996	1997	1998
Workers with insured status[1]	Million	140.4	150.9	164.0	167.5	169.1	170.7	172.9	174.8	177.0	179.1
Male	Million	76.6	80.7	86.5	87.9	88.5	89.1	90.0	90.9	91.8	92.7
Female	Million	63.8	70.1	77.5	79.6	80.6	81.6	82.9	84.0	85.3	86.4
Under 25 years old	Million	25.7	22.0	21.3	20.1	19.5	19.0	18.8	18.5	18.5	18.7
25 to 34 years old	Million	36.5	40.1	41.6	40.8	40.3	39.8	39.4	38.8	38.1	37.2
35 to 44 years old	Million	23.0	29.9	36.4	38.1	38.9	39.7	40.5	41.3	41.9	42.3
45 to 54 years old	Million	18.6	19.2	22.8	25.6	26.8	28.2	29.5	30.7	31.9	33.1
55 to 59 years old	Million	9.3	9.0	8.7	9.0	9.3	9.5	9.7	10.1	10.7	11.2
60 to 64 years old	Million	8.2	8.8	8.8	8.5	8.5	8.4	8.4	8.5	8.7	8.9
65 to 69 years old	Million	7.0	7.5	8.2	8.2	8.2	8.1	8.1	8.1	8.0	7.9
70 years old and over	Million	12.1	14.3	16.3	17.3	17.7	18.1	18.5	18.8	19.3	19.6
Workers reported with—											
Taxable earnings[2]	Million	113	120	134	134	136	138	141	144	147	. . .
Maximum earnings[2]	Million	10	8	8	8	8	8	8	9	9	. . .
Earnings in covered employment[2]	Bil. dol	1 329	1 942	2 704	2 916	3 023	3 169	3 359	3 568	3 853	. . .
Reported taxable[2]	Bil. dol	1 178	1 725	2 359	2 533	2 636	2 785	2 920	3 076	3 292	. . .
Percent of total	Percent	88.6	88.8	87.2	86.8	87.2	87.9	86.9	86.2	85.5	. . .
Average per worker:											
Total earnings[2]	Dollars	11 761	16 125	20 227	21 776	22 205	22 929	23 814	24 863	26 258	. . .
Taxable earnings[2]	Dollars	10 430	14 326	17 642	18 911	19 364	20 152	20 700	21 431	22 440	. . .
Annual maximum taxable earnings[3]	Dollars	25 900	39 600	51 300	55 500	57 600	60 600	61 200	62 700	65 400	68 400
Contribution rates for OASDHI:[4]											
Each employer and employee	Percent.	6.13	7.05	7.65	7.65	7.65	7.65	7.65	7.65	7.65	7.65
Self-employed[5]	Percent.	8.10	14.10	15.30	15.30	15.30	15.30	15.30	15.30	15.30	15.30
SMI monthly premium[6]	Dollars	9.60	15.50	28.60	31.80	36.60	41.10	46.10	42.50	43.80	43.80

1. Estimated number fully insured for retirement and/or survivor benefits as of end of year.
2. Includes self-employment.
3. The maximum taxable earnings for HI was $130 200 in 1992 and 135 000 in 1993. Beginning 1994 upper limit on earnings subject to HI taxes was repealed.
4. As of January 1, 1999 each employee and employer pays 7.65 percent and the self-employed pay 15.3 percent.
5. Self-employed pays 11.8 percent in 1985. The additional amount is supplied from general revenues. Beginning 1990, self-employed pays 15.3 percent, and half of the tax is deductible for income tax purposes and for computing self-employment income subject to social security tax.
6. 1980, as of July 1; beginning 1985. As of January 1, 1999, the monthly premium is $45.50.
Source: U.S. Social Security Administration, Annual Statistical Supplement to the Social Security Bulletin; and unpublished data.

Series HH-2 Private Pension Plans—Summary, by Type of Plan: 1980 to 1995

("Pension plan" is defined by the Employee Retirement Income Security Act (ERISA) as "any plan, fund, or program which was heretofore or is hereafter established or maintained by an employer or an employee organization, or by both, to the extent that such plan (a) provides retirement income to employees, or (b) results in a deferral of income by employees for periods extending to the termination of covered employment or beyond, regardless of the method of calculating the contributions made to the plan, the method of calculating the benefits under the plan, or the method of distributing benefits from the plan." A defined benefit plan provides a definite benefit formula for calculating benefit amounts - such as a flat amount per year of service or a percentage of salary times years of service. A defined contribution plan is a pension plan in which the contributions are made to an individual account for each employee. The retirement benefit is dependent upon the account balance at retirement. The balance depends upon amounts contributed, investment experience, and, in the case of profit sharing plans, amounts which may be allocated to the account due to forfeitures by terminating employees. Employee Stock Ownership Plans (ESOP) and 401(k) plans are included among defined contribution plans. Data are based on Form 5500 series reports filed with the Internal Revenue Service)

Item	Unit	Total				Defined contribution plan				Defined benefit plan			
		1980	1985	1990	1995	1980	1985	1990	1995	1980	1985	1990	1995
Number of plans[1]	1 000	488.9	632.1	712.3	693.4	340.8	462.0	599.2	623.9	148.1	170.2	113.1	69.5
Total participants[2][3]	Million	57.9	74.7	76.9	87.5	19.9	35.0	38.1	47.7	38.0	39.7	38.8	39.7
Active participants[2][4]	Million	49.0	62.3	61.8	66.2	18.9	33.2	35.5	42.7	30.1	29.0	26.3	23.5
Contributions[5]	Bil. dol	66.2	95.1	98.8	158.8	23.5	53.1	75.8	117.4	42.6	42.0	23.0	41.4
Benefits[6]	Bil. dol	35.3	101.9	129.4	183.0	13.1	47.4	63.0	97.9	22.1	54.5	66.4	85.1

1. Excludes all plans covering only one participant.
2. Includes double counting of workers in more than one plan.
3. Total participants include active participants, vested separated workers, and retirees.
4. Any workers currently in employment covered by a plan and who are earning or retaining credited service under a plan. Includes any nonvested former employees who have not yet incurred breaks in service.
5. Includes both employer and employee contributions.
6. Benefits paid directly from trust and premium payments made from plan to insurance carriers. Excludes benefits paid directly by insurance carriers.
Source: U.S. Dept. of Labor, Pension and Welfare Benefits Administration, Private Pension Plan Bulletin, winter 1996 and unpublished data.

Series HH-3   State Unemployment Insurance—Summary: 1980 to 1997

(3 356 represents 3 356 000. Includes unemployment compensation for state and local government employees where covered by state law)

Item	Unit	1980	1985	1990	1991	1992	1993	1994	1995	1996	1997
Insured unemployment, avg. weekly	1 000	3 356	2 617	2 522	3 342	3 245	2 751	2 670	2 572	2 596	2 323
Percent of covered employment[1]	Percent	3.9	2.9	2.4	3.1	3.1	2.6	2.5	2.3	2.3	2.0
Percent of civilian unemployed	Percent	43.9	31.5	35.8	38.7	33.8	30.8	33.4	34.7	35.9	34.5
Unemployment benefits, avg. weekly	Dollars	100	128	162	170	174	180	182	187	189	193
Percent of weekly wage	Percent	36.6	35.3	36.0	36.4	35.4	36.0	35.7	35.5	34.5	33.5
Weeks compensated	Million	149.0	119.3	116.0	155.1	150.2	125.6	123.4	118.3	119.0	106.6
Beneficiaries, first payments	1 000	9 992	8 372	8 629	10 075	9 243	7 884	7 959	8 035	7 995	7 325
Average duration of benefits[2]	Weeks	14.9	14.2	13.4	15.4	16.2	15.9	15.5	14.7	14.9	14.6
Claimants exhausting benefits	1 000	3 072	2 572	2 323	3 472	3 838	3 204	2 977	2 662	2 739	2 485
Percent of first payment[3]	Percent	33.2	31.2	29.4	34.8	39.9	39.2	36.3	34.3	33.4	32.8
Contributions collected[4]	Bil. dol	11.4	19.3	15.2	14.5	17.0	19.8	21.8	22.0	21.6	21.2
Benefits paid	Bil. dol	14.2	14.7	18.0	25.5	25.1	21.8	21.5	21.2	21.8	19.7
Funds available for benefits[5]	Bil. dol	6.6	10.1	37.9	30.5	25.8	28.0	31.3	35.4	38.6	43.8
Average employer contribution rate[6]	Percent	2.4	3.1	2.0	1.9	2.2	2.5	2.6	2.4	2.3	2.1

1. Insured unemployment as percent of average covered employment in preceding year.
2. Weeks compensated divided by first payment.
3. Based on first payments for 12-month period ending June 30.
4. Contributions from employers; also employees in states which tax workers.
5. End of year. Sum of balances in state clearing accounts, benefit-payment accounts, and state accounts in Federal unemployment trust funds.
6. As percent of taxable wages.
Source: U.S. Employment and Training Administration, Unemployment Insurance Financial Handbook, annual.

Series HH-4 Elementary and Secondary Schools—Teachers and Pupil-Teacher Ratios With Projections: 1960 to 1998

(In thousands (1 600 represents 1 600 000), except ratios. As of fall. Data are for full-time equivalents. Schools are classified by type of organization, rather than by grade group; elementary includes kindergarten and secondary includes junior high)

Item	Total			Public			Private		
	Total	Elementary	Secondary	Total	Elementary	Secondary	Total	Elementary	Secondary
Number of teachers:									
1960	1 600	991	609	1 408	858	550	192	133	59
1970	2 292	1 283	1 009	2 059	1 130	929	233	153	80
1975	2 453	1 353	1 100	2 198	1 181	1 017	255	172	83
1980	2 485	1 401	1 084	2 184	1 189	995	301	212	89
1985	2 549	1 483	1 066	2 206	1 237	969	343	246	97
1988	2 668	1 604	1 064	2 323	1 353	970	345	251	94
1989	2 734	1 662	1 072	2 357	1 387	970	377	275	102
1990	2 753	1 680	1 073	2 398	1 426	972	355	254	101
1991	2 787	1 713	1 074	2 432	1 459	973	355	254	101
1992	2 822	1 752	1 070	2 459	1 492	967	363	260	103
1993	2 870	1 775	1 095	2 504	1 513	991	366	262	104
1994	2 926	1 794	1 132	2 552	1 528	1 024	373	266	108
1995	2 978	1 814	1 164	2 598	1 546	1 053	380	269	111
1996	3 053	1 856	1 197	2 666	1 582	1 084	387	274	113
1997, prel	3 103	1 882	1 222	2 710	1 604	1 106	394	278	116
1998, proj	3 126	1 894	1 233	2 728	1 612	1 116	399	281	117
Pupil-teacher ratio:									
1960	26.4	29.4	21.4	25.8	28.4	21.7	30.7	36.1	18.6
1970	22.4	24.6	19.5	22.3	24.3	19.8	23.0	26.5	16.4
1975	20.3	21.7	18.6	20.4	21.7	18.8	19.6	21.5	15.7
1980	18.6	20.1	16.6	18.7	20.4	16.8	17.7	18.8	15.0
1985	17.6	19.1	15.6	17.9	19.5	15.8	16.2	17.1	14.0
1988	17.0	18.6	14.7	17.3	19.0	14.9	15.2	16.1	12.8
1989	16.8	18.4	14.3	17.2	19.0	14.6	14.2	15.1	11.7
1990	16.9	18.5	14.3	17.2	19.0	14.6	14.7	16.1	11.3
1991	17.0	18.5	14.5	17.3	18.9	14.9	14.6	16.0	11.1
1992	17.1	18.4	14.8	17.4	18.8	15.2	14.8	16.2	11.3
1993	17.1	18.5	14.7	17.4	18.9	15.1	14.9	16.3	11.5
1994	17.1	18.6	14.7	17.3	18.9	15.1	15.0	16.4	11.4
1995	17.0	18.6	14.5	17.3	18.9	14.8	15.0	16.5	11.4
1996	16.8	18.4	14.3	17.1	18.8	14.6	14.9	16.4	11.5
1997, prel	16.7	18.3	14.2	17.0	18.6	14.5	14.9	16.3	11.4
1998, proj	16.9	18.5	14.4	17.2	18.9	14.7	14.9	16.3	11.4

Source: U.S. National Center for Education Statistics, Digest of Education Statistics, annual.

Series HH-5   Educational Attainment, by Race, Hispanic Origin, and Sex: 1960 to 1998

(In percent. For persons 25 years old and over. 1960, 1970, and 1980 as of April 1 and based on sample data from the censuses of population. Other years as of March and based on the Current Population Survey)

Year	All races[1]		White		Black		Asian and Pacific Islander		Hispanic[2]	
	Male	Female	Male	Female	Male	Female	Male	Female	Male	Female
COMPLETED 4 YEARS OF HIGH SCHOOL OR MORE										
1960	39.5	42.5	41.6	44.7	18.2	21.8	...	...	...	...
1965	48.0	49.9	50.2	52.2	25.8	28.4	...	...	...	...
1970	51.9	52.8	54.0	55.0	30.1	32.5	...	...	37.9	34.2
1975	63.1	62.1	65.0	64.1	41.6	43.3	...	...	39.5	36.7
1980	67.3	65.8	69.6	68.1	50.8	51.5	...	...	67.3	65.8
1985	74.4	73.5	76.0	75.1	58.4	60.8	...	...	48.5	47.4
1990	77.7	77.5	79.1	79.0	65.8	66.5	84.0	77.2	50.3	51.3
1995[3]	81.7	81.6	83.0	83.0	73.4	74.1	...	...	52.9	53.8
1996[3]	81.9	81.6	82.7	82.8	74.3	74.2	86.0	80.7	53.0	53.3
1997[3]	82.0	82.2	82.9	83.2	73.5	76.0	...	...	54.9	54.6
1998[3]	82.8	82.9	83.6	83.8	75.2	76.7	...	...	55.7	55.3
COMPLETED 4 YEARS OF COLLEGE OR MORE										
1960	9.7	5.8	10.3	6.0	2.8	3.3	...	...	...	...
1965	12.0	7.1	12.7	7.3	4.9	4.5	...	...	...	...
1970	13.5	8.1	14.4	8.4	4.2	4.6	...	...	7.8	4.3
1975	17.6	10.6	18.4	11.0	6.7	6.2	...	...	8.3	4.6
1980	20.1	12.8	21.3	13.3	8.4	8.3	...	...	9.4	6.0
1985	23.1	16.0	24.0	16.3	11.2	11.0	...	...	9.7	7.3
1990	24.4	18.4	25.3	19.0	11.9	10.8	44.9	35.4	9.8	8.7
1995[3]	26.0	20.2	27.2	21.0	13.6	12.9	...	...	10.1	8.4
1996[3]	26.0	21.4	26.9	21.8	12.4	14.6	46.4	37.3	10.3	8.3
1997[3]	26.2	21.7	27.0	22.3	12.5	13.9	...	...	10.6	10.1
1998[3]	26.5	22.4	27.3	22.8	13.9	15.4	...	...	11.1	10.9

1. Includes other races, not shown separately.
2. Persons of Hispanic origin may be of any race.
3. Beginning 1995, persons who are high school graduates and those with a BA degree or higher.
Source: U.S. Census Bureau, U.S. Census of Population, 1960, 1970, and 1980, Vol. 1; and Current Population Reports P20-459, P20-493, P20-505, P20-513; and unpublished data.

Series HH-6 Scholastic Assessment Test (SAT) Scores and Characteristics of College-Bound Seniors: 1967 to 1998

(For school year ending in year shown. Data are for the SAT I: Reasoning Tests. SAT I: Reasoning Test replaced the SAT in March 1994. Scores between the two tests have been equated to the same 200-800 scale and are thus comparable. Scores for 1995 and prior years have been recentered and revised)

Type of test and characteristic	Unit	1967	1970	1975	1980	1985	1990	1995	1996	1997	1998
AVERAGE TEST SCORES[1]											
Verbal, total[2]	Point	543	537	512	502	509	500	504	505	505	505
Male	Point	540	536	515	506	514	505	505	507	507	509
Female	Point	545	538	509	498	503	496	502	503	503	502
Math, total[2]	Point	516	512	498	492	500	501	506	508	511	512
Male	Point	535	531	518	515	522	521	525	527	530	531
Female	Point	495	493	479	473	480	483	490	492	494	496
PARTICIPANTS											
Total[3]	1 000	...	...	996	922	977	1,026	1,068	1,085	1,127	1,173
Male	Percent	...	...	49.9	48.2	48.3	47.8	46.4	46.5	46.1	46.2
White	Percent	...	...	86.0	82.1	81.0	73.0	69.2	68.7	68.0	67.0
Black	Percent	...	...	7.9	9.1	7.5	10.0	10.7	10.8	10.8	11.0
Obtaining scores[1] of											
600 or above:											
Verbal	Percent	...	...	...	...	...	20.3	21.9	21.1	20.9	21.0
Math	Percent	...	...	...	...	...	20.4	23.4	22.7	23.4	23.7
Below 400:											
Verbal	Percent	...	...	...	...	...	17.3	16.4	15.9	16.1	16.1
Math	Percent	...	...	...	...	...	15.8	16.0	16.0	15.2	15.3
Selected intended area of study:											
Business and commerce	Percent	...	...	11.5	18.6	21.0	20.9	13.3	12.8	12.8	13.6
Engineering	Percent	...	...	6.7	11.1	11.7	10.2	8.8	8.5	8.4	8.6
Social science	Percent	...	...	7.7	7.8	7.5	12.6	11.6	11.3	11.0	10.5
Education	Percent	...	...	9.1	6.1	4.7	7.5	8.1	8.2	8.6	8.9

1. Minimum score, 200; maximum score, 800.
2. 1967 and 1970 are estimates based on total number of persons taking SAT.
3. 996 represents 996,000.
Source: College Entrance Examination Board, New York, NY, National College-Bound Senior, annual (copyright).

Series HH-7 Libraries—Number, by Type: 1980 to 1997

Type	1980	1985	1990	1997	Type	1980	1985	1990	1997
Total[1]	31 564	32 323	34 613	37 591	Junior college	1 191	1 188	1 233	1 270
United States	28 638	29 843	30 761	33 108	Colleges, universities	3 400	3 846	3 360	3 430
Public	8 717	8 849	9 060	9 815	Departmental	1 489	1 824	1 454	1 452
Public branches	5 936	6 330	5 833	6 435	Law, medicine, religious	269	531	501	491
Special[2]	7 649	7 530	9 051	9 898	Government	1 260	1 574	1 735	1 897
Medicine	1 674	1 667	1 861	1 900	Armed Forces	485	526	489	363
Religious	913	839	946	1 010	Outlying areas	113	114	110	...
Law[3]	417	435	647	1 153					
Academic	4 591	5 034	4 593	4 700					

1. Includes Canadian libraries and libraries in regions administered by the United States, not shown separately. Data are exclusive of elementary and secondary school libraries. Law libraries with fewer than 10 000 volumes are included only if they specialize in a particular field.
2. Includes other types of special libraries, not shown separately. Increase between 1980 and 1990 is due mainly to revised criteria for identifying special libraries and improved methods of counting.
3. Increase in 1997 due to increased effort in identifying special libraries.
Source: R.R. Bowker Co., New York, NY, The Bowker Annual: Library and Book Trade Almanac and American Library Directory, annual. (Copyright by Reed Elsevier Inc.)

Series HH-8 Foreign (Nonimmigrant) Student Enrollment in College: 1976 to 1998

(For fall of the previous year. (179 represents 179 000))

Region of origin	Enrollment (1,000)									Percent enrolled in-					
										Engineering		Science[1]		Business	
	1976	1980	1985	1990	1994	1995	1996	1997	1998	1980	1996	1980	1996	1980	1996
All regions	179	286	342	387	449	453	454	458	481	25	16	8	8	16	21
Africa	25	36	40	25	21	21	21	22	23	20	14	9	8	19	20
Nigeria	11	16	18	4	2	2	2	2	2	19	11	9	10	22	18
Asia[2]	97	165	200	245	294	292	290	291	308	32	19	8	9	16	22
China: Taiwan	11	18	23	31	37	36	33	30	31	17	18	15	6	17	25
Hong Kong	12	10	10	11	14	13	12	11	10	22	15	9	4	26	37
India	10	9	15	26	35	34	32	31	34	31	36	16	9	21	15
Indonesia	1	2	7	9	11	12	13	12	13	27	21	7	2	21	45
Iran	20	51	17	7	4	3	3	2	2	45	31	7	17	11	7
Japan	7	12	13	30	44	45	46	46	47	7	3	5	4	19	18
Malaysia	2	4	22	14	14	14	14	15	15	13	31	14	3	22	36
Saudi Arabia	3	10	8	4	4	4	4	4	5	30	29	4	4	14	14
South Korea	3	5	16	22	31	34	36	37	43	17	12	11	8	15	16
Thailand	7	7	7	7	9	11	12	13	15	17	17	6	3	26	40
Europe	14	23	33	46	62	65	67	68	72	15	9	9	9	14	22
Latin America[3]	30	42	49	48	45	47	47	50	51	20	13	8	7	14	23
Mexico	5	6	6	7	8	9	9	9	10	16	16	7	6	11	22
Venezuela	5	10	10	3	4	4	4	5	5	30	16	8	5	11	25
North America	10	16	16	19	23	23	24	24	23	8	5	6	7	13	11
Canada	10	15	15	18	22	23	23	23	22	8	5	6	7	12	11
Oceania	3	4	4	4	4	4	4	4	4	5	5	7	7	16	16

1. Physical and life sciences.
2. Includes countries not shown separately.
3. Includes Central America, Caribbean, and South America.
Source: Institute of International Education, New York, NY, Open Doors, annual (copyright).

Series HH-9 Institutions of Higher Education—Charges: 1985 to 1998

(In dollars. Estimated. For the entire academic year ending in year shown. Figure are average charges per full-time equivalent student. Room and board are based on full-time students)

Academic control and year	Tuition and required fees[1]				Board rates[2]				Dormitory charges			
	All institutions	2-yr. colleges	4-yr. colleges	Other 4-yr. schools	All institutions	2-yr. colleges	4-yr. colleges	Other 4-yr. schools	All institutions	2-yr. colleges	4-yr. colleges	Other 4-yr. schools
Public:												
1985	971	584	1 386	1 117	1 241	1 302	1 276	1 201	1 196	921	1 237	1 200
1990	1 356	756	2 035	1 608	1 635	1 581	1 728	1 561	1 513	962	1 561	1 554
1991	1 454	824	2 159	1 707	1 691	1 594	1 767	1 641	1 612	1 050	1 658	1 655
1992	1 624	937	2 410	1 933	1 780	1 612	1 852	1 745	1 731	1 074	1 789	1 782
1993	1 782	1 025	2 604	2 192	1 841	1 668	1 982	1 761	1 756	1 106	1 856	1 787
1994	1 942	1 125	2 820	2 360	1 880	1 681	1 993	1 828	1 873	1 190	1 897	1 958
1995	2 057	1 192	2 977	2 499	1 949	1 712	2 108	1 866	1 959	1 232	1 992	2 044
1996	2 179	1 239	3 151	2 660	2 020	1 681	2 192	1 937	2 057	1 297	2 104	2 133
1997	2 271	1 276	3 323	2 778	2 111	1 789	2 282	2 025	2 148	1 339	2 187	2 232
1998 est	2 365	1 318	3 489	2 876	2 180	1 864	2 380	2 076	2 243	1 419	2 280	2 338
Private:												
1985	5 315	3 485	6 843	5 135	1 462	1 294	1 647	1 405	1 426	1 424	1 753	1 309
1990	8 174	5 196	10 348	7 778	1 948	1 811	2 339	1 823	1 923	1 663	2 411	1 774
1991	8 772	5 570	11 379	8 389	2 074	1 989	2 470	1 943	2 063	1 744	2 654	1 889
1992	9 434	5 752	12 192	9 053	2 252	2 090	2 727	2 098	2 221	1 789	2 860	2 038
1993	9 942	6 059	13 055	9 533	2 344	1 875	2 825	2 197	2 348	1 970	3 018	2 151
1994	10 572	6 370	13 874	10 100	2 434	1 970	2 946	2 278	2 490	2 067	3 277	2 261
1995	11 111	6 914	14 537	10 653	2 509	2 023	3 035	2 362	2 587	2 233	3 469	2 347
1996	11 864	7 094	15 605	11 297	2 606	2 098	3 218	2 429	2 738	2 371	3 680	2 473
1997	12 498	7 236	16 552	11 871	2 663	2 181	3 142	2 520	2 878	2 537	3 826	2 602
1998 est	13 013	7 536	17 197	12 388	2 742	2 321	3 224	2 608	2 990	2 624	4 001	2 717

1. For in-state students.
2. Beginning 1990, rates reflect 20 meals per week, rather than meals served 7 days a week.
Source: U.S. National Center for Education Statistics, Digest of Education Statistics, annual.

Series HH-10 Quantity of Books Sold and Value of U.S. Domestic Consumer Expenditures: 1982 to 1997

(Includes all titles released by publishers in the United States and imports which appear under the imprints of American publishers. (1 732 represents 1 732 000 000). Multivolume sets, such as encyclopedias, are counted as one unit)

Type of publication and market area	Units sold (mil.)					Consumer expenditures (mil. dol.)				
	1982	1985	1990	1995	1997	1982	1985	1990	1995	1997
Total[1]	1 723	1 788	2 005	2 186	2 144	9 889	12 611	19 043	25 154	26 450
Hardbound, total	646	694	824	827	758	6 190	7 969	11 789	15 011	15 343
Softbound, total	1 077	1 094	1 181	1 359	1 386	3 699	4 642	7 254	10 143	11 107
Trade	459	553	705	813	759	2 484	3 660	6 498	9 340	9 173
Adult	315	360	403	465	424	2 028	2 871	4 777	7 060	6 832
Juvenile	144	193	301	348	335	456	789	1 721	2 280	2 341
Religious	144	134	130	148	157	706	926	1 362	1 792	1 958
Professional	106	110	131	146	146	1 630	2 043	2 957	4 153	4 465
Bookclubs	133	130	108	123	134	510	582	705	949	1 113
Elhi text	233	234	209	237	275	1 067	1 415	1 948	2 384	2 866
College text	115	110	137	142	154	1 388	1 575	2 319	2 708	3 110
Mail order publications	134	121	138	92	83	581	650	752	578	539
Mass market paperbacks—rack-sized	382	382	433	470	419	1 102	1 244	1 775	2 322	2 220
General retailers	756	829	1 010	1 145	1 078	3 743	5 103	8 465	11 888	11 958
College stores	224	225	255	274	274	1 910	2 309	3 403	4 311	4 698
Libraries and institutions[2]	80	80	88	97	96	888	1 090	1 592	2 111	2 210
Schools[2]	262	260	244	273	309	1 313	1 685	2 365	2 896	3 388
Direct to consumers	319	300	304	289	291	1 889	2 214	2 901	3 544	3 820
Other	82	94	104	108	96	146	210	316	404	378

1. Types of publications include university press publications and subscription reference works, not shown separately.
2. Elhi libraries included in schools.
Source: Book Industry Study Group, Inc., New York, NY, Book Industry Trends, 1998, annual (copyright).

Series HH-11 Boy Scouts and Girl Scouts—Membership and Units: 1970 to 1998

(In thousands (6 287 represents 6 287 000). Boy Scouts as of Dec. 31; Girl Scouts as of Sept. 30. Includes Puerto Rico and outlying areas)

Item	1970	1975	1980	1985	1990	1993	1994	1995	1996	1997	1998
BOY SCOUTS OF AMERICA											
Membership	6 287	5 318	4 318	4 845	5 448	5 354	5 378	5 457	5 629	5 835	6 043
Boys	4 683	3 933	3 207	3 755	4 293	4 165	4 188	4 256	4 399	4 574	4 756
Adults	1 604	1 385	1 110	1 090	1 155	1 189	1 190	1 201	1 230	1 262	1 287
Total units (packs, troops, posts, groups)	157	150	129	134	130	128	129	132	135	139	143
GIRL SCOUTS OF THE U.S.A.											
Membership	3 922	3 234	2 784	2 802	3 269	3 438	3 363	3 318	3 390	3 525	3 567
Girls	3 248	2 723	2 250	2 172	2 480	2 612	2 561	2 534	2 584	2 671	2 708
Adults	674	511	534	630	788	826	802	784	807	855	858
Total units (troops, groups)	164	159	154	166	202	221	218	215	219	223	226

Source: Boy Scouts of America, National Council, Irving, TX, Annual Report; and Girl Scouts of the United States of America, New York, NY, Annual Report.

Series HH-12 Performing Arts—Selected Data: 1985 to 1997

(Sales, receipts, and expenditures in millions of dollars (209 represents $209 000 000). For season ending in year shown, except as indicated)

Item	1985	1989	1990	1991	1992	1993	1994	1995	1996	1997
Legitimate theater:[1]										
Broadway shows:										
New productions	33	33	39	28	39	35	38	33	39	36
Attendance (mil.)	7.3	8.1	8.0	7.3	7.4	7.9	8.1	9.0	9.5	10.6
Playing weeks[2][3]	1 078	1 093	1 062	971	905	1 019	1 061	1 118	1 144	1 349
Gross ticket sales	209	262	282	267	293	328	356	406	436	499
Broadway road tours:										
Attendance (mil.)	8.2	8.3	11.1	13.0	13.0	15.0	16.0	16.0	18.1	18.0
Playing weeks	993	869	944	1 152	1 171	1 296	1 249	1 242	1 345	1 334
Gross ticket sales	226	256	367	450	503	626	705	701	796	782
Nonprofit professional theatres:[4]										
Companies reporting	217	192	185	184	182	177	231	215	228	197
Gross income	234.7	349.0	307.6	333.9	359.1	342.5	455.1	444.4	450.7	565.0
Earned income	146.1	224.6	188.4	202.6	222.5	209.7	277.4	281.2	274.0	349.9
Contributed income	88.6	124.4	119.2	131.3	136.6	132.8	177.7	163.1	176.7	215.1
Gross expenses	239.3	349.2	306.3	336.7	365.6	349.3	460.2	444.9	439.5	526.6
Productions	2 710	2 469	2 265	2 277	2 310	2 319	2 929	2 646	3 074	2 295
Performances	52 341	53 263	46 131	48 695	46 184	44 933	59 542	56 608	56 954	51 453
Total attendance (mil.)	14.2	18.7	15.2	16.9	16.0	16.5	20.7	18.6	17.1	17.2
OPERA America professional member companies:[5]										
Number of companies reporting[6]	97	101	98	98	100	85	86	88	83	91
Expenses[6]	216.4	311.7	321.2	346.7	371.8	389.5	404.9	435.0	466.7	534.1
Performances[7]	1 909	2 429	2 336	2 283	2 424	1 945	1 982	2 251	2 019	2 137
Total attendance (mil.)[7][8]	6.7	7.4	7.5	7.6	7.3	5.5	6.0	6.5	6.5	6.9
Main season attendance (mil.)[7][9]	3.3	4.0	4.1	4.3	4.3	3.6	3.7	3.9	3.9	4.0
Symphony orchestras:[10]										
Concerts	19 573	20 630	18 931	18 074	19 778	18 389	17 795	29 328	28 887	26 906
Attendance (mil.)	24.0	25.8	24.7	26.7	26.3	24.0	24.4	30.9	31.1	31.9
Gross revenue	252.4	353.2	377.5	394.5	414.0	430.5	442.5	536.2	558.9	575.5
Concert income	168.6	231.0	253.3	273.8	284.1	294.1	303.6	368.6	383.7	390.5
Endowment income	(NA)	46.8	52.1	52.5	55.3	59.7	60.4	76.2	79.9	91.4
Other earned income	83.8	75.4	72.1	68.2	74.6	76.8	78.5	91.4	95.3	93.5
Operating expenses	426.1	583.5	621.7	662.2	683.0	689.9	710.0	858.8	892.4	937.1
Artistic personnel	231.9	310.2	327.3	355.8	398.9	378.8	389.9	464.7	473.9	487.1
Concert production	69.2	89.0	104.3	110.3	117.2	114.3	129.3	160.6	166.0	175.1
Advertising and promotion	32.5	47.5	51.3	57.3	58.3	63.1	67.3	75.2	82.9	90.8
General and administrative	51.3	68.4	73.3	75.6	76.2	73.6	74.4	87.2	88.2	91.6
Other	41.3	68.4	65.6	63.2	32.4	60.1	49.1	71.1	81.5	92.5
Support	188.1	249.0	257.8	281.2	279.6	293.0	293.1	351.0	382.8	401.1
Tax supported grants	42.2	54.5	55.6	58.3	49.1	48.0	46.4	55.5	57.6	54.5
Private sector support	145.9	194.5	202.1	222.9	230.5	245.0	246.7	295.5	325.3	346.6
Development expenses	20.8	30.9	31.4	36.7	36.0	38.0	37.9	38.8	42.8	44.9
Net support	167.3	218.2	226.4	244.6	243.6	255.0	255.2	312.2	340.0	356.2

1. Source: The League of American Theaters and Producers, Inc., New York, NY.
2. All shows (new productions and holdovers from previous seasons).
3. Eight performances constitute one playing week.
4. Source: Theatre Communications Group, New York, NY. For years ending on or prior to Aug. 31.
5. Source: OPERA America, Washington, DC. For years ending on or prior to Aug 31.
6. United States companies.
7. Prior to 1993, United States and Canadian companies; beginning 1993, US companies only.
8. Includes educational performances, outreach, etc.
9. For paid performances.
10. Source: American Symphony Orchestra League, Inc., Washington, DC. For years ending Aug. 31. Prior to 1995 represents 254 U.S. orchestras; beginning 1995, represents all U.S. orchestras, excluding college/university and youth orchestras. Also, beginning 1995, data based on 1 200 orchestras; prior data based on 254.
Source: Compiled from sources listed in footnotes.

Series HH-13   Fire Losses—Total and Percent Change: 1980 to 1997

(5 579 represents 5 579 000 000. Includes allowance for uninsured and unreported losses but excludes losses to government property and forests. Represents incurred losses)

Year	Total (mil. dol.)	Per capita[1]	Year	Total (mil. dol.)	Per capita[1]	Year	Total (mil. dol.)	Per capita[1]
1980	5 579	24.56	1986	8 488	35.21	1992	13 588	53.29
1981	5 625	24.53	1987	8 504	34.96	1993	11 331	43.96
1982	5 894	25.61	1988	9 626	39.11	1994	12 778	49.09
1983	6 320	27.20	1989	9 514	38.33	1995	11 887	45.24
1984	7 602	32.35	1990	9 495	38.07	1996	12 544	47.30
1985	7 753	32.70	1991	11 302	44.83	1997	11 372	42.49

1. Based on U.S. Census Bureau estimated resident population as of July 1.
Source: Insurance Information Institute, New York, NY, Insurance Facts, annual (copyright).

Series HH-14   Federal Prosecutions of Public Corruption: 1980 to 1996

(As of Dec. 31. Prosecution of persons who have corrupted public office in violation of Federal Criminal Statutes)

Prosecution status	1980	1985	1987	1988	1989	1990	1991	1992	1993	1994	1995	1996
Total:[1] Indicted	727	1 157	1 276	1 274	1 348	1 176	1 452	1 189	1 371	1 165	1 051	984
Convicted	602	997	1 081	1 067	1 149	1 084	1 194	1 081	1 362	969	878	902
Awaiting trial	213	256	368	288	375	300	346	380	403	332	323	244
Federal officials: Indicted	123	563	651	629	695	615	803	624	627	571	527	456
Convicted	131	470	545	529	610	583	665	532	595	488	438	459
Awaiting trial	16	90	118	86	126	103	149	139	133	124	120	64
State officials: Indicted	72	79	102	66	71	96	115	84	113	99	61	109
Convicted	51	66	76	69	54	79	77	92	133	97	61	83
Awaiting trial	28	20	26	14	18	28	42	24	39	17	23	40
Local officials: Indicted	247	248	246	276	269	257	242	232	309	248	236	219
Convicted	168	221	204	229	201	225	180	211	272	202	191	190
Awaiting trial	82	49	89	79	122	98	88	91	132	96	89	60

1. Includes individuals who are neither public officials nor employees but who were involved with public officials or employees in violating the law, not shown separately.
Source: U.S. Department of Justice, Federal Prosecutions of Corrupt Public Officials, 1970-1980 and Report to Congress on the Activities and Operations of the Public Integrity Section, annual.

Series HH-15   Adults on Probation, in Jail or Prison, or on Parole: 1980 to 1997

(As of December 31, except jail counts as June 30)

Year	Total[1]	Probation	Jail	Prison	Parole	Male	Female
1980	1 840 400	1 118 097	[2]182 288	319 598	220 438	...	...
1981	2 006 600	1 225 934	[2]195 085	360 029	225 539	...	...
1982	2 192 600	1 357 264	207 853	402 914	224 604	...	...
1983	2 475 100	1 582 947	221 815	423 898	246 440	...	...
1984	2 689 200	1 740 948	233 018	448 264	266 992	...	...
1985	3 011 400	1 968 712	254 986	487 593	300 203	2 606 000	405 500
1986	3 239 400	2 114 621	272 735	526 436	325 638	2 829 100	410 300
1987	3 459 600	2 247 158	294 092	562 814	355 505	3 021 000	438 600
1988	3 714 100	2 356 483	341 893	607 766	407 977	3 223 000	491 100
1989	4 055 600	2 522 125	393 303	683 367	456 803	3 501 600	554 000
1990	4 348 000	2 670 234	403 019	743 382	531 407	3 746 300	601 700
1991	4 535 600	2 728 472	424 129	792 535	590 442	3 913 000	622 600
1992	4 762 600	2 811 611	441 781	850 566	658 601	4 050 300	712 300
1993	4 944 000	2 903 061	455 500	909 381	676 100	4 215 800	728 200
1994	5 141 300	2 981 022	479 800	990 147	690 371	4 377 400	763 900
1995	5 335 100	3 077 861	499 300	1 078 542	679 421	4 546 400	828 100
1996	5 475 000	3 161 030	510 400	1 127 528	676 045	...	...
1997, total[3]	5 690 700	3 261 888	557 974	1 185 800	685 033	...	...

1. Totals may not add due to individuals having multiple correctional statuses.
2. Estimated.
3. Totals may not add due to rounding.
Source: U.S. Bureau of Justice Statistics, Correctional Populations in the United States, annual.

Series HH-16   Immigration Border Patrol and Investigation Activities: 1980 to 1995

(For fiscal years ending in year shown. See text, Section 9, State and Local Government)

Item	Unit	1980	1985	1989	1990	1991	1992	1993	1994	1995
BORDER PATROL										
Border patrol agents:										
Authorized number	Number	2 484	3 228	4 804	4 852	4 968	4 948	4 143	4 559	5 259
On duty	Number	2 329	3 023	3 857	4 360	4 312	4 759	3 991	4 226	4 881
Border patrol obligations	Mil. dol.	82.5	141.9	246.4	261.1	29d.5	325.8	354.5	376.8	457.2
Persons apprehended[1]	1 000	766.6	1 272.4	906.5	1 123.2	1 152.7	1 221.9	1 281.7	1 046.6	1 336.5
Deportable aliens located[2]	1 000	759.4	1 262.4	893.0	1 103.4	1 132.9	1 199.6	1 263.5	1 031.7	1 324.2
Mexican	1 000	734.2	1 218.7	832.2	1 054.8	1 095.1	1 168.9	1 230.1	999.9	1 293.5
Canadian	1 000	5.3	5.9	5.3	5.7	6.7	6.2	5.2	3.4	3.5
Other	1 000	19.9	37.8	55.5	42.8	31.1	24.4	28.1	28.4	27.2
Number of seizures	Number	1 920	7 827	10 789	17 275	14 261	11 391	10 995	9 134	9 327
Value of seizures	Mil. dol.	116.1	122.0	1 212.7	843.6	950.2	1 247.9	1 383	1 598	733.0
Narcotics	Mil. dol.	110.3	119.8	1 191.5	797.8	910.1	1 216.8	1 338	1 556	686.6
INVESTIGATIONS										
Deportable aliens located	1 000	150.9	83.9	61.1	64.1	63.6	57.4	60.4	61.6	68.9
Mexican	1 000	83.3	48.3	33.1	35.8	35.5	36.2	38.8	40.1	46.3
Canadian	1 000	1.5	1.1	0.5	0.4	0.5	0.4	0.4	0.5	0.5
Other	1 000	66.1	34.5	28.5	30.0	29.7	20.8	21.1	21.1	22.0

1. Covers deportable aliens located and U.S. citizens engaged in smuggling or other immigration violations.
2. Beginning 1989, includes apprehension by the anti smuggling unit.
Source: U.S. Immigration and Naturalization Service, Statistical Yearbook, annual; and unpulibhsed data.

SECTION

J

SECTION

LAND, WATER AND CLIMATE

LAND, WATER AND CLIMATE

Highlights

1 When the United States became a republic, its boundaries were unclear. Its territorial claims were based on several treaties that were subject to interpretation. The boundaries themselves were poorly marked and expanded or receded depending on the status of the Indian Wars. From 1781 to 1867, the federal government acquired millions of acres of public domain. From 1781 to 1902, 7 of the original 13 states relinquished their claims to the so-called "Western lands" to the federal government. In 1788, the state of Maryland ceded the present area of the District of Columbia. Between 1810 and 1867, title to the remaining area west of the Mississippi River (except the state of Texas) and to Florida passed to the federal government. The annual report to the General Land Office in 1850 contained the first reference to the areas of the states and territories, although the methods used to obtain the measurements was not indicated. In 1881, the Bureau of the Census initiated the first effort to obtain an accurate and detailed area measurement of the United States. This was revised in 1940 in *Areas of the United States,* which presented land and water areas, as well as state, municipal and county boundaries. Differences in land area figures over time reflect improvements in cartography that made possible a more accurate determination of the outer limits as well as inclusion or exclusion of certain bodies of water. For the 1990 census, area measurements were calculated by computer based on the information contained in a single database, the TIGER (Topologically Integrated Geographic Encoding and Referencing) File. As result, the number of inland water areas increased when coverage was extended to inland bodies of water of at least 40 acres and streams with a width of at least one-eighth of a statute mile. An inventory of the nation's land resources by type of use/cover was conducted by the Soil Conservation Service from 1982 to 1987 and its results were published in 1987 in the *National Inventory of Land Resources.*

2 The state with the largest land area and largest water area is Alaska. Alaska's water area of 85,051 square miles is larger than the land area of all but 11 states.

3 The highest point in the United States is Mount McKinley in Alaska at 20,310 feet. The lowest point is Death Valley in California at -282 feet.

4 The five Great Lakes—Michigan, Superior, Huron, Erie and Ontario (including only those portions under the jurisdiction of the United States)—account for 58,178 square miles of water areas. The largest inland lakes outside the Great Lakes are Great Salt Lake (1,836 square miles) and Green Bay (1,396 square miles).

5 The Mississippi, America's longest river, is 2,340 miles long. It has an average discharge at its mouth of 593,000 cubic feet per second and a drainage area of 1,150,000 square miles. There are nine other rivers longer than 1,000 miles: Missouri (2,540 miles), Yukon (1,980 miles), St. Lawrence (1,900 miles), Arkansas (1,460 miles), Atchafalaya (1,420 miles), Ohio (1,310 miles), Red (1,290 miles), Columbia (1,240 miles), and Snake (1,040 miles).

6 Of the 2,271,343,000 acres of land in the United States, 563,081,000 acres, or 24.8%, is federal land. The percentage of federal land is highest in Nevada (79.8%), Utah (64.3%), Idaho (62.3%), and Wyoming (49.5%). It is lowest in Iowa (0.1%), Connecticut and Delaware (0.2% each), Rhode Island (0.5%), New York (0.6%), Kansas and Maine (0.7%), Massachusetts (1.0%), Ohio, Nebraska and Illinois (1.1% each) and Texas (1.2%).

7 In 1995 total water withdrawal (all water withdrawn from natural reservoirs, lakes, rivers, etc. for human consumption and industrial use) per day in the United States was 402 billion gallons, or 1,500 gallons per capita. The largest water use was for irrigation (134 billion gallons per day), followed by electric utilities (190 billion gallons per day), public supply (43 billion gallons per day), and industrial use (26 billion gallons per day). Of total water withdrawals, 19.3% is ground water and 80.7% surface water.

8 In 1997, 8,624 oil spills were reported, 2,341 in the Gulf of Mexico, 505 in the Pacific Ocean, 87 in the Atlan-

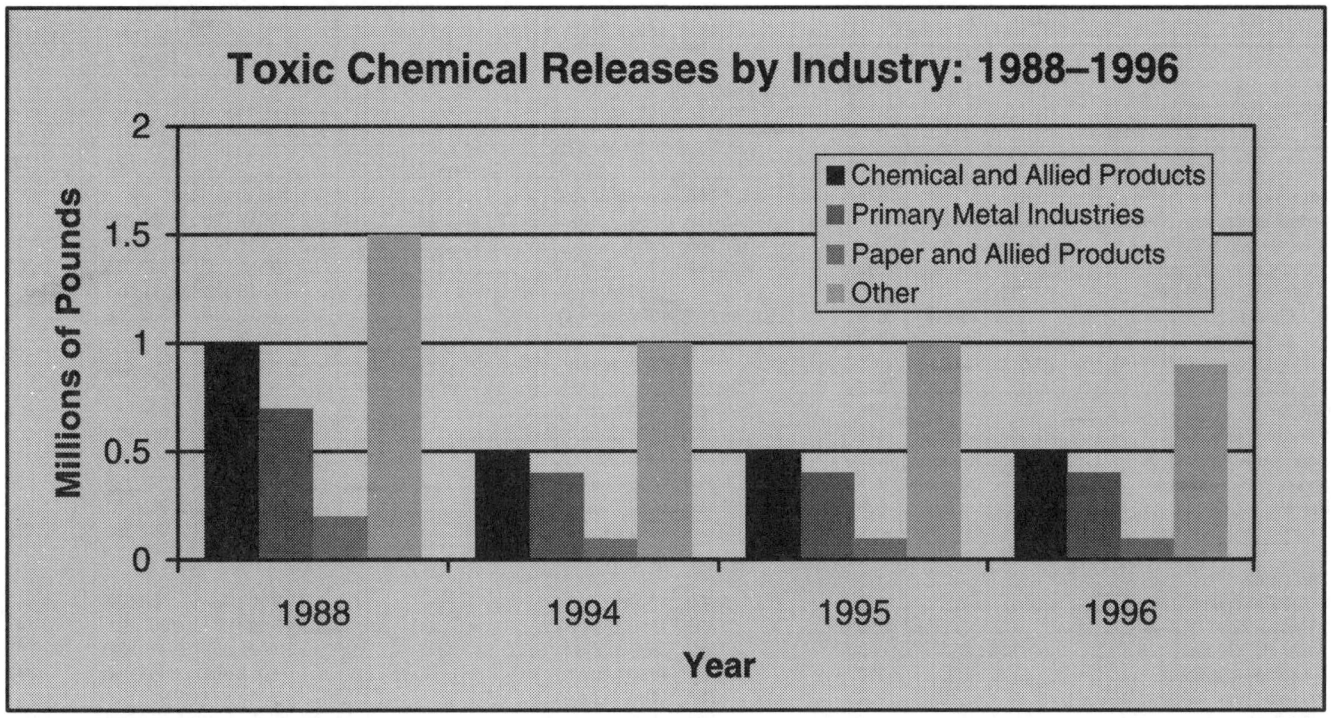

Toxic Chemical Releases by Industry: 1988–1996

tic Ocean, 156 in the Great Lakes, and 1,821 in rivers and canals.

9 The principal agency for environmental monitoring in the United States is the Council on Environmental Quality (CEQ), and the principal agency for pollution abatement is the Environmental Protection Agency (EPA). CEQ reports data on environmental conditions in its annual *Environmental Quality.* The National Ambient Air Quality Standards (NAAQS) are set by the EPA for particulate matter, sulfur dioxide, petrochemical oxidants (now called ozone), carbon monoxide, and nitrogen dioxide. Environmental quality has steadily improved in the United States since the 1970s. In 1997, sulfur dioxide decreased to 20,369,000 tons from 31,161,000 tons in 1970; volatile organic compounds to 19,214,000 tons from 30,817,000 tons; carbon monoxide to 87,451,000 tons from 128,761,000 tons, lead to 3,915,000 tons from 220,869,000 tons; and particulate matter down to 8,428,000 tons from 13,190,000 tons. Only nitrogen dioxide increased, rising from 21,639,000 tons in 1970 to 23,582,000 tons in 1997.

10 Between 1980 and 1995, there were 252 violations nationwide of fecal coliform bacteria count in rivers and streams and 21 violations relating to levels of dissolved oxygen below 5 milligrams in water. The number is indicative of the amount of sewage contained in drinking water.

11 In 1997 217 million tons of waste were generated nationwide, or 4.4 pounds per capita per day. Of these 60.8 million tons were recycled and recovered. Paper and paperboard accounted for 38.6 of recycled and recovered materials. The Northeast leads in curbside recycling programs,

serving 83% of the population. The percentage of population served through recycling programs is lowest in the South at 35%.

12 In 1998, there were 1,258 hazardous waste sites in the United States, of which New Jersey had the most at 105 sites, followed by Pennsylvania (94), New York (80), and California (73).

13 In 1999, the United States had 569 species of endangered (those in immediate danger of becoming extinct) plants, 61 species of endangered mammals, 75 species of endangered birds, and 14 species of endangered reptiles. On the threatened species list (those likely to become endangered in the foreseeable future), were 8 species of mammals, 15 species of birds, 21 species of reptiles, and 135 species of plants.

14 The number of tornadoes and storms have increased in the past 20 years. In 1997, there were 1,148 tornadoes (compared to 656 in 1987 and 701 in 1988) and 117 flash floods (compared to 70 in 1987). The number of North Atlantic tropical storms and hurricanes varied widely over the years. Between 1987 and 1997, there were 113 tropical storms and hurricanes in the Atlantic coastal states.

15 The lowest temperature on record in the United States was -44°F in Bismarck, North Dakota. The city with the most precipitation is Mobile, Alabama, with 63.96 inches, but Juneau, Alaska, has the most rainy days— 222—in a year. Juneau also holds the record for the highest average annual snowfall: 99.6 inches.

Series J 1-2. Territorial Expansion and Land and Water Area of the United States: 1790 to 1990

(In square miles)

Accession	Territorial expansion		Year	Area		
	Date	Gross area (land and water)[1]		Gross[1] area	Land	Water[1]
		1		2	2a	2b
Total	**1970**	**3 628 066**	United States			
United States............................	. . .	3 615 122	1990..	3 717 796	3 536 278	181 518
Territory in 1790[2]........................	. . .	888 685	1980..	3 618 770	3 539 289	79 481
Louisiana Purchase......................	1803	827 192	1970 (April 1).................................	3 615 122	3 536 855	78 267
By treaty with Spain:			1960 (April 1).................................	3 615 123	3 540 911	74 212
Florida	1819	58 560	1950 (April 1).................................	3 615 211	3 552 206	63 005
Other areas	1819	13 443				
			Coterminous U.S.[7]			
Texas......................................	1845	390 143				
Oregon	1846	285 580	1960 (April 1).................................	3 002 261	2 968 054	54 207
Mexican Cession..........................	1848	529 017	1950 (April 1).................................	3 022 387	2 974 726	47 661
Gadsden Purchase	1853	29 640	1940 (April 1).................................	3 022 387	2 977 128	45 259
Alaska......................................	1867	586 412	1930 (April 1).................................	3 022 387	2 977 128	45 259
Hawaii......................................	1898	6 450	1920 (Jan. 1).................................	3 022 387	2 969 451	52 936
			1910 (April 15)...............................	3 022 387	2 969 565	52 822
Other areas:						
The Philippines[3]........................	1898	115 600	1900 (June 1).................................	3 022 387	2 969 834	52 553
Puerto Rico..............................	1899	3 435	1890 (June 1).................................	3 022 387	2 969 640	52 747
Guam......................................	1899	212	1880 (June 1).................................	3 022 387	2 969 640	52 747
American Samoa........................	1900	76	1870 (June 1).................................	3 022 387	2 969 640	52 747
Canal Zone[4]	1904	553	1860 (June 1).................................	3 022 387	2 969 640	52 747
Corn Islands[5]	1914	4	1850 (June 1).................................	2 992 747	2 940 042	52 705
Virgin Islands of the U.S.	1917	133				
Trust Territory of the Pacific Islands[6]....................			1840 (June 1).................................	1 788 006	1 749 462	38 544
	1947	8 489	1830 (June 1).................................	1 788 006	1 749 462	38 544
All other	. . .	42	1820 (Aug. 7).................................	1 788 006	1 749 462	38 544
			1810 (Aug. 6).................................	1 716 003	1 681 828	34 175
			1800 (Aug. 4).................................	888 811	864 746	24 065
			1790 (Aug. 2).................................	888 811	864 746	24 065

1. Water area 1790–1980 includes inland water only. 1990 data reflect new database and include coastal water (42,528 square miles) and Great Lakes (60,052 square miles).
2. Includes that part of drainage basin of Red River of the North, south of 49th parallel, sometimes considered part of Louisiana Purchase.
3. Not included in total. Ceded by Spain in 1898, the Philippines constituted a territorial possession of the United States until 1946. Granted independence July 4, 1946.
4. Under jurisdiction of United States in accordance with treaty of Nov. 18, 1903, with Republic of Panama.
5. Included in total for 1970. Leased (1914) from Republic of Nicaragua for 99 years, but returned April 25, 1971.
6. Under trusteeship with the United States as administering authority. See Trusteeship Agreement for the Former Japanese Mandated Islands (Documentary Supplement No.1) of the Security Council of the United Nations which became effective on July 18, 1947.
7. Excludes Alaska and Hawaii.

Series J 92-103. Estimated Water Use: 1900 to 2000

(In billions of gallons, daily average)

Year	Total water use	Total irrigation[1]	Total public water utilities	Self-supplied use		
				Total rural domestic[2]	Total industrial and miscellaneous[3]	Total steam electric utilities
	92	94	96	98	100	102
1995	402	134	43	8.9	26	190
1990	408	137	41	7.9	30	195
1985	399	137	38	7.8	31	187
1980	440	150	34	5.6	45	210
1975	420	140	29	4.9	45	200
1974	373	125	29	4.5	63	145
1973	361	124	29	4.5	61	142
1972	350	122	28	4.4	59	135
1971	338	120	27	4.4	57	128
1970	370	130	27	4.35	47	170
1969	403	156.82	26.60	6.82	83.44	129.62
1968	395	154.64	26.20	6.74	80.88	126.94
1967	387	152.46	25.80	6.66	78.32	124.26
1966	379	150.28	25.40	6.58	75.76	121.58
1965	310	120	24	4.08	46	84.54
1964	361.94	145.48	24.40	6.40	70.80	114.86
1963	352.18	142.86	23.80	6.30	68.40	110.82
1962	344.48	141.16	23.31	6.22	66.62	107.17
1961	334.72	138.54	22.71	6.12	64.22	103.13
1960*	322.90	135.00	22.00	6.00	61.20	98.70
1958	299.26	127.52	19.72	5.76	56.40	89.86
1955	263.80	116.30	16.30	5.40	49.20	76.60
1950	202.70	100.00	14.10	4.60	38.10	45.90
1946	165.74	86.44	12.00	3.50	33.00	30.80
1945	170.46	83.06	12.00	3.20	41.00	31.20
1944	178.43	80.65	12.00	3.18	48.00	34.60
1940	136.43	71.03	10.10	3.10	29.00	23.20
1930	110.50	60.20	8.00	2.90	21.00	18.40
1920	91.54	55.94	6.00	2.40	18.00	9.20
1910	66.44	39.04	4.70	2.20	14.00	6.50
1900	40.19	20.19	3.00	2.00	10.00	5.00

* Denotes first year for which figures include Alaska and Hawaii.
1. Total take, including delivery losses but not including reservoir evaporation.
2. Rural farm and nonfarm household and garden use, and water for farm stock and dairies.
3. For 1900-1960, includes manufacturing industries, mineral industries, rural commercial industries, air conditioning, resorts, hotels, motels, military and other state and federal agencies and other miscellaneous uses; thereafter, includes manufacturing, mining and mineral processing, ordnance and construction.

Series J 268-278. Tornadoes, Floods, and Tropical Cyclones: 1886 to 1997

Year	Tornadoes Lives lost				Floods		North Atlantic tropical cyclones (including hurricanes)	
	Number	Total	Most in a single tornado	$500,000 and over in property loss	Lives lost	Property loss ($1,000)	Total reaching U.S. coast	Lives lost in United States
	268	270	271	273	274	275	276	278
1997	1 148	67	27	...	117	...	7	4
1996	1 170	25	5	...	131	...	13	33
1995	1 235	30	6	...	80	...	19	29
1994	1 082	69	22	...	91	...	7	38
1993	1 176	33	7	...	103	...	8	9
1992	1 298	39	12	...	62	...	7	26
1991	1 132	39	17	...	61	...	8	17
1990	1 133	53	29	91	142	...	14	10
1989	856	50	21	60	85	415	11	56
1988	702	32	5	48	31	114	12	6
1987	656	59	30	38	70	1 490	7	...
1986	764	15	3	75	80	4 000	6	...
1985	684	94	18	69	304	3 000	11	9
1984	907	122	16	125	126	4 000	2	4
1983	931	34	3	95	200	4 100	2	22
1982	1 046	64	10	92	155	3 500	1	...
1981	783	24	5	55	90	1 000	2	...
1980	866	28	5	92	97	1 500	2	2
1979	852	84	42	73	100	4 000	5	11
1978	788	53	16	59	120	1 000	2	35
1977	852	43	22	46	212	1 393	1	...
1976	835	44	5	46	187	1 000	2	9
1975	920	60	9	42	114	1 051	1	21
1974	947	361	34	107	121	576	1	1
1973	1 102	87	7	76	105	859	1	5
1972	741	27	6	29	540	3 449	3	121
1971	888	156	58	35	74	258	5	8
1970	649	73	26	30	135	225 453	4	11
1969	604	66	32	19	297	902 654	3	256
1968	661	131	34	32	31	339 399	3	9
1967	912	116	33	41	34	375 218	2	18
1966	570	99	58	17	31	117 004	2	54
1965	899	298	44	41	119	788 046	2	75
1964	713	73	22	22	100	651 642	6	49
1963	461	31	5	16	39	177 946	1	11
1962	658	28	17	10	19	75 237	1	4
1961	682	51	16	22	52	154 033	3	46
1960	618	47	16	12	32	92 976	5	65
1959	589	58	21	5	25	141 255	7	24
1958	565	66	19	9	47	218 255	1	2
1957	864	191	44	29	82	360 303	5	395
1956	532	83	25	25	42	64 688	2	21
1955	593	125	80	14	302	995 491	5	218
1954	549	35	6	9	55	106 842	4	193
1953	437	516	116	25	40	122 204	6	2
1952	236	230	57	19	54	254 064	2	3
1951	272	34	6	13	51	1 028 741	1	...
1950	199	70	18	9	93	176 050	4	19
1949	249	212	58	13	48	93 931	3	4
1948	183	140	33	13	82	229 959	4	3
1947	165	313	169	8	55	272 328	7	53
1946	106	78	15	7	28	70 813	4	...
1945	121	210	69	11	91	165 798	5	7
1944	169	275	100	9	33	101 079	4	64
1943	152	58	5	8	107	199 732	4	16
1942	167	384	65	10	68	98 507	3	8

See footnote at end of chart.

Series J 268-278. Tornadoes, Floods, and Tropical Cyclones: 1886 to 1997—Cont'd.

Year	Tornadoes Lives lost				Floods		North Atlantic tropical cyclones (including hurricanes)	
	Number	Total	Most in a single tornado	$500,000 and over in property loss	Lives lost	Property loss ($1,000)	Total reaching U.S. coast	Lives lost in United States
	268	**270**	**271**	**273**	**274**	**275**	**276**	**278**
1941	118	53	25	1	47	39 524	4	10
1940	124	65	18	2	60	40 467	3	51
1939	152	87	27	3	83	13 834	3	3
1938	213	183	32	6	180	101 098	4	600
1937	147	29	5	. . .	142	440 738	4	. . .
1936	151	552	216	6	142	282 549	7	9
1935	180	70	11	. . .	236	127 127	2	414
1934	147	47	6	3	88	10 362	5	17
1933	258	362	34	9	33	36 679	7	63
1932	151	394	37	2	11	10 295	5	. . .
1931	94	36	6	1	. . .	2 808	2	. . .
1930	192	179	41	6	14	15 850	1	. . .
1929	197	274	40	4	89	68 098	2	3
1928	203	92	14	7	15	44 611	3	1 836
1927	163	540	92	10	423	347 656	1	. . .
1926	111	144	23	. . .	16	23 468	4	269
1925	119	794	689	3	36	9 923	2	6
1924	130	376	85	12	. . .	. . .	3	2
1923	102	109	23	1	. . .	. . .	4	. . .
1922	108	135	16	5	. . .	. . .	1	. . .
1921	105	202	61	3	. . .	. . .	2	5
1920	87	498	87	10	. . .	. . .	3	2
1919	64	206	59	2	. . .	. . .	2	287
1918	81	135	36	5	. . .	. . .	2	34
1917	121	509	101	9	. . .	. . .	1	5
1916	90	150	30	1	. . .	. . .	8	107
1915	. . .	. . .	. . .	. . .	. . .	. . .	4	600
1914	. . .	. . .	. . .	. . .	. . .	. . .	1	(1)
1913	. . .	. . .	. . .	. . .	. . .	. . .	3	(1)
1912	. . .	. . .	. . .	. . .	. . .	. . .	4	12
1911	. . .	. . .	. . .	. . .	. . .	. . .	2	17
1910	. . .	. . .	. . .	. . .	. . .	. . .	2	13
1909	. . .	. . .	. . .	. . .	. . .	. . .	7	404
1908	. . .	. . .	. . .	. . .	. . .	. . .	2	(1)
1907	. . .	. . .	. . .	. . .	. . .	. . .	3	(1)
1906	. . .	. . .	. . .	. . .	. . .	. . .	6	285
1905	. . .	. . .	. . .	. . .	. . .	. . .	2	(1)
1904	. . .	. . .	. . .	. . .	. . .	. . .	3	(1)
1903	. . .	. . .	. . .	. . .	. . .	. . .	2	9
1902	. . .	. . .	. . .	. . .	. . .	. . .	3	(1)
1901	. . .	. . .	. . .	. . .	. . .	. . .	6	10
1900	. . .	. . .	. . .	. . .	. . .	. . .	3	. . .
1899	. . .	. . .	. . .	. . .	. . .	. . .	4	. . .
1898	. . .	. . .	. . .	. . .	. . .	. . .	6	. . .
1897	. . .	. . .	. . .	. . .	. . .	. . .	4	. . .
1896	. . .	. . .	. . .	. . .	. . .	. . .	4	. . .
1895	. . .	. . .	. . .	. . .	. . .	. . .	4	. . .
1894	. . .	. . .	. . .	. . .	. . .	. . .	3	. . .
1893	. . .	. . .	. . .	. . .	. . .	. . .	7	. . .
1892	. . .	. . .	. . .	. . .	. . .	. . .	3	. . .
1891	. . .	. . .	. . .	. . .	. . .	. . .	4	. . .
1890	. . .	. . .	. . .	. . .	. . .	. . .	. . .	. . .
1889	. . .	. . .	. . .	. . .	. . .	. . .	4	. . .
1888	. . .	. . .	. . .	. . .	. . .	. . .	6	. . .
1887	. . .	. . .	. . .	. . .	. . .	. . .	4	. . .
1886	. . .	. . .	. . .	. . .	. . .	. . .	7	. . .

1. Not reported, believed to be small number.

Series JJ-1 Municipal Solid Waste Generation, Recovery, and Disposal: 1980 to 1997

(In millions of tons (151.5 represents 151 500 000), except as indicated. Covers post-consumer residential and commercial solid wastes which comprise the major portion of typical municipal collections. Excludes mining, agricultural and industrial processing, demolition and construction wastes, sewage sludge, and junked autos and obsolete equipment wastes. Based on material-flows estimating procedure and wet weight as generated)

Item and material	1980	1990	1991	1992	1993	1994	1995	1996	1997
Waste generated	151.5	205.2	204.6	208.9	211.8	214.2	211.4	209.2	217.0
Per person per day (lb.)	3.7	4.5	4.4	4.5	4.5	4.5	4.4	4.3	4.4
Materials recovered	14.5	33.6	37.0	40.6	43.8	50.8	55.0	57.4	60.8
Per person per day (lb.)	0.35	0.7	0.8	0.9	0.9	1.1	1.1	1.2	1.2
Combustion for energy recovery	2.7	29.7	30.1	30.5	30.9	31.2	34.5	36.1	36.7
Per person per day (lb.)	0.06	0.7	0.7	0.7	0.7	0.7	0.7	0.7	0.8
Combustion without energy recovery.	11.0	2.2	2.2	2.2	1.6	1.3	1.0	. . .	. . .
Per person per day (lb.)	0.27	0.05	0.05	0.05	0.03	0.03	0.02	. . .	. . .
Landfill, other disposal	123.3	139.7	135.3	135.7	135.5	130.9	120.8	115.7	119.5
Per person per day (lb.)	2.97	3.1	2.9	2.9	2.9	2.8	2.5	2.4	2.4
Percent distribution of generation:									
Paper and paperboard	36.1	35.4	34.7	35.5	36.6	37.7	38.6	38.1	38.6
Glass	9.9	6.4	6.2	6.3	6.4	6.2	6.1	5.9	5.5
Metals	9.6	8.1	8.1	7.7	7.5	7.6	7.5	7.7	7.7
Plastics	5.2	8.3	8.7	8.8	9.0	9.0	8.9	9.4	9.9
Rubber and leather	2.8	2.8	2.9	2.8	2.7	2.9	2.9	3.0	3.0
Textiles	1.7	2.8	3.0	3.2	3.2	3.4	3.5	3.7	3.8
Wood	4.4	6.0	6.2	5.9	5.8	5.3	4.9	5.2	5.3
Food wastes	8.7	10.1	10.2	10.1	10.0	10.0	10.3	10.4	10.1
Yard wastes	18.2	17.1	17.1	16.8	15.7	14.7	14.0	13.3	12.8
Other wastes	3.4	3.0	3.1	2.9	3.0	3.2	3.3	3.3	3.3

Source: Franklin Associates, Ltd., Prairie Village, KS, Characterization of Municipal Solid Waste in the United States: 1998. Prepared for the U.S. Environmental Protection Agency.

Series JJ-2   National Air Pollutant Emissions: 1970 to 1997

(In thousands of tons, except as indicated. PM-10 = Particulate matter of less than 10 microns. Methodologies to estimate data for 1970 to 1984 period and 1985 to present emissions differ. Beginning with 1985, the estimates are based on a modified National Acid Precipitation Assessment Program inventory)

Year	PM-10	PM-10, fugitive dust[1]	Sulfur dioxide	Nitrogen dioxide	Volatile organic componds	Carbon monoxide	Lead
1970	13 190	. . .	31 161	21 639	30 817	128 761	220 869
1975	7 803	. . .	28 011	23 151	25 895	115 968	159 659
1980	7 287	. . .	25 905	24 875	26 167	116 702	74 153
1984	6 220	. . .	23 470	23 172	25 572	114 262	42 217
1985	4 695	40 889	23 230	23 488	24 227	115 644	22 890
1986	4 553	46 582	22 544	23 329	23 480	110 437	14 763
1987	4 492	38 041	22 308	22 806	23 193	108 879	7 681
1988	5 424	55 851	22 767	24 526	24 167	117 169	7 053
1989	4 590	48 650	22 907	24 057	22 383	104 447	5 468
1990	5 425	24 419	23 678	23 436	20 935	95 794	4 975
1991	5 329	24 122	23 056	23 520	21 063	97 790	4 168
1992	5 515	23 865	22 818	23 789	20 642	94 400	3 808
1993	3 680	24 196	22 476	24 046	20 830	94 526	3 911
1994	5 294	25 461	21 878	24 345	21 465	98 854	4 043
1995	4 306	22 454	19 189	23 768	20 558	89 151	3 924
1996	8 481	24 716	19 812	23 465	19 293	90 929	3 910
1997	8 428	25 153	20 369	23 582	19 214	87 451	3 915

1. Sources such as agricultural tilling, construction, mining and quarrying, paved roads, unpaved roads, and wind erosion.

Table 4-2. National Air Pollutant Emissions 1970 to 1991

SECTION K

AGRICULTURE

SECTION K
AGRICULTURE
Highlights

1 Annual agricultural statistics have been published by the Department of Agriculture since May 1, 1863. They are now compiled by the Statistical Reporting Service and the Economic Research Service. Since 1840, Census of Agriculture has been taken every 10 years. Beginning in 1925, a mid-decade Census of Agriculture has also been taken, based on mailed questionnaires. The first census was limited in scope to domestic animals, production of principal crops, and the value of wool and dairy products. Number of farms, acreage, and value of farmland were first included in 1850, farm tenure in 1880, and classification of farmland by use in 1925.

2 The definition of a farm has varied from census to census. Before 1954, the cutoff was three acres with annual output valued at $150 or more, but farms smaller than three acres were included if the value of output reached the same level. Between 1925 and 1945, farms included places of three or more acres on which there were agricultural operations and places of less than three acres with an annual output of $250 or more. Between 1910 and 1920, the definition was even more liberal, including farms smaller than three acres with less than $250 in output, if they required the continuous services of one person. In 1860 and 1900, there were no acreage or value limits. In 1870, 1880, and 1890, farms smaller than three acres were included only if the value of output exceeded $500. In the census of 1850, no acreage qualification was given, but there was a floor of $100 for value of products. In 1959 the acreage limit was raised to 10 and the value limit to $250 for smaller farms. For the 1974, 1978, 1982 and 1986 Censuses of Agriculture, a farm was defined as any place which $1,000 or more of agricultural products were produced and/or sold.

3 Estimates of farm population are equally problematic. Since 1960, farm population has been defined as all persons living in rural territory on places of 10 or more acres producing at least $50 worth of agricultural produce. The principal characteristics of farm population are its higher age profile, higher outflow, and higher birth rates. The classification of farm operator was first made in the Census of 1900. It designates a person who operates a farm as an owner, salaried employee, tenant, renter or sharecropper. Because of the decreasing importance of the cropper sys-

tem in the South, croppers have not been classified since 1959. Since 1880, farms have been classified by tenure, and since 1900, by race of the owner.

4 Estimates of farm income were started in 1924 on a crop-year basis. Only scattered data on farm income are available for the period before 1910. Willford I. King provides some data for census years from 1850 in *The Wealth and Income of the People of the United States*; The National Industrial Conference Board's *National Income in the United States, 1799 to 1938* provides decennial projections going back to 1800, and the Department of Agriculture's *Gross Farm Income and Indices of Farm Production and Prices in the United States, 1869-1937* extends back to 1869.

5 For many crops, estimates of acreage, production, and prices began in 1866 when the Department of Agriculture began making regular reports. These data are found in *Agricultural Statistics, Crop Production* and *Crop Values*. Data on livestock have been published since 1867, based on the decennial and quintennial Censuses of Agriculture.

6 Early development of the dairy industry is indicated by the export statistics of 1890, which showed the New England states, New York, and Pennsylvania producing considerable amounts of butter and cheese in excess of their consumption requirements. By the middle of the 19th Century, milk cows were distributed as far west as southern Wisconsin, eastern Iowa, western Missouri and Arkansas and the eastern third of Texas. By 1860, they had spread to the Pacific coast states. Before 1850, milk, butter and cheese were produced mainly on farms. Factory cheese production began shortly after 1850; the first condensery was established in 1856 and the first first commercial creamery in 1861. Unsweetened condensed milk was first produced in 1885.

7 The share of the farm sector in the economy has steadily declined as the United States moved into the postindustrial age. In 1998, agriculture contributed only 2% of the $7.9 trillion economy. Although the United States is in many ways the granary of the world, it employs fewer people in that sector today than it did in 1990. The number of

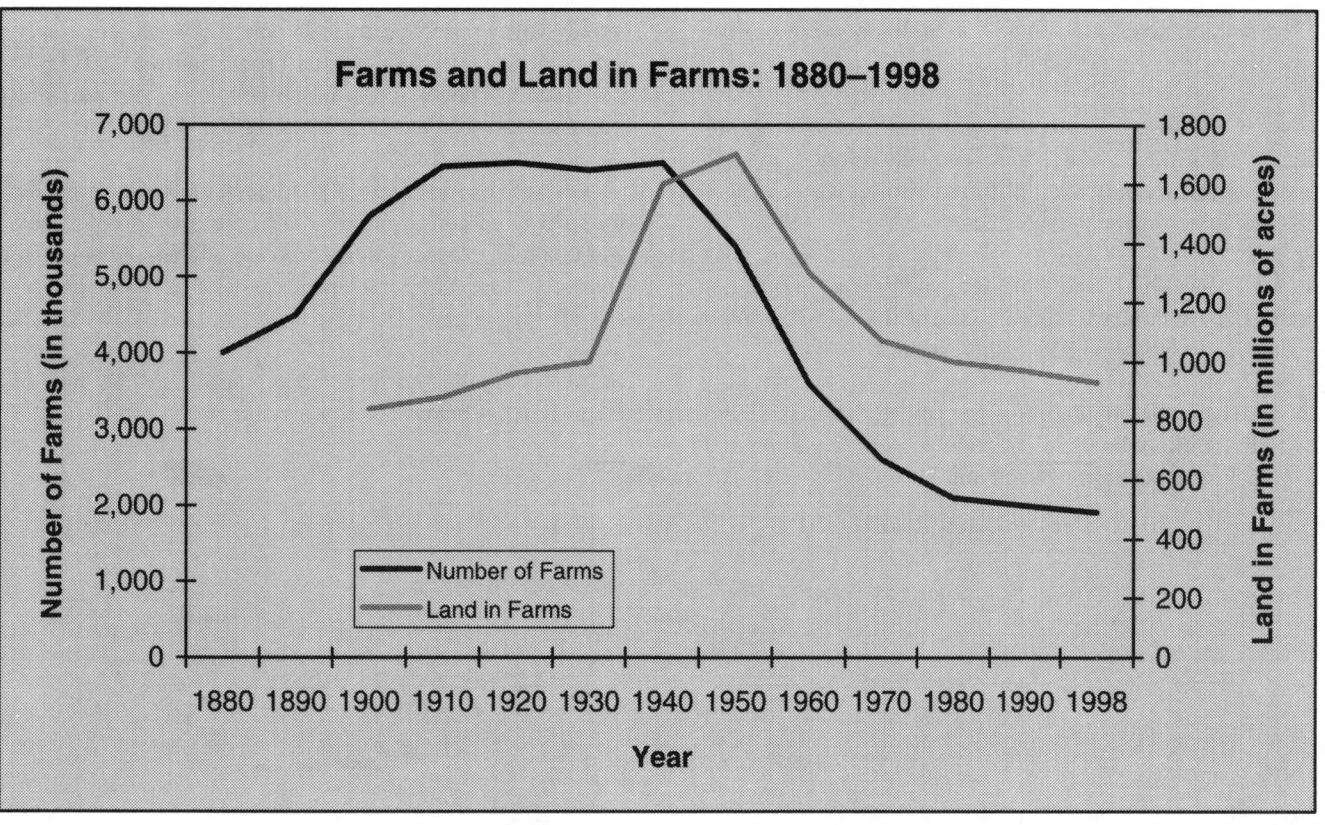

Farms and Land in Farms: 1880–1998

farms has declined from 2.088 million in 1987 to 1.912 million in 1997. Although the land in farms has declined from 964.5 million acres to 931.8 million acres, harvested cropland has increased from 282.2 million acres to 309.4 million acres. Gross farm output grew at a slower pace than other sectors of the economy, reaching $225.3 billion in 1997.

8 Texas has the most land in farms (131.3 million acres), followed by Montana (58.6 million acres), New Mexico (45.8 million acres), Kansas (46.1 million acres), and Nebraska (45.5 million acres). Arizona leads in the average size of farms with 5.173 acres. Texas leads in the gross value of agricultural output with $77.351 billion, followed by California with $69.768 billion and Illinois $56.475 billion. Texas and Nebraska lead in cattle, California and Wisconsin in dairy products, and Iowa and Illinois in corn and soybean.

9 Agriculture is one of the strongest export sectors and has always shown a positive trade balance. In 1998, agriculture had a trade balance of $14.8 billion with exports valued at $51.8 billion (8% of all exports) and imports of $37.1 billion. The United States accounts for 39.4% of the world production of corn and 50.8% of soybeans. In exports, it accounts for 28.5% of the wheat, 64.3% of corn, 66.3% of soybeans, and 33.5% of cotton.

10 By cash receipts from farm marketings, the five principal U.S. crops are corn, soybean, vegetables, wheat and

cotton, which together account for 60% of value (corn is considered a cereal, while only sweet corn is considered a vegetable). The most popular vegetable is the potato, followed by the tomato. The most popular fruit is the orange, followed by the grape.

11 The Balance Sheet of the Farming Sector was first attempted in 1944. In 1997, it showed assets of $1.089 trillion of which real estate accounted for $849 billion.

12 Foreign ownership of U. S. agricultural land has been steadily increasing. Of foreign owned acreage, 91.3% is in farms of 1,000 acres or more. The largest share of foreign agricultural holdings in the United States belongs to Canada, United Kingdom, France, Germany and Switzerland, in that order.

13 Irrigated lands are found primarily in the West and South. California led all states in this respect with 7.596 million acres under irrigation, or 24.8% of all cropland, followed by Idaho (23.1%), Florida (14.5%), and Nebraska (12.5%). Irrigation accounted for withdrawals of 134 billion gallons of water per day.

14 Farms that produce less than $10,000 annually account for 50.4% of the number of farms, but only 13.9% of the acreage and 1.5% of the value of sales. Farms that produce more than $10,000 in sales account for 49.6% of the number of farms, 86.1% of the acreage and 98.5% of sales. In 1998, there were 84,002 corporate farms owning

131.5 million acres and selling $56.9 billion worth of farm products.

15 California is the nation's principal fruit grower, producing 19 of the 31 major fruits and nuts. Florida, in second place grows only six. California also grows 12 of the 20 leading commercial vegetables.

16 Production of red meat and poultry was 78.6 billion pounds in 1998, of which beef accounted for 25.76 million pounds and poultry 33.358 million pounds.

17 The cattle population of the United States in 1999 was 98.5 million, hog and pig population 62.2 million and the chicken population 424 million.

18 Milk production in 1998 was 157.4 billion pounds valued at $24.52 billion. Butter production was 1.082 billion pounds, cheese 7.502 billion pounds, yogurt 1.616 billion pounds and ice cream 1.146 billion pounds.

19 New exotic styles of food have created a demand for spices and herbs, almost all of them imported. In 1998, 223,000 tons of spices were imported, including pepper, sesame seed, capsicum, cinnamon, cassia, ginger root and cumin.

20 Nearly 30% of farm workers are Hispanic, most of them living at below poverty levels.

Series K 1-16. Farm Population, Farms, Land in Farms and Value of Farm Property and Real Estate: 1850 to 1998

(Census figures in italics)

Year	Farm population — Total (1 000)[3] (col 1)	Farm population — Percent of total population[3] (col 2)	Number of farms (1 000) (col 4)	Land in farms — Total (1 000 acres) (col 5)	Land in farms — Average acreage per farm (acres)[1] (col 7)	Value of land and building (mil. dollars)[2] (col 11)
1998	...	...	2 192	954 000	435	...
1997	...	...	2 191	956 000	436	870
1996	...	...	2 191	959 000	438	...
1995	...	...	2 196	963 000	438	...
1994	...	...	2 198	966 000	440	...
1993	...	...	2 202	969 000	440	...
1992	...	1.9	2 108	979 000	464	687
1991	4 632	1.9	2 117	982 000	464	...
1990	4 591	1.9	2 140	987 000	461	658 451
1989	4 801	2.0	2 171	991 000	457	659 381
1988	4 951	2.1	2 197	995 000	453	626 909
1987	4 986	2.1	2 213	999 000	451	597 110
1986	5 226	2.2	2 250	1 005 000	447	597 600
1985	5 355	2.3	2 293	1 012 000	441	719 398
1984	5 754	2.5	2 334	1 018 000	436	793 700
1983	5 787	2.5	2 379	1 023 000	430	804 800
1982	5 628	2.5	2 407	1 028 000	427	843 300
1981	5 850	2.6	2 440	1 034 000	424	843 700
1980	6 051	2.8	2 440	1 039 000	426	763 285
1979	6 241	2.8	2 437	1 042 000	428	653 100
1978	6 501	3.0	2 436	1 045 000	429	553 000
1977	7 806	3.6	2 456	1 048 000	427	495 000
1976	8 253	3.8	2 497	1 054 000	422	416 800
1975	8 864	4.2	2 521	1 059 000	420	358 600
1974	9 264	4.4	2 795	1 084 000	388	326 600
1973	9 472	4.5	2 823	1 088 000	385	266 200
1972	9 610	4.6	2 860	1 092 000	382	238 700
1971	9 425	4.8	2 902	1 097 000	378	...
1970	9 712	4.8	2 954	1 102 769	373	208 214
1969	10 307	5.1	2 730	1 063 346	390	[3]206 751
1968	10 454	5.3	3 071	1 115 231	363	193 703
1967	10 875	5.5	3 162	1 123 456	355	182 456
1966	11 595	5.9	3 257	1 131 844	348	172 532
1965	12 363	6.4	3 356	1 139 597	340	160 942
1964	12 954	6.8	3 158	1 110 185	352	[3]159 932
1963	13 367	7.1	3 572	1 151 572	322	143 834
1962	14 313	7.7	3 685	1 161 383	314	137 956
1961	14 803	8.1	3 821	1 169 899	306	131 752
1950	23 048	15.3	[3]5 388	[3]1 161 420	[3]216	[3]75 462
1949	24 194	16.3	5 722	1 155 174	202	76 623
1948	24 383	16.7	5 803	1 151 784	199	73 664
1947	25 829	18.0	5 871	1 148 394	196	68 463
1946	25 403	18.0	5 926	1 145 003	193	61 046
1945	24 420	17.5	5 859	1 141 615	195	46 389
1944	24 815	18.0	6 003	1 125 461	187	46 200
1943	26 186	19.2	6 089	1 109 308	182	41 604
1942	28 914	21.5	6 202	1 093 155	176	37 547
1941	30 118	22.6	6 293	1 077 002	171	34 400
1940	30 547	23.2	[3]6 102	[3]1 065 114	[3]175	[3]33 758
1939	30 840	23.6	6 441	1 059 582	165	34 074
1938	30 980	23.9	6 527	1 058 315	162	35 170
1937	31 266	24.3	6 636	1 057 047	159	35 213
1936	31 737	24.8	6 739	1 055 780	157	34 260
1935	32 161	25.3	6 812	1 054 515	155	32 859
1934	32 305	25.6	6 776	1 040 963	154	32 201
1933	32 393	25.8	6 741	1 027 415	152	30 802
1932	31 388	25.2	6 687	1 013 865	152	37 180
1931	30 845	24.9	6 608	1 000 317	151	43 730
1930	30 529	24.9	[3]6 295	[3]991 112	[3]157	[3]47 994
1929	30 580	25.2	6 512	974 277	150	47 985
1928	30 548	25.4	6 470	961 787	149	47 532
1927	30 530	25.7	6 458	949 297	147	47 680
1926	30 979	26.5	6 462	936 806	145	149 000
1925	31 190	27.0	6 372	924 319	145	49 468
1924	31 177	27.5	3 480	930 628	144	50 487
1923	31 490	28.2	6 492	936 941	144	52 629
1922	32 109	29.3	6 500	943 253	145	54 050
1921	32 123	29.7	6 511	949 566	146	61 523
1920	31 974	30.1	[3]6 454	[3]958 677	[3]149	[3]66 446
1919	31 200	29.7	6 506	948 169	146	54 533
1918	31 950	30.6	6 488	940 461	145	49 980
1917	32 430	31.5	6 478	932 752	144	45 524
1916	32 530	32.0	6 463	925 044	143	42 264
1915	32 440	32.4	6 458	917 335	142	39 590
1914	32 320	32.8	6 447	909 627	141	39 579
1913	32 270	33.4	6 437	901 918	140	38 456

See footnotes at end of chart.

Series K 1-16. Farm Population, Farms, Land in Farms and Value of Farm Property and Real Estate: 1850 to 1998—Cont'd.

(Census figures in italics)

Year	Farm population — Total (1 000)[3]	Percent of total population[3]	Number of farms (1 000)	Land in farms[1] — Total (1 000 acres)	Average acreage per farm (acres)	Value of land and building (mil. dollars)[2]
	1	2	4	5	7	11
1960	*15 635	*8.7	3 962	1 176 946	297	130 169
1959	16 592	9.4	*3 711	*508	*303	[3]129 005
1958	17 128	9.9	4 233	1 184 944	280	115 934
1957	17 656	10.4	4 372	1 191 340	273	110 422
1956	18 712	11.2	4 514	1 197 080	265	102 934
1955	19 078	11.6	4 654	1 201 900	258	98 172
1954	19 019	11.8	4 782	1 158 192	242	97 583
1953	19 874	12.5	4 984	1 205 740	242	96 535
1952	21 748	13.9	5 198	1 204 930	232	95 078
1951	21 890	14.2	5 428	1 203 500	222	86 586
1912	32 210	33.9	6 430	894 209	139	37 298
1911	32 110	34.3	6 425	886 501	138	36 042
1910	32 077	34.9	[3]6 366	[3]881 431	[3]139	[3]34 885
1900	29 875	41.9	[3]5 740	[3]841 202	[3]147	[3]16 614
1890	24 771	42.3	4 565	623 219	137	13 279
1880	21 973	43.8	4 009	536 082	134	10 197
1870	...	...	2 660	407 735	153	7 444
1860	...	...	2 044	407 213	199	6 645
1850	...	...	1 449	293 561	203	3 272

* Except as indicated by footnote 3, denotes first year for which figures include Alaska and Hawaii. Excludes District of Columbia.
1. Intercensal estimates derived from straight-line interpolation. Excludes District of Columbia.
2. Census years as of date of enumeration. All other years as of March 1. Excludes District of Columbia.
3. Includes Alaska and Hawaii.

Series K 162-173. Farms and Land in Farms, by Size of Farm: 1880 to 1997

(Farms in thousands, land in farms in thousands of acres)

Year	Total	Under 10 acres	50-99 acres	1 000 acres and over	Year	Total	Under 10 acres	50-99 acres	1 000 acres and over
	162	163	168	173		162	163	168	173
Number of Farms					Land in Farms				
1997	1 912	154	295	176	1987	964 500	7 000	22 500	602 000
1996	. . .	. . .	. . .	. . .	1982	. . .	. . .	. . .	. . .
1995	. . .	. . .	. . .	. . .	1978	986 800	7 000	24 800	599 900
1994	. . .	. . .	. . .	. . .	1974	1 014 800	6 000	25 900	600 400
1993	. . .	. . .	. . .	. . .	1969	1 063 346	568	33 620	578 412
1992	1 925	166	283	173	1964	1 110 185	778	39 590	584 847
1991	. . .	. . .	. . .	. . .	1959	1 123 508	1 053	47 950	554 631
1987	2 088	183	311	169	1954[1]	1 158 192	2 260	62 725	531 482
1982	2 241	188	344	163	1950	[3]1 162 643	2 443	75 647	494 856
1978	2 258	151	356	161	1945[1]	1 141 615	2 805	83 206	460 006
1974	2 314	128	385	155	1940	1 065 114	2 679	93 336	365 772
1969	2 730	162	460	151	1935[1]	1 054 515	3 057	104 016	309 701
1964	3 158	183	542	145	1930	990 112	1 922	98 700	276 667
1959	3 711	244	658	136	1925[1]	924 319	2 097	101 906	224 472
1954[1]	4 782	484	864	130	1920	[4]958 677	1 600	105 631	220 636
1950	5 388	489	1 048	121	1910[1]	[4]881 431	. . .	103 121	167 082
1945[1]	5 859	595	1 157	113	1900	841 202	1 482	98 600	200 324
1940	6 102	509	1 291	101					
1935[1]	6 812	571	1 444	89					
1930	6 295	362	1 375	81					
1925[1]	6 372	379	1 421	63					
1920	6 454	[2]292	1 475	67					
1910[1]	6 362	335	1 438	50					
1900	5 740	268	1 366	47					
1890	4 565	150	1 122	32					
1880	4 009	139	1 033	29					

1. Excludes Alaska and Hawaii.
2. Excludes Alaska.
3. Based on sample; therefore differs from series K 5.
4 Total includes Alaska and Hawaii.

Series K 195-203. Farmers' Marketing and Purchasing Cooperatives Number, Memberships and Business: 1913 to 1998

(Fiscal-year data)

Year	Cooperatives listed			Estimated memberships (1,000)			Estimated business, net[1] (mil. dollars)		
	Total	Marketing and related	Farm Supply	Total	Marketing and related	Farm supply	Total	Marketing and related[2]	Farm Supply
	195	196	197	198	199	200	201	202	203
1998	3 651	2 304	1 347	3 353	1 579	1 774	104 667	80 115	24 551
1997	3 791	2 405	1 386	3 424	1 681	1 743	106 670	81 490	25 181
1996	3 884	2 481	1 403	3 664	1 869	1 795	106 182	82 529	23 653
1995	4 006	2 548	1 458	3 767	1 922	1 846	93 818	72 605	21 213
1994	4 174	2 678	1 496	3 986	2 050	1 936	89 309	68 531	20 779
1993	4 244	2 697	1 547	4 023	2 046	1 977	82 872	63 654	19 218
1992	4 315	2 697	1 618	4 072	2 051	2 020	79 284	60 771	18 513
1991	4 494	2 805	1 689	4 058	2 033	2 025	76 636	58 720	17 916
1990	4 663	2 946	1 717	4 119	2 114	2 006	77 266	60 178	17 088
1989	4 799	2 996	1 803	4 134	2 099	2 035	72 129	55 222	16 907
1988	4 937	3 101	1 836	4 195	2 053	2 142	66 430	51 006	15 424
1987	5 109	3 168	1 941	4 440	2 158	2 282	60 318	46 047	14 271
1986	5 369	3 398	1 971	4 600	2 290	2 310	58 395	43 300	15 095
1985	5 625	3 589	2 036	4 781	2 383	2 398	65 601	48 961	16 641
1984	5 782	3 646	2 136	4 842	2 445	2 397	73 047	56 078	16 969
1983	5 989	3 781	2 208	4 955	2 402	2 553	66 755	50 812	15 943
1982	6 125	3 826	2 299	5 136	2 469	2 666	69 150	52 788	16 362
1981	6 211	3 855	2 356	5 335	2 479	2 856	71 534	54 475	17 059
1980	6 293	3 924	2 369	5 379	2 574	2 804	66 254	50 120	16 134
1979	6 445	3 938	2 507	5 627	2 567	3 060	56 268	42 747	13 521
1978	6 600	4 050	2 550	5 695	2 632	3 063	47 305	36 253	11 052
1977	6 736	4 143	2 593	5 758	2 692	3 066	43 584	33 027	10 557
1976	7 533	4 804	2 731	5 906	2 850	3 056	40 104	30 692	9 412
1975	7 645	4 916	2 729	6 123	3 151	2 972	41 342	32 682	8 660
1974	7 755	4 977	2 778	6 106	3 133	2 973	35 366	27 602	7 764
1973	7 854	5 053	2 801	6 128	3 140	2 988	25 991	20 076	5 915
1972	7 797	5 016	2 781	6 147	3 156	2 991	21 665	16 925	4 740
1971	7 995	5 264	2 731	6 158	3 130	3 028	20 556	16 210	4 340
1970	7 790	5 015	2 775	6 355	3 133	3 222	19 080	15 207	3 873
1969	7 747	4 954	2 793	6 364	3 175	3 189	17 396	13 796	3 600
1968	7 940	5 105	2 835	6 445	3 259	3 186	17 034	13 513	3 521
1967	8 125	5 254	2 871	6 502	3 333	3 169	16 557	13 218	3 339
1966	8 329	5 380	2 949	6 826	3 672	3 154	15 608	12 523	3 085
1965	8 583	5 498	3 085	7 082	3 831	3 251	14 742	11 832	2 910
1964	8 847	5 621	3 226	7 080	3 655	3 425	14 354	11 522	2 832
1963	8 907	5 696	3 211	7 219	3 623	3 596	13 842	11 138	2 704
1962	9 039	5 833	3 206	7 099	3 464	3 635	13 024	10 463	2 561
1961	9 163	5 941	3 222	7 203	3 523	3 680	12 409	9 937	2 472
1960	9 345	6 048	3 297	7 273	3 673	3 600	12 036	9 628	2 408
1959*	9 658	6 271	3 387	7 559	3 915	3 644	11 747	9 376	2 371
1958	9 735	6 352	3 383	7 486	3 943	3 543	10 753	8 566	2 187
1957	9 891	6 518	3 373	7 673	4 184	3 489	10 379	8 233	2 146
1956	9 894	6 519	3 375	7 732	4 288	3 444	9 756	7 710	2 046
1955	9 903	6 557	3 346	7 604	4 281	3 323	9 642	7 620	2 022
1954	10 072	6 698	3 374	7 608	4 355	3 252	9 475	7 497	1 978
1953	10 128	6 750	3 378	7 475	4 336	3 139	9 521	7 508	2 013
1952	10 179	6 855	3 324	7 364	4 331	3 033	9 410	7 491	1 919
1951	10 064	6 781	3 283	7 091	4 212	2 879	8 147	6 462	1 685
1950	10 035	6 922	3 113	6 584	4 075	2 509	8 726	7 083	1 643
1949	10 075	6 993	3 082	6 384	3 973	2 411	9 320	7 700	1 620
1948	10 135	7 159	2 976	5 890	3 630	2 260	8 635	7 195	1 440
1947	10 125	7 268	2 857	5 436	3 378	2 058	7 116	6 005	1 111
1946	10 150	7 378	2 772	5 010	3 150	1 860	6 070	5 147	923
1945	10 150	7 400	2 750	4 505	2 895	1 610	5 645	4 835	810
1944	10 300	7 522	2 778	4 250	2 730	1 520	5 160	4 430	730
1943	10 450	7 708	2 742	3 850	2 580	1 270	3 780	3 180	600
1942	10 550	7 824	2 726	3 600	2 430	1 170	2 840	2 360	480
1941	10 600	7 943	2 657	3 400	2 420	980	2 280	1 911	369
1936	10 500	8 388	2 112	3 660	2 710	950	1 840	1 586	254
1931	11 950	10 362	1 588	3 000	2 608	392	2 400	2 185	215
1926	10 803	9 586	1 217	2 700	2 453	247	2 400	2 265	135
1921	7 374	6 476	898	. . .	. . .	. . .	1 256	1 198	58
1915	5 424	5 149	275	651	592	59	636	624	12
1913	3 099	2 988	111	. . .	. . .	. . .	310	304	6

* Denotes first year for which figures include Alaska and Hawaii.
1. Data for years to 1951 are not entirely comparable due to revisions in statistical procedure.
2. Includes services related to marketing or supply purchasing.

Series K 204-219. Balance Sheet of the Farming Sector: 1940 to 1998

(In billions of dollars. As of December 31 beginning 1980; before then January 1. Excludes Alaska and Hawaii)

	Assets							Claims		
		Physical								
			Non-real estate							
Year	Total	Real estate	Livestock and poultry[1]	Machinery and motor vehicles	Crops stored on and off farm[2]	Household equipment and furnishings	Investment in cooperatives	Total	Total liability	Proprietors' equities
	204	205	206	207	208	209	212	213	214	219
1998	1 064.5	822.0	62.0	88.6	30.1	. . .	31.8	1 064.3	172.9	891.4
1997	1 051.6	808.4	67.0	89.0	32.2	. . .	31.7	1 051.4	165.0	886.0
1996	1 003.9	769.5	60.0	89.0	31.7	. . .	31.3	1 003.9	156.0	848.0
1995	967.0	741.0	58.0	89.0	27.4	. . .	31.4	967.0	151.0	816.0
1994	935.5	704.0	68.0	88.0	23.3	. . .	30.7	935.5	147.0	789.0
1993	906.0	674.0	73.0	86.0	23.3	. . .	30.8	906.0	142.0	764.0
1992	870.0	643.0	71.0	88.6	24.0	. . .	29.4	870.0	139.0	731.0
1991	845.0	626.0	68.0	86.0	22.0	. . .	28.7	845.0	139.0	706.0
1990	841.5	620.0	69.1	86.3	23.2	46.3	27.6	841.0	138.0	704.0
1989	814.4	601.0	66.2	84.1	23.9	42.2	26.1	814.4	138.0	677.0
1988	801.1	595.5	62.2	81.2	23.3	37.0	25.1	801.1	137.0	661.7
1987	772.6	578.9	58.0	80.0	17.5	32.9	25.3	772.4	144.0	628.2
1986	724.4	542.3	47.8	81.5	18.3	28.7	24.4	724.4	157.0	567.0
1985	773.0	586.0	46.3	83.0	22.9	27.8	24.3	773.0	178.0	595.0
1980	983.0	783.0	80.0	86.9	32.8	19.4	19.3	983.0	167.0	816.0
1979	873.4	655.0	51.3	85.1	28.0	16.0	18.3	873.4	136.5	736.9
1978	736.3	554.7	31.9	76.9	24.4	13.8	15.2	736.3	119.3	617.0
1977	664.2	496.4	29.0	71.0	22.1	12.1	14.9	664.2	102.7	561.6
1976	576.3	418.1	29.4	64.0	21.3	11.7	13.4	576.3	90.8	485.5
1975	577.0	420.6	29.4	63.1	21.1	11.7	12.8	577.0	91.5	485.5
1974	478.5	327.7	42.4	44.2	22.0	12.3	10.8	478.5	74.1	404.4
1973	394.8	267.3	34.1	39.3	14.5	11.9	9.7	394.8	65.3	327.5
1972	351.8	239.6	27.3	35.6	11.8	10.8	8.8	351.8	59.1	292.7
1971	314.9	213.0	23.7	33.8	10.7	10.1	7.6	314.9	61.1	253.8
1970	305.8	207.1	23.5	31.8	10.9	9.7	7.2	305.8	58.1	247.7
1969	294.8	201.5	20.2	30.9	10.6	9.6	6.8	294.8	54.6	240.2
1968	280.1	192.0	18.8	29.5	9.6	9.0	6.5	280.1	50.4	229.7
1967	266.8	181.8	18.9	27.3	10.0	8.4	6.2	266.8	45.7	221.1
1966	253.8	172.2	17.6	25.8	9.7	8.6	5.9	253.8	41.6	212.2
1965	237.2	160.9	14.4	24.7	9.2	8.6	5.6	237.2	37.6	199.6
1964	229.2	152.1	15.8	23.9	9.8	8.8	5.4	229.2	34.9	194.3
1963	221.4	143.8	17.3	23.4	9.3	9.0	5.0	221.4	31.7	189.7
1962	212.8	138.0	16.4	22.5	8.8	9.1	4.8	212.8	28.7	184.1
1961	204.2	131.8	15.5	22.2	8.0	8.9	4.5	204.2	26.2	178.0
1960	203.5	130.2	15.2	22.7	7.7	9.6	4.2	203.5	24.8	178.7
1959	202.1	124.4	17.7	21.8	9.3	9.8	3.9	202.1	23.6	178.5
1958	185.8	115.9	13.9	20.2	7.6	9.9	3.7	185.8	20.4	165.4
1957	177.9	110.4	11.0	20.2	8.3	10.0	3.5	177.9	19.3	158.6
1956	169.6	102.9	10.6	19.3	8.4	10.5	3.2	169.6	18.8	150.8
1955	165.1	98.2	11.2	18.6	9.6	10.0	3.1	165.1	17.6	147.5
1954	161.2	95.0	11.7	18.4	9.2	9.9	2.9	161.2	16.9	144.3
1953	164.3	96.5	14.8	17.4	9.0	9.9	2.7	164.3	16.1	148.2
1952	167.0	95.1	19.5	16.7	8.8	10.3	2.5	167.0	14.7	152.3
1951	151.5	86.6	17.1	14.1	7.9	9.7	2.3	151.5	13.1	138.4
1950	132.5	75.3	12.9	12.2	7.6	8.6	2.1	132.5	12.4	120.1
1949	134.9	76.6	14.4	10.1	8.6	9.1	1.9	134.9	11.4	123.5
1948	127.9	73.7	13.3	7.4	9.0	8.5	1.7	127.9	9.3	118.6
1947	116.4	68.5	11.9	5.3	7.1	7.7	1.5	116.4	8.5	107.9
1946	103.5	61.0	9.7	5.4	6.3	6.1	1.4	103.5	8.0	95.5
1945	94.2	53.9	9.0	6.5	6.7	5.6	1.2	94.2	8.3	85.9
1944	84.6	48.2	9.7	5.4	6.1	5.3	1.1	84.6	8.9	75.7
1943	73.7	41.6	9.6	4.9	5.1	5.0	1.0	73.7	10.0	63.7
1942	62.9	37.5	7.1	4.0	3.8	4.9	.9	62.9	10.5	52.4
1941	55.0	34.4	5.3	3.3	3.0	4.2	.9	55.0	10.4	44.6
1940	52.9	33.6	5.1	3.1	2.7	4.2	.8	52.9	10.0	42.9

1. Beginning 1961, excludes horses and mules.
2. Includes crops held on farms and crops held off farms by farmers as security for CCC loans.

See footnotes at end of chart.

Series K 256-285.   Farm Income and Expenses: 1910 to 1998

(In millions of dollars, except as indicated)

Year	Net income of farm operators from farming	Realized gross farm income	Cash receipts from marketings			Government payments	Value of farm products consumed in farm households	Gross rental value of farm dwellings
			Total	Crops	Livestock and livestock products			
	259	264	265	266	267	268	269	270
1998	44 089	233 059	222 780	110 222	94 539	12 200	498	10 814
1997	48 622	238 669	227 500	111 075	96 535	7 500	530	10 092
1996	54 925	235 741	217 450	106 182	92 956	7 300	438	9 851
1995	37 212	210 743	205 800	100 954	87 101	7 300	506	9 410
1994	49 234	216 076	198 200	93 085	88 178	7 900	554	9 025
1993	44 533	204 758	200 300	87 447	90 445	13 400	594	8 070
1992	47 918	200 534	188 600	85 684	85 636	9 200	617	7 200
1991	38 600	191 950	184 359	82 077	85 786	8 200	642	7 155
1990	44 700	198 000	169 517	80 297	89 220	9 300	700	7 339
1989	45 300	191 900	179 900	76 800	84 100	10 887	700	7 164
1988	40 600	174 500	171 900	71 600	79 400	14 480	700	7 116
1987	39 700	168 400	165 100	65 800	76 000	16 747	700	4 900
1986	31 000	156 100	152 800	63 700	71 600	11 813	900	4 600
1985	28 600	161 200	157 900	74 300	69 800	7 704	900	4 700
1984	26 100	168 000	156 100	69 900	72 900	8 400	1 000	4 900
1983	14 200	153 900	151 100	67 200	69 600	9 300	1 000	12 600
1982	23 800	164 100	151 300	72 300	70 300	3 500	1 100	13 100
1981	26 900	166 300	146 000	72 500	69 200	1 900	1 200	12 600
1980	16 100	149 300	143 300	71 700	68 000	1 300	1 200	11 000
1979	27 400	150 700	135 100	62 300	69 200	1 400	1 300	9 300
1978	25 200	128 400	117 300	53 200	59 200	3 000	1 200	8 100
1977	19 900	108 800	99 300	48 600	47 600	1 800	1 200	7 300
1976	18 682	101 812	94 780	48 668	46 112	734	1 334	5 973
1975	25 500	100 600	90 700	45 800	43 100	800	1 100	5 400
1974	26 130	98 340	92 449	51 090	41 359	531	1 295	4 687
1973	33 349	98 911	87 068	41 132	45 936	2 607	1 104	3 913
1972	18 171	70 119	61 190	25 520	35 670	3 961	831	3 474
1971	14 194	60 603	52 859	22 276	30 583	3 145	732	3 226
1970	16 825	57 925	50 522	20 907	29 615	3 717	773	2 913
1969	16 856	55 550	48 143	19 541	28 602	3 794	750	2 863
1968	14 825	50 897	44 117	18 620	25 497	3 462	732	2 586
1967	14 882	48 998	42 693	18 434	24 259	3 079	745	2 481
1966	16 253	49 740	43 294	18 373	24 921	3 277	817	2 352
1965	14 987	44 926	39 350	17 392	21 958	2 463	813	2 300
1964	12 266	42 567	37 233	17 377	19 856	2 181	930	2 223
1963	13 206	42 271	37 398	17 435	19 963	1 696	1 016	2 161
1962	13 215	41 258	36 356	16 294	20 062	1 747	1 076	2 079
1961	12 987	39 771	35 089	15 660	19 429	1 493	1 176	2 012
1960	12 079	38 088	34 154	15 208	18 946	702	1 250	1 981
1959	11 454	37 468	33 511	14 648	18 863	682	1 318	1 957
1958	13 500	37 911	33 456	14 229	19 227	1 089	1 505	1 861
1957	11 325	34 001	29 714	12 338	17 376	1 016	1 484	1 787
1956	11 444	34 274	30 401	14 038	16 363	554	1 585	1 734
1955	11 464	33 138	29 490	13 523	15 967	229	1 678	1 741
1954	12 503	33 589	29 832	13 556	16 276	257	1 789	1 711
1953	13 088	34 986	31 001	14 078	16 923	213	2 007	1 765
1952	15 051	36 759	32 528	14 290	18 238	275	2 220	1 736
1951	15 987	37 055	32 858	13 239	19 619	286	2 304	1 607
1950	13 673	32 271	28 461	12 356	16 105	283	2 063	1 464
1949	12 780	31 628	27 805	12 396	15 409	185	2 230	1 408
1948	17 664	34 722	30 227	13 098	17 129	257	2 733	1 505
1947	15 354	34 146	29 620	13 093	16 527	314	2 765	1 447
1946	15 068	29 539	24 802	11 016	13 786	772	2 662	1 303
1945	12 312	25 813	21 663	9 655	12 008	742	2 356	1 052

Series K 256-285.   Farm Income and Expenses: 1910 to 1998—Cont'd.

(In millions of dollars, except as indicated)

Year	Net income of farm operators from farming	Realized gross farm income	Realized gross income from farming			Government payments	Value of farm products consumed in farm households	Gross rental value of farm dwellings
			Cash receipts from marketings					
			Total	Crops	Livestock and livestock products			
	259	264	265	266	267	268	269	270
1944	11 705	24 448	20 536	9 185	11 351	776	2 181	955
1943	11 736	23 397	19 620	8 127	11 493	645	2 253	879
1942	9 853	18 794	15 565	6 526	9 039	650	1 758	821
1941	6 490	13 851	11 111	4 619	6 492	544	1 429	767
1940	4 482	11 059	8 382	3 469	4 913	723	1 210	744
1939	4 414	10 585	7 872	3 336	4 536	763	1 209	741
1938	4 361	10 149	7 723	3 200	4 523	446	1 235	745
1937	6 005	11 367	8 864	3 924	4 940	336	1 434	733
1936	4 308	10 756	8 391	3 649	4 742	278	1 394	693
1935	5 278	9 696	7 120	2 977	4 143	573	1 320	683
1934	2 923	8 568	6 357	3 021	3 336	446	1 125	640
1933	2 555	7 107	5 332	2 486	2 846	131	1 030	614
1932	2 032	6 405	4 748	1 996	2 752	...	993	664
1931	3 344	8 421	6 381	2 540	3 841	...	1 265	775
1930	4 259	11 472	9 055	3 868	5 187	...	1 552	865
1929	6 152	13 938	11 312	5 130	6 182	...	1 713	913
1928	5 981	13 598	10 991	4 956	6 035	...	1 724	883
1927	5 699	13 336	10 733	5 125	5 608	...	1 725	878
1926	5 937	13 302	10 558	4 875	5 683	...	1 875	869
1925	6 734	13 716	11 021	5 545	5 476	...	1 827	868
1924	4 855	12 785	10 225	5 413	4 812	...	1 706	854
1923	5 068	12 167	9 545	4 865	4 680	...	1 772	850
1922	4 343	11 059	8 575	4 300	4 275	...	1 717	767
1921	3 370	10 573	8 058	4 106	3 952	...	1 746	769
1920	7 795	15 944	12 600	6 644	5 956	...	2 509	835
1919	9 078	17 918	14 538	7 603	6 935	...	2 556	824
1918	8 887	16 547	13 467	6 974	6 493	...	2 341	739
1917	8 304	13 410	10 736	5 642	5 094	...	2 003	671
1916	4 570	9 744	7 746	4 035	3 711	...	1 384	614
1915	4 307	8 147	6 392	3 263	3 129	...	1 192	563
1914	4 181	7 793	6 036	2 899	3 137	...	1 228	529
1913	3 728	7 978	6 238	3 077	3 161	...	1 222	518
1912	4 456	7 710	6 008	3 095	2 913	...	1 204	498
1911	3 371	7 213	5 584	2 905	2 679	...	1 165	464
1910	4 176	7 495	5 780	2 929	2 851	...	1 270	445

Series K 256-285. Farm Income and Expenses: 1910 to 1995—Cont'd.

(In millions of dollars, except as indicated)

		Expenses of agricultural production									
		Operating expenses (excluding hired labor)									
Year	Total	Feed purchased	Livestock purchased	Seed purchased[1]	Fertilizer and lime	Repairs	Miscellaneous[2]	Taxes on farm property	Wages paid hired farm labor[3]	Interest on farm mortgage debt	Net rent to nonfarm landlords
	271	273	274	275	276	277	278	280	281	282	283
1995	175 600	24 500	12 600	5 500	10 000	9 400	34 300	6 900	16 300	12 800	10 900
1994	167 600	22 600	13 200	5 400	9 200	9 200	31 200	6 700	15 300	11 900	11 500
1993	160 500	21 400	14 600	5 200	8 400	9 200	28 200	6 300	15 000	10 800	10 900
1992	152 500	20 100	13 600	4 900	8 300	8 500	24 900	6 200	14 000	11 200	10 800
1991	153 300	19 300	14 100	5 100	8 700	8 600	22 500	5 900	13 900	12 200	9 900
1990	144 300	20 700	14 700	3 600	7 100	7 300	18 800	5 600	12 500	14 500	8 200
1989	140 200	21 000	13 100	3 600	7 200	7 300	19 200	5 100	11 100	14 700	7 900
1988	133 900	20 400	12 800	3 400	6 900	6 800	17 200	4 800	10 400	14 700	7 400
1987	128 700	17 500	11 800	3 300	6 500	6 800	17 500	4 900	10 000	15 000	7 300
1986	125 100	17 500	9 800	3 200	6 800	6 400	15 500	4 600	9 500	16 500	6 100
1985	132 400	16 900	9 200	3 100	7 500	6 400	16 500	4 500	10 000	18 600	7 700
1984	141 900	19 400	9 500	3 400	8 400	6 400	16 900	4 300	9 400	21 100	8 100
1983	139 600	20 600	8 800	2 700	7 100	6 500	17 100	4 500	8 900	21 400	5 200
1982	140 300	18 600	9 700	3 200	8 000	6 400	15 500	4 000	9 400	21 800	5 500
1981	139 400	20 900	9 000	3 400	9 400	7 000	12 400	4 200	8 900	19 900	6 200
1980	133 100	21 000	10 700	3 200	9 500	7 100	11 800	3 900	9 300	16 300	6 100
1979	123 300	19 300	13 000	2 900	7 400	7 300	11 500	3 900	9 000	13 100	6 200
1978	103 200	16 000	10 200	2 600	6 600	6 600	9 500	3 600	8 300	10 200	4 000
1977	89 000	14 000	7 100	2 500	6 500	5 800	6 700	3 700	8 000	8 500	3 400
1976	83 130	14 370	5 871	2 537	6 141	9 096	12 586	3 607	7 037	3 852	4 220
1975	75 100	12 900	5 000	2 100	6 700	4 500	5 600	3 200	6 600	6 400	4 000
1974	72 210	14 513	5 131	2 082	5 808	6 659	10 178	3 096	6 036	3 044	5 100
1973	65 562	13 224	8 065	1 617	3 354	5 229	8 836	2 888	5 232	2 495	5 679
1972	52 809	8 397	6 668	1 115	2 690	4 708	8 312	2 815	4 594	2 132	3 491
1971	47 806	8 049	5 123	1 072	2 633	4 707	7 650	2 704	4 367	1 905	2 246
1970	41 091	7 189	4 345	829	2 222	5 031	5 132	2 957	3 643	1 717	1 302
1969	38 759	6 602	4 219	737	2 084	4 896	4 732	2 732	3 299	1 599	1 297
1968	36 209	5 894	3 676	672	2 130	4 831	4 451	2 515	3 047	1 477	1 307
1967	34 775	6 472	3 391	678	2 124	4 495	4 068	2 275	2 878	1 343	1 305
1966	33 406	6 324	3 498	626	1 952	4 227	3 854	2 108	2 889	1 205	1 442
1965	30 933	5 749	2 913	637	1 754	4 073	3 628	1 943	2 849	1 077	1 328
1964	29 481	5 715	2 420	566	1 701	3 940	3 515	1 833	2 913	952	1 223
1963	29 688	6 128	2 917	553	1 570	3 942	3 315	1 763	2 990	846	1 193
1962	28 639	5 575	3 106	521	1 474	3 944	3 135	1 684	2 961	759	1 132
1961	27 125	5 121	2 730	521	1 373	3 858	2 936	1 597	2 977	686	1 109
1960	26 352	4 923	2 502	510	1 315	3 966	2 829	1 502	2 923	628	1 010
1959	26 106	4 744	2 693	491	1 291	4 069	2 724	1 401	2 882	572	1 011
1958	25 236	4 541	2 702	508	1 206	3 921	2 517	1 306	2 842	521	1 161
1957	23 294	4 035	1 934	510	1 166	3 917	2 332	1 242	2 734	482	1 029
1956	22 374	3 894	1 610	519	1 166	3 785	2 307	1 178	2 641	442	1 109
1955	21 889	3 880	1 539	566	1 185	3 600	2 204	1 141	2 615	402	1 057
1954	21 577	3 906	1 563	525	1 209	3 506	2 077	1 084	2 596	371	1 159
1953	21 275	3 770	1 320	551	1 178	3 541	2 106	1 060	2 736	345	1 214
1952	22 630	4 331	1 918	594	1 184	3 506	2 142	1 033	2 857	318	1 421
1951	22 252	4 144	2 437	551	1 064	3 282	2 064	983	2 921	291	1 368
1950	19 410	3 283	2 004	518	975	2 975	1 763	919	2 811	264	1 233
1949	17 982	3 024	1 529	543	895	2 896	1 702	872	2 806	243	1 107
1948	18 790	3 996	1 589	581	826	2 818	1 580	806	2 990	232	1 370
1947	17 032	3 746	1 379	514	755	2 468	1 421	733	2 783	225	1 455
1946	14 500	3 022	1 170	428	683	2 054	1 185	617	2 532	219	1 401
1945	13 062	2 738	1 011	435	657	1 689	1 081	557	2 299	221	1 064
1944	12 333	2 427	812	440	576	1 608	1 071	499	2 202	230	1 043
1943	11 608	2 135	908	406	505	1 465	1 026	477	2 027	246	1 044
1942	10 040	1 625	877	301	417	1 289	937	466	1 631	272	890
1941	7 781	1 089	635	203	334	1 132	875	463	1 249	284	647

See footnotes at end of chart.

Series K 256-285. Farm Income and Expenses: 1910 to 1995—Cont'd.

(In millions of dollars, except as indicated)

		Expenses of agricultural production									
		Operating expenses (excluding hired labor)						Taxes on farm property	Wages paid hired farm labor[3]	Interest on farm mortgage debt	Net rent to nonfarm landlords
Year	Total	Feed purchased	Livestock purchased	Seed purchased[1]	Fertilizer and lime	Repairs	Miscellaneous[2]				
	271	273	274	275	276	277	278	280	281	282	283
1940	6 858	998	517	197	306	1 038	784	451	1 029	293	448
1939	6 266	732	465	169	273	959	759	456	988	305	379
1938	5 920	557	368	206	258	907	726	448	979	320	318
1937	6 178	805	332	194	279	879	732	452	988	341	380
1936	5 642	755	283	147	261	749	664	440	868	364	383
1935	5 116	528	312	108	188	717	647	434	775	396	347
1934	4 715	542	183	104	176	608	663	424	679	430	256
1933	4 358	422	199	65	120	554	669	438	617	472	158
1932	4 483	348	193	79	118	521	730	510	669	526	55
1931	5 537	448	253	117	202	635	834	589	914	553	136
1930	6 944	791	362	124	297	785	914	648	1 177	570	321
1929	7 664	919	504	122	300	886	998	651	1 300	582	486
1928	7 757	977	588	134	318	827	1 001	636	1 290	590	496
1927	7 462	892	465	140	267	787	986	620	1 302	593	520
1926	7 372	891	396	142	298	774	1 033	599	1 330	598	425
1925	7 347	988	382	136	299	711	1 021	589	1 267	612	470
1924	7 447	1 116	313	120	264	654	1 030	583	1 248	647	520
1923	7 054	819	304	111	263	637	1 027	590	1 251	679	430
1922	6 614	676	319	109	234	557	1 027	583	1 127	680	368
1921	6 638	710	202	123	249	550	1 052	586	1 170	653	304
1920	8 837	1 254	422	178	390	695	1 263	556	1 790	574	504
1919	8 331	1 097	567	138	358	615	1 143	454	1 515	476	928
1918	7 507	1 106	522	132	311	536	1 024	361	1 337	417	859
1917	6 092	614	414	122	232	464	863	339	1 127	379	825
1916	4 836	517	260	76	193	395	715	304	904	341	534
1915	4 167	411	207	62	165	343	639	284	815	314	403
1914	4 029	414	215	62	195	297	648	261	804	296	355
1913	3 974	406	250	62	175	289	634	257	804	276	340
1912	3 833	419	217	74	161	278	606	225	789	252	343
1911	3 582	350	188	65	168	251	588	215	758	225	331
1910	3 531	426	199	56	152	251	558	195	755	203	320

1. Includes bulbs plants and trees.
2. Includes interest on non-real estate debt, marketing, charges, net insurance premiums (crop, fire, wind and hail) and miscellaneous supplies and services purchased.
3. Includes value of perquisites.

Series K 358-360. Consumer Expenditures, Farm Value and Marketing Bill for All Farm Food Products Purchased by Domestic Civilian Consumers: 1913 to 1997

(In billions of dollars)

Year	Consumer expenditures[1]	Farm value	Marketing bill	Year	Consumer expenditures[1]	Farm value	Marketing bill	Year	Consumer expenditures[1]	Farm value	Marketing bill
	358	**359**	**360**		**358**	**359**	**360**		**358**	**359**	**360**
1997	561.1	120.0	441.1	1967	84.8	27.3	57.5	1939[4]	13.4	5.2	8.2
1996	546.7	122.2	424.5	1966	82.8	28.1	54.7	1938	13.4	5.2	8.2
1995	529.5	113.8	415.7	1965	77.6	25.5	52.1	1937	14.2	6.0	8.2
1994	512.2	109.6	402.6	1964	47.6	23.4	51.2	1936	14.3	5.8	8.5
1993	489.2	109.6	379.6	1963	71.5	22.6	48.9	1935	13.8	5.2	8.6
1992	474.5	105.1	369.4	1962	69.3	22.4	46.9	1935[4]	12.9	5.0	7.9
1991	465.1	101.6	363.5	1961	67.1	22.0	45.1	1934	12.5	4.3	8.2
1990	440.8	106.6	334.2	1960	65.9	21.7	44.2	1933	10.9	3.6	7.3
1989	419.4	103.8	315.6	1959	63.1	20.9	42.2	1932	10.6	3.4	7.2
1988	398.8	96.8	301.9	1958	61.0	21.5	39.5	1931	13.1	4.7	8.4
1987	375.5	90.4	285.1	1957	58.3	21.4	37.9	1930	16.2	6.3	9.9
1986	359.6	88.8	270.8	1956	55.5	19.2	36.3	1929[4]	18.0	7.5	10.5
1985	345.4	86.4	259.0	1955	53.1	18.7	34.4	1929	17.1	7.2	9.9
1984	332.0	89.8	242.2	1954	51.1	18.8	32.3	1928	16.3	6.9	9.4
1983	315.0	85.3	229.7	1953	51.0	19.5	31.5	1927	16.2	9.7	9.5
1982	298.9	81.4	217.5	1952	50.9	20.4	30.5	1926	16.4	7.0	9.4
1981	287.7	83.2	204.5	1951	49.2	20.5	28.7	1925	15.7	6.8	8.9
1980	264.4	81.7	182.7	1950	44.0	18.0	26.0	1924	14.5	5.9	8.6
1979	245.2	79.2	166.0	1949	43.4	17.4	26.0	1923	14.0	5.6	8.4
1978	216.9	69.5	147.4	1948	44.8	19.9	24.9	1922	12.9	5.2	7.7
1977	189.3	57.3	132.0	1947[2]	41.9	19.3	22.6	1921	12.6	5.1	7.5
1976	180.9	57.5	123.4	1947[3]	36.5	18.7	17.8	1920	16.5	7.4	9.1
1975	167.0	55.6	111.4	1946	30.8	15.7	15.6	1919	15.2	7.6	7.6
1974	152.3	55.8	96.5	1945	24.4	12.6	12.5	1918	13.2	6.9	6.3
1973	136.7	51.0	85.7	1944	22.5	11.6	11.4	1917	12.4	6.1	6.3
1972	120.3	39.3	81.0	1943	22.3	11.4	11.1	1916	9.5	4.4	5.1
1971	. . .	. . .	. . .	1942	19.8	9.3	10.5	1915	8.0	3.6	4.4
1970	101.6	33.1	68.5	1941	16.3	7.1	9.2	1914	7.9	3.6	4.3
1969	95.3	32.1	63.2	1940	14.1	5.6	8.5	1913	7.4	3.6	3.9
1968	90.1	29.0	61.1	1939	15.3	5.4	9.9				

1. For 1913-1947, consumer expenditures for farm food eaten away from home are based on retail food store prices.
2. Comparable with later years. Beginning 1947, a new series based on 1958 benchmark estimate.
3. Comparable with earlier years.
4. Revised figures according to the commodity flow method; comparable to 1947-1970 data based on 1958 benchmark estimate.

Series K 496-501. Acreages of Harvested Crops, by Use, and Indexes of Cropland Used for Crops and Crop Production Per Acre: 1910 to 1998

(Excludes Alaska and Hawaii)

Year	Acreages of harvested crops, by use (million acres)			Year	Acreages of harvested crops, by use (million acres)			Year	Acreages of harvested crops, by use (million acres)		
	Total	Export products	Products for domestic use		Total	Export products	Products for domestic use		Total	Export products	Products for domestic use
	496	497	499		496	497	499		496	497	499
1998	344	...	...	1968	303	54	249	1938	349	22	279
1997	349	...	...	1967	308	69	239	1937	347	29	266
1996	346	...	...	1966	295	69	226	1936	323	18	251
1995	332	...	...	1965	298	76	222	1935	345	20	269
1994	339	...	...	1964	301	74	227	1934	304	20	227
1993	330	...	...	1963	300	77	223	1933	340	28	253
1992	337	...	...	1962	295	66	229	1932	371	35	276
1991	337	...	...	1961	303	67	¹232	1931	365	36	267
1990	322	83	239	1960	324	64	255	1930	369	39	265
1989	318	103	215	1959	324	61	257	1929	365	44	254
1988	297	118	179	1958	324	44	273	1928	361	49	242
1987	302	106	196	1957	324	48	268	1927	358	49	236
1986	325	96	229	1956	324	60	255	1926	359	54	229
1985	342	81	263	1955	340	47	283	1925	360	44	238
1984	348	96	252	1954	346	37	298	1924	355	53	221
1983	306	124	182	1953	348	31	304	1923	354	47	223
1982	362	113	249	1952	349	36	298	1922	355	50	219
1981	366	129	237	1951	344	59	267	1921	359	66	206
1980	352	137	215	1950	345	50	276	1920	360	60	210
1979	348	115	232	1949	360	45	293	1919	364	56	217
1978	337	113	224	1948	356	52	280	1918	362	62	208
1977	344	112	232	1947	355	42	287	1917	349	44	213
1976	337	97	240	1946	352	45	278	1916	340	53	195
1975	336	100	236	1945	354	42	280	1915	340	49	198
1974	328	99	229	1944	362	25	301	1914	334	57	185
1973	321	96	225	1943	357	21	299	1913	333	43	198
1972	294	91	203	1942	348	13	296	1912	329	42	196
1971	305	62	243	1941	344	12	292	1911	330	40	200
1970	297	72	225	1940	341	8	290	1910	325	37	200
1969	294	61	233	1939	331	23	263				

1. 1961 and earlier, does not include feed for horses and mules.

Series K 502-516.   Corn and Wheat Acreage and Production: 1839 to 1999

(Census figures in italics)

Year	Corn for all purposes Acreage harvested	Production	All wheat for grain Acreage harvested	Production	Year	Corn for all purposes Acreage harvested	Production	All wheat for grain Acreage harvested	Production
	502	503	506	507		502	503	506	507
	1,000 acres	Million bushels	1,000 acres	Million bushels		1,000 acres	Million bushels	1,000 acres	Million bushels
1999	70 500	9 437	53 900	2 302	1930	101 465	2 080	62 637	887
1998	72 600	9 759	59 000	2 550	*1929*	*97 742*	*¹2 131*	*62 000*	*801*
1997	72 700	9 207	62 800	2 481	1929	97 805	2 516	63 392	824
1996	72 600	9 233	62 800	2 277	1928	100 336	2 666	59 226	914
1995	65 200	7 400	61 000	2 183	1927	98 357	2 616	59 628	875
1994	72 500	10 050	61 800	2 321	1925	101 331	2 798	52 443	669
1993	62 900	6 337	62 700	2 396	1926	99 452	2 547	56 616	832
1992	72 100	9 477	62 800	2 467	*1924*	*98 402*	*¹1 824*	*50 862*	*801*
1991	68 800	7 475	57 800	1 980	1924	100 420	2 223	52 463	842
1990	67 000	7 934	69 300	2 730	1923	101 123	2 875	56 920	759
1989	69 700	7 525	62 200	2 037	1922	100 345	2 707	61 397	847
1988	58 300	4 929	53 200	1 812	1921	103 155	2 928	64 566	819
1987	59 500	7 131	55 900	2 108	1920	101 359	3 071	62 358	843
1986	69 200	8 253	60 700	2 087	*1919*	*¹87 778*	*¹2 346*	*73 099*	*945*
1985	75 200	8 877	64 700	2 425	1919	98 145	2 679	73 700	952
1984	71 900	7 674	66 900	2 595	1918	102 195	2 441	61 068	904
1983	51 500	4 175	61 400	2 420	1917	110 893	2 908	46 787	620
1982	72 700	8 235	77 900	2 765	1916	100 561	2 425	53 510	635
1981	74 500	8 119	80 600	2 785	1915	100 623	2 829	60 303	1 009
1980	73 000	6 639	71 100	2 381	1914	97 796	2 524	55 613	897
1979	72 400	7 939	62 454	2 134	1913	100 206	2 273	52 012	751
1978	70 275	7 087	56 942	1 798	1912	101 451	2 948	48 413	720
1977	70 872	6 425	66 461	2 036	1911	101 393	2 475	49 894	618
1976	71 300	6 266	70 771	2 142	1910	102.267	2 853	45 793	625
1975	67 505	5 829	69 391	2 122	*1909*	*¹98 386*	*¹2 552*	*44 263*	*683*
1974	65 405	4 701	65 368	1 782	1909	100 200	2 611	44 262	684
1973	62 143	5 671	54 148	1 711	1908	95 285	2 567	45 102	643
1972	57 421	5 573	47 284	1 545	1907	96 094	2 614	44 139	629
1971	64 047	5 641	47 674	1 618	1906	95 624	3 033	46 230	741
1970	66 222	¹4 099	44 141	1 370	1905	95 746	2 954	46 306	706
1969²	*60 402*	*¹4 357*	*45 373*	*1 328*	1904	95 228	2 687	43 155	556
1969	63 360	¹4 583	47 577	1 460	1903	93 555	2 515	48 456	663
1968	64 603	¹4 393	55 262	1 576	1902	97 177	2 774	46 244	687
1967	69 978	¹4 760	58 771	1 522	1901	94 422	1 716	50 847	763
1966	65 828	¹4 117	49 867	1 312	1900	94 852	2 662	49 203	599
1965	64 565	¹4 084	49 560	1 316	*1899*	*¹94 917*	*¹2 666*	*52 589*	*659*
1964	*63 515*	*¹3 361*	*47 958*	*1 218*	1899	94 591	2 646	52 342	655
1964	65 388	¹3 484	49 762	1 283	1898	87 784	2 351	50 506	768
1963	68 317	¹4 019	45 506	1 147	1897	89 965	2 288	43 413	606
1962	64 474	¹3 606	43 688	1 092	1896	89 074	2 671	40 828	523
1961	65 405	¹3 598	51 571	1 232	1895	90 479	2 535	38 998	542
1960	80 678	4 314	51 879	1 355	1894	80 069	1 615	40 167	542
1959³	*79 616*	*¹3 697*	*49 567*	*1 056*	1893	79 832	1 900	40 790	506
1959	81 902	4 197	51 716	1 118	1892	76 914	1 897	42 979	612
1958	72 224	3 725	53 047	1 457	1891	78 855	2 336	41 090	678
1957	71 864	3 400	43 754	956	1890	74 785	1 650	36 686	449
1956	75 247	3 445	49 768	1 005	*1889*	*¹72 088*	*¹2 122*	*33 580*	*468*
1955	79 367	3 220	47 290	926	1889	77 656	2 294	36 098	504
1954	*78 123*	*¹2 613*	*51 362*	*909*	1888	77 474	2 251	34 969	424
1954	80 186	3 058	54 356	984	1887	73 296	1 605	36 873	491
1953	80 459	3 210	67 840	1 173	1886	73 911	1 783	36 312	514
1952	80 940	3 292	71 130	1 306	1885	71 854	2 058	35 095	400
1951	80 729	2 926	61 873	988	1884	68 834	1 948	38 485	571
1950	81 818	3 075	61 607	1 019	1883	68 168	1 652	35 587	439
1949	*83 337*	*¹2 778*	*71 163*	*1 007*	1882	66 157	1 755	36 496	552
1949	85 595	3 238	75 910	1 098	1881	63 026	1 245	36 795	406

See footnotes at end of chart.

Series K 502-516. Corn and Wheat Acreage and Production: 1839 to 1999—Cont'd.

(Census figures in italics)

Year	Corn for all purposes		All wheat for grain		Year	Corn for all purposes		All wheat for grain	
	Acreage harvested	Production	Acreage harvested	Production		Acreage harvested	Production	Acreage harvested	Production
	502	**503**	**506**	**507**		**502**	**503**	**506**	**507**
	1,000 acres	*Million bushels*	*1,000 acres*	*Million bushels*		*1,000 acres*	*Million bushels*	*1,000 acres*	*Million bushels*
1948	84 778	3 605	72 418	1 295	1880	62 545	1 707	38 096	502
1947	82 888	2 355	74 519	1 359	*1879*	*¹62 369*	*¹1 755*	*35 430*	*459*
1946	87 585	3 217	67 105	1 152	1879	62 229	1 752	35 347	459
1945	87 625	2 869	65 167	1 108	1878	59 659	1 565	33 379	449
1944	*92 259*	*¹2 788*	*58 286*	*1 033*	1877	58 799	1 516	27 963	396
1944	94 014	3 088	59 749	1 060	1876	55 277	1 478	28 283	309
1943	92 060	2 966	51 355	844	1875	52 446	1 450	28 382	314
1942	87 367	3 069	49 773	969	1874	47 640	1 059	27 310	356
1941	85 357	2 652	55 935	942	1873	44 084	1 008	24 866	322
1940	86 429	2 457	53 273	815	1872	43 584	1 279	22 962	271
1939	*86 991*	*¹2 311*	*50 527*	*709*	1871	42 002	1 142	22 230	272
1939	88 279	2 581	52 669	741	1870	38 388	1 125	20 945	254
1938	92 160	2 549	69 197	920	*1869*	. . .	*¹761*	. . .	*288*
1937	93 930	2 643	64 169	874	1869	35 833	782	21 194	290
1936	93 154	1 506	49 125	630	1868	35 116	920	19 140	246
1935	95 974	2 299	51 305	628	1867	32 116	794	16 738	211
1934	*87 476*	*¹1 169*	*41 943*	*513*	1866	30 017	731	15 408	170
1934	92 193	1 449	43 347	526	*1859*	. . .	*¹839*	. . .	*173*
1933	105 918	2 398	49 424	552	*1849*	. . .	*¹592*	. . .	*100*
1932	110 577	2 930	57 851	756	*1839*	. . .	*¹378*	. . .	*85*
1931	106 866	2 576	57 704	942					

1. Corn harvested for grain only.
2. Not comparable with previous censuses; data for farms with farm product sales of $2 500 or more.
3. Beginning 1959, census data include Alaska and Hawaii.

Series K 517-531. Soybeans and Sorghum Grain Acreage and Production: 1909 to 1999

(Census figures in italics)

Year	Soybeans for beans Acreage harvested 520	Production 521	Sorghum grain Acreage harvested 523	Production 524	Year	Soybeans for beans Acreage harvested 520	Production 521	Sorghum grain Acreage harvested 523	Production 524
	1,000 acres	*Million bushels*	*1,000 acres*	*Million bushels*		*1,000 acres*	*Million bushels*	*1,000 acres*	*Million bushels*
1999	72 476	2 642	8 544	595	1951	13 615	283.8	8 544	163
1998	70 400	2 741	7 723	519	1950	13 807	299.2	10 346	234
1997	69 100	2 689	9 160	633	*1949*	*10 148*	*212.4*	*6 602*	*148*
1996	63 300	2 380	11 800	795	1949	10 482	234.2	6 325	141
1995	61 600	2 174	8 300	459	1948	10 682	227.2	7 317	131
1994	60 800	2 514	8 900	645	1947	11 411	186.5	5 480	93
1993	57 300	1 871	8 900	534	1946	9 932	203.4	6 669	106
1992	58 200	2 190	12 100	875	1945	10 740	193.2	6 324	96
1991	58 000	1 986	9 800	585	*1944*	*. . .*	*187.7*	*9 386*	*185*
1990	56 500	1 926	9 100	573	1944	10 245	192.1	9 061	178
1989	59 500	1 924	11 100	615	1943	10 397	190.1	6 889	110
1988	57 400	1 549	9 000	577	1942	9 894	187.5	5 991	110
1987	57 200	1 938	10 500	731	1941	5 889	107.2	6 015	114
1986	59 400	2 007	13 900	942	1940	4 807	78.0	6 374	86
1985	61 600	2 099	16 800	1 120	*1939*	*4 274*	*87.6*	*4 760*	*53*
1984	66 100	1 861	15 400	866	1939	4 315	90.1	4 693	52
1983	62 500	1 636	10 000	488	1938	3 035	61.9	4 699	67
1982	69 400	2 190	14 100	835	1937	2 586	46.2	4 915	70
1981	66 200	1 989	13 700	876	1936	2 359	33.7	2 793	30
1980	67 800	1 798	12 500	579	1935	2 915	48.9	4 597	58
1979	70 566	2 268	12 901	809	*1934*	*. . .*	*23.0*	*2 396*	*19*
1978	63 343	1 870	13 561	748	1934	1 556	23.2	2 370	19
1977	57 612	1 762	14 092	793	1933	1 044	13.5	4 354	54
1976	49 358	1 288	14 723	720	1932	1 001	15.2	4 400	66
1975	53 579	1 547	15 355	753	1931	1 141	17.3	4 443	72
1974	51 341	1 216	13 809	623	1930	1 074	13.9	3 477	38
1973	55 667	1 548	15 706	923	*1929*	*. . .*	*8.7*	*3 522*	*49*
1972	45 698	1 271	13 368	809	1929	708	9.4	3 523	50
1971	42 701	1 176	16 301	876	1928	579	7.9	4 115	77
1970	42 056	1 123.7	13 568	684	1927	568	6.9	4 260	81
1969[1]	*38 550*	*1 041.5*	*13 437*	*730*	1926	466	5.2	4 211	71
1969	40 982	1 126.3	. . .	. . .	1925	415	4.9	3 917	57
1968	41 104	1 103.1	13 890	731	*1924*	*. . .*	*. . .*	*3 519*	*61*
1967	39 767	976.1	14 988	755	1924	448	4.9	3 526	59
1966	36 546	928.5	12 813	715	1923	. . .	. . .	4 204	62
1965	34 449	845.6	13 029	673	1922	. . .	. . .	3 369	50
1964	*29 844*	*669.7*	*11 742*	*490*	1921	. . .	. . .	3 700	71
1964	30 793	700.9	11 168	463	1920	. . .	. . .	4 027	88
1963	28 615	699.2	13 326	585	*1919*	*113*	*1.1*	*3 630*	*74*
1962	27 608	669.2	11 571	510	1919	. . .	. . .	3 619	72
1961	27 003	678.6	10 985	480	1918	. . .	. . .	. . .	. . .
1960	23 655	555.1	15 601	620	1917	. . .	. . .	. . .	. . .
1959[2]	*22 080*	*515.6*	*15 406*	*555*	1916	. . .	. . .	. . .	. . .
1959	22 631	532.9	14 561	508	1915	. . .	. . .	. . .	. . .
1958	23 993	580.3	16 524	581	1914	. . .	. . .	. . .	. . .
1957	20 857	483.4	19 682	568	1913	. . .	. . .	. . .	. . .
1956	20 620	449.3	9 209	205	1912	. . .	. . .	. . .	. . .
1955	18 620	373.7	12 891	243	1911	. . .	. . .	. . .	. . .
1954	*16 444*	*324.1*	*11 718*	*236*	1910	. . .	. . .	. . .	. . .
1954	17 047	341.1	11 304	224	*1909*	*2*	*(Z)*	*. . .*	*. . .*
1953	*14 829*	*269.2*	*6 295*	*116*					
1952	14 435	298.8	5 326	91					

Z Less than 50 000.
1. Not comparable with previous census; data for farms with farm products sales of $2 500 or more in 1969.
2. Beginning 1959, census data include Alaska and Hawaii.

Series K 532-537. Irish Potatoes and Sweet Potatoes—Acreage, Production and Price: 1849 to 1998

(Census figures in italics. Prices are those received by growers)

Year	Irish potatoes — Acreage harvested 532 (1 000 acres)	Irish potatoes — Production 533 (1 000 cwt.)	Year	Irish potatoes — Acreage harvested 532 (1 000 acres)	Irish potatoes — Production 533 (1 000 cwt.)	Year	Irish potatoes — Acreage harvested 532 (1 000 acres)	Irish potatoes — Production 533 (1 000 cwt.)
1998	1 394	477 760	1951	1 348	195 776	1909	3 675	234 100
1997	1 354	46 700	1950	1 698	259 112	1908	3 417	183 148
1996	1 426	499 260	*1949*	*1 515*	*219 917*	1907	3 333	199 875
1995	1 400	444 000	1949	1 755	240 950	1906	3 254	204 876
1994	1 400	467 000	1948	1 981	269 937	1905	3 263	180 421
1993	1 300	429 000	1947	2 001	233 391	1904	3 208	209 695
1992	1 300	425 000	1946	2 527	292 389	1903	3 079	165 770
1991	1 400	418 000	1945	2 664	251 639	1902	3 077	177 941
1990	1 400	402 000	*1944*	*2 537*	*213 928*	1901	2 950	124 447
1989	1 300	370 000	1944	2 780	230 356	1900	2 997	155 813
1988	1 300	356 000	1943	3 239	275 332	*1899*	*2 939*	*163 997*
1987	1 300	389 000	1942	2 671	221 339	1899	2 939	163 541
1986	1 200	362 000	1941	2 693	213 418	1898	2 877	144 209
1985	1 300	407 000	1940	2 832	226 152	1897	2 809	118 904
1984	...	...	*1939*	*2 645*	*190 999*	1896	2 968	157 641
1983	1 243	334 000	1939	2 813	205 423	1895	3 090	181 269
1982	1 267	355 000	1938	2 870	213 509	1894	2 869	118 614
1981	1 232	341 000	1937	3 055	225 869	1893	2 614	122 534
1980	1 155	301 000	1936	2 960	194 373	1892	2 519	114 120
1979	1 270	342 000	1935	3 469	227 337	1891	2 633	158 170
1978	1 371	365 000	*1934*	*3 582*	*242 052*	1890	2 557	102 065
1977	1 359	355 000	1934	3 599	243 889	*1889*	*2 601*	*130 528*
1976	1 375	358 000	1933	3 423	205 922	1889	2 603	130 760
1975	1 264	322 000	1932	3 568	224 815	1888	2 604	143 785
1974	1 392	342 000	1931	3 490	230 590	1887	2 466	95 769
1973	1 307	300 000	1930	3 139	206 290	1886	2 393	117 045
1972	1 254	296 000	*1929*	*3 945*	*193 480*	1885	2 335	118 286
1971	1 391	319 000	1929	3 030	200 035	1884	2 307	124 789
1970	1 420	325 588	1928	3 499	256 349	1883	2 373	136 253
1969[1]	*1 261*	*273 644*	1927	3 182	221 786	1882	2 216	118 390
1969	1 413	311 903	1926	2 811	192 964	1881	2 036	76 544
1968	1 376	293 984	1925	2 810	177 880	1880	1 968	99 095
1967	1 457	305 334	*1924*	*2 911*	*211 477*	*1879*	*(2)*	*101 675*
1966	1 464	306 902	1924	3 106	230 500	1879	1 961	101 663
1965	1 384	291 169	1923	3 378	219 814	1878	1 879	86 018
1964	*1 174*	*221 874*	1922	3 901	249 224	1877	1 878	104 221
1964	1 272	241 076	1921	3 598	195 187	1876	1 783	73 567
1963	1 323	271 158	1920	3 301	221 342	1875	1 789	107 887
1962	1 347	264 810	*1919*	*3 253*	*174 293*	1874	1 654	78 668
1961	1 480	293 166	1919	3 300	178 405	1873	1 543	77 698
1960	1 386	257 104	1918	3 597	207 668	1872	1 559	80 144
1959[3]	*1 200*	*224 140*	1917	3 801	239 192	1871	1 496	80 833
1959	1 331	245 272	1916	3 274	162 233	1870	1 443	64 725
1958	1 428	266 897	1915	3 433	202 056	*1869*	*...*	*86 002*
1957	1 359	242 522	1914	3 417	220 949	1869	1 479	86 759
1956	1 371	245 792	1913	3 477	199 468	1868	1 400	72 175
1955	1 405	224 696	1912	3 505	243 729	1867	1 289	59 798
1954	*1 211*	*204 113*	1911	3 532	181 628	1866	1 225	66 969
1954	1 413	219 547	1910	3 644	205 231	*1859*	*...*	*66 660*
1953	1 536	231 679	*1909*	*3 669*	*233 527*	*1849*	*...*	*39 479*
1952	1 397	211 095						

1. Not comparable with previous censuses; data for farms with farm products sales of $2 500 or more.
2. Acreage reporting incomplete: 13 states reported 911 325 acres of Irish potatoes; 23 states 444 817 acres of sweet potatoes.
3. Beginning 1959, census data include Alaska and Hawaii.

Series K 538-549.   Rice Acreage and Production: 1895 to 1999

(Census figures in italics)

Year	Rice Acreage harvested 538 (1 000 acres)	Rice Production 539 (1 000 cwt.)	Year	Rice Acreage harvested 538 (1 000 acres)	Rice Production 539 (1 000 cwt.)	Year	Rice Acreage harvested 538 (1 000 acres)	Rice Production 539 (1 000 cwt.)	Year	Rice Acreage harvested 538 (1 000 acres)	Rice Production 539 (1 000 cwt.)
1999	3 600	210 458	*1969[1]*	*2 131*	*91 544*	*1944*	*1 394*	*29 270*	*1919*	*917*	*16 195*
1998	3 300	188 000	1969	2 128	90 838	1944	1 480	30 974	1919	1 083	19 310
1997	3 100	183 000	1968	2 353	104 075	1943	1 472	29 264	1918	1 101	17 999
1996	2 800	172 000	1967	1 970	89 379	1942	1 457	29 082	1917	953	15 621
1995	3 100	174 000	1966	1 967	85 020	1941	1 214	23 095	1916	843	17 795
1994	3 300	198 000	1965	1 793	76 281	1940	1 069	24 495	1915	740	11 748
1993	2 800	156 000	*1964*	*1 815*	*75 824*	*1939*	*852*	*19 732*	1914	646	10 565
1992	3 100	180 000	1964	1 786	73 166	1939	1 045	24 328	1913	722	10 894
1991	2 800	155 000	1963	1 771	70 269	1938	1 076	23 628	1912	643	10 665
1990	2 800	156 000	1962	1 773	66 045	1937	1 099	24 040	1911	636	10 198
1989	2 700	155 000	1961	1 589	54 198	1936	981	22 419	1910	666	11 129
1988	2 900	160 000	1960	1 595	54 591	1935	817	17 753	*1909*	*620*	*10 246*
1987	2 300	130 000	*1959[2]*	*1 617*	*54 403*	*1934*	*706*	*14 831*	1909	662	10 614
1986	2 400	134 000	1959	1 586	53 647	1934	812	17 571	1908	596	10 079
1985	2 500	135 000	1958	1 415	44 760	1933	798	16 943	1907	563	9 338
1984	2 800	139 000	1957	1 340	42 935	1932	874	18 729	1906	505	7 999
1983	2 200	100 000	1956	1 569	49 459	1931	965	20 076	1905	457	7 217
1982	3 300	154 000	1955	1 826	55 902	1930	966	20 218	1904	574	8 647
1981	3 800	183 000	*1954*	*2 498*	*65 284*	*1929*	*743*	*15 137*	1903	547	8 590
1980	3 300	146 000	1954	2 550	64 193	1929	860	17 790	1902	545	6 541
1979	2 869	132 000	1953	2 159	52 834	1928	972	19 725	1901	423	5 702
1978	2 970	133 000	1952	1 997	48 193	1927	1 027	20 024	1900	361	4 407
1977	2 249	99 000	1951	1 996	46 089	1926	1 016	18 911	*1899*	*351*	*4 386*
1976	2 480	116 000	1950	1 637	38 820	1925	853	14 866	1899	338	4 029
1975	2 818	128 000	*1949*	*1 819*	*40 251*	*1924*	*744*	*13 286*	1898	314	3 737
1974	2 531	112 000	1949	1 858	40 769	1924	838	14 689	1897	290	3 084
1973	2 170	93 000	1948	1 804	38 275	1923	874	14 957	1896	270	2 340
1972	1 818	85 000	1947	1 708	35 217	1922	1 053	18 748	1895	292	3 341
1971	1 818	86 000	1946	1 582	32 497	1921	990	17 673			
1970	1 815	83 754	1945	1 499	30 668	1920	1 299	23 242			

1. Not comparable with previous censuses; data for farms with farm products sales of $2 500 or more.
2. Beginning 1959, census data include Alaska and Hawaii.

Series K 550-563. Hay, Cotton, and Tobacco Acreage and Production: 1790 to 1999

(Census figures in italics)

	Hay [1]		Cotton		Tobacco			Hay [1]		Cotton		Tobacco	
Year	Acreage harvested	Production	Acreage harvested	Production	Acreage harvested	Production	Year	Acreage harvested	Production	Acreage harvested	Production	Acreage harvested	Production
	550	551	553	554	561	562		550	551	553	554	561	562
	1 000 acres	*Million tons*	*1 000 acres*	*1 000 bales*	*1 000 acres*	*Million pounds*		*1 000 acres*	*Million tons*	*1 000 acres*	*1 000 bales*	*1 000 acres*	*Million pounds*
1999	63 800	159	13 400	16 960	644	1 275	1944	*73 402*	*95*	*18 962*	*11 838*	...	...
1998	60 000	151	10 700	13 900	717	1 500	1944	77 639	103	19 617	12 230	1 750	1 951
1997	61 100	153	13 400	18 800	836	1 787	1943	77 004	103	21 610	11 427	1 458	1 406
1996	61 200	150	12 900	18 900	733	1 519	1942	74 827	108	22 602	12 817	1 377	1 408
1995	59 800	154	16 000	17 900	663	1 270	1941	73 136	96	22 236	10 744	1 307	1 262
1994	58 800	150	13 300	19 700	671	1 583	1940	73 058	96	23 861	12 566	1 410	1 460
1993	59 700	147	12 800	16 100	746	1 614	1939	*61 229*	*74*	*22 811*	*11 481*	...	...
1992	59 900	146	11 100	16 200	784	1 722	1939	69 243	87	23 805	11 817	2 000	1 881
1991	61 834	152	12 900	17 000	763	1 664	1938	68 175	91	24 248	11 943	1 601	1 386
1990	61 000	146	11 700	15 500	733	1 626	1936	67 732	70	29 755	12 399	1 441	1 163
1989	65 100	126	9 500	12 200	700	1 367	1937	66 001	83	33 623	18 946	1 753	1 569
1988	60 100	148	11 900	15 400	600	1 370	1935	68 550	90	27 509	10 638	1 439	1 302
1987	62 400	156	10 000	14 800	800	1 189	1934	*63 156*	*54*	*26 754*	*9 472*	...	...
1986	62 300	155	8 500	9 700	600	1 166	1934	65 387	60	26 866	9 636	1 273	[3] 1 085
1985	60 400	149	10 200	13 400	700	1 512	1933	68 439	75	29 383	13 047	1 739	1 372
1984	61 400	151	10 400	13 000	800	1 728	1932	70 412	84	35 891	13 003	1 405	1 018
1983	59 700	141	7 300	7 800	800	1 429	1931	68 160	75	38 704	17 097	1 988	1 565
1982	59 800	149	9 700	12 000	900	1 994	1930	67 947	75	42 444	13 932	2 124	1 648
1981	59 600	143	13 800	15 600	1 000	2 064	1929	*67 823*	*82*	*43 228*	*14 574*	...	...
1980	58 900	131	13 200	11 100	900	1 786	1929	69 531	87	43 232	14 825	1 980	1 533
1979	61 666	148	12 831	14 600	827	1 527	1928	67 185	84	42 434	14 477	1 864	1 373
1978	61 515	142	12 370	10 900	948	2 024	1927	72 131	98	38 342	12 956	1 556	1 211
1977	60 658	131	13 275	14 400	958	1 913	1926	68 795	76	44 608	17 978	1 628	1 289
1976	60 311	120	10 914	10 600	1 045	2 136	1925	70 105	79	44 386	16 105	1 751	1 376
1975	61 324	132	8 796	8 300	1 086	2 182	1924	*74 692*	*88*	*39 204*	*13 683*	...	...
1974	60 195	126	12 547	11 500	963	1 990	1924	74 459	91	39 501	13 630	1 702	1 245
1973	61 828	134	11 970	13 000	887	1 742	1923	73 545	89	35 550	10 140	1 855	1 518
1972	59 821	129	12 984	14 000	842	1 749	1922	75 432	95	31 361	9 755	1 616	1 254
1971	61 405	129	11 471	10 000	838	1 705	1921	73 070	85	28 678	7 945	1 340	1 005
1970	62 911	127	11 160	10 166	899	1 908	1920	73 033	92	34 408	13 429	1 935	1 509
1969 [2]	*53 204*	*112*	*11 496*	*10 360*	...	...	1919	*70 936*	*89*	*33 740*	*11 376*	...	...
1969	62 053	128	11 055	9 990	920	1 804	1919	73 156	92	32 906	11 141	1 959	1 444
1968	62 693	126	10 160	10 925	880	1 710	1918	71 909	82	35 038	12 018	1 720	1 445
1967	64 667	126	7 997	7 443	960	1 968	1917	71 017	85	32 245	11 284	1 616	1 326
1966	65 140	121	9 552	9 555	974	1 887	1916	72 918	99	33 071	11 448	1 483	1 207
1965	67 684	126	13 615	14 951	977	1 855	1915	69 518	91	29 951	11 172	1 419	1 157
1964	*65 295*	*116*	*13 917*	*14 734*	...	...	*1914*	*67 337*	*83*	*35 615*	*16 112*	*1 258*	*1 037*
1964	67 375	119	14 055	15 144	1 078	2 228	1913	66 873	77	35 206	14 153	1 284	992
1963	66 428	118	14 212	15 294	1 176	2 344	1912	67 395	86	32 557	13 703	1 335	1 117
1962	67 563	122	15 569	14 827	1 224	2 315	1911	65 885	65	34 916	15 694	1 133	941
1961	67 376	117	15 634	14 318	1 174	2 061	1910	68 332	75	31 508	11 609	1 398	1 142
1960	67 313	118	15 309	14 272	1 142	1 944	1909	*68 227*	*87*	*32 044*	*10 649*	...	...
1959 [3]	*63 549*	*107*	*14 649*	*13 914*	...	...	1909	68 703	87	30 555	10 005	1 292	1 054
1959	66 266	111	15 117	14 558	1 153	1 796	1908	51 487	72	31 091	13 241	1 009	836
1958	70 547	120	11 849	11 512	1 078	1 736	1907	49 833	66	30 729	11 106	1 042	886
1957	71 912	120	13 558	10 964	1 122	1 668	1906	48 650	60	31 404	13 274	1 123	973
1956	72 292	108	15 615	13 310	1 364	2 176	1905	48 333	67	27 753	10 576	1 103	939
1955	74 956	113	16 928	14 721	1 495	2 193	1904	47 480	66	30 377	13 438	1 026	857
1954	*69 940*	*104*	*18 858*	*12 921*	...	...	*1903*	*46 650*	*64*	*27 762*	*9 851*	*1 212*	*976*
1954	73 721	108	19 251	13 697	1 668	2 244	1902	44 716	59	27 561	10 630	1 189	960
1953	74 997	108	24 341	16 465	1 633	2 059	1901	43 555	53	27 050	9 508	1 098	886
1952	75 147	106	25 921	15 139	1 772	2 256	1900	42 488	50	24 886	10 124	1 086	852
1951	75 063	110	26 949	15 149	1 780	2 332	1899	*61 691*	*79*	*24 275*	*9 535*	...	...
1950	75 150	104	17 843	10 014	1 599	2 030	1899	43 395	54	24 163	9 346	1 102	870
1949	*67 470*	*89*	*26 599*	*15 419*	...	...	1898	*43 083*	*60*	*24 715*	*11 278*	*1 116*	*909*
1949	72 821	97	27 439	16 128	1 623	1 969	1897	42 396	56	25 131	10 899	978	703
1948	71 817	96	22 911	14 877	1 554	1 980	1896	40 971	51	23 230	8 533	1 038	760
1947	74 666	101	21 330	11 860	1 852	2 107							
1946	73 741	100	17 584	8 640	1 960	1 315							
1945	76 697	107	17 029	9 015	1 821	1 991							

See footnotes at end of chart.

Series K 550-563. Hay, Cotton, and Tobacco Acreage and Production: 1790 to 1999—Cont'd.
(Census figures in italics)

Year	Hay¹ Acreage harvested	Hay¹ Production	Cotton Acreage harvested	Cotton Production	Tobacco Acreage harvested	Tobacco Production	Year	Hay Production	Cotton Production	Year	Cotton Production	Year	Cotton production
	550	551	553	554	561	562		551	554		554		562
	1 000 acres	Million tons	1 000 acres	1 000 bales	1 000 acres	Million pounds		Million tons	1 000 bales		1 000 bales		1 000 bales
1893	42 083	53	20 256	7 493	1 096	767	1865	...	2 094	1835	1 062	1810	178
1892	41 328	53	18 869	6 700	1 039	757	1864	...	299	1834	962	1809	172
1891	40 350	51	21 503	9 035	955	747	1863	...	449	1833	931	1808	157
1890	39 613	51	20 937	8 653	851	648	1862	...	1 597	1832	816	1807	167
1889	*52 949*	*67*	*20 175*	*7 473*	*...*	*...*	1861	...	4 491	1831	805	1806	167
1889	38 867	50	20 191	7 473	758	525	1860	...	3 841	1830	732	1805	146
1888	37 411	47	19 520	6 938	891	661	*1859*	*19*	*5 387*	1829	764	1804	136
1887	36 480	42	18 793	7 047	722	469	1859	...	4 508	1828	680	1803	126
1886	35 771	45	18 370	6 505	848	609	1858	...	3 758	1827	565	1802	115
1885	34 507	43	17 922	6 576	815	611	1857	...	3 012	1826	732	1801	100
1884	33 448	43	16 849	5 682	754	580	1856	...	2 874	1825	533	1800	73
1883	32 077	44	16 295	5 713	750	509	1855	...	3 221	1824	450	1799	42
1882	30 373	39	15 638	6 949	744	579	1854	...	2 708	1823	387	1798	31
1881	28 619	35	16 483	5 456	698	426	1853	...	2 766	1822	439	1797	23
1880	27 011	33	15 921	6 606	650	469	1852	...	3 130	1821	377	1796	21
1879	*30 631*	*35*	*14 480*	*5 755*	*...*	*...*	1851	...	2 799	1820	335	1795	17
1879	26 641	31	14 474	5 756	633	472	1850	...	2 136	1819	349	1794	17
1878	25 627	33	13 539	5 074	651	455	*1849*	*14*	*2 469*	1818	262	1793	10
1877	24 749	30	12 606	4 773	789	621	1849	...	2 066	1817	272	1792	6
1876	23 986	29	11 747	4 474	625	466	1848	...	2 615	1816	259	1791	4
1875	22 662	26	11 348	4 631	746	609	1847	...	2 128	1815	209	1790	3
1874	21 861	25	10 753	3 836	378	217	1846	...	1 604	1814	146		
1873	21 597	24	10 998	4 168	513	382	1845	...	1 806	1813	157		
1872	21 081	24	9 580	3 933	492	385	1844	...	2 079	1812	157		
1871	20 270	22	8 285	2 974	420	327	1843	...	1 750	1811	167		
1870	19 719	21	9 238	4 352	424	345	1842	...	2 035				
1869	*...*	*27*	*...*	*3 012*	*...*	*...*	1841	...	1 398				
1869	19 310	25	7 751	3 011	395	264	1840	...	1 348				
1868	19 568	23	6 973	2 366	369	286	*1839*	*10*	*1 976*				
1867	18 641	23	7 864	2 520	370	260	1839	...	1 654				
1866	18 250	21	7 666	2 097	394	316	1838	...	1 093				
							1837	...	1 428				
							1836	...	1 129				

1. All hay, 1909-1970; tame hay prior to 1909.
2. Annual production estimates prior to 1962 are shown in 500-pound gross-weight bales; beginning 1962, 480-pound net-weight bales. Figures for census years are shown in running bales, and are not comparable with annual production estimates; the net weight per running bale was 383 pounds in 1839; 496.1 pounds in 1944; 482.0 pounds in 1954; 501.1 pounds in 1964; and 503.6 pounds in 1969.
3. Includes 26.5 million pounds that were not utilized due to Agricultural Adjustment Act.

Series K 564-582. Livestock—Number, Value Per Head, Production and Price: 1867 to 1999

(Census figures in italics. All figures are as of January 1 except for 1870, 1880, 1890, 1900 (June 1); 1910 (April 15); 1930, 1940, 1950 (April 1); 1954, 1959 (October-November); 1964 (November-December); and 1969 (December 31))

	Number on farms and value per head							Number on farms and value per head					
	All cattle		Hogs		Stock sheep			All cattle		Hogs		Stock sheep	
Year	Number	Value per head	Number	Value per head	Number	Value per head	Year	Number	Value per head	Number	Value per head	Number	Value per head
	564	**565**	**566**	**567**	**568**	**569**		**564**	**565**	**566**	**567**	**568**	**569**
	1 000 head	Dollars	1 000 head	Dollars	1 000 head	Dollars		1 000 head	Dollars	1 000 head	Dollars	1 000 head	Dollars
1999	99 100	594.0	59 407	72.0	7 200	88.0	1930 [2]	*63 896*	...	*56 288*	...	*56 975*	...
1998	99 700	603.0	61 200	82.0	7 800	102.0	1930	61 003	56.36	55 705	13.45	45 577	9.00
1997	101 700	525.0	56 100	94.00	8 000	96.00	1929	58 877	58.47	59 042	12.93	43 481	10.71
1996	103 500	503.0	58 200	70.70	8 500	86.50	1928	57 322	50.63	61 873	13.17	40 689	10.36
1995	102 800	615.0	59 700	53.20	9 000	74.70	1927	58 178	39.98	55 496	17.19	38 067	9.79
1994	101 000	659.0	57 900	74.90	9 800	69.90	1926	60 576	36.80	52 105	15.66	35 719	10.53
1993	99 200	649.0	58 200	71.20	10 200	70.60	1925	*60 760*	...	*50 854*	...	*35 590*	...
1992	97 600	630.0	57 600	68.80	10 800	61.20	1925	63 373	31.72	55 770	13.15	34 469	9.63
1991	96 400	653.0	54 500	85.40	11 200	65.60	1924	65 996	32.11	66 576	10.30	32 859	7.94
1990	95 800	614.0	53 800	79.10	11 400	79.30	1923	67 546	31.66	69 304	12.29	32 597	7.50
1989	98 100	580.0	55 500	66.30	10 900	82.40	1922	68 795	30.39	59 749	10.58	33 365	4.79
1988	99 600	523.0	54 400	76.00	10 900	90.00	1921	68 714	39.07	58 942	13.63	35 426	6.34
1987	102 100	407.0	51 000	91.90	10 600	75.70	1920	*66 640*	...	*59 346*	...	*35 034*	...
1986	105 400	391.0	52 300	69.90	10 100	67.40	1920	70 400	52.64	60 159	20.00	37 328	10.59
1985	109 600	402.0	54 100	75.00	10 700	61.10	1919	72 094	54.65	64 326	22.18	38 360	11.49
1984	113 400	396.0	56 700	58.80	11 600	52.10	1918	73 040	50.01	62 931	19.69	36 704	11.76
1983	115 000	406.0	54 500	89.90	12 100	51.80	1917	70 979	43.34	57 578	11.82	35 246	7.06
1982	115 400	415.0	58 700	70.10	13 000	57.10	1916	67 438	40.10	60 596	8.48	36 260	5.10
1981	114 400	473.0	64 500	74.70	12 900	69.90	1915	63 849	40.67	56 600	9.95	36 263	4.39
1980	111 200	502.0	67 300	56.00	12 700	78.20	1914	59 461	38.97	52 853	10.51	38 059	3.91
1979	110 900	403.0	60 400	83.20	12 400	72.10	1913	56 592	33.07	53 747	9.89	40 544	3.87
1978	116 400	232.0	56 500	63.20	12 400	51.60	1912	55 675	27.68	55 394	7.99	42 972	3.42
1977	122 800	206.0	54 900	47.00	12 700	42.50	1911	57 225	27.22	55 366	9.33	46 055	3.93
1976	128 000	190.0	49 300	80.40	13 300	37.30	1910	*61 804*	...	*58 186*	...	*52 448*	...
1975	132 000	159.0	54 700	44.90	14 500	30.50	1910	58 993	24.54	48 072	9.05	46 939	4.06
1974	127 800	293.0	60 600	60.40	16 300	32.80	1909	60 774	21.99	52 508	6.45	47 098	3.42
1973	121 500	252.0	59 000	42.00	17 600	26.70	1908	61 989	20.92	58 388	5.99	45 095	3.87
1972	117 900	208.0	62 400	28.50	18 700	22.90	1907	63 754	20.91	56 543	7.54	43 460	3.81
1971	114 600	184.0	67 300	23.50	19 700	23.60	1906	65 009	19.65	53 633	6.07	41 965	3.51
1970	112 303	180.0	¹ 56 655	¹ 39.00	17 411	24.70	1905	66 111	18.39	53 176	5.89	40 410	2.77
1969	*106 381*	...	*55 455*	...	*21 611*	...	1904	*66 442*	*19.69*	*51 623*	*6.08*	*41 908*	*2.55*
1969	109 885	158.0	¹ 60 632	¹ 30.501	8 332	22.00	1903	66 004	21.55	48 100	7.69	44 436	2.62
1968	109 152	149.0	58 777	28.30	19 105	19.20	1902	64 418	21.48	17 858	6.95	46 196	2.62
1967	108 645	149.0	53 249	33.20	20 661	19.70	1901	62 576	22.68	50 681	6.08	46 126	2.96
1966	108 862	133.0	47 414	45.20	21 456	19.70	1900	*67 719*	...	*62 868*	...	*61 504*	...
1965	109 000	113.0	50 792	24.50	21 843	15.80	1900	59 739	26.50	51 055	5.36	46 065	2.97
1964	*105 558*	...	*54 080*	...	*25 472*	...	1899	*55 927*	*24.53*	*51 558*	*4.67*	*42 688*	*2.80*
1964	107 903	127.0	56 757	23.40	23 455	14.00	1898	52 868	22.79	53 282	4.70	40 097	2.51
1963	104 488	142.0	57 993	27.50	25 122	14.40	1897	50 447	18.62	51 232	4.36	38 891	1.84
1962	100 369	140.0	56 619	27.50	26 719	12.90	1896	49 205	17.86	49 154	4.50	39 609	1.71
1961 *	97 700	134.0	55 560	27.20	28 320	14.60	1895	49 510	16.56	47 628	5.09	41 827	1.57
1960	96 236	137.0	59 026	18.50	28 849	16.50	1894	51 713	16.84	46 522	6.06	43 414	1.97
1959	*92 534*	...	*67 949*	...	*33 945*	...	1893	*55 119*	*17.00*	*43 652*	*6.37*	*44 567*	*2.64*
1959	93 322	153.0	58 045	32.00	28 108	20.30	1892	58 126	16.81	45 165	4.65	44 628	2.60
1958	91 176	120.0	51 517	30.20	27 167	19.40	1891	59 968	16.49	47 435	4.24	43 882	2.51
1957	92 860	91.6	51 897	24.70	26 348	14.90	1890	*57 649*	...	*57 427*	...	*40 876*	...
1956	95 900	88.1	55 354	17.70	26 890	14.30	1890	60 104	16.95	48 130	4.80	42 693	2.29
1955	96 592	88.2	50 474	30.60	27 137	14.90	1889	59 178	18.77	44 508	5.81	42 365	2.14
1954	*95 027*	...	*57 093*	...	*31 619*	...	1888	*58 599*	*19.39*	*42 134*	*5.12*	*43 011*	*2.06*
1954	95 679	92.0	45 114	36.60	27 079	13.80	1887	56 602	21.18	42 563	4.60	44 217	2.05
1953	94 241	128.0	51 755	26.10	27 593	15.70	1886	54 868	22.20	45 457	4.30	46.654	1.95
1952	88 072	179.0	62 117	29.90	27 944	28.00	1885	52 463	24.40	47 330	5.06	49 620	2.19
1951	82 083	160.0	62 269	33.30	27 251	26.50	1884	49 804	25.26	45 961	5.64	51 101	2.40
1950	*76 762*	...	*55 722*	...	*31 387*	...	1883	47 387	23.87	43 440	6.74	50 935	2.53

See footnotes at end of chart.

Series K 564-582. Livestock—Number, Value Per Head, Production and Price: 1867 to 1999—Cont'd.

(Census figures in italics. All figures are as of January 1 except for 1870, 1880, 1890, 1900 (June 1); 1910 (April 15); 1930, 1940, 1950 (April 1); 1954, 1959 (October-November); 1964 (November-December); and 1969 (December 31))

Year	Number on farms and value per head						Year	Number on farms and value per head					
	All cattle		Hogs		Stock sheep			All cattle		Hogs		Stock sheep	
	Number	Value per head	Number	Value per head	Number	Value per head		Number	Value per head	Number	Value per head	Number	Value per head
	564	**565**	**566**	**567**	**568**	**569**		**564**	**565**	**566**	**567**	**568**	**569**
1950........	77 963	124.0	58 937	27.10	26 182	17.80	1882	45 738	20.93	42 566	6.00	48 883	2.35
1949........	76 830	135.0	56 257	38.30	26 940	17.00	1881	44 501	18.67	43 076	4.80	47 371	2.35
1948........	77 171	117.0	54 590	42.90	29 486	15.00	*1880*	*39 676*	. . .	*49 773*	. . .	*42 192*	. . .
1947........	80 554	97.5	56 810	36.00	31 805	12.20	1880	43 347	17.80	44 327	4.40	44 867	2.18
1946........	82 235	76.2	61 306	24.00	35 525	9.57	1879	41 420	16.96	43 767	3.15	41 678	2.01
1945........	82 654	. . .	46 735	. . .	41 224	. . .	1878	39 396	19.05	43 375	4.89	38 942	2.12
1945........	*85 573*	*66.9*	*59 373*	*20.60*	*39 609*	*8.45*	1877	37 333	18.38	39 333	5.68	38 147	2.03
1944........	85 334	68.4	82 741	17.50	44 270	8.68	1876	36 140	18.76	35 715	5.97	37 477	2.20
1943........	81 204	69.3	73 881	22.50	48 196	9.68	1875	35 361	18.96	35 834	4.65	37 237	2.39
1942........	76 025	55.0	60 607	15.60	49 346	8.66	1874	34 821	19.51	38 377	3.93	36 234	2.33
1941........	71 755	43.2	54 353	8.34	47 441	6.77	1873	33 830	20.50	39 794	3.60	35 782	2.60
1940 [2]......	*60 675*	. . .	*34 037*	. . .	*40 129*	. . .	1872	33 078	21.64	39 296	3.96	34 312	2.51
1940........	68 309	40.6	61 175	7.78	46 266	6.35	1871	32 107	24.71	36 688	5.48	34 063	2.10
1939........	66 029	38.44	50 012	11.18	45 463	5.74	*1870*	*23 821*	. . .	*25 135*	. . .	*28 478*	. . .
1938........	65 249	36.58	44 525	11.26	44 972	6.13	1870	31 082	22.84	33 781	5.64	36 449	1.87
1937........	66 098	34.06	43 083	11.89	45 251	6.02	1869	30 060	20.74	32 570	4.60	39 802	1.65
1936........	67 847	34.06	42 075	12.71	45 435	6.35	1868	29 238	18.30	33 304	3.23	43 808	1.83
1935........	*68,284*	. . .	*37 213*	. . .	*48 358*	. . .	1867	28 636	19.13	34 489	3.95	44 997	2.40
1935 [3]......	68 846	20.20	39 066	6.31	46 139	4.33							
1934 [3]......	74 369	17.78	58 621	4.09	48 244	3.77							
1933 [3]......	70 280	19.74	62 127	4.21	47 303	2.91							
1932........	65 801	26.39	59 301	6.13	47 682	3.44							
1931........	63 030	38.99	54 835	11.35	47 720	5.40							

* Denotes first year for which figures include Alaska and Hawaii.
1. December 1, preceding year.
2. Excludes spring-born calves, pigs and lambs.
3. Government purchases included in figures for all cattle, 1935 and 1934; for hogs, 1933.

Series K 583-594. Meat Slaughtering, Production: 1899 to 1999

Year	Beef		Veal		Pork		Lamb and mutton	
	Cattle slaughtered [1]	Production, dressed weight	Calves slaughtered [1]	Production, dressed weight	Hogs slaughtered [1]	Production, dressed weight	Lambs and sheep slaughtered [1]	Production, dressed weight
	583	**584**	**586**	**587**	**589**	**590**	**592**	**593**
	1 000 head	*Mil. lb.*	*1 000 head*	*Mil. lb.*	*1 000 head*	*Mil. lb.*	*1 000 head*	*Mil. lb.*
1999	. . .	26 385	. . .	233	. . .	19 300	. . .	247
1998	. . .	25 760	. . .	261	. . .	19 011	. . .	251
1997	. . .	25 490	. . .	334	. . .	17 274	. . .	251
1996	. . .	25 527	. . .	379	. . .	17 116	. . .	269
1995	. . .	25 225	. . .	318	. . .	17 849	. . .	287
1994	34 300	24 386	1 200	293	95 800	17 697	5 000	310
1993	33 500	23 049	1 200	286	93 300	17 087	5 300	337
1992	33 100	23 204	1 400	322	95 200	17 282	5 600	354
1991	32 900	22 916	1 500	306	88 400	15 999	5 800	364
1990	33 400	22 743	1 800	327	85 400	15 354	5 700	363
1989	34 100	23 087	2 200	355	89 000	15 813	5 600	347
1988	35 300	20 589	2 600	396	88 100	15 684	5 400	335
1987	35 900	23 600	2 900	429	81 400	14 400	5 300	316
1986	37 600	24 400	3 500	524	80 000	14 100	5 800	337
1985	36 600	23 728	3 500	515	84 900	14 807	6 300	359
1984	37 900	23 600	3 400	495	85 600	14 800	6 900	380
1983	37 000	23 200	3 200	454	88 100	15 200	6 800	376
1982	36 200	22 500	3 100	448	82 800	14 200	6 600	365
1981	35 300	22 400	2 900	436	92 500	15 900	6 200	338
1980	34 100	21 643	2 700	400	97 200	16 617	5 700	318
1979	34 000	21 400	2 900	434	90 200	15 500	5 200	293
1978	40 000	24 200	4 300	632	78 400	13 400	5 500	309
1977	42 400	25 300	5 700	834	78 400	13 200	6 600	351
1976	43 200	26 000	5 500	853	74 900	12 400	6 900	371
1975	41 500	24 000	5 400	873	69 800	11 500	8 100	410
1974	37 300	23 100	3 200	486	83 100	13 800	9 000	465
1973	34 000	21 277	2 400	357	77 800	12 751	9 800	514
1972	36 100	22 387	3 200	459	85 700	13 631	10 500	543
1971	35 900	21 868	3 800	546	95 600	14 783	11 000	555
1970	35 354	21 651	4 204	588	86 962	13 427	10 802	551
1969	35 574	21 126	5 010	673	84 958	12 946	10 923	550
1968	35 414	20 846	5 613	734	86 401	13 055	12 119	602
1967	34 295	20 184	6 107	792	83 421	12 572	13 034	646
1966	34 171	19 694	6 861	910	75 325	11 328	13 003	650
1965	33 171	18 699	7 788	1 020	76 394	11 132	13 300	651
1964	31 678	18 429	7 632	1 013	86 284	12 503	14 895	715
1963	28 070	16 428	7 204	929	87 117	12 419	16 147	770
1962	26 911	15 298	7 857	1 015	83 424	11 819	17 168	808
1961	26 471	15 300	8 080	1 044	81 970	11 399	17 537	832
1960	26 029	14 728	8 615	1 109	84 150	11 598	16 240	768
1959	23 723	13 580	8 072	1 008	87 606	11 993	15 528	738
1958	24 368	13 330	9 738	1 086	76 822	10 454	14 495	688
1957	27 068	14 202	12 353	1 526	78 636	10 424	5 292	707
1956	27 755	14 462	12 999	1 632	85 064	11 200	16 328	741
1955	26 587	13 569	12 864	1 578	81 051	10 990	16 553	758
1954	25 889	12 963	13 270	1 647	71 495	9 870	16 255	734
1953	24 465	12 407	12 200	1 546	74 368	10 006	16 321	729
1952	18 625	9 650	9 388	1 169	86 572	11 527	14 304	648
1951	17 084	8 837	8 902	1 059	85 540	11 481	11 416	521
1950	18 614	9 534	10 501	1 230	79 263	10 714	13 244	597
1949	18 765	9 439	11 398	1 334	74 997	10 286	13 780	603
1948	19 177	9 075	12 378	1 423	70 869	10 055	17 371	747
1947	22 404	10 432	13 726	1 605	74 001	10 502	18 706	799
1946	19 824	9 373	12 176	1 443	76 115	11 136	22 788	968
1945	21 694	10 276	13 657	1 664	71 891	10 697	24 639	1 054
1944	19 844	9 112	14 242	1 738	98 068	13 304	25 355	1 024
1943	17 845	8 571	9 940	1 167	95 226	13 640	27 073	1 104

See footnotes at end of chart.

Series K 583-594. Meat Slaughtering, Production: 1899 to 1999—Cont'd.

Year	Beef		Veal		Pork		Lamb and mutton	
	Cattle slaughtered [1]	Production, dressed weight	Calves slaughtered [1]	Production, dressed weight	Hogs slaughtered [1]	Production, dressed weight	Lambs and sheep slaughtered [1]	Production, dressed weight
	583	**584**	**586**	**587**	**589**	**590**	**592**	**593**
	1 000 head	*Mil. lb.*	*1 000 head*	*Mil. lb.*	*1 000 head*	*Mil. lb.*	*1 000 head*	*Mil. lb.*
1942	18 033	8 843	9 718	1 151	78 547	10 876	25 585	1 042
1941	16 419	8 082	9 252	1 036	71 397	9 528	22 309	923
1940	14 958	7 175	9 089	981	77 610	10 044	21 571	876
1939	14 621	7 011	9 191	991	66 561	8 660	21 614	872
1938	14 822	6 908	9 306	994	58 927	7 680	22 423	897
1937	15 254	6 798	10 304	1 108	53 715	6 951	21 455	852
1936 [2]	15 897	7 358	10 008	1 075	58 730	7 474	21 555	854
1935 [2]	14 566	6 608	9 580	1 023	46 011	5 919	22 000	877
1934 [2]	15 071	[3] 8 343	10 106	1 246	68 760	8 397	20 444	851
1933 [4]	13 107	6 440	8 564	891	73 270	9 234	21 833	852
1932	11 980	5 789	7 970	822	71 425	8 923	23 043	884
1931	12 096	6 009	8 057	823	69 233	8 739	23 133	885
1930	12 056	5 917	7 761	792	67 272	8 482	21 125	825
1929	12 038	5 871	7 406	761	71 012	8 833	17 483	682
1928	12 028	5 771	7 651	773	72 889	9 041	17 076	663
1927	13 413	6 395	8 478	867	66 195	8 430	16 113	629
1926	14 781	7 089	9 354	955	62 585	7 966	16 444	639
1925	14 704	6 878	9 936	989	65 508	8 128	15 430	603
1924	14 750	6 877	9 804	972	76 809	9 149	15 578	597
1923	14 283	6 721	9 327	916	77 508	9 483	15 146	588
1922	13 706	6 588	8 832	852	66 201	8 145	14 373	553
1921	12 428	6 022	8 394	820	61 818	7 697	16 742	639
1920	13 470	6 306	8 481	842	61 502	7 648	13 984	538
1919	15 027	6 756	8 201	819	65 795	8 477	15 784	590
1918	17 093	7 726	7 485	760	65 100	8 349	13 220	506
1917	15 741	7 239	7 372	744	56 500	7 055	12 128	463
1916	13 793	6 460	6 628	655	67 000	8 207	15 160	585
1915	12 901	6 075	6 054	590	62 000	7 616	15 576	605
1914	12 676	6 017	5 927	569	55 000	6 824	18 035	693
1913	12 939	6 182	6 305	608	57 000	6 979	18 375	706
1912	13 386	6 234	6 828	662	55 500	6 822	19 131	735
1911	13 817	6 549	6 855	666	57 000	6 961	18 177	693
1910	14 140	6 647	6 917	667	48 215	6 087	15 332	597
1909	14 135	6 915	6 864	660	54 986	6 557	15 464	608
1908	13 569	6 662	6 546	637	63 463	7 535	14 200	559
1907	13 886	6 544	6 395	626	56 527	7 059	13 799	553
1906	13 456	6 537	6 187	598	54 698	6 793	13 800	543
1905	13 096	6 504	5 731	556	54 433	6 629	13 100	530
1904	12 257	6 176	5 076	491	52 072	6 387	13 100	538
1903	12 266	6 240	5 044	492	48 548	6 067	13 800	563
1902	11 751	5 649	4 854	476	48 306	5 936	13 700	534
1901	11 526	5 814	4 318	422	53 898	6 357	13 200	548
1900	10 792	5 628	4 105	397	51 885	6 329	12 000	493
1899	. . .	5 522	. . .	387	. . .	6 310	. . .	487

1. Excludes inspected, noninspected, retail and farm slaughter.
2. Excludes cattle and calves purchased for slaughter for Federal Surplus Relief Corporation from June 1934-Feb. 1935 and for Aug. 1936; excludes also cattle thus purchased for Sept. 1936.
3. Includes slaughter under the Emergency Government Relief Purchase Program in 1934-1935.
4. Excludes purchases on government account for the Emergency Hog Production Control Program from Aug. 22-Oct. 7, 1933.

Series K 595-608. Cows Kept for Milk on Farms, Milk Produced, Manufactured Dairy Products: 1849 to 1998

(Census figures in italics)

Year	Number of cows and heifers 2 years old and over kept for milk Jan. 1 (595) 1 000 head	Milk produced on farms during year (597) Millions pounds	Butter [1] (598) Millions pounds	Cheese [2] (599) Millions pounds	Evaporated and condensed milk [3] (600) Millions pounds	Ice cream (601) Millions gallons	Year	Number of cows and heifers 2 years old and over kept for milk Jan. 1 (595) 1 000 head	Milk produced on farms during year (597) Millions pounds	Butter [1] (598) Millions pounds	Cheese [2] (599) Millions pounds	Evaporated and condensed milk [3] (600) Millions pounds	Ice cream (601) Millions gallons
1998	9 158	157 000	1 082	7 502	...	937	1923	22 138	...	1 993	471	1 585	214
1997	9 252	156 000	1 151	7 330	...	914	1922	21 851	...	1 870	432	1 281	191
1996	9 372	154 000	1 174	7 218	492	879	1921	21 456	...	1 748	434	1 324	175
1995	9 466	155 000	1 264	6 917	503	862	*1920*	*19 675*	...	...	...	...	...
1994	9 494	154 000	1 296	6 735	565	876	1920	21 455	...	1 574	423	1 413	171
1993	9 581	151 000	1 315	6 528	557	866	1919	21 545	67 124	1 647	486	1 883	153
1992	9 688	151 000	1 365	6 488	599	875	1918	21 536	...	1 503	415	1 619	143
1991	9 826	148 000	1 336	6 055	560	863	1917	21 212	...	1 644	472	1 391	106
1990	9 993	148 000	1 302	6 059	615	824	1916	20 752	...	1 793	422	1 196	94
1989	10 046	144 000	1 295	5 615	545	831	1915	20 270	...	1 751	440	1 028	...
1988	10 300	145 000	1 208	5 572	612	882	1914	19 821	...	1 685	367	883	72
1987	10 300	143 000	1 104	5 344	597	928	1913	19 580	...	1 608	359	787	...
1986	10 800	143 000	1 202	5 209	602	924	1912	19 517	...	1 592	323	701	...
1985	11 000	143 000	1 248	5 081	656	901	1911	19 422	...	1 762	345	624	...
1984	10 800	135 000	1 103	4 674	666	894	*1910*	*20 625*	...	...	...	...	...
1983	11 000	140 000	1 299	4 819	710	882	1910	19 450	...	1 706	355	556	...
1982	11 000	136 000	1 257	4 542	754	852	1909	19 201	64 211	1 622	313	495	30
1981	10 800	133 000	1 228	3 984	758	832	1908	18 992	...	1 763	313	450	...
1980	10 800	128 000	1 145	3 984	740	830	1907	18 629	...	1 537	286	410	...
1979	10 800	123 000	985	3 717	810	811	1906	18 230	...	1 545	292	373	...
1978	10 900	122 000	994	3 520	798	815	1905	17 823	...	1 667	327	339	...
1977	11 000	123 000	1 086	3 359	827	810	1904	17 485	...	1 540	331	308	12
1976	11 100	120 000	979	3 319	942	818	1903	17 217	...	1 485	323	279	...
1975	11 100	115 000	984	2 811	938	837	1902	16 992	...	1 401	318	252	...
1974	11 300	115 000	952	2 897	...	783	1901	16 708	...	1 575	362	228	...
1973	11 600	115 000	919	2 685	...	774	*1900*	*17 136*	...	...	...	...	...
1972	11 800	120 000	1 102	2 605	1 131	770	1900	16 544	...	1 540	324	207	...
1971	11 900	119 000	1 144	2 374	1 187	766	1897	15 382	...	1 533	311	...	...
1970	13 838	117 149	1 143	2 204	1 517	763	1896	15 266	...	1 604	240	...	...
1969	*11 175*	...	...	...	...	...	1895	15 230	...	1 297	234	...	...
1969	14 152	116 345	1 129	1 990	1 776	766	1894	15 237	...	1 063	257	...	...
1968	14 644	117 234	1 175	1 938	1 800	773	1893	15 164	...	1 047	254	...	...
1967	15 198	118 769	1 238	1 919	1 886	745	1892	15 177	...	1 058	318	...	...
1966	15 987	119 892	1 128	1 854	2 196	751	1891	15 133	...	1 091	293	...	...
1965	16 981	124 173	1 346	1 755	2 178	757	*1890*	*16 512*	...	...	...	...	...
1964	*14 623*	...	...	...	...	...	1890	15 000	...	1 171	318	...	...
1964	17 647	126 967	1 469	1 724	2 395	739	1889	14 706	44 807	1 292	301	45	1
1963	18 379	125 202	1 454	1 632	2 369	718	1888	14 350	...	978	286	...	...
1962	18 963	126 251	1 579	1 592	2 409	704	1887	13 888	...	978	268	...	...
1961	* 19 271	125 707	1 536	1 635	2 632	699	1886	13 478	...	989	244	...	...
1960	19 527	* 123 109	* 1 436	* 1 478	* 2 666	* 700	1885	13 213	...	933	260	...	...
1959 [4]	*16 522*	...	...	...	...	...	1884	12 883	...	869	275	...	...
1959	20 132	121 989	1 411	1 383	2 743	699	1883	12 571	...	844	281	...	...
1958	21 265	123 220	1 486	1 399	2 752	658	1882	12 234	...	743	261	...	...
1957	22 325	124 628	1 533	1 407	2 872	651	1881	11 977	...	803	304	...	...
1956	22 921	124 860	1 553	1 388	2 953	641	*1880*	*12 443*	...	...	...	...	...
1955	23 462	122 945	1 545	1 367	2 922	629	1880	11 754	...	816	270	...	...
1954	*20 183*	...	...	...	...	...	1879	11 486	...	807	243	13	(Z)
1954	23 896	122 094	1 628	1 383	2 845	597	1878	11 222	...	726	303	...	...
1953	23 549	120 221	1 607	1 344	2 875	605	1877	11 004	...	696	235	...	...

See footnotes at end of chart.

Series K 595-608.   Cows Kept for Milk on Farms, Milk Produced, Manufactured Dairy Products: 1849 to 1998—Cont'd.

(Census figures in italics)

Year	Number of cows and heifers 2 years old and over kept for milk Jan. 1	Milk produced on farms during year	Production of dairy products				Year	Number of cows and heifers 2 years old and over kept for milk Jan. 1	Milk produced on farms during year	Production of dairy products			
			Butter [1]	Cheese [2]	Evaporated and condensed milk [3]	Ice cream				Butter [1]	Cheese [2]	Evaporated and condensed milk [3]	Ice cream
	595	**597**	**598**	**599**	**600**	**601**		**595**	**597**	**598**	**599**	**600**	**601**
	1 000 head	*Millions pounds*	*Millions pounds*	*Millions pounds*	*Millions pounds*	*Millions gallons*		*1 000 head*	*Millions pounds*	*Millions pounds*	*Millions pounds*	*Millions pounds*	*Millions gallons*
1952.....	23 060	114 671	1 402	1 170	3 165	593	1876	10 821	...	677	214	...	...
1951.....	23 568	114 681	1 443	1 161	3 228	569	1875	10 714	...	556	233	...	...
1950.....	*21 233*	...	...	...	...	...	1874	10 562	...	585	206	...	...
1950.....	23 853	116 602	1 648	1 191	3 205	554	1873	10 348	...	566	212	...	...
1949.....	23 862	116 103	1 688	1 199	3 106	558	1872	10 191	...	434	187	...	...
1948.....	24 615	112 671	1 504	1 098	3 755	576	1871	9 941	...	470	164	...	...
1947.....	25 842	116 814	1 640	1 183	3 630	631	*1870*.....	*8 935*	...	...	...	...	...
1946.....	26 521	117 697	1 502	1 106	3 333	714	1870	9 672	...	412	181	...	...
1945.....	*22 803*	...	...	...	...	...	1869	9 205	...	514	163	4	(Z)
1945.....	27 770	119 828	1 699	1 117	4 126	477	1868	8 705	...	...	...	...	...
1944.....	27 704	117 023	1 818	1 017	3 750	445	1867	8 263	...	...	...	...	...
1943.....	27 138	117 017	2 015	993	3 344	412	1866	...	...	...	...	...	...
1942.....	26 313	118 533	2 130	1 112	3 782	464	1865	...	...	...	...	...	...
1941.....	25 453	115 088	2 268	956	3 555	390	1864	...	...	...	...	...	...
1940.....	*21 937*	...	...	...	...	...	1863	...	...	...	...	...	...
1940.....	24 940	109 412	2 240	785	2 731	318	1862	...	...	...	...	...	...
1939.....	24 600	106 792	2 210	710	2 367	306	1861	...	...	...	...	...	...
1938.....	24 466	105 807	2 252	726	2 322	286	*1860*.....	*8 586*	...	...	...	...	...
1937.....	24 649	101 908	2 135	653	2 131	291	1860	...	...	...	...	...	...
1936.....	25 196	102 410	2 168	650	2 270	259	1859	...	...	460	104	...	(Z)
1935.....	*24 582*	...	...	...	...	...	1858	...	...	...	...	...	...
1935.....	26 082	101 205	2 211	628	2 032	219	1857	...	...	...	...	...	...
1934.....	26 931	101 621	2 286	587	1 908	192	1856	...	...	...	...	...	...
1933.....	25 936	104 762	2 375	548	1 899	162	1855	...	...	...	...	...	...
1932.....	24 896	103 810	2 307	491	1 780	168	1854	...	...	...	...	...	...
1931.....	23 820	103 029	2 239	499	1 682	226	1853	...	...	...	...	...	...
1930.....	*21 124*	...	...	...	...	...	1852	...	...	...	...	...	...
1930.....	23 032	100 158	2 149	510	1 761	255	1851	...	...	...	...	...	...
1929.....	22 440	98 988	2 184	499	1 849	277	*1850*.....	*6 385*	...	...	...	...	...
1928.....	22 231	95 843	2 120	479	1 604	254	1850	...	...	...	...	...	...
1927.....	22 251	95 172	2 188	462	1 576	251	1849	...	...	313	106	...	...
1926.....	22 410	93 325	2 132	468	1 456	238							
1925.....	*20 900*	...	...	...	...	...							
1925.....	22 575	90 699	2 082	503	1 548	240							
1924.....	22 331	89 240	2 066	474	1 507	213							

* Denotes first year for which figures include Alaska and Hawaii.
Z Less than 500,000 gallons.
1. Farm and factory production combined.
2. Includes all types of cheese except cottage, pot and bakers' cheese; full-skim American cheese excluded since 1908. Farm output not estimated since 1926.
3. For 1919-1970 includes all evaporated and condensed whole milk as compiled by the former Bureau of Agricultural Economics and Agricultural Marketing Service. Prior to 1919, includes total production of all condensed and evaporated milk as interpolated from census enumerations.
4. Beginning 1959, census figures include Alaska and Hawaii.

Series K 609-623. Poultry and Eggs—Number, Production and Price: 1909 to 1998

(Census figures in italics and as of April 15, 1910; April 1, 1930, 1940, 1950 and 1954; January 1, 1920, 1925, 1935 and 1945; October-November, 1959; November-December, 1964; and December 31, 1969)

| Year | Chickens | | | Broilers | | Eggs | | Turkeys |
	Number, Jan. 1	Value per head, Jan. 1	Price per pound [1]	Number produced	Price per pound [1]	Number produced	Price per dozen [1]	Number, Jan. 1 [2]
	609	610	613	614	616	617	618	619
	Millions	*Dollars*	*Cents*	*Millions*	*Cents*	*Millions*	*Cents*	*Millions*
1998	424	2.69	8.0	7 974	39.3	79 764	65.5	284
1997	410	2.72	7.7	7 764	37.7	77 515	70.3	301
1996	393	2.65	6.7	7 598	38.1	76 452	74.9	303
1995	388	2.41	6.5	7 326	34.4	74 592	62.4	293
1994	386	2.34	7.6	7 018	35.0	74 136	61.4	287
1993	380	2.37	10.0	6 694	34.0	71 900	63.4	288
1992	371	2.26	8.6	6 402	31.8	70 500	57.6	289
1991	364	2.30	7.2	6 137	30.8	69 000	67.8	285
1990	353	2.29	9.3	5 864	32.6	67 900	70.9	282
1989	357	2.16	14.9	5 517	36.6	67 200	68.9	261
1988	356	2.04	9.2	5 238	33.1	69 700	52.8	242
1987	380	1.87	11.0	5 004	28.7	70.400	54.7	240
1986	373	1.87	12.5	4 649	34.5	68 400	61.6	207
1985	370	1.90	14.8	4 470	30.1	68 400	57.2	185
1984	374	2.02	15.9	4 283	33.7	68 232	72.3	171
1983	365	1.96	12.7	4 184	28.6	68 172	61.1	171
1982	379	1.85	10.3	4 149	26.9	69 720	59.5	165
1981	385	1.89	11.1	4 148	28.4	69 828	63.1	171
1980	392	1.88	11.0	3 963	27.7	69 700	56.3	165
1979	401	1.81	14.4	3 951	26.0	69 204	58.3	3 705
1978	397	1.75	12.4	3 613	26.3	67 152	52.2	3 370
1977	387	1.69	12.0	3 400	23.6	64 608	55.6	3 038
1976	378	1.70	12.9	3 283	23.6	64 512	58.3	3 069
1975	380	1.74	9.9	2 950	26.3	64 632	52.4	3 014
1974	384	1.70	9.7	2 993	21.5	65 616	53.2	2 970
1973	413	1.52	15.1	3 008	. . .	67.000	52.5	3 553
1972	406	1.28	9.0	. . .	. . .	70 000	30.9	3 303
1971	433	1.21	7.7	. . .	. . .	70 000	31.4	7 701
1970	434	1.35	8.8	2 987	13.6	70 312	37.6	6 769
1969	*371*	*1.31*	. . .	. . .	. . .	. . .	. . .	. . .
1969	420	1.21	9.7	2 789	15.2	69 086	40.0	6 604
1968	425	1.14	8.2	2 620	14.2	69 270	34.0	7 301
1967	429	1.20	7.9	2 592	13.3	70 031	31.2	7 817
1966	393	1.21	9.7	2 571	15.3	66 484	39.1	6 905
1965	394	1.17	8.9	2 334	15.0	65 692	33.7	6 105
1964	*343*	*1.17*	. . .	. . .	. . .	. . .	. . .	. . .
1964	382	1.16	9.2	2 161	14.2	65 215	33.8	5 996
1963	376	1.16	10.0	2 102	14.6	63 500	34.5	6 374
1962	377	1.15	10.2	2 023	15.2	63 569	33.8	6 423
1961	[3] 366	[3] 1.25	[3] 10.1	1 991	13.9	[3] 62 423	[3] 35.6	7 008
1960	369	1.06	12.2	1 795	16.9	61 602	36.1	5 633
1959 [4]	[4] *351*	[4] *1.06*	. . .	. . .	. . .	. . .	. . .	. . .
1959	*387*	*1.26*	*11.0*	*1 737*	*16.1*	*63 335*	*31.4*	*6 105*
1958	*374*	*1.26*	*14.0*	*1 660*	*18.5*	*61 607*	*38.5*	*5 612*
1957	391	1.17	13.7	1 448	18.9	61 026	35.9	5 828
1956	384	1.26	16.0	1 344	19.6	61 113	39.3	4 937
1955	391	1.05	18.6	1 092	25.2	59 526	39.5	4 917
1954	*376*	*1.04*	. . .	. . .	. . .	. . .	. . .	[5] *2 278*
1954	397	1.43	16.8	1 048	23.1	58 933	36.6	4 956
1953	398	1.41	22.1	947	27.1	57 891	47.7	5 086
1952	427	1.53	22.1	861	28.8	58 068	41.6	5 725
1951	431	1.46	25.0	789	28.5	58 063	47.7	5 037
1950	*343*	*1.09*	. . .	. . .	. . .	. . .	. . .	*2 849*
1950	457	1.36	22.2	631	27.4	58 954	36.3	5 124

See footnotes at end of chart.

Series K 609-623. Poultry and Eggs—Number, Production and Price: 1909 to 1998—Cont'd.

(Census figures in italics and as of April 15, 1910; April 1, 1930, 1940, 1950 and 1954; January 1, 1920, 1925, 1935 and 1945; October-November, 1959; November-December, 1964; and December 31, 1969)

Year	Chickens Number, Jan. 1	Value per head, Jan. 1	Price per pound [1]	Broilers Number produced	Price per pound [1]	Eggs Number produced	Price per dozen [1]	Turkeys Number, Jan. 1 [2]
	609	610	613	614	616	617	618	619
	Millions	Dollars	Cents	Millions	Cents	Millions	Cents	Millions
1949	431	1.66	25.4	513	28.2	56 154	45.2	4 622
1948	500	1.44	30.1	371	36.0	54 899	47.2	3 959
1947	467	1.44	26.5	310	32.3	55 384	45.3	5 879
1946	523	1.27	27.6	293	32.7	55 962	37.6	7 862
1945	433	1.23	...	...	...	...	...	...
1945	516	1.21	25.9	366	29.5	56 221	37.7	7 082
1944	582	1.18	23.7	274	28.8	58 537	32.5	7 294
1943	542	1.04	24.3	285	28.6	54 547	37.1	6 584
1942	477	.83	18.7	228	22.9	48 610	30.0	7 447
1941	423	.65	15.6	192	18.4	41 894	23.5	7 150
1940	338	.56	...	...	...	...	...	4 362
1940	438	.60	13.0	143	17.3	39 707	18.0	8 569
1939	419	.70	13.2	106	17.0	38 843	17.4	6 489
1938	390	.76	14.8	82	19.0	37 356	20.3	6 096
1937	424	.66	16.0	68	21.4	37 564	21.3	6 358
1936	403	.75	15.0	53	20.6	34 534	21.8	5 731
1935	372	.52	...	...	...	...	...	5 382
1935	390	.54	14.9	43	20.0	33 609	23.4	5 499
1934	434	.42	11.1	34	19.3	34 429	17.0	6 309
1933	445	.45	9.5	...	...	35 514	13.8	6 852
1932	437	.62	11.7	...	...	36 298	14.2	5 946
1931	450	.70	15.8	...	...	38 532	17.6	5 318
1930	379	.85	...	...	...	...	...	...
1930	468	.93	18.4	...	...	39 067	23.7	5 969
1929	449	.91	22.8	...	...	37 921	29.8	5 541
1928	475	.86	21.4	...	...	38 659	28.1	...
1927	461	.91	20.2	...	...	38 627	25.1	...
1926	438	.89	22.1	...	...	37 248	28.9	...
1925	409	.93	...	...	...	...	...	...
1925	435	.79	20.5	...	...	34 969	30.4	...
1924	435	.76	19.4	...	...	34 592	26.7	...
1923	415	.75	...	...	...	35 000	26.5	...
1922	395	.81	...	...	...	33 000	25.0	...
1921	370	.89	...	...	...	30 800	28.3	...
1920	360	1.04	...	...	...	...	...	3 627
1920	381	.97	...	...	...	29 700	43.5	...
1919	391	.96	...	...	...	30 500	41.3	...
1918	363	.77	...	...	...	28 000	36.0	...
1917	359	.59	...	...	...	27 700	31.8	...
1916	369	.49	...	...	...	28 800	22.1	...
1915	379	.46	...	...	...	29 900	19.4	...
1914	367	.49	...	...	...	27 900	20.5	...
1913	365	.47	...	...	...	28 100	19.4	...
1912	367	.42	...	...	...	28 300	20.2	...
1911	382	.46	...	...	...	29 400	17.5	...
1910	280	.50	...	...	...	...	...	3 689
1910	356	.47	...	...	...	27 000	20.9	...
1909	340	.44	...	...	...	25 300	20.0	...

1. Average annual price received by farmers.
2. Beginning 1980, data are for breeder hens, and only 26 major producer states.
3. Beginning 1961, Department of Agriculture data include Alaska and Hawaii.
4. Beginning 1959, census data include Alaska and Hawaii.
5. Data for October-November.

Series KK 1. Gross Farm Product—Summary: 1980 to 1997

(In billions of dollars (142.9 represents $142 900 000 000). For definition of gross product, see text, Section 14, Income. Minus sign (-) indicates decrease)

Item	1980	1985	1989	1990	1991	1992	1993	1994	1995	1996	1997
CURRENT DOLLARS											
Farm output, total	142.9	152.7	177.2	185.6	180.3	187.7	186.5	202.9	196.7	222.1	225.3
Cash receipts from farm marketings	140.3	136.3	166.7	172.3	170.4	172.2	181.7	180.9	194.1	201.7	207.2
Farm housing	5.1	5.0	5.0	5.1	5.2	5.3	5.5	5.8	5.9	6.1	6.3
Farm products consumed on farms	1.2	0.9	0.7	0.7	0.6	0.6	0.5	0.5	0.5	0.4	0.5
Other farm income	2.4	4.6	4.9	4.8	5.1	4.6	4.9	4.9	5.5	6.3	7.1
Change in farm inventories	-6.1	5.8	-	2.6	-1.1	5.0	-6.2	10.8	-9.3	7.6	4.3
Less: Intermediate goods and services purchased [1]	86.8	85.6	101.0	106.0	107.3	107.1	113.5	119.4	124.4	130.5	135.1
Equals: Gross farm product	56.1	67.1	76.2	79.6	72.9	80.6	73.0	83.5	72.3	91.6	90.2
Less: Consumption of fixed capital	18.7	20.7	21.1	21.8	22.4	23.2	23.4	23.7	24.8	25.8	26.6
Indirect business tax [2]	3.0	3.3	3.9	4.4	4.4	4.5	4.4	4.8	5.1	5.1	5.5
Plus: Subsidies to operators	1.0	6.3	9.3	7.5	6.8	7.7	11.3	6.6	6.1	6.1	6.2
Equals: Farm national income	35.5	49.4	60.5	61.0	52.9	60.5	56.5	61.5	48.4	66.9	64.4
CHAINED (1992) DOLLARS [3]											
Farm output, total	144.5	163.6	169.7	177.0	178.7	187.7	182.4	199.4	190.7	195.7	208.3
Cash receipts from farm marketings	146.3	149.3	159.7	164.0	168.9	172.2	177.9	178.2	188.8	177.3	191.0
Farm housing	7.4	6.2	5.6	5.6	5.5	5.3	5.2	5.2	5.2	5.1	5.0
Farm products consumed on farms	1.4	1.1	0.7	0.6	0.6	0.6	0.5	0.5	0.5	0.4	0.4
Other farm income	2.4	4.7	4.5	4.7	5.0	4.6	4.8	4.8	5.0	5.3	6.2
Change in farm inventories	-7.0	6.9	-	2.5	-1.7	5.0	-7.3	11.7	-11.0	7.1	4.3
Less: Intermediate goods and services purchased [1]	102.0	96.6	104.1	106.2	107.1	107.1	111.4	114.7	118.5	116.9	118.2
Equals: Gross farm product	46.7	66.9	65.9	70.8	71.6	80.6	71.0	85.0	72.0	78.6	90.3

- Represents zero.
1. Includes rent paid to nonoperator landlords.
2. Includes nontax liability.
3. See text, Section 14, Income.

SOURCE: U.S. Bureau of Economic Analysis, National Income and Product Accounts of the United States 1929-94, Vol. 2; and Survey of Current Business, August 1998.

Series KK 2. Agricultural Exports and Imports—Value: 1980 to 1998

(In billions of dollars, except percent (23.9 represents $23 900 000 000). Includes Puerto Rico. Excludes forest products and distilled liquors; includes crude rubber and similar gums (now mainly plantation products). Includes shipments under foreign aid programs)

Year	Trade balance	Exports domestic products	Percent of all exports	Imports for consumption	Percent of all imports	Year	Trade balance	Exports, domestic products	Percent of all exports	Imports for consumption	Percent of all imports
1980	23.9	41.2	18	17.4	7	1993	17.7	42.9	10	25.2	4
1985	9.1	29.0	13	20.0	6	1994	19.2	46.2	10	27.1	4
1989	18.2	40.1	12	21.9	5	1995	26.0	56.3	10	30.3	4
1990	16.6	39.5	11	22.9	5	1996	26.8	60.4	10	33.7	4
1991	16.5	39.4	10	22.9	5						
						1997	21.0	57.2	9	36.3	4
1992	18.3	43.1	10	24.8	5	1998	14.8	51.8	8	37.1	4

SOURCE: U.S. Dept. of Agriculture, Economic Research Service, U.S. Agricultural Trade Update, February 26, 1999; and Foreign Agricultural Trade of the United States, calendar year supplements. Also in Agricultural Statistics, annual.

FORESTRY AND FISHERIES

SECTION L
FORESTRY AND FISHERIES
Highlights

1 The National Forest Service is the largest landowner in the United States and oversees the National Forest System, which covers more than 231 million acres. A forest is defined as land that is at least 10% stocked by forest trees of any size. The states with the largest forest areas are California (24.434 million acres), Alaska (24.233 million acres), Idaho (21.694 million acres), Montana (19.101 million acres), and Oregon (17.496 million acres).

2 Data on lumber were first collected by the Census Office (later the Census Bureau) in 1810. Subsequent statistics were published by this agency for 1819, decennially for 1839 to 1899, and annually from 1904 to 1954, except in 1905, 1906, 1913, 1915 to 1918, 1920 and 1948. Current data are reported in *An Analysis of the Timber Situation in the United States, 1989-2040; Forest Statistics of the United States, U. S. Timber Production, Trade, Consumption and Price Statistics, 1960-1988;* and the annual *Land Areas of the National Forest System.*

3 The total forest area of the United States in 1992 was 754 million acres of which 360 million acres were in private hands, 116 million acres were federally owned or managed, and 29 million acres were owned by states, counties and municipalities. Of the total acreage, 168 million acres were in the Northeast, 212 million acres in the South, 142 million acres in the Rockies, and 217 million acres in the West. The net volume of growing stock was 786 billion cubic feet, of which softwood accounted for 450 billion cubic feet.

4 The most popular hardwood is Douglas fir, and the most popular softwood is oak. However, stumpage prices for Southern pine are generally higher than those for Douglas fir because it is favored by carpenters and construction people.

5 The GDP of timber-related industry was $97.8 billion in 1997, of which paper and allied products accounted for $55 billion and timber and wood products for $42.8 billion. Logging, sawmills, millwork and veneer and wood products industries employed 738,700 persons and paper, paper-board and other paper products industries employed 630,600 persons. In 1997, domestic production of industrial roundwood was 15.361 billion cubic feet; lumber, 7.120 billion cubic feet; plywood and veneer, 1.211 billion cubic feet; and pulp products 5.794 billion cubic feet.

6 The total production of paper and paperboard in 1997 was 96.9228 million short tons, of which paper accounted for 44.679 million short tons. The United States consumes double its annual production of newsprint of 6.304 million metric tons, importing the balance from Canada and Scandinavia.

7 The first comprehensive statistical study of fisheries and fishery industries was produced for the year 1880 by the U. S. National Museum with the cooperation of the Commission of Fisheries and the Superintendent of the Tenth Census. The next general survey was conducted by the Bureau of the Census in 1908, followed by one in 1931 and another in 1950. Since then, annual data have been available for all coastal areas. Annual surveys are also made of the Mississippi River and its tributaries. Extended data are available for landing at the important fishing ports for certain species and for canned and industrial fishery products. Current fishery data are published in the *Current Fishery Statistics* and *Fisheries of the United States* by the National Marine Fisheries Service. Statistics on commercial landed catches of fish are shown as round, salable weight of recoverable meat. Data do not include catches made for personal use by hobby fishermen, or landings by foreign fishing vessels.

8 The fishing species most often caught are whiting, cod, flounder, haddock, herring, lobster, mackerel, and ocean perch in the New England states; menhaden, oysters, and crabs in the Middle Atlantic and Chesapeake Bay states; shrimp, menhaden, and mullet in the South Atlantic and Gulf states; lake trout and white fish in the Great Lakes states; tuna, salmon, sardine, halibut, and mackerel in the Pacific coast states; tuna in Hawaii; and salmon, halibut, and herring in Alaska.

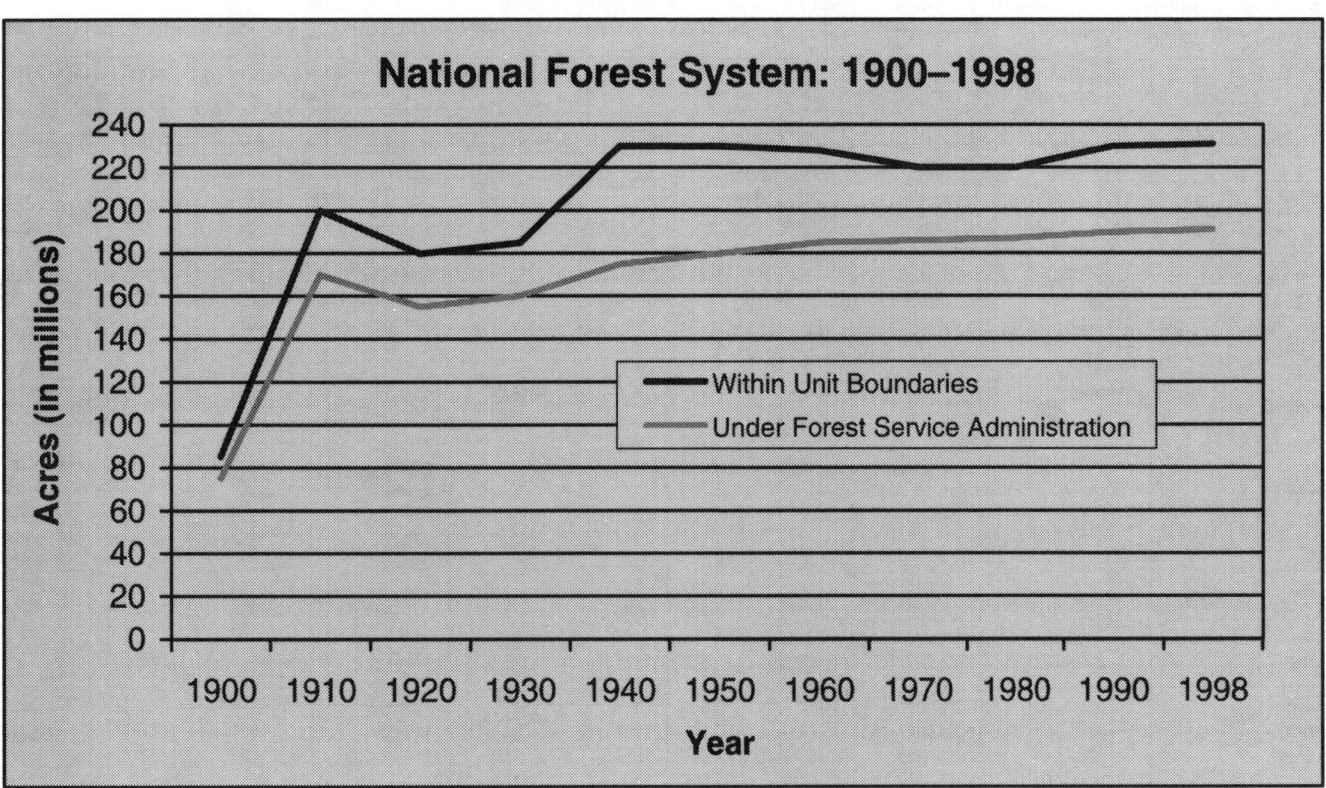

National Forest System: 1900–1998

Legend: Within Unit Boundaries; Under Forest Service Administration

9 The total fish catch in 1997 was 9.845 billion pounds valued at $3.466 billion. Of these, shellfish accounted for 1.448 billion pounds worth $1.744 billion. Menhaden and pollock account for about half the fish catch, but salmon has the highest dollar value ($242.5 million). Among shellfish, shrimp ($544.056 million) and crabs ($429,547 million) have the highest dollar value. The largest fishing ports (on the basis of landed fish) are Dutch Harbor in Alaska, Pascagoula-Moss Point in Mississippi, Kodiak in Alaska, and Empire-Venice in Louisiana. The largest fishing port (on the basis of value of fish catch) is New Bedford, Massachusetts. In 1997, 1.565 million pounds of fish were canned and shrimp overtook tuna as the fish in most abundant supply.

10 Aquaculture has become a major sector of fishing industry producing 598.5 million pounds of catfish and 57.1 million pounds of trout per year.

Series L 10-14. National Forest System Areas and Purchases: 1905 to 1997

(Forest area data as of June 30; includes Alaska and Puerto Rico. Forest purchases for years ending June 30; includes Puerto Rico)

Year	Gross area of national forests and other lands [1] Within unit boundaries	Under Forest Service administration	Gross area approved for national forest purchase Total area	Total price
	10	11	12	13
	1 000 acres	*1 000 acres*	*Acres*	*$1 000*
1997	231 864	191 813	...	...
1996	...	...	...	...
1995	...	...	...	...
1994	...	...	...	
1993	...	...	...	...
1992	231 502	191 453	...	...
1991	...	...	...	...
1990	231 000	191 000	51 000	24 000
1989	231 000	191 000	99 000	34 000
1988	230 000	191 000	42 000	235 000
1987	230 000	191 000	87 000	38 000
1986	230 000	191 000	23 000	7 000
1985	230 000	191 000	16 000	6 900
1984	230 000	191 000	8 000	4 200
1983	230 000	191 000	7 000	2 400
1982	230 000	191 000	2 000	1 500
1981	230 000	191 000	111 000	50 400
1980	226 000	187 000	42 000	27 900
1979	226 000	187 000	58 000	30 200
1978	226 000	188 000	51 000	22 500
1977	226 000	188 000	45 000	16 600
1976	226 000	188 000	43 000	12 300
1975	226 000	188 000	12 000	3 300
1974	226 000	187 000	25 000	6 000
1973	226 000	187 000	117 000	17 500
1972	225 000	187 000	79 000	14 752
1971	225 000	187 000	32 000	4 467
1970	226 064	186 900	92 437	11 539
1969	226 045	186 632	126 341	12 353
1968	226 502	186 921	112 767	9 413
1967	227 721	186 799	104 507	7 037
1966	226 519	186 497	171 947	13 307
1965	226 434	186 577	28 507	1 364
1964	225 743	186 476	40 873	1 600
1963	225 584	186 316	24 698	1 795
1962	225 613	186 324	22 556	964
1961	226 110	186 385	10 355	236
1960	226 623	185 772	7 845	114
1959	227 359	185 805	8 716	224
1958	231 080	188 042	10 463	722
1957	231 293	188 013	17 519	416
1956	232 118	188 117	21 376	372
1955	235 728	188 120	18 665	192
1954	235 694	188 138	17 761	109
1953	229 112	181 568	7 969	99
1952	229 165	181 293	10 181	106
1951	229 258	181 255	25 317	265

Year	Gross area of national forests and other lands [1] Within unit boundaries	Under Forest Service administration	Gross area approved for national forest purchase Total area	Total price
	10	11	12	13
	1 000 acres	*1 000 acres*	*Acres*	*$1 000*
1950	229 341	181 205	61 078	532
1949	229 175	180 895	60 719	464
1948	228 936	180 528	103 490	739
1947	228 810	180 264	380 471	2 190
1946	228 760	179 726	...	...
1945	228 703	179 381	5	1
1944	228 643	179 101	9	1
1943	228 633	178 508	8 759	38
1942	228 725	178 340	243 522	1 103
1941	228 309	177 653	195 818	805
1940	228 174	176 779	553 077	2 203
1939	228 784	176 494	534 138	2 275
1938	227 280	175 238	800 113	2 713
1937	226 621	174 405	425 637	2 124
1936	197 435	165 979	2 891 040	11 535
1935	188 292	163 310	3 661 848	14 991
1934	188 037	162 591	4 206 817	10 018
1933	186 837	162 009	667 314	1 221
1932	186 215	161 361	83 086	206
1931	185 252	160 788	547 945	1 944
1930	183 976	160 091	538 048	1 468
1929	184 565	159 751	464 177	1 787
1928	184 404	159 481	261 107	1 996
1927	183 938	158 800	135 088	726
1926	184 124	158 759	191 725	737
1925	184 126	158 395	247 067	1 187
1924	182 817	157 503	130 290	425
1923	182 100	157 237	79 923	348
1922	181 800	156 837	242 169	826
1921	181 820	156 666	112 397	499
1920	180 300	156 032	101 428	451
1919	174 261	153 933	103 355	657
1918	175 951	155 375	185 199	848
1917	176 340	155 220	175 463	853
1916	176 089	155 400	54 898	316
1915	184 506	162 773	282 900	1 618
1914	185 321	163 849	391 114	1 940
1913	186 617	165 517	425 717	2 005
1912	187 406	165 027	287 698	1 627
1911	190 608	168 165	...	...
1910	192 931	168 029	...	...
1909	194 505	172 230	...	...
1908	167 977	147 820	...	...
1907	150 832	132 732	...	...
1906	106 994	94 159	...	...
1905	85 693	75 352	...	...

1. On January 2, 1954, some 6,910,000 acres of land utilization project lands were transferred to the Forest Service for administration.

Series L 72-86. Domestic Production, Net Imports and Apparent Consumption of Industrial Timber Products in Roundwood Equivalent: 1900 to 1997

(In millions of cubic feet. Excludes fuelwood)

Year	Total			Domestic production of lumber	Domestic production of plywood and veneer	Domestic production of pulp products	Logs	
	Domestic production	Net Imports	Apparent consumption				Imports	Exports
	72	73	74	75	78	81	85	86
1997	15 361	4 154	17 201	7 120	1 211	5 794	20	422
1996	14 664	4 045	16 527	7 072	1 297	5 795	18	278
1995	14 501	3 988	16 275	6 826	1 314	5 847	13	250
1994	14 904	3 649	16 287	6 880	1 268	5 417	18	354
1993	14 632	3 464	15 816	6 660	1 257	5 391	15	326
1992	14 994	3 104	15 628	6 864	1 265	5 463	7	351
1991	14 780	2 873	15 153	6 677	1 226	5 434	2	331
1990	15 413	3 000	15 986	7 213	1 368	5 353	4	288
1988	14 985	1 245	16 230	6 920	1 630	4 885	15	825
1987	14 670	1 925	16 595	6 990	1 650	4 670	15	705
1986	13 845	2 075	15 920	6 545	1 505	4 545	15	620
1985	12 515	2 270	14 785	5 665	1 420	4 165	20	655
1984	12 725	2 105	14 830	5 770	1 400	4 355	30	600
1983	12 065	1 600	13 665	5 370	1 365	4 165	30	565
1982	10 910	1 020	11 930	4 635	1 135	3 980	20	550
1981	10 710	1 665	11 775	4 395	1 180	4 125	20	435
1980	12 120	900	13 020	5 300	1 175	4 390	25	560
1979	12 510	1 520	14 030	5 680	1 370	4 110	25	665
1978	12 235	1 910	14 145	5 825	1 460	3 745	20	585
1977	11 965	1 515	13 480	5 730	1 425	3 645	30	525
1976	11 815	970	12 785	5 475	1 355	3 805	15	555
1975	10 575	530	11 105	4 890	1 165	3 485	15	455
1974	11 540	950	12 490	5 095	1 150	4 220	15	455
1973	11 925	1 395	13 325	5 670	1 320	3 755	5	575
1972	11 440	1 515	12 960	5 535	1 300	3 520	10	535
1971	11 310	1 565	12 875	5 715	1 225	3 560	15	360
1970	11 115	1 065	12 180	5 355	1 065	3 835	25	430
1969	11 000	1 375	12 370	5 535	1 050	3 585	15	375
1968	11 025	1 275	12 305	5 630	1 120	3 385	15	405
1967	10 410	1 205	11 615	5 360	1 030	3 190	15	310
1966	10 645	1 430	12 075	5 645	1 030	3 190	15	220
1965	10 540	1 385	11 930	5 670	1 030	3 095	10	190
1964	10 170	1 315	11 485	5 635	960	2 865	10	170
1963	9 560	1 360	10 920	5 355	870	2 670	15	150
1962	9 035	1 415	10 450	5 120	800	2 565	20	85
1961	8 745	1 250	9 995	4 945	765	2 475	20	75
1960	8 920	1 220	10 145	5 080	705	2 575	20	45
1959	9 390	1 345	10 735	5 745	720	2 355	20	35
1958	8 530	1 185	9 715	5 160	615	2 165	15	30
1957	8 615	1 155	9 770	5 100	560	2 350	25	25
1956	9 620	1 330	10 950	5 920	590	2 475	30	30
1955	9 225	1 270	10 495	5 785	575	2 200	35	25
1954	8 755	1 190	9 945	5 635	480	1 960	35	25
1953	8 790	1 230	10 020	5 710	475	1 910	40	20
1952	8 775	1 160	9 935	5 820	435	1 810	30	10
1951	8 740	1 205	9 950	5 780	390	1 825	35	15
1950	8 525	1 380	9 910	5 905	345	1 500	45	10
1949	7 355	935	8 290	5 000	320	1 275	30	10
1948	8 375	1 090	9 465	5 750	290	1 470	45	10
1947	8 090	815	8 905	5 500	275	1 370	30	10
1946	7 705	810	8 515	5 295	255	1 260	25	(Z)
1945	6 605	685	7 290	4 365	250	1 140	25	5
1944	7 455	555	8 010	5 115	270	1 160	25	5
1943	7 560	565	8 125	5 325	280	1 030	20	5
1942	8 085	705	8 790	5 645	305	1 130	30	5

See footnote at end of chart.

Series L 72-86. Domestic Production, Net Imports and Apparent Consumption of Industrial Timber Products in Roundwood Equivalent: 1900 to 1997—Cont'd.

(In millions of cubic feet. Excludes fuelwood)

Year	Total			Domestic production of lumber	Domestic production of plywood and veneer	Domestic production of pulp products	Logs	
	Domestic production	Net Imports	Apparent consumption				Imports	Exports
	72	73	74	75	78	81	85	86
1941	8 055	650	8 705	5 680	265	1 075	55	5
1940	6 990	420	7 410	4 845	235	930	35	10
1939	6 370	535	6 905	4 470	210	725	. . .	. . .
1938	5 570	470	6 040	3 860	195	595	. . .	. . .
1937	6 360	610	6 980	4 505	195	640	. . .	. . .
1936	5 990	560	6 540	4 295	165	555	. . .	. . .

Year	Total			Domestic production of lumber	Domestic production of plywood and veneer	Domestic production of pulp products
	Domestic production	Net Imports	Apparent consumption			
	72	73	74	75	78	81
1935	5 090	420	5 515	3 565	145	485
1934	4 340	355	4 695	2 925	130	430
1933	4 040	345	4 385	2 665	125	415
1932	3 400	305	3 705	2 100	120	350
1931	4 600	335	4 945	3 105	125	400
1930	6 305	400	6 705	4 560	155	395
1929	8 045	330	8 375	6 020	200	445
1928	7 670	290	7 960	5 710	175	400
1927	7 780	340	8 115	5 790	175	380
1926	8 215	375	8 595	6 180	145	400
1925	8 350	360	8 710	6 375	135	345
1924	8 250	285	8 530	6 140	115	340
1923	8 535	345	8 880	6 375	115	340
1922	7 605	290	7 895	5 480	90	340
1921	6 560	165	6 730	4 505	75	260
1920	7 770	205	7 975	5 440	80	360
1919	7 725	125	7 850	5 370	105	330
1918	7 310	180	7 490	4 955	95	335
1917	7 940	170	8 110	5 570	90	245
1916	8 530	165	8 695	6 185	90	325
1915	8 020	135	8 150	5 750	85	300
1914	8 565	15	8 550	6 290	85	265
1913	9 170	165	9 005	6 835	80	260
1912	9 330	145	9 185	6 990	80	250
1911	9 020	150	8 870	6 680	80	240
1910	9 295	80	9 215	6 910	90	220
1909	9 275	50	9 225	6 910	80	230
1908	8 725	80	8 645	6 520	70	205
1907	9 555	115	9 440	7 145	65	235
1906	9 225	95	9 130	7 145	60	225
1905	8 625	90	8 535	6 755	35	195
1904	8 490	150	8 340	6 675	20	190
1903	8 215	140	8 075	6 445	15	175
1902	7 880	60	7 820	6 180	10	160
1901	7 580	110	7 470	5 930	5	150
1900	7 285	140	7 140	5 680	5	135

Z Less than 2.5 million cubic feet.

Series L 87-97. Per Capita Consumption of Timber Products, by Major Product: 1900 to 1988
(Cubic feet per persons)

Year	All products	Industrial roundwood					Fuelwood
		Total	Lumber	Plywood and veneer	Pulp products	Miscellaneous products [1]	
	87	88	89	91	93	95	96
1988	79.5	65.9	34.2	6.9	22.7	2.1	13.6
1987	81.0	68.0	36.3	7.2	22.4	2.0	12.9
1986	78.8	65.9	35.0	6.7	22.2	2.0	12.9
1985	76.2	61.8	32.2	6.5	21.1	1.9	14.4
1984	77.9	62.6	31.9	6.3	22.3	1.9	15.3
1983	72.0	58.2	29.5	6.2	20.5	1.9	13.8
1982	65.7	51.3	24.9	5.2	19.3	1.9	14.4
1981	66.9	52.8	25.6	5.4	20.2	1.6	14.0
1980	70.8	57.2	28.3	5.5	21.4	1.8	13.6
1979	74.4	64.3	33.7	6.8	21.9	1.8	10.1
1978	67.7	64.6	34.1	7.5	21.2	1.8	3.1
1977	65.1	62.1	32.9	7.4	19.9	1.8	2.9
1976	62.2	59.4	30.1	7.0	20.5	1.8	2.8
1975	54.0	51.4	25.8	5.9	17.9	1.8	2.6
1974	61.5	58.9	28.0	5.9	23.1	1.9	2.5
1973	65.7	63.3	32.5	7.2	21.7	1.9	2.4
1972	64.3	62.1	32.3	7.4	20.4	1.9	2.3
1971	63.7	61.0	31.2	6.9	20.6	2.2	2.4
1970	62.1	59.5	29.8	6.0	21.5	2.1	2.6
1969	64.1	61.0	31.3	6.0	21.5	2.2	3.1
1968	64.8	61.3	31.9	6.4	20.2	2.4	3.5
1967	62.4	58.5	30.1	5.7	20.0	2.6	3.9
1966	65.8	61.5	32.0	5.8	20.7	2.9	4.3
1965	66.1	61.4	32.7	5.8	20.0	2.9	4.7
1964	65.0	59.9	32.9	5.5	18.7	2.8	5.1
1963	63.3	57.7	32.0	5.0	17.9	2.7	5.6
1962	62.0	56.0	30.9	4.7	17.8	2.5	6.0
1961	61.0	54.4	29.9	4.5	17.3	2.7	6.6
1960	63.3	56.1	30.8	4.2	18.2	2.8	7.2
1959	68.2	60.4	35.2	4.4	17.6	3.0	7.8
1958	64.0	55.5	31.9	3.8	16.5	3.2	8.5
1957	65.9	56.8	31.6	3.5	18.2	3.4	9.1
1956	74.6	64.8	37.5	3.7	19.9	3.6	9.8
1955	73.8	63.3	37.5	3.7	18.1	3.8	10.5
1954	72.3	61.0	36.8	3.1	16.8	4.0	11.3
1953	74.5	62.6	37.7	3.1	17.3	4.2	12.0
1952	75.8	63.0	38.7	2.8	16.9	4.4	12.7
1951	78.6	64.2	38.9	2.6	17.8	4.7	14.4
1950	80.0	65.1	41.8	2.3	15.6	5.1	14.9
1949	74.6	55.7	34.5	2.1	14.1	5.0	18.9
1948	81.9	63.7	40.5	2.0	15.3	5.8	18.2
1947	79.8	61.2	38.1	1.8	14.7	6.5	18.6
1946	78.4	59.4	38.1	1.8	13.3	6.3	18.9
1945	73.2	51.9	31.9	1.7	12.3	6.0	21.3
1944	78.6	57.6	37.7	1.9	11.5	6.5	21.1
1943	79.9	59.5	39.6	1.9	11.3	6.7	20.4
1942	86.3	65.1	43.1	2.2	12.3	7.4	21.2
1941	91.9	65.0	43.4	1.9	11.9	7.7	26.9
1940	85.3	55.8	36.4	1.7	10.4	7.3	29.4
1939	84.8	52.8	33.7	1.6	10.1	7.4	32.0
1938	79.8	46.5	29.2	1.5	8.7	7.1	33.3
1937	85.8	54.2	34.1	1.5	10.7	7.9	31.6
1936	84.3	51.1	32.7	1.2	9.4	7.6	33.3
1935	78.8	43.4	27.0	1.1	8.3	7.0	35.5
1934	75.3	37.1	21.8	1.0	7.6	6.8	38.2
1933	74.8	34.9	20.1	1.0	7.2	6.6	39.8
1932	69.6	29.7	15.9	.9	6.3	6.7	39.9
1931	75.3	39.9	23.9	1.0	7.2	7.8	35.4

See footnote at end of chart.

Series L 87-97. Per Capita Consumption of Timber Products, by Major Product: 1900 to 1988—Cont'd.
(Cubic feet per persons)

| Year | All products | Industrial roundwood | | | | | | Fuelwood |
		Total	Lumber	Plywood and veneer	Pulp products	Miscellaneous products [1]	
	87	**88**	**89**	**91**	**93**	**95**	**96**
1930	85.3	54.5	35.6	1.2	7.9	9.7	30.8
1929	94.8	68.8	47.3	1.6	8.5	11.3	26.0
1928	92.8	66.1	45.1	1.5	8.0	11.5	26.8
1927	95.1	68.2	46.9	1.4	7.8	12.1	26.9
1926	99.3	73.2	51.4	1.2	7.9	12.7	26.1
1925	103.1	75.2	54.0	1.2	7.1	12.9	27.8
1924	104.4	74.7	52.4	1.0	6.8	14.5	29.6
1923	109.5	79.4	56.3	1.0	6.8	15.2	30.2
1922	105.9	71.7	49.2	.8	6.3	15.4	34.2
1921	101.4	62.0	40.8	.7	4.7	15.9	39.4
1920	113.1	74.9	50.5	.8	5.9	17.7	38.2
1919	113.5	74.7	50.6	1.0	4.9	18.2	38.8
1918	112.7	71.7	47.6	.9	4.8	18.4	41.1
1917	117.5	78.4	53.9	.9	5.0	18.7	39.1
1916	124.1	85.3	60.6	.9	4.9	18.9	38.8
1915	120.6	81.1	56.9	.8	4.6	18.8	39.6
1914	126.4	86.3	61.7	.9	4.4	19.4	40.1
1913	131.5	92.6	67.0	.8	4.3	20.5	38.9
1912	135.8	96.4	70.3	.8	4.1	21.1	39.5
1911	137.4	94.5	68.0	.9	4.0	22.5	43.0
1910	142.0	99.7	72.5	1.0	3.8	22.5	42.3
1909	144.2	101.9	74.7	.9	3.7	22.7	42.3
1908	142.3	97.5	71.7	.8	3.2	21.8	44.8
1907	152.5	108.5	79.7	.7	3.9	24.3	44.0
1906	152.6	106.9	81.7	.7	3.5	21.1	45.7
1905	150.2	101.8	78.8	.4	3.1	19.6	48.3
1904	152.6	101.5	78.7	.2	3.0	19.5	51.1
1903	154.2	100.2	77.6	.2	2.9	19.5	54.0
1902	155.6	98.7	76.6	.1	2.7	19.3	56.8
1901	156.2	96.3	74.5	.1	2.4	19.2	59.9
1900	156.9	93.8	72.3	.1	2.2	19.2	63.1

1. Includes cooperage logs, poles and piling, fence posts, hewn ties, round mine timbers, box bolts, excelsior bolts, chemical wood, shingle bolts and miscellaneous items.

Series L 166-177. Paper and Board Domestic Production, Apparent Consumption, and Waste Paper Consumption: 1809 to 1997

(In thousands short tons)

Year	Paper and board			Year	Paper and board			Year	Paper and board		
	Domestic production	Apparent consumption [1]	Waste paper consumption		Domestic production	Apparent consumption [1]	Waste paper consumption		Domestic production	Apparent consumption [1]	Waste paper consumption
	172	174	175		172	174	175		172	174	175
1997	96 828	...	...	1961	35 749	40 312	9 018	1925	9 002	10 417	...
1996	92 195	...	...	1960	34 444	39 138	9 032	1924	7 930	9 281	...
1995	91 352	...	...	1959	34 015	38 725	9 414	1923	7 871	9 194	...
1994	90 897	...	...	1958	30 823	35 119	8 671				
1993	86 693	...	...					1922	6 875	7 865	...
				1957	30 666	35 268	8 493	1921	5 333	6 027	...
1992	84 701	...	...	1956	31 441	36 496	8 836	1920	7 185	7 640	...
1991	81 234	84 800	23 500	1955	30 178	34 719	9 041	1919	5 966	6 253	1 854
1990	80 445	86 700	21 700	1954	26 876	31 379	7 857	1918	5 938	6 275	...
1989	78 400	85 200	20 200	1953	26 605	31 360	8 531	1917	5 804	6 054	...
1988	78 100	85 600	19 700					1916	...	...	...
				1952	24 418	29 017	7 881	1915	...	...	...
1987	78 000	83 600	18 700	1951	26 047	30 561	9 071	1914	5 153	5 395	1 510
1986	72 700	79 800	17 900	1950	24 375	29 011	7 956	1913	...	...	...
1985	68 700	76 100	16 400	1949	20 315	24 694	6 600				
1984	70 600	77 300	16 700	1948	21 897	26 082	7 585	1912	...	...	...
1983	66 900	71 400	15 600					1911	...	...	...
				1947	21 102	24 749	8 009	1910	...	...	...
1982	61 200	64 900	14 600	1946	19 278	22 510	7 278	1909	4 121	4 103	984
1981	64 400	64 100	15 000	1945	17 371	19 665	6 800	1908	...	...	...
1980	63 600	67 200	14 900	1944	17 183	19 445	6 859				
1979	67 000	72 700	15 400	1943	17 036	19 437	6 368	1907	...	...	...
1978	64 300	70 400	14 800					1906	...	...	...
				1942	17 084	19 780	5 495	1905	...	...	...
1977	62 100	66 500	14 100	1941	17 762	20 421	6 075	1904	3 107	3 029	589
1976	60 500	64 300	13 600	1940	14 484	16 757	4 668	1903	...	...	...
1975	52 800	56 000	11 700	1939	13 510	15 949	4 366				
1974	61 100	65 500	14 000	1938	11 381	13 542	...	1902	...	...	...
1973	61 800	67 400	14 100					1901	...	...	...
				1937	12 837	16 028	...	1900	...	...	...
1972	59 500	64 500	12 925	1936	11 976	14 651	...	1899	2 168	2 168	...
1971	55 100	59 700	12 100	1935	10 479	12 758	3 587	1889	935	...	...
1970	53 516	58 057	10 594	1934	9 187	11 289	...				
1969	54 187	59 003	10 939	1933	9 190	10 916	...	1879	452	...	...
1968	51 245	55 664	10 222					1869	[2] 386	...	...
				1932	7 998	9 727	...	1859	127	...	...
1967	46 926	51 945	9 888	1931	9 382	11 347	...	1849	[2] 78	...	...
1966	47 113	52 680	10 564	1930	10 169	12 319	...	1839	[2] 38	...	...
1965	44 080	49 102	10 231	1929	11 140	13 411	3 842				
1964	41 703	46 384	9 843	1928	10 403	12 451	...	1819	[2] 12	...	...
1963	39 230	43 715	9 613					1809	[2] 3	...	...
				1927	10 002	11 925	...				
1962	37 541	42 216	9 075	1926	9 794	11 584	...				

1. Beginning 1929, includes changes in newsprint stocks.
2. Estimated from values reported by the Bureau of the Census.

Series L 192-198. Newsprint Production, Shipments, Consumption, Stocks, Imports and Price: 1935 to 1996

(In thousands of metric tons, except as indicated)

Year	Production	Shipments from mills	Consumption[2]	Imports	Year	Production	Shipments from mills	Consumption by publishers	Imports
	192	**193**	**194**	**197**		**192**	**193**	**194**	**197**
1996	6 304	. . .	11 256	. . .	1963	2 218	2 208	5 585	5 413
1995	6 352	. . .	11 826	. . .	1962	2 154	2 162	5 577	5 474
1994	6 336	. . .	11 535	. . .	1961	2 094	2 086	5 461	5 435
1993	6 412	. . .	11 505	. . .	1960	2 038	2 031	5 532	5 412
1992	6 424	6 464	11 268	. . .	1959	1 964	1 963	5 328	5 255
1991	6 206	6 152	12 126	. . .	1958	1 758	1 761	4 950	4 884
1990	5 997	6 007	12 241	. . .	1957	1 826	1 817	5 149	5 218
1989	5 523	5 515	12 241	8 765	1956	1 717	1 715	5 209	5 567
1988	5 427	5 415	12 244	8 592	1955	1 552	1 550	5 045	5 164
1987	5 300	5 310	12 303	8 976	1954	1 211	1 213	4 684	4 995
1986	5 107	5 115	11 873	8 589	1953	1 084	1 088	4 669	5 006
1985	4 924	4 927	11 507	8 472	1952	1 147	1 143	4 551	5 036
1984	5 025	5 065	11 349	7 899	1951	1 125	1 125	4 511	4 963
1983	4 688	4 674	10 529	6 919	1950	1 015	1 017	4 542	4 864
1982	4 574	4 525	10 107	5 925	1949	900	898	4 257	4 640
1981	4 753	4 735	10 165	6 329	1948	867	867	4 010	4 395
1980	4 239	4 234	10 088	7 280	1947	826	832	3 565	3 958
1979	4 096	4 100	11 240	7 223	1946	771	762	3 136	3 492
1978	3 768	3 779	10 874	7 484	1945	724	725	2 455	2 669
1977	3 870	3 866	10 230	6 559	1944	720	723	2 351	2 491
1976	3 736	3 728	9 611	6 569	1943	805	803	2 720	2 637
1975	3 348	3 347	8 395	5 847	1942	953	951	2 835	2 921
1971	3 296	3 288	7 057	6 835	1941	1 015	1 021	2 947	2 982
1970[1]	3 142	3 136	8 805	6 635	1940	1 013	1 013	2 856	2 763
1969	3 232	3 233	7 344	6 790	1939	939	945	2 730	2 615
1968	2 935	2 946	7 025	6 463	1938	820	817	2 653	2 275
1967	2 620	2 602	6 907	6 599	1937	946	945	2 956	3 317
1966	2 408	2 405	6 898	6 991	1936	921	917	2 939	2 752
1965	2 180	2 183	6 387	6 323	1935	912	917	2 663	2 383
1964	2 261	2 273	6 031	5 954					

1. For this and earlier years, thousands of short tons.
2. 1970 to date, all users; previously, publishers.

Series L 224-235. Yield and Value of Domestic Fisheries, Imports and Exports: 1880 to 1997

Year	Yield (mil. lb.) Domestic			Value (mil. dol.)			Year	Yield (mil. lb.) Domestic			Value (mil. dol.)		
	Total	For human food	For industrial use	Domestic total	Total imports [1]	Total exports [1]		Total	For human food	For industrial use	Domestic total	Total imports [1]	Total exports [1]
	224	**225**	**226**	**229**	**230**	**233**		**224**	**225**	**226**	**229**	**230**	**233**
1997	9 845	7 248	2 597	3 467	...	...	1953	4 487	2 519	1 968	356.1	245.5	27.9
1996	9 565	7 476	2 090	3 487	...	...							
1995	9 788	7 667	2 121	3 770	...	...	1952	4 432	2 778	1 654	363.6	240.4	21.9
1994	10 461	7 936	2 525	3 807	...	...	1951	4 433	3 048	1 385	364.8	212.5	35.7
1993	10 467	8 214	2 253	3 471	...	...	1950	4 901	3 307	1 594	347.4	198.3	27.5
							1949	4 804	3 305	1 499	342.7	151.6	35.1
1992	9 637	7 618	2 019	3 678	...	...	1948	4 513	3 146	1 367	371.1	156.6	24.4
1991	9 484	7 031	2 453	3 308	...	...							
1990	9 404	7 041	2 362	3 522	9 048	5 639	1947	4 349	3 020	1 329	312.0	110.0	52.8
1989	8 463	6 204	2 259	3 238	9 604	4 707	1946	4 467	3 049	1 418	313.0	129.7	40.0
1988	7 192	4 588	2 604	3 520	8 872	2 275	1945	4 598	3 167	1 431	269.9	101.3	38.5
							1944	4 533	2 865	1 668	213.0	78.4	35.9
1987	6 896	3 946	2 950	3 115	8 818	1 660	1943	4 162	2 737	1 425	204.0	67.2	48.5
1986	6 031	3 393	2 638	2 763	7 626	1 356							
1985	6 258	3 294	2 964	2 326	6 679	1 084	1942	3 875	2 683	1 192	170.3	39.6	31.9
1984	6 438	3 320	3 118	2 350	5 883	949	1941	4 900	3 062	1 838	129.0	41.0	22.0
1983	6 439	3 238	3 201	2 355	5 129	1 021	1940	4 060	2 675	1 385	96.1	41.8	17.8
							1939	4 445	2 713	1 732	97.6	46.0	14.2
1982	6 367	3 285	3 082	2 390	4 523	1 059	1938	4 254	2 639	1 615	94.2	39.3	14.4
1981	5 977	3 547	2 430	2 388	4 206	1 157							
1980	6 482	3 654	2 828	2 237	3 648	1 006	1937	4 353	2 703	1 650	101.4	50.6	14.6
1979	6 267	3 318	2 949	2 234	3 809	1 084	1936	4 826	2 854	1 972	94.8	41.9	13.2
1978	6 028	3 177	2 851	1 854	3 086	906	1935	4 135	2 583	1 552	82.8	36.2	14.4
							1934	4 104	2 434	1 670	76.8	30.8	13.8
1977	5 271	2 592	2 319	1 554	2 634	520	1933	2 997	2 087	911	61.1	305	8.3
1976	5 388	2 775	2 613	1 349	2 328	385							
1975	4 877	2 465	2 412	977	1 637	305	1932	2 612	1 864	748	56.0	29.6	7.8
1974	4 967	2 496	2 471	932	1 711	262	1931	2 630	2 129	501	77.0	43.0	11.6
1973	4 858	2 398	2 460	937	1 583	299	1930	3 224	2 478	746	109.0	50.8	17.3
							1929	3 491	2 601	890	125.8	66.6	23.8
1972	4 806	2 435	2 371	748	1 494	158	1928	3 061	2 370	691	114.3	58.9	21.2
1971	4 969	2 400	2 569	643	1 074	139							
1970	4 917	2 537	2 380	613.1	1 037.4	117.5	1927	2 806	2 172	634	111.5	55.6	18.7
1969	4 337	2 321	2 016	526.5	844.3	104.5	1926	2 871	2 198	673	106.7	50.1	20.3
1968	4 160	2 347	1 814	497.3	822.7	67.8	1925	2 891	2 029	862	105.1	49.0	21.3
							1924	2 461	1 874	587	...	46.3	20.9
1967	4 055	2 368	1 687	439.6	707.9	82.2	1923	2 726	1 807	919	...	...	...
1966	4 366	2 573	1 794	472.3	719.7	84.8							
1965	4 777	2 587	2 190	445.7	600.9	69.5	1922	2 619	1 677	942	...	...	...
1964	4 541	2 497	2 044	389.5	564.2	64.2	1921	2 255	1 451	804	...	...	...
1963	4 847	2 556	2 291	377.2	500.7	56.6	1917	2 676	...	...	71.1	...	...
							1908	2 053	...	...	62.7	...	...
1962	5 354	2 540	2 814	396.4	489.8	35.7	1907	1 930	...	...	60.9	...	...
1961	5 187	2 490	2 697	362.2	400.6	34.7							
1960	4 942	2 498	2 444	353.6	363.3	44.2	1906	2 046	...	...	59.3	...	...
1959	5 122	2 369	2 753	346.1	370.1	44.2	1905	2 002	...	...	57.3	...	...
1958	4 747	2 651	2 096	373.3	330.8	31.0	1892	1 652	...	...	40.7	...	...
							1891	1 709	...	...	42.3	...	...
1957	4 789	2 475	2 314	353.7	299.3	36.0	1890	1 758	...	...	41.3	...	...
1956	5 268	2 690	2 578	372.2	282.7	39.5							
1955	4 809	2 579	2 230	338.9	258.9	40.0	1889	1 685	...	...	39.0	...	...
1954	4 762	2 705	2 057	359.3	252.4	31.5	1880	1 706	...	...	39.1	...	...

1. Fish as fish products. Includes Puerto Rico; beginning 1955, imports also include landings of tuna by foreign vessels in American Samoa, and imports of tuna into U.S. outlying areas.

260

Series L 254-261.   Fisheries—Employment, Fishing Craft and Establishments: 1930 to 1992

Year	Persons employed (1 000)		Craft utilized				Fishery shore establishments
	Total	Fishermen	Total	Vessels [1]	Motorboats	Other boats	
	254	255	257	258	259	260	261
1992	...	...	...	...	...	...	4 900
1991	...	...	...	...	...	...	4 600
1989	...	...	111 000	36 000	75 000	...	4 500
1988	364	274	110 000	32 000	78 000	...	4 600
1987	359	256	93 000	23 000	68 000	2 000	4 200
1986	347	247	128 000	38 000	88 000	2 000	4 000
1985	351	239	130 000	24 000	104 000	2 000	4 000
1984	340	230	127 000	24 000	102 000	1 000	4 000
1983	333	223	127 000	21 000	105 000	1 000	3 900
1982	314	216	123 000	20 000	102 000	1 000	3 600
1981	303	198	115 000	20 000	93 000	2 000	3 600
1980	296	193	113 000	19 000	93 000	1 000	3 600
1979	267	184	103 000	18 000	84 000	1 000	3 400
1978	257	172	104 000	18 000	84 000	2 000	3 300
1977	269	173	104 000	11 000	84 000	2 000	3 600
1976	266	174	103 000	17 000	84 000	2 000	3 600
1975	260	168	103 000	16 000	85 000	2 000	3 600
1974	253	161	101 000	16 000	83 000	2 000	3 500
1973	243	149	90 000	15 000	72 000	2 000	3 600
1972	...	...	91 000	...	...	...	3 700
1971	230	139	86 000	14 000	71 000	2 000	3 800
1970	227	140	88 400	13 300	73 100	2 000	3 735
1969	220	132	77 057	12 018	56 889	8 150	4 207
1968	217	128	81 614	13 150	66 654	1 810	3 967
1967	220	132	81 328	12 874	66 075	2 379	4 053
1966	224	136	82 122	12 677	66 941	2 504	4 187
1965	215	129	79 532	12 311	63 828	3 393	4 189
1964	212	128	76 412	11 808	60 945	3 659	4 121
1963	216	128	77 973	11 928	62 090	3 955	4 194
1962	217	126	70 733	11 511	54 406	4 816	4 135
1961	222	130	77 487	11 964	60 118	5 405	4 138
1960	224	130	77 057	12 018	56 889	8 150	4 207
1959	222	129	75 301	12 109	54 735	8 457	4 372
1958	227	129	75 291	11 496	54 821	8 974	4 402
1957	235	138	77 970	11 671	56 434	9 865	4 322
1956	248	145	82 300	11 300	52 000	19 000	4 000
1955	241	144	83 292	11 796	58 218	13 278	4 124
1954	246	145	82 090	11 179	51 814	19 097	4 012
1953	254	153	86 681	10 621	48 067	27 993	3 904
1952	254	152	88 136	11 065	46 291	30 780	3 843
1951	...	155	89 791	11 242	45 749	32 800	...
1950	263	161	92 310	11 496	46 067	34 747	3 883
1940	215	125	71 810	5 562	31 055	35 193	3 055
1930	199	120	77 772	4 374	35 437	37 961	2 995

1. 5 net tons and over.

Series LL 1.   Forest and Timberland Area, Sawtimber and Stock: 1970 to 1992

(As of Jan. 1. 754 acres represents 754 000 000 acres)

Year and region	Total forest land (mil. acres)	Timberland, ownership [1]				Sawtimber, net volume [3]		Growing stock, net volume [4]	
		All ownerships (mil. acres)	Federally owned or managed [2] (mil. acres)	State, county, and municipal (mil. acres)	Private (mil. acres)	Total (bil. bd. ft.)	Softwood (bil. bd. ft.)	Total (bil. cu. ft.)	Softwood (bil. cu. ft.)
United States, 1970	754	504	116	29	360	2 587	2 035	694	458
North......................................	. . .	154	11	18	126	295	81	146	39
South	. . .	203	15	3	185	569	302	191	87
Rocky Mountains	. . .	65	42	2	20	398	384	101	95
Pacific Coast.........................	. . .	82	47	5	29	1 325	1 268	257	238
United States, 1987	731	485	97	34	354	2 853	2 040	766	453
North......................................	165	154	11	19	124	459	126	190	48
South	203	197	16	4	177	781	388	245	106
Rocky Mountains	142	61	39	3	20	411	394	108	100
Pacific Coast.........................	220	72	31	8	32	1 202	1 132	223	199
United States, 1992	737	490	97	35	358	2 992	2 047	786	450
North......................................	168	158	11	19	127	540	137	207	51
South	212	199	16	4	179	842	389	251	103
Rocky Mountains	140	63	40	3	20	415	397	110	101
Pacific Coast.........................	217	70	30	8	32	1 196	1 124	218	195

1. Timberland is forest land that is producing or is capable of crops of industrial wood and not withdrawn from timber utilization by statute or administrative regulation. Areas qualifying as timberland have the capability of producing in excess of 20 cubic feet per acre per year of industrial wood in natural stands. Currently inaccessible and inoperable areas are included.
2. Includes Indian lands.
3. Sawtimber is timber suitable for sawing into lumber. Live trees of commercial species containing at least one 12-foot sawlog or two noncontinguous 8-foot logs, and meeting regional specifications for freedom from defect. Softwood trees must be at least 9.0-inches diameter, and hardwood trees must be at least 11.0-inches diameter at 4½ feet above ground. International ¼-inch rule.
4. Live trees of commercial species meeting specified standards of quality or vigor. Cull trees are excluded. Includes only trees 5.0-inches diameter or larger at 4 1/1 feet above ground.

SOURCE: U.S. Forest Service, Forest Resources of the United States, 1992.

SECTION M

MINERALS
Highlights

1 The principal source for minerals data is the *Minerals Yearbook* published annually since 1932 to 1933 by the U.S. Bureau of Mines. For earlier years, the same data are provided by the *Minerals Resources of the United States*, which was published from 1882 until 1932 by the U. S. Geological Survey. Since 1977, mineral fuel data have been collected and published by the Energy Information Administration.

2 Censuses of mineral industries have been conducted by the Bureau of the Census at various intervals since 1840. Since 1967, the census has been conducted every fifth year for years ending in 2 and 7.

3 Because of poor husbandry of natural resources and unbridled consumption habits, the United States is losing its commanding position in the production of major minerals. It now accounts for more than one-half of world production in only mica among nonmetals and molybdenum among metals. Its share of world production is more than 40% in magnesium, 30% in phosphate rock, 20% in sulfur, natural gas, aluminum and lead and more than 10% in coal, crude oil, gypsum, feldspar, copper and gold. The United States is 100% dependent on foreign suppliers for columbium, strontium, manganese and bauxite; 88% for the platinum group, 85% for tantalum, 80% for cobalt, and barite; 78% for tungsten, 77% for chromium, 74% for nickel, 73% for tin, 70% for barium, 67% for potassium, 57% for antimony, 54% for cadmium, 52% for selenium 45% for titanium, 35% for zinc, 26% for aluminum, and 18% for copper and iron and steel.

4 In 1997, there were 26,100 mining establishments (of which 5,600 have 20 or more employees) employing 550,000 workers. The value added in mining was $113.621 billion, of which oil and gas extraction accounted for $80.016 billion. Nevada leads all states in mineral production with $3.1 billion, followed by California ($2.97 billion), Arizona ($2.82 billion), and Georgia ($2.140 billion).

5 The federal government maintains the world's largest stockpile of strategic minerals. In 1997, they included 104,000 tons of tin, 39.152 million troy oz of silver, 38 million pounds of cobalt, 2.691 million tons of manganese, 82 million pounds of tungsten, 244 million tons of zinc, 37,000 tons of titanium, 440,000 troy oz of platinum, 1.128 million tons of chromium and 3.751 million carats of diamonds.

6 The United States is the world's largest exporter of coal, producing 1.090 billion tons of coal, or 20.9% of world production. The United States is the second largest producer of coal; the first is China. The most significant coal mining states are Wyoming, Kentucky and West Virginia. The number of mines has declined to 1,828 in 1997 from 5,598 in 1980, and the number of miners from 225,00 to 82,000 during the same period.

7 Proved U.S. reserves of oil may last for 10 years at current rates of production. The United States fares better in natural gas with reserves of 169 trillion cubic feet. U.S. production of natural gas accounts for 23% of the world total, making it the world's second largest natural gas producer, after Russia. U.S. production of crude oil in 1998 was 2.282 billion barrels of which Alaska alone accounted for 429 million barrels and offshore wells for 607 million barrels. U. S. dependence on foreign oil, which was significantly reduced in the 1970s, is once again rising. Imports of foreign oil has increased to 3.178 billion barrels compared to 1.921 billion barrels in 1980. The number of oil wells drilled, which peaked in 1985 at close to 70,000, dropped to fewer than 30,000 in 1998. There were 163 operating refineries in 1998, down from 319 in 1980. The refineries total output was 6.190 billion barrels, of which motor gasoline was a little less than half. Natural gas production was 19.865 trillion cubic feet of which Louisiana and Texas together accounted for 59%. Oklahoma and New Mexico are the other major producers.

8 The 1998 prices of major minerals are far below those prevailing in1980. Copper dropped from $1.01 per pound to 80 cents; platinum from $677 per troy oz. to $406; gold from $613 per oz. to $300; silver from $20.63 per oz to $5.1 and tin from $8.46 per pound to $3.77.

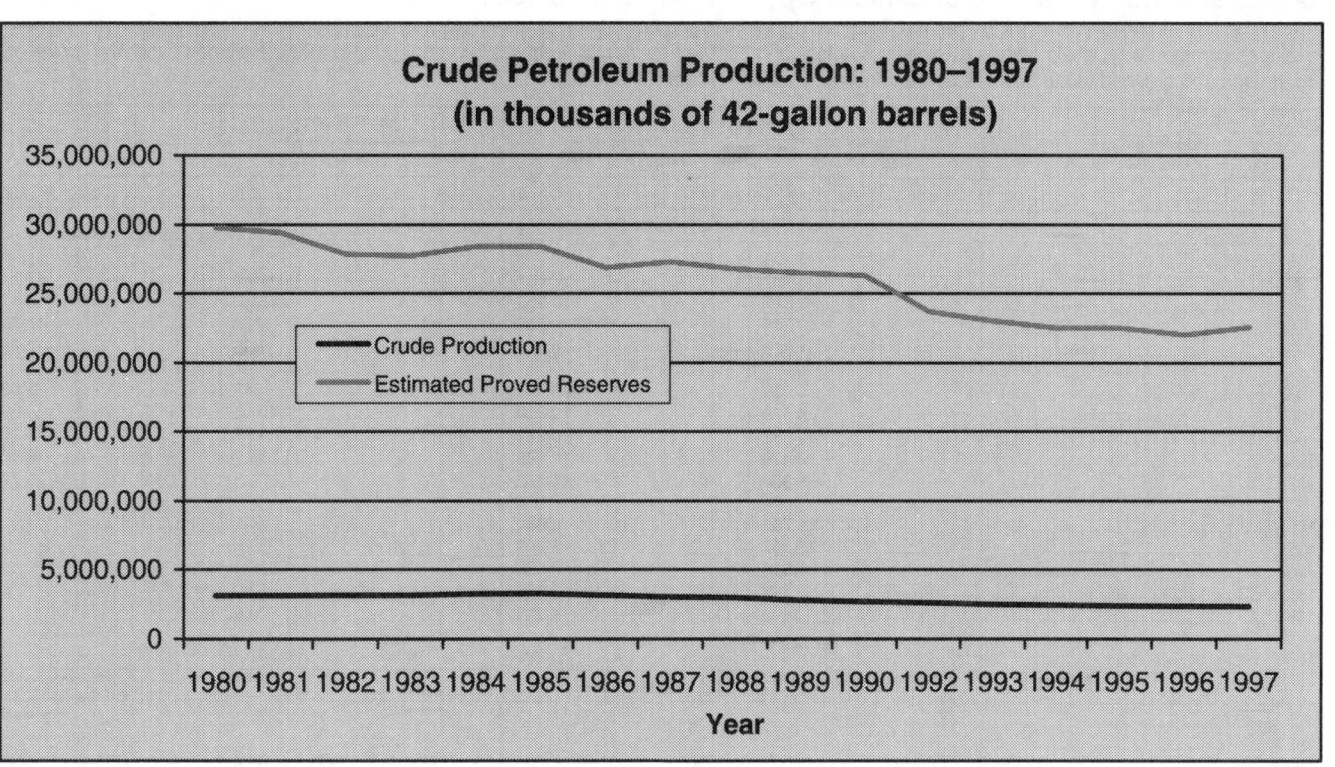

Crude Petroleum Production: 1980–1997
(in thousands of 42-gallon barrels)

Series M 1-12. Summary of Mineral Operations: 1840 to 1997

(From Census of Mined Industries. In general, includes data for mining operations at manufacturing establishments. For all years prior to 1935, excludes common clay, shale and pea (except as noted) and contract service operations; for years prior to 1929, excludes sand and gravel operations and crushed stone quarries at manufacturing plants, except as indicated)

Industry group and year	Number of establishments	Value added in mining (mil. dol.)	Production and development workers (1 000)	Capital expenditures (mil. dol.)
	1	4	5	11
ALL MINERAL OPERATIONS				
1997	26 100	. . .	. . .	. . .
1992	30 787	113 621	415.0	17 179
1987	33 617	110 959	451.0	15 418
1982	42 241	188 055	762	47 753
1977	31 359	68 013	593	17 718
1972	25 269	26 471	443	5 026
1967 [1]	28 579	19 330	401.6	4 058
1963	40 532	16 231	501.7	3 268
1958	37 958	13 685	585.2	2 807
1954	38 858	11 752	667.8	2 728
1939 [2]	24 703	2 680	774.1	. . .
1919	22 347	2 399	989.8	. . .
1909	25 698	928	961.1	. . .
1902 [3]	52 123	628	[4] 582.0	. . .
1889	. . .	336	[5] 529.6	. . .
1880	. . .	221	[5] 301.2	. . .
METAL MINING				
1997	. . .	. . .	. . .	. . .
1993	. . .	. . .	. . .	. . .
1992	1 023	6 724	42.0	1 580
1987	1 027	4 610	34.0	899
1982	1 434	3 215	. . .	. . .
1977	1 206	3 504	. . .	. . .
1972	. . .	2 382	. . .	. . .
1967 [1]	1 155	1 557	55.4	340
1963	1 614	1 418	62.2	231
1958	2 351	1 180	70.8	215
1954	3 668	[6] 1 084	82.7	222
1939 [2]	[7] 2 164	417	89.8	. . .
1929 [2,8]	1 799	496	115.8	. . .
1919 [9]	2 739	413	138.2	. . .
1909 [10]	7 834	267	164.9	. . .
1902 [3]	7 730	168	[4] 123.2	. . .
1889	. . .	132	104.2	. . .
1880	4 048	104	62.6	. . .
1870	2 969	41	[5] 39.9	. . .
1860	7 462	37	[5] 53.6	. . .
COAL MINING				
1997	. . .	. . .	. . .	. . .
1992	3 069	17 252	108.0	1 943
1987	3 905	17 068	129.0	1 665
1982	5 087	18 631	. . .	. . .
1977	5 451	11 266	. . .	. . .
1972	. . .	3 754	. . .	. . .
1967 [1]	4 484	2 091	115.1	341
1963	7 374	1 727	129.0	233
1958	8 188	1 780	183.8	205
1954	8 301	1 621	233.0	131
1939 [2]	[7] 6 468	765	454.1	. . .
1935 [2,11]	[12] 6 661	[12] 730	527.9	. . .
1929 [2]	5 193	1 141	601.6	. . .
1919	6 924	1 252	693.8	. . .
1909	4 765	462	657.8	. . .
1902 [2,3]	6 017	328	[4] 350.8	. . .
1889 [2]	[13] 12 552	138	291.5	. . .
1880 [2]	[14] 8 419	84	[5] 180.0	. . .
1870 [2]	1 566	68	[5] 94.8	. . .
1860 [2]	622	17	[5] 36.5	. . .

See footnotes at end of chart.

Series M 1-12. Summary of Mineral Operations: 1840 to 1997—Cont'd.

(From Census of Mined Industries. In general, includes data for mining operations at manufacturing establishments. For all years prior to 1935, excludes common clay, shale and pea (except as noted) and contract service operations; for years prior to 1929, excludes sand and gravel operations and crushed stone quarries at manufacturing plants, except as indicated)

Industry group and year	Number of establishments	Value added in mining (mil. dol.)	Production and development workers (1 000)	Capital expenditures (mil. dol.)
	1	4	5	11
COAL MINING (CONTINUED)				
1850 [2]	510	7	[5] 15.1	...
1840 [2]	...	...	[5] 6.8	...
OIL AND GAS EXTRACTION				
1997	...	...	...	...
1992	20 891	80 016	188.0	12 519
1987	22 910	80 049	206.0	11 717
1982	29 974	159 937	...	...
1977	18 447	48 587	...	...
1972	...	17 612	...	...
1967 [1]	16 358	13 394	167.2	3 005
1963	21 242	11 020	192.0	2 552
1958	18 522	9 032	214.0	2 194
1954	17 591	[2, 15] 7 674	235.5	2 228
1939 [2]	10 909	[15] 1 242	149.0	...
1919 [2]	9 970	614	93.7	...
1909	8 202	112	37.6	...
1902 [3]	[16] 31 736	59	[4] 22.4	...
1889	...	15	26.9	...
1880 [17]	...	18	[5] 11.5	...
1870	2 314	18	[5] 4.5	...
1860 [18]	64	2	[5] .9	...

1. First year that data for single unit establishments without paid employees were excluded from the census. For 1963, for mining as a whole, included 6 543 such establishments, accounting for approximately 3 percent of value added. The number of such establishments in 1963 for metal mining was 460; for coal mining, 1 347; for oil and gas extraction, 3 714; and for nonmetallic minerals (except fuels), 1 022.
2. Excludes Alaska.
3. Operators of mineral properties reported an average of 8 527 employees performing contract service operations for metal mines; 6 906 for coal mines; 12 143 for oil and gas field operations; and 592 for nonmetallic minerals (except fuels). These are not included in the employment series shown.
4. Figures for average employment converted to a 300-day basis for establishments operating for a shorter period.
5. "All other" employees included with production and exploration workers.
6. Excludes uranium-radium-vanadium ores industry.
7. Represents number of mining operations and service establishments.
8. Except for number of establishments, includes 27 nonproducing establishments in the nonmetallic minerals mining industries.
9. Except for number of establishments, excludes 1 chromite mine in Alaska.
10. Except for number of establishments, includes 2 producing and 18 nonproducing establishments in the nonmetallic minerals mining industries.
11. Represents producing operations only.
12. Excludes anthracite stripping services.
13. Includes 9 920 "Local mines and farmers' banks," producing about 2 percent of all bituminous coal and lignite, for which no data are available on labor and expenditures.
14. Includes 5 148 bituminous coal and lignite mines, producing coal valued at $1.1 million, representing "irregular" operations for which no other data are available.
15. For 1954 and 1939, no data obtained on value of gas received for processing at natural gas liquids plants or on value of residue gas sold or transferred. However, for 1954, estimated value (prior to processing) of natural gas liquids contained in such gas was included with value of natural gas liquids received for processing and used in computing value added. No figures for value of residue gas are included in the value of shipments and receipts shown for 1954. For 1939, cost of supplies, purchases for resale, and purchased fuels and electric energy for all oil and gas extraction industries include estimated cost of such items and subcontract work to oil and gas field services industries, for which such data were not requested in 1939. These estimates used in computing value added for such industries. For Alaska in 1958 and 1954, cost of supplies, purchased fuels and electric energy, contract work, and purchased machinery installed exceeded value of shipments and capital expenditures.
16. Represents number of operating companies.
17. Excludes natural gas operations.
18. Reported as "oil, coal" and probably includes some refining as well as production of crude petroleum, or may represent primarily recovery of oil from coal.

Series M 13-37. Value of Mineral Products, in Current Dollars: 1880 to 1998

(In millions of dollars)

Year	Mineral products	Fuels					Nonmetals (except fuels)			
		Total [1]	Bituminous coal and lignite	Pennsylvania anthracite	Petroleum	Natural gas	Total [1]	Portland cement	Raw clay	Lime
	13	14	15	16	17	18	20	21	22	24
1998	...	83 601	19 668	174	24 792	39 082	...	...	...	...
1997	147 204	106 524	19 777	165	40 576	46 098	27 606	5 710	1 670	1 200
1996	145 206	106 197	19 691	177	43 561	42 858	25 994	5 310	1 710	1 170
1995	123 486	84 783	19 469	187	35 006	30 241	24 679	4 920	1 730	1 100
1994	122 015	86 815	19 908	168	31 920	34 819	23 100	4 460	1 600	1 020
1993	125 265	93 265	18 624	141	35 625	38 834	21 200	3 920	1 480	965
1992	127 486	95 453	20 856	120	41 846	32 555	20 496	3 500	1 482	950
1991	...	...	21 598	...	...	30 300	19 617	3 343	1 505	891
1990	141 608	108 144	22 415	138	53 801	31 789	20 891	3 683	1 620	902
1989	123 603	96 378	21 268	142	44 071	30 627	20 357	3 592	1 515	852
1988	119 102	89 088	20 827	159	37 479	30 287	19 805	3 576	1 401	818
1987	123 840	97 499	21 050	157	46 930	29 008	18 894	3 647	1 202	786
1986	117 408	93 944	21 001	190	39 632	23 717	17 647	3 760	1 095	758
1985	168 154	144 847	22 063	215	78 871	43 343	17 678	3 817	1 011	809
1984	179 176	156 026	22 750	200	84 100	48 490	17 173	3 810.4	1 037.2	811.2
1983	168 848	147 748	20 110	210	83 050	43 570	15 263	3 315.7	931.1	757.6
1982	179 042	159 395	22 620	230	90 030	45 560	14 150	3 084.4	825.1	696.2
1981	187 187	161 899	21 510	240	99 400	39 510	16 446	3 515.6	988.8	884.2
1980	146 750	121 612	20 197	259	67 930	32 090	16 213	3 613	899	843
1979	106 856.7	82 888.6	18 243	183.7	39 453.4	24 115.1	15 449	3 650.4	846.1	862.5
1978	86 241.2	86 241	14 486.3	207.1	28 477.8	18 084.9	13 525.7	3 239.6	717.3	749.7
1977	77 112.0	60 182	13 705.2	184.8	25 790.7	15 825.0	11 702	2 727.6	579.2	666.5
1976	69 216.3	52 919	13 189.5	209.2	24 229.5	11 571.8	10 616	2 330.4	528.7	609.0
1975	62 190	47 781	12 472.5	198.5	23 116.1	8 945.1	9 494	2 015.6	424.6	523.8
1974	55 172	40 937	9 502	144.7	21 580.5	1 072.2	8 682	1 992.7	422.5	473.7
1973	36 788	25 012	5 050	90.0	13 057.9	668.8	7 413	1 810.3	354.1	365.8
1972	32 217	22 084	4 561.9	85.2	11 706.5	4 203.2	6 492	1 588.2	303	339.3
1971	30 732	21 258	3 901.4	103.4	11 692.9	4 096.5	6 068	1 421.3	274.4	308.1
1970	29 790	20 153	3 772	105	11 174	3 746	5 711	[2] 1 336	[3] 268	286
1969	26 921	17 965	2 797	94	10 427	3 456	5 624	[2] 1 354	[3] 264	281
1968	24 971	16 820	2 546	97	9 795	3 169	5 448	1 295	[3] 247	250
1967	23 729	16 195	2 555	96	9 376	2 899	5 206	1 211	[3] 224	240
1966	22 968	15 088	2 421	101	8 726	2 703	5 176	1 227	[3]222	240
1965	21 524	14 047	2 276	122	8 158	2 495	4 933	1 221	[3] 205	233
1964	20 612	13 623	2 166	149	8 017	2 388	4 623	1 209	[3] 193	223
1963	19 635	13 317	2 013	154	7 966	2 328	4 316	1 157	[3] 181	199
1962	18 838	12 784	1 892	134	7 774	2 145	4 117	1 129	[3] 163	187
1961	18 230	12 357	1 845	140	7 566	1 996	3 946	1 106	[3] 157	177
1960	18 032	12 142	1 950	147	7 420	1 790	3 868	1 089	[3] 162	173
1959	17 381	11 950	1 966	172	7 473	1 557	3 861	1 145	[3] 160	164
1958	16 649	11 589	1 996	188	7 380	1 317	3 466	1 039	[3] 143	121
1957	18 233	12 709	2 504	228	8 079	1 202	3 387	961	[3] 156	135
1956	17 490	11 741	2 412	237	7 297	1 084	3 391	989	[3] 163	136
1955	15 911	10 780	2 092	206	6 870	978	3 076	884	[3] 140	127
1954	14 170	9 919	1 770	248	6 425	883	2 733	763	[3] 123	102
1953	14 418	10 257	2 248	299	6 327	775	2 350	698	[3] 125	112
1952	13 396	9 616	2 283	380	5 785	624	2 163	638	[3] 131	95
1951	13 529	9 779	2 622	406	5 690	543	2 079	612	[3] 129	97
1950	11 862	8 689	2 497	392	4 963	409	1 822	538	[3] 95	83
1949	10 580	7 920	2 134	358	4 675	344	1 559	475	79	69
1948	12 273	9 502	2 990	467	5 245	333	1 552	446	85	75
1947	9 610	7 188	2 620	413	3 578	275	1 338	357	74	63
1946	7 062	5 090	1 836	413	2 443	212	1 243	297	[3] 61	51
1945	6 231	4 569	1 768	324	2 094	191	888	175	[3] 43	46
1944	6 310	4 574	1 811	355	2 033	190	836	152	37	49
1943	5 931	4 028	1 585	307	1 809	177	916	202	40	49
1942	5 623	3 568	1 374	272	1 643	154	1 056	287	27	44

See footnotes at end of chart.

Series M 13-37. Value of Mineral Products, in Current Dollars: 1880 to 1998—Cont'd.

(In millions of dollars)

Year	Mineral products	Fuels					Nonmetals (except fuels)			
		Total [1]	Bituminous coal and lignite	Pennsylvania anthracite	Petroleum	Natural gas	Total [1]	Portland cement	Raw clay	Lime
	13	14	15	16	17	18	20	21	22	24
1941	5 107	3 228	1 125	240	1 602	139	989	251	27	43
1940	4 198	2 662	879	205	1 385	120	784	193	20	34
1939	3 808	2 423	728	187	1 294	120	754	184	17	30
1938	3 518	2 436	679	181	1 373	114	622	157	13	24
1937	4 265	2 798	864	198	1 513	123	711	171	18	30
1936	3 606	2 405	771	227	1 200	119	685	173	16	27
1935	2 942	2 013	658	210	961	110	564	115	22	
1934	2 744	1 947	628	244	905	106	520	118	17	
1933	2 050	1 413	446	207	608	97	432	86	14	
1932	2 000	1 460	407	222	680	99	412	83	12	
1931	2 578	1 620	589	296	551	108	671	143	19	
1930	3 980	2 500	795	355	1 070	147	973	231	26	
1929	4 908	2 940	953	386	1 280	158	1 166	255	33	
1928	4 484	2 666	934	394	1 055	140	1 163	279	36	
1927	4 698	2 875	1 030	421	1 173	127	1 201	282	39	
1926	5 311	3 371	1 183	474	1 448	125	1 219	281	42	
1925	4 812	2 910	1 060	328	1 285	112	1 187	281	43	
1924	4 754	2 899	1 063	477	1 023	254	1 174	266	40	
1923	5 252	3 317	1 515	507	978	240	1 157	260	40	
1922	4 183	2 738	1 275	274	895	222	921	208	33	
1921	3 828	2 703	1 200	452	815	175	780	182	25	
1920	6 084	4 193	2 130	434	1 361	196	1 025	196	38	
1919	4 007	2 511	1 161	365	760	161	752	147	29	
1918	4 563	2 736	1 492	336	704	154	648	114	27	
1917	4 131	2 238	1 249	284	523	142	666	123	24	
1916	2 993	1 333	665	202	331	120	554	105	19	
1915	2 078	973	502	185	179	101	429	75	14	
1914	1 870	993	493	188	214	94	431	81	13	
1913	2 092	1 088	565	195	237	88	467	90	15	
1912	1 921	946	518	178	164	85	430	70	14	
1911	1 675	836	451	175	134	75	407	67	14	
1910	1 707	828	469	160	128	71	410	69	14	
1909	1 571	746	405	149	128	63	386	54	14	
1908	1 417	716	374	158	129	55	325	44	11	
1907	1 667	789	451	164	120	54	376	56	13	
1906	1 492	652	381	132	92	47	362	55	12	
1905	1 313	602	335	142	84	42	319	36	11	
1904	1 167	584	305	139	101	38	274	26	10	
1903	1 215	634	352	152	95	36	272	32	9	
1902	1 018	469	291	76	71	31	254	25	9	
1901	960	442	236	113	66	27	219	16	8	
1900	914	406	221	86	76	24	188	13	7	
1899	798	341	168	88	65	20	185	13	7	
1898	631	268	133	75	44	15	151	10	7	
1897	574	254	120	79	41	14	128	8	6	
1896	573	268	115	82	59	13	120	6	6	
1895	555	268	116	82	58	13	126	5	7	
1894	498	236	108	78	36	14	127	5	8	

See footnotes at end of chart.

Series M 13-37.   Value of Mineral Products, in Current Dollars: 1880 to 1998—Cont'd.

(In millions of dollars)

Year	Mineral products	Fuels					Nonmetals (except fuels)		
		Total [1]	Bituminous coal and lignite	Pennsylvania anthracite	Petroleum	Natural gas	Total [1]	Portland cement	Lime
	13	14	15	16	17	18	20	21	24
1893...........................	480	252	123	86	29	14	70	4	(4)
1892...........................	524	248	125	82	26	15	90	5	(4)
1891...........................	504	237	117	74	31	16	83	5	(4)
1890...........................	499	231	110	66	35	19	81	5	(4)
1889...........................	456	208	95	66	27	21	83	5	8
1888...........................	476	231	102	89	18	23	80	5	25
1887...........................	448	217	98	85	19	16	77	6	23
1886...........................	389	185	78	76	20	10	67	4	21
1885...........................	374	183	82	77	19	5	62	3	20
1884...........................	355	166	77	66	21	1	58	4	18
1883...........................	383	186	82	77	26	(Z)	61	4	19
1882...........................	378	170	76	71	24	(Z)	64	4	22
1881...........................	340	150	60	64	25	. . .	61	3	20
1880...........................	301	120	53	42	25	. . .	56	2	19

See footnotes at end of chart.

Series M 13-37. Value of Mineral Products, in Current Dollars: 1880 to 1998—Cont'd.

(In millions of dollars)

	Nonmetals (except fuels)						Metals						
Year	Sand [5] and gravel	Stone [5] (incl. slate)	Phosphate rock	Salt	Sulfur	Total [1]	Iron ore	Copper	Lead	Zinc	Gold	Silver	Molybdenum
	25	26	27	28	29	30	31	32	33	34	35	36	37
1998	...	...	1 131	...	...	...	...	...	...				
1997	4 778	8 295	1 076	993	...	13 074	1 890	4 580	460	860	3 850	338	...
1996	4 500	7 410	1 060	1 060	...	13 015	1 770	4 610	459	674	4 090	262	456
1995	4 400	6 970	947	1 000	207	14 024	1 730	5 640	359	756	3 950	259	651
1994	4 230	6 620	839	990	162	12 100	1 580	4 430	298	619	4 050	253	284
1993	3 980	6 030	759	893	101	10 800	1 640	5 640	249	497	3 840	227	165
1992	3 766	5 775	1 058	803	159	11 537	1 732	4 610	308	674	3 662	229	209
1991	3 196	5 382	1 109	802	272	10 950	1 674	4 580	344	602	3 386	240	250
1990	3 686	5 822	1 075	827	335	12 442	1 741	4 311	491	847	3 650	329	348
1989	3 659	5 326	1 083	777	379	11 868	1 840	4 324	356	499	3 269	355	427
1988	3 514	5 558	888	680	431	10 209	1 717	3 764	315	324	2 831	349	271
1987	3 367	5 439	793	684	387	7 447	1 503	2 262	247	200	2 216	280	179
1986	3 107	4 228	897	665	509	5 817	1 473	1 671	165	170	1 377	189	241
1985	2 812	4 225	1 237	740	574	5 269	2 077	1 633	174	202	771	242	348
1984	2 621.2	3 910.5	1 182.2	675.1	546.1	5 977	...	1 608.4	181.3	270.8	742.5	361.8	326.8
1983	2 270.2	3 474.8	1 021.1	597.1	414.2	5 837	1 938.5	1 751.5	214.7	251.2	829.5	496.7	166.6
1982	1 997.8	3 056.0	950.3	671.4	434.7	5 517	1 491.7	1 840.9	288.6	257.1	551	320	504.1
1981	2 260.3	3 275.4	1 438.0	637.6	715.7	8 842	2 914.7	2 886.4	350.8	306.9	633.9	427.9	945.5
1980	2 289.0	3 394.0	1 257.0	656.0	721.0	8 921.0	2 544	2 667	515	262	594	667	1 344
1979	2 427.0	3 399.0	1 045.7	538.4	449.4	8 519.1	2 814	2 955.7	609.9	219.8	298.3	422	871.1
1978	2 302.0	2 885.7	928.8	499.3	279.9	6 296.0	2 388	1 990.3	393.5	206.9	193.3	212.7	607.9
1977	2 028.0	2 456.9	821.7	451.6	294.7	5 228.0	1 417.4	2 009.3	363.8	309.3	163.2	176.3	450.4
1976	1 774.0	2 221.0	949.4	431.0	300.0	5 681.3	1 860.1	2 235.0	281.6	358.5	131.3	149.3	333.5
1975	1 340.3	2 120.3	1 122.2	368.1	304.8	4 914.9	1 620.6	1 814.8	267.2	366.1	169.9	154.4	259.3
1974	1 451.1	2 186.2	501.4	360.8	241.1	5 562.0	1 386.4	2 469.0	208.7	359.0	180	159	234.7
1973	1 359.4	1 990.5	238.7	306.1	138.6	4 362.0	1 163.7	2 044.3	196.5	197.0	115	96.8	217.7
1972	1 199.5	1 683.3	207.9	296.7	132.8	3 641.0	950.3	1 704.7	186.0	169.8	84.9	62.7	170.5
1971	1 148.9	1 601.3	203.8	303.6	118.2	3 406	891	1 583	159.6	161.8	61.6	64.2	164.9
1970	1 116	1 475	203	304	152	3 926	942	1 984	179	164	63	80	190
1969	1 070	1 425	209	288	177	3 332	929	1 468	152	162	72	75	174
1968	1 020	1 318	251	272	268	2 703	836	1 008	95	143	58	70	151
1967	981	1 240	266	251	252	2 333	818	729	89	152	55	50	134
1966	985	1 261	261	230	201	2 703	854	1 034	99	166	63	56	144
1965	957	1 204	193	216	165	2 544	801	957	94	178	60	51	121
1964	893	1 135	161	201	121	2 366	802	813	75	156	51	47	97
1963	847	1 068	140	185	99	2 002	678	747	55	123	51	45	91
1962	795	1 026	134	175	109	1 937	618	757	44	116	54	40	69
1961	751	947	131	160	120	1 927	651	699	54	107	54	32	88
1960	720	953	117	161	117	2 022	724	693	58	112	58	28	87
1959	729	912	99	156	123	1 570	514	506	59	98	56	28	65
1958	653	827	94	141	111	1 594	569	515	63	84	61	31	50
1957	600	825	88	149	124	2 137	866	654	97	123	63	35	68
1956	602	[6] 775	98	136	166	2 358	750	939	111	149	64	35	64
1955	536	[6] 715	75	123	177	2 055	749	745	101	127	66	34	67
1954	503	[6] 622	87	105	155	1 518	526	493	89	102	64	33	64
1953	374	489	77	78	150	1 811	790	532	90	125	69	34	52
1952	345	473	72	71	117	1 617	590	448	126	223	58	36	41
1951	330	448	65	70	112	1 671	630	449	134	249	61	36	36
1950	293	402	63	60	106	1 351	483	378	116	179	74	38	38
1949	246	352	51	54	86	1 101	378	297	130	149	62	31	19
1948	252	340	51	54	90	1 219	391	362	140	168	62	34	20
1947	213	298	47	52	85	1 084	318	356	111	153	64	32	15
1946	171	243	31	45	66	729	215	173	49	82	51	19	12
1945	129	185	24	44	61	774	244	185	46	80	33	21	24
1944	125	181	21	44	56	900	257	237	50	99	36	25	28
1943	153	189	19	42	47	987	269	258	52	102	49	29	38
1942	188	211	17	38	50	999	279	257	59	110	131	40	47

See footnotes at end of chart.

Series M 13-37.   Value of Mineral Products, in Current Dollars: 1880 to 1998—Cont'd.

(In millions of dollars)

Year	Nonmetals (except fuels)					Total [1]	Metals						
	Sand [5] and gravel	Stone [5] (incl. slate)	Phosphate rock	Salt	Sulfur		Iron ore	Copper	Lead	Zinc	Gold	Silver	Molybdenum
	25	**26**	**27**	**28**	**29**	**30**	**31**	**32**	**33**	**34**	**35**	**36**	**37**
1941	147	203	16	34	54	890	250	228	54	98	209	51	26
1940	111	166	12	26	41	752	189	205	43	74	210	49	17
1939	106	165	12	25	36	631	159	148	40	51	196	44	22
1938	86	145	13	23	27	460	74	110	31	42	178	41	18
1937	97	152	13	24	44	756	208	202	52	72	168	56	21
1936	90	147	11	23	35	516	132	112	36	49	153	49	12
1935	62	91	11	22	29	365	83	63	25	36	126	33	7
1934	61	102	10	23	29	277	66	39	22	31	108	21	7
1933	53	84	8	22	30	205	64	29	19	26	65	8	4
1932	58	92	6	20	20	128	13	34	15	12	51	7	1
1931	86	141	9	22	25	287	74	95	29	22	50	9	2
1930	115	187	14	25	36	507	146	181	57	47	47	20	2
1929	133	214	13	27	44	802	197	353	85	81	46	33	2
1928	119	208	12	27	38	655	156	263	73	72	46	34	2
1927	116	210	11	25	38	622	151	221	84	74	45	34	2
1926	111	201	11	25	37	721	174	244	109	92	48	39	1
1925	108	187	12	26	29	715	161	238	114	84	50	46	1
1924	97	174	10	26	25	682	151	214	91	67	52	44	(Z)
1923	91	172	12	28	26	778	241	211	76	69	52	60	(Z)
1922	65	131	10	27	22	524	158	128	52	40	49	56	. . .
1921	56	114	12	25	17	344	90	65	36	20	50	53	. . .
1920	66	142	25	30	30	866	285	222	76	73	51	61	(Z)
1919	46	103	12	27	10	744	197	239	45	66	60	64	(Z)
1918	38	88	8	27	28	1 179	244	471	77	90	69	66	1
1917	35	88	8	20	24	1 228	238	515	94	119	84	59	(Z)
1916	30	84	6	14	12	1 107	182	474	76	151	93	49	(Z)
1915	23	80	5	12	5	677	101	243	48	114	101	37	(Z)
1914	24	83	10	10	6	446	72	153	40	35	95	40	(Z)
1913	24	90	12	10	6	538	131	190	36	38	89	40	. . .
1912	23	84	12	9	5	537	107	205	35	45	93	39	. . .
1911	21	83	12	8	5	432	87	137	35	31	97	33	. . .
1910	21	83	11	8	5	470	141	137	33	27	96	31	. . .
1909	18	77	11	8	5	439	110	142	30	25	100	28	. . .
1908	13	72	11	8	4	376	82	124	26	18	95	28	. . .
1907	14	77	11	8	5	501	132	174	37	26	90	37	. . .
1906	13	72	9	7	3	477	101	177	38	24	94	38	. . .
1905	11	69	7	6	3	392	75	139	29	24	88	34	. . .
1904	6	64	7	6	1	309	43	104	26	19	80	33	. . .
1903	1	64	5	5	1	309	66	96	24	17	74	29	. . .
1902	1	60	5	6	1	295	65	80	22	15	80	29	. . .
1901	. . .	52	5	7	1	299	49	101	22	12	79	33	. . .
1900	. . .	41	5	7	(Z)	319	67	101	23	11	79	36	. . .
1899	. . .	39	5	7	(Z)	272	35	97	18	15	71	33	. . .
1898	. . .	32	3	6	(Z)	213	22	65	15	11	64	32	. . .
1897	. . .	30	3	5	(Z)	193	19	59	14	8	57	32	. . .
1896	. . .	27	3	4	(Z)	185	23	50	11	6	53	40	. . .
1895	. . .	29	4	4	(Z)	161	18	41	10	6	47	36	. . .
1894	. . .	30	3	5	(Z)	136	14	34	10	5	40	31	. . .
1893	. . .	36	4	4	(Z)	158	19	36	12	6	36	47	. . .
1892	. . .	52	3	6	(Z)	186	33	40	14	8	33	56	. . .
1891	. . .	50	4	5	(Z)	184	32	36	15	8	33	58	. . .
1890	. . .	50	3	5	(Z)	187	35	41	13	7	33	57	. . .
1889	. . .	46	3	4	(Z)	164	33	31	12	6	33	47	. . .
1888	. . .	29	2	4	(Z)	164	29	38	13	5	33	43	. . .
1887	. . .	28	2	4	(Z)	153	34	25	13	5	33	41	. . .

See footnotes at end of chart.

Series M 13-37. Value of Mineral Products, in Current Dollars: 1880 to 1998—Cont'd.

(In millions of dollars)

	Nonmetals (except fuels)						Metals						
Year	Sand [5] and gravel	Stone [5] (incl. slate)	Phosphate rock	Salt	Sulfur	Total [1]	Iron ore	Copper	Lead	Zinc	Gold	Silver	Molybdenum
	25	26	27	28	29	30	31	32	33	34	35	36	37
1886	. . .	22	2	5	(Z)	138	28	18	12	4	35	39	. . .
1885	. . .	21	4	5	(Z)	129	19	18	10	3	32	43	. . .
1884	. . .	21	2	4	(Z)	130	21	19	10	3	31	42	. . .
1883	. . .	22	2	4	(Z)	136	26	19	12	3	30	40	. . .
1882	. . .	23	2	4	(Z)	144	31	17	13	4	32	41	. . .
1881	. . .	24	2	4	(Z)	130	24	13	11	3	35	38	. . .
1880	. . .	22	1	5	(Z)	125	23	13	10	3	36	35	. . .

Z Less than $500 000.
1. Includes additional mineral products not shown separately; therefore, components frequently will not add to group totals.
2. Excludes natural and slag cement.
3. Value of clays used in cement is included here, but excluded from total nonmetals (series M 20) to avoid duplication.
4. Not available separately; included with value of stone (series M 26).
5. Beginning 1954, sand and sandstone (ground) included in series M 25 (sand and gravel) and M 26 (stone), respectively.
6. Includes value of stone used for cement or lime, excluded from total nonmetals (series M 20) to avoid duplication.

Series M 76-92. Production and Calculated Consumption of Mineral Energy Fuels and Electricity from Water Power, in B.t.u.s.: 1800 to 1970

(In trillions of British thermal units. A British thermal unit (B.t.u.) is the quantity of heat required to raise the temperature of one pound of water 1°F. at or near its point of maximum density)

Year	Production					Calculated consumption				
	Mineral fuels				Electricity from water power at prevailing central station equivalent	Mineral fuels				Electricity from water power at prevailing central station equivalent
	Total[1]	Bituminous coal	Crude petroleum	Natural gas, wet		Total[2]	Bituminous coal	Crude petroleum	Natural gas, dry	
	76	77	79	80	81	83	84	86	88	90
1970	59 174	15 001	19 772	24 154	2 630	64 565	12 712	22 367	22 029	2 650
1969	55 947	13 957	18 886	22 838	2 648	62 174	12 509	21 796	21 020	2 659
1968	54 096	13 664	18 593	21 548	2 349	59 291	12 401	21 091	19 580	2 342
1967	52 402	13 904	18 100	20 087	2 347	55 841	11 982	20 208	18 250	2 344
1966	49 745	13 507	16 925	18 984	2 062	54 282	12 205	19 315	17 393	2 073
1965	46 977	13 017	15 930	17 652	2 059	51 247	11 580	18 506	16 098	2 058
1964	45 683	12 418	15 691	17 138	1 886	49 298	10 899	18 194	15 648	1 907
1963	44 188	11 712	15 741	16 271	1 768	47 507	10 353	18 174	14 843	1 767
1962	42 071	10 782	15 495	15 365	1 816	45 577	9 826	17 822	14 121	1 821
1961	40 627	10 308	15 185	14 691	1 656	43 621	9 502	17 348	13 228	1 680
1960	39 939	10 662	14 664	14 135	1 608	42 906	9 693	16 861	12 699	1 657
1959	39 128	10 581	14 662	13 361	1 551	41 547	9 332	16 686	11 990	1 591
1958	37 599	10 663	14 154	12 244	1 592	40 058	9 366	16 250	10 995	1 636
1957	40 675	12 800	15 346	11 885	1 422	40 154	10 640	16 960	10 416	1 551
1956	40 343	13 013	15 344	11 252	1 435	40 213	11 142	16 994	9 834	1 487
1955	37 722	12 080	14 445	10 532	1 360	38 296	10 941	15 956	9 232	1 407
1954	33 916	10 262	13 427	9 488	1 360	34 875	9 512	14 830	8 548	1 388
1953	35 554	11 981	13 671	9 116	1 413	36 147	11 182	14 912	8 156	1 439
1952	35 249	12 231	13 282	8 705	1 466	34 962	10 971	14 248	7 760	1 496
1951	36 209	13 982	13 037	8 106	1 424	35 321	12 285	13 867	7 248	1 454
1950	32 937	13 527	11 449	6 841	1 415	32 552	11 900	12 304	6 150	1 440
1949	29 151	11 472	10 683	5 911	1 425	30 039	11 673	11 402	5 289	1 449
1948	34 490	15 707	11 717	5 615	1 369	32 487	13 622	12 085	5 033	1 393
1947	33 758	16 522	10 771	5 012	1 296	31 709	14 600	11 065	4 518	1 326
1946	30 133	13 989	10 057	4 550	1 406	29 048	13 110	10 270	4 089	1 446
1945	30 891	15 134	9 939	4 423	1 442	30 055	14 661	10 199	3 973	1 486
1944	31 759	16 233	9 732	4 176	1 344	30 434	15 447	9 923	3 775	1 387
1943	29 575	15 463	8 733	3 839	1 304	29 095	15 557	8 538	3 481	1 347
1942	28 278	15 267	8 043	3 436	1 136	26 720	14 149	7 987	3 102	1 177
1941	26 198	13 471	8 133	3 162	934	25 650	12 893	8 343	2 851	975
1940	24 208	12 072	7 849	2 979	880	22 991	11 290	7 662	2 726	917
1939	21 753	10 345	7 337	2 763	838	20 717	9 854	7 327	2 539	872
1938	19 911	9 132	7 043	2 565	866	18 981	8 811	6 921	2 348	899
1937	23 093	11 673	7 419	2 684	871	21 846	11 286	7 004	2 468	905
1936	21 679	11 504	6 378	2 411	812	20 577	10 697	6 426	2 221	841
1935	18 997	9 756	5 780	2 136	806	18 276	9 336	5 799	1 974	831
1934	18 104	9 415	5 267	1 970	698	17 216	9 008	5 136	1 819	721
1933	16 985	8 741	5 253	1 733	711	16 171	8 323	5 143	1 600	729
1932	15 663	8 114	4 554	1 729	713	15 666	8 041	4 830	1 594	726
1931	18 331	10 011	4 936	1 869	668	18 107	9 743	5 304	1 715	692
1930	21 367	12 249	5 208	2 148	752	21 503	11 921	6 148	1 969	785
1929	28 852	14 017	5 842	2 118	816	22 909	13 612	5 894	1 942	847
1928	21 997	13 120	5 229	1 734	854	21 491	13 069	5 474	1 588	890
1927	22 424	13 565	5 227	1 598	776	21 013	13 095	5 027	1 465	815
1926	23 088	15 020	4 471	1 452	728	21 730	13 954	4 876	1 335	765
1925	20 939	13 625	4 430	1 314	668	20 198	13 079	4 641	1 212	701
1924	20 309	12 672	4 141	1 263	648	19 768	12 681	4 228	1 170	685
1923	22 524	14 792	4 248	1 113	685	20 958	13 598	4 419	1 032	727
1922	16 529	11 063	3 234	843	643	16 540	11 185	3 390	785	675
1921	16 666	10 897	2 739	732	620	15 754	10 266	3 016	682	656
1920	20 627	14 899	2 569	883	738	19 007	13 325	3 027	827	775
1919	17 441	12 206	2 195	802	718	16 792	11 688	[3] 2 159	793	766
1918	20 529	15 180	2 064	775	701	19 686	14 588	1 911	771	750
1917	19 787	14 457	1 945	855	700	18 842	13 835	1 755	850	755

See footnote at end of chart.

Series M 76-92. Production and Calculated Consumption of Mineral Energy Fuels and Electricity from Water Power, in B.t.u.s.: 1800 to 1970—Cont'd.

(In trillions of British thermal units. A British thermal unit (B.t.u.) is the quantity of heat required to raise the temperature of one pound of water 1°F. at or near its point of maximum density)

	Production					Calculated consumption				
	Mineral fuels				Electricity from water power at prevailing central station equivalent	Mineral fuels				Electricity from water power at prevailing central station equivalent
Year	Total[1]	Bituminous coal	Crude petroleum	Natural gas, wet		Total[2]	Bituminous coal	Crude petroleum	Natural gas, dry	
	76	77	79	80	81	83	84	86	88	90
1916	17 944	13 166	1 744	810	681	17 052	12 631	1 497	807	729
1915	16 163	11 597	1 630	676	659	15 385	11 134	1 411	673	691
1914	15 559	11 075	1 541	636	636	14 858	10 703	1 320	632	676
1913	16 927	12 535	1 441	626	609	16 074	12 034	1 210	620	645
1912	15 833	11 793	1 293	604	585	15 093	11 402	1 058	594	615
1911	14 763	10 635	1 279	551	565	14 027	10 245	1 040	544	597
1910	14 836	10 928	1 215	547	539	14 261	10 654	1 007	540	539
1909	13 587	9 949	1 062	517	513	13 018	9 685	844	511	513
1908	12 295	8 713	1 035	432	476	11 762	8 478	820	427	476
1907	13 917	10 343	963	437	441	13 390	10 079	781	432	441
1906	11 946	8 983	734	418	414	11 507	8 793	555	411	414
1905	11 386	8 255	781	377	386	10 983	8 091	610	372	386
1904	10 171	7 301	679	333	354	9 816	7 155	534	330	354
1903	10 205	7 408	583	319	321	9 924	7 315	449	317	321
1902	8 685	6 818	515	301	289	8 426	6 733	364	299	289
1901	8 316	5 917	402	283	264	7 996	5 808	250	281	264
1900	7 643	5 563	369	254	250	7 322	5 431	229	252	250
1895	5 467	3 540	307	147	. . .	5 265	3 511	168	147	90
1890	4 619	2 916	266	257	. . .	4 475	2 903	156	257	22
1885	3 063	1 880	127	82	. . .	2 962	1 883	40	82	. . .
1880	2 210	1 330	152	. . .	. . .	2 150	1 337	96	. . .	. . .
1875	1 494	856	51	. . .	. . .	1 451	862	11	. . .	. . .
1870	1 074	536	31	. . .	. . .	1 059	545	11	. . .	. . .
1865	645	324	14	. . .	. . .	642	358	10	. . .	. . .
1860	519	237	3	. . .	. . .	521	243	3	. . .	. . .
1855	417	198	. . .	. . .	. . .	421	205	. . .	. . .	. . .
1850	216	106	. . .	. . .	. . .	219	110	. . .	. . .	. . .
1845	122	55	. . .	. . .	. . .	. . .	. . .	. . .	. . .	. . .
1840	64	35	. . .	. . .	. . .	. . .	. . .	. . .	. . .	. . .
1835	47	28	. . .	. . .	. . .	. . .	. . .	. . .	. . .	. . .
1830	23	17	. . .	. . .	. . .	. . .	. . .	. . .	. . .	. . .
1825	12	11	. . .	. . .	. . .	. . .	. . .	. . .	. . .	. . .
1820	9	9	. . .	. . .	. . .	. . .	. . .	. . .	. . .	. . .
1815	7	7	. . .	. . .	. . .	. . .	. . .	. . .	. . .	. . .
1810	5	5	. . .	. . .	. . .	. . .	. . .	. . .	. . .	. . .
1805	4	4	. . .	. . .	. . .	. . .	. . .	. . .	. . .	. . .
1800	3	3	. . .	. . .	. . .	. . .	. . .	. . .	. . .	. . .

1. Includes production from Pennsylvania anthracite coal, not shown separately.
2. Includes production from Pennsylvania anthracite, net imports of petroleum products, and natural gas liquids, not shown separately.
3. 1919 and earlier, includes the net imports of petroleum.

Series M 138-142. Crude Petroleum—Production, Value, and Proved Reserves: 1859 to 1998

(In thousands of 42-gallon barrels, except as indicated)

Year	Production	Average value at well per bbl. dollars	Estimated proved reserves, Dec. 31
	138	139	142
1998	2 282 000	10.88	...
1997	2 355 000	17.23	22 550 000
1996	2 366 000	18.46	22 020 000
1995	2 406 000	14.62	22 400 000
1994	2 432 000	13.19	22 500 000
1993	2 499 000	14.25	23 000 000
1992	2 617 000	15.99	23 700 000
1991	...	...	
1990	2 685 000	20.03	26 300 000
1989	2 785 000	15.86	26 500 000
1988	2 979 000	12.58	26 800 000
1987	3 047 000	15.40	27 300 000
1986	3 168 000	12.51	26 900 000
1985	3 275 000	24.09	28 400 000
1984	3 250 000	25.88	28 400 000
1983	3 171 000	26.19	27 735 000
1982	3 157 000	28.52	27 858 000
1981	3 129 000	31.77	29 426 000
1980	3 146 000	21.59	29 800 000
1979	3 121 000	12.64	29 810 000
1978	3 178 000	9.00	27 804 000
1977	3 009 000	8.57	29 486 000
1976	2 976 000	8.19	30 942 000
1975	3 057 000	7.67	32 700 000
1974	3 203 000	6.87	34 250 000
1973	3 361 000	3.89	35 300 000
1972	3 455 000	3.39	36 339 000
1971	3 454 000	3.39	38 063 000
1970	3 517 450	3.18	39 001 000
1969	3 371 751	3.09	29 632 000
1968	3 329 042	2.94	30 707 000
1967	3 216 715	2.92	31 377 000
1966	3 027 763	2.88	31 452 000
1965	2 848 514	2.86	31 352 000
1964	2 786 822	2.88	30 991 000
1963	2 752 723	2.89	30 970 000
1962	2 676 189	2.90	31 389 000
1961	2 621 758	2.89	31 759 000
1960	2 574 933	2.88	31 613 000
1959	2 574 590	2.90	31 719 000
1958	2 448 937	3.01	30 536 000
1957	2 616 901	3.09	30 300 000
1956	2 617 283	2.79	30 434 649
1955	2 484 428	2.77	30 012 170
1954	2 314 988	2.77	29 560 746
1953	2 357 082	2.68	28 944 828
1952	2 289 836	2.53	27 960 554

Year	Production	Average value at well per bbl. dollars	Estimated proved reserves, Dec. 31
	138	139	142
1951	2 247 711	2.53	27 468 031
1950	1 973 574	2.51	25 268 398
1949	1 841 940	2.54	24 649 489
1948	2 020 185	2.60	23 280 444
1947	1 856 987	1.93	21 487 685
1946	1 733 939	1.41	20 873 560
1945	1 713 655	1.22	20 826 813
1944	1 677 904	1.21	20 453 231
1943	1 505 613	1.20	20 064 152
1942	1 386 645	1.19	20 082 793
1941	1 402 228	1.14	19 559 296
1940	1 353 214	1.02	19 024 515
1939	1 264 962	1.02	18 483 012
1938	1 214 355	1.13	17 348 146
1937	1 279 160	1.18	15 507 268
1936	1 099 687	1.09	13 063 400
1935	996 596	.97	12 400 000
1934	908 065	1.00	12 177 000
1933	905 656	.67	12 000 000
1932	785 159	.87	12 300 000
1931	851 081	.65	13 000 000
1930	898 011	1.19	13 600 000
1929	1 007 323	1.27	13 200 000
1928	901 474	1.17	11 000 000
1927	901 129	1.30	10 500 000
1926	770 874	1.88	8 800 000
1925	763 743	1.68	8 500 000
1924	713 940	1.43	7 500 000
1923	732 407	1.34	7 600 000
1922	557 531	1.61	7 600 000
1921	472 183	1.73	7 800 000
1920	442 929	3.07	7 200 000
1919	378 367	2.01	6 700 000
1918	355 928	1.98	6 200 000
1917	335 316	1.56	5 900 000
1916	300 767	1.10	5 900 000
1915	281 104	.64	5 500 000
1914	265 763	.81	5 400 000
1913	248 446	.95	5 500 000
1912	222 935	.74	5 400 000
1911	220 449	.61	5 000 000
1910	209 557	.61	4 500 000
1909	183 171	.70	4 200 000
1908	178 527	.72	4 000 000
1907	166 095	.72	3 900 000
1906	126 494	.73	3 800 000
1905	134 717	.62	3 800 000

Year	Production	Average value at well per bbl. dollars	Estimated proved reserves, Dec. 31
	138	139	142
1904	117 081	.86	3 600 000
1903	100 461	.94	3 400 000
1902	88 767	.80	3 200 000
1901	69 389	.96	3 000 000
1900	63 621	1.19	2 900 000
1899	57 071	1.13	2 500 000
1898	55 364	.80	...
1897	60 476	.68	...
1896	60 960	.96	...
1895	52 892	1.09	...
1894	49 344	.72	...
1893	48 431	.60	...
1892	50 515	.51	...
1891	54 293	.56	...
1890	45 824	.77	...
1889	35 164	.77	...
1888	27 612	.65	...
1887	28 283	.67	...
1886	28 065	.71	...
1885	21 859	.88	...
1884	24 218	.85	...
1883	23 450	1.10	...
1882	30 350	.78	...
1881	27 661	.92	...
1880	26 286	.94	...
1879	19 914	.86	...
1878	15 397	1.17	...
1877	13 350	2.38	...
1876	9 133	2.52	...
1875	12 163	1.35	...
1874	10 927	1.17	...
1873	9 894	1.83	...
1872	6 293	3.64	...
1871	5 205	4.34	...
1870	5 261	3.86	...
1869	4 215	5.64	...
1868	3 646	3.62	...
1867	3 347	2.41	...
1866	3 598	3.74	...
1865	2 498	6.59	...
1864	2 116	8.06	...
1863	2 611	3.15	...
1862	3 057	1.05	...
1861	2 114	.49	...
1860	500	9.59	...
1859	2	16.00	...

SECTION N

CONSTRUCTION AND HOUSING

Highlights

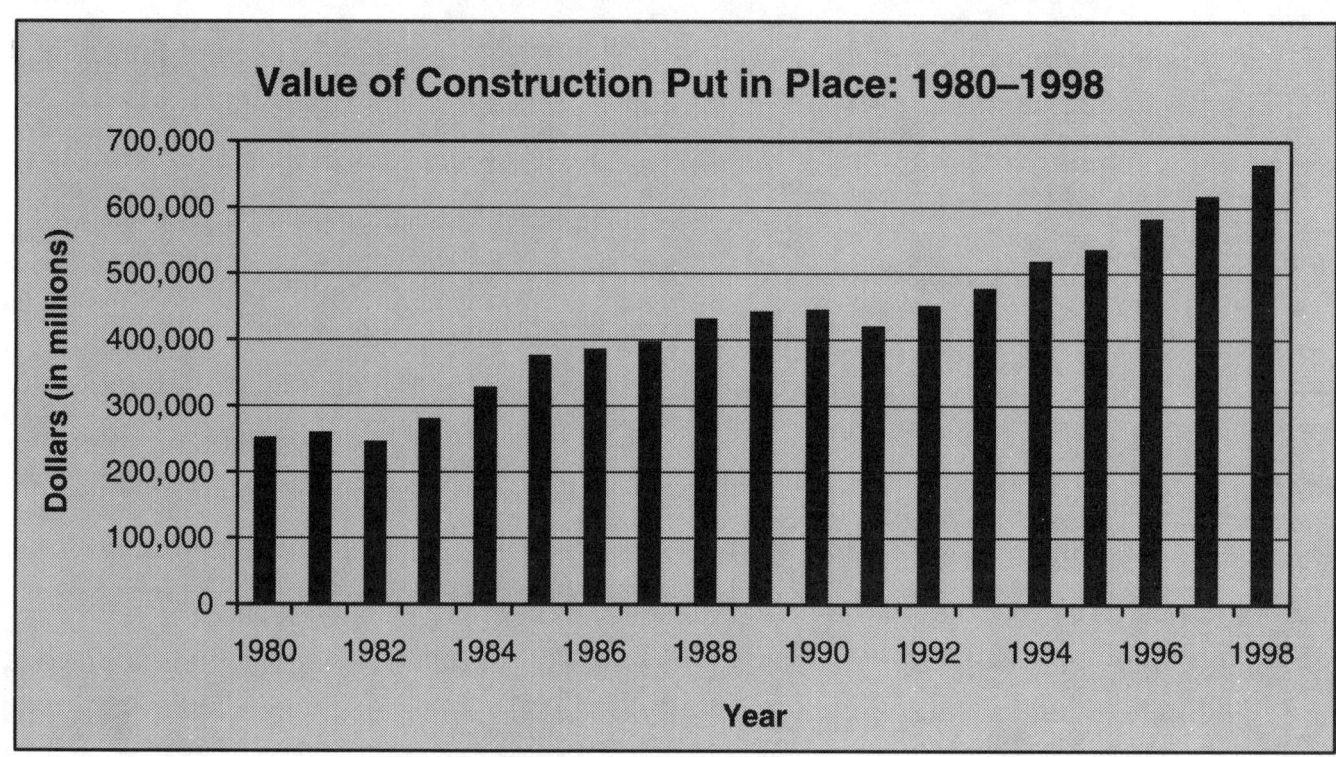

Value of Construction Put in Place: 1980–1998

1 Housing and construction statistics were collected and published by the Department of Labor until 1959 when the Department of Commerce assumed that responsibility. The Bureau of the Census issues a variety of publications providing data in these fields, including *Current Construction Reports, Housing Starts and Housing Completions, New One Family Houses Sold and for Sale, Price Indexes of New One-Family Houses Sold, Housing Units Authorized by Building Permits, Expenditures for Residential Upkeep and Improvements, Value of New Construction Put in Place,* and *Current Housing Reports.* Other sources include the F. W. Dodge division of McGraw-Hill, the National Association of Home Builders, and the National Association of Realtors. Censuses of the construction industry were first conducted by the Bureau of the Census for 1929, 1935, and 1939; beginning in 1967, a census has been taken every five years, in years ending 2 and 7.

2 From 1850 to 1930, the Bureau of the Census collected some housing data as part of its censuses of population and agriculture. Beginning in 1940, separate censuses of housing have been taken at 10-year intervals. Beginning in 1970, information on structural characteristics of housing have been included in the censuses.

3 In 1997, 631,595 businesses were involved in construction, with a total value of business equaling $832.489 billion. In 1998, the value of new construction was $665.446 billion, of these, private buildings and structures accounting for $520.073 billion of that amount (of which $294.326 billion was for residential buildings). Private construction included $189.453 billion worth of single-family homes, up from $108.737 billion in 1990. Churches and religious buildings saw the biggest increase, doubling in value from $3.5 billion to 6.7 billion in the 1990s.

4 Sales of one-family homes rose to 804,000 in 1998 compared to 545,000 in 1980. Of these, 88,000 were luxury homes valued at $300,000 or more. Median prices of new private one-family homes increased to $152,500 nationwide, reversing a decade-old trend. The prices are highest in the Northeast ($200,000) and lowest in the South ($135,800). The highest home prices are found in Honolulu, San Francisco, Orange County, California, and New York–Northern New Jersey–Long Island. The least expensive homes are found in Oklahoma City, San Antonio, Tulsa, Louisville, Omaha, Des Moines and Baton Rouge.

5 In 1998, the total number of housing units in the United States was 117.282 million, of which 68,638,000 were owner-occupied and 34,896,000 were rented.

6 Home ownership is part of the American dream, but as of 1998, only 66.3% of the population achieved that dream. Home ownership is highest in South Carolina (76.6%), Minnesota (75.4%) and Kentucky (75.1%). It is lowest in Hawaii and New York because of the high cost of first-time ownership.

7 Average monthly mortgage payments jumped from $329 in 1976 to $1,212 in 1998, and from 24% of personal income to 32.3% during the same period of time.

8 Of the 1.160 million new one-family homes completed and sold in 1998, 91% carry a mortgage, 32% have a floor space of 2,400 ft or more, 33% have more than four bedrooms, 70% are heated with gas, 83% have central air conditioning, 61% have a fireplace and 86% have a garage.

9 In 1997, the median rent for an apartment nationwide was $724, and 58.4% of the apartments had a rent of $850 or more.

10 Blacks and Hispanics have a lower home ownership rate than Whites. White home ownership is 70.3%, while only 45.2% of Blacks and 42.5% of Hispanics own homes. The majority of Blacks and Hispanics live in apartments.

11 In 1998, 46.1% of home buyers were first-time buyers; whole down payment was only 12.8% of the sale price.

12 In 1995, there were 4,579,000 commercial buildings in the United States of which 309,000 were educational, 285,000 food service establishments, 105,000 hospitals and healthcare centers, 158,000 hotels and motels, 705,000 office buildings, 326,000 public assembly buildings, 580,000 warehouses, and 269,000 churches and religious worship centers.

13 Although the quality of American housing has steadily improved during the 20th Century, 1.673 million homes have no bathrooms, 920,000 have signs of mice and rats, 1.168 million have holes in floors, 40,000 have no electrical wiring, and 9.667 million have water leakages.

Series N 1-29. Value of New Private and Public Construction Put in Place: 1964 to 1999

(In millions of dollars)

Year	Total construction	Private construction						Farm nonresidetial	Public utilities
		Total	Residential buildings			Nonresidential buildings			
			Total	New housing units	Improvements	Total	Industrial	Total	Total
	1	2	3	4	5	7	8		12
1999	764 233	591 561	348 826	249 536	99 290	195 776	34 894	4 451	39 607
1998	711 759	552 236	314 607	223 983	90 624	190 711	40 484	4 284	40 028
1997	656 630	501 749	289 014	198 063	90 951	172 990	36 739	3 815	33 638
1996	613 535	474 273	281 115	191 113	90 002	153 912	36 220	3 658	33 156
1995	555 591	425 658	247 351	171 404	75 947	136 541	34 024	3 014	35 859
1994	539 232	419 038	258 561	176 389	82 172	120 289	28 952	3 226	34 071
1993	493 260	377 300	225 067	150 911	74 156	110 635	26 482	3 392	34 925
1992	463 661	347 814	199 393	135 070	64 323	105 646	29 029	2 398	36 807
1991	432 592	322 483	166 251	114 575	51 676	116 570	31 424	2 753	33 966
1990	476 778	369 300	191 103	132 137	58 966	143 506	33 636	2 801	28 933
1989	477 502	379 328	204 255	143 232	61 023	139 953	28 786	2 531	30 129
1988	462 012	367 277	204 496	142 391	62 105	130 854	23 203	2 394	27 412
1987	446 643	355 994	199 652	142 668	56 984	123 247	21 210	2 605	27 862
1986	433 454	348 872	190 677	135 169	55 508	120 917	20 984	2 072	32 931
1985	403 416	325 601	160 520	115 888	44 632	127 466	24 139	2 197	32 692
1984	370 190	299 952	155 015	114 616	40 399	107 680	20 901	3 161	32 191
1983	311 887	248 437	125 833	94 961	30 872	87 069	19 454	3 255	30 817
1982	279 332	216 268	84 676	57 001	27 675	92 690	26 082	3 692	33 942
1981	289 070	224 378	99 241	69 424	29 817	85 569	25 413	4 612	33 688
1980	273 936	210 290	100 381	69 629	30 752	72 480	20 522	5 274	30 905
1979	272 873	216 228	116 444	89 272	27 172	64 765	22 034	5 588	27 978
1978	239 867	189 721	109 838	85 601	24 237	48 824	16 155	5 209	24 567
1977	200 501	157 418	92 004	72 231	19 773	38 245	11 309	4 431	21 437
1976	172 132	128 153	68 273	50 771	17 502	34 628	10 473	3 971	20 204
1975	152 635	109 342	51 581	36 317	15 264	35 409	11 659	3 731	17 553
1974	155 170	117 038	55 967	43 420	12 547	39 889	11 454	3 249	16 933
1973	153 781	121 433	65 085	54 619	10 466	37 639	9 021	2 525	15 272
1972	139 126	109 096	60 693	50 095	10 598	32 375	6 730	1 785	13 301
1971	122 414	92 715	48 514	38 670	9 844	29 307	7 754	1 916	11 985
1970	105 890	77 982	35 863	27 059	8 804	28 171	9 316	1 875	11 127
1969	104 944	77 151	37 214	29 224	7 990	27 741	9 600	1 689	9 766
1968	96 824	69 386	34 172	26 723	7 449	23 811	8 492	1 598	9 232
1967	87 221	61 844	28 737	21 541	7 196	23 117	8 400	1 702	7 834
1966	85 753	61 907	28 611	21 811	6 800	24 238	9 261	1 484	7 090
1965	81 886	59 966	30 235	23 846	6 389	21 896	7 182	1 387	6 032
1964	75 097	54 893	30 526	24 098	6 428	17 385	5 028	1 331	5 314

Series N 1-29. Value of New Private and Public Construction Put in Place: 1964 to 1999—Cont'd.

(In millions of dollars)

Year	Public construction	Buildings		Nonresidential buildings		Military facilities	Highways, roads and streets	Sewer and water systems	Conservation and development
	Total	Total	Residential	Industrial	Educational				
	19		20	22	23	25	26	27	28
1999	172 673	77 690	5 618	925	39 725	2 111	53 532	18 783	6 003
1998	159 523	73 277	5 124	1 010	36 234	2 529	48 515	16 998	5 447
1997	154 882	71 867	5 230	999	34 385	2 556	44 105	16 811	5 739
1996	139 263	63 471	5 048	1 389	28 590	2 591	39 464	15 416	6 008
1995	129 933	57 754	4 698	1 508	25 783	3 011	37 616	13 129	6 308
1994	120 193	49 446	3 835	1 465	20 361	2 318	37 419	13 347	6 363
1993	115 960	48 559	4 011	1 718	19 129	2 453	34 299	13 948	5 937
1992	115 847	49 986	4 138	1 876	20 647	2 502	33 106	14 825	5 952
1991	110 109	47 406	3 587	1 824	19 203	1 837	32 042	15 020	5 011
1990	107 478	43 615	3 808	1 434	16 055	2 665	32 105	15 185	4 686
1989	98 174	38 235	3 441	1 300	14 696	3 520	28 747	13 993	5 098
1988	94 735	35 193	3 292	1 413	12 823	3 579	29 126	13 840	4 768
1987	90 648	32 216	3 268	1 457	10 627	4 324	27 073	13 402	5 531
1986	84 582	30 528	3 029	1 657	10 456	3 868	25 318	11 465	4 926
1985	77 815	27 466	2 893	1 968	9 084	3 235	23 741	9 995	5 126
1984	70 238	23 949	2 651	1 828	7 833	2 839	21 556	9 324	4 909
1983	63 450	21 832	2 617	1 809	6 904	2 544	17 904	7 820	5 054
1982	63 064	21 203	2 277	1 632	7 606	2 205	17 274	8 795	5 286
1981	64 691	20 776	2 347	1 655	7 936	1 964	18 405	8 960	5 462
1980	63 646	20 427	1 983	1 441	8 902	1 880	18 209	9 857	5 178
1979	56 646	17 661	1 656	1 112	7 806	1 647	17 088	8 083	4 678
1978	50 146	16 129	1 384	932	6 654	1 502	14 169	7 349	4 494
1977	43 083	14 578	1 478	838	6 215	1 429	1 2460	5 710	3 966
1976	43 980	15 690	1 263	672	7 245	1 630	12 371	6 147	3 868
1975	43 293	15 912	1 356	687	7 776	1 389	13 147	5 710	3 261
1974	38 132	14 788	1 006	564	7 310	1 186	12 065	4 063	2 741
1973	32 348	12 842	941	454	6 647	1 167	10 505	3 021	2 311
1972	30 030	11 351	874	389	5 718	1 088	10 429	2 777	2 170
1971	29 699	11 223	1 136	402	5 561	901	10 657	2 826	2 097
1970	27 908	10 473	1 106	316	5 619	717	9 982	2 636	1 907
1969	27 793	11 065	1 046	358	5 867	877	9 251	2 678	1 780
1968	27 437	10 271	746	351	6 061	808	9 321	3 065	1 973
1967	25 377	9 823	709	249	5 988	695	8 591	2 328	2 124
1966	23 846	8 759	655	208	5 333	727	8 405	2 366	2 194
1965	21 920	7 751	603	226	4 284	830	7 550	2 461	2 019
1964	20 203	6 997	567	223	3 790	910	7 133	2 281	1 750

Series N 78-89. Value of Construction Contracts Awarded (Dodge), by Class of Construction: 1901 to 1998

(In millions of dollars. Includes new structures and alteration to existing structures. Figures for 1901-1909 are for New England states only; 1910-1922, for 27 states except as noted; 1923-1924, for 36 states; 1925-1955, for 37 states; 1956-1969, for 48 states; thereafter, for 50 states.)

Year	Total	Nonresidential buildings									Residential buildings	Non-building construction
		Total	Commercial	Industrial	Educational and science	Hospital	Public buildings	Religious	Social and recreational	Miscellaneous		
	78	79	80	81	82	83	84	85	86	87	88	89
1998	375 300	134 000	63 900	10 100	26 900	10 800	6 000	3 800	9 300	3 100	173 000	68 200
1997	358 400	136 500	58 600	14 100	27 800	11 500	6 900	3 700	9 800	4 000	152 600	69 400
1996	331 800	120 300	51 800	13 100	22 900	11 100	6 300	2 900	8 100	4 000	146 400	65 100
1995	306 500	114 200	46 600	13 800	22 900	10 800	6 300	2 800	7 100	3 800	127 800	64 400
1994	296 700	101 500	40 800	11 200	21 000	10 500	6 100	2 500	6 500	3 000	133 600	61 600
1993	271 500	88 800	34 200	9 000	19 300	10 500	3 900	2 400	6 800	2 600	123 900	58 900
1992	252 200	87 000	32 800	8 900	17 600	10 900	5 800	2 500	5 500	3 100	110 600	54 600
1991	230 800	86 200	32 700	8 300	19 000	9 600	6 200	2 400	5 100	3 000	94 400	50 200
1990	246 000	95 400	44 800	8 400	16 600	9 200	5 700	2 200	5 300	3 100	100 900	49 700
1989	271 300	106 100	53 600	12 700	15 900	8 800	5 200	2 000	5 000	2 900	116 200	49 000
1988	262 200	97 900	51 600	9 500	14 100	8 200	4 400	2 200	4 700	3 200	116 200	48 100
1987	259 000	98 800	53 700	8 600	13 200	9 000	4 700	2 100	4 300	3 200	114 100	46 100
1986	249 300	91 600	52 400	7 300	11 700	7 900	3 200	2 100	4 200	2 800	115 600	42 100
1985	235 600	92 100	54 600	8 100	10 000	7 800	3 100	2 000	4 000	2 500	102 100	41 400
1984	214 300	82 100	48 200	7 900	8 500	7 400	2 700	1 700	3 300	2 400	95 300	36 900
1983	194 100	67 900	38 300	5 400	7 100	8 500	2 100	1 500	2 900	2 100	88 400	37 800
1982	157 100	64 600	32 300	9 600	6 800	8 000	1 900	1 200	2 800	2 000	55 000	37 500
1981	157 300	65 500	35 200	9 300	6 600	6 400	1 400	1 200	3 400	2 000	56 300	35 400
1980	151 800	56 900	27 700	9 200	7 400	5 400	1 600	1 200	2 700	1 700	60 400	34 500
1979	168 400	50 200	24 400	7 600	6 300	4 800	1 600	1 300	4 100	(3)	74 600	43 700
1978	159 900	45 000	20 600	9 200	5 700	3 800	1 500	1 200	3 000	(3)	74 900	39 900
1977	139 700	35 100	13 600	5 400	5 200	4 500	2 300	1 000	3 300	(3)	62 000	42 600
1976	110 100	30 000	10 200	4 500	4 900	4 500	2 100	900	3 000	(3)	44 200	35 900
1975	92 700	31 600	9 200	6 800	5 900	3 700	2 100	800	3 100	(3)	31 300	29 800
1974	93 700	33 200	11 800	5 600	6 300	3 800	2 100	800	2 800	(3)	33 600	27 000
1973	99 300	31 400	12 800	4 800	5 100	3 300	2 000	700	2 700	(3)	45 700	22 100
1972	88 885	. . .	11 369	3 005	4 760	3 516	1 490	640	1 237	1 003	42 882	18 983
1971	80 188	. . .	9 610	2 619	5 649	3 188	1 493	603	1 296	1 131	34 714	19 883
1970	68 294	24 455	9 056	3 664	5 253	2 811	1 007	575	1 137	952	24 837	19 001
1969	68 294	25 949	9 786	3 915	5 543	2 817	1 154	674	1 116	944	25 633	16 710
1968	61 732	22 513	7 645	3 768	5 347	2 114	1 112	778	954	795	24 838	14 382
1967	54 514	20 139	6 080	3 701	5 216	1 873	959	793	834	683	21 155	13 220
1966	50 150	19 393	5 835	3 623	4 939	1 721	939	825	855	656	17 827	12 930
1965	49 272	17 219	5 457	3 064	4 164	1 515	842	783	800	596	21 248	10 805
1964	47 330	15 522	4 572	2 970	3 554	1 625	789	814	599	598	20 565	11 244
1963	45 546	14 377	4 445	2 274	3 314	1 485	964	755	648	493	20 502	10 667
1962	41 303	13 010	4 216	2 086	3 060	1 079	677	811	704	377	18 039	10 255
1961	37 135	12 115	3 797	1 814	3 015	985	671	805	623	403	16 123	8 897
1960	36 318	12 240	3 725	2 114	3 005	832	679	789	631	464	15 105	8 973
1959	36 269	11 387	3 496	1 880	2 666	865	605	799	601	474	17 150	7 732
1958	35 090	10 948	3 197	1 400	2 907	879	655	746	500	664	14 696	9 446
1957	32 173	11 293	3 267	2 168	2 936	870	470	699	429	455	13 039	7 841
1956	31 612	11 208	3 140	2 381	2 883	678	428	681	422	595	12 862	7 542
1955	24 632	8 497	2 359	1 878	2 134	475	301	551	270	530	11 072	5 063
1954	20 596	7 110	1 816	1 274	2 063	519	249	486	252	452	9 344	4 142
1953	18 804	6 956	1 489	2 051	1 720	434	203	385	222	452	7 840	4 008
1952	18 070	6 695	979	2 558	1 472	444	233	318	153	538	7 963	3 412
1951	17 151	6 823	915	2 883	1 335	581	158	299	136	515	7 605	2 723
1950	16 592	5 182	1 209	1 142	1 180	655	124	336	261	274	8 832	2 578
1949	11 826	3 644	885	559	824	555	119	276	222	204	5 706	2 476
1948	11 121	3 666	975	840	725	405	84	245	232	161	5 299	2 155
1947	9 175	2 716	785	941	392	192	73	118	122	92	4 569	1 890
1946	7 490	2 716	773	1 317	221	131	25	68	93	88	3 142	1 631
1945	3 299	1 850	346	1 027	100	113	16	35	60	153	563	885

Series N 78-89. Value of Construction Contracts Awarded (Dodge), by Class of Construction: 1901 to 1998—Cont'd.

(In millions of dollars. Includes new structures and alteration to existing structures. Figures for 1901-1909 are for New England states only; 1910-1922, for 27 states except as noted; 1923-1924, for 36 states; 1925-1955, for 37 states; 1956-1969, for 48 states; thereafter, for 50 states.)

Year	Total	Nonresidential buildings									Residential buildings	Non-building construction
		Total	Commercial	Industrial	Educational and science	Hospital	Public buildings	Religious	Social and recreational	Miscellaneous		
	78	**79**	**80**	**81**	**82**	**83**	**84**	**85**	**86**	**87**	**88**	**89**
1944........	1 994	899	81	473	69	59	12	12	33	161	348	746
1943........	3 274	1 424	121	766	62	111	25	7	58	274	868	982
1942........	8 255	3 897	302	2 228	148	185	102	24	101	808	1 818	2 541
1941........	6 007	2 316	471	1 182	141	89	89	53	78	214	1 954	1 738
1940........	4 004	1 295	318	442	147	94	80	46	63	104	1 597	1 112
1939........	3 551	966	247	175	201	83	110	38	82	29	1 334	1 251
1938........	3 197	1 072	216	121	334	116	114	36	108	28	986	1 139
1937........	2 913	1 156	297	314	223	82	105	37	84	15	905	852
1936........	2 675	960	249	198	219	74	102	28	75	14	802	914
1935........	1 845	681	165	109	168	47	98	24	55	16	479	685
1934........	1 543	551	151	116	112	37	56	18	46	15	249	743
1933........	1 256	417	99	128	39	37	51	18	27	19	249	589
1932........	1 351	488	123	44	81	48	118	27	34	13	280	583
1931........	3 093	1 141	311	116	223	121	181	53	99	36	811	1 141
1930........	4 523	1 822	616	257	366	163	140	93	117	71	1 101	1 599
1929........	5 751	2 425	929	546	370	152	121	106	147	55	1 916	1 410
1928........	6 628	2 438	885	509	390	165	76	128	219	67	2 788	1 402
1927........	6 303	2 439	933	376	369	163	80	157	261	102	2 573	1 291
1926........	6 381	2 418	921	471	373	133	67	149	252	52	2 671	1 292
1925........	6 006	2 202	872	327	419	111	55	153	253	12	2 748	1 057

Year	Total	Nonresidential buildings				Residential buildings	Non-building construction	Year	Total	Year	Total
		Total [1]	Commercial	Industrial	Public and institutional						
	78	**79**	**80**	**81**	**83-87**	**88**	**89**		**78**		**78**
1924	4 479	1 583	591	233	721	2 052	844	1914.................	775	1904.................	97
1923	3 992	1 456	518	313	601	1 736	801	1913.................	917	1903.................	104
1922	3 344	1 395	496	278	599	1 340	609	1912.................	923	1902.................	119
1921	2 355	998	332	153	461	879	479	1911.................	828	1901.................	120
1920 [2]	2 564	1 394	444	555	345	570	600	1910.................	859		
1919 [2]	2 580	1 213	406	498	266	849	517	1909.................	166		
1918	1 767	...	...	...	...	305	...	1908.................	112		
1917	1 691	...	...	...	...	355	...	1907.................	129		
1916	1 413	...	...	...	...	483	...	1906.................	125		
1915	978	...	...	...	...	418	...	1905.................	107		

1. Includes theaters, not shown separately.
2. 25 states only. Totals for 27 states are 1919, 2 699; 1920, 2 635.
3. From 1973-1979, included in series N 26.

Series N 170. Mobile Home Shipments: 1947 to 1998

(A mobile home is a moveable dwelling, 10 feet or more wide and 35 feet or more long, designed to be towed on its own chassis and without need of permanent foundation. Excluded are travel trailers, motor homes, and modular housing. See source for information on sampling variability of data.)

Year	Mobile home shipments	Year	Mobile home shipments	Year	Mobile home shipments	Year	Mobile home shipments
	170		**170**		**170**		**170**
1998	331 000	1984	287 900	1971	497 000	1958	102 000
1997	296 500			1970	401 190	1957	119 300
1996	319 700	1983	278 100	1969	412 690	1956	124 330
1995	310 700	1982	234 100			1955	111 900
1994	286 100	1981	229 200	1968	317 950	1954	76 000
		1980	233 700	1967	240 360		
1993	242 500	1979	279 900	1966	217 300	1953	76 900
1992	212 000			1965	216 470	1952	83 000
1991	174 300	1978	279 900	1964	191 320	1951	67 300
1990	195 400	1977	257 500			1950	63 100
1989	202 800	1976	249 600	1963	150 840	1949	46 200
		1975	229 300	1962	118 000		
1988	224 300	1974	332 000	1961	90 200	1948	85 500
1987	239 200			1960	103 700	1947	60 000
1986	256 100	1973	567 000	1959	120 500		
1985	283 400	1972	576 000				

Source: U.S. Census Bureau, Current Construction Reports, Series C 20, Housing Starts, monthly.

Series N 186. Low-Rent Public Housing Units: 1947 to 1993

(Low-rent public housing units cover those units subsidized by U.S. Department of Housing and Urban Development under annual contributions contracts, including new, conventional and turnkey units and existing housing either acquired or leased. Includes Puerto Rico and Virgin Islands)

Year	Total low-rent public housing (1 000)[1]	Year	Total low-rent public housing (1 000)[1]	Year	Total low-rent public housing (1 000)[1]	Year	Total low-rent public housing (1 000)[1]
	186		**186**		**186**		**186**
1993	1 324.7	1980	1 321.1	1968	923.7	1957	534.6
1992	1 323.3	1979	1 332.9	1967	850.2	1956	533.6
1991	1 320.0			1966	778.2	1955 [2]	489.7
1990	1 305.3	1978	1 224.8	1965	735.7	1954	455.7
1989	1 205.0	1977	1 308.8	1964	714.3		
		1976	1 305.4			1953	455.2
1988	1 448.8	1975	1 316.7	1963	682.3	1952	436.8
1987	1 443.0	1974	1 314.0	1962	646.6	1951	404.8
1986	1 365.1			1961	624.1	1950 [2]	302.1
1985	1 378.0	1973	1 323.6	1960	593.3	1949	204.9
1984	1 368.7	1972	1 260.2	1959	585.2		
		1971	1 175.9			1948	193.8
1983	1 483.3	1970	1 155.3	1958	557.2	1947	192.0
1982	1 432.2	1969	1 034.7				
1981	1 404.0						

1. As of December 31.
2. Excludes units which have been sold to mutual housing associations, limited dividend corporations (PWA), and homestead associations on which HUD has mortgages for collection.

Series N 200-215. Value of Gross and Net Stocks of Residential Structures in Current Dollars: 1925 to 1993

(In billions of constant 1970 dollars)

	Gross stocks of residential structures						Gross stocks of residential structures					
	Total, all types	Private nonfarm		Farm	Private non-housekeeping	Mobile homes		Total, all types	Private nonfarm		Farm	Private non-housekeeping	Mobile homes
Year		1-4 unit	5 or more unit				Year		1-4 unit	5 or more unit			
	200	**201**	**202**	**205**	**206**	**207**		**200**	**201**	**202**	**205**	**206**	**207**
1993.....	8 798	7 164	1 015	172	34	147	1957.....	618.4	517.7	40.1	37.0	10.5	2.3
1991.....	7 869	6 345	974	167	32	129	1956.....	593.7	496.0	39.0	36.4	10.2	1.9
1990.....	7 543	6 075	933	163	32	124	1955.....	556.7	463.4	37.4	35.0	9.8	1.5
1989.....	7 152	5 744	916	164	32	103	1954.....	517.1	427.7	35.7	34.0	9.5	1.3
1988.....	6 662	5 337	854	159	30	101	1953.....	498.8	410.5	35.1	34.0	9.5	1.2
1987.....	6 376	5 100	819	159	30	94	1952.....	486.8	398.1	35.0	34.0	9.7	1.0
1986.....	5 817	4 643	743	153	28	93	1951.....	465.0	378.6	34.0	33.8	9.6	.8
1985.....	5 706	4 566	701	150	27	104	1950.....	428.4	347.8	32.1	32.2	9.3	.7
1984.....	4 815	3 764	655	134	26	88	1949.....	386.2	312.0	29.6	29.4	8.9	.6
1983.....	4 522	3 534	606	131	25	86	1948.....	369.3	297.8	28.5	28.5	8.8	.5
1982.....	4 292	3 353	569	129	25	82	1947.....	342.6	274.4	26.8	27.5	8.6	.3
1981.....	4 211	3 294	554	130	25	78	1946.....	286.7	228.8	22.9	23.3	7.5	.1
1980.....	4 380	3 502	522	136	24	79	1945.....	243.4	194.8	19.9	18.9	6.5	(Z)
1979.....	3 494	2 735	452	114	22	66	1944.....	226.2	181.3	18.5	17.2	6.2	...
1978.....	3 135	2 455	402	106	20	57	1943.....	211.5	168.2	17.2	16.8	5.8	...
1977.....	2 627	2 052	336	91	18	49	1942.....	195.1	155.4	15.8	15.8	5.5	...
1976.....	2 274	1 771	292	82	16	42	1941.....	179.3	144.3	14.7	14.2	5.1	...
1975.....	2 017	1 567	259	75	14	37	1940.....	162.9	131.3	13.5	12.9	4.7	...
1974.....	1 862	1 446	239	71	14	34	1939.....	151.4	121.7	12.6	12.3	4.5	...
1973.....	1 801	1 429	199	60	42	30	1938.....	146.4	117.5	12.1	12.3	4.3	...
1972.....	1 573	1 261	163	55	35	24	1937.....	142.3	114.0	11.8	12.1	4.2	...
1971.....	1 395	1 127	135	51	31	19	1936.....	132.2	105.9	10.9	11.3	4.0	...
1970.....	1 284.7	1 050.2	111.1	50.5	27.9	16.0	1935.....	121.8	97.5	10.0	10.6	3.7	...
1969.....	1 197.3	983.4	100.3	47.7	25.6	13.4	1934.....	119.3	95.4	9.8	10.5	3.6	...
1968.....	1 094.4	903.3	88.4	44.3	23.4	10.9	1933.....	114.2	91.2	9.4	10.2	3.4	...
1967.....	1 010.6	836.5	79.0	42.6	21.2	9.1	1932.....	109.1	86.9	9.0	9.9	3.3	...
1966.....	941.8	782.1	72.5	39.5	19.4	7.9	1931.....	122.2	97.1	10.1	11.3	3.7	...
1965.....	888.9	739.8	67.0	39.5	16.7	6.9	1930.....	140.5	111.6	11.5	13.2	4.2	...
1964.....	848.0	707.2	62.2	38.4	16.3	5.9	1929.....	147.4	117.1	12.0	14.0	4.3	...
1963.....	807.5	675.1	57.2	38.3	14.9	5.0	1928.....	143.6	113.8	11.3	14.4	4.1	...
1962.....	765.7	641.3	52.2	38.0	13.6	4.4	1927.....	136.3	108.1	10.1	14.4	3.7	...
1961.....	731.6	614.1	48.2	37.9	12.6	3.9	1926.....	131.6	105.3	8.2	14.6	3.5	...
1960.....	713.5	600.8	45.6	37.7	11.9	3.6	1925.....	127.8	101.7	8.2	14.8	3.1	...
1959.....	689.0	579.8	43.9	37.6	11.4	3.2							
1958.....	645.1	540.9	41.6	37.2	10.8	2.7							

Z Less than $0.05 billion.

Series N 216-231.   Mean Age of Stocks of Residential Structures: 1925 to 1994
(In years)

Year	Gross stocks of residential structures						Year	Gross stocks of residential structures					
	Total, all types	Private nonfarm		Farm	Private non-housekeeping	Mobile homes		Total, all types	Private nonfarm		Farm	Private non-housekeeping	Mobile homes
		1-4 unit	5 or more unit						1-4 unit	5 or more unit			
	216	217	218	221	222	223		216	217	218	221	222	223
1994	24.0	24.4	21.8	43.2	. . .	11.0	1957	29.4	28.4	29.5	47.3	20.7	3.4
1993	24.0	24.4	21.8	43.2	. . .	11.1	1956	29.6	28.6	29.3	47.0	21.2	3.5
1991	23.8	24.3	20.3	42.9	23.9	11.0	1955	30.0	29.0	29.0	46.8	21.6	3.8
1990	23.6	24.2	19.8	43.2	23.6	10.7	1954	30.5	29.6	28.6	46.6	21.8	4.0
1989	23.7	24.3	19.1	43.6	23.4	8.7	1953	30.9	30.1	28.2	46.4	21.9	3.8
1988	23.7	24.4	18.8	43.5	23.1	8.5	1952	31.3	30.6	27.8	46.3	21.8	3.6
1987	23.7	24.5	18.6	43.2	22.7	8.4	1951	31.6	31.0	27.4	46.2	21.6	3.3
1986	23.8	24.7	18.4	43.1	22.3	8.3	1950	32.1	31.5	27.0	46.2	21.3	2.8
1985	23.7	24.3	18.7	43.4	22.0	9.2	1949	32.8	32.4	27.0	46.2	21.1	2.3
1984	24.9	26.3	18.1	46.0	21.6	7.9	1948	33.2	32.9	27.0	46.3	20.8	1.6
1983	25.0	26.3	18.1	45.8	21.0	7.8	1947	33.7	33.5	26.9	46.5	20.4	1.2
1982	25.0	26.3	17.9	45.5	20.4	7.7	1946	34.1	33.9	26.6	46.5	20.0	.8
1981	24.8	26.1	17.6	45.5	19.9	7.4	1945	34.2	34.1	26.1	46.4	19.7	.5
1980	23.2	23.9	17.8	42.8	19.3	7.7	1944	33.6	33.5	25.3	45.6	19.1	. . .
1979	24.6	25.9	17.1	45.4	18.7	6.7	1943	33.0	32.9	24.5	44.8	18.4	. . .
1978	24.6	25.9	16.9	45.6	18.1	6.4	1942	32.5	32.2	23.7	44.1	17.7	. . .
1977	24.7	26.1	16.7	45.8	17.5	6.2	1941	32.1	31.8	23.0	43.5	17.2	. . .
1976	24.9	26.3	16.4	46.0	17.0	5.8	1940	32.0	31.7	22.4	43.0	16.7	. . .
1975	24.9	26.4	16.0	46.0	16.5	5.4	1939	31.9	31.6	21.9	42.4	16.3	. . .
1974	24.8	26.3	15.6	46.0	16.1	4.9	1938	31.6	31.4	21.4	42.0	15.8	. . .
1973	26.8	27.2	15.9	49.8	11.5	4.1	1937	31.3	31.0	20.8	41.6	15.4	. . .
1972	26.8	27.3	16.9	49.6	11.6	4.1	1936	30.9	30.6	20.2	41.2	14.9	. . .
1971	27.1	27.4	18.1	49.4	11.6	4.2	1935	30.4	30.2	19.5	40.8	14.3	. . .
1970	27.6	27.7	19.7	49.0	11.5	4.2	1934	29.9	29.6	18.7	40.3	13.7	. . .
1969	27.6	27.5	20.4	49.1	11.5	4.2	1933	29.2	28.9	17.9	39.7	13.0	. . .
1968	27.6	27.4	21.3	49.1	11.6	4.3	1932	28.5	28.2	17.0	39.0	12.4	. . .
1967	27.7	27.4	22.0	49.0	11.9	4.4	1931	27.8	27.5	16.1	38.4	11.7	. . .
1966	27.7	27.3	22.4	49.0	12.2	4.3	1930	27.3	27.0	15.4	37.8	11.0	. . .
1965	27.7	27.2	23.1	48.8	12.8	4.2	1929	26.8	26.5	14.8	37.4	10.7	. . .
1964	27.9	27.3	24.0	48.7	13.6	4.1	1928	26.6	26.2	14.7	37.0	10.4	. . .
1963	28.1	27.4	25.3	48.5	14.6	4.1	1927	26.6	26.2	15.0	36.6	10.3	. . .
1962	28.3	27.5	26.8	48.3	15.9	4.1	1926	26.8	26.3	15.8	36.3	10.4	. . .
1961	28.5	27.6	27.9	48.2	16.9	3.9	1925	27.0	26.4	16.7	35.9	10.8	. . .
1960	28.7	27.7	28.8	48.0	18.0	3.6							
1959	28.9	27.8	29.2	47.8	19.0	3.4							
1958	29.2	28.2	29.5	47.5	19.9	3.4							

Series N 238-245. Occupied Housing Units and Tenure of Homes: 1890 to 1997

Year [1]	Total occupied housing units (1 000)	Tenure of homes		Number of renter occupied (1 000)	Year [1]	Total occupied housing units (1 000)	Tenure of homes		Number of renter occupied (1 000)
		Owner occupied					Owner occupied		
		Number (1 000)	Percent				Number (1 000)	Percent	
	238	242	243	244		238	242	243	244
1997	99 487	65 487	65.8	34 000	1973	69 337	41 653	64.4	24 684
1995	97 693	63 544	65.0	34 150	1970 [2]	63 450	39 885	62.9	23 565
1993	94 724	61 252	64.7	33 472	1960 *	53 024	32 796	61.9	20 227
1990	91 947	59 025	64.2	32 923	1956 [3]	49 874	30 121	60.4	19 753
1987	90 888	58 164	64.0	32 724	1950	42 826	23 560	55.0	19 266
1985	88 425	56 145	63.5	32 280	1945 [3]	37 600	20 009	53.2	17 591
1983	84 638	54 742	64.7	29 914	1940	34 855	15 196	43.6	19 659
1981	83 175	54 342	65.3	28 833	1930	29 905	14 002	47.8	15 320
1980	80 390	51 795	64.4	28 595	1920	24 353	10 867	45.6	12 944
1979	78 572	51 411	65.4	27 160	1910	20 256	9 084	45.9	10 698
1978	77 167	50 283	59.4	26 884	1900	15 964	7 205	46.7	8.224
1977	75 280	48 765	59.2	26 515	1890	12 690	6 066	47.8	6 624
1976	74 005	47 904	64.7	26 101					
1975	72 523	46 867	64.6	25 656					
1974	62 562	42 157	67.4	20 405					

* Denotes first year for which figures include Alaska and Hawaii.
1. Figures for 1956 are for December 31; figures for 1945 are for November 1; figures for decennial years 1890 to 1970 are for census dates.
2. Farm-nonfarm breakdown will not add to total; "Total" figures were revised as a result of errors found after the tabulations were completed.
3. These figures are not comparable with other years; based on sample surveys.

Series N 246-258. Housing Units Vacancy Rates, by Region: 1950 to 1998

(In percent. Annual averages, except as noted.)

Year	Homeowner vacancy rate					Rental vacancy rate				
	United States	Northeast	Midwest	South	West	United States	Northeast	Midwest	South	West
	249	250	251	252	253	254	255	256	257	258
1998	1.7	1.5	1.4	2.0	1.7	7.9	6.7	7.9	9.6	6.7
1997	1.6	1.6	1.2	1.9	1.8	7.7	6.7	8.0	9.1	6.6
1996	1.6	1.6	1.3	1.8	1.7	7.8	7.4	7.9	8.6	7.2
1995	1.5	1.5	1.3	1.7	1.7	7.6	7.2	7.2	8.3	7.5
1994	1.5	1.5	1.1	1.7	1.6	7.4	7.1	6.8	8.0	7.1
1993	1.4	1.3	1.1	1.7	1.4	7.3	7.0	6.6	7.9	7.4
1992	1.5	1.3	1.2	1.7	1.9	7.4	6.9	6.7	8.2	7.1
1991	1.7	1.5	1.3	2.2	1.7	7.4	6.9	6.7	8.9	6.5
1990	1.7	1.6	1.3	2.1	1.8	7.2	6.1	6.4	8.8	6.6
1989	1.8	1.5	1.4	2.2	1.6	7.4	4.7	6.8	9.7	7.1
1988	1.6	1.6	1.2	1.9	1.6	7.7	4.8	6.9	10.1	7.7
1987	1.7	1.2	1.4	2.0	1.8	7.7	4.1	6.8	10.9	7.3
1986	1.6	1.0	1.5	2.1	1.6	7.3	3.9	6.9	10.1	7.1
1985	1.7	1.0	1.6	2.1	2.1	6.5	3.5	5.9	9.1	6.2
1984	1.7	.8	1.6	2.0	2.0	5.9	3.7	5.9	7.9	5.2
1983	1.5	1.0	1.5	1.8	1.8	5.9	4.0	6.1	6.9	5.2
1982	1.5	1.0	1.6	1.6	1.9	5.3	3.7	6.3	5.8	5.4
1981	1.4	1.1	1.4	1.3	1.7	5.0	3.7	5.9	5.4	5.1
1980	1.4	1.1	1.6	1.3	1.6	5.4	4.2	6.0	6.0	5.2
1979	1.1	.9	1.1	1.1	1.3	5.0	4.0	5.1	5.8	4.9
1978	1.0	.8	1.0	1.3	1.0	5.0	4.8	4.8	5.5	4.8
1977	1.2	.9	.9	1.7	0.9	5.2	5.1	5.1	5.7	5.0
1976	1.2	1.0	1.0	1.6	1.2	5.6	4.7	5.6	6.4	5.4
1975	1.2	1.0	1.0	1.5	1.5	6.0	4.1	5.7	7.7	6.2
1974	1.2	.8	1.0	1.5	1.5	6.2	4.2	6.1	8.0	6.2
1973	1.0	.7	.9	1.2	1.2	5.8	3.9	5.9	7.1	6.3
1972	1.0	.8	1.0	1.2	1.1	5.6	3.3	6.1	7.0	6.0
1971	1.0	1.0	1.2	2.0	1.9	5.4	3.0	5.7	7.3	5.7
1970	1.0	.8	1.0	1.2	1.1	5.3	2.7	5.8	7.2	5.6
1969	1.0	.8	.9	1.2	1.2	5.5	3.0	5.7	7.2	6.1
1968	1.1	.8	1.0	1.4	1.3	5.9	3.7	5.4	7.5	7.1
1967	1.3	.7	1.0	1.7	2.0	6.8	4.8	5.7	8.0	8.9
1966	1.4	.9	1.0	1.8	2.1	7.7	5.3	6.5	8.5	10.9
1965	1.5	1.0	1.2	2.0	1.9	8.3	5.6	7.2	9.0	11.9
1964	1.5	1.1	1.3	1.9	1.8	8.3	5.2	7.9	9.1	11.0
1963	1.5	1.0	1.4	1.9	1.9	8.3	5.1	8.7	9.2	10.2
1962	1.4	1.1	1.2	1.7	1.6	8.1	4.7	9.0	9.9	9.5
1961	1.4	1.1	1.2	1.7	1.3	8.7	4.9	9.3	10.4	10.7
1960 *	.3	1.0	1.2	1.6	1.4	8.1	4.9	8.3	9.5	11.0
1959	1.2	1.0	1.1	1.2	1.4	7.0	3.9	7.1	9.4	8.5
1958	1.2	1.0	1.4	1.0	1.2	6.5	3.8	7.3	7.9	7.5
1957	1.0	.7	.9	.9	1.3	5.6	3.4	5.4	6.7	7.4
1956	1.0	.9	.8	1.0	1.4	6.1	3.1	5.6	8.1	8.7
1950 [1]	.9	...	...	...	...	...	...	...	...	...

* Denotes first year for which figures include Alaska and Hawaii.
1. As of April.

Series N 273-277. Residential Nonfarm Mortgage Debt Outstanding, by Type of Property: 1925 to 1999

(In billions of dollars. As of December 31.)

Year	Home mortgages	Multi-family residential mortgages	Year	Home mortgages	Multi-family residential mortgages	Year	Home mortgages	Multi-family residential mortgages	Year	Home mortgages	Multi-family residential mortgages
	273	276		273	276		273	276		273	276
1999	4 790.7	373.0	1979	861.5	134.8	1959	129.6	18.7	1939	16.3	5.6
1998	4 358.4	330.9	1978	743.8	124.9	1958	116.7	16.6	1938	15.8	4.4
1997	3 971.5	302.9	1977	633.6	114.0	1957	106.9	14.6	1937	15.5	4.5
1996	3 719.2	289.1	1976	540.3	105.7	1956	98.3	14.1	1936	15.4	4.6
1995	3 510.5	273.5	1975	477.7	100.6	1955	87.5	13.5	1935	15.4	4.8
1994	3 329.7	265.9	1974	438.2	100.0	1954	75.0	12.7	1934	15.6	5.1
1993	3 146.5	266.2	1973	402.9	93.1	1953	65.7	12.1	1933	15.4	5.7
1992	2 981.1	269.3	1972	360.1	82.8	1952	58.1	11.5	1932	16.7	6.0
1991	2 814.5	281.7	1971	320.9	70.1	1951	51.5	10.6	1931	18.1	6.2
1990	2 646.5	285.6	1970	294.4	60.1	1950	44.9	9.3	1930	18.9	6.5
1989	2 404.5	285.9	1969	280.2	53.2	1949	37.4	7.8	1929	18.9	6.0
1988	2 175.7	273.5	1968	262.1	48.3	1948	33.1	6.7	1928	17.9	5.4
1987	1 940.4	257.7	1967	245.0	44.8	1947	28.0	5.8	1927	16.4	5.0
1986	1 737.7	238.3	1966	231.8	41.3	1946	22.9	5.3	1926	14.8	4.6
1985	1 533.5	205.0	1965	218.5	38.2	1945	18.6	4.9	1925	13.0	4.2
1984	1 332.8	185.5	1964	201.3	34.6	1944	17.9	5.6			
1983	1 197.1	160.7	1963	184.0	30.0	1943	17.8	5.8			
1982	1 079.5	145.7	1962	167.4	26.7	1942	18.2	5.8			
1981	1 038.4	142.0	1961	153.3	23.6	1941	18.4	5.9			
1980	964.7	142.3	1960	140.8	20.8	1940	17.4	5.7			

Series NN-1. Net Stock of Residential Capital: 1985 to 1997

(In billions of dollars. End-of-year estimates)

Item	1985	1988	1989	1990	1991	1992	1993	1994	1995	1996	1997
Total residential capital [1]	4 683.3	5 737.1	6 054.7	6 295.7	6 407.8	6 749.5	7 152.5	7 643.5	7 964.4	8 378.2	8 791.1
By type of owner and legal form of organization:											
Private	4 578.2	5 602.7	5 911.1	6 147.3	6 258.5	6 591.4	6 983.1	7 465.8	7 779.0	8 185.5	8 590.9
Corporate	55.6	65.3	67.1	68.6	69.4	72.3	74.0	76.1	78.3	81.5	84.3
Noncorporate	4 522.6	5 537.4	5 844.0	6 078.7	6 189.1	6 519.1	6 909.2	7 389.6	7 700.7	8 104.0	8 506.6
Government	105.1	134.4	143.6	148.4	149.3	158.2	169.4	177.7	185.4	192.7	200.2
Federal	32.0	46.2	50.3	51.4	50.1	52.9	56.1	58.7	61.1	63.2	65.3
State and local	73.1	88.3	93.3	97.0	99.2	105.3	113.3	119.1	124.3	129.5	134.9
By tenure group:											
Owner-occupied	3 254.0	4 043.9	4 298.3	4 494.3	4 597.9	4 870.7	5 211.9	5 629.7	5 899.7	6 241.1	6 587.8
Farm	128.6	142.5	146.9	151.2	152.0	156.8	162.2	170.7	175.1	180.0	184.7
Nonfarm	3 125.3	3 901.4	4 151.4	4 343.1	4 445.9	4 713.9	5 049.6	5 459.0	5 724.7	6 061.1	6 403.1
Tenant-occupied	1 302.3	1 534.0	1 587.1	1 626.7	1 634.7	1 694.1	1 743.4	1 807.1	1 849.9	1 914.4	1 972.3
Farm	5.6	6.3	6.4	6.7	6.7	6.9	7.3	7.8	8.1	8.4	8.6
Nonfarm	1 296.7	1 527.7	1 580.7	1 620.1	1 628.0	1 687.2	1 736.2	1 799.3	1 841.8	1 906.0	1 963.7

1. Includes stocks of other nonfarm residential capital, which consists of dormitories, fraternity and sorority houses, and nurses' homes.

SOURCE: U.S. Bureau of Economic Analysis, *Survey of Current Business*, monthly, September 1998 issue.

Series NN-2.   New Privately-Owned Housing Units Started—Selected Characteristics: 1970 to 1998

[In thousands (1 434 represents 1 434 000. Census regions.)]

Year	Total units	Structures with-			Region				Condominium units [1]		
		One unit	2 to 4 units	5 or more units	Northeast	Midwest	South	West	Total	Single-family	Multi-family
1970	1 434	813	85	536	218	294	612	311	. . .	. . .	. . .
1973	2 045	1 132	118	795	277	440	899	429	241	69	172
1974	1 338	888	68	382	183	317	553	285	175	46	130
1975	1 160	892	64	204	149	294	442	275	65	20	45
1976	1 538	1 162	86	289	169	400	569	400	95	30	64
1977	1 987	1 451	122	414	202	465	783	538	118	41	77
1978	2 020	1 433	125	462	200	451	824	545	156	42	114
1979	1 745	1 194	122	429	178	349	748	470	198	43	156
1980	1 292	852	110	331	125	218	643	306	186	35	150
1981	1 084	705	91	288	117	165	562	240	181	36	145
1982	1 062	663	80	320	117	149	591	205	170	40	130
1983	1 703	1 068	113	522	168	218	935	382	276	77	199
1984	1 750	1 084	121	544	204	243	866	436	291	96	194
1985	1 742	1 072	93	576	252	240	782	468	225	79	146
1986	1 805	1 179	84	542	294	296	733	483	214	80	134
1987	1 621	1 146	65	409	269	298	634	420	196	73	123
1988	1 488	1 081	59	348	235	274	575	404	148	53	95
1989	1 376	1 003	55	318	179	266	536	396	118	37	82
1990	1 193	895	37	260	131	253	479	329	75	22	53
1991	1 014	840	36	138	113	233	414	254	60	21	39
1992	1 200	1 030	31	139	127	288	497	288	74	35	40
1993	1 288	1 126	29	133	126	298	562	302	86	45	41
1994	1 457	1 198	35	224	138	329	639	351	96	48	48
1995	1 354	1 076	34	244	118	290	615	331	93	47	47
1996	1 477	1 161	45	271	132	322	662	361	107	53	54
1997	1 474	1 134	44	296	137	304	670	363	110	56	54
1998	1 617	1 271	43	303	148	330	743	395	113	59	54

1. Type of ownership under which the owners of the individual housing units are also joint owners of the common areas of the building or community. Includes a small number of cooperatively-owned units.

SOURCE: U.S. Census Bureau, Current Construction Reports, Series C20, Housing Starts, monthly.

Series NN-3. Existing One-Family Houses Sold and Price, by Region: 1970 to 1998

(Based on data (adjusted and aggregated to regional and national totals) reported by participating real estate multiple listing services Census regions. The median is the middle value when each item in the group is ranked according to size.)

Year	Houses sold (1 000)					Median sales price (dol.)				
	Total	Northeast	Midwest	South	West	Total	Northeast	Midwest	South	West
1970	1 612	251	501	568	292	23 000	25 700	20 100	22 200	24 300
1972	2 252	361	630	788	473	26 700	29 800	23 900	26 400	28 400
1973	2 334	367	674	847	446	28 900	32 800	25 300	29 000	31 000
1974	2 272	354	645	839	434	32 000	35 800	27 700	32 200	34 800
1975	2 476	370	701	862	543	35 300	39 300	30 100	34 800	39 600
1976	3 064	439	881	1 033	712	38 100	41 800	32 900	36 500	46 100
1977	3 650	515	1 101	1 231	803	42 900	44 400	36 700	39 800	57 300
1978	3 986	516	1 144	1 416	911	48 700	47 900	42 200	45 100	66 700
1979	3 827	526	1 061	1 353	887	55 700	53 600	47 800	51 300	77 400
1980	2 973	403	806	1 092	672	62 200	60 800	51 900	58 300	89 300
1981	2 419	353	632	917	516	66 400	63 700	54 300	64 400	96 200
1982	1 990	354	490	780	366	67 800	63 500	55 100	67 100	98 900
1983	2 697	477	692	1 004	524	70 300	72 200	56 600	69 200	94 900
1984	2 829	478	720	1 006	624	72 400	78 700	57 100	71 300	95 800
1985	3 134	561	806	1 063	704	75 500	88 900	58 900	75 200	95 400
1986	3 474	635	922	1 145	773	80 300	104 800	63 500	78 200	100 900
1987	3 436	618	892	1 163	763	85 600	133 300	66 000	80 400	113 200
1988	3 513	606	865	1 224	817	89 300	143 000	68 400	82 200	124 900
1989 [1]	3 325	490	832	1 185	818	89 500	127 700	71 800	84 400	127 100
1990	3 219	458	809	1 193	759	92 000	126 400	75 300	85 100	129 600
1991	3 186	463	812	1 173	737	97 100	129 100	79 500	88 500	135 300
1992	3 479	521	913	1 242	802	99 700	128 900	83 000	91 500	131 500
1993	3 786	550	967	1 386	882	103 100	129 100	86 000	94 300	132 500
1994	3 916	552	965	1 436	962	107 200	129 100	89 300	95 700	139 400
1995	3 888	547	945	1 433	964	110 500	126 700	94 800	97 700	141 000
1996	4 196	584	986	1 511	1 116	115 800	127 800	101 000	103 400	147 100
1997	4 381	606	1 005	1 596	1 174	121 800	131 800	107 000	109 600	155 200
1998	4 970	662	1 130	1 868	1 309	128 400	135 900	114 300	116 200	164 800

1. Beginning 1989 data not comparable to earlier years due to rebenchmarking.

SOURCE: NATIONAL ASSOCIATION OF REALTORS, Washington, DC, prior to 1990, Home Sales, monthly, and Home Sales Yearbook: 1990; (copyright); thereafter, Real Estate Outlook; Market Trends & Insights, monthly (copyright).

P

MANUFACTURING

SECTION P
MANUFACTURING
Highlights

1 Manufacturing is defined as the mechanical or chemical transformation of inorganic and organic substances into new products or the assembly of component parts of products. Manufacturing activities were classified from 1947 through 1997 according to the *Standard Industrial Classification (SIC) Manual* published by the Office of Management and Budget. First issued in 1939, it was revised in 1945, 1957, 1972 and 1987. Beginning 1997 the Manual was replaced with a new system called North American Industry Classification System (NAICS).

2 The basic source of data on manufactures has been the *Census of Manufactures* conducted by the Bureau of the Census, beginning in 1809. A census was taken at 10-year intervals thereafter until 1899 (with the exception of 1829), at five-year intervals from 1904 to 1919, and biennially from 1921 to 1939. It was suspended during World War II but resumed in 1947. Legislation enacted in 1948 provided for a Census of Manufactures every five years with annual sample surveys for interim years. The *Annual Survey of Manufactures* (ASM) is based on a sample of 55,000 establishments out of an approximate total of 200,000. The scope of the census has varied from one census to another. From 1849 to 1899, the minimum size limit of factories was output valued at $500 or more. It was raised to $5,000 or more for 1929 to 1937. Beginning in 1947, the criterion was employment of one or more persons at any time during the census year. However, these changes have not appreciably affected the historical comparability of the census figures except for the data on the number of establishments. There have also been numerous changes in the definition of manufacturing industries. When the changes result in the omission of an entire industry, the adjustments are generally carried back through the previous censuses. Furthermore, the treatment of nonproduction workers has not been consistent over the years. Personnel in manufacturing industries engaged in distribution and construction have been reported separately since 1939, but not before. Officers of corporations are included as employees, but not proprietors and partners of unincorporated firms, for whom no data have been collected since 1963. Another difference concerns value added in manufacturing. The standard formula for calculating value added by manufacture since 1958 differs from the one used for 1954 and previous years. Prior

to 1958, value added by an establishment was calculated by subtracting the cost of materials, supplies, containers, fuels, electrical energy, and contract work from the value of shipments. This was known as unadjusted value added. Beginning in 1958, the formula was changed to adjusted value added which includes two elements: (1) value added by merchandising (the difference between the sales value and the cost of merchandise sold without further manufacture, processing, and assembly); and (2) an adjustment in the net change in finished goods and work-in-process inventories between the beginning and the end of the year. This concept should not be confused with the National Income Originating in Manufacturing, which is obtained by subtracting from the value of shipments not only the cost of materials, but also other costs such as depreciation charges, state and local taxes, allowances for bad debts, and purchases of services from nonmanufacturing enterprises (engineering and management consultants, advertising, telephone, insurance, royalties, patent fees, etc.). It is therefore a net concept of value added in manufacturing and generally exceeds the latter by about a third.

3 The value added in manufacturing in 1996 was $1.749 trillion or $143,782 per worker, $69.96 per production worker hour and $5.39 per dollar of wages. The operation ratio of payroll to value added was 36.9.

4 The GDP in manufacturing in 1997 was $1.378 trillion of which durable goods accounted for $784 billion and nondurable goods for $594 billion. The largest manufacturing sectors in value were industrial machinery $158.9 billion, chemicals $158.8 billion, electronic and electric equipment, $157.3 billion, food $118.5 billion, fabricated metal products $99.3 billion, and printing and publishing, $98.4 billion.

5 In 1996 manufacturing employed 12.169 million workers and their total wages amounted to $324.496 billion or $26,666 per worker ($12.98 per hour).

6 The most industrialized state in the Union is California with value of shipments in 1996 $368.329 billion, followed by Texas ($284.151 billion), Ohio ($232.721 billion), Michi-

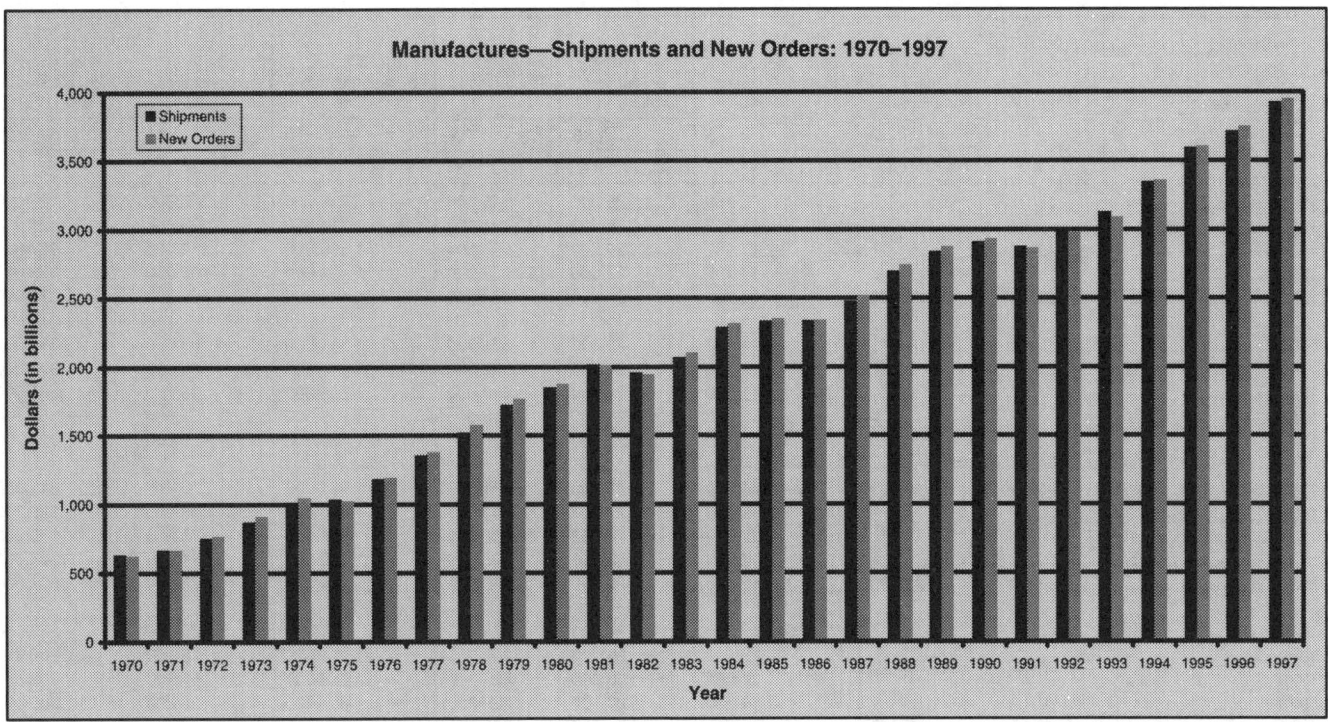

Manufactures—Shipments and New Orders: 1970–1997

gan ($205.744 billion), Illinois ($196.845 billion), Pennsylvania ($165.889 billion) and New York ($163.697 billion).

7 Based on 1992 = 100, the national industrial production index was 131.4 in 1998 and manufacturing index 135.1. The fastest growing sectors since 1992 were computers which jumped to 650.4 and electrical machinery (291.5). The only sector that lost ground was leather and leather products which ended 1998 with 75.3.

8 Net manufacturing sales in 1998 were $3.934 trillion, net profit $318 billion and net profit after taxes $238 billion.

9 While the sales of wine, whiskey, and distilled spirits have declined, those of beer have increased from 193 million barrels to 199 million barrels. There were 1,504 beer breweries in the United States in 1996 compared to 86 in 1980. Production of distilled spirits was 104 million gallons (236 million gallons in 1980), whiskey (69 million gallons compared to 87 million gallons in 1980) and wines (412 million gallons compared to 982 million gallons in 1980).

10 Official antismoking campaigns seem to have had no significant effect on cigarette production and consump-

tion. In 1997 cigarette production was slightly higher at 720 billion compared to 714 billion in 1980. However, consumption per person has declined to 2,000 annually in 1997 compared to 4,000 in 1980.

11 Iron and steel were once the bellwether of manufacturing but it no longer has that role. Nevertheless, United States is a major producer of steel mill products, producing 131 million tons in 1998, up from 97.8 million tons in 1990.

12 Computer industry, hardly 20 years old, has become one of the most dynamic sectors. There are 172 computer manufactures that produced 20.124 million computers in 1997 valued at $49.606 billion. Of these 13.473 million were personal computers.

13 Home electronic equipment sales have increased from $43 billion in 1990 to $76 billion in 1998. Of these home office products, as telephones, answering devices, word processors, fax machines, and home security systems accounted for $1.756 billion.

14 Toy industry shipments totaled $20.321 billion of which dolls accounted for $2.085 billion, activity toys for $2.097 billion and games and puzzles for $1.506 billion.

Series P 1-12. Manufactures Summary: 1849 to 1996

Year	Establishments		Production workers engaged in manufacturing (1 000) [1]	Man-hours, production workers (mil.)	Total payroll (mil. dol.)	Value added by manufacture [2] (mil. dol.)	Capital expenditures, new (mil. dol.)	End-of-year inventories (mil. dol.)
	Total	With 20 or more employees						
	1	2	5	6	7	10	11	12
FACTORIES, EXCLUDING HAND AND NEIGHBORHOOD INDUSTRIES								
1996	...	...	12 169	25 000	645 100	1 749 700	139 300	427 000
1995	...	...	12 253	25 100	624 400	1 711 400	128 400	421 000
1994	...	...	11 947	24 600	593 600	1 598 000	112 000	397 000
1993	...	...	11 700	23 800	573 000	1 483 000	103 000	383 000
1992	382 000	125 000	11 641	23 600	559 000	1 425 200	103 200	374 000
1991	...	...	11 700	23 400	529 000	1 341 000	103 000	380 000
1990	...	...	12 200	24 500	532 000	1 347 000	105 000	393 000
1989	...	...	12 500	24 900	519 000	1 325 000	98 700	381 000
1988	...	...	12 400	24 800	503 000	1 269 000	81 600	362 000
1987	369 000	126 000	12 280	24 300	476 000	1 166 000	78 600	333 000
1986	...	...	11 800	23 200	451 000	1 035 000	76 400	311 000
1985	...	...	12 200	23 700	443 000	1 000 000	83 100	322 000
1984	...	...	12 600	24 600	429 000	984 000	75 300	330 000
1983	...	...	12 200	23 600	395 000	882 000	61 900	308 000
1982	358 000	123 000	12 400	23 500	380 000	824 000	75 000	307 000
1981	...	...	13 500	26 200	379 000	838 000	78 600	279 000
1980	...	...	13 900	26 700	350 000	774 000	70 100	262 000
1979	...	...	14 500	28 300	329 000	748 000	61 500	239 000
1978	...	...	14 200	27 700	299 000	657 000	55 200	209 000
1977	360 000	119 000	13 700	26 700	264 000	585 000	47 500	188 000
1976	...	...	13 100	25 400	233 000	511 000	40 700	170 000
1975	...	...	12 600	24 100	210 000	442 000	37 300	158 000
1974	...	...	14 000	27 200	208 000	452 000	35 700	...
1973	...	...	14 200	28 100	193 000	404 000	27 000	125 000
1972	321 000	114 000	13 500	26 700	174 000	354 000	24 100	108 000
1971	...	...	12 900	25 300	156 000	314 000	20 900	102 000
1970	...	...	13 258	26 669	141 886	300 228	22 164	101 285
1969	...	...	14 358	28 600	142 645	304 441	22 291	98 206
1968	...	...	14 041	28 157	132 568	285 059	20 613	90 505
1967	305 680	107 138	13 955	27 838	123 481	261 984	21 503	84 406
1966	...	...	13 827	28 103	117 157	250 880	20 236	77 721
1965	...	...	13 076	26 568	106 643	226 940	16 615	68 009
1964	...	...	12 403	25 246	98 685	206 194	13 294	63 211
1963	306 617	99 352	12 232	24 509	93 283	192 083	11 370	59 913
1962	...	...	12 127	24 270	89 819	179 071	10 436	58 067
1961	...	...	11 779	23 289	83 677	164 281	9 780	54 744
1960	...	...	12 210	24 174	83 673	163 999	10 098	53 560
1959	...	...	12 273	24 444	81 204	161 536	9 140	52 552
1958	299 017	95 278	11 681	22 679	73 875	141 541	9 544	49 947
1957	...	...	12 839	25 208	76 315	147 838	12 144	...
1956	...	...	13 131	26 089	74 015	144 909	11 233	...
1955	...	...	12 954	25 898	69 097	135 023	8 233	...
1954	286 814	90 470	12 372	24 334	62 963	117 032	8 201	40 341
1953	285 000	...	13 501	27 066	66 493	121 659	8 048	...
1952	267 000	...	12 706	25 618	59 598	109 162	7 883	...
1951	262 000	...	12 509	25 264	54 742	102 086	7 782	...
1950	260 000	...	11 779	23 717	46 643	89 750	5 041	...
1949	...	...	11 016	21 770	41 482	75 367	5 067	...
1947	240 807	...	11 918	24 317	39 696	74 291	5 998	26 129
1939 [3]	173 802	...	7 808	...	[4] 12 706	24 487	...	9 632
1937	166 794	...	8 569	...	12 830	25 174	...	9 863
1935	167 916	...	7 204	...	9 565	18 553	...	...
1933	139 325	...	5 788	...	[5] 6 238	14 008	...	...
1931	171 450	...	6 163	...	...	18 601	...	...
1929	206 663	...	8 370	...	14 284	30 591	...	...
1927	187 629	...	7 848	...	13 123	26 325	...	...

See footnotes at end of chart.

Series P 1-12. Manufactures Summary: 1849 to 1996—Cont'd.

Year	Establishments		Production workers engaged in manufacturing (1 000) [1]	Man-hours, production workers (mil.)	Total payroll (mil. dol.)	Value added by manufacture [2] (mil. dol.)	Capital expenditures, new (mil. dol.)	End-of-year inventories (mil. dol.)
	Total	With 20 or more employees						
	1	2	5	6	7	10	11	12
1925	183 877	...	7 871	...	12 958	25 668	...	...
1923	192 096	...	8 194	...	12 997	24 570	...	...
1921	192 059	...	6 476	...	9 870	17 253	...	...
1919	270 231	...	8 465	...	12 427	23 842	...	...
1914	268 436	...	6 602	...	5 016	9 386	...	...
1909	264 810	...	6 262	...	4 106	8 160	...	...
1904	213 444	...	5 182	...	2 991	6 019	...	...
1899	204 754	...	4 502	...	2 259	4 647	...	...
FACTORIES AND HAND AND NEIGHBORHOOD INDUSTRIES								
1899	509 490	...	5 098	...	2 596	5 475	...	...
1889	353 864	...	4 129	...	2 209	4 102	...	...
1879	253 852	...	2 733	...	...	1 973	...	...
1869	252 148	...	2 054	...	...	1 395	...	...
1859	140 433	...	1 311	...	...	854	...	...
1849	123 025	...	957	...	...	464	...	...

1. The Bureau of Labor Statistics annual averages for employment in manufacturing indicates 1943 as the year of maximum employment, with 15 147 000 production workers.
2. For 1849-1933, cost of contract work was not subtracted from value of products in calculating value added by manufacture. For 1935-1953, value added by manufacture represents unadjusted value added; beginning 1954, it represents adjusted value, which includes the change during the year in finished goods and work-in-process inventories.
3. Except as noted, figures have been revised by retabulation of returns to exclude data for establishments classified as manufacturing in 1939 but as nonmanufacturing beginning 1947. Value added by manufacture in 1939, prior to revision and on a basis comparable with prior years, was $24.7 billion.
4. Figures revised on basis of estimates rather than by retabulation of 1939 reports. Estimates made as follows: For nonproduction employees, by multiplying the retabulated figure for number of production workers by the ratio of all employees to production workers computed from unrevised 1939 data; for salaries and wages, by multiplying the retabulated wage figure by the ratio for salaries and wages also derived from the unrevised 1939 data.
5. Excludes data for salaried officers of corporations and their salaries; therefore, not strictly comparable with figures for other years.

Series P 74-92. Value of Manufactures' Shipments, Inventories and Orders: 1947 to 1997

(In billions of dollars, except ratios. As of December 31, except shipments are for calendar year)

Year	Total shipments	Inventories Total	Ratio of inventories to sales [1]	Total new orders	Total unfilled orders	Year	Total shipments	Inventories Total	Ratio of inventories to sales [1]	Total new orders	Total unfilled orders
	74	**77**	**80**	**87**	**90**		**74**	**77**	**80**	**87**	**90**
1997	3 929	446	1.36	3 952	532	1971	671	102	1.76	672	107
1996	3 715	427	1.39	3 749	509	1970	630.7	101.4	1.90	620.0	73.8
1995	3 375	421	1.42	3 608	475	1969	642.7	96.6	1.76	643.7	84.5
1994	3 370	384	1.40	3 383	452	1968	603.4	90.5	1.76	606.1	85.4
1993	3 102	370	1.46	3 068	438						
						1967	557.4	84.4	1.77	561.2	83.9
1992	2 934	373	1.55	2 899	472	1966	538.4	77.7	1.73	550.9	79.8
1991	2 826	380	1.64	2 812	508	1965	492.0	68.0	1.66	502.0	67.2
1990	2 917	382	1.60	2 924	524	1964	448.0	63.0	1.69	455.4	58.0
1989	2 840	377	1.62	2 889	518	1963	420.4	60.0	1.71	424.0	50.2
1988	2 682	361	1.64	2 724	469						
						1962	397.4	58.0	1.75	396.1	47.0
1987	2 475	333	1.64	2 513	427	1961	371.0	55.0	1.77	373.0	48.0
1986	2 336	318	1.66	2 342	390	1960 *	370.0	54.0	1.74	361.4	46.0
1985	2 334	330	1.72	2 348	384	1959	363.0	52.5	1.74	368.1	54.1
1984	2 288	334	1.78	2 315	370	1958	327.4	50.0	1.83	323.0	49.0
1983	2 071	308	1.80	2 105	343						
						1957	345.0	52.0	1.81	330.2	53.3
1982	1 960	307	1.91	1 947	309	1956	333.0	51.0	1.83	341.0	67.5
1981	2 018	280	1.74	2 015	323	1955	318.0	45.2	1.71	329.1	60.0
1980	1 853	262	1.61	1 876	326	1954	280.2	42.0	1.80	267.8	48.2
1979	1 727	239	1.61	1 771	303	1953	298.0	44.2	1.79	282.4	60.3
1978	1 523	209	1.55	1 580	259						
						1952	271.0	42.0	1.84	278.4	75.5
1977	1 358	188	1.58	1 381	202	1951	260.4	39.2	1.80	287.0	67.0
1976	1 186	175	1.66	1 194	180	1950	223.4	32.0	1.70	241.3	41.2
1975	1 039	160	1.77	1 023	171	1949	193.1	26.5	1.65	187.4	24.0
1974	1 018	158	1.86	1 047	187	1948	217.3	29.0	1.59	212.3	31.0
1973	875	124	1.63	913	158						
						1947	186.0	26.1	.69	183.1	34.3
1972	756	108	1.58	770	120						

* Denotes first year for which figures include Alaska and Hawaii.
1. Ratios of average inventories to average monthly sales.

Series P 93-106. Manufacturing Corporations—Sales, Profits and Stockholders' Equity: 1947 to 1998

In billions of dollars)

	All manufacturing corporations					All manufacturing corporations			
		Net profits					Net profits		
Year	Sales (net)	Before federal income taxes	After federal income taxes	Stockholders' equity [2]	Year	Sales (net)	Before federal income taxes	After federal income taxes	Stockholders' equity [2]
	93	94	95	96		93	94	95	96
998	3 934	314	234	1 482.5	1972	850	63	36	343.4
997	3 922	331	244	1 462.7	1971	751	53	31	320.8
996	3 758	307	225	1 340.0	1970	708.8	48.1	28.6	306.8
995	3 528	275	198	1 240.6	1969 [1]	694.6	58.1	33.2	289.9
994	3 256	244	175	1 110.1					
					1968	631.9	55.4	32.1	265.9
993	3 015	118	83	1 039.7	1967	575.4	47.8	29.0	247.6
992	2 890	31	22	1 034.7	1966	554.2	51.8	30.9	230.3
991	2 761	99	66	1 064.1	1965	492.2	46.5	27.5	211.7
990	2 811	160	112	1 043.8	1964	443.1	39.6	23.2	199.8
989	2 745	189	136	999.0					
					1963	412.7	34.9	19.5	189.7
988	2 596	216	155	957.6	1962	389.9	31.9	17.7	181.4
987	2 378	173	116	900.9	1961	356.4	27.5	15.3	172.6
986	2 221	129	83	874.7	1960	345.7	27.5	15.2	165.4
985	2 331	137	88	866.2	1959	338.0	29.7	16.3	157.1
984	2 335	166	108	864.2					
					1958	305.3	22.7	12.7	147.4
983	2 114	133	86	812.8	1957	320.0	28.2	15.4	141.1
982	2 039	108	71	770.2	1956	307.3	29.8	16.2	131.6
981	2 145	158	101	743.4	1955	278.4	28.6	15.1	120.1
980	1 913	145	92	668.1	1954	248.5	20.9	11.2	113.1
979	1 742	154	99	600.5					
					1953	265.9	24.4	11.3	108.2
978	1 496	133	81	540.5	1952	250.2	22.9	10.7	103.7
977	1 328	115	70	496.7	1951	245.0	27.4	11.9	98.3
976	1 203	105	65	462.7	1950	181.9	23.2	12.9	83.3
975	1 065	80	49	423.4	1949	154.9	14.4	9.0	77.6
974	1 061	92	59	395.0					
					1948	165.6	18.4	11.5	72.2
973	1 017	81	48	374.1	1947	150.7	16.6	10.1	65.1

. Beginning 1969, includes newspapers.
. Average equity for the year, using four end-of-quarter figures.

TRANSPORTATION

1 The first transportation agency in the United States, the Office of Road Inquiry, was created in 1894, "to make inquiries in regard to the systems of road management throughout the United States, to make investigations in regard to the best methods of roadmaking, to prepare publications on this subject suitable for publication." It was succeeded by the Office of Public Roads and Rural Engineering in 1916 and by the Bureau of Public Roads in 1918 (called Public Roads Administration between 1939 and 1949). The Bureau was transferred to the Department of Transportation in 1966 and its functions assigned to the Federal Highways Administration. The first survey of highway mileage, revenues and expenditures was made in 1904, followed by others in 1909 and 1914.

2 In 1912 Congress authorized $500,000 for an experimental program of rural post road construction. However, it was not until the Federal Aid Road Act of 1916 that the Federal–State Highway Program was established on an ongoing basis. In 1921, Congress authorized designation of a system of principal interstate and intercounty roads, limited to 7% of the rural mileage then existing. The Federal Aid Highway Act of 1944 specifically authorized the use of funds for highways in urban areas. In addition, the Act provided for the designation of a Federal Aid secondary system and a national system of interstate highways. Under President Dwight Eisenhower, the Federal Aid Highway Act of 1956 established the goal of a 41,000-mile interstate system, which forms the basis of the U.S. road transportation system today. In 1995 Congress abolished the Federal Aid Highway Systems and replaced it with the National Highway System (NHS). Roads are classified as (1) arterial highways, (2) collector facilities that link arterials and lower systems, and (3) local roads.

3 The principal sources of highway and motor transport data are the *Highway Statistics* of the Federal Highway Administration, the *Transport Statistics of the United States* published by the Interstate Commerce Commission, various surveys and censuses conducted by the U.S. Bureau of the Census, *Factbook* of the U.S. National Highway Traffic

Safety Administration, *Motor Vehicle Facts and Figures* published by the Motor Vehicle Manufacturers Association, *Accident Facts* published by the National Safety Council, and *Transportation in America* published by the Eno Foundation for Transportation.

4 The first Federal highway was the Great National Pike, also known as the Cumberland Road, which was built in sections from 1806 to 1840 between Cumberland, Maryland, and Vandalia, Illinois. The total construction cost was $6.821 million.

5 The first hardsurfaced road in what is now the United States was built by the Dutch in 1663. It ran for 100 miles from Pahaquarry Mines in New Jersey to Kingston, New York. The first toll road was the Little River Turnpike built in 1785 from Alexandria, Virginia, to Snicker's Gap, a pass through the Blue Ridge Mountains leading to the Shenandoah Valley.

6 Of the total passenger traffic of 1.968 trillion passenger miles in 1997 private automobiles handled 2.476 trillion passenger miles, air public carriers 453 billion passenger miles, buses 30 billion passenger miles and railroads 14 billion passenger miles. Of the total freight traffic of 3.622 trillion ton miles, railroads carried 1.421 trillion ton miles, trucks 1.051 trillion ton miles and inland waterways 508 billion ton miles.

7 11,562,916 tons of commodities were shipped in the United States in 1997. Of these trucks handled 7,992,437 tons, rail 1,480,692 tons, and inland waterways 538,197 tons.

8 Transportation accidents and deaths are closely monitored by the National Highway Traffic Safety Administration. In 1997 there were 6,764,000 motor vehicle accidents and 42,000 deaths , 2,397 railroad acidents and 602 deaths, 148 air carried accidents and 93 deaths, 1,858 general aviation accidents and 660 deaths, 8,044 recreational boating

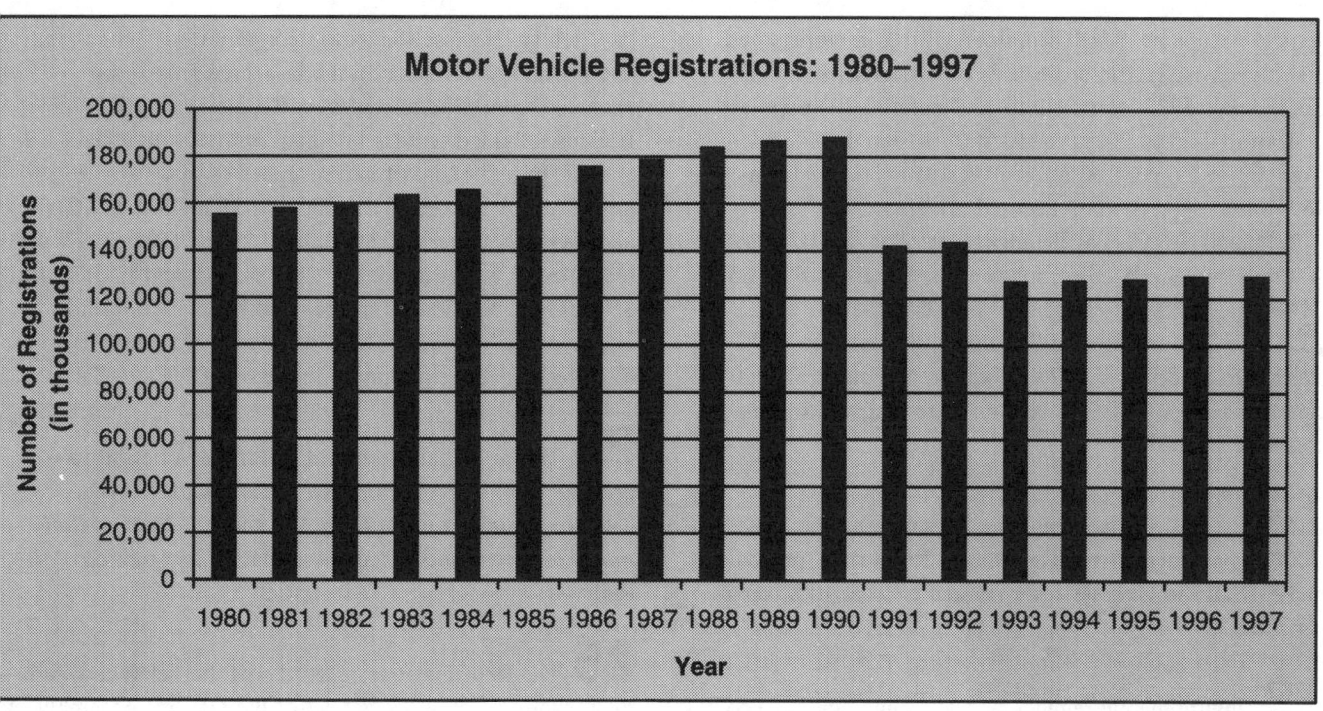

Motor Vehicle Registrations: 1980–1997

ccidents and 819 deaths, and 15,151 rail rapid transit accidents and 77 deaths.

9 The total highway mileage in the United States in 1997 was 3,944,597 miles of which interstates accounted for 6,048 miles, other arterial roads 378,451 miles, collector oads 793,120 miles, local roads 2,718,166 miles, urban oads 836,109 miles and rural roads 3,108,408 miles. The ongest road system in in Texas (296,551 miles), followed y California (170,598 miles). By pavement condition, 5% of the roads are above average, 42% average and 23% elow average.

10 Highways are generally paid for by issuing bonds which are then redeemed by imposing tolls and imposts on ighway users. In 1995 imposts on highway users totaled 97.2 billion while total highway debt outstanding was 68.73 billion.

11 In 1997 motor vehicle registrations totaled 07,754,000, of which automobiles (including taxicabs) ccounted for 129.749,000 and motor cycles 3,786,000. California has the largest number of motor vehicles (24.9 million). New car sales in 1997 was 8,259,000 (6,924,000 of hem domestic) and new truck sales 7,121,000. Foreign car nanufacturers have captured 16% of the U. S. market and .5% of the truck market.

12 The United States manufactured 6,083,000 cars and ,716,000 trucks in 1996. Of the 123.2 million cars in use, 6.2% is under five years, 26.9% between 6 and 8 years,

23.3% between 9 and 11 years and 26.8% more than 12 years. Of the 70.2 million trucks in use 18.6% is over 12 years. In 1995 7.414 million cars and 2.918 million trucks were retired or condemned.

13 In 1997 the United States had 698,000 buses of which 403,000 were publicly owned.

14 In 1997 there were 438,800 recreational vehicles, including 139,300 motorized homes, 131,600 travel trailers, and 10,300 truck campers in the United States.

15 In 1990, 84,215,000 commuted by automobile to work, 15,378,000 carpooled, and only 5.2% used public transportation and 3,406,000 worked at home. The average travel time to work was 22.4 minutes.

16 Roadway congestion measured in annual person hours of delay is 66,280 per freeway nationwide, costing $1.055 billion in delay and fuel costs, or $630 per driver and $485 per capita. The worst road congestion is in Los Angeles (684,410 hours), followed by New York (611,420 hours), Chicago (250,840 hours), Washington (231,080 hours), San Francisco (202,985 hours), and Houston (150,240 hours)

17 In 1997 there were 35 million motor vehicle accidents of which 13.8 million occurred on the road involving 16 million cars, 7.7 million trucks and 138,000 motor cycles. Fatalities numbered 41,900 of which 33,600 were vehicle occupants, 5,300 pedestrians, 2,100 motorists and 800 bicyclists. Traffic death rates have decreased significantly since 1972 from 26.2 to 15.7 per 100,000 population, from 44.5 to 20.6 per 100,000 registered vehicles, from 4.3 to 1.6 per 100 million vehicle miles and from 46.1 to 23.0 per 100,000 licensed drivers.

By state, Nevada has the highest fatality rate at 4.0 per 100 million vehicle miles, followed by Mississippi at 3.5. Of the 41,900 fatalities, 21,989 were in passenger cars, 10,224 in light trucks, and 717 in heavy trucks. In 1995 57,883 drunk drivers, 25.7% of whom had blood alcohol concentrations of .10% or greater, were involved in fatal crashes.

18 The cost of operating an automobile has increased from 27.95 cents per mile in 1980 to 53.08 cents per mile in 1997. Of the variable costs gas and oil cost 10.8 cents per mile.

19 Environmental regulations and technology have combined to reduce substantially the average fuel consumption of a car and increase the average number of miles per gallon. The domestic motor fuel consumption in 1996 was 146.7 billion gallons, up from 92.3 billion gallons in 1970. The average fuel consumption was 531 gallons per car, 1,414 gallons per bus and 4,205 gallons per truck. The average miles per gallon for cars has increased from 13.5 miles in 1970 to 21.3 miles in 1996.

20 In 1997 U. S. cars traveled a total of 1.5 trillion miles, buses 6.8 billion miles and trucks 850 billion miles. The average annual car mileage is 14,200. In 1993, 6.433 million traffic citations were issued. More than one-quarter of all U. S. drivers exceed the speed limit of 65 miles per hour.

21 In 1997 there were 5,973 mass transit systems (including 2,250 motor bus systems) carrying 8.558 million people. Buses carried 5.199 billion, heavy rail 2.430 billion, light rail 263 million and commuter rail 357 million. There were 17 Class I Intercity motor carriers (down from 48 in 1980). Their operating revenue has declined from $1.397 billion in 1980 to $1.0 billion.

22 In 1997 the trucking industry had a fleet of 346,000 trucks and 784,000 truck–tractors with revenues of $183.153 billion.

23 Railroad companies reporting to the Interstate Commerce Commission (ICC) are divided into four groups: (1) Regular line-haul, (2) Switching and terminal, (3) Private

or Circular (because they are reported on brief circulars), and (4) unofficial. Data on the last three groups are excluded from official statistics. Beginning in 1911, the ICC also divided regular line-haul railroads into Class I, II and III. Initially Class I had revenues of more than $1 million, Class II between $100,000 and $1 million and Class had revenues under $100,000. In 1978 the categories were redefined with thresholds for Classes I, II, and III raised to $50 million, $10 to $50 million and below $10 million respectively. In 1982 the ICC adopted a procedure to adjust the threshold for inflation on the basis of 1978 dollars.

24 The principal sources of information on railways prior to 1890 is Poor's *Manual of Railroads.* Current data are contained in *Railway Age* and *Yearbook of Railroad Facts* published by the Association of American Railroads.

25 The first interstate railroad was the Petersburg Railroad, chartered by a special act of the General Assembly of Virginia in 1830 and by a special act of the North Carolina legislature in 1831. It ran for 59 miles along the north bank of the Roanoke River from Petersburg, Virginia, to Blakeley, North Carolina. The first railroad for the commercial transportation of passengers and freight was the Baltimore and Ohio Railroad Company, incorporated in 1827.

26 U. S. railroads have downsized in the last decade, resulting in only nine Class I railroads with 178,000 employees (compared to 23 Class I railroads with 302,000 employees. The total rail line mileage was 133,000 railroad line owned and 225,000 railroad track owned. Railroads had operating revenues of $33.118 billion (of which freight generated $32.2 billion) and operating expenditures of $27.291 billion, leaving a net income of $5.827 billion. AMTRAK carried 20.2 billion passengers and had a revenue of $792 million.

27 The principal sources of information on water transportation are *Waterborne Commerce of the United States* issued by the Corps of Engineers of the Department of the Army, *Merchant Fleets of the World* issued by the U. S. Maritime Administration, *The Bulletin* issued by the American Bureau of Shipping, and *World Fleet Statistics* issued by Lloyd's Register of Shipping. Historical statistics on merchant shipping are found in a variety of sources, including *Merchant Marine Statistics, 1924-1965,* Congressional Documents, such as publications of the Maritime Commission, especially *Ocean-Going Merchant Fleets of Principal Maritime Nations,* and the censuses of water transportation conducted by the Bureau of the Census and its predecessors. The first census for 1880 was limited to steam vessels (excluding fishing vessels), and those of 1916 and 1926 provided data for all vessels over 5 tons. Changes in maritime law on admeasurement (a determination or comparison of measurements) of gross tonnage have also affected the data. Gross tonnage is a measurement of space, not weight in which 100 cubic feet (95 cubic feet before 1865) equals one ton. Also, an act of 1874 excluded canalboat and unrigged tonnage from the totals. Other measurements used over the years included duty tonnage (tonnage on which duties were collected), district tonnage (reported by district collectors of customs), registered tonnage and net tonnage.

28 The United States has five major waterways systems: Atlantic Coast, Gulf Coast, Pacific Coast, Mississippi River and Great Lakes. The Mississippi River with 707.1 million tons accounts for more than two third of the total freight carried in these systems.

29 Of the total world gross tonnage of merchant ships of 507.873 million, the U. S. share is only 12.024 million. The global merchant fleet consists of 84,264 ships of which only 5,289 are registered in the United States. Of the world total of 27,730 vessels of over 1,000 gross tons, the United States owns 473 placing it in the 19th rank just below Indonesia. Of the 473 ships, 156 are tankers and 12 are cruise ships.

30 The output of U. S. shipyards has been falling since 1970, bringing shipbuilding, one of the oldest industrial activities in the United States, to the verge of extinction. In 1999 private shipyards employed 99,900 workers compared to 178,000 in 1980 and had only five ships under construction, compared to 69 in 1980.

31 Only scattered data on air transportation are available for the years before 1926. Regular collection of national statistics began with the establishment in that year of an Aeronautical Branch in the Department of Commerce. The Civil Aeronautics Act of 1938 created the Civil Aeronautics Authority, reorganized in 1940 into two separate entities: The Civil Aeronautics Board and Civil Aeronautics Administration. In 1958, the latter's functions were transferred to the Federal Aviation Agency which, in turn, was made a part of the Department of Transportation and Renamed the Federal Aviation Administration (FAA). The FAA's annual *Statistical Handbook of Civil Aviation* is the principal source of data in this field. Air Transportation data are also presented annually in Air Transport Facts and Figures, published by the *Air Transport Association of America*. A major development in 1978 was the Airline Deregulation Act which encouraged competition among airlines and also blurred the distinction between domestic and international operators.

32 In 1997 there were 11,364 establishments engaged in air transportation with 360,000 employees and revenues of $48.623 billion and 9,245 establishments engaged in water transportation with 180,000 employees and revenues of $36.304 billion.

33 The scheduled airline industry covers certificated route air carriers, commercial operators with large aircraft and commuter airlines. In 1997 these airlines had 598.9 billion passengers against an available seat-miles of 860.6 billion miles. There were 8.157 million aircraft departures. Total operating revenue was $109.535 billion and operating expenditures were $100.924 billion, leaving a net profit of $5.195 billion. The airline industry employed 586,500 persons, including 60,400 pilots.

34 In 1997 Atlanta Hartsfield International Airport overtook O'Hare Airport in Chicago as the top in passengers enplaned. In order, the cities with the top airports in passengers enplaned after Atlanta and Chicago are Dallas, Los Angeles, San Francisco, Denver, Detroit, Phoenix, Las Vegas, St. Louis, Newark, Minneapolis, Houston, Miami, Seattle–Tacoma, Orlando, Boston, Charlotte, New York La Guardia, and New York JFK.

35 There are only two major players in the aircraft industry: Boeing and McDonnell Douglas. In 1998 Boeing was the larger with 350 orders for civil jet transport aircraft. McDonnell Douglas had 103.

36 In 1998 there were 48 aircraft accidents, but only one fatality.

37 In 1997 there were 18,345 airports in the United States of which 4,626 were heliports and 13,211 private airports. During this same period, there were 200,000 active aircraft, of which 7,600 were owned by air carriers. Of the 616,000 pilots, commercial pilots numbered 125,000. Women make up only 5.8% of all pilots.

38 In 1998 U. S. aircraft shipments totaled 3,400 units worth $56.1 billion. Of these, large transports numbered 530, general aviation aircraft 2,030, and helicopters 340.

39 International transportation transactions of the United States, covering ocean and air travel and freight, profitable since 1990, became unprofitable in 1998. In that year, total receipts were $45.5 billion and total payments $50.2 billion.

40 The percentage of on-time arrivals and departures in U.S. airports has been steadily improving. The national average was 79.4% for the former and 82.8% for the latter. Cincinnati led in both areas at 86.2% and 90.3% respectively.

41 There were 7,994 complaints against U. S. airlines in 1998. The most common complaints were flight problems, customer service, ticketing and boarding, baggage and refunds.

42 In 1997 there were 180,000 miles of pipeline valued at $30.665 billion and delivering 12.1 billion barrels of petroleum.

Series Q 1-11. Volume of Domestic Intercity Passenger Traffic, by Type of Transport: 1950 to 1997

(In billions of passenger miles. Airways, prior to 1959, and other types of transportation, prior to 1960, exclude Alaska and Hawaii. A passenger-mile is the movement of one passenger for the distance of one mile. Comprises public and private traffic, both revenue and nonrevenue)

Year	Total traffic, volume	Private automobiles, volume	Airways [1], volume	Buses [2], volume	Railroads [3], volume	Year	Total traffic, volume	Private automobiles, volume	Airways [1], volume	Buses [2], volume	Railroads [3], volume
	1	2	4	6	8		1	2	4	6	8
1997	2 476	1 968	453	30	14	1972	1 300	1 129	133	26	9
1996	2 405	1 917	435	29	13	1971	1 230	1 071	120	26	9
1995	2 337	1 881	404	28	14	1970	1 185	1 026	119	25	11
1994	...	...	...	...	...	1969	1 138	977	120	25	12
1993	2 126	1 718	370	23	14	1968	1 079	936	101	25	13
1992	2 079	1 675	367	24	14	1967	1 021	890	87	25	15
1991	2 012	1 623	351	24	14	1966	971	856	69	25	17
1990	2 054	1 660	358	23	13	1965	920	818	58	24	18
1989	2 012	1 627	347	24	13	1964	896	802	49	23	18
1988	1 968	1 586	346	23	13	1963	853	766	43	23	19
1987	1 897	1 521	341	23	12	1962	818	736	37	22	20
1986	1 808	1 452	320	24	12	1961	791	714	35	20	21
1985	1 744	1 418	291	24	11	1960	784	706	34	19	22
1984	1 739	1 437	263	27	12	1959	765	687	33	20	22
1983	1 647	1 364	245	27	11	1958	760	685	29	21	24
1982	1 609	1 344	227	27	11	1957	748	670	28	21	26
1981	1 574	1 319	216	27	12	1956	751	670	26	25	29
1980	1 557	1 300	219	27	11	1955	716	637	23	25	29
1979	1 590	1 322	228	28	12	1954	673	597	20	26	29
1978	1 602	1 362	203	26	11	1953	655	576	17	28	32
1977	1 529	1 316	177	26	10	1952	575	496	15	29	35
1976	1 460	1 260	164	25	11	1951	535	458	13	27	35
1975	1 354	1 171	148	25	10	1950	508	438	10	26	32
1974	1 331	1 143	146	28	10						
1973	1 341	1 163	143	26	9						

1. Includes domestic commercial revenue service and private, pleasure and business flying.
2. Excludes school buses.
3. Includes electric railways.

Series Q 12-22.   Volume of Domestic Intercity Freight Traffic, by Type of Transport: 1939 to 1997

(In billions of ton-miles. Motor vehicles and airways, prior to 1959, and other types of transportation, prior to 1960, exclude Alaska and Hawaii, except as noted. A ton-mile is the movement of one ton (2 000 pounds) of freight for the distance of one mile. Comprises public and private traffic, both revenue and nonrevenue)

Year	Total traffic, volume	Railroads [1], volume	Motor vehicles, volume	Inland water-ways [2], volume	Oil pipelines, volume	Airways [3], volume	Year	Total traffic, volume	Railroads [1], volume	Motor vehicles, volume	Inland water-ways [2], volume	Oil pipelines, volume	Airways [3], volume
	12	13	15	17	19	21		12	13	15	17	19	21
1997	3 622	1 421	1 051	508	628	14	1967	1 776	742	389	281	361	2.6
1996	3 540	1 426	977	498	631	13	1966	1 759	762	381	281	333	2.3
1995	3 407	1 375	921	497	601	13	1965	1 651	721	359	262	306	1.9
1994	...	...	...	...	...	...	1964	1 556	679	356	250	269	1.5
1993	3 105	1 183	871	367	572	12	1963	1 469	644	336	234	253	1.3
1992	3 009	1 138	815	474	571	11	1962	1 387	616	309	223	238	1.3
1991	2 886	1 078	758	462	578	10	1961	1 326	586	296	210	233	.9
1990	2 855	1 071	735	462	577	11.0	1960	1 330	595	285	220	229	.8
1989	2 807	1 048	716	449	584	10.0	1959	1 303	599	279	197	227	.7
1988	2 793	1 034	704	434	612	9.3	1958	1 231	575	256	189	211	.6
1987	2 640	972	661	411	587	8.7	1957	1 354	645	254	232	223	.6
1986	2 494	889	627	393	578	7.3	1956	1 376	677	249	220	230	.6
1985	2 458	895	610	382	564	7.0	1955	1 298	655	223	217	203	.6
1984	2 497	935	605	382	568	6.6	1954	1 144	578	213	174	179	.4
1983	2 337	841	575	359	556	5.9	1953	1 232	643	217	[4] 202	170	.4
1982	2 252	810	520	351	566	5.1	1952	1 172	651	195	168	158	.4
1981	2 430	924	527	410	564	5.0	1951	1 209	686	188	[4] 182	152	.4
1980	2 487	932	555	407	588	5.0	1950	1 094	628	173	163	129	.3
1979	2 573	927	608	425	608	4.8	1949	947	567	125	139	115	.2
1978	2 467	868	599	409	586	4.8	1948	1 086	689	115	[4] 162	120	.2
1977	2 307	834	555	368	546	4.2	1947	1 060	707	102	147	105	.2
1976	2 202	800	510	373	515	3.9	1946	944	643	82	124	96	.1
1975	2 066	759	454	342	507	4.0	1945	1 072	736	67	143	127	.1
1974	2 213	860	495	348	506	3.9	1944	1 136	795	58	150	133	.1
1973	2 232	858	505	358	507	4.0	1943	1 076	780	57	142	98	.1
1972	2 071	783	470	339	476	3.7	1942	973	689	60	149	75	(Z)
1971	1 953	746	445	315	444	3.5	1941	811	521	81	140	68	(Z)
1970	1 936	771	412	319	431	3.3	1940	651	412	62	118	59	(Z)
1969	1 895	774	404	303	411	3.2	1939	575	370	53	96	56	(Z)
1968	1 839	757	396	291	391	2.9							

Z Less than 50 million ton-miles.
1. Includes electric railways express and mail.
2. Includes Great Lakes. Includes Alaska for all years and Hawaii beginning 1959.
3. Domestic revenue service only. Includes express mail and excess baggage.
4. Part of this increase resulted from coverage of waterways previously existing but not covered.

Series Q 50-63. Mileage of Rural Roads and Municipal Streets: 1921 to 1997

Year	Total mileage		Year	Total mileage		Year	Total mileage		Year	Total mileage	
	Total	Rural roads		Total	Rural roads		Total	Rural roads		Total	Rural roads
	50	51		50	51		50	51		50	51
	1 000 miles	1 000 miles		1 000 miles	1 000 miles		1 000 miles	1 000 miles		1 000 miles	1 000 miles
1997	3 959	3 116	1977	3 867	3 180	1957	3 453	2 952	1937	3 245	2 894
1996	3 934	3 100	1976	3 857	3 209	1956	3 430	2 945	1936	3 267	2 920
1995	3 912	3 093	1975	3 838	3 199	1955	3 418	2 954	1935	3 310	3 032
1994	3 906	3 093	1974	3 816	3 178	1954	3 395	2 941	1934	3 309	3 034
1993	3 905	3 102	1973	3 807	3 176	1953	3 366	2 925	1933	3 286	3 029
1992	3 902	3 117	1972	3 787	3 173	1952	3 343	2 925	1932	3 296	3 040
1991	3 889	3 139	1971	3 759	3 166	1951	3 326	2 925	1931	3 291	3 036
1990	3 880	3 123	1970	3 730	3 169	1950	3 313	2 922	1930	3 259	3 009
1989	3 877	3 123	1969	3 710	3 162	1949	3 322	2 934	1929	3 272	3 024
1988	3 871	3 132	1968	3 684	3 152	1948	3 323	2 929	1928	3 262	3 016
1987	3 874	3 164	1967	3 705	3 184	1947	3 326	2 933	1927	3 257	3 013
1986	3 880	3 178	1966	3 698	3 188	1946	3 316	2 934	1926	3 242	3 000
1985	3 862	3 171	1965	3 690	3 009	1945	3 319	2 939	1925	3 246	3 006
1984	3 892	3 218	1964	3 644	3 003	1944	3 311	2 932	1924	3 243	3 004
1983	3 880	3 217	1963	3 620	3 002	1943	3 311	2 930	1923	3 233	2 996
1982	3 866	3 226	1962	3 600	3 005	1942	3 309	2 925	1922	3 196	2 960
1981	3 853	3 221	1961	3 573	2 995	1941	3 309	2 926	1921	3 160	2 925
1980	3 955	3 331	1960	3 546	2 989	1940	3 287	2 920			
1979	3 918	3 224	1959 *	3 511	2 974	1939	3 274	2 913			
1978	3 885	3 190	1958	3 479	2 959	1938	3 257	2 898			

* Denotes first year for which figures include Alaska and Hawaii.

Series Q 69-81.   Class I Intercity Motor Carriers of Passengers and Property: 1939 to 1997
(Carriers subject to ICC regulations)

| | Carriers of passengers | | | | | | | Carriers of passengers | | | | | |
Year	Carriers reporting [1]	Operating revenue	Expenses	Net income after income taxes	Vehicles in service [2]	Vehicle miles, passenger	Year	Carriers reporting [1]	Operating revenue	Expenses	Net income after income taxes	Vehicles in service [2]	Vehicle miles, passenger
	69	70	71	72	73	74		69	70	71	72	73	74
		Mil. dol.	*Mil. dol.*	*Mil. dol.*		*Millions*			*Mil. dol.*	*Mil. dol.*	*Mil. dol.*	*Millions*	
1997	17	1 000	948	-2	...	...	1967	177	670	591	52	15 406	997
1996	17	912	878	13	...	...	1966	166	644	550	54	14 298	988
1995	20	917	899	-9	...	...	1965	156	607	514	52	13 287	947
1994	20	870	919	-67	...	...	1964	161	655	570	52	16 157	1 056
1993	21	928	880	14	...	...	1963	148	610	529	48	³ 13 608	1 009
1992	21	938	874	21	...	...	1962	151	589	511	43	³ 13 873	998
1991	21	980	967	162	...	...	1961	144	485	423	31	³ 11 036	865
1990	21	943	1 015	-180	...	...	1960 *	143	463	405	28	12 680	843
1989	20	1 205	1 133	12	...	...	1959	143	439	380	29	³ 10 763	810
1988	21	1 122	1 059	...	...	...	1958	136	410	366	20	³ 10 791	816
1987	32	1 079	1 081	-21	...	...	1957	144	407	371	20	³ 11 301	867
1986	29	1 117	1 082	36	8 300	495	1956	145	377	343	17	³ 11 032	859
1985	43	1 233	1 168	53	8 400	567	1955	146	362	331	16	13 127	859
1984	43	1 255	1 254	43	7 000	585	1954	155	363	331	15	³ 12 314	887
1983	45	1 276	1 283	26	7 300	591	1953	161	395	354	18	³ 12 940	972
1982	50	1 447	1 416	37	8 100	717	1952	160	395	348	22	³ 13 106	975
1981	45	1 453	1 381	61	8 400	732	1951	166	393	345	25	³ 13 431	1 011
1980	48	1 397	1 318	90	8 600	781	1950	172	351	315	19	14 566	959
1979	45	1 200	1 143	57	8 200	754	1949	262	380	346	20	³ 14 863	1 066
1978	43	1 021	983	41	8 500	726	1948	260	401	351	31	³ 15 290	1 130
1977	42	969	924	40	8 300	754	1947	253	367	313	33	³ 14 149	1 056
1976	78	975	937	32	...	...	1946	254	381	299	50	³ 13 168	1 043
1975	77	942	880	56	9 700	835	1945	231	378	265	32	³ 12 865	931
1974	81	933	859	61	13 800	886	1944	194	375	245	36	³ 12 019	905
1973	75	815	738	58	12 794	850	1943	157	344	214	37	³ 11 000	832
1972	74	775	690	59	12 122	845	1942	136	251	164	24	³ 9 677	702
1971	71	758	664	65	12 896	856	1941	132	149	120	20	³ 7 891	556
1970	71	722	639	52	13 282	871	1940	135	115	98	15	³ 6 678	482
1969	70	677	594	56	12 992	869	1939	149	113	95	20	³ 6 408	466
1968	173	695	613	61	15 398	977							

* Denotes first year for which figures include Alaska and Hawaii.
1. Excludes carriers subject to ICC jurisdiction engaged preponderantly in local or suburban service and carriers engaged in transpsortation of both property and passengers.
2. Regular route intercity and local.
3. Excludes intercity service.

Series Q 136-147. Public Highway Debt—Long-Term Highway Obligations of State and Local Governments: 1945 to 1995

In millions of dollars. Data are for varying calendar fiscal years. Excludes duplicated and interunit. Municipal obligations include data for all municipalities and other political subdivisions urban in character)

Year	Debt issued Total [1] [136]	State [137]	Local Total	County and local rural [138]	Municipal [139]	Debt redeemed Total [2] [140]	State [141]	Local Total	County and local rural [142]	Municipal [143]	Total debt outstanding [144]
1995	11 306	4 718	6 587	...	...	5 635	2 940	2 695	...	...	68 733
1994	10 833	5 739	5 094	...	...	6 103	3 622	2 481	...	...	63 062
1993	14 178	10 035	4 143	...	...	10 823	8 082	2 741	...	...	58 373
1992	12 988	9 460	3 528	...	...	7 665	5 388	2 277	...	...	53 539
1991	9 516	6 252	3 264	800	1 420	6 138	4 352	1 786	375	1 033	47 892
1990	5 838	3 277	2 561	580	1 600	5 158	2 041	3 117	750	950	44 514
1989	5 900	3 775	2 125	650	1 522	3 729	2 813	916	618	925	43 834
1988	4 594	2 702	1 892	567	1 310	2 774	1 547	1 227	353	986	41 663
1987	6 898	4 395	2 503	451	1 424	4 924	3 221	1 713	349	711	39 843
1986	9 803	5 873	3 930	1 200	1 150	5 313	3 755	1 558	432	825	37 869
1985	8 194	5 397	2 797	1 387	1 283	4 606	3 835	771	378	779	33 379
1984	3 151	1 715	...	524	912	2 411	1 507	...	216	688	27 964
1983	2 566	1 072	...	475	1 019	2 172	1 191	...	303	678	27 224
1982	3 155	1 555	...	350	1 250	1 831	1 146	...	185	500	27 285
1981	2 574	965	...	305	1 204	2 464	1 579	...	201	684	25 961
1980	2 094	1 128		276	690	1 706	1 022		209	475	25 851
1979	1 904	941		279	684	1 751	960		177	614	25 463
1978	1 883	942		238	703	1 593	934		170	469	25 327
1977	2 230	1 183		339	708	1 648	960		178	510	25 037
1976	2 224	1 402		198	564	1 567	920		172	475	24 455
1975	2 239	1 412		222	605	1 492	908		166	418	23 801
1974	1 657	846		230	581	1 445	887		163	395	23 016
1973	2 066	1 216		250	600	1 367	883		140	344	22 963
1972	2 459	1 672		241	546	1 270	783		148	339	22 264
1971	3 341	2 649		196	496	1 281	815		145	321	21 068
1970	1 886	1 305		174	407	1 252	782		152	318	19 107
1969	2 022	1 351		241	430	1 122	705		137	280	18 572
1968	1 991	1 377		241	373	1 071	657		136	278	17 672
1967	1 633	1 012		194	427	965	540		136	289	16 749
1966	1 680	1 156		158	366	915	519		126	270	16 080
1965	1 070	586		169	315	855	459		123	273	15 316
1964	1 097	634		156	307	752	381		116	255	15 114
1963	981	458		114	409	732	382		114	236	14 773
1962	1 535	1 017		184	334	679	340		110	229	14 537
1961	1 272	718		153	401	665	330		117	218	13 718
1960	1 206	680		190	336	616	300		96	220	13 166
1959 *	1 158	669		153	336	610	308		92	210	12 576
1958	1 352	913		140	299	543	252		94	197	12 278
1957	1 200	702		123	375	535	253		92	190	11 422
1956	1 439	1 067		105	267	438	190		97	151	10 659
1955	1 174	646		205	323	421	191		89	141	9 658
1954	2 684	2 317		94	273	433	168		109	156	8 905
1953	1 353	1 038		119	196	344	139		86	119	6 654
1952	1 102	797		100	205	339	157		78	104	5 645
1951	790	535		79	176	349	156		82	111	4 883
1950	652	400		90	162	322	143		83	96	4 436
1949	533	254		98	181	[3] 261	106		81	84	[3] 4 077
1948	476	270		83	123	[3] 266	117		79	78	[3] 3 797
1947	608	80		107	122	[3] 258	115		78	75	[3] 3 589
1946	[3] 161	55		49	62	[3] 261	124		78	72	[3] 3 538
1945	[3] 49	11		22	20	[3] 258	115		87	78	[3] 3 640

Denotes first year for which figures include Alaska and Hawaii.

. Excludes refunding issues.

. Excludes redemptions by refunding.

. Duplicated and interunit obligations have been excluded from totals only.

Series Q 148-162. Motor Vehicle Sales from U.S. Factories, Motor Vehicle Registrations, and Motor Fuel Usage Consumption: 1900 to 1997

(Number sold includes sales of military vehicles)

Year	Motor-vehicle factory sales — Number of passenger cars	Motor-vehicle factory sales — Number of motor trucks and buses [1]	Motor-vehicle registrations — Total	Motor-vehicle registrations — Automobiles	Motor-fuel consumption — Total	Motor-fuel consumption — Passenger vehicles
	148	150	152	153	156	159
	1 000	1 000	1 000	1 000	Mil. gal.	Mil. gal.
1997	6 070	6 153	207 754	129 749	. . .	. . .
1996	6 140	5 776	206 365	129 728	146 700	68 900
1995	6 310	5 713	201 530	128 387	143 800	68 100
1994	6 549	5 640	198 045	127 883	140 800	67 900
1993	5 962	4 895	194 063	127 327	137 300	67 000
1992	5 685	4 062	190 362	144 213	132 900	65 400
1991	5 407	3 387	188 136	142 956	128 600	64 300
1990	6 050	3 725	188 798	133 700	130 800	69 600
1989	6 807	4 062	187 261	143 081	131 900	73 900
1988	7 105	4 121	184 397	141 252	130 100	73 300
1987	7 085	3 821	179 044	137 324	127 500	73 300
1986	7 516	3 393	176 191	135 431	125 200	73 200
1985	8 002	3 357	171 654	131 864	121 300	71 500
1984	7 621	3 075	166 200	128 100	118 700	70 600
1983	6 739	2 414	163 900	126 200	116 100	70 300
1982	5 049	1 906	159 600	123 700	113 400	69 100
1981	6 255	1 701	158 300	123 100	114 500	69 100
1980	6 400	1 667	155 796	121 601	115 000	70 000
1979	8 419	3 037	151 900	118 500	122 100	77 300
1978	9 165	3 706	148 400	116 600	125 100	81 700
1977	9 201	3 441	142 100	112 300	119 600	80 400
1976	8 500	2 979	138 500	110 200	115 700	79 700
1975	6 713	2 272	132 900	106 700	109 000	74 100
1974	7 331	2 727	129 900	104 800	106 300	75 100
1973	9 658	2 980	125 700	102 000	110 500	78 700
1972	8 824	2 447	118 800	97 100	105 100	73 500
1971	8 585	2 053	113 000	92 700	97 600	69 500
1970	6 546.8	1 692.4	108 407.3	89 279.8	92 300	67 700
1969	8 223.7	1 923.1	105 096.6	86 861.3	92 240	63 395
1968	8 822.1	1 896.0	100 884.7	83 591.6	87 154	59 456
1967	7 436.7	1 539.4	96 930.9	80 414.1	81 911	56 020
1966	8 598.3	1 731.0	93 962.0	78 122.9	78 979	54 208
1965	9 305.5	1 751.8	90 357.6	75 257.5	75 312	51 169
1964	7 751.8	1 540.4	86 301.2	71 982.7	72 097	48 431
1963	7 637.7	1 462.7	82 713.7	69 055.4	68 760	46 084
1962	6 933.2	1 240.1	79 173.3	66 108.2	66 101	44 608
1961	5 542.7	1 133.8	75 958.2	63 417.3	64 534	42 863
1960	6 674.7	1 194.4	73 868.6	61 682.3	63 210	41 996
1959 *	5 591.2	1 137.3	71 354.4	59 453.9	61 715	40 879
1958	4 257.8	877.2	68 296.5	56 890.5	58 589	38 904
1957	6 113.3	1 107.1	67 124.9	55 917.8	56 954	37 594
1956	5 816.1	1 104.4	65 148.2	54 210.9	55 149	36 128
1955	7 920.1	1 249.1	62 688.7	52 144.7	52 565	34 319
1954	5 558.8	1 042.1	58 505.3	48 468.4	49 118	31 670
1953	6 116.9	1 206.2	56 217.4	46 429.2	47 381	30 384
1952	4 320.7	1 218.1	53 262.4	43 823.0	45 037	28 735
1951	5 338.4	1 426.8	51 912.7	42 688.3	42 473	26 910
1950	6 665.8	1 337.1	49 161.6	40 339.0	39 860	25 037
1949	5 119.4	1 134.1	44 690.2	36 457.9	36 440	23 645
1948	3 909.2	1 376.2	41 085.5	33 355.2	34 329	22 149
1947	3 558.1	1 239.4	37 841.4	30 849.3	31 680	20 864
1946	2 148.6	940.9	34 373.0	28 217.0	28 876	19 502
1945	69.5	655.6	31 035.4	25 796.9	22 046	14 023
1944	.6	737.5	30 479.3	25 566.4	19 292	11 805
1943	.1	699.6	30 888.1	36 009.0	18 642	11 424
1942	222.8	818.6	33 003.6	27 972.8	22 438	[2] 14 974
1941	3 779.6	1 060.8	34 894.1	29 624.2	26 429	18 502
1940	3 717.3	754.9	32 453.2	27 465.8	24 038	16 759
1939	2 888.5	700.3	31 009.9	26 226.3	22 571	15 826
1938	2 019.5	488.8	29 813.7	25 250.4	21 311	15 069
1937	3 929.2	891.0	30 058.8	25 467.2	21 115	15 018
1936	3 679.2	782.2	28 506.8	24 182.6	19 561	14 026
1935	3 273 8	697.3	26 546.1	22 257.8	17 637	. . .
1934	2 160.8	576.2	25 261.7	21 544.7	16 557	. . .
1933	1 560.5	329.2	24 159.2	20 657.2	15 367	. . .
1932	1 103.5	228.3	24 391.0	20 901.4	15 427	. . .
1931	1 948.1	432.2	26 093.9	22 396.2	16 621	. . .
1930	2 787.4	575.3	26 749.8	23 034.7	15 777	. . .
1929	4 455.1	881.9	26 704.8	23 120.8	15 051	. . .
1928	3 775.4	583.3	24 688.6	21 362.2	13 090	. . .
1927	2 936.5	464.7	23 303.4	20 193.3	11 936	. . .
1926	3 692.3	608.6	22 200.1	19 267.9	10 552	. . .
1925	3 735.1	530.6	20 068.5	17 481.0	9 143	. . .
1924	3 185.8	416.6	17 612.9	15 436.0	7 809	. . .
1923	3 624.7	409.2	15 102.1	13 253.0	6 313	. . .
1922	2 274.1	269.9	12 273.5	10 704.0	5 014	. . .
1921	1 468.0	148.0	10 493.6	9 212.1	4 064	. . .
1920	1 905.5	321.7	9 239.1	8 131.5	3 448	. . .
1919	1 651.6	224.7	7 576.8	6 679.1	2 747	. . .
1918	943.4	227.2	6 160.4	5 554.9	. . .	. . .
1917	1 745.7	128.1	5 118.5	4 727.4	. . .	. . .
1916	1 525.5	92.1	3 617.9	3 367.8	. . .	. . .
1915	895.9	74.0	2 490.9	2 332.4	. . .	. . .
1914	548.1	24.9	1 763.0	1 664.0	. . .	. . .
1913	461.5	23.5	1 258.0	1 190.3	. . .	. . .
1912	356.0	22.0	944.0	901.5	. . .	. . .
1911	199.3	10.6	639.5	618.7	. . .	. . .
1910	181.0	6.0	468.5	548.3	. . .	. . .
1909	123.9	3.2	312.0	305.9	. . .	. . .
1908	63.5	1.5	198.4	194.4	. . .	. . .
1907	43.0	1.0	143.2	140.3	. . .	. . .
1906	33.2	.8	108.1	105.9	. . .	. . .
1905	24.2	.7	78.8	77.4	. . .	. . .
1904	22.1	.7	55.2	54.5	. . .	. . .
1903	11.2	. . .	32.9	32.9	. . .	. . .
1902	9.0	. . .	23.0	23.0	. . .	. . .
1901	7.0	. . .	14.8	14.8	. . .	. . .
1900	4.1	. . .	8.0	8.0	. . .	. . .

* Denotes first year for which figures include Alaska and Hawaii.
1. A substantial portion of the number of trucks and buses consists of chassis only, without bodies.
2. Beginning 1942, includes travel by military vehicles.

Series Q 199-207. Miles of Travel by Motor Vehicles: 1921 to 1997

(In million vehicle-miles)

Year	Total travel, all motor vehicles	Passenger cars[1]	Trucks and combinations[1]	Average miles per vehicle[1] Passenger cars[1]	Average miles per vehicle[1] Trucks and combinations[1]	Year	Total travel, all motor vehicles	Passenger cars[1]	Trucks and combinations[1]	Average miles per vehicle[1] Passenger cars[1]	Average miles per vehicle[1] Trucks and combinations[1]
	199	202	204	206	207		199	202	204	206	207
1997	2 560 000	1 512 000	1 041 000	11 600	27 000	1957	647 004	523 000	118 000	9 300	10 800
1996	2 486 000	1 480 000	1 000 000	11 300	26 100	1956	631 161	515 000	112 000	9 500	10 500
1995	2 423 000	1 448 000	968 000	11 000	26 500	1955	605 646	493 000	109 000	9 400	10 600
1994	2 358 000	1 416 000	935 000	10 800	25 800	1954	561 963	453 000	105 000	9 300	10 700
1993	2 296 000	1 385 000	906 000	10 500	26 300	1953	544 433	435 000	105 000	9 400	11 000
1992	2 247 000	1 381 000	860 000	10 600	25 400	1952	513 581	410 000	99 000	9 400	10 800
1991	2 172 000	1 367 000	799 000	10 300	24 200	1951	491 093	392 000	95 000	9 200	10 500
1990	2 148 000	1 418 000	721 000	10 300	23 600	1950	458 246	365 000	89 000	9 100	10 300
1989	2 096 000	1 412 000	679 000	10 200	22 900	1949	424 461	342 000	78 000	9 400	9 700
1988	2 025 000	1 380 000	639 000	10 000	22 500	1948	397 957	319 000	74 000	9 600	9 900
1987	1 921 000	1 325 000	591 000	9 700	23 300	1947	370 894	301 000	66 000	9 800	9 600
1986	1 834 000	1 780 000	551 000	9 500	22 100	1946	340 880	281 000	56 000	10 000	9 300
1985	1 774 000	1 256 000	514 000	9 400	20 600	1945	250 173	200 000	46 000	7 800	9 100
1984	1 720 000	1 236 000	480 000	9 200	22 600	1944	212 713	167 000	42 000	6 500	8 900
1983	1 653 000	1 204 000	444 000	9 100	21 100	1943	208 192	162 000	43 000	6 200	9 000
1982	1 592 000	1 172 000	417 000	9 100	19 900	1942	268 224	218 000	47 000	7 800	9 500
1981	1 556 000	1 144 000	408 000	8 900	19 000	1941	333 612	276 000	55 000	9 300	10 600
1980	1 527 000	1 122 000	399 000	8 800	18 700	1940	302 188	250 000	50 000	9 100	10 200
1979	1 529 000	1 122 000	401 000	9 100	18 500	1939	285 402	236 000	47 000	9 000	10 100
1978	1 548 000	1 154 000	385 000	9 500	18 000	1938	271 177	224 000	45 000	8 900	10 000
1977	1 477 000	1 116 000	346 000	9 500	16 700	1937	270 110	224 000	44 000	8 800	9 800
1976	1 412 000	1 084 000	312 000	9 400	15 400	1936	252 128	209 000	41 000	8 600	9 600
1975	1 330 000	1 040 000	282 000	9 300	15 200	1935	228 568	...	...	...	...
1974	1 286 000	1 013 000	262 000	9 200	15 000	1934	215 563	...	...	...	...
1973	1 309 000	1 051 000	256 000	9 900	15 400	1933	200 642	...	...	...	...
1972	1 268 000	1 026 000	229 000	10 200	14 800	1932	200 517	...	...	...	...
1971	1 186 300	970 000	204 000	10 100	14 100	1931	216 151	...	...	...	...
1970	1 120 705	920 000	185 000	10 000	13 600	1930	206 320	...	...	...	...
1969	1 070 575	885 000	172 000	9 900	13 500	1929	197 720	...	...	...	...
1968	1 015 649	850 000	161 000	9 900	12 400	1928	172 856	...	...	...	...
1967	961 553	811 000	149 000	9 800	12 800	1927	158 453	...	...	...	...
1966	930 497	777 000	143 000	9 700	12 500	1926	140 735	...	...	...	...
1965	887 640	723 000	160 000	9 600	10 900	1925	122 346	...	...	...	...
1964	846 500	696 000	146 000	9 700	10 400	1924	104 838	...	...	...	...
1963	805 423	662 000	139 000	9 600	10 400	1923	84 995	...	...	...	...
1962	766 852	627 000	135 000	9 500	10 600	1922	67 697	...	...	...	...
1961	737 535	604 000	129 000	9 500	10 500	1921	55 027	...	...	...	...
1960	718 845	587 000	127 000	9 500	10 700						
1959 *	700 478	572 000	125 000	9 600	10 700						
1958	664 653	540 000	120 000	9 500	10 800						

* Denotes first year for which figures include Alaska and Hawaii.

1. Columns 202 and 206 exclude vans, pick-ups, and SUVs. These are included in column 204 along with trucks. Column 207 includes only trucks.

Series Q 208-223.   Motor Vehicle Deaths and Death Rates: 1913 to 1997

(Rates are deaths per 100 000 population)

Year	All ages		Year	All ages		Year	All ages	
	Number	Rate [1]		Number	Rate [1]		Number	Rate [1]
	208	**209**		**208**	**209**		**208**	**209**
1997........................	43 200	15.7	1976........................	47 000	21.2	1956........................	39 628	25.1
1996........................	43 300	15.8	1975........................	45 900	20.7	1955........................	38 426	24.6
1995........................	43 400	15.9	1974........................	46 400	21.4	1954........................	35 586	23.0
1994........................	42 500	15.6	1973........................	55 500	25.8	1953........................	37 955	24.9
1993........................	41 900	15.6						
			1972........................	56 300	26.2	1952........................	37 794	25.0
1992........................	41 000	15.4	1971........................	54 000	26.5	1951........................	36 996	24.6
1991........................	43 500	16.5	1970........................	54 633	25.3	1950........................	34 763	23.3
1990........................	46 800	17.9	1969........................	55 791	27.6	1949........................	31 701	21.5
1989........................	47 100	18.4	1968........................	55 200	28.8	1948........................	32 259	22.3
1988........................	49 100	19.2						
			1967........................	52 924	27.8	1947........................	32 697	23.0
1987........................	48 300	19.1	1966........................	53 041	28.3	1946........................	33 411	24.0
1986........................	47 900	19.1	1965........................	49 163	26.5	1945........................	28 076	21.4
1985........................	45 900	18.4	1964........................	47 700	26.1	1944........................	24 282	18.3
1984........................	46 200	18.7	1963........................	43 564	24.3	1943........................	23 823	17.7
1983........................	44 600	18.2						
			1962........................	40 804	23.1	1938-1942 avg.	33 549	25.5
1982........................	46 000	19.0	1961........................	38 091	22.0	1933-1937 avg.	36 313	29.3
1981........................	51 400	21.5	1960........................	38 137	22.4	1928-1932 avg.	30 900	26.4
1980........................	53 200	22.6	1959........................	37 910	22.7	1923-1927 avg.	21 700	19.6
1979........................	53 500	22.8	1958........................	36 981	22.5	1918-1922 avg.	12 500	12.3
1978........................	52 400	22.7						
			1957........................	38 702	24.1	1913-1917 avg.	6 700	7.0
1977........................	49 500	22.1						

1. Based on populations standardized for age (base 1940) to remove influence of changes in age distribution.

Series Q 224-232. Motor Vehicle Accidents—Number and Deaths, by Type of Accident: 1913 to 1997

Year	Total motor vehicle accidents (1 000)	Traffic deaths [1]					Traffic death rates	
		Total	Non-collision accidents	Collision accidents			Per 10 000 motor vehicles	Per 100 million vehicle miles
				With other motor vehicles	With pedestrians	With fixed objects		
	224	**225**	**226**	**227**	**228**	**229**	**231**	**232**
1997	13 800	43 200	4 200	21 300	5 700	10 800	2.1	1.6
1996	11 200	43 300	4 500	19 500	5 800	12 300	2.1	1.7
1995	10 700	43 400	4 400	19 000	6 400	12 100	2.1	1.7
1994	11 200	42 500	4 400	18 900	6 300	11 500	2.1	1.7
1993	11 900	41 900	4 200	18 300	6 400	11 500	2.1	1.7
1992	. . .	41 000	4 100	17 600	6 300	11 700	2.1	1.7
1991	11 300	43 500	4 700	18 200	6 600	12 600	2.2	1.9
1990	11 500	46 800	4 900	19 900	7 300	13 100	2.4	2.1
1989	12 800	47 100	5 000	20 000	7 600	12 600	2.3	2.2
1988	20 600	49 100	5 300	20 900	7 700	13 400	2.5	2.3
1987	20 800	48 300	5 200	20 700	7 500	13 200	2.5	2.4
1986	17 700	47 900	13 100	20 800	8 900	3 300	2.5	2.5
1985	19 300	45 900	12 600	19 900	8 500	3 200	2.4	2.5
1984	18 800	46 200	12 600	20 300	8 600	3 000	2.8	2.6
1983	18 300	44 600	12 200	19 200	8 200	3 100	2.7	2.6
1982	18 100	46 000	12 600	19 800	8 400	3 200	2.9	2.8
1981	18 000	51 400	14 200	22 200	9 400	3 600	3.4	3.2
1980	17 900	53 200	14 700	23 000	9 700	3 700	3.5	3.3
1979	18 100	53 500	15 200	22 200	9 700	3 500	3.5	3.3
1978	18 300	52 400	14 500	22 400	9 600	3 600	3.5	3.3
1977	17 600	49 500	13 700	20 200	9 100	3 400	3.4	3.3
1976	16 800	47 000	13 000	20 100	8 600	3 200	3.4	3.3
1975	16 500	45 900	12 700	19 500	8 400	3 100	3.4	3.4
1974	15 600	46 400	12 800	19 700	8 500	3 100	3.6	3.5
1973	16 600	55 500	15 600	23 600	10 200	3 800	4.4	4.1
1972	17 000	56 300	15 800	23 900	10 300	3 900	4.4	4.3
1971	16 400	54 000	13 700	23 300	10 600	7 100	4.8	4.7
1970	16 000	54 633	[2] 15 400	23 200	9 900	[2] 3 800	4.9	4.9
1969	15 500	55 791	15 700	23 700	10 100	3 900	5.2	5.2
1968	14 600	54 862	17 400	22 400	9 900	2 700	5.3	5.4
1967	13 700	52 924	16 700	22 000	9 400	2 350	5.4	5.5
1966	13 600	53 041	16 300	22 200	9 400	2 500	5.5	5.7
1965	13 200	49 163	14 900	20 800	8 900	2 200	5.4	5.5
1964	12 300	47 700	14 600	19 600	9 000	2 100	5.5	5.6
1963	11 500	43 564	13 800	17 600	8 200	1 900	5.2	5.4
1962	11 000	40 804	12 900	16 400	7 900	1 750	5.1	5.3
1961	10 400	38 091	12 200	14 700	7 650	1 700	5.0	5.2
1960	10 400	38 137	11 900	14 800	7 850	1 700	5.1	5.3
1959 *	10 200	37 910	11 800	14 900	7 850	1 600	5.3	5.4
1958	10 000	36 981	11 600	14 200	7 650	1 650	5.4	5.6
1957	10 200	38 702	11 800	15 400	7 850	1 700	5.7	6.0
1956	10 300	39 628	13 000	15 200	7 900	1 600	6.1	6.3
1955	9 900	38 426	12 100	14 500	8 200	1 600	6.1	6.3
1954	9 550	35 586	11 500	12 800	8 000	1 500	6.1	6.3
1953	9 900	37 955	12 200	13 400	8 750	1 500	6.7	7.0
1952	9 500	37 794	11 900	13 500	8 900	1 450	7.1	7.4
1951	9 400	36 996	11 200	13 100	9 150	1 400	7.1	7.5
1950	8 300	34 763	10 600	11 650	9 000	1 300	7.1	7.6
1949	7 600	31 701	9 100	10 500	8 800	1 100	7.1	7.5
1948	8 200	32 259	8 950	10 200	9 950	1 000	7.9	8.1
1947	8 400	32 697	8 800	9 900	10 450	1 000	8.6	8.8
1946	6 150	33 411	8 900	9 400	11 600	950	9.7	9.8
1945	5 500	28 076	6 600	7 150	11 000	800	9.1	11.2
1944	4 800	24 282	5 600	5 700	9 900	700	8.0	11.4
1943	4 400	23 823	5 690	5 300	9 900	700	7.7	11.4

See footnotes at end of chart.

Series Q 224-232. Motor Vehicle Accidents—Number and Deaths, by Type of Accident: 1913 to 1997—Cont'd.

Year	Total motor vehicle accidents (1 000)	Traffic deaths [1]					Traffic death rates	
		Total	Non-collision accidents	Collision accidents			Per 10 000 motor vehicles	Per 100 million vehicle miles
				With other motor vehicles	With pedestrians	With fixed objects		
	224	**225**	**226**	**227**	**228**	**229**	**231**	**232**
1942	5 200	28 309	6 740	7 300	10 650	850	8.6	10.6
1941	7 000	39 969	9 450	12 500	13 550	1 350	11.5	12.0
1940	6 100	34 501	7 800	10 100	12 700	1 100	10.6	11.4
1939	5 700	32 386	7 900	8 700	12 400	1 000	10.4	11.4
1938	5 800	32 582	7 350	8 900	12 850	940	10.9	12.0
1937	7 000	39 643	9 690	10 320	15 500	1 160	13.2	14.7
1936	...	38 089	9 410	9 500	15 250	1 060	13.4	15.1
1935	...	36 369	9 720	8 750	14 350	1 010	13.7	15.9
1934	...	36 101	9 820	8 110	14 480	1 040	14.3	16.8
1933	...	31 363	8 680	6 470	12 840	900	13.0	15.6
1932	...	29 500	7 000	6 070	11 490	800	12.2	16.1
1931	...	33 700	7 850	6 820	13 370	870	13.0	17.0
1930	...	32 900	8 730	5 880	12 900	720	12.4	17.4
1929	...	31 200	8 430	5 400	12 250	620	11.8	17.3
1928	...	28 000	7 360	4 310	11 420	540	11.4	17.4
1927	...	25 800	7 280	3 430	10 820	500	11.2	17.7
1926	...	23 400	...	...	...	...	10.6	18.0
1925	...	21 900	...	...	...	...	11.0	17.9
1924	...	19 400	...	...	...	...	11.0	...
1923	...	18 400	...	...	...	...	12.2	...
1922	...	15 300	...	...	...	...	...	...
1921	...	13 900	...	...	...	...	...	...
1920	...	12 500	...	...	...	...	...	...
1919	...	11 200	...	...	...	...	...	...
1918	...	10 700	...	...	...	...	...	...
1917	...	10 200	...	...	...	...	...	...
1916	...	8 200	...	...	...	...	...	...
1915	...	6 600	...	...	...	...	...	...
1914	...	4 700	...	...	...	...	...	...
1913	...	4 200	...	...	...	...	...	...

1. Totals may not quite equal sums of various types because totals for most types are estimated and these have been rounded.
2. Data based on improved reporting procedure; therefore not entirely comparable with other years.

Series Q 235-250. Public Transit Mileage, Equipment, Passengers and Passenger Revenue: 1922 to 1997

Year	Equipment owned Dec. 31			Total revenue and nonrevenue passengers (millions)	Passenger revenue (mil. dol.)	Employees (1 000)	Employee payroll (mil. dol.)
	Heavy rail	Trolley buses	Motor buses				
	238	239	240	241	246	247	248
1997	10 242	859	72 170	8 558	7 599	340	9 060
1996	10 201	871	67 874	7 975	7 417	306	8 687
1995	10 157	885	67 107	7 763	6 801	311	8 213
1994	10 138	877	68 123	7 949	6 756	304	8 224
1993	10 261	851	64 850	...	6 351	299	7 932
1992	10 245	907	63 080	...	6 152	279	7 671
1991	10 331	752	60 377	...	6 037	276	7 395
1990	10 419	832	59 753	8 799	5 891	273	7 325
1989	10 506	725	58 919	8 931	5 420	272	6 898
1988	10 539	710	62 572	8 666	5 225	276	6 675
1987	10 168	671	63 017	8 735	5 114	277	6 324
1986	10 386	680	66 218	8 777	5 113	278	6 119
1985	9 326	676	64 258	8 636	4 575	270	5 843
1984	9 083	664	67 294	8 829	4 448	263	5 488
1983	9 943	686	62 093	7 889	3 172	195	3 921
1982	9 867	763	62 114	7 741	3 077	194	3 731
1981	9 801	751	60 393	7 964	2 701	193	3 494
1980	9 641	823	59 411	8 567	2 557	187	3 281
1979	9 522	725	54 490	8 130	2 436	178	3 025
1978	9 567	593	52 866	7 616	2 271	165	2 741
1977	9 639	645	51 968	7 286	2 280	163	2 547
1976	9 714	685	52 382	7 081	2 161	163	2 404
1975	9 608	703	50 811	6 972	1 861	160	2 236
1974	9 403	718	48 700	6 935	1 940	153	1 967
1973	9 387	794	48 286	6 660	1 798	141	1 624
1972	9 423	1 030	49 075	6 567	1 729	138	1 455
1971	9 325	1 037	49 150	6 847	1 741	139	1 393
1970	10 600	1 050	49 700	7 332	1 639.1	138	1 274
1969	10 665	1 082	49 600	7 803	1 554.7	141	1 184
1968	10 745	1 185	50 000	8 019	1 470.2	144	1 110
1967	10 645	1 244	50 180	8 172	1 457.4	146	1 055
1966	10 680	1 326	50 130	8 083	1 385.4	144	995
1965	10 664	1 453	49 600	8 253	1 340.1	145	964
1964	10 614	1 865	49 200	8 328	1 326.0	145	917
1963	10 634	2 155	49 400	8 400	1 316.3	147	892
1962	11 084	3 161	48 800	8 695	1 330.2	149	878
1961	11 419	3 593	49 000	8 883	1 320.9	152	856
1960	11 866	3 826	49 600	9 395	1 334.9	156	857
1959 *	11 983	4 297	49 500	9 557	1 308.0	159	832
1958	12 201	4 848	50 100	9 732	1 282.2	165	831
1957	12 759	5 412	50 800	10 389	1 319.8	177	840
1956	13 225	5 748	51 400	10 941	1 351.1	186	852
1955	14 532	6 157	52 400	11 529	1 358.9	198	864
1954	15 600	6 598	54 000	12 392	1 410.0	211	895
1953	17 234	6 941	54 700	13 902	1 448.6	220	913
1952	19 176	7 180	55 980	15 119	1 438.1	227	903
1951	20 604	7 071	57 660	16 125	1 411.6	232	872
1950	22 986	6 504	56 820	17 246	1 386.8	240	835
1949	24 728	6 366	57 035	19 008	1 419.7	253	841
1948	26 280	5 687	58 540	21 368	1 416.8	261	829
1947	30 158	4 707	56 917	22 540	1 324.2	266	790
1946	33 479	3 916	52 450	23 372	1 331.5	261	713
1945	36 377	3 711	49 670	23 254	1 313.7	242	632
1944	37 199	3 561	48 400	23 017	1 296.9	242	599
1943	37 505	3 501	47 100	22 000	1 235.6	239	554
1942	37 508	3 385	46 000	18 000	979.1	219	462
1941	37 670	3 029	39 300	14 085	758.8	205	386

See footnote at end of chart.

Series Q 235-250. Public Transit Mileage, Equipment, Passengers and Passenger Revenue: 1922 to 1997—Cont'd.

Year	Equipment owned Dec. 31			Total revenue and nonrevenue passengers (millions)	Passenger revenue (mil. dol.)	Employees (1 000)	Employee payroll (mil. dol.)
	Heavy rail	Trolley buses	Motor buses				
	238	**239**	**240**	**241**	**246**	**247**	**248**
1940	37 662	2 802	35 000	13 098	701.5	203	360
1939	40 372	2 184	32 600	12 837	681.5	202	352
1938	42 605	2 032	28 500	12 645	662.9	202	344
1937	45 312	1 655	27 500	13 246	689.7	209	348
1936	48 103	1 136	23 900	13 146	685.5	206	328
1935	50 466	578	23 800	12 226	642.3	204	311
1934	54 118	441	18 700	12 038	. . .	204	303
1933	58 124	310	17 200	11 327	. . .	201	287
1932	. . .	. . .	. . .	12 025	. . .	. . .	. . .
1931	. . .	. . .	. . .	13 924	. . .	. . .	. . .
1930	. . .	. . .	. . .	15 567	. . .	. . .	. . .
1929	. . .	. . .	. . .	16 985	. . .	. . .	. . .
1928	. . .	. . .	. . .	16 989	. . .	. . .	. . .
1927	. . .	. . .	. . .	17 201	. . .	. . .	. . .
1926	. . .	. . .	. . .	17 234	. . .	. . .	. . .
1925	. . .	. . .	. . .	16 651	. . .	. . .	. . .
1924	. . .	. . .	. . .	16 301	. . .	. . .	. . .
1923	. . .	. . .	. . .	16 311	. . .	. . .	. . .
1922	. . .	. . .	. . .	15 735	. . .	. . .	. . .

* Denotes first year for which figures include Alaska and Hawaii.

Series Q 251-263. Oil Pipelines Operated and Oil Originated: 1921 to 1997

Year	Miles of line operated	Total oil delivered out of system	Investment in carrier property	Net income	Year	Miles of line operated	Total oil delivered out of system	Investment in carrier property	Net income
	251	254	258	263		251	254	258	263
		Mil. bbl.	Mil. dol.	Mil. dol.			Mil. bbl.	Mil. dol.	Mil. dol.
1997	160 000	12 481	50	2 255	1957	145 236	4 472	2 843	159
1996	169 000	12 635	47	2 372	1956	142 686	4 458	2 716	178
1995	177 000	12 862	46	2 670	1955	140 374	4 039	2 586	153
1994	159 000	12 159	46	2 148	1954	138 962	3 705	2 501	124
1993	164 000	12 219	44	1 763	1953	133 900	3 627	2 312	109
1992	164 000	11 447	43	2 061	1952	132 715	3 359	2 064	97
1991	172 000	11 496	42	1 788	1951	131 457	3 201	1 822	82
1990	168 000	11 378	25 828	2 340	1950	128 589	2 740	1 656	81
1989	169 000	11 281	24 638	2 227	1949	124 984	2 448	1 498	58
1988	171 000	11 484	24 332	2 505	1948	124 092	2 697	1 381	57
1987	168 000	11 194	21 353	2 475	1947	119 298	2 474	1 225	53
1986	170 000	11 002	22 384	2 051	1946	116 544	2 260	1 106	56
1985	171 000	10 745	21 605	2 431	1945	113 351	2 365	1 043	66
1984	174 000	10 224	19 397	2 545	1944	111 615	2 389	1 001	66
1983	168 000	10 310	22 255	2 353	1943	108 783	2 077	965	61
1982	173 000	10 181	21 942	2 162	1942	106 485	1 764	919	57
1981	172 800	10 223	21 250	2 031	1941	105 435	1 642	885	79
1980	173 000	10 600	19 752	1 912	1940	100 156	1 407	842	80
1979	169 800	11 140	18 990	1 648	1939	98 681	...	830	81
1978	161 600	10 768	17 654	1 696	1938	95 938	...	808	93
1977	154 500	10 019	16 736	478	1937	96 612	...	803	103
1976	169 900	9 742	13 684	595	1936	93 926	...	774	92
1975	171 000	9 391	10 740	456	1935	92 037	...	763	78
1974	169 000	9 132	8 038	330	1934	93 070	...	758	84
1973	170 100	9 416	7 000	408	1933	93 724	...	766	106
1972	172 100	8 847	6 749	415	1932	92 782	...	764	112
1971	175 000	8 183	6 305	314	1931	93 090	...	845	121
1970	175 735	8 147	5 786	312	1930	88 728	...	773	124
1969	170 824	7 745	5 379	273	1929	85 796	...	741	142
1968	169 307	7 269	5 139	262	1928	81 676	...	659	117
1967	165 478	6 800	4 745	[1] 261	1927	76 070	...	609	93
1966	163 155	6 238	4 433	236	1926	72 846	...	539	80
1965	161 412	5 864	4 178	218	1925	70 009	...	511	88
1964	159 583	5 565	4 040	210	1924	68 185	...	496	72
1963	156 812	5 322	3 915	201	1923	64 760	...	432	63
1962	155 053	5 109	3 518	204	1922	57 349	...	382	59
1961	153 737	4 923	3 407	181	1921	55 260	...	365	34
1960 *	151 968	4 783	3 300	169					
1959	149 159	4 659	3 197	183					
1958	144 354	4 317	2 949	162					

* Denotes first year for which figures include Alaska and Hawaii.
1. After extraordinary and period items.

Series Q 284-312. Railroad Mileage and Equipment: 1890 to 1997

(Includes intercorporate duplications. Unless otherwise noted, covers Class I, II and III railroads, except that prior to 1908 includes switching and terminal companies where applicable)

Year ending x	Total mileage of track	Total locomotives in service [2]	Passenger-train cars in service, railroad only	Freight-train cars in service [3] Number	Average capacity [4]	Year ending x	Total mileage of track	Total locomotives in service [2]	Passenger-train cars in service, railroad only	Freight-train cars in service [3] Number	Average capacity [4]
	288	295	301	304	305		288	295	301	304	305
Dec. 31					Tons	Dec. 31 (cont'd.)					Tons
1997	225 000	19 684	...	568 000	...	1942	399 627	44 671	38 446	1 773 735	50.5
1996	228 000	19 269	...	571 000	...	1941	403 625	44 375	38 334	1 732 673	50.3
1995	228 000	18 812	...	583 000	...	1940	405 975	44 333	38 308	1 684 171	50.0
1994	232 000	18 505	...	591 000	...	1939	408 350	45 172	38 977	1 680 519	49.7
1993	236 000	18 161	...	587 000	...	1938	411 324	46 544	39 931	1 731 096	49.4
1992	238 000	18 004	...	605 000	...	1937	414 572	47 555	40 949	1 776 428	49.2
1991	242 000	18 344	...	633 000	87.9	1936	416 381	48 009	41 390	1 790 043	48.8
1990	239 000	18 835	...	659 000	87.5	1935	419 228	49 541	42 426	1 867 381	48.3
1989	249 000	19 015	...	682 000	87.8	1934	422 401	51 423	44 884	1 973 247	48.0
1988	251 000	19 364	2 332	725 000	86.4	1933	425 664	54 228	47 677	2 072 632	47.5
1987	254 000	19 358	2 350	749 000	85.0	1932	428 402	56 732	50 598	2 184 690	47.0
1986	256 000	20 790	2 307	799 000	84.1	1931	429 823	58 652	52 096	2 245 904	47.0
1985	257 000	22 932	2 502	867 000	83.2	1930	429 883	60 189	53 584	2 322 267	46.9
1984	264 000	22 548	2 580	948 000	83.4	1929	429 054	61 257	53 838	2 323 683	46.3
1983	270 000	25 838	2 610	1 007 000	82.4	1928	427 750	63 311	54 800	2 346 751	45.8
1982	275 000	27 073	3 736	1 039 000	81.6	1927	424 737	65 348	55 729	2 378 800	45.5
1981	278 000	27 808	3 945	1 111 000	80.5	1926	421 341	66 847	56 855	2 403 967	45.1
1980	290 000	28 094	4 347	1 168 000	78.5	1925	417 954	68 098	56 814	2 414 083	44.8
1979	300 000	27 900	2 400	1 148 000	77.7	1924	415 028	69 486	57 451	2 411 627	44.3
1978	322 000	27 000	2 400	1 201 000	76.9	1923	412 993	69 414	57 159	2 379 131	43.8
1977	321 000	29 700	5 700	1 275 000	75.5	1922	409 359	68 518	56 827	2 352 483	43.1
1976	314 000	29 600	5 600	1 309 000	73.8	1921	407 531	69 122	56 950	2 378 510	42.5
1975	324 000	28 210	6 471	1 359 000	72.9	1920	403 580	68 942	56 102	2 388 424	42.4
1974	354 000	30 110	7 080	1 373 000	71.4	1919	403 891	68 977	56 290	2 426 889	41.9
1973	354 000	29 926	7 363	1 387 000	70.5	1918	402 343	67 936	56 611	2 397 943	41.6
1972	356 000	29 338	7 763	1 411 000	69.6	1917	400 353	66 070	55 939	2 379 472	41.5
1971	359 194	29 185	8 869	1 441 000	68.4	1916	397 014	65 595	55 193	2 329 475	40.9
1970	360 330	29 122	11 378	1 453 708	67.1	June 30					
1969	364 915	29 090	12 630	1 464 194	65.8						
1968	366 238	29 448	14 816	1 484 571	64.3	1916	394 944	65 314	54 774	2 343 378	40.5
1967	368 030	29 874	17 822	1 510 963	63.4	1915	391 142	66 502	55 810	2 341 567	39.7
1966	370 104	30 124	18 974	1 523 741	61.4	1914	387 208	67 012	54 492	2 349 734	39.1
1965	370 636	30 061	20 022	1 515 169	59.8	1913	379 508	65 597	52 717	2 298 478	38.3
1964	372 300	30 296	21 510	1 517 564	58.2	1912	371 238	63 463	51 583	2 229 163	37.4
1963	374 522	30 506	22 616	1 542 456	56.8	1911	362 824	62 463	49 906	2 208 997	36.9
1962	376 290	30 701	23 430	1 581 213	56.3	1910	351 767	60 019	47 179	2 148 478	35.9
1961	379 415	30 889	24 433	1 635 342	55.7	1909	342 351	58 219	45 664	2 086 835	35.3
1960 *..	* 381 745	* 31 178	* 25 746	* 1 690 396	* 55.4	1908	333 646	57 698	45 292	2 100 784	34.9
1959	383 912	31 539	27 419	1 708 116	55.0	1907	327 975	55 388	43 973	1 991 557	33.8
1958	385 264	31 616	28 999	1 755 775	54.8	1906	317 083	51 672	42 262	1 837 914	32.2
1957	386 978	32 391	29 564	1 777 557	54.5	1905	306 797	48 357	40 713	1 731 409	30.8
1956	389 668	32 593	30 817	1 738 631	54.0	1904	297 073	46 743	39 752	1 692 194	30.1
1955	390 965	33 533	32 118	1 723 747	53.7	1903	283 822	43 871	38 140	1 653 782	29.4
1954	392 580	35 033	33 035	1 761 386	53.7	1902	274 196	41 225	36 987	1 546 101	...
1953	393 736	37 251	34 106	1 801 874	53.5	1901	265 352	39 584	35 969	1 464 328	...
1952	394 631	39 697	34 942	1 783 352	53.2	1900	258 784	37 663	34 713	1 365 531	...
1951	395 831	42 473	36 326	1 777 878	52.9	1899	250 143	36 703	33 850	1 295 510	...
1950	396 380	42 951	37 359	1 745 778	52.6	1898	245 334	36 234	33 595	1 248 826	...
1949	397 232	43 272	38 006	1 778 811	52.4	1897	242 013	35 986	33 626	1 221 730	...
1948	397 203	44 474	39 406	1 785 067	51.9	1896	239 140	35 950	33 003	1 221 887	...
1947	397 355	44 344	39 057	1 759 758	51.5	1895	233 276	35 699	33 112	1 196 119	...
1946	398 037	45 511	38 697	1 768 400	51.3	1894	229 796	35 492	33 018	1 205 169	...

See footnotes at end of chart.

Series Q 284-312. Railroad Mileage and Equipment: 1890 to 1997—Cont'd.

(Includes intercorporate duplications. Unless otherwise noted, covers Class I, II and III railroads, except that prior to 1908 includes switching and terminal companies where applicable)

Year ending x	Total mileage of track	Equipment [1]		Freight-train cars in service [3]		Year ending x	Total mileage of track	Equipment [1]		Freight-train cars in service [3]	
		Total locomotives in service [2]	Passenger-train cars in service, railroad only	Number	Average capacity [4]			Total locomotives in service [2]	Passenger-train cars in service, railroad only	Number	Average capacity [4]
	288	**295**	**301**	**304**	**305**		**288**	**295**	**301**	**304**	**305**
Dec. 31					*Tons*	Dec. 31 (cont'd.)					*Tons*
1945	398 054	46 253	38 633	1 787 073	51.1	1893	221 864	34 788	31 384	1 013 307	. . .
1944	398 437	46 305	38 217	1 797 012	50.8	1892	211 051	33 136	28 876	966 998	. . .
1943	398 730	45 406	38 331	1 784 472	50.7	1891	207 446	32 139	27 949	947 300	. . .
						1890	199 876	30 140	26 820	918 491	. . .

* Denotes first year for which figures include Alaska and Hawaii.
1. Includes switching and terminal companies.
2. For 1890-1927, number of locomotives; for 1928, number of units, except for steam locomotives. (A unit is the least number of wheel bases together with superstructure capable of independent propulsion, but not necessarily equipped with an independent control.)
3. Excludes caboose cars.
4. For 1916-1956, represents steam locomotives and freight cars of class I railroads, excluding switching and terminal companies; for 1957-1967, includes all class I locomotives, excluding switching and terminal companies.

Series Q 331-345. Railroad Freight Traffic: 1912 to 1997

(In thousands of tons of 2,000 pounds)

Year ending x	Total revenue freight originated (Class I railroads) in carloads	Year ending x	Total revenue freight originated (Class I railroads) in carloads	Year ending x	Total revenue freight originated (Class I railroads) in carloads	Year ending x	Total revenue freight originated (Class I railroads) in carloads
	332		332		332		332
Dec. 31							
1997	1 585 000	1974	1 530 000	1952	1 343 294	1930	1 123 530
1996	1 611 000	1973	1 532 000	1951	1 467 023	1929	1 303 048
1995	1 550 000			1950	1 343 308	1928	1 248 989
1994	1 470 000	1972	1 448 000	1949	1 213 911		
1993	1 397 000	1971	1 391 000	1948	1 488 612	1927	1 243 171
		1970	1 484 110			1926	1 296 651
1992	1 399 000	1969	1 472 620	1947	1 514 985	1925	1 206 655
1991	1 383 000	1968	1 430 441	1946	1 342 230	1924	1 146 747
1990	1 425 000			1945	1 404 080	1923	1 234 692
1989	1 403 000	1967	1 406 668	1944	1 471 366		
1988	1 429 000	1966	1 447 852	1943	1 462 314	1922	980 516
		1965	1 386 090			1921	898 191
1987	1 372 000	1964	1 353 117	1942	1 403 612	1920	[1] 1 202 219
1986	1 306 000	1963	1 283 382	1941	1 209 559	1919	[1] 1 045 148
1985	1 312 100			1940	994 728	1918	1 209 957
1984	1 429 400	1962	1 231 415	1939	886 794		
1983	1 292 600	1961	1 191 154	1938	757 470	1917	1 210 247
1982	1 268 600	1960	1 237 575			1916	[1] 1 150 456
1981	1 453 000	1959	1 228 277	1937	998 398	June 30	
1980	1 492 400	1958	1 185 951	1936	942 538		
1979	1 502 100			1935	775 588	1916	[1] 878 761
1978	1 390 400	1957	1 374 884	1934	750 951	1915	[1] 982 892
		1956	1 440 937	1933	684 592	1914	[1] 1 026 817
1977	1 394 700	1955	1 389 346			1913	[1] 889 999
1976	1 370 000	1954	1 217 005	1932	630 989	1912	[1] 866 398
1975	1 395 100	1953	1 376 046	1931	871 412		

1. Includes the following amounts of unassigned carload tonnage (thousands): 1911, 35 199; 1912, 32 266; 1913, 15 617; 1914, 14 671; 1915, 2 268; 1916, 1 367; and 1919, 338.

Series Q 438-448.   Merchant Vessels Completed by U.S. Shipyards: 1914 to 1994

(Tons in thousands. Represents self-propelled steel vessels of 2 000 gross tons and over for domestic use. Excludes Alaska and Hawaii.)

Year	Merchant vessels		Cargo			Tanker		
	Number	Gross tons	Number	Gross tons	Deadweight	Number	Gross tons	Deadweight
	438	**439**	**443**	**444**	**445**	**446**	**447**	**448**
1994	1	17	...	...	...	1	17	22
1993	X	X	X	X	X	X	X	X
1992	3	44	1	32	29	2	12	16
1988	4	153	3	58	63	1	95	209
1987	4	153	3	58	63	1	95	209
1986	5	215	2	66	53	3	149	271
1985	8	172	4	113	97	4	59	92
1984	5	118	X	X	X	5	118	210
1983	13	376	6	228	219	7	148	277
1982	11	337	6	221	219	5	116	226
1981	12	275	2	53	73	10	222	358
1980	10	375	6	105	114	4	270	354
1979	15	1 149	4	53	47	11	1 096	1 901
1978	14	912	2	27	30	12	885	1 392
1977	17	884	2	25	37	15	859	1 585
1976	16	615	4	57	76	12	558	1 176
1975	15	452	3	65	71	12	387	742
1974	20	697	11	314	402	9	383	759
1973	24	734	18	419	450	6	315	653
1972	13	357	7	151	187	6	206	415
1971	14	394	6	151	170	8	243	473
1970	13	342	6	120	134	7	222	427
1969	22	418	14	217	247	8	201	381
1968	21	319	18	256	291	3	63	113
1967	12	143	12	143	150	X	X	X
1966	13	146	12	125	161	1	21	36
1965	13	173	11	121	154	2	52	92
1964	15	213	10	104	123	4	95	166
1963	35	418	23	250	289	6	117	200
1962	27	392	23	265	303	3	113	186
1961	25	369	18	190	224	7	179	298
1960	26	410	15	134	163	11	276	456
1959	30	714	3	40	73	26	668	1 095
1958	30	572	5	48	67	21	463	759
1957	19	297	3	8	6	16	289	457
1956	8	113	2	7	15	6	106	169
1955	9	119	7	84	95	2	35	55
1954	39	585	11	106	159	27	475	764
1953	45	570	22	212	234	22	354	555
1952	31	399	17	170	289	8	127	202
1951	10	148	4	29	43	4	71	116
1950	26	405	3	27	44	23	378	609
1949	33	541	X	X	X	33	541	863
1948	24	159	17	92	159	6	52	88
1947	39	247	28	154	224	3	19	36
1946	83	646	66	487	729	8	82	121
1945	1 041	7 615	807	5 336	7 206	188	1 770	2 787
1944	1 463	11 403	1 175	8 455	11 858	240	2 486	3 955
1943	1 661	12 486	1 410	10 103	14 921	231	2 163	3 420
1942	724	5 393	652	4 679	6 843	61	612	982
1941	95	749	61	423	598	28	268	424
1940	53	445	31	227	335	16	149	238
1939	28	241	14	92	128	11	119	193
1938	24	181	6	39	56	18	142	228
1937	15	122	X	X	X	15	122	192
1936	8	63	X	X	X	8	63	105
1935	2	19	X	X	X	2	19	30
1934	2	10	2	10	15	X	X	X

See footnote at end of chart.

Series Q 438-448.   Merchant Vessels Completed by U.S. Shipyards: 1914 to 1994—Cont'd.
(Tons in thousands. Represents self-propelled steel vessels of 2 000 gross tons and over for domestic use. Excludes Alaska and Hawaii.)

Year	Merchant vessels		Cargo			Tanker		
	Number	Gross tons	Number	Gross tons	Deadweight	Number	Gross tons	Deadweight
	438	**439**	**443**	**444**	**445**	**446**	**447**	**448**
1933............................	4	50	X	X	X	X	X	X
1932............................	15	145	2	16	22	X	X	X
1931............................	14	151	X	X	X	5	42	70
1930............................	18	164	2	16	24	11	97	161
1929............................	8	65	5	33	49	1	9	15
1928............................	7	72	X	X	X	4	28	44
1927............................	19	155	9	73	104	3	30	50
1926............................	8	54	2	16	26	1	9	15
1925............................	12	84	9	65	92	X	X	X
1924............................	12	84	4	34	48	1	7	11
1923............................	18	117	9	68	110	2	16	23
1922............................	19	168	10	78	156	6	48	71
1921............................	183	1 359	57	317	485	104	786	1 158
1920............................	467	2 396	375	1 758	2 696	80	538	778
1919............................	723	3 370	679	3 086	4 680	42	273	395
1918............................	414	1 770	375	1 508	2 283	34	232	339
1917............................	125	642	92	414	627	32	218	314
1916............................	74	370	49	201	300	24	163	247
1915............................	24	128	17	88	131	4	20	30
1914............................	26	135	17	88	130	8	45	67

X Represents zero.

Series Q 449-458. Shipbuilding in Private Shipyards—Summary: 1949 to 1999

(Tons in thousands; gross tons for commercial vessels, light displacement tons for naval vessels. Covers steel self-propelled vessels 1 000 tons or more)

Year	Commercial vessels			Naval vessels		
	Under construction Jan. 1	Contracted for	Delivered	Under construction Jan. 1	Contracted for	Delivered
	449	451	453	454	456	458
1999	5	6	1	46	42	4
1998	12	5	5	42	46	13
1997	14	12	4	46	42	8
1996	10	14	1	46	46	11
1995	3	10	1	57	46	17
1994	1	3	1	60	57	15
1993	1	1	...	82	73	19
1992	3	1	3	90	82	18
1991 [1]	3	3	...	91	90	14
1990	X	3	X	95	87	15
1989	X	X	X	105	98	23
1988	X	X	X	83	105	10
1987	6	X	4	79	83	16
1986	7	6	1	85	79	20
1985	10	7	3	100	85	26
1984	10	10	5	111	100	22
1983	21	10	15	105	111	21
1982	35	21	17	93	105	18
1981	49	35	22	91	93	26
1980	69	49	23	99	91	19
1979	70	69	21	102	99	16
1978	60	30	19	91	25	14
1977	72	13	25	88	15	12
1976	79	16	22	76	20	8
1975	96	79	19	63	76	3
1974	97	24	24	56	16	9
1973	88	43	34	57	7	8
1972	59	48	19	64	14	21
1971	49	24	14	82	15	33
1970 Number	49	49	13	108	6	32
Tons	1 388	580	370	621	132	166
1969 Number	63	8	22	133	6	31
Tons	1 495	309	416	701	80	159
1968 Number	64	23	24	134	15	16
Tons	1 211	613	329	686	153	138
1967 Number	48	29	13	147	8	21
Tons	596	740	162	745	50	109
1966 Number	45	16	13	106	54	13
Tons	513	244	161	573	246	74
1965 Number	47	16	18	101	23	18
Tons	550	166	203	537	158	122
1964 Number	45	18	16	83	39	21
Tons	517	244	223	450	195	108
1963 Number	54	25	34	71	29	17
Tons	648	291	422	2 383	148	81
1962 Number	66	15	27	67	19	15
Tons	859	174	285	362	99	76
1961 Number	57	34	25	59	24	16
Tons	789	2 438	369	2 403	132	173
1960 Number	60	23	25	52	19	12
Tons	979	270	404	334	115	39
1959 Number	75	19	32	55	13	16
Tons	1 514	196	717	335	63	64
1958 Number	93	22	31	46	17	8
Tons	2 156	176	573	281	78	24
1957 Number	84	35	23	55	14	23
Tons	1 855	751	320	286	100	114
1956 Number	25	68	9	42	22	9
Tons	312	1 715	126	247	87	49

See footnotes at end of chart.

Series Q 449-458. Shipbuilding in Private Shipyards—Summary: 1949 to 1999—Cont'd.

(Tons in thousands; gross tons for commercial vessels, light displacement tons for naval vessels. Covers steel self-propelled vessels 1 000 tons or more)

Year	Commercial vessels			Naval vessels		
	Under construction Jan. 1	Contracted for	Delivered	Under construction Jan. 1	Contracted for	Delivered
	449	**451**	**453**	**454**	**456**	**458**
1955 Number	15	18	8	44	13	14
Tons	225	196	105	307	93	146
1954 Number	48	7	38	31	26	13
Tons	672	122	564	212	138	48
1953 Number	92	4	45	45	2	16
Tons	1 298	19	570	254	16	51
1952 Number	96	27	31	31	18	6
Tons	1 222	478	397	158	107	14
1951 Number	29	77	10	11	22	1
Tons	411	987	148	42	170	765
1950 Number	39	16	26	11	X	X
Tons	636	181	415	42	X	X
1949 Number	71	5	34	21	X	7
Tons	1 130	72	539	194	X	58

X Represents zero.
1. Figures from 1971-1991 include just the total number of vessels built.
2. Tonnages revised.

Series Q 473-480. Merchant Vessels Launched and Owned—World and United States: 1895 to 1996

(Vessels of 100 gross tons and over. Excludes sailing ships, nonpropelled craft, and all ships built of wood. Figures for 1895 to 1935 represent annual average 5-year span beginning with the year shown; for example, the figure shown for 1895 is the annual average for 1895 to 1899, that for 1900, the annual average for 1900 to 1904, etc.)

	World				United States			
	Launched		Registered		Launched		Registered	
Year	Number	Gross tons (1 000)	Number	Gross tons (1 000)	Number	Gross tons (1 000)	Number	Gross tons (1 000)
	473	474	475	476	477	478	479	480
1996	1 745	25 881	84 264	507 873	29	24	5 289	12 024
1995	1 856	22 565	82 890	490 662	30	14	5 292	12 760
1994	1 789	19 612	80 676	475 859	28	29	5 270	13 665
1993	1 505	20 025	80 655	457 915	30	14	5 646	14 087
1992	1 506	18 633	79 845	444 305	27	54	5 737	18 228
1991	1 574	16 095	80 030	436 027	17	9	6 222	20 291
1990	1 672	15 885	78 336	423 627	16	15	6 348	21 328
1989	1 593	13 236	76 100	410 481	10	4	6 375	20 588
1988	1 575	10 909	75 680	403 406	60	11	6 442	20 832
1987	1 528	12 259	75 240	403 498	29	164	6 427	20 178
1986	1 634	16 845	75 266	404 910	36	223	6 496	19 901
1985	1 964	18 157	76 395	416 269	66	180	6 447	19 518
1984	2 210	18 334	76 068	418 682	73	84	6 441	19 292
1983	2 276	15 911	76 106	422 590	159	381	6 437	19 358
1982	2 312	16 820	75 151	424 742	204	216	6 133	19 111
1981	2 269	16 932	73 864	420 835	223	360	5 869	18 908
1980	2 412	13 101	73 832	419 911	205	555	5 579	18 464
1979	2 466	14 289	71 129	413 021	182	1 352	5 088	17 542
1978	2 618	18 194	69 020	406 002	151	1 033	4 746	16 188
1977	2 796	27 532	67 945	393 678	129	1 012	4 740	15 300
1976	2 723	33 922	63 611	371 612	143	815	4 035	14 810
1975	2 730	34 202	61 501	341 780	127	476	3 801	14 491
1974	2 949	33 541	58 957	310 934	233	733	3 566	14 337
1973	2 999	30 409	57 347	289 532	277	964	3 539	14 818
1972	2 776	26 749	55 251	267 965	292	482	3 305	14 951
1971	2 645	24 860	52 997	246 840	242	482	3 070	16 211
1970	2 814	20 980	52 444	227 490	156	375	2 983	18 463
1969	2 819	19 315	48 246	211 294	174	400	2 972	19 507
1968	2 798	16 908	45 343	193 770	199	441	3 049	19 623
1967	2 778	15 780	42 234	181 709	231	242	3 115	20 286
1966	2 561	14 307	40 822	170 730	191	167	3 140	20 750
1965	2 280	12 216	39 628	159 979	130	270	3 224	21 478
1964	2 147	10 264	38 602	152 584	80	276	3 344	22 380
1963	2 001	8 539	37 310	145 438	78	294	3 506	23 082
1962	1 901	8 375	36 364	139 549	90	449	3 542	23 220
1961	1 990	7 940	35 465	135 477	59	343	3 728	24 184
1960	2 020	8 356	34 056	129 339	60	485	3 845	24 781
1959	1 808	8 746	33 924	124 494	47	597	3 964	25 227
1958	1 936	9 270	32 857	117 578	64	732	4 054	25 526
1957	1 950	8 501	31 421	109 778	54	359	4 116	25 843
1956	1 815	6 670	30 620	104 720	50	169	4 157	26 074
1955	1 437	5 315	29 967	100 069	26	73	4 225	26 343
1954	1 223	5 251	29 766	96 899	46	477	4 404	27 252
1953	1 134	5 095	29 174	92 826	68	528	4 431	27 144
1952	1065	4 394	28 751	89 636	64	468	4 458	27 139
1951	1 002	3 639	28 374	86 678	58	164	4 484	27 226
1950	990	3 489	27 922	83 996	51	437	4 531	27 404
1949	899	3 126	27 194	81 954	66	633	4 605	27 707
1948	840	2 303	26 479	79 714	49	126	4 807	29 060
1947	741	2 093	. . .	. . .	61	163	. . .	. . .
1946	655	2 108	. . .	. . .	95	501	. . .	. . .
1945	1 311	7 189	. . .	. . .	880	5 968	. . .	. . .
1944	1 690	11 157	. . .	. . .	1 237	9 332	. . .	. . .
1943	2 067	13 881	. . .	. . .	1 620	11 577	. . .	. . .

See footnote at end of chart.

Series Q 473-480.   Merchant Vessels Launched and Owned—World and United States: 1895 to 1996—Cont'd.

(Vessels of 100 gross tons and over. Excludes sailing ships, nonpropelled craft, and all ships built of wood. Figures for 1895 to 1935 represent annual average 5-year span beginning with the year shown; for example, the figure shown for 1895 is the annual average for 1895 to 1899, that for 1900, the annual average for 1900 to 1904, etc.)

	World				United States			
	Launched		Registered		Launched		Registered	
Year	Number	Gross tons (1 000)	Number	Gross tons (1 000)	Number	Gross tons (1 000)	Number	Gross tons (1 000)
	473	**474**	**475**	**476**	**477**	**478**	**479**	**480**
1942.............................	1 285	7 812	. . .	. . .	861	5 671	. . .	. . .
1941.............................	489	2 487	. . .	. . .	184	1 035	. . .	. . .
1940.............................	495	1 754	. . .	. . .	167	579	. . .	. . .
1939.............................	1 040	2 595	31 186	69 440	117	244	3 270	11 874
1935.............................	(1)	(1)	30 979	64 886	(1)	(1)	3 585	12 773
1930.............................	484	1 020	32 713	69 608	25	83	4 105	13 947
1925.............................	873	2 469	32 905	65 638	74	159	4 790	15 314
1920.............................	942	2 582	31 484	57 281	99	315	5 381	15 997
1915.............................	1 637	4 616	30 643	49 246	605	2 217	3 180	5 846
1910.............................	1 426	2 588	29 943	41 884	140	222	3 380	5 018
1905.............................	1 474	2 218	29 574	35 949	206	352	3 457	3 996
1900.............................	1 611	2 354	27 840	28 957	242	347	3 135	2 750
1895.............................	1 205	1 844	30 288	25 086	155	200	3 200	2 165

1. 1935 figures have been combined with 1939 figures.

Series Q 487-502. United States Flag Merchant Vessels, Steam and Motor: 1934 to 1998

(Dead-weight tonnage in thousands. As of end of fiscal year, except as indicated. Covers ocean-going vessels of 1 000 gross tons and over engaged in foreign and domestic trade, and inactive vessels. Excludes special types and vessels employed on Great Lakes)

Year and type of vessel	All vessels		Active vessels				Year and type of vessel	All vessels		Active vessels			
			Foreign trade		Total domestic trade					Foreign trade		Total domestic trade	
	Number	Tons	Number	Tons	Number	Tons		Number	Tons	Number	Tons	Number	Tons
	487	488	491	492	493	494		487	488	491	492	493	494
1998	473	16 853	81	3 082	124	6 826	1975	891	17 608	267	6 204	205	5 687
Cargo	106	3 675	60	2 522	29	752	Cargo	612	8 175	228	3 901	49	832
Tanker	156	9 415	5	185	86	5 922	Tanker	279	9 433	39	2 303	156	4 855
1996	509	18 585	97	3 714	127	7 017	1974	965	17 334	305	6 909	202	5 169
Cargo	125	1 803	5	56	5	85	Cargo	594	7 981	241	4 082	53	800
Tanker	181	11 028	18	855	92	6 286	Tanker	275	8 739	60	2 793	148	4 362
1994	564	21 126	134	5 479	134	7 727	1973	1 051	17 297	312	6 618	196	4 725
Cargo	145	2 097	18	282	...	...	Cargo	658	8 320	237	3 749	59	796
Tanker	210	13 048	31	2 039	106	7 147	Tanker	273	8 220	71	2 832	135	3 916
1992	619	23 254	112	4 944	161	8 741	1972	1 233	18 412	262	4 683	201	4 881
Cargo	191	2 444	11	175	4	76	Cargo	792	9 366	224	3 452	57	751
Tanker	226	14 993	23	1 803	121	7 847	Tanker	283	8 047	33	1 185	143	4 124
1990	635	24 262	131	5 119	158	8 624	1971	1 478	20 474	321	5 273	236	5 418
Cargo	199	2 456	27	426	2	24	Cargo	1 014	11 515	279	3 955	65	829
Tanker	233	15 649	23	1 637	121	7 850	Tanker	293	7 848	33	1 232	169	4 576
1989	661	24 457	164	7 251	158	8 967	1970	1 780	23 290	386	5 775	245	5 368
Cargo	422	8 726	125	3 883	32	697	Cargo	1 302	14 298	344	4 605	68	837
Tanker	239	15 731	39	3 368	126	8 270	Tanker	301	7 835	32	1 076	175	4 518
1988	684	25 677	170	7 356	177	10 339	1969	2 013	25 079	447	6 021	199	4 062
Cargo	433	8 887	128	3 861	42	875	Cargo	1 521	16 462	398	5 100	69	823
Tanker	251	16 790	42	3 495	135	9 464	Tanker	305	7 403	29	734	128	3 228
1987	724	25 114	135	4 702	170	9 581	1968	2 101	25 699	481	6 332	242	4 934
Cargo	470	9 040	97	2 528	40	881	Cargo	1 581	16 993	421	5 180	65	797
Tanker	254	16 074	38	2 174	130	8 700	Tanker	315	7 363	38	952	176	4 133
1986	738	24 499	156	5 475	168	9 474	1967	2 209	26 560	460	6 037	233	4 654
Cargo	484	9 106	123	3 468	37	775	Cargo	1 670	17 843	400	4 936	66	810
Tanker	254	15 393	33	2 007	131	8 699	Tanker	317	7 263	36	860	166	3 840
1985	748	24 439	161	5 448	171	9 168	1966	2 292	27 393	494	6 576	248	4 825
Cargo	485	8 792	129	3 623	36	659	Cargo	1 739	18 565	420	5 093	83	1 050
Tanker	263	15 647	32	1 825	135	8 909	Tanker	328	7 352	48	1 250	164	3 771
1984	749	23 965	160	5 432	183	9 606	1965	2 425	28 755	512	6 877	217	3 953
Cargo	477	7 876	122	3 108	41	813	Cargo	1 840	19 561	440	5 249	92	1 056
Tanker	272	16 089	38	2 324	142	8 793	Tanker	349	7 636	54	1 475	124	2 892
1983	819	24 737	184	5 700	204	10 335	1964	2 598	30 084	584	7 271	295	5 504
Cargo	517	7 991	141	3 281	40	660	Cargo	1 959	20 612	509	5 971	100	1 137
Tanker	302	16 746	43	2 419	164	9 675	Tanker	368	7 685	43	1 010	194	4 362
1982	828	24 108	197	5 141	224	11 308	1963	2 691	30 753	587	7 344	299	5 479
Cargo	524	7 597	171	3 426	42	651	Cargo	2 013	21 047	512	5 979	103	1 157
Tanker	304	16 511	26	1 715	182	10 657	Tanker	388	7 784	45	1 095	195	4 318
1981	863	24 477	216	5 141	235	10 951	1962	2 716	30 954	543	6 616	340	5 951
Cargo	550	7 919	184	3 530	40	667	Cargo	2 018	21 024	482	5 554	115	1 233
Tanker	313	16 558	32	1 611	195	10 284	Tanker	409	8 006	32	803	223	4 703
1980	863	23 979	227	6 619	257	11 259	1961	2 810	31 525	415	5 066	182	3 107
Cargo	553	7 872	195	3 826	46	713	Cargo	2 086	21 575	365	4 135	64	642
Tanker	310	16 107	32	2 793	211	10 546	Tanker	424	7 941	33	781	118	2 465
1979	871	22 997	276	10 109	208	7 629	1960	2 934	32 601	558	6 541	372	5 926
Cargo	566	7 844	204	3 886	40	597	Cargo	2 204	22 813	479	5 265	148	1 589
Tanker	305	15 153	72	6 223	168	7 032	Tanker	425	7 750	45	972	222	4 323
1978	841	21 253	266	8 484	221	7 721	1959	3 047	33 565	533	5 935	375	5 912
Cargo	552	7 807	204	3 829	46	685	Cargo	2 347	24 333	473	5 189	142	1 512
Tanker	289	13 446	62	4 655	175	7 036	Tanker	412	7 283	24	422	231	4 386
1977	841	19 468	281	6 817	214	7 442	1958	3 047	33 316	551	6 208	356	5 369
Cargo	566	7 850	240	4 336	44	646	Cargo	2 425	25 125	487	5 348	133	1 366
Tanker	275	11 618	41	2 481	170	6 796	Tanker	384	6 553	28	516	220	3 973
1976	843	17 989	294	7 770	194	5 136	1957	3 032	32 900	721	8 406	399	5 595
Cargo	521	7 519	230	4 140	50	731	Cargo	2 450	25 412	611	6 649	161	1 675
Tanker	263	10 086	59	3 586	143	4 399	Tanker	352	5 894	72	1 393	325	3 891

See footnotes at end of chart.

Series Q 487-502. United States Flag Merchant Vessels, Steam and Motor: 1934 to 1998—Cont'd.

(Dead-weight tonnage in thousands. As of end of fiscal year, except as indicated. Covers ocean-going vessels of 1 000 gross tons and over engaged in foreign and domestic trade, and inactive vessels. Excludes special types and vessels employed on Great Lakes)

Year and type of vessel	All vessels		Active vessels				Year and type of vessel	All vessels		Active vessels			
			Foreign trade		Total domestic trade					Foreign trade		Total domestic trade	
	Number	Tons	Number	Tons	Number	Tons		Number	Tons	Number	Tons	Number	Tons
	487	**488**	**491**	**492**	**493**	**494**		**487**	**488**	**491**	**492**	**493**	**494**
1956................	3 150	34 052	644	7 538	402	5 639	1941..................	1 168	10 096	471	4 052	663	5 836
Cargo	2 511	26 007	524	5 688	149	1 569	Cargo	716	5 472	358	2 966	333	2 340
Tanker..........	392	6 363	82	1 489	252	4 061	Tanker...........	358	4 083	70	739	286	3 331
1955................	3 235	35 017	601	6 992	425	5 880	1940..................	1 300	11 019	425	3 749	693	5 893
Cargo	2 560	26 539	492	5 383	160	1 650	Cargo	790	6 020	291	2 443	350	2 438
Tanker..........	426	6 790	70	1 248	264	4 220	Tanker...........	370	4 126	68	791	297	3 273
1954................	3 333	35 860	623	7 299	398	5 324	1939..................	1 398	11 699	319	2 804	772	6 499
Cargo	2 636	26 435	489	5 226	154	1 581	Cargo	851	6 364	193	1 619	415	2 921
Tanker..........	445	7 730	95	1 713	239	3 719	Tanker...........	384	4 256	48	565	304	3 343
1953................	3 349	36 255	629	7 390	437	5 725	1938..................	1 422	11 814	366	3 301	694	5 718
Cargo	2 630	27 228	461	4 890	167	1 638	Cargo	882	6 557	213	1 808	379	2 629
Tanker..........	462	6 988	128	2 122	265	4 064	Tanker	373	4 149	77	931	266	2 888
1952................	3 350	36 081	782	9 052	395	5 190	1937..................	1 517	12 335	426	3 643	805	6 608
Cargo	2 629	27 210	582	6 177	135	1 302	Cargo	975	7 231	275	2 286	446	3 058
Tanker..........	461	6 827	156	2 481	259	3 884	Tanker...........	357	3 900	52	604	299	3 252
1951................	3 386	36 336	988	11 245	426	5 333	1936..................	1 563	12 323	430	3 714	776	5 958
Cargo	2 650	27 376	743	7 892	176	1 721	Cargo	1 007	7 405	250	2 087	442	2 961
Tanker..........	470	6 893	199	3 129	245	3 587	Tanker	355	3 637	76	857	267	2 684
1950................	3 408	36 526	711	8 353	434	5 474	1935..................	1 637	12 809	434	3 748	709	5 425
Cargo	2 846	28 927	505	5 367	177	1 708	Cargo	1 065	7 847	253	2 096	390	2 624
Tanker..........	479	6 959	161	2 597	251	3 737	Tanker...........	355	3 615	73	850	251	2 504
1949................	3 379	36 228	1 004	11 416	382	4 628	1934..................	1 673	12 986	438	3 753	657	4 993
Cargo	2 799	28 442	813	8 626	156	1 437	Cargo	1 079	7 946	258	2 168	336	2 194
Tanker..........	501	7 177	148	2 415	222	3 178	Tanker...........	361	3 652	69	763	248	2 499
1948................	3 490	36 774	1 246	13 767	477	5 785							
Cargo	2 887	28 674	1 023	10 592	198	1 832							
Tanker..........	526	7 499	182	2 818	272	3 925							
1947 [1]..............	3 696	38 882	1 603	17 238	511	6 413							
Cargo	2 977	29 206	1 434	14 779	194	1 782							
Tanker..........	624	8 934	137	2 200	311	4 606							
1946 [2]..............	4 852	50 263	1 890	20 592	442	4 807							
Cargo	3 829	36 675	1 607	16 200	226	1 910							
Tanker..........	906	12 785	268	4 264	206	2 858							

1. Data as of December 31.
2. Data as of September 30.

Series Q 506-517. Net Tonnage Capacity of Vessels Entered and Cleared: 1826 to 1995

In thousands of net tons. For years ending September 20, 1826-1842; June 30, 1843-1918; December 31 thereafter. Excludes domestic trade. Includes Alaska, Hawaii, Puerto Rico and, beginning 1935, the Virgin Islands)

	Vessels entered						Vessels cleared					
	All ports			Seaports [1]			All ports			Seaports [1]		
Year	Total	U.S. vessels	Foreign vessels	Total	U.S. vessels	Foreign vessels	Total	U.S. vessels	Foreign vessels	Total	U.S. vessels	Foreign vessels
	506	507	508	509	510	511	512	513	514	515	516	517
1995	539 000	32 000	507 000	514 000	30 000	484 000	540 000	33 000	508 000	517 000	31 000	485 000
1994	527 000	35 000	492 000	503 000	33 000	469 000	532 000	36 000	496 000	508 000	34 000	473 000
1993	515 000	35 000	480 000	493 000	33 000	460 000	519 000	36 000	483 000	497 000	35 000	462 000
1992	515 000	37 000	478 000	493 000	36 000	457 000	519 000	38 000	481 000	496 000	37 000	460 000
1991	516 000	39 000	476 000	494 000	38 000	455 000	521 000	40 000	480 000	498 000	39 000	459 000
1990	589 000	41 000	548 000	564 000	40 000	524 000	592 000	43 000	550 000	566 000	41 000	525 000
1989	587 000	44 000	543 000	558 000	42 000	516 000	590 000	45 000	545 000	561 000	44 000	517 000
1988	556 000	47 000	509 000	527 000	46 000	481 000	561 000	49 000	512 000	531 000	47 000	484 000
1987	518 000	48 000	470 000	492 000	47 000	445 000	521 000	49 000	472 000	495 000	48 000	447 000
1986	489 000	49 000	439 000	463 000	48 000	415 000	491 000	51 000	441 000	466 000	49 000	417 000
1985	441 000	53 000	398 000	426 000	52 000	374 000	461 000	55 000	438 000	435 000	53 000	382 000
1984	459 000	53 000	406 000	429 000	51 000	378 000	468 000	54 000	414 000	414 000	51 000	387 000
1983	442 000	62 000	380 000	416 000	60 000	355 000	449 000	62 000	387 000	423 000	60 000	363 000
1982	438 000	59 000	379 000	412 000	57 000	355 000	448 000	60 000	388 000	421 000	58 000	363 000
1981	470 000	56 000	414 000	439 000	54 000	385 000	477 000	56 000	420 000	446 000	54 000	392 000
1980	492 000	52 000	440 000	460 000	50 000	410 000	487 000	54 000	433 000	456 000	51 000	405 000
1979	499 000	45 000	454 000	462 000	42 000	420 000	497 000	48 000	449 000	459 000	44 000	415 000
1978	487 000	37 000	420 000	423 000	34 000	376 000	447 000	34 000	413 000	412 000	31 000	381 000
1977	440 000	34 000	406 000	407 000	31 000	376 000	430 000	34 000	395 000	397 000	31 000	366 000
1976	401 000	33 000	368 000	370 000	31 000	339 000	404 000	34 000	370 000	374 000	32 000	342 000
1975	355 000	32 000	323 000	326 000	30 000	297 000	363 000	34 000	329 000	334 000	31 000	303 000
1974	346 000	36 000	311 000	322 000	32 000	289 000	352 000	37 000	315 000	327 000	33 000	294 000
1973	344 000	33 000	312 000	314 000	31 000	283 000	348 000	35 000	313 000	317 000	33 000	285 000
1972	295 000	25 000	271 000	267 000	23 000	244 000	300 000	27 000	273 000	271 000	25 000	246 000
1971	256 000	24 000	232 000	229 000	22 000	207 000	258 000	24 000	234 000	231 000	23 000	208 000
1970	254 154	26 239	227 915	226 666	24 234	202 431	253 136	26 953	226 183	225 925	24 898	201 027
1969	238 085	26 662	211 423	213 008	25 264	187 741	237 986	27 235	210 758	212 746	25 738	187 013
1968	229 850	30 389	199 465	203 664	27 456	176 210	230 324	31 198	199 126	204 086	28 244	175 839
1967	220 681	30 830	189 848	195 871	26 990	168 848	220 231	30 827	189 404	195 845	27 089	168 756
1966	217 894	31 487	486 407	191 684	28 621	163 063	219 437	32 738	186 699	193 433	29 925	163 507
1965	209 000	34 041	174 960	183 724	30 919	152 806	208 736	34 016	174 721	183 540	31 048	152 492
1964	199 330	34 956	164 373	174 625	30 909	143 715	202 262	35 337	166 924	177 636	31 409	146 225
1963	186 700	33 300	153 400	165 124	29 677	135 447	187 539	34 106	153 433	166 103	30 440	135 663
1962	178 334	33 774	144 560	158 606	29 963	128 644	178 953	34 165	144 788	159 330	30 337	128 993
1961	166 548	31 144	135 404	148 955	28 266	120 688	168 878	31 941	136 936	151 295	29 062	122 233
1960	162 765	30 189	132 575	145 828	26 708	119 119	166 715	31 280	135 434	149 778	27 649	122 127
1959	154 213	26 417	127 796	137 845	21 897	115 947	155 505	26 623	128 883	139 262	22 042	117 221
1958	149 097	26 842	122 255	136 291	23 642	112 648	148 816	26 449	122 366	136 102	23 324	112 778
1957	162 925	35 898	127 027	146 144	31 189	114 956	162 578	35 118	127 460	145 954	30 569	115 385
1956	147 844	36 247	111 598	130 767	31 254	99 514	148 269	36 317	111 952	131 391	31 510	99 881
1955	128 405	34 321	94 084	113 807	30 407	83 400	129 368	34 407	94 961	114 806	30 615	84 192
1954	109 524	33 860	75 664	97 198	30 133	67 065	109 899	33 579	76 321	97 674	29 969	67 706
1953	112 559	39 319	73 240	97 344	34 969	62 375	112 935	39 188	73 747	97 627	34 775	62 852
1952	116 375	45 223	71 152	101 263	40 732	60 532	114 797	43 726	71 071	99 703	39 273	60 429
1951	108 086	44 571	63 515	93 974	40 482	53 192	110 236	46 763	63 472	96 257	43 024	53 233
1950	86 629	35 376	51 251	73 451	31 757	41 693	87 829	36 043	51 778	74 785	32 510	42 269
1949	85 700	41 251	44 451	74 701	37 626	37 076	84 286	39 681	44 604	73 063	36 136	36 927
1948	90 927	47 726	43 199	76 910	43 270	33 640	89 449	45 775	43 667	75 714	41 348	34 358
1947	93 796	53 627	40 170	80 889	49 044	31 844	97 160	54 088	43 072	84 508	49 558	34 949
1946	80 258	53 045	27 213	69 520	49 143	20 378	77 225	49 124	28 101	66 376	45 113	21 263
1945	94 021	61 375	32 646	81 182	56 499	24 682	94 559	61 460	33 099	81 452	56 332	25 120
1944	81 860	48 071	33 789	66 305	42 196	24 109	87 385	53 050	34 335	71 717	46 919	24 798
1943	61 084	29 292	31 792	44 739	24 508	20 231	66 716	33 862	33 034	50 232	28 826	21 406
1942	43 942	13 611	30 331	28 258	10 326	17 932	47 706	16 354	31 352	31 976	13 149	18 827
1941	59 061	20 940	38 121	42 616	16 767	25 849	62 596	21 869	40 726	46 142	17 701	28 441

See footnotes at end of chart.

Series Q 506-517. Net Tonnage Capacity of Vessels Entered and Cleared: 1826 to 1995—Cont'd.

(In thousands of net tons. For years ending September 20, 1826-1842; June 30, 1843-1918; December 31 thereafter. Excludes domestic trade. Includes Alaska, Hawaii, Puerto Rico and, beginning 1935, the Virgin Islands)

	Vessels entered						Vessels cleared					
	All ports			Seaports [1]			All ports			Seaports [1]		
Year	Total	U.S. vessels	Foreign vessels	Total	U.S. vessels	Foreign vessels	Total	U.S. vessels	Foreign vessels	Total	U.S. vessels	Foreign vessels
	506	507	508	509	510	511	512	513	514	515	516	517
1940	58 544	19 220	39 324	45 393	15 740	29 652	62 171	20 248	41 923	48 996	16 766	32 230
1939	68 992	17 769	51 223	57 973	14 553	43 421	70 306	18 156	52 150	59 218	14 903	44 316
1938	70 516	19 020	51 496	59 223	15 899	43 324	71 286	18 829	52 456	60 064	15 742	44 322
1937	71 560	19 527	52 033	59 890	16 747	43 233	72 880	19 938	52 942	61 177	17 134	44 043
1936	65 972	20 682	45 290	55 038	17 510	37 528	66 066	20 069	45 997	55 381	16 967	38 414
1935	64 612	22 372	42 240	54 289	18 893	35 395	64 887	22 126	42 761	54 722	18 651	36 071
1934	63 787	23 192	40 594	53 132	19 186	33 946	63 702	22 799	40 903	53 162	18 901	34 261
1933	60 936	22 488	38 448	51 564	19 051	32 513	61 287	22 434	38 853	52 083	19 093	32 990
1932	64 837	24 278	40 559	55 229	20 643	34 587	64 446	23 865	40 582	54 900	20 204	34 695
1931	72 782	26 907	45 875	60 427	21 499	38 929	73 501	26 854	46 647	61 204	21 417	39 787
1930	81 253	31 866	49 387	66 499	24 620	41 879	81 307	31 560	49 747	66 500	24 154	42 346
1929	82 602	32 241	50 361	66 853	25 208	41 645	82 343	31 927	50 416	67 030	25 045	41 985
1928	80 211	31 285	48 926	62 809	22 991	39 818	80 667	31 734	48 933	63 331	23 180	40 151
1927	74 310	29 289	45 021	58 921	22 001	36 920	75 440	29 793	45 647	59 759	22 078	37 681
1926	76 933	26 890	50 043	63 759	21 091	42 668	79 041	28 532	50 509	65 583	22 234	43 349
1925	69 378	27 947	41 431	55 636	21 148	34 487	70 229	27 808	42 421	57 160	21 394	35 766
1924	68 292	29 628	38 664	54 726	22 462	32 264	68 910	30 092	38 818	55 294	22 896	32 397
1923	66 319	27 725	38 594	52 775	20 984	31 791	66 624	27 932	38 692	53 215	21 305	31 910
1922	65 191	31 738	33 453	51 701	23 633	28 068	64 839	31 759	33 080	51 799	23 755	28 044
1921	62 285	31 185	31 100	49 958	24 402	25 556	62 665	30 181	32 484	50 423	23 432	26 991
1920	64 104	32 119	31 985	51 531	26 225	25 306	67 817	34 053	33 764	54 980	27 875	27 106
1919	46 702	21 933	24 769	36 381	16 224	20 157	51 257	24 992	26 265	40 751	19 133	21 617
1918 [2]	45 456	19 284	26 173	31 101	11 256	19 845	46 014	19 206	26 808	31 869	11 280	20 589
1917	50 472	18 725	31 747	36 521	10 898	25 623	52 077	19 146	32 931	38 094	11 339	26 755
1916	51 550	17 928	33 622	37 744	9 446	28 298	52 423	17 902	34 521	38 946	9 763	29 182
1915	46 710	13 275	33 435	35 032	6 830	28 202	46 885	13 418	33 467	35 458	7 110	28 347
1914	53 389	13 730	39 659	40 052	5 436	34 616	53 183	13 740	39 443	39 743	5 185	34 558
1913	50 639	13 073	37 567	37 973	5 241	32 732	51 152	13 946	37 206	37 566	5 289	32 277
1912	46 158	11 257	34 901	34 659	4 572	30 087	46 417	11 703	34 713	34 706	4 794	29 912
1911	42 675	9 693	32 982	32 457	4 302	28 155	42 437	9 753	32 684	32 299	4 427	27 871
1910	40 236	8 888	31 347	30 917	4 214	26 703	39 706	8 809	30 897	30 510	4 196	26 314
1909	39 058	8 771	30 287	30 243	4 403	25 840	38 196	8 492	29 705	29 604	4 215	25 389
1908	38 539	7 473	30 066	30 444	4 314	26 130	38 282	8 435	29 846	30 198	4 288	25 910
1907	36 622	8 116	28 507	29 248	3 924	25 324	35 990	8 093	27 898	28 499	3 797	24 702
1906	34 155	7 613	26 543	27 401	4 023	23 379	33 784	7 581	26 204	26 970	3 923	23 047
1905	30 983	7 081	23 903	24 793	4 120	20 673	31 158	7 203	23 955	25 020	4 259	20 760
1904	29 952	6 679	23 273	24 111	3 806	20 305	30 016	6 641	23 374	24 192	3 836	20 356
1903	31 094	6 907	24 187	24 698	3 881	20 817	31 316	6 975	24 341	24 823	3 931	20 892
1902	30 654	6 961	23 693	24 361	4 020	20 342	30 444	6 822	23 623	24 242	3 956	20 287
1901	29 768	6 381	23 387	24 791	3 980	20 811	29 820	6 417	23 403	24 889	4 020	20 870
1900	28 163	6 136	22 027	23 534	3 974	19 559	28 281	6 209	22 072	23 618	4 006	19 612
1899	26 111	5 341	20 770	21 963	3 333	18 631	26 266	5 472	20 794	22 177	3 463	18 714
1898	25 579	5 240	20 339	21 700	3 362	18 338	25 748	5 111	20 637	21 892	3 231	18 661
1897	23 760	5 525	18 235	20 003	3 611	16 391	23 709	5 618	18 091	19 878	3 637	16 241
1896	20 989	5 196	15 793	17 453	3 673	13 779	21 415	5 330	16 085	17 819	3 741	14 078
1895	19 295	4 473	14 822	16 725	3 677	13 049	19 751	4 504	15 246	17 024	3 616	13 408
1894	19 990	4 655	15 335	17 025	3 649	13 376	20 272	4 740	15 532	17 306	3 747	13 560
1893	19 582	4 359	15 223	16 679	3 493	13 186	19 761	4 403	15 357	16 825	3 537	13 288
1892	21 013	4 470	16 543	18 180	3 747	14 434	21 161	4 536	16 625	18 258	3 751	14 507
1891	18 204	4 381	13 823	15 394	3 670	11 724	18 261	4 455	13 805	15 411	3 716	11 695
1890	18 107	4 083	14 024	15 366	3 405	11 961	18 149	4 067	14 082	15 429	3 390	12 039
1889	15 952	3 724	12 228	13 312	3 128	10 184	16 343	3 988	12 355	13 672	3 342	10 329
1888	15 393	3 367	12 026	12 956	2 914	10 042	15 669	3 415	12 254	13 252	2 944	10 308
1887	15 816	3 366	12 451	13 532	2 871	10 661	15 753	3 259	12 494	13 511	2 771	10 740
1886	15 136	3 232	11 904	12 230	2 762	9 468	15 328	3 303	12 024	12 413	2 806	9 607

See footnotes at end of chart.

Series Q 506-517. Net Tonnage Capacity of Vessels Entered and Cleared: 1826 to 1995—Cont'd.

(In thousands of net tons. For years ending September 20, 1826-1842; June 30, 1843-1918; December 31 thereafter. Excludes domestic trade. Includes Alaska, Hawaii, Puerto Rico and, beginning 1935, the Virgin Islands)

Year	Vessels entered						Vessels cleared					
	All ports			Seaports [1]			All ports			Seaports [1]		
	Total	U.S. vessels	Foreign vessels	Total	U.S. vessels	Foreign vessels	Total	U.S. vessels	Foreign vessels	Total	U.S. vessels	Foreign vessels
	506	507	508	509	510	511	512	513	514	515	516	517
1885	15 305	3 132	12 173	12 287	2 709	9 578	15 515	3 232	12 283	12 496	2 809	9 688
1884	15 069	3 202	11 867	12 085	2 821	9 264	15 205	3 237	11 968	12 206	2 845	9 361
1883	16 382	3 256	13 126	13 361	2 835	10 526	16 541	3 307	13 234	13 565	2 895	10 670
1882	17 601	3 341	14 260	14 656	2 968	11 688	17 757	3 318	14 439	14 846	2 936	11 911
1881	18 319	3 254	15 066	15 631	2 919	12 711	18 470	3 376	15 094	15 794	3 040	12 754
1880	18 011	3 437	14 574	15 251	3 140	12 111	18 043	3 397	14 646	15 296	3 078	12 218
1879	16 193	3 415	12 778	13 768	3 050	10 718	16 075	3 464	12 611	13 617	3 071	10 545
1878	14 464	3 642	10 821	11 531	3 009	8 521	14 808	3 872	10 935	11 844	3 196	8 647
1877	13 455	3 663	9 791	10 406	2 958	7 449	13 442	3 765	9 677	10 389	3 043	7 345
1876	12 511	3 611	8 899	9 716	2 928	6 788	12 655	3 732	8 923	9 839	3 037	6 802
1875	11 693	3 574	8 119	9 143	2 887	6 256	11 897	3 737	8 160	9 341	3 061	6 279
1874	13 092	3 894	9 198	10 010	2 915	7 095	13 189	3 982	9 207	10 058	2 961	7 097
1873	11 696	3 613	8 083	8 395	2 443	5 951	11 822	3 757	8 065	8 515	2 574	5 941
1872	10 806	3 712	7 095	7 770	2 585	5 185	10 734	3 682	7 051	7 739	2 598	5 141
1871	10 009	3 743	6 266	6 994	2 604	4 391	9 898	3 747	6 152	6 918	2 635	4 283
1870	9 156	3 486	5 670	6 270	2 452	3 818	9 169	3 507	5 662	6 362	2 530	3 832
1869	8 750	3 403	5 348	6 032	2 459	3 573	7 754	3 381	4 373	6 114	2 502	3 612
1868	8 046	3 551	4 495	5 572	2 466	3 106	8 279	3 718	4 561	5 811	2 625	3 186
1867	7 774	3 422	4 319	2 533	2 146	3 121	7 885	3 420	4 465	5 501	2 270	3 230
1866	7 782	3 372	4 410	2 008	1 891	3 117	7 822	3 383	4 438	5 161	2 030	3 131
1865	6 161	2 944	3 217	3 827	1 615	2 212	6 620	3 025	3 595	4 161	1 710	2 450
1864	6 538	3 066	3 471	4 167	1 655	2 512	6 832	3 091	3 741	4 279	1 662	2 617
1863	7 255	4 615	2 640	4 205	2 308	1 898	7 511	4 447	3 064	4 343	2 266	2 077
1862	7 363	5 118	2 245	4 191	2 629	1 562	7 339	4 962	2 377	4 205	2 568	1 637
1861	7 241	5 024	2 218	4 559	3 025	1 534	7 151	4 889	2 262	4 410	2 874	1 536
1860	8 275	5 921	2 354	5 000	3 302	1 698	8 790	6 166	2 624	5 257	3 501	1 756
1859	7 806	5 366	2 540	4 913	3 328	1 585	7 916	5 297	2 618	4 867	3 315	1 552
1858	6 605	4 396	2 209	4 338	3 051	1 587	7 803	4 490	3 313	4 436	3 128	1 309
1857	7 186	4 721	2 465	4 843	3 482	1 361	7 071	4 581	2 490	4 882	3 483	1 398
1856	6 872	4 385	2 487	4 464	3 194	1 270	7 000	4 538	2 462	4 695	. . .	. . .
1855	5 945	3 861	2 084	4 178	. . .	. . .	6 179	4 069	2 110	4 435	. . .	. . .
1854	5 884	3 752	2 132	4 343	. . .	. . .	6 019	3 911	2 108	4 524	. . .	. . .
1853	6 282	4 004	2 278	4 157	. . .	. . .	6 066	3 767	2 299	4 289	. . .	. . .
1852	5 293	3 236	2 057	3 926	. . .	. . .	5 278	3 231	2 048	. . .	. . .	. . .
1851	4 993	3 054	1 939	3 466	. . .	. . .	5 130	3 201	1 930	. . .	. . .	. . .
1850	3 749	2 573	1 176	3 013	. . .	. . .	4 361	2 633	1 728	3 167	. . .	. . .
1849	4 369	2 658	1 711	2 890	. . .	. . .	4 429	2 754	1 676	. . .	. . .	. . .
1848	3 799	2 393	7 105	2 503	. . .	. . .	3 865	2 461	1 404	. . .	. . .	. . .
1847	3 322	2 101	1 220	2 429	. . .	. . .	3 379	2 202	1 177	. . .	. . .	. . .
1846	3 111	2 151	960	2 022	. . .	. . .	3 189	2 221	968	. . .	. . .	. . .
1845	2 946	2 035	911	2 011	. . .	. . .	2 984	2 054	930	. . .	. . .	. . .
1844	2 894	1 977	917	1 897	. . .	. . .	2 918	2 011	907	. . .	. . .	. . .
1843	1 678	1 144	535	. . .	. . .	. . .	1 792	1 268	524	. . .	. . .	. . .
1842	2 243	1 510	733	. . .	. . .	. . .	2 277	1 536	740	. . .	. . .	. . .
1841	2 368	1 632	736	. . .	. . .	. . .	2 371	1 634	737	. . .	. . .	. . .
1840	2 289	1 577	712	1 788	. . .	. . .	2 353	1 647	706	1 861	. . .	. . .
1839	2 116	1 491	625	. . .	. . .	. . .	2 090	1 478	612	. . .	. . .	. . .
1838	1 895	1 303	592	. . .	. . .	. . .	2 013	1 409	604	. . .	. . .	. . .
1837	2 065	1 300	766	. . .	. . .	. . .	2 023	1 267	756	. . .	. . .	. . .
1836	1 936	1 255	680	. . .	. . .	. . .	1 990	1 316	674	. . .	. . .	. . .
1835	1 994	1 353	641	. . .	. . .	. . .	2 031	1 401	631	. . .	. . .	. . .
1834	1 643	1 075	568	. . .	. . .	. . .	1 712	1 134	578	. . .	. . .	. . .
1833	1 608	1 111	497	. . .	. . .	. . .	1 639	1 142	497	. . .	. . .	. . .
1832	1 343	950	393	. . .	. . .	. . .	1 362	975	388	. . .	. . .	. . .
1831	1 405	923	482	. . .	. . .	. . .	1 244	973	272	. . .	. . .	. . .

See footnotes at end of chart.

Series Q 506-517. Net Tonnage Capacity of Vessels Entered and Cleared: 1826 to 1995—Cont'd.

(In thousands of net tons. For years ending September 20, 1826-1842; June 30, 1843-1918; December 31 thereafter. Excludes domestic trade. Includes Alaska, Hawaii, Puerto Rico and, beginning 1935, the Virgin Islands)

Year	Vessels entered						Vessels cleared					
	All ports			Seaports [1]			All ports			Seaports [1]		
	Total	U.S. vessels	Foreign vessels	Total	U.S. vessels	Foreign vessels	Total	U.S. vessels	Foreign vessels	Total	U.S. vessels	Foreign vessels
	506	**507**	**508**	**509**	**510**	**511**	**512**	**513**	**514**	**515**	**516**	**517**
1830	1 099	967	132	...	...	...	1 105	972	133	...	...	...
1829	1 004	873	131	...	...	...	1 078	945	133	...	...	...
1828	1 019	868	150	...	...	...	1 048	897	151	...	...	...
1827	1 056	918	138	...	...	...	1 112	981	131	...	...	...
1826	1 048	942	106	...	...	...	1 052	953	99	...	...	...

1. Comprises all ports except northern border ports.
2. As of June 30; figures (in thousands of tons) for July-Dec. are as follows: Series Q 506, 25 029; series Q 507, 11 006; series Q 508, 14 023; series Q 512, 25 472; series Q 513, 11 223; and series Q 514, 14 249.

Series Q 577-590.   U.S. Scheduled Airline Industry: 1926 to 1997

(As of December 31 or for years ending December 31. Data include intra-Alaska carriers beginning 1941 for series Q 586 and Q 587; 1948 for series Q 582; and 1961 for series Q 581)

Year	Number of operators	Aircraft in service [1]	Persons employed	Revenue miles flown (1 000)	Revenue passengers carried, unduplicated [2] (1 000)	Revenue passenger-miles flown (millions)	Ton-miles flown Express and freight (1 000)	Mail (1 000)	Fuel consumed [11] (mil. gal.)	Average available seats	Average speed (m.p.h.)
	577	578	581	582	584	585	586	587	588	589	590
Domestic											
1997	...	...	586 500	...	598 900	605 400	17 959 000	...	...	...	...
1996	...	...	564 400	...	581 200	578 700	15 301 000	...	...	...	...
1995	...	...	547 000	...	547 800	540 700	14 578 000	...	...	...	...
1994	...	...	539 800	...	528 800	519 400	13 792 000	...	...	...	...
1993	...	...	537 100	...	488 500	489 700	11 944 000	...	...	...	...
1992	...	...	540 400	...	475 100	478 600	11 130 000	...	...	...	...
1991	...	...	533 600	...	452 300	448 000	10 225 000	...	...	...	...
1990	60	4 665	545 000	4 491 000	466 000	457 900	10 600 000	2 004 000	16 252	151.9	408
1989	62	4 477	507 000	4 193 000	454 000	432 700	10 275 000	1 911 000	15 624	152.1	406
1988	66	4 439	481 000	4 141 000	455 000	423 300	9 632 000	1 837 000	15 094	153.1	409
1987	68	4 231	457 000	3 988 000	448 000	404 500	8 260 000	1 758 000	14 461	152.9	413
1986	74	3 799	422 000	3 725 000	419 000	366 500	7 344 000	1 081 000	13 682	153.4	409
1985	86	2 860	355 000	3 320 000	382 000	336 400	6 020 000	1 659 000	12 603	152.5	409
1984	87	2 692	345 000	3 133 000	345 000	305 100	6 566 000	1 618 000	11 470	153.7	414
1983	84	2 618	329 000	2 809 000	319 000	281 800	6 092 000	1 480 000	10 526	154.1	415
1982	98	2 468	330 000	2 699 000	294 000	259 600	5 482 000	1 404 000	10 268	153.0	408
1981	98	2 523	350 000	2 703 000	286 000	248 800	5 686 000	1 374 000	10 810	147.2	403
1980	72	2 505	371 000	2 816 000	297 000	255 200	5 742 000	1 342 000	11 311	143.1	405
1979	52	2 466	341 000	2 791 000	317 000	262 000	5 964 000	1 225 000	11 369	139.9	406
1978	34	2 345	329 000	2 520 000	275 000	226 800	5 818 000	1 181 000	10 534	140.0	409
1977	32	2 234	314 000	2 419 000	240 000	193 200	4 109 000	1 039 000	10 296	136.9	408
1976	32	2 271	303 000	2 320 000	223 000	179 000	3 855 000	1 001 000	9 832	134.1	406
1975	33	2 260	290 000	2 241 000	205 000	162 800	4 796 000	1 109 000	9 507	130.4	403
1974	31	2 244	305 000	2 258 000	208 000	162 900	3 760 000	1 016 000	9 546	127.7	402
1973	33	2 361	312 000	2 448 000	202 000	161 900	3 692 000	1 048 000	10 671	123.8	404
1972	37	2 361	305 000	2 376 000	191 000	152 406	3 354 000	1 049 000	9 985	118.1	404
1971	38	2 389	285 000	2 378 000	173 000	132 687	3 023 000	1 154 000	9 841	115.3	405
1970	33	2 437	242 206	2 013 484	153 408	104 156	1 966 009	705 711	[11] 10 083	110.4	350
1969	33	2 423	255 386	2 000 269	158 405	102 717	1 916 472	801 416	27	109.8	394
1968	38	2 317	244 742	1 715 857	145 774	87 508	1 578 992	564 084	113	100.8	373
1967	39	2 194	223 381	1 462 240	128 479	75 487	1 314 409	405 352	223	94.4	354
1966	40	2 027	196 298	1 178 458	105 789	60 591	1 108 691	291 277	332	91.2	320
1965	40	1 896	169 952	1 088 112	92 073	51 887	943 128	225 992	448	89.2	314
1964	40	1 863	153 243	957 575	79 139	44 141	743 963	189 782	507	86.1	297
1963	40	1 832	143 112	888 793	69 366	38 457	603 725	174 439	554	83.4	287
1962	40	1 831	138 673	827 694	60 738	33 623	554 599	166 801	696	79.4	274
1961	41	1 867	136 987	795 165	56 900	31 062	454 142	150 452	743	72.9	253
1960	42	1 594	133 717	820 756	56 352	30 567	386 933	135 923	922	65.5	235
1959	39	1 596	132 042	841 925	54 955	29 308	344 728	120 308	1 142	58.7	223
1958	39	1 546	119 746	784 200	48 297	25 375	294 018	107 018	1 188	55.8	220
1957	40	1 494	119 333	791 265	48 761	25 379	268 791	100 218	1 165	53.7	215
1956	40	1 347	103 489	694 050	41 738	22 399	247 255	94 523	1 005	52.4	213
1955	42	1 212	95 548	627 336	38 025	19 852	229 966	88 751	912	51.2	208
1954	43	1 175	84 765	556 880	32 343	16 802	189 765	82 768	776	50.1	206
1953	44	1 139	84 651	525 374	28 721	14 794	179 063	74 106	692	46.1	198
1952	46	1 078	79 687	465 477	25 010	12 559	162 047	70 443	588	42.7	191
1951	49	981	72 898	411 878	22 652	10 590	144 790	64 734	...	39.6	185
1950	52	960	61 903	369 826	17 345	8 007	152 223	47 740	418	37.5	180
1949	51	913	59 886	355 501	15 081	6 752	123 603	41 889	375	35.0	179
1948	39	878	60 416	338 217	13 168	5 976	102 360	38 198	332	32.4	172
1947	27	810	58 998	325 054	12 890	6 105	64 637	33 086	294	30.0	168
1946	23	674	69 182	309 889	12 213	5 945	38 590	32 969	236	25.3	160
1945	19	421	50 313	208 969	6 576	3 360	22 175	65 103	135	19.7	155
1944	18	288	31 198	138 732	4 046	2 177	16 974	51 146	90	19.1	156

See footnotes at end of chart.

Series Q 577-590.   U.S. Scheduled Airline Industry: 1926 to 1997—Cont'd.

(As of December 31 or for years ending December 31. Data include intra-Alaska carriers beginning 1941 for series Q 586 and Q 587; 1948 for series Q 582; and 1961 for series Q 581)

Year	Number of operators	Aircraft in service [1]	Persons employed	Revenue miles flown (1 000)	Revenue passengers carried, unduplicated [2] (1 000)	Revenue passenger-miles flown (millions)	Ton-miles flown Express and freight (1 000)	Ton-miles flown Mail (1 000)	Fuel consumed [11] (mil. gal.)	Average available seats	Average speed (m.p.h.)
	577	578	581	582	584	585	586	587	588	589	590
Domestic											
1943	18	204	29 654	105 355	3 020	1 632	15 618	36 067	65	18.3	...
1942	19	186	26 910	111 341	3 137	1 418	11 896	21 167	69	17.9	...
1941	19	370	19 223	134 406	[3] 3 464	1 385	5 257	13 108	82	17.5	...
1940	19	369	15 984	110 101	[3] 2 523	1 052	3 476	10 118	66	16.5	...
1939	[4] 18	[4] 276	[4] 10 639	82 925	[3] 1 561	683	2 713	8 611	47	14.7	...
1938	[5] 16	[5] 260	[5] 9 008	68 610	[3] 1 077	480	2 182	7 449	38	13.9	...
1937	22	291	7 586	66 791	[3] 887	412	2 162	6 698	34	12.5	...
1936	24	280	7 079	64 307	...	[6] 439	1 866	5 741	31	10.7	...
1935	26	363	5 945	55 918	...	[6] 316	1 098	4 133	27	10.3	...
1934	24	423	4 201	41 526	...	[6] 190	[7] 597	[8] 2 237	19	8.9	...
1933	25	418	4 369	49 256	...	[6] 175	[7] 423	[9] 2 568	22	7.6	...
1932	32	456	4 020	45 894	...	[6] 127	[7] 290	[9] 2 701	20	6.6	...
1931	39	490	4 314	43 109	...	[6] 107	[7] 221	[9] 3 140	16	...	...
1930	43	497	2 778	32 645	...	[6] 85	[7] 101	...	12	...	...
1929	38	442	1 958	22 729	...	...	[7] 70	...	6	...	...
1928	34	268	[10] 1 496	10 528	...	...	[7] 59	...	2	...	...
1927	18	...	...	5 856	...	...	[7] 13	...	1	...	...
1926	13	...	...	4 318	...	...	[7] 1	...	1	...	...

1. Figures for 1961-1970 for domestic airlines are for total aircraft in service, domestic and international.
2. Duplication has been eliminated where the same passengers were carried on more than one route of an air carrier, but still exists where the same passengers were carried by more than one air carrier.
3. Computed by CAA from reports of duplicated revenue passengers.
4. Excludes Marine Airlines.
5. Excludes Colonial and Marine Airlines.
6. Includes nonrevenue passenger miles flown.
7. Excludes Colonial Airlines, Inc., and Hawaiian Airlines, Ltd.
8. Excludes 224 236 ton-miles flown by U.S. Army.
9. Excludes Colonial Airlines, Inc.
10. Includes employees of Pan American Airways.
11. Shows gasoline prior to 1970; jet fuel beginning in 1970.

Series Q 604-623. Airports, Aircraft, Pilots and Miles Flown: 1927 to 1997

(As of December 31 or for years ending December 31, except as noted. Includes Alaska, Hawaii and outlying areas for all years)

Year	Airports and landing fields [1]		Total civil aircraft [2]	Certified airplane pilots [3]			
	Total	Lighted		Total	Airline transport	Commercial	Private
	604	**605**	**606**	**607**	**608**	**609**	**610**
1997	18 345	4 832	200 000	616 000	131 000	125 000	248 000
1996	18 292	4 847	198 600	622 000	127 000	129 000	254 000
1995	18 224	4 838	195 500	639 000	124 000	134 000	261 000
1994	18 343	4 830	281 000	654 000	117 000	139 000	284 000
1993	18 317	4 842	279 000	665 000	117 000	143 000	284 000
1992	17 846	4 831	277 000	683 000	116 000	146 000	288 000
1991	17 581	4 811	275 500	692 000	112 000	148 000	293 000
1990	17 490	4 822	275 900	703 000	108 000	149 000	299 000
1989	17 446	4 443	274 800	700 000	102 000	145 000	293 000
1988	17 327	4 890	272 700	694 000	97 000	143 000	300 000
1987	17 015	4 922	275 100	700 000	91 000	144 000	301 000
1986	16 582	4 954	275 700	709 000	87 000	148 000	306 000
1985	16 318	4 941	274 900	710 000	83 000	152 000	311 000
1984	16 075	4 889	271 500	722 000	79 000	155 000	322 000
1983	16 029	4 878	264 900	718 000	75 000	159 000	319 000
1982	15 831	4 844	259 000	733 000	73 000	165 000	322 000
1981	15 476	4 795	261 600	764 000	70 000	169 000	329 000
1980	15 161	4 738	259 400	827 000	70 000	183 000	357 000
1979	14 746	4 631	251 500	815 000	64 000	182 000	343 000
1978	14 574	4 567	236 800	799 000	56 000	186 000	338 000
1977	14 117	4 483	215 300	784 000	50 000	189 000	327 000
1976	13 770	4 362	205 900	744 000	45 000	188 000	309 000
1975	13 251	4 171	196 300	728 000	43 000	189 000	306 000
1974	13 062	3 999	188 000	734 000	41 000	192 000	306 000
1973	12 700	3 880	179 800	715 000	38 000	182 000	299 000
1972	12 405	3 827	170 800	751 000	38 000	196 000	321 000
1971	12 070	3 759	166 800	741 000	36 000	192 000	313 000
1970	11 261	3 554	154 450	732 729	34 430	186 821	303 779
1969	11 050	3 430	190 749	720 028	31 442	176 585	299 491
1968	10 470	3 312	179 285	691 695	28 607	164 458	281 728
1967	10 126	3 149	166 598	617 931	25 817	150 135	253 312
1966	9 673	2 988	155 132	548 757	23 917	131 539	222 427
1965	9 566	2 878	142 078	479 770	22 440	116 665	196 393
1964	9 490	2 773	137 189	431 041	21 572	108 428	175 574
1963	8 814	2 672	129 975	378 700	20 269	96 341	152 209
1962	8 084	2 481	124 273	830 220	23 220	275 495	531 505
1961	7 715	2 299	117 904	804 707	22 042	268 707	513 958
1960	6 881	2 133	111 580	783 232	20 985	262 437	499 810
1959	6 426	1 943	105 309	758 368	19 364	255 377	483 627
1958	6 018	1 809	98 893	731 078	18 303	245 541	467 234
1957	6 412	1 713	93 189	702 519	16 900	237 149	448 470
1956	7 028	1 399	87 531	669 079	15 295	221 096	432 688
1955	6 839	1 247	85 320	643 201	13 700	211 142	418 359
1954	6 977	1 108	92 067	613 695	13 341	201 441	398 913
1953	[4] 6 760	[4] 1 050	91 102	585 974	12 757	195 363	377 854
1952	6 042	1 858	89 313	581 218	11 357	193 575	376 286
1951	6 237	. . .	88 545	580 574	10 813	197 900	371 861
1950	6 403	1 670	92 809	. . .	. . .	. . .	. . .
1949	6 484	1 480	92 622	525 174	9 025	187 769	328 380
1948	6 414	1 521	95 997	[5] 491 306	[5] 7 762	[5] 176 846	[5] 306 699
1947	5 759	1 447	94 821	[6] 433 241	[6] 7 059	[6] 181 912	[6] 244 270
1946	4 490	1 019	81 002	400 061	7 654	203 251	189 156
1945	4 026	1 007	37 789	296 895	5 815	162 873	128 207
1944	3 427	964	27 919	183 383	3 046	68 449	111 888
1943	2 769	859	27 180	173 206	2 315	63 940	106 951
1942	2 809	700	27 170	166 626	2 177	55 760	108 689
1941	2 484	662	26 013	129 947	1 587	34 578	93 782
1940	2 331	776	17 928	69 829	1 431	18 791	49 607

See footnotes at end of chart.

PROPERTY OF GERMANNA
COMMUNITY COLLEGE LIBRARY

Series Q 604-623.   Airports, Aircraft, Pilots and Miles Flown: 1927 to 1997—Cont'd.

(As of December 31 or for years ending December 31, except as noted. Includes Alaska, Hawaii and outlying areas for all years)

Year	Airports and landing fields [1]		Total civil aircraft [2]	Certified airplane pilots [3]			
	Total	Lighted		Total	Airline transport	Commercial	Private
	604	**605**	**606**	**607**	**608**	**609**	**610**
1939..............................	2 280	735	13 772	33 706	1 197	11 677	20 832
1938..............................	2 374	719	11 159	22 983	1 159	7 839	13 985
1937..............................	2 299	720	10 836	17 681	1 064	6 411	10 206
1936..............................	2 342	705	9 229	15 952	842	7 288	7 822
1935..............................	2 368	698	9 072	14 805	736	7 362	6 707
1934..............................	2 297	664	8 322	13 949	676	7 484	5 789
1933..............................	2 188	626	9 284	13 960	554	7 635	5 771
1932..............................	2 117	701	10 324	18 594	[7] 330	7 967	10 297
1931..............................	2 093	680	10 780	17 739	. . .	8 513	9 226
1930..............................	1 782	640	9 818	15 280	. . .	7 847	7 433
1929..............................	1 550	. . .	9 922	10 430	. . .	6 165	4 265
1928..............................	1 364	. . .	5 104	4 887	. . .	. . .	. . .
1927..............................	1 036	. . .	2 740	1 572	. . .	. . .	. . .

1. Includes seaplane bases, heliports, and beginning 1954, military fields having joint civil-military use. Prior to 1954, all military fields are included.
2. 1946-1952 includes gliders. Beginning 1950 and until 1994, includes active and inactive aircraft; 1995 to 1997, active aircraft only.
3. Beginning 1963, data are for active certified airplane pilots only. Also beginning 1963, total includes student, helicopter, glider, and other pilots, not shown separately.
4. As of Mar. 1, 1954.
5. As of May 1, 1949.
6. As of Apr. 1, 1948.
7. Airline transport rating became effective May 5, 1932.

Series Q 624-637.   Air Transportation Accidents: 1927 to 1998

Year	Domestic scheduled air carriers [1,2] Total accidents	Number of fatal accidents	Total passenger fatalities	Year	Domestic scheduled air carriers [1,2] Total accidents	Number of fatal accidents	Total passenger fatalities	Year	Domestic scheduled air carriers [1,2] Total accidents	Number of fatal accidents	Total passenger fatalities
	624	625	626		624	625	626		624	625	626
1998	48	1	1	1973	32	6	217	1948	56	5	83
1997	49	4	8	1972	43	7	186	1947	44	8	199
1996	38	5	380	1971	39	6	194	1946	33	9	75
1995	36	3	168	1970	31	1	X	1945	40	8	76
1994	20	4	239	1969	37	7	132	1944	30	5	48
1993	23	1	1	1968	44	11	258	1943	23	2	22
1992	16	4	33	1967	43	8	226	1942	23	5	55
1991	25	4	62	1966	50	4	59	1941	27	4	35
1990	22	6	39	1965	55	6	205	1940	30	3	35
1989	25	8	131	1964	45	6	106	1939	28	2	9
1988	28	3	285	1963	39	4	48	1938	23	5	25
1987	32	4	231	1962	35	5	158	1937	42	5	40
1986	21	2	5	1961	56	5	124	1936	65	8	44
1985	17	4	197	1960	62	[3] 10	326	1935	58	8	15
1984	14	1	4	1959	61	9	209	1934	71	8	17
1983	23	4	15	1958	42	4	114	1933	100	9	8
1982	15	3	233	1957	44	4	32	1932	108	16	19
1981	25	4	4	1956	55	4	143	1931	118	13	25
1980	15	X	X	1955	[4] 45	8	156	1930	88	9	24
1979	18	5	352	1954	[5] 49	4	16	1929	124	21	14
1978	19	4	16	1953	37	5	86	1928	85	11	14
1977	18	2	75	1952	44	6	46	1927	25	4	1
1976	21	2	36	1951	45	11	142				
1975	29	2	122	1950	39	4	96				
1974	43	7	460	1949	35	8	96				

X Represents zero.
1. From 1927 to 1994, includes scheduled revenue operators only. Beginning 1995, including all flights by U.S. air carriers operating under 14 CFR 121.
2. Figures between 1980 and 1990 represent both domestic and international flights.
3. Includes two midair collisions nonfatal to air carrier occupants.
4. Excludes sabotage disaster at Longmont, Colo., on Nov. 1, 1955 in which five crew members and 39 passengers were fatally injured.
5. Includes one ground collision between two air carrier aircrafts, one in scheduled passenger service and one in other revenue operations.

Series QQ 1.   Freight Carried on Major U.S. Waterways: 1975 to 1997

(In millions of tons [3.2 represents 3 200 000])

Item	1975	1980	1985	1990	1993	1994	1995	1996	1997
Atlantic intracoastal waterway	3.2	4.0	3.1	4.2	3.8	3.7	3.5	4.3	3.6
Great Lakes	193.8	183.5	148.1	167.1	159.6	175.3	177.7	181.8	188.6
Gulf intracoastal waterway	97.0	94.5	102.5	115.5	114.9	117.6	117.9	118.0	118.1
Mississippi River system [1]	453.4	584.2	527.8	659.6	660.4	693.3	710.1	701.8	707.1
Mississippi River mainstream	311.2	441.5	384.0	475.6	475.1	496.8	520.2	505.6	504.7
Ohio River system [2]	171.4	179.3	203.9	260.0	257.2	270.5	267.6	270.9	274.9
Columbia River	38.1	49.2	42.4	51.4	51.2	50.9	57.1	51.2	52.7
Snake River	2.0	5.1	3.5	4.8	5.3	5.9	6.8	5.7	6.1

1. Main channels and all tributaries of the Mississippi, Illinois, Missouri and Ohio Rivers.
2. Main channels and all navigable tributaries and embayments of the Ohio, Tennessee, and Cumberland Rivers.

SOURCE: U.S. Army Corps of Engineers, Waterborne Commerce of the United States, annual.

Series QQ 2.   U.S. Aircraft Shipments: 1980 to 1998

(Value in millions of dollars [18 929 represents $18 929 000 000])

Year	Total		Civil						Military	
			Large transports		General aviation [1]		Helicopters			
	Units	Value	Units	Value	Units	Value	Units	Value	Units	Value
1980	14 677	18 929	387	9 895	11 877	2 486	1 366	656	1 047	5 892
1985	3 610	27 269	278	8 448	2 029	1 431	384	506	919	16 884
1990	3 321	38 585	521	22 215	1 144	2 007	603	254	1 053	14 109
1993	2 585	41 166	408	24 133	964	2 144	258	113	955	14 776
1994	2 309	36 568	309	18 124	928	2 357	308	185	764	15 902
1995	2 436	33 658	256	15 263	1 077	2 842	292	194	811	15 359
1996	2 232	36 247	269	17 564	1 130	3 127	278	193	555	15 363
1997, est.	2 814	45 315	374	25 810	1 569	4 674	346	231	525	14 600
1998, est.	3 400	56 150	530	37 000	2 030	5 300	340	240	500	13 610

1. Excludes off-the-shelf military aircraft.

SOURCE: U.S. Department of Commerce International Trade Administration, Internet site <http://www.ita.doc.gov/industry/tai/green/trends.htm>.

Series QQ 3. Top 40 Airports in 1997—Passengers Enplaned: 1987 and 1997

(In thousands [448 914 represents 448 914 000], except rank. For calendar year. Airports ranked by total passengers enplaned 1997)

Airport	1987 Total	1987 Rank	1997 Total	1997 Rank	Airport	1987 Total	1987 Rank	1997 Total	1997 Rank
All airports, total	448,914	...	574 612	...	New York (John F. Kennedy), NY	10 140	10	9 731	20
Top 40 airports	327 563	...	445 113	...	Philadelphia, PA	6 603	23	9 714	21
Atlanta (Hartsfield Intl), GA	22 649	2	32 677	1	Salt Lake City, UT	4 729	28	9 427	22
Chicago (O'Hare), IL	26 122	1	31 123	2	Pittsburgh, PA	8 156	16	9 224	23
Dallas/Ft. Worth, TX	19 905	3	27 256	3	Honolulu, HI	7 773	17	8 939	24
Los Angeles, CA	18 970	4	22 596	4	Cincinnati, OH	3 265	35	7 638	25
San Francisco, CA	13 117	6	16 858	5	Washington (National), DC	7 113	18	7 010	26
Denver, CO	15 594	5	16 006	6	San Diego, CA	4 901	27	6 719	27
Detroit (Wayne County), MI	9 254	13	14 773	7	Baltimore, MD	4 010	31	6 311	28
Phoenix (Sky Harbor Intl), AZ	8 785	14	14 650	8	Portland, OR	2 834	39	6 233	29
Las Vegas (McCarran Intl), NV	6 836	21	14 011	9	Tampa, FL	4 682	29	5 901	30
St. Louis (Lambert-St Louis), MO	9 727	11	13 956	10	Cleveland, OH	3 103	36	5 580	31
Newark, NJ	11 289	8	13 783	11	Ft. Lauderdale, FL	3 929	33	5 426	32
Minneapolis/St. Paul, MN	8 310	15	13 775	12	Kansas City, MO	4 481	30	5 143	33
Houston (Intercontinental), TX	6 929	20	12 708	13	Washington (Dulles Intl), DC	4 917	26	4 970	34
Miami, FL	9 342	12	12 073	14	San Jose, CA	2 807	40	4 874	35
Seattle-Tacoma, WA	6 826	22	11 758	15	San Juan, PR	2 995	37	4 721	36
Orlando, FL	7 075	19	11 745	16	Chicago (Midway), IL	2 541	41	4 392	37
Boston (Logan Intl), MA	10 255	9	10 453	17	Oakland, CA	1 918	54	4 378	38
Charlotte (Douglas Municipal), NC	6 021	24	10 358	18	New Orleans, LA	3 311	34	4 199	39
New York (La Guardia), NY	11 326	7	9 868	19	Memphis, TN	5 023	25	4 156	40

SOURCE: U.S. Bureau of Transportation Statistics, Office of Airline Information, Airport Activity Statistics of Certificates Route Air Carriers, Calendar Year 1997 and the Federal Aviation Administration Airport Activity Statistics, 1987.

Series QQ 4. Petroleum Pipeline Companies—Characteristics: 1980 to 1997

([173 represents 173 000]. Covers pipeline companies operating in interstate commerce and subject to jurisdiction of Federal Energy Regulatory Commission)

Item	Unit	1980	1985	1990	1992	1993	1994	1995	1996	1997
Miles of pipeline, total	1 000	173	171	168	164	164	159	177	169	160
Gathering lines	1 000	36	35	32	29	29	30	35	32	31
Trunk lines	1 000	136	136	136	136	135	128	142	137	130
Total deliveries	Mil. bbl	10 600	10 745	11 378	11 447	12 219	12 159	12 862	12 635	12 481
Crude oil	Mil. bbl	6 405	6 239	6 563	6 541	6 708	6 785	6 952	6 975	6 795
Products	Mil. bbl	4 195	4 506	4 816	4 906	5 511	5 373	5 910	5 660	5 686
Total trunk line traffic	Bil. bbl-miles	3 405	3 342	3 500	3 428	3 051	3 566	3 619	3 734	3 683
Crude oil	Bil. bbl-miles	1 948	1 842	1 891	1 853	1 382	1 823	1 899	1 912	1 901
Products	Bil. bbl-miles	1 458	1 500	1 609	1 575	1 669	1 743	1 720	1 822	1 782
Carrier property value	Mil. dol	19 752	21 605	25 828	27 106	31 625	26 363	27 460	28 043	30 655
Operating revenues	Mil. dol	6 356	7 461	7 149	7 154	6 931	7 281	7 711	7 321	7 215
Net income	Mil. dol	1 912	2 431	2 340	2 061	1 763	2 148	2 670	2 372	2 255

SOURCE: PennWell Publishing Co., Houston, Texas, Oil & Gas Journal, annual (copyright).

Series QQ 5.   Cost of Owning and Operating an Automobile: 1980 to 1997

Item	Unit	1980	1990	1992	1993	1994	1995	1996	1997
Cost per mile [1]	Cents	27.95	40.96	45.77	45.14	46.65	48.91	51.43	53.08
Cost per 10 000 miles [1]	Dollars	2 795	4 096	4 577	4 514	4 665	4 891	5 143	5 308
Variable cost	Cents/mile	7.62	8.40	9.10	9.30	9.20	10.00	10.10	10.80
Gas and oil	Cents/mile	5.86	5.40	6.00	6.00	5.60	6.00	5.90	6.60
Maintenance	Cents/mile	1.12	2.10	2.20	2.40	2.50	2.60	2.80	2.80
Tires	Cents/mile	0.64	0.90	0.90	0.90	1.10	1.40	1.40	1.40
Fixed cost	Dollars	. . .	. . .	3 667	3 584	3 745	3 891	4 133	4 228
Insurance	Dollars	490	675	747	724	697	716	782	809
License and registration	Dollars	82	165	179	183	204	211	229	220
Depreciation	Dollars	1 038	2 357	2 780	2 883	2 988	3 099	3 208	3 268
Finance charge	Dollars	423	680	832	696	695	729	778	793

1. Beginning 1990, not comparable to previous data.

SOURCE: American Automobile Manufacturers Association Inc., Detroit, MI, Motor Vehicle Facts and Figures, annual (copyright).

Series QQ 6.   Domestic Motor Fuel Consumption, by Type of Vehicle: 1970 to 1996

(Comprises all fuel types used for propulsion of vehicles under state motor fuels laws. Excludes Federal purchases for military use. Minus sign (-) indicates decrease)

Year	Fuel consumption					Avg. fuel consumption per vehicle (gal.)			Avg. miles per gallon		
	All vehicles (bil. gal.)	Aug. annual percent change [1]	Cars [2] (bil. gal.)	Buses [3] (bil. gal.)	Trucks [4] (bil. gal.)	Cars [2]	Buses [3]	Trucks [4]	Cars [2]	Buses [3]	Trucks [4]
1970	92.3	5.4	67.7	0.8	11.3	688	2 172	2 467	13.5	5.5	5.5
1975	109.0	2.5	74.1	1.1	14.6	619	2 279	2 722	14.0	5.8	5.6
1980	115.0	-5.9	70.0	1.0	20.0	507	1 926	3 447	16.0	6.0	5.4
1981	114.5	-0.4	69.1	1.1	20.3	496	1 938	3 565	16.4	5.9	5.3
1982	113.4	-0.9	69.1	1.0	20.4	496	1 756	3 647	16.8	5.9	5.5
1983	116.1	2.4	70.3	0.9	20.8	497	1 507	3 769	17.0	5.9	5.6
1984	118.7	2.3	70.6	0.8	21.4	495	1 398	3 967	17.3	5.7	5.7
1985	121.3	2.2	71.5	0.8	21.4	505	1 405	3 570	17.5	5.4	5.8
1986	125.2	3.2	73.2	0.9	21.8	507	1 496	3 821	17.4	5.3	5.8
1987	127.5	1.8	73.3	0.9	22.5	500	1 527	3 937	18.0	5.8	5.9
1988	130.1	2.0	73.3	0.9	22.9	487	1 524	3 736	18.7	5.8	6.0
1989	131.9	1.4	73.9	0.9	23.5	486	1 519	3 776	18.9	6.0	6.1
1990	130.8	-0.8	69.6	0.9	24.5	461	1 428	3 953	20.2	6.4	6.0
1991	128.6	-1.7	64.3	0.9	25.0	443	1 369	4 047	21.1	6.7	6.0
1992	132.9	3.3	65.4	0.9	25.5	455	1 362	4 210	20.9	6.6	6.0
1993	137.3	3.3	67.0	0.9	26.2	462	1 420	4 309	20.5	6.6	6.1
1994	140.8	2.5	67.9	1.0	27.7	462	1 438	4 102	20.7	6.6	6.1
1995	143.8	2.1	68.1	1.0	29.0	530	1 412	4 315	21.1	6.6	6.1
1996	146.7	2.0	68.9	1.0	29.5	531	1 414	4 205	21.3	6.6	6.2

1. From prior year, except 1970, change from 1965.
2. Includes taxicabs. The format used to report some vehicle types was changed. In previous years, some other two-axle four-tire vehicles were included in the passenger car category. Other two-axle four-tire vehicles are now separate from the truck category.
3. Includes school buses.
4. Includes combinations.

SOURCE: U.S. Federal Highway Administration, Highway Statistics Summary to 1985, and Highway Statistics, annual.

Series QQ 7. Motor Vehicle Production and Trade: 1980 to 1996

(8 010 represents 8 010 000)

Item	Unit	1980	1990	1991	1992	1993	1994	1995	1996
United States....................................	1 000..........	8 010	9 784	8 811	9 702	10 898	12 263	11 985	11 799
Passenger car production	1 000..........	6 376	6 078	5 439	5 664	5 981	6 614	6 351	6 083
Truck and bus production........................	1 000..........	1 634	3 706	3 372	4 038	4 917	5 649	5 635	5 716
Imports:									
Passenger cars (new) [1,2]	1 000..........	3 116	3 945	3 736	3 575	3 808	4 097	4 114	4 064
Canada	1 000..........	595	1 220	1 196	1 200	1 468	1 591	1 678	1 688
Germany, Federal Republic of	1 000..........	339	245	172	206	184	188	207	234
Japan	1 000..........	1 992	1 868	1 789	1 637	1 597	1 593	1 387	1 191
Trucks and buses (new) [2]	1 000..........	747	766	716	777	722	708	662	688
Japan	1 000..........	483	302	283	197	154	170	90	52
All-terrain vehicles......................	1 000..........	. . .	100	. . .	. . .	. . .	. . .	. . .	. . .
Motorcycles, total [3]	1 000..........	1 120	169	. . .	. . .	. . .	. . .	. . .	. . .
Import value:									
Passenger cars (new) [1]	Mil. dol.	16 675	45 716	45 564	46 729	52 208	61 367	64 526	66 916
Trucks and buses, (new) [1]	Mil. dol.	1 985	8 155	8 221	10 000	10 104	10 909	11 792	12 381
Motorcycles [3,4]	Mil. dol.	1 142	361	. . .	. . .	. . .	. . .	. . .	. . .
Exports, number:									
Passenger cars (new) [1]	1 000..........	617	794	755	851	864	1 019	989	974
Trucks and buses (new) exports..................	1 000..........	186	159	208	161	181	274	254	316
Export value [1,5]	Mil. dol.	16 015	38 086	. . .	. . .	. . .	. . .	. . .	. . .
Passenger cars (new) [5]	Mil. dol.	3 932	9 708	9 886	11 893	12 476	14 591	14 251	14 392
Trucks and buses (new) [5]	Mil. dol.	2 977	2 845	3 388	3 073	3 399	5 238	5 209	6 246
Parts and accessories [6]	Mil. dol.	9 106	24 996	. . .	. . .	. . .	. . .	. . .	. . .
Factory sales:									
Passenger cars	1 000..........	6 400	6 050	5 407	5 685	5 962	6 549	6 310	6 140
Trucks and buses	1 000..........	1 667	3 725	3 387	4 062	4 895	5 640	5 713	5 776
Retail sales:									
Passenger cars (new) [1]	1 000..........	8 979	9 300	8 175	8 213	8 518	8 991	8 635	8 527
Domestics [7]	1 000..........	6 581	6 897	6 137	6 277	6 742	7 255	7 129	7 254
Imports [8]........................	1 000..........	2 398	2 403	2 038	1 937	1 776	1 735	1 506	1 273
Trucks and buses [9]	1 000..........	2 232	4 261	3 606	4 247	5 000	5 658	5 691	6 132
Light duty (up to 14 000 GVW) [10]..............	1 000..........	1 964	3 984	3 621	4 264	5 015	5 673	5 703	. . .
Med. duty (14 001-26 000 GVW) [10]...........	1 000..........	92	71	50	57	64	69	80	. . .
Heavy duty (over 26 000 GVW) [10]............	1 000..........	176	207	171	192	239	284	308	. . .
Under 6 000 pounds	1 000..........	985	2 866	2 719	3 212	3 754	4 132	4 031	4 398
Utility	1 000..........	51	490	549	666	721	1 130	1 258	1 392
Van........................	1 000..........	79	31	17	21	18	12	12	18
Minivan (cargo)	1 000..........	. . .	83	66	63	70	82	73	64
Station wagon (truck chassis)................	1 000..........	. . .	112	110	201	321	-	-	-
Mini-passenger carrier	1 000..........	. . .	750	706	840	1 002	1 132	1 113	1 098
6 000 to 10 000 pounds [11]	1 000..........	975	1 097	876	1 021	1 232	1 506	1 631	1 690
Utility	1 000..........	108	68	37	51	60	72	144	243
Van........................	1 000..........	172	254	203	241	279	275	274	254
Pickup, conventional	1 000..........	546	568	476	524	647	883	967	936
Station wagon (truck chassis)................	1 000..........	39	85	55	80	115	125	109	137
10 001 pounds and over	1 000..........	271	298	242	275	330	388	428	. . .

- Represents zero.
1. Based on data from U.S. Dept. of Commerce.
2. Includes other countries, not shown separately.
3. Source: Motorcycle Industry Council, Inc., Irvine, CA. Data from U.S. Dept. of Commerce. Excludes mopeds/motorized bicycles and all-terrain vehicles. Excludes moped imports (motorcycle imports less than 51 cc's) from all countries (except Japan).
4. Represents c.i.f. value.
5. Covers assembled and unassembled vehicles.
6. Includes rubber tires and tubes and used vehicles.
7. Includes domestic models produced in Canada and Mexico.
8. Excludes domestic models produced in Canada.
9. Excludes motorcoaches and light-duty imports from foreign manufactures. Includes imports sold by franchised dealers of U.S. manufacturers. Starting in 1987, includes sales of trucks over 10 000 lbs. GVW by foreign manufacturers.
10. Gross vehicle weight (fully loaded vehicle).
11. Includes vehicles, not shown separately.

Series QQ 8. Volume of Domestic Intercity Freight and Passenger Traffic, by Type of Transport: 1980 to 1997

(Freight traffic in bil. ton-miles; passenger traffic in bil. passenger-miles. A ton-mile is the movement of 1 ton [2 000 pounds] of freight for the distance of 1 mile. A passenger-mile is the movement of one passenger for the distance of 1 mile. Comprises public and private traffic, both revenue and nonrevenue)

Type of transport	Traffic volume						Percent distribution					
	1980	1985	1990	1995	1996	1997	1980	1985	1990	1995	1996	1997
Freight traffic, total	2 487	2 458	2 895	3 407	3 540	3 622	100.0	100.0	100.0	100.0	100.0	100.0
Railroads.............................	932	895	1 091	1 375	1 426	1 421	37.5	38.0	35.6	37.9	37.6	38.1
Truck:												
ICC truck	242	250	311	401	428	466	9.7	9.9	10.4	11.0	11.3	11.8
Non-ICC truck.....................	313	360	424	520	549	585	12.6	11.8	14.9	15.1	15.6	16.0
Water:												
Rivers/canals.....................	311	306	390	406	408	413	12.5	12.8	13.0	13.3	13.0	12.0
Great Lakes.....................	96	76	85	91	90	95	3.9	4.0	2.7	2.5	2.5	2.7
Oil pipelines	588	564	584	601	631	628	23.6	23.2	23.1	19.9	19.5	19.1
Domestic airways [1]	5	7	10	13	13	14	0.2	0.2	0.3	0.3	0.4	0.4
Passenger traffic, total..............	1 468	1 636	2 034	2 337	2 405	2 476	100.0	100.0	100.0	100.0	100.0	100.0
Private automobiles	1 210	1 310	1 639	1 881	1 917	1 968	82.5	82.7	79.4	81.3	81.3	81.3
Domestic airways [2]	15	12	13	10	11	13	1.0	14.7	-	0.6	0.5	0.5
Air, public carrier...........................	204	278	346	404	435	453	13.9	-	-	16.3	16.5	16.5
Bus [3].................................	27	24	23	28	29	30	1.9	1.8	1.4	1.1	1.1	1.1
Railroads [4]...........................	11	11	13	14	13	14	0.7	0.7	0.7	0.7	0.7	0.6

- Represents zero.
1. Revenue service only for scheduled and nonscheduled carriers, with small section 418 all-cargo carriers included. Includes express mail, and excess baggage.
2. Includes general aviation (mostly private business) flying.
3. Excludes school and urban transit buses.
4. Includes intercity (Amtrak) and rail commuter service.

SOURCE: Eno Transportation Foundation, Inc., Lansdowne VA, Transportation in America, annual (copyright).

Series QQ 9. Highway Mileage, Vehicle Miles of Travel, Accidents, and Fatalities, 1980 to 1997, and by Type of Highway System, 1997

Year and type of system	Highway mileage (1 000)	Vehicle miles of travel (bil.)	Daily vehicle of highway miles per mile	Fatal accidents		Nonfatal injury accidents		Fatalities [2]	
				Number	Rate [1]	Number (1 000)	Rate [1]	Number	Rate [1]
1980.............................	3 857	1 527	1 082	45 284	2.96	2 008	131	51 091	3.35
1985.............................	3 862	1 774	1 259	39 168	2.21	2 219	125	43 825	2.47
1986.............................	3 880	1 835	1 298	41 062	2.23	2 254	123	46 087	2.51
1987.............................	3 874	1 921	1 361	41 434	2.15	2 294	119	46 390	2.41
1988.............................	3 871	2 026	1 430	42 119	2.08	2 302	114	47 087	2.32
1989.............................	3 877	2 096	1 489	40 718	1.93	2 384	113	45 582	2.16
1990.............................	3 880	2 148	1 516	39 779	1.85	2 501	116	44 529	2.07
1991.............................	3 889	2 172	1 530	36 895	1.70	2.210	102	41 462	. . .
1992.............................	3 902	2 240	1 568	34 928	1.56	2 216	99	39 235	1.75
1993.............................	3 905	2 297	1 611	35 750	1.56	. . .	. . .	40 115	1.75
1994.............................	3 907	2 360	1 655	36 223	1.53	. . .	. . .	40 676	1.72
1995.............................	3 912	2 423	. . .	37 221	1.54	2 335	96	41 798	1.73
1996.............................	3 919	2 482	. . .	37 351	1.50	2 411	97	41 907	1.69
1997.............................	3 945	2 560	. . .	37 280	1.46	2 400	94	41 967	1.64

1. Rate per 100 million vehicle miles of travel.
2. Represents fatalities occurring within 30 days of accident. Excludes nontraffic accidents which, for example, occur outside the rights-of-way or other boundaries of roads that are open for public use.

SOURCE: U.S. Federal Highway Administration, Fatal and Injury Accident Rates on Public Roads in the United States, annual.

Series QQ 10. Motor Vehicle Registrations: 1980 to 1997

(In thousands [155 796 represents 155 796 000]. Compiled principally from information obtained from state authorities, but it was necessary to draw on other sources and to make numerous estimates in order to complete series. Includes Alaska and Hawaii)

Item	1980	1990	1993	1994	1995	1996	1997
All motor vehicles......................	155 796	188 798	194 063	198 045	201 530	206 365	207 754
Private and commercial	153 265	185 541	190 643	194 532	197 941	202 714	204 079
Publicly owned..............................	2 531	3 257	3 421	3 514	3 589	3 651	3 674
Automobiles [1].....................................	121 601	133 700	127 327	127 883	128 387	129 728	129 749
Private and commercial	120 743	132 164	125 844	126 397	126 900	128 439	128 450
Publicly owned..............................	857	1 536	1 484	1 486	1 487	1 289	1 299
Buses..	529	627	654	670	686	697	698
Private and commercial	254	275	276	283	288	291	294
Publicly owned..............................	275	351	378	388	398	406	403
Trucks [1]...	33 667	54 470	66 082	69 491	72 458	75 940	77 307
Private and commercial	32 268	53 101	64 523	67 852	70 754	73 984	75 335
Publicly owned..............................	1 399	1 369	1 559	1 639	1 704	1 956	1 972

1. Trucks include pickups, panels and delivery vans. Beginning 1985, personal passenger vans, passenger minivans and utility-type vehicles are no longer included in automobiles but are included in trucks.

SOURCE: U.S. Federal Highway Administration, Highway Statistics, annual.

Series QQ 11. Motor Vehicle Travel, by Type of Vehicle and by Speed: 1970 to 1997

(Travel in billions of vehicle-miles, except as indicated [1 110 represents 1 110 000 000 000]. Travel estimates based on automatic traffic recorder data. Speed trend data for 1970 were collected by several state highway agencies, normally during summer months; beginning Oct. 1975, all states have monitored speeds at locations on several highway systems Monitoring Program)

Year	Vehicle-miles of travel (bil.)				Avg. miles per vehicle (1 000)			Motor vehicle speed on rural interstate				
					Passenger vehicles			Citations recorded (1 000) [2]	Avg. speed (miles per hour)	Percent of vehicles exceeding-		
	Total	Cars [1]	Buses	Trucks	Cars [1]	Buses	Trucks			55 mph	60 mph	65 mph
1970..............................	1 110	917	4.5	186	10.3	12.0	9.9	200	63.8	87	69	44
1980..............................	1 527	1 122	6.1	291	8.8	11.5	10.4	667	57.5	66	25	7
1985..............................	1 775	1 256	4.5	391	9.4	7.5	10.5	8 449	59.5	75	44	17
1986..............................	1 835	1 280	4.7	424	9.5	7.9	10.8	8 549	59.7	76	46	18
1987..............................	1 921	1 325	5.3	457	9.7	8.9	11.1	7 992	59.7	74	46	19
1988..............................	2 026	1 380	5.5	502	10.0	8.9	11.5	7 566	59.5	74	46	19
1989..............................	2 096	1 412	5.7	536	10.2	9.1	11.7	7 488	60.1	77	49	22
1990..............................	2 144	1 418	5.7	575	10.3	9.1	11.9	7 511	60.4	78	50	23
1991..............................	2 172	1 367	5.8	649	10.3	9.1	12.2	7 594	59.9	76	48	21
1992..............................	2 247	1 381	5.8	707	10.6	9.0	12.4	7 004	61.2	81	56	28
1993..............................	2 296	1 385	6.1	746	10.5	9.4	12.4	6 433	60.8	78	51	24
1994..............................	2 358	1 416	6.4	765	10.8	9.6	12.2	...	...	...	...	...
1995..............................	2 423	1 448	6.4	790	11.0	9.3	12.0	...	...	...	...	...
1996..............................	2 486	1 480	6.6	817	13.9	9.4	11.8	...	...	...	...	...
1997..............................	2 560	1 512	6.8	850	14.2	9.8	12.1	...	...	...	...	...

1. Includes motorcycles.
2. Citations issued for 55 mph violations.

SOURCE: U.S. Federal Highway Administration, Highway Statistics Summary, annual.

COMMUNICATIONS

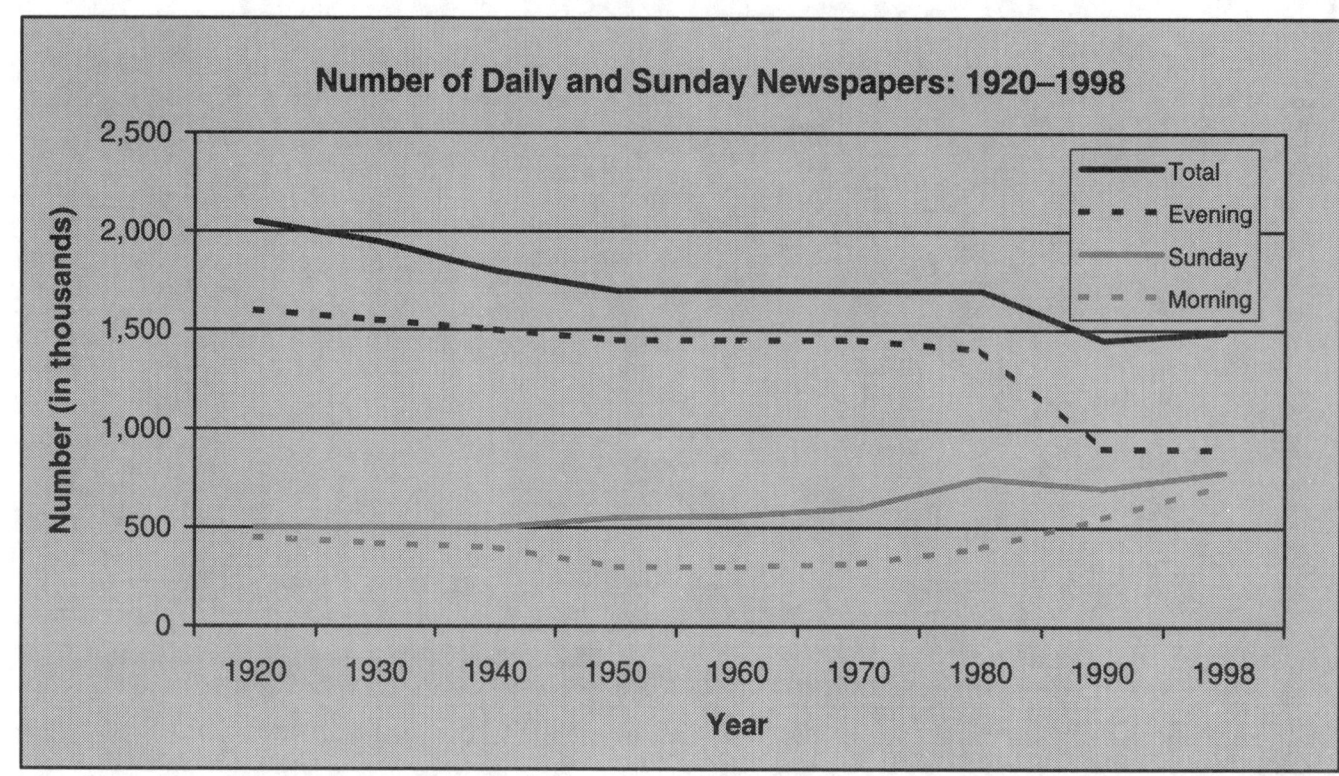

Number of Daily and Sunday Newspapers: 1920–1998

Legend:
- Total
- Evening
- Sunday
- Morning

Y-axis: Number (in thousands) — 0, 500, 1,000, 1,500, 2,000, 2,500

X-axis: Year — 1920, 1930, 1940, 1950, 1960, 1970, 1980, 1990, 1998

1 Communication systems are regulated primarily by the Federal Communications Commission and also by the Interstate Commerce Commission. The bulk of the regional telephone services are provided by the so-called Baby Bells, but the telecommunications industry has been transformed beyond recognition by new communications technology. There is no longer any distinction between local and regional providers and carriers and national ones, and all communications companies are engaged not only in telephones but also in video, internet, satellites, data transmission, cellulars, interactives and a host of other new services. AT&T continues to be the largest communications company, closely followed by MCI (owned by Worldcom) and Sprint. Until the 1980s AT&T was a virtual monopoly, controlling virtually all local and interstate facilities and services. Through Western Union, it controlled production facilities as well. The number of companies within AT&T (known as American Bell Telephone Company until 1900)

varied from time to time. At its peak in 1915–1916, it included 39 companies, but subsequent consolidations reduced it to 25. At the time of its breakup, it included 21 totally owned and controlled regional companies (AT&T owned 100% of the outstanding shares, although these companies operated under their own names), one subsidiary of one of these regional companies, two companies in which it had substantial minority interests (Cincinnati Bell and Southern New England Telephone Company), Bell Telephone Laboratories, and Western Electric Company.

2 An interesting footnote in the history of U. S. communications is the story of the rise and fall of Western Union Telegraph. Founded in 1851 as the New York and Mississippi Valley Printing and Telegraph Company, it emerged within a few decades as the sole telegraph company in the United States. Western Union developed close contractual ties with the railways, constructing telegraph pole lines along railroad rights-of-way and using railroad stations and personnel for pickup and delivery of telegraph messages. Western Union's most serious rival was the Postal Telegraph which was acquired in the 1880s by Mackay's Commercial Cable Company (later IT&T). Postal Telegraph merged with the Western Union in 1943, but shortly thereafter telegraph was rendered obsolete by other modern forms of communication.

3 Another 19th century technological breakthrough that became obsolete was the submarine cable. The first successful cable linking North America with Europe was laid in 1866. The first telegraph rate on cable (presumably from New York to London) was $100 for 100 words. Subsequently, it was reduced, first to $50 and later to $25. By 1868, the rate had fallen to $15.75 and by 1885 to $4.00. By 1916 the New York to London rate was $17 cents per word. Radio was not a significant factor in overseas communication until the Radio Corporation of America entered the field as successor to the Marconi Company, which was the first company to utilize and market the invention of wireless.

4 Among all forms of communications, Federal control has been most effective in radio and television. In 1912 the Department of Commerce was given authority to license radio equipment, operators and broadcast stations which began operation in 1921. On February 23, 1927, Congress established the Federal Radio Commission; its powers were transferred to the Federal Communications Commission (FCC) in 1934.

5 Statistics on radio and television are provided in the annual reports of the FCC as well as its *Statistics of the Communications Industry*. Unlike the telephone and telegraph, radio and television are not common carriers (public utilities that are subject to strict government supervision) and therefore are not subject to rate or earnings regulation. Statistics on radio and television broadcasting stations are presented in terms of licensed and authorized stations, the former generally referring to operating stations. FM radio was authorized as a regular service in 1941; in the same year the first commercial station was licensed. Noncommercial FM is a separate service with a specific spectrum allocation. Television was first authorized on a regular commercial basis on July 1, 1941, and two stations in New York were the first to begin operations. Time series broadcast advertising were first developed by L. D. H. Weld of McCann–Erickson Advertising Agency and continued after his death in 1946 by Hans Zeisel and others.

6 The first mail service was started in the Colonies in 1673 between New York and Boston, a distance of 260 miles. The trip took two weeks on horseback; much of that time was spent waiting for ferries. Mail was not inexpensive. At a time when a decent day's wage was 50 cents, a letter from New York to Philadelphia cost $3.50 and from New York to Williamsburg, Virginia, $11.50. The first postage rates were fixed by the Continental Congress in 1782. In the early days the recipient rather than the sender paid the postage. In 1847 postage stamps were introduced and in 1885 compulsory prepayment for all domestic letter mail was established. Postcards were introduced in 1898. It was not until 1863 that mail was divided into classes. Local rates were often improvised because no one knew for sure how much it cost to transport mail. The first letter rate on the Pony Express (which operated between Missouri and California during 1860 and 1861) was $5 for a half ounce; it was later reduced to $2 and then $1. Rates continued to fall well into the 20th century, reaching their lowest in 1928 and 1946 when a first-class postage stamp cost only five cents. Postage rates have been rising since then, while telephone rates have done the opposite. In 1915 it cost $20.70 to call New York from San Francisco but only five cents to mail a letter; in 1999 it cost only 7 cents for the same long distance call (for one minute), but 33 cents to mail a letter.

7 Since 1970, contrary to popular perceptions and prejudices against "snail mail," the U. S. Postal Service has become one of the most efficient and productive businesses in the nation. Although the number of post offices is down from 30,754 in 1975 to 27,952 in 1998, the number of pieces of mail handled grew from 89.3 billion to 197.943 billion, the number of employees from 667,000 to 905,000 and operating revenues from $19.253 billion to $60.116 billion during the same period.

8 A book has never been properly defined, but according to UNESCO it is any printed and bound publication longer than 49 pages that is not a periodical. Book publishing statistics, compiled from a number of sources, are not strictly comparable over time and may vary depending on what is included as well as what is excluded. The legal requirement of copyright and deposit of copies with the Library of Congress ensures that the publication of the vast majority of books is documented. The International Standard Book Number (ISBN) system also has the same effect, although compliance is voluntary.

9 There are only approximately 500 publishers in the United States with over 20 employees each. The book title output, the most important industry indicator, has increased from 46,738 in 1990 to 64,711 in 1997. The subjects with most titles are sociology and economics (9,968), fiction (8,329), medicine (4,045), science (3,918), religion (3,820) and history (3,692). Average hardcover prices have gone up from $24.64 in 1980 to $50.27, and trade paperback prices from $8.60 to $22.56.

10 Slightly different trends are found in the newspaper and periodical publishing industry. The number of daily newspapers have declined from 1,744 in 1980 to 1,527 in 1998, although the number of periodicals decreased from

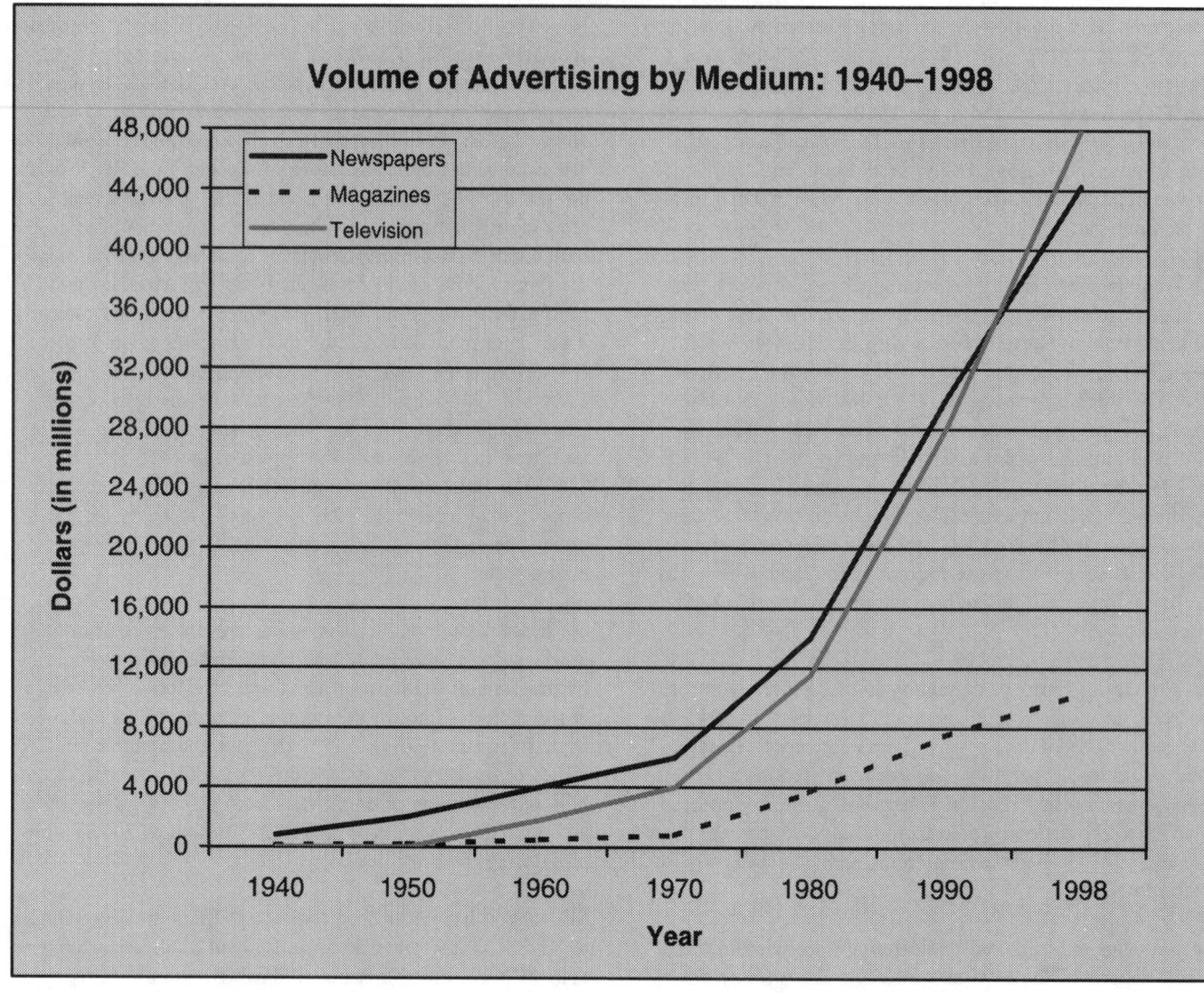

Volume of Advertising by Medium: 1940–1998

10,236 to 12,036 during the same period. Fewer people read newspapers in 1998 than in 1970. Total circulation of dailies has fallen from 62.1 million to 56.2 million during this period. In per capita terms, the circulation has fallen from 0.30 to 0.21. Per capita circulation is highest in Colorado (0.40) and lowest in Mississippi and Georgia (0.14).

11 Total advertising expenditures in all media were $200.3 billion. The share of each medium is determined by the nature of the special audience that is being addressed. For newspapers it is 22%, television (23.9%), magazines (5.1%), radio (7.2%), Yellow Pages (5.9%), direct mail (19.7%), business papers (2.1%), and outdoor (0.7%).

12 In 1998 there were 10,845 cable television systems with 64.4 million subscribers. Pay television has 70.1 million subscribers and pay cable 47.3 million subscribers. The average monthly rate for cable television is $27.43 and that for pay cable $8.20.

13 The total value of recording media shipments (including CDs, cassettes, and albums) was $13.723 billion in 1998.

14 Deregulation of the telecommunications industry has encouraged competition. In 1997 there were 3,604 service providers (including 2,066 local service providers) and the gross sectoral revenue had grown to $231.1 billion. There are 194 million access lines handling 522 billion local calls and 101 billion toll calls. There are 621 long-distance carriers with 159 million presubscribed lines. International calls numbered 4.229 billion. The telecommunications industry had operating revenues in 1997 of $256.1 billion and operating expenses of $212.4 billion, leaving a net revenue of $43.626 billion.

15 There are 3,073 cellular telephone systems with 69.2 million subscribers.

16 The United States is fast approaching total saturation in the utilization of all media. Access to telephones is 93.9%, radio 99%, and television 98.4%. Only cable is behind at 66.5%.

Series R 93-105. Radio and Television Stations, Sets Produced and Households With Sets: 1921 to 1997

(Figures as of June 30, except for census figures in italics, which are as of April 1)

Year	Standard broadcast (AM) 93	Frequency modulation (FM), commercial 94	Television (TV), commercial 96	Systems 98	Total subscribers (households) (1 000) 99	Radio sets (1 000) 104	Television sets (1 000) 105
1997	4 762	5 542	1 177	10 950	65 900	98 000	97 000
1996	4 857	5 419	1 174	11 119	64 600	98 000	96 000
1995	4 150	5 730	1 161	11 218	63 000	98 000	95 000
1994	4 913	5 109	1 145	11 214	60 500	98 000	94 000
1993	4 994	4 971	1 137	11 217	58 800	97 300	93 000
1992	4 961	4 785	1 118	11 075	57 200	96 600	92 000
1991	4 985	4 570	1 099	10 704	55 800	95 500	93 000
1990	4 987	4 392	1 092	...	...	94 400	92 000
1989	4 975	4 269	1 061	...	47 800	92 800	90 000
1988	4 932	4 155	1 028	8 500	43 800	91 100	89 000
1987	4 902	4 041	968	7 900	41 000	89 900	87 000
1986	4 863	3 944	919	7 600	37 500	88 100	86 000
1985	4 718	3 875	883	6 644	31 300	87 100	85 000
1984	4 754	3 716	841	6 200	30 000	86 700	84 000
1983	4 733	3 527	813	5 600	25 000	...	83 300
1982	4 668	3 380	777	4 825	21 000	...	81 500
1981	4 634	3 349	756	4 375	18 300	...	79 900
1980	4 589	3 282	734	4 225	15 500	78 600	76 000
1979	4 511	3 036	723	4 150	14 100	...	74 500
1978	4 459	2 922	714	3 875	13 000	...	72 900
1977	4 474	3 007	697	3 832	11 900	...	71 200
1976	...	...	701	3 681	10 800	...	69 600
1975	4 463	2 767	706	3 506	9 800	71 400	69 000
1974	4 305	2 413	694	3 158	8 700	...	...
1973	4 295	2 278	692	2 991	7 300	...	...
1972	4 273	2 229	690	2 841	6 000	...	...
1971	4 250	2 122	688	2 639	5 300	...	...
1970	4 288	2 126	691	2 490	4 500	62 000	59 550
1970	...	...	...	...	...	*2 46 108*	*60 594*
1969	4 254	2 018	680	2 260	3 600	60 600	58 250
1968	4 203	1 850	655	2 000	2 800	58 500	56 670
1967	4 135	1 708	626	1 770	2 100	57 500	55 130
1966	4 075	1 515	613	1 570	1 575	57 000	53 850
1965	4 025	1 343	589	1 325	1 275	55 200	52 700
1964	3 976	1 181	582	1 200	1 085	54 000	51 600
1963	3 860	1 120	581	1 000	950	52 300	50 300
1962	3 745	1 012	571	800	850	51 305	48 855
1961	3 602	889	553	700	725	50 695	47 200
1960	3 483	741	579	640	650	50 193	45 750
1960	...	...	...	...	...	*48 504*	*46 312*
1959	3 377	622	566	560	550	* 49 450	* 43 950
1958	3 253	548	556	525	450	48 500	41 924
1957	3 079	530	519	500	350	47 600	38 900
1956	2 896	530	496	450	300	46 800	34 900
1955	2 732	540	458	400	150	45 900	30 700
1954	2 583	553	402	300	65	45 100	26 000
1953	2 458	580	198	150	30	44 800	20 400
1952	2 355	629	108	70	14	42 800	15 300
1951	2 281	649	107	...	...	41 900	10 320
1950	2 144	691	104	...	...	40 700	3 875
1950	...	...	...	...	...	*40 411*	*5 030*
1949	2 066	737	69	...	...	39 300	940
1948	2 034	1 020	108	...	...	37 623	172
1947	1 795	918	66	...	...	35 900	14
1946	1 215	511	30	...	...	33 998	8

See footnotes at end of table.

Series R 93-105. Radio and Television Stations, Sets Produced and Households With Sets: 1921 to 1997—Cont'd.

(Figures as of June 30, except for census figures in italics, which are as of April 1)

Year	Operating broadcast stations [1]			Cable television		Households with x	
	Standard broadcast (AM)	Frequency modulation (FM), commercial	Television (TV), commercial	Systems	Total subscribers (households) (1 000)	Radio sets (1 000)	Television sets (1 000)
	93	94	96	98	99	104	105
1945....................	955	53	9	. . .	. . .	33 100	. . .
1944....................	924	52	9	. . .	. . .	32 500	. . .
1943....................	912	48	8	. . .	. . .	30 800	. . .
1942 [3]	925	42	10	. . .	. . .	30 600	. . .
1941....................	897	49	2	. . .	. . .	29 300	. . .

Year	Operating broadcast stations (AM)	Households with radio sets (1 000)	Year	Operating broadcast stations (AM)	Households with radio sets (1 000)	Year	Operating broadcast stations (AM)	Households with radio sets (1 000)
	93	104		93	104		93	104
1940...........	847	28 500	1933...........	598	19 250	1927...........	681	6 750
1940...........	. . .	*28 048*	*1932*...........	*604*	*18 450*	1926...........	528	4 500
1939...........	778	27 500				1925...........	571	2 750
1938...........	743	26 667	1931...........	612	16 700	1924...........	530	1 250
1937...........	704	24 500	1930...........	618	13 750	1923...........	556	466
			1930...........	. . .	12 049			
1936...........	656	22 869	1929...........	606	10 250	1922...........	30	60
1935...........	623	21 456	1928...........	677	8 000	1921...........	[4] 1	. . .
1934...........	593	20 400						

* Denotes first year for which figures include Alaska and Hawaii.
X Represents zero.
1. Includes Alaska, Hawaii, Puerto Rico, Guam and Virgin Islands for all years. Prior to 1948, the FCC did not keep records on the number of stations on the air. Therefore, data for 1933-1948 are for authorized stations and may include a number that were not actually on the air.
2. In 1970 census of housing, only battery-operated radios were enumerated.
3. Authorization of new radio stations and production of radio receivers for commercial use halted from April 1942 until October 1945.
4. First station to receive regular license as of Sept. 15; other stations in operation experimentally.

Series R 106-122. Radio Advertising Expenditures, Finances and Employment: 1935 to 1990

Year	Advertising expenditures (mil. dol.)				Year	Advertising expenditures (mil. dol.)			
	Total	Network	National spot	Local		Total	Network	National spot	Local
	106	**107**	**108**	**109**		**106**	**107**	**108**	**109**
1990	8 726	482	1 635	6 609	1962	736	46	233	457
1989	8 323	476	1 547	6 300	1961	683	43	221	510
1988	7 798	425	1 418	5 955					
1987	7 206	413	1 330	5 463	1960	692	43	222	428
1986	6 949	423	1 348	5 178	1959	656	44	206	406
					1958	619	58	190	372
1985	6 490	365	1 335	4 790	1957	618	64	187	368
1984	5 817	320	1 197	4 300	1956	567	61	161	346
1983	5 210	296	1 038	3 876					
1982	4 670	255	923	3 492	1955	545	84	134	326
1981	4 230	230	879	3 129	1954	559	114	135	309
					1953	611	141	146	324
1980	3 702	183	779	2 740	1952	624	162	142	321
1979	3 310	161	685	2 484	1951	606	180	138	289
1978	3 052	147	620	2 285					
1977	2 634	137	546	1 951	1950	605	196	136	273
1976	2 330	105	518	1 707	1949	571	203	123	245
					1948	562	211	121	230
1975	1 980	83	436	1 461	1947	506	201	106	199
1974	1 837	69	405	1 363	1946	454	200	98	157
1973	1 690	70	380	1 240					
1972	1 555	75	400	1 080	1945	424	198	92	134
1971	1 386	58	387	935	1944	394	192	87	114
					1943	314	157	71	86
1970	1 308	56	371	881	1942	260	129	59	73
1969	1 264	59	368	837	1941	247	125	52	70
1968	1 190	63	360	767					
1967	1 031	64	310	657	1940	216	113	42	60
1966	1 010	64	308	638	1939	184	99	35	50
					1938	167	89	34	44
1965	917	60	275	582	1937	165	89	28	48
1964	846	59	256	531	1936	122	76	23	24
1963	789	56	243	490	1935	113	63	15	35

Series R 123-139.   Television Advertising Expenditures, Finances and Employment: 1949 to 1998

Year	Advertising expenditures (mil. dol.)				Year	Advertising expenditures (mil. dol.)			
	Total	Network	National spot	Local		Total	Network	National spot	Local
	123	**124**	**125**	**126**		**123**	**124**	**125**	**126**
1998	47 990	13 735	10 675	12 295	1973	4 460	1 968	1 377	1 115
1997	44 519	13 020	9 999	11 436	1972	4 091	1 804	1 318	969
1996	42 484	13 081	9 803	10 944	1971	3 520	1 575	1 150	795
1995	37 828	11 600	9 119	9 985	1970	3 596	1 658	1 234	704
1994	35 435	10 942	8 993	9 464	1969	3 585	1 678	1 253	654
1993	31 698	10 209	7 800	8 435	1968	3 231	1 523	1 131	577
1992	30 450	10 249	7 551	8 079	1967	2 909	1 455	988	466
1991	28 189	9 533	7 110	7 565	1966	2 823	1 393	988	442
1990	28 405	9 383	7 788	7 856	1965	2 515	1 237	892	386
1989	26 891	9 110	7 354	7 812	1964	2 289	1 132	806	351
1988	25 686	9 172	7 147	7 270	1963	2 032	1 025	698	309
1987	23 904	8 500	6 846	6 833	1962	1 897	976	629	292
1986	22 081	8 342	6 570	6 514	1961	1 691	887	548	263
1985	21 022	8 060	6 004	5 714	1960	1 627	820	527	281
1984	19 848	8 318	5 488	5 084	1959	1 529	776	486	267
1983	16 759	6 955	4 827	4 345	1958	1 387	742	397	248
1982	14 636	6 144	4 364	3 765	1957	1 286	690	352	244
1981	12 650	5 575	3 730	3 345	1956	1 225	643	329	253
1980	11 469	5 130	3 269	2 967	1955	1 035	550	260	225
1979	10 154	4 599	2 873	2 682	1954	809	422	207	180
1978	8 955	3 975	2 607	2 373	1953	606	320	146	141
1977	7 612	3 466	2 204	1 948	1952	454	256	94	104
1976	6 721	2 857	2 154	1 710	1951	332	181	70	82
1975	5 263	2 306	1 623	1 334	1950	171	85	31	55
1974	4 851	2 145	1 495	1 211	1949	58	29	9	19

Series R 140-148. Safety and Special Radio Stations Authorized, by Class: 1913 to 1996

(As of June 30. Includes Alaska, Hawaii, Puerto Rico and outlying area.)

Year	Amateur and disaster services	Aviation services	Industrial services	Land transportation services	Marine services	Public safety services	Year	Amateur and disaster services	Aviation services	Industrial services	Land transportation services	Marine services	Public safety services
	140	141	143	144	145	146		140	141	143	144	145	146
1996¹	664 000	140 000	392 000	16 000	642 000	127 000	1951	90 587	34 061	9 551	4 253	29 544	9 129
1995¹	864 000	140 000	394 000	18 000	642 000	127 000	1950	87 967	23 794	6 099	3 495	24 921	7 607
1994	652 000	192 000	795 000	40 000	686 000	252 000	1949	81 675	27 227	4 266	3 588	20 004	5 700
1993	628 000	199 000	828 000	41 000	664 000	251 000	1948	78 434	20 858	2 855	3 122	15 024	4 903
1992	583 000	210 000	840 000	41 000	634 000	245 000	1947	75 000	15 943	1 787	1 692	11 955	4 620
1991	535 000	241 000	854 000	41 000	641 000	240 000	1946	70 000	6 205	702	156	8 676	4 760
1990	495 700	250 900	864 800	40 100	622 900	234 500	1945	60 000	3 793	576	...	...	4 446
1989	467 300	251 200	873 900	40 400	620 400	228 500	1944	60 000	3 445	468	...	6 817	4 144
1988	439 100	248 500	875 600	40 100	605 400	221 400	1943	60 000	3 553	386	...	6 609	3 772
1987	432 600	247 700	871 100	40 000	573 700	212 600	1942	60 000	4 713	356	...	...	3 455
1986	423 700	244 300	864 400	39 800	561 200	207 100	1941	60 000	3 000	306	...	5 822	2 967
1985	415 400	245 700	811 300	37 700	525 300	194 500	1940	56 295	2 099	340	...	4 945	2 334
1984	413 200	245 300	767 900	35 800	497 500	184 200	1939	53 558	1 824	307	...	4 036	1 536
1983	413 200	245 300	767 900	35 800	497 500	184 200	1938	49 911	1 460	232	...	3 516	662
1982	410 600	238 000	649 000	34 400	434 700	166 200	1937	47 444	1 212	221	...	2 422	535
1981	385 200	234 900	605 000	32 500	402 000	158 500	1936	46 850	812	195	...	2 219	403
1980	389 900	231 600	504 900	28 000	398 300	137 100	1935	45 561	678	146	...	2 157	298
1979	375 500	227 000	513 900	29 400	371 200	147 000	1934	46 390	671	129	...	2 195	220
1978	369 300	216 100	426 800	27 500	345 200	136 800	1933	41 555	646	121	...	2 192	152
1977	340 900	207 800	357 900	25 400	315 000	127 200	1932	30 374	579	134	...	2 225	123
1976	292 800	188 500	277 100	23 000	262 600	105 900	1931	22 739	463	130	...	2 392	91
1975	276 800	184 400	244 600	22 600	250 700	92 600	1930	18 994	281	...	...	2 173	20
1974	273 780	172 466	231 158	21 696	243 276	86 411	1929	16 829	131	...	...	...	12
1973	279 505	167 121	195 132	20 753	238 596	75 865	1928	16 928	...	...	...	...	...
1972	284 235	161 223	171 387	18 318	238 415	66 209	1927	16 926	...	...	...	...	...
1971	286 118	158 328	140 146	16 851	218 527	57 726	1926	14 902	...	...	...	1 954	...
1970	283 461	150 955	222 500	22 262	206 251	72 215	1925	15 000	...	...	...	1 901	4
1969	285 175	143 997	204 266	21 291	186 295	67 730	1924	15 540	...	...	...	2 741	3
1968	282 525	140 799	185 046	20 016	164 000	63 160	1923	16 570	...	...	...	...	3
1967	279 093	122 568	169 417	18 613	143 612	58 831	1922	...	...	...	...	...	...
1966	285 600	105 133	152 315	16 914	137 469	54 839	1921	...	...	...	...	...	...
1965	280 343	109 897	141 360	15 635	114 075	50 888	1920	5 719	...	...	...	...	1
1964	280 818	107 557	124 347	14 815	161 593	47 389	1919	...	...	...	...	...	...
1963	270 838	106 202	107 796	14 089	143 227	43 168	1918	...	...	...	...	...	...
1962	251 659	106 923	93 073	13 278	127 633	38 676	1917	...	...	...	...	...	...
1961	234 681	92 779	77 773	12 075	110 433	36 658	1916	...	...	...	...	...	1
1960	228 206	91 180	64 804	11 452	97 411	32 906	1915	...	...	...	...	...	...
1959	205 588	77 682	49 679	10 625	84 947	29 363	1914	...	...	...	...	...	...
1958	187 362	62 684	39 978	10 190	72 514	26 512	1913	1 312	...	...	...	701	...
1957	165 908	49 699	35 711	9 592	63 844	23 270							
1956	154 337	48 745	30 597	8 990	56 915	20 718							
1955	142 387	43 855	24 854	7 668	50 714	18 415							
1954	124 324	40 154	21 598	6 891	46 299	15 697							
1953	111 579	39 315	17 378	5 922	40 357	13 631							
1952	113 163	32 603	13 680	5 027	35 500	11 143							

1. Wireless bureau stations authorized; may not be comparable with previous years. In column 140, the number is that identified as "amateur." The categories shown here do not include microwave, 220 MHz, 800/900 MHz, broadcast auxiliary, general mobile, and interactive data.

Series R 163-171.   Postal Service—Post Offices, Revenues and Expenditures, Postage Stamps, Stamped Envelopes and Postal Cards Issued, and Pieces of Mail Handled: 1789 to 1999

(In thousands, except number of post offices. For years ending June 30. Includes Alaska, Hawaii, Puerto Rico and all outlying areas except the Canal Zone)

Year	Post offices [1]	Revenues [2]	Expenditures [2]	Pieces of matter of all kinds handled	Year	Post offices [1]	Revenues [2]	Expenditures [2]	Pieces of matter of all kinds handled
	163	164	165	169		163	164	165	169
1999	27 893	62 755 000	60 631 000	201 576 000	1939	44 327	745 955	784 550	26 444 846
1998	27 952	60 116 000	57 778 000	196 905 000	1938	44 586	728 634	772 308	26 041 979
1997	26 060	58 331 000	54 873 000	190 888 000	1937	44 877	726 201	772 743	25 801 279
1996	28 189	56 544 000	53 113 000	188 440 000	1936	45 230	665 343	753 616	23 571 315
1995	28 392	54 509 000	50 730 000	180 734 000	1935	45 686	$630 795	$696 503	22 331 752
1994	28 657	49 576 000	48 455 000	178 039 000	1934	46 506	586 733	630 733	20 625 827
1993	28 837	47 986 000	46 322 000	171 200 000	1933	47 641	587 631	699 887	19 868 456
1992	28 837	47 105 000	45 653 000	166 400 000	1932	48.159	588 172	793 684	24 306 744
1991	28 912	44 202 000	43 291 000	165 912 000	1931	48 733	656 463	802 485	26 544 352
1990	28 959	$40 074 000	$40 490 000	166 301 000	1930	49 063	705 484	803 667	27 887 823
1989	29 083	38 920 000	38 370 000	161 600 000	1929	49 482	696 948	782 344	27 951 548
1988	29 203	35 939 000	36 119 000	161 000 000	1928	49 944	693 634	725 700	26 837 005
1987	29 319	32 297 000	32 520 000	153 900 000	1927	50 266	683 122	714 577	26 686 556
1986	29 344	31 021 000	30 716 000	147 400 000	1926	50 601	659 820	679 704	25 483 529
1985	29 557	28 956 000	29 207 000	140 100 000	1925	50 957	599 591	639 282	. . .
1984	29 750	26 474 000	26 357 000	131 500 000	1924	51 266	572 949	587 377	. . .
1983	29 990	24 699 000	24 083 000	119 400 000	1923	51 613	532 828	556 851	23 054 832
1982	30 155	23 628 000	22 826 000	114 000 000	1922	51 950	484 854	545 644	. . .
1981	30 242	20 781 000	21 369 000	110 100 000	1921	52 168	463 491	620 994	. . .
1980	30 326	19 253 000	19 413 000	106 311 000	1920	52 641	437 150	454 323	. . .
1979	30 449	17 999 000	17 529 000	99 800 000	1919	53 084	[3] 436 239	362 498	. . .
1978	30 518	15 841 000	16 220 000	98 900 000	1918	54 347	[3] 388 976	324 834	. . .
1977	30 521	14 622 000	15 310 000	92 200 000	1917	55 414	329 726	319 839	. . .
1976	30 521	12 747 000	13 923 000	89 800 000	1916	55 935	312 058	306 204	. . .
1975	30 754	11 590 000	12 578 000	89 300 000	1915	56 380	287 248	298 546	. . .
1974	31 000	10 857 000	11 295 000	90 100 000	1914	56 810	287 935	283 544	. . .
1973	31 385	9 913 000	9 926 000	89 700 000	1913	58 020	266 620	262 068	18 567 445
1972	31 686	9 347 000	9 522 000	87 200 000	1912	58 729	246 744	248 525	17 588 659
1971	31 947	8 751 000	8 955 000	87 000 000	1911	59 237	237 880	237 649	16 900 552
1970	32 002	7 701 695	7 867 269	84 881 833	1910	59 580	224 129	229 977	14 850 102
1969	32 064	7 025 898	7 168 489	82 004 501	1909	60 144	203 562	221 004	14 004 577
1968	32 260	6 423 515	6 543 920	79 516 731	1908	60 704	191 479	208 352	13 364 069
1967	32 626	5 101 982	6 249 027	78 366 572	1907	62 658	183 585	190 238	12 255 666
1966	33 121	4 784 186	5 726 523	75 607 302	1906	65 600	167 933	178 450	11 361 091
1965	33 624	4 483 390	5 275 840	71 873 166	1905	68 131	152 827	167 399	10 187 506
1964	34 040	4 276 123	4 927 825	69 676 477	1904	71 131	143 582	152 362	9 502 460
1963	34 498	3 879 128	4 698 528	67 852 738	1903	74 169	134 224	138 784	8 887 467
1962	34 797	3 557 041	4 331 617	66 493 190	1902	75 924	121 848	124 786	8 085 447
1961	34 955	3 423 059	4 249 414	64 932 859	1901	76 945	111 631	115 555	7 424 390
1960	35 238	3 276 588	3 873 953	63 674 604	1900	76 688	102 354	107 740	7 129 990
1959	35 750	3 035 232	3 640 368	61 247 220	1899	75 000	95 021	101 632	6 576 310
1958	36 308	2 550 221	3 440 810	60 129 911	1898	73 570	89 013	98 054	6 214 447
1957	37 012	2 496 614	3 044 438	59 077 633	1897	71 022	82 665	94 077	5 781 002
1956	37 515	2 419 354	2 883 305	56 441 216	1896	70 360	82 499	90 933	5 693 719
1955	38 316	2 349 477	2 712 150	55 233 564	1895	70 064	76 983	87 180	5 134 281
1954	39 405	2 268 517	2 667 664	52 213 170	1894	69 805	75 080	84 994	4 919 090
1953	40 609	2 091 714	2 742 126	50 948 156	1893	68 403	75 897	81 582	5 021 841
1952	40 919	1 947 316	2 666 860	49 905 875	1892	67 119	70 930	76 981	4 776 575
1951	41 193	1 776 816	2 341 399	46 908 410	1891	64 329	65 932	73 060	4 369 900
1950	41 464	1 677 487	2 222 949	45 063 737	1890	62 401	60 882	66 260	4 005 408
1949	41 607	1 571 851	2 149 322	43 555 108	1889	58 999	56 176	62 317	3 860 200
1948	41 695	1 410 971	1 687 805	40 280 374	1888	57 376	52 695	56 458	3 576 100
1947	41 760	1 299 141	1 504 799	37 427 706	1887	55 157	48 838	53 006	3 495 100
1946	41 751	1 224 572	1 353 654	36 318 158	1886	53 614	43 948	51 005	3 747 000

See footnotes at end of table.

Series R 163-171. Postal Service—Post Offices, Revenues and Expenditures, Postage Stamps, Stamped Envelopes and Postal Cards Issued, and Pieces of Mail Handled: 1789 to 1999—Cont'd.

(In thousands, except number of post offices. For years ending June 30. Includes Alaska, Hawaii, Puerto Rico and all outlying areas except the Canal Zone)

Year	Post offices [1]	Revenues [2]	Expenditures [2]	Pieces of matter of all kinds handled	Year	Post offices [1]	Revenues [2]	Expenditures [2]	Pieces of matter of all kinds handled
	163	164	165	169		163	164	165	169
1945	41 792	1 314 240	1 145 002	37 912 067	1885	51 252	42 561	50 046	...
1944	42 161	1 112 877	1 068 987	34 930 685	1884	48 434	43 326	47 225	...
1943	42 654	966 227	952 529	32 818 262	1883	46 820	45 509	43 283	...
1942	43 358	859 817	873 950	30 117 633	1882	46 231	41 876	40 482	...
1941	43 739	812 828	836 859	29 235 791	1881	44 512	36 785	39 593	...
1940	44 024	766 949	807 629	27 749 467					
1939	44 327	745 955	784 550	26 444 846					

See footnotes at end of table.

Series R 163-171. Postal Service—Post Offices, Revenues and Expenditures, Postage Stamps, Stamped Envelopes and Postal Cards Issued, and Pieces of Mail Handled: 1789 to 1999—Cont'd.

(In thousands, except number of post offices. For years ending June 30. Includes Alaska, Hawaii, Puerto Rico and all outlying areas except the Canal Zone)

Year	Post offices [1]	Revenues [2]	Expenditures [2]	Year	Post offices [1]	Revenues [2]	Expenditures [2]
	163	164	165		163	164	165
1880	42 989	33 315	36 543	1833	10 127	2 617	2 930
1879	40 588	30 042	33 450	1832	9 205	2 259	2 266
1878	38 253	29 278	34 165	1831	8 686	1 998	1 936
1877	37 345	27 532	33 486				
1876	36 383	28 644	33 263	1830	8 450	1 851	1 933
				1829	8 004	1 707	1 782
1875	35 547	26 791	33 611	1828	7 530	1 660	1 690
1874	34 294	26 471	32 126	1827	7 300	1 525	1 470
1873	33 244	22 997	29 085	1826	6 150	1 448	1 367
1872	31 863	21 915	26 658				
1871	30 345	20 037	24 390	1825	5 677	1 307	1 229
				1824	5 182	1 198	1 188
1870	28 492	18 880	23 999	1823	4 043	1 130	1 157
1869	27 106	17 314	23 698	1822	4 709	1 117	1 168
1868	26 481	16 292	22 731	1821	4 650	1 059	1 165
1867	25 163	15 237	19 235				
1866	29 389	14 387	15 352	1820	4 500	1 112	1 161
				1819	4 000	1 205	1 118
1865	28 882	14 556	13 695	1818	3 618	1 230	1 036
1864	28 878	12 438	12 645	1817	3 459	1 003	917
1863	29 047	11 164	11 314	1816	3 260	962	804
1862	28 875	8 300	11 125				
1861	28 586	8 349	13 607	1815	3 000	1 043	748
				1814	2 670	730	727
1860	28 498	8 518	14 875	1813	2 708	703	631
1859	28 539	7 968	15 754	1812	2 610	649	540
1858	27 977	7 487	12 722	1811	2 403	587	499
1857	26 586	7 354	11 508				
1856	25 565	6 921	10 405	1810	2 300	552	496
				1809	2 012	507	498
1855	24 410	6 642	9 968	1808	1 944	461	463
1854	23 548	6 256	8 577	1807	1 848	479	454
1853	22 320	5 241	7 983	1806	1 710	446	417
1852	20 910	5 185	7 108				
1851	19 796	6 411	6 278	1805	1 558	421	377
				1804	1 405	389	338
1850	18 417	5 500	5 213	1803	1 258	352	322
1849	16 749	4 705	4 479	1802	1 114	327	282
1848	16 159	4 555	4 327	1801	1 025	320	255
1847	15 146	3 880	3 980				
1846	14 601	3 487	4 076	1800	903	281	214
				1799	677	265	188
1845	14 183	4 290	4 321	1798	639	233	179
1844	14 103	4 237	4 299	1797	554	214	150
1843	13 814	4 296	4 375	1796	468	195	132
1842	13 733	4 547	4 628				
1841	13 778	4 408	4 500	1795	453	161	118
				1794	450	129	90
1840	13 468	4 544	4 718	1793	209	105	72
1839	12 780	4 485	4 637	1792	195	67	55
1838	12 519	4 239	4 431	1791	89	46	37
1837	11 767	4 102	3 288				
1836	11 091	3 408	2 842	1790	75	38	32
				1789	75	[4] 8	[4] 8
1835	10 770	2 994	2 757				
1834	10 693	2 824	2 911				

1. Excludes branches and stations.
2. Accounting basis changed from cash to accrual basis in 1954; from accrual basis to accrued cost basis in 1963.
3. For 1918 and 1919, includes $44,500,000 and $71,392,000, respectively, war-tax revenue accruing from increased postage.
4. For three months only.

Series R 172-187. Postal Service—Revenues, Expenses and Volume of Mail, by Classes of Mail, and Employees: 1926 to 1999

(In millions, except employees in thousands. Includes Alaska, Hawaii, Puerto Rico and all outlying areas except the Canal Zone. Series R 174 also includes airmail from 1971 on)

Year	First-class mail [1,2], pieces	Second-class mail, pieces	Third-class mail, pieces	Fourth-class mail, pieces	Post Office employees	Year	First-class mail [1,2], pieces	Second-class mail, pieces	Third-class mail, pieces	Fourth-class mail, pieces	Post Office employees
	174	**177**	**180**	**183**	**187**		**174**	**177**	**180**	**183**	**187**
1999	101 937	10 274	85 662	1 063	906	1962	35 333	8 090	17 837	1 024	588
1998	101 434	10 317	82 875	1 023	905	1961	34 289	7 966	17 569	978	582
1997	99 660	10 411	77 254	988	893	1960	33 235	7 535	17 910	1 016	563
1996	98 216	10 126	71 626	949	886						
1995	96 296	10 194	71 112	936	875	1959	32 274	7 099	16 978	1 038	550
						1958	32 218	7 148	15 849	1 170	538
1994	95 333	10 228	69 416	872	852	1957	31 561	6 888	15 702	1 184	521
1993	92 200	10 300	65 773	744	818	1956	30 078	6 915	14 676	1 173	509
1992	90 800	10 300	62 547	764	819	1955	28 713	6 740	15 050	1 136	512
1991	90 300	10 400	...	...	808						
1990	89 917	10 680	63 725	663	809	1954	27 085	6 483	13 866	1 195	507
						1953	27 257	6 762	12 004	1 245	507
1989	85 826	10 523	62 779	626	817	1952	26 502	6 956	11 630	1 257	524
1988	82 381	10 448	81 970	649	824	1951	25 578	6 520	10 534	1 235	498
1987	78 933	10 324	59 734	615	791	1950	24 500	6 265	10 343	1 179	501
1986	76 252	10 588	55 049	602	785						
1985	72 517	10 380	52 170	576	744	1949	23 206	6 987	9 389	1 209	518
						1948	21 948	6 344	8 188	1 143	503
1984	68 507	9 522	48 249	599	702	1947	20 665	6 124	6 803	1 067	471
1983	64 320	9 220	40 735	568	679	1946	20 059	5 832	6 055	994	487
1982	62 271	9 527	36 719	597	675	1945	21 009	5 522	5 446	1 028	436
1981	61 476	9 956	33 607	590	670						
1980	60 276	10 220	30 381	633	667	1944	20 510	4 635	4 409	961	390
						1943	...	...	...	...	374
1979	57 976	8 400	27 513	614	663	1942	16 972	4 571	5 435	779	360
1978	56 020	8 691	26 330	691	656	1941	15 989	4 607	6 075	738	361
1977	53 668	8 673	24 050	762	655	1940	15 224	4 577	5 556	712	353
1976	52 459	8 899	22 514	759	679						
1975	52 482	9 713	21 867	801	702	1939	14 657	4 310	5 181	693	349
						1938	14 226	4 377	5 272	670	345
1974	52 929	8 838	22 537	859	710	1937	13 882	4 529	5 356	685	332
1973	52 291	9 034	22 689	893	701	1936	12 731	4 353	4 674	618	324
1972	50 293	9 494	21 908	914	706	1935	12 498	4 138	4 030	573	309
1971	51 493	9 604	20 532	968	729						
1970	48 640	9 351	19 974	977	741	1934	11 557	3 956	3 612	531	314
						1933	10 878	3 869	3 753	530	322
1969 [3]	46 411	9 206	19 622	1 031	739	1932	14 598	4 552	3 641	617	333
1968	43 183	8 907	20 665	1 039	731	1931	15 824	4 857	4 100	766	339
1967	41 998	8 711	20 985	1 070	717	1930	16 901	4 968	4 325	837	340
1966	40 422	8 634	20 305	1 066	675						
1965	38 068	8 600	19 454	1 045	596	1928	16 706	4 678	3 838	752	337
						1927	16 284	4 753	4 062	743	332
1964	36 943	8 559	18 599	1 066	585	1926	15 266	4 658	3 962	770	329
1963	35 833	8 227	18 407	1 076	587						

1. For 1926-1929, domestic airmail included with first class mail.
2. Includes airmail from 1971.
3. In fiscal year 1969, the department changed from a fully distributed cost system to an attributable cost system.

Series R 188-190. Postal Rates for First-Class Mail, Letters and Postal Cards: 1861 to 1999

(First-class mail as a mail category not officially established until 1863. Ship and steamboat letters, 1792-1863, carried special rates)

Year of rate change	Letters, nonlocal	Postal cards (cents)	Year of rate change	Letters, nonlocal	Postal cards (cents)	Year of rate change	Letters, nonlocal	Postal cards (cents)
	188	**189**		**188**	**189**		**188**	**189**
1999......	0.33	0.22	1985	22¢ per oz.	14	1952	3¢ per oz.	2
1998......	. . .	. . .	1982 [2]	20¢ per oz.	13	1940	(1)	(1)
1997......	. . .	. . .	1981	18¢ per oz.	12	1932	3¢ per oz.	1
1996......	. . .	. . .	1978	15¢ per oz.	10	1919	2¢ per oz.	1
1995......	0.32	0.20	1975	. . .	9	1917	3¢ per oz.	2
1994......	. . .	. . .	1974	10¢ per oz.	8	1885	2¢ per oz.	1
1993......	. . .	. . .	1971	8¢ per oz.	6	1883	2¢ per ½ oz.	1
1992......	. . .	. . .	1968-1970	6¢ per oz.	5	1872	3¢ per ½ oz.	[3] 1
1991......	29¢ per oz.	19	1963	5¢ per oz.	4	1863 [4]	3 per ½ oz.	. . .
1988......	25¢ per oz.	15	1953, Aug. 1......	4¢ per oz.	3	1861 [5]	(4)	. . .

1. The 1940 rate change provided that the three-cent letter rate was not to apply to first-class matter for local delivery or for delivery within a county with a population of more than 1 million people if it was entirely within a corporate city.
2. From November 1981.
3. Government postal cards first authorized in 1872.
4. A uniform rate regardless of distance, a free city delivery service and a letter unit of ½ ounce instead of the former "single letter" were inaugurated.
5. Rate between any point in the U.S. east of the Rocky Mountains and any state or territory on the Pacific.

Series R 192-217. New Books and New Editions Published, by Subject: 1880 to 1998

Year	Total books published [1]	Agriculture	Art	Biography	Business	Education	Fiction	General works	History	Home Economics	Juvenile	Language
							New Books					
	192	195	196	197	198	199	200	201	202	203	204	205
1998	56 129	801	1 685	2 657	1 456	1 224	7 096	2 237	3 108	1 200	3 381	840
1997	64 796	871	1 912	3 069	1 657	1 438	7 963	3 159	3 713	1 533	3 381	1 056
1996	68 175	675	2 033	3 007	1 788	1 595	8 573	3 027	3 576	1 447	5 353	898
1995	62 039	673	2 168	2 658	1 843	1 526	7 605	2 751	2 999	1 395	5 678	732
1994	51 663	532	1 621	2 197	1 616	1 310	5 415	2 208	2 507	1 004	5 321	700
1993	49 756	558	1 540	2 071	1 442	1 247	5 419	1 870	2 317	881	5 469	699
1992	49 276	565	1 392	2 007	1 367	1 184	5 690	2 153	2 322	826	5 144	617
1991	48 146	523	1 283	2 120	1 421	1 129	5 424	1 886	2 331	789	5 111	566
1991	41 223	468	1 119	1 890	1 298	973	4 199	1 684	2 107	721	4 555	521
1990	46 738	514	1 262	1 957	1 191	1 039	5 764	1 760	2 243	758	5 172	649
1989	53 446	562	1 569	2 193	1 569	1 054	5 941	2 332	2 563	949	5 413	586
1988	55 483	666	1 602	2 250	1 647	1 113	5 564	2 475	3 260	1 057	4 954	628
1987	56 057	652	1 693	2 259	1 462	1 081	6 298	2 620	2 882	1 168	4 642	699
1986	52 637	564	1 697	2 152	1 604	1 029	5 578	2 484	2 471	1 103	4 516	668
1985	50 070	536	1 545	1 953	1 518	1 085	5 105	2 905	2 327	1 228	3 801	632
1984	51 058	507	1 836	2 098	1 696	1 052	5 413	3 021	2 257	1 306	3 128	670
1983	53 280	572	1 896	2 135	1 636	1 059	5 470	2 767	2 296	1 325	3 197	669
1982	46 935	439	1 722	1 752	1 327	1 046	5 419	2 398	2 177	1 099	3 049	576
1981	48 793	474	1 693	1 860	1 342	1 172	5 655	1 743	2 321	1 108	3 102	761
1980	42 377	461	1 691	1 891	1 185	1 011	2 835	1 643	2 220	879	2 659	529
1979	45 182	538	2 021	2 042	1 362	1 121	3 264	1 471	2 160	897	3 052	560
1978	41 216	552	1 483	1 891	1 248	1 063	3 693	1 310	2 016	845	2 909	458
1977	42 780	594	1 795	2 104	1 077	1 194	3 681	1 448	2 022	795	2 918	556
1976	35 141	477	1 369	1 714	843	899	3 458	1 034	1 934	690	2 210	409
1975	39 372	456	1 561	1 968	820	1 038	3 805	1 113	1 823	728	2 292	438
1974	40 846	391	1 525	2 197	925	1 161	3 562	1 191	1 292	828	2 592	441
1973	39 351	382	1 377	2 325	762	1 618	3 688	1 187	1 598	669	2 042	458
1972	38 053	390	1 470	1 986	684	1 292	3 260	1 048	1 629	596	2 526	479
1971	37 692	324	1 246	1 797	700	1 250	3 430	1 012	1 978	477	2 223	536
1970	36 071	200	852	735	658	842	1 998	568	1 010	235	2 472	339
1969	29 579	216	856	718	566	721	1 816	508	1 191	267	1 321	355
1968	30 387	191	930	786	644	917	1 822	521	1 048	245	2 318	387
1967	[2] 28 762	218	844	783	509	871	1 981	426	1 015	203	2 390	382
1966	30 050	212	779	819	478	886	1 699	410	959	219	2 375	459
1965	28 595	214	763	455	437	789	1 615	384	909	241	2 473	385
1964	28 451	209	776	697	411	934	1 703	361	834	188	2 533	414
1963	25 784	219	664	680	396	777	1 859	346	847	205	2 605	334
1962	21 904	215	590	667	308	559	1 787	279	812	156	2 328	226
1961	18 060	194	539	622	286	461	1 645	231	796	143	1 513	248
1960	15 012	121	422	746	240	308	1 642	233	695	155	1 628	. . .
1959	[3] 14 876	101	354	671	327	368	1 675	326	750	141	1 540	. . .
1958	13 462	122	409	608	283	276	1 592	213	750	142	1 424	. . .
1957	13 142	120	304	699	266	254	1 433	360	773	115	1 420	. . .
1956	12 538	103	283	676	222	229	1 500	305	521	159	1 384	. . .
1955	12 589	125	305	735	228	231	1 459	315	572	205	1 372	. . .
1954	11 901	111	285	687	196	223	1 512	339	529	192	1 193	. . .
1953	12 050	126	265	710	225	201	1 495	360	495	197	1 264	. . .
1952	11 840	114	267	650	180	238	1 354	336	454	237	1 094	. . .
1951	11 255	105	272	586	180	229	1 329	329	435	186	982	. . .
1950	11 022	111	317	538	190	209	1 211	262	456	150	907	. . .

See footnotes at end of table.

Series R 192-217.   New Books and New Editions Published, by Subject: 1880 to 1998—Cont'd.

Year	Total books published [1]	Year	Total books published [1]	Year	Total books published [1]	Year	Total books published [1]	Year	Total books published [1]	Year	Total books published [1]
	192		**192**		**192**		**192**		**192**		**192**
1949	10 892	1937	10 912	1925	9 574	1913	12 230	1901	8 141	1890	4 559
1948	9 897	1936	10 436	1924	9 012	1912	10 903			1889	4 014
1947	9 182			1923	8 863	1911	[5] 11 123	1900	6 356	1888	4 631
1946	7 735	1935	8 766	1922	8 638			1899	5 321	1887	4 437
		1934	8 198	1921	8 329	1910	13 470	1898	4 886	1886	4 676
1945	6 548	1933	8 092			1909	10 901	1897	4 928		
1944	6 970	1932	9 035	1920	8 422	1908	9 254	1896	5 703	1885	4 030
1943	8 325	1931	10 307	1919	8 594	1907	9 620			1884	4 088
1942	9 525			1918	9 237	1906	7 139	1895	5 469	1883	3 481
1941	11 112	1930	10 027	1917	10 060			1894	4 484	1882	3 472
		1929	10 187	1916	10 445	1905	8 112	1893	5 134	1881	2 991
1940	11 328	1928	10 354			1904	8 391	1892	4 862		
1939	10 640	1927	10 153	1915	9 734	1903	7 865	1891	4 665	1880	2 076
1938	11 067	1926	9 925	1914	12 010	1902	7 833				

See footnotes at end of table.

Series R 192-217. New Books and New Editions Published, by Subject: 1880 to 1998—Cont'd.

Year							New Books					
	Law	Literature	Medicine	Music	Philosophy, psychology	Poetry, drama	Religion	Science	Sociology, economics	Sports, recreation	Technology	Travel
	206	**207**	**208**	**209**	**210**	**211**	**212**	**213**	**214**	**215**	**216**	**217**
1998	1 189	2 369	3 676	408	2 104	1 125	3 153	3 432	8 970	1 367	1 999	652
1997	1 390	2 729	4 136	433	2 321	1 545	3 857	3 942	10 064	1 691	2 765	809
1996	1 357	3 082	4 223	461	2 333	1 566	3 803	3 725	10 528	1 751	2 629	745
1995	1 230	2 525	3 510	479	2 068	1 407	3 324	3 323	9 362	1 591	2 470	722
1994	1 108	2 356	3 147	364	1 741	1 065	2 730	3 021	8 038	1 161	2 085	556
1993	1 143	2 169	3 094	377	1 764	1 004	2 633	2 678	7 502	1 146	2 247	487
1992	1 063	2 227	3 234	346	1 806	899	2 540	2 729	7 432	1 113	2 152	468
1991	1 177	2 087	3 027	300	1 766	890	2 389	2 710	7 241	1 063	2 421	492
1991	967	1 903	2 710	275	1 611	821	2 059	2 427	5 508	893	2 089	425
1990	896	2 049	3 014	289	1 683	874	2 285	2 742	7 042	973	2 092	495
1989	1 096	2 298	3 447	375	2 058	1 128	2 586	3 288	7 971	1 077	2 690	701
1988	1 343	2 272	3 900	329	1 955	1 270	2 746	3 743	8 247	1 099	2 694	669
1987	1 544	2 358	3 995	352	1 845	1 236	2 850	3 658	8 115	1 263	2 756	629
1986	1 385	2 145	3 445	356	1 689	1 278	2 788	3 360	7 912	1 192	2 698	543
1985	1 349	1 964	3 579	364	1 559	1 166	2 564	3 304	7 441	1 154	2 526	465
1984	1 406	2 006	3 554	387	1 554	1 164	2 482	3 236	7 794	1 299	2 639	551
1983	1 756	1 957	4 002	417	1 578	1 234	2 433	3 620	8 470	1 335	2 994	562
1982	1 451	1 742	3 229	346	1 465	1 049	2 075	3 124	7 449	1 191	2 328	482
1981	1 448	1 777	3 788	398	1 465	1 183	2 278	3 375	7 801	1 264	2 313	472
1980	1 102	1 686	3 292	357	1 429	1 179	2 055	3 109	7 152	971	2 337	504
1979	1 218	1 749	3 257	389	1 377	1 361	2 325	3 156	7 715	1 122	2 391	634
1978	1 065	1 800	2 788	439	1 367	1 297	2 180	2 877	6 465	1 160	1 896	414
1977	948	1 866	2 833	373	1 372	1 437	2 121	3 015	6 814	1 119	2 218	480
1976	698	1 405	2 128	302	1 192	1 307	1 748	2 342	5 960	1 034	1 489	499
1975	915	1 904	2 282	305	1 374	1 501	1 778	2 942	6 590	1 225	1 720	794
1974	1 031	2 285	2 281	273	1 368	1 626	1 851	3 049	6 640	1 132	1 593	1 612
1973	756	2 307	2 002	336	1 406	1 917	1 826	2 714	6 565	1 082	1 347	1 587
1972	716	2 525	1 839	402	1 164	1 484	1 705	2 586	6 415	941	1 425	1 491
1971	661	2 986	1 655	402	1 354	1 494	1 567	2 697	6 095	890	1 309	1 609
1970	355	1 349	1 144	217	843	973	1 315	1 955	3 867	583	930	848
1969	363	1 348	928	227	678	944	1 278	1 999	3 216	585	884	802
1968	432	1 301	1 022	210	669	791	1 511	2 011	3 107	501	1 072	885
1967	392	1 172	935	165	633	739	1 502	1 835	2 761	391	1 051	769
1966	316	1 185	1 007	207	629	728	1 477	2 079	2 632	441	1 091	732
1965	291	1 166	871	183	582	775	1 428	1 850	2 372	474	942	635
1964	256	1 038	876	156	528	681	1 441	1 923	2 445	452	939	747
1963	269	861	752	139	505	578	1 459	1 648	1 932	427	960	595
1962	219	771	688	137	436	505	1 174	1 309	1 603	367	780	532
1961	203	617	595	114	433	517	1 098	1 193	1 289	381	665	455
1960	303	560	388	82	496	404	983	833	651	233	⁴ 574	372
1959	245	630	445	93	505	395	984	814	566	204	585	298
1958	245	495	393	89	467	373	941	781	494	201	443	271
1957	252	477	359	73	480	378	883	697	416	195	316	291
1956	221	570	334	88	425	337	810	531	448	160	404	294
1955	240	529	407	85	362	423	747	623	443	175	355	290
1954	226	493	345	69	386	389	774	522	463	201	325	230
1953	196	485	328	58	425	412	725	522	467	194	294	280
1952	236	518	350	71	427	424	715	513	478	168	311	264
1951	223	445	336	80	393	400	636	521	430	151	287	230
1950	228	510	312	88	380	453	626	499	447	153	366	221

1. 1880-1919 includes pamphlets; 1920-1928, pamphlets included in total only; thereafter, pamphlets excluded entirely.
2. Beginning 1967, counting methods were revised; prior years not strictly comparable with subsequent years.
3. Beginning 1959, data not strictly comparable with previous years because of change in definition of "book."
4. Prior to 1961, includes military.
5. Agrees with source; however, figures for components do not add to total shown.

Series R 224-231. Newspapers—Number and Circulation of Daily and Sunday Newspapers: 1920 to 1998

(Circulation in thousands. Figures as of October 1 of each year)

Year	Total		Daily newspapers				Sunday newspapers	
			Morning		Evening			
	Number	Circulation	Number	Circulation	Number	Circulation	Number	Circulation
	224	**225**	**226**	**227**	**228**	**229**	**230**	**231**
1998	1 489	56 200	721	4 560	781	10 500	898	60 100
1997	1 509	56 700	705	45 400	816	11 300	903	60 500
1996	1 520	57 000	686	44 800	846	12 200	890	60 800
1995	1 533	58 200	656	44 300	891	13 900	888	61 500
1994	1 548	59 300	635	43 400	935	15 900	886	62 300
1993	1 556	59 800	623	43 100	954	16 700	884	62 600
1992	1 570	60 100	596	42 400	996	17 800	891	62 200
1991	1 586	60 700	571	41 500	1 042	19 200	875	62 100
1990	1 611	62 300	559	41 300	1 084	21 000	863	62 600
1989	1 626	62 600	530	40 700	1 125	21 800	847	62 000
1988	1 642	62 700	529	40 400	1 141	22 200	840	61 500
1987	1 645	62 800	511	39 100	1 166	23 700	820	60 100
1986	1 657	62 500	499	37 400	1 188	25 100	802	58 900
1985	1 676	62 800	482	36 400	1 220	26 400	798	58 800
1984	1 688	63 100	458	35 400	1 257	27 700	783	57 500
1983	1 701	62 600	446	33 800	1 284	28 800	772	56 700
1982	1 711	62 500	434	33 200	1 310	29 300	768	56 300
1981	1 731	61 400	408	30 600	1 352	30 900	755	55 200
1980	1 745	62 200	387	29 400	1 388	32 800	736	54 700
1979	1 763	62 200	382	28 600	1 405	33 600	720	54 400
1978	1 756	62 000	355	27 700	1 419	34 300	696	54 000
1977	1 753	61 495	347	26 742	1 424	34 753	668	52 429
1976	1 762	60 977	346	25 858	1 435	35 119	650	51 565
1975	1 756	60 700	339	25 500	1 436	35 200	639	51 100
1974	1 768	61 877	340	26 145	1 449	35 732	641	51 679
1973	1 774	63 147	343	26 524	1 451	36 623	634	51 717
1972	1 761	62 510	337	26 078	1 441	36 432	603	49 339
1971	1 749	62 231	339	26 116	1 425	36 115	590	49 665
1970	[1] 1 748	62 108	334	25 934	1 429	36 174	586	49 217
1969	[1] 1 758	62 060	333	25 812	1 443	36 248	585	49 675
1968	[1] 1 752	62 535	328	25 838	1 443	36 697	578	49 693
1967	[1] 1 749	62 561	327	25 282	1 438	36 279	573	49 224
1966	[1] 1 754	61 397	324	24 806	1 444	36 592	578	49 282
1965	[1] 1 751	60 358	320	24 107	1 444	36 251	562	48 600
1964	[1] 1 763	60 412	323	24 365	1 452	36 048	561	48 383
1963	[1] 1 754	58 905	311	23 459	1 453	35 446	550	46 830
1962	[1] 1 760	59 849	318	24 563	1 451	35 286	558	48 888
1961	[1] 1 761	59 261	312	24 094	1 458	35 167	558	48 216
1960	[1] 1 763	58 882	312	24 029	1 459	34 853	563	47 699
1959	[1] 1 755	58 300	306	23 547	1 455	34 753	564	47 848
1958	[1] 1 751	57 418	307	23 161	1 456	34 258	556	46 955
1957	[1] 1 755	57 805	309	23 171	1 453	34 635	544	47 044
1956	[1] 1 761	57 102	314	22 492	1 454	34 610	546	47 162
1955	[1] 1 760	56 147	316	22 183	1 454	33 964	541	46 448
1954	[1] 1 765	55 072	317	21 705	1 448	33 367	544	46 176
1953	1 785	54 472	327	21 412	1 458	33 060	544	45 949
1952	1 786	53 951	327	21 160	1 459	32 791	545	46 210
1951	1 773	54 018	319	21 223	1 454	32 795	543	46 279
1950	1 772	53 829	322	21 266	1 450	32 563	549	46 582
1949	1 780	52 846	329	21 005	1 451	31 841	546	46 399
1948	1 781	52 285	328	21 082	1 453	31 203	530	46 308
1947	1 769	51 673	328	20 762	1 441	30 911	511	45 151
1946	1 763	50 928	334	20 546	1 429	30 382	497	43 665
1945	1 749	48 384	330	19 240	1 419	29 144	485	39 680
1944	1 744	45 955	338	18 059	1 406	27 896	481	37 946
1943	1 754	44 393	333	17 078	1 421	27 315	467	37 292

See footnotes at end of table.

Series R 224-231. Newspapers—Number and Circulation of Daily and Sunday Newspapers: 1920 to 1998—Cont'd.

(Circulation in thousands. Figures as of October 1 of each year)

Year	Total		Daily newspapers				Sunday newspapers	
			Morning		Evening			
	Number	Circulation	Number	Circulation	Number	Circulation	Number	Circulation
	224	**225**	**226**	**227**	**228**	**229**	**230**	**231**
1942	1 787	43 375	345	17 111	1 442	26 264	474	35 294
1941	1 857	42 080	377	16 519	1 480	25 561	510	33 436
1940	1 878	41 132	380	16 114	1 498	25 018	525	32 371
1939	1 888	39 671	383	. . .	1 505	. . .	524	31 519
1938	1 936	39 572	398	. . .	1 538	. . .	523	30 481

Year	Daily newspapers				Sunday newspapers	
	Total					
	Number	Circulation	Number of morning	Number of evening	Number	Circulation
	224	**225**	**226**	**228**	**230**	**231**
1937............................	1 983	41 419	406	1 577	539	30 957
1936............................	1 989	40 292	405	1 584	520	29 962
1935............................	1 950	38 156	390	1 560	518	28 147
1934............................	1 929	36 709	385	1 544	505	26 545
1933............................	1 911	35 175	378	1 533	506	24 041
1932............................	1 913	36 408	380	1 533	518	24 860
1931............................	1 923	38 761	384	1 539	513	25 702
1930............................	1 942	39 589	388	1 554	521	26 413
1929............................	1 944	39 426	381	1 563	528	26 880
1928............................	1 939	37 973	397	1 542	522	25 772
1927............................	1 949	37 967	411	1 538	526	25 469
1926............................	2 001	36 002	425	1 576	545	24 435
1925............................	2 008	33 739	427	1 581	548	23 355
1924............................	2 014	32 999	429	1 585	539	22 220
1923............................	2 036	31 454	426	1 610	547	21 463
1922............................	2 033	29 780	426	1 607	546	19 713
1921............................	2 028	28 424	427	1 601	545	19 041
1920............................	2 042	27 791	437	1 605	522	17 084

1. Total is adjusted to account for "all-day" papers listed in both morning and evening figures. Circulations are divided between morning and evening totals.

Series R 232-243.   Newspapers and Periodicals: 1935 to 1999
(Data refer to year of compilation of the Directory, i.e., generally to year preceding year shown)

Year	Newspapers				Periodicals					
	Total	Semi-weekly	Weekly	Daily	Total	Weekly	Semi-monthly	Monthly	Bi-monthly	Quarterly
	232	233	234	235	237	238	239	240	241	242
1999	10 521	560	7 471	1 647	9 893	388	260	3 447	2 220	3 429
1998	10 504	557	7 267	1 461	12 036	382	262	3 378	2 184	3 366
1997	10 042	558	7 191	1 582	8 530	350	139	3 067	1 943	2 893
1996	10 466	612	7 655	1 537	9 843	442	307	3 554	2 216	3 280
1995	12 246	705	9 011	1 710	11 179	513	216	4 067	2 568	3 621
1994	12 513	661	9 067	1 831	12 136	487	209	4 494	2 475	3 370
1993	12 597	639	9 177	1 850	11 863	485	199	4 545	2 359	3 199
1992	11 339	562	8 293	1 755	11 143	466	371	4 326	2 143	3 024
1991	11 689	574	8 546	1 781	11 239	511	412	4 340	2 116	2 861
1990	11 471	579	8 420	1 788	11 092	553	435	4 239	2 087	2 758
1989	10 457	567	7 622	1 773	11 556	828	622	4 445	1 880	2 513
1988	10 088	555	7 438	1 745	11 229	880	619	4 192	1 558	2 245
1987	9 031	510	6 750	1 646	11 593	1 400	858	4 031	1 402	1 984
1986	9 144	495	6 857	1 651	11 328	1 383	789	4 066	1 387	1 895
1985	9 134	517	6 811	1 701	11 090	1 367	801	4 088	1 361	1 759
1984	9 151	525	6 798	1 711	10 809	1 376	658	4 096	1 348	1 711
1983	9 205	508	6 855	1 735	10 952	1 626	724	4 108	1 307	1 627
1982	9 183	498	6 806	1 740	10 688	1 672	689	4 078	1 237	1 554
1981	9 676	508	7 238	1 747	10 873	1 921	667	4 199	1 193	1 484
1980	9 620	537	7 159	1 744	10 236	1 716	645	3 985	1 114	1 444
1979	9 827	543	7 357	1 744	9 719	1 764	594	3 850	1 045	1 261
1978	10 538	569	7 980	1 783	9 582	1 827	541	3 846	1 031	1 172
1977	11 089	550	8 506	1 811	9 732	1 882	548	4 019	1 043	1 149
1976	11 298	511	8 735	1 813	9 872	1 915	557	4 144	1 058	1 161
1975	11 400	506	8 824	1 819	9 657	1 918	537	4 087	1 009	1 093
1974	11 296	523	8 711	1 806	9 755	2 027	529	4 123	942	1 164
1973	11 324	459	8 804	1 792	9 630	2 022	506	4 107	925	1 148
1972	11 299	398	8 682	1 809	9 062	1 606	493	4 093	852	1 106
1971	11 350	412	8 888	1 818	9 657	1 873	544	4 277	1 005	1 124
1970	11 383	423	8 903	1 838	9 573	1 856	589	4 314	957	1 108
1969	11 336	413	8 855	1 833	9 434	1 787	587	4 353	899	1 084
1968	11 293	387	8 858	1 833	9 400	1 796	606	4 331	899	1 078
1967	11 307	366	8 915	2 026	9 238	1 808	573	¹ 4 296	859	1 051
1966	12 365	382	9 785	1 972	10 002	1 884	335	4 796	912	1 119
1965	11 383	357	8 989	1 843	8 990	1 716	550	¹ 4 195	876	1 030
1964	12 332	390	9 761	1 963	9 798	1 724	334	4 847	910	1 065
1963	12 295	391	9 739	1 974	9 643	1 792	313	4 744	858	1 025
1962	12 293	376	9 774	1 970	9 483	1 740	305	4 705	826	1 030
1961	12 285	361	9 783	1 968	9 275	1 656	301	4 634	801	998
1960 *	11 315	324	8 979	1 854	8 422	1 580	527	¹ 4 113	743	895
1959	12 294	359	9 812	1 977	9 004	1 592	302	4 577	712	950
1958	12 207	332	9 768	1 969	8 927	1 705	292	4 490	676	914
1957	12 299	354	9 854	1 946	8 722	1 681	288	4 457	639	842
1956	12 256	338	9 813	1 963	8 718	1 748	283	4 450	614	831
1955	11 415	324	9 126	1 860	7 648	1 602	503	¹ 3 782	608	674
1954	12 398	328	9 960	1 999	8 092	1 584	260	4 218	604	695
1953	12 645	346	10 173	2 009	7 792	1 494	242	4 115	598	673
1952	12 833	341	10 381	1 998	7 711	1 485	246	4 118	558	665
1951	13 009	362	10 514	2 018	7 635	1 491	239	4 132	517	633
1950	12 115	337	9 794	1 894	6 960	1 443	416	¹ 3 694	436	604
1949	12 814	326	10 386	2 014	7 570	1 537	244	4 073	458	635
1948	12 900	301	10 511	2 001	7 346	1 498	262	3 970	412	576
1947	12 877	284	10 523	2 003	7 083	1 394	272	3 805	401	609
1946	12 804	286	10 424	2 020	6 693	1 331	253	3 595	345	595
1945	12 791	283	10 430	2 004	6 569	1 359	246	3 503	309	578
1944	12 889	308	10 504	2 006	6 672	1 456	226	3 500	285	588
1943	13 456	356	10 967	2 043	7 040	1 489	215	3 826	274	596
1942	14 100	408	11 474	2 131	7 374	1 609	248	3 983	288	601

See footnotes at end of table.

Series R 232-243. Newspapers and Periodicals: 1935 to 1999—Cont'd.
(Data refer to year of compilation of the Directory, i.e., generally to year preceding year shown)

Year	Newspapers				Periodicals					
	Total	Semi-weekly	Weekly	Daily	Total	Weekly	Semi-monthly	Monthly	Bi-monthly	Quarterly
	232	233	234	235	237	238	239	240	241	242
1941	14 284	397	11 617	2 153	7 141	1 449	222	3 966	277	595
1940	13 314	368	10 860	2 086	6 432	1 399	427	¹ 3 466	241	538
1939	14 213	380	11 516	2 216	6 846	1 408	213	3 821	250	563
1938	14 112	383	11 421	2 242	6 412	1 220	202	3 663	219	530
1937	14 336	401	11 592	2 272	6 320	1 251	253	3 512	203	530
1936	13 928	368	11 288	2 189	6 670	1 546	216	3 622	197	497
1935	14 091	369	11 438	2 197	6 546	1 484	203	3 608	196	493

Denotes first year for which figures include Alaska and Hawaii.
¹. Includes fortnightly.

Series RR 1. Cable Television—Systems and Subscribers: 1970 to 2000
(Subscribers in thousands (4 500 represents 4 500 000), except percent. Estimated)

Year (As of Jan. 1)	Systems	Subscribers	Year (As of Jan. 1)	Systems	Subscribers	Subscriber size group	Number of [1]- Systems	Number of [1]- Subscribers	Percent of [1]- Systems	Percent of [1]- Subscribers
1970	2 490	4 500	1989	9 050	47 500	1999, total [2]	10 466	66 054	100	100
1975	3 506	9 800	1990	9 575	50 000	50 000 and over	279	33 600	3	50
1980	4 225	16 000	1991	10 704	51 000	20 000 to 49 999	442	13 976	4	21
1982	4 825	21 000	1992	11 075	53 000	10 000 to 19 999	481	6 982	5	11
1983	5 600	25 000	1993	11 100	55 000	5 000 to 9 999	651	4 516	6	7
1984	6 200	30 000	1994	11 200	57 000	3 500 to 4 999	394	1 740	4	3
1985	6 600	32 000	1995	11 126	58 000	1 000 to 3 499	1 842	3 469	18	6
1986	7 600	37 500	1996	11 119	60 280	500 to 999	1 324	956	13	2
1987	7 900	41 100	1997	10 950	64 050	250 to 499	1 290	463	12	1
1988	8 500	44 000	1998	10 845	64 170	Less than 250	3 051	352	29	1
			1999	10 700	65 500					
			2000	10 400	66 500					

1. As of October 1.
2. Total number of systems includes 844 not available by subscriber size-group.

Series RR 3. Public Television Programming: 1984 to 1996
(For October through September seasons. General programming is directed at the general community. Instructional programming is directed at students in the classroom or otherwise in the general context of formal education)

Item	1984	1986	1988	1990	1992	1994	1996
Stations broadcasting	303	305	322	341	349	349	352
Number of broadcasters [1]	169	178	186	193	198	198	201
Average annual hours per broadcaster	5 542	5 650	6 135	6 392	6 303	6 500	6 758
BROADCAST HOURS, PERCENT DISTRIBUTION							
Program content	100	100	100	100	100	100	100
General	88	86	85	86	90	92	92
News and public affairs [2]	14	16	16	18	17	19	19
Information and skills	26	30	32	32	29	27	29
Cultural	20	21	18	19	18	16	17
General children's and youth's	8	7	6	6	15	20	20
Sesame Street	15	11	12	11	11	9	8
Other	6	2	1	1	1	1	1
Instructional [3]	13	15	16	14	12	9	8
Children and youth	12	...	...	...	9	6	5
Adult	1	...	...	...	3	3	3
Producer	100	100	100	100	100	100	100
Local	6	5	5	5	4	5	5
Any public TV source	44	38	27	32	31	33	36
U.S. Coproduction [4]	3	3	10	10	6	6	6
Children's TV Workshop	16	529	16	15	14	12	9
Independent producer	9	(5)	19	19	25	26	27
Foreign producer, international coproduction	13	15	14	12	11	10	10
Commercial producer	3	6	4	4	5	5	4
Other	5	4	4	3	4	4	4
Distributor	100	100	100	100	100	100	100
Local distribution only	6	5	6	6	5	4	5
Public broadcasting service	65	64	62	59	63	63	63
Regional public television network	13	14	18	24	23	23	25
Other	16	17	14	11	9	9	8

1. Beginning 1988, only broadcasters in the 50 U.S. States were surveyed. In prior years, the stations in the outlying areas were also included.
2. Beginning 1986, this category includes "Business or Consumer."
3. Some general audience programs with instructional applications were double counted if aired during school hours when school was in session. The Electric Company was one such program.
4. Prior to 1986, "Consortium".
5. Independent producer included with Children's TV Workshop for 1986.

SOURCE: Corporation for Public Broadcasting, Washington, DC, Programming Survey, biennial.

Series RR 4. Cellular Telephone Industry: 1990 to 1999

(Calendar year data, except as noted (5 283 represents 5 283 000). Based on a survey mailed to all cellular, personal communications services, and enhanced special mobile radio systems. For 1998 data, the universe was 3 073 systems and the response rate was 94 percent)

Item	Unit	1990	1992	1993	1994	1995	1996	1997	1998	1999
Systems..........................	Number	751	1 506	1 529	1 581	1 627	1 740	2 228	3 073	3 518
Subscribers......................	1 000	5 283	11 033	16 009	24 134	33 786	44 043	55 312	69 209	86 047
Cell sites [1]	Number	5 616	10 307	12 805	17 920	22 663	30 045	51 600	65 887	81 698
Employees........................	Number	21 382	34 348	39 775	53 902	68 165	84 161	109 387	134 754	155 817
Service revenue	Mil. dol.	4 548	7 822	10 891	14 229	19 081	23 635	27 486	33 133	40 018
Roamer revenue [2]............	Mil. dol.	456	974	1 360	1 830	2 542	2 781	2 974	3 501	4 085
Capital investment............	Mil. dol.	6 282	11 262	13 946	18 939	24 080	32 574	46 058	60 543	71 265
Average monthly bill [3]	Dollars	80.90	68.68	61.48	56.21	51.00	47.70	42.78	39.43	41.24
Average length of call [3].....	Minutes	2.20	2.58	2.41	2.24	2.15	2.32	2.31	2.39	2.38

1. The basic geographic unit of a wireless PCS or cellular system. A city or county is divided into smaller "cells," each of which is equipped with a low-powered radio transmitter/receiver. The cells can vary in size depending upon terrain, capacity demands, etc. By controlling the transmission power, the radio frequencies assigned to one cell can be limited to the boundaries of that cell. When a wireless PCS or cellular phone moves from one cell toward another, a computer at the Switching Office monitors the movement and at the proper time, transfers or hands off the phone call to the new cell and another radio frequency.
2. Service revenue generated by subscribers' calls outside of their system areas.
3. As of December 31.

Series RR 5. Telecommunications Industry—Carriers and Revenue: 1993 to 1998

(Revenue in millions of dollars (165 342 represents $165 342 000 000). Data based on carrier filings to the FCC. Because of reporting changes, data for 1997 are not strictly comparable with previous years; see source for details)

Category	Carriers						Telecommunications revenue					
	1993	1994	1995	1996	1997	1998	1993	1994	1995	1996	1997	1998
Total [1]	2 709	2 847	3 058	3 832	3 604	4 144	165 342	174 890	190 076	211 782	231 168	246 392
Local service providers	1 464	1 574	1 675	2 028	2 066	2 239	95 595	99 011	103 792	109 273	108 568	113 369
Incumbent local exchange carriers (ILECs).............	1 281	1 347	1 347	1 376	1 410	1 348	95 228	98 431	102 820	107 905	105 154	108 234
Pay telephone providers........................	163	197	271	533	509	615	175	300	349	357	933	1 101
Competitors of ILECs..............	20	30	57	119	147	276	191	281	623	1 011	2 481	4 034
CAPs and CLECs [2]	20	30	57	94	129	212	191	281	623	1 011	1 919	3 348
Local resellers..................	(3)	(3)	(3)	8	11	54	(3)	(3)	(3)	(3)	206	410
Other local exchange carriers...........	(3)	(3)	(3)	13	3	10	(3)	(3)	(3)	(3)	157	36
Private carriers.................	(3)	(3)	(3)	(3)	2	(NA)	(3)	(3)	(3)	(3)	112	147
Shared tenant service providers.......	(3)	(3)	(3)	4	2	(NA)	(3)	(3)	(3)	(3)	87	93
Wireless service providers [4]......................	924	907	930	1 217	969	1 258	10 179	14 197	18 627	25 900	33 030	37 032
Telephony [5]......................	798	790	792	853	732	808	9 215	13 259	17 208	23 778	29 944	33 139
Paging service providers.............	126	117	138	200	137	303	(3)	(3)	(3)	(3)	2 861	3 161
Toll service providers..............	321	366	453	587	569	647	64 393	70 466	76 447	86 896	89 570	95 992
Interexchange carriers........................	83	97	130	149	151	171	61 118	66 381	70 938	79 057	79 080	83 443
Operator service providers..................	35	29	25	27	32	24	695	536	500	461	603	590
Prepaid service providers.....................	(3)	(3)	8	16	18	20	(3)	(3)	16	238	519	888
Satellite service carriers.................	(3)	(3)	(3)	22	13	13	(3)	(3)	(3)	(3)	1 011	473
Toll resellers...................	171	206	260	345	340	388	1 869	2 840	4 220	6 564	8 010	9 885
Other toll carriers................	32	34	30	28	15	31	711	709	773	577	348	710

1. Revenue data include adjustments, not shown separately. Through 1996, revenue data include some non-telecommunications revenue, formerly reported as local exchange wireless revenue.
2. Competitive access providers and competitive local exchange carriers.
3. Data not available separately.
4. Includes specialized mobile radio services and other services, not shown separately.
5. Cellular service, personal communications service, and specialized mobile radio.

SOURCE: U.S. Federal Communications Commission, Trends in Telephone Service, February 1999.

Series RR 6. Utilization of Selected Media: 1970 to 1997

(62.0 represents 62 000 000)

Item	Unit	1970	1980	1985	1990	1992	1993	1994	1995	1996	1997
Households with-											
Telephone service [1]	Percent	87.0	93.0	91.8	93.3	93.9	94.2	93.9	93.9	93.8	93.9
Radio [2]	Millions	62.0	78.6	87.1	94.4	96.6	97.3	98.0	98.0	98.0	98.0
Percent of total households	Percent	98.6	99.0	99.0	99.0	99.0	99.0	99.0	99.0	99.0	99.0
Average number of sets	Number	5.1	5.5	5.5	5.6	5.6	5.6	5.6	5.6	5.6	5.6
Television [3]	Millions	59	76	85	92	92	93	94	95	96	97
Percent of total households	Percent	95.3	97.9	98.1	98.2	98.3	98.3	98.3	98.3	98.3	98.4
Television sets in homes	Millions	81	128	155	193	192	201	211	217	223	229
Average number of sets per home	Number	1.4	1.7	1.8	2.1	2.1	2.2	2.2	2.3	2.3	2.4
Color sets	Millions	21	63	78	90	91	92	93	94	95	97
Cable television [4]	Millions	4	15	36	52	55	57	59	60	63	64
Percent of TV households	Percent	6.7	19.9	42.8	56.4	60.2	61.4	62.4	63.4	65.3	66.5
VCRs [4]	Millions	. . .	1	18	63	69	72	74	77	79	82
Percent of TV households	Percent	. . .	1.1	20.8	68.6	75.0	77.1	79.0	81.0	82.2	84.2
Commercial radio stations: [2]											
AM	Number	4 323	4 589	[5] 4 718	4 987	4 961	4 994	4 913	4 150	4 857	4 762
FM	Number	2 196	3 282	[5] 3 875	4 392	4 785	4 971	5 109	5 730	5 419	5 542
Television stations: [6] Total	Number	862	1 011	1 182	1 442	1 481	1 506	1 512	1 532	1 533	1 574
Commercial [3]	Number	677	734	883	1 092	1 118	1 137	1 145	1161	1 174	1 177
VHF	Number	501	516	520	547	551	552	561	562	554	588
UHF	Number	176	218	363	545	567	585	584	599	620	619
Cable television:											
Systems [6]	Number	2 490	4 225	6 844	9 575	11 075	11 217	11 214	11 218	11 119	10 950
Households served [7]	Millions	4.5	17.7	39.9	54.9	57.2	58.8	60.5	63.0	64.6	65.9
Daily newspaper circulation [8]	Millions	62	62	63	62	60	60	59	57	57	57

1. For occupied housing units. 1970 and 1980 as of April 1; all other years as of March. Source: U.S. Census Bureau, 1970 and 1980 Census of Housing, Vol. 1; thereafter Federal Communications Commission, Trends in Telephone Service, July 1998.
2. As of December 31, except as noted. Source: Radio Advertising Bureau, New York, NY, through 1992, Radio Facts, annual, (copyright); beginning 1993, Radio Marketing Guide and Fact Book for Advertisers, annual, (copyright). Number of stations on the air compiled from Federal Communications Commission reports.
3. 1970, as of September of prior year; all other years as of January of year shown. Excludes Alaska and Hawaii. Source: Television Bureau of Advertising, Inc., Trends in Television, annual (copyright).
4. As of February. Excludes Alaska and Hawaii. Source: See footnote 3.
5. As of February 1986.
6. As if January 1. Source: Warren Publishing, Washington DC, Television and Cable Factbook (copyright).
7. Source: Nielsen Media Research, Nielsen Station Index, November diary estimates (copyright).
8. As of September 30. Source: Editor & Publisher, Co., New York, NY, Editor & Publisher International Year Book, annual (copyright).

SOURCE: Compiled from sources mentioned in footnotes.

Series RR 7. Recording Media—Manufacturers' Shipments and Value: 1982 to 1998

(577.4 represents 577 400 000. Domestic shipments based on reports of manufacturers representing more than 85 percent of the market. Domestic value data based on list prices of records and other media)

Medium	1982	1985	1990	1993	1994	1995	1996	1997	1998
UNIT SHIPMENTS [1] (mil.)									
Total [2]	577.4	653.0	865.7	955.6	1 122.7	1 112.7	1 137.2	1 063.4	1 124.3
CDs	. . .	22.6	286.5	495.4	662.1	722.9	778.9	753.1	847.0
CD singles	. . .	. . .	1.1	7.8	9.3	21.5	43.2	66.7	56.0
Cassettes	182.3	339.1	442.2	339.5	345.4	272.6	225.3	172.6	158.5
Cassette singles	. . .	. . .	87.4	85.6	81.1	70.7	59.9	42.2	26.4
Albums-LPs and EPs	243.9	167.0	11.7	1.2	1.9	2.2	2.9	2.7	3.4
Vinyl singles	137.2	120.7	27.6	15.1	11.7	10.2	10.1	7.5	5.4
Music video	. . .	. . .	9.2	11.0	11.2	12.6	16.9	18.6	27.2
VALUE (mil. dol.)									
Total [2]	3 641.6	4 378.8	7 541.1	10 046.6	12 068.0	12 320.3	12 533.8	12 236.8	13 723.5
CDs	. . .	389.5	3 451.6	6 511.4	8 464.5	9 377.4	9 934.7	9 915.1	11 416.0
CD singles	. . .	. . .	6.0	45.8	56.1	110.9	184.1	272.7	213.2
Casettes	1 384.5	2 411.5	3 472.4	2 915.8	2 976.4	2 303.6	1 905.3	1 522.7	1 419.9
Cassette singles	. . .	. . .	257.9	298.5	274.9	236.3	189.3	133.5	94.4
Albums-LPs and EPs	1 925.1	1 280.5	86.5	10.6	17.8	25.1	36.8	33.3	34.0
Vinyl singles	283.0	281.0	94.4	51.2	47.2	46.7	47.5	35.6	25.7
Music video	. . .	. . .	172.3	213.3	231.1	220.3	236.1	323.9	508.0

1. Net units, after returns.
2. Includes discontinued media.

SOURCE: Recording Industry Association of America, Washington, DC, Internet site <http://www.riaa.com> (accessed March 30, 1999).

SECTION

S

ENERGY

SECTION S

ENERGY

Highlights

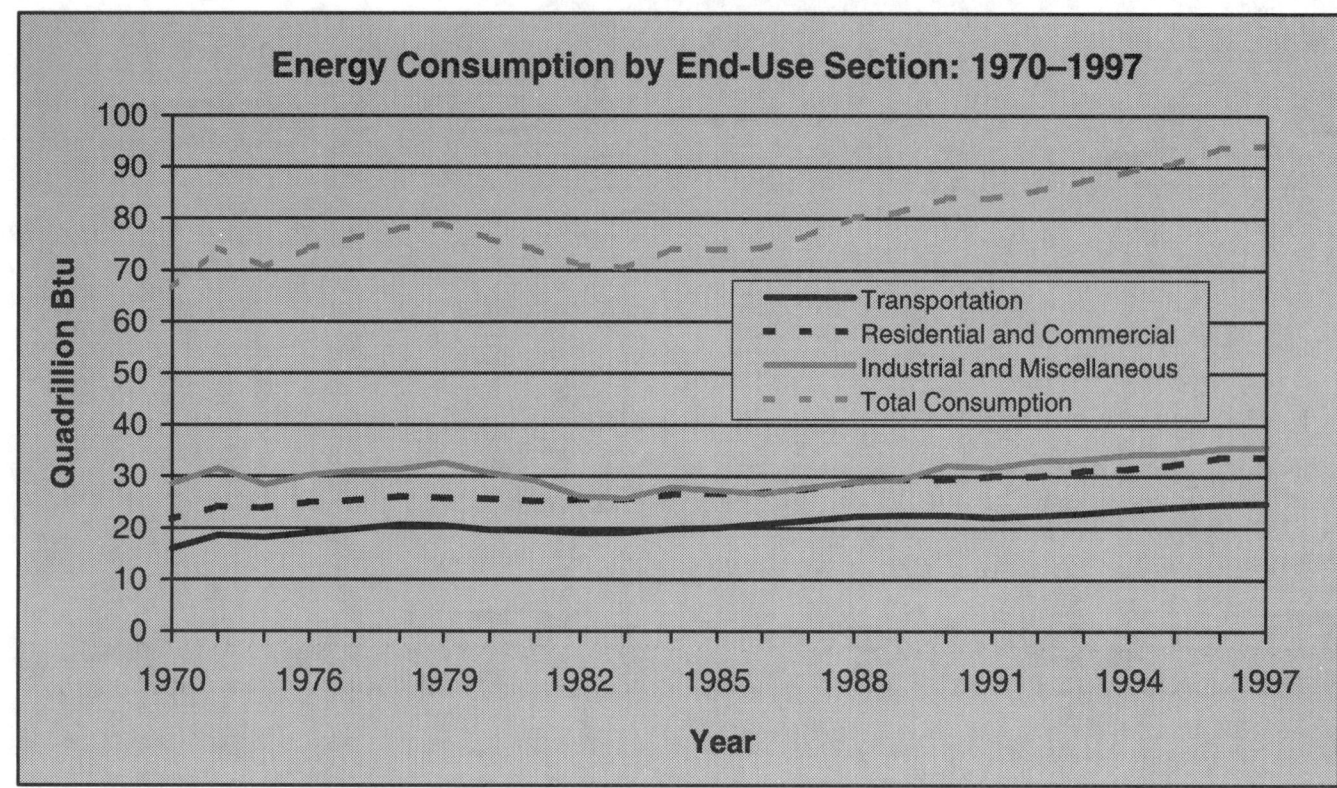

Energy Consumption by End-Use Section: 1970–1997

y-axis: Quadrillion Btu — 0, 10, 20, 30, 40, 50, 60, 70, 80, 90, 100

x-axis: Year — 1970, 1976, 1979, 1982, 1985, 1988, 1991, 1994, 1997

Legend:
- Transportation
- Residential and Commercial
- Industrial and Miscellaneous
- Total Consumption

1 Data on the production of electric energy have been available since the beginning of the first commercial production in 1882, but because of the changing bases of measurement and variations in coverage, the information is difficult to evaluate for the years before 1920. The Bureau of the Census conducted censuses of the light and power industries at five-year intervals from 1902 to 1937. The *Electrical World* (McGraw-Hill) and the National Electric Light Association also published considerable data on this early period. Early data on capacity have to be converted from horsepower (hp) to kilowatts (kW) to be comparable. Data on generation also were often reported without allowance for kWhs used in generation, and end uses were reported by appliances (such as lamps) rather than as kWh. These variations in measurements, classification, and coverage often resulted in differences as high as 25%. Generators in mobile equipment, such as ships, railroads and barges, are also unaccounted for in the totals.

2 The principal sources of data on energy are the Energy Information Administration, the Edison Electric Institute, and the American Gas Association. Among the EIA annuals are *Annual Energy Review, Electric Power Annual, Natural Gas Annual, Petroleum Supply Annual, State Energy Data Report, State Energy Price and Expenditure Report, Financial Statistics of Selected Electric Utilities, Performance Profiles of Major Energy Producers, Annual Energy Outlook,* and *International Energy Annual.* The Edison Electric Institute produces the *Statistical Yearbook of Electric Utility Industry* and the *Year-End Summary of the Electric Power Situation in the United States* while the American Gas Association publish *Gas Facts.*

3 Energy data were presented formerly in widely varying units, but increasingly are being converted to a common thermal unit, the BTU (British Thermal Unit). A BTU is the amount of energy required to raise the temperature of 1 pound of water 1 degree Farhrenheit at or near 39.2 degrees F. The conversion factors are as follows:

	Production	Consumption
Petroleum (barrel)	5.800 million BTU	5.586 million BTU
Coal (short ton)	21.278 million BTU	20.852 million BTU
Natural Gas (cubic feet)	1,028 BTU	1,028 BTU
Nuclear Power (kWh)	10,676 BTU	10,676 BTU
Geothermal Power (kWh)	20,914 BTU	20,914 BTU
Fossil Fuel (kWh)	10,272 BTU	10,272 BTU

4 Of the total consumption of 90.42 quadrillion BTU in 1998, 40% is derived from petroleum, 24.1% from natural gas, 23.4% from coal, 8% from nuclear power, and 4.5% from renewable sources, such as hydroelectric, geothermal, and biofuels. The United States is more or less self-sufficient in the major energy sources except petroleum of which it imports 18.35 quadrillion BTU.

5 The share of coal in both production and consumption has shown remarkable growth. Its production has increased from 14.61 quadrillion BTU in 1970 to 23.58 quadrillion BTU and its consumption from 21.26 quadrillion BTU to 21.20 quadrillion BTU. Other alternative forms of energy, once touted as the wave of the future, have yet to make an impact on the energy picture.

6 By end-use consumption, residential and commercial use account for 35.8% of total energy, industrial use for 37.9% and transportation for 26.3%.

7 Energy prices rose steeply from 1970 to 1985 and since then have stabilized. The average fuel price per million BTU was $1.65 in 1970, $8.40 in 1985 and $8.28 in 1995.

8 In 1993 the average single-family detached home consumed 121 million BTU at a cost of $1,452 per year. Of total consumption, natural gas accounted for 3.77 quadrillion BTU, electricity for 2.34 quadrillion BTU, and fuel oil for 0.78 quadrillion BTU.

9 The United States has had a negative trade balance in both natural gas and crude oil since 1970. Crude oil imports have reached 3.121 billion barrels in 1998 compared to 483 million barrels in 1970. Of the total imports OPEC countries supply 1.492 billion barrels and non-OPEC countries 1.458 billion barrels.

10 There are 110 nuclear power plants in the United States in 32 states. Illinois has the most with 13. Total generation of electric power is 628.644 billion kWh or 20.1% of total. The United States accounts for slightly less than one-third of the 362 nuclear plants worldwide.

11 Electric utilities generate 3.123 trillion kWh and sell 3.140 trillion kWh. Of total generation, 34.4% goes to residential customers.

12 The gas utility industry had 59,802,000 customers, (of which 54,998,000 were residential), sales of 8.913 quadrillion BTU and revenues of $511.5 billion.

13 The Strategic Petroleum Reserve grew from 7.6 million barrels in 1977 to 585.69 million barrels in 1990, equivalent to 83 days of crude oil imports.

14 Solar collectors have yet to realize their potential as inexpensive energy producers. The number of solar collector manufacturers has dropped from a high of 225 in 1984 to 29 in 1997 and total shipments from 17,191,000 sq ft to 8,138,000 square feet.

15 Developed water power in the United States generated 73.5 million kWh in 1997. The Pacific region produced one-half of the total.

Series S 1-14. Total Horsepower of All Prime Movers: 1849 to 1992

(In thousands)

Year	Total [10]	Automotive [1]	Nonautomotive Total [10]	Factories [2]	Mines	Railroad [3]	Merchant ships [9] powered	Farms [4]	Electric central stations	Aircraft
	1	2	3	6	7	8	9	11	13	14
1992	35 300 000	33 431 000	1 869 000	68 000	47 000	50 000	29 000	352 000	1 057 000	266 000
1991	34 962 000	33 158 000	1 804 000	67 000	48 000	50 000	27 000	355 000	991 000	266 000
1990	34 958 000	33 158 000	1 800 000	67 000	48 000	50 000	28 000	356 000	1 043 000	267 000
1989	34 579 000	32 790 000	1 789 000	65 000	47 000	50 000	28 000	356 000	976 000	267 000
1988	34 200 000	32 415 000	1 785 000	65 000	47 000	53 000	28 000	356 000	969 000	267 000
1987	33 266 000	31 488 000	1 778 000	65 000	47 000	53 000	29 000	357 000	958 000	269 000
1986	32 660 000	30 893 000	1 767 000	65 000	47 000	56 000	29 000	358 000	942 000	270 000
1985	32 529 000	30 792 000	1 737 000	65 000	47 000	58 000	29 000	358 000	912 000	268 000
1984	31 819 000	30 117 000	1 702 000	65 000	47 000	61 000	30 000	359 000	886 000	254 000
1983	31 337 000	29 662 000	1 675 000	64 000	47 000	62 000	29 000	356 000	877 000	240 000
1982	30 495 000	28 852 000	1 643 000	64 000	48 000	64 000	29 000	352 000	854 000	232 000
1981	29 507 000	27 909 000	1 598 000	64 000	48 000	65 000	29 000	345 000	835 000	212 000
1980	28 922 000	27 362 000	1 564 000	64 000	48 000	63 000	28 000	345 000	806 000	210 000
1979	28 162 000	26 617 000	1 545 000	63 000	48 000	62 000	26 000	342 000	803 000	201 000
1978	27 379 000	25 892 000	1 487 000	63 000	48 000	64 000	25 000	335 000	754 000	198 000
1977	26 469 000	25 025 000	1 444 000	62 000	47 000	62 000	23 000	328 000	728 000	194 000
1976	25 507 000	24 339 000	1 393 000	61 000	47 000	64 000	22 000	324 000	692 000	184 000
1975	25 100 000	23 752 000	1 348 000	60 000	47 000	62 000	22 000	318 000	654 000	185 000
1974	24 516 000	23 224 000	1 292 000	59 000	46 000	61 000	21 000	315 000	605 000	185 000
1973	24 262 000	23 029 000	1 233 000	58 000	46 000	57 000	20 000	308 000	562 000	182 000
1972	22 913 000	21 736 000	1 175 000	57 000	46 000	57 000	21 000	305 000	508 000	181 000
1971	21 862 000	20 732 000	1 130 000	56 000	45 000	56 000	21 000	300 000	473 000	179 000
1970	20 408 000	19 325 000	1 083 000	54 000	45 000	54 000	22 000	[6] 288 500	435 000	183 000
1969	19 115 000	18 075 000	1 040 250	53 000	44 000	53 000	19 000	[6] 302 000	404 000	165 000
1968	17 912 144	16 937 725	974 419	52 000	43 400	57 607	20 413	290 600	371 756	137 158
1967	17 050 693	16 152 371	898 322	51 000	42 500	49 067	21 493	273 606	342 918	116 093
1966	15 959 175	15 101 836	857 339	49 700	41 200	47 098	22 622	274 227	323 800	96 864
1965	15 096 332	14 306 300	790 023	48 400	40 300	43 838	24 015	269 822	307 025	54 600
1964	14 272 244	13 512 653	759 591	47 000	39 327	46 548	23 175	258 451	287 111	55 154
1963	13 413 072	12 713 712	699 360	45 770	37 000	46 390	23 890	217 928	273 085	52 758
1962	12 586 417	11 930 000	656 417	44 600	[2] 36 300	46 694	22 867	204 740	249 059	49 516
1961	11 611 311	10 972 210	639 101	43 250	[2] 35 400	47 453	23 046	205 463	235 746	46 000
1960	11 007 889	10 366 880	641 009	42 000	34 700	46 856	23 890	237 020	217 173	36 534
1955	7 158 229	6 632 121	526 108	35 579	[7] 30 768	60 304	[8] 24 155	[7] 207 742	137 576	[8] 25 779
1952	5 736 886	5 361 386	375 500	35 045	9 523	101 690	23 207	73 590	103 453	22 941
1950	4 754 038	4 403 617	350 421	32 921	8 500	110 969	[8] 23 423	57 533	87 965	[8] 22 000
1940	2 773 316	2 511 312	262 004	21 768	7 332	92 361	[8] 9 408	57 472	53 542	7 455
1939	. . .	2 400 000	. . .	21 239	7 149	90 500	10 000	40 750	52 115	6 000
1930	1 663 944	1 426 568	237 376	19 519	5 620	109 743	9 115	28 610	43 427	3 382
1929	. . .	1 424 980	. . .	19 328	5 450	111 881	9 017	27 261	40 014	3 091
1920	453 450	280 900	172 550	19 422	5 146	80 182	6 508	21 443	17 050	. . .
1919	. . .	230 432	. . .	19 432	5 112	76 660	6 229	20 796	15 250	. . .
1910	138 810	24 686	114 124	16 697	4 473	51 308	3 098	10 460	6 228	. . .
1909	. . .	7 714	. . .	16 393	4 401	48 491	2 750	9 311	5 225	. . .
1900	63 952	100	63 852	10 309	2 919	24 501	1 663	4 009	1 350	. . .
1899	. . .	32	. . .	9 633	2 754	21 835	1 542	3 420	1 200	. . .
1890	44 086	. . .	44 086	6 308	1 445	16 980	1 124	1 452	447	. . .
1889	. . .	. . .	. . .	5 939	1 300	16 440	1 078	1 233	120	. . .
1880	26 314	. . .	26 314	3 664	715	8 592	741	668	. . .	. . .
1879	. . .	. . .	. . .	3 411	650	7 720	703	605	. . .	. . .
1870	16 931	. . .	16 931	2 453	380	4 462	632	. . .	. . .	. . .
1869	. . .	. . .	. . .	2 346	350	4 100	624	. . .	. . .	. . .
1860	13 763	. . .	13 763	1 675	170	2 156	515	. . .	. . .	. . .
1859	. . .	. . .	. . .	1 600	150	1 940	503	. . .	. . .	. . .
1850	8 495	. . .	8 495	1 150	60	586	325	. . .	. . .	. . .
1849	. . .	. . .	. . .	1 100	50	435	305	. . .	. . .	. . .

* Denotes first year for which figures include Alaska and Hawaii.
1. Includes passenger cars, trucks, buses and motorcycles.
2. Excludes electric motors.
3. Beginning 1965, not strictly comparable with earlier years.
4. Excludes horses and other work animals.
5. Includes private planes and commercial airlines.
6. Includes windmills.
7. Beginning 1955, not strictly comparable with earlier years.
8. Includes Alaska and Hawaii.
9. Beginning 1975, includes sailing vessels, which supplied 1,000 HP in 1970. At their high point in 1860, sailing vessels provided 597,000 HP.
10. Includes horsepower supplied by work animals and windmills, not shown separately. At their high point in 1920, work animals provided 22,430 HP. At their high point in 1930, windmills supplied 200,000 HP.

Series S 32-43. Net Production of Electric Energy, by Electric Utility and Industrial Generating Plants, by Type of Plant: 1902 to 1997

(In millions of kilowatt hours)

Year	Total utility and industrial				Year	Total utility and industrial			
	Total	Hydro	Steam	Internal combustion		Total	Hydro	Steam	Internal combustion
	32	**33**	**34**	**35**		**32**	**33**	**34**	**35**
1997	3 123 000	. . .	. . .	. . .	1952	463 055	109 708	344 695	8 652
1996	3 077 000	328 000	2 018 000	49 000	1951	433 358	104 376	321 705	7 277
1995	2 995 000	294 000	1 977 000	44 000	1950	388 674	100 884	281 000	6 790
1994	2 911 000	244 000	1 982 000	36 000	1949	345 066	94 773	244 429	5 864
1993	2 883 000	265 000	1 964 000	25 000	1948	336 808	86 992	243 730	6 086
1992	2 797 000	240 000	1 908 000	21 000	1947	307 400	83 066	218 985	5 349
1991	2 825 000	276 000	1 905 000	22 000	1946	269 609	83 150	181 825	4 634
1990	2 805 000	280 000	1 916 000	22 000	1945	271 255	84 747	181 708	4 800
1989	2 784 000	265 000	1 950 000	29 000	1944	279 252	78 905	195 664	4 956
1988	2 704 000	223 000	1 921 000	22 000	1943	267 540	79 077	183 952	4 511
1987	2 572 000	250 000	1 837 000	18 000	1942	233 146	69 133	159 725	4 288
1986	2 487 000	291 000	1 756 000	15 000	1941	208 306	55 357	149 157	3 792
1985	2 470 000	281 000	1 778 000	16 000	1940	179 907	51 659	124 941	3 307
1984	2 416 000	321 000	1 742 000	17 000	1939	161 308	47 691	110 635	2 982
1983	2 310 000	332 000	1 668 000	14 000	1938	141 955	48 394	93 561	. . .
1982	2 241 000	309 000	1 633 000	14 000	1937	146 476	48 272	98 204	. . .
1981	2 295 000	261 000	1 736 000	22 000	1936	136 006	42 750	93 256	. . .
1980	2 286 000	276 000	1 726 000	24 000	1935	118 935	42 253	76 682	. . .
1979	2 247 000	280 000	1 680 000	28 000	1934	110 404	35 922	74 482	. . .
1978	2 206 000	280 000	1 613 000	31 000	1933	102 655	36 730	65 925	. . .
1977	2 124 000	220 000	1 619 000	29 000	1932	99 359	35 998	63 361	. . .
1976	2 038 000	284 000	1 534 000	24 000	1931	109 373	32 106	77 267	. . .
1975	1 918 000	300 000	1 417 000	22 000	1930	114 637	34 874	79 763	. . .
1974	1 867 000	301 000	1 414 000	32 000	1929	116 747	37 038	79 709	. . .
1973	1 860 000	272 000	1 552 000	30 000	1928	108 069	37 297	70 772	. . .
1972	1 752 000	275 000	1 441 000	29 000	1927	101 390	32 924	68 466	. . .
1971	1 614 000	266 000	1 319 000	22 000	1926	94 222	30 355	63 867	. . .
1970	1 639 771	250 699	1 345 252	13 820	1925	84 666	26 112	58 554	. . .
1969	1 552 757	253 468	1 285 448	13 841	1924	75 892	24 138	51 754	. . .
1968	1 436 029	225 874	1 196 587	13 568	1923	71 399	23 421	47 978	. . .
1967	1 317 301	224 978	1 079 508	12 844	1922	61 204	21 262	39 942	. . .
1966	1 249 444	197 938	1 038 645	12 861	1921	53 125	18 732	34 393	. . .
1965	1 157 583	196 984	947 890	12 709	1920	56 559	20 311	36 248	. . .
1964	1 083 741	180 301	890 887	12 553	1917	43 429	13 948	29 481	. . .
1963	1 011 417	168 990	830 285	12 142	1912	24 752	7 387	17 365	. . .
1962	946 526	172 086	763 313	11 127	1907	14 121	4 003	10 118	. . .
1961	881 495	155 630	716 161	9 705	1902	5 969	2 166	3 803	. . .
1960	844 188	149 515	683 941	10 733					
1959 *	797 567	141 500	645 164	10 903					
1958	724 752	143 614	571 037	10 101					
1957	716 356	133 358	571 405	11 593					
1956	684 804	125 237	548 306	11 261					
1955	629 010	116 236	502 388	10 386					
1954	544 645	111 640	423 151	9 854					
1953	514 169	109 617	394 726	9 826					

* Denotes first year for which figures include Alaska and Hawaii.

Series S 95-107. Consumption of Fuels by Electric Utilities: 1920 to 1997

Year	Net generation, by fuel					Fuel consumed		Gas
	Total [1]	Coal	Fuel oil	Gas	Nuclear	Coal	Oil	
	95	96	97	98	99	101	102	103
	Millions of kilowatt hours	Millions of kilowatt hours	Millions of kolowatt hours	Millions of kilowatt hours	Millions of kilowatt hours	1 000 short tons	1 000 42-gallon barrels	Millions of cubic feet
1997	3 123 000	1 789 479	78 075	284 193	627 723	900 000	125 000	2 968 000
1996	3 077 000	1 753 890	61 540	276 930	676 940	875 000	113 000	2 732 000
1995	2 995 000	1 653 240	59 900	308 485	673 875	829 000	102 000	3 197 000
1994	2 911 000	1 635 982	902 241	291 100	640 420	817 000	155 000	2 987 000
1993	2 883 000	1 640 427	100 905	259 470	611 196	814 000	169 000	2 682 000
1992	2 797 000	1 574 711	89 504	262 918	618 137	780 000	152 000	2 766 000
1991	2 825 000	1 550 925	110 175	262 725	613 025	772 000	189 000	2 789 000
1990	2 808 000	1 557 000	117 000	263 000	577 000	772 000	196 000	2 776 000
1989	2 519 000	1 554 000	158 000	267 000	529 000	767 000	267 000	2 787 000
1988	2 481 000	1 541 000	149 000	253 000	527 000	758 000	250 000	2 636 000
1987	2 322 000	1 464 000	118 000	273 000	455 000	718 000	201 000	2 844 000
1986	2 197 000	1 386 000	137 000	249 000	414 000	685 000	232 000	2 602 000
1985	2 189 000	1 402 000	100 000	292 000	384 000	694 000	175 000	3 044 000
1984	2 095 000	1 342 000	120 000	297 000	328 000	664 000	206 000	3 111 000
1983	1 978 000	1 259 000	144 000	274 000	294 000	625 000	247 000	2 911 000
1982	1 932 000	1 192 000	147 000	305 000	283 000	594 000	251 000	3 226 000
1981	2 034 000	1 203 000	206 000	346 000	273 000	597 000	352 000	3 640 000
1980	2 286 000	1 162 000	246 000	346 000	251 000	569 000	421 000	3 682 000
1979	1 968 000	1 076 000	303 000	329 000	255 000	527 000	523 000	3 491 000
1978	1 926 000	977 000	364 000	305 000	276 000	482 000	636 000	3 188 000
1977	1 904 000	985 000	358 000	306 000	251 000	477 000	624 000	3 191 000
1976	1 754 000	945 000	320 000	295 000	191 000	448 000	556 000	3 081 000
1975	1 618 000	853 000	289 000	300 000	173 000	406 000	506 000	3 158 000
1974	1 566 000	830 000	299 000	320 000	114 000	392 000	536 000	3 429 000
1973	1 588 000	849 000	313 000	341 000	83 000	390 000	560 000	3 644 000
1972	1 478 000	773 000	273 000	376 000	54 000	352 000	494 000	3 977 000
1971	1 348 000	. . .	. . .	. . .	. . .	328 000	396 000	3 993 000
1970	1 284 153	706 102	182 488	372 884	21 797	320 818	335 514	3 931 966
1969	1 191 989	706 110	137 847	333 279	13 928	310 641	251 027	3 487 642
1968	1 106 952	684 905	104 276	304 433	12 528	297 779	188 642	3 147 909
1967	992 847	630 483	89 271	264 806	7 655	274 185	161 278	2 746 352
1966	949 594	613 475	78 926	251 151	5 520	266 477	140 949	2 609 949
1965	861 401	570 926	64 801	221 559	3 657	244 788	115 203	2 321 101
1964	806 917	526 230	56 954	220 038	3 343	225 425	101 141	2 322 896
1963 *	751 038	493 927	52 001	201 602	3 212	211 332	93 314	2 144 473
1962	684 031	450 249	46 983	184 301	2 270	193 238	85 768	1 965 974
1961	640 189	421 871	47 120	169 286	1 692	182 121	85 736	1 825 117
1960	607 660	403 067	46 105	157 970	518	176 634	85 340	1 724 762
1959	572 071	378 424	46 840	146 619	188	168 423	88 263	1 628 509
1958	504 662	344 366	40 372	119 759	165	155 724	77 668	1 372 853
1957	501 108	346 386	40 500	114 212	10	160 769	79 693	1 336 141
1956	478 487	338 503	35 947	104 037	. . .	158 279	72 711	1 239 311
1955	433 786	301 363	37 138	95 285	. . .	143 759	75 274	1 153 280
1954	364 354	239 146	31 520	93 688	. . .	118 385	66 745	1 165 498
1953	337 042	218 846	38 404	79 791	. . .	115 897	82 238	1 034 272
1952	293 640	195 437	29 750	68 453	. . .	107 071	67 218	910 117
1951	270 531	185 204	28 712	56 616	. . .	105 768	63 945	763 898
1950	232 813	. . .	. . .	. . .	. . .	91 871	75 420	628 919
1949	200 965	. . .	. . .	. . .	. . .	83 963	66 301	550 121
1948	199 796	. . .	. . .	. . .	. . .	99 586	42 345	478 097
1947	176 983	. . .	. . .	. . .	. . .	89 531	45 309	373 054
1946	144 555	. . .	. . .	. . .	. . .	72 197	36 316	306 942
1945	142 331	. . .	. . .	. . .	. . .	74 725	20 228	326 212
1944	153 868	. . .	. . .	. . .	. . .	80 084	20 862	358 784
1943	143 785	. . .	. . .	. . .	. . .	77 301	17 986	301 937
1942	121 585	. . .	. . .	. . .	. . .	66 257	15 236	235 208
1941	113 272	. . .	. . .	. . .	. . .	62 668	20 177	201 763

See footnotes at end of table.

Series S 95-107. Consumption of Fuels by Electric Utilities: 1920 to 1997—Cont'd.

Year	Net generation, by fuel					Fuel consumed		
	Total [1]	Coal	Fuel oil	Gas	Nuclear	Coal	Oil	Gas
	95	96	97	98	99	101	102	103
	Millions of kilowatt hours	Millions of kilowatt hours	Millions of kolowatt hours	Millions of kilowatt hours	Millions of kilowatt hours	1 000 short tons	1 000 42-gallon barrels	Millions of cubic feet
1940	93 963	. . .	. . .	. . .	. . .	51 474	16 325	180 096
1939	83 628	. . .	. . .	. . .	. . .	44 539	17 139	188 878
1938	69 255	. . .	. . .	. . .	. . .	38 394	12 942	165 504
1937	74 502	. . .	. . .	. . .	. . .	42 929	13 829	169 127
1936	69 823	. . .	. . .	. . .	. . .	40 085	14 079	154 084
1935	56 688	. . .	. . .	. . .	. . .	32 715	11 257	124 118
1934	54 418	. . .	. . .	. . .	. . .	34 414	10 258	127 071
1933	48 170	. . .	. . .	. . .	. . .	28 543	9 606	101 985
1932	46 422	. . .	. . .	. . .	. . .	28 056	7 583	107 103
1931	58 014	. . .	. . .	. . .	. . .	36 115	7 922	138 458
1930	59 583	. . .	. . .	. . .	. . .	40 278	8 805	119 553
1929	59 154	. . .	. . .	. . .	. . .	41 827	9 783	112 353
1928	49 622	. . .	. . .	. . .	. . .	38 042	6 818	77 155
1927	46 660	. . .	. . .	. . .	. . .	38 199	6 552	62 485
1926	43 472	. . .	. . .	. . .	. . .	36 842	8 999	52 647
1925	39 443	. . .	. . .	. . .	. . .	35 615	9 794	45 472
1924	34 963	. . .	. . .	. . .	. . .	32 790	16 060	47 301
1923	32 088	. . .	. . .	. . .	. . .	33 636	13 925	29 340
1922	26 561	. . .	. . .	. . .	. . .	29 193	12 443	24 996
1921	22 343	. . .	. . .	. . .	. . .	26 604	11 505	21 701
1920	23 495	. . .	. . .	. . .	. . .	31 640	12 690	22 136

* Denotes first year for which figures include Alaska and Hawaii.
1. Excludes generations by wood and waste fuels. Beginning 1961, includes limited output by use of wood, waste and geothermal power, as follows, in million kw.-hr: 220 in 1961; 228 in 1962, 296 in 1963, 352 in 1964, 458 in 1965, 522 in 1966, 632 in 1967, 811 in 1968, 935 in 1969, and 882 in 1970.

Series S 160-175. Developed and Underdeveloped Water Power, by Geographic Division: 1920 to 1997

(In thousands of kilowatts. As of December 31)

Year	Developed water power [1]							
	United States	New England	Middle Atlantic	North Central	South Atlantic	South Central	Mountain	Pacific
	160	**161**	**162**	**163**	**164**	**165**	**166**	**167**
1997	73 500	2 000	5 600	4 200	6 800	8 700	10 000	36 200
1996	74 800	2 000	5 000	4 200	6 800	8 600	10 000	38 300
1995	74 200	1 900	4 900	4 300	6 700	8 600	9 500	38 300
1994	74 100	1 900	4 900	4 300	6 700	8 600	9 500	38 200
1993	74 000	1 900	4 900	4 300	6 700	8 600	9 500	38 100
1992	74 100	1 900	4 900	4 300	6 700	8 600	9 500	38 000
1991	73 600	1 900	4 900	4 300	6 700	8 600	9 400	37 800
1990	73 000	1 900	4 900	4 200	6 700	8 600	9 200	37 500
1989	71 800	1 900	4 800	4 200	6 700	8 300	8 900	37 000
1988	71 300	1 900	4 800	4 200	6 600	8 300	8 500	37 100
1987	70 800	1 800	4 700	4 100	6 700	8 200	8 300	36 800
1986	69 600	1 700	4 600	4 100	6 700	8 200	8 200	36 100
1985	68 800	1 700	4 500	4 000	6 500	8 200	8 100	35 800
1984	67 700	1 600	4 300	3 900	6 100	8 000	8 100	35 700
1983	66 800	1 600	4 300	3 900	6 000	8 100	7 900	35 000
1982	65 900	1 500	4 300	4 000	5 900	7 900	7 700	34 600
1981	65 500	1 500	4 300	3 800	6 000	7 900	7 700	34 300
1980	64 400	1 500	4 300	3 700	5 900	7 900	7 400	33 700
1979	63 300	1 500	4 200	3 800	5 900	7 700	7 300	33 000
1978	61 000	1 500	4 200	3 800	5 800	7 600	7 300	30 800
1977	59 200	1 500	4 200	3 800	5 800	7 900	7 100	29 000
1976	58 600	1 500	4 200	3 700	5 800	7 800	7 100	28 500
1975	57 000	1 500	4 200	3 700	5 800	7 800	6 900	27 200
1974	55 400	1 500	4 200	3 700	5 700	7 700	6 700	26 000
1973	54 974	1 490	4 246	3 704	5 467	7 578	6 665	25 824
1972	53 778	1 510	4 252	3 660	5 470	7 386	6 235	25 265
1971	53 404	1 511	4 252	3 670	5 473	7 321	6 219	24 958
1970	51 952	1 473	4 264	3 664	5 265	7 170	6 202	23 914
1969	50 248	1 495	4 231	3 718	5 271	6 951	6 097	22 481
1968	48 741	1 487	4 243	3 665	5 255	6 874	6 095	21 122
1967	45 826	1 491	4 247	3 703	5 349	6 350	6 083	18 425
1966	44 288	1 487	4 246	3 625	5 184	6 298	6 022	17 426
1965	42 948	1 488	4 237	3 460	4 700	6 088	5 551	17 424
1964	41 827	1 491	4 237	3 302	4 635	5 851	5 218	17 093
1963	40 230	1 497	4 218	3 197	4 600	5 419	4 845	16 454
1962	37 835	1 508	4 239	2 942	4 099	5 164	4 773	15 110
1961	36 193	1 518	3 852	2 618	3 795	4 897	4 821	14 694
1960	33 180	1 520	2 472	2 522	3 773	4 695	4 621	13 578
1959	* 31 794	1 513	2 475	2 369	3 788	4 697	4 511	* 12 439
1958	30 089	1 521	2 113	2 376	3 732	4 697	4 157	11 592
1957	27 761	1 528	1 600	2 277	3 732	4 674	3 785	10 165
1956	26 386	1 388	1 479	2 243	3 611	4 524	3 701	9 440
1955	25 742	1 385	1 789	1 905	3 536	4 524	3 706	8 898
1954	24 238	1 335	1 750	1 783	3 423	4 418	3 629	7 901
1953	23 055	1 282	1 704	1 620	3 212	4 371	3 438	7 425
1952	21 416	1 262	1 707	1 564	2 834	4 054	3 181	6 814
1951	19 871	1 254	1 677	1 559	2 785	3 547	2 627	6 421
1950	18 675	1 239	1 678	1 530	2 767	3 195	2 286	5 980
1949	17 662	1 202	1 687	1 469	2 687	2 993	2 202	5 423
1948	16 635	1 192	1 668	1 437	2 662	2 731	2 056	4 888
1947	15 956	1 165	1 662	1 435	2 662	2 618	2 026	4 387
1946	15 828	1 167	1 669	1 434	2 663	2 618	2 008	4 269
1945	14 912	895	1 591	1 300	2 222	2 592	2 002	4 309
1944	14 586	894	1 593	1 303	2 086	2 393	2 003	4 314
1943	13 884	893	1 587	1 314	2 085	2 151	1 924	3 929
1942	12 842	891	1 596	1 294	2 084	1 936	1 784	3 256

See footnotes at end of table.

Series S 160-175. Developed and Underdeveloped Water Power, by Geographic Division: 1920 to 1997—Cont'd.

(In thousands of kilowatts. As of December 31)

Year	Developed water power [1]							
	United States	New England	Middle Atlantic	North Central	South Atlantic	South Central	Mountain	Pacific
	160	**161**	**162**	**163**	**164**	**165**	**166**	**167**
1941	11 817	855	1 589	1 280	1 912	1 588	1 692	2 902
1940	11 224	858	1 588	1 219	1 882	1 397	1 612	2 668
1939	11 004	833	1 563	1 204	1 803	1 279	1 581	2 741
1938	10 657	824	1 561	1 204	1 728	1 223	1 381	2 736
1937	10 176	832	1 550	1 147	1 710	1 114	1 160	2 662
1936	10 037	832	1 533	1 111	1 709	1 079	1 152	2 622
1935	9 399	804	1 517	1 071	1 678	924	792	2 613
1934	9 345	767	1 489	1 071	1 680	924	782	2 631
1933	9 334	768	1 489	1 065	1 680	916	791	2 624
1932	9 258	768	1 457	1 058	1 634	954	788	2 599
1931	9 091	762	1 338	1 056	1 635	945	788	2 566
1930	8 585	753	1 290	881	1 603	882	784	2 391
1929	7 831	554	1 218	879	1 351	841	680	2 308
1928	7 702	557	1 205	862	1 346	840	679	2 213
1927	6 802	496	1 151	842	963	700	673	1 977
1926	6 405	474	1 115	835	945	618	592	1 826
1925	5 922	415	1 027	813	878	482	570	1 738
1924	5 024	381	905	741	760	280	544	1 413
1923	4 507	350	766	705	659	248	520	1 259
1922	4 128	337	757	664	534	195	509	1 132
1921	3 902	314	741	632	536	187	494	998
1920	3 704	291	662	629	589	174	487	872

See footnotes at end of table.

Series S 160-175. Developed and Underdeveloped Water Power, by Geographic Division: 1920 to 1997—Cont'd.

(In thousands of kilowatts. As of December 31)

Year	Undeveloped water power [1]							
	United States	New England	Middle Atlantic	North Central	South Atlantic	South Central	Mountain	Pacific
	168	**169**	**170**	**171**	**172**	**173**	**174**	**175**
1997	64 100	3 900	3 600	4 300	6 800	6 000	18 000	21 500
1996	70 000	4 400	4 800	4 600	7 300	6 600	19 100	22 900
1995	71 000	4 400	4 900	4 800	7 200	6 900	18 800	24 000
1994	73 500	4 400	4 900	4 800	7 200	7 000	19 100	26 100
1993	73 600	4 400	4 900	4 800	7 200	7 000	19 100	26 200
1992	73 600	4 400	4 900	4 800	7 200	7 000	19 100	26 200
1991	73 300	4 400	4 900	4 800	7 100	7 000	19 100	26 000
1990	73 900	4 400	5 100	4 800	7 000	7 000	19 400	26 200
1989	75 200	4 500	5 200	4 800	7 100	7 200	19 300	27 100
1988	75 800	4 500	5 800	4 800	7 200	7 300	19 400	26 900
1987	76 100	4 300	5 800	4 900	7 200	7 600	20 000	26 300
1986	74 400	4 300	5 200	4 800	7 300	8 100	19 200	26 100
1985	76 400	4 400	5 400	4 900	7 400	8 100	19 400	26 800
1984	76 400	4 500	5 400	4 900	8 100	8 100	18 200	27 200
1983	77 300	4 600	5 400	4 800	8 400	8 100	18 200	27 800
1982	79 100	4 500	5 400	4 800	8 500	8 200	18 500	29 200
1981	108 700	4 600	5 300	5 400	8 900	7 300	20 600	56 600
1980	129 900	4 700	5 100	5 400	9 600	8 000	34 200	62 900
1979	110 500	3 000	4 400	3 600	8 100	6 700	20 800	63 900
1978	109 900	2 800	4 600	3 900	8 500	6 300	17 800	66 000
1977	102 700	3 300	4 500	3 400	7 000	5 100	17 600	61 800
1976	109 900	3 200	4 100	3 500	7 100	5 500	19 000	67 500
1975	113 700	3 300	4 300	3 500	8 400	5 800	19 600	68 800
1974	118 500	3 200	4 300	7 400	9 300	6 000	21 800	66 400
1973	119 202	3 327	4 301	5 606	9 066	6 625	21 829	68 448
1972	126 078	3 315	4 301	5 647	8 965	6 841	25 518	71 491
1971	125 203	3 318	4 269	5 634	9 059	6 906	26 174	69 843
1970	127 990	3 330	4 455	5 966	9 556	7 089	26 655	70 939
1969	128 900	3 300	4 545	5 892	9 708	7 054	26 923	71 478
1968	129 709	3 302	4 545	5 892	9 716	7 063	26 923	72 268
1967	130 444	3 304	4 514	5 619	9 468	7 008	26 891	73 640
1966	130 640	3 312	4 332	5 312	9 812	7 031	26 822	74 019
1965	124 087	3 240	4 986	5 497	9 977	7 343	26 530	66 514
1964	117 793	3 125	4 950	5 691	10 017	7 549	27 253	59 208
1963 *	115 734	3 128	5 179	5 866	9 903	8 023	26 652	56 983
1962	116 100	3 100	5 200	6 800	11 000	8 200	26 900	54 900
1961	112 700	2 800	5 700	9 000	8 900	8 100	24 100	54 100
1960	114 200	2 900	7 600	9 400	8 400	8 500	23 600	53 800
1959	* 114 287	2 858	7 465	9 591	8 388	8 499	23 243	* 54 243
1958	93 783	2 708	7 869	9 323	8 393	7 854	23 141	34 495
1957	90 242	2 728	8 382	8 967	7 645	7 480	21 245	33 795
1956	90 102	2 728	8 012	9 000	7 586	7 721	21 333	33 722
1955	86 895	2 589	8 023	9 335	7 943	7 213	20 668	31 127
1954	82 804	2 990	6 395	9 211	8 058	7 035	20 105	29 010
1953	85 562	3 122	6 449	9 412	8 281	7 464	21 618	29 216
1952	87 992	3 233	3 415	9 480	8 677	7 784	21 895	30 508
1951	86 174	3 239	3 598	8 117	8 255	8 168	22 089	29 708
1950	87 604	3 250	6 572	8 119	8 151	8 304	23 440	29 768
1949	88 070	3 249	6 503	8 192	8 184	8 374	23 426	30 142
1948	. . .	. . .	. . .	. . .	. . .	. . .	. . .	. . .
1947	77 130	3 348	5 175	7 309	7 462	7 446	17 755	28 635
1946	. . .	. . .	. . .	. . .	. . .	. . .	. . .	. . .

* Denotes first year for which figures include Alaska and Hawaii.
1. Nameplate capacity of existing installations only. Includes capacity at electric utility and industrial plants, but excludes pumped storage capacity. Prior to 1946, includes capacity at electric utility plants only.

Series S 190-204. Gas Utility Industry—Customers, Sales, and Revenues, by Type of Service: 1932 to 1997

Year	Customers [1] (1 000)				Sales [2] (mil. therms [3])				Revenues [2] (mil. dol.)			
	Total	Residential	Commercial	Industrial	Total	Residential	Commercial	Industrial	Total	Residential	Commercial	Industrial
	190	191	192	193	195	196	197	198	200	201	202	203
1997	59 802	54 998	4 593	173	89 130	50 210	22 440	15 240	51 517	33 068	12 666	5 284
1996	59 820	54 968	4 616	183	95 320	51 980	23 950	17 910	51 115	32 022	12 726	5 821
1995	58 728	53 955	4 530	181	90 940	47 360	22 040	19 300	46 381	28 741	11 410	5 652
1994	57 960	53 243	4 474	181	94 800	49 720	23 510	20 090	49 864	30 563	12 254	6 475
1993	57 028	52 358	4 428	181	100 210	50 540	23 970	24 040	49 847	29 787	12 076	7 351
1992	56 132	51 525	4 397	165	99 060	46 940	22 090	27 720	46 178	26 702	10 865	7 913
1991	55 174	50 634	4 322	168	96 050	45 500	21 980	26 310	44 647	25 729	10 669	7 576
1990	54 293	49 830	4 249	214	98 460	44 710	21 940	30 110	45 174	25 014	10 610	8 997
1989	53 356	48 980	4 161	215	105 510	47 980	23 220	32 430	47 493	26 172	11 074	9 666
1988	52 422	48 133	4 060	220	107 050	46 950	23 060	35 440	46 162	24 828	10 681	10 113
1987	51 576	47 362	3 980	234	105 430	43 850	21 560	38 480	45 492	23 622	10 271	11 069
1986	50 704	46 583	3 892	229	111 250	43 810	22 390	43 380	51 201	24 759	11 274	14 495
1985	49 971	45 929	3 616	226	126 160	45 130	23 380	56 350	63 293	26 864	12 722	23 086
1984	49 325	45 367	3 730	228	131 620	46 280	23 960	59 910	67 496	27 485	13 205	26 094
1983	48 799	44 894	3 676	229	128 580	44 500	22 980	59 700	65 837	26 173	12 659	26 315
1982	48 415	44 552	3 631	232	141 830	47 700	24 710	67 950	63 200	23 700	11 666	27 200
1981	47 947	44 149	3 564	234	153 750	46 100	23 760	82 390	56 110	19 180	9 286	27 124
1980	47 223	43 489	3 498	236	154 130	48 260	24 530	79 570	48 303	17 432	8 183	22 215
1979	46 478	42 821	3 423	234	154 400	50 830	24 860	74 550	38 947	14 833	6 624	16 961
1978	45 789	42 183	3 370	236	147 480	51 070	25 000	68 410	32 150	12 939	5 696	13 065
1977	45 274	41 682	3 371	220	143 410	49 460	24 090	67 110	28 303	11 541	4 980	11 385
1976	44 942	41 338	3 371	233	148 140	50 140	24 230	71 070	23 701	9 941	4 075	9 374
1975	44 555	40 950	3 367	237	148 630	49 910	23 870	68 370	19 101	8 445	3 302	6 745
1974	44 267	40 628	3 392	249	160 000	48 650	22 930	81 530	15 242	6 899	2 539	5 391
1973	43 715	40 119	3 332	209	164 840	49 940	22 830	83 720	12 990	6 247	2 174	4 198
1972	42 955	39 431	3 261	209	170 820	51 440	22 790	87 770	12 465	6 096	2 064	3 943
1971	42 241	38 788	3 199	205	166 800	50 400	21 560	86 430	11 355	5 635	1 829	3 568
1970	41 482	38 097	3 131	199	160 435	49 237	20 066	84 392	10 283	5 207	1 620	3 181
1969	40 854	37 538	3 074	193	153 916	48 204	18 781	81 358	9 480	4 883	1 459	2 919
1968	39 930	36 691	3 004	188	144 724	45 527	17 049	75 951	8 781	4 567	1 315	2 675
1967	39 077	35 915	2 934	181	134 883	43 653	15 776	70 143	8 261	4 383	1 224	2 461
1966	38 228	35 142	2 868	174	128 591	41 754	14 628	66 533	7 870	4 195	1 135	2 335
1965	37 338	34 341	2 790	166	119 803	39 990	13 448	61 465	7 407	4 030	1 054	2 148
1964	36 463	33 551	2 712	159	115 912	38 697	12 735	59 120	7 133	3 895	998	2 049
1963	35 551	32 711	2 640	162	107 663	36 680	11 366	54 381	6 727	3 728	910	1 906
1962	34 683	31 893	2 598	156	102 348	35 369	10 929	51 001	6 445	3 603	874	1 796
1961	33 831	31 118	2 529	147	95 890	33 210	9 881	47 856	5 993	3 377	789	1 658
1960 *	33 054	30 418	2 458	141	92 877	31 881	9 198	47 094	5 617	3 177	723	1 563
1959 [4]	32 066	29 530	2 364	136	87 917	29 739	8 275	45 631	5 065	2 870	633	1 431
1958	31 242	28 786	2 287	134	80 285	28 125	7 649	40 764	4 568	2 658	571	1 229
1957	30 476	28 101	2 211	132	77 034	25 985	6 989	40 476	4 134	2 379	506	1 150
1956	29 536	27 241	2 141	125	72 541	24 643	6 558	38 687	3 850	2 237	471	1 066
1955	28 479	26 283	2 048	121	66 586	22 387	6 029	35 351	3 450	2 007	424	938
1954	27 528	25 398	1 990	112	61 026	20 031	5 405	33 096	3 049	1 783	378	821
1953	26 705	24 647	1 926	107	56 073	18 033	4 980	30 373	2 716	1 574	339	739
1952	25 850	23 852	1 869	104	52 392	17 348	4 929	27 990	2 466	1 457	321	639
1951	24 953	23 042	1 787	101	48 222	16 205	4 559	35 522	2 228	1 335	294	557
1950	24 001	22 146	1 739	100	42 090	13 839	4 104	22 887	1 948	1 177	266	480
1949	23 035	21 264	1 657	97	35 790	11 827	3 724	18 979	1 689	1 031	238	396
1948	22 245	20 562	1 571	94	33 885	11 153	3 535	17 981	1 579	958	221	377
1947	21 416	19 835	1 474	91	29 882	10 087	3 107	15 792	1 396	862	191	326
1946	20 636	19 157	1 377	87	26 379	8 482	2 630	14 602	1 213	754	161	284
1945	19 977	18 607	1 278	80	25 868	7 749	2 497	14 523	1 153	705	149	281
1944	19 585	18 320	1 177	82	25 120	7 313	2 208	14 635	1 108	667	133	293
1943	19 064	17 838	1 141	77	23 415	7 001	2 083	13 582	1 064	648	128	277
1942	18 734	17 511	1 137	78	20 849	6 679	1 990	11 723	994	623	127	238
1941	18 126	16 904	1 137	78	19 009	5 862	1 650	11 206	914	575	114	220
1940	17 600	16 381	1 138	73	17 235	5 823	1 598	9 544	872	573	112	182

See footnotes at end of table.

Series S 190-204.   Gas Utility Industry—Customers, Sales, and Revenues, by Type of Service: 1932 to 1997—Cont'd.

Year	Customers [1] (1 000)				Sales [2] (mil. therms [3])				Revenues [2] (mil. dol.)			
	Total	Residential	Commercial	Industrial	Total	Residential	Commercial	Industrial	Total	Residential	Commercial	Industrial
	190	**191**	**192**	**193**	**195**	**196**	**197**	**198**	**200**	**201**	**202**	**203**
1939..........	17 128	15 926	1 121	73	15 927	5 289	1 469	8 768	814	538	105	156
1938..........	16 876	15 697	1 094	75	14 682	4 956	1 380	7 941	777	523	101	145
1937..........	16 605	15 466	1 056	74	15 773	4 987	1 382	9 041	802	528	100	167
1936..........	16 170	15 026	1 058	77	14 693	4 784	1 369	8 280	770	516	97	151
1935..........	15 819	14 725	1 014	72	12 924	4 445	1 211	7 221	727	503	91	130
1934..........	15 512	14 440	990	74	12 063	4 202	1 102	6 699	703	494	87	119
1933..........	15 195	14 141	978	68	10 531	4 237	1 150	5 114	680	495	88	95
1932..........	15 532	14 452	999	73	10 441	4 672	1 193	4 534	723	537	93	91

* Denotes first year for which figures include Alaska and Hawaii.
1. Yearly averages.
2. Excludes sales for resale.
3. A therm is equivalent to 100 000 British thermal units. A B.t.u is the quantity of heat required to raise the temperature of one pound of water 1°F. at or near its point of maximum density.
4. Includes Hawaii.

Series SS 1. Energy Supply and Disposition, by Type of Fuel: 1970 to 1998

(In quadrillion British thermal units (Btu). For Btu conversion factors, see text, this section)

Type of fuel	1970	1973	1975	1980	1985	1990	1994	1995	1996	1997	1998
Production	62.07	62.06	59.86	64.76	64.87	167.87	67.46	67.76	68.92	69.04	69.16
Crude oil [2]	20.4	19.49	17.73	18.25	18.99	15.57	14.1	13.89	13.72	13.66	13.22
Natural gas liquids	2.51	2.57	2.37	2.25	2.24	2.18	2.39	2.44	2.53	2.5	2.41
Natural gas	21.67	22.19	19.64	19.91	16.98	18.36	19.35	19.1	19.3	19.39	19.47
Coal	14.61	13.99	14.99	18.6	19.33	22.46	22.07	21.98	22.65	23.16	23.58
Nuclear electric power	0.24	0.91	1.9	2.74	4.15	6.16	6.84	7.18	7.17	6.68	7.16
Hydroelectric power	2.63	2.86	3.16	2.9	2.97	[3] 2.94	2.55	3.06	3.42	3.52	3.19
Geothermal	(Z)	0.04	0.07	0.11	0.2	[1] 0.18	0.15	0.1	0.11	0.12	0.11
Biofuels [4]	(Z)	(Z)	(Z)	(Z)	(Z)	[1] 2.63	2.84	2.85	2.94	2.72	...
Net trade [5]	-5.73	12.68	11.75	12.25	7.87	14.08	18.57	17.89	19.26	20.89	21.82
Exports	2.66	2.05	2.36	3.72	4.23	4.91	4.13	4.58	4.71	4.63	4.32
Coal	1.94	1.43	1.76	2.42	2.44	2.77	1.88	2.32	2.37	...	...
Natural gas	0.07	0.08	0.07	0.05	0.06	0.09	0.16	0.16	0.16	...	...
Petroleum	0.55	0.49	0.44	1.16	1.66	1.82	1.99	1.99	2.06	...	...
Imports	8.39	14.73	14.11	15.97	12.1	18.99	22.7	22.47	23.96	25.53	26.15
Coal	(Z)	-1.42	-1.74	-2.39	-2.39	-2.71	-1.69	-2.14	-2.19	-2.01	-1.81
Natural gas	0.82	0.98	0.9	0.96	0.9	1.46	2.52	2.75	2.85	2.9	3.04
Petroleum [6]	2.81	6.88	8.71	10.59	6.38	12.54	15.13	15.43	16.08	17.65	18.35
Consumption	66.43	74.28	70.55	75.96	73.98	81.28	85.6	87.21	90.04	90.63	90.42
Petroleum [7]	29.52	34.84	32.73	34.2	30.92	33.55	34.74	34.66	35.86	36.38	36.57
Natural gas [8]	21.79	22.51	19.95	20.39	17.83	19.3	21.29	22.16	22.56	22.54	21.84
Coal	12.26	12.97	12.66	15.42	17.48	19.1	19.54	19.61	20.51	21.02	21.2
Nuclear electric power	0.24	0.91	1.9	2.74	4.15	6.16	6.84	7.18	7.17	6.68	7.16
Renewable energy	2.67	3.06	3.29	3.23	3.61	6.17	6.28	6.85	7.39	...	...
Hydroelectric power [9]	2.65	2.98	3.19	3.09	3.37	2.93	2.97	3.41	3.78	3.82	3.45
Geothermal	0.01	0.04	0.07	0.11	0.2	0.18	0.15	0.1	0.11	0.12	0.11
Biofuels [4]	(Z)	-	-	0.01	0.02	0.02	0.02	0.02	0.02	0.02	0.02

- Represents or rounds to zero.
Z Less than 50 trillion.
1. There is a discontinuity in this time series between 1989 and 1990 due to the expanded coverage of nonelectric utility use of renewable energy beginning in 1990.
2. Includes lease condensate.
3. There is a discontinuity in this time series between 1989 and 1990; beginning in 1990, pumped storage is removed and expanded coverage of industrial use of hydroelectric power is included.
4. Includes wood, wood waste, peat, wood liquors, railroad ties, pitch, wood sludge, municipal solid waste, agricultural waste, straw, tires, landfill gases, fish oils, and/or other waste.
5. Exports minus imports.
6. Includes imports of crude oil for the Strategic Petroleum Reserve, which began in 1977. Includes imports of unfinished oils and natural gas plant liquids.
7. Petroleum products supplied, including natural gas plant liquids and crude oil burned as fuel.
8. Includes supplemental gaseous fuels.
9. Includes net imports of electricity.

SOURCE: U.S. Energy Information Administration, Annual Energy Review through 1989; thereafter, Monthly Energy Review, March 1999.

Series SS 2.   Selected Energy Indicators—Summary: 1970 to 1997

(Btu = British thermal unit. For Btu conversion factors, see text, this section. Minus sign (-) indicates decrease)

Item	1970	1973	1975	1980	1985	1990	1991	1992	1993	1994	1995	1996	1997
AVERAGE ANNUAL PERCENT CHANGE [1]													
Gross domestic product [2]	3.3	1.9	-0.2	-0.1	0.7	1.2	-0.9	2.7	2.3	3.4	2.0	2.7	3.7
Energy production, total [3,4]	4.6	-0.2	-1.8	0.3	-0.3	6.8	-0.5	-0.7	-2.4	3.4	0.5	1.8	-
Crude oil [5]	4.2	-0.9	-4.7	0.2	0.2	-3.4	0.8	-3.1	-4.9	-2.7	-1.5	-1.2	-1.1
Natural gas	6.4	-0.0	-6.1	-0.2	-1.2	2.8	-0.7	0.8	1.1	4.0	-1.3	1.0	0.9
Coal	2.2	-0.2	3.4	1.2	-0.4	5.1	-3.9	(Z)	-6.5	8.8	-0.4	3.0	2.3
Energy consumption, total [3,4]	4.6	1.4	-2.6	-0.8	-0.0	3.3	-0.1	1.8	2.1	2.1	1.8	3.3	0.4
Petroleum products	4.8	1.9	-3.1	-1.6	-0.1	-1.9	-2.1	2.1	0.9	2.6	-0.2	3.4	1.2
Natural gas (dry)	6.5	-0.3	-6.0	-0.3	-0.7	-0.5	1.6	2.6	3.4	2.2	4.0	1.8	0.1
Coal	1.1	2.4	-1.2	0.5	0.5	0.9	-1.7	2.4	3.2	1.0	0.3	4.5	2.0
PER CAPITA [6] (mil. Btu)													
Energy production	304	294	278	285	273	284	279	274	265	272	270	273	-
Energy consumption	327	351	327	335	310	338	333	336	339	343	346	354.0	352.0
Energy consumption per dollar of GDP [2] (1 000 Btu)	19.6	19.0	18.2	16.5	13.9	13.7	13.8	13.7	13.7	13.5	13.5	13.6	13.1

- Represents zero.
Z less than .05 percent.
1. Represents percent change from immediate prior year; for example, 1970, change from 1965. Percent change derived from Btu values.
2. Gross domestic product in chained (1992) dollars. For definition of chained, see text, Section 14, Income.
3. Includes types of fuel or power, not shown separately.
4. Due to a lack of consistent historical data, some renewable energy sources are not included.
5. Includes lease condensate.
6. Based on resident population estimated as of July 1.

SOURCE: U.S. Energy Information Administration, Annual Energy Review, and Monthly Energy Review.

Series SS 3.   Energy Prices: 1980 to 1997

Product	Unit	1980	1990	1991	1992	1993	1994	1995	1996	1997
Crude oil domestic first purchase price:										
Nominal	Dol./bbl	21.6	20.0	16.5	16.0	14.3	13.2	14.6	18.5	17.2
Real [1]	Dol./bbl	35.8	21.4	17.0	16.0	13.9	12.6	13.6	16.8	15.3
Motor gasoline	Cents/gal	122.1	121.7	119.6	119.0	117.3	117.4	120.5	128.8	129.1
Leaded regular	Cents/gal	119.1	114.9	. . .	. . .	. . .	. . .	. . .	. . .	. . .
Unleaded regular	Cents/gal	124.5	116.4	114.0	112.7	110.8	111.2	114.7	123.1	123.4
Premium	Cents/gal	. . .	134.9	132.1	131.6	130.2	130.5	133.6	141.3	141.6
Natural gas, residential	Dol./1 000 cu. ft.	3.7	5.8	5.8	5.9	6.2	6.4	6.1	6.3	6.9
Heating oil, residential	Cents/gal	161.3	113.6	104.7	93.4	88.8	84.3	80.6	90.1	. . .
Coal, all	Dol./short tons	28.8	30.5	30.0	29.4	28.6	28.0	27.0	26.5	26.2
Electricity, total	Cents/kilowatthour	4.7	6.6	6.7	6.8	6.9	6.9	6.9	6.9	6.9
Uranium, domestic purchases	Dol./lb	. . .	15.7	13.7	13.5	13.1	10.3	11.1	13.8	12.9

1. In chained (1992) dollars, calculated by using gross domestic product implicit price deflators.

SOURCE: U.S. Energy Information Administration, Annual Energy Review.

Series SS 4. Crude Oil and Refined Products—Summary: 1973 to 1998

(Barrels of 42 gallons. Data are averages)

Year	Crude oil products (1 000 bbl. per day)					Refined oil products (1 000 bbl. per day)			Total all imports [2] (1 000 bbl. per day)	Crude oil stocks [3]	
	Input to refineries	Domestic production	Imports		Exports	Domestic demand	Imports	Exports		Total	Strategic reserve
			Total [1]	Strategic reserve							
1973	12 431	9 208	3 244	. . .	2	17 308	3 012	229	6 256	242	. . .
1974	12 133	8 774	3 477	. . .	3	16 653	2 635	218	6 112	265	. . .
1975	12 442	8 375	4 105	. . .	6	16 322	1 951	204	6 056	271	. . .
1976	13 416	8 132	5 287	. . .	8	17 461	2 026	215	7 313	285	. . .
1977	14 602	8 245	6 615	21	50	18 431	2 193	193	8 807	348	7
1978	14 739	8 707	6 356	161	158	18 847	2 008	204	8 363	376	67
1979	14 648	8 552	6 519	67	235	18 513	1 937	236	8 456	430	91
1980	13 481	8 597	5 263	44	287	17 056	1 646	258	6 909	466	108
1981	12 470	8 572	4 396	256	228	16 058	1 599	367	5 996	594	230
1982	11 774	8 649	3 488	165	236	15 296	1 625	579	5 113	644	294
1983	11 685	8 688	3 329	234	164	15 231	1 722	575	5 051	723	379
1984	12 044	8 879	3 426	197	181	15 726	2 011	541	5 437	796	451
1985	12 002	8 971	3 201	118	204	15 726	1 866	577	5 067	814	493
1986	12 716	8 680	4 178	48	154	16 281	2 045	631	6 224	843	512
1987	12 854	8 349	4 674	73	151	16 665	2 004	613	6 678	890	541
1988	13 246	8 140	5 107	51	155	17 283	2 295	661	7 402	890	560
1989	13 401	7 613	5 843	56	142	17 325	2 217	717	8 061	921	580
1990	13 409	7 355	5 894	27	109	16 988	2 123	748	8 018	908	586
1991	13 301	7 417	5 782	-	116	16 714	1 844	885	7 627	893	569
1992	13 411	7 171	6 083	10	89	17 033	1 805	861	7 888	893	575
1993	13 613	6 847	6 787	15	98	17 237	1 833	904	8 620	922	587
1994	13 866	6 662	7 063	12	99	17 718	1 933	843	8 996	929	592
1995	13 973	6 560	7 230	-	95	17 725	1 605	855	8 835	895	592
1996	14 195	6 465	7 508	-	110	18 309	1 971	871	9 478	850	566
1997	14 662	6 452	8 225	-	108	18 620	1 936	896	10 162	868	563
1998	14 837	6 243	8 550	-	110	18 684	1 832	821	10 382	894	571

- Represents zero.
1. Includes Strategic Petroleum Reserve.
2. Crude oil (including Strategic Petroleum Reserve imports) plus refined products.
3. End of year.

SOURCE: U.S. Energy Information Administration, Monthly Energy Review.

Series SS 5. Electric Utility Sales and Average Prices, by End-Use Sector: 1970 to 1997

(Prior to 1980, covers Class A and B privately-owned electric utilities; thereafter, Class A utilities whose electric operating revenues were $100 million or more during the previous year)

Year	Sales (bil. kWh)				Average price of electricity sold (cents per kWh)							
					Current dollars				Constant (1992) dollars [2]			
	Total [1]	Residential	Commercial	Industrial	Total [1]	Residential	Commercial	Industrial	Total [1]	Residential	Commercial	Industrial
1970	1 392	466	307	571	1.7	2.2	2.1	1.0	5.6	7.2	6.9	3.3
1973	1 713	579	388	686	2.0	2.5	2.4	1.3	5.7	7.1	6.8	3.7
1975	1 747	588	403	688	2.9	3.5	3.5	2.1	6.9	8.3	8.3	5.0
1980	2 094	717	488	815	4.7	5.4	5.5	3.7	7.8	9.0	9.1	6.1
1981	2 147	722	514	826	5.5	6.2	6.3	4.3	8.3	9.4	9.5	6.5
1982	2 086	730	526	745	6.1	6.9	6.9	5.0	8.7	9.8	9.8	7.1
1983	2 151	751	544	776	6.3	7.2	7.0	5.0	8.6	9.8	9.6	6.8
1984	2 286	780	583	838	6.3	7.2	7.1	4.8	8.3	9.5	9.4	6.3
1985	2 324	794	606	837	6.4	7.4	7.3	5.0	8.2	9.4	9.3	6.4
1986	2 369	819	631	831	6.4	7.4	7.2	4.9	7.9	9.2	8.9	6.1
1987	2 457	850	660	858	6.4	7.4	7.1	4.8	7.7	8.9	8.5	5.8
1988	2 578	893	699	896	6.4	7.5	7.0	4.7	7.4	8.7	8.1	5.5
1989	2 647	906	726	926	6.5	7.6	7.2	4.7	7.2	8.5	8.0	5.2
1990	2 713	924	751	946	6.6	7.8	7.3	4.7	7.1	8.3	7.8	5.0
1991	2 762	955	766	947	6.7	8.0	7.5	4.8	6.9	8.2	7.7	4.9
1992	2 763	936	761	973	6.8	8.2	7.7	4.8	6.8	8.2	7.7	4.8
1993	2 861	995	795	977	6.9	8.3	7.7	4.8	6.7	8.1	7.5	4.7
1994	2 935	1 008	820	1 008	6.9	8.4	7.7	4.8	6.6	8.0	7.3	4.6
1995	3 013	1 043	863	1 013	6.9	8.4	7.7	4.7	6.4	7.8	7.1	4.4
1996	3 098	1 082	887	1 030	6.9	8.4	7.6	4.6	6.3	7.6	6.9	4.2
1997	3 120	1 072	913	1 036	6.9	8.5	7.6	4.6	6.1	7.6	6.8	4.1

1. Includes other sectors not shown separately.
2. Based on the GDP implicit price deflator.

SOURCE: U.S. Energy Information Administration, Annual Energy Review.

Series SS 6. Nuclear Power Plants—Number, Capacity, and Generation: 1980 to 1997

Item	1980	1985	1988	1989	1990	1991	1992	1993	1994	1995	1996	1997
Operable generating units [1]	71	96	109	111	112	111	109	110	109	109	109	107
Net summer capability [1, 2] (mil. kW)	51.8	79.4	94.7	98.2	99.6	99.6	99.0	99.0	99.1	99.5	100.8	100.8
Net generation (bil. kWh)...	251.1	383.7	527.0	529.4	576.9	612.6	618.8	610.3	640.4	673.4	674.7	629.4
Percent of total electric utility generation............	11.0	15.5	19.5	19.0	20.5	21.7	22.1	21.2	22.0	22.5	21.9	20.1
Capacity factor [3]..	56.3	58.0	63.5	62.2	66.0	70.2	70.9	70.5	73.8	77.4	76.3	70.8

1. As of year-end.
2. Net summer capability is the peak steady hourly output that generating equipment is expected to supply to system load, exclusive of auxiliary and other power plant, as demonstrated by test at the time of summer peak demand.
3. Weighted average of monthly capacity factors. Monthly factors are derived by dividing actual monthly generation by the maximum possible generation for the month (hours in month times net maximum dependable capacity).

SOURCE: U.S. Energy Information Administration, Annual Energy Review and Monthly Energy Review March 1996.

DISTRIBUTION AND SERVICES

DISTRIBUTION AND SERVICES

Highlights

1 The *Survey of Current Business,* issued by the Bureau of Economic Analysis, is the principal source of data on domestic trade and services. Financial data relating to this sector appear in the *Statistics of Income* published by the Internal Revenue Service. Censuses of retail and wholesale trade have been taken at various intervals since 1929. Limited coverage of service industries started in 1933. Beginning with the 1963 Census, legislation has provided that a census of each area be conducted every five years, in years ending with 2 or 7. The industries covered in the censuses and surveys are classified in the three divisions defined in the *Standard Industrial Classification Manual:* retail trade, wholesale trade and services. The purview of the censuses has varied over the years so that some of the data is incomparable over time. Since 1954, data for nonemployer establishments have been published separately and establishments with no paid employees are excluded from wholesale trade. Since 1977, sales taxes and finance charges have been excluded from sales figures. After 1987, the number of establishments was defined as those in business at any time during the year, rather than at the end of the year as defined previously. From 1987, hospitals are included among services, but government operated services are excluded. In 1982 and 1987, data were not collected from educational institutions nor from services run by labor unions or political organizations. Beginning in 1982, each leased department in a store was classified separately, rather than consolidated with the store as before. Current retail and wholesale trade data appear in the *Monthly Retail Trade Report* and the *Monthly Wholesale Trade Report* respectively.

2 Since 1990 the share of GDP of retail and wholesale trade has remained fairly stable at between 15.2% and 15.5%. The share of services has gone up slightly from 18.4% to 20.2%. Among services, the largest sectors in dollar value are health services ($447 billion), business services ($318.5 billion) and legal services ($100 billion).

3 Retail trade is the most visible and ubiquitous of all businesses. In 1996 there were 1.579 million of them, divided as follows:

Building materials and hardware	64,700
Department stores	10,800
Other merchandise stores	25,500
Food stores	179,300
Automotive dealers and service stations	202,000
Clothing and apparel stores	132,700
Furniture and home furnishing	115,700
Eating and drinking places	466,400
Drug stores	43,200
Liquor stores	28,800
Sporting goods	25,200
Book stores	13,100
Jewelry stores	27,700
Gift and novelties shops	36,100
Florists	26,700

Retail trade employed 21.487 million people with a payroll of $317.7 billion. The annual gross sales revenues of retail establishments were $2.456 trillion. Wholesale trade had 453,184 establishments with sales of $4.055 trillion and 5.82 million employees. Retail sales per capita were $9,984 in 1997.

4 Chains or multiunit stores numbered 528,000 in 1992 accounting for 58.3% of all sales and 91.8% of general merchandise sales. Chain stores account for more than half of all retail sales in drug and proprietary goods, shoes, food and groceries, and apparel and accessories.

5 In terms of annual sales, automotive dealers lead with $661.4 billion, followed by food stores $443 billion, department stores $278.6 billion, eating and drinking places $247 billion, drug stores $105.7 billion. The smallest in sales are bookstores with $13 billion.

6 The gross margin in sales is highest for apparel stores at 41.6% and lowest for automotive dealers at 18.3%. The relative figures are 26.7% for food stores, 32.4% for department stores, 35.3% for furniture stores and 31% for building materials stores.

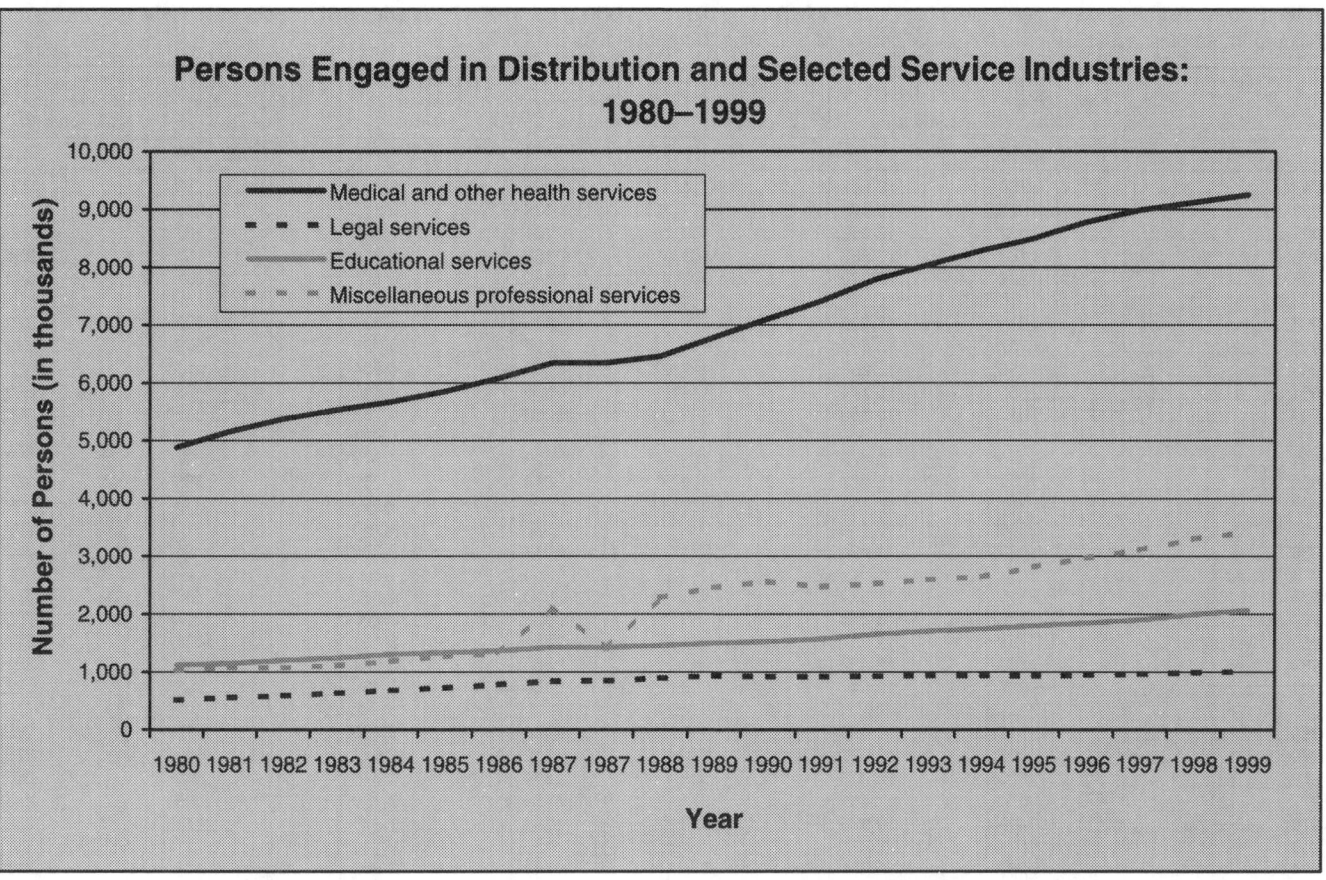

Persons Engaged in Distribution and Selected Service Industries: 1980–1999

Legend:
- Medical and other health services
- Legal services
- Educational services
- Miscellaneous professional services

Y-axis: Number of Persons (in thousands)

X-axis: Year (1980 1981 1982 1983 1984 1985 1986 1987 1987 1988 1989 1990 1991 1992 1993 1994 1995 1996 1997 1998 1999)

7 The 24,100 supermarkets have sales of $307.5 billion and account for 71.5% of all food sales.

8 Of the $94.5 billion worth of alcoholic beverages sold in 1997 $42.6% were consumed in bars, taverns, and restaurants.

9 U.S. mail order sales reached $219.9 billion, of which business products and services accounted for $78 billion.

10 In 1998 there were 43,661 shopping centers in the United States, with 5.333 billion square feet of gross leasable area and retail sales of $1.032 trillion. California with 5,887 shopping centers has the most followed by Florida with 3,278, and Texas with 2,976.

11 In 1992 there were 1,825,000 service industries subject to Federal Income Tax and 209,000 service firms exempt from Federal Income Tax. Health services are the most numerous with 442,000 firms.

12 According to the *Encyclopedia of Associations*, there were 22,901 associations in the United States compared with 14,726 in 1980. Trade, business and commercial associations (3,755) are the most numerous followed by medical (2,453), public affairs (2,113), social welfare (1,934), cultural (1,918), hobbies (1,548), scientific and engineering (1,381) and religious (1,230). The largest association in the United States is the AARP (American Association of Retired Persons), which had more than 22 million members. The largest professional society is the American Psychological Association with over 77,000 members.

13 The growth of the computer industry is reflected in the number of establishments for computer programming and data processing. In 1992 there were 223,600 firms specializing in this field with sales of $104.6 billion.

14 With growing leisure time, amusement and recreation services have burgeoned in both conventional and unconventional areas. Physical fitness centers earn in $4.1 billion, entertainers $13.054 billion, video tape rentals $5.495 billion and motion picture related services $40.168 billion.

Series T 15-28. Persons Engaged in Distribution and Selected Service Industries: 1869 to 1997

(In thousands. Data represent man-years of full-time equivalent by persons working for wages or salaries and by active proprietors or unincorporated businesses devoting the major portion of their time to the business)

Year	Wholesale trade	Retail trade [1]	Hotels and other lodging places	Personal services	Miscellaneous business services	Automobile repair, services and garages [1]	Miscellaneous repair services
	15	**16**	**17**	**18**	**19**	**20**	**21**
1999	6 734	19 643	1 711	1 206	8 797	1 273	366
1998	6 621	19 063	1 647	1 176	8 169	1 215	368
1997	6 462	18 759	1 603	1 161	7 525	1 182	360
1996	6 280	18 383	1 561	1 163	6 876	1 136	358
1995	6 201	18 030	1 522	1 140	6 372	1 061	343
1994	5 971	17 308	1 479	1 118	5 794	1 005	320
1993	5 787	16 692	1 441	1 094	5 338	962	340
1992	5 856	16 258	1 427	1 068	4 934	911	324
1991	5 851	16 124	1 444	1 050	4 642	909	320
1990	6 013	16 560	1 493	1 060	4 782	955	368
1989	6 064	16 472	1 463	1 029	4 543	922	353
1988	5 841	15 981	1 402	1 014	4 255	886	334
1987 [2]	5 707	15 468	1 332	1 026	3 939	849	309
1987 [3]	5 686	15 489	1 332	1 073	4 763	849	309
1986	5 550	14 921	1 271	1 017	4 374	796	309
1985	5 508	14 527	1 222	993	4 042	780	311
1984	5 388	13 788	1 162	951	3 700	707	306
1983	5 103	12 821	1 071	891	3 199	638	277
1982	5 140	12 457	1 043	863	2 981	619	281
1981	5 237	12 541	1 033	850	2 936	598	291
1980	5 112	12 425	997	824	2 783	591	285
1979	5 065	12 527	970	832	2 617	600	278
1978	4 826	12 213	929	814	2 378	566	256
1977	4 574	11 481	877	783	2 138	509	235
1976	4 408	10 975	858	753	1 973	474	222
1975	4 260	10 501	834	741	1 845	444	211
1974	4 342	10 465	828	750	1901	440	213
1973	4 230	10 281	807	773	1 805	433	200
1972	4 005	9 764	750	771	1 634	397	182
1971	3 891	9 524	722	816	1 519	379	172
1970	3 864	9 329	706	858	1 525	365	176
1969	3 782	9 180	691	900	1 483	353	174
1968	3 668	8 867	659	908	1 359	340	170
1967	3 585	8 541	635	905	1 278	331	168
1966	3 501	8 301	604	877	1 170	320	158
1965	3 372	7 941	569	846	1 050	306	147
1964	3 268	7 643	538	809	960	291	139
1963	3 193	7 364	509	793	884	277	136
1962	3 161	7 198	484	780	833	265	133
1961	3 130	7 040	472	774	767	260	130
1960	3 132	7 100	474	780	721	258	131
1959	3 069	6 900	459	771	661	243	124
1958	3 017	6 698	450	775	599	226	115
1957	3 041	6 811	459	792	572	219	125
1956	3 031	6 781	449	788	521	211	119
1955	2 891	6 570	442	783	464	198	114
1954	2 821	6 405	440	787	426	189	110
1953	2 830	6 482	451	805	411	193	120
1952	2 784	6 384	444	815	379	194	126
1951	2 715	6 275	438	825	350	191	122
1950	2 559	5 942	428	818	322	196	111
1949	2 528	5 805	434	826	307	208	114
1948 [2]	2 586	5 852	451	855	306	223	126
1948 [3]	2 428	6 477	453	852	369	. . .	126
1947	2403	6280	461	863	351	. . .	116
1946	2 215	6 011	462	857	324	. . .	107
1945	1 868	5 070	417	746	264	. . .	84
1944	1 771	4 896	420	731	243	. . .	81
1943	1 752	4 926	412	756	229	. . .	78
1942	1 857	4 966	404	750	236	. . .	66

See footnotes at end of table.

Series T 15-28. Persons Engaged in Distribution and Selected Service Industries: 1869 to 1997—Cont'd.

(In thousands. Data represent man-years of full-time equivalent by persons working for wages or salaries and by active proprietors or unincorporated businesses devoting the major portion of their time to the business)

Year	Wholesale trade	Retail trade [1]	Hotels and other lodging places	Personal services	Miscellaneous business services	Automobile repair, services and garages [1]	Miscellaneous repair services
	15	16	17	18	19	20	21
1941	1 952	5 075	404	718	241	...	64
1940	1 840	4 686	388	661	225	...	57
1939	1 776	4 389	377	597	220	...	58
1938	1 707	4 216	373	616	208	...	58
1937	1 706	4 340	373	647	204	...	57
1936	1 550	4 034	349	613	201	...	57
1935	1 443	3743	327	575	172	...	56
1934	1 406	3 576	313	549	172	...	56
1933	1 275	3 197	266	513	147	...	56
1932	1 279	3 217	282	525	141	...	56
1931	1 418	3 656	331	566	137	...	57
1930	1 571	3 980	371	606	153	...	58
1929	1 631	4 215	387	617	157	...	59
1919	1 233	3 977	...	...	...	...	...
1909	1 034	3 177	...	...	...	...	...
1899	783	2 218	...	...	...	...	...
1889	397	1 775	...	...	...	...	...
1879	250	1 087	...	...	...	...	...
1869	169	716	...	...	...	...	...

1. For 1948 and prior year, "Automobile repair, services and garages" included with "Retail trade."
2. Comparable with later years.
3. Comparable with earlier years.

Series T 79-196. Retail Establishments, Sales and Persons: 1929 to 1998

	All establishments			Establishments with payroll		
		Sales				
		Amount	Per capita		Payroll, entire year, amount (mil. dol.)	Paid employees, workweek ended nearest Nov. 15
Year	Number	(mil. dol.)		Number		
	79	**80**	**81**	**82**	**84**	**87**
1998	...	2 696 000	9 984	...	...	...
1997	...	2 566 000	9 588	1 566 000	293 578	21 349 000
1996	...	2 461 000	9 281	1 579 300	317 700	21 487 000
1995	...	2 329 000	8 865	1 566 000	293 578	21 349 000
1994	...	2 230 000	8 567	...	...	...
1993	...	2 074 000	8 046	...	...	...
1992	2 672 000	1 952 000	7 653	1 551 500	265 300	19 777 000
1991	...	1 856 000	7 361	...	...	...
1990	...	1 845 000	7 395	1 529 700	241 700	19 815 000
1989	...	1 759 000	7 127	1 495 000	228 600	19 335 000
1988	...	1 656 000	6 774	1 472 900	...	...
1987 [1]	1 992 000	1 540 000	6 328	1 504 000	177 500	17 780 000
1987 [2]	...	...	...	1 379 000	177 700	17 793 000
1986	...	...	...	1 441 200	193 000	17 550 000
1985	...	1 375 000	5 779	1 406 800	179 000	16 852 000
1982	1 573 000	1 066 000	4 599	1 324 000	123 600	14 468 000
1980	...	957 000	4 213	1 222 900	...	15 047 000
1977	1 567 000	723 000	3 291	1 304 000	85 900	13 040 000
1972 [1]	1 665 000	457 000	2 186	1 265 000	55 400	11 211 000
1972 [2]	1 934 500	470 800	...	1 286 500	56 400	11 359 600
1967	1 763 324	310 214	1 557	1 191 546	36 175	9 380 616
1963 *	1 707 931	244 202	1 294	1 206 087	27 632	8 410 199
1958	1 788 325	199 646	1 152	1 180 641	21 589	7 911 081
1954	1 721 650	169 968	1 054	1 124 040	18 199	7 124 331
1948 [2]	1 688 479	128 849	882	1 118 692	...	...
1948 [3]	1 769 540	130 521	866	1 100 223	13 568	6 918 061
1939	1 770 355	42 042	321	1 017 062	4 529	4 821 806
1935	1 587 718	32 791	258	...	3 568	[4] 3 898 258
1933	1 526 119	25 037	199	...	2 910	[4] 2 703 325
1929	1 476 365	48 330	396	...	5 044	[4] 4 286 516

* Denotes first year for which figures include Alaska and Hawaii.
1. Comparable with later years.
2. Comparable with earlier years.
3. Average annual number of full-time and part-time for year; comparable figure for 1939 is 4 600 217.

Series T 245-271. Retail Store Sales, by Kind of Business: 1929 to 1998

(In millions of dollars. Includes nonstores)

				Durable goods stores					Nondurable goods stores		
				Furniture and appliance group		Lumber, building, hardware group				Apparel group	
Year	All stores	Total sales [1]	Passenger car, other automotive dealers	Furniture, home furnishings stores	Household appliance, T.V., radio stores	Lumber, building materials dealers [2]	Hardware stores	Total sales [1]	Total	Shoe stores
	245	**246**	**247**	**250**	**251**	**252**	**253**	**255**	**256**	**260**
1998..........	2 695 900	1 132 500	661 400	76 200	71 600	127 000	15 300	1 563 400	124 000	20 900
1997..........	2 566 200	1 058 200	625 700	71 600	64 000	116 100	14 600	1 508 000	117 800	20 400
1996..........	2 461 200	1 008 500	599 700	66 000	60 700	106 200	14 400	1 452 700	114 600	20 000
1995..........	2 329 300	939 700	556 700	62 300	57 200	98 200	14 100	1 389 600	110 900	19 300
1994..........	2 229 900	882 100	521 800	59 900	50 100	94 600	14 000	1 347 800	110 000	19 100
1993..........	2 074 500	777 500	456 900	49 500	40 700	82 400	13 200	1 297 000	107 200	18 200
1992..........	1 951 600	703 600	406 900	52 300	35 800	75 400	12 700	1 248 000	104 200	18 100
1991..........	1 855 900	650 000	372 600	55 700	33 600	68 200	12 100	1 206 000	97 400	17 500
1990 [3,9]......	1 844 600	668 800	387 600	50 500	33 000	70 300	12 500	1 175 800	95 800	18 000
1990 [4,10]......	1 807 200	654 800	382 000	51 600	33 000	66 800	13 300	1 152 500	94 700	17 900
1989..........	1 741 700	652 200	383 600	51 100	32 400	67 000	12 600	1 089 600	91 400	17 200
1988..........	1 651 400	627 400	371 600	47 500	30 500	66 600	11 900	1 024 000	84 900	15 400
1987..........	1 542 100	576 600	342 900	44 500	27 100	61 300	11 000	965 500	79 300	14 600
1986..........	1 450 300	541 500	326 300	43 000	27 000	56 500	10 700	908 900	75 600	13 900
1985..........	1 375 000	498 100	303 200	38 300	25 100	50 800	10 500	876 900	70 200	13 100
1984..........	1 297 000	464 300	277 000	35 100	24 000	49 800	9 500	832 700	66 900	10 300
1983..........	1 174 300	396 500	232 800	31 000	19 700	42 400	9 000	777 800	60 300	9 800
1982..........	1 072 100	336 700	193 200	27 000	15 700	35 200	8 700	735 400	55 300	9 100
1981..........	1 041 300	325 100	182 400	27 400	15 300	35 700	8 400	716 300	53 000	9 500
1980..........	957 400	299 200	164 100	26 300	14 000	35 000	8 300	658 100	49 300	10 500
1979..........	899 100	306 400	178 600	25 600	12 700	36 300	7 900	592 800	44 600	7 800
1978..........	806 800	280 400	167 900	22 500	10 700	31 900	6 600	526 400	41 100	6 600
1977..........	725 200	248 700	150 000	20 300	10 000	27 100	6 100	476 500	35 600	5 700
1976..........	657 400	217 800	129 800	18 000	9 200	22 500	5 400	439 600	33 700	5 000
1975..........	588 100	183 000	106 600	16 200	8 300	18 000	5 100	405 200	31 300	4 600
1974..........	541 000	169 400	96 500	16 300	7 600	17 800	4 500	371 600	28 900	4 400
1973..........	509 500	172 900	103 300	15 200	7 400	17 200	4 100	336 600	27 700	4 500
1972..........	449 100	148 400	88 500	13 700	6 800	15 000	3 900	300 700	24 100	4 000
1971 [3,10]......	406 200	128 800	77 400	11 600	6 100	12 900	3 400	277 400	22 100	3 700
1971 [4]......	408 900	131 800	72 500	11 000	6 200	13 700	3 600	277 000	20 800	3 500
1970..........	375 527	114 288	59 388	10 483	6 073	11 995	3 351	261 239	19 810	3 501
1969..........	362 935	115 517	63 091	10 523	5 693	11 630	3 367	247 418	19 866	3 618
1968..........	339 324	110 245	60 660	10 227	5 235	10 984	. . .	229 079	19 265	3 196
1967..........	313 809	100 173	53 966	. . .	. . .	9 781	2 894	213 636	18 123	. . .
1966..........	303 956	98 301	54 144	. . .	. . .	9 769	2 804	205 655	17 291	. . .
1965..........	284 128	94 186	53 484	. . .	. . .	9 731	2 657	189 942	15 765	. . .
1964..........	261 870	84 593	46 029	. . .	. . .	9 089	2 505	177 277	15 295	. . .
1963..........	246 666	79 927	43 609	. . .	. . .	9 169	2 399	166 739	14 233	. . .
1962..........	235 563	74 894	40 472	. . .	. . .	9 017	2 401	160 669	14 164	. . .
1961 [3]......	218 992	67 302	34 695	. . .	. . .	8 697	2 358	151 690	13 614	. . .
1961 [4]......	218 811	66 968	34 523	. . .	. . .	8 316	2 495	151 843	13 601	. . .
1960 *........	219 529	70 560	37 038	. . .	. . .	8 567	2 655	148 969	13 631	2 437
1959..........	215 413	71 608	36 901	. . .	. . .	9 086	2 737	143 805	13 239	2 330
1958..........	200 353	63 409	31 577	6 636	3 688	8 154	2 653	136 944	12 559	2 222
1957..........	200 002	68 352	36 298	6 601	3 983	7 950	2 737	131 650	12 277	2 091
1956..........	189 729	65 810	34 050	6 568	4 099	8 312	2 893	123 919	11 610	2 068
1955..........	183 851	66 978	36 267	6 116	3 939	8 242	2 788	116 873	10 791	2 009
1954..........	169 135	58 173	29 962	5 291	3 788	7 433	2 702	110 962	10 147	1 809
1953..........	169 094	60 371	31 489	5 136	3 989	7 715	2 706	108 723	10 256	1 736
1952..........	162 353	55 270	26 393	5 255	3 671	7 572	2 628	107 083	10 633	1 693
1951..........	156 548	54 479	26 282	5 095	3 509	7 470	2 738	102 069	10 209	1 684
1950..........	147 213	54 275	27 405	4 997	3 798	7 155	2 526	92 938	9 485	1 556
1949..........	133 783	44 983	22 211	4 284	2 956	5 648	2 248	88 800	9 493	1 498
1948..........	133 619	42 888	19 212	4 503	2 853	6 007	2 398	90 731	9 971	1 510
1947..........	122 406	37 542	16 198	4 167	2 593	5 204	2 171	84 864	9 467	1 487

See footnotes at end of table.

Series T 245-271. Retail Store Sales, by Kind of Business: 1929 to 1998—Cont'd.

(In millions of dollars. Includes nonstores)

Year	All stores	Total sales [1]	Passenger car, other automotive dealers	Furniture, home furnishings stores	Household appliance, T.V., radio stores	Lumber, building materials dealers [2]	Hardware stores	Total sales [1]	Total	Shoe stores
				Durable goods stores				**Nondurable goods stores**		
				Furniture and appliance group		Lumber, building, hardware group			Apparel group	
	245	246	247	250	251	252	253	255	256	260
1946 [3]	104 802	28 231	10 912	3 366	1 766	3 935	1 836	76 571	9 054	1 417
1946 [4]	102 488	27 570	10 647	3 264	1 575	4 106	1 911	74 918	8 880	1 377
1945	78 034	16 026	5 000	2 101	639	2 502	1 237	62 008	7 689	1 140
1944	70 208	13 952	4 420	1 848	462	2 102	1 030	56 266	6 704	1 001
1943	63 235	12 221	3 768	1 692	415	2 024	903	51 014	6 158	969
1942	57 212	12 320	3 404	1 776	594	2 332	973	44 892	5 089	914
1941	55 274	17 213	8 185	1 780	796	2 442	905	38 061	4 137	726
1940	46 375	13 576	6 429	1 386	625	2 023	712	32 799	3 451	632
1939	42 042	11 312	5 025	1 200	533	1 761	629	30 730	3 259	617
1938	38 053	9 475	3 909	1 014	476	1 530	563	28 578	2 998	591
1937	42 150	12 048	5 568	1 254	592	1 739	651	30 102	3 323	636
1936	38 339	10 751	5 102	1 082	533	1 463	576	27 588	3 102	586
1935	32 791	8 321	3 863	852	438	1 105	467	24 470	2 656	511
1933	24 517	5 384	2 142	646	313	854	311	19 133	1 930	425
1929	48 459	15 610	6 432	1 813	942	2 621	706	32 849	4 241	807

See footnotes at end of table.

Series T 245-271. Retail Store Sales, by Kind of Business: 1929 to 1998—Cont'd.

(In millions of dollars. Includes nonstores)

| Year | Drug and proprietary stores | Eating and drinking places | Grocery stores | Gasoline service stations | General merchandise groups | | | | | Liquor stores |
| | | | | | Total [1] | Department stores, excl. mail order | Mail order, (catalog sales) [7] | Variety stores | Other general merchandise | |
	261	**262**	**264**	**265**	**266**	**267**	**268**	**269**	**270**	**271**
1998	105 700	247 000	414 600	149 600	353 500	278 600	. . .	11 900	62 900	25 000
1997	98 200	236 200	403 000	158 500	331 500	261 200	. . .	11 500	58 800	24 000
1996	90 500	228 200	397 000	157 600	313 200	244 500	. . .	10 600	58 100	22 700
1995	84 700	222 100	385 000	149 600	298 000	231 100	. . .	9 900	57 000	21 700
1994	81 300	217 100	376 500	143 900	282 300	217 400	. . .	9 500	55 400	21 900
1993	79 600	213 700	365 700	138 300	264 600	200 500	. . .	9 000	55 100	21 600
1992	77 800	200 200	358 100	137 000	246 400	186 400	. . .	9 500	50 500	21 700
1991	75 500	194 400	354 300	137 300	226 700	172 900	. . .	8 300	45 500	22 500
1990 [3,9]	70 600	190 100	348 200	138 500	215 500	165 800	4 700	8 300	41 400	20 800
1990 [4,10]	68 600	182 000	338 700	131 700	211 900	170 700	4 700	7 300	33 900	20 800
1989	62 500	173 900	324 000	117 800	204 400	164 400	4 700	7 400	32 700	20 000
1988	57 400	166 900	307 200	107 900	191 800	155 100	4 400	7 200	29 500	19 600
1987	54 100	153 500	291 000	104 800	182 000	147 200	4 100	7 100	27 700	19 800
1986	50 500	139 400	280 800	102 100	169 200	137 800	4 300	7 400	24 000	19 900
1985	47 000	127 900	269 500	113 300	158 600	126 400	4 700	8 500	23 800	19 500
1984	44 200	124 100	252 900	101 000	153 600	129 300	4 700	9 100	15 300	19 500
1983	40 100	114 700	239 100	98 900	139 400	116 600	4 400	8 600	14 200	19 000
1982	36 200	104 400	230 100	97 100	128 700	107 200	4 400	8 300	13 200	18 100
1981	33 700	98 000	220 100	102 800	125 400	103 500	4 400	8 300	13 500	17 600
1980	31 000	90 100	205 600	94 100	109 000	85 500	4 300	7 800	15 700	16 900
1979	28 200	82 000	184 900	73 300	109 300	89 200	4 200	7 900	12 200	15 100
1978	25 400	71 700	163 800	59 700	103 200	84 400	4 000	7 300	11 500	13 600
1977	23 200	63 300	147 800	56 500	90 700	73 600	6 800	7 100	. . .	13 000
1976	21 600	57 200	138 200	52 000	81 800	65 700	6 100	7 200	. . .	12 400
1975	19 900	51 100	129 200	47 500	78 400	62 100	5 600	8 000	. . .	11 800
1974	18 400	44 700	117 200	43 000	71 200	55 400	5 400	7 700	. . .	11 000
1973	17 000	40 400	103 500	37 000	67 400	52 600	5 000	7 400	. . .	10 200
1972	15 300	36 200	91 700	33 400	60 900	47 300	4 300	7 200	. . .	9 700
1971 [3,10]	14 400	32 900	85 300	30 900	55 500	43 100	4 300	6 600	. . .	9 200
1971 [4]	13 700	31 100	82 800	29 200	68 100	42 000	4 300	7 000	. . .	9 200
1970	13 366	29 689	79 756	27 994	61 320	37 295	3 853	6 959	. . .	7 980
1969	12 224	26 970	77 942	25 909	57 606	35 659	3 538	6 426	. . .	7 384
1968	11 458	25 285	67 925	24 526	54 493	33 323	3 256	6 152	. . .	6 969
1967	10 721	23 473	. . .	22 739	49 820	29 589	. . .	. . .	. . .	6 409
1966	9 988	22 098	. . .	21 792	46 961	27 868	. . .	. . .	. . .	6 081
1965	9 186	20 201	. . .	20 611	42 299	25 014	. . .	. . .	. . .	5 674
1964	8 476	18 462	. . .	19 196	38 289	22 224	. . .	. . .	. . .	5 410
1963	8 068	17 194	. . .	18 319	34 232	. . .	. . .	. . .	. . .	5 138
1962	7 917	16 434	. . .	17 644	32 537	. . .	. . .	. . .	. . .	4 892
1961 [3]	7 629	15 549	. . .	17 007	29 874	. . .	. . .	. . .	. . .	4 433
1961 [4]	7 752	16 488	50 369	17 959	25 059	. . .	. . .	. . .	. . .	4 927
1960 *	7 538	16 146	48 610	17 588	24 085	. . .	. . .	. . .	. . .	4 893
1959	7 150	15 618	46 132	16 793	23 420	. . .	. . .	. . .	(5)	4 743
1958	6 600	14 792	44 547	15 757	21 667	12 563	1 536	3 609	3 943	4 439
1957	6 325	14 787	42 444	15 070	21 157	. . .	1 477	3 523	4 254	4 212
1956	5 775	14 317	39 180	13 738	20 762	11 327	1 407	3 423	4 605	3 944
1955	5 232	13 662	36 919	12 411	20 100	10 882	1 331	3 295	4 592	3 546
1954	4 940	13 127	34 993	11 443	18 857	10 272	1 222	3 027	4 336	3 415
1953	4 790	13 003	33 623	10 536	19 006	10 370	1 327	3 095	4 214	3 325
1952	4 717	12 688	32 238	9 976	18 694	10 277	1 339	2 996	4 082	3 165
1951	4 547	12 207	30 346	9 151	18 202	10 095	1 309	2 859	3 939	2 975
1950	4 205	11 158	26 886	8 240	17 275	9 649	1 258	2 632	3 736	2 669
1949	4 074	10 994	25 248	7 590	16 339	9 083	1 178	2 555	3 523	2 598
1948	4 050	11 218	25 215	7 077	17 170	9 579	1 328	2 556	3 707	2 711

See footnotes at end of table.

Series T 245-271.   Retail Store Sales, by Kind of Business: 1929 to 1998—Cont'd.

(In millions of dollars. Includes nonstores)

					Nondurable goods stores					
						General merchandise groups				
Year	Drug and proprietary stores	Eating and drinking places	Grocery stores	Gasoline service stations	Total [1]	Department stores, excl. mail order	Mail order, (catalog sales) [7]	Variety stores	Other general merchandise	Liquor stores
	261	262	264	265	266	267	268	269	270	271
1947	3 904	11 183	22 907	5 979	16 088	9 108	1 194	2 363	3 423	2 782
1946 [3]	3 759	11 152	18 980	4 922	14 755	8 431	976	2 197	3 151	2 823
1946 [4]	3 723	10 619	18 640	4 511	14 724	9 183		2 158	3 383	2 688
1945	3 155	9 575	14 593	3 284	11 802	7 092		1 845	2 865	2 288
1944	2 924	8 305	13 665	2 812	11 076	6 488		1 774	2 814	1 926
1943	2 628	7 216	12 481	2 628	10 162	5 889		1 642	2 631	1 557
1942	2 213	5 699	11 368	3 089	9 204	5 389		1 536	2 279	1 212
1941	1 847	4 570	9 312	3 466	7 973	4 862		1 320	1 791	854
1940	1 636	3 787	8 169	2 970	6 859	4 128		1 153	1 578	681
1939	1 563	3 529	7 722	2 822	6 475	3 872		1 080	1 523	586
1938	1 474	3 188	7 187	2 696	6 145	. . .	. . .	1 015	1 536	539
1937	1 527	3 293	7 266	2 641	6 673	. . .	. . .	1 025	1 755	558
1936	1 409	2 748	6 850	2 318	6 366	. . .	. . .	967	1 731	475
1935	1 233	2 395	6 352	1 968	5 730	2 833	386	873	1 638	328
1933	1 066	1 434	5 004	1 532	4 982	. . .	. . .	756	1 766	17
1929	1 690	2 132	7 353	[8] 1 787	9 015	3 903	447	904	3 761	. . .

* Denotes first year for which figures include Alaska and Hawaii.
1. Totals include subclasses not shown separately.
2. Includes lumber yards; building materials dealers; and paint, plumbing and electrical stores.
3. Comparable with later years.
4. Comparable with earlier years.
5. No longer available separately; included in total for group.
6. Includes nonstores, i.e., establishments selling merchandise primarily through coin-operated vending machines, house-to-house canvass and mail orders.
7. Includes sales made by mail order catalog desks located within department stores of mail order firms.
8. Excludes garages primarily selling gasoline and oil.
9. Based on 1987 Standard Industrial Classification (SIC) codes.
10. Based on 1972 Standard Industrial Classification (SIC) codes.

Series T 274-371. Wholesale Establishments, Sales, Operating Expenses and Persons Engaged: 1929 to 1997

(Sales, inventories and payroll in millions of dollars; paid employees and active proprietors in thousands)

Year	All wholesale establishments [1]				Merchant wholesalers			
	Number	Sales	Payroll, entire year	Paid employees [2]	Number	Sales	Operating expenses (percent)	Inventories, end of year
	274	275	277	278	280	281	282	283
1997	518 200	4 212 312	234 445	6 507	440 200	2 498 395	. . .	273 000
1996	. . .	. . .	. . .	. . .	. . .	2 420 700	. . .	256 200
1995	. . .	. . .	. . .	. . .	. . .	2 265 700	. . .	253 100
1994	. . .	. . .	. . .	. . .	. . .	2 075 700	. . .	234 900
1993	. . .	. . .	. . .	. . .	. . .	1 940 200	. . .	215 900
1992	495 500	3 238 520	173 272	5 791	414 800	1 847 274	. . .	207 700
1987 [3]	469 500	2 524 727	133 359	5 596	391 000	1 478 169	. . .	165 300
1987 [4]	466 700	2 523 688	133 153	5 581	388 100	1 477 132	. . .	. . .
1982	435 100	1 997 895	95 209	4 985	353 100	1 159 334	. . .	118 800
1977	382 800	1 258 400	58 290	4 397	307 300	676 058	. . .	72 300
1972 [3]	369 800	695 224	36 893	4 026	290 000	353 919	. . .	39 800
1972 [4]	348 200	683 659	35 887	3 878	. . .	. . .	. . .	. . .
1967	311 464	459 476	23 922	3 519	212 993	206 055	13.5	21 463
1963 *	308 177	358 386	18 101	3 089	208 997	157 392	13.5	14 992
1958	285 996	284 977	13 199	2 791	190 492	122 060	13.4	11 253
1954	250 322	233 976	10 868	2 555	163 157	100 103	13.0	9 492
1948 [3]	216 099	180 577	7 734	2 305	129 117	76 533	11.5	7 056
1948 [4]	243 366	188 689	7 991	2 383	146 518	79 767	11.6	7 207
1939 [5]	190 379	53 766	2 511	[6] 1 553	100 961	22 538	13.1	2 621
1935	176 756	42 803	2 022	[6] 1 261	88 931	17 662	7.6	2 068
1933 [5]	163 583	30 010	1 659	[6] 1 188	82 844	12 960	15.0	1 971
1929 [5]	163 830	65 378	2 922	[6] 1 550	79 840	29 556	11.7	3 383

* Denotes first year for which figures include Alaska and Hawaii.
1. Beginning 1954, excludes ready-mixed concrete distributors, no longer part of wholesale trade but included in selected service trade.
2. Data on paid employees is for work week ended nearest Nov. 15 for 1929-1963 and for work week ended nearest Mar. 12 for 1967-1997.
3. Comparable with later years.
4. Comparable with earlier years.
5. Data for series T 274-279 for 1939, 1933, and 1929 are revised; revised data for other series for these years not available.
6. Average annual number of full-time and part-time employees.

Series T 391-443. Selected Service Establishments and Receipts: 1933 to 1992

(Receipts and payroll in millions of dollars; paid employees and active proprietors in thousands. Paid employees for work week ended nearest Nov. 15 for 1933-1963, and for work week ended nearest March 12 for 1967-1992.)

Year	Number of establishments [4]	Receipts, all establishments	Payroll, entire year	Paid employees	Year	Number of establishments [4]	Receipts, all establishments	Payroll, entire year	Paid employees
	391	393	398	400		391	393	398	400
1992	1 825 000	1 202 613	452 697	19 290	1954	785 589	23 508	6 534	2 362
1987	1 626 000	772 194	289 807	16 055					
1982	1 339 200	426 982	158 625	11 106	1948 [2]	617 002	13 230	. . .	. . .
1977	725 000	164 200	56 055	6 337	1948 [3]	665 475	13 296	4 164	2 100
1972 [1]	684 000	103 200	33 400	5 305	1939 [2]	656 482	4 872	1 384	1 497
					1939 [3]	646 028	3 420	1 070	[4] 1 102
1972 [2]	569 928	84 754	27 002	4 671	1935	631 309	3 001	. . .	. . .
1967	1 187 814	60 542	17 524	[1] 3 841					
1963 *	1 061 673	44 586	12 192	3 262	1933	502 416	2 761	702	[4] 657
1958	975 250	32 376	9 006	2 889					

* Denotes first year for which figures include Alaska and Hawaii.
1. Comparable with later years.
2. Comparable with earlier years.
3. Average annual number of full-time and part-time employees.
4. "Number of establishments" includes only establishments with payroll after 1967.

Series T 444-471. Volume of Advertising, by Medium: 1935 to 1998
(In millions of dollars)

Year	Total [1]	National [1]	Local [1]	Newspapers			Magazines	
				Total	National	Local	Total	Weeklies
	444	445	446	447	448	449	450	451
1998	200 320	118 000	82 320	44 245	5 390	38 855	10 360	4 040
1997	187 529	110 232	77 297	41 670	5 016	36 654	9 821	3 850
1996	175 230	103 040	72 190	38 402	4 400	34 002	9 010	3 581
1995	162 930	95 360	67 570	36 317	3 996	32 321	8 580	3 347
1994	151 680	88 250	63 430	34 356	3 906	30 450	7 916	3 140
1993	139 540	80 795	58 745	32 025	3 620	28 405	7 357	2 850
1992	132 650	76 710	55 940	30 737	3 602	27 135	7 000	2 739
1991	124 470	73 270	54 200	30 409	3 685	26 724	6 524	2 670
1990	128 640	72 780	72 780	32 281	3 867	28 414	6 803	2 864
1989	123 390	68 990	54 940	32 368	3 720	28 648	6 716	2 813
1988	118 050	65 610	52 440	31 197	3 586	27 611	6 072	2 646
1987	109 650	60 625	49 025	29 412	3 494	25 918	5 607	2 445
1986	102 140	56 850	45 290	26 990	3 376	23 614	5 317	2 327
1985	94 750	53 355	41 395	25 170	3 352	21 818	5 155	2 297
1984	87 820	49 690	38 130	23 522	3 081	20 441	4 932	2 224
1983	75 850	42 525	33 325	20 582	2 734	17 848	4 233	1 917
1982	66 580	37 785	28 795	17 694	2 452	15 242	3 710	1 659
1981	60 430	33 890	26 540	16 528	2 259	14 269	3 533	1 598
1980	53 550	29 815	23 735	14 794	1 963	12 831	3 149	1 418
1979	48 780	26 695	22 085	13 863	1 770	12 093	2 932	1 327
1978	43 330	23 720	19 610	12 214	1 541	10 673	2 597	1 158
1977	38 120	21 055	17 056	11 132	1 677	9 455	2 162	903
1976	33 720	18 585	15 135	9 910	1 502	8 408	1 789	748
1975	27 900	15 200	12 700	8 234	1 109	7 125	1 465	612
1974	26 780	14 755	12 025	8 001	1 194	6 807	1 504	630
1973	25 080	13 755	11 325	7 595	1 111	6 484	1 448	583
1972	23 130	12 940	10 190	7 008	1 103	5 905	1 440	610
1971	20 500	11 720	8 780	6 215	1 125	5 090	1 405	630
1970	19 600	11 485	8 115	5 745	1 014	4 731	1 323	617
1969	19 482	11 518	7 964	5 753	1 059	4 694	1 376	662
1968	18 127	10 883	7 244	5 265	990	4 275	1 318	657
1967	16 866	10 250	6 616	4 942	936	4 006	1 280	651
1966	16 670	10 213	6 457	4 896	975	3 920	1 291	658
1965	15 255	9 398	5 857	4 457	869	3 587	1 199	610
1964	14 155	8 745	5 410	4 148	848	3 300	1 108	583
1963	13 107	8 148	4 959	3 904	765	3 039	1 034	540
1962	12 381	7 683	4 698	3 681	782	2 900	973	519
1961	11 845	7 270	4 575	3 623	802	2 821	924	508
1960	11 932	7 296	4 636	3 703	836	2 867	941	525
1959	11 255	6 835	4 420	3 546	826	2 720	866	478
1958	10 302	6 331	3 971	3 193	769	2 424	767	425
1957	10 311	6 253	4 057	3 283	810	2 474	814	451
1956	9 905	5 926	3 979	3 236	789	2 447	795	440
1955	9 194	5 407	3 788	3 088	743	2 345	729	396
1954	8 164	4 812	3 352	2 695	635	2 060	668	363
1953	7 755	4 521	3 235	2 645	643	2 002	667	351
1952	7 156	4 096	3 060	2 473	562	1 910	616	325
1951	6 426	3 701	2 725	2 258	549	1 709	574	297
1950	5 710	3 257	2 453	2 076	533	1 542	515	261
1949	5 202	2 965	2 237	1 916	476	1 440	493	245
1948	4 864	2 776	2 088	1 750	394	1 356	513	258
1947	4 260	2 487	1 772	1 475	336	1 139	493	246
1946	3 364	1 963	1 401	1 158	248	911	427	202
1945	2 875	1 775	1 099	921	211	710	365	188
1944	2 724	1 669	1 054	888	197	691	324	173
1943	2 496	1 452	1 045	900	182	718	275	154
1942	2 156	1 212	944	798	144	654	199	107
1941	2 236	1 259	977	844	165	680	214	117

See footnotes at end of table.

Series T 444-471.   Volume of Advertising, by Medium: 1935 to 1998—Cont'd.
(In millions of dollars)

| Year | Total [1] | National [1] | Local [1] | Newspapers | | | Magazines | |
				Total	National	Local	Total	Weeklies
	444	**445**	**446**	**447**	**448**	**449**	**450**	**451**
1940	2 088	1 163	925	815	163	652	198	104
1939	1 980	1 086	895	793	153	640	180	88
1938	1 004	1 031	873	782	150	632	169	75
1937	2 072	1 103	969	873	173	700	193	83
1936	1 902	1 003	899	844	171	673	162	67
1935	1 690	859	831	762	152	610	136	54

See footnotes at end of table.

Series T 444-471. Volume of Advertising, by Medium: 1935 to 1998—Cont'd.

(In millions of dollars)

Year	Magazines		Television			
	Women's	Monthlies	Total [2]	Network	Spot, national	Spot, local
	452	**453**	**455**	**456**	**457**	**458**
1998	2 705	3 615	47 990	13 735	10 675	12 295
1997	2 576	3 395	44 519	13 020	9 999	11 436
1996	2 303	3 126	42 484	13 081	9 803	10 944
1995	2 236	2 997	37 828	11 600	9 119	9 985
1994	2 106	2 670	35 435	10 942	8 993	9 464
1993	2 009	2 498	31 698	10 209	7 800	8 435
1992	1 853	2 408	30 450	10 249	7 551	8 079
1991	1 671	2 183	28 189	9 533	7 110	7 565
1990	1 713	2 226	28 405	9 383	7 758	7 856
1989	1 710	2 193	26 841	9 110	7 354	7 612
1988	1 504	1 922	25 686	9 172	7 147	7 270
1987	1 417	1 745	23 904	8 500	6 846	6 833
1986	1 376	1 614	22 881	8 342	6 570	6 514
1985	1 294	1 564	21 022	8 060	6 004	5 714
1984	1 209	1 499	19 848	8 318	5 488	5 084
1983	1 056	1 260	16 759	6 955	4 827	4 345
1982	904	1 147	14 636	6 144	4 364	3 765
1981	853	1 082	12 650	5 575	3 730	3 345
1980	782	949	11 469	5 130	3 269	2 967
1979	730	875	10 154	4 599	2 873	2 682
1978	672	767	8 955	3 925	2 607	2 373
1977	565	694	7 612	3 460	2 204	1 948
1976	457	584	6 721	2 857	2 154	1 710
1975	368	485	5 263	2 306	1 623	1 334
1974	372	502	4 851	2 145	1 495	1 211
1973	362	503	4 460	1 968	1 377	1 115
1972	368	462	4 091	1 804	1 318	969
1971	340	406	3 520	1 575	1 150	795
1970	301	374	3 665	1 712	1 247	706
1969	308	374	3 585	1 678	1 253	654
1968	284	342	3 231	1 523	1 131	577
1967	282	312	2 889	1 455	968	466
1966	280	316	2 823	1 393	988	442
1965	269	282	2 515	1 237	892	386
1964	231	260	2 289	1 132	806	351
1963	218	244	3 032	1 025	698	309
1962	200	223	1 897	976	629	292
1961	187	200	1 691	887	548	256
1960	184	200	1 590	783	527	281
1959	168	185	1 494	740	486	267
1958	151	158	1 354	709	397	248
1957	164	161	1 265	670	352	244
1956	166	153	1 207	625	329	253
1955	161	133	1 025	540	260	225
1954	152	114	809	422	207	180
1953	158	118	606	320	146	141
1952	149	101	454	256	94	104
1951	144	95	332	181	70	82
1950	129	88	171	85	31	55
1949	129	84	58	29	9	19
1948	133	87	. . .	. . .	. . .	. . .
1947	133	85	. . .	. . .	. . .	. . .
1946	127	76	. . .	. . .	. . .	. . .
1945	97	59	. . .	. . .	. . .	. . .
1944	82	51	. . .	. . .	. . .	. . .
1943	65	39	. . .	. . .	. . .	. . .
1942	51	28	. . .	. . .	. . .	. . .
1941	52	32	. . .	. . .	. . .	. . .

See footnotes at end of table.

Series T 444-471.   Volume of Advertising, by Medium: 1935 to 1998—Cont'd.

(In millions of dollars)

Year	Magazines		Television			
	Women's	Monthlies	Total [2]	Network	Spot, national	Spot, local
	452	**453**	**455**	**456**	**457**	**458**
1940..	49	34	. . .	. . .	. . .	. . .
1939..	48	32	. . .	. . .	. . .	. . .
1938..	52	31	. . .	. . .	. . .	. . .
1937..	60	38	. . .	. . .	. . .	. . .
1936..	57	30	. . .	. . .	. . .	. . .
1935..	52	25	. . .	. . .	. . .	. . .

See footnotes at end of table.

Series T 444-471.   Volume of Advertising, by Medium: 1935 to 1998—Cont'd.

(In millions of dollars)

Year	Radio				Year	Radio			
	Total	Network	Spot	Local		Total	Network	Spot	Local
	459	**460**	**461**	**462**		**459**	**460**	**461**	**462**
1998	14 455	585	2 660	11 210	1966	1 010	64	308	638
1997	13 491	560	2 455	10 476	1965	917	60	275	582
1996	12 269	523	2 135	9 611	1964	846	59	256	531
1995	11 338	480	1 959	8 899					
1994	10 529	463	1 902	8 164	1963	789	56	243	490
					1962	736	46	233	457
1993	9 457	458	1 657	7 342	1961	683	43	221	510
1992	8 654	424	1 505	6 725	1960	692	43	222	428
1991	8 476	490	1 575	6 411	1959	656	44	206	406
1990	8 726	482	1 635	6 609					
1989	8 323	476	1 547	6 300	1958	619	58	190	372
					1957	618	64	187	368
1988	7 798	425	1 418	5 955	1956	567	61	161	346
1987	7 206	413	1 330	5 463	1955	545	84	134	326
1986	6 949	423	1 348	5 178	1954	559	114	135	309
1985	6 490	365	1 335	4 790					
1984	5 817	320	1 197	4 300	1953	611	141	146	324
					1952	624	162	142	321
1983	5 210	296	1 038	3 876	1951	606	180	138	289
1982	4 670	255	923	3 492	1950	605	196	136	273
1981	4 230	230	879	3 129	1949	571	203	123	245
1980	3 702	183	779	2 740					
1979	3 310	161	685	2 484	1948	562	211	121	230
					1947	506	201	106	199
1978	3 052	147	620	2 285	1946	454	200	98	157
1977	2 634	137	546	1 951	1945	424	198	92	134
1976	2 330	105	518	1 707	1944	394	192	87	114
1975	1 980	83	436	1 461					
1974	1 837	69	405	1 363	1943	314	157	71	86
					1942	260	129	59	73
1973	1 690	70	380	1 240	1941	247	125	52	70
1972	1 555	75	400	1 080	1940	216	113	42	60
1971	1 386	58	387	935	1939	184	99	35	50
1970	1 308	56	371	881					
1969	1 264	59	368	837	1938	167	89	34	44
					1937	165	89	28	48
1968	1 190	63	360	767	1936	122	76	23	24
1967	1 031	64	310	657	1935	113	63	15	35

See footnotes at end of table.

Series T 444-471. Volume of Advertising, by Medium: 1935 to 1998—Cont'd.

(In millions of dollars)

Year	Direct mail	Year	Direct mail	Year	Direct mail	Year	Direct mail
	464		**464**		**464**		**464**
1998	39 470	1982	(3)	1966	2 461	1950	803
1997	36 890	1981	(3)	1965	2 324	1949	756
1996	34 509	1980	7 596	1964	2 184		
1995	32 866	1979	(3)			1948	689
1994	29 638			1963	2 078	1947	580
		1978	(3)	1962	1 933	1946	334
1993	27 266	1977	(3)	1961	1 850	1945	290
1992	25 391	1976	(3)	1960	1830	1944	326
1991	24 460	1975	(3)	1959	1 688		
1990	23 370	1974	(3)			1943	322
1989	21 945			1958	1 589	1942	329
		1973	(3)	1957	1 471	1941	353
1988	21 115	1972	(3)	1956	1 419	1940	334
1987	19 111	1971	(3)	1955	1 299	1939	333
1986	17 145	1970	2 734	1954	1 202		
1985	15 500	1969	2 670			1938	324
1984	(3)			1953	1 099	1937	333
		1968	2 612	1952	1 024	1936	319
1983	(3)	1967	2 488	1951	924	1935	282

1. Includes farm publications, yellow pages, business papers, Internet, outdoor, and miscellaneous, not shown separately.
2. Includes syndication and cable, not shown separately.
3. Not shown separately, but included in national totals.

Series TT-1.   Retail Trade—Summary: 1972 to 1992

(1 665 represents 1 665 000. 1972 through 1982 based on 1972 Standard Industrial Classification (SIC) code; beginning 1987 based on 1987 SIC code. Comparability of data over time is affected by changes in the SIC code)

Item	Unit	1972	1977	1982	1987	1992
Firms, total [1]	1 000	1 665	1 567	1 573	1 992	2 212
Multiunit establishments [1,2]	1 000	301	343	415	498	528
Establishments, total [1]	1 000	1 780	1 855	1 923	2 420	2 672
With payroll	1 000	1 265	1 304	1 324	1 504	1 526
With sales of $1 000 000 or more [3]	1 000	74	119	193	259	326
Consumer Price Index: [4]						
All items	1982-84 = 100	41.8	60.6	96.5	113.6	140.3
All commodities	1982-84 = 100	44.5	64.2	97.0	107.7	129.1
Sales	Bil. dol.	457	723	1 066	1 540	1 949
By establishments with payroll	Bil. dol.	440	700	1 039	1 493	1 895
By multiunit establishments [2]	Bil. dol.	202	341	567	844	1 137
Percent of total sales	Percent	44.0	47.1	53.2	54.8	58.3
Percent of multiunit sales by 100-or-more establishment multiunits	Percent	55.8	55.8	54.5	54.6	57.0
In 1987 dollars [6]	Bil. dol.	1 042	1 170	1 175	1 540	1 669
Percent of sales by corporations [3]	Percent	76.4	79.8	84.6	88.9	89.9
Per capita sales: [7]						
Current dollars	Dollars	2 186	3 291	4 601	6 357	7 643
Constant (1987) dollars [6]	Dollars	4 978	5 325	5 073	6 357	6 544
Sales as percent of personal income	Percent	46.6	45.2	39.6	40.5	37.9
Payroll, entire year	Bil. dol.	55.4	85.9	123.6	177.5	222.9
Percent of sales [8]	Percent	12.6	12.3	11.9	11.9	11.8
Paid employees, March 12 pay period	1 000	11 211	13 040	14 468	17 780	18 407

1. Through 1982, represents the number of establishments and firms in business at the end of year. Beginning 1987, represents the number of establishments and firms in business at any time during year.
2. Establishments of firms that operate at two or more locations.
3. Through 1982, represents establishments with and without payroll. Beginning 1987, represents only establishments with payroll.
4. Source: U.S. Bureau of Labor Statistics (BLS), Monthly Labor Review. Beginning 1982, CPI-U annual averages. CPI-U is a CPI for all urban consumers which covers approximately 80 percent of the total population. The CPI-U includes, in addition to wage earners and clerical workers, groups which historically have been excluded from CPI coverage, such as professional, managerial, and technical workers; the self-employed; short-term workers; the unemployed; and retirees and others not in the labor force. For further detail on the CPI, see the BLS Handbook of Methods, Bulletin 2490, Chapter 17.
5. Prior to 1982, data provided for percent of multiunit sales by 101-or-more establishment units.
6. Based on implicit price deflators for retail sales supplied by U.S. Bureau of Economic Analysis.
7. Based on estimated resident population as of July 1.
8. Covers only establishments with payroll.

SOURCE: Except as noted, U.S. Census Bureau, Census of Retail Trade, 1972, RC72-S-1; 1977, RC77-52; 1982, RC82-A-52 and RC82-I-1; 1987, RC87-A-52, RC87-N-1, and RC87-S-1; and 1992, RC92-A-52, RC92-N-1, and RC92-S-1.

Series TT-2. Retail Foodstores—Number and Sales, by Type: 1990 to 1997

(254.4 represents 254 400) except as indicated)

Type of foodstore	Number [1] (1 000)					Sales [2] (bil. dol.)					Percent distribution			
											Number		Sales	
	1990	1994	1995	1996	1997	1990	1994	1995	1996	1997	1990	1997	1990	1997
Total	254.4	248.3	247.3	246.3	245.3	368.3	399.3	410.5	421.0	429.8	100.0	100.0	100.0	100.0
Grocery stores..........................	172.9	165.6	164.3	163.0	161.7	348.2	378.6	385.0	397.0	403.0	67.7	65.9	94.5	93.8
Supermarkets [3]	f25.0	24.6	24.1	23.8	24.1	260.1	289.0	293.2	302.5	307.5	9.9	9.8	70.6	71.5
Conventional	13.7	12.0	11.1	10.8	11.1	90.7	81.5	68.9	69.2	59.2	5.7	4.5	24.6	13.8
Superstore [4]	5.8	6.5	6.8	7.1	7.3	87.6	107.6	116.7	127.0	132.9	2.2	3.0	23.8	30.9
Warehouse [5]	3.4	2.9	2.7	2.4	2.2	33.1	27.7	26.0	24.3	22.2	1.3	0.9	9.0	5.2
Combination food and drug [6]...........	1.6	2.4	2.7	2.4	2.8	34.8	51.7	59.3	61.3	64.7	0.5	1.1	9.4	15.1
Superwarehouse [7]...........................	0.3	0.5	0.6	0.5	0.5	12.6	16.2	17.8	15.3	11.9	0.2	0.2	3.4	2.8
Hypermarket [8]	0.1	0.2	0.2	0.2	0.2	1.3	4.3	4.5	5.4	16.6	(Z)	0.1	0.4	3.9
Convenience stores [9]	59.2	61.5	62.1	62.7	62.1	37.0	40.3	37.4	38.8	42.0	19.1	25.3	10.0	9.8
Superette [10]...................	88.7	79.6	78.1	76.5	75.5	51.1	49.2	54.4	55.7	53.5	38.6	30.8	13.9	12.4
Specialized food stores [11]	81.5	82.7	83.0	83.3	83.6	20.1	20.7	22.4	24.0	26.8	32.3	34.1	5.5	6.2

Z Less than 0.05 percent.
1. Estimated.
2. Includes nonfood items.
3. A grocery store, primarily self-service in operation, providing a full range of departments, and having at least $2.5 million in annual sales in 1985 dollars.
4. Contains greater variety of products than conventional supermarkets, including specialty and service departments, and considerable nonfood (general merchandise) products.
5. Contains limited product variety and fewer services provided, incorporating case lot stocking and shelving practices.
6. Contains a pharmacy, a nonprescription drug department, and a greater variety of health and beauty aids than that carried by conventional supermarkets.
7. A larger warehouse store that offers expanded product variety and often service meat, deli, or seafood departments.
8. A very large store offering a greater variety of general merchandise—like clothes, hardware, and seasonal goods—and personal care products than other grocery stores.
9. A small grocery store selling a limited variety of food and nonfood products, typically open extended hours.
10. A grocery store, primarily self-service in operation, selling a wide variety of food and nonfood products with annual sales below $2.5 million (1985 dollars).
11. Primarily engaged in the retail sale of a single food category such as meat and seafood stores and retail bakeries.

SOURCE: U.S. Dept. of Agriculture, Economic Research Service, Food Marketing Review, annual.

SECTION U

INTERNATIONAL TRANSACTIONS AND FOREIGN COMMERCE
Highlights

1 The first edition of the *Statistical Abstract of the United States,* published in 1879, was almost wholly devoted to foreign trade and shipping. Data on imports of gold, silver coins and bullion took up 11 of its 154 pages and nearly 100 pages were devoted to imports and exports. The section on exports showed that the major U. S. exports were raw cotton and wheat, which together accounted for 38% of all exports. In the early years of the republic, international trade and transactions loomed large in the public economy and received considerable attention from statisticians, because at that time the United States was more heavily dependent on foreign markets than it has been in the 20th century. Records of foreign trade have been kept by the Treasury Department since August 1, 1789, (in a more or less complete fashion), although they do not show the value of commerce with each country. However, Edward Ely, author of *International Trade Statistics*, observes that the United States may be said to have an adequate set of of import and export statistics only since about 1821. No information was compiled on the amounts of articles that were imported free of duty or on imports subject to specific rates of duty. The total dollar value of imports from 1795 to 1801 was apparently estimated by the Secretary of the Treasury, and the figures for 1790 to 1794 and from 1802 to 1820 were apparently estimated many years later. The adequacy of these early records, of course, depends on the use made of them. Some of the earliest records were not published officially, and scholars have had to rely on other sources, particularly, *A View of the United States of America* by Tench Coxe, A *Statistical Manual of the United States of America* by Samuel Blodgett, Jr., *A Statistical View of Commerce of the United States of America* by Timothy Pitkin, and the *History of Domestic and Foreign Commerce of the United States* by Emory Johnson.

2 Foreign trade data are subject to a variety of special statistical problems. The record of gold movements, in particular, has been subject to considerable error because of smuggling. The Civil War Introduced two special difficulties. Because the ports of the Southern States stopped furnishing reports to the Treasury in 1861, exports of cotton are based on estimates derived from records of recipient countries. A second difficulty was introduced in 1862 when the United States abandoned its specie backing for its money. The dollar fluctuated against foreign currencies and gold with each reverse or success of the Northern forces. While exports or reexports continued to be valued in specie (dollars of a fixed parity to gold), domestic exports were recorded in mixed values from 1862 until the resumption of specie payment in 1879. A third problem affecting the comparability of trade statistics arose between 1934 and 1953 when the foreign exchange value of the dollar was allowed to depreciate as a result of the restriction placed on gold shipments to foreign countries. World War II introduced such complications as Lend-Lease, surplus property disposal after the war, and economic and military aid.

3 In 1820, Congress established the Division of Commerce and Navigation in the Register of the Treasury. Collectors of Customs were required to compile and transmit annual reports to that office on trade and navigation with foreign countries. Beginning in 1821, these reports were consolidated and published annually in *Commerce and Navigation of the United States*. In 1866, Congress established the Bureau of Statistics and charged it with the collection of data on all articles imported, exported or reexported classified by countries of destination. Since 1866, monthly trade statistics have been published in addition to annual data.

4 Balance of international payments data for the period 1790 to 1918 are derived basically from private authors. They illustrate U. S. foreign relations, territorial expansion, immigration and the cost of wars and the Civil War. For example, $600,000 was paid in 1794 and 1796 to the Barbary pirates; $11.2 million was paid to France in 1803 for the Louisiana Purchase; $15 million was paid to Mexico between 1849 and 1852 for territory now constituting Arizona, New Mexico, California, Nevada, Utah and Colorado; $10 million to Mexico between 1854 and 1856 for

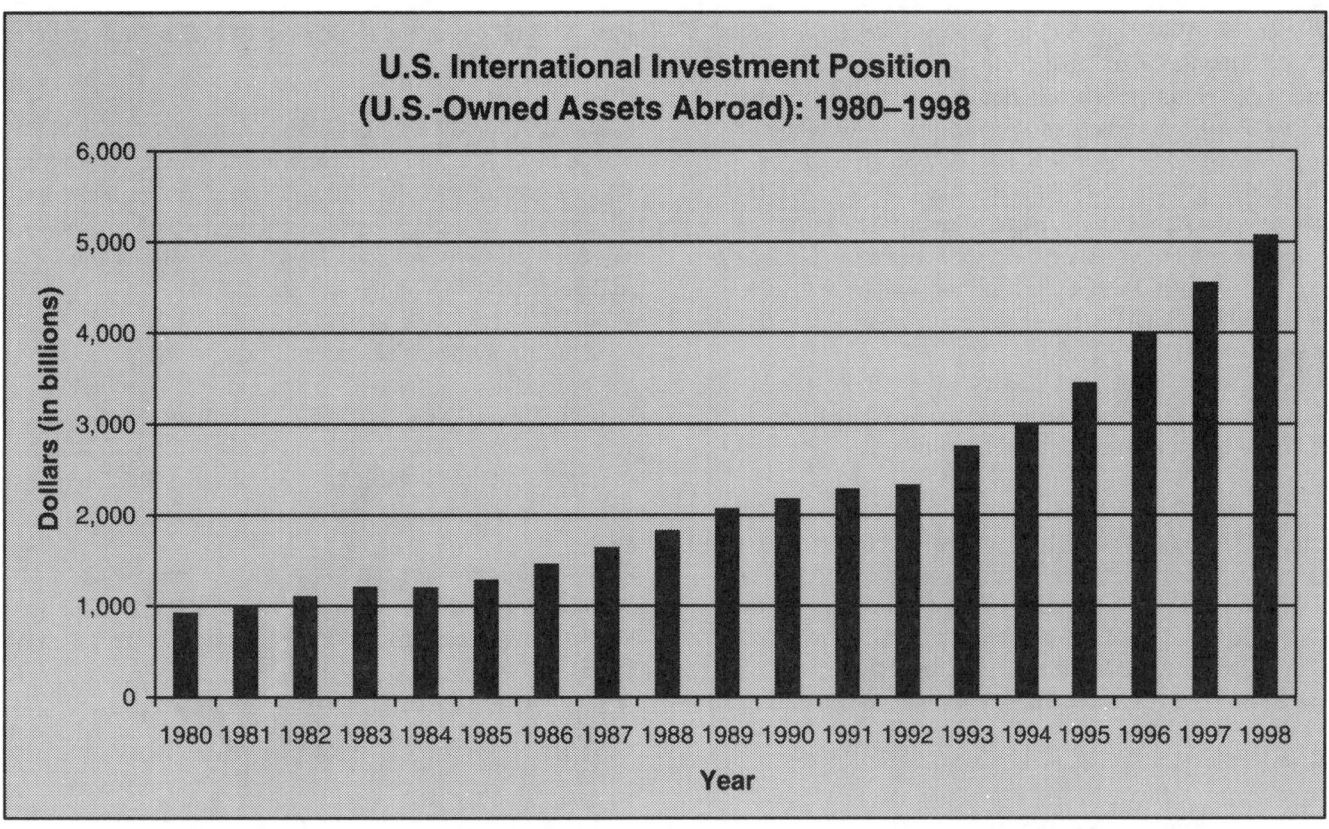

U.S. International Investment Position (U.S.-Owned Assets Abroad): 1980–1998

the Gadsden Purchase; $7.1 million to Russia in 1869 for Alaska; and $20 million to Spain in 1898 for the Philippines, Guam, and Puerto Rico. Similarly, the United States received $5.5 million from France in 1836-38 as indemnity for losses suffered during the Napoleonic Wars, as well as $15.5 million from Great Britain for losses suffered from British privateers during the Civil War. After World War II, the United States became a grantor, providing extensive grants and credits to its allies in the Cold War. Data for foreign aid programs are presented by the Agency for International Development.

5 Exports and imports constitute the backbone of foreign trade. The Bureau of the Census compiles export data primarily from the Shippers' Export Declarations that are required to be filed with customs officials for shipments leaving the United States. Import data are compiled from various required customs forms as well. The data suffer from serious underreporting because of the exclusion of low-valued shipments exported and imported. For exports, the minimum is $2,500 and for imports $1,250. Data for shipments below these limits are estimated, and such estimates may have a wide margin of error. Low value shipments are believed to represent less than 2.5% of U. S. exports and 4% of U.S. imports. Since 1982, import prices have been based on customs values and export prices on f.a.s. (free alongside ship) values at the U. S. port of export.

6 Since 1983 foreign assets in the United States have exceeded U.S. assets abroad by a considerable margin. In 1998 foreign assets in the United States were $7.485 trillion, and U.S. assets abroad were $5.947 trillion at market value. Similarly, the United States runs a deficit on current accounts in international transactions, with exports worth $1.192 trillion and imports of $1.368 trillion. Generally, the United States has a negative balance in transactions with almost all countries. Exceptions are France and Netherlands. The U.S. has a shortfall in merchandise trade which is partially offset by a surplus on net private service transactions and travel and transportation receipts. These receipts amounted to $156 billion in 1997.

7 Foreign direct investment in the United States rose from $83 billion in 1980 to $403.7 billion in 1990 and $811.756 billion in 1998. The United Kingdom is the largest single direct investor in the United States with $$151.335 billion, followed by Japan with $132.659 billion, Netherlands $96.904 billion, Germany with $85.045 billion, France with $62.167 billion, Switzerland $54.011 billion, Luxembourg with $20.214 billion, Australia with $14.755 billion, Sweden with $14.564 billion and Ireland with $13.227 billion.

8 Of U.S. foreign investment of $980.565 billion in 1998, developing countries accounted for only 39.5%. Of the investment in developing countries, Latin America accounted for 20%, Africa for 1.3%, Middle East, 1% and Asia and the Pacific for 16.5%.

9 Between 1966 and 1998 the United States has extended $285.2 billion as grants and credits to foreign countries. Grants and credits to Western Europe, Western hemisphere and the Pacific have tapered off since the 1980s while those to Eastern Europe, Near East and South Asia and Africa have grown. In 1998, grants and credits to Western Europe were $258 million, Eastern Europe $17.85 billion, Near East and South Asia $4. 979 billion, Africa $1.277 billion, Far East and Pacific $735 million and Western Hemisphere $987 million.

10 Total economic and military aid in 1996 totaled $13.035 billion of which economic aid accounted for $9.170 billion and military aid $3.864 billion.

11 Israel receives the most military and economic aid from the United States. In 1997 military aid totaled $1.8 billion and economic aid $1.2 billion. Israel received 46% of all military assistance and 23% of all economic assistance. All of Africa received less assistance than Israel as all of Latin America, Asia, Western Europe and Eastern Europe. Egypt also receives heavy military and economic assistance, $1.3 billion of the former and $810.7 million of the latter.

12 The United States has always maintained a healthy balance in services, unlike in merchandise trade. In 1998 it had a balance of $79.398 billion. In merchandise trade, it had a surplus in trade in agricultural products ($16.3 billion) but a massive deficit of $194.2 billion in manufactured goods and $47 billion in mineral fuels.

13 California leads all states in exports with $95.768 billion, followed by Texas ($78.875 billion), Washington ($38.249 billion), New York ($37.383 billion), Michigan ($28.977 billion), Illinois ($28.914 billion), Ohio ($24.851 billion), Florida ($24.452 billion), Louisiana ($16.836 billion) and Pennsylvania ($15.974 billion).

14 California also leads in agricultural exports with $7.694 billion, followed by Iowa ($4.146 billion), Illinois ($3.748 billion), Nebraska ($3.308 billion) and Texas ($3.054 billion).

Series U 1-25. U.S. Exports and Imports of Goods and Services and Income Receipts and Payments: 1790 to 1998

(In millions of dollars, balance of payments basis. Totals include components not shown separately. For fiscal years, 1790-1900; thereafter, calendar years)

Year	Exports of goods and services and income receipts [1]				Imports of goods and services and income receipts			
	Total	Goods [2]	Travel	Income on U.S.-owned assets	Total	Goods [2]	Direct military expenditures	Income payments on foreign-owned assets in U.S.[3]
	1	2	4	6	8	9	12	13
1998	1 119 422	670 324	71 286	256 511	1 364 531	917 178	12 841	257 547
1997	1 194 283	679 702	73 426	255 554	1 294 029	876 366	11 698	244 494
1996	1 075 874	612 057	69 809	222 054	1 159 111	803 327	11 061	198 634
1995	1 006 576	575 845	63 395	209 741	1 081 976	749 574	10 043	184 692
1994	868 867	502 398	58 417	163 895	949 212	668 590	10 217	142 792
1993	776 933	456 832	57 875	132 725	821 877	589 441	12 086	105 123
1992	749 324	440 352	54 742	130 631	762 035	536 458	13 835	104 349
1991	730 387	416 913	48 385	147 924	734 524	490 981	16 409	121 058
1990	708 881	389 307	43 007	170 570	759 189	498 337	17 531	139 728
1989	650 494	361 451	36 205	160 270	721 307	477 368	15 313	139 177
1988	567 862	320 330	29 434	135 718	663 741	447 189	15 604	116 179
1987	457 053	250 208	23 563	107 190	594 443	409 766	14 950	91 553
1986	407 098	223 344	20 385	96 156	530 142	368 425	13 950	78 893
1985	387 612	215 915	17 762	98 542	483 769	338 083	13 108	72 819
1984	399 913	219 926	17 177	108 819	473 923	332 422	12 516	73 756
1983	356 106	201 799	10 947	90 000	377 488	268 900	13 089	53 614
1982	366 983	211 157	12 393	91 747	355 975	247 642	12 460	56 583
1981	380 928	237 044	12 913	86 529	364 196	265 067	11 564	53 626
1980	344 440	224 250	10 588	72 606	333 774	249 750	10 851	42 532
1979	287 905	184 439	8 441	63 834	281 677	212 007	8 294	32 961
1978	220 516	142 075	7 183	42 088	229 880	176 002	7 352	21 680
1977	184 655	120 816	6 150	32 354	...	151 907	5 823	14 217
1976	172 090	114 745	5 742	29 375	...	124 228	4 895	13 311
1975	157 936	107 088	4 697	25 351	...	98 185	4 795	12 564
1974	148 484	98 306	4 032	27 587	...	103 811	5 032	12 084
1973	113 050	71 410	3 412	21 808	99 997	70 499	4 629	9 655
1972	81 986	49 381	2 817	14 765	79 237	55 797	4 784	6 572
1971	72 384	43 319	2 534	12 707	66 414	45 579	4 819	5 435
1970	68 387	42 469	2 331	11 748	59 901	39 866	4 852	5 515
1969	60 132	36 414	2 043	10 913	53 998	35 807	4 856	4 869
1968	54 911	33 626	1 775	9 367	48 671	32 991	4 535	3 378
1967	49 353	30 666	1 646	8 021	41 476	26 886	4 378	2 747
1966[4]	46 454	29 310	1 590	7 528	38 468	25 493	3 764	2 481
1966[5]	43 277	29 287	1 590	7 581	38 108	25 463	3 764	2 206
1965	39 408	26 438	1 380	7 092	32 310	21 496	2 952	1 797
1964	37 281	25 478	1 207	6 399	28 715	18 647	2 880	1 524
1963	32 603	22 252	1 015	5 539	26 646	17 011	2 961	1 386
1962	30 507	20 779	957	5 219	25 382	16 218	3 105	1 167
1961	28 772	20 107	947	4 604	23 173	14 519	2 998	1 050
1960	27 490	19 650	919	3 939	23 383	14 744	3 087	1 098
1959	23 652	16 458	902	3 586	23 342	15 310	3 107	860
1958	23 217	16 414	825	3 287	20 861	12 952	3 435	703
1957	26 653	19 562	785	3 263	20 752	13 291	3 216	675
1956	23 772	17 556	705	3 100	19 627	12 803	2 949	606
1955	19 945	14 424	654	2 817	17 795	11 527	2 901	520
1954	17 889	12 929	595	2 555	15 930	10 353	2 642	443
1953	17 078	12 412	574	2 215	16 546	10 975	2 615	483
1952	18 122	13 449	550	2 120	15 766	10 838	2 054	445
1951	18 864	14 243	473	2 154	15 047	11 176	1 270	434
1950	13 893	10 203	419	1 839	12 001	9 081	576	379
1949	15 834	12 213	392	1 615	9 616	6 874	621	342
1948	16 861	13 265	334	1 553	10 343	7 557	799	291
1947	19 819	16 097	364	1 303	8 202	5 973	455	256
1946	14 792	11 764	271	978	6 985	5 067	493	222

See footnotes at end of table.

Series U 1-25. U.S. Exports and Imports of Goods and Services and Income Receipts and Payments: 1790 to 1998—Cont'd.

(In millions of dollars, balance of payments basis. Totals include components not shown separately. For fiscal years, 1790-1900; thereafter, calendar years)

	Exports of goods and services and income receipts [1]				Imports of goods and services and income receipts			
Year	Total	Goods [2]	Travel	Income on U.S.-owned assets	Total	Goods [2]	Direct military expenditures	Income payments on foreign-owned assets in U.S.[3]
	1	2	4	6	8	9	12	13
1945	16 273	12 473	162	734	10 232	5 245	2 434	231
1944	21 438	16 969	117	573	8 986	5 043	1 982	161
1943	19 134	15 115	84	509	8 096	4 599	1 763	155
1942	11 769	9 187	82	514	5 356	3 499	953	158
1941	6 896	5 343	70	544	4 486	3 416	162	187
1940	5 355	4 124	95	564	3 636	2 698	61	210
1939	4 432	3 347	135	541	3 366	2 409	46	230
1938	4 336	3 243	130	585	3 045	2 173	41	200
1937	4 553	3 451	135	577	4 256	3 181	41	295
1936	3 539	2 590	117	569	2 424	2 546	38	270
1935	3 265	2 404	101	521	3 137	2 462	41	155
1934	2 975	2 238	81	437	2 374	1 763	34	135
1933	2 402	1 736	66	427	2 044	1 510	41	115
1932	2 474	1 667	65	527	2 067	1 343	47	135
1931	3 641	2 494	94	766	3 125	2 120	48	220
1930	5 448	3 929	129	1 040	4 416	3 104	49	295
1929	7 034	5 347	139	1 139	5 886	4 463	50	330
1928	6 842	5 249	121	1 080	5 465	4 159	44	275
1927	6 456	4 982	114	981	5 383	4 240	38	240
1926	6 381	4 922	110	953	5 555	4 500	43	200
1925	6 348	5 011	83	912	5 261	4 291	39	170
1924	5 911	4 741	77	762	4 560	3 684	36	140
1923	5 494	4 266	71	840	4 652	3 866	33	130
1922	4 954	3 929	61	670	3 957	3 184	42	105
1921	5 505	4 586	76	445	3 383	2 572	65	105
1920	10 264	8 481	67	596	6 741	5 384	123	120
1919	10 776	8 891	56	719	5 908	3 995	757	130
1918	7 272	6 432	44	450	4 814	3 103	1 018	100
1917	7 072	6 398	34	350	3 597	3 006	...	100
1916	6 029	5 560	22	250	2 927	2 423	...	118
1915	3 948	3 686	24	200	2 200	1 813	...	136
1914	2 445	2 230	39	145	2 389	1 815	...	200
1913	2 816	2 600	50	137	2 442	1 829	...	210
1912	2 738	2 532	49	123	2 481	1 866	...	197
1911	2 405	2 228	41	114	2 131	1 576	...	190
1910	2 160	1 995	38	108	2 114	1 609	...	172
1909	2 013	1 857	41	100	1 987	1 522	...	164
1908	2 022	1 880	39	89	1 595	1 159	...	160
1907	2 192	2 021	35	87	1 896	1 469	...	153
1906	2 052	1 921	27	86	1 756	1 365	...	148
1905	1 859	1 751	18	76	1 561	1 215	...	145
1904	1 657	1 563	13	70	1 378	1 062	...	141
1903	1 663	1 575	9	67	1 323	1 019	...	139
1902	1 550	1 473	9	57	1 292	996	...	137
1901	1 651	1 585	8	47	1 213	912	...	135
1900 [4]	1 686	1 623	8	38	1 179	869	...	137
1900 [5]	1 578	1 534	19	...	1 149	894	...	144
1899	1 400	1 363	17	...	973	735	...	124
1898	1 340	1 301	16	...	896	653	...	133
1897	1 173	1 136	15	...	1 041	803	...	127
1896	1 082	1 048	15	...	1 048	816	...	122
1895	888	855	14	...	1 015	774	...	126
1894	981	943	20	...	883	692	...	113
1893	1 021	974	26	...	1 140	898	...	139

See footnotes at end of table.

Series U 1-25. U.S. Exports and Imports of Goods and Services and Income Receipts and Payments: 1790 to 1998—Cont'd.

(In millions of dollars, balance of payments basis. Totals include components not shown separately. For fiscal years, 1790-1900; thereafter, calendar years)

Year	Exports of goods and services and income receipts [1]				Imports of goods and services and income receipts			
	Total	Goods [2]	Travel	Income on U.S.-owned assets	Total	Goods [2]	Direct military expenditures	Income payments on foreign-owned assets in U.S.[3]
	1	2	4	6	8	9	12	13
1892	1 122	1 084	14	. . .	1 142	888	. . .	143
1891	1 035	997	13	. . .	1 124	875	. . .	134
1890	960	921	15	. . .	1 109	866	. . .	125
1889	880	841	14	. . .	1 046	817	. . .	118
1888	786	750	14	. . .	1 013	791	. . .	107
1887	810	774	14	. . .	967	759	. . .	98
1886	817	781	15	. . .	894	698	. . .	93
1885	830	792	17	. . .	818	635	. . .	86
1884	862	822	15	. . .	921	730	. . .	90
1883	915	875	13	. . .	927	748	. . .	89
1882	859	824	7	. . .	915	747	. . .	84
1881	971	936	6	. . .	834	672	. . .	88
1880	963	929	7	. . .	848	694	. . .	79
1879	813	784	5	. . .	612	469	. . .	78

See footnotes at end of table.

Series U 1-25. U.S. Exports and Imports of Goods and Services and Income Receipts and Payments: 1790 to 1998—Cont'd.

(In millions of dollars, balance of payments basis. Totals include components not shown separately. For fiscal years, 1790-1900; thereafter, calendar years)

	Exports of goods and services and income receipts [1]			Imports of goods and services and income receipts		
Year	Total	Goods [2]	Travel	Total	Goods [2] adjusted	Income payments on foreign-owned assets in U.S. [3]
	1	2	4	8	9	13
1878	813	780	4	595	462	76
1877	716	687	3	614	475	86
1876	654	620	4	634	478	96
1875	623	590	3	722	556	99
1874	707	669	3	767	593	102
1873	675	631	2	856	683	99
1872	578	539	4	824	662	86
1871	603	564	6	704	557	84
1870	507	473	3	608	475	80
1869	395	365	2	567	450	69
1868	428	395	2	505	382	67
1867	401	369	1	550	430	58
1866	481	446	1	572	459	51
1865	279	261	...	343	256	45
1864	304	288	...	418	339	34
1863	313	287	1	328	260	31
1862	272	248	1	272	211	30
1861	303	261	1	406	344	24
1860	438	401	2	438	376	25
1859	384	358	1	416	352	23
1858	350	326	2	334	293	15
1857	385	366	2	416	375	15
1856	359	329	2	378	327	23
1855	303	279	2	325	272	22
1854	314	281	4	377	316	20
1853	258	231	4	333	279	16
1852	232	211	4	265	221	15
1851	251	219	4	271	225	13
1850	166	153	4	210	185	12
1849	166	146	3	173	154	12
1848	174	155	2	188	161	12
1847	181	160	2	178	151	9
1846	133	114	2	143	126	9
1845	135	115	1	138	120	9
1844	126	112	1	126	111	7
1843	101	85	1	81	66	7
1842	119	105	1	119	102	8
1841	136	122	1	148	130	8
1840	160	133	1	134	109	12
1839	135	121	1	188	165	14
1838	128	109	1	135	116	10
1837	133	118	2	161	144	9
1836	141	129	2	209	194	9
1835	132	122	1	166	153	7
1834	116	105	1	140	129	6
1833	101	90	1	119	110	5
1832	101	88	1	112	103	5
1831	97	82	1	112	103	4
1830	86	74	1	79	71	5
1829	83	73	...	83	75	5
1828	84	73	1	97	89	4
1827	98	83	...	90	80	5
1826	91	78	...	95	85	5
1825	112	100	...	106	96	5
1824	90	77	...	90	81	5
1823	89	75	...	87	78	5
1822	83	73	...	92	83	5

See footnotes at end of table.

Series U 1-25. U.S. Exports and Imports of Goods and Services and Income Receipts and Payments: 1790 to 1998—Cont'd.

(In millions of dollars, balance of payments basis. Totals include components not shown separately. For fiscal years, 1790-1900; thereafter, calendar years)

| Year | Exports of goods and services and income receipts [1] | | Imports of goods and services and income receipts | | |
| | Total | Goods [2] | Total | Goods [2] | Income payments on foreign-owned assets in U.S.[3] |
	1	2	8	9	13
1821	76	66	72	63	5
1820	84	70	84	75	5
1819	91	72	105	94	6
1818	116	95	141	128	6
1817	103	89	113	102	7
1816	105	84	163	151	5
1815	81	55	96	85	4
1814	11	8	20	16	3
1813	45	32	30	22	4
1812	75	39	96	83	3
1811	114	63	78	61	5
1810	117	68	110	91	6
1809	88	55	76	61	6
1808	55	26	71	58	5
1807	162	109	167	146	5
1806	148	105	155	137	4
1805	134	97	144	128	4
1804	114	81	102	87	5
1803	88	59	80	67	4
1802	98	75	91	78	5
1801	134	95	132	114	5
1800	107	74	108	93	5
1799	111	80	96	81	6
1798	83	62	84	72	6
1797	79	57	90	77	5
1796	94	67	97	84	5
1795	72	48	85	73	4
1794	55	36	46	36	5
1793	43	28	42	33	5
1792	32	23	40	33	4
1791	29	21	37	31	4
1790	29	21	30	24	4

1. Prior to 1946, includes transfers of goods and services under U.S. military grant programs.
2. Imports include receipts from military cash and credit transactions, from 1790 through 1966. From 1966 (later version) to date, goods exports and imports exclude certain military components and include other adjustments.
3. Net for 1790-1900.
4. Comparable with later years.
5. Comparable with earlier years.

Series U 26-39. International Investment Position of the United States: 1843 to 1998

(Value at yearend in billions of dollars)

Year	U.S.-owned assets abroad [1]			Total foreign-owned assets in U.S.[1]	Year	U.S.-owned assets abroad [1]			Total foreign-owned assets in U.S.[1]
	Total [2]	Private	U.S. government [2]			Total [2]	Private	U.S. government [2]	
	26	27	32	33		26	27	32	33
1998	5 079.1	4 846.3	232.8	6 190.9	1965	120.4	81.5	38.8	58.8
1997	4 557.9	4 336.9	221.0	5 528.4	1964	114.7	75.9	38.8	56.9
1996	4 008.9	3 762.0	246.9	4 605.4					
1995	3 452.0	3 190.9	261.1	3 966.6	1963	103.9	66.6	37.4	51.5
1994	2 998.6	2 751.3	247.3	3 310.5	1962	96.5	60.1	36.4	46.3
					1961	92.0	55.6	36.4	46.0
1993	2 753.6	2 505.3	248.3	3 060.6	1960	85.6	49.3	36.3	40.9
1992	2 331.7	2 101.2	230.5	2 762.9	1959	82.2	44.8	37.4	39.1
1991	2 286.5	2 045.8	240.6	2 595.7					
1990	2 179.0	1 920.0	259.0	2 424.3	1958	79.2	41.1	38.1	34.4
1989	2 070.9	1 815.5	255.4	2 330.4	1957	76.4	36.9	39.5	30.7
					1956	70.8	33.4	37.4	30.5
1988	1 829.7	1 597.6	232.1	2 008.1	1955	65.1	29.1	35.9	27.8
1987	1 646.5	1 393.5	253.1	1 726.5	1954	62.4	26.6	35.8	25.0
1986	1 469.4	1 237.7	231.7	1 505.6					
1985	1 287.4	1 079.7	207.7	1 233.1	1953	60.2	23.8	36.4	21.9
1984	1 204.9	1 012.9	192.0	1 044.2	1952	59.1	22.7	36.4	20.8
					1951	56.4	20.8	35.6	18.7
1983	1 211.0	1 006.2	204.8	912.7	1950	54.4	19.0	35.4	17.6
1982	1 108.4	888.1	220.3	779.5	1949	53.9	16.9	37.0	14.8
1981	1 001.7	806.2	195.5	661.9					
1980	929.8	692.8	237.0	569.0	1948	52.5	16.3	36.2	14.4
1979	786.7	584.6	202.1	469.8	1947	48.3	14.9	33.4	13.8
					1946	39.4	13.5	25.9	15.2
1978	621.2	498.6	122.6	414.8	1945	36.9	14.7	22.2	17.0
1977	512.3	410.3	101.9	340.8	1940	34.3	12.2	22.1	13.5
1976 [3]	457.0	367.9	89.1	292.1					
1976 [4]	347.2	282.4	64.8	263.6	1935	23.6	13.5	10.1	6.4
1975	295.1	237.1	58.0	220.9	1931	20.1	15.9	4.2	3.8
					1930	21.5	17.2	4.3	8.4
1974	255.7	201.5	54.2	197.0	1927	17.9	13.8	4.1	6.6
1973	226.1	165.3	60.8	163.1	1924	15.1	10.9	4.2	3.9
1972	200.6	145.7	54.9	149.4					
1971	180.8	130.5	50.3	123.1	1919	9.7	7.0	2.7	3.3
1970	166.9	120.2	46.7	97.7	1914 (June 30)	5.0	3.5	1.5	7.2
					1908	2.5	2.5	...	6.4
1969	158.1	110.4	47.7	90.8	1897	.7	.7	...	3.4
1968	146.8	102.5	44.3	81.2	1869	.1	.1	...	1.5
1967	134.7	93.6	41.1	69.7					
1966	125.2	86.4	38.8	60.4	1843	(Z)	...	...	.2

Z Less than 50 million.

1. From 1976 to the present, direct investment is valued at current (i.e., replacement) cost. Previously, it was valued at book value (historical cost).
2. Beginning 1914, includes U.S. monetary gold stock.
3. Comparable with later years.
4. Comparable with earlier years.

Series U 41-46. Value of Direct Investment in Foreign Countries, by Area: 1929 to 1998

(In millions of dollars, historical cost basis)

Year	Total, all areas	Canada	Latin America and other Western Hemisphere	Western Europe [1]	Year	Total, all areas	Canada	Latin America and other Western Hemisphere	Western Europe [1]
	41	42	43	44		41	42	43	44
1998	1 014 012	101 871	200 477	528 113	1972	94 337	25 771	13 667	30 817
1997	871 316	96 031	178 505	420 108	1971	86 198	24 105	12 982	27 740
1996	795 195	89 592	155 925	389 378	1970	78 178	22 790	12 252	24 516
1995	699 015	83 498	131 377	344 596	1969	71 016	21 127	11 694	21 650
1994	612 893	74 221	116 478	297 133					
					1968	64 983	19 535	11 033	19 407
1993	564 283	69 922	59 302	285 735	1967	59 491	18 102	10 270	17 926
1992	502 063	68 690	54 339	248 744	1966	54 799	17 017	9 876	16 234
1991	467 844	70 711	48 546	235 163	1965	49 474	15 318	9 441	13 985
1990	430 521	69 508	43 348	214 739	1964	44 480	13 855	8 742	12 129
1989	370 091	65 548	62 727	175 213					
					1963	40 736	13 044	8 712	10 340
1988	335 893	62 656	53 506	157 077	1962	37 276	12 133	8 474	8 930
1987	314 307	57 783	47 551	150 439	1961	34 717	11 602	8 286	7 742
1986	259 582	49 994	34 790	122 165	1960	31 865	11 197	7 481	6 691
1985	230 250	46 909	28 261	105 171	1959	29 827	10 310	8 120	5 323
1984	211 480	46 730	24 627	91 589					
					1958	27 409	9 470	7 773	4 573
1983	207 203	44 339	24 133	92 178	1957	25 394	8 769	7 434	4 151
1982	221 343	44 509	31 175	99 877	1956	22 505	7 795	6 844	3 561
1981	226 359	45 129	30 020	101 514	1955	19 395	6 761	6 031	3 002
1980	215 375	45 119	38 761	96 287	1954	17 631	6 043	5 741	2 643
1979	187 658	40 662	22 792	85 056					
					1953	16 253	5 349	5 589	2 375
1978	167 804	37 071	21 467	69 553	1952	14 721	4 641	5 355	2 153
1977	149 848	35 200	18 882	60 930	1951	12 979	3 969	4 818	1 989
1976	136 809	33 838	17 125	55 139	1950	11 788	3 579	4 445	1 733
1975	124 050	31 038	16 394	49 305	1940	7 000	2 103	2 771	1 420
1974	118 819	28 404	14 597	44 782					
					1936	6 691	1 952	2 847	1 245
1973	103 675	25 541	13 527	38 255	1929	7 528	2 010	3 519	1 353

1. Western Europe includes Eastern Europe for 1929, 1936, and 1940 but excludes Turkey for 1936 and 1940.

Series U 47-74. Value of Foreign Direct Investment in the United States, by Area and Industry: 1937 to 1998

(In millions of dollars, historical cost basis. Book value at year end. Covers U.S. business enterprises, including real estate investments, in which there was a foreign interest or ownership of 25 percent or more)

Year	All areas				Canada			
	Total [1]	Petroleum	Manufacturing	Finance and insurance	Total [1]	Petroleum	Manufacturing	Finance and insurance
	47	**48**	**49**	**50**	**51**	**52**	**53**	**54**
1998	793 748	51 729	334 898	167 484	74 143	2 526	26 507	18 162
1997	689 834	42 632	271 287	154 307	65 144	3 199	24 251	15 033
1996	598 021	43 483	245 662	124 919	54 836	3 220	23 096	13 384
1995	535 553	34 907	214 504	119 333	45 618	3 241	20 320	10 900
1994	480 667	32 290	189 459	91 099	41 219	3 097	17 439	8 364
1993	464 110	31 740	166 397	74 733	40 143	2 455	15 306	8 168
1992	427 566	37 555	158 873	48 780	37 843	2 443	15 598	7 235
1991	419 108	40 051	157 115	44 748	36 834	2 468	15 716	7 354
1990	403 735	38 004	159 998	58 437	27 733	1 417	9 327	7 325
1989	373 763	37 201	151 820	58 215	28 686	1 233	9 934	7 227
1988	314 754	36 006	122 582	44 010	26 566	1 181	9 730	5 769
1987	263 394	37 815	93 865	39 455	24 684	1 088	8 085	5 797
1986	220 414	29 094	71 963	34 978	20 318	1 432	6 108	4 283
1985	184 615	28 270	59 584	27 429	17 131	1 589	4 607	4 008
1984	164 583	25 400	51 802	24 881	15 286	1 544	4 115	3 245
1983	137 061	18 209	47 665	10 934	11 434	1 391	3 313	1 061
1982	124 677	17 660	44 065	17 933	11 708	1 550	3 500	1 801
1981	90 421	18 005	29 976	12 574	9 883	1 387	3 519	818
1980	83 046	12 200	32 993	12 027	12 162	1 817	5 227	1 612
1979	54 462	9 906	20 876	7 575	7 154	943	3 615	505
1978	42 471	7 762	17 202	5 231	6 180	723	3 213	397
1977	34 595	6 573	14 030	4 544	5 650	710	3 077	367
1976	30 770	5 921	12 620	2 943	5 907	676	3 386	422
1975	27 662	6 213	11 386	3 152	5 352	596	3 061	341
1974	22 421	5 979	10 685	2 864	4 930	468	2 966	342
1973	18 284	4 649	8 559	2 854	4 044	296	2 430	320
1972	14 868	3 272	7 262	2 911	3 466	243	2 201	353
1971	13 914	3 139	6 722	2 553	3 335	207	2 013	330
1970	13 270	2 992	6 140	2 256	3 117	190	1 836	324
1969	11 818	2 493	5 344	2 189	2 834	132	1 644	352
1968	10 815	2 261	4 475	2 305	2 659	100	1 413	376
1967	9 923	1 885	4 181	2 193	2 575	99	1 397	354
1966	9 054	1 740	3 789	2 072	2 439	98	1 342	386
1965	8 797	1 710	3 478	2 169	2 388	208	1 219	370
1964	8 363	1 621	3 213	2 181	2 284	205	1 129	382
1963	7 944	1 513	3 018	2 045	2 183	213	1 063	337
1962	7 612	1 419	2 885	1 943	2 064	212	1 015	269
1961	7 392	1 325	2 754	2 025	1 989	194	975	274
1960	6 910	1 238	2 611	1 810	1 934	203	932	246
1959	6 604	1 184	2 471	1 734	1 896	207	907	227
1958	6 115	1 099	2 232	1 660	1 835	214	863	222
1957	5 710	1 043	2 083	1 496	1 773	211	816	208
1956	5 459	937	1 940	1 534	1 690	200	775	196
1955	5 076	853	1 759	1 499	1 542	196	711	179
1954	4 633	776	1 582	1 371	1 427	192	651	168
1953	4 251	706	1 451	1 219	1 350	168	611	162
1952	3 945	552	1 377	1 170	1 218	90	592	149
1951	3 658	466	1 274	1 105	1 119	62	525	150
1950	3 391	405	1 138	1 065	1 029	56	468	153
1941	2 312	222	714	521	530	. . .	. . .	. . .
1937	1 882	283	729	412	463	. . .	. . .	. . .

See footnote at end of table.

Series U 47-74. Value of Foreign Direct Investment in the United States, by Area and Industry: 1937 to 1998—Cont'd.

(In millions of dollars, historical cost basis. Book value at year end. Covers U.S. business enterprises, including real estate investments, in which there was a foreign interest or ownership of 25 percent or more)

Year	Europe				United Kingdom			
	Total [1]	Petroleum	Manufacturing	Finance and insurance	Total [1]	Petroleum	Manufacturing	Finance and insurance
	55	56	57	58	59	60	61	62
1998	528 601	46 008	251 750	105 481	143 165	30 069	54 765	18 581
1997	433 876	30 526	200 042	92 969	130 883	13 202	55 682	23 156
1996	370 843	29 194	176 309	71 960	121 582	11 060	58 675	21 021
1995	332 374	24 039	156 543	67 908	116 272	9 275	56 703	21 821
1994	294 035	23 947	138 751	53 074	98 732	9 489	47 334	14 615
1993	287 084	29 396	124 454	46 895	102 351	9 963	42 783	19 927
1992	255 570	29 167	115 215	28 550	90 931	11 080	40 818	12 436
1991	256 053	31 436	114 248	27 715	100 085	14 068	41 924	13 391
1990	256 496	31 197	125 568	30 329	108 055	15 310	52 955	13 139
1989	242 961	32 476	120 132	31 609	105 511	16 545	51 798	11 859
1988	208 942	33 499	95 641	27 121	95 698	19 522	41 708	11 256
1987	181 006	35 700	74 300	26 336	75 519	17 950	30 372	9 801
1986	144 181	26 139	56 016	21 787	55 935	11 758	16 500	10 163
1985	121 413	25 636	45 841	17 022	43 555	12 155	11 687	6 483
1984	108 211	23 142	39 083	15 945	38 387	10 991	9 179	5 485
1983	92 936	16 326	36 866	8 450	32 152	5 955	9 221	3 777
1982	83 193	15 071	33 032	12 601	28 447	5 444	8 504	5 661
1981	60 510	14 937	21 995	8 841	15 576	-165	6 109	4 330
1980	54 688	10 137	21 953	8 673	14 105	-257	6 159	3 350
1979	37 403	8 010	13 952	5 529	9 796	199	3 547	2 432
1978	29 180	6 569	11 717	3 575	7 638	492	3 014	1 596
1977	23 754	5 523	9 267	3 076	6 397	486	2 305	1 425
1976	20 162	4 999	7 426	2 637	5 802	602	1 963	1 211
1975	18 584	5 478	6 673	2 088	6 331	. . .	1 833	932
1974	14 627	3 871	7 143	2 181	6 188	1 650	2 476	1 363
1973	12 504	3 438	5 828	2 261	5 649	1 377	2 250	1 506
1972	11 087	3 011	4 836	2 335	4 987	1 297	1 719	1 567
1971	10 336	2 893	4 455	2 047	4 853	1 270	1 615	1 326
1970	9 554	2 777	4 091	1 805	4 127	1 220	1 391	1 141
1969	8 510	2 322	3 530	1 766	3 496	829	1 176	1 143
1968	7 750	2 146	2 941	1 855	3 409	749	1 076	1 239
1967	7 005	1 772	2 669	1 758	3 156	612	1 009	1 189
1966	6 273	1 620	2 335	1 611	2 864	558	906	1 075
1965	6 076	1 481	2 167	1 724	2 852	511	839	1 176
1964	5 819	1 404	2 005	1 723	2 796	498	812	1 154
1963	5 491	1 306	1 881	1 640	2 665	480	779	1 085
1962	5 245	1 203	1 797	1 611	2 474	416	762	1 023
1961	5 129	1 125	1 708	1 690	2 484	381	750	1 091
1960	4 707	1 028	1 611	1 504	2 248	339	722	953
1959	4 452	972	1 501	1 451	2 167	316	698	927
1958	4 070	885	1 332	1 384	2 024	283	640	889
1957	3 753	832	1 248	1 238	1 881	271	611	794
1956	3 598	737	1 155	1 289	1 833	227	566	841
1955	3 369	657	1 040	1 272	1 749	204	510	836
1954	3 049	584	925	1 158	1 590	180	460	751
1953	2 751	538	836	1 014	1 422	163	419	647
1952	2 575	462	782	977	1 345	137	395	626
1951	2 410	404	747	912	1 273	118	388	583
1950	2 228	349	669	870	1 168	95	337	554
1941	1 569	. . .	. . .	. . .	712	. . .	. . .	. . .
1937	1 337	. . .	. . .	. . .	833	. . .	. . .	. . .

1. Includes industries not shown separately: Mining and smelting, transportation and utilities, trade and miscellaneous.

Series U 187-200.   Value of Exports and Imports: 1790 to 1998

(In millions of dollars. For years ending September 30, 1790-1842; June 30, 1843-1915, thereafter, calendar years)

| | Merchandise [1] | | | | | Merchandise [1] | | | |
| | Exports and re-exports | | | | | Exports and re-export: | | | |
Year	Total	Exports of U.S. merchandise	Total general imports	Excess of exports (+) or imports (−)	Year	Total	Exports of U.S. merchandise	Total general imports	Excess of exports (+) or imports (−)
	190	**191**	**193**	**196**		**190**	**191**	**193**	**196**
1998	682 100	659 000	911 900	− 229 800	1893	848	831	866	− 19
1997	689 200	662 600	870 700	− 181 500	1892	1 030	1 016	827	+ 203
1996	625 100	597 700	795 300	− 170 200	1891	884	872	845	+ 40
1995	584 700	553 200	743 400	− 158 700	1890	858	845	789	+ 69
1994	512 600	486 000	663 300	− 150 600	1889	742	730	745	− 3
1993	465 100	441 400	580 700	− 115 600	1888	696	684	724	− 28
1992	448 200	412 900	532 700	− 84 500	1887	716	703	692	+ 24
1991	421 900	400 900	488 100	− 66 200	1886	680	666	635	+ 44
1990	393 600	375 100	495 300	− 101 700	1885	742	727	578	+ 165
1989	363 800	349 400	473 400	− 109 600	1884	741	725	668	+ 73
1988	322 400	310 000	441 000	− 118 600	1883	824	804	723	+ 101
1987	254 100	243 900	406 200	− 152 100	1882	751	733	725	+ 26
1986	217 300	206 400	370 000	− 152 700	1881	902	884	643	+ 260
1985	213 100	206 900	345 300	− 132 100	1880	836	824	668	+ 168
1984	217 900	212 100	325 700	− 107 900	1879	710	698	446	+ 265
1983	200 500	196 000	258 000	− 57 500	1878	695	681	437	+ 258
1982	212 300	207 100	244 000	− 31 800	1877	602	590	451	+ 151
1981	233 700	228 900	261 000	− 27 300	1876	540	526	461	+ 80
1980	220 600	216 500	244 900	− 24 200	1875	513	499	533	− 20
1979	181 900	178 600	209 500	− 27 600	1874	596	569	567	+ 19
1978	143 700	141 000	174 800	− 31 100	1873	522	505	642	− 120
1977	121 200	118 900	150 400	− 29 200	1872	444	428	627	− 182
1976	115 200	113 500	123 500	− 8 300	1871	443	428	520	− 77
1975	107 700	106 100	98 500	+ 9 100	1870	393	377	436	− 43
1974	98 100	96 500	102 600	− 4 500	1869	286	275	418	− 131
1973	70 800	69 700	69 500	+ 1 300	1868	282	269	357	− 75
1972	49 200	48 400	55 600	− 6 400	1867	295	290	396	− 101
1971	43 500	42 900	45 600	− 2 000	1866	349	338	435	− 86
1970	43 224	42 590	39 952	+ 3 272	1865	166	137	239	− 73
1969	38 006	37 462	36 043	+ 1 964	1864	159	144	316	− 158
1968	34 636	34 199	33 226	+ 1 410	1863	204	186	243	− 39
1967	31 526	31 142	26 812	+ 4 714	1862	191	180	189	+ 1
1966	30 320	29 884	25 542	+ 4 777	1861	220	205	289	− 70
1965	27 470	27 127	21 364	+ 6 105	1860	334	316	354	− 20
1964	26 508	26 156	18 684	+ 7 824	1859	293	278	331	− 38
1963	23 347	23 062	17 138	+ 6 209	1858	272	251	263	+ 9
1962	21 700	21 431	16 380	+ 5 320	1857	294	279	348	− 55
1961	20 999	20 755	14 714	+ 6 286	1856	281	166	310	− 29
1960	20 575	20 375	14 654	+ 5 922	1855	219	193	258	− 39
1959	17 634	17 451	15 207	+ 2 427	1854	237	215	298	− 61
1958	17 910	17 745	12 792	+ 5 118	1853	203	190	264	− 60
1957	20 850	20 671	12 982	+ 7 868	1852	167	155	207	− 40
1956	19 090	18 940	12 615	+ 6 475	1851	189	179	211	− 22
1955	15 547	15 419	11 384	+ 4 163	1850	144	135	174	− 29
1954	15 110	14 981	10 215	+ 4 894	1849	140	132	141	− 1
1953	15 774	15 652	10 873	+ 4 900	1848	138	130	149	− 10
1952	15 201	15 049	10 717	+ 4 483	1847	157	151	122	+ 34
1951	15 032	14 879	10 967	+ 4 065	1846	110	102	118	− 8
1950	10 275	10 142	8 852	+ 1 423	1845	106	98	113	− 7
1949	12 051	11 936	6 622	+ 5 429	1844	106	100	103	+ 3
1948	12 653	12 532	7 124	+ 5 529	1843 [5]	83	78	42	+ 40
1947	[2] 14 430	14 252	5 756	+ 8 673	1842	100	92	96	+ 4
1946	[2] 9 738	9 500	4 942	+ 4 796	1841	112	104	123	− 11
1945	[2] 9 806	9 585	[3] 4 159	+ 5 646	1840	124	112	98	+ 25
1944	[2] 14 259	14 162	[3] 3 929	+ 10 330	1839	112	102	156	− 44

See footnotes at end of table.

Series U 187-200.   Value of Exports and Imports: 1790 to 1998—Cont'd.

(In millions of dollars. For years ending September 30, 1790-1842; June 30, 1843-1915, thereafter, calendar years)

	Merchandise [1]					Merchandise [1]			
	Exports and re−exports					Exports and re−export:			
Year	Total	Exports of U.S. merchandise	Total general imports	Excess of exports (+) or imports (−)	Year	Total	Exports of U.S. merchandise	Total general imports	Excess of exports (+) or imports (−)
	190	191	193	196		190	191	193	196
1943	12 965	12 842	3 381	+9 583	1838	105	96	96	+9
1942	8 079	8 003	[3] 2 756	+5 323	1837	111	94	130	−19
1941	5 147	5 020	3 345	+1 802	1836	124	107	177	−52
1940	4 021	3 934	2 625	+1 396	1835	115	100	137	−22
1939	3 177	3 123	2 318	+859	1834	102	81	109	−6
1938	3 094	3 057	1 960	+1 134	1833	88	70	101	−14
1937	3 349	3 299	3 084	+265	1832	82	62	95	−14
1936	2 456	2 419	2 423	+33	1831	72	59	96	−24
1935	2 283	2 243	2 047	+235	1830	72	59	63	+9
1934	2 133	2 100	1 655	+478	1829	67	55	67	(Z)
1933	1 675	1 647	1 450	+225	1828	64	50	81	−17
1932	1 611	1 576	1 323	+288	1827	74	58	71	+3
1931	2 424	2 378	2 091	+334	1826	73	52	78	−5
1930	3 843	3 781	3 061	+782	1825	91	67	90	+1
1929	5 241	5 157	4 399	+842	1824	69	51	72	−3
1928	5 128	5 030	4 091	+1 037	1823	68	47	72	−4
1927	4 865	4 759	4 185	+681	1822	61	50	80	−19
1926	4 809	4 712	4 431	+378	1821	55	41	55	(Z)
1925	4 910	4 819	4 227	+683	1820	70	52	74	−5
1924	4 591	4 498	3 610	+981	1819	70	51	87	−17
1923	4 167	4 091	3 792	+375	1818	93	74	122	−28
1922	3 832	3 765	3 113	+719	1817	88	68	99	−12
1921	4 485	4 379	2 509	+1 976	1816	82	65	147	−65
1920	8 228	8 080	5 278	+2 950	1815	53	46	113	−60
1919	7 920	7 750	3 904	+4 016	1814	7	7	13	−6
1918	6 149	6 048	3 031	+3 118	1813	28	25	22	+6
1917	6 234	6 170	2 952	+3 281	1812	39	30	77	−39
1916	5 483	5 423	2 392	+3 091	1811	61	45	53	+8
1915 [4]	2 769	2 716	1 674	+1 094	1810	67	42	85	−19
1914	2 365	2 330	1 894	+471	1809	52	31	59	−7
1913	2 466	2 429	1 813	+653	1808	22	9	57	−35
1912	2 204	2 170	1 653	+551	1807	108	49	139	−30
1911	2 049	2 014	1 527	+522	1806	102	41	129	−28
1910	1 745	1 710	1 557	+188	1805	96	42	121	−25
1909	1 663	1 638	1 312	+351	1804	78	41	85	−7
1908	1 861	1 835	1 194	+666	1803	56	42	65	−9
1907	1 881	1 854	1 434	+446	1802	72	36	76	−4
1906	1 744	1 718	1 227	+517	1801	93	46	111	−18
1905	1 519	1 492	1 118	+401	1800	71	32	91	−20
1904	1 461	1 435	991	+470	1799	79	33	79	(Z)
1903	1 420	1 392	1 026	+394	1798	61	28	69	−7
1902	1 382	1 355	903	+478	1797	51	24	75	−24
1901	1 488	1 460	823	+665	1796	59	32	81	−23
1900	1 394	1 371	850	+545	1795	48	40	70	−22
1899	1 227	1 204	697	+530	1794	33	27	35	−2
1898	1 231	1 210	616	+615	1793	26	24	31	−5
1897	1 051	1 032	765	+286	1792	21	19	32	−11
1896	883	863	780	+103	1791	19	19	29	−10
1895	808	793	732	+76	1790	20	...	23	−3
1894	892	869	655	+237					

Z Less than $500 000 or less than −$500 000.
1. Includes gold and silver prior to 1821. Beginning 1961, includes exports and imports of uranium, thorium and related products; beginning 1968, includes silver ore and bullion.
2. Figures which include estimates of civilian supplies shipped to occupied areas through U.S. Armed Forces and other relief agencies are as follows (in millions of dollars); 1944, 14 414; 1945, 10 560; 1946, 10 184; 1947, 15 338.
3. Does not add due to revisions not carried to detail.
4. Figures for six-month period July 1, 1915-Dec. 31, 1915, are as follows: Series U 190, 1 853; series U 191, 1 820; series U 193; series U 196, 940.
5. Period beginning Oct. 1, 1842, and ending June 30, 1843.

Series U 317-334.   Value of Exports (Including Re-exports) of U.S. Merchandise, by Country of Destination: 1790 to 1998

(In millions of dollars. Figures shown here are mixed values for 1862-1879. For years ending September 30, 1790-1842; June 30, 1843-1915; thereafter, calendar years. Beginning 1961, includes uranium, thorium and related products. Beginning 1869, includes silver ores, base bullion and refined bullion)

Year	America			Europe			Japan [3]
	Canada [1]	Mexico	Brazil	United Kingdom	France	Germany [2]	
	319	321	322	325	326	327	331
1998	156 307	79 010	15 157	39 070	17 728	26 641	57 887
1997	151 766	71 388	15 914	36 425	15 964	24 458	65 548
1996	134 210	56 791	12 717	30 962	14 455	23 495	67 606
1995	127 226	46 292	11 439	28 856	14 245	22 394	64 342
1994	114 438	50 843	8 101	26 899	13 618	19 229	53 487
1993	100 444	41 581	6 058	26 438	13 267	18 932	47 892
1992	90 594	40 592	5 751	22 800	14 593	21 249	47 813
1991	85 150	33 276	6 154	22 064	15 365	21 317	48 147
1990	83 866	28 279	5 048	23 490	13 665	18 760	48 580
1989	78 809	24 982	4 804	20 837	11 579	16 956	44 494
1988	71 622	20 643	4 289	18 404	10 133	14 331	37 732
1987	59 814	14 582	4 040	14 114	7 943	11 748	28 249
1986	55 512	12 392	3 885	11 418	7 216	10 561	26 882
1985	53 287	13 635	3 140	11 273	6 096	9 050	22 631
1984	51 777	11 992	2 640	12 210	6 037	9 084	23 575
1983	43 345	9 082	2 557	10 621	5 961	8 737	21 894
1982	37 887	11 817	3 423	10 645	7 110	9 291	20 966
1981	44 602	17 789	3 798	12 439	7 341	10 227	21 823
1980	40 331	15 145	4 343	12 694	7 485	10 960	20 790
1979	37 599	9 847	3 442	10 635	5 587	8 478	17 581
1978	30 540	6 680	2 981	7 116	4 166	6 957	12 885
1977	27 738	4 822	2 490	5 951	3 503	5 989	10 529
1976	25 677	4 990	2 809	4 801	3 446	5 731	10 145
1975	22 948	5 141	3 056	4 527	3 031	5 194	9 563
1974	21 281	4 855	3 088	4 574	2 942	4 985	10 679
1973	16 146	2 937	1 916	3 564	2 263	3 756	8 313
1972	13 070	1 982	1 243	2 658	1 609	2 808	4 963
1971	10 903	1 620	966	2 369	1 373	2 831	4 055
1970	9 596	1 704	840	2 536	1 483	2 741	4 652
1969	9 137	1 450	672	2 335	1 195	2 142	3 490
1968	8 072	1 378	705	2 289	1 095	1 709	2 954
1967	7 165	1 222	547	1 960	1 025	1 706	2 695
1966	6 661	1 180	575	1 737	1 007	1 674	2 364
1965	5 642	1 104	341	1 615	971	1 649	2 080
1964	4 915	1 107	402	1 532	990	1 606	2 009
1963	4 251	873	405	1 213	813	1 582	1 844
1962	4 045	821	449	1 128	735	1 581	1 574
1961	3 826	828	545	1 206	704	1 343	1 837
1960	3 810	831	464	1 487	699	1 272	1 447
1959	3 825	755	435	1 097	483	878	1 079
1958	3 539	904	567	905	570	887	987
1957	4 041	917	512	1 162	708	1 330	1 319
1956	4 149	860	326	982	829	943	998
1955	3 404	719	273	1 006	536	617	683
1954	2 966	649	507	808	783	505	693
1953	3 197	663	379	826	1 236	363	686
1952	3 003	683	597	787	1 013	450	633
1951	2 693	730	739	1 000	843	523	601
1950	2 039	526	365	548	475	441	418
1949	1 959	468	383	700	497	822	468
1948	1 944	522	497	644	591	863	325
1947	2 114	630	643	1 103	817	128	60
1946	1 442	505	356	855	709	83	102
1945	1 178	307	219	2 193	472	2	1
1944	1 441	264	218	5 243	18	(Z)	. . .

See footnotes at end of table.

Series U 317-334. Value of Exports (Including Re-exports) of U.S. Merchandise, by Country of Destination: 1790 to 1998—Cont'd.

(In millions of dollars. Figures shown here are mixed values for 1862-1879. For years ending September 30, 1790-1842; June 30, 1843-1915; thereafter, calendar years. Beginning 1961, includes uranium, thorium and related products. Beginning 1869, includes silver ores, base bullion and refined bullion)

Year	America			Europe			Japan [3]
	Canada [1]	Mexico	Brazil	United Kingdom	France	Germany [2]	
	319	321	322	325	326	327	331
1943	1 444	187	156	4 505	...	...	2
1942	1 334	148	105	2 529	1	...	...
1941	994	159	148	1 637	2	(Z)	60
1940	713	97	111	1 011	252	(Z)	227
1939	489	83	80	505	182	46	232
1938	468	62	62	521	134	107	240
1937	509	109	69	536	165	126	289
1936	384	76	49	440	129	102	204
1935	323	66	44	433	117	92	203
1934	302	55	40	383	116	109	210
1933	211	38	30	312	122	140	143
1932	241	32	29	288	112	134	135
1931	396	52	29	456	122	166	156
1930	689	116	54	678	224	278	165
1929	948	134	109	848	266	410	259
1928	915	116	100	847	241	467	288
1927	837	109	89	840	229	482	258
1926	739	135	95	973	264	364	261
1925	649	145	87	1 034	280	470	230
1924	624	135	65	983	282	440	253
1923	652	120	46	882	272	317	267
1922	577	110	43	856	267	316	222
1921	594	222	58	942	225	372	238
1920	972	208	157	1 825	676	311	378
1919	734	131	115	2 279	893	93	366
1918	887	98	57	2 061	931	...	274
1917	829	111	66	2 009	341	(Z)	186
1916	605	54	48	1 887	861	2	109
1915	301	34	26	912	369	29	41
1914	345	39	30	594	106	345	51
1913	415	54	43	597	146	332	58
1912	329	53	35	564	135	307	53
1911	270	61	27	577	135	287	37
1910	216	58	23	506	118	250	22
1909	163	50	18	515	109	235	27
1908	167	56	19	581	116	277	41
1907	183	66	19	608	114	257	39
1906	157	58	15	583	98	235	38
1905	141	46	11	523	76	194	52
1904	131	46	11	537	84	215	25
1903	123	42	11	524	77	194	21
1902	110	40	10	549	72	173	21
1901	106	36	12	631	79	192	19
1900	95	35	12	534	83	187	29
1899	88	25	12	512	61	156	17
1898	84	21	13	541	95	155	20
1897	65	23	12	483	58	125	13
1896	60	19	14	406	47	98	8
1895	53	15	15	387	45	92	5
1894	57	13	14	431	55	92	4
1893	47	20	12	421	47	84	3
1892	43	14	14	499	99	106	3
1891	38	15	14	445	61	93	5
1890	40	13	12	448	50	86	5

See footnotes at end of table.

Series U 317-334. Value of Exports (Including Re-exports) of U.S. Merchandise, by Country of Destination: 1790 to 1998—Cont'd.

(In millions of dollars. Figures shown here are mixed values for 1862-1879. For years ending September 30, 1790-1842; June 30, 1843-1915; thereafter, calendar years. Beginning 1961, includes uranium, thorium and related products. Beginning 1869, includes silver ores, base bullion and refined bullion)

	America			Europe			Japan [3]
Year	Canada [1]	Mexico	Brazil	United Kingdom	France	Germany [2]	
	319	321	322	325	326	327	331
1889	41	11	9	383	46	68	5
1888	36	10	7	362	39	56	4
1887	35	8	8	366	57	59	3
1886	33	8	7	348	42	62	3
1885	38	8	7	398	47	62	3
1884	44	13	9	386	51	61	3
1883	44	17	9	425	59	66	3
1882	37	15	9	408	50	54	3
1881	38	11	9	481	94	70	1
1880	29	8	9	454	100	57	3
1879	30	7	8	349	90	57	3
1878	37	7	9	387	55	55	2
1877	37	6	8	346	45	58	1
1876	33	6	7	336	40	51	1
1875	35	6	8	317	34	50	2
1874	42	6	8	345	43	63	1
1873	33	6	7	317	34	62	1
1872	29	6	6	265	31	41	1
1871	32	8	6	273	27	35	1
1870	25	6	6	248	46	42	1
1869	23	5	6	185	33	38	1
1868	24	6	6	198	26	31	1
1867	21	5	5	225	34	22	1
1866	24	5	6	288	51	22	1
1865	29	16	6	103	11	20	(Z)
1864	27	9	5	97	13	13	(Z)
1863	28	9	5	128	14	14	(Z)
1862	21	2	4	86	20	10	(Z)
1861	23	2	5	108	15	11	(Z)
1860	23	5	6	169	39	15	(Z)
1859	28	3	6	133	30	15	(Z)
1858	24	3	5	129	28	12	(Z)
1857	24	4	5	135	32	15	(Z)
1856	29	4	5	128	35	13	...
1855	28	3	4	92	29	9	(Z)
1854	24	3	4	117	25	9	...
1853	12	4	4	103	22	7	...
1852	10	2	3	81	19	6	...
1851	12	2	3	101	21	6	...
1850	10	2	3	71	18	5	...
1849	8	2	3	78	13	3	...
1848	8	4	3	67	15	4	...
1847	7	1	3	87	19	5	...
1846	7	2	3	46	14	5	...
1845	6	1	3	45	12	6	...
1844	6	2	3	49	13	4	...
1843 [4]	3	1	2	41	12	4	...
1842	6	2	3	40	17	5	...
1841	6	2	3	47	18	5	...
1840	6	3	2	55	20	4	...
1839	4	3	2	57	18	3	...
1838	2	2	2	52	15	3	...
1837	3	4	2	52	19	4	...
1836	3	6	2	58	21	4	...

See footnotes at end of table.

Series U 317-334. Value of Exports (Including Re-exports) of U.S. Merchandise, by Country of Destination: 1790 to 1998—Cont'd.

(In millions of dollars. Figures shown here are mixed values for 1862-1879. For years ending September 30, 1790-1842; June 30, 1843-1915; thereafter, calendar years. Beginning 1961, includes uranium, thorium and related products. Beginning 1869, includes silver ores, base bullion and refined bullion)

Year	America			Europe			Japan [3]
	Canada [1]	Mexico	Brazil	United Kingdom	France	Germany [2]	
	319	321	322	325	326	327	331
1835	3	9	2	52	19	4	...
1834	3	5	2	44	15	5	...
1833	4	5	3	32	14	3	...
1832	3	3	2	29	12	4	...
1831	3	6	2	31	6	3	...
1830	3	5	2	26	11	2	...
1829	2	2	2	24	10	3	...
1828	2	3	2	20	9	3	...
1827	2	4	2	26	11	3	...
1826	2	6	2	21	11	2	...
1825	3	6	2	37	10	3	...
1824	2	...	2	21	10	2	...
1823	2	...	1	22	9	3	...
1822	2	...	1	24	6	3	...
1821	2	...	1	19	6	2	...
1820	...	...	...	24	8	3	...
1819	...	...	...	24	9	4	...
1818	...	...	...	38	12	3	...
1817	...	...	...	33	9	3	...
1816	...	...	...	30	10	4	...
1815	...	...	...	18	7	2	...
1814	...	...	...	...	(Z)	...	...
1813	...	...	...	...	4	(Z)	...
1812	...	...	...	6	3	...	...
1811	...	...	...	14	2	(Z)	...
1810	...	...	...	12	(Z)	2	...
1809	...	...	...	6	...	2	...
1808	...	...	...	3	3	(Z)	...
1807	...	...	...	23	13	3	...
1806	...	...	...	16	11	6	...
1805	...	...	...	15	13	4	...
1804	...	...	...	13	9	6	...
1803	...	...	...	18	4	4	...
1802	...	...	...	16	8	6	...
1801	...	...	...	31	4	11	...
1800	...	...	...	19	(Z)	8	...
1799	...	...	...	19	...	18	...
1798	...	...	...	12	1	15	...
1797	...	...	...	6	4	10	...
1796	...	...	...	17	3	10	...
1795	...	...	...	6	8	10	...
1794	...	...	...	6	1	5	...
1793	...	...	...	6	2	2	...
1792	...	...	...	5	2	1	...
1791	...	...	...	6	1	(Z)	...
1790	...	...	...	7	1	(Z)	...

Z less than $500 000.
1. Prior to 1873, data are for trade with British North American Provinces which is a somewhat larger area than the Dominion of Canada. In the year ending June 30, 1873, the U.S. traded with British North American Provinces the following amounts: exports, $34.6 million and imports, $37.6 million. Beginning 1950, includes Newfoundland and Labrador.
2. Prior to January 1952, East and West Germany; thereafter, only West Germany.
3. Beginning 1954, excludes Ryukyu Islands. No records available prior to 1855.
4. For nine months.

Series U 335-352. Value of General Imports, by Country of Origin: 1821 to 1998

(In millions of dollars. For years ending September 30, 1790-1842; June 30, 1843-1915; thereafter, calendar years. Beginning 1961, includes uranium, thorium and related products)

Year	America			Europe			Japan [3]
	Canada [1]	Mexico	Brazil	United Kingdom	France	Germany [2]	
	337	339	340	343	344	345	349
1998	173 256	94 708	10 122	34 792	24 077	49 823	121 981
1997	168 200	85 937	9 625	32 659	20 636	43 121	121 663
1996	155 893	74 297	8 762	28 892	18 630	38 943	115 218
1995	145 349	61 685	8 830	26 898	17 209	36 844	123 479
1994	128 948	49 493	8 708	25 063	16 699	31 749	119 149
1993	111 216	39 917	7 479	21 730	15 279	28 562	107 246
1992	98 630	35 211	7 609	20 093	14 797	28 820	97 414
1991	91 141	31 194	6 727	18 520	13 333	26 229	91 583
1990	91 380	30 157	7 898	20 188	13 124	28 162	89 684
1989	87 953	27 162	8 410	18 319	13 013	24 971	93 553
1988	81 398	23 277	9 324	18 042	12 509	26 503	89 802
1987	71 085	20 271	7 865	17 341	10 730	27 069	84 575
1986	68 253	17 302	6 813	15 396	10 129	25 124	81 911
1985	69 006	19 132	7 526	14 937	9 482	20 239	68 783
1984	66 478	18 020	7 621	14 492	8 113	16 996	57 135
1983	52 130	16 776	4 946	12 470	6 025	12 695	41 183
1982	46 477	15 566	4 285	13 095	5 545	11 975	37 744
1981	46 414	13 765	4 475	12 835	5 851	11 379	37 612
1980	41 459	12 580	3 715	9 842	5 265	11 693	30 714
1979	38 046	8 800	3 118	8 028	4 768	10 995	26 248
1978	33 525	6 094	2 826	6 514	4 051	9 962	24 458
1977	29 599	4 694	2 241	5 141	3 032	7 238	18 550
1976	26 237	3 598	1 737	4 254	2 509	5 592	15 504
1975	21 747	3 066	1 467	3 773	2 164	5 410	11 425
1974	22 286	3 386	1 705	4 023	2 305	6 429	12 456
1973	17 715	2 306	1 189	3 657	1 732	5 345	9 676
1972	14 907	1 632	942	2 987	1 369	4 250	9 064
1971	12 692	1 262	762	2 499	1 088	3 651	7 259
1970	11 092	1 209	670	2 194	942	3 127	5 875
1969	10 384	1 029	617	2 120	842	2 603	4 888
1968	9 005	910	670	2 058	842	2 721	4 054
1967	7 107	749	559	1 710	690	1 955	2 999
1966	6 125	750	600	1 786	698	1 976	2 963
1965	4 833	638	512	1 405	625	1 341	2 414
1964	4 239	643	535	1 143	495	1 171	1 768
1963	3 829	594	562	1 079	431	1 003	1 498
1962	3 660	578	541	1 005	428	962	1 358
1961	3 270	538	562	898	485	856	1 055
1960	2 901	443	570	993	396	897	1 149
1959	3 042	435	628	1 137	462	920	1 029
1958	2 674	454	565	864	308	629	666
1957	2 907	430	700	766	256	607	601
1956	2 894	401	745	726	236	494	558
1955	2 653	397	633	616	202	366	432
1954	2 377	328	682	501	157	278	279
1953	2 462	355	768	543	186	277	262
1952	2 386	410	808	485	167	212	229
1951	2 275	326	911	466	263	233	205
1950	1 960	315	715	335	132	104	182
1949	1 551	243	552	228	61	45	82
1948	1 593	246	514	290	73	32	63
1947	1 127	247	446	205	47	6	35
1946	883	232	408	158	63	3	81
1945	1 125	231	311	90	13	1	(Z)
1944	1 260	204	293	84	(Z)	(Z)	(Z)
1943	1 024	192	228	105	(Z)	(Z)	(Z)

See footnotes at end of table.

Series U 335-352.   Value of General Imports, by Country of Origin: 1821 to 1998—Cont'd.

(In millions of dollars. For years ending September 30, 1790-1842; June 30, 1843-1915; thereafter, calendar years. Beginning 1961, includes uranium, thorium and related products)

Year	America			Europe			Japan [3]
	Canada [1]	Mexico	Brazil	United Kingdom	France	Germany [2]	
	337	339	340	343	344	345	349
1942	717	124	165	134	1	(Z)	(Z)
1941	554	98	184	136	5	3	78
1940	424	76	105	155	37	5	158
1939	340	56	107	149	62	52	161
1938	260	49	98	118	54	65	127
1937	398	60	121	203	76	92	204
1936	376	49	102	200	65	80	172
1935	286	42	100	155	58	78	153
1934	232	36	91	115	61	69	119
1933	185	31	83	111	50	78	128
1932	174	37	82	75	45	74	134
1931	266	48	110	135	79	127	206
1930	402	80	131	210	114	117	279
1929	503	118	208	330	171	255	432
1928	489	125	221	349	159	222	384
1927	475	138	203	358	168	201	402
1926	476	169	235	383	152	198	401
1925	454	179	222	413	157	164	384
1924	399	167	179	366	148	139	340
1923	416	140	143	404	150	161	347
1922	364	132	120	357	143	117	354
1921	335	119	96	239	142	80	251
1920	612	179	228	514	166	89	415
1919	495	149	234	309	124	11	410
1918	452	159	98	149	60	(Z)	302
1917	414	130	145	280	99	(Z)	254
1916	237	105	132	305	109	6	182
1915	160	78	99	256	77	91	99
1914	161	93	101	294	141	190	107
1913	121	78	120	296	137	189	92
1912	109	66	124	273	125	171	81
1911	101	57	101	261	115	163	79
1910	95	59	108	271	132	169	66
1909	79	48	98	209	108	144	70
1908	75	47	75	190	102	143	68
1907	73	57	98	246	128	162	69
1906	68	51	80	210	108	135	53
1905	62	46	100	176	90	118	52
1904	52	44	76	166	81	109	47
1903	55	41	67	190	90	120	44
1902	48	40	79	166	83	102	38
1901	42	29	71	143	75	100	29
1900	39	29	58	160	73	97	33
1899	31	23	58	118	62	84	27
1898	32	19	62	109	53	70	25
1897	40	19	69	168	68	111	24
1896	41	17	71	170	66	94	26
1895	37	16	79	159	62	81	24
1894	31	29	79	107	48	69	19
1893	38	34	76	183	76	96	27
1892	35	28	119	156	69	83	24
1891	39	27	83	195	77	97	19
1890	39	23	59	186	78	99	21
1889	43	21	60	178	70	82	17
1888	43	17	54	178	71	78	19
1887	38	15	53	165	68	81	17

See footnotes at end of table.

Series U 335-352. Value of General Imports, by Country of Origin: 1821 to 1998—Cont'd.

(In millions of dollars. For years ending September 30, 1790-1842; June 30, 1843-1915; thereafter, calendar years. Beginning 1961, includes uranium, thorium and related products)

Year	America			Europe			Japan [3]
	Canada [1]	Mexico	Brazil	United Kingdom	France	Germany [2]	
	337	339	340	343	344	345	349
1886	37	11	42	154	63	69	15
1885	37	9	45	137	57	63	12
1884	38	9	50	163	71	65	11
1883	44	8	44	189	98	57	15
1882	51	8	49	196	89	56	14
1881	38	8	53	174	70	53	14
1880	33	7	52	211	69	52	15
1879	26	5	39	109	51	36	10
1878	25	5	43	107	43	35	7
1877	24	5	43	114	48	33	14
1876	29	5	45	123	51	35	15
1875	28	5	42	155	60	40	8
1874	34	4	44	180	52	44	6
1873	37	4	39	237	34	61	8
1872	36	4	30	249	43	46	7
1871	33	3	31	221	28	25	5
1870	36	3	25	152	43	27	3
1869	29	2	25	159	30	25	3
1868	26	2	24	132	25	22	2
1867	25	1	19	172	29	27	3
1866	49	2	17	202	23	26	2
1865	33	6	10	85	7	10	(Z)
1864	30	6	14	142	11	14	(Z)
1863	17	3	11	113	11	13	(Z)
1862	19	1	13	75	8	14	(Z)
1861	23	1	18	105	32	15	(Z)
1860	24	2	21	138	43	19	(Z)
1859	19	1	22	126	41	18	(Z)
1858	16	1	17	89	33	14	(Z)
1857	22	1	21	127	46	15	(Z)
1856	21	1	19	122	49	15	(Z)
1855	15	1	15	106	32	13	(Z)
1854	9	1	14	146	36	17	. . .
1853	7	1	15	130	33	14	. . .
1852	5	1	12	89	25	8	. . .
1851	5	1	12	93	31	10	. . .
1850	5	1	9	75	27	9	. . .
1849	2	1	8	58	24	8	. . .
1848	3	1	8	60	28	6	. . .
1847	1	(Z)	7	48	24	4	. . .
1846	1	1	7	45	24	3	. . .
1845	1	1	6	45	21	3	. . .
1844	1	1	7	41	17	2	. . .
1843 [4]	(Z)	1	4	12	5	1	. . .
1842	1	1	6	34	17	2	. . .
1841	1	1	6	46	24	2	. . .
1840	1	1	5	33	16	3	. . .
1839	2	1	5	65	32	5	. . .
1838	1	1	3	36	16	3	. . .
1837	2	1	5	45	21	6	. . .
1836	2	1	7	76	32	5	. . .
1835	1	1	6	60	22	4	. . .
1834	1	1	5	41	15	3	. . .
1833	1	1	5	38	13	2	. . .
1832	1	1	4	37	12	3	. . .
1831	1	1	2	44	14	4	. . .

See footnotes at end of table.

Series U 335-352.   Value of General Imports, by Country of Origin: 1821 to 1998—Cont'd.

(In millions of dollars. For years ending September 30, 1790-1842; June 30, 1843-1915; thereafter, calendar years. Beginning 1961, includes uranium, thorium and related products)

| Year | America | | | Europe | | | Japan [3] |
| | Canada [1] | Mexico | Brazil | United Kingdom | France | Germany [2] | |
	337	339	340	343	344	345	349
1830	(Z)	1	2	24	8	2	...
1829	(Z)	1	2	25	9	2	...
1828	(Z)	1	3	33	9	3	...
1827	(Z)	1	2	30	8	2	...
1826	(Z)	1	2	26	8	3	...
1825	(Z)	1	2	37	11	3	...
1824	(Z)	...	2	28	7	2	...
1823	(Z)	...	1	28	6	2	...
1822	(Z)	...	1	35	6	2	...
1821	(Z)	...	1	24	4	1	...

Z Less than $500 000.
1. Prior to 1873, data are for trade with British North American Provinces which is a somewhat larger area than the Dominion of Canada. In the year ending June 30, 1873, the U.S. traded with British North American Provinces the following amounts: exports, $34.6 million and imports, $37.6 million. Beginning 1947, includes Newfoundland and Labrador.
2. Prior to January 1952, East and West Germany; thereafter, 1952-1990, West Germany only; 1991 to date, united Germany.
3. Beginning 1954, excludes Ryukyu Islands. No records available prior to 1855.
4. For nine months.

Series UU 1.   U.S. Foreign Economic and Military Aid Programs: 1980 to 1997

(In millions of dollars. For years ending September 30. Economic aid shown here represents U.S. economic aid—not just aid under the Foreign Assistance Act. Major components in recent years include AID, Food for Peace, Peace Corps, and paid-in subscriptions to international financial institutions, such as IBRD, and IDB. Annual figures are gross unadjusted program figures)

Year and region	Total economic and military aid	Economic aid			Military aid		
		Total	Loans	Grants	Total	Loans	Grants
1980	9 695	7 573	1 993	5 580	2 122	1 450	672
1981	10 550	7 305	1 460	5 845	3 245	2 546	699
1982	12 324	8 129	1 454	6 675	4 195	3 084	1 111
1983	14 202	8 603	1 619	6 984	5 599	3 932	1 667
1984	15 524	9 038	1 621	7 417	6 486	4 401	2 085
1985	18 128	12 327	1 579	10 748	5 801	2 365	3 436
1986	16 739	10 900	1 330	9 570	5 839	1 980	3 859
1987	14 488	9 386	1 138	8 248	5 102	953	4 149
1988	13 792	8 961	852	8 109	4 831	763	4 068
1989	14 688	9 860	694	9 166	4 828	410	4 418
1990	15 727	10 834	756	10 078	4 893	404	4 489
1991	16 663	11 904	354	11 550	4 760	428	4 332
1992	15 589	11 242	494	10 748	4 347	345	4 002
1993	28 196	24 054	462	23 593	4 143	855	3 288
1994	15 870	11 940	887	11 053	3 931	770	3 161
1995	15 108	11 295	190	11 105	3 813	558	3 255
1996	13 559	9 589	329	9 260	3 970	544	3 426
1997, total	13 035	9 170	218	8 952	3 864	298	3 566
Near East	5 414	2 279	30	2 249	3 135	—	3 135
Sub Saharan Africa	1 172	1 156	42	1 114	16	—	16
Latin America	752	741	40	701	11	—	11
Asia	606	599	81	518	7	—	7
Europe	884	508	10	498	376	298	78
New Independent States	563	559	15	544	4	—	4
Oceania and other	21	20	—	20	1	—	1
Nonregional	3 622	3 307	—	3 307	315	—	315

— Represents zero or rounds to zero.

SOURCE: U.S. Agency for International Development, U.S. Overseas Loans and Grants and Assistance From International Organizations, annual.

1 As President Coolidge is reported to have said, "The business of America is business." This business is conducted by more than 14 million firms, but data on the total number and size distribution of firms must be used with caution. There has never been a satisfactory definition of a firm, and the boundary between self-employment and a firm is tenuous at best. In addition, there are problems with inactive or partly active firms and seasonal firms. This problem is compounded when an effort is made to group firms into industrial categories whose boundaries are arbitrary and too tidy for real life. There are activities that defy known categories. Because small firms dominate the business landscape and because many small firms are on the boundary line, a slight difference in method may generate a considerable change in the total. If, however, the focus is on activity and output rather than number, then the unequal size distribution of firms becomes a statistical advantage because it permits a more efficient sample design at lower cost. Similarly, mergers and acquisitions, changes in public taste, and cyclical economic fluctuations all help to distort the structural profile of American business in ways of which statisticians may not be aware.

2 The principal sources of business data are official and nonofficial. Official sources include the *Survey of Current Business* published by the Bureau of Economic Analysis and the Statistics of Income produced by the Internal Revenue Service. Unofficial sources include publications of Dun & Bradstreet, including *Business Failure Record*.

3 Business firms are conventionally divided into the categories of corporation, partnership and proprietorship. Of the total 23.083 million business firms in the United States in 1996 proprietorships were the most numerous (16.955 million), partnerships the least numerous (1.654 million) and corporations in the middle (4.631 million). However in terms of receipts and income, corporations accounted for the lion's share with $14.89 trillion, followed by partnerships ($1.042 trillion) and proprietorships $843 billion. The order was slightly different in net income. Corporations had a net income of $806 billion, proprietorships $177 billion, and partnerships $145 billion.

4 In 1996 U.S. corporations had assets of $28.642 trillion of which $1.097 trillion was in cash and $1.825 trillion in real estate, In the same year they had liabilities of $28.642 trillion of which $5.979 billion was in short-term and long-term debt. Net worth of all corporations was $9.495 trillion and net income $987 billion.

5 In terms of assets by corporate sectors FIRE (finance, insurance and real estate) leads with $17.360 trillion, followed by manufacturing ($5.425 trillion), transportation ($2.069 trillion), and wholesale and retail trade ($2.016 trillion). The same rank order prevails in net income, where FIRE has $299.1 billion, manufacturing $286.1 billion, transportation and public utilities $75.4 billion and wholesale and retail trade $73.4 billion. The smallest sector is agriculture which has assets of $94.1 billion and net income of $2.6 billion.

6 In terms of assets of more than $250 million, FIRE has 5,151 corporations, manufacturing has 1,417, wholesale and retail trade has 586, and transportation and public utilities 453. Agriculture is the last with 21.

7 The business sector employs 102.199 million persons, and its annual payroll is $2.849 trillion. Retail trade has the most number of establishments (2,461,000) and the most number of employees (35.750 million) and the largest payroll ($933 billion). Wholesale trade is second in terms of establishments (1,579,000) and employees (21.487 million), but manufacturing has the second largest payroll at $660 billion.

8 Between 1989 and 1995 3.400,089 new firms were born in the United States and 3,092,984 firms died. In 1998 84,342 new businesses were launched and 71,857 businesses folded. The rate of business failure is highest in paper and allied products manufacturing, where it is 830 per 10,000 firms. Transportation and public utilities has a failure rate of 115, apparel and textile manufacturing 103 and construction 102.

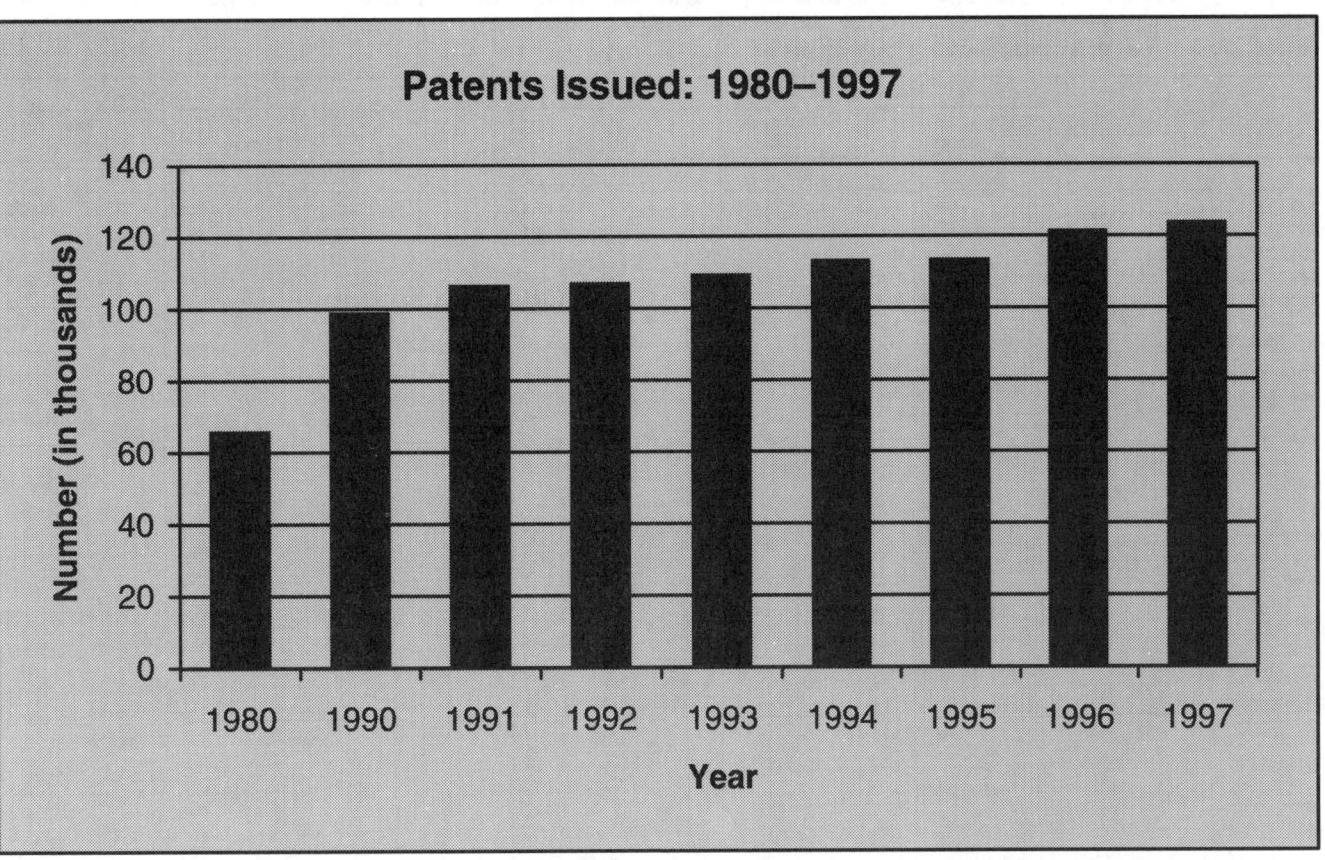

Patents Issued: 1980–1997

9 Wholesale and retail trade and services dominate small business. Of the total 6,738,541 small business firms, 2,461,235 are in services, 1,579,264 are in retail trade and 531,200 in wholesale trade. Together, these three sectors make up 67.8% of all small business firms.

10 The 5,888, 883 women-owned firms had annual sales of $642.484 billion, 53% are in services and 18.5% in retail trade.

11 There were 1.411 million bankruptcies in the United States in 1998 compared to 858,100 in 1995, 1.042 million in 1996 and 1.317 million in 1997.

12 The Small Business Administration extended loans valued at $10.177 billion to 52,700 small firms. Minority business loans accounted for $2.177 billion.

13 Reflecting a booming economy, there were 9,634 mergers and acquisitions in 1998 valued at $2.480 trillion. Foreign interests acquired 483 U.S. companies valued at $232.5 billion, and U.S. companies acquired 746 overseas companies valued at $127.8 billion. Domestic mergers and acquisitions activity was most prominent in banking where 253 companies were acquired for $241.6 billion, followed by telecommunications (101 companies for $206.6 billion) and oil and gas (147 companies for $118.1 billion).

14 In 1997 233,000 patent applications were filed, and 124,100 patents were granted. Of the patents issued 112,000 were for inventions. Of the new patents, 27,640 were for electronic equipment, 23,547 for machinery and 17,210 for chemicals. In the same year 224,400 trademark applications were filed, and 112,500 new trademarks were issued.

15 In 1997 9,194 new consumer products were introduced into the marketplace. Of these 3,793 were foods, 1,205 beverages, 3,492 health and beauty products, 366 household products, and 216 pet products.

16 Gross private domestic investment has risen from $829.2 billion in 1989 to $1.256 trillion in 1997.

17 In 1998 549 corporations with assets of more than $1 billion had assets over $3.018 trillion and net profit of $184.707 billion. The 500 largest corporations gave a 30.5% return to investors.

18 In 1997 U.S. multinational companies had assets of $7.805 trillion, sales of $4.497 trillion and a work force of 18.755 million.

Series V 1-12. Proprietorships, Partnerships and Corporations—Number, Receipts: 1939 to 1996

(Number in thousands; money figures in billions of dollars. Based on sample of unaudited tax returns filed for accounting periods ending between July 1 of year shown and June 30 of following year)

Year	Proprietorships [1]		Partnerships		Corporations	
	Number	Business receipts	Number	Total receipts	Number	Total receipts
	4	5	7	8	10	11
1996	16 955	843	1 654	1 042	4 631	15 526
1995	16 424	807	1 581	854	4 474	14 539
1994	16 154	791	1 493	731	4 342	13 360
1993	15 848	757	1 468	627	3 965	12 270
1992	15 495	737	1 485	571	3 869	11 742
1991	15 181	713	1 515	539	3 803	11 436
1990	14 783	731	1 554	541	3 717	11 410
1989	14 298	693	1 635	524	3 628	10 935
1988	13 679	672	1 654	464	3 563	10 265
1987	13 091	611	1 648	411	3 612	9 582
1986	12 394	559	1 703	379	3 429	8 669
1985	11 929	540	1 714	349	3 277	8 398
1984	11 262	516	1 644	375	3 171	7 861
1983	10 704	465	1 542	291	2 999	7 135
1982	10 106	434	1 514	297	2 926	7 025
1981	9 585	427	1 461	272	2 812	7 026
1980	8 932	411	1 380	286	2 711	6 361
1979	...	...	1 300	258	2 557	5 599
1978	...	...	1 234	219	2 377	4 715
1977	...		1 153	177	2 242	4 128
1976	...	...	1 096	160	2 082	3 635
1975	7 221	274	1 073	147	2 024	3 199
1974	...	...	1 062	139	1 966	3 090
1973	...	...	1 039	124	1 905	2 558
1972	...	...	992	104	1 813	2 171
1971	...	...	959	100	1 733	1 906
1970	9 399	238	936	93	1 665	1 751
1969	9 429	234	920	87	1 659	1 680
1968	9 212	222	918	83	1 542	1 508
1967	9 126	211	906	80	1 534	1 375
1966	9 087	207	923	80	1 469	1 307
1965	9 078	199	914	75	1 424	1 195
1964	9 193	189	922	75	1 374	1 087
1963	9 136	182	924	73	1 323	1 009
1962	9 193	178	932	74	1 268	949
1961	9 242	171	939	75	1 190	873
1960	9 090	171	941	74	1 141	849
1959	9 142	176	949	78	1 074	817
1958	8 800	163	954	78	990	735
1957	8 738	163	971	82	940	720
1956	8 973	...	...	...	886	680
1955	8 239	139	...	...	807	642
1954	7 786	...	...	...	723	555
1953	7 715	144	959	79	698	558
1952	6 873	...	...	...	672	531
1951	7 340	132	...	...	652	517
1950	6 865	...	...	...	629	458
1949	6 901	110	...	...	615	393
1948	7 208	...	...	...	594	411
1947	6 624	101	889	60	552	368
1946	6 944	...	...	...	491	289
1945	5 689	79	627	47	421	255
1944	6 134	66	...	...	412	262
1943	5 121	58	...	...	421	250
1942	...	...	...	...	443	218
1941	3 169	38	...	...	469	190
1940	2 018	31	...	...	473	148
1939	1 052	24	271	13	470	133

1. Through 1970, individually owned businesses and farms; thereafter, nonfarm businesses.

Series V 20-30. Business Formation and Business Failures: 1857 to 1998

Year	Total concerns in business (1 000)	New business corporations (number)	Business failure rate [2]	Total number of failures	Total current liabilities (mil. dol.)
	20	21	23	24	27
1998	...	...	76	71 857	23 868
1997	...	799 000	89	84 342	24 802
1996	...	786 000	80	71 931	29 569
1995	...	767 000	82	71 128	37 284
1994	...	742 000	86	71 558	28 978
1993	8 966	707 000	109	86 133	47 756
1992	8 805	667 000	110	97 069	94 318
1991	8 218	629 000	107	88 140	96 825
1990	8 039	647 000	74	60 747	56 130
1989	7 694	677 000	65	50 361	44 261
1988	5 804	685 000	98	57 098	39 126
1987	6 004	685 000	102	61 111	34 724
1986	5 119	702 000	120	61 616	44 724
1985	4 990	663 000	115	57 078	36 937
1984	4 885	635 000	107	52 078	29 269
1983	2 851	602 000	110	31 334	16 073
1982	2 806	566 000	68	24 908	15 611
1981	2 745	581 000	61	16 794	6 955
1980	2 780	532 000	42	11 742	4 635
1979	2 708	525 000	28	7 564	2 667
1978	2 786	478 000	24	6 619	2 656
1977	2 793	438 000	28	7 919	3 095
1976	2 782	376 000	35	9 628	3 011
1975	2 679	326 000	43	11 432	4 380
1974	2 591	319 000	38	9 915	3 053
1973	2 567	329 000	36	9 345	2 299
1972	2 490	317 000	38	9 566	2 000
1971	2 466	288 000	42	10 326	1 917
1970	2 442	264 209	44	10 748	1 888
1969	2 444	274 267	37	9 154	1 142
1968	2 481	233 635	39	9 636	941
1967	2 519	206 569	49	12 364	1 265
1966	2 520	200 010	52	13 061	1 386
1965	2 527	203 897	53	13 514	1 322
1964	2 524	197 724	53	13 501	1 329
1963	2 544	186 404	56	14 374	1 353
1962	2 589	182 057	61	15 872	1 214
1961	2 641	181 535	64	17 075	1 090
1960	2 708	182 713	57	15 445	939
1959	2 708	193 067	52	14 053	693
1958	2 675	150 781	56	14 964	728
1957	2 652	137 112	52	13 739	615
1956	2 629	141 163	48	12 686	563
1955	2 633	139 915	42	10 969	449
1954	2 632	117 411	42	11 086	463
1953	2 997	102 706	33	8 862	394
1952	2 637	92 946	29	7 611	283
1951	2 608	83 778	31	8 058	260
1950	2 687	93 092	34	9 162	248
1949	2 679	85 640	34	9 246	308
1948	2 550	96 346	20	5 250	235
1947	2 405	112 897	14	3 474	205
1946	2 142	132 916	5	1 129	67
1945	1 909	...	4	809	30
1944	1 855	...	7	1 222	32
1943	2 023	...	16	3 221	45
1942	2 152	...	45	9 405	101

Year	Total concerns in business (1 000)	Business failure rate [2]	Total number of failures	Total current liabilities (mil. dol.)
	20	23	24	27
1935	1 983	62	12 244	311
1934	1 974	61	12 091	334
1933 [3]	1 961	100	19 859	458
1932	2 077	154	31 822	928
1931	2 125	133	28 285	736
1930	2 183	122	26 355	668
1929	2 213	104	22 909	483
1928	2 199	109	23 842	490
1927	2 172	106	23 146	520
1926	2 158	101	21 773	409
1925	2 113	100	21 214	444
1924	2 047	100	20 615	543
1923	1 996	93	18 718	539
1922	1 983	120	23 676	624
1921	1 927	102	19 652	627
1920	1 821	48	8 881	295
1919	1 711	37	6 451	113
1918	1 708	59	9 982	163
1917	1 733	80	13 855	182
1916	1 708	100	16 993	196
1915	1 675	133	22 156	302
1914	1 655	118	18 280	358
1913	1 617	98	16 037	273
1912	1 564	100	15 452	203
1911	1 525	88	13 441	191
1910	1 515	84	12 652	202
1909	1 486	87	12 924	154
1908	1 448	108	15 690	222
1907	1 418	83	11 725	197
1906	1 393	77	10 682	119
1905	1 357	85	11 520	103
1904	1 320	92	12 199	144
1903	1 281	94	12 069	155
1902	1 253	93	11 615	117
1901	1 219	90	11 002	113
1900	1 174	92	10 774	138
1899	1 148	82	9 337	91
1898	1 106	111	12 186	131
1897	1 059	125	13 351	154
1896	1 152	133	15 088	226
1895	1 209	112	13 197	173
1894	1 114	123	13 885	173
1893	1 193	130	15 242	347
1892	1 173	89	10 344	114
1891	1 143	107	12 273	190
1890	1 111	99	10 907	190
1889	1 051	103	10 882	149
1888	1 047	103	10 679	124
1887	994	97	9 634	168
1886	970	101	9 834	115
1885	920	116	10 637	134
1884	905	121	10 638	226
1883	864	106	9 184	173
1882	822	82	6 738	102
1881	782	71	5 582	81

See footnotes at end of chart.

Series V 20-30. Business Formation and Business Failures: 1857 to 1998—Cont'd.

Year	Total concerns in business (1 000)	New business corporations (number)	Business failures[1] Business failure rate[2]	Business failures[1] Total number of failures	Business failures[1] Total current liabilities (mil. dol.)	Year	Total concerns in business (1 000)	Business failures[1] Business failure rate[2]	Business failures[1] Total number of failures	Business failures[1] Total current liabilities (mil. dol.)
	20	21	23	24	27		20	23	24	27
1941	2 171	. . .	55	11 848	136					
1940	2 156	. . .	63	13 619	167					
1939 [3]	2 116	. . .	70	14 768	183					
1938	2 102	. . .	61	12 836	247					
1937	2 057	. . .	46	9 490	183					
1936	2 010	. . .	48	9 607	203					

Year	Total concerns in business (1 000)	Business failures[1] Business failure rate[2]	Business failures[1] Total number of failures	Business failures[1] Total current liabilities (mil. dol.)	Year	Total concerns business (1 000)	Business failures[1] Business failure rate[2]	Business failures[1] Total number of failures	Business failures[1] Total current liabilities (mil. dol.)
	20	23	24	27		20	23	24	27
1880..............	747	63	4 735	66	1868...............	. . .	. . .	2 608	64
1879..............	702	95	6 658	98	1867...............	. . .	. . .	2 780	97
1878..............	661	158	10 478	234	1866...............	. . .	. . .	1 505	54
1877..............	637	139	8 872	191					
1876..............	639	142	9 092	191	1865...............	. . .	. . .	530	18
					1864...............			520	9
1875..............	603	128	7 740	201	1863...............	. . .	. . .	495	8
1874..............	559	104	5 830	155	1862...............	. . .	. . .	1 652	23
1873..............	494	105	5 183	229	1861...............	. . .	. . .	6 993	207
1872..............	500	81	4 069	121					
1871..............	457	64	2 915	85	1860...............	. . .	. . .	3 676	80
					1859...............	230	170	3 913	64
1870..............	427	83	3 546	88	1858...............	. . .	. . .	4 225	96
1869..............	. . .	. . .	2 799	75	1857...............	204	242	4 932	292

1. Commercial and industrial failures only. Excludes failures of banks and railroads and, beginning 1933, of real estate, insurance, holding and financial companies, steamship lines, travel agencies, etc.
2. Failure rate per 10 000 listed enterprises.
3. Series revised; not strictly comparable with earlier data.
Source: Dunn & Bradstreet Corp., Wilton, CT, "Monthly Failure Report."

Series V 38-40. Recorded Mergers and Acquisitions: 1895 to 1998

(Merger values in millions of dollars. Prior to 1980, only manufacturing and mining.)

Year	Recorded mergers (FTC) 38	Value of recorded mergers (Eis) 40
1998	9 634	2 480 200
1997	8 770	1 610 300
1996	5 639	1 059 300
1995	4 981	895 800
1994	4 383	524 900
1993	3 722	420 400
1992	3 502	125 300
1991	3 446	141 500
1990	4 239	205 600
1989	3 752	316 800
1988	2 970	218 800
1987	2 479	198 800
1986	2 497	223 100
1985	1 719	149 600
1984	. . .	126 000
1983	. . .	53 000
1982	. . .	61 000
1981	. . .	70 000
1980	. . .	33 000
1979	519	12 867
1978	610	10 724
1977	590	8 670
1976	559	6 279
1975	439	4 950
1974	602	4 466
1973	874	3 149

Year	Recorded mergers (FTC) 38	Value of recorded mergers (Eis) 40
1972	911	1 885
1971	1 011	2 480
1970	1 351	5 904
1969	2 307	. . .
1968	2 407	. . .
1967	1 496	. . .
1966	995	. . .
1965	1 008	3 254
1964	854	. . .
1963	861	. . .
1962	853	. . .
1961	954	. . .
1960	844	1 535
1959	835	. . .
1958	589	. . .
1957	585	. . .
1956	673	. . .
1955	683	. . .
1954	387	. . .
1953	295	. . .
1952	288	. . .
1951	235	. . .
1950	219	. . .
1949	126	. . .
1948	223	. . .
1947	404	. . .

Year	Recorded merges (FTC) 38	Value of recorded mergers (Nelson) 40
1946	419	. . .
1945	333	. . .
1944	324	. . .
1943	213	. . .
1942	118	. . .
1941	111	. . .
1940	140	. . .
1939	87	. . .
1938	110	. . .
1937	124	. . .
1936	126	. . .
1935	130	. . .
1934	101	. . .
1933	120	. . .
1932	203	. . .
1931	464	. . .
1930	799	1 757
1929	1 245	1 993
1928	1 058	1 653
1927	870	727
1926	856	1 135
1925	554	721
1924	368	466
1923	311	1 171
1922	309	502
1921	487	430

Year	Recorded mergers (FTC) 38	Value of recorded mergers (Nelson) 40
1920	760	809
1919	438	777
1918	. . .	254
1917	. . .	679
1916	. . .	470
1915	. . .	158
1914	. . .	160
1913	. . .	176
1912	. . .	322
1911	. . .	210
1910	. . .	257
1909	. . .	89
1908	. . .	188
1907	. . .	185
1906	. . .	378
1905	. . .	243
1904	. . .	110
1903	. . .	298
1902	. . .	911
1901	. . .	2 053
1900	. . .	442
1899	. . .	2 263
1898	. . .	651
1897	. . .	120
1896	. . .	25
1895	. . .	41

SOURCE: 1980-1998: Thompson Financial Securities Data, Newark, NJ; Securities Data Company, Newark, NJ; and MRL Publishing Company, Philadelphia, PA. Prior to 1979: Moody's Investor Service, Inc. and Standard and Poor's Corp.

Series V 108-140. Corporate Assets, Liabilities, Receipts, Deductions, and Profits for All Industries: 1926 to 1996

(In millions of dollars, except number of tax returns)

Year	Number of corporate tax returns	Total assets	Total liabilities [1]	Total receipts	Total compiled deductions	Net income
	108	109	117	129	132	136
1996	4 631 000	28 642 000	28 642 000	15 526 000	14 728 000	806 000
1995	4 474 000	26 014 000	26 014 000	14 539 000	13 821 000	714 000
1994	4 342 000	23 446 000	23 446 000	13 360 000	12 775 000	577 000
1993	3 965 000	21 816 000	21 816 000	12 270 000	11 765 000	498 000
1992	3 869 000	20 002 000	20 002 000	11 742 000	11 330 000	402 000
1991	3 803 000	19 030 000	19 030 000	11 436 000	11 087 000	345 000
1990	3 717 000	18 190 000	18 190 000	11 410 000	11 033 000	371 000
1989	3 628 000	17 647 000	17 647 000	10 935 000	10 545 000	389 000
1988	3 563 000	16 568 000	16 568 000	10 265 000	9 853 000	413 000
1987	3 612 000	15 311 000	15 311 000	9 582 000	9 244 000	328 000
1986	3 429 000	14 163 000	14 163 000	8 669 000	8 395 000	270 000
1985	3 277 000	12 773 000	12 773 000	8 398 000	8 158 000	240 000
1984	3 171 000	11 107 000	11 107 000	7 861 000	7 629 000	233 000
1983	2 999 000	10 201 000	10 201 000	7 135 000	6 945 000	188 000
1982	2 926 000	9 358 000	9 358 000	7 024 000	6 869 000	154 000
1981	2 812 000	8 547 000	8 547 000	7 026 000	6 814 000	214 000
1980	2 711 000	7 617 000	7 617 000	6 361 000	6 125 000	235 900
1979	2 557 000	6 835 000	6 835 000	5 598 700	5 315 700	283 000
1978	2 377 000	6 014 000	6 014 000	4 714 600	4 467 000	247 400
1977	2 242 000	5 326 000	5 326 000	4 128 300	3 908 900	219 500
1976	2 082 000	4 721 000	4 721 000	3 635 500	3 448 900	186 600
1975	2 024 000	4 287 000	4 287 000	3 198 600	3 052 700	146 000
1974	1 966 000	4 016 000	4 016 000	3 089 700	2 941 500	148 200
1973	1 905 000	3 649 000	3 649 000	2 557 700	2 435 000	122 600
1972	1 813 000	3 257 000	3 257 000	2 171 200	2 071 700	99 500
1971	1 733 300	2 889 000	2 889 000	1 906 000	1 824 000	81 900
1970	1 665 477	2 634 707	2 634 707	1 750 728	1 682 779	67 949
1969	1 658 820	2 445 328	2 445 628	1 680 482	1 598 348	82 135
1968	1 541 670	2 215 625	2 215 625	1 507 786	1 420 309	87 477
1967	1 534 360	2 010 443	2 010 443	1 374 599	1 295 348	79 520
1966	1 468 725	1 844 775	1 844 775	1 306 518	1 225 225	81 293
1965	1 423 980	1 723 524	1 723 524	1 194 601	1 119 860	74 742
1964	1 373 517	1 585 619	1 585 619	1 086 739	1 023 680	63 059
1963	1 323 187	1 481 236	1 481 236	1 008 743	953 006	55 737
1962	1 268 042	1 388 127	1 388 127	949 305	898 463	50 842
1961	1 190 286	1 289 516	1 289 516	873 178	826 144	47 034
1960	1 140 574	1 206 662	1 206 662	849 132	804 633	44 499
1959	1 074 120	1 136 668	1 136 668	816 800	769 145	47 655
1958	990 381	1 064 481	1 064 481	735 338	696 114	39 224
1957	940 147	996 400	996 400	720 414	675 340	45 073
1956	827 916	948 951	948 951	673 493	626 309	47 184
1955	746 962	888 621	888 621	634 508	586 907	47 601
1954	667 856	805 300	805 300	547 001	510 515	36 486
1953	640 073	761 877	1761 877	551 984	512 402	39 582
1952	615 698	721 864	721 864	525 011	486 504	38 507
1951	596 385	647 524	647 524	511 849	468 354	43 495
1950	569 961	598 369	598 369	452 523	409 988	42 535
1949	554 573	543 562	543 562	387 636	359 505	28 130
1948	536 833	525 136	525 136	405 430	371 182	34 248
1947	496 821	494 615	494 625	361 521	330 314	31 207
1946	440 750	454 705	454 705	283 917	258 893	25 025
1945	374 950	441 461	441 461	252 636	231 417	21 220
1944	363 056	418 324	418 324	258 880	232 426	26 454
1943	366 870	389 524	389 524	245 796	217 863	27 933
1942	383 534	360 018	360 018	213 777	190 497	23 280
1941	407 053	340 452	340 452	186 137	169 546	16 592
1940	413 716	320 478	320 478	145 427	135 955	9 472
1939	412 759	306 801	306 801	130 365	123 129	7 236

See footnotes at end of chart.

Series V 108-140. Corporate Assets, Liabilities, Receipts, Deductions, and Profits for All Industries: 1926 to 1996—Cont'd.

(In millions of dollars, except number of tax returns)

Year	Number of corporate tax returns	Total assets	Total liabilities [1]	Total receipts	Total compiled deductions	Net income
	108	109	117	129	132	136
1938.................................	411 941	300 022	300 022	117 596	113 452	4 144
1937.................................	416 902	303 357	303 357	138 907	131 130	7 777
1936.................................	415 654	303 180	303 180	126 269	118 651	7 618
1935.................................	415 205	303 150	303 150	112 098	106 599	5 500
1934.................................	410 626	301 307	301 307	99 095	96 058	3 037
1933.................................	388 564	268 206	268 206	82 148	82 787	[2] (639)
1932.................................	392 021	280 083	280 083	79 701	83 211	[2] (3 511)
1931.................................	381 088	296 497	296 497	105 238	105 725	[2] (487)
1930.................................	403 173	334 002	334 002	[2]	[2]	[2]
1929.................................	398 815	335 775	335 778	[2]	[2]	[2]
1928.................................	384 548	307 218	307 218	[2]	[2]	[2]
1927.................................	379 156	287 542	287 542	[2]	[2]	[2]
1926.................................	359 449	262 179	262 179	[2]	[2]	[2]

1. Includes capital.
2. Loss.

Series VV 1. Manufacturing Corporations—Number, Assets, and Profits, by Asset Size: 1980 to 1998

(Corporations and assets as of end of 4th quarter; profits for entire year. Based on complete canvass. For a complete canvass, the asset value was $25 million in 1980 and raised in 1988 to $50 million. Asset sizes less than these values are sampled, except as noted. For details regarding methodology, see source for first quarter, 1988)

Year	Unit	Total	Under [1] $10 mil.	$10-$25 mil.	$25-$50 mil.	$50-$100 mil.	$100-$250 mil.	$250 mil.-$1 bil.	$1 bil. and over
Corporations:									
1980	Number	...	...	1 777	941	590	491	369	244
1985	Number	...	...	...	896	744	608	428	281
1989	Number	...	...	...	...	781	750	579	347
1990	Number	...	...	...	...	834	774	597	367
1991	Number	...	...	...	...	868	799	608	373
1992	Number	...	...	...	...	881	829	621	387
1993	Number	...	...	...	...	956	843	648	407
1994	Number	...	...	...	...	983	903	712	417
1995	Number	...	...	...	...	574	639	727	447
1996	Number	...	...	...	...	532	620	745	484
1997	Number	...	...	...	...	470	615	748	529
1998	Number	...	...	...	...	416	531	753	549
Assets:									
1980	Mil. dol.	1 384 474	126 639	43 569	34 930	41 963	75 284	179 959	882 129
1985	Mil. dol.	1 932 766	153 883	64 324	52 669	58 019	96 748	208 403	1 298 720
1989	Mil. dol.	2 503 761	144 774	73 493	56 554	68 146	117 228	282 595	1 760 971
1990	Mil. dol.	2 629 458	142 498	74 477	55 914	72 554	123 967	287 512	1 872 536
1991	Mil. dol.	2 688 422	140 056	70 567	58 549	72 694	127 748	295 743	1 923 066
1992	Mil. dol.	2 798 625	143 766	70 446	65 718	75 967	132 742	302 287	2 007 698
1993	Mil. dol.	2 904 869	149 763	72 854	61 243	81 389	134 388	317 774	2 087 457
1994	Mil. dol.	3 080 231	148 751	81 505	66 405	82 116	138 950	358 100	2 204 404
1995	Mil. dol.	3 345 229	155 618	87 011	68 538	87 262	159 133	370 263	2 417 403
1996	Mil. dol.	3 574 407	163 928	87 096	69 722	93 205	156 702	398 651	2 605 102
1997	Mil. dol.	3 746 797	167 921	87 398	76 034	85 186	157 130	397 559	2 775 570
1998	Mil. dol.	3 998 804	170 618	88 430	69 450	86 850	148 164	417 209	3 018 082
Net profit: [2]									
1980	Mil. dol.	92 443	7 770	2 235	1 904	2 479	4 532	11 485	62 041
1985	Mil. dol.	87 647	8 601	2 551	2 305	2 819	3 628	7 312	60 431
1989	Mil. dol.	135 141	10 378	5 171	2 920	3 092	4 415	11 665	97 501
1990	Mil. dol.	110 128	8 527	5 160	2 769	2 661	3 525	7 110	80 377
1991	Mil. dol.	66 407	6 820	4 271	2 564	1 704	1 707	5 027	44 316
1992	Mil. dol.	22 085	9 567	4 748	3 245	3 034	4 553	5 919	-8 979
1993	Mil. dol.	83 156	11 195	5 415	3 439	3 218	3 584	4 555	51 750
1994	Mil. dol.	174 874	14 131	7 057	4 072	4 996	6 745	14 626	123 250
1995	Mil. dol.	198 151	13 224	5 668	3 767	5 771	7 000	16 549	146 172
1996	Mil. dol.	224 869	15 802	6 872	4 266	5 664	7 935	16 059	168 271
1997	Mil. dol.	244 505	17 948	8 383	4 153	4 675	7 074	18 433	183 836
1998	Mil. dol.	237 661	18 302	6 409	3 754	4 734	5 607	14 147	184 707

1. Beginning 1986, excludes estimates for corporations with less than $250 000 in assets at time of sample selection. Prior periods include estimates for corporations in this size category.
2. After taxes.

SOURCE: U.S. Census Bureau, Quarterly Financial Report for Manufacturing, Mining and Trade Corporations.

Series VV 2. Business Cycle Expansions and Contractions—Months of Duration: 1919 to 1997

(A trough is the low point of a business cycle; a peak is the high point. Contraction or recession is the period from peak to subsequent trough; expansion is the period from trough to subsequent peak. Business cycle reference dates are determined by the National Bureau of Economic Research, Inc.)

Business cycle				Contraction (trough from previous peak)	Expansion (trough to peak)	Length of cycle	
Trough		Peak				Trough from previous trough	Peak from previous peak
Month	Year	Month	Year				
March	1919	January	1920	[1] 7	10	[2] 51	[1] 17
July	1921	May	1923	18	22	28	40
July	1924	October	1926	14	27	36	41
November	1927	August	1929	13	21	40	34
March	1933	May	1937	43	50	64	93
June	1938	February	1945	13	80	63	93
October	1945	November	1948	8	37	88	45
October	1949	July	1953	11	45	48	56
May	1954	August	1957	10	39	55	49
April	1958	April	1960	8	24	47	32
February	1961	December	1969	10	106	34	116
November	1970	November	1973	11	36	117	47
March	1975	January	1980	16	58	52	74
July	1980	July	1981	6	12	64	18
November	1982	July	1990	16	92	28	108
March	1991	. . .	. . .	8	. . .	100	. . .
Average, all cycles:							
1854 to 1991 (31 cycles)				18	35	53	[3] 53
1854 to 1919 (16 cycles)				22	27	48	[4] 49
1919 to 1945 (six cycles)				18	35	53	53
1945 to 1991 (nine cycles)				11	50	61	61
Average, peacetime cycles:							
1854 to 1991 (26 cycles)				19	29	48	[5] 48
1854 to 1919 (14 cycles)				22	24	46	[6] 47
1919 to 1945 (5 cycles)				20	26	46	45
1945 to 1991 (7 cycles)				11	43	53	53

1. Previous peak: August 1918.
2. Previous trough: December 1914.
3. 30 cycles.
4. 15 cycles.
5. 25 cycles.
6. 13 cycles.

SOURCE: National Bureau of Economic Research, Inc., Cambridge, MA, unpublished data.

Series VV 3. Composite Indexes of Economic Cyclical Indicators: 1980 to 1997

Item	Unit	1980	1990	1994	1995	1996	1997
Leading index, composite	1992 = 100	89.3	99.2	101.3	100.8	102.0	103.8
Average weekly hours, manufacturing	Hours	39.7	40.8	41.9	41.6	41.6	42.0
Average weekly initial claims for unemployment insurance	1,000...................	488.9	385.9	342.0	358.3	351.6	319.4
Manufacturers' new orders, consumer goods and materials (1992 dol.)........	Mil. dol.	96 153	118 017	136 312	139 592	142 199	151 576
Vendor performance, slower deliveries diffusion index	Percent	40.6	47.9	60.1	52.8	50.5	53.9
Manufacturers' new orders, nondefense capital goods (1992 dol.)............	Mil. dol.	27 142	34 598	34 629	38 783	42 066	45 195
Building permits, new private housing units...............................	1 000.................	1 246.4	1 155.1	1 366.9	1 335.8	1 419.1	1 444.6
Stock prices, 500 common stocks	1941-43 = 100	118.8	334.6	460.3	541.6	670.8	872.7
Money supply, M2 (1992 dol.)...	Bil. dol.	2 636	3 476	3 328	3 321	3 414	3 517
Interest rate spread, 10-year treasury bonds less Federal funds...........	Percent	-1.9	0.5	2.9	0.7	1.1	0.9
Index of consumer expectations	Percent	56.8	70.2	83.8	83.2	85.7	97.7
Coincident index, composite	1992 = 100	80.1	100.2	106.1	109.6	112.6	116.4
Employees on nonagricultural payrolls	Millions...............	90 418	109 404	114 131	117 187	119 590	122 677
Personal income less transfer payments (1992 dol.)	Bil. dol.	3 371	4 422	4 581	4 713	4 890	5 078
Industrial production	1992 = 100	79.7	98.9	109.2	114.5	118.5	124.4
Manufacturing and trade sales (1992 dol.)	Bil. dol.	434 290	562 978	627 972	652 755	675 345	714 249
Lagging index, composite	1992 = 100	103.7	106.8	100.2	103.5	104.4	104.7
Average duration of unemployment	Weeks.................	11.9	12.0	18.8	16.6	16.7	15.8
Inventories to sales ratio, manufacturing and trade...........................	Ratio	1.5	1.5	1.4	1.4	1.4	1.4
Labor cost per unit of output, manufacturing	Percent	10.0	4.2	-2.5	-1.3	-1.2	0.9
Average prime rate	Percent	15.3	10.0	7.1	8.8	8.3	8.4
Commercial and industrial loans (1992 dol.)	Bil. dol.	345 348	566 029	463 454	517 670	535 297	556 275
Consumer installment credit to personal income ratio............................	Ratio	15.2	16.4	15.6	17.0	17.9	17.9
Consumer price index for services...	Percent	14.6	5.8	3.0	3.5	3.3	2.8

SOURCE: The Conference Board, New York, NY 10022-6601, Business Cycle Indicators, monthly (copyright).

Series VV 4. Small Business Administration Loans to Small Businesses: 1980 to 1996

(For fiscal year ending in year shown; see text, Section 9, State and Local Government. A small business must be independently owned and operated, must not be dominant in its particular industry, and must meet standards set by the Small Business Administration as to its annual receipts or number of employees. Loans include both direct and guaranteed loans to small business establishments. Does not include Disaster Assistance Loans)

Loans approved	Unit	1980	1985	1989	1990	1991	1992	1993	1994	1995	1996
Loans, all businesses	1 000.........	31.7	19.3	17.0	18.8	20.6	26.4	29.4	40.4	60.1	52.7
Loans, minority-owned businesses	1 000.........	6.0	2.8	2.4	2.4	3.1	3.9	4.5	6.8	10.4	9.1
Percent of all business loans..................	Percent......	19	15	14	13	15	15	15	18	19	19
Value of total loans [1]	Mil. dol.	3 858	3 217	3 490	4 354	4 861	6 596	7 591	9 527	9 854	10 177
Minority business loans [2]	Mil. dol.	470	324	385	473	764	1 033	1 178	1 754	1 885	2 124

1. Includes both SBA and bank portions of loans.
2. SBA direct loans and guaranteed portion of bank loans only.

SOURCE: U.S. Small Business Administration, Management Information Summary, unpublished data.

Series VV 5. Minority-Owned Firms—Comparison of Business Ownership by Minority Group and Gender: 1987 and 1992

(Based on the 1987 Standard Industrial Classification (SIC). Data includes individual proprietorships, partnerships, and subchapter S corporations. Detail may not add to total due to rounding)

Sex and race	Firms		Percent change, 1987-1992	Percent of total		Sales/receipts		Percent change, 1987-1992	Percent of total	
	1987	1992		1987	1992	1987 (mil. dol.)	1992 (mil. dol.)		1987	1992
All minorities...........	1 213 750	1 965 565	61.9	...	...	77 840	202 011	160.0	...	...
Men...........................	825 441	1 248 130	51.2	68.0	63.5	59 847	152 245	154.9	76.9	75.4
Women.....................	388 309	717 435	84.8	32.0	36.5	17 993	49 767	176.6	23.1	24.6
Black............................	424 165	620 912	46.4	34.9	31.6	19 763	32 197	62.9	25.4	15.9
Men...........................	265 887	343 666	29.3	21.9	17.5	13 232	23 688	77.1	17.0	11.7
Women.....................	158 278	277 246	75.2	13.0	14.1	6 531	8 510	30.3	8.4	4.2
Hispanic.........................	422 373	771 708	82.7	34.8	39.3	24 732	72 824	194.5	31.8	36.0
Men...........................	307 348	525 330	70.9	25.3	26.7	20 403	55 645	172.2	26.2	27.5
Women.....................	115 025	246 378	114.2	9.5	12.5	4 328	17 180	297.0	5.6	8.5
API/AIAN [1]:										
Men...........................	258 514	397 779	53.9	21.3	20.2	26 700	74 856	180.4	34.3	37.1
Women.....................	118 197	208 647	76.5	9.7	10.6	7 336	24 853	238.8	9.4	12.3

1. API/AIAN = Asian, Pacific Islander, American Indian, and Alaska Native.

SOURCE: U.S. Census Bureau, Survey of Minority-Owned Businesses, Summary 1992, Series MB92-4.

Series VV 6. Establishments, Employees, and Payroll, by Industry: 1980 to 1996

(4 543 represents 4 543 000. Beginning 1990, data are based on the 1987 Standard Industrial Classification (SIC). Prior to 1990, data are based on the 1972 SIC)

Industry	Establishments (1 000)				Employees (1 000)				Payroll (bil. dol.)			
	1980	1990	1995	1996	1980	1990	1995	1996	1980	1990	1995	1996
All industries [1]	4 543	6 176	6 613	6 739	74 844	93 476	100 335	102 199	1 035	2 104	2 666	2 849
Agricultural services [2]	46	85	108	113	290	531	630	664	3	9	12	13
Mining...	30	30	27	27	994	723	627	574	22	27	26	26
Construction......................................	418	578	634	658	4 473	5 239	5 039	5 207	75	132	147	161
Manufacturing	319	378	390	393	21 165	19 173	18 613	18 558	355	544	631	660
Transportation [3]...............................	168	235	285	295	4 623	5 592	5 924	6 057	88	166	201	212
Wholesale trade...............................	385	476	518	531	5 211	6 328	6 606	6 665	89	181	227	240
Retail trade.......................................	1 223	1 530	1 568	1 579	15 047	19 815	21 085	21 487	124	242	300	318
Finance and insurance [4]	421	545	628	650	5 295	6 956	6 998	7 194	77	197	256	285
Services	1 278	2 059	2 386	2 461	17 186	28 800	34 707	35 750	197	599	864	933

1. Includes nonclassifiable establishments not shown separately.
2. Includes forestry and fisheries.
3. Includes public utilities.
4. Includes real estate.

SOURCE: U.S. Census Bureau, County Business Patterns, annual.

PRODUCTIVITY AND TECHNOLOGICAL DEVELOPMENT

PRODUCTIVITY AND TECHNOLOGICAL DEVELOPMENT

Highlights

1 Productivity is the ratio of output to input expressed in a number of ways. The most common is output per unit of labor. Work in the field of productivity is carried on by many organizations, particularly the Bureau of Labor Statistics and the National Bureau of Economic Research. Labor productivity also reflects the state of the technology, availability of capital and physical resources, efficiency of management, quality of training, and other factors. Productivity may be affected by the specific year chosen as the weight base, because items that increase most in volume output are those with price declines or lower price increases. Productivity series also suffer from certain statistical limitations because they do not measure the quality of the output.

2 Copyright, or that body of exclusive rights granted to authors by law, is the oldest of such protective statutes for intellectual property. The first U.S. copyright law of 1790 applied only to maps, charts and books. Amendments extended the protection to prints (1802); musical compositions (1831); dramatic compositions ((1856); photographs (1865); paintings, drawings, sculpture, and models or designs for works of fine arts ((1870); performed music (1897); motion pictures and photoplays (1912); performance rights in nondramatic literary works (1952); and electronic books (1978). The original term of copyright was 15 years, with the privilege of renewal for another 14. In 1831, the first term was increased to 28 years, and in 1909 the second term was also increased to 28 years. Under current copyright law works are protected for the author's life plus 70 years after the author's death; for works made for hire, the duration of the copyright will be 95 years from publication or 120 years from creation—whichever is shorter. Before 1891, only residents or citizens of the United States could obtain copyrights. The Act of 1891 extended the privilege to citizens of other countries with which the United States had reciprocal copyright agreements, as well as countries that adhered to international copyright conventions (such as the Universal Copyright Convention of 1952) to which the United States was also a party.

3 A patent is a grant by the government to an inventor and his or her heirs and assigns of the right to exclude others from making, using, or selling the invention without proper authorization. Patents may be obtained for any new and "useful" machine, composition of matter, or process, subject to the requirements of law. Since 1946, inventions used solely in the utilization of fissionable materials have been unpatentable. Patents have been issued by the Federal government since 1790. The first body in charge of issuing patents (known as the Patent Board, or the Patent Commission, or the Commission for the Promotion of Useful Arts) had three members: Thomas Jefferson, Henry Knox, and Edmund Randolph. The responsibility for administering patent laws was vested in the Department of State. The first U. S. patent was issued to Samuel Hopkins of Vermont on July 31, 1790, for a process for making potash and pearl ashes. The patent bore the signatures of George Washington, Thomas Jefferson, and Edmund Randolph. Only three patents were issued in the first year. In 1833, the head of the Patent Office recommended to President Andrew Jackson that his office be abolished because "everything that could possibly be invented has already been invented." From 1790 to 1861, the term of a patent was 14 years. After 1861 it could be extended for an additional seven years. Since 1861, the term of a patent on an invention has been fixed at 17 years, with extensions possible only by a special act of Congress. Patents are numbered serially, beginning with the first patent issued after the Act of July 4, 1836.

4 The Federal Trademark Law of 1870 was based on the patent and copyright clause of the Constitution, instead of the interstate and foreign commerce clause, and was found unconstitutional in 1879. The Trademark Law of 1881 was limited to marks used in foreign commerce, but it was extended to interstate commerce by the Act of 1905. The Act of 1920 permitted the registration of a secondary class of marks not previously registrable. It was superseded by the Act of 1946, which granted registrations for a term of

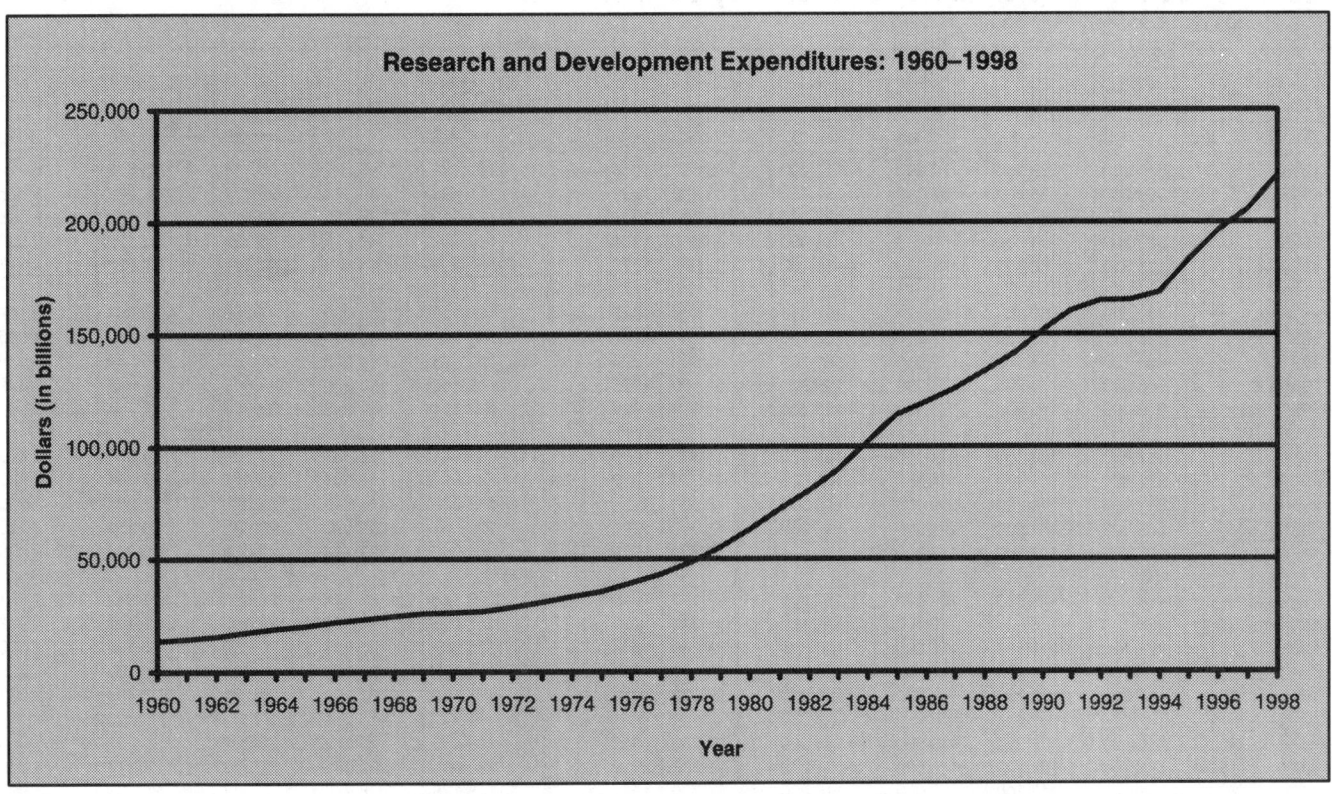

Research and Development Expenditures: 1960–1998

20 years with a possible renewal for successive 20-year terms.

5 National estimates of funds for research and development (R&D) for the four major sectors of the economy have been made by the National Science Foundation since 1953. The data cover basic and applied research as well as development. The last include processes, materials, methods and prototypes. The Federal budget provides data on expenditures and/or obligations for research and development on an agency basis.

6 Total R&D expenditures in 1998 amounted to $220.617 billion compared to $13.669 billion in 1960. Of current expenditures, the Federal government share is $66.6 billion, industry share $143.714 billion, universities' share $4.914 billion, and other nonprofits' share $7.139 billion. Of the Federal government share, 46.8% is borne by the Department of Defense. The United States spends 2.54% of its GDP on R&D, more than any other developed nation.

7 Of R&D expenditures in universities, 55.8% is spent on life sciences. Basic research takes up 68% and applied R&D the balance. The Johns Hopkins University ranks No. 1 in receipt of Federal funds for R&D, a position it has occupied for many decades. The University of Washington, MIT and Stanford University are the runners up.

8 In 1996 there were 4.885 million scientists and engineers, of whom scientists numbered 665,700, computer professionals 932,800, engineers 1.382 million, technicians 1.235 million, and computer programmers 568,000.

9 Of the 39,058 persons who received doctorates in scientific fields in 1997, 28.2% were foreign nationals (10% Asian) and 41% were females.

10 Total NASA expenditures on space-related programs in 1999 were $13.665 billion of which launch vehicles and payload operations accounted for $3.209 billion and mission support $2.699 billion.

11 Between 1981 and 1999 the United States has successfully launched 94 space shuttle launches, including 26 named Discovery,

12 The United States has a commanding lead in the number of Nobel scientists. Of the total 448 Nobel Prizes awarded since 1901, the United States has 190, more than double that of the second-ranking United Kingdom.

Series W 82-95. Copyright Registrations, by Type: 1870 to 1998

(Categories reclassified in 1978 and thereafter)

Year	Total copyright registrations [1]	Total books and pamphlets [2]	Periodicals	Musical compositions	Renewals, all classes [3]	Year	Total copyright registrations [1]	Total books and pamphlets [2]	Periodicals	Musical compositions	Renewals, all classes [3]
	82	83	85	88	95		82	83	85	88	95
1998	558 600	189 300	72 600	142 400	25 400	1933	137 424	40 694	35 464	26 846	6 411
1997	569 200	176 400	83 300	154 400	28 600	1932	151 735	46 576	39 177	29 264	5 888
1996	550 400	187 200	83 400	133 500	23 700	1931	164 642	46 855	42 415	31 488	5 998
1995	609 200	196 000	88 700	163 600	30 600	1930	172 792	47 248	43 939	32 129	5 937
1994	530 300	162 600	75 100	136 100	33 300	1929	161 959	44 040	44 161	27 023	4 948
1993	564 900	185 800	82 600	152 300	37 700	1928	193 914	50 095	47 364	26 897	5 447
1992	606 200	190 200	92 900	162 100	49 100	1927	184 000	47 801	41 475	25 282	4 686
1991	663 700	193 800	109 200	191 200	52 300	1926	177 635	73 455	41 169	25 484	4 029
1990	643 500	179 700	111 500	185 300	51 800	1925	165 848	65 670	40 880	25 548	3 309
1989	618 300	153 800	133 900	197 200	38 600	1924	162 694	61 982	39 806	26 734	3 433
1988	565 300	158 100	114 000	159 500	43 800	1923	148 946	55 561	37 104	24 900	2 689
1987	582 200	153 900	131 000	161 600	45 500	1922	138 633	46 307	35 471	27 381	2 726
1986	561 000	148 200	130 000	156 300	45 300	1921	135 280	41 245	34 074	31 054	2 206
1985	539 800	154 500	120 000	147 900	43 800	1920	126 562	39 090	28 935	29 151	2 112
1984	502 700	147 200	113 600	...	37 300	1919	113 003	37 710	25 083	26 209	1 906
1983	488 200	135 300	106 100	127 800	39 100	1918	106 728	33 617	25 822	21 849	1 857
1982	468 100	116 300	112 400	125 400	36 300	1917	111 438	33 552	26 467	20 115	1 992
1981	471 100	119 000	118 500	125 000	34 200	1916	115 967	32 897	26 553	20 644	1 628
1980	464 700	119 200	117 900	120 200	33 000	1915	115 193	31 926	24 938	21 406	1 326
1979	429 000	122 800	109 600	108 300	27 000	1914	123 154	31 891	24 134	28 493	1 231
1978	415 700	112 900	110 900	114 800	21 200	1913	119 495	29 572	23 002	26 292	1 065
1977	452 700	122 100	106 500	131 200	31 000	1912	120 931	29 286	22 580	26 777	1 349
1976	411 000	113 200	96 000	118 500	27 700	1911	115 198	26 970	23 393	25 525	928
1975	401 300	111 900	95 100	114 800	28 200	1910	109 074	24 740	21 608	24 345	1 007
1974	372 800	104 800	92 200	104 500	25 500	1909	120 131	32 533	21 195	26 306	...
1973	353 600	104 500	88 600	95 300	23 100	1908	119 742	30 191	22 409	28 427	...
1972	344 600	103 200	84 700	97 500	23 200	1907	123 829	30 879	23 078	31 401	...
1971	329 696	96 124	84 491	95 202	20 835	1906	117 704	29 261	23 163	26 435	...
1970	316 466	88 432	83 862	88 949	23 316	1905	113 374	29 860	22 591	24 595	...
1969	301 258	83 603	80 706	83 608	25 667	1904	103 130	27 824	21 496	23 110	...
1968	303 451	85 189	81 773	80 479	25 774	1903	97 979	27 466	22 625	21 161	...
1967	294 406	80 910	81 647	79 291	23 499	1902	92 978	24 272	21 071	19 706	...
1966	286 866	77 300	77 963	76 805	25 464	1901	92 351	...	...	...	...
1965	293 617	76 098	78 307	80 881	23 520	1900	94 798	...	...	...	...
1964	278 987	71 618	74 611	75 256	22 574	1899	80 968	...	...	...	...
1963	264 845	68 445	69 682	72 583	20 164	1898	75 545	...	...	...	...
1962	254 776	66 571	67 523	67 612	19 274	1897	75 000	...	...	...	...
1961	247 014	62 415	66 251	65 500	18 194	1896	72 470	...	12 892	20 951	...
1960	243 926	60 034	64 204	65 558	21 393	1895	67 572	...	12 155	18 563	...
1959	241 735	55 967	62 246	70 707	21 533	1894	62 762	...	12 149	18 460	...
1958	238 935	57 242	60 691	66 515	22 593	1893	58 956	...	11 094	16 273	...
1957	225 807	53 503	59 724	59 614	21 473	1892	54 735	...	10 327	14 649	...
1956	224 908	53 942	58 576	58 330	20 926	1891	48 908	...	9 477	11 688	...
1955	224 732	54 414	59 448	57 527	19 519	1890	42 794	...	8 164	9 132	...
1954	222 665	51 763	60 667	58 213	18 508	1889	40 985	...	7 646	8 958	...
1953	218 506	49 059	59 371	59 302	17 101	1888	38 225	...	7 086	8 066	...
1952	203 705	46 083	56 509	51 538	16 690	1887	35 083	...	6 708	7 744	...
1951	200 354	47 125	55 129	48 319	16 372	1886	31 241	...	6 089	7 514	...
1950	210 564	50 456	55 436	52 309	14 531	1885	28 411	...	6 060	6 808	...
1949	201 190	47 422	54 163	48 210	13 675	1884	26 893	...	5 570	6 241	...
1948	238 121	48 811	59 699	72 339	15 816	1883	25 274	...	5 489	6 280	...
1947	230 215	49 525	58 340	68 709	13 201	1882	22 918	...	4 612	6 143	...
1946	202 144	42 356	48 289	63 367	12 516	1881	21 075	...	4 339	5 578	...
1945	178 848	35 688	45 763	57 835	11 367	1880	20 686	...	4 369	5 628	...
1944	169 269	35 952	44 364	52 087	10 247	1879	18 125	...	3 608	4 688	...
1943	160 795	36 889	42 995	48 348	9 650	1878	15 798	...	3 424	3 772	...
1942	182 232	45 157	45 145	50 023	11 488	1877	15 758	...	...	...	...
1941	180 647	46 040	42 207	49 135	10 342	1876	14 882	...	...	...	...

See footnotes at end of chart.

Series W 82-95. Copyright Registrations, by Type: 1870 to 1998—Cont'd.

(Categories reclassified in 1978 and thereafter)

Year	Total copyright registrations [1]	Total books and pamphlets [2]	Periodicals	Musical compositions	Renewals, all classes [3]	Year	Total copyright registrations [1]	Total books and pamphlets [2]	Periodicals	Musical compositions	Renewals, all classes [3]
	82	83	85	88	95		82	83	85	88	95
1940...........	176 997	50 125	40 173	37 975	10 207	1875...........	15 927	. . .	. . .	. . .	. . .
1939...........	173 135	49 901	38 307	40 961	10 177	1874...........	16 283	. . .	. . .	. . .	. . .
1938...........	166 248	49 156	39 249	35 334	9 940	1873...........	15 352	. . .	. . .	. . .	. . .
1937...........	154 424	45 504	38 053	31 821	8 589	1872...........	14 164	. . .	. . .	. . .	. . .
1936...........	156 962	47 667	38 418	33 250	8 180	1871...........	12 688	. . .	. . .	. . .	. . .
1935...........	142 031	43 134	36 351	27 459	6 661	1870 [4]........	5 600	. . .	. . .	. . .	. . .
1934...........	139 047	40 658	35 819	27 001	6 989						

1. Prior to 1941, commercial prints and labels not included in total; jurisdiction moved to copyright office in 1940.
2. Prior to 1927, contributions to periodicals included with books and pamphlets. Includes computer software and machine readable works.
3. Prior to 1941, excludes renewals of commercial prints and labels.
4. July-December.

Series W 96-106. Patent Applications Filed and Patents Issued, by Type and Patentee: 1790 to 1997

Year	Patent applications filed					Patents issued						
	Inventions	Designs	Botanical plants	Total [1]	Individuals	Inventions			Designs	Botanical plants	To residents of foreign countries
						Corporations		U.S. government [2]			
						U.S.	Foreign				
	96	97	98	99	100	101	102	103	104	105	106
1997	215 300	16 500	600	124 100	17 600	50 200	42 900	900	11 400	400	54 200
1996	195 200	15 200	700	121 700	18 200	48 700	41 500	900	11 400	400	52 400
1995	212 400	15 400	500	113 800	17 400	44 000	39 100	1 000	11 700	400	49 400
1994	189 900	15 800	500	113 600	17 300	44 000	38 800	1 300	11 100	500	49 300
1993	174 700	13 600	400	109 700	16 500	41 800	38 800	1 200	10 600	400	48 700
1992	173 100	13 100	400	107 400	17 300	40 300	38 700	1 200	9 300	300	48 700
1991	164 300	13 100	400	106 800	18 100	39 200	38 100	1 200	9 600	400	49 000
1990	164 500	11 300	400	90 400	17 300	36 100	36 000	1 000	8 000	300	46 200
1989	152 800	12 600	400	95 500	17 900	38 700	38 000	900	6 100	600	47 900
1988	139 800	11 300	400	77 900	14 300	31 400	31 400	700	5 700	400	39 700
1987	127 900	11 200	400	83 000	15 300	33 800	32 900	1 000	6 000	200	41 700
1986	122 400	9 900	300	70 900	13 300	29 600	27 000	1 000	5 500	200	34 900
1985	117 000	9 600	200	71 700	12 900	31 300	26 400	1 100	5 100	200	33 900
1984	111 300	8 700	300	67 200	12 300	30 100	23 600	1 200	4 900	200	30 500
1983	103 700	8 100	300	56 900	10 500	25 700	19 600	1 000	4 600	200	25 400
1982	109 600	8 200	200	57 900	11 900	25 800	19 200	1 000	4 900	200	25 600
1981	106 400	7 400	200	65 800	14 100	29 500	21 000	1 100	4 700	200	26 500
1980	104 300	7 800	200	61 800	13 300	29 400	18 200	1 000	3 900	100	25 400
1979	100 500	7 500	200	48 900	9 300	23 800	14 800	900	3 100	100	18 200
1978	100 900	7 500	200	66 100	14 300	31 300	19 300	1 200	3 900	200	25 100
1977	100 900	7 300	200	65 300	14 000	31 500	18 200	1 500	3 900	200	23 900
1976	102 300	7 100	200	70 200	14 100	34 400	19 900	1 800	4 600	200	26 100
1975	101 014	6 292	150	71 994	17 192	34 577	18 344	1 881	4 282	150	25 391
1974	102 206	4 780	130	76 275	18 083	37 807	18 686	1 699	4 303	261	25 632
1973	103 695	5 425	118	74 139	16 929	38 615	16 513	2 082	4 033	132	22 638
1972	98 928	5 867	135	74 808	17 729	38 890	16 414	1 775	2 901	199	23 293
1971	104 566	6 211	155	78 316	17 299	43 022	16 048	1 947	3 156	71	22 850
1970	102 868	5 996	188	64 427	13 511	36 896	12 294	1 726	3 214	52	17 872
1969	98 386	5 496	111	67 557	14 772	38 847	12 188	1 750	3 335	103	17 573
1968	93 136	5 171	95	59 102	13 555	34 886	9 172	1 489	3 352	72	13 722
1967	87 872	4 744	103	65 652	15 647	38 353	9 895	1 757	3 165	85	14 711
1966	88 293	4 853	104	68 406	16 018	41 634	9 222	1 532	3 188	114	14 008
1965	94 632	5 413	105	62 857	16 063	37 158	8 096	1 540	3 424	120	12 782
1964	87 597	5 259	120	47 376	12 504	27 836	5 854	1 182	2 686	128	9 168
1963	85 724	4 968	145	45 679	12 525	26 632	5 501	1 021	2 965	129	8 736
1962	85 029	4 897	151	55 691	15 470	32 560	6 380	1 281	2 300	91	10 255
1961	83 100	4 714	107	48 368	13 383	28 351	5 161	1 473	2 487	108	8 384
1960	79 590	4 525	131	47 170	13 069	28 187	4 670	1 244	2 543	116	7 850
1959	78 594	4 879	114	52 408	16 017	29 888	5 081	1 422	2 768	101	8 340
1958	77 495	4 923	134	48 330	15 706	27 116	4 230	1 278	2 374	120	7 395
1957	74 197	4 714	101	42 744	15 154	23 255	3 372	963	2 362	129	6 282
1956	74 906	4 824	104	46 817	16 643	25 502	3 690	982	2 977	101	6 646
1955	77 188	5 764	118	30 432	11 914	16 084	1 744	689	2 713	103	4 065
1954	77 185	5 465	95	33 809	12 531	18 319	2 301	658	2 536	101	4 433
1953	72 284	5 450	99	40 468	16 284	21 230	2 294	658	2 713	78	4 331
1952	64 554	4 993	84	43 616	18 538	22 340	2 035	695	2 959	101	5 635
1951	60 438	4 279	71	44 326	19 192	22 305	2 163	659	4 163	58	4 888
1950	67 264	6 739	105	43 040	18 960	21 782	1 660	622	4 718	89	4 408
1949	67 592	6 998	70	35 131	14 957	18 536	1 127	485	4 450	93	3 105
1948	68 740	7 048	59	23 963	9 812	13 124	628	652	3 968	44	1 984
1947	75 443	7 644	92	20 139	7 784	11 448	669	155	2 102	52	1 617
1946	81 056	10 698	72	21 803	7 444	13 486	585	147	2 778	56	1 656
1945	67 846	8 066	52	25 695	8 981	15 665	580	87	3 524	17	2 112
1944	54 190	5 063	42	28 053	9 636	16 769	645	106	2 914	38	2 564
1943	45 493	2 986	41	31 054	11 654	18 022	524	48	2 228	47	2 625
1942	45 549	4 218	60	38 449	14 534	22 019	1 286	62	3 728	65	3 943

See footnotes at end of table.

Series W 96-106. Patent Applications Filed and Patents Issued, by Type and Patentee: 1790 to 1997—Cont'd.

Year	Patent applications filed				Patents issued						
						Inventions					To residents of foreign countries
						Corporations		U.S.			
	Inventions	Designs	Botanical plants	Total [1]	Individuals	U.S.	Foreign	government [2]	Designs	Botanical plants	
	96	97	98	99	100	101	102	103	104	105	106
1941	52 339	7 203	67	41 109	16 322	22 632	2 112	43	6 486	62	5 311
1940	60 863	8 530	91	42 238	17 627	22 165	2 406	40	6 145	85	6 148
1939	64 093	7 137	76	43 073	18 583	21 800	2 640	50	5 592	45	6 338
1938	66 874	8 084	48	38 061	16 304	19 635	2 063	59	5 026	41	5 776
1937	65 324	7 207	45	37 683	15 995	19 831	1 824	33	5 136	55	5 638
1936	62 599	6 478	66	39 782	16 639	21 207	1 903	33	4 556	49	5 734
1935	58 117	5 728	72	40 618	17 757	20 821	2 018	22	3 864	45	5 980
1934	56 643	4 399	28	44 420	19 731	22 529	2 131	29	2 919	32	6 489
1933	56 558	3 600	27	48 774	22 713	23 667	2 343	51	2 411	33	7 170
1932	67 006	4 345	46	53 458	26 274	24 822	2 325	37	2 942	46	7 376
1931	79 740	4 190	37	51 756	26 618	23 149	1 961	28	2 438	5	6 897
1930	89 554	4 182	16	45 226	23 726	19 700	1 800	...	2 710	...	6 085
1929	89 752	4 520	...	45 267	25 367	18 500	1 400	...	2 905	...	5 921
1928	87 603	4 761	...	42 357	23 357	17 800	1 200	...	3 182	...	5 218
1927	87 219	4 473	...	41 717	25 417	15 100	1 200	...	2 387	...	4 918
1926	81 365	4 343	...	44 733	28 633	15 200	900	...	2 897	...	5 103
1925	80 208	4 082	...	46 432	30 332	14 800	1 300	...	2 819	...	5 347
1924	87 987	3 635	...	42 574	29 174	12 400	1 000	...	2 670	...	4 723
1923	76 783	3 550	...	38 616	27 016	10 800	800	...	1 927	...	4 133
1922	83 962	4 763	...	38 369	27 369	10 300	700	...	1 609	...	4 455
1921	87 467	5 596	...	37 798	27 098	9 860	840	...	3 265	...	3 963
1920	81 915	4 660	...	37 060	...	...	...	...	2 481	...	3 762
1919	76 710	3 627	...	36 797	...	...	...	...	1 521	...	3 687
1918	57 347	2 234	...	38 452	...	...	...	...	1 206	...	2 883
1917	67 590	3 545	...	40 935	...	...	...	...	1 505	...	3 209
1916	68 075	2 684	...	43 892	31 742	11 540	610	...	1 745	...	3 767
1915	67 138	2 734	...	43 118	...	...	...	...	1 538	...	4 334
1914	67 774	2 454	...	39 892	...	...	...	...	1 711	...	4 595
1913	68 117	2 060	...	33 917	...	...	...	...	1 677	...	4 212
1912	68 968	1 850	...	36 198	...	...	...	...	1 341	...	4 498
1911	67 370	1 534	...	32 856	24 756	7 580	520	...	1 004	...	4 058
1910	63 293	1 155	...	35 141	...	...	...	...	636	...	3 719
1909	64 408	1 234	...	36 561	...	...	...	...	679	...	3 812
1908	60 142	1 131	...	32 735	...	...	...	...	755	...	3 338
1907	57 679	896	...	35 859	...	...	...	...	589	...	3 866
1906	55 471	806	...	31 170	24 750	6 040	380	...	620	...	3 471
1905	54 034	781	...	29 775	...	...	...	...	486	...	3 292
1904	51 168	818	...	30 258	...	...	...	...	553	...	3 285
1903	49 289	770	...	31 029	...	...	...	...	536	...	3 763
1902	48 320	1 170	...	27 119	...	...	...	...	639	...	3 499
1901	43 973	2 361	...	25 546	20 896	4 370	280	...	1 729	...	3 402
1900	39 673	2 225	...	24 644	...	...	...	...	1 754	...	3 483
1899	38 937	2 400	...	23 278	...	...	...	...	2 137	...	2 311
1898	33 915	1 843	...	20 377	...	...	...	...	1 799	...	2 752
1897	45 661	2 150	...	22 067	...	...	...	...	1 620	...	2 221
1896	42 077	1 828	...	21 822	...	...	...	...	1 441	...	2 027
1895	39 145	1 463	...	20 856	...	...	...	...	1 108	...	2 049
1894	36 987	1 357	...	19 855	...	...	...	...	927	...	2 166
1893	37 293	1 060	...	22 750	...	...	...	...	899	...	2 473
1892	29 514	1 130	...	22 647	...	...	...	...	816	...	2 051
1891	39 418	1 025	...	22 312	...	...	...	...	835	...	1 928
1890	39 884	1 046	...	25 313	...	...	...	...	886	...	2 105
1889	39 607	857	...	23 324	...	...	...	...	723	...	2 003
1888	34 713	971	...	19 551	...	...	...	...	832	...	1 536
1887	37 420	1 041	...	20 403	...	...	...	...	948	...	1 466
1886	35 161	645	...	21 767	...	...	...	...	594	...	1 489

See footnotes at end of table.

Series W 96-106. Patent Applications Filed and Patents Issued, by Type and Patentee: 1790 to 1997—Cont'd.

Year	Patent applications filed			Total [1]	Individuals	Patents issued					To residents of foreign countries
						Inventions					
						Corporations		U.S. government [2]			
	Inventions	Designs	Botanical plants			U.S.	Foreign		Designs	Botanical plants	
	96	97	98	99	100	101	102	103	104	105	106
1885	34 697	862	. . .	23 285	. . .	. . .	. . .	. . .	769	. . .	1 549
1884	34 192	1 230	. . .	19 118	. . .	. . .	. . .	. . .	1 150	. . .	1 284
1883	33 073	1 238	. . .	21 162	. . .	. . .	. . .	. . .	1 017	. . .	1 259
1882	30 270	948	. . .	18 091	. . .	. . .	. . .	. . .	858	. . .	1 135
1881	24 878	678	. . .	15 500	. . .	. . .	. . .	. . .	565	. . .	995
1880	21 761	634	. . .	12 903	. . .	. . .	. . .	. . .	514	. . .	786
1879	20 059	. . .	. . .	12 125	. . .	. . .	. . .	. . .	591	. . .	648

See footnotes at the end of table.

Series W 96-106. Patent Applications Filed and Patents Issued, by Type and Patentee: 1790 to 1997—Cont'd.

Year	Inventions, patent applications filed [3]	Patents issued			Year	Inventions, patent applications filed [3]	Patents issued		
		Inventions	Designs	To residents of foreign countries			Inventions	Designs	To residents of foreign countries
	96	99	104	106		96	99	104	106
1878	20 260	12 345	590	581	1856	4 960	2 302	107	31
1877	20 308	12 920	699	590	1855	4 435	1 881	70	41
1876	21 425	14 169	802	787	1854	3 328	1 755	57	35
1875	21 638	13 291	915	563					
1874	21 602	12 230	886	547	1853	2 673	844	86	26
					1852	2 639	885	109	20
1873	20 414	11 616	747	493	1851	2 258	752	90	17
1872	18 246	12 180	884	581	1850	2 193	883	83	20
1871	19 472	11 659	903	522	1849	1 955	984	49	17
1870	19 171	12 137	737	644					
1869	19 271	12 931	506	377	1848	1 628	583	46	14
					1847	1 531	495	60	21
1868	20 420	12 526	445	337	1846	1 272	566	59	19
1867	21 276	12 277	325	275	1845	1 246	473	17	12
1866	15 269	8 863	294	244	1844	1 045	478	12	20
1865	10 664	6 088	221	181					
1864	6 932	4 630	139	181	1843	819	493	14	8
					1842	761	488	1	11
1863	6 014	3 773	176	125	1841	847	490	...	21
1862	5 038	3 214	195	80	1840	765	458	...	19
1861	4 643	3 020	142	83	1839	[4] 800	404	...	10
1860	7 653	4 357	183	49					
1859	6 225	4 160	107	47	1838	[4] 900	514	...	17
					1837	[4] 650	426	...	7
1858	5 364	3 455	102	28	1836	[4,5] 400	[5] 103	...	8
1857	4 771	2 674	113	45	1836	...	[6] 509	...	...

Year	Patents issued for inventions	Year	Patents issued for inventions	Year	Patents issued for inventions
	99		99		99
1835	752	1819	156	1803	97
1834	630	1818	222	1802	65
1833	586	1817	174	1801	44
1832	474	1816	206		
1831	573			1800	41
		1815	173	1799	44
1830	544	1814	210	1798	28
1829	447	1813	181	1797	51
1828	368	1812	238	1796	44
1827	331	1811	215		
1826	323			1795	12
		1810	223	1794	22
1825	304	1809	203	1793	20
1824	228	1808	158	1792	11
1823	173	1807	99	1791	33
1822	200	1806	63		
1821	168			1790	3
		1805	57		
1820	155	1804	84		

1. Since 1942, includes patents issued to Alien Property Custodian, not shown separately.
2. Excludes patents issued to Alien Property Custodian.
3. Applications for reissue included with inventions, 1836-1876; design applications included with inventions, 1836-1879.
4. Estimate.
5. From July 4 to end of year.
6. To July 4.

Series W 107-108. Trademarks Registered and Renewed: 1870 to 1997

Year	Registered	Renewed	Year	Registered	Renewed	Year	Registered	Renewed	Year	Registered
	107	108		107	108		107	108		107
1997	112 500	7 400	1964	20 087	2 702	1932	9 603	1 587	1900	1 721
1996	93 700	7 700	1963	19 740	2 655	1931	11 400	1 643	1899	1 649
1995	85 600	6 900				1930	13 246	1 661	1898	1 238
1994	63 900	6 200	1962	17 023	2 809	1929	14 514	1 750		
1993	80 600	6 300	1961	16 595	3 358	1928	14 133	2 049	1897	1 671
			1960	18 434	3 933				1896	1 813
1992	80 200	5 600	1959	18 709	3 272	1927	14 579	3 063	1895	1 829
1991	46 600	5 800	1958	15 351	3 070	1926	14 955	4 273	1894	1 806
1990	53 600	7 200				1925	13 815	2 278	1893	1 677
1989	55 300	7 800	1957	17 480	3 488	1924	15 727	227		
1988	47 400	6 900	1956	20 753	3 756	1923	14 834	251	1892	1 737
			1955	18 207	4 268				1891	1 762
1987	47 300	4 100	1954	15 946	3 491	1922	12 793	254	1890	1 415
1986	46 700	5 100	1953	15 610	3 103	1921	11 636	117	1889	1 229
1985	65 800	5 900				1920	10 268	73	1888	1 059
1984	48 600	5 400	1952	16 172	3 419	1919	4 208	64		
1983	40 500	6 200	1951	17 376	3 350	1918	4 061	38	1887	1 133
			1950	16 817	3 564				1886	1 029
1982	42 400	6 000	1949	15 968	3 788	1917	5 339	52	1885	1 067
1981	42 700	5 900	1948	11 472	5 056	1916	6 791	55	1884	1 021
1980	18 900	5 900				1915	6 262	57	1883	902
1979	20 500	5 400	1947	8 976	6 139	1914	6 817	48		
1978	29 600	5 500	1946	8 106	5 725	1913	5 065	. . .	1882	947
			1945	7 490	4 210				1881	834
1977	25 900	6 100	1944	6 025	4 052	1912	5 020	. . .	1880	349
1976	26 300	6 800	1943	5 595	3 835	1911	4 205	. . .	1879	872
1975	30 931	6 132				1910	4 239	. . .	1878	1 455
1974	28 099	5 513	1942	6 795	2 894	1909	4 184	. . .		
1973	26 112	5 397	1941	8 530	2 765	1908	5 191	. . .	1877	1 216
			1940	9 974	2 547				1876	959
1972	23 252	5 637	1939	10 521	1 398	1907	7 878	. . .	1875	1 138
1971	21 019	6 213	1938	10 204	1 051	1906	10 568	. . .	1874	559
1970	21 745	6 076				1905	4 490	. . .	1873	492
1969	20 613	6 176	1937	11 242	1 524	1904	2 158	. . .		
1968	21 528	4 646	1936	10 722	1 888	1903	2 186	. . .	1872	491
			1935	10 886	1 874				1871	486
1967	20 036	3 801	1934	11 362	2 445	1902	2 006	. . .	1870	121
1966	20 259	3 585	1933	9 130	1 671	1901	1 928	. . .		
1965	18 501	3 165								

Series W 109-125. Funds Expended for Performance of Research and Development and Basic Research, by Sector and Major Function: 1953 to 1998

(Basic research, applied research, and development; amounts in millions of dollars)

				By performance sector									
				Industry		Universities and colleges					Other nonprofit institutions		
Year	Total funds	Percent federal as source	Federal government	Federal funds	Industry funds	Federal funds	Industry funds	Universities and colleges funds [1]	Other nonprofit institutions funds [1]	FFRDC's [2]	Federal funds	Industry funds	Other funds [3]
	109	110	111	112	113	114	115	116	117	118	119	120	121
1998	220 617	...	16 936	22 481	140 847	15 247	1 829	4 974	1 778	5 529	3 219	1 038	1 671
1997	205 561	...	16 585	22 061	128 276	14 582	1 717	4 667	1 708	5 459	2 996	960	1 605
1996	196 011	33.6	10 574	21 356	121 015	13 962	1 604	4 322	1 663	5 362	2 896	901	1 562
1995	183 045	35.0	17 133	21 178	108 652	13 470	1 506	4 112	1 626	5 388	2 848	827	1 528
1994	168 586	36.1	16 432	20 261	97 131	12 840	1 431	3 904	1 589	5 305	2 900	762	1 493
1993	165 188	36.3	16 532	20 844	94 591	12 133	1 374	3 654	1 509	5 289	2 839	737	1 418
1992	166 697	36.2	15 690	24 660	96 654	11 090	1 291	5 018	1 395	5 249	3 550	750	1 350
1991	160 096	37.7	15 238	26 372	90 580	10 230	1 205	4 835	1 307	5 079	3 300	700	1 250
1990	145 450	44.0	16 100	31 200	73 000	9 250	1 100	4 450	1 200	4 800	2 850	600	1 100
1989	140 486	44.6	15 121	31 366	70 233	8 972	984	3 948	1 083	4 729	2 500	550	1 000
1988	133 741	46.0	14 281	32 306	65 583	8 181	870	3 473	941	4 531	2 200	500	875
1987	125 352	46.2	13 413	30 752	61 403	7 333	789	3 200	831	4 206	2 200	450	775
1986	119 529	45.4	13 535	27 891	59 932	6 702	699	2 790	735	3 895	2 250	425	675
1985	113 818	45.8	12 945	27 196	57 043	6 056	559	2 376	695	3 523	2 400	375	650
1984	101 139	45.1	11 572	23 396	51 404	5 423	475	2 104	615	3 150	2 100	325	570
1983	89 139	45.8	10 582	20 680	44 588	4 983	388	1 929	577	2 737	1 850	275	550
1982	80 317	46.1	9 141	19 059	39 952	4 749	326	1 683	503	2 479	1 625	250	550
1981	71 912	46.4	8 425	16 382	35 476	4 559	288	1 523	448	2 486	1 550	225	550
1980	62 610	47.1	7 632	14 029	30 476	4 104	236	1 334	403	2 246	1 450	200	500
1979	54 933	48.8	7 417	12 518	25 708	3 595	193	1 200	373	1 935	1 350	180	464
1978	48 129	49.6	6 811	11 189	22 115	3 059	170	1 037	359	1 717	1 100	165	407
1977	42 783	50.5	6 012	10 485	19 340	2 726	139	888	314	1 384	987	150	358
1976	38 581	50.6	5 710	9 285	17 392	2 501	123	815	285	1 147	925	120	278
1975	35 196	51.6	5 397	8 605	15 559	2 291	113	743	258	987	875	115	253
1974	32 677	51.2	4 815	8 199	14 617	2 032	96	671	218	865	822	111	231
1973	30 581	53.3	4 619	8 131	13 068	2 041	86	613	200	817	690	105	211
1972	28 296	55.5	4 482	8 010	11 512	1 839	75	576	186	764	653	101	198
1971	27 336	54.9	4 156	7 685	10 647	1 724	70	1 099	177	716	732	100	230
1970	26 545	55.6	3 853	7 779	10 283	1 648	61	961	166	737	748	90	220
1969	26 169	57.0	3 501	8 451	9 867	1 595	60	895	145	725	640	81	209
1968	25 119	59.5	3 493	8 560	8 869	1 572	55	841	131	719	608	73	198
1967	23 613	61.1	3 396	8 365	8 020	1 409	48	753	119	673	577	66	187
1966	22 264	62.8	3 220	8 332	7 216	1 262	42	673	108	630	546	59	176
1965	20 439	63.8	3 093	7 740	6 445	1 073	41	615	93	629	498	53	159
1964	19 214	65.3	2 838	7 720	5 792	916	41	555	83	629	450	47	143
1963	17 371	64.6	2 279	7 270	5 360	760	41	485	73	530	380	48	145
1962	15 665	63.4	2 098	6 435	5 029	613	40	424	66	470	310	45	135
1961	14 552	63.7	1 874	6 240	4 668	500	40	371	58	410	240	41	110
1960	13 730	63.7	1 726	6 081	4 428	405	40	328	52	360	180	40	90
1959	12 540	64.3	1 640	5 635	3 983	306	39	290	47	338	140	35	87
1958	10 870	62.5	1 374	4 759	3 630	254	39	257	42	293	111	31	80
1957	9 912	61.7	1 220	4 335	3 396	229	34	230	38	240	95	30	65
1956	8 483	57.3	1 040	3 328	3 277	213	29	204	34	194	84	30	50
1955	6 279	55.9	905	2 180	2 460	169	25	185	30	180	75	28	42
1954	5 738	54.7	1 020	1 750	2 320	160	22	167	28	141	67	25	38
1953 [4]	5 207	53.0	1 010	1 430	2 200	138	19	151	26	121	60	20	32

1. Includes state and local government funds received by these institutions and used for research and development.
2. Federally Funded Research and Development Centers administered by individual universities and colleges and by university consortia.
3. Includes estimates for independent nonprofit hospitals and voluntary health agencies.
4. Calendar year data for industry and nonprofit institutions combined with federal and university data for fiscal year 1953 (July 1952-June 1953).

Series WW 1. Worldwide Successful Space Launches: 1957 to 1998
(Criterion of success is attainment of earth orbit or earth escape)

Country	Total, 1957-98	1957-64	1965-69	1970-74	1975-79	1980-84	1985-89	1990-94	1995	1996	1997	1998
Total	3 969	289	586	555	607	605	550	466	75	73	86	77
Soviet Union/CIS [1]	2 572	82	302	405	461	483	447	283	32	25	28	24
United States	1 158	207	279	139	126	93	61	122	27	33	37	34
Japan	54	—	—	5	10	12	11	9	2	1	2	2
ESA [2]	107	—	—	—	1	8	21	33	11	10	12	11
China	55	—	—	2	6	6	9	15	2	3	6	6
France	10	—	4	3	3	—	—	—	—	—	—	—
India	8	—	—	—	—	3	—	3	—	1	1	—
Israel	3	—	—	—	—	—	1	1	1	—	—	—
Australia	1	—	1	—	—	—	—	—	—	—	—	—
United Kingdom	1	—	—	1	—	—	—	—	—	—	—	—

— Represents zero.
1. Commonwealth of Independent States.
2. European Space Agency. Includes launches by Arianespace.

SOURCE: Library of Congress, Congressional Research Service, Science Policy Research Division, Space Activities of the United States, CIS, and Other Launching Countries/Organizations 1957-1994, July 31, 1995; and forthcoming report.

Series WW 2. Federal Outlays for General Science, Space, and Other Technology: 1970 to 2004
(In billions of dollars, [4.5 represents $4 500 000 000]. For fiscal years ending in year shown; see text, Section 9, State and Local Governments)

Year	Current dollars			Constant (1992) dollars		
	Total	General science/basic research	Space and other technologies	Total	General science/basic research	Space and other technologies
1970	4.5	0.9	3.6	16.0	3.4	12.6
1975	4.0	1.0	3.0	10.0	2.6	7.4
1980	5.8	1.4	4.5	10.0	2.4	7.6
1982	7.2	1.6	5.6	10.4	2.3	8.1
1983	7.9	1.6	6.3	10.9	2.3	8.6
1984	8.3	1.8	6.5	11.0	2.4	8.6
1985	8.6	2.0	6.6	11.1	2.6	8.5
1986	9.0	2.2	6.8	11.2	2.8	8.5
1987	9.2	2.2	7.0	11.2	2.7	8.4
1988	10.8	2.4	8.4	12.6	2.8	9.8
1989	12.8	2.6	10.2	14.4	2.9	11.4
1990	14.4	2.8	11.6	15.6	3.1	12.6
1991	16.1	3.1	13.0	16.5	3.2	13.3
1992	16.4	3.5	12.8	16.4	3.5	12.8
1993	17.0	3.9	13.1	16.4	3.8	12.6
1994	16.2	3.8	12.4	15.1	3.6	11.5
1995	16.7	4.1	12.6	15.2	3.7	11.5
1996	16.7	4.0	12.7	14.8	3.5	11.2
1997	17.1	4.1	13.1	15.0	3.6	11.4
1998	18.2	5.3	12.9	15.4	4.5	10.9
1999, est.	18.5	5.7	12.8	15.5	4.8	10.8
2000, est.	18.5	6.2	12.3	15.3	5.2	10.1
2001, est.	18.9	6.5	12.4	15.5	5.4	10.1
2002, est.	19.1	6.7	12.4	15.5	5.4	10.1
2003, est.	19.3	6.7	12.5	15.3	5.3	9.9
2004, est.	19.3	6.7	12.6	14.9	5.2	9.7

SOURCE: U.S. Office of Management and Budget, Budget of the United States, Historical Tables, Fiscal Year 2000, annual.

Series WW 3.   R&D Expenditures: 1960 to 1998

(In millions of dollars, (13 669 represents $13 669 000 000) except as indicated. For calendar years)

Year	Total	Sources of funds					Objective (percent of total)			Character of work		
		Federal Government	Industry	Universities/ colleges	Nonprofit	Non-Federal Government [1]	Defense related [2]	Space related [3]	Other	Basic research	Applied research	Development
1960	13 669	8 879	4 516	66	122	88	53	3	44	1 256	3 059	9 355
1961	14 514	9 441	4 757	72	146	98	50	6	44	1 476	3 115	9 924
1962	15 577	10 086	5 123	82	177	109	49	7	44	1 780	3 688	10 110
1963	17 446	11 582	5 456	93	195	122	42	14	45	2 060	3 855	11 531
1964	19 053	12 726	5 887	108	198	135	37	19	44	2 358	4 189	12 507
1965	20 192	13 147	6 548	130	221	146	33	21	46	2 618	4 361	13 214
1966	22 010	14 117	7 330	156	249	158	32	20	48	2 886	4 638	14 486
1967	23 279	14 511	8 144	190	267	166	35	14	50	3 113	4 838	15 328
1968	24 646	14 956	9 006	219	286	178	35	14	52	3 361	5 141	16 144
1969	25 965	15 213	10 010	228	311	203	35	11	54	3 471	5 448	17 046
1970	26 235	14 970	10 446	251	340	228	33	10	56	3 567	5 742	16 926
1971	26 910	15 183	10 823	282	364	259	33	10	58	3 698	5 817	17 395
1972	28 661	15 976	11 713	308	389	276	33	8	59	3 829	6 098	18 734
1973	30 905	16 563	13 296	331	417	298	32	7	61	4 051	6 662	20 193
1974	33 238	17 193	14 882	380	470	314	29	7	64	4 439	7 312	21 488
1975	35 565	18 437	15 823	424	542	340	28	7	65	4 827	8 048	22 691
1976	39 314	20 179	17 698	463	608	367	27	8	65	5 291	8 964	25 059
1977	43 233	21 988	19 637	541	683	384	27	7	66	5 925	9 653	27 655
1978	48 582	24 279	22 456	651	768	429	26	6	68	6 841	10 695	31 047
1979	55 269	27 100	26 092	760	841	477	25	6	70	7 736	12 073	35 460
1980	63 076	29 857	30 926	877	911	505	24	5	70	8 651	13 724	40 701
1981	72 190	33 666	35 956	1 031	974	564	24	5	70	9 741	16 389	46 060
1982	80 633	37 113	40 705	1 159	1 037	619	26	5	69	10 658	18 261	51 714
1983	89 742	41 362	45 274	1 329	1 135	642	28	4	68	11 859	20 323	57 560
1984	101 940	46 319	52 225	1 463	1 228	706	29	3	68	13 176	22 481	66 284
1985	114 344	52 493	58 013	1 680	1 365	793	30	3	67	14 510	25 389	74 444
1986	119 907	54 475	61 079	1 944	1 466	942	32	3	65	16 885	27 225	75 796
1987	125 841	58 254	62 669	2 215	1 658	1 044	32	3	65	18 213	27 819	79 809
1988	133 463	59 930	68 076	2 441	1 880	1 135	30	3	66	19 381	29 466	84 614
1989	141 550	60 301	75 091	2 774	2 136	1 248	28	4	68	21 477	32 304	87 767
1990	151 655	61 456	83 374	3 096	2 367	1 361	25	4	70	22 556	34 981	94 118
1991	160 521	60 564	92 484	3 411	2 585	1 477	23	5	73	26 630	38 699	95 193
1992	164 933	60 694	96 404	3 558	2 770	1 507	22	4	74	27 044	37 996	99 894
1993	165 188	60 351	96 702	3 654	2 928	1 554	22	4	74	28 115	37 325	99 749
1994	168 586	60 700	99 324	3 904	3 081	1 576	20	4	76	28 917	36 643	103 024
1995	183 045	63 102	110 985	4 112	3 154	1 692	19	5	77	28 756	40 973	113 316
1996	196 011	63 215	123 520	4 322	3 225	1 730	18	4	78	31 545	43 057	121 410
1997, prel.	205 561	64 865	130 952	4 667	3 314	1 764	17	4	79	32 978	45 982	126 601
1998, prel.	220 617	66 636	143 714	4 974	3 449	1 845	16	4	80	34 426	49 753	136 438

1. Non-Federal R&D expenditures to university and college performers.
2. R&D spending by the Department of Defense, including space activities, and a portion of the Department of Energy funds.
3. For the National Aeronautics and Space Administration only.

SOURCE: U.S. National Science Foundation, National Patterns of R&D Resources, annual.

Series WW 4. Nobel Prize Laureates in Selected Sciences: 1901 to 1997

(Presented by location of award-winning research and by date of award)

Country	1901-1997				1901-1930	1931-1945	1946-1960	1961-1975	1976-1990	1991-1996	1997
	Total	Physics	Chemistry	Physiology/ Medicine							
Total	448	154	129	165	93	49	74	92	98	35	7
United States	190	67	44	79	6	14	38	41	63	24	4
United Kingdom	71	21	26	24	15	11	14	20	9	1	1
Germany [1]	61	17	29	15	27	11	4	8	7	3	—
France	25	11	7	7	13	2	—	5	2	2	1
Soviet Union.......................	10	7	1	2	2	—	4	3	1	—	—
Japan	4	3	1	—	—	—	1	2	1	—	—
Other countries	87	28	21	38	30	11	13	13	15	5	1

— Represents zero.
1. Between 1946 and 1991, data are for the former West Germany only.

SOURCE: U.S. National Science Foundation, unpublished data.

SECTION X

FINANCIAL MARKETS AND INSTITUTIONS

FINANCIAL MARKETS AND INSTITUTIONS
Highlights

1 Financial markets and institutions not only influence but also drive the U.S. economy. Financial data summarize the types of claims, liabilities, and assets, and also illustrate how lending and borrowing are related to income and expenditure flows. They are derived from banking statistics, Treasury accounts, census data, tax returns, balance of payments and security market reports. The data present a picture of the distribution of wealth ownership and of the major components of national wealth. Financial data also provide information on the structure of debt—who owes what to whom—which has a bearing on corporate and private spending decisions. Other types of data cover savings, investments, money supplies, U.S. government securities, bonds and mortgages and corporate equities.

2 Money supply, broadly defined, includes both bank deposits and currency. Prior to 1934, gold was also a part of means of payments, but in January of that year it was withdrawn from circulation. Until 1971, gold served as a means of settlement of international accounts and until 1968 as domestic reserve money. At present gold is held solely by the Treasury Department. Private gold holdings are forbidden except in limited amounts for licensed purposes. U. S. residents may purchase, hold, or sell foreign and domestic gold coins minted before April 5, 1933 but those minted after that date may be held only by collectors. From 1873 to 1907, gold coins in circulation in the United States were included in the estimates of the Annual Report of the Director of the Mint. In 1934, gold coins worth $287 million were still in circulation, but they disappeared from circulation immediately after the U. S. dollar was taken off the gold standard. Following the enactment of the Old Series Currency Adjustment Act of 1961, both gold and silver certificates were retired.

3 The chief money market in the country is New York City. The New York money market comprises a number of markets with differences in rates corresponding to differences in the supply of funds relative to demand. These markets are called "open" markets because transactions on them are usually made on an impersonal basis with the borrower and lender dealing through agents. In contrast, in a "customer" market, borrower and lender deal directly with each other, and transactions are often made on a personal basis.

4 Although investment companies date back to the 19th century. they became popular only after the rise of mutual funds. A mutual fund is a company that combines the funds of many investors whose investment goals are similar, and which invests those funds in a wide variety of securities. Different mutual funds have different investment objectives, management policies, and degrees of risk. Some emphasize capital growth, others, current income; still others are highly speculative. Mutual funds are technically known as open-end investment companies because they are always ready to redeem outstanding shares at the request of the investor. They are regulated by both federal and state governments. The major federal statues governing them are the Securities Act of 1933, the Securities Exchange Act of 1934, and the Investment Company Act of 1940.

5 The banking system of the United States has evolved over two centuries. Banks are in part regulated by state governments and part by the federal government. Supervision and regulation of banks are the primary responsibility of the chartering authorities—the Comptroller of Currency in the case of national banks organized under the Federal law of 1863 and state officials in the case of state banks. Two other federal entities with additional supervisory authority have been superimposed on the banking system: the Federal Reserve System, which was established in 1914 to exercise central banking functions, and the Federal Deposit Insurance Corporation created in 1933 to insure bank deposits. The Federal Reserve System includes all national banks and those state banks that choose to join voluntarily. Insurance of bank deposits is obligatory for all banks belonging to the Federal Reserve System and optional for others. Prior to the National Banking Act of 1863, the only official banking statistics were compiled by the Treasury Department and were based on reports submitted voluntarily by the banks. No data on state banks were included in these reports, but the Act of 1873 authorized the Comptroller to obtain data about nonnational banks from state authorities.

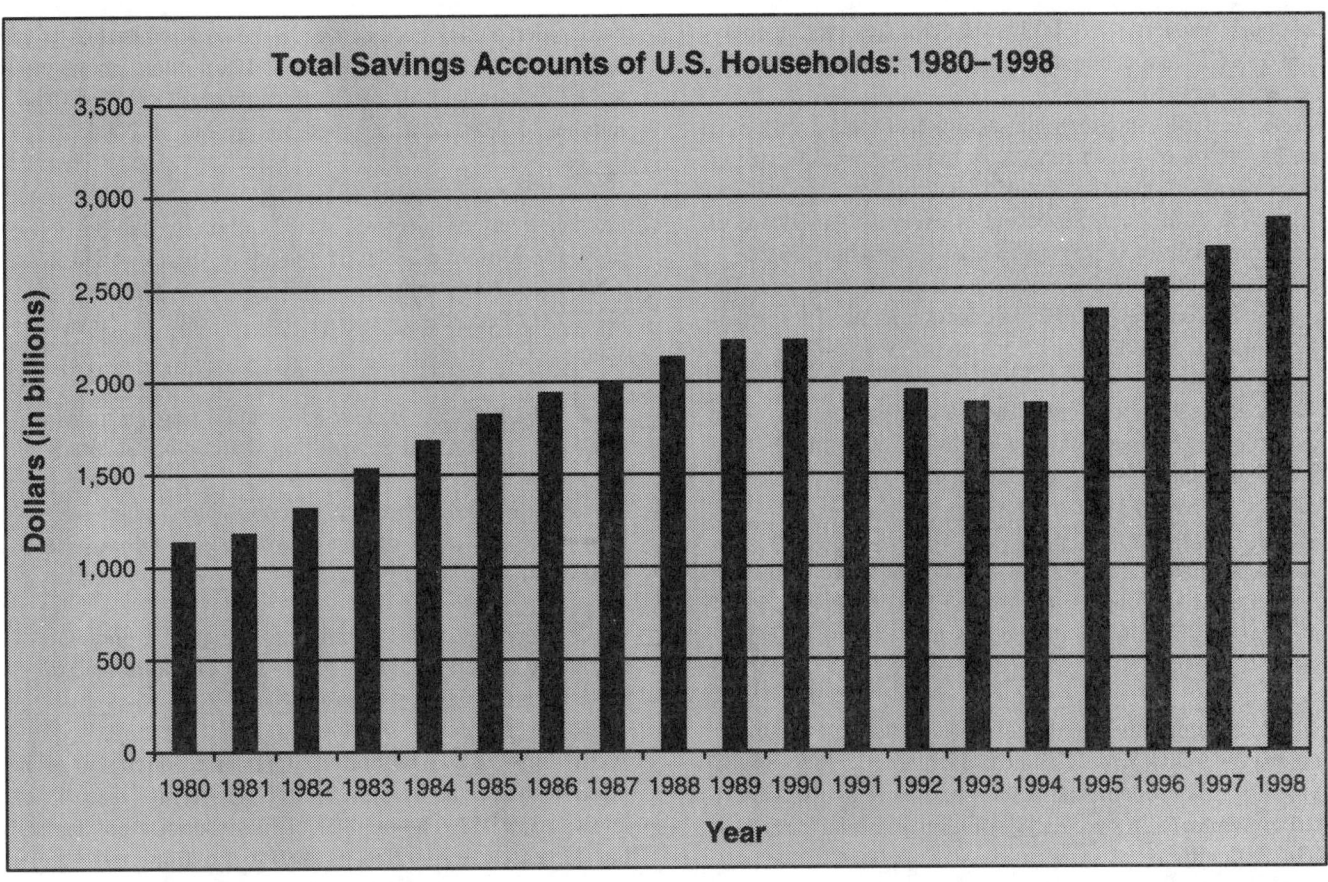

Total Savings Accounts of U.S. Households: 1980–1998

Although coverage was improved, it was far from complete because many banks operated outside the state system, and some states had no departments to collect the information. Efforts to promote uniformity in bank statistics culminated in 1947 when a standardized balance-sheet form was approved and adopted by the federal and state banking agencies. To provide more adequate historical banking statistics comparable to those available beginning 1947, a revised retrospective series was published in 1959 under the title All-Bank Statistics 1896-1955. This series covered number of banks, principal assets and liabilities for major classes of banks, and data for individual states and outlying territories.

6 The first bank chartered by Congress was the Bank of North America in Philadelphia founded in 1781. The Bank of the United States was sponsored by the Federalist Party and chartered in 1791 in Philadelphia. Secretary of the Treasury, Alexander Hamilton, used it as a fiscal agent—a depository bank for government funds. Its charter expired in 1811 and was not renewed by Congress. The Second Bank of the United States was authorized in 1816 and opened in 1817. Its 20-year charter was not renewed either. It failed in 1841 and was liquidated in 1856.

7 There are three sources of primary data about life insurance: Reports of the state insurance departments; commercial publishers, such as A. M. Best Company; and trade associations, such as the American Life Insurance Association.

8 The first life insurance company was the Corporation for the Relief of Poor and Distressed Presbyterian Ministers and of the Poor and Distressed Widows and Children of Presbyterian Ministers, incorporated in 1859 in Philadelphia. The first health insurance company was the Massachusetts Health Insurance Company of Boston, founded in 1847. The first accident insurance company was Travelers Insurance Company of Hartford, chartered in 1863. It issued the first automobile insurance policy in 1898 to Dr. Truman J. Martin of Buffalo—the one-year premium was $11.25. The first fire insurance company to receive a charter was the Philadelphia Contributorship for the Insurance of Houses from Loss by Fire in 1868.

9 Savings institutions are primarily involved in credit extension in the form of mortgage loans. Statistics on savings institutions are collected by the U.S. Office of Thrift Supervision. The Financial Institutions Reform, Recovery and Enforcement Act of 1989 authorized the establishment of the Resolution Trust Corporation (RTC), which is responsible for the disposal of assets from failed savings institutions.

10 In 1997 the Finance, Insurance and Real Estate (FIRE) sector contributed 19% to the GDP, or $1.448 trillion. Of the total 650,100 institutions in this sector, 67,400 were commercial banks, 16,100 savings institutions, 19,000 personal credit institutions, 21,900 mortgage brokers, 45,600 securities and commodities dealers, 41,800 life insurance carriers, 127,300 insurance brokers and agents and 252,600 real estate agents and operators.

11 In 1998 American households had total liabilities of $6.25 trillion of which mortgages made up $4.106 trillion and consumer credit $1.334 trillion. Home mortgages made up 65.7% of all debt. Seven out of every 10 Americans carried some debt of which 39.1% had a mortgage, 46.2% installment debt, 43.8% credit card debt. Of total debt 7% was in car loans and 2.6% in education loans. The median ratio of debt to family income was 16.3% in 1995.

12 Reflecting the general health of the economy, delinquency rates on loans have fallen from 5.98% in 1990 to 2.21% in 1998. The highest delinquency rate is for credit cards at 4.76% in 1998.

13 Foreign banks have increased their share of the U.S. financial market since 1980 from 11.9% of assets to 21.2% in 1997 and from 6.6% of deposits in 1980 to 17.6% in 1997.

14 Although the number of federal and state credit unions has fallen from 17,350 in 1980 to 10,995 in 1998, they have more members in 1998 and more assets. Credit union membership was 73.539 million and total assets $388.691 billion.

15 The number of credit cards in use 1.499 billion held by 157 million cardholders, or an average of nine cards per cardholder. Retail store cards are the most numerous at 652 million followed by bank cards at 458 million, phone cards at 183 million and oil company cards at 105 million. The number of debit cards reached 353 million in 2000.

16 The total volume of trading on the New York Stock Exchange has risen from $11.562 billion in 1980 to $171.188 billion in 1998. The value of shares traded in 1998 was $7.395 trillion. The volume of trading in NASDAQ Securities was $202 billion, and the value of shares $5.759 trillion.

17 In 1998 there were 7,314 mutual funds with assets of $5.525 trillion and 206 million shareholder accounts.

18 Individual Retirement Account (IRA) plans had a total value of $1.347 trillion of which $483 billion was held by mutual funds.

19 New Jersey has the highest automobile premium of any state, $1,126 annually. The lowest premium paid is $436 annually in North Dakota.

20 In 1997 373 million life insurance policies were in effect with a value of $13.196 trillion. Average size of policy was $56,044. The number of life insurance companies has decreased from 1,928 in 1980 to 1,620 in 1997.

Series X 114-147. Financial Assets and Liabilities of Households, Personal Trusts, and Nonprofit Organizations: 1945 to 1998

(In billions of dollars)

		Financial assets									
		Deposits			Credit market instruments						
						U.S. government securities					
Year	Total[1]	Total	Demand deposits and currency	Total savings accounts	Total	Total	Agency issues	Savings bonds	Corporate and foreign bonds	Mortgages	Total corporate equities
	114	115	116	117	120	121	124	125	128	129	130
1998	30 121	4 089	424	2 882	1 738	650	340	187	475	102	6 280
1997	27 020	3 790	423	2 725	1 795	749	367	187	461	105	5 333
1996	23 908	3 538	438	2 556	1 969	911	344	187	463	108	4 528
1995	21 751	3 365	505	2 388	1 938	859	265	185	461	111	3 995
1994	17 997	3 104	722	1 883	1 932	1 084	407	180	198	187	2 913
1993	17 538	3 060	713	1 888	1 526	702	199	172	142	177	3 088
1992	16 465	3 080	635	1 957	1 523	699	237	157	107	166	2 810
1991	15 584	3 109	511	2 021	1 447	600	194	138	105	162	2 469
1990	13 969	3 253	516	2 227	2 004	822	330	126	195	226	2 008
1989	13 806	3 200	497	2 226	1 738	739	308	118	65	213	2 205
1988	12 222	3 051	479	2 137	1 517	622	212	110	52	182	1 877
1987	11 235	2 864	480	2 005	1 297	492	136	101	91	165	1 751
1986	11 063	2 719	507	1 946	1 086	552	66	93	96	147	1 845
1985	9 707	2 484	381	1 830	1 027	448	91	80	19	127	1 700
1984	9 118	2 332	368	1 686	917	495	52	75	48	151	1 321
1983	8 429	2 051	355.7	1 537.6	739.4	328	59.5	71.5	45.8	183.8	1 466.2
1982	7 641	1 871	315.9	1 323.8	662.3	277.3	51.1	68.3	45.7	191.7	1 274.8
1981	7 030	1 709	299.4	1 187.1	603.7	264.8	56.5	68.2	50.4	171.2	1 134.3
1980	6 607	1 517	260.0	1 141.0	523.0	241.0	47.0	73.0	31.0	107.0	1 111.0
1979	5 746	1 360	228.4	1 181.1	552.5	243.0	53.6	79.9	71.6	123.0	906.9
1978	5 007	1 244	218.9	1 103.9	473.1	172.9	33.3	80.7	63.2	106.0	791.9
1977	4 472	1 125	192.0	992.4	385.6	146.8	29.8	76.8	65.3	91.4	634.6
1976	4 206	1 011	174.8	884.2	365.1	141.2	24.4	72.0	65.2	79.8	708.9
1975	3 713	901	170.4	719.6	354.7	138.7	12.5	67.4	60.9	76.2	646.9
1974	3 252	822	173.9	694.7	278.5	118.2	30.5	62.9	53.8	38.9	525.2
1973	3 282	761	170.2	635.6	256.4	105.3	21.1	50.8	56.8	38.1	744.4
1972	3 274	691	554.1	554.1	. . .	. . .	. . .	. . .	. . .	. . .	. . .
1971	2 859	609	135.1	471.4	218.5	89.0	. . .	53.9	47.5	43.8	. . .
1970	2 567	532	126.5	422.4	236.1	100.4	17.4	51.4	39.8	42.5	763.1
1969	2 472	484	120.4	377.8	225.7	104.8	14.8	51.1	27.4	40.2	775.5
1968	2 506	479	116.7	371.8	192.9	92.7	10.5	51.5	21.7	38.4	874.4
1967	2 240	440	104.1	341.5	180.0	88.2	9.0	51.1	16.8	36.6	754.6
1966	1 989	394	92.9	306.8	179.9	89.0	7.9	50.2	12.8	35.7	595.5
1965	1 965	373	90.3	287.5	162.8	80.7	4.0	49.6	11.3	34.3	667.9
1964	1 798	339	82.5	259.5	158.7	79.0	3.8	49.0	10.0	35.1	588.7
1963	1 645	311	77.9	232.1	154.0	77.0	3.3	48.0	9.5	34.8	514.9
1962	1 547	280	74.1	207.5	148.5	73.0	2.9	46.9	9.7	34.5	437.8
1961	1 504	254	72.5	181.8	149.0	72.7	2.6	46.4	10.3	33.5	501.6
1960	1 359	238	70.2	165.3	146.0	73.5	2.7	45.6	9.8	31.8	396.1
1959	1 310	224	69.9	153.8	140.3	73.3	3.0	45.9	9.4	29.9	402.7
1958	1 230	210	68.0	142.1	130.0	67.8	1.5	47.7	9.5	28.1	374.0
1957	1 099	194	65.6	128.0	128.6	70.7	1.9	48.2	8.5	25.8	267.7
1956	1 088	183	66.9	115.9	123.5	70.4	1.2	50.1	7.4	23.9	305.4
1955	1 019	172	65.3	106.3	117.6	69.2	.9	50.2	6.6	22.4	286.7
1954	931	163	64.5	97.5	109.4	66.6	.3	50.0	5.5	21.2	235.0
1953	852	152	62.9	88.3	107.8	68.6	.4	49.4	5.6	20.0	162.4
1952	834	143	61.8	80.0	104.6	68.3	.3	49.2	5.7	19.0	170.4
1951	805	133	59.7	72.2	102.7	68.1	.2	49.1	6.0	18.3	156.4
1950	738	124	56.5	67.3	101.3	69.1	.2	49.6	4.9	17.4	133.7
1949	688	119	54.3	64.8	103.3	69.6	.1	49.3	7.5	16.7	109.5
1948	666	119	56.2	62.1	101.0	68.6	.2	47.8	7.7	15.9	100.2
1947	642	119	58.9	59.9	99.1	68.2	.1	46.2	8.1	14.8	101.3
1946	602	116	60.3	56.4	96.7	67.1	(Z)	44.2	8.7	13.5	103.5
1945	562	114	56.4	50.1	97.2	68.3	-.1	42.9	9.6	12.0	111.6

See footnote at end of table.

Series X 114-147. Financial Assets and Liabilities of Households, Personal Trusts, and Nonprofit Organizations: 1945 to 1998—Cont'd.

(In billions of dollars)

	Financial assets (continued)				Liabilities							
						Credit market instruments						
Year	Life insurance reserves	Pension fund reserves	Security credit	Miscellaneous	Total	Total	Home mortgages	Installment consumer credit	Other consumer credit	Bank loans	Security credit	Trade credit
	133	134	135	136	137	138	139	141	142	143	145	146
1998	707	8 770	274	322	6 250	5 958	4 106	1 334	...	67	152	121
1997	665	7 981	215	312	5 739	5 472	3 737	1 264	...	57	131	117
1996	611	6 568	163	301	5 357	5 135	3 498	1 212	...	48	94	109
1995	566	5 821	128	292	5 004	4 804	3 275	1 123	...	55	79	103
1994	488	5 061	108	281	4 821	4 641	3 156	984	...	36	73	89
1993	468	4 975	103	264	4 464	4 292	2 970	867	...	20	76	80
1992	433	4 516	76	251	4 143	4 002	2 788	803	...	11	53	72
1991	406	4 138	87	234	3 920	3 785	2 614	797	...	9	55	64
1990	377	2 963	62	217	4 008	3 898	2 848	748	61	43	39	55
1989	352	2 848	53	202	3 609	3 502	2 473	731	64	52	43	49
1988	326	2 451	41	188	3 292	3 189	2 228	675	69	40	44	44
1987	300	2 182	39	171	2 972	2 875	1 970	620	74	42	42	40
1986	274	2 054	39	166	2 739	2 635	1 693	586	137	52	60	31
1985	257	1 795	35	133	2 395	2 296	1 484	527	75	44	51	34
1984	246	1 513	18	117	2 150	2 074	1 344	453	109	37	35	26
1983	240.8	1 321.7	19.3	92.5	1 975.7	1 887.5	1 239.0	396.1	96.9	38.4	48.1	24.0
1982	232.8	1 122.7	16.0	85.3	1 778.7	1 712.1	1 133.3	355.8	85.9	34.4	28.8	22.2
1981	225.6	941.2	12.7	78.5	1 679.3	1 619.2	1 084.8	335.7	80.7	31.2	25.6	19.8
1980	216.0	916.0	16.0	74.0	1 485.0	1 430.0	974.0	302.0	53.0	30.0	25.0	17.0
1979	210.7	622.1	11.3	40.6	1 375.8	1 326.9	875.9	311.3	70.9	23.2	22.9	14.6
1978	188.6	530.1	8.8	59.0	1 209.7	1 164.3	762.3	275.6	64.3	22.7	22.2	9.1
1977	180.8	477.7	7.1	50.3	1 026.1	985.5	653.9	216.6	43.3	36.2	20.5	11.8
1976	172.1	431.8	6.3	44.9	890.4	854.5	566.1	185.5	38.7	30.9	17.2	10.5
1975	166.5	405.6	4.5	40.6	808.0	778.8	507.7	172.3	50.9	13.7	12.1	9.4
1974	157.5	313.7	4.6	35.1	702.2	677.4	411.2	156.1	34.0	21.2	10.7	7.3
1973	150.3	307.8	4.8	32.8	661.1	634.8	379.0	147.4	33.0	24.7	13.1	6.8
1972	143.9	...	5.0	31.3	587.4	560.2	348.2	...	...	...	...	...
1971	134.8	256.2	4.9	28.7	523.8	500.4	316.4	137.2	...	24.4	17.9	...
1970	130.3	237.4	2.2	26.3	483.6	463.2	273.1	101.2	25.6	21.9	10.0	5.3
1969	125.0	216.8	2.6	23.8	461.9	440.6	260.4	98.2	24.3	20.4	11.9	4.7
1968	120.0	206.2	3.5	21.6	430.8	407.9	244.1	89.9	23.3	17.5	14.4	4.2
1967	115.4	185.2	2.7	19.8	395.8	375.8	229.4	80.9	21.2	14.4	12.3	3.7
1966	110.6	163.2	1.6	18.2	372.2	356.2	219.0	77.5	20.0	12.2	9.0	3.3
1965	105.9	153.7	1.7	17.0	349.4	333.8	206.4	71.3	19.0	11.9	9.2	3.0
1964	101.1	137.3	1.2	15.7	319.3	305.1	191.1	62.7	17.6	10.5	8.4	2.8
1963	96.6	122.8	1.2	14.8	291.2	277.2	175.1	55.5	16.3	9.1	8.6	2.5
1962	92.4	109.5	1.2	14.3	264.1	252.4	160.4	48.7	15.1	8.6	6.6	2.4
1961	88.6	103.5	1.2	13.8	243.1	231.6	147.7	43.9	14.1	8.1	6.7	2.2
1960	85.2	90.7	1.1	13.3	226.2	216.3	136.8	43.0	13.2	7.2	5.4	2.1
1959	82.0	82.1	1.0	12.8	208.4	198.6	126.0	39.2	12.3	6.7	5.5	2.1
1958	78.5	72.4	1.2	12.3	186.4	177.2	113.4	33.6	11.5	5.7	5.5	1.8
1957	75.5	62.6	.9	12.0	174.0	166.1	104.6	33.9	11.1	5.0	4.4	1.6
1956	72.7	56.6	.9	11.7	161.2	153.2	95.8	31.7	10.6	4.8	4.8	1.5
1955	69.3	50.4	.9	11.4	144.8	137.1	84.6	28.9	9.9	4.4	4.8	1.4
1954	66.3	42.6	1.0	10.9	124.1	117.4	72.4	23.6	8.9	4.1	4.1	1.3
1953	63.6	37.4	.7	10.6	111.8	106.3	63.8	23.0	8.4	3.7	3.0	1.2
1952	60.7	32.4	.7	10.0	98.7	93.8	56.1	19.4	8.1	3.5	2.6	1.1
1951	57.8	27.5	.8	9.3	87.1	82.7	49.7	15.3	7.4	4.3	2.4	.9
1950	55.0	24.0	.9	8.7	77.4	73.0	42.6	14.7	6.8	3.8	2.5	.9
1949	52.1	20.1	.6	8.4	63.2	59.7	35.2	11.6	5.8	2.7	1.8	.8
1948	49.4	17.2	.6	8.0	54.9	51.8	31.1	9.0	5.5	2.5	1.5	.7
1947	46.5	14.8	.6	7.6	46.3	43.1	26.1	6.7	4.9	2.3	1.8	.7
1946	43.4	12.5	.7	7.1	38.7	35.2	21.8	4.2	4.2	2.3	2.2	.6
1945	39.6	11.0	.6	6.3	34.1	28.1	18.0	2.5	3.2	1.8	4.9	.5

Z Less than $50 million or less than -$50 million.

1. Includes the following major categories not shown separately: equity in noncorporate business ($4.415 billion in 1998); investment in bank personal trust ($1.001 billion in 1998); money market fund shares, a component of deposits ($726 billion in 1998).

Series X 410-419. Money Stock—Currency, Deposits, Bank Vault Cash and Gold: 1867 to 1998

(In billions of dollars. December data)

Year	Currency held by the public 410	Demand deposits adjusted, commercial 412	M₁ Money supply[1] 414	M₂ Money supply (M₁ plus time[2] deposits) 415	Year	Currency held by the public 410	Demand deposits adjusted, commercial banks 412	M₁ Money supply[1] 414	M₂ Money supply (M plus time[2] deposits) 415
1998	459	377	1 097	4 381	1938	5.55	24.97	30.52	58.0
1997	424	396	1 074	4 029	1937	5.59	25.32	30.91	55.4
1996	394	403	1 081	3 813	1936	5.23	24.32	29.55	56.3
1995	372	389	1 127	3 642	1935	4.80	21.08	25.88	51.2
1994	354	384	1 150	3 499	1934	4.63	17.23	21.86	46.0
1993	322	385	1 129	3 484	1933	5.09	14.82	19.91	41.5
1992	293	340	1 024	3 431	1932	4.92	16.19	21.11	44.8
1991	267	290	896	3 377	1931	4.16	19.98	24.14	48.0
1990	247	277	824	3 278	1930	3.73	22.03	25.76	53.7
1989	223	279	792	3 158	1929	3.90	22.74	26.64	54.9
1988	212	287	787	2 994	1928	3.89	22.49	26.38	55.5
1987	197	287	750	2 831	1927	3.98	22.12	26.10	53.4
1986	181	302	725	2 732	1926	4.00	22.18	26.18	50.9
1985	168	267	620	2 495	1925	3.96	21.70	25.66	50.4
1984	156	244	552	2 310	1924	3.96	19.71	23.67	47.0
1983	146	238	521	2 126	1923	3.96	18.97	22.93	43.6
1982	133	234	475	1 910	1922	3.69	17.98	21.67	41.8
1981	123	231	437	1 755	1921	4.04	17.47	21.51	37.6
1980	115	261	409	1 599	1920	4.48	19.25	23.73	40.0
1979	106	253	381	1 473	1919	4.02	17.77	21.79	38.6
1978	97	254	357	1 366	1918	2.76	16.20	18.96	33.6
1977	89	240	330	1 277	1917	2.17	14.91	17.08	30.2
1976	81	224	306	1 152	1916	2.17	12.53	14.70	26.9
1975	74	214	287	1 016	1915	1.93	10.55	12.48	23.0
1974	68	207	274	902	1914	1.91	...	...	20.2
1973	62	203	263	855	1913	1.89	...	...	19.6
1972	57	199	249	802	1912	1.82	...	...	19.0
1971	53	183	228	710	1911	1.76	...	...	18.0
1970	47.69	162.30	214.3	626.4	1910	1.74	...	...	16.8
1969	44.82	156.94	203.9	587.9	1909	1.71	...	...	16.2
1968	41.97	148.47	197.4	566.8	1908	1.76	...	...	15.0
1967	39.37	138.38	183.3	524.8	1907	1.72	...	...	14.0
1966	37.48	133.58	172.0	480.2	1906	1.63	...	...	13.8
1965	35.26	128.54	167.8	459.2	1905	1.50	...	...	12.8
1964	33.49	123.74	160.3	424.7	1904	1.44	...	...	11.6
1963	31.55	119.74	153.3	393.2	1903	1.42	...	...	11.0
1962	30.09	116.91	147.8	362.7	1902	1.34	...	...	10.4
1961	29.10	114.82	145.2	335.5	1901	1.27	...	...	9.6
1960	28.99	112.62	140.7	312.4	1900	1.21	...	...	8.5
1959	28.90	114.38	140.0	297.8	1899	1.10	...	...	8.0
1958	28.37	109.98	138.35	284.2	1898	1.00	...	...	7.0
1957	28.26	108.48	136.75	262.8	1897	.92	...	...	6.2
1956	27.98	108.05	136.02	251.6	1896	.89	...	...	6.0
1955	27.63	106.79	134.44	240.9	1895	.91	...	...	6.1
1954	27.52	102.75	130.27	229.4	1894	.93	...	...	5.8
1953	27.78	100.64	128.34	215.7	1893	1.00	...	...	5.7
1952	26.70	98.52	125.22	205.2	1892	.96	...	...	6.0
1951	25.53	93.67	119.23	192.5	1891	.96	...	...	5.4
1950	25.05	89.08	114.14	181.6	1890	.93	...	...	5.3
1949	25.50	85.67	111.16	173.9	1889	.87	...	...	4.8
1948	26.07	86.24	112.31	171.7	1888	.85	...	...	4.6
1947	26.58	85.22	111.79	168.5	1887	.83	...	...	4.5
1946	28.48	79.98	103.46	161.6	1886	.78	...	...	4.2
1945	25.33	73.91	99.23	150.9	1885	.80	...	...	3.9
1944	21.22	64.12	85.34	130.6	1884	.84	...	...	3.8
1943	16.35	55.89	72.24	112.5	1883	.87	...	...	3.8
1942	11.54	43.82	55.36	90.9	1882	.84	...	...	3.5
1941	8.40	38.12	46.52	75.9	1881	.78	...	...	3.1
1940	6.76	32.89	39.65	69.6					
1939	6.04	28.11	34.15	63.0					

Series X 410-419. Money Stock—Currency, Deposits, Bank Vault Cash and Gold: 1867 to 1998—Cont'd.

(In billions of dollars. December data)

Year	Currency held by the public	M_2 Money supply (M_1 plus time deposits)
	410	415
1880...........................	.67	2.7
1879...........................	.58	2.3
1878...........................	.54	2.4
1877...........................	.54	2.5
1876...........................	.53	2.5
1875...........................	.54	2.4
1874...........................	.54	2.3
1873...........................	.56	2.3
1872...........................	.55	2.2
1871...........................	.54	1.9
1870...........................	.54	1.7
1869...........................	.55	1.6
1868...........................	.54	1.5
1867...........................	.58	1.6

1. Currency, demand deposits, other checkable deposits, and travelers' checks.
2. Includes M_1 plus household savings and time deposits, and retail money market funds. Prior to 1948, it does not include deposits at savings and loan associations. From 1882 to 1906, M_2 shows June data; from 1867 to 1881, January or February data.
Source: Federal Reserve Board; St. Louis Federal Reserve Bank; and M. Friedman and A. Schwartz, A Monetary History of the United States.

Series X 444-455. Money Market Rates: 1890 to 1998

(Percent per annum. Open market rates in New York City)

Year	Prime commercial paper, 4 to 6 months [1]	Finance company paper, placed directly, 3- to 6-months [2]	Prime bankers' acceptances, 90 days [1]	U.S. government securities [3], 3-month bills [4], rate on new issues	Federal Reserve Bank of New York discount rate Low	High	Year	Prime commercial paper, 4 to 6 months [1]	Prime bankers' acceptances, 90 days [1]	U.S. government securities [3], 3-month bills [4], rate on new issues	Federal Reserve Bank of New York discount rate Low	High
	445	446	449	450	454	455		445	449	450	454	455
1998	8.35	...	5.39	4.81	4.50	5.00	1941	.53	.44	.103	1.00	1.00
1997	8.44	...	5.54	5.07	5.00	5.00	1940	.56	.44	.014	1.00	1.00
1996	8.27	...	5.31	5.02	5.00	5.25	1939	.59	.44	.023	1.00	1.00
1995	8.83	...	5.81	5.51	4.75	5.25						
1994	7.15	...	4.56	4.29	3.00	4.75	1938	.81	.44	.053	1.00	1.00
							1937	.94	.43	.447	1.00	1.50
1993	6.00	...	3.13	3.02	3.00	3.00	1936	.75	.15	.143	1.150	1.50
1992	6.25	...	3.62	3.45	3.00	3.50	1935	.75	.13	.137	1.50	1.50
1991	8.46	...	5.70	5.42	3.50	6.50	1934	1.02	.25	.256	1.50	2.00
1990	10.01	7.87	7.93	7.51	6.50	7.00						
1989	10.87	8.72	8.87	8.12	6.50	7.00	1933	1.73	.63	.252	2.00	3.50
							1932	2.73	1.28	.879	2.50	3.50
1988	9.32	7.38	7.56	6.68	6.00	6.50	1931	2.64	1.57	1.402	1.50	3.50
1987	8.21	6.54	6.75	5.82	5.50	6.00	1930	3.59	2.48	...	2.00	4.50
1986	8.33	6.38	6.38	5.98	5.50	7.50	1929	5.85	5.03	...	4.50	6.00
1985	9.93	7.77	7.91	7.48	7.50	8.00						
1984	12.04	9.73	10.17	9.58	8.00	9.00	1928	4.85	4.09	...	3.50	5.00
							1927	4.11	3.45	...	3.50	4.00
1983	10.79	8.70	8.91	8.63	8.50	8.50	1926	4.34	3.59	...	3.50	4.00
1982	14.85	11.23	11.89	10.69	8.50	12.00	1925	4.02	3.29	...	3.00	3.50
1981	18.87	14.08	15.34	14.03	12.00	14.00	1924	3.98	2.98	...	3.00	4.50
1980	15.26	11.49	12.67	11.51	10.00	13.00						
1979	12.67	10.47	11.04	10.04	10.50	12.00	1923	5.07	4.09	...	4.00	4.50
							1922	4.52	3.51	...	4.00	4.50
1978	9.06	7.80	8.11	7.22	10.00	12.00	1921	6.62	5.28	...	4.50	7.00
1977	6.83	5.49	5.60	5.27	7.00	9.50	1920	7.50	6.06	...	4.75	7.00
1976	6.84	5.20	5.19	4.99	5.75	6.00	1919	5.37	4.37	...	4.00	4.75
1975	7.86	6.15	6.29	5.84	6.25	7.25						
1974	10.81	8.65	9.89	7.89	7.75	8.00	1918	6.02	4.19	...	3.50	4.00
							1917	5.07	...	...	3.00	3.50
1973	8.15	7.40	8.08	7.04	5.00	8.50	1916	3.84	...	...	3.00	4.00
1972	4.69	4.52	4.47	4.07	...	...	1915	4.01	...	...	4.00	5.00
1971	5.11	4.91	4.85	4.34	4.25	5.25	1914	5.47	...	...	5.00	6.00
1970	7.72	7.23	7.31	6.458	5.50	6.00						
1969	7.83	7.16	7.61	6.677	5.50	6.00	1913	6.20	...	...	...	...
							1912	5.41	...	...	...	...
1968	5.90	5.69	5.75	5.339	4.50	5.50	1911	4.75	...	...	...	...
1967	5.10	4.89	4.75	4.321	4.00	4.50	1910	5.72	...	...	...	...
1966	5.55	5.42	5.36	4.881	4.50	4.50	1909	[6]4.67	...	...	...	...
1965	4.38	4.27	4.22	3.954	4.00	4.50						
1964	3.97	3.83	3.77	3.549	3.50	4.00	1908	[6] 5.00	...	...	...	...
							1907	[6] 6.66	...	...	...	...
1963	3.55	3.40	3.36	3.157	3.00	3.50	1906	6.25	...	...	...	...
1962	3.26	3.07	3.01	2.778	3.00	3.00	1905	5.18	...	...	...	...
1961	2.97	2.68	2.81	2.378	3.00	3.00	1904	5.14	...	...	...	...
1960	3.85	3.54	3.51	2.928	3.00	4.00						
1959	3.97	3.82	3.49	3.405	2.50	4.00	1903	6.16	...	...	...	...
							1902	5.81	...	...	...	...
1958	2.46	2.12	2.04	1.839	1.75	3.00	1901	5.40	...	...	...	...
1957	3.81	3.55	3.45	3.267	3.00	3.50	1900	5.71	...	...	...	...
1956	3.31	3.06	2.64	2.658	2.50	3.00	1899	5.50	...	...	...	...
1955	2.18	1.97	1.71	1.753	1.50	2.50						
1954	1.58	1.42	1.35	.953	1.50	2.00	1898	5.34	...	...	...	...
							1897	4.72	...	...	...	...
1953	2.52	2.33	1.87	1.931	1.75	2.00	1896	7.02	...	...	...	...
1952	2.33	2.16	1.75	1.766	1.75	1.75	1895	5.80	...	...	...	...
1951	2.16	1.87	1.60	1.552	1.75	1.75	1894	5.22	...	...	...	...
1950	1.45	1.41	1.15	1.218	1.50	1.75						
1949	1.49	1.46	1.13	1.102	1.50	1.50	1893	7.64	...	...	...	...
							1892	5.40	...	...	...	...
1948	1.44	1.34	1.11	1.040	1.00	1.50	1891	6.48	...	...	...	...
1947	1.03	.94	.87	.594	1.00	1.00	1890	6.91	...	...	...	...
1946	.81	...	.61	.375	[5] .50	1.00						
1945	.75	...	.44	.375	[5] .50	1.00						
1944	.73	...	.44	.375	[5] .50	1.00						
1943	.69	...	.44	.373	[5] .50	1.00						
1942	.66	...	.44	.326	[5] .50	1.00						

1. Averages of weekly prevailing rates through 1934; averages of the most representative daily offering rates quoted by dealers thereafter.
2. Averages of the most representative daily offering rates published by finance companies, for varying maturities in the 90-170 day range.
3. Yields are averages computed from daily closing bid prices.
4. Bills quoted on bank discount rate basis.
5. Preferential rate on advances secured by government securities.
6. Includes one or more interpolated items.

Series X 474-486. Bond and Stock Yields: 1900 to 1998
(Percent per annum)

	Bonds				Common stocks, Dividend-price ratio[1]		Bonds				Common stocks, Dividend-price ratio[1]
Year	U.S. government	Municipal high grade	Corporate Aaa (Moody's)	Preferred stocks		Year	U.S. government	Municipal high grade	Corporate Aaa (Moody's)	Preferred stocks	
	474	475	477	478	483		474	475	477	478	483
1998	5.69	5.12	6.53	...	1.49	1948	2.44	2.40	2.82	4.15	5.77
1997	6.67	5.55	7.27	...	1.77	1947	2.25	2.01	2.61	3.79	5.12
1996	6.80	5.76	7.37	...	2.19	1946	2.19	1.64	2.53	3.53	3.93
1995	6.93	5.95	7.59	...	2.56	1945	2.37	1.67	2.62	3.70	4.17
1994	7.41	6.18	7.97	...	2.82	1944	2.48	1.86	2.72	3.99	4.83
1993	6.45	5.63	7.22	...	2.78	1943	2.47	2.06	2.73	4.06	4.89
1992	7.52	6.41	8.14	...	2.99	1942	2.46	2.36	2.83	4.31	6.64
1991	8.16	6.89	8.77	...	3.24	1941	2.05	2.10	2.77	4.08	6.23
1990	8.74	7.25	9.32	8.96	3.61	1940	2.26	2.50	2.84	4.14	5.26
1989	8.58	7.24	9.26	9.04	3.45	1939	2.41	2.76	3.01	4.19	4.14
1988	8.98	7.74	9.71	9.23	3.64	1938	2.61	2.91	3.19	4.34	4.30
1987	8.64	7.73	9.38	8.37	3.08	1937	2.74	3.10	3.26	4.45	4.63
1986	8.14	7.38	9.02	8.76	3.48	1936	2.69	3.07	3.24	4.33	3.50
1985	10.75	9.18	11.37	10.49	4.25	1935	2.79	3.40	3.60	4.63	4.01
1984	11.99	10.15	12.71	11.59	4.64	1934	3.12	4.03	4.00	5.29	4.07
1983	10.84	9.47	12.04	11.02	4.40	1933	3.31	4.71	4.49	5.75	4.22
1982	12.23	11.57	13.79	12.53	5.81	1932	3.68	4.65	5.01	6.13	7.13
1981	12.87	11.23	14.17	12.36	5.20	1931	3.34	4.01	4.58	5.04	5.93
1980	10.81	8.51	11.94	10.60	5.26	1930	3.29	4.07	4.55	4.95	4.45
1979	8.74	6.39	9.63	9.11	5.47	1929	3.60	4.27	4.73	5.12	3.36
1978	7.89	5.90	8.73	8.25	5.28	1928	3.33	4.05	4.55	5.12	...
1977	7.06	5.56	8.02	7.61	4.62	1927	3.34	3.98	4.57	5.51	...
1976	6.78	6.49	8.43	7.98	3.77	1926	3.68	4.08	4.73	5.78	...
1975	6.98	6.89	8.83	8.36	4.31	1925	3.86	4.09	4.88	5.90	...
1974	6.98	6.09	8.57	8.24	4.47	1924	4.06	4.20	5.00	6.08	...
1973	6.30	5.18	7.44	7.23	3.06	1923	4.36	4.25	5.12	6.12	...
1972	5.63	5.27	7.01	6.89	2.84	1922	4.30	4.23	5.10	6.14	...
1971	5.74	5.70	7.12	6.75	3.14	1921	5.09	5.09	5.97	6.80	...
1970	6.59	6.51	8.04	7.22	3.97[1]	1920	5.32	4.98	6.12	6.79	...
1969	6.10	5.81	7.03	6.41	3.42	1919	4.73	4.46	5.49	6.31	...
1968	5.25	4.51	6.18	5.78	3.22	1918	...	4.50	...	6.70	...
1967	4.85	3.98	5.51	5.34	3.35	1917	...	4.20	...	6.42	...
1966	4.66	3.82	5.13	4.97	3.57	1916	...	3.94	...	6.19	...
1965	4.21	3.27	4.49	4.33	3.06	1915	...	4.16	...	6.48	...
1964	4.15	3.22	4.40	4.32	3.00	1914	...	4.12	...	6.49	...
1963	4.00	3.23	4.26	4.30	3.17	1913	...	4.22	...	6.57	...
1962	3.95	3.18	4.33	4.50	3.37	1912	...	4.02	...	6.27	...
1961	3.90	3.46	4.35	4.66	3.07	1911	...	3.98	...	6.28	...
1960	4.01	3.73	4.41	4.75	3.60	1910	...	3.97	...	6.30	...
1959	4.07	3.95	4.38	4.69	3.31	1909	...	3.78	...	...	...
1958	3.43	3.56	3.79	4.54	4.01	1908	...	3.93	...	...	...
1957	3.47	3.60	3.89	4.63	4.33	1907	...	3.86	...	...	...
1956	3.08	2.93	3.36	4.25	4.07	1906	...	3.57	...	...	...
1955	2.84	2.53	3.06	4.01	4.05	1905	...	3.40	...	...	...
1954	2.55	2.37	2.90	4.02	4.75	1904	...	3.45	...	...	...
1953	2.94	2.72	3.20	4.27	5.49	1903	...	3.38	...	...	...
1952	2.68	2.19	2.96	4.13	5.49	1902	...	3.20	...	...	...
1951	2.57	2.00	2.86	4.11	6.11	1901	...	3.13	...	...	...
1950	2.32	1.98	2.62	3.85	6.28	1900	...	3.12	...	...	...
1949	2.31	2.21	2.66	3.97	6.62						

1. From 1971 to 1998: Standard and Poor's composite. Prior to 1971, Moody's composite. In 1970, the yield according to Standard and Poor's was 3.83 percent.

Series X 517-530. Market Value and Volume of Sales of Stocks and Bonds on Registered Securities Exchanges: 1935 to 1997

(In millions)

Year	All exchanges		New York Stock Exchange		Year	All exchanges		New York Stock Exchange	
	Market value, all sales	Shares of stocks	Market value, all sales	Shares of stocks		Market value, all sales	Shares of stocks	Market value, all sales	Shares of stocks
	517	**519**	**524**	**526**		**517**	**519**	**524**	**526**
1997	6 879	159 700	5 848	138 800	1965	93 325	2 587	76 878	1 809
1996	4 735	125 700	4 013	108 200	1964	75 328	2 045	63 284	1 482
1995	3 690	106 400	3 078	90 100	1963	66 157	1 838	56 564	1 351
1994	2 966	90 500	2 483	76 700					
1993	2 734	82 800	2 278	68 700	1962	56 564	1 664	49 019	1 187
					1961	66 068	2 010	54 785	1 292
1992	2 149	65 500	1 759	53 300	1960	46 901	1 389	39 552	958
1991	1 903	58 000	1 534	47 700	1959	53 877	1 605	45 368	1 039
1990	$1 751 000	53 338	$1 394 000	43 829	1958	39 962	1 400	34 351	999
1989	2 010 000	54 239	1 581 000	44 140					
1988	1 702 000	52 533	1 380 000	44 018	1957	33 360	1 292	28 686	914
					1956	36 360	1 182	31 064	784
1987	2 492 000	63 771	1 987 000	50 038	1955	39 261	1 212	34 038	820
1986	1 868 000	48 338	1 453 000	39 258	1954	29 156	1 053	25 267	749
1985	1 260 000	37 046	1 024 000	30 222	1953	17 488	716	15 010	520
1984	1 004 000	30 456	815 000	25 150					
1983	1 023 000	30 146	816 000	24 253	1952	18 179	732	15 531	522
					1951	22 127	863	19 013	643
1982	658 000	22 423	514 000	18 203	1950	22 840	857	19 735	655
1981	533 000	15 910	416 000	12 843	1949	11 443	516	9 674	380
1980	522 000	15 480	398 000	12 390	1948	13 749	570	11 731	413
1979	323 000	10 850	252 000	8 675					
1978	269 000	9 483	211 000	7 617	1947	12 541	512	10 617	358
					1946	20 001	802	16 675	531
1977	198 000	7 023	157 000	5 613	1945	18 112	744	15 190	496
1976	207 000	7 036	165 000	5 649	1944	11 780	464	10 089	342
1975	167 000	6 231	143 000	5 051	1943	10 986	485	9 457	362
1974	125 000	4 846	106 000	3 822					
1973	187 000	5 732	155 000	4 337	1942	5 570	220	4 796	169
					1941	7 603	310	6 408	230
1972	215 000	6 310	169 000	4 496	1940	9 726	372	8 223	283
1971	195 000	5 916	155 000	4 265	1939	13 347	467	11 488	366
1970	136 465	4 539	107 649	3 213	1938	13 927	542	12 306	424
1969	180 877	4 963	133 173	3 174					
1968	202 772	5 312	149 395	3 299	1937	23 709	837	20 769	614
					1936	27 283	956	23 323	702
1967	168 258	4 504	160 791	2 886	1935 [1]	19 115	662	16 138	499
1966	127 914	3 188	102 754	2 205					

1. Stock and bond sales for New York Stock Exchange and New York Curb Exchange, January to March, exclude stopped sales; stock sales for these exchanges also exclude odd-lot sales.

Series X 536-539. Net Assets, Sales and Redemptions of Mutual Funds: 1940 to 1998

(In millions of dollars)

Year	Number of funds	Net assets	Sales	Redemptions	Year	Number of funds	Net assets	Sales	Redemptions
	536	537	538	539		536	537	538	539
1998	7 314	5 525 000	7 230 000	6 649 000	1967	204	44 701	1 377	743
1997	6 684	4 468 000	5 800 000	5 324 000	1966	182	34 829	924	426
1996	6 293	3 539 000	4 675 000	4 267 000	1965	170	35 220	1 228	512
1995	5 761	2 820 000	3 602 000	3 315 000	1964	160	29 116	958	411
1994	5 357	2 161 000	3 077 000	2 929 000	1963	165	25 214	648	387
1993	4 558	2 075 000	3 189 000	2 905 000	1962	169	21 270	510	285
1992	3 850	1 646 000	2 751 000	2 548 000	1961	170	22 788	813	263
1991	3 427	1 396 000	2 037 000	1 879 000	1960	161	17 025	481	192
1990	3 122	1 069 000	1 566 000	1 471 000	1959	155	15 817	541	171
1989	2 918	982 000	1 445 000	1 327 000	1958	151	13 242	482	174
1988	2 718	810 000	1 177 000	1 167 000	1957	143	8 714	331	95
1987	2 323	770 000	1 252 000	1 179 000	1956	135	9 046	342	90
1986	1 843	716 000	1 206 000	1 016 000	1955	125	7 837	290	92
1985	1 531	496 000	954 000	665 000	1954	115	6 109	270	98
1984	1 246	371 000	680 000	607 000	1953	110	4 146	160	56
1983	1 026	293 000	548 000	566 000	1952	110	3 931	214	49
1982	857	282 900	547 800	565 800	1951	103	3 129	194	62
1981	669	241 400	472 200	362 600	1950	98	2 530	135	82
1980	564	135 000	248 000	217 000	1949	91	1 973	125	40
1979	524	94 500	119 300	86 800	1948	87	1 505	75	34
1978	505	55 800	37 200	31 500	1947	80	1 409	67	28
1977	477	48 500	17 100	16 700	1946	74	1 311	82	31
1976	452	51 000	13 700	16 400	1945	73	1 284	92	29
1975	426	45 800	10 100	9 600	1944	68	882	52	16
1974	431	35 800	5 300	3 900	1943	68	653	116	51
1973	421	46 500	4 400	5 700	1942	68	486	73	25
1972	410	59 800	4 900	6 600	1941	68	401	53	45
1970	356	47 618	1 230	765	1940	. . .	447	. . .	. . .
1969	269	48 290	1 503	846					
1968	240	52 677	1 994	1 027					

Series X 551-560. Short- and Intermediate-Term Consumer Credit, by Major Types: 1919 to 1998

In millions of dollars. Estimated credit as of end of year)

Year	Total credit outstanding	Installment credit	Automobile paper	Total noninstallment credit outstanding	Year	Total credit outstanding	Installment credit	Automobile paper	Total noninstallment credit outstanding
	551	552	553	557		551	552	553	557
1998	1 308 400	...	447 200	...	1958	45 129	33 642	14 152	11 487
1997	1 233 100	...	413 400	...	1957	44 971	33 868	15 340	11 103
1996	1 181 900	...	392 300	...	1956	42 334	31 720	14 420	10 614
1995	1 095 700	...	364 200	...	1955	38 830	28 906	13 460	9 924
1994	960 700	...	327 900	...	1954	32 464	23 568	9 809	8 896
1993	839 100	...	288 100	...	1953	31 393	23 005	9 835	8 388
1992	779 900	...	262 700	...	1952	27 520	19 403	7 733	8 117
1991	777 300	729 400	267 900	47 900	1951	22 712	15 294	5 972	7 418
1990	794 400	735 100	284 600	59 300	1950	21 471	14 703	6 074	6 768
1989	781 200	718 900	290 700	62 300	1949	17 364	11 590	4 555	5 774
1988	731 200	664 000	284 200	67 100	1948	14 447	8 996	3 018	5 451
1987	681 900	610 500	265 900	71 400	1947	11 598	6 695	1 924	4 903
1986	649 100	573 000	247 400	76 100	1946	8 384	4 172	981	4 212
1985	592 100	518 300	210 200	73 800	1945	5 665	2 462	455	3 203
1984	511 300	442 600	173 600	68 700	1944	5 111	2 176	397	2 935
1983	431 200	369 000	143 600	62 200	1943	4 901	2 136	355	2 765
1982	383 100	325 800	125 900	57 300	1942	5 983	3 166	742	2 817
1981	366 900	311 300	119 000	55 600	1941	9 172	6 085	2 458	3 087
1980	350 300	298 200	112 000	52 100	1940	8 338	5 514	2 071	2 824
1979	383 300	312 000	116 400	71 300	1939	7 222	4 503	1 497	2 719
1978	337 900	273 600	101 600	64 300	1938	6 370	3 686	1 099	2 684
1977	289 200	230 600	82 900	58 600	1937	6 948	4 118	1 494	2 830
1976	248 900	193 500	67 700	55 400	1936	6 375	3 747	1 372	2 628
1975	223 100	172 000	57 200	51 100	1935	5 190	2 817	992	2 373
1974	213 400	164 600	54 300	48 800	1934	4 218	1 999	614	2 219
1973	203 100	155 100	53 800	48 000	1933	3 885	1 723	493	2 162
1972	177 700	133 200	47 900	44 500	1932	4 026	1 672	356	2 354
1971	138 400	111 300	38 700	27 100	1931	5 315	2 463	684	2 852
1970	126 802	101 161	35 490	25 641	1930	6 351	3 022	986	3 329
1969	122 469	98 169	36 602	24 300	1929	7 116	3 524	1 384	3 592
1968	113 191	89 890	34 130	23 301	1928	6 258	2 935	1 134	3 323
1967	102 132	80 926	30 724	21 206	1927	5 344	2 319	765	3 025
1966	97 543	77 539	30 556	20 004	1926	5 227	2 363	977	2 864
1965	90 314	71 324	28 619	18 990	1925	4 715	2 115	914	2 600
1964	80 268	62 692	24 934	17 576	1924	4 025	1 646	670	2 379
1963	71 739	55 486	22 254	16 253	1923	3 652	1 368	526	2 284
1962	63 821	48 720	19 381	15 101	1922	3 166	1 047	295	2 119
1961	57 982	43 891	17 135	14 091	1921	2 966	919	317	2 047
1960	56 141	42 968	17 658	13 173	1920	2 964	969	376	1 995
1959	51 544	39 247	16 420	12 297	1919	2 642	800	304	1 842

Series X 716-724.   Number of Banking Offices, by Deposit Insurance Status: 1900 to 1998

Year[1]	All banking offices	Commercial bank offices[2]					Mutual savings banks offices[2][4]	
		Total	Member banks[2][3]		Nonmember banks		Total	Insured[5]
			National	State[4][5]	Insured	Non-insured		
	716	**717**	**718**	**719**	**720**	**721**	**722**	**723**
1998	84 857	70 719	37 414	11 250	22 055	...	14 138	14 138[6]
1997	84 194	69 463	36 690	10 440	22 333	...	14 731	14 731[6]
1996	83 074	67 316	33 559	9 997	23 760	...	15 758	15 758[6]
1995	81 929	66 454	31 644	10 777	24 033	...	15 475	15 475[6]
1994	70 284	65 594	31 633	9 365	24 596	...	...	...
1993	68 664	64 078	30 879	8 760	24 439	...	...	...
1992	67 777	63 903	31 064	8 207	24 632	...	...	3 874
1991	67 783	64 006	31 771	7 678	24 557	...	...	3 777
1990	66 945	62 753	31 279	6 922	24 959	...	3 785	3 785
1989	64 570	60 796	30 019	6 736	24 041	...	3 774	3 774
1988	63 960	60 200	29 270	6 493	24 437	...	3 760	3 760
1987	62 914	59 423	28 744	6 452	24 227	...	3 491	3 491
1986	61 897	58 565	28 218	6 324	24 023	...	3 332	3 332
1985	60 890	57 764	27 844	6 010	23 910	...	3 126	3 126
1984	60 067	57 010	27 037	5 772	23 535	666	3 057	2 728
1983	59 050	55 960	26 080	5 866	23 380	634	3 090	2 760
1982	57 913	54 829	24 867	6 054	23 314	594	3 084	2 733
1981	59 348	55 749	25 221	6 193	23 788	547	3 599	3 217
1980	57 232	53 649	24 217	5 768	23 186	478	3 583	3 066
1979	54 926	51 588	23 307	5 856	21 993	432	3 338	2 840
1978	52 608	49 602	22 731	5 725	20 730	416	3 006	2 517
1977	50 645	47 914	22 294	5 610	19 619	391	2 781	2 302
1976	48 653	46 100	21 459	5 695	18 578	368	2 553	2 125
1975	47 239	44 917	21 073	5 453	18 043	348	2 322	1 897
1974	45 011	42 890	20 437	5 281	16 884	288	2 121	1 706
1973	42 593	40 620	19 567	5 127	15 673	253	1 973	1 562
1972	40 377	38 538	18 571	5 073	14 643	251	1 839	1 437
1971	38 588	36 903	17 871	4 947	13 864	221	1 685	1 310
1970	36 910	35 330	17 142	4 798	13 159	231	1 580	1 222
1969	35 340	33 858	16 384	4 683	12 546	245	1 482	1 137
1968	34 100	32 691	15 700	4 827	11 919	245	1 409	1 072
1967	32 983	31 652	14 940	4 983	11 470	259	1 331	1 001
1966	31 934	30 673	14 404	4 867	11 103	299	1 261	944
1965	30 776	29 556	13 776	4 738	10 723	319	1 220	911
1964	29 549	28 370	12 937	4 751	10 356	326	1 179	876
1963	28 197	27 064	12 032	4 684	10 012	336	1 133	832
1962	26 865	25 768	11 140	4 549	9 718	361	1 097	797
1961	25 839	24 782	10 554	4 453	9 407	368	1 057	757
1960	24 954	23 954	10 036	4 265	9 253	400	1 000	706
1959	*24 094	*23 130	*9 514	4 206	*9 001	*409	964	586
1958	23 305	22 361	9 109	4 120	8 693	439	944	546
1957	22 699	21 772	8 795	3 969	8 545	463	927	535
1956	22 123	21 230	8 459	3 884	8 405	482	893	480
1955	21 494	20 638	8 055	3 785	8 263	535	856	454
1954	20 982	20 147	7 844	3 598	8 132	573	835	439
1953	20 608	19 810	7 602	3 536	8 062	610	798	411
1952	20 288	19 513	7 465	3 436	7 947	665	775	383
1951	20 003	19 244	7 309	3 365	7 879	691	759	367
1950	19 709	18 966	7 188	3 271	7 766	741	742	346
1949	19 465	18 735	7 060	3 216	7 679	780	730	333
1948	19 234	18 520	6 956	3 156	7 582	826	714	325
1947	19 046	18 342	6 875	3 096	7 521	850	704	318
1946	18 863	18 165	6 794	3 022	7 464	885	698	306
1945	18 781	18 096	6 831	2 963	7 397	905	685	293
1944	18 741	18 058	6 840	2 866	7 430	922	683	291
1943	18 646	17 965	6 782	2 744	7 487	952	681	279
1942	18 562	17 878	6 675	2 619	7 602	982	683	91

See footnotes at end of table.

Series X 716-724. Number of Banking Offices, by Deposit Insurance Status: 1900 to 1998—Cont'd.

Year[1]	All banking offices	Commercial bank offices[2]					Mutual savings banks offices[2][4]	
		Total	Member banks[2][3]		Nonmember banks		Total	Insured[5]
			National	State[4][5]	Insured	Non-insured		
	716	**717**	**718**	**719**	**720**	**721**	**722**	**723**
1941	18 524	17 841	6 682	2 514	7 742	903	683	84
1940	18 561	17 875	6 683	2 344	7 892	956	686	84
1939	18 663	17 980	6 705	2 177	8 099	999	683	75
1938	18 774	18 084	6 723	2 106	8 226	1 029	690	64
1937	18 927	18 236	6 745	2 075	8 342	1 074	691	67
1936	19 066	18 373	6 723	2 032	8 440	1 178	693	67
1935	19 153	18 455	6 715	1 953	8 562	1 225	698	67
1934	19 196	18 491	6 705	1 961	[8]9 825		705	(7)
1933	17 940	17 236	6 275	1 817	[8]9 144		704	(7)
1932	. . .	20 997	7 231		13 766		. . .	. . .
1931	. . .	22 842	7 478		15 364		. . .	. . .
1930	. . .	25 694	8 075		17 619		. . .	. . .
1929	. . .	27 379	8 398		18 981		. . .	. . .
1928	. . .	28 106	8 563		19 543		. . .	. . .
1927	. . .	28 714	8 482		20 232		. . .	. . .
1926	. . .	29 454	8 327		21 127		. . .	. . .
1925	. . .	30 163	8 366		21 797		. . .	. . .
1924	. . .	30 482	8 299		22 183		. . .	. . .
1923	. . .	30 931	8 383		22 548		. . .	. . .
1922	. . .	31 259	8 384		22 875		. . .	. . .
1921	. . .	31 243	8 222		23 021		. . .	. . .
1920	. . .	30 368	8 088		22 280		. . .	. . .
1915	. . .	26 660	7 624		19 036		. . .	. . .
1910	. . .	22 034	7 150		14 884		. . .	. . .
1905	. . .	15 032	5 669		9 363		. . .	. . .
1900	. . .	8 857	3 736		5 121		. . .	. . .

* Denotes first year for which figures include Alaska and Hawaii.
1. For 1925, 1926 and 1932, figures are as of December; for earlier years they are as of different dates for banks and branches: for banks, 1927-1931 and 1923-1924, as of December; for 1915-1922, as of June; for branches, 1924 and 1927-1931, as of June; prior to 1924, not for any uniform month.
2. Comparability of figures for classes of banks is affected somewhat by changes in Federal Reserve membership, deposit insurance status and reserve classifications of cities and individual banks, and by mergers, etc.
3. Federal deposit insurance is compulsory for member banks of the Federal Reserve System.
4. None in Alaska and Hawaii.
5. Member commercial banks exclude, and mutual savings banks include, mutual savings banks which are members of the Federal Reserve System as follows: 3, in 1941-1959, 2 in 1960 and 1 in 1961-1970.
6. Includes the offices of former savings and loan associations which were merged with mutual savings into a new legal category, called Savings Institutions, sometimes referred to as "thrifts."
7. In 1947, the series was revised.
8. Federal insurance of bank deposits did not become effective until Jan. 1, 1934, and the number of nonmember banking offices by insurance status is not available prior to 1935.

Series X 741-755.   Bank Suspensions—Number and Deposits of Suspended Banks: 1864 to 1996

Year[1]	Total number of suspensions	Total deposits of suspended banks[2] (mil. dol.)	Year[1]	Total number of suspensions	Total deposits of suspended banks[2] (mil. dol.)	Year[1]	Total number of suspensions	Year[1]	Total number of suspensions
	741	748		741	748		741		741
1996............	5	. . .	1965............	9	45	1915............	152	1887............	25
1995............	6	. . .	1964............	8	24	1914............	151	1886............	20
1994............	13	. . .	1963............	2	23	1913............	105	1885............	46
1993............	49	. . .	1962............	3	4	1912............	80	1884............	63
1992............	122	. . .				1911............	87	1883............	33
			1961............	9	10				
1991............	127	. . .	1960............	2	8	1910............	63	1882............	22
1990............	169	14 489	1959............	3	3	1909............	79	1881............	11
1989............	207	24 097	1956-1960	20	45	1908............	155	1880............	18
1988............	221	37 215	1951-1955	23	70	1907............	91	1879............	37
1987............	203	8 568				1906............	53	1878............	140
			1947-1950	23	33				
1986............	145	6 597	1941-1946	49	[3]59	1905............	80	1877............	99
1985............	120	8 059	1934-1940	[4]448	[5]477	1904............	128	1876............	59
1984............	80	29 883	1933[5]............	4 004	3 601	1903............	52	1875............	28
1983............	48	5 442	1932............	1 456	725	1902............	54	1874............	57
1982............	42	9 908				1901............	69	1873............	41
			1931............	2 294	1 691				
1981............	10	3 826	1930............	1 352	869	1900............	36	1872............	19
1980............	10	5 216	1929............	659	231	1899............	36	1871............	10
1979............	10	110	1928............	499	143	1898............	67	1870............	3
1978............	7	854	1927............	669	199	1897............	145	1869............	7
1977............	6	205				1896............	155	1868............	14
			1926............	976	260				
1976............	17	865	1925............	618	168	1895............	124	1867............	8
1975............	14	340	1924............	775	210	1894............	89	1866............	7
1974............	4	1 575	1923............	646	150	1893............	496	1865............	6
1973............	3	21	1922............	367	93	1892............	83	1864............	2
1972............	2	57				1891............	62		
			1921............	505	172				
1971............	3	5	1920............	168	. . .	1890............	37		
1970............	7	53	1919............	63	. . .	1889............	18		
1969............	9	40	1918............	47	. . .	1888............	33		
1968............	3	23							
1967............	4	11	1917............	49	. . .				
			1916............	52	. . .				
1966............	8	106							

1. For 1864-1891, all series except mutual savings banks are for year ending June 30; for mutual saving banks the date is not specified in the source. For 1892-1920, for all banks other than private figures are for calendar year; for private banks, figures vary in ending date of reporting year as follows: 1892, June 30; 1893 (14 months), Aug. 31; 1894-1899, Aug. 31; 1900-1919, June 30; and 1920 (18 months), Dec. 31. For 1921-1970, all series are for calendar years.
2. Excludes deposits for seven noninsured banks, for which data were unavailable.
3. Excludes deposits for one foreign-owned bank closed in 1941 by order of the federal government, requiring disbursements by the corporation.
4. Excludes one noninsured bank placed in receivership in 1934 with no deposits at time of closing.
5. Excludes deposits for two cases requiring disbursements by the corporation; one bank in voluntary liquidation in 1937, one noninsured bank in 1938 with insured deposits at date of suspensions, its insurance status having been terminated prior to suspension.
6. Figures not wholly comparable with earlier years.

Series X 834-844. Selected Data for Savings Institutions: 1990 to 1998; Data for Savings and Loan Associations: 1900 to 1989[1]

(Includes Alaska, Guam, Hawaii, Puerto Rico and Virgin Islands)

Year	Number of associations	Total assets (mil. dol.)	Year	Number of associations	Total assets (mil. dol.)	Year	Number of associations	Total assets (mil. dol.)	Year	Number of associations	Total assets (mil. dol.)
	834	835		834	835		834	835		834	835
1998	1 687	1 088 000	1973	5 200	271 900	1948	6 011	13 028	1923	10 744	3 943
1997	1 780	1 026 000	1972	5 300	243 100	1947	6 045	11 687	1922	10 009	3 343
1996	1 924	1 028 000	1971	5 500	206 000	1946	6 093	10 202	1921	9 255	2 891
1995	2 030	1 026 000	1970	5 669	176 183	1945	6 149	8 747	1920	8 633	2 520
1994	2 152	1 009 000	1969	5 835	162 149	1944	6 279	7 458	1919	7 788	2 127
1993	2 262	1 001 000	1968	5 947	152 890	1943	6 498	6 604	1918	7 484	1 898
1992	2 390	1 030 000	1967	6 036	143 534	1942	6 941	6 150	1917	7 269	1 769
1991	2 561	1 113 000	1966	6 112	133 933	1941	7 211	6 049	1916	7 072	1 599
1990	2 815	1 259 000	1965	6 185	129 580	1940	7 521	5 733	1915	6 806	1 484
1989	2 271	756 000	1964	6 222	119 355	1939	8 006	5 597	1914	6 616	1 358
1988	2 554	933 000	1963	6 248	107 559	1938	8 762	5 632	1913	6 429	1 248
1987	2 886	974 000	1962	6 289	93 605	1937	9 225	5 682	1912	6 273	1 138
1986	3 084	962 000	1961	6 246	82 135	1936	10 042	5 772	1911	6 099	1 031
1985	3 233	948 000	1960	6 320	71 476	1935	10 266	5 875	1910	5 869	932
1984	3 362	902 000	1959	6 223	63 530	1934	10 744	6 406	1909	5 713	856
1983	3 502	773 400	1958	6 207	55 139	1933	10 596	7 018	1908	5 599	784
1982	3 825	707 600	1957	6 169	48 138	1932	10 915	7 737	1907	5 424	732
1981	4 292	664 200	1956	6 136	42 875	1931	11 442	8 417	1906	5 316	673
1980	4 613	630 000	1955	6 071	37 656	1930	11 777	8 829	1905	5 264	629
1979	4 684	579 000	1954	6 037	31 633	1929	12 342	8 695	1904	5 265	600
1978	4 725	523 600	1953	6 012	26 733	1928	12 666	8 016	1903	5 308	580
1977	4 761	459 200	1952	6 004	22 660	1927	12 804	7 179	1902	5 299	577
1976	4 821	391 900	1951	5 995	19 222	1926	12 626	6 334	1901	5 302	565
1975	4 931	338 200	1950	5 992	16 893	1925	12 403	5 509	1900	5 356	571
1974	5 086	295 500	1949	5 983	14 622	1924	11 844	4 766			

1. The Financial Institutions Reform, Recovery and Enforcement Act of 1989 merged savings and loan associations and mutual savings banks into a single category called Savings Institutions, sometimes referred to as Thrifts.

Series X 864-878. Federal and State—Chartered Credit Unions—Number, Members, Savings, Loans and Total Assets: 1925 to 1998

(As of end of year)

Year	Operating credit unions		Number of members (1 000's)		Members' savings (mil. dol.)		Outstanding loans (mil. dol.)		Total assets (mil. dol.)	
	Federal	State[1]	Federal	State[1]	Federal[2]	State[3]	Federal	State[1]	Federal[2]	State[1]
	865	**866**	**868**	**869**	**871**	**872**	**874**	**875**	**877**	**878**
1998	6 814	4 181	43 865	29 674	202 651	137 347	144 849	100 890	231 904	156 787
1997	6 981	4 257	43 491	27 921	187 822	119 359	140 104	92 117	215 104	136 004
1996	7 152	4 240	43 546	25 652	180 969	105 743	134 127	79 661	206 095	120 193
1995	7 329	4 358	42 163	24 927	170 300	99 838	120 514	71 606	193 781	112 860
1994	7 498	4 493	40 837	24 295	160 226	94 797	110 090	65 769	182 529	106 937
1993	7 696	4 621	39 756	23 997	153 506	93 482	94 640	57 695	172 854	104 316
1992	7 908	4 686	38 124	23 238	145 637	87 371	87 350	52 192	162 066	96 312
1991	8 229	4 731	37 081	21 619	130 164	75 626	84 150	49 268	149 940	83 133
1990	8 511	4 349	36 241	19 454	117 892	62 082	83 029	44 102	130 073	68 133
1989	8 821	4 550	35 612	18 858	109 653	57 658	80 272	42 373	120 666	63 175
1988	9 118	4 760	34 438	18 519	104 431	55 217	73 766	39 977	114 565	60 740
1987	9 401	4 934	32 067	17 999	96 346	52 083	64 104	35 436	105 190	56 972
1986	9 758	4 935	31 041	17 636	87 954	48 097	55 305	30 834	95 484	52 244
1985	10 125	4 920	29 579	15 689	71 616	37 917	48 241	26 168	78 188	41 525
1984	10 548	4 645	28 170	15 205	57 927	26 327	42 132	19 951	63 657	29 188
1983[4]	10 962	4 915	28 798	14 278	49 889	24 850	33 201	17 215	54 482	27 479
1982	11 426	8 464	26 105	20 393	41 352	33 236	28 192	23 454	45 494	36 886
1981	11 951	8 746	25 449	19 620	35 248	28 971	27 238	23 156	39 181	32 596
1980	12 440	9 025	24 519	19 235	36 263	29 480	26 350	22 633	40 092	33 143
1979	12 738	9 274	24 790	18 409	31 831	25 628	25 547	23 677	36 468	29 524
1978	12 759	9 443	23 259	17 461	29 803	23 715	27 687	23 715	34 760	27 588
1977	12 750	9 580	20 427	16 375	25 576	21 120	22 718	19 389	29 688	24 500
1976	12 757	9 775	18 624	15 129	21 130	17 968	18 311	15 999	24 396	20 640
1975	12 737	9 871	17 066	14 196	17 530	15 522	14 869	13 300	20 209	17 804
1974	12 748	10 105	15 870	13 581	14 371	13 148	12 730	11 702	16 715	15 233
1973	12 688	10 191	14 666	12 886	12 598	11 914	11 109	10 650	14 569	13 806
1972	12 708	10 354	13 572	12 118	10 956	10 622	9 424	9 239	12 514	12 275
1971	12 717	10 536	12 702	11 382	9 191	9 167	8 071	8 081	10 553	10 569
1970	12 977	10 679	11 966	10 853	7 629	7 894	6 969	7 137	8 861	9 089
1969	12 921	10 838	11 302	10 326	6 713	7 027	6 329	6 630	7 794	8 124
1968	12 584	10 794	10 509	9 720	5 986	6 326	5 398	5 895	6 902	7 310
1967	12 210	10 787	9 874	9 189	5 421	5 682	4 677	5 204	6 208	6 568
1966	11 941	10 644	9 272	8 651	4 944	5 127	4 324	4 769	5 669	5 938
1965	11 543	10 521	8 641	8 115	4 538	4 682	3 865	4 233	5 166	5 385
1964	11 278	10 452	8 092	7 530	4 017	4 208	3 349	3 699	4 559	4 800
1963	10 955	10 346	7 500	7 080	3 453	3 711	2 911	3 260	3 917	4 213
1962	10 632	10 337	7 008	6 745	3 020	3 311	2 561	2 917	3 430	3 758
1961	10 271	10 296	6 543	6 336	2 673	2 966	2 245	2 607	3 028	3 354
1960	9 905	10 151	6 087	5 971	2 344	2 637	2 021	2 381	2 670	2 989
1959	9 447	9 961	5 643	5 677	2 075	2 366	1 667	2 051	2 353	2 676
1958	9 030	9 740	5 210	5 329	1 812	2 057	1 380	1 698	2 035	2 312
1957	8 735	9 314	4 898	4 964	1 589	1 792	1 257	1 521	1 789	2 021
1956	8 350	8 763	4 502	4 549	1 366	1 548	1 049	1 277	1 529	1 742
1955	7 806	8 258	4 032	4 121	1 135	1 312	863	1 071	1 267	1 476
1954	7 227	7 713	3 599	3 757	931	1 109	682	870	1 033	1 237
1953	6 578	6 986	3 255	3 380	768	923	574	734	854	1 041
1952	5 925	6 324	2 853	3 035	597	758	415	570	662	854
1951	5 398	5 886	2 464	2 732	457	622	300	447	505	694
1950	4 984	5 587	2 127	2 483	362	522	264	416	406	900
1949	4 495	5 402	1 820	2 271	285	445	186	329	316	511
1948	4 058	5 271	1 628	2 121	235	395	138	261	258	443
1947	3 845	5 097	1 446	1 894	192	341	91	189	210	381
1946	3 761	4 954	1 302	1 718	160	291	57	131	173	322
1945	3 757	4 858	1 217	1 626	141	243	35	91	153	282
1944	3 815	4 907	1 306	1 630	134	221	34	87	144	254
1943	3 938	5 124	1 312	1 721	117	206	35	87	127	228

See footnotes at end of table.

Series X 864-878. Federal and State—Chartered Credit Unions—Number, Members, Savings, Loans and Total Assets: 1925 to 1998—Cont'd.

(As of end of year)

Year	Operating credit unions		Number of members (1 000's)		Members' savings (mil. dol.)		Outstanding loans (mil. dol.)		Total assets (mil. dol.)	
	Federal	State[1]	Federal	State[1]	Federal[2]	State[3]	Federal	State[1]	Federal[2]	State[1]
	865	**866**	**868**	**869**	**871**	**872**	**874**	**875**	**877**	**878**
1942...........................	4 145	5 400	1 357	1 797	110	193	43	106	120	221
1941...........................	4 228	5 506	1 409	1 908	97	190	69	151	106	217
1940...........................	3 756	5 175	1 128	1 700	66	157	56	135	73	181
1939...........................	3 182	4 677	851	1 459	43	126	38	111	48	146
1938...........................	2 760	3 977	632	1 237	27	100	24	84	30	118
1937...........................	2 313	3 128	484	1 056	18	80	16	62	19	97
1936...........................	1 751	2 734	310	854	9	59	7	52	9	74
1935...........................	772	2 122	119	523	2	36	2	34	2	48
1934...........................	39	2 028	3	427	(Z)	28	(Z)	28	(Z)	40
1933...........................	. . .	1 772	. . .	360	. . .	23	. . .	26	. . .	35
1932...........................	. . .	1 472	. . .	301	. . .	22	. . .	25	. . .	31
1931...........................	. . .	1 244	. . .	286	. . .	. . .	. . .	. . .	. . .	34
1929...........................	. . .	868	. . .	265	. . .	. . .	. . .	. . .	. . .	. . .
1925...........................	. . .	176	. . .	108	. . .	. . .	. . .	. . .	. . .	. . .

Z Less than $500 000.
1. Reports not received from all operating credit unions.
2. Data for 1935-1944, partly estimated.
3. Includes members' deposits.
4. Beginning 1983, excludes state-insured, privately insured and noninsured state chartered credit unions.

Series X 879-889.   Life Insurance Companies and Life Insurance in Force in the United States, by Type: 1815 to 1997

(As of December 31)

Year	Policies (mil.)	Life insurance in force Value (mil. dol.)					Average size policy in force (dol.)	
		Total	Ordinary	Group[1]	Industrial[2]	Credit[3]	Ordinary	Group
	880	**882**	**883**	**884**	**885**	**886**	**887**	**888**
1997	373	13 196 000	7 689 000	5 277 000	18 000	212 000	56 044	32 221
1996	372	12 590 000	7 294 000	5 067 000	18 000	211 000	52 285	32 577
1995	393	11 638 000	6 816 000	4 603 000	18 000	201 000	45 090	27 051
1994	390	11 057 000	6 407 000	4 442 000	19 000	189 000	45 870	26 338
1993	363	11 105 000	6 428 000	4 456 000	20 000	200 000	45 770	31 430
1992	366	10 406 000	5 942 000	4 241 000	21 000	202 000	42 960	29 930
1991	375	9 986 000	5 678 000	4 058 000	22 000	228 000	41 450	28 760
1990	389	9 393 000	5 367 000	3 754 000	24 000	248 000	37 910	26 630
1989	394	8 694 000	4 940 000	3 469 000	24 000	260 000	34 410	24 510
1988	391	8 020 000	4 512 000	3 232 000	26 000	251 000	31 390	23 410
1987	395	7 452 000	4 139 000	3 043 000	27 000	243 000	28 510	22 380
1986	391	6 720 000	3 658 000	2 801 000	27 000	234 000	25 540	20 720
1985	386	6 053 000	3 247 000	2 562 000	28 000	216 000	22 780	19 720
1984	385	5 500 000	2 888 000	2 392 000	30 000	190 000	19 970	18 780
1983	387	4 966 000	2 544 000	2 220 000	31 000	171 000	17 380	17 530
1982	389	4 477 000	2 217 000	2 066 000	33 000	161 000	15 140	16 630
1981	400	4 064 000	1 978 000	1 889 000	35 000	162 000	13 310	15 400
1980	402	3 541 000	1 761 000	1 579 000	38 000	165 000	11 920	13 410
1979	407	3 222 000	1 586 000	1 419 000	37 800	179 300	10 890	12 350
1978	401	2 870 000	1 425 000	1 244 000	38 100	163 100	10 010	11 260
1977	390	2 583 000	1 289 000	1 115 000	39 000	139 400	9 240	10 550
1976	382	2 343 000	1 178 000	1 003 000	39 200	123 600	8 610	10 010
1975	380	2 140 000	1 083 000	905 000	39 400	112 000	8 090	9 360
1974	380	1 985 000	1 009 000	827 000	39 400	109 600	7 690	8 840
1973	369	1 778 000	928 000	708 000	40 600	101 200	7 230	8 010
1972	365	1 628 000	849 000	631 000	40 000	108 800	6 790	7 730
1971	357	1 503 000	788 000	581 000	39 200	95 000	6 440	7 170
1970	355	1 402 123	734 730	551 357	38 644	77 392	6 105	6 905
1969	351	1 284 529	682 453	488 864	38 614	74 598	5 773	6 473
1968	346	1 183 354	633 392	442 778	38 827	68 357	5 453	6 074
1967	336	1 079 821	584 570	394 501	39 215	61 535	5 150	5 733
1966	331	984 689	541 022	345 945	39 663	58 059	4 938	5 356
1965	320	900 554	499 638	308 078	39 818	53 020	4 662	5 056
1964	308	797 808	457 868	253 620	39 833	46 487	4 382	4 637
1963	299	730 623	420 808	229 477	39 672	40 666	4 136	4 494
1962	290	675 977	391 048	209 950	39 638	35 341	3 932	4 323
1961	286	629 493	366 141	192 794	39 451	31 107	3 766	4 167
1960*	282	586 448	341 881	175 903	39 563	29 101	3 597*	4 034
1959	275	542 128	317 158	160 163	39 809	24 998	3 424	3 875
1958	267	493 561	288 607	144 772	39 646	20 536	3 227	3 736
1957	266	458 359	264 949	133 905	40 139	19 366	3 041	3 580
1956	261	412 630	238 348	117 399	40 109	16 774	2 853	3 361
1955	251	372 332	216 812	101 345	39 682	14 493	2 721	3 202
1954	237	333 719	198 599	86 410	38 664	10 046	2 619	3 018
1953	229	304 259	185 007	72 913	37 781	8 558	2 530	2 755
1952	219	276 591	170 875	62 913	36 448	6 355	2 452	2 667
1951	210	253 140	159 109	54 398	34 870	4 763	2 378	2 535
1950	202	234 168	149 116	47 793	33 415	3 844	2 319	2 478
1949	194	213 672	138 862	40 207	32 087	2 516	2 264	2 330
1948	187	201 208	131 158	37 068	31 253	1 729	2 240	2 280
1947	182	186 035	122 393	32 026	30 406	1 210	2 200	2 050
1946	173	170 066	112 818	27 206	29 313	729	2 150	2 060
1945	163	151 762	101 550	22 172	27 675	365	2 100	1 930
1944	159	145 771	95 085	23 922	26 474	290	2 080	1 860
1943	151	137 158	89 596	22 413	24 874	275	2 080	1 760

See footnotes at end of table.

Series X 879-889. Life Insurance Companies and Life Insurance in Force in the United States, by Type: 1815 to 1997—Cont'd.

(As of December 31)

Year	Policies (mil.)	Life insurance in force Value (mil. dol.)					Average size policy in force (dol.)	
		Total	Ordinary	Group[1]	Industrial[2]	Credit[3]	Ordinary	Group
	880	**882**	**883**	**884**	**885**	**886**	**887**	**888**
1942	144	127 721	85 139	19 316	22 911	355	2 090	1 740
1941	140	122 178	82 525	17 359	21 825	469	2 100	1 710
1940	134	115 530	79 346	14 938	20 866	380	2 130	1 700
1939	131	111 569	77 121	13 641	20 500	307	2 130	1 790
1938	129	108 927	75 772	12 503	20 396	256	2 150	1 890
1937	128	107 794	74 836	12 638	20 104	216	2 180	1 710
1936	124	102 653	72 361	11 291	18 863	138	2 160	1 670
1935	121	98 464	70 684	10 208	17 471	101	2 160	1 590
1934	117	96 677	70 094	9 472	17 036	75	2 210	1 710
1933	115	96 246	70 872	8 681	16 630	63	2 260	1 780
1932	116	101 559	75 898	8 923	16 669	69	2 380	1 860
1931	124	106 970	79 514	9 736	17 635	85	2 420	1 730
1930	124	106 413	78 576	8 901	17 963	73	2 460	1 700
1929	123	102 086	75 686	8 994	17 349	57	2 470	1 590
1928	116	92 590	68 430	7 889	16 231	40	2 410	1 580
1927	110	84 775	63 334	6 333	15 078	30	2 400	1 450
1926	104	77 642	58 453	5 362	13 803	24	2 350	1 400
1925	97	69 475	52 892	4 247	12 318	18	2 270	1 340
1924	90	61 327	47 283	3 127	10 905	12	2 200	1 280
1923	83	55 097	43 077	2 393	9 618	9	2 160	1 180
1922	76	48 342	38 053	1 795	8 486	8	2 090	1 150
1921	70	43 944	34 777	1 527	7 633	7	2 040	1 070
1920	65	40 540	32 018	1 570	6 948	4	1 990	960
1919	60	32 971	25 783	1 092	6 092	4	1 860	920
1918	53	27 924	21 818	630	5 474	2	1 840	840
1917	49	25 243	19 868	349	5 026	(3)	1 830	780
1916	45	22 853	18 081	155	4 617	. . .	1 800	780
1915	41	21 029	16 650	100	4 279	. . .	1 800	830
1914	39	19 737	15 661	65	4 011	. . .	1 810	970
1913	37	18 683	14 827	31	3 825	. . .	1 810	910
1912	34	17 301	13 709	13	3 579	. . .	1 800	1 080
1911	31	16 125	12 772	(Z)	3 353	. . .	1 790	. . .
1910	29	14 908	11 783	. . .	3 125	. . .	1 830	. . .
1909	27	13 878	10 960	. . .	2 918	. . .	1 830	. . .
1908	25	13 085	10 450	. . .	2 635	. . .	1 850	. . .
1907	24	12 639	10 103	. . .	2 536	. . .	1 860	. . .
1906	23	12 285	9 871	. . .	2 414	. . .	1 870	. . .
1905	22	11 863	9 585	. . .	2 278	. . .	1 880	. . .
1904	20	11 165	9 059	. . .	2 106	. . .	1 930	. . .
1903	19	10 217	8 264	. . .	1 953	. . .	1 970	. . .
1902	17	9 369	7 594	. . .	1 775	. . .	2 020	. . .
1901	16	8 369	6 766	. . .	1 603	. . .	2 040	. . .
1900	14	7 573	6 124	. . .	1 449	. . .	2 160	. . .
1899	12	6 822	5 547	. . .	1 275	. . .	2 210	. . .
1898	11	6 053	4 952	. . .	1 101	. . .	2 310	. . .
1897	10	5 555	4 563	. . .	992	. . .	2 340	. . .
1896	9	5 207	4 323	. . .	884	. . .	2 420	. . .
1895	9	4 988	4 170	. . .	818	. . .	2 440	. . .
1894	. . .	4 847	4 048	. . .	799	. . .	. . .	. . .
1893	. . .	4 609	3 948	. . .	661	. . .	. . .	. . .
1892	. . .	4 267	3 685	. . .	582	. . .	. . .	. . .
1891	. . .	3 868	3 388	. . .	481	. . .	. . .	. . .
1890	. . .	3 522.2	3 094.7	. . .	427.5	. . .	. . .	. . .
1889	. . .	3 122.6	2 758.1	. . .	364.5	. . .	. . .	. . .
1888	. . .	2 742.0	2 437.8	. . .	304.2	. . .	. . .	. . .

See footnotes at end of table.

Series X 879-889. Life Insurance Companies and Life Insurance in Force in the United States, by Type: 1815 to 1997—Cont'd.

(As of December 31)

Year	Policies (mil.)	Life insurance in force Value (mil. dol.)					Average size policy in force (dol.)	
		Total	Ordinary	Group[1]	Industrial[2]	Credit[3]	Ordinary	Group
	880	882	883	884	885	886	887	888
1887..................................	. . .	2 456.3	2 201.8	. . .	254.5	. . .	. . .	. . .
1886..................................	. . .	2 096.9	1 899.1	. . .	197.8	. . .	. . .	. . .

Year	Value of life insurance in force (mil. dol.)			Year	Value of life insurance in force (mil. dol.)	
	Total	Ordinary	Industrial[2]		Total	Ordinary
	882	883	885		882	883
1885..................................	2 007.1	1 861.3	145.8	1850..................................	97.1	97.1
1884..................................	1 995.9	1 884.8	111.1	1849..................................	. . .	. . .
1883..................................	1 872.1	1 784.9	87.2	1848..................................	. . .	. . .
1882..................................	1 720.8	1 664.6	56.2	1847..................................	. . .	. . .
1881..................................	1 606.5	1 573.0	33.5	1846..................................	. . .	. . .
1880..................................	1 522.7	1 502.2	20.5	1845..................................	14.5	14.5
1879..................................	1 474.9	1 469.5	5.4	1844..................................	. . .	. . .
1878..................................	1 519.7	1 517.7	2.0	1843..................................	. . .	. . .
1877..................................	1 512.1	1 511.1	1.0	1842..................................	. . .	. . .
1876..................................	1 690.6	1 690.2	.4	1841..................................	. . .	. . .
1875..................................	1 873.9	1 873.9	. . .	1840..................................	4.7	4.7
1874..................................	1 947.6	1 947.6	. . .	1839..................................	. . .	. . .
1873..................................	2 040.8	2 040.8	. . .	1838..................................	. . .	. . .
1872..................................	2 079.2	2 079.2	. . .	1837..................................	. . .	. . .
1871..................................	2 083.0	2 083.0	. . .	1836..................................	. . .	. . .
1870..................................	2 006.1	2 006.1	. . .	1835..................................	2.8	2.8
1869..................................	1 824.8	1 824.8	. . .	1834..................................	. . .	. . .
1868..................................	1 534.6	1 534.6	. . .	1833..................................	. . .	. . .
1867..................................	1 168.0	1 168.0	. . .	1832..................................	. . .	. . .
1866..................................	874.2	874 2	. . .	1831..................................	. . .	. . .
1865..................................	589.9	589.9	. . .	1830..................................	.6	.6
1864..................................	404.3	404.3	. . .	1829..................................	. . .	. . .
1863..................................	276.1	276 1	. . .	1828..................................	. . .	. . .
1862..................................	191.8	191.8	. . .	1827..................................	. . .	. . .
1861..................................	173.3	173.3	. . .	1826..................................	. . .	. . .
1860..................................	173.3	173.3	. . .	1825..................................	.2	.2
1859..................................	151.7	151.7	. . .	1824..................................	. . .	. . .
1858..................................	130.5	130.5	. . .	1823..................................	. . .	. . .
1857..................................	120.6	120.6	. . .	1822..................................	. . .	. . .
1856..................................	106.5	106.5	. . .	1821..................................	. . .	. . .
1855..................................	106.0	106.0	. . .	1820..................................	.1	.1
1854..................................	94.0	94.0	. . .	1819..................................	. . .	. . .
1853..................................	. . .	. . .	. . .	1818..................................	. . .	. . .
1852..................................	. . .	. . .	. . .	1817..................................	. . .	. . .
1851..................................	. . .	. . .	. . .	1816..................................	. . .	. . .
				1815..................................	(Z)	(Z)

* Denotes first year for which figures include Alaska and Hawaii.
Z Less than $50 000 or less than $500 000.
1. Initial year 1911.
2. First weekly premium policy issued 1873; industrial agency system introduced 1875.
3. Initial year 1917.

Series X 957-962. Subscription or Premium Income and Benefit Expenditures of Private Health Insurance: 1948 to 1996

(In millions of dollars)

Year	Subscription or premium income	Total benefit expenditures	Year	Subscription or premium income	Total benefit expenditures	Year	Subscription or premium income	Total benefit expenditures
	957	**958**		**957**	**958**		**957**	**958**
1996	137 100	113 800	1979	35 800	29 600	1963	8 054	6 980
1995	133 900	110 100	1978	32 700	26 400	1962	7 411	6 344
1994	129 300	106 300	1977	28 700	22 100	1961	6 673	5 965
1993	124 700	103 600	1976	24 500	20 200	1960	5 841	4 996
1992	125 000	104 800	1975	20 800	16 500	1959	5 139	4 399
1991	116 400	97 600	1974	17 900	13 600	1958	4 498	3 877
1990	112 900	92 500	1973	16 100	11 900	1957	4 144	3 474
1989	108 000	89 400	1972	14 800	10 600	1956	3 624	3 015
1988	98 200	83 000	1971	12 777	9 497	1955	3 150	2 536
1987	84 100	72 500	1970	17 185	15 744	1954	2 756	2 179
1986	75 500	64 300	1969	14 658	13 069	1953	2 405	1 919
1985	75 200	60 000	1968	12 861	11 310	1952	1 993	1 604
1984	70 400	56 000	1967	11 105	9 545	1951	1 660	1 353
1983	63 200	51 700	1966	10 564	9 142	1950	1 292	992
1982	58 300	49 200	1965	10 001	8 729	1949	1 015	767
1981	49 000	41 600	1964	8 984	7 832	1948	862	606
1980	43 700	37 000						

Series XX 1. Electronic Funds Transfer Volume: 1980 to 1998

(Electronic funds transfer cover automated teller machine (ATM) transactions and transactions at point-of-sale (POS) terminals. Point-of-sale terminals are electronic terminals in retail stores that allow a customer to pay for goods through a direct debit to a customer's account at the bank)

Item	Unit	1980	1985	1990	1993	1994	1995	1996	1997	1998
Total number of transactions	Million	...	3 579	5 942	8 135	8 958	10 464	11 830	12 362	12 960
ATM transactions	Million	...	3 565	5 751	7 705	8 334	9 689	10 684	10 920	11 160
POS transactions	Million	...	14	191	430	624	775	1 146	1 442	1 800
ATM terminals, total[1]	1 000	18.5	60.0	80.2	94.8	109.1	122.7	139.1	165.0	187.0
Monthly transactions per terminal	Number	5 405	4 951	5 980	6 772	6 459	6 580	6 399	5 515	4 977
Shared terminals	1 000	...	35.5	75.3	92.6	108.1	122.6	139.0	165.0	187.0
Proprietary terminals	1 000	...	24.5	4.9	2.3	1.0	0.1	0.1	...	...
POS terminals, total[2]	1 000	...	...	53	155	341	529	875	1 300	1 700

1. As of September.
2. As of June.
Source: Faulkner & Gray, Chicago, IL, Faulkner & Gray/EFT Network Data Book-1998 September 26 1997 and unpublished data (copyright).

Series XX 2. Credit Cards—Holders, Numbers, Spending, and Debt: 1990 to 1997

(122 represents 122 000 000)

Type of credit card	Cardholders (mil.)		Number of cards (mil.)		Credit card spending (bil. dol.)		Credit card debt (bil. dol.)	
	1990	1997	1990	1997	1990	1997	1990	1997
Total[1]	122	149	1 013	1 387	467	1 080	243	560
Bank[2]	79	100	213	403	243	678	154	397
Oil company	85	79	123	109	28	38	3	4
Phone	97	116	141	173	14	19	2	2
Retail store	96	108	459	614	75	121	51	88
Travel and entertainment[3]	16	23	28	31	85	160	20	33
Other[4]	10	7	49	57	22	64	13	36

1. Cardholders may hold more than one type of card.
2. Visa and MasterCard credit cards. Excludes debit cards.
3. Includes American Express and Diners Club.
4. Includes Air Travel Card, automobile rental, Discover (except for cardholders), and miscellaneous cards.
Source: HSN Consultants Inc., Oxnard, CA, The Nilson Report, twice-monthly. (Copyright used by permission.)

Series XX 3. Stock Prices and Yields: 1990 to 1998

(Closing values as of end of December, except as noted)

Index	1990	1993	1994	1995	1996	1997	1998
STOCK PRICES							
Standard & Poor's indices:[1]							
S&P 500 composite (1941-43 = 10)	330.2	466.5	459.3	615.9	740.7	970.4	1 229.20
Industrials	387.1	543.9	548.9	719.7	870.0	1 121.40	1 479.20
Utilities	144.8	176.4	151.9	201.7	198.8	235.8	259.6
S&P 400 Midcap Index (1982 = 100)	100.0	179.4	169.4	217.8	255.6	333.4	392.3
Russell indices:[2]							
Russell 1000 (Dec. 31, 1986 = 130)	171.22	250.71	244.65	328.89	393.75	513.79	642.87
Russell 2000 (Dec. 31, 1986 = 135)	132.16	258.59	250.36	315.97	362.61	437.02	421.96
Russell 3000 (Dec. 31, 1986 = 140)	180.85	270.13	263.44	351.91	419.44	543.05	664.27
N.Y. Stock Exchange common stock index							
Composite (Dec. 31, 1965 = 50)	180.49	259.08	250.94	329.51	392.3	511.19	596.05
Yearly high	201.55	261.16	267.78	331.73	401.08	515.24	601.76
Yearly low	161.76	235.15	241.79	249.86	320.9	386.36	462.69
Industrial (Dec. 31, 1965 = 50)	223.60	315.26	318.1	413.29	494.38	630.38	743.65
Transportation (Dec. 31, 1965 = 50)	141.49	270.48	222.46	301.96	352.3	466.25	482.38
Utility (Dec. 31, 1965 = 100)	182.60	229.92	198.41	252.9	259.91	335.19	445.94
Finance (Dec. 31, 1965 = 50)	122.07	216.82	195.8	274.25	351.17	495.96	521.42
American Stock Exchange Composite Index							
(Dec. 29, 1996 = 550)	. . .	. . .	. . .	550	572.34	684.61	688.99
NASDAQ composite index (Feb. 5, 1971 = 100)	373.8	776.8	752	1 052.10	1 291.00	1 570.40	2 192.70
Industrial	406.1	805.8	753.8	964.7	1 109.60	1 221.00	1 304.30
Insurance	451.8	920.6	925.9	1 292.60	1 465.40	1 798.00	1 796.80
Bank	254.9	689.4	697.1	1 009.40	1 273.50	2 083.20	1 838.00
Dow-Jones and Co., Inc.:							
Composite (65 stocks)	920.6	1 381.00	1 274.40	1 693.20	2 025.80	2 607.40	2 870.80
Industrial (30 stocks)	2 633.70	3 754.10	3 834.40	5 117.10	6 448.30	7 908.30	9 181.40
Transportation (20 stocks)	910.2	1 762.30	1 455.00	1 981.00	2 255.70	3 256.50	3 149.30
Utility (15 stocks)	209.7	229.3	181.5	225.4	232.5	273.1	312.3
Wilshire 5000 equity index							
(Dec. 31, 1980 = 1404.596)	3 101.40	4 657.80	4 540.60	6 057.20	7 274.20	9 298.20	11 317.50
COMMON STOCK YIELDS (percent)							
Standard & Poor's composite index (500 stocks):[3]							
Dividend-price ratio[4]	3.61	2.78	2.82	2.56	2.19	1.77	1.34
Earnings-price ratio[5]	6.47	4.46	5.83	6.09	5.24	4.57	3.10

1. The S&P 500 composite index includes 400 industrial stocks, 20 transportation, 40 public utility, and 40 financial stocks. The S&P Midcap Index shows the 400 largest capitalization stocks in the United States after the S&P 500.
2. The Russell 1000 and 3000 indices show respectively the 1 000 and 3 000 largest capitalization stocks in the United States. The Russell 2000 index shows the 2 000 largest capitalization stocks in the United States after the first 1 000.
3. Source: U.S. Council of Economic Advisers, Economic Report of the President, annual.
4. Aggregate cash dividends (based on latest known annual rate) divided by aggregate market value based on Wednesday closing prices. Averages of monthly figures.
5. Averages of quarterly ratios which are ratio of earnings (after taxes) for 4 quarters ending with particular quarter to price index for last day of that quarter.
Source: Except as noted, Global Financial Data, Alhambra, CA, "GFD Standard and Poor's Sectors;" ⟨http://www.globalfindata.com/tbspsect.htm⟩; "US Stock Market Capitalization Indices;" ⟨http://www.globalfindata.com/tbcap.htm⟩; and "Global Financial Data Dow Jones Industrial Average;" ⟨http://www.globalfindata.com/tbdjia.htm⟩; (all accessed 19 April 1999) and unpublished data (copyright).

Series XX 4. Assets of Private and Public Pension Funds, by Type of Fund: 1980 to 1998

(In billions of dollars. As of end of year. Except for corporate equities, represents book value. Excludes social security trust funds and U.S. government pension funds)

Type of pension fund	1980	1985	1990	1993	1994	1995	1996	1997	1998
Total, all types...........................	882	1 887	3 125	4 344	4 531	5 275	5 964	7 033	8 076
Private funds	685	1 488	2 205	3 088	3 237	3 757	4 249	4 939	5 732
Insured..	172	260	596	836	885	1 002	1 095	1 234	1 401
Noninsured[1][2]	513	1 228	1 608	2 252	2 352	2 755	3 155	3 706	4 331
Credit market instruments[2]	151	331	491	615	661	717	769	835	953
U.S. Government securities[2]	51	196	289	351	402	444	470	503	562
Treasury..	32	138	198	240	272	299	315	334	362
Corporate and foreign bonds	78	97	146	209	201	207	228	256	301
Corporate equities.............................	232	516	595	992	996	1 238	1 491	1 864	2 232
Mutual fund shares	7	11	29	116	150	221	321	438	564
Unallocated insurance contracts[3]	. . .	132	189	207	210	211	220	235	262
State and local pension funds[2]	197	399	920	1 256	1 294	1 518	1 715	2 094	2 344
Credit market instruments[2]	147	252	424	433	456	483	529	566	633
U.S. government securities[2]	40	124	224	231	246	271	299	317	336
Treasury	21	83	140	163	171	176	191	205	195
Corporate and foreign bonds...............................	92	107	172	167	168	163	180	199	245
Corporate equities	44	120	293	531	543	753	956	1 306	1 593

1. Covers all pension funds of corporations, nonprofit organizations, unions, and multi-employer groups. Also includes deferred profit-sharing plans and Federal Employees Retirement System (FERS) Thrift Savings Fund. Excludes health, welfare, and bonus plans.
2. Includes other types of assets not shown separately.
3. Assets held at life insurance companies (e.g., guaranteed investment contracts (GICs), variable annuities).
Source: Board of Governors of the Federal Reserve System, Flow of Funds Accounts, March 1999 quarterly diskettes. Data are also published in the quarterly Z.1 release.

Series XX 5. Securities Listed on New York Stock Exchange: 1980 to 1998

(As of December 31, except cash dividends are for calendar year (602 represent $602 000 000)

Item	Unit	1980	1985	1990	1991	1992	1993	1994	1995	1996	1997	1998
BONDS												
Number of issuers	Number	1 045	1 010	743	705	636	574	583	564	563	533	474
Number of issues	Number	3 057	3 856	2 912	2 727	2 354	2 103	2 141	2 097	2 064	1 965	1 858
Face value	Bil. dol	602	1 327	1 689	2 219	2 009	2 342	2 526	2 773	2 845	2 625	2 554
STOCKS												
Companies	Number	1 570	1 541	1 774	1 885	2 088	2 361	2 570	2 675	2 907	3 047	3 114
Number of issues	Number	2 228	2 298	2 284	2 426	2 658	2 904	3 060	3 126	3 285	3 358	3 382
Shares listed	Billion	33.7	52.4	90.7	99.6	115.8	131.1	142.3	154.7	176.9	207.1	239.3
Market value	Bil. dol	1 243	1 950	2 820	3 713	4 035	4 541	4 448	6 013	7 300	9 413	10 864
Average price	Dollars	36.87	37.20	31.08	37.27	34.83	34.65	31.26	38.86	41.26	45.45	45.40
Cash dividends on common stock[1]	Bil. dol	53.1	74.2	103.2	123.4	109.7	120.2	130.0	147.0	150.6	159.4	179.0

1. Beginning 1990 estimate based on average annual yield of the NYSE composite index.
Source: New York Stock Exchange, Inc., New York, NY, Fact Book annual (copyright).

Seires XX 6. Sales of Stocks and Options on Registered Exchanges: 1980 to 1997

(522 represents $522 000 000 000. Excludes over-the-counter trading)

Exchange	Unit	1980	1985	1990	1991	1992	1993	1994	1995	1996	1997
Market value of all sales, all exchanges[1][2]	Bil. dol	522	1 260	1 752	1 903	2 149	2 734	2 966	3 690	4 735	6 879
New York	Bil. dol	398	1 024	1 394	1 534	1 759	2 278	2 483	3 078	4 013	5 848
American	Bil. dol	47	38	65	67	69	83	83	105	131	204
Chicago	Bil. dol	21	79	74	77	87	107	98	114	136	213
CBOE[3]	Bil. dol	28	38	81	74	63	65	87	107	130	179
Pacific	Bil. dol	13	40	53	63	65	70	70	94	108	151
Philadelphia	Bil. dol	11	23	41	39	49	55	51	59	68	89
STOCKS											
Shares sold, all exchanges[2]	Billion	15.5	37.0	53.3	58.0	65.5	82.8	90.5	106.4	125.7	159.7
New York	Billion	12.4	30.2	43.8	47.7	53.3	68.7	76.7	90.1	108.2	138.8
American	Billion	1.7	2.1	3.1	3.1	3.6	4.5	4.3	4.8	5.3	6.2
Chicago	Billion	0.6	2.3	2.5	2.7	3.0	3.8	3.5	3.9	4.2	6.0
Pacific	Billion	0.4	1.4	1.7	2.1	2.3	2.1	2.1	2.7	3.0	3.2
Market value, all exchanges[2]	Bil. dol	476	1 200	1 612	1 776	2 032	2 610	2 817	3 507	4 511	6 559
New York	Bil. dol	398	1 023	1 390	1 532	1 758	2 276	2 482	3 076	4 011	5 847
American	Bil. dol	35	26	36	40	42	54	56	73	86	139
Chicago	Bil. dol	21	79	74	77	87	107	98	114	136	213
Pacific	Bil. dol	11	37	45	63	58	62	59	79	92	123

1. Includes market value of stocks, rights, warrants, and options trading beginning 1990.
2. Includes other registered exchanges, not shown separately.
3. Chicago Board Options Exchange, Inc.
4. Includes voting trust certificates, American DepositoryReceipts, and certificate of deposit for stocks.
Source: U.S. Securities and Exchange Commission, SEC Monthly Statistical Review (discontinued Feb. 1989); and unpublished data.

SECTION Y

GOVERNMENT

1 Although the United States was founded as a democracy, it took more than 200 years for its electoral mechanisms to evolve from a highly elite, nondemocratic format to their present state. For the first 100 or so years, each state determined for itself who its voters were and how they should be enrolled and permitted to vote. Over the years, Constitutional amendments, Congressional legislation, and judicial decisions applied certain constraints to the states' discretion in specified areas of legal procedure pertaining to elections. In the South, for example, fraudulent stuffing of boxes, suppression of returns, and other irregularities were fairly common from after the Civil War until well into the 20th century. As late as the 1940s Lyndon Johnson's victory in his first Senate race was attributed to such practices. Originally, only free white males were enfranchised. Women were universally enfranchised in 1920, but a number of states gave women suffrage earlier: Wyoming, as a territory, in 1869; Colorado in 1893; Utah in 1896; Idaho in 1897; Washington and California in 1911; Oregon, Arizona and Kansas in 1913; Montana and Nevada in 1914; Illinois in 1916; and Michigan and New York in 1918. Blacks were enfranchised in 1870 by the 15th Amendment to the U.S. Constitution but were handicapped in the South by a number of procedural and technical restrictions designed to keep them away from the ballot box. In the 1960s, the Civil Rights Act made such restrictions unconstitutional. Until 1928 citizenship was not a requirement for voting and aliens voted freely in many states. Because of the difficulty in estimating the number of foreign-born males in the population, the electoral data for years before and after 1928 are not strictly comparable.

2 Article II, Section I of the U.S. Constitution delineates the method for the election of the President of the United States—the establishment of an electoral college in each state. The method of casting the electoral votes was modified in 1804 by the adoption of the 12th Amendment to the U.S. Constitution. With a few exceptions, presidential electors have been chosen by direct popular vote since 1828, although state legislators still have the right to choose the electors. On four occasions in U.S. history, the entire electoral vote of a state remained uncast for technical reasons.

3 The number of members of the U.S. House of Representatives is fixed by Congress at the time of each apportionment and is based on the population of each state as shown in the decennial censuses. No change in total house membership has been made since 1912, except to allot one representative each to Hawaii and Alaska when they attained statehood. Membership was increased to 437 in 1960, but reverted to 435 after 1962. Prior to the passage of the 14th Amendment, Native Americans were excluded from the census and only three out of five slaves were included. Prior to 1850, apportionment ratios were chosen arbitrarily. From 1850 to 1900, it was by dividing the total population by a predetermined number of representatives; from 1910 on, it was by dividing the eligible population by a fixed number of representatives.

4 In any given place, an American lives under at least five governments: federal, state, county, township and school district. In addition, there are many offshoots, such as single-function and multiple-function districts, authorities, and commissions and boards with varying degrees of autonomy and budgetary powers. When Willliam Anderson's monograph, *The Units of Government in the United States,* was published in 1934 there were 175,418 governments in the country. It declined to 155,116 in 1942 and to 83,237 by 1987. This was mainly a result of mergers or eliminations of school districts, which decreased in number from 108,579 in 1942 to 14,721 in 1987. Complete censuses of government covering structure, personnel, expenditure, revenues, and debt were conducted in 1932, 1942 and 1957 and at five year intervals thereafter. Earlier censuses were held decennially, from 1850 to 1890 and for 1902, 1912, and 1922, but were much narrower in scope. These censuses differ not only in scope but also in basic concepts and classifications, thus affecting their comparability. Statistics on government employment and payroll have been published by the Bureau of Labor Statistics since 1955; from 1940 to 1955, they were published by the Bureau of the Census. Data for municipalities are for city, borough, village, and—except in New England, New York and Wisconsin—town governments. Data for school districts are restricted to independent districts and do not include school systems operated by state, city, county, or township governments.

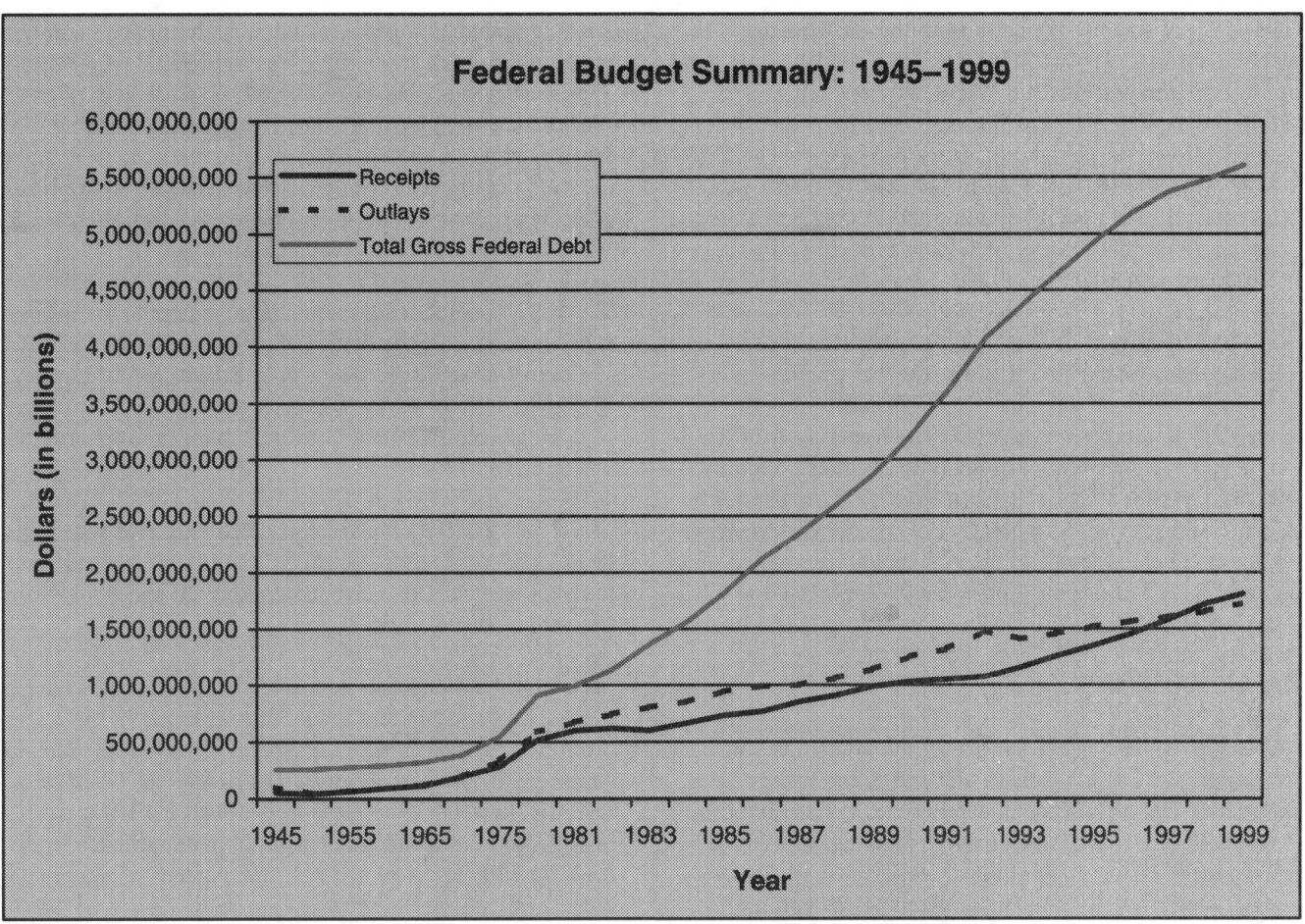

Federal Budget Summary: 1945–1999

5 The first Federal budget of 1789-1791 showed net revenues of $4.399 million, of which all but $20,000 were derived from customs duties. The budget remained under $100 million until 1863 when under the financial strains of the Civil War it rose to $112 million. It crossed the $1 billion mark in 1917, again during wartime; the $100 billion mark in 1963 as the Vietnam War was escalating; and the $1 trillion mark in 1990. As a percentage of GDP, it inched up from 16% in 1950 to 25.2% in 1992. In 1997 it showed a surplus for the first time since 1960, and surpluses are forecast for the foreseeable future "as far as the eye can see." The Unified Federal Budget concept was introduced in 1968 to incorporate reforms recommended by the Presidential Commission on Budget Concepts. Under the Unified Budget, trust funds were included in the Federal Budget to show the total impact of government spending on the economy.

6 When income tax was introduced in 1913, the effective rate was 0.4% for a family in the $5,000 annual earnings range and only 6% for a family earning over $1 million (in 1912 dollars). The total number of returns in 1913 was 357,598. Before the introduction of income tax, 54% of internal revenue collections was from alcohol and 20% from tobacco.

7 Under George Washington, the entire executive staff consisted of two people. In 1815 the number of Federal employees rose to 4,837 of whom 535 worked in Washington, D.C.

8 For a number of years there were two categories of public debt: public debt and the debt subject to the debt limit. The public debt originates from the Treasury Department but excludes debt incurred by public agencies, such as the Tennessee Valley Authority. Gross Public Debt(GPD) is a new concept that includes both Public and Agency debt. Approximately three-fourths of the GPD is owed to the public; the rest is a paper debt consisting of surpluses of trust funds invested by the government in public debt securities. Interest payments on this part of the debt are paid from one account within the budget to another account also within the budget and therefore do not affect the budget surplus or deficit. Because the Federal Reserve System is an independent body outside the Federal budget, the U.S. government pays the Federal Reserve interest on money borrowed from it for budgetary purposes. Debt held by the system is shown as debt held by the public, and interest paid to the system affects budget surplus or deficit. In years of heavy borrowing, the government has to pay billions of dollars in interest, thus adding to the deficit, and vice versa. However, since 1947, the Fed has made annual payments to the Treasury from its surplus, which, in turn, arises primarily as a result of interest payments made by the Treasury. The public debt in 1791 was $75.463 million or $19.21 per capita. By the time of the Civil War it had been reduced to $2.85 per capita. The Civil War and the half century following saw growth in public debt, but it decreased to the very low level of $11.99 per capita by the start of World War I. Thereafter it rose steadily, crossing the $1,000 per capita mark in 1944. In 1998 the the GPD was $5.614 trillion, or $21,000 per capita.

9 The Department of War (now the Department of Defense) was established in 1789. The Navy started functioning in 1794 and a separate Navy Department was authorized and organized in 1798. The Department of the Air Force was set up in 1947 under the National Security Act. The Marine Corps was founded in 1775, disbanded in 1783, and reactivated in 1794. In 1794, under George Washington, the defense force of the new republic consisted of an army of 3,813 persons (including 235 officers) and a Navy of 1,856 persons (including 150 officers). The total military budget was $2.639 million for the Army and $61,000 for the Navy.

10 The United States has one of the lowest rates of voter participation in elections and one of the highest rates of political apathy among all democracies (as measured by voter turnout for elections, number of citizens running for office, membership in political parties, etc.) Generally, presidential election years draw more voters to the polling booths than mid-term election years. Even so, only 50.1% of eligible voters turn out in average presidential years. The highest percentage of voting age population participating in a presidential election was 62.8% in 1960. In Congressional elections, the percentage is much lower, approximately one-third.

11 The power of incumbency on Congress is illustrated by the fact that 94.0% of all representatives and 90.5% of all senators in presidential election years and 97.8% of all representatives in presidential election years and 89.7% of senators in mid term election years are reelected.

12 The women and minority share of both the House and the Senate has increased since the 1980s. The number of women has increased from 19 in the House and two in the Senate in 1981 to 47 in the House and eight in the Senate in 1996. Similarly, the number of Blacks grew from 17 in the House and none in the Senate to 40 in the House and none in the Senate in 1996. The members of both houses are now older than the members in 1981. There are 53 members in the House and one member in the Senate below age 40, compared to 94 and nine, respectively in 1981. The Senators tend to be even older. There were 17 members over age 70 in 1996, compared to six in 1981.

13 The number of measures enacted by Congress has declined since 1972, primarily because many private bills are being bundled together as omnibus bills. The number of measures enacted, 1995-1996, was only 337 compared to 736 in 1979-1980. Nevertheless, both representatives and senators are working more than they used to, working for a fewer number of days in each session, but a greater number of hours per day. On average, a representative worked for 2,445 hours annually or 8.4 hours per day and a senator for 2,876 hours annually or 9.8 hours per day.

14 The number of Democratic governors is the lowest it has been since 1901, with Republican governors in 31 states, including all the major ones except for California. The governor elected in 1998 with the highest percentage of popular votes was Bill Graves, Republican of Kansas who received 73.4%.

15 In 1975 Republicans controlled only five state legislatures and Democrats controlled 37. In 1997 control was fairly even, with Democrats controlling 20 and Republicans 18, with 11 states divided.

16 Of the 493,830 local elected officials at the county, municipal, township and school district levels in 1992, 405905, 82% were white, 2.3% were black and the remainder were of other racial origin. The number of black elected officials nationwide grew from 1,469 in 1970 to 8,617 in 1997 and the number of Hispanic public officials from 3,147 in 1985 to 5,459 in 1994. The number of women elected officials at the state level grew to 1,617 in 1998, compared to 1,375 in 1990.

17 Of the total voting-age population only one third register and only 54.2% voted in presidential election years and 41.9% in congressional election years. More white voters register and vote than black voters and the 4% gap between these two categories of voters has remained despite efforts to bring more blacks into the political stream. By states, the highest percentage of voters was 67.7% in Maine and the lowest 46.2% in Texas.

18 Seven states do not have state income tax: Alaska, Florida, Nevada, South Dakota, Texas, Washington and Wyoming. Illinois, Indiana, Massachusetts, Michigan and Pennsylvania have flat rates,while Colorado, Rhode Island and Vermont have taxes calculated as a percentage of Federal tax liability.

19 Total lottery ticket sales reached $35.5 billion in 1997. Only 10 states do not have lotteries: Alabama, Alaska, Arkansas, Louisiana, Nebraska, Nevada, New Mexico, North Dakota, Oklahoma, and South Carolina.

20 State and local governments generate almost as much revenue as the Federal government: $1.513 trillion for the former compared to $1.572 trillion for the latter. State and local revenues rely more on sales taxes and less on direct income taxes than the Federal government. Pat-

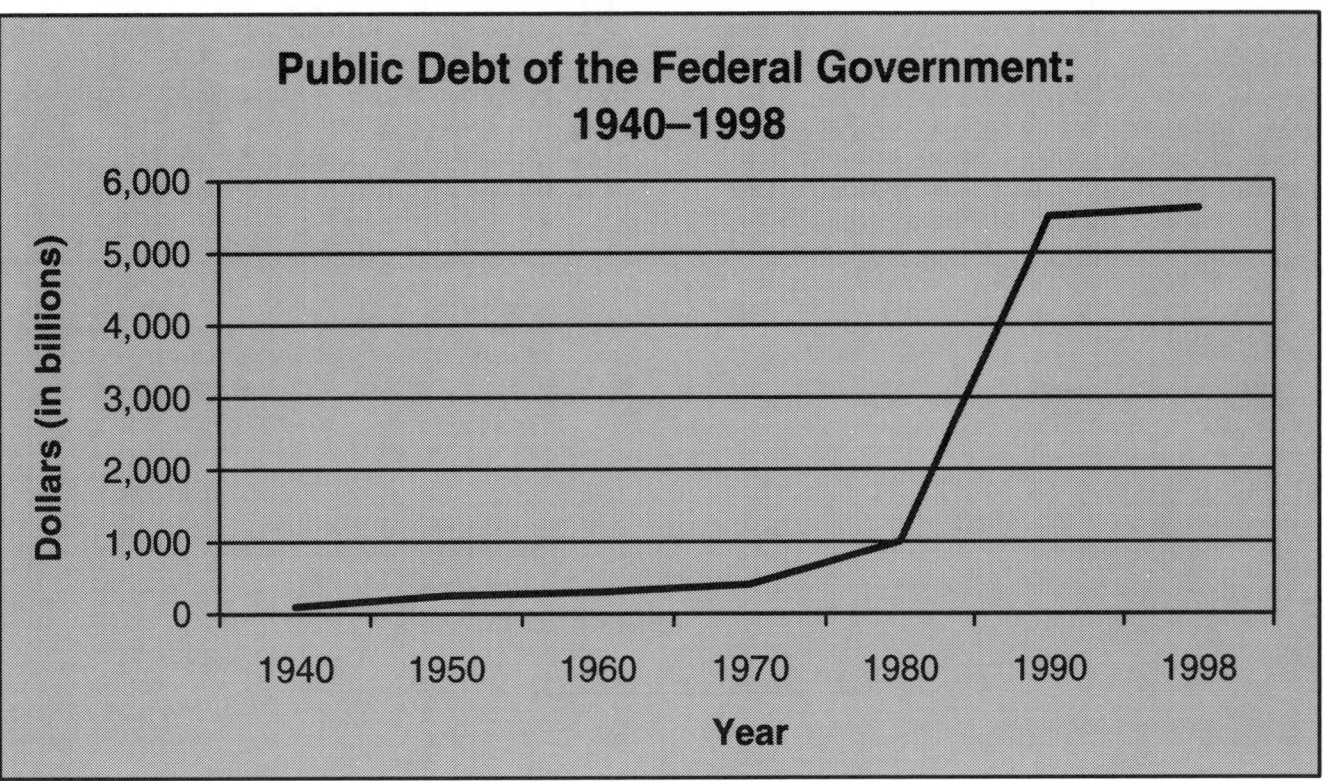

Public Debt of the Federal Government: 1940–1998

terns of expenditure are also different, with state and local governments spending more on education, highways and similar services and less on national defense, environment, and general interest on public debt than the Federal government. State and local governments spend $447 billion on salaries and wages compared to $162 billion for the Federal government.

21 Total Federal grants in aid to state and local governments has risen from $24.065 billion in 1970 to $262.164 billion in 1999. This represents 15.2% of Federal outlays and 3.0% of the GDP The two largest components of Federal aid are Medicaid ($101 billion) and Aid to Children and Families ($32.427 billion).

22 In 1996 Americans paid $209.440 billion in property taxes and $248.993 billion in sales taxes. State and local expenditures reached $1.393 trillion ($5,256 per capita) of which education was the largest component with $398 billion. Total state and local debt was $1.169 trillion, or $4,411 per capita.

23 Honolulu, Hawaii, is the lowest taxed city in the nation, with an effective property tax rate per $100 of 0.39. Newark, New Jersey is the highest with an effective property tax rate per $100 of 3.91.

24 New York City has the largest city budget in the United States, with revenues of $49.292 billion and expenditures of $48.018 billion in 1996. Among counties Los Angeles occupies the same position, with revenues of $13.988 billion and expenditures of $12.421 billion.

25 In 1997, the Federal government employed 2.807 million civilians and state and local governments 16.733 million. Monthly payroll is $9.7 billion for the Federal government and $39.412 billion for state and local governments.

26 The Federal budget, estimated at $1.806 trillion for 1999, will soon exceed $2 trillion a year by 2002. For the first time since 1960, the budget had a surplus in both 1998 and 1999. As a percentage of the GDP, the Federal budget has remained at a stable and healthy 19.7%, the lowest since 1970. Th Gross Federal Debt stood at $5.6 trillion in 1999 or 64.2% of GDP, a lower percentage than in any year since 1993.

27 Americans paid a total of $868 billion in individual income taxes to the federal government, making up approximately half of all revenues. Social insurance and retirement receipts made up another $608.824 billion.

28 By agencies and units of administration, the largest segment of the Federal budget was the $385.9 billion spent by the Treasury, followed by $375.5 billion by HUD, and $263.5 billion by the Department of Defense.

29 The Federal Defense budget reached $320.2 billion, the highest in the past 40 years except for 1993, 1992, 1990 and 1989. As a percentage of GDP, it has declined from 9.3% in 1960 to 3.2% in 1999. Military downsizing has led to a substantial reduction in personnel from 3,693,000 in 1990 to 3,081,000 in 1997. The United States accounts for 32.1% of military expenditures throughout the world.

30 The United States is a major arms exporter. In 1996 it sold $23.5 billion worth of arms to various countries, more than half of all sales worldwide. Between 1994 and 1996 the United States sold $67.2 billion worth of arms.

31 In 1997 227,258 U. S. military personnel were on active military duty abroad, including 35,663 in Korea, 60,053 in Germany, 41,257 in Japan, and 8,170 in Bosnia.

32 The number of veterans in 1998 was 25,062,000 of which war veterans numbered 19.207 million.

Series Y 79-83. Electoral and Popular Vote Cast for President, by Political Party: 1789 to 1996

(Excludes unpledged tickets and minor candidates polling under 10,000 votes through 1968. Includes only the two leading minority party candidates after 1968. Various party labels may have been used by a candidate in different states; the more important of these are listed below)

Year	No. of states	Presidential candidate	Political party	Vote cast Electoral	Vote cast Popular
	79	80	81	82	83
1996..	50	Bill Clinton	Democratic	379	47 402 000
		Robert Dole	Republican	159	39 199 000
		H. Ross Perot	Independent	X	8 085 000
		Ralph Nader	Green	X	685 000
1992..	50	Bill Clinton	Democratic	370	44 409 000
		George Bush	Republican	168	39 104 000
		H. Ross Perot	Independent	X	19 742 000
		Andre Marrou	Libertarian	X	292 000
1988..	50	George Bush	Republican	426	48 886 000
		Michael Dukakis	Democratic	111	41 809 000
		Ron Paul	Libertarian	X	432 000
		Lenora B. Fulani	New Alliance	X	217 000
1984..	50	Ronald Reagan	Republican	525	54 455 000
		Walter Mondale	Democratic	13	37 577 000
		David Bergland	Libertarian	X	228 000
		Lyndon H. LaRouche	Independent	X	79 000
1980..	50	Ronald Reagan	Republican	489	43 904 000
		Jimmy Carter	Democratic	49	35 484 000
		John Anderson	Independent	X	5 720 000
		Ed Clark	Libertarian	X	921 000
1976..	50	Jimmy Carter	Democratic	297	40 831 000
		Gerald Ford	Republican	240	39 148 000
		Eugene McCarthy	Independent	X	757 000
		Roger McBride	Libertarian	X	173 000
1972..	50	Richard Nixon	Republican	520	47 170 000
		George McGovern	Democratic	17	29 170 000
		John Schmitz	American	X	1 099 000
		Benjamin Spock	People's	X	79 000
1968..	50	Richard M. Nixon	Republican	301	31 785 480
		Hubert H. Humphrey	Democratic	191	31 275 166
		George C. Wallace	American Independent	46	9 906 473
		Henning A. Blomen	Socialist Labor	X	52 588
		Dick Gregory	[1]	X	47 133
		Fred Halstead	Socialist Workers	X	41 388
		Eldridge Cleaver	Peace and Freedom	X	36 563
		Eugene J. McCarthy	[2]	X	25 552
		E. Harold Munn	Prohibition	X	15 123
1964..	50	Lyndon B. Johnson	Democratic	486	43 129 566
		Barry M. Goldwater	Republican	52	27 178 188
		Eric Hass	Socialist Labor	X	45 219
		Clifton DeBerry	Socialist Workers	X	32 720
		E. Harold Munn	Prohibition	X	23 267
1960..	50	John F. Kennedy	Democratic	[3]303	34 226 731
		Richard M. Nixon	Republican	219	34 108 157
		Eric Hass	Socialist Labor	X	47 522
		Rutherford L. Decker	Prohibition	X	46 203
		Orval E. Faubus	National States' Rights	X	44 977
		Farrell Dobbs	Socialist Workers	X	40 165
		Charles L. Sullivan	Constitution	X	18 162
1956..	48	Dwight D. Eisenhower	Republican	457	35 590 472
		Adlai E. Stevenson	Democratic	[4]73	26 022 752
		T. Coleman Andrews	States' Rights	X	111 178
		Eric Hass	Socialist Labor	X	44 450
		Enoch A. Holtwick	Prohibition	X	41 937
1952..	48	Dwight D. Eisenhower	Republican	442	33 936 234
		Adlai E. Stevenson	Democratic	89	27 314 992
		Vincent Hallinan	Progressive	X	140 023
		Stuart Hamblen	Prohibition	X	72 949
		Eric Hass	Socialist Labor	X	30 267
		Darlington Hoopes	Socialist	X	20 203
		Douglas A. MacArthur	Constitution	X	17 205
		Farrell Dobbs	Socialist Workers	X	10 312

See footnotes at end of table.

Series Y 79-83. Electoral and Popular Vote Cast for President, by Political Party: 1789 to 1996—Cont'd.

(Excludes unpledged tickets and minor candidates polling under 10,000 votes through 1968. Includes only the two leading minority party candidates after 1968. Various party labels may have been used by a candidate in different states; the more important of these are listed below)

Year	No. of states	Presidential candidate	Political party	Vote cast	
				Electoral	Popular
	79	**80**	**81**	**82**	**83**
1948...	48	Harry S. Truman	Democratic	303	24 179 345
		Thomas E. Dewey	Republican	189	21 991 291
		Strom Thurmond	States' Rights	39	1 176 125
		Henry Wallace	Progressive	X	1 157 326
		Norman Thomas	Socialist	X	139 572
		Claude A. Watson	Prohibition	X	103 900
		Edward A. Teichert	Socialist Labor	X	29 241
		Farrell Dobbs	Socialist Workers	X	13 614
1944...	48	Franklin D. Roosevelt	Democratic	432	25 606 585
		Thomas E. Dewey	Republican	99	22 014 745
		Norman Thomas	Socialist	X	80 518
		Claude A. Watson	Prohibition	X	74 758
		Edward A. Teichert	Socialist Labor	X	45 336
1940...	48	Franklin D. Roosevelt	Democratic	449	27 307 819
		Wendell L. Willkie	Republican	82	22 321 018
		Norman Thomas	Socialist	X	99 557
		Roger Q. Babson	Prohibition	X	57 812
		Earl Browder	Communist	X	46 251
		John W. Aiken	Socialist Labor	X	14 892
1936...	48	Franklin D. Roosevelt	Democratic	523	27 752 869
		Alfred M. Landon	Republican	8	16 674 665
		William Lemke	Union	X	882 479
		Norman Thomas	Socialist	X	187 720
		Earl Browder	Communist	X	80 159
		D. Leigh Colvin	Prohibition	X	37 847
		John W. Aiken	Socialist Labor	X	12 777
1932...	48	Franklin D. Roosevelt	Democratic	472	22 809 638
		Herbert C. Hoover	Republican	59	15 758 901
		Norman Thomas	Socialist	X	881 951
		William Z. Foster	Communist	X	102 785
		William D. Upshaw	Prohibition	X	81 869
		Verne L. Reynolds	Socialist Labor	X	33 276
		William H. Harvey	Liberty	X	53 425
1928...	48	Herbert C. Hoover	Republican	444	21 391 993
		Alfred E. Smith	Democratic	87	15 016 169
		Norman Thomas	Socialist	X	267 835
		Verne L. Reynolds	Socialist Labor	X	21 603
		William Z. Foster	Workers	X	21 181
		William F. Varney	Prohibition	X	20 106
1924...	48	Calvin Coolidge	Republican	382	15 718 211
		John W. Davis	Democratic	136	8 385 283
		Robert M. LaFollette	Progressive	13	4 831 289
		Herman P. Faris	Prohibition	X	57 520
		Frank T. Johns	Socialist Labor	X	36 428
		William Z. Foster	Workers	X	36 386
		Gilbert O. Nations	American	X	23 967
1920...	48	Warren G. Harding	Republican	404	16 143 407
		James M. Cox	Democratic	127	9 130 328
		Eugene V. Debs	Socialist	X	919 799
		P.P. Christensen	Farmer-Labor	X	265 411
		Aaron S. Watkins	Prohibition	X	189 408
		James E. Ferguson	American	X	48 000
		W.W. Cox	Socialist Labor	X	31 715

See footnotes at end of table.

Series Y 79-83. Electoral and Popular Vote Cast for President, by Political Party: 1789 to 1996—Cont'd.

(Excludes unpledged tickets and minor candidates polling under 10,000 votes through 1968. Includes only the two leading minority party candidates after 1968. Various party labels may have been used by a candidate in different states; the more important of these are listed below)

Year	No. of states	Presidential candidate	Political party	Vote cast Electoral	Vote cast Popular
	79	80	81	82	83
1916	48	Woodrow Wilson	Democratic	277	9 127 695
		Charles E. Hughes	Republican	254	8 533 507
		A.L. Benson	Socialist	X	585 113
		J. Frank Hanly	Prohibition	X	220 506
		Arthur E. Reimer	Socialist Labor	X	13 403
1912	48	Woodrow Wilson	Democratic	435	6 296 547
		Theodore Roosevelt	Progressive	88	4 118 571
		William H. Taft	Republican	8	3 486 720
		Eugene V. Debs	Socialist	X	900 672
		Eugene W. Chafin	Prohibition	X	206 275
		Arthur E. Reimer	Socialist Labor	X	28 750
1908	46	William H. Taft	Republican	321	7 675 320
		William J. Bryan	Democratic	162	6 412 294
		Eugene V. Debs	Socialist	X	420 793
		Eugene W. Chafin	Prohibition	X	253 840
		Thomas L Hisgen	Independence	X	82 872
		Thomas E. Watson	People's	X	29 100
		August Gillhaus	Socialist Labor	X	14 021
1904	45	Theodore Roosevelt	Republican	336	7 628 461
		Alton B. Parker	Democratic	140	5 084 223
		Eugene V. Debs	Socialist	X	402 283
		Silas C. Swallow	Prohibition	X	258 536
		Thomas E. Watson	People's	X	117 183
		Charles H. Corregan	Socialist Labor	X	31 249
1900	45	William McKinley	Republican	292	7 218 491
		William J. Bryan	Democratic[5]	155	6 356 734
		John C. Wooley	Prohibition	X	208 914
		Eugene V. Debs	Socialist	X	87 814
		Wharton Barker	People's	X	50 373
		Joseph F. Malloney	Socialist Labor	X	39 739
1896	45	William McKinley	Republican	271	7 102 246
		William J. Bryan	Democratic[5]	176	6 492 559
		John M. Palmer	National Democratic	X	133 148
		Joshua Levering	Prohibition	X	132 007
		Charles H. Matchett	Socialist Labor	X	36 274
		Charles E. Bentley	Nationalist	X	13 969
1892	44	Grover Cleveland	Democratic	277	5 555 426
		Benjamin Harrison	Republican	145	5 182 690
		James B. Weaver	People's	22	1 029 846
		John Bidwell	Prohibition	X	264 133
		Simon Wing	Socialist Labor	X	21 164
1888	38	Benjamin Harrison	Republican	233	5 447 129
		Grover Cleveland	Democratic	168	5 537 857
		Clinton B. Fisk	Prohibition	X	249 506
		Anson J. Streeter	Union Labor	X	146 935
1884	38	Grover Cleveland	Democratic	219	4 879 507
		James G. Blaine	Republican	182	4 850 293
		Benjamin F. Butler	Greenback-Labor	X	175 370
		John P. St. John	Prohibition	X	150 369
1880	38	James A. Garfield	Republican	214	4 453 295
		Winfield S. Hancock	Democratic	155	4 414 082
		James B. Weaver	Greenback-Labor	X	308 578
		Neal Dow	Prohibition	X	10 305
1876	38	Rutherford B. Hayes	Republican	185	4 036 572
		Samuel J. Tilden	Democratic	184	4 284 020
		Peter Cooper	Greenback	X	81 737

See footnotes at end of table.

Series Y 79-83. Electoral and Popular Vote Cast for President, by Political Party: 1789 to 1996—Cont'd.

(Excludes unpledged tickets and minor candidates polling under 10,000 votes through 1968. Includes only the two leading minority party candidates after 1968. Various party labels may have been used by a candidate in different states; the more important of these are listed below)

Year	No. of states	Presidential candidate	Political party	Vote cast	
				Electoral	Popular
	79	**80**	**81**	**82**	**83**
1872	37	Ulysses S. Grant	Republican	286	3 596 745
		Horace Greeley	Democratic	(6)	2 843 446
		Charles O'Connor	Straight Democratic	X	29 489
		Thomas A. Hendricks	Independent Democratic	42	...
		B. Gratz Brown	Democratic	18	...
		Charles J. Jenkins	Democratic	2	...
		David Davis	Democratic	1	...
		(Not voted)	...	17	...
1868	37	Ulysses S. Grant	Republican	214	3 013 421
		Horatio Seymour	Democratic	80	2 706 829
		(Not voted)	...	23	...
1864	36	Abraham Lincoln	Republican	212	2 206 938
		George B. McClellan	Democratic	21	1 803 787
		(Not voted)	...	81	...
1860	33	Abraham Lincoln	Republican	180	1 865 593
		J.C. Breckinridge	Democratic (S)	72	848 356
		Stephen A. Douglas	Democratic	12	1 382 713
		John Bell	Constitutional Union	39	592 906
1856	31	James Buchanan	Democratic	174	1 832 955
		John C. Fremont	Republican	114	1 339 932
		Millard Fillmore	American	8	871 731
1852	31	Franklin Pierce	Democratic	254	1 601 117
		Winfield Scott	Whig	42	1 385 453
		John P. Hale	Free Soil	X	155 825
1848	30	Zachary Taylor	Whig	163	1 360 967
		Lewis Cass	Democratic	127	1 222 342
		Martin Van Buren	Free Soil	X	291 263
1844	26	James K. Polk	Democratic	170	1 338 464
		Henry Clay	Whig	105	1 300 097
		James G. Birney	Liberty	X	62 300
1840	26	William H. Harrison	Whig	234	1 274 624
		Martin Van Buren	Democratic	60	1 127 781
1836	26	Martin Van Buren	Democratic	170	765 483
		William H. Harrison	Whig	73	...
		Hugh L. White	Whig	26	[7] 739 795
		Daniel Webster	Whig	14	...
		W.P. Mangum	Anti-Jackson	11	...
1832	24	Andrew Jackson	Democratic	219	687 502
		Henry Clay	National Republican	49	530 189
		William Wirt	Anti-Masonic	7	...
		John Floyd	Nullifiers	11	...
		(Not voted)	...	2	...
1828	24	Andrew Jackson	Democratic	178	647 286
		John Q. Adams	National Republican	83	508 064
1824	24	John Q. Adams	No distinct party	[8]84	108 740
		Andrew Jackson	designations	[8]99	153 544
		Henry Clay	...	37	47 136
		W.H. Crawford	...	41	46 618
1820	24	James Monroe	Republican	231	...
		John Q. Adams	Independent-Republican	1	...
		(Not voted)	...	3	...

See footnotes at end of table.

Series Y 79-83. Electoral and Popular Vote Cast for President, by Political Party: 1789 to 1996—Cont'd.

(Excludes unpledged tickets and minor candidates polling under 10,000 votes through 1968. Includes only the two leading minority party candidates after 1968. Various party labels may have been used by a candidate in different states; the more important of these are listed below)

Year	No. of states	Presidential candidate	Political party	Vote cast	
				Electoral	Popular
79	79	80	81	82	83
1816	19	James Monroe	Republican	183	...
		Rufus King	Federalist	34	...
		(Not voted)	...	4	...
1812	18	James Madison	Democratic-Republican	128	...
		DeWitt Clinton	Fusion	89	...
		(Not voted)	...	1	...
1808	17	James Madison	Democratic-Republican	122	...
		C.C. Pinckney	Federalist	47	...
		George Clinton	Independent-Republican	6	...
		(Not voted)	...	1	...
1804	17	Thomas Jefferson	Democratic-Republican	162	...
		C.C. Pinckney	Federalist	14	...
1800 [9]	16	Thomas Jefferson	Democratic-Republican	73	...
		Aaron Burr	Democratic-Republican	73	...
		John Adams	Federalist	65	...
		C.C. Pinckney	Federalist	64	...
		John Jay	Federalist	1	...
1796 [9]	16	John Adams	Federalist	71	...
		Thomas Jefferson	Democratic-Republican	68	...
		Thomas Pinckney	Federalist	59	...
		Aaron Burr	Anti-Federalist	30	...
		Samuel Adams	Democratic-Republican	15	...
		Oliver Ellsworth	Federalist	11	...
		George Clinton	Democratic-Republican	7	...
		John Jay	Independent-Federalist	5	...
		James Iredell	Federalist	3	...
		George Washington	Federalist	2	...
		John Henry	Independent	2	...
		S. Johnston	Independent-Federalist	2	...
		C.C. Pinckney	Independent-Federalist	1	...
1792 [9]	15	George Washington	Federalist	132	...
		John Adams	Federalist	77	...
		George Clinton	Democratic-Republican	50	...
		Thomas Jefferson	...	4	...
		Aaron Burr	...	1	...
1789 [9]	10	George Washington	...	69	...
		John Adams	...	34	...
		John Jay	...	9	...
		R.H. Harrison	...	6	...
		John Rutledge	...	6	...
		John Hancock	...	4	...
		George Clinton	...	3	...
		Samuel Huntington	...	2	...
		John Milton	...	2	...
		James Armstrong	...	1	...
		Benjamin Lincoln	...	1	...
		Edward Telfair	...	1	...
		(Not voted)	...	12	...

X Represents zero.
1. Total vote for Gregory includes write-in votes as well as votes for the Freedom and Peace Party, the Peace Freedom Alternative, the Peace and Freedom Party and the New Party.
2. Total vote for McCarthy includes write-in votes as well as votes for the Alternative in November Party and the New Party.
3. Six Democratic electors in Alabama, all eight unpledged Democratic electors in Mississippi and one Republican elector in Oklahoma voted for Senator Harry F. Byrd.
4. One Democratic elector in Alabama voted for Walter Jones.
5. Includes a variety of joint tickets with People's Party electors committed to Bryan.
6. Greeley died shortly after the election and presidential electors supporting him cast their votes as indicated, including three for Greeley, which were not counted.
7. Whig tickets were pledged to various candidates in various states.
8. No candidate having a majority in the electoral college, the election was decided in the House of Representatives.
9. Prior to the election of 1804, each elector voted for two candidates for president; the one receiving the highest number of votes, if a majority, was declared elected president, the next highest, vice president. This provision was modified by adoption of the 12th amendment, which was declared ratified by the legislatures of three-fourths of the states in a proclamation of the Secretary of State, Sept. 25, 1804.

Series Y 135-186. Popular Vote Cast for President, by State and Political Party: 1836 to 1996

(In thousands. Rep.-Republican; Dem.-Democratic; Ind.-Independent. Vote listed is normally that of the highest candidate for presidential elector for each party. Democratic vote in 1896 and 1900 includes a variety of joint elector tickets with the People's Party, and party totals generally include votes cast for the presidential candidate under other designations than that of the party itself)

Series No.	State	1996 Total	1996 Rep.	1996 Dem.	1996 Ind.	1992 Rep.	1992 Dem.	1992 Ind.	1988 Total	1988 Rep.	1988 Dem.	1984 Total	1984 Rep.	1984 Dem.
135	**United States**	104 425	39 104	44 909	19 742	38 117	43 682	19 217	91 595	48 886	41 809	92 653	54 455	37 577
136	Alabama	...	804	690	183	797	686	180	1 378	816	550	1 442	873	552
137	Alaska	...	102	78	73	73	57	50	200	119	73	208	138	62
138	Arizona	...	572	543	354	543	521	339	1 172	703	454	1 026	681	334
139	Arkansas	...	337	506	99	331	495	97	828	467	349	884	535	339
140	California	...	3 631	5 121	2 296	3 338	4 812	2 144	9 887	5 055	4 702	9 505	5 467	3 923
141	Colorado	...	563	630	366	557	625	362	1 372	728	621	1 295	822	455
142	Connecticut	...	578	682	349	574	681	348	1 443	750	677	1 467	891	570
143	Delaware	...	102	126	59	102	125	59	250	140	109	255	152	102
144	District of Columbia	...	21	193	10	...	...	...	...	...	...	...	...	...
145	Florida	...	2 173	2 073	1 053	2 131	2 051	1 040	4 302	2 619	1 657	4 180	2 730	1 449
146	Georgia	...	995	1 009	310	985	1 002	366	1 810	1 081	715	1 776	1 069	707
147	Hawaii	...	137	179	53	136	178	52	354	159	192	336	185	147
148	Idaho	...	203	137	130	201	136	129	409	254	147	411	298	109
149	Illinois	...	1 734	2 453	841	1 717	2 378	832	4 559	2 311	2 216	4 819	2 707	2 086
150	Indiana	...	989	848	456	978	839	451	2 169	1 298	861	2 233	1 377	841
151	Iowa	...	505	586	253	503	583	251	1 226	545	671	1 320	703	606
152	Kansas	...	450	390	312	443	386	312	993	554	423	1 022	677	333
153	Kentucky	...	617	665	204	617	661	203	1 323	734	580	1 369	822	540
154	Louisiana	...	733	816	211	729	815	210	1 628	884	717	1 707	1 037	652
155	Maine	...	207	263	207	207	261	205	555	307	244	553	337	215
156	Maryland	...	707	989	281	671	941	271	1 714	876	826	1 676	880	788
157	Massachusetts	...	805	1 319	631	803	1 315	630	2 633	1 195	1 401	2 559	1 311	1 240
158	Michigan	...	1 555	1 871	825	1 585	1 854	819	3 669	1 965	1 676	3 802	2 252	1 530
159	Minnesota	...	748	1 021	563	734	994	549	2 007	962	1 109	2 084	1 033	1 036
160	Mississippi	...	488	400	86	478	391	83	932	558	364	941	852	352
161	Missouri	...	811	1 054	519	810	1 051	517	2 094	1 085	1 002	2 123	1 274	849
162	Montana	...	144	155	107	143	153	106	366	190	169	384	232	147
163	Nebraska	...	344	217	174	338	214	171	661	398	259	652	460	188
164	Nevada	...	176	189	133	171	185	129	350	206	133	287	189	92
165	New Hampshire	...	202	209	121	199	207	120	451	282	164	389	267	120
166	New Jersey	...	1 357	1 436	522	1 303	1 361	504	3 100	1 743	1 320	3 218	1 934	1 261
167	New Mexico	...	213	262	92	209	255	90	521	270	244	514	307	202
168	New York	...	2 347	3 444	1 091	2 240	3 244	1 028	6 486	3 082	3 348	6 807	3 665	3 120
169	North Carolina	...	1 135	1 114	358	1 122	1 103	353	2 134	1 237	890	2 175	1 346	824
170	North Dakota	...	136	99	71	133	97	69	297	167	128	309	200	104
171	Ohio	...	1 894	1 985	1 036	1 876	1 964	1 024	4 394	2 417	1 940	4 548	2 679	1 825
172	Oklahoma	...	593	473	320	592	473	319	1 171	678	483	1 256	862	385
173	Oregon	...	476	621	354	393	524	307	1 202	560	616	1 227	686	536
174	Pennsylvania	...	1 792	2 239	903	1 777	2 223	895	4 536	2 300	2 195	4 845	2 584	2 228
175	Rhode Island	...	132	213	105	121	198	94	405	178	225	410	212	197
176	South Carolina	...	578	480	139	572	475	137	986	606	371	969	616	344
177	South Dakota	...	137	125	73	136	124	73	313	165	146	318	200	116
178	Tennessee	...	841	934	200	840	933	199	1636	947	680	1 712	990	712
179	Texas	...	2 496	2 282	1 355	2 460	2 278	1 349	5 427	3 037	2 353	5 398	3 433	1 949
180	Utah	...	323	183	203	320	182	202	647	428	207	630	469	155
181	Vermont	...	88	134	66	85	125	61	243	124	116	235	136	96
182	Virginia	...	1 151	1 039	349	1 146	1 033	344	2 192	1 309	860	2 147	1 337	796
183	Washington	...	731	993	542	609	855	470	1 865	904	934	1 884	1 052	807
184	West Virginia	...	242	331	109	236	324	105	653	341	310	736	405	328
185	Wisconsin	...	931	1 041	544	926	1 035	542	2 192	1 047	1 127	2 212	1 199	996
186	Wyoming	...	79	68	51	79	67	51	177	107	67	189	133	53

See footnotes at end of table.

Series Y 135-186. Popular Vote Cast for President, by State and Political Party: 1836 to 1996—Cont'd.

(In thousands. Rep.-Republican; Dem.-Democratic; Ind.-Independent. Vote listed is normally that of the highest candidate for presidential elector for each party. Democratic vote in 1896 and 1900 includes a variety of joint elector tickets with the People's Party, and party totals generally include votes cast for the presidential candidate under other designations than that of the party itself)

Series No.	State	1980			1976			1972		
		Total	Rep.	Dem.	Total	Rep.	Dem.	Total	Rep.	Dem.
135	**United States**	**86 515**	**43 904**	**35 484**	**81 556**	**39 148**	**40 831**	**77 719**	**47 170**	**29 170**
136	Alabama	1342	654	637	1 183	504	659	1 006	729	257
137	Alaska	158	86	42	124	72	44	95	55	33
138	Arizona	874	530	247	743	419	296	623	403	109
139	Arkansas	838	403	398	768	268	499	651	449	200
140	California	8 587	4 525	3 084	7 867	3 882	3 742	8 368	4 602	3 476
141	Colorado	1 184	652	368	1 082	584	460	954	597	330
142	Connecticut	1 406	677	542	1 382	719	648	1 384	811	555
143	Delaware	236	111	106	236	110	123	236	140	92
144	District of Columbia	...	...	...	...	...	...	...	...	...
145	Florida	3 687	2 047	1 419	3 151	1 470	1 636	2 583	1 858	718
146	Georgia	1 597	654	891	1 467	484	979	1 175	881	290
147	Hawaii	303	130	136	291	140	147	270	169	101
148	Idaho	437	291	110	344	204	127	310	199	81
149	Illinois	4 750	1 981	2 358	4 719	2 364	2 271	4 723	2 788	1 913
150	Indiana	2 242	1 256	844	2 220	1 184	1 015	2 126	1 405	709
151	Iowa	1 318	676	509	1 279	633	620	1 226	706	496
152	Kansas	980	567	326	958	503	430	916	620	270
153	Kentucky	1 295	635	616	1 167	532	616	1 067	676	371
154	Louisiana	1 549	793	708	1 278	587	661	1 051	687	298
155	Maine	523	239	221	483	236	232	417	256	161
156	Maryland	1 540	681	726	1 440	673	760	1 354	829	506
157	Massachusetts	2 524	1 058	1 054	2 548	1 030	1 429	2 459	1 112	1 333
158	Michigan	3 910	1 915	1 662	3 654	1 894	1 697	3 490	1 962	1 459
159	Minnesota	2 052	873	954	1 950	819	1 070	1 742	898	802
160	Mississippi	893	441	429	769	367	381	646	505	127
161	Missouri	2 100	1 074	931	1 954	927	998	1 856	1 154	697
162	Montana	364	207	118	329	174	149	318	184	120
163	Nebraska	641	420	167	608	360	234	576	406	170
164	Nevada	248	155	67	202	101	92	182	116	66
165	New Hampshire	384	222	109	340	186	148	334	214	116
166	New Jersey	2 976	1 547	1 147	3 014	1 510	1 445	2 997	1 846	1 102
167	New Mexico	457	251	168	418	211	201	386	236	141
168	New York	6 202	2 894	2 728	6 534	3 101	3 390	7 166	4 193	2 951
169	North Carolina	1 856	915	876	1 679	742	927	1 519	1 055	439
170	North Dakota	302	194	79	297	153	136	281	174	100
171	Ohio	4 284	2 207	1 752	4 112	2 001	2 012	4 095	2 442	1 559
172	Oklahoma	1 150	696	402	1 092	546	532	1 030	759	247
173	Oregon	1 182	571	457	1 030	492	490	928	487	393
174	Pennsylvania	4 562	2 262	1 938	4 621	2 206	2 329	4 592	2 715	1 797
175	Rhode Island	416	155	198	411	181	228	416	220	195
176	South Carolina	894	442	430	803	346	451	674	477	187
177	South Dakota	328	198	104	301	152	147	307	166	140
178	Tennessee	1 618	788	783	1 476	634	826	1 201	813	357
179	Texas	4 542	2 511	1 881	4 072	1 953	2 082	3 471	2 299	1 154
180	Utah	604	440	124	541	338	182	478	324	126
181	Vermont	213	95	82	188	102	81	187	117	68
182	Virginia	1 866	990	752	1 697	837	814	1 457	988	439
183	Washington	1 742	865	650	1 556	778	717	1 471	837	568
184	West Virginia	738	334	367	751	315	436	762	485	277
185	Wisconsin	2 273	1 089	982	2 104	1 005	1 040	1 853	989	810
186	Wyoming	177	111	49	156	93	62	146	100	44

See footnotes at end of table.

Series Y 135-186. Popular Vote Cast for President, by State and Political Party: 1836 to 1996—Cont'd.

(In thousands. Rep.-Republican; Dem.-Democratic; Ind.-Independent. Vote listed is normally that of the highest candidate for presidential elector for each party. Democratic vote in 1896 and 1900 includes a variety of joint elector tickets with the People's Party, and party totals generally include votes cast for the presidential candidate under other designations than that of the party itself)

Series No.	State	1968 Total	1968 Rep.	1968 Dem.	1964 Total	1964 Rep.	1964 Dem.	1960 Total	1960 Rep.	1960 Dem.
135	**United States**	**73 212**	**31 785**	**31 275**	**70 645**	**27 178**	**43 130**	**68 838**	**34 108**	**34 277**
136	Alabama	1 050	147	197	690	479	. . .	570	238	324
137	Alaska	83	38	35	67	23	44	61	31	30
138	Arizona	487	267	171	481	243	238	398	221	177
139	Arkansas	620	191	188	560	243	314	429	185	215
140	California	7 252	3 468	3 244	7 058	2 879	4 172	6 507	3 260	3 224
141	Colorado	811	409	335	777	297	476	736	402	331
142	Connecticut	1 256	557	622	1 219	391	826	1 223	566	657
143	Delaware	214	97	89	201	78	123	197	96	100
144	District of Columbia	171	31	140	199	29	170	. . .	. . .	. . .
145	Florida	2 188	887	677	1 854	906	949	1 544	795	749
146	Georgia	1 250	380	334	1 139	617	523	733	274	459
147	Hawaii	236	91	141	207	44	163	185	92	92
148	Idaho	291	165	89	292	144	149	300	162	139
149	Illinois	4 620	2 175	2 040	4 703	1 906	2 797	4 757	2 369	2 378
150	Indiana	2 124	1 068	807	2 092	911	1 171	2 135	1 175	952
151	Iowa	1 168	619	477	1 185	449	733	1 274	722	551
152	Kansas	873	479	303	858	387	464	929	561	363
153	Kentucky	1 056	462	398	1 046	373	670	1 124	603	522
154	Louisiana	1 097	258	310	896	509	387	808	231	407
155	Maine	393	169	217	381	119	262	422	241	181
156	Maryland	1 235	518	538	1 116	385	731	1 055	490	566
157	Massachusetts	2 332	767	1 469	2 345	550	1 786	2 469	977	1 487
158	Michigan	3 306	1 371	1 593	3 203	1 060	2 137	3 318	1 620	1 687
159	Minnesota	1 589	659	858	1 554	560	991	1 542	758	780
160	Mississippi	655	89	151	409	357	53	298	74	108
161	Missouri	1 810	812	791	1 818	654	1 164	1 934	962	972
162	Montana	274	139	114	279	113	164	278	142	135
163	Nebraska	537	321	171	584	277	307	613	381	233
164	Nevada	154	73	61	135	56	79	107	52	55
165	New Hampshire	297	155	131	288	104	184	296	158	138
166	New Jersey	2 875	1 325	1 264	2 848	964	1 868	2 773	1 363	1 385
167	New Mexico	327	170	130	329	133	194	311	154	156
168	New York	6 792	3 008	3 378	7 166	2 244	4 913	7 291	3 446	3 830
169	North Carolina	1 587	627	464	1 425	625	800	1 369	655	713
170	North Dakota	248	139	95	258	108	150	278	154	124
171	Ohio	3 960	1 791	1 701	3 969	1 471	2 498	4 162	2 218	1 944
172	Oklahoma	943	450	302	932	413	520	903	533	370
173	Oregon	820	408	359	786	283	501	776	408	367
174	Pennsylvania	4 748	2 090	2 259	4 823	1 674	3 131	5 007	2 440	2 556
175	Rhode Island	385	122	247	390	75	315	406	148	258
176	South Carolina	667	254	197	525	309	216	387	189	198
177	South Dakota	281	150	118	293	130	163	306	178	128
178	Tennessee	1 249	473	351	1 144	509	635	1 052	557	481
179	Texas	3 079	1 228	1 267	2 627	959	1 663	2 311	1 121	1 168
180	Utah	423	239	157	401	182	220	375	205	169
181	Vermont	161	85	70	163	55	108	167	98	69
182	Virginia	1 361	590	442	1 042	481	558	771	405	362
183	Washington	1 304	589	616	1 259	470	780	1 242	629	599
184	West Virginia	754	308	374	792	254	538	838	396	442
185	Wisconsin	1 692	810	749	1 692	638	1 050	1 729	895	831
186	Wyoming	127	71	45	143	62	81	141	77	63

See footnotes at end of table.

Series Y 135-186. Popular Vote Cast for President, by State and Political Party: 1836 to 1996—Cont'd.

(In thousands. Rep.-Republican; Dem.-Democratic; Ind.-Independent. Vote listed is normally that of the highest candidate for presidential elector for each party. Democratic vote in 1896 and 1900 includes a variety of joint elector tickets with the People's Party, and party totals generally include votes cast for the presidential candidate under other designations than that of the party itself)

Series No.	State	1956			1952			1948		
		Total	Rep.	Dem.	Total	Rep.	Dem.	Total	Rep.	Dem.
135	**United States**	**62 034**	**35 590**	**26 023**	**61 551**	**33 936**	**27 315**	**48 794**	**21 991**	**24 179**
136	Alabama	497	196	281	426	149	275	215	41	X
138	Arizona	290	177	113	261	152	109	177	78	95
139	Arkansas	407	186	213	405	177	226	242	51	150
140	California	5 466	3 028	2 420	5 142	2 897	2 198	4 022	1 895	1 913
141	Colorado	657	394	258	630	380	246	515	240	267
142	Connecticut	1 117	712	405	1 097	611	482	884	438	423
143	Delaware	178	98	79	174	90	83	139	70	68
145	Florida	1 126	644	480	989	544	445	578	194	282
146	Georgia	670	223	445	656	199	457	419	77	255
148	Idaho	273	167	106	276	181	95	215	102	107
149	Illinois	4 407	2 623	1 776	4 481	2 457	2 014	3 984	1 961	1 995
150	Indiana	1 975	1 183	784	1 955	1 136	802	1 656	821	808
151	Iowa	1 235	729	502	1 269	809	452	1 038	494	522
152	Kansas	866	567	296	896	616	273	789	423	352
153	Kentucky	1 054	572	476	993	495	496	823	341	467
154	Louisiana	618	329	244	652	307	345	416	73	136
155	Maine	352	249	102	352	232	119	265	150	112
156	Maryland	933	560	373	902	499	395	597	295	287
157	Massachusetts	2 349	1 393	948	2 383	1 292	1 084	2 107	909	1 152
158	Michigan	3 080	1 714	1 360	2 799	1 552	1 231	2 110	1 039	1 003
159	Minnesota	1 340	719	618	1 379	763	608	1 212	484	693
160	Mississippi	248	61	144	286	113	173	192	5	19
161	Missouri	1 833	914	918	1 892	959	930	1 579	655	917
162	Montana	271	155	116	265	157	106	224	97	119
163	Nebraska	577	378	199	610	422	188	489	265	224
164	Nevada	97	56	41	82	51	32	62	29	31
165	New Hampshire	267	177	90	273	166	107	231	121	108
166	New Jersey	2 484	1 607	850	2 419	1 374	1 016	1 950	981	895
167	New Mexico	254	147	106	239	132	106	187	80	105
168	New York	7 096	4 346	2 748	7 128	3 953	3 105	6 177	2 841	2 780
169	North Carolina	1 166	575	591	1 211	558	653	791	259	459
170	North Dakota	254	157	97	270	192	77	221	115	96
171	Ohio	3 702	2 263	1 440	3 701	2 100	1 600	2 936	1 446	1 453
172	Oklahoma	859	474	386	949	518	431	722	269	453
173	Oregon	736	406	329	695	421	271	524	261	243
174	Pennsylvania	4 577	2 585	1 982	4 581	2 416	2 146	3 735	1 902	1 752
175	Rhode Island	388	226	162	414	211	203	328	136	189
176	South Carolina	301	76	136	341	168	173	143	5	34
177	South Dakota	294	172	122	294	204	90	250	130	118
178	Tennessee	939	462	457	893	446	444	550	203	270
179	Texas	1 955	1 081	860	2 076	1 103	969	1 250	303	824
180	Utah	334	216	118	330	194	135	276	124	149
181	Vermont	153	110	43	154	110	43	123	76	46
182	Virginia	698	386	268	620	349	269	419	172	201
183	Washington	1 151	620	523	1 103	599	493	905	386	476
184	West Virginia	831	449	382	874	420	454	749	316	429
185	Wisconsin	1 551	955	587	1 607	980	622	1 277	591	647
186	Wyoming	124	75	50	129	81	48	101	48	52

See footnotes at end of table.

Series Y 135-186. Popular Vote Cast for President, by State and Political Party: 1836 to 1996—Cont'd.

(In thousands. Rep.-Republican; Dem.-Democratic; Ind.-Independent. Vote listed is normally that of the highest candidate for presidential elector for each party. Democratic vote in 1896 and 1900 includes a variety of joint elector tickets with the People's Party, and party totals generally include votes cast for the presidential candidate under other designations than that of the party itself)

Series No.	State	1944			1940			1936		
		Total	Rep.	Dem.	Total	Rep.	Dem.	Total	Rep.	Dem.
135	**United States**	**47 969**	**22 015**	**25 607**	**49 891**	**22 321**	**27 308**	**45 643**	**16 675**	**27 753**
136	Alabama	245	45	199	294	42	251	276	35	238
138	Arizona	138	56	81	150	54	95	124	33	87
139	Arkansas	213	64	149	200	42	157	179	32	147
140	California	3 521	1 513	1 989	3 269	1 351	1 878	2 638	836	1 767
141	Colorado	505	269	234	549	280	266	489	181	295
142	Connecticut	832	391	435	782	361	418	691	279	382
143	Delaware	125	57	68	136	61	75	128	54	70
145	Florida	483	143	339	485	126	359	327	78	249
146	Georgia	328	57	268	313	24	265	293	37	255
148	Idaho	208	100	107	235	107	128	200	66	126
149	Illinois	4 036	1 939	2 079	4 218	2 047	2 150	3 957	1 570	2 283
150	Indiana	1 672	876	781	1 783	899	874	1 651	692	935
151	Iowa	1 053	547	500	1 215	632	579	1 143	488	622
152	Kansas	734	442	287	860	489	365	859	394	462
153	Kentucky	868	392	473	968	410	557	923	370	539
154	Louisiana	349	68	282	372	52	320	330	37	293
155	Maine	296	155	141	321	164	156	304	169	126
156	Maryland	608	293	315	660	270	385	625	231	390
157	Massachusetts	1 961	921	1 035	2 027	940	1 077	1 840	769	943
158	Michigan	2 205	1 084	1 107	2 086	1 040	1 033	1 805	700	1 017
159	Minnesota	1 126	527	590	1 251	596	644	1 130	350	699
160	Mississippi	180	12	169	176	7	168	162	4	157
161	Missouri	1 572	761	807	1 834	871	958	1 829	698	1 111
162	Montana	207	93	113	248	100	146	231	64	160
163	Nebraska	563	330	233	616	352	264	608	248	347
164	Nevada	54	25	30	53	21	32	44	12	32
165	New Hampshire	230	110	120	235	110	125	218	105	108
166	New Jersey	1 964	961	988	1 974	945	1 016	1 819	719	1 084
167	New Mexico	152	71	81	183	79	104	169	62	106
168	New York	6 317	2 988	3 304	6 302	3 027	3 252	5 596	2 181	3 293
169	North Carolina	791	263	527	823	214	609	839	223	616
170	North Dakota	220	119	100	281	155	124	274	73	163
171	Ohio	3 153	1 582	1 571	3 320	1 587	1 733	3 012	1 128	1 747
172	Oklahoma	722	319	401	826	349	474	750	245	501
173	Oregon	480	225	249	481	220	258	414	123	267
174	Pennsylvania	3 795	1 835	1 940	4 078	1 890	2 171	4 138	1 690	2 354
175	Rhode Island	299	123	175	321	139	182	310	125	164
176	South Carolina	103	5	91	100	2	95	115	2	114
177	South Dakota	232	135	97	308	177	131	296	126	160
178	Tennessee	511	200	309	523	169	352	477	147	328
179	Texas	1 144	192	816	1 117	212	905	850	103	742
180	Utah	248	98	150	248	93	154	217	65	150
181	Vermont	125	72	54	143	78	64	144	81	62
182	Virginia	388	145	242	347	109	236	335	98	235
183	Washington	856	362	487	794	322	462	692	207	460
184	West Virginia	716	323	393	868	372	496	830	325	503
185	Wisconsin	1 339	675	650	1 403	679	705	1 259	381	803
186	Wyoming	101	52	49	112	53	59	103	39	63

See footnotes at end of table.

Series Y 135-186. Popular Vote Cast for President, by State and Political Party: 1836 to 1996—Cont'd.

(In thousands. Rep.-Republican; Dem.-Democratic; Ind.-Independent. Vote listed is normally that of the highest candidate for presidential elector for each party. Democratic vote in 1896 and 1900 includes a variety of joint elector tickets with the People's Party, and party totals generally include votes cast for the presidential candidate under other designations than that of the party itself)

Series No.	State	1932 Total	Rep.	Dem.	1928 Total	Rep.	Dem.	1924 Total	Rep.	Dem.
135	**United States**	**39 732**	**15 759**	**22 810**	**36 812**	**21 392**	**15 016**	**29 086**	**15 718**	**8 385**
136	Alabama	242	35	205	249	121	128	165	43	113
138	Arizona	118	36	79	91	53	39	74	31	26
139	Arkansas	219	27	190	202	78	123	139	41	85
140	California	2 266	848	1 324	1 797	1 162	614	1 282	733	106
141	Colorado	457	190	251	392	254	133	342	195	75
142	Connecticut	594	288	282	553	297	252	400	246	110
143	Delaware	113	57	54	105	69	35	90	52	33
145	Florida	275	69	206	254	144	102	109	31	62
146	Georgia	256	20	234	231	65	130	166	30	123
148	Idaho	187	71	109	154	100	53	148	70	24
149	Illinois	3 408	1 433	1 882	3 107	1 769	1 313	2 470	1 453	577
150	Indiana	1 575	677	862	1 421	848	563	1 272	703	492
151	Iowa	1 037	414	598	1 010	624	379	972	537	160
152	Kansas	790	348	423	713	514	193	662	408	156
153	Kentucky	983	395	581	941	558	381	814	397	376
154	Louisiana	269	19	249	216	51	165	122	25	93
155	Maine	298	167	129	262	180	81	192	138	42
156	Maryland	511	184	314	528	301	224	359	162	148
157	Massachusetts	1 580	737	800	1 578	776	793	1 130	703	281
158	Michigan	1 665	740	872	1 372	965	397	1 160	875	152
159	Minnesota	1 003	364	601	971	561	396	822	421	56
160	Mississippi	146	5	140	152	26	125	112	8	100
161	Missouri	1 610	565	1 025	1 501	834	663	1 310	648	575
162	Montana	216	75	127	194	113	79	174	74	34
163	Nebraska	570	201	359	547	346	198	464	219	137
164	Nevada	41	13	29	32	18	14	27	11	6
165	New Hampshire	206	104	101	197	115	81	165	99	57
166	New Jersey	1 630	775	806	1 548	925	616	1 086	675	298
167	New Mexico	151	54	95	118	70	48	114	55	49
168	New York	4 689	1 938	2 535	4 406	2 193	2 090	3 264	1 820	951
169	North Carolina	712	208	498	635	349	286	482	191	284
170	North Dakota	256	72	178	240	131	107	199	95	14
171	Ohio	2 610	1 228	1 302	2 508	1 628	864	2 016	1 176	478
172	Oklahoma	705	188	516	618	394	219	528	226	256
173	Oregon	369	136	214	320	205	109	279	143	68
174	Pennsylvania	2 859	1 454	1 296	3 160	2 055	1 077	2 145	1 401	409
175	Rhode Island	266	115	147	237	118	119	210	125	77
176	South Carolina	104	2	102	69	3	63	51	1	49
177	South Dakota	288	99	184	262	3 158	103	204	101	27
178	Tennessee	390	127	259	353	195	157	301	131	159
179	Texas	856	98	753	708	367	340	656	130	483
180	Utah	207	85	117	177	95	81	157	77	47
181	Vermont	137	79	56	135	90	44	103	80	16
182	Virginia	298	91	204	305	165	140	224	73	140
183	Washington	615	209	353	501	336	157	422	220	43
184	West Virginia	744	331	405	643	376	264	584	289	257
185	Wisconsin	1 115	348	707	1 017	544	450	841	321	68
186	Wyoming	97	40	54	83	53	29	80	42	13

See footnotes at end of table.

Series Y 135-186.   Popular Vote Cast for President, by State and Political Party: 1836 to 1996—Cont'd.

(In thousands. Rep.-Republican; Dem.-Democratic; Ind.-Independent. Vote listed is normally that of the highest candidate for presidential elector for each party. Democratic vote in 1896 and 1900 includes a variety of joint elector tickets with the People's Party, and party totals generally include votes cast for the presidential candidate under other designations than that of the party itself)

Series No.	State	1920			1916			1912		
		Total	Rep.	Dem.	Total	Rep.	Dem.	Total	Rep.	Dem.
135	**United States**	**26 748**	**16 143**	**9 130**	**18 531**	**8 534**	**9 128**	**15 037**	**3 487**	**6 297**
136	Alabama	234	75	156	131	29	99	118	10	82
138	Arizona	67	37	30	58	21	33	23	3	10
139	Arkansas	183	72	106	168	47	112	124	24	69
140	California	943	625	229	1 000	463	466	678	4	283
141	Colorado	292	173	105	294	102	179	266	58	114
142	Connecticut	366	229	121	214	107	100	190	68	75
143	Delaware	95	53	40	52	26	25	49	16	23
145	Florida	145	45	91	81	15	56	52	4	36
146	Georgia	149	43	106	160	11	128	121	6	94
148	Idaho	136	89	47	135	55	70	106	33	34
149	Illinois	2 095	1 420	534	2 193	1 153	950	1 146	254	405
150	Indiana	1 263	696	511	719	341	334	654	151	282
151	Iowa	895	635	228	515	279	221	492	120	185
152	Kansas	570	369	185	628	276	314	365	75	144
153	Kentucky	919	452	456	520	242	270	453	116	219
154	Louisiana	126	39	88	93	6	80	79	4	60
155	Maine	198	136	59	136	70	64	130	27	51
156	Maryland	428	236	181	262	117	138	232	55	113
157	Massachusetts	994	681	277	532	269	248	489	156	174
158	Michigan	1 038	756	231	647	338	284	548	151	150
159	Minnesota	736	519	143	387	180	179	334	64	106
160	Mississippi	82	12	69	86	4	80	64	2	57
161	Missouri	1 332	727	575	787	369	398	699	208	331
162	Montana	179	109	57	178	67	101	80	19	28
163	Nebraska	383	248	120	287	118	159	249	54	109
164	Nevada	27	15	10	33	12	18	20	3	8
165	New Hampshire	159	958	63	89	44	44	88	33	35
166	New Jersey	904	611	257	494	269	211	434	89	179
167	New Mexico	106	58	47	67	31	34	49	18	20
168	New York	2 899	1 871	781	1 706	869	759	1 588	455	656
169	North Carolina	538	233	305	290	121	168	244	29	144
170	North Dakota	204	160	37	115	53	55	86	23	30
171	Ohio	2 021	1 182	780	1 164	514	604	1 037	278	425
172	Oklahoma	489	248	218	292	97	148	253	91	119
173	Oregon	239	144	80	262	127	120	137	35	47
174	Pennsylvania	1 853	1 218	504	1 297	704	522	1 218	273	396
175	Rhode Island	168	107	55	88	45	40	78	28	30
176	South Carolina	67	2	34	64	2	62	50	1	48
177	South Dakota	182	111	36	129	64	59	117	X	49
178	Tennessee	428	219	207	273	117	153	253	60	133
179	Texas	486	115	288	373	65	287	302	29	220
180	Utah	146	82	57	143	54	84	112	42	37
181	Vermont	90	68	21	64	40	23	63	23	15
182	Virginia	231	87	142	154	49	103	137	23	90
183	Washington	399	223	84	381	167	183	322	70	87
184	West Virginia	510	282	221	290	143	140	264	57	113
185	Wisconsin	701	499	113	447	221	192	400	131	164
186	Wyoming	55	35	17	52	22	28	42	15	15

See footnotes at end of table.

Series Y 135-186. Popular Vote Cast for President, by State and Political Party: 1836 to 1996—Cont'd.

(In thousands. Rep.-Republican; Dem.-Democratic; Ind.-Independent. Vote listed is normally that of the highest candidate for presidential elector for each party. Democratic vote in 1896 and 1900 includes a variety of joint elector tickets with the People's Party, and party totals generally include votes cast for the presidential candidate under other designations than that of the party itself)

Series No.	State	1908			1904			1900		
		Total	Rep.	Dem.	Total	Rep.	Dem.	Total	Rep.	Dem.
135	**United States**	**14 884**	**7 675**	**6 412**	**13 521**	**7 628**	**5 084**	**13 968**	**7 218**	**6 357**
136	Alabama....................	105	26	74	109	22	80	160	56	97
139	Arkansas...................	152	57	88	117	48	64	128	45	81
140	California..................	387	214	127	332	205	89	303	165	125
141	Colorado	264	124	127	244	135	100	221	93	123
142	Connecticut..............	190	113	68	191	111	73	180	103	74
143	Delaware...................	48	25	22	44	24	19	42	23	19
145	Florida	49	11	31	39	8	27	40	7	28
146	Georgia	132	41	72	130	24	84	121	34	81
148	Idaho	98	53	36	73	48	18	58	27	29
149	Illinois	1 155	630	451	1 076	633	238	1 132	598	503
150	Indiana	721	319	338	682	369	274	663	335	310
151	Iowa	495	275	201	486	308	149	530	308	209
152	Kansas	376	197	161	329	213	86	352	186	131
153	Kentucky	490	235	244	436	205	217	468	227	235
154	Louisiana..................	76	9	64	54	5	48	68	14	54
155	Maine	106	67	35	97	65	28	108	66	38
156	Maryland	239	117	116	224	109	109	264	136	122
157	Massachusetts	457	266	156	445	258	166	415	239	157
158	Michigan...................	538	333	175	520	362	134	544	316	211
159	Minnesota	30	196	109	293	217	55	316	190	113
160	Mississippi................	67	4	60	59	3	53	58	6	51
161	Missouri....................	716	347	347	644	321	296	684	314	352
162	Montana...................	69	32	29	64	35	22	64	25	37
163	Nebraska...................	67	127	131	226	139	53	241	122	114
164	Nevada.....................	25	11	11	12	7	4	10	4	6
165	New Hampshire	90	53	34	90	54	34	92	55	35
166	New Jersey................	467	265	183	432	245	165	401	222	165
168	New York..................	1 638	870	667	1 618	860	684	1 548	822	678
169	North Carolina............	252	115	137	208	82	124	292	133	158
170	North Dakota..............	95	58	33	70	53	14	58	36	21
171	Ohio	1 122	572	503	1 004	600	345	1 040	544	475
172	Oklahoma..................	256	107	127	. . .	. . .	. . .	. . .	. . .	. . .
173	Oregon.....................	111	63	38	90	60	17	84	47	33
174	Pennsylvania..............	1 265	746	447	1 237	841	338	1 173	713	424
175	Rhode Island..............	72	44	25	69	42	25	57	34	20
176	South Carolina	66	4	62	56	3	53	51	4	47
177	South Dakota	115	68	40	101	72	22	96	55	40
178	Tennessee	257	118	136	243	105	132	274	123	145
179	Texas	298	69	218	233	51	167	422	131	268
180	Utah	109	61	43	102	62	33	93	47	45
181	Vermont	53	40	11	52	40	10	56	13	13
182	Virginia	137	53	83	131	48	81	264	116	156
183	Washington	184	106	58	145	102	28	108	57	45
184	West Virginia..............	258	138	111	240	133	101	221	120	99
185	Wisconsin..................	454	248	167	443	280	124	442	266	159
186	Wyoming...................	36	21	15	31	20	9	25	14	10

See footnotes at end of table.

Series Y 135-186. Popular Vote Cast for President, by State and Political Party: 1836 to 1996—Cont'd.

(In thousands. Rep.-Republican; Dem.-Democratic; Ind.-Independent. Vote listed is normally that of the highest candidate for presidential elector for each party. Democratic vote in 1896 and 1900 includes a variety of joint elector tickets with the People's Party, and party totals generally include votes cast for the presidential candidate under other designations than that of the party itself)

Series No.	State	1896			1892			1888		
		Total	Rep.	Dem.	Total	Rep.	Dem.	Total	Rep.	Dem.
135	**United States**	**13 907**	**7 102**	**6 493**	**12 061**	**5 183**	**5 555**	**11 383**	**5 447**	**5 538**
136	Alabama	195	56	130	233	9	138	175	57	117
139	Arkansas	140	38	101	148	47	88	157	60	86
140	California	299	147	123	270	118	118	250	125	118
141	Colorado	187	26	159	96	39	X	91	50	37
142	Connecticut	174	110	57	165	77	82	154	75	75
143	Delaware	32	17	13	37	18	19	30	13	16
145	Florida	46	11	31	35	. . .	30	67	27	40
146	Georgia	156	59	93	221	48	129	142	40	100
148	Idaho	30	6	23	19	9	. . .	. . .	. . .	. . .
149	Illinois	1 088	607	465	874	399	426	748	370	348
150	Indiana	637	324	306	552	254	263	537	263	261
151	Iowa	521	289	224	443	220	196	404	212	180
152	Kansas	336	159	172	325	157	-	331	183	103
153	Kentucky	446	218	218	341	136	148	344	155	184
154	Louisiana	101	22	77	114	26	88	116	31	85
155	Maine	118	80	35	116	63	48	128	74	50
156	Maryland	251	137	105	213	93	114	211	100	106
157	Massachusetts	402	279	106	391	203	177	345	184	152
158	Michigan	546	293	237	467	223	202	475	236	213
159	Minnesota	342	194	140	268	123	101	262	143	104
160	Mississippi	70	5	63	53	1	41	115	29	85
161	Missouri	74	305	364	542	228	268	521	236	262
162	Montana	53	10	42	44	19	18	. . .	. . .	. . .
163	Nebraska	223	103	115	200	87	24	203	108	80
164	Nevada	10	2	8	11	3	1	12	7	5
165	New Hampshire	84	57	21	89	46	42	91	46	43
166	New Jersey	371	221	134	336	156	171	304	144	152
168	New York	1 424	820	551	1 337	609	655	1 320	650	363
169	North Carolina	330	154	175	278	101	133	286	135	148
170	North Dakota	47	26	21	36	18	. . .	. . .	. . .	. . .
171	Ohio	1 014	526	477	851	405	405	839	416	395
173	Oregon	97	49	45	78	35	14	62	33	27
174	Pennsylvania	1 194	728	427	1 003	516	452	998	526	447
175	Rhode Island	55	37	14	53	27	24	41	22	18
176	South Carolina	66	7	59	71	13	55	80	14	66
177	South Dakota	83	41	41	71	35	9	. . .	. . .	. . .
178	Tennessee	318	149	164	266	101	136	304	139	159
179	Texas	539	163	369	423	75	240	364	94	236
180	Utah	78	13	65	. . .	. . .	. . .	. . .	. . .	. . .
181	Vermont	64	51	10	56	38	16	63	45	17
182	Virginia	295	135	155	292	113	164	304	150	152
183	Washington	94	39	52	88	37	30	. . .	. . .	. . .
184	West Virginia	202	105	94	171	80	84	159	78	79
185	Wisconsin	447	268	166	371	171	177	355	177	155
186	Wyoming	21	10	10	17	8	. . .	. . .	. . .	. . .

See footnotes at end of table.

Series Y 135-186. Popular Vote Cast for President, by State and Political Party: 1836 to 1996—Cont'd.

(In thousands. Rep.-Republican; Dem.-Democratic; Ind.-Independent. Vote listed is normally that of the highest candidate for presidential elector for each party. Democratic vote in 1896 and 1900 includes a variety of joint elector tickets with the People's Party, and party totals generally include votes cast for the presidential candidate under other designations than that of the party itself)

Series No.	State	1884			1880			1876		
		Total	Rep.	Dem.	Total	Rep.	Dem.	Total	Rep.	Dem.
135	**United States**	**10 053**	**4 850**	**4 880**	**9 217**	**4 453**	**4 414**	**8 422**	**4 037**	**4 284**
136	Alabama..................	154	59	93	152	56	91	172	69	103
139	Arkansas....................	126	51	73	109	42	61	97	39	58
140	California....................	197	102	89	164	80	80	156	79	76
141	Colorado	64	36	28	54	28	25	. . .	. . .	. . .
142	Connecticut.................	137	66	67	133	67	64	122	59	62
143	Delaware......................	30	13	17	29	14	15	24	11	13
145	Florida.........................	60	28	32	52	24	28	48	24	24
146	Georgia.......................	143	48	94	157	54	103	181	51	130
149	Illinois.........................	673	337	312	622	318	277	553	277	259
150	Indiana........................	495	239	245	471	232	226	430	107	214
151	Iowa	377	197	178	323	184	106	295	174	112
152	Kansas	66	154	90	201	122	60	124	78	38
153	Kentucky.....................	276	118	153	267	106	149	260	97	160
154	Louisiana....................	109	46	63	103	38	65	146	75	71
155	Maine	130	72	52	144	74	65	116	66	50
156	Maryland.....................	16	86	97	173	79	94	164	72	92
157	Massachusetts............	303	147	122	283	165	112	259	150	109
158	Michigan......................	403	193	150	353	185	132	317	167	141
159	Minnesota	190	112	70	151	94	53	124	73	49
160	Mississippi..................	121	44	78	116	34	76	165	53	112
161	Missouri......................	441	203	236	397	154	209	351	145	202
163	Nebraska.....................	134	77	54	87	55	29	58	32	17
164	Nevada........................	13	7	6	18	9	10	20	10	9
165	New Hampshire	84	43	39	86	45	41	80	42	39
166	New Jersey..................	261	123	128	246	121	123	220	104	116
168	New York.....................	1 167	562	563	1 104	556	535	1 016	490	522
169	North Carolina.............	268	125	143	241	116	125	234	108	125
171	Ohio............................	785	400	368	725	375	341	659	331	323
173	Oregon........................	53	27	25	41	21	20	30	15	14
174	Pennsylvania...............	900	473	395	875	445	107	755	385	362
175	Rhode Island...............	33	19	12	29	18	11	26	16	11
176	South Carolina............	93	22	70	171	58	112	183	92	91
178	Tennessee	259	124	134	243	108	130	223	90	133
179	Texas..........................	326	93	226	241	57	156	151	45	106
181	Vermont	59	40	17	65	46	18	65	44	20
182	Virginia.......................	285	139	145	212	84	97	237	96	141
184	West Virginia...............	132	63	67	113	46	57	100	42	57
185	Wisconsin....................	320	161	146	266	144	114	257	130	124

See footnotes at end of table.

Series Y 135-186.   Popular Vote Cast for President, by State and Political Party: 1836 to 1996—Cont'd.

(In thousands. Rep.-Republican; Dem.-Democratic; Ind.-Independent. Vote listed is normally that of the highest candidate for presidential elector for each party. Democratic vote in 1896 and 1900 includes a variety of joint elector tickets with the People's Party, and party totals generally include votes cast for the presidential candidate under other designations than that of the party itself)

Series No.	State	1872			1868			1864		
		Total	Rep.	Dem.	Total	Rep.	Dem.	Total	Rep.	Dem.
135	**United States**	**6 460**	**3 597**	**2 843**	**5 720**	**3 013**	**2 707**	**4 011**	**2 207**	**1 804**
136	Alabama	170	90	79	149	76	72	. . .	. . .	. . .
139	Arkansas	79	41	38	41	22	19	. . .	. . .	. . .
140	California	96	54	41	109	55	54	106	62	44
142	Connecticut	96	50	46	99	51	48	87	45	42
143	Delaware	22	11	10	19	8	11	17	8	9
145	Florida	33	18	15	. . .	. . .	. . .	. . .	. . .	. . .
146	Georgia	143	63	76	160	57	103	. . .	. . .	. . .
149	Illinois	430	242	185	448	250	198	348	190	159
150	Indiana	350	186	164	344	177	167	280	150	130
151	Iowa	205	132	71	194	120	74	135	86	48
152	Kansas	100	67	33	44	30	14	21	17	4
153	Kentucky	189	89	100	155	39	116	90	27	63
154	Louisiana	129	72	57	114	33	80	. . .	. . .	. . .
155	Maine	91	61	29	113	70	42	109	64	45
156	Maryland	135	67	68	93	30	62	70	37	32
157	Massachusetts	199	133	65	196	136	59	175	127	49
158	Michigan	222	139	79	226	129	97	160	89	72
159	Minnesota	91	56	35	72	44	28	42	25	17
160	Mississippi	129	82	47	. . .	. . .	. . .	. . .	. . .	. . .
161	Missouri	271	119	151	152	87	66	104	73	31
163	Nebraska	25	17	8	15	10	6	. . .	. . .	. . .
164	Nevada	15	8	6	12	6	5	16	10	7
165	New Hampshire	69	37	31	68	38	31	69	36	33
166	New Jersey	168	92	77	163	80	83	129	34	68
168	New York	830	441	387	850	420	430	731	369	362
169	North Carolina	165	95	70	181	97	85	. . .	. . .	. . .
171	Ohio	529	282	244	519	280	239	471	266	206
173	Oregon	20	12	8	22	11	11	18	10	8
174	Pennsylvania	562	349	213	656	342	314	574	296	277
175	Rhode Island	19	14	5	20	13	6	23	14	9
176	South Carolina	95	72	23	108	62	45	. . .	. . .	. . .
178	Tennessee	181	86	95	82	57	25	. . .	. . .	. . .
179	Texas	116	48	68	. . .	. . .	. . .	. . .	. . .	. . .
181	Vermont	52	41	11	56	44	12	56	42	13
182	Virginia	185	93	92	. . .	. . .	. . .	. . .	. . .	. . .
184	West Virginia	62	32	30	49	29	20	34	23	10
185	Wisconsin	192	105	86	194	109	85	145	80	63

See footnotes at end of table.

Series Y 135-186. Popular Vote Cast for President, by State and Political Party: 1836 to 1996—Cont'd.

(In thousands. Rep.-Republican; Dem.-Democratic; Ind.-Independent. Vote listed is normally that of the highest candidate for presidential elector for each party. Democratic vote in 1896 and 1900 includes a variety of joint elector tickets with the People's Party, and party totals generally include votes cast for the presidential candidate under other designations than that of the party itself)

Series No.	State	1860			1856			1852		
		Total	Rep.	Dem.	Total	Rep.	Dem.	Total	Whig	Dem.
135	**United States**	**4 690**	**1 866**	**1 383**	**4 045**	**1 340**	**1 833**	**3 162**	**1 385**	**1 601**
136	Alabama	90	...	14	75	...	47	44	15	27
139	Arkansas	54	...	5	33	...	22	20	7	12
140	California	120	39	38	110	21	53	77	36	41
142	Connecticut	80	43	17	81	43	35	67	30	33
143	Delaware	16	4	1	14	...	8	13	6	6
145	Florida	13	...	...	11	...	6	7	3	4
146	Georgia	107	...	12	99	...	57	62	17	35
149	Illinois	337	171	158	239	96	106	155	65	80
150	Indiana	272	139	116	235	94	119	184	81	95
151	Iowa	128	70	55	90	44	36	35	16	18
153	Kentucky	146	1	26	133	...	70	111	57	54
154	Louisiana	51	...	8	43	...	22	36	17	19
155	Maine	101	63	30	110	67	39	82	33	42
156	Maryland	93	2	6	87	...	39	75	35	40
157	Massachusetts	169	107	34	167	108	39	125	53	45
158	Michigan	155	88	65	126	72	52	83	34	42
159	Minnesota	35	22	12	...	...	...	...	...	...
160	Mississippi	69	...	4	59	...	34	45	18	27
161	Missouri	165	17	59	106	...	58	69	30	39
165	New Hampshire	66	38	26	70	37	32	51	15	29
166	New Jersey	121	58	63	100	28	47	84	39	44
168	New York	677	363	314	597	276	196	525	235	263
169	North Carolina	96	...	3	85	...	48	79	39	40
171	Ohio	443	232	187	386	187	171	353	153	169
173	Oregon	14	5	3	...	...	...	...	...	...
174	Pennsylvania	476	268	17	460	148	231	386	179	199
175	Rhode Island	20	12	8	20	11	7	17	8	9
178	Tennessee	144	...	11	140	...	74	115	59	57
179	Texas	63	34	...	48	...	32	20	5	15
181	Vermont	45	2	9	51	40	11	44	22	13
182	Virginia	167	2	16	150	...	90	133	59	74
185	Wisconsin	152	86	65	120	66	53	62	21	32
186	Wyoming	...	...	...	...	...	...	...	...	...

See footnotes at end of table.

Series Y 135-186. Popular Vote Cast for President, by State and Political Party: 1836 to 1996—Cont'd.

(In thousands. Rep.-Republican; Dem.-Democratic; Ind.-Independent. Vote listed is normally that of the highest candidate for presidential elector for each party. Democratic vote in 1896 and 1900 includes a variety of joint elector tickets with the People's Party, and party totals generally include votes cast for the presidential candidate under other designations than that of the party itself)

Series No.	State	1848			1844			1840		
		Total	Whig	Dem.	Total	Whig	Dem.	Total	Whig	Dem.
135	**United States**	2 879	1 361	1 222	2 701	1 300	1 338	2 412	1 275	1 128
136	Alabama	62	30	31	63	26	37	63	29	34
139	Arkansas	17	8	9	15	6	10	12	5	7
142	Connecticut	62	30	27	65	33	30	57	32	25
143	Delaware	12	6	6	12	6	6	11	6	5
145	Florida	7	4	3	. . .	. . .	. . .	. . .	. . .	. . .
146	Georgia	92	48	45	86	42	44	72	40	32
149	Illinois	125	53	56	108	46	59	93	46	47
150	Indiana	153	70	75	140	68	70	117	65	52
151	Iowa	22	10	11	. . .	. . .	. . .	. . .	. . .	. . .
153	Kentucky	115	67	49	113	61	52	91	59	33
154	Louisiana	34	18	15	27	13	14	19	11	8
155	Maine	87	35	40	85	34	46	93	47	46
156	Maryland	72	38	34	69	36	33	62	34	29
157	Massachusetts	134	61	35	130	68	52	126	73	52
158	Michigan	65	24	31	56	24	28	44	23	21
160	Mississippi	52	26	27	46	20	26	37	20	17
161	Missouri	73	33	40	73	31	41	53	23	30
165	New Hampshire	50	15	28	49	18	27	59	26	33
166	New Jersey	78	40	37	76	38	37	64	33	31
168	New York	456	219	114	486	232	238	442	226	213
169	North Carolina	80	44	36	82	43	39	79	46	34
171	Ohio	329	139	155	312	155	149	273	148	124
174	Pennsylvania	369	185	173	331	160	167	288	144	144
175	Rhode Island	11	7	4	12	7	5	9	5	3
178	Tennessee	122	64	58	120	60	60	108	60	48
179	Texas	17	5	12	. . .	. . .	. . .	. . .	. . .	. . .
181	Vermont	48	23	11	49	27	18	51	32	18
182	Virginia	92	45	47	96	45	51	86	43	44
185	Wisconsin	39	14	15	. . .	. . .	. . .	. . .	. . .	. . .

See footnotes at end of table.

Series No.	State	1836			Series No.	State	1836		
		Total	Whig	Dem.			Total	Whig	Dem.
135	**United States**	1 505	740	765	160	Mississippi	20	10	10
136	Alabama	37	17	21	161	Missouri	18	7	11
139	Arkansas	4	1	2	165	New Hampshire	25	6	19
142	Connecticut	38	19	19	166	New Jersey	52	26	26
143	Delaware	9	5	4	168	New York	306	139	167
146	Georgia	47	24	23	169	North Carolina	50	24	27
149	Illinois	33	15	18	171	Ohio	203	106	97
150	Indiana	74	41	32	174	Pennsylvania	179	87	91
153	Kentucky	69	37	33	175	Rhode Island	6	3	3
154	Louisiana	7	4	4	178	Tennessee	62	36	26
155	Maine	38	15	23	181	Vermont	35	21	14
156	Maryland	48	26	22	182	Virginia	54	23	30
157	Massachusetts	78	42	35					
158	Michigan	12	6	7					

X Represents zero.

Series Y 189-198. Congressional Bills, Acts and Resolutions: 1789 to 1996

(Excludes simple and concurrent resolutions)

Period of session	Congress	Measures introduced			Measures passed		
		Total	Bills	Joint resolutions	Total	Total public	Total private
		189	**190**	**191**	**192**	**193**	**196**
Jan. 1995-Oct. 1996	104	6 808	6 545	263	337	333	4
Jan. 1993-Dec. 1994	103	8 544	7 883	661	473	465	8
Jan. 1991-Oct. 1992	102	6 775	6 212	563	609	589	20
Jan. 1989-Oct. 1990	101	6 664	5 977	687	666	650	16
Jan. 1987-Oct. 1988	100	9 588	8 515	1 073	761	713	48
Jan. 1985-Oct. 1986	99	9 885	8 697	1 188	483	466	17
Jan. 1983-Oct. 1984	98	11 156	10 134	1 022	677	623	54
Jan. 1981-Dec. 1982	97	11 490	10 582	908	529	473	56
Jan. 1979-Dec. 1980	96	12 583	11 722	861	736	613	123
Jan. 1977-Oct. 1978	95	19 387	18 045	1 342	803	633	170
Jan. 1975-Oct. 1976	94	21 096	19 762	1 334	729	588	141
Jan. 1973-Dec. 1974	93	23 296	21 950	1 446	774	651	123
Jan. 1971-Oct. 1972	92	22 969	21 363	1 606	768	607	161
Jan. 1969-Jan. 1971	91	26 303	24 631	1 672	941	695	246
Jan. 1967-Oct. 1968	90	26 460	24 786	1 674	1 002	640	362
Jan. 1965-Oct. 1966	89	24 003	22 483	1 520	1 283	810	473
Jan. 1963-Oct. 1964	88	17 480	16 079	1 401	1 026	666	360
Jan. 1961-Oct. 1962	87	18 376	17 230	1 146	1 569	885	684
Jan. 1959-Sept. 1960	86	18 261	17 230	1 031	1 292	800	492
Jan. 1957-Aug. 1958	85	19 112	18 205	907	1 720	936	784
Jan. 1955-July 1956	84	17 687	16 782	905	1 921	1 028	893
Jan. 1953-Dec. 1954	83	14 952	14 181	771	1 783	781	1 002
Jan. 1951-July 1952	82	12 730	12 062	668	1 617	594	1 023
Jan. 1949-Jan. 1951	81	14 988	14 219	769	2 024	921	1 103
Jan. 1947-Dec. 1948	80	10 797	10 108	689	1 363	906	457
Jan. 1945-Aug. 1946	79	10 330	9 748	582	1 625	733	892
Jan. 1943-Dec. 1944	78	8 334	7 845	489	1 157	568	589
Jan. 1941-Dec. 1942	77	11 334	10 793	541	1 485	850	635
Jan. 1939-Jan. 1941	76	16 105	15 174	931	1 662	1 005	657
Jan. 1937-June 1938	75	16 156	15 120	1 036	1 759	919	840
Jan. 1935-June 1936	74	18 754	17 819	935	1 724	987	737
March 1933-June 1934	73	14 370	13 774	596	975	539	436
Dec. 1931-March 1933	72	21 382	20 501	881	843	516	327
April 1929-March 1931	71	24 453	23 652	801	1 522	1 009	513
Dec. 1927-March 1929	70	23 897	23 238	659	1 722	1 145	577
Dec. 1925-March 1927	69	23 799	23 250	549	1 423	879	544
Dec. 1923-March 1925	68	17 462	16 884	578	996	707	289
April 1921-March 1923	67	19 889	19 133	756	930	654	276
May 1919-March 1921	66	21 967	21 222	745	594	470	124
May 1917-Dec. 1919	65	22 594	21 919	675	453	405	48
Dec. 1915-March 1917	64	30 052	29 438	614	684	458	226
March 1913-March 1915	63	30 053	29 367	686	700	417	283
April 1911-March 1913	62	38 032	37 459	573	716	530	186
March 1909-March 1911	61	44 363	43 921	442	884	595	289
Dec. 1907-March 1909	60	38 388	37 981	407	646	411	235
March 1905-March 1907	59	34 879	34 524	355	7 024	775	6 249
March 1903-March 1905	58	26 851	26 504	347	4 041	575	3 466
March 1901-March 1903	57	25 460	25 007	453	2 790	480	2 310
Dec. 1899-March 1901	56	20 893	20 409	484	1 942	443	1 499
March 1897-March 1899	55	18 463	17 817	646	1 437	552	885
Dec. 1895-March 1897	54	14 585	14 114	471	948	434	514
March 1893-March 1895	53	12 226	11 796	430	711	463	248
Dec. 1891-March 1893	52	14 893	14 518	375	722	398	324
March 1889-March 1891	51	19 630	19 163	467	2 251	611	1 640
Dec. 1887-March 1889	50	17 078	16 664	414	1 824	570	1 254

Series Y 189-198.   Congressional Bills, Acts and Resolutions: 1789 to 1996—Cont'd.

(Excludes simple and concurrent resolutions)

Period of session	Congress	Measures introduced			Measures passed		
		Total	Bills	Joint resolutions	Total	Total public	Total private
		189	**190**	**191**	**192**	**193**	**196**
March 1885-March 1887	49	15 002	14 618	384	1 452	424	1 028
Dec. 1883-March 1885	48	11 443	10 961	482	969	284	685
March 1881-March 1883	47	10 704	10 194	510	761	419	342
March 1879-March 1881	46	10 067	9 481	586	650	372	278
March 1877-March 1879	45	8 735	8 413	322	746	303	443
March 1875-March 1877	44	6 230	6 001	229	580	278	302
March 1873-March 1875	43	6 434	6 252	182	859	415	444
March 1871-March 1873	42	5 943	5 725	218	1 012	531	481
March 1869-March 1871	41	5 314	4 466	848	769	470	299
April 1867-March 1869	40	3 723	3 003	720	765	354	411
March 1865-March 1867	39	2 348	1 864	484	714	427	287
March 1863-March 1865	38	1 708	1 402	306	515	411	104
March 1861-March 1863	37	1 661	1 370	291	521	428	93
March 1859-March 1861	36	1 746	1 595	151	370	157	213
March 1857-March 1859	35	1 686	1 544	142	312	129	183
Dec. 1855-March 1857	34	1 608	1 515	93	433	157	276
March 1853-March 1855	33	1 660	1 552	108	540	188	352
March 1851-March 1853	32	1 167	1 011	156	306	137	169
March 1849-March 1851	31	1 080	978	102	167	109	58
Dec. 1847-March 1849	30	1 433	1 305	128	446	176	270
March 1845-March 1847	29	1 051	956	95	303	142	161
Dec. 1843-March 1845	28	1 085	979	106	279	142	137
March 1841-March 1843	27	1 210	1 146	64	524	201	323
Dec. 1839-March 1841	26	1 122	1 081	41	147	55	92
March 1837-March 1839	25	1 631	1 566	65	532	150	382
Dec. 1835-March 1837	24	1 107	1 055	52	459	144	315
Dec. 1833-March 1835	23	993	946	47	390	128	262
Dec. 1831-March 1833	22	1 000	976	24	462	191	271
March 1829-March 1831	21	856	842	14	369	152	217
Dec. 1827-March 1829	20	632	612	20	235	134	101
March 1825-March 1827	19	622	609	13	266	153	113
Dec. 1823-March 1825	18	498	481	17	335	141	194
Dec. 1821-March 1823	17	492	492	. . .	238	136	102
Dec. 1819-March 1821	16	480	480	. . .	208	117	91
March 1817-March 1819	15	507	507	. . .	257	156	101
Dec. 1815-March 1817	14	465	465	. . .	298	173	125
March 1813-March 1815	13	400	400	. . .	273	185	88
March 1811-March 1813	12	406	406	. . .	209	170	39
March 1809-March 1811	11	348	348	. . .	119	94	25
Oct. 1807-March 1809	10	266	266	. . .	105	88	17
March 1805-March 1807	9	219	219	. . .	106	90	16
Oct. 1803-March 1805	8	217	217	. . .	111	93	18
March 1801-March 1803	7	161	161	. . .	95	80	15
Dec. 1799-March 1801	6	157	157	. . .	112	100	12
March 1797-March 1799	5	234	234	. . .	155	137	18
June 1795-March 1797	4	132	132	. . .	85	75	10
March 1793-March 1795	3	122	122	. . .	127	103	24
March 1791-March 1793	2	105	105	. . .	77	65	12
March 1789-March 1791	1	144	144	. . .	118	108	10

Series Y 199-203. Congressional Bills Vetoed: 1789 to 1997

Period	President	Vetoed bills			Vetoes sustained	Bills passed over veto
		Total	Regular	Pocket		
		199	**200**	**201**	**202**	**203**
1993-1997	Clinton	20	20	. . .	19	1
1989-1992	Bush	44	29	15	43	1
1981-1989	Reagan	78	39	39	69	9
1977-1981	Carter	31	13	18	29	2
1974-1977	Ford	66	48	18	54	12
1969-1974	Nixon	43	26	17	36	7
1963-1969	L. Johnson	30	16	14	30	. . .
1961-1963	Kennedy	21	12	9	21	. . .
1953-1961	Eisenhower	181	73	108	179	2
1945-1953	Truman	250	180	70	238	12
1933-1945	F. Roosevelt	635	372	263	626	9
1929-1933	Hoover	37	21	16	34	3
1923-1929	Coolidge	50	20	30	46	4
1921-1923	Harding	6	5	1	6	. . .
1913-1921	Wilson	44	33	11	38	6
1909-1913	Taft	39	30	9	38	1
1901-1909	T. Roosevelt	82	42	40	81	1
1897-1901	McKinley	42	6	36	42	. . .
1893-1897	Cleveland	170	42	128	165	5
1889-1893	B. Harrison	44	19	25	43	1
1885-1889	Cleveland	414	304	110	412	2
1881-1885	Arthur	12	4	8	11	1
1881	Garfield	. . .	. . .	. . .	. . .	. . .
1877-1881	Hayes	13	12	1	12	1
1869-1877	Grant	93	45	48	89	4
1868-1869	A. Johnson	29	21	8	14	15
1861-1865	Lincoln	6	2	4	6	. . .
1857-1861	Buchanan	7	4	3	7	. . .
1853-1857	Pierce	9	9	. . .	4	5
1850-1853	Filmore	. . .	. . .	. . .	. . .	. . .
1849-1850	Taylor	. . .	. . .	. . .	. . .	. . .
1845-1849	Polk	3	2	1	3	. . .
1841-1845	Tyler	10	6	4	9	1
1841	W. H. Harrison	. . .	. . .	. . .	. . .	. . .
1837-1841	Van Buren	1	. . .	1	1	. . .
1829-1837	Jackson	12	5	7	12	. . .
1825-1829	John Q. Adams	. . .	. . .	. . .	. . .	. . .
1817-1825	Monroe	1	1	. . .	1	. . .
1809-1817	Madison	7	5	2	7	. . .
1801-1809	Jefferson	. . .	. . .	. . .	. . .	. . .
1797-1801	John Adams	. . .	. . .	. . .	. . .	. . .
1789-1797	Washington	2	2	. . .	2	. . .

Series Y 204-210. Political Party Affiliation in Congress and the Presidency: 1789 to 1997

(Letter symbols for political parties: Ad = "Administration"; AM = Anti-Masonic; C = Coalition; D = Democratic; DR = Democratic-Republican; F = Federalist; J = Jacksonian; NR = National Republican; Op = "Opposition"; R = Republican; U = Unionist; W = Whig. Figures are for the beginning of the first session of each Congress, except as noted.)

Year	Congress	House		Senate		President
		Majority party	Principal minority party	Majority party	Principal minority party	
		204	**205**	**207**	**208**	**210**
1997[1]	105th	R-226	D-207	R-55	D-45	D-Clinton
1996[1]	104th	R-236	D-197	R-53	D-46	D-Clinton
1995	104th	R-230	D-204	R-52	D-48	D-Clinton
1993-1994	103d	D-258	R-176	D-57	R-43	D-Clinton
1991-1992	102d	D-267	R-167	D-56	R-44	R-Bush
1989-1990	101st	D-259	R-174	D-55	R-45	R-Bush
1987-1988	100th	D-258	R-177	D-55	R-45	R-Reagan
1985-1986	99th	D-252	R-182	R-53	D-47	R-Reagan
1983-1984	98th	D-269	R-165	R-54	D-46	R-Reagan
1981-1982	97th	D-243	R-192	R-53	D-46	R-Reagan
1979-1980	96th	D-276	R-157	D-58	R-41	D-Carter
1977-1978	95th	D-292	R-143	D-61	R-38	D-Carter
1975-1976	94th	D-291	R-144	D-60	R-37	R-Ford
1973-1974	93d	D-239	R-192	D-56	R-42	R-Nixon
1971-1972	92d	D-254	R-180	D-54	R-44	R-Nixon
1969-1970	91st	D-245	R-189	D-57	R-43	R-Nixon
1967-1968	90th	D-246	R-187	D-64	R-36	D-L. Johnson
1965-1966	89th	D-295	R-140	D-68	R-32	D-L. Johnson
1963-1964	88th	D-258	R-177	D-67	R-33	D-L. Johnson D-Kennedy
1961-1962	87th	D-263	R-174	D-65	R-35	D-Kennedy
1959-1960[2]	86th	D-283	R-153	D-64	R-34	R-Eisenhower
1957-1958	85th	D-233	R-200	D-49	R-47	R-Eisenhower
1955-1956	84th	D-232	R-203	D-48	R-47	R-Eisenhower
1953-1954	83d	R-221	D-211	R-48	D-47	R-Eisenhower
1951-1952	82d	D-234	R-199	D-49	R-47	D-Truman
1949-1950	81st	D-263	R-171	D-54	R-42	D-Truman
1947-1948	80th	R-245	D-188	R-51	D-45	D-Truman
1945-1946	79th	D-242	R-190	D-56	R-38	D-Truman
1943-1944	78th	D-218	R-208	D-58	R-37	D-F. Roosevelt
1941-1942	77th	D-268	R-162	D-66	R-28	D-F. Roosevelt
1939-1940	76th	D-261	R-164	D-69	R-23	D-F. Roosevelt
1937-1938	75th	D-331	R-89	D-76	R-16	D-F. Roosevelt
1935-1936	74th	D-319	R-103	D-69	R-25	D-F. Roosevelt
1933-1934	73d	D-310	R-117	D-60	R-35	D-F. Roosevelt
1931-1933	72d	D-220	R-214	R-48	D-47	R-Hoover
1929-1931	71st	R-267	D-167	R-56	D-39	R-Hoover
1927-1929	70th	R-237	D-195	R-49	D-46	R-Coolidge
1925-1927	69th	R-247	D-183	R-56	D-39	R-Coolidge
1923-1925	68th	R-225	D-205	R-51	D-43	R-Coolidge
1921-1923	67th	R-301	D-131	R-59	D-37	R-Harding
1919-1921	66th	R-240	D-190	R-49	D-47	D-Wilson
1917-1919	65th	D-216	R-210	D-53	R-42	D-Wilson
1915-1917	64th	D-230	R-196	D-56	R-40	D-Wilson
1913-1915	63d	D-291	R-127	D-51	R-44	D-Wilson
1911-1913	62d	D-228	R-161	R-51	D-41	R-Taft
1909-1911	61st	R-219	D-172	R-61	D-32	R-Taft
1907-1909	60th	R-222	D-164	R-61	D-31	R-T. Roosevelt
1905-1907	59th	R-250	D-136	R-57	D-33	R-T. Roosevelt
1903-1905	58th	R-208	D-178	R-57	D-33	R-T. Roosevelt
1901-1903	57th	R-197	D-151	R-55	D-31	R-T. Roosevelt R-McKinley
1899-1901	56th	R-185	D-163	R-53	D-26	R-McKinley
1897-1899	55th	R-204	D-113	R-47	D-34	R-McKinley
1895-1897	54th	R-244	D-105	R-43	D-39	D-Cleveland
1893-1895	53d	D-218	R-127	D-44	R-38	D-Cleveland
1891-1893	52d	D-235	R-88	R-47	D-39	R-B. Harrison

See footnotes at end of table.

Series Y 204-210. Political Party Affiliation in Congress and the Presidency: 1789 to 1997—Cont'd.

(Letter symbols for political parties: Ad = "Administration"; AM = Anti-Masonic; C = Coalition; D = Democratic; DR = Democratic-Republican; F = Federalist; J = Jacksonian; NR = National Republican; Op = "Opposition"; R = Republican; U = Unionist; W = Whig. Figures are for the beginning of the first session of each Congress, except as noted.)

Year	Congress	House		Senate		President
		Majority party	Principal minority party	Majority party	Principal minority party	
		204	**205**	**207**	**208**	**210**
1889-1891	51st	R-166	D-159	R-39	D-37	R-B. Harrison
1887-1889	50th	D-169	R-152	R-39	D-37	D-Cleveland
1885-1887	49th	D-183	R-140	R-43	D-34	D-Cleveland
1883-1885	48th	D-197	R-118	R-38	D-36	R-Arthur
1881-1883	47th	R-147	D-135	R-37	D-37	R-Arthur R-Garfield
1879-1881	46th	D-149	R-130	D-42	R-33	R-Hayes
1877-1879	45th	D-153	R-140	R-39	D-36	R-Hayes
1875-1877	44th	D-169	R-109	R-45	D-29	R-Grant
1873-1875	43d	R-194	D-92	R-49	D-19	R-Grant
1871-1873	42d	R-134	D-104	R-52	D-17	R-Grant
1869-1871	41st	R-149	D-63	R-56	D-11	R-Grant
1867-1869	40th	R-143	D-49	R-42	D-11	R-A. Johnson
1865-1867	39th	U-149	D-42	U-42	D-10	R-A. Johnson R-Lincoln
1863-1865	38th	R-102	D-75	R-36	D-9	R-Lincoln
1861-1863	37th	R-105	D-43	R-31	D-10	R-Lincoln
1859-1861	36th	R-114	D-92	D-36	R-26	D-Buchanan
1857-1859	35th	D-118	R-92	D-36	R-20	D-Buchanan
1855-1857	34th	R-108	D-83	D-40	R-15	D-Pierce
1853-1855	33d	D-159	W-71	D-38	W-22	D-Pierce
1851-1853	32d	D-140	W-88	D-35	W-24	W-Fillmore
1849-1851	31st	D-112	W-109	D-35	W-25	W-Fillmore W-Taylor
1847-1849	30th	W-115	D-108	D-36	W-21	D-Polk
1845-1847	29th	D-143	W-77	D-31	W-25	D-Polk
1843-1845	28th	D-142	W-79	W-28	D-25	W-Tyler
1841-1843	27th	W-133	D-102	W-28	D-22	W-Tyler W-W. H. Harrison
1839-1841	26th	D-124	W-118	D-28	W-22	D-Van Buren
1837-1839	25th	D-108	W-107	D-30	W-18	D-Van Buren
1835-1837	24th	D-145	W-98	D-27	W-25	D-Jackson
1833-1835	23d	D-147	AM-53	D-20	NR-20	D-Jackson
1831-1833	22d	D-141	NR-58	D-25	NR-21	D-Jackson
1829-1831	21st	D-139	NR-74	D-26	NR-22	D-Jackson
1827-1829	20th	J-119	Ad-94	J-28	Ad-20	C-J. Q. Adams
1825-1827	19th	Ad-105	J-97	Ad-26	J-20	C-J. Q. Adams
1823-1825	18th	DR-187	F-26	DR-44	F-4	DR-Monroe
1821-1823	17th	DR-158	F-25	DR-44	F-4	DR-Monroe
1819-1821	16th	DR-156	F-27	DR-35	F-7	DR-Monroe
1817-1819	15th	DR-141	F-42	DR-34	F-10	DR-Monroe
1815-1817	14th	DR-117	F-65	DR-25	F-11	DR-Madison
1813-1815	13th	DR-112	F-68	DR-27	F-9	DR-Madison
1811-1813	12th	DR-108	F-36	DR-30	F-6	DR-Madison
1809-1811	11th	DR-94	F-48	DR-28	F-6	DR-Madison
1807-1809	10th	DR-118	F-24	DR-28	F-6	DR-Jefferson
1805-1807	9th	DR-116	F-25	DR-27	F-7	DR-Jefferson
1803-1805	8th	DR-102	F-39	DR-25	F-9	DR-Jefferson
1801-1803	7th	DR-69	F-36	DR-18	F-13	DR-Jefferson
1799-1801	6th	F-64	DR-42	F-19	DR-13	F-John Adams
1797-1799	5th	F-58	DR-48	F-20	DR-12	F-John Adams
1795-1797	4th	F-54	DR-52	F-19	DR-13	F-Washington
1793-1795	3d	DR-57	F-48	F-17	DR-13	F-Washington
1791-1793	2d	F-37	DR-33	F-16	DR-13	F-Washington
1789-1791	1st	Ad-38	Op-26	Ad-17	Op-9	F-Washington

1. As of beginning of second session.
2. Excludes Hawaii; two senators (1-R, 1-D) and one representative (D) seated August 1959.

Series Y 272-289. Public Employees, by Type of Government: 1940 to 1997

(In thousands. As of October 31 except as noted)

Year	All governments	Federal [1] (civilian)	Total state and local	Total state	Total local	Local [2] Total municipalities	Total counties	School districts
	272	273	274	277	280	283	285	287
1997	19 540	2 807	16 733	4 733	12 000	...	...	...
1996	...	...	...	...	...	...	...	...
1995	19 521	2 895	16 626	4 719	11 906	...	...	...
1994	19 420	2 952	16 468	4 694	11 775	...	...	...
1993	18 823	2 999	15 824	4 673	11 151	2 644	2 270	...
1992	18 745	3 047	15 698	4 595	11 103	2 665	2 253	5 134
1991	18 554	3 103	15 452	4 521	10 930	2 662	2 196	5 045
1990	18 369	3 105	15 263	4 503	10 760	2 642	2 167	4 950
1989	17 879	3 114	14 765	4 365	10 400	2 569	2 085	4 774
1988	17 588	3 112	14 476	4 236	10 240	2 570	2 024	4 679
1987	17 212	3 091	14 121	4 116	10 005	2 493	1 963	4 627
1986	16 933	3 019	13 913	4 068	9 846	2 494	1 926	4 502
1985	16 690	3 021	13 669	3 984	9 685	2 467	1 891	4 416
1984	16 436	2 942	13 494	3 898	9 595	2 434	1 872	4 387
1983	16 034	2 875	13 159	3 816	9 344	2 424	1 811	4 211
1982	15 918	2 848	13 071	3 747	9 324	2 460	1 804	4 182
1981	15 968	2 865	13 103	3 726	9 377	2 469	1 808	4 222
1980	16 213	2 898	13 315	3 753	9 562	2 561	1 853	4 270
1979	15 971	2 869	13 102	3 699	9 403	2 553	1 804	4 200
1978	15 628	2 885	12 743	3 539	9 204	2 509	1 768	4 113
1977	15 459	2 848	12 611	3 491	9 120	2 469	1 761	4 127
1976	15 012	2 843	12 169	3 343	8 826	2 107	1 448	3 272
1975	14 973	2 890	12 084	3 271	8 813	2 506	1 563	3 969
1974	14 628	2 874	11 754	3 155	8 599	2 127	1 343	3 183
1973	14 139	2 786	11 353	3 013	8 339	2 109	1 318	3 074
1972	14 759	2 795	10 964	2 957	8 007	2 029	1 242	2 981
1971	13 316	2 872	10 444	2 832	7 612	1 960	1 153	2 865
1970	13 028	2 881	10 147	2 755	7 392	2 244	1 229	3 316
1969	12 685	2 969	9 716	2 614	7 102	2 165	1 163	3 176
1968	12 342	2 984	9 358	2 495	6 864	2 112	1 151	3 028
1967	11 867	2 993	8 874	2 335	6 539	1 993	1 077	2 919
1966	11 388	2 861	8 527	2 211	6 316	1 971	1 043	2 850
1965	10 589	2 588	8 001	2 028	5 973	1 884	979	2 598
1964	10 064	2 528	7 536	1 873	5 663	1 817	936	2 436
1963	9 736	2 548	7 188	1 775	5 413	1 782	875	2 300
1962	9 388	2 539	6 849	1 680	5 169	1 696	862	2 161
1961	9 100	2 484	6 616	1 625	4 992	1 734	821	2 049
1960	8 808	2 421	6 387	1 527	4 860	1 692	788	1 921
1959 *	8 487	2 399	6 088	1 454	4 634	1 636	767	1 820
1958	8 297	2 405	5 892	1 408	4 484	1 594	738	1 752
1957 [3]	8 047	2 439	5 608	1 300	4 307	1 539	726	1 651
1956	7 685	2 410	5 275	1 268	4 007	1 485	674	1 533
1955	7 432	2 378	5 054	1 199	3 855	1 436	648	1 455
1954	7 232	2 373	4 859	1 149	3 710	1 420	628	1 365
1953	7 048	2 385	4 663	1 082	3 580	1 382	597	1 293
1952	7 105	2 583	4 522	1 060	3 461	1 341	573	1 234
1951	6 802	2 515	4 287	1 070	3 218	1 297	505	1 136
1950	6 402	2 117	4 285	1 057	3 228	1 311	500	1 102
1949	6 203	2 047	4 156	1 037	3 119	1 281	476	1 056
1948	6 042	2 076	3 966	963	3 002	1 249	469	986
1947	5 791	2 002	3 789	909	2 880	1 202	434	962
1946	6 001	2 434	3 567	804	2 762	1 155	417	934
1945	6 556	3 375	3 181	...	...	...	...	...
1944	6 537	3 365	3 172	...	...	...	...	...
1943	6 358	3 166	3 192	...	...	...	...	...
1942	5 915	2 664	3 251	...	...	...	...	...
1941	4 970	1 598	3 372	...	...	...	...	...
1940	4 474	1 128	3 346	...	...	...	...	...

* Denotes first year for which figures include Alaska and Hawaii.
1. Includes federal civilian employees outside continental United States. Prior to 1953, figures as of September 30.
2. Local government data, except for 1067, 1962 and 1967, are subject to sampling variation.
3. As of April 30.

Series Y 335-338. Summary of Federal Government Finances—Administrative Budget: 1789 to 1939

(In thousands of dollars. For 1789-1842, years ending December 31; 1844-1939, June 30; 1843 figures are for January 1-June 30)

Year	Budget receipts [1]	Budget expendi-tures [2]	Surplus or deficit [3] (-)	Total public debt [4]	Year	Budget receipts [1]	Budget expendi-tures [2]	Surplus or deficit [3] (-)	Total public debt [4]
	335	336	337	338		335	336	337	338
1939	4 979 066	8 841 224	-3 862 158	40 439 532	1884	348 520	244 126	104 394	1 625 307
1938	5 588 012	6 764 628	-1 176 617	37 164 740	1883	398 288	265 408	132 879	1 721 959
1937	4 955 613	7 733 033	-2 777 421	36 424 614	1882	403 525	257 981	145 544	1 856 916
1936	3 997 059	8 421 608	-4 424 549	33 778 543	1881	360 782	260 713	100 069	2 019 286
1935	3 705 956	6 497 008	-2 791 052	28 700 893	1880	333 527	267 643	65 884	2 090 909
1934	3 014 970	6 644 602	-3 629 632	27 053 141	1879	273 827	266 948	6 879	2 298 913
1933	1 996 844	4 958 496	-2 601 652	22 538 673	1878	257 764	236 964	20 800	2 159 418
1932	1 923 892	4 659 182	-2 735 290	19 487 002	1877	281 406	241 334	40 072	2 107 760
1931	3 115 557	3 577 434	-461 877	16 801 281	1876	294 096	265 101	28 995	2 130 846
1930	4 057 884	3 320 211	737 673	16 185 310	1875	288 000	274 623	13 377	2 156 277
1929	3 861 589	3 127 199	734 391	16 931 088	1874	304 979	302 634	2 345	2 159 933
1928	3 900 329	2 961 245	939 083	17 604 293	1873	333 738	290 345	43 393	2 151 210
1927	4 012 794	2 857 429	1 155 365	18 511 907	1872	374 107	277 518	96 589	2 209 991
1926	3 795 108	2 929 964	865 144	19 643 216	1871	383 324	292 177	91 147	2 322 052
1925	3 640 805	2 923 762	717 043	20 516 194	1870	411 255	309 654	101 602	2 436 453
1924	3 871 214	2 907 847	963 367	21 250 813	1869	370 944	322 865	48 078	2 545 111
1923	3 852 795	3 140 287	712 508	22 349 707	1868	405 638	377 640	28 298	2 583 446
1922	4 025 901	3 289 404	736 496	22 963 382	1867	490 634	357 543	133 091	2 650 168
1921	5 570 790	5 061 785	509 005	23 977 451	1866	558 033	520 809	37 223	2 755 764
1920	6 648 898	6 357 677	291 222	24 299 321	1865	333 715	1 297 555	-963 841	2 677 929
1919	5 130 042	18 492 665	-13 362 623	25 484 506	1864	264 627	865 323	-600 696	1 815 831
1918	3 645 240	12 677 359	-9 032 120	12 455 225	1863	112 697	714 741	-602 043	1 119 774
1917	1 100 500	1 953 857	-853 357	2 975 619	1862	51 987	474 762	-422 774	524 178
1916	761 445	712 967	48 478	1 225 146	1861	41 510	66 547	-25 037	90 582
1915	683 417	746 093	-62 676	1 191 264	1860	56 065	63 131	-7 066	64 844
1914	725 117	725 525	-408	1 188 235	1859	53 486	69 071	-15 585	58 498
1913	714 463	714 864	-401	1 193 048	1858	46 655	74 185	-27 530	44 913
1912	692 609	689 881	2 728	1 193 839	1857	68 965	67 796	1 170	28 701
1911	701 833	691 202	10 631	1 153 985	1856	74 057	69 571	4 486	31 974
1910	675 512	693 617	-18 105	1 146 940	1855	65 351	59 743	5 608	35 588
1909	604 320	693 744	-89 423	1 148 315	1854	73 800	58 045	15 755	42 244
1908	601 862	659 196	-57 334	1 177 690	1853	61 587	48 184	13 403	59 805
1907	665 860	579 129	86 732	1 147 178	1852	49 847	44 195	5 652	66 199
1906	594 984	570 202	24 782	1 142 523	1851	52 559	47 709	4 850	68 305
1905	544 275	567 279	-23 004	1 132 357	1850	43 603	39 543	4 060	63 453
1904	541 087	583 660	-42 573	1 136 259	1849	31 208	45 052	-13 844	63 062
1903	561 881	517 006	44 875	1 159 406	1848	35 736	45 377	-9 641	47 045
1902	562 478	485 234	77 244	1 178 031	1847	26 496	57 281	-30 786	38 827
1901	587 685	524 617	63 068	1 221 572	1846	29 700	27 767	1 933	15 550
1900	567 241	520 861	46 380	1 263 417	1845	29 970	22 937	7 033	15 925
1899	515 961	605 072	-89 112	1 436 701	1844	29 321	22 338	6 984	23 462
1898	405 321	443 369	-38 047	1 232 743	1843	8 303	11 858	-3 555	32 743
1897	347 722	365 774	-18 052	1 226 794	1842	19 976	25 206	-5 230	20 201
1896	338 142	352 179	-14 037	1 222 729	1841	16 860	26 522	-9 706	13 594
1895	324 729	356 195	-31 466	1 096 913	1840	19 480	24 318	-4 837	5 351
1894	306 355	367 525	-61 170	1 016 898	1839	31 483	26 899	4 584	3 573
1893	385 820	383 478	2 342	961 432	1838	26 303	33 865	-7 562	10 434
1892	354 938	345 023	9 914	968 219	1837	24 954	37 243	-12 289	3 308
1891	392 612	365 774	26 839	1 005 807	1836	50 827	30 868	19 959	337
1890	403 081	318 041	85 040	1 122 397	1835	35 430	17 573	17 857	38
1889	387 050	299 289	87 761	1 249 471	1834	21 792	18 628	3 164	38
1888	379 266	267 925	111 341	1 384 632	1833	33 948	23 018	10 931	4 760
1887	371 403	267 932	103 471	1 465 485	1832	31 866	17 289	14 577	7 012
1886	336 440	242 483	93 957	1 555 660	1831	28 527	15 248	13 279	24 322
1885	323 691	260 227	63 464	1 578 551					

See footnotes of end of table.

Series Y 335-338.   Summary of Federal Government Finances—Administrative Budget: 1789 to 1939—Cont'd.

(In thousands of dollars. For years ending June 30. Data for 1929-1953 are consolidated cash statement figures; for 1954-1970, unified budget figures. For 1789-1842, years ending December 31; 1844-1939, June 30; 1843 figures are for January 1-June 30)

Year	Budget receipts [1]	Budget expenditures [2]	Surplus or deficit [3] (-)	Total public debt [4]	Year	Budget receipts [1]	Budget expenditures [2]	Surplus or deficit [3] (-)	Total public debt [4]
	335	336	337	338		335	336	337	338
1830	24 844	15 143	9 701	39 123	1810	9 384	8 157	1 228	48 006
1829	24 828	15 203	9 624	48 565	1809	7 773	10 281	-2 507	53 173
1828	24 764	16 395	8 369	58 421	1808	17 061	9 932	7 128	57 023
1827	22 966	16 139	6 827	67 475	1807	16 398	8 354	8 044	65 196
1826	25 260	17 036	8 225	73 987	1806	15 560	9 804	5 756	69 218
1825	21 841	15 857	5 984	81 054	1805	13 561	10 506	3 054	75 723
1824	19 381	20 327	-945	83 788	1804	11 826	8 719	3 107	82 312
1823	20 541	14 707	5 834	90 270	1803	11 064	7 852	3 212	86 427
1822	20 232	15 000	5 232	90 876	1802	14 996	7 862	7 134	77 055
1821	14 573	15 811	-1 237	93 547	1801	12 935	9 395	3 541	80 713
1820	17 881	18 261	-380	89 987	1800	10 849	10 786	63	83 038
1819	24 603	21 464	3 140	91 016	1799	7 547	9 666	-2 120	82 976
1818	21 585	19 825	1 760	95 530	1798	7 900	7 677	224	78 409
1817	33 099	21 844	11 255	103 467	1797	5 689	6 134	2 555	79 229
1816	47 678	30 587	17 091	123 492	1796	8 378	5 727	2 651	82 064
1815	15 729	32 709	-16 979	127 335	1795	6 115	7 540	-1 425	83 762
1814	11 182	34 721	-23 539	99 834	1794	5 432	6 991	-1 559	80 748
1813	14 340	31 682	-17 341	81 488	1793	4 653	4 482	171	78 427
1812	9 801	20 281	-10 480	55 963	1792	3 670	5 080	-1 410	80 359
1811	14 424	8 058	6 365	45 210	1789-1791	4 419	4 269	150	77 228

1. Excludes receipts from borrowing. Prior to 1913, total receipts; thereafter, net receipts.
2. Excludes debt repayment. Prior to 1913, total expenditures; thereafter, net expenditures.
3. Receipts compared with expenditures.
4. As of end of period.

Series Y 339-342.   Summary of Federal Government Finances: 1940 to 1999

(For years ending June 30. Data for 1940-1953 are consolidated cash statement figures; for 1954-1992, unified budget figures.)

Year	Receipts	Outlays	Surplus or deficit (-)	Total gross Federal debt	Year	Receipts	Outlays	Surplus or deficit (-)	Total gross Federal debt
	339	**340**	**341**	**342**		**339**	**340**	**341**	**342**
1999	1 806 334	1 727 071	79 263	5 614 934	1969	187 800 000	184 500 000	3 200 000	367 100 000
1998	1 721 798	1 652 552	69 246	5 478 724	1968	153 700 000	178 800 000	-25 200 000	369 800 000
1997	1 579 292	1 601 232	-21 940	5 369 707	1967	149 600 000	158 300 000	-8 700 000	341 300 000
1996	1 453 062	1 560 512	-107 450	5 181 934	1966	130 900 000	134 700 000	-3 800 000	329 500 000
1995	1 351 830	1 515 729	-163 899	4 921 018	1965	116 800 000	118 400 000	-1 600 000	323 200 000
1994	1 258 627	1 461 731	-203 104	4 643 705	1964	112 700 000	118 600 000	-5 900 000	316 800 000
1993	1 154 401	1 409 414	-255 013	4 351 416	1963	106 600 000	111 300 000	-4 800 000	310 800 000
1992	1 075 706 000	1 475 439 000	-399 733 000	4 077 510 000	1962	99 700 000	106 800 000	-7 100 000	303 300 000
1991	1 054 264 000	1 323 011 000	-268 746 000	3 598 993 000	1961	94 400 000	97 800 000	-3 400 000	292 900 000
1990	1 031 308 000	1 251 778 000	-220 470 000	3 206 347 000	1960	92 500 000	92 200 000	300 000	290 900 000
1989	990 691 000	1 144 169 000	-206 132 000	2 867 538 000	1959	79 200 000	92 100 000	-12 900 000	287 800 000
1988	908 954 000	1 064 140 000	-193 897 000	2 600 760 000	1958	79 600 000	82 600 000	-2 900 000	279 700 000
1987	854 143 000	1 003 911 000	-169 257 000	2 345 578 000	1957	80 000 000	76 700 000	3 200 000	272 400 000
1986	769 091 000	990 336 000	-237 898 000	2 120 082 000	1956	74 500 000	70 500 000	4 100 000	272 800 000
1985	734 057 000	946 391 000	-221 623 000	1 816 974 000	1955	65 500 000	68 500 000	-3 000 000	274 400 000
1984	666 457 000	851 846 000	-185 586 000	1 564 110 000	1954	69 700 000	70 900 000	-1 200 000	270 800 000
1983	600 562 000	808 380 000	-207 977 000	1 371 164 000	1953	71 500 000	76 800 000	-5 300 000	266 000 000
1982	617 766 000	745 755 000	-120 003 000	1 136 798 000	1952	68 000 000	(Z)	259 100 000	. . .
1981	599 272 000	678 249 000	-73 916 000	994 298 000	1951	53 400 000	45 800 000	7 600 000	255 300 000
1980	517 112 000	590 920 000	-72 689 000	908 503 000	1950	40 900 000	43 000 000	-2 200 000	256 900 000
1979	463 302 000	530 464 000	-38 178 000	828 923 000	1949	41 600 000	40 600 000	1 000 000	252 600 000
1978	399 561 000	458 729 000	-54 902 000	776 602 000	1948	45 400 000	36 500 000	8 900 000	252 000 000
1977	355 559 000	409 203 000	-49 745 000	706 398 000	1947	43 500 000	36 900 000	6 600 000	257 100 000
1976	298 060 000	371 779 000	-70 499 000	628 970 000	1946	43 500 000	61 700 000	-18 200 000	271 000 000
1975	279 090 000	332 332 000	-55 260 000	541 925 000	1945	50 200 000	95 200 000	-45 000 000	260 100 000
1974	263 224 000	269 359 000	-7 971 000	483 893 000	1944	47 800 000	94 000 000	-46 100 000	204 100 000
1973	230 799 000	245 707 000	-15 403 000	466 291 000	1943	25 100 000	78 900 000	-53 800 000	142 600 000
1972	207 309 000	230 681 000	-26 423 000	435 936 000	1942	15 100 000	34 500 000	-19 400 000	79 200 000
1971	187 139 000	210 172 000	-26 052 000	408 176 000	1941	9 200 000	14 000 000	-4 800 000	57 500 000
1970	193 700 000	196 600 000	-2 800 000	382 600 000	1940	6 900 000	9 600 000	-2 700 000	50 700 000

Z less than $50 million.

Series Y 393-401. Individual Federal Income Tax Returns: 1944 to 1996

(In thousands of dollars, except number of returns)

Income Year	Total number of returns	Returns with adjusted gross income		Income Year	Total number of returns	Returns with adjusted gross income	
		Taxable income	Income tax (after credits)			Taxable income	Income tax (after credits)
	393	**398**	**399**		**393**	**398**	**399**
1996	120 351 000	3 089 700 000	658 200 000	1966	70 160 425	286 296 994	56 087 084
1995	118 218 000	2 813 800 000	588 400 000	1965	67 596 300	255 082 124	49 529 695
1994	115 943 000	2 598 000 000	534 900 000	1964	65 375 601	229 875 078	47 152 855
1993	114 602 000	2 453 500 000	502 800 000	1963	63 943 236	209 090 323	48 203 580
1992	113 605 000	2 395 700 000	476 200 000	1962	62 712 386	195 320 479	44 902 840
1991	114 730 000	2 284 100 000	448 400 000	1961	61 499 420	181 779 732	42 224 498
1990	113 717 000	2 263 600 000	447 200 000	1960	61 027 931	171 627 771	39 464 156
1989	112 136 000	2 173 346 000	432 940 000	1959	60 271 297	166 540 616	38 645 299
1988	109 708 000	2 069 967 000	412 870 000	1958	59 085 182	149 337 414	34 335 652
1987	106 996 000	1 850 597 000	369 203 000	1957	59 825 121	149 363 077	34 393 639
1986	103 045 000	1 947 025 000	367 287 000	1958	59 085 182	149 337 414	34 335 652
1985	101 660 000	1 820 741 000	325 710 000	1956	59 197 004	141 532 061	32 732 132
1984	99 400 000	1 701 400 000	301 900 000	1955	58 250 188	128 020 111	29 613 722
1983	96 300 000	1 544 900 000	274 200 000	1954	56 747 008	115 331 301	26 665 753
1982	95 300 000	1 473 300 000	277 600 000	1953	57 838 184	. . .	29 430 659
1981	95 400 000	1 410 900 000	284 100 000	1952	56 528 817	. . .	27 802 831
1980	93 902 000	1 279 985 000	250 341 000	1951	55 447 009	. . .	24 227 780
1979	92 700 000	1 157 200 000	213 300 000	1950	53 060 098	. . .	18 374 922
1978	89 800 000	1 062 200 000	186 700 000	1949	51 814 124	. . .	14 538 141
1977	86 600 000	939 000 000	158 500 000	1948	52 072 006	. . .	15 441 529
1976	84 700 000	674 900 000	140 800 000	1947	55 099 008	. . .	18 076 281
1975	82 200 000	595 500 000	124 500 000	1946	52 816 547	. . .	16 075 913
1974	83 300 000	573 600 000	123 500 000	1945	49 932 783	. . .	17 050 378
1973	80 700 000	511 900 000	107 900 000	1944	47 111 495	. . .	16 216 401
1972	77 570 000	444 600 000	93 354 000				
1971	74 573 000	413 400 000	85 253 000				
1970	74 279 831	400 859 064	83 909 314				
1969	75 834 388	388 153 971	86 568 215				
1968	73 728 708	352 799 662	76 637 902				
1967	71 651 909	315 108 212	62 919 958				

Series Y 402-411. Individual Federal Income Tax Returns: 1913 to 1943

Income Year	Total number of returns with net income [1]	Income Year	Total number of returns with net income [1]	Income Year	Total number of returns with net income [1]
	402		**402**		**402**
1943	43 506 553	1932	3 877 430	1922	6 787 481
1942	36 456 110	1931	3 225 924	1921	6 662 176
1941	26 770 089	1930	3 707 509	1920	7 259 944
1940	14 598 074	1929	4 044 327	1919	5 332 760
1939	7 570 320				
		1928	4 070 851	1918	4 425 114
1938	6 150 776	1927	4 101 547	1917	3 472 890
1937	6 301 833	1926	4 138 092	1916	437 036
1936	5 418 499	1925	4 171 051	1915	336 652
1935	4 575 012	1924	7 369 788		
1934	4 049 420			1914	357 515
		1923	7 698 321	1913 [2]	357 598
1933	3 723 558				

1. Includes fiduciary returns with net income filed on Form 1040, 1913-1936.
2. Data pertain to last 10 months of year.

Series Y 493-504.   Public Debt of the Federal Government: 1853 to 1999

(End of fiscal year)

Year	Interest-bearing principal of public debt outstanding [1]	U.S. savings bonds	Treasury bills [2]	Notes [3]
	497	500	502	503
	1,000 dollars	Million dollars	Million dollars	Million dollars
1999	5 606 087 000	...	...	...
1998	5 478 724 000	180 186	637 648	2 009 115
1997	5 369 707 000	182 665	701 909	2 122 172
1996	5 181 934 000	184 147	761 232	2 098 670
1995	4 921 018 000	181 181	742 462	1 980 343
1994	4 643 705 000	176 413	697 295	1 867 507
1993	4 351 416 000	167 024	658 381	1 734 161
1992	4 002 136 000	148 266	634 287	1 566 349
1991	3 598 498 000	133 512	564 589	1 387 717
1990	3 211 000 000	122 000	482 000	1 218 000
1989	2 836 000 000	114 000	407 000	1 133 000
1988	2 600 000 000	106 000	398 000	1 090 000
1987	2 348 000 000	97 000	378 300	1 005 100
1986	2 123 000 000	85 600	410 700	896 900
1985	1 821 000 000	77 000	384 000	776 000
1984	1 560 000 000	72 800	356 800	661 700
1983	1 376 000 000	70 000	340 700	557 500
1982	1 141 000 000	67 300	277 900	442 900
1981	996 000 000	68 000	223 400	363 600
1980	906 000 000	73 000	200 000	311 000
1979	819 000 000	80 400	161 400	274 200
1978	767 000 000	79 800	160 900	267 900
1977	698 000 000	75 400	156 100	241 700
1976	619 000 000	69 700	161 200	191 800
1975	532 000 000	65 000	129 000	150 000
1974	473 000 000	61 900	105 000	128 400
1973	456 000 000	59 400	100 100	117 800
1972	425 400 000	56 000	94 600	113 400
1971	396 300 000	53 000	86 700	104 800
1970	369 025 522	51 281	78 050	97 821
1969	351 729 445	51 711	69 039	82 761
1968	344 400 507	51 712	65 580	73 793
1967	322 285 952	51 213	64 899	49 774
1966	315 431 055	50 537	57 348	50 987
1965	313 112 817	50 043	54 537	52 699
1964	307 356 562	49 299	51 028	67 436
1963	301 953 731	48 314	69 891	52 328
1962	294 442 001	47 607	56 518	65 464
1961	285 671 609	47 514	50 062	56 257
1960	283 241 183	47 544	51 065	51 483
1959	281 833 362	50 503	65 860	27 314
1958	274 697 560	51 984	55 326	20 416
1957	268 485 563	54 622	43 893	30 973
1956	269 883 068	57 497	37 111	35 952
1955	271 741 538	58 365	33 350	42 642
1954	268 909 767	58 061	37 920	37 039
1953	263 946 018	57 886	35 561	34 878
1952	256 862 861	57 685	45 642	25 575
1951	252 851 765	57 572	23 123	43 624
1950	255 209 353	57 536	31 951	28 876
1949	250 761 637	56 260	40 964	8 456
1948	250 063 348	53 274	36 345	15 769
1947	255 113 412	51 367	41 071	13 702
1946	268 110 842	49 035	51 843	24 972
1945	256 356 616	45 586	51 177	33 633

Year	Interest-bearing principal of public debt outstanding [1]	U.S. savings bonds	Treasury bills [2]	Notes [3]
	497	500	502	503
	1,000 dollars	Million dollars	Million dollars	
1944	199 543 355	34 606	43 557	26 962
1943	135 380 306	21 256	28 425	16 663
1942	71 968 418	10 188	5 604	9 703
1941	48 387 400	4 314	1 603	5 698
1940	42 376 496	2 905	1 302	6 383
1939	39 885 970	1 868	1 308	7 243
1938	36 575 926	1 238	1 154	9 147
1937	35 800 109	800	2 303	10 617
1936	32 988 790	316	2 354	11 381
1935	27 645 241		2 053	10 023
1934	26 480 488		2 921	6 653
1933	22 157 643		3 063	4 548
1932	19 161 274		3 341	1 261
1931	16 519 589		2 246	452
1930	15 921 892		1 420	1 626
1929	16 638 941		1 640	2 267
1928	17 317 694		1 252	2 582
1927	18 252 665		686	1 986
1926	19 383 771		453	1 799
1925	20 210 907		533	2 740
1924	20 981 242		808	4 148
1923	22 007 044		1 031	4 441
1922	22 710 338		1 829	4 916
1921	23 738 900		2 700	4 920
1920	24 062 500		2 769	5 075
1919	25 236 947		3 625	4 422
1918	12 197 508		1 706	369
1917	2 712 549		273	27
1916	971 563		...	4
1915	969 759		...	...
1914	967 953		...	...
1913	965 707		...	...
1912	963 777		...	...
1911	915 353		...	...
1910	913 317		...	...
1909	913 317		...	...
1908	897 504		14	...
1907	894 834		(Z)	...
1906	895 159		(Z)	...
1905	895 158		(Z)	...
1904	895 157		(Z)	...
1903	914 541		(Z)	...
1902	931 070		(Z)	...
1901	987 141		(Z)	...
1900	1 023 479		(Z)	...
1899	1 046 049		(Z)	...
1898	847 367		(Z)	...
1897	847 365		(Z)	...
1896	847 364		(Z)	...
1895	716 202		(Z)	...
1894	635 042		(Z)	...
1893	585 037		(Z)	...
1892	585 029		(Z)	...
1891	610 529		(Z)	...
1890	711 313		(Z)	...

See footnotes at end of table.

Series Y 493-504. Public Debt of the Federal Government: 1853 to 1999—Cont'd.

(End of fiscal year)

Year	Interest-bearing principal of public debt outstanding [1]	Selected Components of interest-bearing debt			Year	Interest-bearing principal of public debt outstanding [1]	Selected Components of interest-bearing debt		
		U.S. savings bonds	Treasury bills [2]	Notes [3]			U.S. savings bonds	Treasury bills [2]	Notes [3]
	497	**500**	**502**	**503**		**497**	**500**	**502**	**503**
	1,000 dollars	*Million dollars*	*Million dollars*	*Million dollars*		*1,000 dollars*	*Million dollars*	*Million dollars*	*Million dollars*
					1889............	815 854		(Z)	. . .
					1888............	936 523		(Z)	. . .
					1887............	1 007 692		(Z)	. . .
					1886............	1 132 014		(Z)	. . .
					1885............	1 182 151		(Z)	. . .
					1884............	1 212 564		(Z)	. . .
					1883............	1 324 229		(Z)	. . .
					1882............	1 449 810		1	. . .
					1881............	1 625 568		1	. . .

Year	Interest-bearing principal of public debt outstanding [1]	Year	Interest-bearing principal of public debt outstanding [1]	Year	Interest-bearing principal of public debt outstanding [1]
	497		**497**		**497**
	1 000 dollars		*1 000 dollars*		*1 000 dollars*
1880	1 709 993	1870	2 035 881	1860	64 683
1879	1 887 716	1869	2 151 495	1859	58 333
1878	1 780 736	1868	2 191 326	1858	44 743
1877	1 697 889	1867	2 238 955	1857	28 503
1876	1 696 685	1866	2 322 116	1856	31 805
1875	1 708 676	1865	2 217 709	1855	35 418
1874	1 724 931	1864	1 360 027	1854	42 045
1873	1 696 484	1863	707 834	1853	59 642
1872	1 800 794	1862	365 356		
1871	1 920 697	1861	90 423		

Z Less than $500 000.
1. Exclusive of bonds issued to Pacific Railways (provision was made by law to secure the Treasury against both principal and interest) and the Navy pension fund (which was not a debt, the principal being the property of the United States). The Statement of the Public Debt included the railroad bonds from issuance and the Navy fund from Sept. 1, 1896, until the statement of June 30, 1890.
2. Includes certificates of indebtedness. Also includes refunding certificates of deposit, 1880-1907, inclusive.
3. Includes old Treasury (War) savings securities from 1918 through 1929.

Series Y 533-566. Federal, State and Local Government Expenditure, Total and Selected Functions: 1902 to 1996

(In millions of dollars)

Year	Total expenditure [1]	General expenditure						
		Total	Total education	Highways	Total public welfare	Health and hospitals	Police	Local fire protection
	533	534	538	542	543	547	549	550
1996 [5]	3 103 120	2 103 162	425 519	79 823	250 726	137 335	51 545	17 709
1995	2 819 860	2 059 994	404 933	77 840	250 356	132 467	47 917	17 009
1994	2 150 224	2 181 518	376 526	72 758	236 033	125 597	45 973	16 123
1993	2 571 896	1 902 481	368 473	68 753	218 655	118 969	43 502	15 797
1992	2 487 885	1 858 519	353 591	67 290	201 956	118 791	41 248	14 358
1991	2 380 686	1 805 522	330 759	65 602	167 681	166 700	38 942	13 796
1990	2 218 793	1 686 774	305 552	61 913	140 734	92 487	35 921	13 186
1988	1 920 413	1 461 857	256 960	55 998	115 125	78 789	30 934	11 753
1987	1 810 006	1 374 297	240 686	52 822	106 277	72 488	28 720	10 910
1986	1 696 208	1 284 261	224 400	49 936	99 665	68 706	26 228	9 587
1985	1 580 997	1 192 375	205 894	45 856	94 811	63 698	24 386	8 917
1984	1 428 100	1 068 400	188 600	40 300	88 400	59 300	21 400	8 200
1983	1 350 900	1 002 400	176 600	37 200	83 900	56 400	20 300	7 600
1982	1 233 500	917 500	165 800	35 100	78 800	53 300	18 500	7 000
1981	1 109 800	827 900	158 000	34 900	74 600	47 300	16 900	6 300
1980	958 700	723 100	143 800	33 700	64 800	43 300	15 200	5 700
1979	832 400	630 700	129 400	29 000	59 100	37 100	13 900	5 100
1978	745 400	564 300	118 800	24 900	54 200	33 000	12 900	4 800
1977	682 500	514 200	110 600	23 300	49 400	30 600	11 800	4 400
1976	625 100	476 100	106 300	24 200	45 100	27 500	10 700	3 900
1975	560 100	433 600	95 000	22 800	39 400	24 900	9 600	3 500
1974	478 300	377 200	81 700	20 200	31 000	21 700	8 300	3 000
1973	436 900	348 500	74 900	18 900	27 000	18 700	7 800	2 800
1972	397 400	321 400	70 000	19 400	23 600	17 000	6 500	2 600
1971	369 400	301 100	64 000	18 400	20 400	14 800	5 700	2 300
1970	332 985	275 017	55 771	16 746	17 517	13 588	4 903	2 024
1969	308 344	255 924	50 377	15 738	14 730	11 930	4 242	1 793
1968	282 645	236 348	43 614	14 654	11 245	10 579	3 700	1 623
1967	257 800	216 888	40 214	14 033	9 592	9 457	3 331	1 499
1966	224 813	189 406	34 837	12 895	6 965	8 362	3 033	1 376
1965	205 550	173 613	29 613	12 348	6 420	7 670	2 792	1 306
1964	196 431	166 088	27 342	11 828	5 880	7 079	2 586	1 222
1963	184 996	156 002	24 480	11 315	5 538	6 646	2 446	1 161
1962	176 240	149 159	22 814	10 508	5 147	6 135	2 326	1 124
1961	164 875	139 161	21 214	9 995	4 779	5 681	2 210	1 087
1960*	151 288	128 600	19 404	9 565	4 462	5 244	2 030	995
1959 [2]	145 748	124 217	18 119	9 726	4 193	5 067	1 880	914
1958	134 931	115 714	16 836	8 702	3 866	4 566	1 769	873
1957	125 463	109 765	15 098	7 931	3 534	4 151	1 623	810
1956	115 796	102 156	14 160	7 035	3 184	3 739	1 486	737
1955	110 717	97 828	12 710	6 520	3 210	3 428	1 358	694
1954	111 332	100 365	11 196	5 586	3 103	3 368	1 254	653
1953	110 054	100 733	10 117	5 053	2 956	3 246	1 160	598
1952	99 847	91 291	9 598	4 714	2 830	3 199	1 080	586
1950	70 334	60 701	9 647	3 872	2 964	2 711	864	488
1948	55 081	50 088	7 721	3 071	2 144	1 934	724	406
1946	79 707	75 582	3 711	1 680	1 435	1 142	549	294
1944	109 947	107 823	2 805	1 215	1 150	857	497	251
1942	45 576	43 483	2 696	1 765	1 285	714	444	236
1940	20 417	18 125	2 827	2 177	1 314	732	386	235
1938	17 675	16 273	2 653	2 150	1 233	678	378	231
1936	16 758	15 835	2 365	1 945	997	592	331	205
1934	12 807	12 086	2 005	1 829	979	535	306	189
1932	12 437	11 748	2 325	1 766	445	583	349	210
1927	11 220	10 590	2 243	1 819	161	431	290	203
1922	9 297	8 854	1 713	1 296	128	352	204	158
1913	3 215	3 022	582	419	57	113	92	76
1902	1 660	1 578	258	175	41	63	50	40

See footnotes at end of table.

Series Y 533-566. Federal, State and Local Government Expenditure, Total and Selected Functions: 1902 to 1996—Cont'd.

(In millions of dollars)

Year	Sewage and solid waste	Total natural resources	Housing and community development	Governmental administration	Interest on general debt[4]	Utility and liquor stores expenditure	Total insurance trust expenditure
	551	**552**	**555**	**557**	**558**	**561**	**562**
1996	42 076	55 561	38 994	[6] 54 991	292 137	95 608	667 042
1995	41 284	54 993	37 787	[6] 52 881	290 195	94 235	665 631
1994	38 497	64 624	35 716	67 504	257 623	91 163	618 244
1993	38 125	62 311	31 121	70 406	253 878	84 361	585 174
1992	32 398	63 650	32 549	67 180	254 968	84 361	545 006
1991	31 014	57 149	33 346	64 181	247 374	81 014	494 160
1990	28 453	96 922	32 430	57 546	237 691	77 801	454 218
1988	23 679	103 789	25 212	48 111	202 437	70 051	388 505
1987	21 323	105 282	21 304	44 125	187 971	68 440	367 269
1986	19 142	79 313	19 210	40 422	181 231	65 297	346 651
1985	17 398	71 152	18 592	37 200	172 708	59 798	328 824
1984	16 200	65 300	17 600	30 100	137 900	55 100	304 700
1983	15 600	54 800	18 500	27 900	132 900	52 800	297 400
1982	14 900	45 500	16 500	24 900	122 000	48 400	267 400
1981	14 900	43 600	13 900	22 500	97 600	43 000	238 900
1980	13 200	35 200	12 100	20 700	76 000	36 200	199 400
1979	11 800	30 300	8 000	18 700	61 800	30 800	170 900
1978	9 900	26 300	6 000	16 700	51 300	26 300	154 800
1977	9 400	22 400	5 600	14 800	44 500	24 200	144 100
1976	8 200	19 400	5 400	13 400	39 600	19 500	129 400
1975	7 500	18 100	5 900	11 900	33 800	17 300	109 200
1974	6 000	17 400	5 900	10 000	30 100	14 400	86 700
1973	5 300	16 700	6 900	4 600	25 100	13 000	75 300
1972	4 700	14 200	5 400	4 000	23 100	11 400	64 600
1971	4 100	13 700	4 500	3 600	21 700	10 300	58 000
1970	3 413	11 469	3 189	6 370	18 411	9 447	48 521
1969	2 969	10 024	2 505	5 563	16 992	8 820	43 600
1968	2 707	9 200	2 841	4 966	14 873	8 170	38 127
1967	2 523	10 145	2 413	4 537	13 406	7 350	33 561
1966	2 571	10 301	2 415	4 105	12 478	7 282	28 126
1965	2 360	10 990	2 198	3 842	11 430	7 058	24 880
1964	2 267	10 042	2 037	3 583	10 649	6 184	24 161
1963	1 996	9 511	1 688	3 362	9 846	5 736	23 260
1962	1 958	10 468	1 701	3 187	9 173	5 453	21 628
1961	1 774	9 756	1 320	3 025	9 309	5 523	20 191
1960 *	1 727	7 087	1 142	2 859	9 332	5 088	17 596
1959 [3]	1 609	7 966	838	2 750	6 959	4 901	16 631
1958	1 505	6 160	801	2 536	7 360	4 693	14 524
1957	1 443	6 137	624	2 405	6 603	4 429	11 269
1956	1 326	6 630	562	2 235	6 297	4 065	9 576
1955	1 142	6 338	611	2 060	5 684	3 886	9 002
1954	1 058	6 377	742	1 997	5 515	3 482	7 484
1953	908	4 816	768	1 866	5 477	3 316	6 006
1952	992	3 252	875	1 801	4 814	3 067	5 489
1950	834	5 005	573	1 555	4 862	2 739	6 894
1948	670	2 223	245	1 325	4 722	2 379	2 614
1946	370	3 111	221	1 163	4 286	1 733	2 392
1944	245	2 731	574	1 087	2 650	1 281	842
1942	229	2 468	622	828	1 591	1 106	986
1940	207	2 730	267	739	1 552	1 324	968
1938	226	2 089	109	725	1 513	848	554
1936	204	2 158	71	662	1 455	701	222
1934	177	1 241	3	533	1 473	528	193
1932	223	326	X	601	1 323	518	171
1927	312	206	1	526	1 348	491	139
1922	189	140	1	439	1 370	359	84
1913	97	44	. . .	256	170	186	7
1902	51	17	. . .	175	97	82	. . .

* Denotes first year for which figures include Alaska and Hawaii.
X Represents zero.
1. To avoid duplication, transactions between governments are excluded.
2. From 1971 to 1990, combines hospitals (547) and health (548).
3. Includes Alaska.
4. Excludes interest on federal securities held by federal agencies and funds.
5. Federal expenditure component is for previous fiscal year.
6. State and local only.

Series Y 652-670. State and Local Government Revenue, by Source: 1902 to 1996
(In millions of dollars)

Year	Total revenue from all sources	Total general revenue	Revenue from state and local sources-General revenue						Charges and miscellaneous
			Taxes						
			Total	Individual income	Corporation income	Sales and gross receipts	Property		
	652	656	657	658	659	660	661		663
1996	1 513 633	987 930	689 038	146 844	32 009	248 993	209 440		298 892
1995	1 417 925	940 733	660 577	137 931	31 406	237 268	203 451		280 156
1994	1 331 442	884 996	625 527	128 810	28 320	223 628	197 140		259 469
1993	1 270 748	842 977	594 300	123 235	26 417	209 649	189 743		248 677
1992	1 185 191	793 399	555 610	115 170	23 595	196 112	178 536		237 789
1991	1 080 862	748 108	525 355	109 341	22 242	185 570	167 999		222 753
1990	1 032 115	712 700	501 619	105 640	23 566	177 885	155 613		211 081
1988	1 776 000	1 299 000	998 000	490 000	118 000	209 000	132 000		301 000
1987	1 678 000	1 236 000	945 000	476 000	107 000	193 000	121 000		291 000
1985	719 686	491 525	349 793	70 097	19 158	126 281	103 757		141 732
1983	1 181 300	878 400	665 600	344 100	51 300	144 700	89 100		213 000
1982	1 146 300	866 400	671 500	348 800	64 200	139 300	82 100		194 900
1980	451 537	299 293	223 463	42 080	13 321	79 927	68 499		75 830
1970	150 106	108 898	86 795	10 812	3 738	30 322	34 054		22 103
1969	132 153	95 397	76 712	8 908	3 180	26 519	30 673		18 686
1968	117 581	84 083	67 572	7 308	2 518	22 911	27 747		16 511
1967	106 581	75 827	61 000	5 826	2 227	20 530	26 047		14 827
1966	97 619	69 822	56 647	4 760	2 038	19 085	24 670		13 175
1965	87 777	62 971	51 243	4 090	1 929	17 118	22 583		11 729
1964	81 455	58 440	47 785	3 791	1 695	15 762	21 241		10 655
1963	74 408	53 606	44 014	3 267	1 505	14 446	19 833		9 593
1962	69 492	50 381	41 554	3 037	1 308	13 494	19 054		8 827
1961	64 531	46 907	38 861	2 613	1 266	12 463	18 002		8 045
1960 *	60 277	43 530	36 117	2 463	1 180	11 849	16 405		7 414
1959 [1]	53 972	38 929	32 379	1 994	1 001	10 437	14 983		6 550
1958	49 262	36 354	30 380	1 759	1 018	9 829	14 047		5 974
1957	45 929	34 320	28 817	1 754	984	9 467	12 864		5 503
1956	41 692	31 332	26 368	1 538	890	8 691	11 749		4 964
1955	37 619	27 942	23 483	1 237	744	7 643	10 735		4 459
1954	35 386	26 046	22 067	1 127	778	7 276	9 967		3 979
1953	33 411	24 437	20 908	1 065	817	6 927	9 375		3 529
1952	31 013	22 615	19 323	998	846	6 357	8 652		3 292
1950	25 639	18 425	15 914	788	593	5 154	7 349		2 511
1948	21 613	15 389	13 342	543	592	4 442	6 126		2 047
1946	15 983	11 501	10 094	422	447	2 986	4 986		1 407
1944	14 333	9 954	8 774	342	451	2 289	4 604		1 180
1942	13 148	9 560	8 528	276	272	2 351	4 537		1 031
1940	11 749	8 664	7 810	224	156	1 982	4 430		854
1938	11 058	8 428	7 605	218	165	1 794	4 440		823
1936	9 360	7 447	6 701	153	113	1 484	4 093		746
1934	8 430	6 662	5 912	80	49	1 008	4 076		750
1932	7 887	7 035	6 164	74	79	752	4 487		871
1927	7 383	7 155	6 087	70	92	470	4 730		1 068
1922	5 169	4 673	4 016	43	58	154	3 321		657
1913	2 030	1 900	1 609	...	...	58	1 332		291
1902	1 048	979	860	...	...	28	706		119

* Denotes first year for which figures include Alaska and Hawaii.
1. Includes Alaska.

Series Y 736-782. State Government Expenditure, by Character and Object, by Function and State Government: 1902 to 1996

(In millions of dollars)

									Direct expenditure by function	
	Direct expenditure by character and object								General expenditure	
			Capital outlay		Assistance and subsidies	Interest on debt	Insurance benefits and repayments	Outstanding debt at end of fiscal year	Total education	Highways
Year	Total	Current operation	Total	Construction						
	738	739	740	741	743	744	745	747	759	763
1996	1 393 714	1 021 155	158 911	116 076	36 154	68 743	108 751	1 169 714	398 859	79 092
1995	1 347 763	985 693	151 440	110 012	36 867	66 423	107 340	1 115 370	378 273	77 109
1994	1 260 642	927 899	137 501	101 992	35 295	64 484	95 462	1 074 660	. . .	. . .
1993	1 210 096	875 924	135 899	100 153	34 664	64 802	98 807	1 017 686	. . .	. . .
1992	1 146 610	823 494	134 521	100 533	33 230	64 789	90 276	970 043	. . .	. . .
1991	1 059 805	762 007	131 650	96 654	30 456	61 533	74 159	915 711	. . .	. . .
1990	972 662	700 131	123 069	89 114	27 227	58 914	63 321	860 584	288 148	61 057
1988	824 507	591 247	104 314	78 592	23 928	52 803	52 216	755 034	242 683	55 621
1987	772 863	550 061	98 276	73 616	23 610	50 101	50 815	718 657	226 658	52 199
1986	715 324	511 378	90 449	67 968	22 588	44 370	46 538	658 875	210 819	49 368
1985	656 188	472 543	79 930	60 685	20 707	38 817	44 191	571 351	192 686	45 022
1984	598 945	433 653	70 651	53 833	19 694	34 439	40 508	506 330	176 108	39 419
1983	565 146	401 967	67 981	53 266	18 684	29 178	47 335	454 501	163 876	36 655
1982	523 023	375 057	66 802	53 668	17 335	24 321	39 508	404 579	154 282	34 520
1981	485 174	343 623	67 596	54 950	16 861	20 511	36 583	363 892	145 784	34 603
1980	432 328	307 811	62 894	51 492	15 222	17 604	28 797	335 603	133 211	33 311
1979	380 374	274 167	53 196	43 326	14 044	15 463	23 504	304 103	119 448	28 440
1978	345 313	249 222	44 769	36 199	13 753	14 044	23 525	284 330	110 758	24 609
1977	323 168	225 650	45 154	36 334	13 077	13 137	26 149	259 658	102 780	23 058
1976	304 229	204 387	46 531	38 299	12 494	11 681	27 954	240 532	97 216	23 907
1975	268 241	180 976	44 824	36 356	11 146	10 087	21 209	219 926	87 858	22 528
1974	225 691	154 810	38 084	30 542	11 290	8 840	12 667	206 616	75 833	19 946
1973	205 336	138 974	35 272	28 251	12 187	7 828	11 074	188 485	69 714	18 615
1972	188 825	125 630	34 237	28 107	11 527	6 893	10 358	174 502	64 886	19 010
1971	170 766	111 829	33 137	26 970	10 104	5 904	9 793	158 827	59 413	18 095
1970	56 163	30 971	13 295	11 185	4 387	1 499	6 010	42 008	13 780	11 044
1969	49 448	27 052	12 701	10 610	3 509	1 275	4 911	39 553	12 304	10 414
1968	44 304	23 379	12 210	10 053	2 960	1 128	4 626	35 666	10 957	9 819
1967	39 704	20 201	11 544	9 550	2 665	1 026	4 268	32 472	9 384	9 423
1966	34 195	16 855	10 193	8 287	2 301	894	3 952	29 564	7 572	8 624
1965	31 465	14 930	9 307	7 600	2 236	822	4 170	27 034	6 181	8 214
1964	29 616	13 492	8 820	7 263	2 175	765	4 364	25 041	5 465	7 850
1963	27 698	12 449	8 110	6 717	2 112	721	4 306	23 176	4 718	7 425
1962	25 495	11 290	7 214	5 960	2 118	635	4 238	22 023	4 270	6 635
1961	24 578	10 384	6 865	5 699	2 044	584	4 701	19 993	3 792	6 230
1960 *	22 152	9 534	6 607	5 509	2 015	536	3 461	18 543	3 396	6 070
1959 [1]	22 436	8 775	7 059	5 937	1 891	453	4 259	16 930	3 093	6 414
1958	19 991	8 161	5 946	5 022	1 813	396	3 675	15 394	2 728	5 507
1957	16 796	7 330	5 163	4 318	1 639	351	2 313	13 738	2 342	4 875
1956	15 148	6 758	4 564	3 872	1 531	311	1 984	12 890	2 138	4 367
1955	14 371	6 234	3 992	3 404	1 482	251	2 411	11 198	1 905	3 899
1954	13 008	5 886	3 347	2 831	1 486	193	2 096	9 600	1 715	3 254
1953	11 466	5 540	2 847	2 472	1 501	162	1 416	7 824	1 634	2 781
1952	10 790	5 173	2 658	2 323	1 402	144	1 413	6 874	1 494	2 556
1950	10 864	4 450	2 237	1 966	1 891	109	2 177	5 285	1 358	2 058
1948	7 897	3 837	1 456	1 268	1 499	86	1 020	3 676	1 081	1 510
1946	4 974	2 701	368	292	663	84	1 158	2 353	518	613
1944	3 319	2 134	330	288	527	101	226	2 776	489	540
1942	3 563	1 827	642	560	466	122	505	3 257	391	790
1940	3 555	1 570	737	643	517	130	601	3 590	375	793
1938	3 082	1 503	701	612	448	128	302	3 343	347	815
1936	2 445	1 192	634	553	416	124	79	3 413	297	754
1934	2 143	985	619	540	356	119	64	2 248	228	738
1932	2 028	982	786	686	83	114	63	2 832	278	843
1927	1 451	762	492	430	43	83	71	1 971	218	514
1922	1 085	562	302	263	122	45	54	1 131	164	303
1913	297	218	48	42	17	14	. . .	379	55	26
1902	136	114	2	2	10	10	. . .	230	17	4

See footnotes at end of table.

Series Y 736-782. State Government Expenditure, by Character and Object, by Function and State Government: 1902 to 1996—Cont'd.

(In millions of dollars)

Year	Total public welfare	Hospitals	Health	Police	Natural resources	Financial administration and general control	Interest on general debt	Utility and liquor stores expenditure	Total insurance trust expenditure
	764	**768**	**769**	**770**	**771**	**773**	**774**	**778**	**779**
1990	107 287	50 412	24 223	30 577	12 330	16 217	49 739	77 801	63 321
1988	86 469	43 452	18 488	26 277	10 238	13 589	44 318	70 052	52 216
1987	80 090	40 108	16 864	24 684	9 738	12 841	41 816	68 440	50 815
1986	73 785	37 958	15 550	22 685	9 074	11 897	37 064	65 297	46 538
1985	69 577	36 000	13 711	20 956	8 357	10 448	32 427	59 800	44 191
1984	64 709	34 142	12 277	19 262	7 421	9 502	28 696	55 062	40 508
1983	59 157	32 452	11 546	17 958	7 082	8 789	24 136	52 812	47 335
1982	56 216	30 245	10 636	16 511	6 567	8 106	20 160	48 412	39 508
1981	52 248	26 330	9 771	14 947	6 175	7 230	17 131	43 016	36 583
1980	45 552	23 787	8 387	13 494	5 509	6 719	14 747	36 191	28 797
1979	40 418	21 039	7 179	12 207	4 706	6 071	12 987	30 846	23 504
1978	37 679	18 648	6 303	11 306	4 225	5 292	11 983	26 277	23 526
1977	34 529	17 542	5 497	10 445	4 049	4 489	11 234	24 191	26 149
1976	32 604	15 726	4 960	9 531	4 662	3 960	10 269	19 542	27 954
1975	27 181	14 432	4 414	8 526	4 223	3 594	8 782	17 285	21 209
1974	24 745	12 493	3 452	7 289	3 661	3 165	7 666	14 406	12 667
1973	23 582	11 112	2 732	6 710	3 278	2 811	6 785	13 035	11 074
1972	21 070	10 293	2 574	5 976	3 110	2 480	5 963	11 414	10 538
1971	18 226	9 086	2 119	5 228	3 082	2 271	5 089	10 300	9 793
1970	8 203	4 002	786	688	2 158	1 720	1 499	1 404	6 010
1969	6 464	3 582	676	585	2 035	1 496	1 275	1 293	4 911
1968	5 122	3 233	599	516	1 954	1 310	1 128	1 233	4 626
1967	4 291	2 857	501	441	1 801	1 175	1 026	1 187	4 268
1966	3 138	2 533	433	385	1 532	1 024	894	1 081	3 952
1965	2 998	2 317	384	348	1 343	948	822	1 022	4 170
1964	2 796	2 127	337	315	1 185	871	765	977	4 364
1963	2 712	2 006	324	297	1 097	830	721	900	4 306
1962	2 509	1 878	283	276	973	763	635	882	4 238
1961	2 311	1 799	260	261	906	726	584	873	4 701
1960 *	2 221	1 664	232	245	842	654	536	907	3 461
1959 [1]	2 124	1 627	223	228	813	619	453	860	4 259
1958	1 944	1 549	211	214	753	569	396	869	3 675
1957	1 826	1 373	198	179	688	531	351	836	2 313
1956	1 603	1 268	202	159	670	477	311	845	1 984
1955	1 600	1 145	193	139	597	447	251	770	2 411
1954	1 548	1 089	187	130	563	419	193	803	2 096
1953	1 534	1 014	170	119	531	399	162	757	1 416
1952	1 410	968	164	106	539	361	144	723	1 413
1950	1 566	788	159	85	468	317	109	654	2 177
1948	962	533	130	65	344	266	86	691	1 020
1946	680	308	116	45	207	192	84	663	1 158
1944	577	253	78	41	164	162	101	426	226
1942	523	235	64	40	159	164	122	288	505
1940	527	236	64	34	144	151	130	224	601
1938	453	209	59	30	128	146	128	204	302
1936	422	180	41	19	93	130	124	143	97
1934	363	167	36	15	85	108	119	70	64
1932	74	181	34	15	119	114	114	. . .	63
1927	40	146	24	7	94	96	83	. . .	71
1922	38	105	20	4	61	69	45	. . .	54
1913	16	47	6	1	14	38	14	. . .	. . .
1902	10	28	4	. . .	9	23	10	2	. . .

* Denotes first year for which figures include Alaska and Hawaii.
1. Includes Alaska.

Series Y 856-903. Selected Characteristics of the Armed Forces, by Major Conflict

(For Revolutionary War, number of personnel serving not known, but estimates range from 184 000 to 250 000; for War of 1812, 286 730 served; for Mexican War, 78 718 served. Dates of the major conflicts may differ from those specified in various laws providing benefits for veterans.)

Series No.	Item	Unit	Civil War [1]	Spanish-American War	World War I	World War II	Korean conflict	Vietnam conflict
856	Personnel serving [2]	1 000	2 213	307	4 735	[3] 16 113	[4] 5 720	[5] 8 744
866	Average duration of service	Months	20	8	12	33	19	23
869	Service abroad: Personnel serving	Percent	. . .	[6] 29	53	73	[7] 56	. . .
870	Average duration [8]	Months	. . .	1.5	6	16	13	. . .
880	Casualties: [9] Battle deaths [2]	1 000	140	(Z)	53	292	34	[10] 47
882	Wounds not mortal [2]	1 000	282	2	204	671	103	[10] 153
862	Draftees: Classified	1 000	777	. . .	24 234	36 677	9 123	[5] 75 717
863	Examined	1 000	522	. . .	3 764	17 955	3 685	[5] 8 611
864	Rejected	1 000	160	. . .	803	6 420	1 189	[5] 3 880
865	Inducted	1 000	46	. . .	2 820	10 022	1 560	[5] 1 759

Z Fewer than 500.
1. Union forces only. Estimates of the number serving in Confederate forces range from 600 000 to 1.5 million.
2. Source U.S. Department of Defense, Selected Manpower Statistics, FY 1988, annual.
3. Covers Dec. 1, 1941 to Dec. 31, 1946.
4. Covers June 25, 1950 to July 27, 1953.
5. Covers Aug. 4, 1964 to Jan. 27, 1973.
6. Army and Marines only.
7. Excludes Navy. Covers July 1950 through Jan. 1955. Far East area only.
8. During hostilities only.
9. For periods covered, see footnotes 3, 4 and 5.
10. Covers Jan. 1, 1961 to Jan. 27, 1973. Includes known military service personnel who have died from combat-related wounds.

Series YY 1. Composition of Congress, by Political Party: 1971 to 1997

(D = Democratic, R = Republican. Data for beginning of first session of each Congress (as of January 3), except as noted. Excludes vacancies at beginning of session)

Year	Party and President	Congress	House			Senate		
			Majority party	Minority party	Other	Majority party	Minority party	Other
1971 [1]	R (Nixon)	92d	D-254	R-180	...	D-54	R-44	2
1973 [1,2]	R (Nixon)	93d	D-239	R-192	1	D-56	R-42	2
1975 [3]	R (Ford)	94th	D-291	R-144	...	D-60	R-37	2
1977 [4]	D (Carter)	95th	D-292	R-143	...	D-61	R-38	1
1979 [4]	D (Carter)	96th	D-276	R-157	...	D-58	R-41	1
1981 [4]	R (Reagan)	97th	D-243	R-192	...	R-53	D-46	1
1983	R (Reagan)	98th	D-269	R-165	...	R-54	D-46	...
1985	R (Reagan)	99th	D-252	R-182	...	R-53	D-47	...
1987	R (Reagan)	100th	D-258	R-177	...	D-55	R-45	...
1989	R (Bush)	101st	D-259	R-174	...	D-55	R-45	...
1991 [5]	R (Bush)	102d	D-267	R-167	1	D-56	R-44	...
1993 [5]	D (Clinton)	103d	D-258	R-176	1	D-57	R-43	...
1995 [5]	D (Clinton)	104th	R-230	D-204	1	R-52	D-48	...
1996 [5,6]	D (Clinton)	104th	R-236	D-197	1	R-53	D-46	...
1997 [5,6]	D (Clinton)	105th	R-226	D-207	2	R-55	D-45	...

1. Senate had one Independent and one Conservative-Republican.
2. House had one Independent-Democrat.
3. Senate had one Independent, one Conservative-Republican, and one undecided (New Hampshire).
4. Senate had one Independent.
5. House had one Independent-Socialist.
6. As of beginning of second session.
Source: U.S. Congress, Joint Committee on Printing, Congressional Directory, annual; beginning 1977, biennial.

Series YY 2. Political Party Financial Activity, by Major Political Party: 1981 to 1998

(In millions of dollars [$39.3 represents $39 300 000]. Covers financial activity during 2-year calendar period indicated. Some political party financial activities, such as building funds and state and local election spending, are not reported to the source. Also excludes contributions earmarked to Federal candidates through the party organizations, since some of those funds never passed through the committees' accounts)

Year and type of committee	Democratic				Republican			
	Receipts net [1]	Disbursements behalf of net [1]	Contributions to candidates	Monies spent on behalf of party's nominees [2]	Receipts net [1]	Disbursements behalf of net [1]	Contributions to candidates	Monies spent on behalf of party's nominees [2]
1981-82	39.3	40.1	1.7	3.3	215.0	214.0	5.6	14.3
1983-84	98.5	97.4	2.6	9.0	297.9	300.8	4.9	20.1
1985-86	64.8	65.9	1.7	9.0	255.2	258.9	3.4	14.3
1987-88	127.9	121.9	1.8	17.9	263.3	257.0	3.4	22.7
1989-90	85.8	90.9	1.5	8.7	206.3	213.5	2.9	10.7
1991-92	177.7	171.9	1.9	28.1	267.3	256.1	3.0	33.9
1993-94, total	143.3	141.8	2.2	21.2	254.4	243.7	3.0	20.6
1995-96, total	281.5	274.8	2.1	22.6	474.0	465.3	3.8	31.0
1997-98, total [3]	189.0	184.3	1.2	27.1	319.6	310.5	2.6	15.7
National committee	64.8	65.3	-	6.0	104.0	105.1	0.4	3.9
Senatorial committee	35.6	35.8	0.3	8.4	53.4	53.7	0.3	-
Congressional committee	25.2	24.7	0.4	3.0	72.7	71.7	0.8	5.1
State and local	63.4	58.5	0.5	9.6	89.4	80.0	1.1	6.7

- Represents zero.
1. Excludes monies transferred between affiliated committees.
2. Monies spent in the general election. Minus sign (-) indicates refunds for expenditures.
3. Excludes "Other national" activity.

SOURCE: U.S. Federal Election Commission, FEC Reports on Financial Activity, Final Report, Party and Non-Party Political Committees, biennial.

Series YY 3. Participation in Elections for President and U.S. Representatives: 1932 to 1998

(As of November. Estimated resident population 21 years old and over, 1932-70, except as noted, and 18 years old and over thereafter; includes Armed Forces. Prior to 1960, excludes Alaska and Hawaii. District of Columbia is included in votes cast for President beginning 1964 and in votes cast for Representative from 1972 to 1992)

Year	Resident population (incl. aliens) of voting age [1] (1 000)	Votes cast				Year	Resident population (incl. aliens) of voting age [1] (1 000)	Votes cast			
		For President [2] (1 000)	Percent of voting-age population	For U.S. Representatives (1 000)	Percent of voting-age population			For President [2] (1 000)	Percent of voting-age population	For U.S. Representatives (1 000)	Percent of voting-age population
1932	75 768	39 758	52.5	37 657	49.7	1966	116 638	...	...	52 908	45.4
1934	77 997	...	...	32 256	41.4	1968	120 285	73 212	60.9	66 288	55.1
1936	80 174	45 654	56.9	42 886	53.5	1970	124 498	...	...	54 173	43.5
1938	82 354	...	...	36 236	44.0	1972	140 777	77 719	55.2	71 430	50.7
1940	84 728	49 900	58.9	46 951	55.4	1974	146 338	...	...	52 495	35.9
1942	86 465	...	...	28 074	32.5	1976	152 308	81 556	53.5	74 422	48.9
1944	85 654	47 977	56.0	45 103	52.7	1978	158 369	...	...	55 332	34.9
1946	92 659	...	...	34 398	37.1	1980	163 945	86 515	52.8	77 995	47.6
1948	95 573	48 794	51.1	45 933	48.1	1982	169 643	...	...	64 514	38.0
1950	98 134	...	...	40 342	41.1	1984	173 995	92 653	53.3	83 231	47.8
1952	99 929	61 551	61.6	57 571	57.6	1986	177 922	...	...	59 619	33.5
1954	102 075	...	...	42 580	41.7	1988	181 956	91 595	50.3	81 786	44.9
1956	104 515	62 027	59.3	58 426	55.9	1990	185 812	...	...	61 513	33.1
1958	106 447	...	...	45 818	43.0	1992	189 524	104 425	55.1	96 239	50.8
1960	109 672	68 838	62.8	64 133	58.5	1994	193 650	...	...	70 781	36.6
1962	112 952	...	...	51 267	45.4	1996	196 507	96 278	49.0	89 863	45.8
1964	114 090	70 645	61.9	65 895	57.8	1998	200 929	...	...	66 033	32.9

1. Population 18 and over in Georgia, 1944-70 and in Kentucky, 1956-70; 19 and over in Alaska and 20 and over in Hawaii, 1960-70.
2. Source: 1932-58, U.S. Congress, Clerk of the House, Statistics of the Presidential and Congressional Election, biennial.

SOURCE: Except as noted, U.S. Census Bureau, Current Population Reports, P25-1085; Congressional Quarterly, Inc., Washington, DC America Votes, biennial (copyright).

Series YY 5. Hispanic Public Officials, by Office, 1985 to 1994, and by State, 1994

(As of September. For states not shown, no Hispanic public officials had been identified)

Year and State	Total	State executives and legislators [1]	County and municipal officials	Judicial and law enforcement	Education and school boards	State	Total	State executives and legislators [1]	County and municipal officials	Judicial and law enforcement	Education and school boards
1985 (Sept.)	3 147	129	1 316	517	1 185	IN	8	1	5	1	1
1986 (Sept.)	3 202	132	1 352	530	1 188	KS	7	5	1	-	1
1987 (Sept.)	3 317	138	1 412	568	1 199	LA	12	3	1	8	-
1988 (Sept.)	3 360	135	1 425	574	1 226	MD	2	-	1	-	1
1989 (Sept.)	3 783	143	1 724	575	1 341	MA	1	-	-	-	1
1990 (Sept.)	4 004	144	1 819	583	1 458	MI	8	-	5	1	2
1991 (Sept.)	4 202	151	1 867	596	1 588	MN	3	2	-	1	-
1992 (Sept.)	4 994	150	1 908	628	2 308	MO	1	-	1	-	-
1993 (Sept.)	5 170	182	2 023	633	2 332	MT	2	-	-	1	1
1994 (Sept.)	5 459	199	2 197	651	2 412	NE	3	-	2	-	1
1994	5 459	199	2 197	651	2 412	NV	4	1	-	1	2
						NJ	37	2	17	1	17
AK	1	1	-	-	-	NM	716	50	410	105	151
AZ	341	11	144	50	136	NY	83	12	13	11	47
AR	2	1	-	-	1	OH	4	-	1	2	-
CA	796	16	349	50	381	OK	1	-	1	-	-
CO	201	9	140	10	42	OR	5	-	3	1	1
CT	26	12	9	-	5	PA	8	1	3	1	3
DE	1	-	1	-	-	RI	1	1	-	-	-
DC	1	-	-	1	-	TX	2 215	41	1 022	389	763
FL	64	16	33	12	3	UT	1	1	-	-	-
HI	2	2	-	-	-	WA	14	2	4	2	6
ID	2	1	1	-	-	WI	2	-	2	-	-
IL	881	7	26	3	[2] 845	WY	3	1	2	-	-

- Represents zero.

1. Includes U.S. Representatives.

2. Includes local school council members in the Chicago area.

SOURCE: National Association of Latino Elected and Appointed Officials, Washington, DC, National Roster of Hispanic Elected Officials, annual.

Series YY 6. Black Elected Officials, by Office, 1970 to 1996, and by State, 1997

(As of January 1997, no Black elected officials had been identified in Hawaii, Idaho, Montana, North Dakota, or Utah)

Year and State	Total	U.S. and state legislatures [1]	City and county offices [2]	Law enforcement [3]	Education [4]	State	Total	U.S. and state legislatures [1]	City and county offices [2]	Law enforcement [3]	Education [4]
1970 (Feb.)......	1 469	179	715	213	362	MD.............	195	38	115	32	10
1980 (July).......	4 890	326	2 832	526	1 206	MA.............	33	7	21	3	2
1985 (Jan.)	6 016	407	3 517	661	1 431	MI.............	333	19	134	51	129
1990 (Jan.)	7 335	436	4 485	769	1 645	MN.............	14	1	3	7	3
1995 (Jan.)	8 385	604	4 954	987	1 840	MS.............	803	46	519	98	140
1996 (Jan.)	8 545	606	5 023	994	1 922	MO.............	188	16	136	14	22
1997 (Jan.)	8 617	617	5 052	996	1 952	NE.............	4	1	2	-	1
						NV.............	16	5	5	4	2
AL	726	36	551	52	87	NH.............	2	2	-	-	-
AK................	1	-	1	-	-	NJ.............	222	14	124	-	84
AZ................	17	4	3	5	5	NM.............	5	2	-	2	1
AR................	484	13	262	60	149	NY.............	311	32	75	78	126
CA................	255	14	72	79	90	NC.............	506	27	354	29	96
CO	20	4	4	10	2	OH.............	231	20	129	30	52
CT................	63	14	38	4	7	OK.............	102	6	76	1	19
DE................	25	4	16	2	3	OR.............	7	4	1	2	-
DC................	147	3	139	-	5	PA.............	162	19	55	58	30
FL................	216	23	146	32	15	RI.............	10	9	1	-	-
GA................	579	48	389	37	105	SC.............	542	35	323	12	172
ID	1	-	-	1	-	TN.............	174	17	108	26	23
IL................	545	26	310	55	154	TX.............	448	18	293	45	92
IN	80	13	51	10	6	UT.............	1	-	-	1	-
IA	11	1	7	1	2	VT.............	1	1	-	-	-
KS	21	7	6	4	4	VA.............	333	15	137	17	164
KY................	58	5	42	5	6	WA.............	23	2	9	10	2
LA	645	35	362	112	136	WV.............	19	2	14	3	-
ME	3	1	2	-	-	WI.............	35	8	17	4	6

- Represents zero.
1. Includes elected state administrators.
2. County commissioners and councilmen, mayors, vice mayors, aldermen, regional officials, and others.
3. Judges, magistrates, constables, marshals, sheriffs, justices of the peace, and others.
4. Members of state education agencies, college boards, school boards, and others.

SOURCE: Joint Center for Political and Economic Studies, Washington, DC, Black Elected Officials: A Statistical Summary, 1993-1997, annual (copyright).

Series YY 9. Members of Congress—Incumbents Reelected: 1964 to 1998

		Representatives							Senators				
			Incumbent candidates							Incumbent candidates			
				Reelected		Defeated in-				Reelected		Defeated in-	
Year	Retirements[1]	Total	Number	Percent of candidates	Primary	General election	Retirements[1]	Total	Number	Percent of candidates	Primary	General election
PRESIDENTIAL-YEAR ELECTIONS												
1964	33	397	344	86.6	8	45	2	33	28	84.8	1	4
1968	23	409	396	96.8	4	9	6	28	20	71.4	4	4
1972	40	390	365	93.6	12	13	6	27	20	74.1	2	5
1976	47	384	368	95.8	3	13	8	25	16	64.0	-	9
1980	34	398	361	90.7	6	31	5	29	16	55.2	4	9
1984	22	411	392	95.4	3	16	4	29	26	89.7	-	3
1988	23	409	402	98.3	1	6	6	27	23	85.2	-	4
1992	65	368	325	88.3	[2] 19	[3] 24	7	28	23	82.1	1	4
1996	50	384	361	94.0	2	21	13	21	19	90.5	1	1
MIDTERM ELECTIONS												
1966	22	411	362	88.1	8	41	3	32	28	87.5	3	1
1970	29	401	379	94.5	10	12	4	31	24	77.4	1	6
1974	43	391	343	87.7	8	40	7	27	23	85.2	2	2
1978	49	382	358	93.7	5	19	10	25	15	60.0	3	7
1982	40	393	354	90.1	[2] 10	29	3	30	28	93.3	-	2
1986	40	394	385	97.7	3	6	6	28	21	75.0	-	7
1990	27	406	390	96.1	1	15	3	32	31	96.9	-	1
1994	48	387	349	90.2	4	34	9	26	24	92.3	-	2
1998	23	404	395	97.8	1	6	5	29	26	89.7	-	3

- Represents zero.
1. Does not include persons who died or resigned before the election.
2. Number of incumbents defeated in primaries by other incumbents due to redistricting: six in 1982 and four in 1992.
3. Five incumbents defeated in general election by other incumbents due to redistricting.

SOURCE: Ornstein, Norman J., Thomas E. Mann, and Michael J. Malbin, Vital Statistics on Congress, 1993-1994, beginning 1995, Beginning 1995, Congressional Quarterly, Inc., Washington, DC, America Votes, biennial (copyright).

Series YY 10. Political Action Committees—Number, by Committee Type: 1980 to 1998
(As of December 31)

Committee type	1980	1985	1990	1993	1994	1995	1996	1997	1998
Total	2 551	3 992	4 172	4 210	3 954	4 016	4 079	3 844	3 798
Corporate	1 206	1 710	1 795	1 789	1 660	1 674	1 642	1 597	1 567
Labor	297	388	346	337	333	334	332	332	321
Trade/membership/health	576	695	774	761	792	815	838	825	821
Nonconnected	374	1 003	1 062	1 121	980	1 020	1 103	931	935
Cooperative	42	54	59	56	53	44	41	42	39
Corporation without stock	56	142	136	146	136	129	123	117	115

SOURCE: U.S. Federal Election Commission, press release of January 1999.

Series YY 11. Internal Revenue Gross Collections, by Source: 1980 to 1997
(For fiscal year ending in year shown)

Source of revenue	Collections (bil. dol.)					Percent of Total				
	1980	1990	1995	1996	1997	1980	1990	1995	1996	1997
All taxes	519	1 078	1 389	1 500	1 623	100.0	100.0	100.0	100.0	100.0
Individual income taxes	288	540	676	745	825	54.9	50.1	48.7	50.1	50.7
Withheld by employers	224	388	534	533	580	43.1	36.0	38.4	35.9	35.7
Employment taxes [1]	128	367	465	492	529	24.7	34.0	33.5	33.1	32.6
Old-age and disability insurance	123	358	455	482	518	23.6	33.2	32.8	32.4	31.9
Unemployment insurance	3	6	6	6	6	0.6	0.6	0.4	0.4	0.4
Corporation income taxes	72	110	174	189	204	13.9	10.2	12.5	12.6	12.6
Estate and gift taxes	7	12	15	18	20	1.3	1.1	1.1	1.2	1.2
Excise taxes	25	49	59	56	59	4.7	4.5	4.2	3.7	3.6

1. Includes railroad retirement, not shown separately.

SOURCE: U.S. Internal Revenue Service, Annual Report, and Bureau of Alcohol, Tobacco, and Firearms, Alcohol and Tobacco Tax Collections.

Series YY 12. Federal Civilian Employment and Annual Payroll, by Branch: 1970 to 1998

(Employment in thousands [2 997 represents 2 997 000]; payroll in millions of dollars [$27 322 represents $27 322 000 000]. Average annual employment. For fiscal year ending in year shown. Includes employees in U.S. territories and foreign countries. Data represent employees in active-duty status, including intermittent employees. Annual employment figures are averages of monthly figures. Excludes Central Intelligence Agency, National Security Agency, and, as of November 1984, the Defense Intelligence Agency, and as of October 1996, the National Imagery and Mapping Agency)

Year	Employment						Payroll				
	Total	Percent of U.S. employed [1]	Executive		Legislative	Judicial	Total	Executive		Legislative	Judicial
			Total	Defense				Total	Defense		
1970	[2] 2 997	3.8	2 961	1 263	29	7	27 322	26 894	11 264	338	89
1971	2 899	3.7	2 861	1 162	31	7	29 475	29 007	11 579	369	98
1972	2 882	3.5	2 842	1 128	32	8	31 626	31 102	12 181	411	112
1973	2 822	3.3	2 780	1 076	33	9	33 240	32 671	12 414	447	121
1974	2 825	3.3	2 781	1 041	35	9	35 661	35 035	12 789	494	132
1975	2 877	3.4	2 830	1 044	37	10	39 126	38 423	13 418	549	154
1976	2 879	3.2	2 831	1 025	38	11	42 259	41 450	14 699	631	179
1977	2 855	3.1	2 803	997	39	12	45 895	44 975	15 696	700	219
1978	2 875	3.0	2 822	987	40	13	49 921	48 899	16 995	771	251
1979	2 897	2.9	2 844	974	40	13	53 590	52 513	18 065	817	260
1980	[3] 2 987	3.0	2 933	971	40	14	58 012	56 841	18 795	883	288
1981	2 909	2.9	2 855	986	40	15	63 793	62 510	21 227	922	360
1982	2 871	2.9	2 816	1 019	39	16	65 503	64 125	22 226	980	398
1983	2 878	2.9	2 823	1 033	39	16	69 878	68 420	23 406	1 013	445
1984	2 935	2.8	2 879	1 052	40	17	74 616	73 084	25 253	1 081	451
1985	3 001	2.8	2 944	1 080	39	18	80 599	78 992	28 330	1 098	509
1986	3 047	2.8	2 991	1 089	38	19	82 598	80 941	29 272	1 112	545
1987	3 075	2.7	3 018	1 084	38	19	85 543	83 797	29 786	1 153	593
1988	3 113	2.7	3 054	1 073	38	21	88 841	86 960	29 609	1 226	656
1989	3 133	2.7	3 074	1 067	38	22	92 847	90 870	30 301	1 266	711
1990	[4] 3 233	2.7	3 173	1 060	38	23	99 138	97 022	31 990	1 329	787
1991	3 101	2.7	3 038	1 015	38	25	104 273	101 965	32 956	1 434	874
1992	3 106	2.6	3 040	1 004	39	27	108 054	105 402	31 486	1 569	1 083
1993	3 043	2.5	2 976	952	39	28	114 323	111 523	32 755	1 609	1 191
1994	2 993	2.4	2 928	900	37	28	116 138	113 264	32 144	1 613	1 260
1995	2 943	2.4	2 880	852	34	28	118 304	115 328	31 753	1 598	1 379
1996	2 881	2.3	2 819	811	32	29	119 321	116 385	31 569	1 519	1 417
1997	2 816	2.2	2 755	768	31	30	119 603	116 693	31 431	1 515	1 396
1998	2 783	2.1	2 721	730	31	31	121 964	118 800	30 315	1 517	1 647

1. Civilian only.
2. Includes 33 000 temporary census workers.
3. Includes 81 116 temporary census workers.
4. Includes 111 020 temporary census workers.

SOURCE: U.S. Office of Personnel Management, Federal Civilian Workforce Statistics-Employment and Trends, bimonthly; and unpublished data.

Series YY 13.　Number of Governmental Units, by Type: 1942 to 1997

Type of government	1942	1952 [1]	1962	1967	1972	1977	1982	1987	1992	1997
Total	155 116	116 807	91 237	81 299	78 269	79 913	81 831	83 237	85 006	87 504
U.S. Government............	1	1	1	1	1	1	1	1	1	1
State government	48	50	50	50	50	50	50	50	50	50
Local governments	155 067	116 756	91 186	81 248	78 218	79 862	81 780	83 186	84 955	87 453
County......................	3 050	3 052	3 043	3 049	3 044	3 042	3 041	3 042	3 043	3 043
Municipal....................	16 220	16 807	18 000	18 048	18 517	18 862	19 076	19 200	19 279	19 372
Township and town......	18 919	17 202	17 142	17 105	16 991	16 822	16 734	16 691	16 656	16 629
School district	108 579	67 355	34 678	21 782	15 781	15 174	14 851	14 721	14 422	13 726
Special district.............	8 299	12 340	18 323	21 264	23 885	25 962	28 078	29 532	31 555	34 683

1. Adjusted to include units in Alaska and Hawaii which adopted statehood in 1959.

Series YY 14.　Governmental Employment and Payrolls: 1980 to 1997

(Employees in thousands [16 213 represents 16 213 000], payroll in millions of dollars [19 935 represents $19 935 000 000]. For 1980 to 1995 as of October; 1997 as of March, 1996 data are not available. Covers full-time and part-time employees. Local government data are estimates subject to sampling variation)

Type of government	1980	1985	1989	1990	1991	1992	1993	1994	1995	1997
EMPLOYEES (1 000)										
Total........................	16 213	16 690	17 879	18 369	18 554	18 745	18 823	19 420	19 521	19 540
Federal (civilian) [1]	2 898	3 021	3 114	3 105	3 103	3 047	2 999	2 952	2 895	2 807
State and local................................	13 315	13 669	14 765	15 263	15 452	15 698	15 824	16 468	16 626	16 733
Percent of total	82	82	83	83	83	84	84	85	85	86
State........................	3 753	3 984	4 365	4 503	4 521	4 595	4 673	4 694	4 719	4 733
Local........................	9 562	9 685	10 400	10 760	10 930	11 103	11 151	11 775	11 906	12 000
Counties........................	1 853	1 891	2 085	2 167	2 196	2 253	2 270	. . .	. . .	. . .
Municipalities	2 561	2 467	2 569	2 642	2 662	2 665	2 644	. . .	. . .	. . .
School districts	4 270	4 416	4 774	4 950	5 045	5 134	. . .	. . .	. . .	. . .
Townships........................	394	392	405	418	415	424	. . .	. . .	. . .	. . .
Special districts........................	484	519	568	585	612	627	. . .	. . .	. . .	. . .
OCTOBER PAYROLLS (mil. dol.)										
Total........................	19 935	28 945	36 763	39 228	41 237	43 120	. . .	. . .	. . .	49 156
Federal (civilian) [1]	5 205	7 580	8 636	8 999	9 687	9 937	. . .	. . .	. . .	9 744
State and local................................	14 730	21 365	28 127	30 229	31 551	33 183	34 540	36 545	37 714	39 412
Percent of total	74	74	77	77	77	77	. . .	. . .	. . .	80
State........................	4 285	6 329	8 443	9 083	9 437	9 828	10 288	10 666	10 927	11 413
Local........................	10 445	15 036	19 684	21 146	22 113	23 355	24 252	25 878	26 787	27 999
Counties........................	1 936	2 819	3 855	4 192	4 404	4 698	4 839	. . .	. . .	. . .
Municipalities	2 951	4 191	5 274	5 564	5 784	6 207	6 328	. . .	. . .	. . .
School districts	4 683	6 746	8 852	9 551	9 975	10 394	. . .	. . .	. . .	. . .
Townships........................	330	446	599	642	664	685	. . .	. . .	. . .	. . .
Special districts........................	546	834	1 104	1 197	1 287	1 370	. . .	. . .	. . .	. . .

1. Includes employees outside the United States.

SOURCE: U.S. Census Bureau, Historical Statistics on Governmental Finances and Employment, and Public Employment, series GE, No. 1, annual; <http://www.census.gov/govs/www/apes.html> (accessed 12 July 1999).

Series YY 15. State and Local Governments—Indebtedness: 1980 to 1996

(In billions of dollars [335.6 represents $335,600,000,000], except per capita. For fiscal year ending in year shown. Local government amounts are estimates subject to sampling variation)

Item	Debt outstanding						Long-term debt		
	Total	Per capita [1] (dol.)	Long-term			Short-term	Net long term	Deb issued	Deb retired
			Local schools [2]	Utilities	All other				
1980: Total	335.6	1 481	32.3	55.2	235.0	13.1	262.9	42.4	17.4
State	122.0	540	3.8	4.6	111.5	2.1	79.8	16.4	5.7
Local	213.6	943	28.5	50.6	123.5	11.0	183.1	25.9	11.7
1985: Total	568.6	2 390	43.8	90.8	414.5	19.6	430.5	101.2	43.5
State	211.9	893	6.7	8.6	193.8	2.8	110.4	41.7	16.4
Local	356.7	1 499	37.1	82.2	220.6	16.8	320.1	59.5	27.2
1990: Total	860.6	3 459	60.4	134.8	646.1	19.3	477.0	108.5	64.8
State	318.3	1 282	4.4	12.3	298.8	2.8	125.5	43.5	22.9
Local	542.3	2 180	56.0	122.4	347.4	16.5	351.5	65.0	42.0
1993: Total	1 016.2	3 943	89.2	157.6	746.8	22.6	617.1	195.0	146.3
State	389.7	1 515	9.4	14.8	361.7	3.9	176.9	77.1	60.7
Local	628.0	2 437	79.8	142.7	385.2	18.9	440.2	118.4	86.3
1994: Total	1 074.7	4 129	143.5	164.9	438.0	26.7	672.8	207.8	166.6
State	411.0	1 582	10.4	16.7	162.0	4.9	200.8	78.5	61.3
Local	663.7	2 550	86.2	148.2	276.0	21.8	472.0	129.3	105.3
1995: Total	1 115.3	4 244	118.2	163.9	756.0	27.0	835.3	129.3	95.1
State	427.2	1 629	11.3	17.0	345.0	6.1	205.3	52.6	37.5
Local	688.1	2 619	107.0	146.9	411.0	20.9	629.9	76.8	57.6
1996: Total	1 169.7	4 411	130.7	170.3	868.8	24.0	890.2	141.1	106.5
State	452.4	1 709	11.2	16.3	424.9	5.8	224.4	60.2	42.4
Local	717.3	2 705	119.5	154.0	443.8	18.2	665.7	80.9	64.1

1. 1980 and 1990 based on enumerated resident population as of April 1; other years based on estimated resident population as of July 1; see Table 2.
2. Includes debt for education activities other than higher education.

SOURCE: U.S. Census Bureau, 1980-90, State and Local Government Finance Estimates, annual; thereafter, <http://www.census.gov/govs/www/estimate.html> (accessed 21 May 1999).

Series YY 16. Federal Grants-in-Aid Summary: 1970 to 1999

([24 065 represents $24 065 000 000], except as indicated. For fiscal year ending in year shown; see text, this section. Minus sign (-) indicates decrease)

| | Current dollars | | | | | | | Constant (1992) dollars | |
| | Total grants (mil. dol.) | Annual percent change [1] | Grants to individuals | | Grants as percent of- | | | Total grants (bil. dol.) | Annual percent change [1] |
Year			Total (mil. dol.)	Percent of total grants	State/local govt. expenditures from own sources [2]	Federal outlays	Gross domestic product		
1970	24 065	19.3	8 717	36.3	30.9	12.3	2.4	86.9	11.8
1975	49 791	14.8	16 752	33.7	36.6	15.0	3.2	126.6	3.3
1980	91 385	9.6	32 619	35.7	42.9	15.5	3.4	155.7	-1.1
1985	105 852	8.5	49 321	46.6	32.0	11.2	2.6	135.6	4.7
1990	135 325	11.0	75 685	57.0	26.9	10.8	2.4	144.7	6.2
1991	154 519	14.2	90 744	59.9	28.3	11.7	2.6	158.6	9.6
1992	178 065	15.2	110 016	63.0	30.7	12.9	2.9	178.1	12.3
1993	193 612	8.7	121 519	64.2	31.5	13.7	3.0	188.6	6.0
1994	210 596	8.8	131 123	64.2	32.7	14.4	3.1	200.5	6.3
1995	224 991	6.8	141 183	64.8	33.5	14.8	3.1	208.5	3.8
1996	227 811	1.3	142 802	64.8	32.8	14.6	3.0	206.7	-1.3
1997	234 160	2.8	144 189	63.6	32.2	14.6	2.9	208.1	0.1
1998	246 093	7.2	155 852	64.2	32.4	14.9	2.9	215.2	4.9
1999, est	262 164	8.1	164 194	62.7	. . .	15.2	3.0	225.2	5.7

1. Average annual percent change from prior year shown. For explanation, see Guide to Tabular Presentation. 1970, change from 1969.
2. Outlays as defined in the national income and product accounts.

SOURCE: U.S. Office of Management and Budget, based on Historical Tables and Analytical Prospectives, Budget of the United States Government, annual.

Series YY 17. Military Personnel on Active Duty, by Location: 1980 to 1997

(In thousands [2 051 represents 2 051 000]. As of end of fiscal year; see text, Section 9, State and Local Government)

Item	1980	1985	1989	1990	1991	1992	1993	1994	1995	1996	1997
Total...................................	2 051	2 151	2 130	2 044	1 986	1 807	1 705	1 611	1 518	1 472	1 439
Shore-based [1]...............................	1 840	1 920	1 884	1 794	1 743	1 589	1 505	1 431	1 351	1 317	1 294
Afloat [2]	211	231	246	252	243	218	200	180	167	155	145
United States [3]...............................	1 562	1 636	1 620	1 437	1 539	1 463	1 397	1 324	1 280	1 231	1 211
Foreign countries............................	488	516	510	609	448	344	308	287	238	240	227

1. Includes Navy personnel temporarily on shore.
2. Includes Marine Corps.
3. Includes outlying areas.

SOURCE: U.S. Dept. of Defense, Selected Manpower Statistics, annual.

Series YY 18. Department of Defense Manpower: 1950 to 1997

(In thousands [1 459 represents 1 459 000]. As of end of fiscal year. Includes National Guard, Reserve, and retired regular personnel on extended or continuous active duty. Excludes Coast Guard. Other officer candidates are included under enlisted personnel)

Year	Total¹,²	Army Total²	Army White	Army Black	Army Officers	Army Enlisted	Navy³ Total²	Navy White	Navy Black	Navy Officers	Navy Enlisted	Marine corps Total²	Marine White	Marine Black	Marine Officers	Marine Enlisted	Air Force Total²	Air Force White	Air Force Black	Air Force Officers	Air Force Enlisted
1950	1 459	593	...	...	73	519	381	...	...	45	333	74	...	...	7	67	411	...	...	57	354
1955	2 935	1 109	...	...	122	986	661	...	...	75	583	205	...	...	18	187	960	...	...	137	823
1960	2 475	873	...	...	101	770	617	...	...	70	545	171	...	...	16	154	815	...	...	130	683
1965	2 654	969	...	...	112	855	670	...	...	78	588	190	...	...	17	173	825	...	...	132	690
1966	3 092	1 200	...	...	118	1 080	743	...	...	80	659	262	...	...	21	241	887	...	...	131	753
1967	3 375	1 442	...	...	144	1 297	750	...	...	82	664	285	...	...	24	262	897	...	...	135	759
1968	3 546	1 570	...	...	166	1 402	764	...	...	85	674	307	...	...	25	283	905	...	...	140	762
1969	3 458	1 512	...	...	173	1 337	774	...	...	85	684	310	...	...	26	284	862	...	...	135	723
1970	3 065	1 323	...	...	167	1 153	691	...	...	81	606	260	...	...	25	235	791	...	...	130	657
1971	2 713	1 124	...	...	149	972	622	...	...	75	542	212	...	...	22	191	755	...	...	126	625
1972	2 322	811	...	...	121	687	587	...	...	73	511	198	...	...	20	178	726	...	...	122	600
1973	2 252	801	...	...	116	682	564	...	...	71	490	196	...	...	19	177	691	...	...	115	572
1974	2 162	783	...	...	106	674	546	...	...	67	475	189	...	...	19	170	644	...	...	110	529
1975	2 128	784	...	...	103	678	535	...	...	66	466	196	...	...	19	177	613	...	...	105	503
1976	2 082	779	...	...	99	678	525	...	...	64	458	192	...	...	19	174	585	...	...	100	481
1977	2 075	782	...	...	98	680	530	...	...	63	462	192	...	...	19	173	571	...	...	96	470
1978	2 062	772	...	...	98	670	530	...	...	63	463	191	...	...	18	172	570	...	...	95	470
1979	2 027	759	...	...	97	657	523	...	...	62	457	185	...	...	18	167	559	...	...	96	459
1980	2 051	777	503	229	99	674	527	436	55	63	460	188	142	39	18	170	558	460	80	98	456
1981	2 083	781	502	232	102	675	540	443	58	65	470	191	145	39	18	172	570	468	83	99	467
1982	2 109	780	504	230	103	673	553	450	62	67	481	192	149	38	19	173	583	476	87	102	476
1983	2 123	780	512	220	106	669	558	462	66	68	485	194	152	37	20	174	592	483	88	105	483
1984	2 138	780	520	215	108	668	565	455	67	69	491	196	153	36	20	176	597	486	89	106	486
1985	2 151	781	523	211	110	667	571	459	70	71	495	198	152	37	20	178	602	488	90	108	489
1986	2 169	781	524	210	110	667	581	464	75	72	504	199	151	38	20	179	608	491	92	109	495
1987	2 174	781	519	212	108	668	587	467	81	72	510	200	150	38	20	179	607	489	92	107	495
1988	2 138	772	507	213	107	660	593	466	85	72	516	197	147	38	20	177	576	462	88	105	467
1989	2 130	770	497	218	107	658	593	461	91	72	516	197	146	38	20	177	571	458	87	104	463
1990	2 044	732	466	213	104	624	579	446	93	72	503	197	145	38	20	177	535	428	82	100	431
1991	1 986	711	452	204	104	603	570	439	92	71	495	194	144	36	20	174	510	409	77	97	409
1992	1 807	610	388	173	95	511	542	415	88	69	468	185	138	32	19	165	470	377	70	90	376
1993	1 705	572	365	158	88	480	510	390	84	66	439	178	134	30	18	160	444	357	65	84	356
1994	1 610	541	344	147	85	452	469	355	78	62	403	174	131	28	18	156	426	341	62	81	341
1995	1 518	509	322	137	83	422	435	326	75	59	372	175	130	28	18	157	400	318	58	78	318
1996	1 472	491	...	...	81	407	417	...	...	57	355	175	...	...	18	157	389	...	...	76	309
1997	1 439	492	...	...	79	408	396	...	...	56	335	174	...	...	18	156	377	...	...	74	299

1. Beginning 1980, excludes Navy Reserve personnel on active duty for Training and Administration of Reserves (TARS). From 1969, the full-time Guard and Reserve.
2. Includes Cadets and other not shown separately.
3. Prior to 1980, includes Navy Reserve personnel on active duty for Training and Administration of Reserves (TARS).

SOURCE: U.S. Dept. of Defense, Selected Manpower Statistics, annual.

Series YY 19. Defense-Related Employment and Spending: 1977 to 1996, and Projections to 2006

(Dollar amounts in billions of chain-weighted 1992 dollars [$4 279.3 represents $4 279 300 000 000)

Item	1977	1987	1996	2002	2006	Change				
						1977-87	1987-96	1996-2002	1996-2006	1987-2006
Spending (bil. dol.):										
Gross domestic product (GDP)	4 279.3	5 648.4	6 911.0	7 739.9	8 539.1	1 369.1	1 262.6	828.9	1 628.1	2 890.7
Defense purchases	266.4	409.2	314.9	265.4	257.3	142.8	-94.3	-49.5	-57.6	-151.9
As percent of GDP:										
Defense purchases	6.2	7.2	4.6	3.4	3.0	1.0	-2.7	-1.1	-1.5	-4.2
Employment, total [1] (1 000)	95 588	116 523	133 884	144 646	152 370	20 935	17 361	10 762	18 485	35 847
Defense-related	4 767	6 942	4 492	3 744	3 595	2 175	-2 450	-748	-897	-3 347
As percent of total employment:										
Defense related	4.99	5.96	3.36	2.59	2.36	0.97	-2.60	-0.77	-1.00	-3.60
Civilian, Defense Dept	1.07	0.96	0.61	0.51	0.49	-0.10	-0.36	-0.10	-0.12	-0.48
Civilian, other gov't	0.02	0.04	0.02	0.01	0.01	0.01	-0.02	-0.01	-0.01	-0.03
Armed Forces	2.17	1.92	1.14	1.00	0.95	-0.25	-0.77	-0.15	-0.20	-0.97
Private	1.73	3.04	1.59	1.07	0.92	1.31	-1.46	-0.52	-0.67	-2.13

1. Total employed, including resident Armed Forces, plus Department of Defense estimates of Armed Forces abroad.

SOURCE: U.S. Bureau of Labor Statistics, Monthly Labor Review, July 1998.

Series YY 20. National Defense Outlays and Veterans Benefits: 1960 to 1999

(For fiscal year ending in year shown. Includes outlays of Department of Defense, Department of Veterans Affairs, and other agencies for activities primarily related to national defense and veterans programs. Minus sign (-) indicates decline)

| Year | National defense and veterans outlays | | | | Average annual percent change [1] | | | Defense outlays, percent of- | |
| | Total outlays (bil. dol.) | Defense outlays | | Veterans outlays (bil. dol.) | Total outlays | Defense outlays | Veterans outlays | Federal outlays | Gross domestic product [2] |
		Current dollars (bil. dol.)	Constant (1992) dollars (bil. dol.)						
1960	53.5	48.1	260.3	5.4	2.5	2.4	3.1	52.2	9.3
1965	56.3	50.6	248.9	5.7	-6.8	-7.6	0.7	42.8	7.4
1966	64.1	58.1	274.0	6.0	13.7	14.8	3.5	43.2	7.7
1967	78.1	71.4	323.4	6.7	22.1	22.9	13.8	45.4	8.8
1968	88.9	81.9	352.2	7.0	13.8	14.7	4.4	46.0	9.4
1969	90.2	82.5	337.4	7.7	1.3	0.7	8.5	44.9	8.7
1970	90.4	81.7	315.4	8.7	0.3	-1.0	13.6	41.8	8.1
1971	88.7	78.9	287.1	9.8	-1.9	-3.5	12.7	37.5	7.3
1972	89.9	79.2	263.7	10.7	1.4	0.4	9.8	34.3	6.7
1973	88.7	76.7	239.6	12.0	1.3	-3.1	12.0	31.2	5.9
1974	92.6	79.3	228.3	13.3	4.6	3.5	11.4	29.5	5.5
1975	103.1	86.5	224.1	16.6	11.2	9.0	24.0	26.0	5.6
1976	108.0	89.6	216.8	18.4	4.8	3.6	11.0	24.1	5.2
1976, TQ [3]	26.3	22.3	52.1	4.0	. . .	. . .	. . .	23.2	4.9
1977	115.2	97.2	216.4	18.0	6.7	8.5	-2.1	23.8	4.9
1978	123.5	104.5	217.4	19.0	7.1	7.5	5.2	22.8	4.7
1979	136.2	116.3	221.9	19.9	10.4	11.3	5.0	23.1	4.7
1980	155.1	134.0	229.4	21.1	13.9	15.2	6.3	22.7	4.9
1981	180.4	157.5	241.8	22.9	16.3	17.6	8.5	23.2	5.2
1982	209.2	185.3	263.6	23.9	15.9	17.6	4.2	24.8	5.8
1983	234.7	209.9	284.0	24.8	12.1	13.3	3.3	26.0	6.1
1984	253.0	227.4	287.4	25.6	7.8	8.3	3.2	26.7	6.0
1985	279.0	252.7	306.1	26.3	10.3	11.1	2.7	26.7	6.2
1986	299.9	273.4	324.7	26.5	7.4	8.2	0.4	27.6	6.2
1987	309.0	282.0	330.0	27.0	3.0	3.1	1.5	28.1	6.1
1988	319.7	290.4	333.9	29.3	3.6	3.0	9.7	27.3	5.9
1989	333.6	303.6	338.3	30.0	4.3	4.5	2.4	26.5	5.7
1990	328.3	299.3	324.6	29.0	-1.6	-1.4	-3.3	23.9	5.3
1991	304.5	273.3	283.3	31.2	-7.2	-8.7	7.6	20.6	4.7
1992	332.3	298.4	298.4	33.9	12.0	12.4	8.0	21.6	4.9
1993	326.6	291.1	286.6	35.5	-1.9	-2.4	4.6	20.7	4.5
1994	319.0	281.6	271.9	37.4	-2.3	-3.3	5.4	19.3	4.1
1995	309.9	272.1	256.8	37.8	-2.9	-3.4	1.1	17.9	3.8
1996	302.7	265.8	242.3	36.9	-2.3	-2.3	-2.4	17.0	3.5
1997	309.8	270.5	241.1	39.3	2.3	1.8	6.5	16.9	3.4
1998	310.3	268.5	236.6	41.8	0.2	-0.7	6.3	16.2	3.2
1999, est	320.2	276.7	240.6	43.5	3.2	3.1	4.1	16.0	3.2

1. Change from prior year shown; for 1960, change from 1955.
2. Represents fiscal year GDP.
3. Transition quarter, July-Sept.

SOURCE: U.S. Office of Management and Budget, Historical Tables, annual.

542

Series YY 22.   Vote Cast for President, by Major Political Party: 1936 to 1996

(Prior to 1960, excludes Alaska and Hawaii; prior to 1964, excludes DC. Vote cast for major party candidates include the votes of minor parties cast for those candidates)

	Candidates for President		Vote cast for President						
				Democratic			Republican		
			Total popular vote [1] (1 000)	Popular vote		Electoral vote	Popular vote		Electoral vote
Year	Democratic	Republican		Number (1 000)	Percent		Number (1 000)	Percent	
1936	F. D. Roosevelt	Landon	45,655	27,757	60.8	523	16,684	36.5	8
1940	F. D. Roosevelt	Willkie	49 900	27 313	54.7	449	22 348	44.8	82
1944	F. D. Roosevelt	Dewey	47 977	25 613	53.4	432	22 018	45.9	99
1948	Truman	Dewey	48 794	24 179	49.6	303	21 991	45.1	189
1952	Stevenson	Eisenhower	61 551	27 315	44.4	89	33 936	55.1	442
1956	Stevenson	Eisenhower	62 027	26 023	42.0	73	35 590	57.4	457
1960	Kennedy	Nixon	68 838	34 227	49.7	303	34 108	49.5	219
1964	Johnson	Goldwater	70 645	43 130	61.1	486	27 178	38.5	52
1968	Humphrey	Nixon	73 212	31 275	42.7	191	31 785	43.4	301
1972	McGovern	Nixon	77 719	29 170	37.5	17	47 170	60.7	520
1976	Carter	Ford	81 556	40 831	50.1	297	39 148	48.0	240
1980	Carter	Reagan	86 515	35 484	41.0	49	43 904	50.7	489
1984	Mondale	Reagan	92 653	37 577	40.6	13	54 455	58.8	525
1988	Dukakis	Bush	91 595	41 809	45.6	111	48 886	53.4	426
1992	Clinton	Bush	104 425	44 909	43.0	370	39 104	37.4	168
1996	Clinton	Dole	96 278	47 402	49.2	379	39 199	40.7	159

1. Include votes for minor party candidates, independents, unpledged electors, and scattered write-in votes.

SOURCE: Congressional Quarterly, Inc., Washington, DC, America at the Polls 2, 1965, and America Votes, biennial (copyright).

Series YY 23.   Vote Cast for Leading Minority Party Candidates for President: 1936 to 1996

(Prior to 1960, excludes Alaska and Hawaii; prior to 1964, excludes D.C.)

Year	Candidate	Party	Popular vote (1 000)	Candidate	Party	Popular vote (1 000)
1936	William Lemke	Union	892	Norman Thomas	Socialist	188
1940	Norman Thomas	Socialist	116	Roger Babson	Prohibition	59
1944	Norman Thomas	Socialist	79	Claude Watson	Prohibition	75
1948	Strom Thurmond	States' Rights	1 176	Henry Wallace	Progressive	1 157
1952	Vincent Hallinan	Progressive	140	Stuart Hamblen	Prohibition	73
1956	T. Coleman Andrews	States' Rights	111	Eric Hass	Socialist Labor	44
1960	Eric Hass	Socialist Labor	48	Rutherford Decker	Prohibition	46
1964	Eric Hass	Socialist Labor	45	Clifton DeBerry	Socialist Workers	33
1968	George Wallace	American Independent	9 906	Henning Blomen	Socialist Labor	53
1972	John Schmitz	American	1 099	Benjamin Spock	People's	79
1976	Eugene McCarthy	Independent	757	Roger McBride	Libertarian	173
1980	John Anderson	Independent	5 720	Ed Clark	Libertarian	921
1984	David Bergland	Libertarian	228	Lyndon H. LaRouche	Independent	79
1988	Ron Paul	Libertarian	432	Lenora B. Fulani	New Alliance	217
1992	H. Ross Perot	Independent	19 742	Andre Marrou	Libertarian	292
1996	H. Ross Perot	Reform Party	8 085	Ralph Nader	Green	685

SOURCE: Congressional Quarterly, Inc. Washington, DC, America at the Polls 1920-1996, 1997; and America Votes, biennial (copyright).

Series YY 24.   Democratic and Republican Percentages of Two-Party Presidential Vote, by Selected Characteristics of Voters: 1992 and 1996

(In percent. Covers citizens of voting age living in private housing units in the contiguous United States. Percentages for Democratic Presidential vote are computed by subtracting the percentage Republican vote from 100 percent; third-party or independent votes are not included as valid data. Data are from the National Election Studies and are based on a sample and subject to sampling variability; for details, see source)

Characteristic	1992		1996		Characteristic	1992		1996	
	Democratic	Republican	Democratic	Republican		Democratic	Republican	Democratic	Republican
Year of birth:					Race:				
1959 or later	58	42	58	42	White	53	47	54	46
1943 to 1958	58	42	58	42	Black	94	6	99	1
1927 to 1942	56	44	56	44					
1911 to 1926	62	38	64	36	Education:				
1895 to 1910	58	42	57	43	Grade school	68	32	82	18
					High school	62	38	60	40
Sex:					College	52	48	49	51
Male	55	45	51	50	Union household	68	32	75	25
Female	61	39	65	35	Non-union household	57	43	54	46

SOURCE: Center for Political Studies, University of Michigan, Ann Arbor, MI, unpublished data (copyright).

Series YY 25. Electoral Vote Cast for President, by Major Political Party—States: 1956 to 1996

(D = Democratic, R = Republican. Composition of Regions: Northeast—ME, VT, NH, MA, CT, RI, NY, PA, Midwest—OH, MI, WI, IL, ND, SD, MN, IA, NE, KS, MO, South—MD, DE, VA, DC, WV, NC, SC, GA, FL, KY, TN, MS, AL, AR, OK, LA, TX, West—AK, HI, CA, OR, WA, NV, ID, MT, WY, CO, NM, AZ, UT)

State	1956[1]	1960[2]	1964	1968[3]	1972[4]	1976[5]	1980	1984	1988[6]	1992	1996
Democratic	73	303	486	191	17	297	49	13	111	370	379
Republican	457	219	52	301	520	240	489	525	426	168	159
Northeast: Democratic	-	121	126	102	14	86	4	-	53	106	106
Republican	133	12	-	24	108	36	118	113	60	-	-
Midwest: Democratic	13	71	149	31	-	58	10	10	29	100	100
Republican	140	82	-	118	145	87	135	127	108	29	29
South: Democratic	60	101	121	45	3	149	31	3	8	68	80
Republican	105	50	47	77	165	20	138	174	168	116	104
West: Democratic	-	10	90	13	-	4	4	-	21	96	93
Republican	79	75	5	82	102	97	98	111	90	23	26
AL	[1] D-10	[2] D-5	R-10	([3])	R-9	D-9	R-9	R-9	R-9	R-9	R-9
AK	. . .	R-3	D-3	R-3	R-3	R-3	R-3	R-3	R-3	R-3	R-3
AZ	R-4	R-4	R-5	R-5	R-6	R-6	R-6	R-7	R-7	R-8	R-8
AR	D-8	D-8	D-6	([3])	R-6	D-6	R-6	R-6	R-6	D-6	D-6
CA	R-32	R-32	D-40	R-40	R-45	R-45	R-45	R-47	R-47	D-54	D-54
CO	R-6	R-6	D-6	R-6	R-7	R-7	R-7	R-8	R-8	D-8	R-8
CT	R-8	D-8	D-8	D-8	R-8	R-8	R-8	R-8	R-8	D-8	D-8
DE	R-3	D-3	D-3	R-3	R-3	D-3	R-3	R-3	R-3	D-3	D-3
DC	. . .	. . .	D-3	D-3	D-3	D-3	D-3	D-3	D-3	D-3	D-3
FL	R-10	R-10	D-14	R-14	R-17	D-17	R-17	R-21	R-21	R-25	D-25
GA	D-12	D-12	R-12	([3])	R-12	D-12	D-12	R-12	R-12	D-13	R-13
HI	. . .	D-3	D-4	D-4	R-4	D-4	D-4	D-4	D-4	D-4	D-4
ID	R-4	R-4	D-4	R-4	R-4	R-4	R-4	R-4	R-4	R-4	R-4
IL	R-27	D-27	D-26	R-26	R-26	R-26	R-26	R-24	R-24	D-22	D-22
IN	R-13	R-13	D-13	R-13	R-13	R-13	R-13	R-12	R-12	R-12	R-12
IA	R-10	R-10	D-9	R-9	R-8	R-8	R-8	R-8	D-8	D-7	D-7
KS	R-8	R-8	D-7	R-7	R-7	R-7	R-7	R-7	R-7	R-6	R-6
KY	R-10	R-10	D-9	R-9	R-9	D-9	R-9	R-9	R-9	D-8	D-8
LA	R-10	D-10	R-10	([3])	R-10	D-10	R-10	R-10	R-10	D-9	D-9
ME	R-5	R-5	D-4	D-4	R-4	R-4	R-4	R-4	R-4	D-4	D-4
MD	R-9	D-9	D-10	D-10	R-10	D-10	D-10	R-10	D-10	D-10	D-10
MA	R-16	D-16	D-14	D-14	D-14	D-14	R-14	R-13	D-13	D-12	D-12
MI	R-20	D-20	D-21	D-21	R-21	R-21	R-21	R-20	R-20	D-18	D-18
MN	R-11	D-11	D-10	D-10	R-10	D-10	D-10	D-10	D-10	D-10	D-10
MS	D-8	([2])	R-7	([3])	R-7	D-7	R-7	R-7	R-7	R-7	R-7
MO	D-13	D-13	D-12	R-12	R-12	D-12	R-12	R-11	R-11	D-11	D-11
MT	R-4	R-4	D-4	R-4	R-4	R-4	R-4	R-4	R-4	D-3	R-3
NE	R-6	R-6	D-5	R-5	R-5	R-5	R-5	R-5	R-5	R-5	R-5
NV	R-3	D-3	D-3	R-3	R-3	R-3	R-3	R-4	R-4	D-4	D-4
NH	R-4	R-4	D-4	R-4	R-4	R-4	R-4	R-4	R-4	D-4	D-4
NJ	R-16	D-16	D-17	R-17	R-17	R-17	R-17	R-16	R-16	D-15	D-15
NM	R-4	D-4	D-4	R-4	R-4	R-4	R-4	R-5	R-5	D-5	D-5
NY	R-45	D-45	D-43	D-43	R-41	D-41	R-41	R-36	D-36	D-33	D-33
NC	D-14	D-14	D-13	[3]R-12	R-13	D-13	R-13	R-13	R-13	R-14	R-14
ND	R-4	R-4	D-4	R-4	R-3	R-3	R-3	R-3	R-3	R-3	R-3
OH	R-25	R-25	D-26	R-26	R-25	D-25	R-25	R-23	R-23	D-21	D-21
OK	R-8	[2] R-7	D-8	R-8	R-8	R-8	R-8	R-8	R-8	R-8	R-8
OR	R-6	R-6	D-6	R-6	R-6	R-6	R-6	R-7	D-7	D-7	D-7
PA	R-32	D-32	D-29	D-29	R-27	D-27	R-27	R-25	R-25	D-23	D-23
RI	R-4	D-4	D-4	D-4	R-4	D-4	D-4	R-4	D-4	D-4	D-4
SC	D-8	D-8	R-8	R-8	R-8	D-8	R-8	R-8	R-8	R-8	R-8
SD	R-4	R-4	D-4	R-4	R-4	R-4	R-4	R-3	R-3	R-3	R-3
TN	R-11	R-11	D-11	R-11	R-10	D-10	R-10	R-11	R-11	D-11	D-11
TX	R-24	D-24	D-25	D-25	R-26	D-26	R-26	R-29	R-29	R-32	R-32
UT	R-4	R-4	D-4	R-4	R-4	R-4	R-4	R-5	R-5	R-5	R-5
VT	R-3	R-3	D-3	R-3	R-3	R-3	R-3	R-3	R-3	D-3	D-3
VA	R-12	R-12	D-12	R-12	[4] R-11	R-12	R-12	R-12	R-12	R-13	R-13
WA	R-9	R-9	D-9	D-9	R-9	[5] R-8	R-9	R-10	D-10	D-11	D-11
WV	R-8	D-8	D-7	D-7	R-6	D-6	D-6	R-6	[6] D-5	D-5	D-5
WI	R-12	R-12	D-12	R-12	R-11	D-11	R-11	R-11	D-11	D-11	D-11
WY	R-3	R-3	D-3	R-3	R-3	R-3	R-3	R-3	R-3	R-3	R-3

- Represents zero.
1. Excludes one electoral vote cast for Walter B. Jones in Alabama.
2. Excludes 15 electoral votes cast for Harry F. Byrd as follows: AL 6, MS 8, and OK 1.
3. Excludes 46 electoral votes cast for American Independent George C. Wallace as follows: AL 10, AR 6, GA 12, LA 10, MS 7, and NC 1.
4. Excludes one electoral vote cast for Libertarian John Hospers in Virginia.
5. Excludes one electoral vote cast for Ronald Reagan in Washington.
6. Excludes one electoral vote cast for Lloyd Bentsen for President in West Virginia.

SOURCE: 1956-72, U.S. Congress, Clerk of the House, Statistics of the Presidential and Congressional Election, quadrennial; 1976-96, Congressional Quarterly, Inc., Washington DC, America Votes, biennial (copyright).

Series YY 26.   Vote Cast for United States Senators, 1996 and 1998, and Incumbent Senators, 1998—States

(D = Democrat; R = Republican)

State	1996 Total (1 000) [1]	1996 Percent for leading party	1998 Total (1 000) [1]	1998 Percent for leading party	Incumbent Senators and year term expires	
Alabama	1 499	R-52.5	1 293	R-63.2	Jeff Sessions (R) 2003	Richard C. Shelby (R) 2005
Alaska	232	R-76.7	222	R-74.5	Frank H. Murkowski (R) 2005	Ted Stevens (R) 2003
Arizona	. . .	. . .	1 013	R-68.7	John McCain (R) 2005	Jon Kyl (R) 2001
Arkansas	846	R-52.7	701	D-55.1	Blanche Lincoln (D) 2005	Tim Hutchinson (R) 2003
California	. . .	. . .	8 315	D-53.1	Barbara Boxer (D) 2005	Dianne Feinstein (D) 2001
Colorado	1 470	R-51.1	1 327	R-62.5	Ben N. Campbell (R) 2005	Wayne Allard (R) 2003
Connecticut	. . .	. . .	964	D-65.1	Christopher J. Dodd (D) 2005	Joseph I. Lieberman (D) 2001
Delaware	276	D-60.0	. . .	. . .	Joseph R. Biden Jr. (D) 2003	William V. Roth Jr. (R) 2001
Florida	. . .	. . .	3 900	D-62.5	Bob Graham (D) 2005	Connie Mack (R) 2001
Georgia	2 259	D-48.9	1 754	R-52.4	Paul Coverdell (R) 2005	Max Cleland (D) 2003
Hawaii	. . .	. . .	398	D-79.2	Daniel K. Akaka (D) 2001	Daniel K. Inouye (D) 2005
Idaho	497	R-57.0	378	R-69.5	Larry E. Craig (R) 2003	Michael D. Crapo (R) 2005
Illinois	4 251	D-56.1	3 395	R-50.3	Peter Fitzgerald (R) 2005	Richard J. Durbin (D) 2003
Indiana	. . .	. . .	1 589	D-63.7	Evan Bayh (D) 2005	Richard G. Lugar (R) 2001
Iowa	1 224	D-51.8	948	R-68.4	Tom Harkin (D) 2003	Charles E. Grassley (R) 2005
Kansas	[2]1 065	R-53.9	727	R-65.3	Sam Brownback (R) 2005	Pat Roberts (R) 2003
Kentucky	1 307	R-55.5	1 145	R-49.7	Jim Bunning (R) 2005	Mitch McConnell (R) 2003
Louisiana [3]	1 700	D-50.2	969	D-64.0	John B. Breaux (D) 2005	Mary Landrieu (D) 2003
Maine	607	R-49.2	. . .	. . .	Susan Collins (R) 2003	Olympia Snowe (R) 2001
Maryland	. . .	. . .	1 507	D-70.5	Barbara A. Mikulski (D) 2005	Paul S. Sarbanes (D) 2001
Massachusetts	2 556	D-52.2	. . .	. . .	Edward M. Kennedy (D) 2001	John F. Kerry (D) 2003
Michigan	3 763	D-58.4	. . .	. . .	Carl Levin (D) 2003	Spencer Abraham (R) 2001
Minnesota	2 183	D-50.3	. . .	. . .	Paul David Wellstone (D) 2003	Rod Grams (R) 2001
Mississippi	879	R-71.0	. . .	. . .	Thad Cochran (R) 2003	Trent Lott (R) 2001
Missouri	. . .	. . .	1 577	R-52.7	Christopher S. Bond (R) 2005	John Ashcroft (R) 2001
Montana	407	D-49.6	. . .	. . .	Max Baucus (D) 2003	Conrad Burns (R) 2001
Nebraska	677	R-56.1	. . .	. . .	Chuck Hagel (R) 2003	J. Robert Kerrey (D) 2001
Nevada	. . .	. . .	436	D-47.9	Harry Reid (D) 2005	Richard H. Bryan (D) 2001
New Hampshire	493	R-49.2	315	R-67.8	Judd Gregg (R) 2005	Robert C. Smith (R) 2003
New Jersey	2 884	D-52.7	. . .	. . .	Robert G. Torricelli (D) 2003	Frank R. Lautenberg (D) 2001
New Mexico	552	R-64.7	. . .	. . .	Jeff Bingaman (D) 2001	Pete V. Domenici (R) 2003
New York	. . .	. . .	4 671	D-54.6	Daniel P. Moynihan (D) 2001	Charles E. Schumer (D) 2005
North Carolina	2 556	R-52.6	2 012	D-51.2	John Edwards (D) 2005	Jesse Helms (R) 2003
North Dakota	. . .	. . .	213	D-63.2	Byron L. Dorgan (D) 2005	Kent Conrad (D) 2001
Ohio	. . .	. . .	3 404	R-56.5	George V. Voinovich (R) 2005	Mike DeWine (R) 2001
Oklahoma	1 183	R-56.7	860	R-66.4	James Inhofe (R) 2003	Don Nickles (R) 2005
Oregon	1 360	R-49.8	1 118	D-61.1	Gordon Smith (R) 2003	Ron Wyden (D) 2005
Pennsylvania	. . .	. . .	2 958	R-61.3	Rick Santorum (R) 2001	Arlen Specter (R) 2005
Rhode Island	363	D-63.5	. . .	. . .	Jack Reed (D) 2003	John H. Chafee (R) 2001
South Carolina	1 161	R-53.4	1 068	D-52.7	Ernest F. Hollings (D) 2005	Strom Thurmond (R) 2003
South Dakota	324	D-51.3	262	D-62.1	Thomas A. Daschle (D) 2005	Tim Johnson (D) 2003
Tennessee	1 779	R-61.4	. . .	. . .	Fred Thompson (R) 2003	Bill Frist (R) 2001
Texas	5 527	R-54.8	. . .	. . .	Kay Bailey Hutchison (R) 2001	Phil Gramm (R) 2003
Utah	. . .	. . .	495	R-64.0	Robert F. Bennett (R) 2005	Orrin G. Hatch (R) 2001
Vermont	. . .	. . .	214	D-72.2	Patrick J. Leahy (D) 2005	James M. Jeffords (R) 2001
Virginia	2 355	R-52.5	. . .	. . .	Charles S. Robb (D) 2001	John W. Warner (R) 2003
Washington	. . .	. . .	1 889	D-58.4	Patty Murray (D) 2005	Slade Gorton (R) 2001
West Virginia	596	D-76.6	. . .	. . .	Robert C. Byrd (D) 2001	John D. Rockefeller IV (D) 2003
Wisconsin	. . .	. . .	1 761	D-50.5	Herb Kohl (D) 2001	Russell Feingold (D) 2005
Wyoming	211	R-54.1	. . .	. . .	Mike Enzi (R) 2003	Craig Thomas (R) 2001

1. Includes vote cast for minor parties.
2. Kansas had elections to fill two Senate seats in 1996. Pat Roberts was elected to fill the full-term seat vacated by the retiring Nancy Kassenbaum. Sam Brownback was elected to fill the short-term seat vacated by Robert Dole, who resigned in 1996 to run for President.
3. Louisiana holds an open-primary election with candidates from all parties running on the same ballot. Any candidate who receives a majority is elected.

SOURCE: Congressional Quarterly, Inc., Washington, DC, America Votes, biennial (copyright).

Series YY 27. Vote Cast for United States Representatives, by Major Political Party—States: 1990 to 1998

(In thousands [61 513 represents 61 513 000], except percent. In each state, totals represent the sum of votes cast in each Congressional District or votes cast for Representative at Large in states where only one member is elected. In all years there are numerous districts within the state where either the Republican or Democratic party had no candidate. In some states the Republican and Democratic vote includes votes cast for the party candidate by endorsing parties)

State	1990 Total [1]	1990 Democratic	1990 Republican	1990 Percent for leading party	1996 Total [1]	1996 Democratic	1996 Republican	1996 Percent for leading party	1998 Total [1]	1998 Democratic	1998 Republican	1998 Percent for leading party
U.S.[2]	61 513	32 565	27 648	D-52.9	89 863	43 626	43 902	R-48.9	65 897	31 482	32 255	R-48.9
AL	1 017	690	315	D-67.9	1 469	656	786	R-53.5	1 215	545	666	R-54.8
AK	192	92	99	R-51.7	234	85	139	R-59.4	223	77	140	R-62.6
AZ	966	345	621	R-64.3	1 356	521	801	R-59.0	1 004	407	574	R-57.1
AR [3]	665	369	296	D-55.5	863	396	456	R-52.8	525	169	320	R-60.9
CA	7 287	3 568	3 347	D-49.0	9 482	4 707	4 292	D-49.6	7 990	4 040	3 510	D-50.6
CO	1 001	504	487	D-50.3	1 461	597	833	R-57.0	1 274	533	716	R-56.2
CT	1 037	489	546	R-52.6	1 294	724	547	D-55.9	954	496	442	D-51.9
DE	177	116	58	D-65.5	267	73	186	R-69.5	181	57	120	R-66.4
DC	160	98	42	D-61.7	. . .	. . .	. . .	. . .	. . .	. . .	. . .	. . .
FL [3, 4]	2 378	1 213	1 163	D-51.0	4 692	2 037	2 640	R-56.3	1 213	581	558	D-47.9
GA	1 394	855	539	D-61.3	2 163	1 011	1 152	R-53.3	1 632	592	1 040	R-63.7
HI	341	216	118	D-63.3	353	196	136	D-55.5	397	261	119	D-65.7
ID	315	183	131	D-58.2	494	194	290	R-58.7	379	169	205	R-54.0
IL	3 077	1 646	1 349	D-53.5	4 128	2 267	1 813	D-54.9	3 215	1 566	1 625	R-50.5
IN	1 514	831	683	D-54.9	2 105	944	1 119	R-53.1	1 576	673	862	R-54.7
IA	792	401	385	D-50.6	1 201	533	650	R-54.1	901	338	552	R-61.3
KS	781	394	387	D-50.4	1 049	425	591	R-56.4	727	272	450	R-61.9
KY	764	353	397	R-52.0	1 238	507	731	R-59.0	1 099	456	637	R-58.0
LA	106	106	-	D-100.0	660	262	398	R-60.3	310	213	97	D-68.7
ME	517	284	233	D-55.0	600	379	211	D-63.2	415	281	125	D-67.7
MD	1 091	566	517	D-51.9	1 639	877	762	D-53.5	1 482	792	690	D-53.5
MA	2 051	1 420	567	D-69.2	2 409	1 585	781	D-65.8	1 742	1 306	413	D-75.0
MI	2 434	1 321	1 089	D-54.3	3 700	1 945	1 679	D-52.6	2 985	1 469	1 438	D-49.2
MN	1 781	1 042	736	D-58.5	2 141	1 180	895	D-55.1	2 040	1 090	863	D-53.5
MS	369	299	69	D-81.2	904	397	488	R-54.0	551	263	232	D-47.7
MO	1 353	728	625	D-53.8	2 116	1 116	833	D-52.8	1 572	788	748	D-50.1
MT	317	157	160	R-50.5	404	175	212	R-52.4	332	147	176	R-53.0
NE	587	277	309	R-52.7	662	204	450	R-68.0	526	105	393	R-74.7
NV	313	144	151	R-48.2	450	173	249	R-55.3	410	79	275	R-67.1
NH	291	141	149	R-51.2	491	221	247	R-50.3	318	124	190	R-59.8
NJ	1 827	837	911	R-49.9	2 823	1 352	1 399	R-49.6	1 815	902	858	D-49.7
NM	359	146	214	R-59.5	548	271	261	D-49.4	498	228	246	R-49.5
NY	3 662	1 830	1 662	D-50.0	5 551	3 041	2 358	D-54.8	4 267	2 278	1 858	D-53.4
NC	2 011	1 076	935	D-53.5	2 514	1 136	1 340	R-53.3	1 904	827	1 014	R-53.3
ND	234	153	81	D-65.2	263	145	114	D-55.1	213	120	88	D-56.2
OH	3 418	1 807	1 590	D-52.9	4 388	2 031	2 192	R-49.9	3 375	1 594	1 752	R-51.9
OK	857	519	338	D-60.6	1 180	430	723	R-61.3	859	314	538	R-62.7
OR	1 053	667	342	D-63.4	1 335	724	558	D-54.3	1 090	631	402	D-57.9
PA	2 851	1 293	1 552	R-54.5	4 316	2 223	2 038	D-51.5	2 896	1 381	1 472	R-50.8
RI	347	182	165	D-52.5	360	241	108	D-66.9	293	204	77	D-69.5
SC	670	383	275	D-57.2	1 057	345	683	R-64.6	974	370	580	R-59.6
SD	257	174	83	D-67.6	323	120	186	R-57.7	259	64	194	R-75.1
TN	717	369	289	D-51.5	1 784	856	889	R-49.8	914	412	470	R-51.4
TX	3 278	1 763	1 498	D-53.8	5 219	2 323	2 785	R-53.4	3 462	1 531	1 787	R-51.6
UT	442	234	191	D-52.9	664	264	386	R-58.2	471	127	304	R-64.6
VT	210	6	83	I-56.0	255	24	83	I-58.1	215	(X)	71	R-32.9
VA	1 153	663	411	D-57.5	2 199	1 027	1 117	R-50.8	1 149	514	542	R-47.2
WA	1 313	696	596	D-53.0	2 174	1 130	1 021	D-52.0	1 858	980	819	D-52.8
WV	375	251	123	D-67.1	522	458	64	D-87.8	351	283	29	D-80.6
WI	1 256	597	652	R-51.9	2 150	1 012	1 121	R-52.1	1 673	762	880	R-52.6
WY	158	71	87	R-55.1	210	86	116	R-55.2	174	67	101	R-57.8

- Represents zero.

1. Includes vote cast for minor parties. Total for 1996 includes results from 431 districts, including 14 where members were elected without major party opposition (7 won by the Republicans and 7 by the Democrats). In four districts (three in Louisiana and one in Florida) candidates ran unopposed and no vote was recorded.
2. Includes vote cast for nonvoting Delegate at Large in District of Columbia, except for 1994 and 1996.
3. State law does not require tabulation of votes for unopposed candidates.
4. In 1990 Districts 8, 10, 12, 13, and 16 were unopposed; in 1994 Districts 4, 10, 13, 14, 18, and 23 were unopposed; in 1996 District 4 was unopposed.

SOURCE: Congressional Quarterly, Inc., Washington, DC, America Votes, biennial (copyright).

Series YY 28. Composition of Congress, by Political Party Affiliation—States: 1989 to 1997

(Figures are for the beginning of the first session [as of January 3], except as noted. Dem. = Democratic; Rep. = Republican)

State	Representatives 101st Cong.,[1] 1989 Dem.	Rep.	102d Cong.,[2] 1991 Dem.	Rep.	103rd Cong.,[2] 1993 Dem.	Rep.	104th Cong.,[2,3,4] 1997 Dem.	Rep.	Senators 101st Cong., 1989 Dem.	Rep.	102d Cong., 1991 Dem.	Rep.	103rd Cong., 1993 Dem.	Rep.	104th Cong.,[3,5] 1997 Dem.	Rep.
U.S.	259	174	267	167	258	176	197	236	55	45	56	44	57	43	46	53
AL............	4	2	5	2	4	3	2	5	2	-	2	-	2	-	-	2
AK............	-	1	-	1	-	1	-	1	-	2	-	2	-	2	-	2
AZ............	1	4	1	4	3	3	1	5	1	1	1	1	1	1	-	2
AR............	3	1	3	1	2	2	2	2	2	-	2	-	2	-	1	1
CA............	27	18	26	19	30	22	29	23	1	1	1	1	2	-	2	-
CO............	3	3	3	3	2	4	2	4	1	1	1	1	1	1	-	2
CT............	3	3	3	3	3	3	4	2	2	-	2	-	2	-	2	-
DE............	1	-	1	-	-	1	-	1	1	1	1	1	1	1	1	1
FL............	10	9	9	10	10	13	8	15	1	1	1	1	1	1	1	1
GA............	9	1	9	1	7	4	3	8	2	-	2	-	1	1	1	1
HI	1	1	2	-	2	-	2	-	2	-	2	-	2	-	2	-
ID	1	1	2	-	1	1	-	2	-	2	-	2	-	2	-	2
IL	14	8	15	7	12	8	10	10	2	-	2	-	2	-	2	-
IN	6	3	8	2	7	3	4	6	-	2	-	2	-	2	-	2
IA............	2	4	2	4	1	4	1	4	1	1	1	1	1	1	1	1
KS............	2	3	2	3	2	2	-	4	-	2	-	2	-	2	-	2
KY	4	3	4	3	4	2	1	5	1	1	1	1	1	1	1	1
LA............	4	4	4	4	4	3	2	5	2	-	2	-	2	-	2	-
ME............	1	1	1	1	1	1	2	-	1	1	1	1	1	1	-	2
MD	6	2	5	3	4	4	4	4	2	-	2	-	2	-	2	-
MA............	10	1	10	1	8	2	10	-	2	-	2	-	2	-	2	-
MI	11	7	11	7	10	6	10	6	2	-	2	-	2	-	1	1
MN	5	3	6	2	6	2	6	2	-	2	1	1	1	1	1	1
MS............	4	1	5	-	5	-	2	3	-	2	-	2	-	2	-	2
MO	5	4	6	3	6	3	5	4	-	2	-	2	-	2	-	2
MT............	1	1	1	1	1	-	-	1	1	1	1	1	1	1	1	1
NE............	1	2	1	2	1	2	-	3	2	-	2	-	2	-	1	1
NV............	1	1	1	1	1	1	-	2	2	-	2	-	2	-	2	-
NH............	-	2	1	1	1	1	-	2	-	2	-	2	-	2	-	2
NJ............	8	6	8	6	7	6	6	7	2	-	2	-	2	-	2	-
NM	1	2	1	2	1	2	-	3	1	1	1	1	1	1	1	1
NY............	21	13	21	13	18	13	18	13	1	1	1	1	1	1	1	1
NC............	8	3	7	4	8	4	6	6	1	1	1	1	-	2	-	2
ND............	1	-	1	-	1	-	1	-	2	-	2	-	2	-	2	-
OH............	11	10	11	10	10	9	8	11	2	-	2	-	2	-	1	1
OK............	4	2	4	2	4	2	-	6	1	1	1	1	1	1	-	2
OR............	3	2	4	1	4	1	4	1	-	2	-	2	-	2	1	1
PA	12	11	11	12	11	10	11	10	-	2	-	2	1	1	-	2
RI	-	2	1	1	1	1	2	-	1	1	1	1	1	1	1	1
SC............	4	2	4	2	3	3	2	4	1	1	1	1	1	1	1	1
SD	1	-	1	-	1	-	-	1	1	1	1	1	1	1	2	-
TN	6	3	6	3	6	3	4	5	2	-	2	-	2	-	-	2
TX	19	8	19	8	21	9	17	13	1	1	1	1	1	1	-	2
UT	1	2	2	1	2	1	-	3	-	2	-	2	-	2	-	2
VT	-	1	-	-	-	-	-	-	1	1	1	1	1	1	1	1
VA	5	5	6	4	7	4	6	5	1	1	1	1	1	1	1	1
WA	5	3	5	3	8	1	3	6	1	1	1	1	1	1	1	1
WV............	4	-	4	-	3	-	3	-	2	-	2	-	2	-	2	-
WI............	5	4	4	5	4	5	5	4	1	1	1	1	2	-	2	-
WY	-	1	-	1	-	1	-	1	-	2	-	2	-	2	-	2

- Represents zero.
1. Alabama and Indiana had one vacancy each.
2. Vermont had one Independent-Socialist Representative.
3. As of beginning of second session.
4. California had one vacancy.
5. Oregon had one vacancy.

SOURCE: U.S. Congress, Joint Committee on Printing, Congressional Directory, biennial; and unpublished data.

548

Series YY 29.   Number of Governors, by Political Party Affiliation: 1970 to 1999
(Reflects figures after inaugurations for each year)

Year	Democratic	Republican	Independent/ other	Year	Democratic	Republican	Independent/ other	Year	Democratic	Republican	Independent/ other
1970	18	32	-	1989	28	22	-	1995	19	30	1
1975	36	13	1	1990	29	21	-	1996	18	31	1
1980	31	19	-	1991 [1]	29	19	2	1997	17	32	1
1985	34	16	-	1992	28	20	2	1998	17	32	1
1987	26	24	-	1993	30	18	2	1999	17	31	1
1988	27	23	-	1994	29	19	2				

- Represents zero.
1. Reflects result of runoff election in Arizona in February 1991.

SOURCE: National Governors' Association, Washington, DC, 1970-87 and 1991-99, Directory of Governors of the American States, Commonwealths & Territories, annual; and 1988-90, Directory of Governors, annual (copyright).

Series YY 30.   Votes Cast for and Governor Elected, by State: 1990 to 1998

(In thousands [1 216 represents 1 216 000], except percent. D = Democratic, R = Republican, I = Independent)

State	1990 Total vote [1]	1990 Percent leading party	1994 Total vote [1]	1994 Percent leading party	1996 Total vote [1]	1996 Percent leading party	1998 Total vote [1]	1998 Percent leading party	Candidate elected at most recent election
AL	1 216	R-52.1	1 202	605	594	R-50.3	1 318	D-57.7	Donald Siegelman
AK	195	I-38.9	213	87	88	D-41.1	220	D-51.3	Tony Knowles
AZ	941	R-52.4	1 129	593	501	R-52.5	1 018	R-60.9	Jane Dee Hull
AR	696	D-57.5	717	288	429	D-59.8	706	R-59.8	Mike Huckabee
CA	7 699	R-49.2	8 659	4 778	3 518	R-55.2	8 385	D-58.0	Gray Davis
CO	1 011	D-61.9	1 116	432	619	D-55.5	1 321	R-49.1	Bill Owens
CT	1 141	I-40.4	1 147	415	375	R-36.2	1 000	R-62.9	John G. Rowland
DE	...	...	...	...	...	...	...	...	Thomas R. Carper
FL	3 531	D-56.5	4 206	2 071	2 135	D-50.8	3 964	R-55.3	Jeb Bush
GA	1 450	D-52.9	1 545	756	789	D-51.1	1 793	D-52.5	Roy Barnes
HI	340	D-59.8	369	108	135	D-36.6	408	D-50.1	Benjamin J. Cayetano
ID	321	D-68.2	413	216	181	R-52.3	381	R-67.7	Dirk Kempthorne
IL	3 257	R-50.7	3 107	1 984	1 070	R-63.9	3 359	R-51.0	George Ryan
IN	...	...	...	...	...	...	...	...	Frank L. O'Bannon
IA	976	R-60.6	997	566	414	R-56.8	956	D-52.3	Tom Vilsack
KS	783	D-48.6	821	526	295	R-64.1	743	R-73.4	Bill Graves
KY [2]	...	...	...	...	...	...	...	...	Paul E. Patton
LA	...	...	...	...	...	...	...	...	Mike Foster
ME	522	R-46.7	511	118	173	I-35.4	421	R-18.9	Angus King
MD	1 111	D-59.8	1 410	702	708	D-50.2	1 536	D-55.1	Parris N. Glendening
MA	2 343	R-50.2	2 164	1 533	612	R-70.9	1 903	R-50.8	Argeo Paul Cellucci
MI	2 565	R-49.8	3 088	1 899	1 188	R-61.5	3 027	R-62.2	John Engler
MN	1 807	R-49.6	1 766	1 094	589	R-62.0	2 091	R-34.3	Jesse Ventura
MS [2]	...	...	...	...	...	...	...	...	Kirk Fordice
MO	...	...	...	...	...	...	...	...	Mel Carnahan
MT	...	...	...	...	...	...	...	...	Marc Racicot
NE	587	D-49.9	580	148	423	D-73.0	545	R-53.9	Mike Johanns
NV	321	D-64.8	371	157	200	D-53.9	434	R-51.6	Kenny Guinn
NH	295	R-60.3	312	218	80	R-69.9	319	D-66.1	Jeanne Shaheen
NJ	2 254	D-61.2	2 506	...	...	R-49.3	2 418	R-46.9	Christine Todd Whitman
NM	411	D-54.6	468	233	187	R-49.8	499	R-54.5	Gary E. Johnson
NY	4 057	D-53.2	5 204	2 539	2 365	R-48.8	4 735	R-54.3	George E. Pataki
NC	...	...	...	...	...	...	...	...	James B. Hunt
ND	...	...	...	...	...	...	...	...	Edward T. Schafer
OH	3 478	R-55.7	3 346	2 402	836	R-71.8	3 354	R-50.0	Bob Taft
OK	911	D-57.4	995	467	295	R-46.9	874	R-57.9	Frank Keating
OR	1 113	D-45.7	1 221	518	622	D-50.9	1 113	D-64.4	John Kitzhaber
PA	3 053	D-67.7	3 585	1 628	1 430	R-45.4	3 025	R-57.4	Tom Ridge
RI	357	D-74.1	361	171	157	R-47.4	306	R-51.0	Lincoln C. Almond
SC	761	R-69.5	934	471	447	R-50.4	1 071	D-53.2	Jim Hodges
SD	257	R-58.9	312	173	126	R-55.4	260	R-64.0	William J. Janklow
TN	790	D-60.8	1 487	807	664	R-54.3	976	R-68.6	Don Sundquist
TX	3 893	D-49.5	4 396	2 351	2 017	R-53.5	3 738	R-68.2	George W. Bush
UT	...	...	...	...	...	...	...	...	Michael O. Leavitt
VT	211	R-51.8	212	40	146	D-68.7	218	D-55.7	Howard Dean
VA	1 789	D-50.1	1 794	...	...	R-58.3	1 736	R-55.8	James S. Gilmore
WA	...	...	...	...	...	...	...	...	Gary Locke
WV	...	...	...	...	...	...	...	...	Cecil H. Underwood
WI	1 380	R-58.2	1 563	1 051	483	R-67.3	1 756	R-59.7	Tommy G. Thompson
WY	160	D-65.4	201	118	81	R-58.7	175	R-55.6	Jim Geringer

1. Includes minor party and scattered votes.
2. Voting years 1987, 1991, and 1995.

SOURCE: Congressional Quarterly, Inc., Washington, DC, America Votes, biennial; and unpublished data (copyright).

Series YY 31. Composition of State Legislatures, by Political Party Affiliation: 1990 to 1996

(Data reflect election results in year shown for most states; and except as noted, results in previous year for other states. Figures reflect immediate results of elections, including holdover members in state houses which do not have all of their members running for re-election. Dem. = Democrat, Rep. = Republican. In general, Lower House refers to body consisting of State Representatives; Upper House, of State Senators)

State	Lower house 1990 [1,2] Dem.	Rep.	1992 [3,4] Dem.	Rep.	1994 [5,6] Dem.	Rep.	1996 [5,6] Dem.	Rep.	Upper house 1990 [1,7] Dem.	Rep.	1992 [3,8] Dem.	Rep.	1994 [5,7] Dem.	Rep.	1996 [9] Dem.	Rep.
U.S.	3 242	2 202	3 186	2 223	2 817	2 603	2 886	2 539	1 186	757	1 132	799	1 021	905	998	931
AL [10]	82	23	82	23	74	31	72	33	28	7	27	8	23	12	22	12
AK [11]	23	17	20	18	17	22	16	24	10	10	10	10	8	12	7	13
AZ [12]	27	33	25	35	22	38	22	38	17	13	12	18	11	19	12	18
AR [11]	90	9	88	11	88	12	86	13	31	4	30	5	28	7	28	6
CA [11]	47	33	47	33	39	40	43	37	25	13	21	16	21	17	25	15
CO [11]	27	38	31	34	24	41	24	41	12	23	16	19	16	19	15	20
CT [12]	87	64	85	64	90	61	97	54	20	16	19	17	17	19	19	17
DE [11]	17	24	18	23	14	27	14	27	15	6	15	6	12	9	13	8
FL [11]	74	46	71	49	63	57	59	61	22	18	20	20	19	21	17	23
GA [12]	145	35	128	51	114	65	106	74	45	11	41	15	35	20	34	22
HI [11]	45	6	47	4	44	7	39	12	22	3	22	3	23	2	23	2
ID [12]	28	56	20	50	13	57	11	59	21	21	12	23	8	27	5	30
IL [11]	72	46	67	51	54	64	60	58	31	28	27	32	26	33	28	31
IN [11]	52	48	55	45	44	56	50	50	24	26	22	28	20	30	19	31
IA [11]	55	45	49	51	36	64	46	54	29	21	27	23	27	23	21	29
KS [11]	63	62	59	66	45	80	48	77	18	22	13	27	13	27	13	27
KY [11]	68	32	71	29	64	36	64	36	27	11	25	13	21	17	20	18
LA [10]	89	16	88	16	86	17	76	28	34	5	33	6	33	6	25	14
ME [12]	97	54	93	58	77	74	81	69	21	14	20	15	16	18	19	15
MD [10]	116	25	116	25	100	41	100	41	38	9	38	9	32	15	32	15
MA [12]	118	37	123	34	125	34	134	25	25	15	31	9	30	10	34	6
MI [11]	61	49	55	55	53	56	58	52	18	20	16	22	16	22	16	22
MN [11]	78	56	85	49	71	63	70	64	46	21	45	22	43	21	42	24
MS [10]	98	23	91	29	89	31	86	33	43	9	37	15	36	14	34	18
MO [11]	99	64	98	65	87	76	88	75	23	11	20	14	19	15	19	15
MT [11]	61	39	47	53	33	67	35	65	29	21	30	20	19	31	16	34
NE	(13)	(13)	(13)	(13)	(13)	(13)	(13)	(13)	(13)	(13)	(13)	(13)	(13)	(13)	(13)	(13)
NV [11]	22	19	27	12	21	21	25	17	10	10	10	11	8	13	9	12
NH [12]	125	268	136	258	112	286	143	255	11	13	11	13	6	18	9	15
NJ [11]	22	58	27	53	28	52	30	50	13	27	16	24	16	24	16	24
NM [11]	49	21	53	17	46	24	42	28	26	16	27	15	27	15	25	17
NY [12]	95	55	100	50	94	56	96	54	26	35	26	35	25	36	26	35
NC [12]	81	39	78	42	52	68	59	61	36	14	39	11	26	24	30	20
ND [11]	48	58	33	65	23	75	26	72	27	26	25	24	20	29	19	30
OH [11]	61	38	53	46	43	56	39	60	12	21	13	20	13	20	12	21
OK [11]	68	33	70	31	65	36	65	36	37	11	37	11	35	13	33	15
OR [11]	28	32	28	32	26	34	29	31	20	10	16	14	11	19	10	20
PA [11]	107	94	105	98	101	102	99	104	24	26	24	25	21	29	20	30
RI [12]	89	11	85	15	84	16	84	16	45	5	39	11	40	10	41	9
SC [11]	79	43	71	52	58	62	53	70	33	13	30	16	29	17	26	20
SD [12]	25	45	28	42	24	46	23	47	17	18	20	15	16	19	13	22
TN [11]	57	42	63	36	59	40	61	38	20	13	19	14	18	15	18	15
TX [11]	93	57	91	58	89	61	82	68	22	9	18	13	17	14	14	16
UT [11]	31	44	26	49	20	55	20	55	10	19	11	18	10	19	9	20
VT [12]	73	75	87	57	86	61	89	57	15	15	14	16	12	18	17	13
VA [11]	58	41	52	47	52	47	53	46	22	18	22	18	22	18	20	20
WA [11]	58	40	65	33	38	60	45	53	24	25	28	21	25	24	23	26
WV [11]	74	26	79	21	69	30	74	25	33	1	32	2	26	8	25	9
WI [11]	58	41	51	47	48	51	47	52	19	14	16	17	16	17	17	16
WY [11]	22	42	19	41	13	47	17	43	10	20	10	20	10	20	9	21

1. Status as of May 1992; reflects results of elections held in LA, KY, MS, and NJ in 1991.
2. Excludes one Independent each for MA, MS, NH, SC, and VA; one Independent Democrat for NH; two Independents for VT; one vacancy each for AR, NV, and SC; two vacancies for PA; four vacancies for MA; and five vacancies for NH.
3. Status as of November 11, 1993.
4. Excludes one Independent each for AR, LA, NH, SC, and VA; two Independents each for AK and MS; four Independents for VT; members of political parties other than Democratic, Republican, or Independent (one in MA, two in VT, and four in NH); one vacancy each for GA, NH, TX, and WI; two vacancies each for CT and MA; and three vacancies for NV.
5. Status as of December 7, 1994.
6. Excludes one Independent each for AK, CA, LA, and VA; two Independents each for MS and VT; four Independents for SC; members of political parties other than Democratic, Republican, or Independent (one each in MA and VT and two in NH); one undecided in GA; and one vacancy each in LA, MI, and WV.
7. Excludes two Independents for CA; and one vacancy for NV.
8. Excludes two Independents for CA; and one vacancy each for CA and PA.
9. Excludes one Independent in ME, two independents in CA, one vacancy in GA, two vacancies in MS, and three vacancies in MN.
10. Members of both houses serve 4-year terms.
11. Upper House members serve 4-year terms and Lower House members serve 2-year terms.
12. Members of both houses serve 2-year terms.
13. Single chamber (unicameral body) of 49 members, elected without party designation.

SOURCE: The Council of State Governments, Lexington, KY, State Elective Officials and the Legislatures, biennial (copyright); thereafter, National Conference of State Legislatures, Denver, CO, unpublished data.

Series YY 32. Political Party Control of State Legislatures, by Party: 1975 to 1997

(As of beginning of year. Until 1972 there were two nonpartisan legislatures in Minnesota and Nebraska. Since then only Nebraska has had a nonpartisan legislature)

Year	Legislatures under-			Year	Legislatures under-			Year	Legislatures under-		
	Democratic control	Split control or tie	Republican control		Democratic control	Split control or tie	Republican control		Democratic control	Split control or tie	Republican control
1975	37	7	5	1985	27	11	11	1993	25	16	8
1977	36	8	5	1987	28	12	9	1994	24	17	8
1979	30	7	12	1989 [2]	28	13	8	1995	18	12	19
1981	28	6	15	1990	29	11	9	1996	16	15	18
1983 [1]	34	4	11	1992	29	14	6	1997	20	11	18

1. Two 1984 midterm recall elections resulted in a change in control of the Michigan State Senate. At the time of the 1984 election, therefore, Democrats controlled 33 legislatures.
2. A party change during the year by a Democratic representative broke the tie in the Indiana House of Representatives, giving the Republicans control of both chambers.

SOURCE: National Conference of State Legislatures, Denver, CO, State Legislatures, periodic.

Series YY 33. Local Elected Officials, by Sex, Race, Hispanic Origin, and Type of Government: 1992

Sex, race, and Hispanic origin	General purpose				Special purpose	
	Total	County	Municipal	Town, township	School district	Special district
Total..	493 830	58 818	135 531	126 958	88 434	84 089
Male..	324 255	43 563	94 808	76 213	54 443	55 228
Female..	100 531	12 525	26 825	27 702	24 730	8 749
Sex not reported......................................	69 044	2 730	13 898	23 043	9 261	20 112
White...	405 905	52 705	114 880	102 676	73 894	61 750
Black...	11 542	1 715	4 566	369	4 222	670
American Indian, Eskimo, Aleut	1 800	147	776	86	564	227
Asian, Pacific Islander............................	514	80	97	16	184	137
Hispanic..	5 859	906	1 701	216	2 466	570
Non-Hispanic..	413 902	53 741	118 618	102 931	76 398	62 214
Race, Hispanic origin not reported.........	74 069	4 171	15 212	23 811	9 570	21 305

SOURCE: U.S. Census Bureau, 1992 Census of Governments, Popularly Elected Officials, (GC92(1)-2).

Series YY 34.   Women Holding State Public Offices, by Office and State: 1998
(As of January)

State	State-wide elective executive office [1]	State legislature	State	State-wide elective executive office [1]	State legislature	State	State-wide elective executive office [1]	State legislature
United States	82	1 617	Kentucky	-	13	North Dakota	4	25
Alabama	3	6	Louisiana	1	17	Ohio	2	29
Alaska	1	8	Maine	-	48	Oklahoma	4	15
Arizona	4	33	Maryland	1	56	Oregon	1	24
Arkansas	2	23	Massachusetts	-	47	Pennsylvania	1	31
California	2	26	Michigan	2	34	Rhode Island	1	39
Colorado	3	37	Minnesota	3	63	South Carolina	1	20
Connecticut	2	54	Mississippi	-	22	South Dakota	4	18
Delaware	4	16	Missouri	2	42	Tennessee	1	18
Florida	1	38	Montana	2	35	Texas	1	33
Georgia	2	40	Nebraska	2	13	Utah	2	18
Hawaii	1	13	Nevada	1	21	Vermont	-	60
Idaho	2	25	New Hampshire	1	131	Virginia	-	22
Illinois	2	45	New Jersey	1	20	Washington	4	58
Indiana	3	29	New Mexico	1	30	West Virginia	-	20
Iowa	1	32	New York	1	43	Wisconsin	-	31
Kansas	2	49	North Carolina	1	30	Wyoming	2	17

- Represents zero.
1. Excludes women elected to the judiciary, women appointed to State cabinet-level positions, women elected to executive posts by the legislature, and elected members of university Board of Trustees or board of education.

SOURCE: Center for the American Woman and Politics, Eagleton Institute of Politics, Rutgers University, New Brunswick, NJ, information releases, (copyright).

Series YY 35.   Public Confidence Levels in Selected Public and Private Institutions: 1996
(Based on a sample survey of 2 719 persons 18 years old and over conducted during the spring and subject to sampling variability; see source)

Institution	Level of confidence				
	A great deal	Quite a lot	Some	Very little	Can't say/ no answer
Religious organizations	23.6	31.1	31.3	12.3	1.7
Higher education (colleges or univ.)	18.3	38.7	28.3	7.5	7.1
Private elementary or secondary education	15.1	35.3	33.4	9.7	6.5
Youth development and recreation organizations	14.8	35.2	32.7	11.6	5.7
Federated charitable appeals	12.6	26.3	34.9	21.6	4.5
Health organizations	10.8	28.2	42.0	15.9	3.1
Environmental organizations	9.4	23.1	41.0	20.3	6.2
Human service organizations	9.1	28.1	42.6	15.1	5.0
Recreational organizations (adult)	7.8	27.5	41.9	13.4	9.4
Arts, culture, & humanities organizations	9.3	26.7	39.8	14.3	9.9
Private and community foundations	7.6	24.0	42.3	13.5	12.6
Public /society benefit organizations [1]	7.5	22.7	43.4	20.8	5.6
International/foreign organizations [2]	6.3	19.1	37.5	24.2	12.8
Small businesses	15.3	40.8	32.6	7.6	3.6
Military	16.9	37.0	31.0	12.1	3.1
Public higher educ. (colleges or univ.)	15.0	36.4	34.2	11.6	2.8
Public elementary or secondary education	13.3	31.7	37.2	15.3	2.4
Organized labor	6.6	17.7	40.9	29.3	5.6
Media (e.g. newspapers, TV, radio)	6.3	22.7	39.5	29.7	1.8
Work-related organizations	6.1	21.5	47.2	17.4	7.9
Major corporations	4.9	18.7	44.2	27.4	4.8
State government	4.1	22.2	44.9	26.4	2.5
Organizations that lobby for a particular cause	4.0	15.7	42.7	29.5	8.1
Political organizations, parties	3.8	10.8	39.2	42.6	3.7
Local government	5.4	25.9	43.3	23.1	2.3
Federal government	5.2	17.5	43.9	31.1	2.2
Congress	3.4	12.4	41.7	39.0	3.5

1. Civil rights, social justice, or community improvement organizations.
2. Culture exchange or relief organizations.

SOURCE: Hodgkinson, Virginia, Murray Weitzman, andthe Gallup Organization, Inc., Giving & Volunteering in the United States: 1996 Edition. (Copyright and published by INDEPENDENT SECTOR, Washington, DC, 1996.)

Series YY 36. Political Party Identification of the Adult Population, by Degree of Attachment, 1972 to 1994, and by Selected Characteristics, 1994

(In percent. Covers citizens of voting-age living in private housing units in the contiguous United States. Data are from the National Election Studies and are based on a sample and subject to sampling variability; for details, see source)

Year and selected characteristic	Total	Strong Democrat	Weak Democrat	Independent Democrat	Independent	Independent Republican	Weak Republican	Strong Republican	Apolitical
1972	100	15	26	11	13	11	13	10	1
1980	100	18	23	11	13	10	14	9	2
1984	100	17	20	11	11	12	15	12	2
1986	100	18	22	10	12	11	15	11	2
1988	100	18	18	12	11	13	14	14	2
1990	100	20	19	12	11	12	15	10	2
1992	100	18	18	14	12	12	14	11	1
1994	100	15	19	13	10	12	15	16	1
1994									
Age:									
17 to 24 year	100	9	20	22	10	8	19	10	1
25 to 34 years old	100	11	19	14	12	11	16	16	1
35 to 44 years old	100	13	18	14	12	11	14	18	-
45 to 54 years old	100	15	16	15	7	16	12	17	1
55 to 64 years old	100	18	22	8	8	16	12	15	-
65 to 74 years old	100	28	17	6	8	13	14	15	-
75 to 99 years old	100	19	26	9	9	5	17	13	2
Sex:									
Male	100	13	17	12	11	14	14	18	1
Female	100	18	21	13	10	9	15	13	1
Race:									
White	100	12	19	12	10	13	16	17	1
Black	100	38	23	20	8	4	2	3	1
Education:									
Grade school	100	26	26	7	13	7	11	6	4
High school	100	15	22	14	13	10	13	11	1
College	100	14	16	13	7	13	16	21	-

- Represents zero.
1. Includes other characteristics, not shown separately.

SOURCE: Center for Political Studies, University of Michigan, Ann Arbor, MI, unpublished data. Data prior to 1988 published in Warren E. Miller and Santa A. Traugott, American National Election Studies Data Sourcebook, 1952-1986, Harvard University Press, Cambridge, MA, 1989 (copyright).

Series YY 37. Political Party Financial Activity, by Major Political Party: 1981 to 1998

(In millions of dollars [$39.3 represents $39 300 000]. Covers financial activity during 2-year calendar period indicated. Some political party financial activities, such as building funds and state and local election spending, are not reported to the source. Also excludes contributions earmarked to Federal candidates through the party organizations, since some of those funds never passed through the committees' accounts)

Year and type of committee	Democratic				Republican			
	Receipts, net [1]	Disbursements, net [1]	Contributions to candidates	Monies spent on behalf of party's nominees [2]	Receipts, net [1]	Disbursements, net [1]	Contributions to candidates	Monies spent on behalf of party's nominees [2]
1981-82	39.3	40.1	1.7	3.3	215.0	214.0	5.6	14.3
1983-84	98.5	97.4	2.6	9.0	297.9	300.8	4.9	20.1
1985-86	64.8	65.9	1.7	9.0	255.2	258.9	3.4	14.3
1987-88	127.9	121.9	1.8	17.9	263.3	257.0	3.4	22.7
1989-90	85.8	90.9	1.5	8.7	206.3	213.5	2.9	10.7
1991-92	177.7	171.9	1.9	28.1	267.3	256.1	3.0	33.9
1993-94, total	143.3	141.8	2.2	21.2	254.4	243.7	3.0	20.6
1995-96, total	281.5	274.8	2.1	22.6	474.0	465.3	3.8	31.0
1997-98, total [3]	189.0	184.3	1.2	27.1	319.6	310.5	2.6	15.7
National committee	64.8	65.3	-	6.0	104.0	105.1	0.4	3.9
Senatorial committee	35.6	35.8	0.3	8.4	53.4	53.7	0.3	-
Congressional committee ...	25.2	24.7	0.4	3.0	72.7	71.7	0.8	5.1
State and local	63.4	58.5	0.5	9.6	89.4	80.0	1.1	6.7

- Represents zero.
1. Excludes monies transferred between affiliated committees.
2. Monies spent in the general election. Minus sign (-) indicates refunds for expenditures.
3. Excludes Other national activity.

SOURCE: U.S. Federal Election Commission, FEC Reports on Financial Activity, Final Report, Party and Non-Party Political Committees, biennial.

Series YY 38. Independent Expenditures for Presidential and Congressional Campaigns: 1985 to 1996

(In thousands of dollars ($10 205 represents $10 205 000). Covers campaign finance activity during 2-year calendar period indicated. An "independent expenditure" is money spent to support or defeat a clearly identified candidate. According to Federal election law, such an expenditure must be made without cooperation or consultation with the candidate or his/her campaign. Independent expenditures are not limited, as are contributions)

Type of office and year	All parties			Democrats		Republicans		Others	
	Total	For	Against	For	Against	For	Against	For	Against
TOTAL									
1985-86	10 205	8 832	1 373	3 450	888	5 376	485	6	-
1987-88	21 341	16 654	4 687	2 865	4 248	13 784	439	6	-
1989-90	5 774	4 177	1 597	1 530	735	2 645	862	2	-
1991-92	11 052	8 710	2 342	3 044	1 483	5 548	847	118	12
1993-94	4 980	3 256	1 724	672	1 119	2 571	590	13	15
1995-96	21 744	11 016	10 728	1 186	6 491	9 714	4 228	116	9
PRESIDENTIAL									
1985-86	841	795	45	76	28	719	17	-	-
1987-88	14 127	10 628	3 499	568	3 352	10 054	146	6	-
1989-90	497	322	174	5	169	318	5	-	-
1991-92	4 431	3 695	736	583	561	3 052	163	60	12
1993-94	112	27	85	12	84	15	(Z)	-	1
1995-96	1 436	601	835	111	761	459	74	31	-
SENATE									
1985-86	5 312	4 331	980	988	632	3 343	348	-	-
1987-88	4 401	3 641	761	831	617	2 810	143	(Z)	-
1989-90	3 506	2 362	1 144	756	428	1 604	716	2	-
1991-92	2 604	1 912	692	1 025	462	886	230	1	-
1993-94	2 627	1 612	1 015	261	476	1 351	539	(Z)	-
1995-96	14 821	7 041	7 780	347	5 499	6 668	2 280	26	1
HOUSE OF REPRESENTATIVES									
1985-86	4 053	3 706	347	2 386	227	1 314	120	6	-
1987-88	2 813	2 385	427	1 466	279	920	149	(Z)	-
1989-90	1 772	1 493	279	770	138	723	141	-	-
1991-92	4 017	3 103	914	1 436	460	1 610	454	57	-
1993-94	2 241	1 617	624	399	559	1 205	51	13	14
1995-96	5 487	3 374	2 113	728	231	2 587	1 874	59	8

- Represents zero.
Z less than $500.

SOURCE: U.S. Federal Election Commission, FEC Index of Independent Expenditures, 1987-88, May 1989; press release of May 19, 1989; and unpublished data.

Series YY 39. Congressional Campaign Finances—Receipts and Disbursements: 1993 to 1998

(Covers all campaign finance activity during 2-year calendar period indicated for primary, general, run-off, and special elections. For 1993-94, relates to 2 045 House of Representatives candidates and 331 Senate candidates; Data have been adjusted to eliminate transfers between all committees within a campaign. For further information on legal limits of contributions, see Federal Election Campaign Act of 1971, as amended)

Item	House of Representatives						Senate					
	Amount (mil. dol.)			Percent distribution			Amount (mil. dol.)			Percent distribution		
	1993-94	1995-96	1997-98	1993-94	1995-96	1997-98	1993-94	1995-96	1997-98	1993-94	1995-96	1997-98
Total receipts [1]	421.3	505.4	493.8	100	100	100	319.1	285.1	287.6	100	100	100
Individual contributions	216.1	276.5	256.0	51	55	52	186.4	167.5	166.8	58	59	58
Other committees	132.4	155.8	158.7	31	31	32	47.2	45.6	48.1	15	16	17
Candidate loans	43.9	42.6	48.2	10	8	10	43.5	40.3	52.3	14	14	18
Candidate contributions	10.3	7.3	5.4	2	1	1	24.9	16.4	1.4	8	6	(Z)
Democrats	216.7	233.1	233.4	51	46	47	133.6	126.5	134.1	42	44	47
Republicans	201.8	266.9	255.8	48	53	52	183.6	157.7	153.0	58	55	53
Others	2.8	5.4	4.5	1	1	1	2.0	0.9	0.4	1	(Z)	(Z)
Incumbents	224.1	281.7	294.4	53	56	60	113.3	81.8	135.5	36	29	47
Challengers	100.6	121.6	96.2	24	24	19	119.2	79.2	113.9	37	28	40
Open seats [2]	96.6	72.2	103.2	23	14	21	86.6	124.1	37.7	27	44	13
Total disbursements	407.2	477.8	452.5	100	95	100	318.8	287.5	287.9	100	100	100
Democrats	213.4	221.1	211.1	46	44	47	136.3	127.4	134.6	43	44	47
Republicans	191.0	251.4	237.2	53	50	52	180.6	159.1	152.9	57	55	53
Others	2.8	5.3	4.2	1	1	1	2.0	0.9	0.4	1	(Z)	(Z)
Incumbents	213.5	258.1	257.2	54	51	57	115.1	85.4	137.3	36	30	48
Challengers	99.1	119.6	94.7	25	24	21	118.3	78.9	112.5	37	27	39
Open seats [2]	94.6	100.2	100.6	21	20	22	85.5	123.1	38.1	27	43	13

Z Less than $50 000 or 0.5 percent.
1. Includes other types of receipts, not shown separately.
2. Elections in which an incumbent did not seek re-election.

SOURCE: U.S. Federal Election Commission, FEC Reports on Financial Activity, Final Report, U.S. Senate and House Campaigns, biennial.

Series YY 40. Contributions to Congressional Campaigns by Political Action Committees (PAC), by Type of Committee: 1981 to 1998

(In millions of dollars [61.1 represents $61 100 000]. Covers amounts given to candidates in primary, general, run-off, and special elections during the 2-year calendar period indicated.)

Type of committee	Total [1]	Democrats	Republicans	Incumbents	Challengers	Open seats [2]
HOUSE OF REPRESENTATIVES						
1981-82	61.1	34.2	26.8	40.8	10.9	9.4
1983-84	75.7	46.3	29.3	57.2	11.3	7.2
1985-86	87.4	54.7	32.6	65.9	9.1	12.4
1987-88	102.2	67.4	34.7	82.2	10.0	10.0
1989-90	108.5	72.2	36.2	87.5	7.3	13.6
1991-92	127.4	85.4	41.7	94.4	12.2	20.8
1993-94	132.4	88.2	43.9	101.4	12.7	18.3
1995-96, total	159.8	79.4	79.7	117.2	21.4	20.1
1997-98, total [3]	162.1	79.1	82.8	127.0	15.2	19.8
Corporate	51.7	16.7	35.0	45.4	2.1	4.2
Trade association [4]	47.5	18.0	29.4	39.0	3.1	5.3
Labor...	37.9	34.5	3.3	26.6	5.4	5.7
Nonconnected [5]	20.2	7.7	12.4	11.7	4.2	4.3
SENATE						
1981-82	22.6	11.2	11.4	14.3	5.2	3.0
1983-84	29.7	14.0	15.6	17.9	6.3	5.4
1985-86	45.3	20.2	25.1	23.7	10.2	11.4
1987-88	45.7	24.2	21.5	28.7	8.0	9.0
1989-90	41.2	20.2	21.0	29.5	8.2	3.5
1991-92	51.2	29.0	22.2	31.9	9.4	10.0
1997-98, total [3]	57.8	24.1	33.6	43.8	6.8	7.2
Corporate	26.3	8.4	17.9	20.6	2.7	3.0
Trade association [4]	14.9	5.5	9.4	11.3	1.6	1.9
Labor...	6.7	6.0	0.7	4.6	1.0	1.1
Nonconnected [5]	7.9	3.3	4.6	5.6	1.3	1.0

1. Includes other parties, not shown separately.
2. Elections in which an incumbent did not seek re-election.
3. Includes other types of political action committees not shown separately.
4. Includes membership organizations and health organizations.
5. Represents "ideological" groups as well as other issue groups not necessarily ideological in nature.

SOURCE: U.S. Federal Election Commission, FEC Reports on Financial Activity, Party and Non-Party Political Committees, Final Report, biennial.

Sources

Unless otherwise indicated, all publications are from the United States Federal Government.

A. Population

Census of Population: General Population Characteristics
Population Profile of the United States

B. Vital Statistics and Health

Monthly Vital Statistics Report
Vital Statistics of the United States

Abortion Service in the United States. *Alan Guttmacher Institute*
Annual Medicare Program Statistics Series
Cancer Incidence and Mortality in the United States
Data on Health Resource Utilization
Data on Health Resources: Manpower and Facilities
Dental Statistics Handbook
Food Consumption: Prices and Expenditures
Healthcare Financing Review
Healthcare Financing Program Statistics
Health United States
Hospital Statistics. *American Hospital Association*
Mental Health
Mental Health Statistics
Morbidity and Mortality Weekly Report
Physician Characteristics and Distribution in the United States
Physicians' Earnings and Expenses. *Medical Economics*
Reference Data on the Profile of Medical Practice. *American Medical Association*
Statistical Bulletin. *Metropolitan Life Insurance Company*
Statistical Summary. *American Nurses' Association*
Teenage Pregnancy in the United States. *Alan Guttmacher Institute*
U.S. Medical Licensure Statistics. *American Medical Association*

C. Migration

Statistical Yearbook of the Immigration and Naturalization Service

D. Labor

Compensation and Working Conditions
Employment and Earnings
Employment, Hours and Earnings, 1909-1990
Employment and Earnings: Characteristics of Families
Employment Benefits in Large and Medium Firms
Employment Benefits in State and Local Governments
Employment Cost Index
Employment in Perspective: Minority Workers
Employment in Perspective: Women in the Labor Force

Employment in the Aerospace Industry. *Aerospace Industries Association*
Employment Outlook. *Bureau of National Affairs*
The Employment Situation
Geographic Profile of Employment and Unemployment
Handbook of Labor Statistics
Job Absence and Turnover. *Bureau of National Affairs*
Key Statistics on Work and Family Issues. *Bureau of National Affairs*
Labor Force Statistics Derived from the Current Population Survey
Major Collective Bargaining Settlements
Major Work Stoppages
Monthly Labor Review
Mass Layoffs
Occupational Employment in Selected Non-Manufacturing Industries
Occupational Illnesses and Injuries in the United States by Industry
Occupational Projections and Training Data
Outlook 2000
Permanent Mass Layoffs and Plant Closings
Productivity Measures for Certain Industries
Real Earnings
Revised Seasonally Adjusted Labor Force Statistics
State and Metropolitan Area Employment and Unemployment
Weekly Wage Earnings of Wage and Salary Workers
White Collar Pay
Work Experiences of the Population
Working Woman: A Chartbook
Farm Labor
Unemployment Insurance Claims

F. National Income and Wealth

Consumer Expenditure Survey
Economic Indicators
Flow of Funds Accounts
National Income and Product Accounts
Statistics of Income Bulletin
Survey of Current Business

G. Consumer Income and Expenditures

Consumer Expenditure Survey
Federal Reserve Bulletin
Individual Income Tax Returns
Local Area Personal Income
Statistics of Income Bulletin

Trends in Family Income, 1970-86
Trends Since 1960 in the Economic Situation of Aged Men and
Women

H. Social Statistics

American Red Cross Annual
Benefits and Beneficiaries under Public Employment Retirement
Systems
Characteristics of Social Security Disability
Insurance Beneficiaries
Compensation Report
Giving USA. *American Association of Fundraising Councils*
Employment and Trends
Income of Population 55 and Over
Private Social Welfare Expenditures
Public Social Welfare Expenditures
Quarterly Public Assistance Statistics
Railway Retirement Board: Monthly Benefit Statistics
Social Security Beneficiaries by State and County
Social Security Bulletin
Social Security Programs in the United States
Supplementary Security Income: State and County Data Annual
Trend Data of Department of Veterans Affairs
Unemployment Insurance Claims
Unemployment Insurance: Financial Data
Workers' Compensation: Coverage, Benefits and Costs

Catholic Schools in America. *National Catholic Education
Association*
Condition of Education
Digest of Education Statistics
Earned Degrees Conferred
Estimates of School Statistics. *National Education Association*
Factbook of Higher Education. *American Council on Education*
Faculty Salaries, Tenure and Benefits
Fall Enrollment in Colleges and Universities
Projections of Education Statistics
Racial, Ethnic and Sex Enrollment Data from Institutions of
Higher Education
Rankings of the States
Revenues and Expenditures for Public Elementary and Secondary
Education
States' Profiles: Financing Public Higher Education. *Research
Associates*
U.S. Catholic Elementary Schools Staffing and Enrollment. *NCEA*
U.S. Catholic Secondary Schools and their Finances. *NCEA*
U.S. Catholic Elementary Schools and their Finances. *NCEA*

American Jewish Yearbook
Churches and Church Membership in the United States. *Glenmary
Research Center*
Yearbook of American and Canadian Churches. *National Council
of Churches*

Boating: A Statistical Report. *National Marine Manufacturers
Association*
Federal Recreation Fee Report
International Air Travel Statistics
International Travel to the United States
National Parks Statistical Abstract
National Parks Index

Public Lands Statistics
Report of the Forest Service
Sporting Goods Market. *National Sporting Goods Association*
Statistics on Outdoor Recreation. *Resources for the Future*
Trends in the Golf Industry. *National Golf Foundation*

Capital Punishment Annual
Census of Jails
Census of State Correctional Facilities
Children in Custody
Crime in the United States
Criminal Victimization in the United States
Drug Abuse and Law Enforcement Statistics
Expenditure and Employment Data for the Criminal Justice
System
Federal Bureau of Prisons Statistical Report
Federal Court Management Statistics
Federal Judicial Workload Statistics
Federal Offenders and Sentences Imposed
Households Touched by Crime
Law Enforcement Officers Killed and Assaulted
National Crime Survey
National Survey of Courts
Parole in the United States
Prisoners in State and Federal Institutions
Sourcebook of Criminal Justice Statistics
State Court Caseload Statistics
Survey of Prison Inmates
Uniform Crime Reports

J. Land, Water and Climate

Air Quality Data
Climatological Data
Environmental Quality
Environmental Trends
Estimated Use of Water in the United States
General Summary of Tornadoes
Hourly Precipitation Data
Local Climatological Data
National Air Quality and Emissions Trends Report
National Inventory of Land Resources
Radiation Data and Reports
State of the Environment Conservation Foundation
Storm Data

K. Agriculture

Agricultural Income and Finance
Agricultural Outlook
Agricultural Price Report
Agricultural Statistics
Crop Production
Crop Values
Economic Indicators of the Farm Sector
Farmline
Fertilizer Use and Price Statistics
Financial Characteristics of U.S. Farms
Food Consumption, Prices and Expenditures
Food Marketing Review
Food Spending in American Households
Foreign Agricultural Trade of the United States

Fruit and Vegetable Reports
Journal of American Agricultural Economics Research
Livestock Production, Disposition and Income
Milk and Dairy Products Reports
Poultry and Egg Reports
Rural Development Perspectives
Stock Reports
U.S. Egg and Poultry Statistics Series
U.S. Rice Distribution Patterns

L. Forestry and Fisheries

Analysis of the Timber Situation in the United States
Aquaculture
Fisheries of the United States
Forest Statistics of the United States
Land Areas of the National Forest System
Marine Recreational Fishery Statistical Survey
Statistical Roundup. *National Forest Products Association*
U.S. Timber Production, Trade, Consumption and Price Statistics

M. Minerals

Annual Energy Review
Annual Statistical Report. *American Iron and Steel Institute*
Census of Mineral Industries
Coal Data Annual
Coal Production
Comparative Oil Company Statistics. *Carl H. Pforzheimer Co.*
Domestic Uranium Mining and Milling Industry
Engineering and Mining Journal
Gas Facts. *American Gas Association*
International Energy Annual
The Iron Age. *Chilton Co.*
Metal Statistics. *American Metal Market*
Mineral Commodity Summaries
Mineral Industry Surveys
Minerals Today
Minerals Yearbook
Monthly Energy Review
Natural Gas Annual
Non-Ferrous Metal Data. *American Bureau of Metal Statistics*
Offshore. *Pennwell Publishing*
Petroleum Supply Annual
Quarterly Coal Report
Quarterly Review of Drilling Statistics. *American Petroleum Institute*
U.S. Crude Oil, Natural Gas and Natural Gas Liquids Reserves
U.S. Petroleum Statistics
Weekly Oil Trends. *Independent Petroleum Association*
Wholesale Oil Prices. *Independent Petroleum Association*

N. Construction and Housing

Census of Housing
Characteristics of Apartments Completed
Construction Potentials. *F.W. Dodge*
Construction Review
Current Construction Reports
Current Housing Reports: Housing Vacancies
Expenditures for Residential Upkeep and Improvements
Home Sales Monthly National Association of Realtors
Housing Starts and Housing Completions

Housing Units Authorized by Building Permits
Market Absorption of Apartments
New One-Family Houses Sold and For Sale
Price Index of New One-Family Houses Sold
Residential Alterations and Repairs
Savings and Home Finance Source Book
Survey of Mortgage Lending Activity
Value of New Construction Put in Place

P. Manufacturing

Aerospace Facts and Figures. *Aerospace Industries Association*
Annual Survey of Manufacturers
Annual Statistical Report. *American Iron and Steel Institute*
Business Statistics
Canned Fruit and Vegetable Pack and Stock
Situation Reports. *National Food Processors Association*
Commercial Helicopter Shipments
Concentration Ratios in Manufacturing Industries
Cotton Production and Distribution
County Business Patterns
Current Industrial Reports
Electronic Market Data Book. *Electronic Industries Association*
Exports from Manufacturing Establishments
Frozen Food Pack Statistics. *American Frozen Food Institute*
Hosiery Statistics. *National Association of Hosiery Manufacturers*
Industrial Production and Capacity Utilization
Manufacturing Production, Capacity and Utilization in Aerospace and Aircraft and Parts. *Aerospace Industries Association*
Manufacturers Shipments, Inventories and Orders
Motor Vehicle Facts and Figures. *Motor Vehicles Manufacturers Association*
Plant and Equipment Expenditures and Plans
Pollution Abatement, Costs and Expenditures
Quarterly Financial Report for Manufacturing, Mining and Trade Corporations
Quarterly Survey of Capital Appropriations. *Conference Board*
Quarterly Survey of Capital Investment and Supply Conditions in Manufacturing
Survey of Current Business
Synthetic Organic Chemicals: U.S. Production and Sales
U.S. Commodity Exports and Imports as Related to Output
U.S. Industrial Outlook

Q. Transportation

Accident Facts
Bus Facts. *American Bus Association*
Drivers Licenses
Factbook of National Highway Safety
Fatal Accident Reporting System
Highway Statistics
Large Class I Household Goods Carriers: Selected Earnings Data
Large Class I Motor Carriers of Passengers: Selected Earnings Data
Large Class I Motor Carriers of Property: Selected Earnings Data
Motor Vehicle Facts and Figures. *Motor Vehicle Manufacturers Association*
Transit Fact Book
Transportation in America. *ENO Foundation*
Transport Statistics in the United States
Truck Inventory

Analysis of Class I Railroads. *Association of American Railroads*
Cars of Revenue Freight Loaded. *Association of American Railroads*
Class I Freight Railroads Selected Earnings Data
Freight Commodity Statistics, Class I Railroads. *Association of American Railroads*
Yearbook of Railroad Facts

Air Carrier Financial Statistics
Air Carrier Industry Scheduled Service Traffic Statistics
Air Traffic Activity
Air Transport Facts and Figures. *Air Transport Association*
Airport Activity Statistics of Certified Route Carriers
Aviation Forecasts
Census of U.S. Civil Aircraft
General Aviation Activity and Avionics Survey
Statistical Data Book. *General Aviation Manufacturers Association*
Statistical Handbook of Aviation
Statistical Report. *Regional Airline Association*
Summary of Passport Statistics
U.S. Civil Airman Statistics Annual
U.S. International Air Transport Statistics

Annual Summary of Merchant Ships Completed in the World. *Lloyd's Register*
Annual Report. *Shipbuilders Council*
The Bulletin. *American Bureau of Shipping*
Bulk Carriers of the World Fleet
Containerized Cargo Statistics
Foreign Flag Merchant Ships Owned by U.S. Parent Companies
Maritime Manpower Report
Merchant Fleets of the World
Merchant Vessels of the United States
Monthly Bulk Commodities Report. *Lake Carriers Association*
New Ship Construction
Statistical Tables. *Lloyd's Register*
Vessel Entrances and Clearances
Waterborne Exports and General Imports

R. Communications

Annual Survey of Communication Services
Book Industry Trends. *Book Industry Study Group*
Market Guide. *Editor and Publisher*
Radio Facts Annual. *Radio Advertising Bureau*
Public Broadcasting: Statistical Brief. *Corporation for Public Broadcasting*
Statistical Trends in Broadcasting. *John Blair*
Statistics of Communications Common Carriers
Statistics of Independent Telephone Industry. *United States Telephone Association*
Television and Cable Factbook. *Warren Publishing*
U.S. Postal Service Cost and Revenue Analysis

S. Energy

Annual Energy Outlook
Basic Petroleum Data Book. *American Petroleum Institute*
Coal Distribution
Coal Production
Comparative Oil Company Statistics. *Carl H. Pforzheimer Co.*

Electric Power Annual
Electric Sales, Revenues and Bills
Energy Conservation Indicators
Financial Statistics of Selected Electric Utilities
Gas Facts. *American Gas Association*
Gas Statistics. *American Gas Association*
International Energy Annual
Key Data on Nuclear Energy
Natural Gas Annual
Performance Profiles of Major Energy Producers
Petroleum Supply Annual
Quarterly Coal Report
Residential Energy Consumption Survey
Residential Transportation Energy Consumption Survey
Short-Term Energy Outlook
Solar Collector Manufacturing Activity
Statistics of Interstate Natural Gas Pipeline Companies
Uranium Industry
Weekly Coal Production

T. Distribution and Services

Annual Retail Trade Report
Annual Wholesale Trade Report
Census of Service Industries
Foodservice Numbers: A Statistical Digest. *National Restaurant Association*
Service Annual Survey
Survey of Current Business
Trends in Hotel Industry. *Pannell, Kerr, Forster*
U.S. Lodging Industry. *Laventhol and Horwath*

U. International Transactions and Foreign Commerce

Containerized Cargo Statistics
Exports/Imports of Aerospace Products
Aerospace Industries Association
Foreign Agricultural Trade of the United States
Guide to Foreign Trade Statistics
Highlights of the U.S. Export and Import Trade
Summary of the U.S. Export and Import Merchandise Trade
U.S. Airborne Exports and General Imports
U.S. Commodity Exports and Imports as Related to Output
U.S. Merchandise Trade Exports and Imports for Consumption
U.S. Trade Performance Outlook Annual
U.S. Overseas Loans and Grants
Waterborne Commerce of the United States

V. Business Enterprise

Annual Report of the Small Business Administration
Business Failure Record Dun and Bradstreet
Business Statistics
Economic Indicators
Economic Road Maps Conference Board
Fortune Directory of the 500 Largest Industrial Corporations
Fortune Directory of the 500 Largest Non-Industrial Corporations
Monthly Business Starts Report Dun and Bradstreet
Monthly New Business Incorporations Dun and Bradstreet
Quarterly Financial Report for Manufacturing, Mining, and Trade Corporations

Statistics of Income: Corporate Income Tax Returns
Survey of Current Business

W. Productivity and Technological Development

Characteristics of Recent Scientists and Engineers
Commissioner of Patents and Trademarks Annual Report
Comparative Analysis of Information on National R&D Expenditures
Federal Funds for Research and Development
Immigrant Scientists and Engineers: Detailed Statistical Tables
International Science and Technology Data Update
National Patterns of R&D Resources
Planned R&D Expenditures of Major U.S. Firms
Research and Development in Industry: Detailed Statistical Report
Science and Engineering Indicators
Science and Technology Data Book
Science and Engineering Personnel
Science and Technology Resources in U.S. Industry
Scientists, Engineers and Technicians in Manufacturing Industries
Scientists, Engineers and Technicians in Non-Manufacturing Industries
Scientists, Engineers and Technicians in Trade and Regulated Industries
Women and Minorities in Science and Engineering

X. Financial Markets and Institutions

Annual Report National Credit Union Administration
Fact Book of National Council of Savings Institutions
Fact Book of New York Stock Exchange
Fact Book of Securities Industry Association
Federal Reserve Bulletin
Flow of Funds Accounts
Insurance Facts. *Insurance Information Institute*
Life Insurance Fact Book. *American Council of Life Insurance*
Life Reports: Life Company Financial Data
Mutual Fund Fact Book. *Investment Company Institute*

Reports of Condition Comptroller of Currency
Savings Institutions Source Book. *U.S. League of Savings Institutions*
SEC Annual Report
Source Book of Health Insurance Data. *Health Insurance Association*
Statistics of Banking Annual
Trust Assets of Insured Commercial Banks
Yearend Statistics National Credit Union Administration

Y. Government

Affirmative Employment Statistics
America Votes Congressional Quarterly
Atlas/Data Abstract for the United States and Selected Areas
Book of the States
Budget of the United States Government
Census of Governments
City Employment
City Government Finances
County Government Employment
County Government Finances
Congressional District Data
Facts and Figures on Government Finance Tax Foundation
Federal Civilian Workforce Statistics: Employment and Trends
Federal Expenditure by States
Government Finances
Local Government Employment in Major County Areas
Local Government Finances in Major County Areas
Monthly Statement of the Public Debt of the United States
Municipal Yearbook
Public Employment
Quarterly Summary of Federal, State and Local Tax Revenue
Selected Manpower Statistics
State Government Finances
Statistics of the Presidential and Congressional Elections
United States Government Annual Report

Index

Page numbers in italics indicate graphs.
Page numbers followed by "t" indicate tables.

GERMANNA COMM COLLEGE LOCUST GROVE VA

3 7218 000 098 975

Re
Hf
20
.K8
20

For Reference

Not to be taken from this room

PROPERTY OF GERMANNA
COMMUNITY COLLEGE LIBRARY